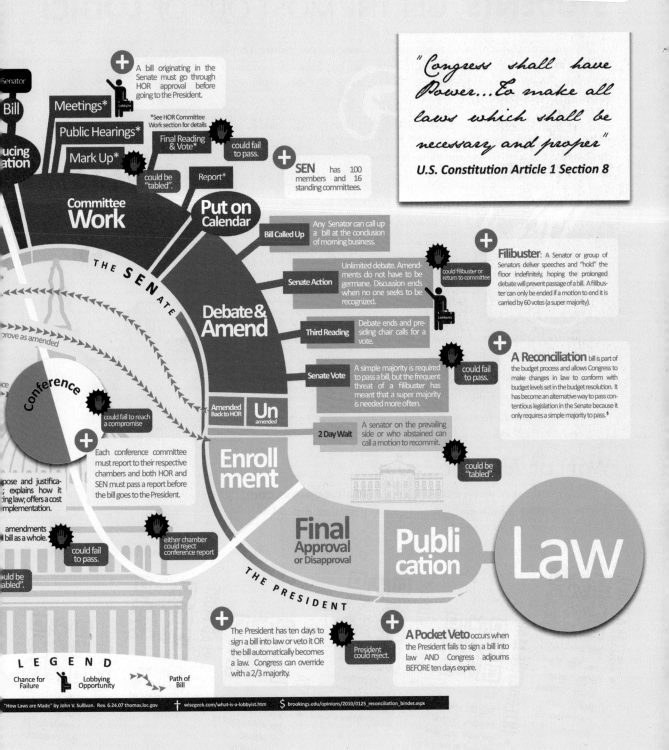

Senator

Bill

Meetings*

Public Hearings*

Mark Up*

ucing
ation

could be
"tabled".

*See HOR Committee
Work section for details

Final Reading
& Vote*

could fail
to pass.

A bill originating in the
Senate must go through
HOR approval before
going to the President.

Report*

SEN has 100
members and 16
standing committees.

"Congress shall have
Power...To make all
laws which shall be
necessary and proper"

U.S. Constitution Article 1 Section 8

Committee Work

Put on Calendar

Bill Called Up

Any Senator can call up
a bill at the conclusion
of morning business.

THE SENATE

Senate Action

Unlimited debate. Amend-
ments do not have to be
germane. Discussion ends
when no one seeks to be
recognized.

could filibuster or
return to committee

Lobbyist

Filibuster: A Senator or group of
Senators deliver speeches and "hold" the
floor indefinitely, hoping the prolonged
debate will prevent passage of a bill. A filibuster can only be ended if a motion to end it is
carried by 60 votes (a super majority).

Debate & Amend

Third Reading

Debate ends and pre-
siding chair calls for a
vote.

rove as amended

Senate Vote

A simple majority is required
to pass a bill, but the frequent
threat of a filibuster has
meant that a super majority
is needed more often.

could fail
to pass.

A Reconciliation bill is part of
the budget process and allows Congress to
make changes in law to conform with
budget levels set in the budget resolution. It
has become an alternative way to pass contentious legislation in the Senate because it
only requires a simple majority to pass. [5]

Conference

could fail to reach
a compromise

Amended
Back to HOR

Un
amended

2 Day Wait

A senator on the prevailing
side or who abstained can
call a motion to recommit.

could be
"tabled".

Each conference committee
must report to their respective
chambers and both HOR and
SEN must pass a report before
the bill goes to the President.

Enroll ment

pose and justifica-
; explains how it
ng law; offers a cost
plementation.

amendments
l bill as a whole."

could fail
to pass.

could reject
conference report

either chamber
could reject
conference report

uld be
abled".

Final Approval or Disapproval

Publi cation

Law

THE PRESIDENT

The President has ten days to
sign a bill into law or veto it OR
the bill automatically becomes
a law. Congress can override
with a 2/3 majority.

President
could reject.

A Pocket Veto occurs when
the President fails to sign a bill into
law AND Congress adjourns
BEFORE ten days expire.

LEGEND

Chance for
Failure

Lobbying
Opportunity

Path of
Bill

"How Laws are Made" by John V. Sullivan. Rev. 6.24.07 thomas.loc.gov   † wisegeek.com/what-is-a-lobbyist.htm $ brookings.edu/opinions/2010/0125_reconciliation_binder.aspx

STUDENTS, GET THE MOST OUT OF LOGIC!

Use your smartphone or tablet to scan the QR codes in every chapter. They'll take you to interesting video clips, political ads, speeches, interactive graphics, and more. (No smartphone? No problem. You can access all of these resources at **logic.cqpress.com**.)

If you don't already have a QR code scanner on your phone or tablet, do a quick search from iPhone's Apple App Store or Android's Google Play to download a free app. Hover the phone's viewer over a QR code and it will activate the following:

- **Watch a Video:** Watch the book's concepts and issues play out in the real world, from a British game show clip to political candidates in debate.

- **Interactive Map:** Explore current trends in state marijuana laws, same-sex marriage, and more.

- **Take a Survey:** Weigh in on issues like gun control and see how your answers compare with those of your peers.

- **Data Update:** See how public approval of Congress and presidential popularity changes from month to month.

- **Read More:** Read recent Supreme Court rulings or deals struck in Congress, well after the book has gone to press.

- **Take a Quiz:** Test your knowledge of each chapter with this mobile-friendly study aid.

Want an **A** on the Exam?

Check out the open-access student study site (**logic.cqpress.com**) for chapter summaries, review questions, interactive quizzes, and eflashcards that will help you prepare for exams. ∎

WATCH A VIDEO

logic.cqpress.com

See how the British game show "Golden Balls" uses the prisoner's dilemma.

INTERACTIVE MAP

logic.cqpress.com

See the effects of party control on vote and seat shares in the fifty states.

TAKE A SURVEY

logic.cqpress.com

Should gun control policy be decided in state capitols or in Washington, DC?

DATA UPDATE

logic.cqpress.com

View the most recent numbers on public approval of Congress.

READ MORE

logic.cqpress.com

Review the complete nine principles of journalism.

TAKE A QUIZ

logic.cqpress.com

Test your knowledge of this chapter.

Three branches of government, two main political parties, thousands of interest groups, millions of voters, and countless media voices can make a confusing jumble out of American politics. Make sense of it all with *The Logic of American Politics.*

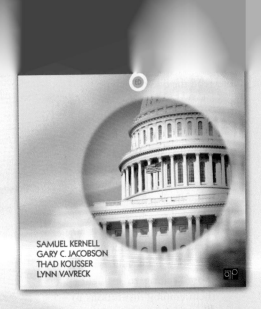

SAMUEL KERNELL
GARY C. JACOBSON
THAD KOUSSER
LYNN VAVRECK

Kernell, Jacobson, Kousser, and Vavreck arm students with the tools they need for understanding institutional design concepts, building their critical thinking skills so they can see that there really is a logic to how the American political system works. Through 15 chapters, *Logic* explores the rules of the game and the way institutions structure the actions and choices of citizens and politicians. Students move beyond trying to memorize details and instead come away with the more lasting and crucial knowledge of why the American political system functions the way it does.

Take a look at the features that provide the framework to understanding American politics.

Chapter-opening vignettes draw in students while effectively pointing to a chapter's main themes.

Blue text highlights passages that apply collective action and institutional design themes, helping to reinforce analytic points.

A set of **feature boxes** strengthen and extend the book's analytic approach:

- **Logic of Politics** boxes examine the design of various political institutions in light of the objectives they were intended to achieve.

- **Strategy and Choice** boxes show how officeholders and those seeking to influence them employ institutions to advance their goals.

- **Politics to Policy** boxes highlight how public policies reflect the institutions that produce them and evaluate institutional capacity to solve the nation's problems.

"I think the analytic framework is well developed throughout the book and is precisely why I assign Logic every semester. I always think that these analytical themes are best introduced in each chapter using short anecdotal stories (especially recent history) and the book is successful in this regard."

—Paul Wohlfarth, University of Maryland

Key terms and suggested reading lists provide an easy way to review and study or explore additional resources for research and writing projects.

Exciting new changes in the sixth edition!

New coauthor Lynn Vavreck, draws on her research and expertise to bring a fresh dimension to the public opinion and media chapters.

A new full-color interior, clean and elegant in design, showcases more than 200 carefully chosen photographs and enhances the display of data in the book's many maps, tables, and figures

Fully updated for recent events and new scholarship the sixth edition reflects the latest developments from landmark Supreme Court rulings to the impact of the 2012 election and the continuing impact of polarization.

Map 4-4   High Concentration of U.S. Hispanics: A Guarantee of Political Influence

Figure 1-2   A Ready Source of Government Revenue: The Income Tax

logic.cqpress.com

Explore a map of the policy patchwork of state marijuana laws.

New QR codes linking students by way of their smartphones to video case studies, data updates, brief surveys, interactive graphics, and quizzes provide mobility, currency, and depth to chapter content.

logic.cqpress.com

Logic supports instructors.

A full set of instructor ancillaries saves time, eases class prep, adds quality multimedia to your course, and offers TAs extra guidance. Click on "instructor's resources" to register and download the materials you need.

- **Test Bank**—more than 900 questions, separated into factual and conceptual multiple choice, short answer, and essay; available with test-generation Respondus software (compatible with course management systems).

- **Author Videos**—interviews with noted political scientists provide expert insight to contemporary topics like divided government, federalism, and elections, helping to make politics relevant and relatable.
- **TA Guide**—a chapter-by-chapter "how-to" for effectively running section discussion, with questions, additional examples, and teaching tips.

- **Downloadable Graphics**—all the book's tables, figures, and maps in PowerPoint and PDF.
- **PowerPoint Slides**—key concepts and instructor notes enhance lectures.
- **A common cartridge** allows you to upload test bank questions, PowerPoint slides, quiz questions, and skill-builder exercises into a range of LMS.

The Modern Presidency

- The powers and role of the modern presidency are a product of the changing place of Washington in national and world affairs.
- Emergence of divided government as "normal state of affairs" in Washington – increases zero-sum political game
- Increasing use of constitutional and unilateral presidential resources
  - Executive Orders
  - Executive privileges
  - Appointments
  - Centralized administration

LOGIC
AMERICAN POLITICS

Logic supports students.

The open-access student study website combines valuable study materials that reinforce key concepts and offers opportunities to put knowledge to the test.

- **Logic of the News**—in blog format with an RSS feed, recent news stories are linked to chapters and placed in analytical context, showing how *Logic*'s themes play out in current events.
- **Study**—chapter summaries with objectives and review questions.

- **Quiz**—multiple-choice questions with automatic feedback.
- **Flashcards**—viewable by definition or by word, with marking and reshuffling.

- **Explore**—annotated web resources.
- **Skillbuilder**—interactive exercises help develop students' social scientific skills.

The Logic of American Politics

The Logic of American Politics

SIXTH EDITION

Samuel Kernell
University of California, San Diego

Gary C. Jacobson
University of California, San Diego

Thad Kousser
University of California, San Diego

Lynn Vavreck
University of California, Los Angeles

⊗SAGE | **CQPRESS**

Los Angeles | London | New Delhi
Singapore | Washington DC

To Dianne, Marty, Kate, and Jeff

The following dedication to James Madison is from the oldest American government textbook we have found: William Alexander Duer's *Outlines of the Constitutional Jurisprudence of the United States*, published in 1833.

To you, Sir, as the surviving member of the august assembly that framed the Constitution, and of the illustrious triumvirate who, in vindicating it from the objections of its first assailants, succeeded in recommending it to the adoption of their country; to you, who, in discharging the highest duties of its administration, proved the stability and excellence of the Constitution, in war as well as in peace, and determined the experiment in favor of republican institutions and the right of self-government; to you, who in your retirement, raised a warning voice against those heresies in the construction of that Constitution which for a moment threatened to impair it; to you, Sir, as alone amongst the earliest and the latest of its defenders,—this brief exposition of the organization and principles of the National Government, intended especially for the instruction of our American youth, is most respectfully, and, in reference to your public services, most properly inscribed.

Columbia College, N.Y.
August 1st, 1833.

Los Angeles | London | New Delhi
Singapore | Washington DC

FOR INFORMATION:

CQ Press

An Imprint of SAGE Publications, Inc.

2455 Teller Road

Thousand Oaks, California 91320

E-mail: order@sagepub.com

SAGE Publications Ltd.

1 Oliver's Yard

55 City Road

London EC1Y 1SP

United Kingdom

SAGE Publications India Pvt. Ltd.

B 1/I 1 Mohan Cooperative Industrial Area

Mathura Road, New Delhi 110 044

India

SAGE Publications Asia-Pacific Pte. Ltd.

3 Church Street

#10-04 Samsung Hub

Singapore 049483

Printed in Canada

A catalog record of this book is available from the Library of Congress.

ISBN 978-1-4522-7649-6

This book is printed on acid-free paper.

Acquisitions Editor: Charisse Kiino

Development Editor: Nancy Matuszak

Production Editor: Laura Barrett

Copy Editor: Melinda Masson

Typesetter: C&M Digitals (P) Ltd.

Proofreader: Stefanie Storholt

Indexer: Teddy Diggs

Cover Designer: Glenn Vogel

Marketing Manager: Erica DeLuca

Permissions Editor: Jennifer Barron

14 15 16 10 9 8 7 6 5 4 3 2

Brief Contents

Detailed Contents

The Nationalization of Politics   PART **1** ■ ■ ■

Chapter 5: Civil Liberties   182

PART ■ 2 ■ ■ The Institutions of Government

Chapter 12: Political Parties   524

GUE OF CONSERVATION VOTERS

ONS

2012 DIRTY DOZ

Dirty Dozen program targets candidates for Congress — regardless of party affiliation — who con
energy and conservation and are running in races in which LCV has a serious chance to affect th
996, more than 60 percent of the Dirty Dozen have been defeated. Check back regularly for new :
Dozen. Click here to view the 2012 State-Level Dirty Dozen candidates.

Y DOZEN

E BUERKLE
ew York 24

DAN BENISHEK
HOUSE : Michigan 01

DAN LUNGREN
HOUSE : California 07

REHBERG
: Montana

FRANCISCO CANSECO
HOUSE : Texas 23

GEORGE ALLEN
SENATE : Virginia

Conclusion PART ■ ■ ■ 4

Chapter 15: The Prospects for Institutional Reform 664

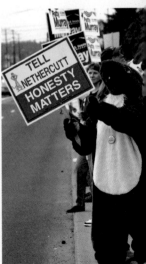

Preface

Since this book's last edition went to press in the summer of 2011, politics in Washington, D.C., and across the nation have changed dramatically, once again. In a landmark decision, the Supreme Court at once upheld the health care reform act that President Obama and his Democratic allies in Congress has passed and, at the same time, reinterpreted the Constitution's "Commerce Clause" to make it much more difficult to pass such sweeping federal legislation in the future. One policy favored by liberals was thus saved while the prospects of future policy victories dimmed. After the Tea Party-fueled fervor of the 2010 midterm election led to a Republican surge that captured the House of Representatives, the nation's political pendulum swung back as Barack Obama won a convincing reelection victory in 2012. Control of the presidency and Congress is yet again divided, with the ideological gulf between the two parties growing every year. These hardened political lines led to a political staring match as 2012 drew to a close and the "fiscal cliff" loomed, with each party waiting for the other to blink by making policy concessions before major spending cuts and tax increases took effect. The deal that Washington's leaders reached on New Year's Day of 2013 saw both sides compromise on tax policy, but did not resolve the nation's long-term budget controversies. The next session of Congress will bring more fiscal deadlines as well as significant debates over immigration reform and gun control, all with no assurances that leaders of the two sharply divided parties will blink.

Our overarching goal in *The Logic of American Politics* is to help students understand the forces that have created conditions like these – partisan polarization, divided government, and judicial intervention – and to see how they shape the choices of political leaders today. We want to help readers discern the rationale embedded in the extraordinary and complex array of American political institutions and practices. To accomplish this goal, we analyze political institutions and practices as (imperfect) solutions to problems facing people who need to act collectively. We highlight recurring obstacles to collective action in various contexts to illuminate the diverse institutional means that American politicians have created to overcome them. These obstacles include the conflict over values and interests, the difficulty of aggregating individual preferences into collective decisions, the need for coordination, and the threat of reneging implicit in every collective undertaking. Stable political communities strengthen their capacity to act collectively and reduce the costs of doing so by fashioning appropriate institutions. These institutions feature majority and plurality rules and procedures that convert votes into representation, delegate authority to agents, and permit some institutional actors to propose courses of action while allocating to others the right to veto proposals. Throughout the book we emphasize the strategic dimension of political action, from the Framers' trade-offs in crafting the Constitution to the efforts of contemporary officeholders to shape policy, so students can understand current institutions as the products of political conflicts, as well as the venues for resolving them.

New challenges pose fresh problems for collective action for which current institutions may seem inadequate. Yet as illustrated by the prolonged response to the September 11, 2001, attacks and, more recently, the tentative regulatory reforms intended to prevent a repeat of the mortgage crisis and near-meltdown of the financial system, reforms are not automatic or easy. The institutions created to deal with the challenges of collective action at one historical moment can continue to shape politics long after those challenges have receded. Therefore, we pay a good deal of attention to the historical development of political institutions, a narrative that reveals politicians and citizens grappling intellectually, as well as politically, with their collective action problems and discovering the institutional means to resolve them.

This book is the product of our nearly forty years of teaching American politics in a way that seeks to go beyond the basics. In this edition, it is refreshed by the addition of Lynn Vavreck as to our author team. An extraordinary scholar and teacher at UCLA who is often called upon by the national media to interpret political events, Professor Vavreck focuses on campaigns, political advertisement, and the links between the economy and politics. She has brought new expertise and energy to many sections of the book, while sharing the approach that has been consistent across *Logic* from the first edition. In addition to introducing students to descriptive facts and fundamental principles, we have sought to help them cultivate an ability to analyze and understand American politics for themselves. Each of us is variously associated with the rational choice school, yet over time our research and teaching have benefited from many of its insights, especially those familiarly referred to as "the new institutionalism." We have found these insights helpful in making sense of American politics in terms that students can grasp intuitively. Having absorbed these ideas into our own scholarly thinking, we employ them here to help students understand what the American political system looks like and why it has assumed its present shape. We will be more timely in our analysis in this and in future editions, because we will now revise the book every two years. Our editions will follow the electoral cycle. Yet rather than rushing to press immediately after an election, as some texts do, we will take time to gather complete data and to reflect. By writing a new edition during and after each election cycle, we can present students with a deeper analysis of each election's lesson for American politics.

ORGANIZATION OF THE BOOK

Our emphasis on the primacy of institutions extends well beyond collecting and processing the preferences of citizens and politicians. In that institutions may structure the choices available to voters and their leaders, we view them as indispensable in explaining public opinion and the strategic behavior of the political organizations that seek to influence and mobilize these preferences. We therefore have adopted a somewhat unorthodox structure for the book. We cover the rules of the game and the formal institutions of government before discussing the "input" side of the political process—public opinion, elections, parties, and interest groups—because we emphasize the way rules and institutions structure the actions and choices of citizens and politicians alike.

The introductory chapter presents the concepts and ideas that form the framework for the subsequent chapters. The core concepts address problems of making and implementing collective choices. Along with traditional concepts that remain indispensable to understanding American politics—such as representation, majority rule, and separation of powers—we introduce students to a number of ideas from economics that political scientists have found increasingly useful for exploring American politics. These include the focal points of coordination, prisoner's dilemma, free riding, tragedy of the commons, transaction costs, principal–agent relations, and public goods. Other concepts, with a more specialized and limited application in our discussion (such as negative agenda control), are presented later in the book, where they are most relevant.

The substantive chapters are arranged in four parts. Part 1 covers the foundational elements of American politics: the Constitution, federalism, civil rights, and civil liberties. The chapters that cover these topics give students an understanding of the political origins and development of the basic structure and rules of the national polity.

Part 2 examines the major formal institutions of national government: Congress, the presidency, the bureaucracy, and the federal judiciary. These chapters reveal how the politics and logic of their development have shaped their current organizational features, practices, and relations with one another.

Part 3 analyzes the institutions that link citizens with government officials, again in terms of their historical development, political logic, and present-day operations. Chapters in this section are devoted to public opinion; voting, campaigns, and elections; political parties; interest groups; and the news media.

The concluding chapter, found in Part 4 evaluates proposals to "reform" American government through the lens of our collective action framework. It begins by describing the obstacles that the Framers placed in the way of any potential changes to the system they designed. Then, the conclusion tells the story of four reform movements—the shift from caucus nominations to primary elections, the enactment of legislative term limits, efforts to increase voter turnout, and the failed move to give the president a line-item veto—viewed as attempts to solve collective action problems. The political fate of each movement, and the ultimate effect of each reform on the operations of government, has been driven by the same logic of American politics described throughout this book.

In elaborating on and reinforcing the themes of the text, we include several sets of boxes in every chapter. The "Logic of Politics" boxes explain the logical rationale or implications of some institutional feature presented in the text. In Chapter 7, "The Presidency," where the text presents the standard descriptive facts about the Constitution's provision for a presidential veto and the frequency with which it has been enlisted over the past two centuries, the adjacent "Logic of Politics" box compares those circumstances in which this "take it or leave it" choice confers real influence on the president in settings where a veto holds little promise for advancing the president's policy preferences. Another set of boxes, "Strategy and Choice," explores how politicians use institutions and respond to the incentives that institutions provide in pursuing their personal or constituencies' interests. In Chapter 6, "Congress," we learn about the accidental origin of that most characteristic of Senate practices, the filibuster, and the strategic considerations that have entrenched it as a crucial and enduring, if often frustrating, feature of Senate life. In Chapter 14, "News Media," we examine how the advent of Wi-Fi brought together government, entrepreneurs, and researchers to solve coordination problems. Rather than devote separate chapters to public policy, we incorporate policy issues throughout the book. "Politics to Policy" boxes explain how policies reflect the underlying political rationale of the institutions that produce them. For example, in Chapter 3, "Federalism," we examine the reasoning that drives an individual health insurance mandate, along with the logic surrounding who – the rich or the poor – pays the largest share of federal and state taxes.

An exciting feature of this edition is that it is our first in full color, bringing to life the photos that we choose so carefully and lending even greater clarity to our charts and figures. Because we constantly collect data from primary sources and work hard to display it clearly for students, having an expanded color palette to draw sharp contrasts and highlight important trends is a luxury that will bring a true pedagogical payoff.

INSTRUCTIONAL FEATURES

The Logic of American Politics includes special features designed to engage students' attention and to help them think analytically about the subject. Thematic questions at the beginning of each chapter preview important themes and set the tone for critical thinking. Each chapter then opens with a story that sets the scene, often dramatically, for the topic at hand. For example, Chapter 14, "The News Media," opens with a case study of the media coverage of the Sago mine disaster and asks students to consider what they would have done if they were reporting from the scene of this tragedy, witnessing ebullient family members yelling "they're alive!" and listening to the town's church bells ringing in the midnight air—all while facing the constraints put on reporters by the 24-hours news cycle and the Internet. Would they have done what Anderson Cooper, *The New York Times*, and the *Washington Post* did? All three reported what they saw happening and made the incorrect inference that the miners had been found alive. In truth, all but one was dead. The pressure to fill an ever-expanding news hole has changed the craft and product of journalism. Chapter 14 explores the implications of this modern news environment for citizens and governance, never forgetting that, in the United States, the vital civic function of informing the public is provided by private, profit-based, competitive businesses.

The introduction offers ideas and concepts that are employed throughout the text. They can be classified under two broad categories: collective action problems and institutional design concepts. Both sets of ideas have deeply informed each chapter's argument. Because this is an introduction to American politics, rather than to political theory, we have intentionally sublimated the analytic ideas in favor of enlisting them to explicate real politics. But be assured that these concepts and theoretical issues are never far beneath the surface of the narrative. To help the student reader spot these concepts when they occasionally break to the surface, we have highlighted these passages in bright blue text. In addition, important terms and concepts throughout the text appear in boldface the first time they are defined. These key terms are listed at the end of each chapter, with page references to their explanations, and are defined in a glossary at the back of the book. To encourage students to continue their studies of American politics beyond the pages of this volume, we have included annotated reading lists at the end of each chapter. Knowing that students today spend far more time on electronic devices than in libraries, this edition also features the innovation of linking to deeper explorations of our concepts through the many QR codes that appear in each chapter. With a wave of their smartphones, students will be able to watch a video of a British game show based on the prisoners' dilemma, view an interactive graphic, or answer a survey question before finding out how others answered it. These QR codes could be used by professors in classes or as parts of assignments, taking advantage of technology to allow teachers and students to tailor the book to their interests.

Review questions from our companion Web site help students review chapter material and to remind them that additional study aids reside on the site. The content for the companion Web site (**logic.cqpress.com**) is rich in exercises and materials that go far beyond the text. Among them is a study guide that includes chapter summaries, learning objectives, and review questions with response boxes so students can e-mail answers directly to their professors. Students also will find interactive quizzes that offer results broken down into questions by type and by chapter section, with the capability to e-mail results to instructors. The Web site sports a "Logic of the News" blog, maintained by one of our PhD candidates, Scott Guenther, where we post important news stories and videos that update topics covered in the text. We also annotate each story and clip to illustrate or extend the themes of the book. Online exercises provide students an interactive introduction to basic social science skills such as reading tables and graphs, analyzing poll results, and interpreting maps. The Web site is just one item in a valuable instructional package that accompanies the text. Instructor's resources (adopters should go to **http://college.cqpress.com/sites/logicir** to register, access, and download) include a test bank, PowerPoint lecture slides, graphics from the book available in PowerPoint and PDF, and extra materials that professors can use throughout their courses, including additional tables and figures. This edition includes a half-dozen five-to-seven-minute videos designed to introduce important themes from the text to the classroom. (Instructors can run these videos directly from the Web site, but if access proves difficult, we can supply copies on DVD.) We also offer a unique guide for running precepts or sections that is geared to graduate student teaching assistants or instructors new to the intro to American government course or teaching *Logic* for the first time. This guide is organized chapter by chapter and offers discussion questions, additional cases and examples that further explain collective action concepts, and a number of group activities. The test bank contains more than a thousand conceptual and factual questions, combining multiple-choice, fill-in-the-blank, short-answer, and essay formats. The extensive lecture materials and the Guide for Teaching Assistants further support classroom instruction.

An outstanding reference is offered to professors who adopt the text (subject to restrictions by the publisher): subscriptions to *CQ Weekly*, the same source that political Washington relies on for nonpartisan coverage and insightful analysis, are available.

ACKNOWLEDGMENTS

Without the help and encouragement of department colleagues, friends, students, and the editorial staff at CQ Press, this book never would have been completed. The book also has benefited from the insightful and astute comments of colleagues at other institutions who took time from their busy schedules to review chapters. We are deeply obliged to everyone who has helped us along the way. In particular, we wish to thank Lawrence Baum, Lee Epstein, Rosalind Gold, Richard Hart, and Vickie Stangl for their assistance in procuring data for tables and figures and clarifying historical events.

Our colleagues and students at the University of California, San Diego, and the University of California, Los Angeles, have contributed to every aspect of the book, often in ways they might not realize, for the way we think about politics is permeated by the intellectual atmosphere they have created and continue to sustain. Leigh Bradberry assisted us in revising those sections covering the judiciary and case law; her expertise and diligence in looking over our shoulders provided an education as well as assistance.

We are indebted to the executive director of the College Publishing Group of CQ Press, Brenda Carter, for her enthusiasm in taking up this project and bringing it to fruition. Charisse Kiino regularly summoned her nonpareil skills as a diplomat, critic, dispatcher, coach, and booster. Nancy Matuszak diligently developed the book's many gangling features, including not only the manuscript but also photographs and cartoons, tables and figures, and citations. She also pulled together a helpful transition guide for new adopters. Melinda Masson cheerfully entered the ring with the authors to wrestle the prose into submission, and Laura Stewart Barrett coordinated the editing and production processes. We also wish to thank Catherine Forrest, who managed production; Paul Pressau, who managed the typesetting and composition; Glenn Vogel who designed the cover; Gail Buschman for the new interior layout; Erica DeLuca and Jennifer Jones for brochures, advertisements, and displays for the professional meetings; and Dwain Smith and Jerry Orvedahl, who worked on the Web site and instructional videos.

Listed below are colleagues across the country who have read and commented on the past four editions and given us an abundance of good advice, much of which we took in writing this revision. Equally essential, they kept us from making many embarrassing mistakes.

Danny M. Adkison, Oklahoma State University

E. Scott Adler, University of Colorado

Scott H. Ainsworth, University of Georgia

Richard Almeida, Francis Marion University

Ellen Andersen, University of Vermont

Phillip J. Ardoin, Appalachian State University

Ross K. Baker, Rutgers University

Lawrence A. Baum, Ohio State University

William T. Bianco, Indiana University

Sarah Binder, Brookings Institution and George Washington University

Christopher Bonneau, University of Pittsburgh

Michael Burton, Ohio University

Suzanne Chod, North Central College

Rosalee Clawson, Purdue University

Ann H. Cohen, Hunter College of The City University of New York

Marty Cohen, James Madison University

Richard S. Conley, University of Florida

Michael Crespin, University of Georgia

Michelle D. Deardorff, Jackson State University

John Domino, Sam Houston State University

Keith Dougherty, University of Georgia

Justin Dyer, University of Missouri

Richard S. Fleisher, Fordham University

John Freemuth, Boise State University

John B. Gilmour, College of William & Mary

Lawrence L. Giventer, California State University–Stanislaus

Brad Gomez, Florida State University

Sanford Gordon, New York University

Paul Gronke, Reed College

Edward B. Hasecke, Wittenberg University

Valerie Heitshusen, Georgetown University

Richard Herrera, Arizona State University

Brian D. Humes, Georgetown University

Jeffery Jenkins, University of Virginia

Paul E. Johnson, University of Kansas

Timothy Johnson, University of Minnesota

Chris Koski, James Madison University

Timothy M. LaPira, James Madison University

Dan Lee, Michigan State University

Joel Lefkowitz, State University of New York–New Paltz

Brad Lockerbie, East Carolina University

Amy Lauren Lovecraft, University of Alaska–Fairbanks

Anthony Madonna, University of Georgia

Forrest A. Maltzman, George Washington University

Wendy Martinek, Binghamton University

John McAdams, Marquette University

Madhavi McCall, San Diego State University

Scott R. Meinke, Bucknell University

Eric Miller, Blinn College, Bryan Campus

Will Miller, Ohio University

William J. Miller, Southeast Missouri State University

Timothy Nokken, Texas Tech University

Bruce I. Oppenheimer, Vanderbilt University

L. Marvin Overby, University of Missouri–Columbia

Justin Phillips, Columbia University

Andrew J. Polsky, Hunter College

Suzanne M. Robbins, George Mason University

Jason Roberts, University of Minnesota

Beth Rosenson, University of Florida

Eric Schicker, University of California–Berkeley

Ronnee Schreiber, San Diego State University

Charles Shipan, University of Michigan

David Shock, Kennesaw State University

James D. Slack, University of Alabama at Birmingham

Charles Anthony Smith, University of California - Irvine

Tara Stricko-Neubauer, Kennesaw State University

Brian Vargus, Indiana University–Purdue University Indianapolis

Charles E. Walcott, Virginia Polytechnic Institute and State University

Hanes Walton Jr., University of Michigan

Wendy Watson, University of North Texas

Christopher Weible, University of Colorado–Denver

Garry Young, George Washington University

Finally, our families. Dianne Kernell, Marty Jacobson, Jeff Lewis and Kate, Will, and Kat Kousser also deserve our gratitude for putting up with what occasionally seemed an interminable drain on our time and attention. We are sure that they are as delighted as we are to have this revision finished.

A Note to Students

PLAN OF THE BOOK

Our analysis of the logic of American politics begins in Chapter 1 with an introduction to the analytical concepts we draw on throughout the text. Although these concepts are straightforward and intuitive, we do not expect you to understand them fully until they have been applied in later chapters. The rest of the text is arranged in four main parts. Part 1 looks at the foundational elements of the political system that are especially relevant to understanding modern American politics. It begins with the constitutional system (Chapter 2, "The Constitution") and then moves on to the relations between the national government and the states (Chapter 3, "Federalism"), the evolution of civil rights and the definition of citizenship (Chapter 4, "Civil Rights"), and the establishment of civil liberties, such as freedom of speech and religion (Chapter 5, "Civil Liberties"). A recurring theme of Part 1 is *nationalization,* the gradual shift of authority from state and local governments to the national government.

Part 2 examines the four basic institutions of America's national government: Congress (Chapter 6), the presidency (Chapter 7), the bureaucracy (Chapter 8), and the federal judiciary (Chapter 9). The development of effective, resourceful institutions at the national level has made it possible for modern-day politicians to tackle problems that in an earlier time they would have been helpless to solve. We explain how all four institutions have evolved along the paths initiated and confined by the Constitution in response to the forces of nationalization and other social and economic changes.

Part 3 surveys the institutions that keep citizens informed about what their representatives are doing and enable them to influence their elected officials through voting and other forms of participation. Chapter 10, "Public Opinion," explores the nature of modern political communication by focusing on the ins and outs of mass public opinion. Chapter 11, "Voting, Campaigns, and Elections," examines the ways in which candidates' strategies and voters' preferences interact at the polls to produce national leaders and, on occasion, create mandates for policies. The Constitution mentions neither political parties nor interest groups, and the Framers were deeply suspicious of both. But they are vital to helping citizens make sense of politics and pursue political goals effectively. In Chapter 12, "Political Parties," and Chapter 13, "Interest Groups," we explain how and why parties and interest groups have flourished as intermediaries between citizens and government officials. President Woodrow Wilson once aptly observed that "news is the atmosphere of politics." Chapter 14 looks at the news media both as channels of communication from elected leaders to their constituents and as independent sources of information about the leaders' performance. The chapter also considers the implications of the rise of the Internet in coordinating the collective efforts of unorganized publics.

Part 4, which consists of Chapter 15, concludes our inquiry by reviewing the biases inherent in the institutions we have examined and considering how to evaluate proposals to reform current political arrangements.

SPECIAL FEATURES

This book contains several special features designed to help you grasp the logic of American politics. At the outset of each chapter are questions that preview important themes and, we hope, will pique your curiosity. To help you more easily spot discussions of collective action problems and institutional design concepts, important passages and analytic points are highlighted in bright blue text. Each chapter opens with a story from the real world of politics that introduces one or more of the central issues to be explored. Within each chapter, thematic boxes labeled "Logic of Politics" consider more fully the logical rationale and implications of certain features of government design that are introduced in the core text. Another set of boxes, "Strategy and Choice," focuses on the sometimes imaginative ways politicians enlist institutions to advance their agendas and their constituents' goals. A third set of thematic boxes, "Politics to Policy," treats some of the public policy issues that have sprung forth from the political process. Additional boxes, tables, figures, photographs, and other visuals clarify and enliven the text. Since these features, including the substantive captions, play an integral role in the presentation and discussion, *you should read them with as much care as you do the text.* Key terms, another feature, appear in boldface when first explained and are grouped together at the end of chapters. Definitions of these terms are listed in the glossary at the back of the book. Finally, to encourage you to pursue more information on topics you find particularly interesting, we have included annotated lists of suggested readings at the end of each chapter. We also feature review questions from the companion Web site to make it easier for you to study and review, as well as to explore a wealth of online resources.

But more lies beyond the covers of this book. Be sure to check out the *Logic of American Politics* Web site (**logic.cqpress.com**), where you will find chapter summaries, review questions, and interactive quizzes that will give you a chance to test and extend your knowledge of the material. The site also features a "Logic of the News" blog that posts current news stories and videos, discussing how the news follows and extends *Logic*'s analysis. In addition, the site offers a wide variety of skill-building exercises that will improve your ability to analyze data, such as a table, figure, or public opinion poll.

Politics, like every significant human endeavor, becomes more intriguing the more deeply it is explored and understood. Our book aims to give you not only a strong basic foundation for understanding political life in the present-day United States but also a glimpse of how intellectually enjoyable it can be to grapple with its puzzles and paradoxes.

1 The Logic of American Politics

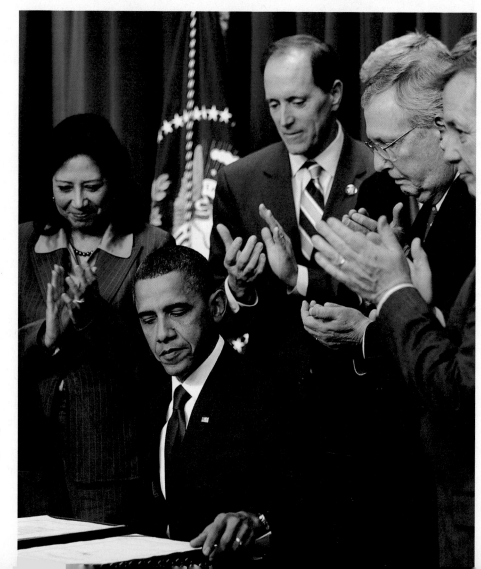

President Barack Obama, flanked by members of Congress, including Republican Senate minority leader Mitch McConnell (second from right), signs the middle-class tax cut bill in December 2010.

- Can politics help people solve their problems?

- In a democracy, do institutions matter? When a majority agrees on a course of action, do the political institutions really affect the majority's ability to achieve its goals?

- Are politicians the servants of the public, as they say in their campaign ads, or are they just self-serving? Why do we need them?

For Democrats there was no way to sugarcoat the 2010 midterm election results. When pressed by reporters for a response, about all President Barack Obama could muster was to acknowledge the "shellacking" his party took. Sixty-four Democrats in the House of Representatives had been defeated, resulting in a Republican takeover of the chamber. Jubilant Republican leaders announced that rescinding the new national health care program would be the first order of business. Thanks to weak Tea Party–sponsored Republican challengers, Democrats had managed to hang on to a slim majority in the Senate. But with the filibuster an ever-present threat, Democratic leaders could only expect success on issues where they could garner significant Republican support. News analyses portrayed President Obama as the next victim in 2012, and generally depicted Democrats as if they were well on their way to becoming an endangered species.

But before the new Congress reintroduced divided government in January 2011, the lame-duck Democratic Congress returned after Thanksgiving to deal with several major, unresolved items on the legislative agenda. Foremost among them was the "Bush tax cut," scheduled to expire on January 1. All politicians prefer to cut taxes, but this one included provisions that had long rankled many Democrats. It sharply reduced estate and income taxes on wealthy citizens. Moreover, extending it would cost the treasury an estimated $900 billion in revenue over the next decade—revenue that some Democrats had already earmarked to pay down a ballooning deficit in the federal budget and relieve pressure to cut spending on social programs favored by Democrats. Finally, ending the tax break appeared easy. All Congress need do was nothing. The law would expire, leaving the new Republican House with the almost impossible task of having to persuade a Democratically controlled Senate and the president to sign on to new legislation reinstating the tax breaks.

Yet within several weeks of convening the late session, the House with its sixty-four exiting Democratic members and the Senate passed a bill extending the tax cut on estates and high incomes for two years. Were President Obama and his party wholly rudderless and unable to withstand Republican demands? How Democrats found themselves reenacting these tax breaks depicts a classic instance of American politics in action. President Obama had railed against income tax breaks for the wealthy during his election campaign, but two years later other, more pressing concerns held his attention. The soon-to-expire law that contained the objectionable tax breaks also included reduced taxes for middle-income earners. Without them, the president's economic advisers warned, the nation's tentative steps out of the deepest recession since the Great Depression would likely halt and possibly even reverse. Moreover, without new legislation two million unemployed citizens would exhaust unemployment benefits in early 2011. These and other expiring Democratic programs sent Obama to the negotiating table with Senate Republicans (who were threatening to filibuster legislation during the lame-duck session) to hammer out a *quid pro quo* whereby each side would get a temporary extension of its preferred program. Within a week, the deal on the massive spending and tax break package was consummated.

On learning of the deal, many liberal Democrats in Congress were incensed and ready to rebel. The president had just removed their one source of revenge against Republicans—for many, their last opportunity to stand up for their principles before leaving office. To add insult to injury, they had no say in the matter. Even many conservative Republicans blanched at the sheer magnitude of the package's cost—$860 billion. They questioned if their leaders had conceded too much to preserve the sacrosanct tax cut. After meeting with the Democratic Party's caucus, in which a single member reportedly defended the president, House Speaker Nancy Pelosi reminded reporters that the brokered bill on which Democratic leaders had not been consulted would, nonetheless, have to pass both chambers and would be unlikely to do so in its current form. Senate Majority Leader Harry Reid, who had barely survived reelection weeks earlier, was only slightly more reserved in expressing his displeasure. He too predicted a final bill with amendments more to the Democrats' liking. Soon thereafter, the Washington press corps dubbed President Obama "rudderless." Weakened by the election, he was caving in to Republican demands.

During the next week, the president made his case to Democratic leaders and the public in a heavily covered press conference. He reminded fellow partisans that neither side could appear to be holding the American public hostage to the partisan fight in Washington. He also noted that the controversial extensions were temporary. They would expire in two years, just in time for the next election cycle. Finally, he recited the list of policies that the other side had grudgingly accepted, which would have stood little chance in the incoming Republican House of Representatives. In the end, Democrats on Capitol Hill continued to grumble, but they passed the deal without changes.

Inevitably, social choices breed conflict, especially when they involve issues that affect the political parties' core constituencies. Through politics, people try to manage such conflicts. Neither side may be thrilled by the process or the results, but when politics succeeds, people of different persuasions agree on a course of action that satisfies them more than what they would have had without it. Try as they may, politics does not always end in success. Resources are too scarce to satisfy the competing claimants, and values prove irreconcilable. And even when the configuration of interests might allow reconciliation, the political process may be deficient. Participants may fail to discover a common ground or suspect that the other side might find a way to renege on their agreements. Under these circumstances, disagreement persists and disputants may even resort to force.[*] Successful politics does not always lead to

---

[*] In 1832 the Prussian general Carl von Clausewitz proclaimed famously that war is "politics by other means." Clausewitz wrote, "War is not merely an act of policy but a true political instrument, a continuation of political intercourse, carried on with other means." Carl von Clausewitz, *On War,* ed. and trans. Michael Howard and Peter Paret (Princeton, NJ: Princeton University Press, 1976), 87.

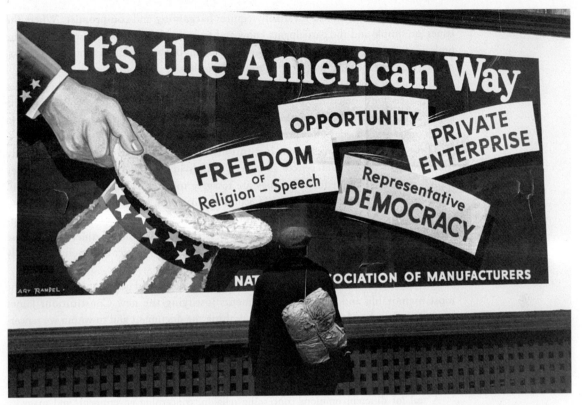

During the Great Depression, when millions of Americans were suddenly impoverished, many critics blamed unfettered capitalism. The National Association of Manufacturers, still a politically active industry association, posted billboards like this one around the country in an effort to bolster support for "private enterprise" by associating it with other fundamental preferences.

happy endings. No one in either political party expressed enthusiasm for the tax deal; yet politics allowed them to find a mutually advantageous exchange.

In more formal terms, **politics** is *the process through which individuals and groups reach agreement on a course of common, or collective,* action—even as they disagree on the intended goals of that action.* This definition covers a great variety of social relations. Parents and teenagers negotiate over use of a family car; bosses and employees haggle over working conditions and pay; and organized crime families jockey over turf for conducting their illicit activities. Politics matters because each party needs to find a solution to its conflict or disagreement. A solution requires parties to cooperate, even when cooperation is costly and difficult to achieve.

---

*This text concentrates on politics in the American national government, but it also draws freely on examples from other settings because the logic embedded in political processes is not confined to matters related to government. Consequently, throughout the text we frequently refer to some generic *collectivity,* whose members engage each other in reaching a *collective decision* either to undertake some *collective action* or to produce some *collective good.* We enlist these general terms whenever we offer a definition, an observation, or a conclusion that has a general application.

Success at politics almost invariably requires **bargaining** and **compromise**. Where the issues are simple and the participants know and trust one another, bargaining, such as the prolonged exchange of proposals and counterproposals between teenagers and their parents, may be all that is needed for the group to reach a collective decision.

Although successful bargaining could lead to the discovery that the contending parties actually agree with each other or possibly to one side's capitulation (such as handing over the keys without any conditions attached), generally it ends in a compromise, or a settlement in which each side concedes some preferences to secure others.

Those who create government institutions (and the political scientists who study them) tend to regard **preferences** as "givens"—individuals and groups know what they want—that must be reconciled if they are to agree to some common course of action. Preferences may reflect the individual's economic situation, religious values, ethnic identity, or some other valued interest. We commonly associate preferences with some perception of self-interest, but they need not be so restrictive. Millions of Americans oppose capital punishment, but surely very few of those who do so expect to benefit personally from such a ban.

Reconciling preferences represents a fundamental problem of governance. In one of the most memorable and instructive statements justifying the new Constitution, James Madison, who played a dominant role in drafting the document and to whom we repeatedly turn for guidance throughout this book, explains that the new government must be devised to represent and reconcile society's many, diverse preferences that are "sown into the nature of man":

> A zeal for different opinions concerning religion, concerning government, and many other points . . . have, in turn, divided mankind into parties, inflamed them with mutual animosity, and rendered them much more disposed to vex and oppress each other than to co-operate for their common good. So strong is this propensity of mankind to fall into mutual animosities, that where no substantial occasion presents itself, the most frivolous and fanciful distinctions have been sufficient to kindle their unfriendly passions and excite their most violent conflicts.[*]

Certainly, Madison's observation appears no less true today than when he wrote it in 1787.

THE IMPORTANCE OF INSTITUTIONAL DESIGN

As participants and preferences multiply and as issues become more complex and divisive, unstructured negotiation rarely yields a collective decision all parties can accept. It may simply require too much time and effort. More crucially, it may expose each side to too great a risk that the other will not live up to its agreements. Fear of reneging may foster

---

[*]This passage is from Madison's *Federalist* No. 10, published initially in 1787 as a newspaper editorial supporting the Constitution's ratification. We shall examine this immensely insightful essay in Chapter 2; it is reprinted in its entirety in the Appendix.

mutual suspicions and lead each side to conclude that "politics" will not work. When this occurs, war may become the preferred alternative. The conflict in the 1990s among Serbs, Croats, and Muslims in Bosnia followed such a dynamic. The collapse of Yugoslavia's communist government in 1990 resurrected ancient enmities among people who had lived peacefully as neighbors for decades. In the absence of effective political **institutions** they could count on to manage potential conflicts, ethnic and religious rivals became trapped in a spiral of mutual suspicion, fear, and hostility. Without a set of rules prescribing a political process for reaching and enforcing collective agreements, they were joining militias and killing one another with shocking brutality within a year. A decade and a half later, European and American forces still police the region as the former Yugoslav states, now separate national governments, strive to build institutions that can replace violence with politics.

Whether at war or simply at odds over the mundane matter of scheduling employee coffee breaks, the parties to a conflict will benefit from prior agreement on rules and procedures for negotiations. Indeed, this theme reappears throughout this book: a stable community, whether a club or a nation-state, endures by establishing rules and procedures for promoting successful collective action. In January 1999, when the Senate turned to the impeachment trial of President Bill Clinton, the stage was set for an escalation of the partisan rancor that had so marred the impeachment proceedings in the House of Representatives. Yet the Senate managed to perform its constitutional responsibility expeditiously and with a surprising degree of decorum thanks to an early, closed-door meeting in which all hundred senators endorsed a resolution that laid out the trial's ground rules. More important, in their desire for partisan and institutional comity, senators gave their majority and minority leaders the right to reject any changes in these rules. Thus members on both sides of the partisan divide could proceed toward a decision without fear that the other side would resort to trickery to get the results it favored. That the Senate would find a way to manage its disagreements is not so surprising. Its leaders take pride in finding collegial ways of containing the potential conflicts that daily threaten to disrupt its business.

Reliance on rules and procedures to reconcile competing preferences is nothing new, of course. In an era of arbitrary kings and aristocrats, republican political theorists understood their value. In a 1656 treatise exploring how institutions might be constructed to allow conflicting interests to find solutions, the English political theorist James Harrington described two young girls who were arguing about how to share a single slice of cake. Suddenly one of the girls proposed a rule: "'Divide,' said one to the other, 'and I will choose; or let me divide, and you shall choose.'" At this moment, Harrington stepped away from his story and seemingly shouted to the reader, "My God! These 'silly girls' have discovered the secret of republican institutions."* With that ingenious rule, both girls were able to pursue their self-interest (the largest possible slice of cake) and yet have the collective decision result in a division both could happily live with.[1]

---

* Actually, Harrington exclaimed, "Mon Dieu!" Note that the lowercase "republican" refers to a form of government, and not the (uppercase) Republican Party. The same case distinction applies to "democratic" and Democratic Party. Both of these forms of government are examined later in the chapter.

Over a hundred years after Harrington's treatise, the Framers of the Constitution spent the entire summer of 1787 in Philadelphia debating what new rules and offices to create for their fledgling government. They were guided by their best guesses about how the alternatives they were contemplating would affect the interests of their states and the preferences of their constituencies (see Chapter 2). The result of their efforts, the Constitution, is a collection of rules fundamentally akin to the one discovered by the girls in Harrington's story. It was intended to reassure diverse interests that they would be better off under the proposed system than they had been under the Articles of Confederation.

The events in Philadelphia remind us that however lofty the goal that gives rise to reform, institutional design is a product of politics. As a result, institutions may confer advantages on some interests over others. Indeed, sometimes one side, enjoying a temporary advantage, will try to permanently implant its preferences in difficult-to-change rules and procedures. The present-day Department of Education, for example, arose from the former Department of Health, Education, and Welfare in 1977 after newly elected Jimmy Carter proposed this split as a reward for early support from teacher organizations who had long regarded a separate department as key to their ability to win increased federal funding for schools and teacher training. The history of this department bears out the wisdom of their strategy. Republican Ronald Reagan followed Carter into the White House with the full intention of returning the education bureaucracy to its former status. But before long the cabinet secretary he appointed to dismantle the department began championing it, as did many Republicans in Congress whose committees oversaw the department's activities and budgets. Nearly three decades later, the Department of Education is entrenched in Washington and has helped implement such education reforms as President George W. Bush's ambitious "No Child Left Behind."

CONSTITUTIONS AND GOVERNMENTS

All organizations are governed by rules and procedures for making and enforcing decisions. Within colleges and universities, the student government, the faculty senate, staff associations, academic departments, and, of course, the university itself follow rules and procedures when transacting regular business. Although rules and procedures go by different names (for example, constitution, bylaw, charter), their purpose is the same: to guide an organization's members in making essentially political decisions— that is, decisions in which the participants initially disagree about what they would like the organization to do.

And what happens when the organization is a nation? Consider the problems: the number of participants is great, the many unsettled issues are complex, and each participant's performance in living up to agreements cannot be easily monitored. Yet, even with their conflicts, entire populations engage in politics every day. Their degree of success depends largely on whether they have developed constitutions and governments that work.

The **constitution** of a nation establishes its governing institutions and *the set of rules and procedures these institutions must (and must not) follow to reach and enforce collective agreements.* A constitution may be a highly formal legal document, such as that of the United States, or it may resemble Britain's unwritten constitution, an informal "understanding" based on centuries of precedents and laws. A **government**, then, consists of these institutions and the legally prescribed process for making and enforcing collective agreements. Governments may assume various forms, including a monarchy, a representative democracy, a theocracy (a government of religious leaders), or a dictatorship.

Authority versus Power

The simple observation that governments are composed of institutions actually says a great deal and implies even more. Government institutions consist of **offices** that confer on their occupants' specific authority and responsibilities. Rules and procedures prescribe how an institution transacts business and what authority relations will link offices together. **Authority** is the acknowledged right to make a particular decision. Only presidents possess the "authority" to nominate federal judges. However, a majority of the Senate's membership retains sole authority to actually "confirm" these appointments and allow the nominees to take office.

Authority is distinguishable from **power**, a related but broader concept we enlist throughout the book. Power refers to an officeholder's actual influence with other officeholders and, as a consequence, over the government's actions. An office's authority will be an important ingredient in its occupant's power, but an officeholder's power includes the skill to deploy that authority when dealing with other officeholders and politicians. President Obama has the authority only to nominate a judge, but whether the Senate confirms his appointment may rest on Obama's persuasiveness with members of the Senate Judiciary Committee, his mobilization of key support groups to lobby undecided senators, and his ability to generate favorable publicity for his candidate and perhaps even unfavorable publicity for opponents.

Institutional Durability

Institutions are by no means immutable, but they tend to be stable and resist change for several reasons. First, with authority assigned to the office, not to the individual holding the office, established institutions persist well beyond the tenure of the individuals who occupy them. A university remains the same institution even though all of its students, professors, and administrators are eventually replaced. Institutions, therefore, contribute a fundamental continuity and orderliness to collective action. Second, the people who are affected by them make plans on the expectation that current arrangements will remain. Imagine how senior college students would react if, during their last semester, their college or university increased the required course units for a degree. Or consider the anxiety that the millions of workers approaching retirement must feel whenever politicians in Washington talk about changing Social Security.* Finally, even those who seek change typically find it hard to agree on a proposed alternative. Virtually everyone endorses some

---

*Hence, in his 2005 State of the Union address President George W. Bush sought emphatically to reassure the most anxious segment of the public approaching retirement—specifically, those over age fifty-five—that his sweeping reform proposal would not apply to them.

reform on national health care policy, but they disagree sharply over its direction. As a result, current arrangements, though preferred by few, if any, members of Congress, have undergone only minor changes.

Sometimes reform is undertaken to make institutions perform more efficiently. During the opening session of the First Congress in 1789, James Madison, while serving as a member of the House of Representatives from Virginia, observed that "in every step the difficulties arising from novelty are severely experienced. . . . Scarcely a day passes without some striking evidence of the delays and perplexities springing merely from the want of precedents." Then, more sanguinely, he predicted that "time will be a full remedy for this evil." And time has proven Madison right. By setting rules and following precedents, the House of Representatives has become a well-regulated machine, allowing members to concentrate on lawmaking.

On other occasions reforms enable institutions to accomplish new collective goals. In 1970 an executive reorganization plan consolidated components of five executive departments and agencies into a single independent agency, the Environmental Protection Agency, with a strong mandate and commensurate regulatory authority to protect the environment. By coordinating their actions and centralizing authority, these formerly dispersed agencies could more effectively monitor and regulate polluting industries. Within agencies new tasks are added to old, until the work outstrips the capacity of existing structures; only then are new offices and procedures created. Before there was the modern White House Office, presidents relied informally on a handful of assistants loaned to them from the executive departments. In the late 1930s Congress, acceding to President Franklin Roosevelt's request, created a separate staff and designated six assistants to the president. Gradually, as presidents took on more responsibilities, the White House Office grew in number and complexity. Today its staff, composed of more than five hundred policy and political specialists, occupies two office buildings. Like rings within a tree, the history of the presidency can be seen in the layers of offices that have accumulated in response to successive demands and challenges. While the changes have been gradual, over time they transformed the office.

The Political System's Logic

The quality of democracy in modern America reflects the quality of its governing institutions. Embedded in these institutions are certain core values, such as the belief that those entrusted with important government authority must periodically stand before the citizenry in elections. Balanced against this ideal of popular rule is the equally fundamental belief that government must protect certain individual liberties even when a majority of the public insists otherwise. Throughout this text we will find politicians and citizens disagreeing on the precise meaning of these basic beliefs and values as they are applied or redefined to fit modern society.

Also embedded in these institutions—initially by the Framers in the Constitution and later by amendment and two centuries of political evolution—is a logic based on principles about how members of a community should engage one another politically to identify and pursue their common goals. Although the Framers did not use the vocabulary of modern political science, they intuitively discerned this logic and realized they must apply it correctly if the "American Experiment" were to succeed.* For us, too, this logic is essential for understanding the behavior of America's political institutions, the politicians who occupy them, and the citizens who monitor and respond to political actions. To that end, the concepts presented in the remainder of this chapter are the keys to "open up" America's political institutions and to reveal their underlying logic. We begin with the problems (or one can think of them as puzzles) that confront all attempts at collective action. Many institutional arrangements have been devised over time to solve these problems. Those we examine here are especially important to America's political system and will appear throughout the book.

COLLECTIVE ACTION PROBLEMS

By virtue of their size and complexity, nations encounter special difficulties in conducting political business. In those nations where citizens participate in decisions through voting and other civic activities, still more complex issues arise. Successful **collective action** (that is, the efforts of a group to reach and implement agreements) challenges participants to figure out what to do and how to do it. The former involves comparing preferences and finding some course of action that sufficient numbers of participants agree is preferable to proposed alternatives or doing nothing. The latter concerns implementation—not just the nuts and bolts of performing some task, but reassuring participants that everyone will share the costs (e.g., taxes) and otherwise live up to agreements.

Even when differences are in principle reconcilable, there is no guarantee that a solution will be discovered and implemented. Two fundamental barriers—coordination problems and prisoner's dilemmas—may block effective collective action. **Coordination** is perhaps the simplest to overcome: members of the group must decide individually what they want, what they are prepared to contribute to the collective enterprise, and how to coordinate their efforts with those of others. A **prisoner's dilemma** arises whenever individuals decide that even though they support some collective undertaking, they are personally better off pursuing an activity that rewards them individually despite undermining the collective effort. Prisoner's dilemmas pervade all of politics, from neighbors petitioning City Hall for a stop sign to legislators collaborating to strike budget deals in Congress. These dilemmas especially interest us because the "solution"—that is, having everyone contribute to the collective undertaking—depends heavily on providing the kinds of incentives to individuals that governments are well suited to provide.

Coordination

A classical music performance offers an education in the costs of coordinating collective action. During a concert the members of a string quartet coordinate their individual performances by spending nearly as much time looking at each other as they do following

---

*They were, after all, contemporaries of Isaac Newton and found in his theory of mechanics inspiration to search for similar natural laws to create a well-functioning polity. With Britain the only real-world model to guide them, which they tended to judge more as a model of what to avoid than to emulate, the Framers depended heavily on carefully reasoned ideas, which took them to Newtonian physics. Consequently, the terms *force, counterweight,* and *balance* were familiarly employed during debates at the Constitutional Convention and by both sides in the Constitution's subsequent ratification campaign.

their music.* Volume, tempo, and ornamentation must all be executed precisely and in tandem. By the end of a successful concert, the effort required is evident on the triumphant musicians' perspiring faces. A symphony orchestra, by contrast, achieves comparable coordination, despite its greater numbers, by retaining one of its members to put aside the musical instrument and take up the conductor's baton. By focusing on the conductor, orchestra members are able to coordinate their playing and produce beautiful music. And at the end of the concert the conductor is the first one to mop a perspiring brow.

Coordination problems increase with the size of a group. Large groups trying to reach a shared goal might emulate the symphony in designating and following a leader. Members of the House of Representatives and the Senate configure procedures to enable Congress to decide policy for the hundreds of issues presented each session. But to achieve the same objective the 435-member House and the 100-member Senate proceed quite differently, following a logic reflecting the size of their organizations. The House delegates to a Rules Committee responsibility for scheduling the flow of legislation onto the floor and setting limits on deliberations and amendments. This important committee becomes the "leader" in setting the body's agenda. The entire House cedes this authority to a committee because coordination is vital if the chamber is to identify and pass the most preferred legislation. By contrast, the smaller Senate has found that it can achieve comparable levels of coordination without having to surrender authority to a specialized committee. Rather, informal discussions among members and party leaders suffice.

When the number of participants desiring to coordinate is really large—say, a state's voters—coordination may generally be unachievable. It explains, after all, why a society's collective decisions are generally delegated to a small group of professionals, namely politicians, who intensively engage one another in structured settings, namely government, in order to discover mutually attractive collective decisions. On some problems simple, self-enforcing rules—such as traffic staying to the right side of the street—might be all that is required. For other kinds of collective choices, institutions severely limit options, allowing like-minded individuals to coordinate easily. Political party nominations offer voters an obvious common choice.

Successful mass coordination occasionally arises even in the absence of institutions channeling individuals' choices. The 2012 presidential primaries saw conservative Republican voters race *en masse* from one candidate to another in search of an alternative—apparently any alternative—to moderate and eventual winner Mitt Romney. As displayed in Figure 1-1, five of Romney's serious challengers for the nomination briefly achieved front-runner status in the public opinion polls. On reaching the top of the pile, each faltered and was quickly discarded by voters in favor of yet another "anyone but Romney" nominee. Eventually, they all stumbled badly, leaving Romney the only viable candidate still in the race. At this point, conservative Republicans switched their mantra to "anyone but Obama" and rallied behind their party's nominee.

Among the several surprising outcomes in this chronology is the alacrity with which Republican voters' preferences switched from one candidate to another. How, for example,

---

*The recent movie *A Late Quartet* (2012) vividly portrays the tremendous coordination costs borne by each member (in the movie, off the stage as well as on).

Figure 1-1 Republicans Pick a Presidential Nominee, 2012

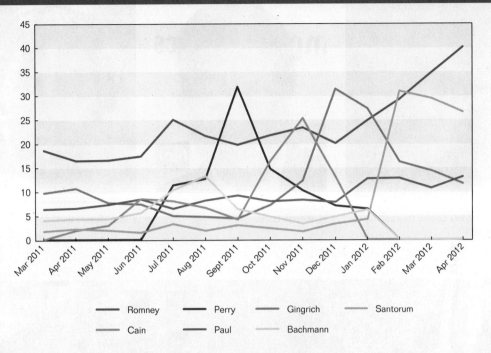

Source: RealClearPolitics.com, 2012 Republican Presidential Nomination, www.realclearpolitics.com/epolls/2012/president/us/republican_presidential_nomination-1452.html#polls.

did so many survey respondents manage to shift from front-runner Rick Perry (after he forgot the names of several government departments he promised to disband) to Herman Cain, who had until Perry's debate fiasco barely registered a blip in the polls? In such instances a critical ingredient of success lies in identifying a common **focal point** to help individuals target their energies toward a common purpose. A focal point is some prominent cue that helps individuals recognize the preferences of others with whom they want to cooperate. A strong debate performance might win some supporters, but equally important, it might identify to all the candidates who will attract the most support. Similarly, a narrow victory in a state delegate caucus could signal the candidate that all like-minded voters should gather behind. Or endorsement by some accepted authority—like the Tea Party—could concentrate support. And so each of these kinds of focal point cues guided conservative Republicans as they settled on a "not Romney" alternative who, shortly thereafter, displayed some fatal flaw that sent them searching for another candidate.

Internet-based social networks offer levels of focal point coordination unimaginable in earlier decades. The rise of the Tea Party through viral videos and blogs and the meteoric growth of the "Occupy" movement in 2012 are among the recent examples of highly coordinated mass behavior arising from focal points. A remarkable example of nearly spontaneously coordinated protest activity occurred in 2006, when a Los Angeles union

Renán Almendárez Coello, "the Latino Howard Stern"

Humberto Luna

Eddie "Tweety Bird" Sotelo

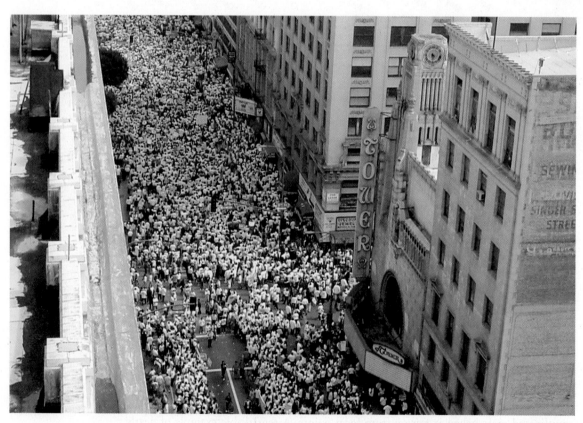

These Los Angeles Spanish-language DJs, among others, are credited with turning out nearly five hundred thousand demonstrators for an immigration reform rally in downtown L.A. in March 2006.

and church organized a protest march against anti-immigrant legislation under consideration by the House of Representatives. The organizers hoped to arouse twenty thousand participants, but after they persuaded several Spanish-radio DJs to publicize the rally, over half a million protesters showed up. The size of the turnout amazed everyone, including the organizers, and the crowd quickly overwhelmed the police force. Clearly, there was a pent-up demand needing only a cue as to when and where everyone would show up.

Coordination problems essentially arise from uncertainty and insufficient information and may prevent collective undertakings even when a great majority agrees on a course of action, such as Republicans' desire to win back the presidency in 2012. We now turn to potentially more problematic challenges to collective action—the problems of the prisoner's dilemma. Unlike a lack of coordination, where mutual ignorance prevents participants from identifying and working together for a common goal, prisoner's dilemma problems find participants privately calculating that they would be better off by not contributing to the collective action even when they wholeheartedly agree with its purpose. Where coordination problems frequently require no more than direction and information, prisoner's dilemmas generally necessitate monitoring and the threat of coercion.

The Prisoner's Dilemma

Since it was first formally introduced in the late 1950s, the prisoner's dilemma has become one of the most widely employed concepts in the social sciences. A casual Google search generated over half a million hits on this phrase, bringing up websites on subjects far afield from political science and economics (where systematic consideration of the concept originated), including psychiatry, evolutionary biology, and drama theory. The prisoner's dilemma depicts a specific tension in social relations, one long intuitively understood by political thinkers. Solving this dilemma fundamentally distinguishes political success and failure and is a cornerstone of our inquiry. What precisely is the prisoner's dilemma, and why is it so important for the study of American politics?

The prisoner's dilemma arises whenever individuals, who ultimately would benefit from cooperating with each other, also have a powerful and irresistible incentive to break the agreement and exploit the other side. Only when each party is confident that the other will live up to an agreement can they successfully break out of the dilemma and work to their mutual advantage.

A simple example of how this works is the original exercise that gives the prisoner's dilemma its name. In the movie stills from the 1941 drama *I Wake Up Screaming* (see photos), homicide detectives are subjecting screen legends Victor Mature and Betty Grable to the prisoner's dilemma. Specifically, each murder suspect is being advised to confess and testify against the other, in return for a lighter prison sentence. The diagram on the next page maps out the likely prison term each faces. Deep down Mature and Grable know the police do not have enough evidence to convict them of murder. All they have to do is stick to their story (i.e., cooperate) and, at worst, they may have to spend six months in jail on a gun possession charge. If both were to confess, each would get a five-year sentence. Each is offered a deal: in exchange for a full confession, the "squealer" will get off scot-free, while the "fall guy" or "sucker" will be convicted and likely receive a ten-year prison term. In the movie both suspects are isolated in their cells for a few days, with the detectives hinting that their partner is

Subjected to the classic prisoner's dilemma interrogation, Victor Mature and Betty Grable turn out to have nothing to confess in this 1941 whodunit *I Wake Up Screaming*. Since its introduction in the 1950s, thousands of articles have enlisted this metaphor to explore the fundamental conflict between what is rational behavior for each member of a group and what is in the best interest of the group as a whole.

"singing like a canary." As the days pass, each begins to recognize the other's character flaws and panics. If Mature squeals, Grable realizes, she must also in order to avoid a ten-year stretch. If, however, she has underestimated his virtues and he holds out, well, that would be unfortunate, but she gains some solace in knowing that her lone confession will be her "get-out-of-jail" card. Of course, Mature, stewing in his cell, reaches the same conclusion. Why this movie presents a genuine dilemma is that *in this setting* confessing offers the best outcome for each suspect, regardless of what the other individual does. So, in the end they both confess and spend the next five years in the slammer.*

		Victor Mature			
		Stays Silent		Confesses	
Betty Grable	Stays Silent	6 months	6 months	10 years	No jail
	Confesses	No jail	10 years	5 years	5 years
		(Grable's sentence is listed first.)			

So what does this dilemma have to do with American politics? Everything. Every successful political exchange must tacitly solve the prisoner's dilemma. Exchanges occur because each side recognizes that it will be better off with a collective outcome rather than trying to

---

* For this reason police have traditionally objected to giving suspects early access to lawyers, who might help the otherwise isolated prisoners coordinate their plan. But this is a different story we will return to in Chapter 5. By the way, the movie offers a happy ending.

act alone. Had Mature and Grable somehow managed to stay silent, their cooperation would have shaved all but six months from their five-year terms. And both knew this. Yet neither could be sure the other confederate would stay silent. To get something worthwhile, both sides must typically give up something of value in return. The moral: unless participants in a collective decision can trust each other to abide by their commitments, they will not achieve a mutually profitable exchange.

How do the Matures and Grables shift the outcome from that quadrant, where neither cooperates, to the one where they both do? One solution involves making reneging and defection very expensive. In some settings this can be achieved informally. For example, politicians who repeatedly make campaign promises that they subsequently fail to act on lose credibility with voters, making them vulnerable to defeat in the next election. Once in office, reneging on an agreement will quickly damage a politician's reputation, and others will refuse to deal with her in the future. Where failure to live up to one's agreements imposes costs down the road, politicians will think twice before doing so.

Another common solution is to create institutions that help parties discover opportunities to profit through cooperation and, most importantly, guarantee that agreements are honored. Here the government's coercive authority is useful. An anthropologist once reported that two tribes in a remote region of New Guinea lived in a state of continual warfare, to the point that many more men from both tribes had died in battle than from natural causes. The anthropologist summed up their dilemma: "In the absence of any central authority, they are condemned to fight forever . . . since for any group to cease defending itself would be suicidal." He added that these tribes might "welcome pacification." One day the distant government in Papua sent a ranger armed with a handgun to establish territorial boundaries between the tribes and rules governing their chance encounters. Suddenly, the decades-long warfare ended. Each side believed the ranger with his single sidearm presented sufficient force to punish any breaches of the peace agreements, and the now-peaceful neighbors began to use politics—not war—to solve their conflicts.[2] Members of a society must be able to engage one another politically. Without confidence that agreements will be enforced, the political process quickly unravels. Participants will balk at undertaking mutual obligations they suspect their bargaining partners will not honor.

In his 1651 treatise on the origin and purposes of government, *Leviathan,* political philosopher Thomas Hobbes examined the straits to which society is reduced when its government is unable to enforce collective obligations and agreements. (See box "Hobbes on Monarchs.") In a famous passage he warned that life would return to "a state of nature . . . solitary, poor, nasty, brutish and short."[3] The mortality rate of New Guinea tribesmen confirmed Hobbes's insight. They were not naturally bellicose; rather, these tribes simply could not trust each other. Thus enforcement succeeded in inducing cooperation, but not by flaunting overwhelming force or imposing a solution on the contending parties. The ranger's presence simply rendered any party's defection more costly than its compliance.

Hopefully, the relevance of the prisoner's dilemma to American politics is becoming clearer. Virtually every policy the government adopts represents a successful resolution of this dilemma. Constituencies and their representatives cooperate to achieve their separate goals—recall our definition of politics on page 3—because institutions have developed to help diverse constituencies discover opportunities for mutual gain through cooperation and, just as importantly, deter them from reneging on their agreements. Like the ranger with a

■ WATCH A VIDEO

logic.cqpress.com
See how the British game show "Golden Balls" uses the prisoner's dilemma.

HOBBES ON MONARCHS

logic of politics

In 1651 Thomas Hobbes argued in *Leviathan*, one of the most important books in political theory, that the English monarch was a necessary guarantor of collective agreements.[1] He proposed that since the king and his offspring derived their wealth directly from the population in taxes and labor, they would pursue the nation's welfare because it would enrich them as well. Even if the monarch were wicked and expropriated too much of the nation's wealth for himself, the citizenry was still better off with him wielding power arbitrarily than if no one had enforcement authority. Restated in the vocabulary of this text, Hobbes argued that monarchs offered a cost-effective means to collective action.

1. Thomas Hobbes, *Leviathan, or The matter, forme, & power of a commonwealth ecclesiasticall and civill* (1651; reprint, Oxford: Clarendon Press, 1958).

handgun from Papua, America's political institutions foster collective action by solving the prisoner's dilemma.

There are failures, to be sure. Some issues simply do not offer mutual gains through cooperation. One party's gain is the other's loss, and politics may break down and give way to force. National policy on rights to abortion frequently becomes just such an issue where irreconcilable preferences seek to control policy. Chapter 4 recounts the most intractable issue of all in American political history—the failure, despite repeated compromise attempts, to come up with a policy on slavery's extension into the territories during the 1850s. This issue was only resolved by the deadliest war of its time.

Even where each side can envision opportunities for mutual gains, American politics is not fail proof. Everyone agrees that in several decades the Social Security program will be unable to provide its current level of benefits for the next generation of retirees. Both Republican and Democratic politicians in Washington want to fix it, and from time to time one side will make an overture to the other. But all of the solutions are costly or unpopular, either requiring hefty new taxes or curtailing benefits. Both political parties worry that as soon as they offer a tough solution, the other side will seek to exploit it and score points in the next election. Until politicians figure out a way to cooperate and share the blame, Social Security reform will remain the proverbial "third rail" of politics: "Touch it and you are dead."*

---

*The third rail metaphor refers to the third rail of subway tracks, the one that carries the electricity.

FREE-RIDER PROBLEM. A form of the prisoner's dilemma that afflicts large groups is the **free-rider problem**. With each individual's contribution to the success of the collective activity quite small and inconsequential, each member will be tempted to free ride—that is, to defect from the agreement by withholding a contribution to the group's undertaking while enjoying the benefits of the collective effort. Of course, such a course of action is available to everyone, with the result that no one actually contributes to a collective enterprise all deem meritorious.

To better understand the critical role of group size to this particular form of prisoner's dilemma, let us return to the collective efforts of our quartet and symphony. Suppose a violinist is tempted to skip practice and party with friends the evening before a performance. As a member of a quartet, the violinist faces powerful incentives to fulfill her obligations. If she performs poorly, her three colleagues will quickly notice, as will music critics and many in the audience. Since each musician's contribution is manifestly vital to the quartet's collective product, all are likely to stay home and practice. Now consider the decision of the would-be partygoer who is a member of the symphony. As one of twenty violinists in the orchestra, each performer's contribution adds only marginally to the collective product, certainly much less than do the contributions of members of the string quartet. This introduces an opportunity to free ride. The symphony musician might be tempted to spend the night on the town knowing that he could still bask in the orchestra's beautiful music.

The free-rider problem arises whenever citizens recognize that their small contribution to the collective enterprise will not affect its success or failure. And because contributing is somewhat costly, they decide not to make the effort. Even those citizens who enthusiastically support an enterprise realize that they (and others) can escape fulfilling their obligations. If many people react this way—and many do—and suspect their neighbors of doing so as well, too few people will contribute to collective endeavors and, thus, some may fail.

During Barack Obama's 2008 presidential campaign "get out the vote" operatives discovered that organizing volunteers into groups of more than ten volunteers reduced the group's success in contacting prospective voters. Instead of crusaders making a difference, they felt like "numbers on a spreadsheet." A lot of them dropped out of the campaign. Having learned this lesson, in 2012 they organized into smaller teams where they could more easily see that their contribution made a difference. As a result, the campaign's voter contact efforts proved more successful.[4]

For many voluntary associations, this strategy is unavailable. With about 10 percent of its regular viewers ever donating to their local PBS affiliate, the public television system requires an annual government subsidy to stay in business. Given the logic of nonparticipation, why does anyone ever contribute to a collective enterprise? Clearly some people find some activities intrinsically rewarding, however minor their contribution. That said, most of the people, most of the time, are inclined to free ride. If a collective effort is to succeed, it must provide potential participants with a private inducement. A few PBS viewers donate to their local station because they want to express their support for public television (or perhaps their disgust with commercial television). But many others are lured into donating by the monthly program guide subscription, license-plate holders, coffee mugs, discount coupon books, and other direct benefits of membership.

WATCH A VIDEO

logic.cqpress.com

Governor
Romney explains
Massachusetts'
health care
mandate.

Governments face many of the same free-riding issues as voluntary associations, but generally they solve them not by rewards and plying individuals with selective benefits but rather by sanctions and, if necessary, force. Immediately after the United States declared war on Japan after the attack on Pearl Harbor, thousands of patriotic young men rushed to the army and navy recruiters. In case they did not, however, Congress passed a draft law. Imagine how few people would pay income taxes if there were no Internal Revenue Service waiting in the wings. Governments also have a variety of other resources at their disposal to induce participation in collective undertakings. One of the most controversial features of the national health care law enacted in 2009 was the requirement that everyone sign up for health care insurance. Failing to do so would result in an extra tax added to the individual's income tax to cover these premiums. Clearly the intuition behind the mandate was that in a setting where no one could be denied insurance coverage, many people would wait until they got sick to sign up. In a sense they would free ride—that is, not contribute to the overall financing of the program—but avail themselves of the collective good whenever they liked.

THE TRAGEDY OF THE COMMONS. Another distinctive and important form of the prisoner's dilemma is the **tragedy of the commons**. It resembles free riding in that the provision of a public good is divorced from its consumption. Where free riding emphasizes efforts of individuals to avoid contributing to the creation or preservation of a public good, tragedy of the commons concentrates on individuals' costless consumption of a public good (the "commons") that results in its ruination. A large number of participants encourages each to renege on contributions to the public good. The difference is that the good already exists and will be destroyed if its exploitation is not brought under control. This dilemma takes its name from another instructive allegory. A number of herdsmen graze their cattle in a common pasture. Gradually they increase the size of their herds, destroying the pasture and with it their livelihood. With each herdsman reasoning that adding one more cow to the herd will increase his income while having negligible impact on the pasture, they all add cattle, and do so repeatedly. The end result is a disaster—eventually, overgrazing strips the pasture of fodder, the cows starve, and the herdsmen go broke.

A real-world analogy is the collapse of the cod fishing industry off New England. Entire communities based their economies on fishing cod in nearby waters, but so many fishermen exploited this resource, without allowing nature to replenish it adequately, that they managed to wipe out the fishery on which their jobs depended.[5] Kansas wheat growers confront the same dilemma when they over-irrigate their fields even while recognizing that they are rapidly depleting the underground aquifer and, consequently, their long-term livelihood. In these and many other examples of overpopulation and pollution, participants find themselves racing toward ruin as they deplete natural resources.

The commons metaphor has broader and timely applications. When patients fail to take their full prescription of antibiotics, they contribute to the emergence of a more resistant strain of bacteria to which everyone could be exposed. The Internet can be thought of as a commons in a variety of respects (see Politics/Policy box on Google's attempt to create a new digital library). Anyone can post information on the Internet, attract Net surfers' attention, and net some revenue as viewers click on accompanying advertising banners. Since high-quality information is costly to produce, many will seek to exploit this commons by creating cheaply produced, low-grade information, making it difficult for quality information to distinguish itself and ask for compensation for its more-costly-to-produce information.*

The trick to avoiding the tragedy of the commons lies in proper institutional design. As with free riding, the solution links the individual's personal interest to provision (in this instance, preservation) of the collective good. A decision to squander or conserve resources must somehow be made to affect each participant's personal welfare. One solution is **regulation**—setting up rules limiting access to the common resource and monitoring and penalizing those who violate

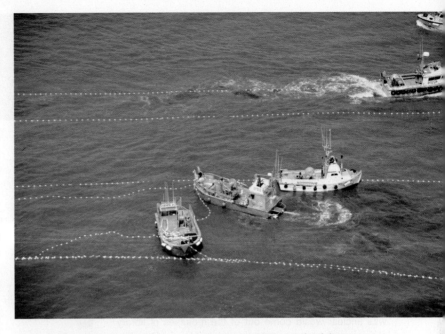

Classic tragedy of the commons scene: too many boats chasing too few fish, not because the skippers are greedy, but in the absence of an agreement, none can afford to stop fishing and surrender the harvest to the others. Here, in the mouth of the Egegik River in Bristol Bay, Alaska, the fleet competes for a limited and concentrated salmon fishery and manages to tangle its nets.

them. The House of Representatives strictly rations access to the floor with rules prescribing time limits to debates and germaneness of motions. But enforcement can be costly, since individuals will be tempted to exploit the collective good if they see their neighbors and colleagues flaunting the rules.

In many settings, a less costly and more effective alternative solution to conserving the commons involves **privatizing** it—that is, converting it from a collective good to a private good. After a second straight disastrous harvest in 1622, the residents of Plymouth Plantation found themselves as close to starvation as at any time since their arrival on the Mayflower. In desperation, the community's leader, William Bradford, announced an end to communal farming. He divided the acreage into family plots and left each family to provide for itself. This ended the famine. As one historian noted, "[T]he change in attitude was stunning. Families were now willing to work much harder than they had ever worked before."[6] After instituting the reform Bradford observed, "The women now went willingly into the field and took their little ones with them to set corn." Confronted with decreasing stock, modern fishery management has increasingly switched from regulations (i.e., catch quotas) to privatization by granting fishermen exclusive access to parts of the

---

*Blog monitoring site Technorati presently tracks traffic to over 6,700 political blogs posted from U.S. sites.

GOOGLE PROPOSES A LIBRARY IN A CLOUD

politics to policy

In 2004 Google unveiled a grandiose plan to digitize every book and make each of them universally available on the Web. It launched the project by announcing agreements with more than a dozen major research universities throughout the world, allowing Google to copy their collections. In effect, the Google project envisioned the creation of a new "commons"–the ability to search every book online and, depending on the copyright, read select passages or the entire book. The benefit to users was obvious. Books long out of print, many out of copyright, and many others "orphans" in that their copyright holder was unclear would come out of the recesses of library storage and become instantly accessible via Google's search engine. Although the concept won widespread support, the project ran into opposition on two fronts. First, other companies–such as Amazon–had their own designs on creating downloadable libraries. Google's plan would give it a huge advantage over others in providing print on demand and other services. Moreover, everyone going to this new "commons" would pass through Google's site, which is loaded with advertising banners.

The second group of critics consisted of authors and publishers. Google anticipated complaints from these producers, and it assured everyone their copyrights were safe. The public could "preview" books by reading a selection of pages, but other pages would be omitted. Those who sued held that Google proposed to offer too much and that, since it had a financial stake in drawing users to its site, it was the inappropriate party to decide what contents of a book would be available. Copyright holders' objections were unabashedly self-interested. After all, those who contribute to the expansion of knowledge should be compensated. Without control over copyright, which the Google plan compromised, authors and publishers would be less likely to undertake books and journals.

Ironically, Google's thoroughly twenty-first-century concept of a "cloud" library conjures up the same issues that afflicted publishing at its founding. It is a history that offers a moral that is arguably more relevant today than at any time during the intervening four centuries. Shortly after the invention and manufacture of the printing press in the early seventeenth century, a class of freelance printers, or publishers, sprang up throughout England. The number of books published exploded. But within a few years authors and publishers experienced a crisis that threatened the future of the industry. Some wily publishers would only "publish" books that already had a market–the same strategy pursued by those who make knockoffs of Coach handbags today. They would reprint a text and, to gain a market edge, attribute authorship to someone famous. Authors and publishers had no legal recourse because the "copyright" had not yet been invented. Their books entered the public domain freely available for anyone to copy. Given the prospect that even a highly successful book would offer publishers little return on their investment, these early printer-publishers petitioned the government for protection. In 1709 the British Parliament decided to privatize this commons in passing the first copyright law, with its title appropriately beginning with "An Act for the Encouragement of Learning." This history raises the following question for the Google project: would reverting to a commons ruin the resource (i.e., knowledge) Google purports to advance?[1]

---

1. In a series of settlements, Google introduced some limitations on access and gave authors a right to remove their books from the proposed digital library. Lawsuits, tentative settlements, and Justice Department antitrust investigations ensued. As of early 2013, Google is continuing its massive undertaking of digitizing books, but what form this commons will take remains unclear.

ocean in the hope that this will motivate them to harvest prudently. Whether regulation or privatization, the solution involves aligning personal gain with promotion of the collective good.

THE COSTS OF COLLECTIVE ACTION

Collective action offers a group benefits its members cannot achieve on their own. But participating in a collective enterprise also entails various costs. The key to successful collective action lies in designing a system that achieves the benefits of a collective effort while minimizing its costs. For example, the Senate, with its 100 members, efficiently accomplishes its business with fewer and less restrictive rules than those required for the much larger, 435-member House of Representatives.

Some of the costs associated with collective enterprises are not hard to spot. An obvious one is each person's monetary contribution to an enterprise—for example, tax payments funding road construction or staffing of a police department. Less obvious are the "overhead" costs of enforcing agreements, such as the ranger's salary in New Guinea or the costs associated with the judicial system and the lawyers needed to ensure that those who enter into business agreements live up to their contracts. Overhead costs also include the government's effort to combat free riding. If people were not inclined to free ride, the federal government could disband the large bureaucracy that goes after tax cheats.

Two kinds of costs that are especially relevant for designing and evaluating institutions are **transaction costs** and **conformity costs**. Though they represent separate aspects of how a community tackles collective enterprises, they often involve a trade-off with one another. In creating institutions to achieve desirable collective goods, a society should collectively weigh the balance between members' private autonomy and the requirements for achieving the collective good.

Transaction Costs

Transaction costs are the time, effort, and resources required to make collective decisions. Consider a student activities committee that selects which band to bring to campus. First, do students want rock, hip-hop, or some other kind of music? Then, what bands are available, how good are they, and what do they charge? Of course, unsatisfactory answers to the second set of questions might return the committee to the first. Once a decision has been made, the bands must be contacted, dates and prices negotiated, and a venue found. The time and effort spent researching available bands, debating preferences, and implementing decisions are all transaction costs of the collective good of campus entertainment.

Transaction costs can pose a formidable barrier to political agreements. These costs rise sharply as the number of participants whose preferences must be taken into account increases. In the absence of institutions for negotiating and implementing collective agreements, these costs might overwhelm the ability of participants to identify and to commit themselves to collective enterprises. With well-designed institutions, however, agreements become easier to make. In the above example the student body greatly reduced its transaction costs by authorizing a committee to make a collective choice for it. Other approaches to mitigating transaction costs involve streamlining rules and procedures. Before the Sixteenth Amendment creating a federal income tax was ratified in 1913, the government did not have a systematic method of taxing citizens. Without it, the nation would have inadequate revenue to finance the many federal programs to which Americans have become accustomed in the last half-century. Though enactment of the income tax undoubtedly required massive transaction costs, once legislators had established a dependable flow of revenue, they could finance new programs by doing little more than tinkering with the tax code. Raising taxes is still not easy, but it is far easier to adjust the tax code up or down than it was to raise revenue before there was a Sixteenth Amendment. Evidence of this can be found in Figure 1-2. Over time, the income tax represents an ever-larger share of government receipts. Reducing the transaction cost of raising federal revenue fueled the dramatic growth in federal policy and programs during the twentieth century.

Figure 1-2 A Ready Source of Government Revenue: The Income Tax

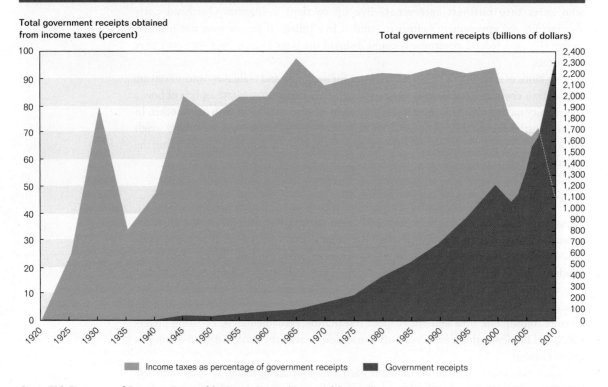

Sources: U.S. Department of Commerce, Bureau of the Census, *Historical Statistics of the United States, Colonial Times to 1970* (White Plains, N.Y.: Kraus International Publications, 1989), Tables Y343–351, Y358–373. Additional data provided by U.S. Department of the Treasury, Bureau of Statistics, *Statistical Abstract of the United States* (Washington, D.C.: Government Printing Office, various years), Tables 358–361.

Note: Total government receipts do not include employment taxes, such as Social Security and Medicare.

SOUTHERN CHIVALRY — ARGUMENT VERSUS CLUB'S.

In 1856, several days after learning of Senator Charles Sumner's fiery speech against admission of Kansas to the Unions as a slave state, South Carolina's Preston Brooks, a member of the House of Representatives, entered the chamber and beat Sumner unconscious. Everyone shocked, no one intervened. Sumner eventually recuperated and returned to the Senate for another eighteen years.

Sometimes, though, high transaction costs are intentionally put in place to make some collective activities more, not less, difficult. Having fashioned a delicately balanced plan of government, the Framers were understandably uninterested in making it easy for some group down the road to rewrite the Constitution. Indeed, the prospect that their labors might soon be undone could have prevented them from reaching agreement in the first place. The Framers ratcheted up the transaction costs of future constitutional change. A proposed amendment to the Constitution must be endorsed by two-thirds of the membership of both houses of Congress and ratified by three-fourths of the states.[*]

Conformity Costs

In negotiating a common course of action, parties advocating competing interests rarely discover that they want precisely the same thing. Politics invariably means compromise. Most of the time there are losers—parties whose preferences receive little accommodation but who must still contribute to a collective undertaking. To the extent collective decisions

---

[*] Alternatively, two-thirds of the state legislatures can ask Congress to call a national convention to propose amendments, but this has never been done.

obligate participants to do something they prefer not to—and all resolutions of the prisoner's dilemma involve this—we refer to this necessity as a *conformity cost.* Conformity costs range from an ordinary task such as paying property taxes to extraordinary sacrifices such as serving in Iraq away from home and family. Rules that require fishermen to stay at the dock during a portion of the fishing season, rules that make a citizen spend part of her income to fund government programs that she opposes, and rules that limit the time allotted a member of Congress for a floor speech all impose conformity costs on individuals in order to achieve a collective goal. Not surprisingly, members of a community prefer minimum conformity costs. But since collective goals never come effortlessly, elected representatives must continually weigh what kinds of and how much costs its citizens are prepared to bear for a particular good. Failure to do so, as Democrats discovered in the 2010 congressional elections shortly after passage of comprehensive health care policy, could find them ushered out of office.

In that transaction and conformity costs generally entail a trade-off, such calculations tend to be complicated: those institutions that minimize transaction costs, making it easy for government to act, may do so by imposing excessive conformity costs. An extreme case would be a dictator, who arbitrarily decides national policies (minimal transaction costs) by insisting that everyone do what he, not they, prefer (maximum conformity costs). At the opposite end of the continuum would be government by consensus. The group does nothing unless everyone agrees to it. Of course, governments based on consensus often have a difficult time undertaking any collective enterprise, although they expend great effort (exorbitant transaction costs) discovering this.

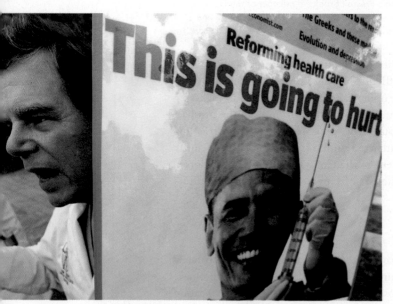

Of the various provisions of the recent health care reform law to which critics have raised objections, the most controversial has been related to imposing conformity costs. Perhaps the most controversial of these provisions is the requirement that everyone purchase health insurance or pay a penalty on their income taxes.

These extreme mixes of transaction and conformity costs might seem far-fetched when referring to national governments, but for many of the Constitution's Framers this was precisely the issue that brought them to Philadelphia. Chapter 2 examines America's unhappy, precarious experience with government by consensus in the decade following independence. The Articles of Confederation, the nation's first constitution, allowed any state to block national action on important policies such as taxes. Moreover, the absence of enforcement authority fostered rampant free riding even when the states could agree on a course of action. Consequently, even in a country with only thirteen participating states—each with one vote in the Confederation Congress—the transaction costs of consensus government proved impossibly difficult and prompted all but one state, Rhode Island, to send delegates to a constitutional convention to create a more viable arrangement.

More commonly, governmental reform occurs within a narrow range of trade-offs between transaction and conformity costs. Rules, procedures, and resources are frequently changed to reduce transaction costs and make government more efficient and decisive. But sometimes the opposite scheme is adopted to prevent abuses. After the civil rights movement and the Vietnam War era, scandals uncovered widespread abuses by the FBI and CIA in spying on civil rights activists (including Martin Luther King) and antiwar leaders. Congress enacted procedures requiring judicial approval before these investigative agencies could undertake wiretaps and other forms of intrusive surveillance of citizens. Such reforms to prevent abuses were adopted with little opposition in Washington and represent a classic instance of increasing transaction costs as a way to hamstring action—in this instance, action taken against those who opposed current government policies. Over the objections of law enforcement officials, the government decided to preserve individuals' freedom of dissent (reduce conformity costs) by jacking up transaction costs on law enforcement officials. After September 11, 2001, the balance shifted back to reducing the transaction costs involved in going after potential terrorists (via the USA PATRIOT Act), and conformity costs increased.

DESIGNING INSTITUTIONS FOR COLLECTIVE ACTION: THE FRAMERS' TOOL KIT

What constitutional arrangements best solve the problems and costs associated with collective action? It depends on what is being decided. If citizens fear that government might intrude too far into their private lives, they might want to add high transaction costs and require consensus to make collective decisions. This perhaps explains why those leaders who feared a shift in power from the states to the new national government clamored for a Bill of Rights to limit the ability of national majorities to demand religious and political conformity. (Their concerns resonated with the broader population and led to the quick adoption of the Bill of Rights as the first amendments to the new Constitution.) If, by contrast, citizens greatly value quick and decisive action, as in defense against an imminent foreign threat, they may favor institutions that minimize transaction costs even at the risk of ceding more authority to leaders than they would normally deem prudent. Clearly, the delegates to the Constitutional Convention—many of them recent veterans with still-fresh memories of the frustrating and nearly failed revolution—harbored both concerns and many variations in between.

In devising the several branches of the national government and its relations with the states, the Framers relied on design principles that instituted varying trade-offs between transaction and conformity costs to fit the purposes of the institutions they were creating. And they sought balance—keeping the branches in "their proper orbits"—so that none would gradually gain a permanent advantage over the others.

By intent, the Constitution provides only a general framework for government. As its institutions have evolved over the past two centuries, the Framers' design principles have shaped their subsequent development. Consequently, the principles, summarized in

TABLE 1-1

The Framers' Tool Kit

Design Principle	Defining Feature	Example
Command	Authority to dictate others' actions	President's commander-in-chief authority
Veto	Authority to block a proposal or stop an action	President's veto; Senate confirmation of the president's appointments; judicial review
Agenda control	Authority to place proposals before others for their decision, as well as preventing proposals from being considered	Congress presenting enrolled bill to president; congressional committees' recommendations to the full chamber
Voting rules	Rules prescribing who votes and the minimum number of votes required to accept a proposal or elect a candidate	Supreme Court decisions; Electoral College; selection of the Speaker of House of Representatives
Delegation	Authority to assign an agent responsibility to act in your behalf	Representation, bureaucracy

Table 1-1, are just as useful for dissecting the internal organization of the modern House of Representatives as they are for studying the Framers' plan. The Framers' tool kit presented below will inform our analyses throughout the text—especially those chapters that delve into the logic of the governmental system.*

Command

This refers to the authority of one actor to dictate the actions of another. Unlike the other design concepts, **command** authority gives its holder comprehensive control of those within the scope of its authority. Command cuts through both coordination and prisoner's dilemma problems by conferring the authority to impose a solution regardless of the preferences of others—a solution that invariably favors the authority's preferences over the preferences of those who must comply with the authority's edicts. So, while command certainly achieves efficiencies in reducing transaction costs, it does so by imposing potentially huge conformity costs on the community. For decades, Cuba's Fidel Castro banned whole genres of music from the radio. For Hobbes (see box "Hobbes on

---

*We do not present this list of design principles as exhaustive. One can think of other principles—such as the principles in the Bill of Rights prohibiting certain classes of government actions—but we do find that the tool kit's principles are indispensable for understanding how America's political institutions work the way they do.

Monarchs," page 16), monarchical command prevented society from deteriorating into anarchy.*

The Framers, and republican theorists before them, sought other institutional arrangements that would enable efficiency, yet minimize the conformity costs imposed by command. Consequently, "command" was rarely used in designing the Constitution. The only provision (Section 2, Article II) that comes close makes the president "the commander in chief of the army and navy." The military, then and now, is the one component of government designed to place a premium on conformity. Any squad member under enemy fire can appreciate the value of not having others in the unit calculating whether to cover for their buddies or to engage in free riding. Soldiers undergo intensive training to instill reflexive obedience to superiors' orders, subordinating their own well-being to that of their unit. Each soldier's place within the hierarchy, or "command structure," is explicitly identified by his or her rank.

The work of government fundamentally differs from that of a squad in battle. The president may be the supreme commander, but the Framers made sure any pretense of command authority ends there. Vivid evidence of their success appears in outgoing president Harry Truman's prediction about his successor, army general Dwight Eisenhower: "He'll sit here, and he'll say, 'Do this! Do that!' And nothing will happen. Poor Ike— it won't be a bit like the Army. He'll find it very frustrating."[†]

BORN TO COMMAND.

OF VETO MEMORY.

HAD I BEEN CONSULTED.

KING ANDREW THE FIRST.

Widely published in opposition Whig newspapers, this cartoon depicts President Andrew Jackson trampling on the Constitution and public works legislation. However imperiously Jackson dealt with the opposition-controlled Congress and the Supreme Court, whose decisions he selectively ignored, the veto in his left hand hardly sufficed to allow him "to rule" the country.

Veto

The **veto** embodies the right of an official or institution to say "no" to a proposal from another official or institution. Like command, the veto is unilateral, allowing its possessors to impose their views regardless of the preferences of others. Yet it is far less potent than command because of one critical difference: it is a "negative" or blocking action that

---

*Moreover, Hobbes argued that in monarchies, the inherited right to rule was not just necessary but also salutary; monarchs had a long-term stake in their subjects' prosperity in order to maximize their own power and prosperity.

[†]According to most contemporary observers, Eisenhower's experiences in office bore out Truman's prediction. According to one description of Ike's sixth year in office, "The President still feels that when he has decided something, that *ought* to be the end of it . . . and when it bounces back undone or done wrong, he tends to react with shocked surprise." Richard E. Neustadt, *Presidential Power and the Modern Presidents* (New York: John Wiley and Sons, 1960), 10.

preserves the status quo.[*] The veto confers little direct advantage in shifting government policy, but in Chapter 7 we find that a president's threat to use it may induce Congress to address the president's objections as it prepares legislation. Moreover, the blocking effects of the veto can be limited by providing those subject to a veto the means of circumventing it. After weighing the pros and cons of giving the president an absolute veto, the Framers backed off and added an override provision. With a two-thirds vote in each chamber, the House of Representatives and Senate can enact a vetoed bill without the president's endorsement. A policy that withstands the huge transaction costs entailed in mustering supermajorities in both chambers has demonstrated its merits and deserves enactment despite the president.[†]

The president's veto is the only explicit use of this instrument in the Constitution, but the Constitution implicitly creates other important veto relationships. Both the House of Representatives and the Senate must agree to identical legislation before it can proceed to the president's desk for his signature (or veto). In effect, then, each legislative chamber holds a veto over the legislation emanating from the other chamber. Yet another unnamed veto resides with the Supreme Court. Shortly after the new government was launched, the Supreme Court claimed the power of *judicial review,* asserting its authority to overturn public laws and executive actions it deemed unconstitutional. (We will discuss fully this important "discovered" authority in Chapters 2, 5, and 9.)

The greater the number of veto holders, the higher the transaction costs in making new policy. Consequently, with its numerous veto holders, the American political system deserves its reputation as being inherently conservative.

Agenda Control

This refers to the right of an actor to set choices for others. The choices might concern legislation, proposed regulations, or any other decision presented to a collectivity. Political parties nominate candidates who define the choices available to voters on Election Day. Those who exercise **agenda control** gain both positive and negative influence over collective decisions. On the positive side an agenda setter can introduce a choice to the collectivity—a senator proposing an amendment to a bill under consideration, for example—which then decides to accept or reject it. Where everyone enjoys this right—when, say, any fellow senator can offer an amendment to any colleague's proposal—access to the agenda will be of little consequence in explaining collective decisions. Agenda control becomes consequential in settings where some members of the group exercise proposal power and others do not. The Constitution requires, for example, that tax bills originate in the House of Representatives, and so the House sets the Senate's agenda on this important topic.

Consider the advantage this right confers. The agenda setter can propose a course of action, while the others are limited to deciding between the proposal or the status quo

---

[*] In fact, many of the Constitution's Framers referred to the veto as a "negative."

[†] All state governors possess some form of veto over legislation; many of these vetoes differ significantly from the president's in allowing the governor to veto parts of bills and flexibility in appropriating expenditures less than those prescribed in the legislation.

(no action). The agenda controller thus *limits* the choices available to the collectivity. Unlike the Senate, where proposal rights are universal, the House has long been governed by rules that empower leaders to set the choices members will vote on. Leaders determine what, if any, amendments will be allowed, and limit the time available for debating alternatives. This procedural authority can have huge consequences. In fact, it probably led to that chamber's impeachment of President Bill Clinton in 1998. In late fall 1998 the Republican-controlled Judiciary Committee sent to the floor articles of impeachment against President Clinton. Republican floor leaders faced a potential problem. They favored impeaching the president as well, but they were fairly certain that a majority of members did not favor this drastic course. Republicans held only a nine-vote majority overall. Moreover, with Democrats appearing unified in opposing impeachment, four to six Republicans informed their leaders that they preferred a softer punishment—specifically, a resolution censuring President Clinton—to impeachment. Yet the Republican leadership's agenda control held a trump card that guaranteed their ultimate success. With the authority to decide which proposals would be available for the members to vote on, the leadership disallowed censure motions and forced Republican fence-sitters to decide between impeachment and no action. In the end the fence-sitters joined their colleagues, and on a nearly perfect party line vote, the House of Representatives impeached the president, even though a majority of the membership preferred censure.[7]

House members confer so much power on their leaders and knowingly bear heavy conformity costs because in the absence of agenda control the transaction costs would be unmanageable. Without leaders orchestrating the chamber's decisions, the institution would be at the mercy of its 435 members—each, like their colleagues in the smaller Senate, jealously protecting and exercising their right to offer any bill or amendment at any time. After members of a reform group in New York branded the majority leader of that state's senate as an autocrat for not letting their favored proposals come to the floor, he responded, "[P]ure nonsense. . . . Talk to the C.E.O. of any company. If you want to act on something, and the company has 212 employees, what are you going to do, have a discussion and let 212 employees do whatever the agenda is? Is that what you do? So you have 212 different agendas. And that is just chaotic, doesn't work. That is Third-World-country stuff."[8]

"It's either this or a country run by lawyers."

Not just another lawyer joke. . . . Clearly the guards prefer the high conformity costs imposed by this hapless leviathan to the transaction costs of more democratic institutions.

© *The New Yorker* Collection 1997; Frank Cotham from cartoonbank.com. All Rights Reserved.

Voting Rules

Any government that aspires to democracy must allow for diverse interests to be expressed in government policy. When members of a collectivity share decision-making authority, the outcomes are determined by some previously agreed-to voting rule. The most prominent option in classical democratic theory is **majority rule**. Normally this term refers to a **simple majority**, or one-half plus one.

Majority rule embodies the hallowed democratic principle of political equality. Equality requires that each citizen's vote carries the same weight and offers all citizens the same opportunity to participate in the nation's civic life. When all votes count the same, majority rule becomes an obvious principle: when disagreements arise, the more widely shared preference should prevail.

Yet majority rule offers no magic balance between transaction and conformity costs. It is just one possible constitutional rule midway between dictatorship and consensus. Governments controlled by popular majorities are less likely to engage in **tyranny**—that is, impose very high conformity costs—than are dictatorships, but this knowledge did not fully reassure the Constitution's Framers. Worried about tyranny by the majority, they carefully constructed institutions that would temper transient passions of majorities in the new government. Separation of powers with checks and balances—two concepts we will examine in detail in the next chapter; different term lengths for members of the House and Senate, the president, and federal judges; and explicit provision for states' rights all make it difficult for majorities to take charge of the new government.

Although majority rule figures prominently in the Constitution, it is explicitly required in only a few instances. A majority of the Electoral College is required to elect the president, although the winner may not necessarily receive a majority of the popular vote, as we saw in the contested presidential election of 2000 when Democratic candidate Al Gore received a half-million more votes than George W. Bush but lost the election.[9] And a quorum, a majority of the membership of the House of Representatives, must be present before the House can conduct business. Much of what the government does requires action by Congress, which, the Framers seemed to assume, would conduct its business by majority vote.

Yet the Constitution permits or tacitly authorizes other voting rules. The Constitution leaves it to the states to specify rules electing members of Congress, and states almost always have preferred the **plurality** rule (the candidate receiving the most votes, regardless of whether the plurality reaches a majority) in deciding winners. Elsewhere in the Constitution **supermajorities** of various amounts are required. If the president vetoes a bill passed by both houses of Congress, two-thirds of the House and of the Senate must vote to override the veto, or the bill is defeated. And in another example of steep transaction costs, three-quarters of the states must agree to any amendments to the Constitution.

Delegation

When individuals or groups authorize someone to make and implement decisions for them, **delegation** occurs. Every time Americans go to the polls, they *delegate* to representatives the responsibility for making collective decisions for them. Similarly, members of the

House of Representatives elect leaders empowered to orchestrate their chamber's business, thereby reducing coordination and other costs of collective action. The House also delegates the task of drafting legislation to standing committees, which are more manageable subsets of members. As in this instance, decisions are frequently delegated in order to control their transaction costs.

Social scientists who analyze delegation note that **principals**, those who possess decision-making authority, may delegate their authority to **agents**, who then exercise it on behalf of the principals. Every spring millions of Americans hire an agent—say, H&R Block—to fill out their tax forms for them and, they hope, save them some money. Similarly, the president (principal) appoints hundreds of staff members (agents) to monitor and promote the administration's interests within the bureaucracy and on Capitol Hill. We will use these terms to identify and illuminate a variety of important political relationships that involve some form of delegation.

Delegation is so pervasive because it addresses common collective action problems. It is indispensable whenever special expertise is required to make and carry out sound decisions. The vast and complex federal bureaucracy requires a full chapter (Chapter 8) to describe and explain—because Congress has pursued so many diverse public policies and delegated their implementation to agencies. A legislature could not possibly administer its policies directly without tying itself in knots. In the next chapter, we will examine the Continental Congress's failed attempts to directly supply Washington's army during the Revolutionary War. The predictable failure resulted in the chronically inadequate provision of essential supplies to the troops. The lesson was not lost on the participants, many of whom served as delegates to the Constitutional Convention in Philadelphia two decades later.

Beyond the need for technical expertise, majorities may sometimes find it desirable politically to delegate decisions. For example, the government allocates space on the frequency band to prevent radio or television stations from interfering with each other's signals. In 1934 Congress stopped allocating frequencies itself, leaving decisions instead to the five members of the Federal Communications Commission. Congress had learned early that assigning frequencies was difficult and politically unrewarding, as its decisions were regularly greeted with charges of favoritism or worse. Congress therefore delegated such decisions to a body of experts while retaining the authority to pass new laws that could override the commission's decisions. Thus Congress retains the ultimate authority to set the nation's technical broadcasting policies when it chooses to exercise it.

Voting Rules of the U.S. Senate*

Motion	Voting Rule
Passage of ordinary bills and amendments	Simple majority of members present and voting
Rule 22 (cloture to set time limit on debate)	Three-fifths of the full Senate (normally sixty votes)
Veto override	Two-thirds of members present and voting
Unanimous consent to take up legislation out of turn	Unanimous agreement of members present

* We will explain these rules fully in Chapter 5.

Finally, almost all enforcement authority—the key to solving prisoner's dilemmas of all types—involves delegation to a policing agent. It might be the IRS, the Securities and Exchange Commission, the Equal Employment Opportunity Commission, or any of the hundreds of other federal, state, and local agencies that make sure that individuals abide by their collective agreements.

Delegation solves some problems for a collectivity, but it introduces others. A principal runs the risk that its agents will use their authority to serve their own rather than the principal's interest. The discrepancy between what a principal would ideally like its agents to do and what they actually do is called **agency loss**. Agency losses might arise "accidentally" by incompetence or the principal's failure to communicate goals clearly. Or losses might reflect the inherent differences between the goals of a principal and its agents. A principal wants its agents to be exceedingly diligent in protecting its interests while asking for very little in return. Agents, on the other hand, prefer to be generously compensated for minimal effort. The balance in most principal-agent relationships lies on a continuum between these extremes. Mild examples of agency loss include various forms of shirking, or "slacking off." Our agents in the legislature might attend to their own business rather than to the public's, nod off in committee meetings, or accept Super Bowl tickets or golf vacations from someone who wants a special favor. Citizens warily appreciate the opportunities available to their agents in Washington to "feather their own nest." So voters are quick to respond to information, typically from opponents who covet the job, suggesting that the incumbent is not serving constituents well. Members of Congress who miss more than a few roll-call votes usually do so at their peril.

So how can a principal determine whether its agents are being faithful when it cannot observe or understand their actions? Car owners face a similar problem when an auto mechanic says the strange engine noise will require replacement of an obscure part costing a month's pay. How do owners know whether to trust the mechanic, especially since they know the mechanic's financial interest clashes with theirs? They could get a second opinion, investigate the mechanic's reputation, or learn more about cars and check for themselves, but all these solutions take time and energy. Governments employ all of these techniques and others to minimize agency loss. Whistle-blower laws generously reward members of the bureaucracy who report instances of malfeasance. Or governments can create an agent who monitors the performance of other agents. Congress has created about eighty inspector general offices within the federal bureaucracy to check and report to the president and Congress on agency failures to perform assigned duties faithfully and honestly. Delegation always entails a trade-off between the benefits of having the agent attend to decisions on the principal's behalf and the costs associated with agency loss and the effort required to monitor the agent's behavior.

A virulent form of agency loss occurs when the agent turns its delegated authority against the principal. This possible scenario arises when principals provide agents with the coercive authority to ward off external threats or to discourage free riding. What prevents these agents—the police, the army, the IRS, the FBI, and many others—from exploiting their advantage not only to enrich but also to entrench themselves by preventing challenges to their authority? Certainly many have. World history—indeed, current affairs—is rife with news of military takeovers, secret police, rigged elections, imprisoned opponents, ethnic cleansing, and national treasuries drained into Swiss bank accounts. Institutions created to minimize transaction costs may, as the trade-off indicates, impose unacceptably high conformity costs.

This risk raises another fundamental question: How much authority can citizens safely surrender in achieving their collective goals? When does delegation become abdication and invite tyranny? As we'll see in Chapter 2, the Constitution's Framers struggled mightily with this conundrum. James Madison regarded this question as critical. "In framing a government," he wrote, "the great difficulty lies in this: you must first enable the government to control the governed; and in the next place oblige it to control itself."[10] How to design government to manage this "great difficulty" preoccupied the Framers of the Constitution, as it did the political philosophers who influenced them.

REPRESENTATIVE GOVERNMENT

Modern democracies blend delegation with majority rule into what is known as **representative government**. Citizens limit their decisions to the selection of government officials who, acting as their agents, deliberate and commit the citizenry to collective enterprises. This form of democracy eliminates the massive confusion that would ensue if large communities tried to craft policies directly, and it frees most citizens from having to attend constantly to civic business. For a large group or society,

"Pigs get fat . . . Hogs get slaughtered!!!!" So wrote Angela Spaccia (salary: $850,000), assistant city manager of Bell, California, to the incoming police chief (salary: $770,000, half of it tax free). To the left of Spaccia in the photo is city manager Robert Rizzo, who awarded himself $1.5 million annually. Rounding out the gallery of indicted city officials are a former city councilman and mayor. Four other city officials also face charges of misappropriating funds and concealing it from the town's citizens.

representative government, through delegation, makes large-scale democracy possible. **Direct democracy**, in which citizens participate directly in collective decision making, is reserved primarily for small communities and organizations.*

---

*Another approach to direct democracy that is adapted to a large electorate is the **referendum**. Nearly half the states allow the legislature to propose a change to the state's laws or constitution, which all the voters subsequently vote on. An alternative and even purer form of direct democracy is the **initiative**, which places a proposal on the ballot when the requisite number of registered voters have signed petitions to place the issue on an election ballot.

Majority Rule versus the Republic

At the time of the adoption of the U.S. Constitution, the idea of majority rule was controversial. The ancient city-state of Athens, one of the few experiments with democracy known at the time, had ended ignominiously in mob rule and ultimately dictatorship. The eighteenth-century political theorists who influenced the Constitution's Framers endorsed a form of government called a **republic**, designed to allow some degree of popular control and also avoid tyranny.[11] The Framers designed the new Constitution to pose formidable transaction costs on collective action. The Framers especially favored some form of veto or "check" of one institution over another. In a republic, voters elect their representatives, but these representatives are constrained in following the majority's dictates by constitutional guarantees for minorities and by institutions and rules requiring exceptionally large majorities for certain decisions.

The notion of an independent, unelected judiciary also challenges the paramount democratic principle of majority rule, but presents no problem for the republican creed. By ratifying the Constitution and retaining the power to amend it, the people may choose to set up an institution independent of the others and unconcerned with short-term swings in public opinion to referee the political process and preserve the values on which the government is founded. In short, republican theorists, who had the allegiance of virtually everyone who attended the Constitutional Convention in 1787, *really* believed in the role of institutions in reaching and preserving agreements. And by making some collective decisions more difficult than others, the Framers consciously built in higher transaction costs, even if they did not use those terms.

Since the American experiment was launched over two hundred years ago, experience with majority rule throughout the world has proved it to be a viable approach to self-governance. Although constitutions written in the twentieth century—such as those in France and Germany—may still divide authority in ways that allow their countries to be referred to as republics, they have dispensed with the elaborate rules and institutions designed to constrain majority rule by ratcheting up transaction costs. Rather than separating the executive from the legislature, most of the world's modern democracies have fused them in **parliamentary government**. Many varieties of parliamentary government exist, but they all lodge decisive authority in a popularly elected legislature, whose actions are not subject to the same severe checks by executive and judicial vetoes. The legislature in turn elects a team of executives called a **cabinet**, one of whose members serves as the premier or prime minister (see Figure 1-3). This system promotes majority rule in the sense that the political party or coalition of parties that controls the legislature controls the executive. In effect parliamentary systems are able to forgo the higher transaction costs embedded in the U.S. Constitution's **separation of powers**. At the same time, as the majority gains the capacity to act on its preferences, those who disagree are obliged to accept the majority's preferences.

Politicians

Another innovation of representative government is elected **politicians**. These professionals specialize in discovering collective enterprises that unite citizens with different values and interests. These elected agents are sometimes called "public servants"—a euphemism they prefer because the self-effacing image tends to allay the public's fears of agency loss.

A much more apt term for a politician, however, is *entrepreneur*. Like entrepreneurs, politicians are deal makers, but instead of putting together financial partnerships and other ventures, they assemble coalitions. A **coalition** is a combination of *unlike*-minded interests who nonetheless agree, for their own distinct reasons, to a common course of action. To win elections, politicians must succeed at building coalitions. Successful candidates persuade a plurality of voters to support them (a common action) by offering different constituencies their own reasons for doing so. For many Americans, the "ideal" politician is a dutiful, selfless public servant who abjures personal or political advantage in pursuit of the public good. But most citizens probably would not be satisfied with such a politician's performance. Where numerous competing interests are well represented and governing power is widely shared, the public is better served with politicians who are more dedicated to solving problems that satisfy the interests of their constituents than to pursuing their personal vision of the good society.

Figure 1-3   Comparing the American and British Constitutional Systems

Throughout the book we will refer to the behavior of politicians as *strategic* when they subordinate their *sincere* preferences to what is best for their constituents in order to achieve results that stand a better chance of success. Every time a politician compromises, defers to a colleague, or decides not to resist certain defeat on an issue, she, knowingly or unknowingly, is behaving strategically. In distributing authority across institutions and by incorporating numerous preferences, the American political system essentially demands that its politicians behave strategically.

Citizens want their politicians to act as faithful agents—diligent custodians of their interests—and yet they fear that, once elected to office, politicians will pursue their own interests and neglect the concerns of the people who put them there. Such fears in the 1990s spawned a movement to limit the number of terms representatives can serve in Congress and in state legislatures. But a politician's responsiveness is linked to the desire to get reelected or to create a firm base for advancing to higher elective office. Thus the term-limit "solution" eliminates the one real device that democracy provides citizens for keeping their agents responsive.

THE WORK OF GOVERNMENT

Given the variety of costs and risks associated with collective action, Americans weigh such undertakings carefully. Among other things, they calculate whether the prospective gains from a collective public effort are sufficiently greater than what they could achieve privately. The vast majority of these calculations favor private action, perhaps explaining why much of what Americans do and consume as individuals has little or nothing to do with government. Their homes, cars, clothes, food, and sources of entertainment fall into a realm called **private goods**—that is, things people buy and consume themselves in a marketplace that supplies these goods according to the demand for them.

What we will discuss in this book is the provision of **public goods**, which everyone participates in supplying—say, through tax dollars—and which anyone can freely consume, as much as he or she desires. Stated another way, the two distinguishing features of all public goods are that their costs are borne collectively and that no one can be excluded from their benefits. An example of a public good is a freeway, which, as its name implies, may be used by anyone. A toll road is a private good because its costs are met by the motorists who pay a fee (toll) for its use. A quintessential public good is national defense. However, in the early 1950s, at the beginning of the Cold War, some fearful homeowners took a "private goods approach" and installed backyard bomb shelters in the event of nuclear attack. They were eventually abandoned as just about everyone accepted the logic of relying on national defense—a public good—to protect them from nuclear assault.

Citizens frequently look to government to provide positive public goods: national defense, public order, a legal system, civil liberties, and public parks. They also count on government to prevent or correct negative public goods such as laws controlling pollution, protecting endangered species, and establishing residential, commercial, and industrial zones. For these tasks, the government enjoys two important advantages: it has sufficient resources to undertake expensive projects, and it has coercive authority to prevent free riding. Many public goods simply could not be produced any other way. Some are too risky financially to attract private investment. What business could afford to build a multibillion-dollar supercollider to research nuclear fusion and, at the project's inception, expect to recover its costs within a period reasonable to shareholders? Other goods offer better value when converted from a private to a public good. The history of fire protection in America is one example (see box "Fire Protection: From a Private to a Public Good").

Another large class of goods and services has a "public good" aspect that justifies the collective provision of essentially private benefits. Earlier we examined a class of mixed policies where government privatizes the "commons" in order to conserve it. Federal and state tax codes are complicated because many of their provisions are intended not to raise revenue, but to motivate the public to contribute to some collective policy goal. Tax deductions or credits for charitable contributions, for contributions to personal retirement accounts, for installing solar heating, for restoring historic homes, and for investing in new equipment are just a few of a long list of federal incentives promoting some collective good.

In reality, most of the goods and services that governments provide cannot be easily sorted into either the private or the public bin. Public education is a classic example. A well-educated citizenry undeniably strengthens the civic and economic life of a society, but public education also bestows substantial *private* benefits on students and educators. The immediate beneficiary of a flu vaccination is the person who received it. But so too is everyone with whom he or she comes into contact, even if only by pushing the same elevator button.

FIRE PROTECTION
From a Private to a Public Good

politics to policy

The history of fire protection in America offers a classic example of the evolution of private goods to a government responsibility. During the nation's colonial era, fire protection assumed the form of an insurance policy. Homeowners subscribed to a local protection service, mounted its identifying shield on the front of the house, and hoped that if they had a fire it would show up.

In many small communities voluntary fire departments formed to turn fire protection into a public good. The coordination problems were resolved, and the service's responsiveness limited the spread of fires across structures. This arrangement worked reasonably well in towns and villages where everyone knew everyone

else. Any "volunteer" who chronically slept through the fire bell might well have found his neighbors doing the same when the bell sounded for his house.

As communities grew and social controls on free riding weakened, voluntary fire protection gave way to government-run, professional fire protection. Typically, governments created a special fire district with taxing authority and hired professional firefighters to supply this public good.

Because the work of modern governments typically belongs in this class of *mixed* goods, public policy is frequently referred to as dealing in **collective goods**. Throughout our discussion we will employ this less restrictive term that includes both true *public goods* and mixed policies that also confer private benefits (see Figure 1-4).

MITIGATING "POPULAR PASSIONS"

The Constitution's Framers, who assembled in Philadelphia during the summer of 1787, did not employ the modern vocabulary of collective action problems, such as prisoner's dilemma or tragedy of the commons. Nor did they formally label and classify their institutional design mechanisms. Yet they were intimately preoccupied with the collective action issues that afflicted society and overwhelmed the capacity of the nation under the Articles of Confederation to solve them. Perhaps most impressive about their deliberations is that, however much they disagreed on the design of the new government, they all understood that the nation's previous failures stemmed from politics and political institutions. Citizens and state governments engaged in rampant free riding, and politicians failed to honor commitments because the institutions made reneging easy and cooperation risky. Americans were trapped in the same fundamental

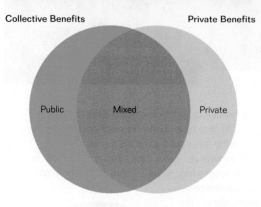

Figure 1-4 Several Types of Goods

Collective Benefits   Private Benefits

Public   Mixed   Private

prisoner's dilemma that ensnared Victor Mature and Betty Grable. The Framers reformed, knowing that the survival of the republic was at stake.[*]

To solve the nation's pervasive collective action problems, the Framers designed a new government that, by modern standards, minimized conformity costs. Some delegates worried that the states were being reduced to minor administrative districts. Others, including James Madison, were far more concerned that self-interested majorities might tyrannize minorities and exploit the public good. The solution to both extremes lay in escalating transaction costs so the new government could better address the nation's collective problems but would possess too little authority to allow self-interested politicians or a majority coalition to turn the power of government against the citizenry. Separation of powers, staggered legislative terms, an unelected judiciary, limited national authority, and the other features explored in the chapters that follow all effectively constrain majority rule. The result is a highly complex constitutional system in which politicians must work hard to introduce even minor changes in national policy. The most appropriate place to begin our examination of *modern* American politics and apply the concepts presented here is at the reorganization of the entire government. In Chapter 2 we turn to the founding of the republic.

NOTA BENE

TAKE A QUIZ

logic.cqpress.com
Test your knowledge of this chapter.

This chapter presents two sets of concepts that our discussion will employ throughout the remainder of the book. The first distinguishes the various kinds of collective action problems that invariably arise both within society and within government whenever differently minded individuals attempt to work together. The second identifies simple institutional design principles that appear in all governmental organizations. For those chapters examining the several branches of government and federalism, problems of collective action and institutional design are naturally more prominent than in the political behavior chapters. Yet these issues arise in every chapter, and when they do, we will highlight the text (including the important topics located in the boxes!) to alert you that the concepts introduced here are being put to work.

---

[*] So too did rival nations abroad that tried to pry the nation apart by pitting states against one another in bidding for trade agreements that would weaken and eventually destroy the national union.

Key Terms

agency loss, 32

agenda control, 28

agents, 31

authority, 7

bargaining, 4

cabinet, 34

coalition, 35

collective action, 9

collective goods, 37

command, 26

compromise, 4

conformity costs, 21

constitution, 6

coordination, 9

delegation, 30

direct democracy, 33

focal point, 11

free-rider problem, 17

government, 7

initiative, 33

institutions, 5

majority rule, 30

offices, 7

parliamentary government, 34

plurality, 30

politicians, 34

politics, 3

power, 7

preferences, 4

principals, 31

prisoner's dilemma, 9

private goods, 36

privatizing, 19

public goods, 36

referendum, 33

regulation, 19

representative government, 33

republic, 34

separation of powers, 34

simple majority, 30

supermajorities, 30

tragedy of the commons, 18

transaction costs, 21

tyranny, 30

veto, 27

Suggested Readings

Safire, William. *Safire's New Political Dictionary.* New York: Ballantine Books, 1993. Arguably, Safire understands the American version of English better than any other modern popular writer. Fortunately, the former presidential speechwriter also has an especially keen eye for politics.

Shepsle, Kenneth A., and Mark S. Bonchek. *Analyzing Politics: Rationality, Behavior, and Institutions.* New York: Norton, 1997. This book, aimed at the undergraduate audience, elaborates on many of the rational choice concepts presented in this chapter.

Stanley, Harold W., and Richard G. Niemi. *Vital Statistics on American Politics, 2009–2010.* Washington, DC: CQ Press, 2009. If the text does not satisfy your appetite for tables and figures, this book, filled with well-organized data about American politics, will.

Tocqueville, Alexis de. *Democracy in America.* Many good paperback translations of Tocqueville are available, but beware of abridged versions in which, invariably, the lively asides and incidental observations are lost.

Review Questions

1. Why can't we solve our disputes through simple bargaining all the time? What factors undermine bargaining in different settings? What can people or governments do to help solve disputes despite these factors?

2. What sorts of institutions are commonly used to manage conflicts in societies? What are some examples of where these institutions have failed?

3. Discuss how the coordination and transaction costs for states changed when the national government moved from the Articles of Confederation to the Constitution.

4. What are principals and agents? When in your life have you been one or the other?

5. What are some examples of public and private goods that you have consumed today? How did you acquire them?

2 The Constitution

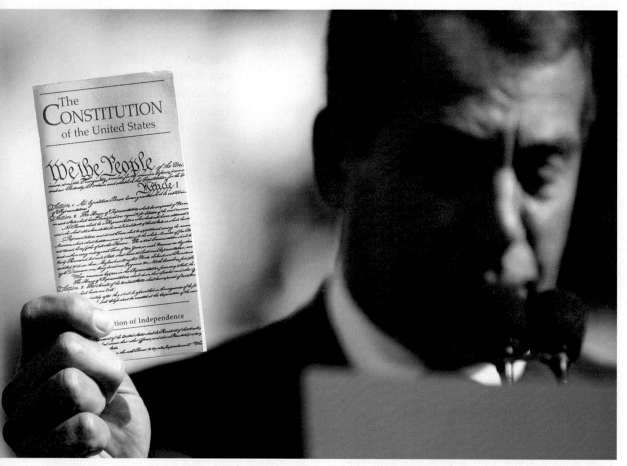

Republican House Speaker John Boehner opens the 112th Congress with a reading of the Constitution—as much in gratitude for the Tea Party movement's impact in the fall's election as an homage to the Constitution.

- The Constitution has not changed much over the past two hundred years. Were the Framers really geniuses, or are Americans simply very lucky?

- Why is America's Constitution so complicated, where even the word *majority* has several different meanings?

- How can the United States call itself a democracy when so many features of its national political system are designed to frustrate majority rule?

The year 1780 was a disastrous one for the American Revolution. Three years into the war the Continental Army, the revolutionary fighting force, teetered on total collapse. In May an entire garrison of five thousand men surrendered to the British at Charleston, South Carolina. In late summer, across the state in Camden, nearly nine hundred Continental soldiers were killed, and one thousand were taken prisoner in a single engagement. When the army regrouped, only seven hundred of the original four thousand men showed up. The fall brought no respite from the army's woes. Indeed, the young nation learned that one of its few illustrious military commanders, General Benedict Arnold, switched sides and became a byword for treason.

By the end of 1780, the American forces, under General George Washington, had shrunk from twenty-six thousand to fifteen thousand. New Year's Day 1781 saw even further deterioration in the campaign—1,300 mutinous Pennsylvania troops, camped in Princeton, New Jersey, demanded Congress give them a year's back pay and an immediate discharge. A congressional committee met the soldiers outside Philadelphia and agreed to some of their demands.

Although all these difficulties appeared to stem from unfit commanders or unwilling troops, the real problem was the fledgling national government, the Continental Congress. It simply was unable to act decisively or rapidly because all matters of consequence (such as taxes) required the approval of all the state governments. And it had virtually no administrative apparatus to implement policy, even those that enjoyed unanimous support. As a result, members of congressional committees sometimes found themselves deadlocked over how many uniforms the army needed. Long into the war the army remained underfed, ill clothed, poorly armed, unpaid (at least in currency of value), and despised by civilians uncompensated for requisitioned supplies. The troops struggled just to survive as a unit. Ultimately, of course, this depleted army had to confront the well-equipped British on the battlefield. During the winter of 1780, General Washington desperately exhorted Congress, "Where are the Men? Where are the provisions? Where are the Cloaths?"

The bitter irony was that many of the desperately needed provisions existed in ample supply. The war was causing shortages, but they were not severe enough to account for the deprivations hampering the army. Nor was the problem the strictly logistical exercise of

Countdown to the Constitution

Date	Event	Colonial Action
1750s	French and Indian War (1754–1763) drains the British treasury	Albany Congress calls for colonial unity (1754)
1760s	Stamp Act enacted by British Parliament (1765)	Stamp Act Congress attended by delegates from nine of the thirteen colonies (1765)
1770s	Tea Act (1773)	Boston Tea Party (1773)
	British adopt Coercive Acts to punish colonies (1774)	First Continental Congress rejects plan of union but adopts Declaration of American Rights denying Parliament's authority over internal colonial affairs (1774)
	Battles of Lexington and Concord (1775)	Second Continental Congress assumes role of revolutionary government (1775); adopts Declaration of Independence (1776)
	Thomas Paine's *Common Sense* (1776) published	Congress adopts Articles of Confederation as constitution for new government (1777)
1780s	British defeat Americans at Camden and Charleston (1780)	
	Hartford Convention (1781)	Articles of Confederation ratified (1781)
	British surrender at Yorktown (1781)	
	Shays's Rebellion (1786)	Constitutional Convention drafts blueprint for new government (1787)
	The Federalist (1787–1788) published	Constitution ratified (1789)

keeping a traveling army supplied. Despite the difficulty of that task, British troops and their German mercenaries were reasonably well provisioned. Undermining the Revolution's cause was an epidemic of free riding by Americans—from political leaders to ordinary soldiers. States agreed to contribute money and supplies but failed to do so in a timely fashion, if at all. Contractors, paid with a currency that was losing about 10 percent of its value every month, sold the American army spoiled food, shoddy clothing, and poorly manufactured arms, and then shortchanged the Continental Army even on those inferior provisions when the suppliers thought they could get away with it. Many recruits enlisted, received their requisitions, and then deserted with their new booty.

Although all of the politicians, merchants, and soldiers involved in the war effort may have been patriots, they were unprepared to shoulder the costs of serving the public good while their neighbors and colleagues conspicuously shirked the same duties. If, as we argued in Chapter 1, the enforcement of contracts and other collective agreements is the fundamental responsibility of government, then we must blame ineffective government for the free riding and other shirking that sap a community's will to achieve its collective goals. General

Washington understood the problem and warned darkly that if the Continental Congress did not soon take charge, "our Independence fails, [our government] will be annihilated, and we must once more return to the Government of Great Britain, and be made to kiss the rod preparing for our correction."[1]

Over the next year Washington continued to endure the government's ineptitude, narrowly avoiding a catastrophic military defeat. Then, with time, the Revolution gained credibility abroad. France, England's archrival, agreed to loan Congress money to continue the war effort and, finally, to commit French naval and land forces to the battlefield. On October 17, 1781, the collaboration paid off with a decisive victory at Yorktown, Virginia, which ended the war.

In what is recognized as America's first political cartoon, Benjamin Franklin depicts the colonies as caught in a classic collective action dilemma. If united, the colonies represent a formidable force for England to reckon with. But if any colony attempts to free ride, the collective effort will survive no better than a dismembered snake.

The year 1783 brought a formal end to the hostilities and independence for the American colonies. But the young nation, still saddled with a government that could not act, was confronted with many of the same problems it had labored under during the revolution. Indeed, many observers feared that independence, won in war, would soon be lost in peace as the nation threatened to unravel into thirteen disputatious nation-states.

In the summer of 1787 fifty-five delegates from all the states except Rhode Island assembled in Philadelphia to consider revising the nation's constitution, known as the Articles of Confederation. (Content with the Articles, the citizens and politicians of Rhode Island feared correctly that their small state would lose influence under any reforms.) General Washington, presiding over this convention, and the twenty other delegates who had served under him in the field knew firsthand the failings of the current government. The rest of the delegates similarly drew on their varied governing experiences, some stretching back into the colonial era, as they worked together first to revise the Articles and then to formulate an entirely new constitution. How did these delegates use their experience and their familiarity with the new nation's struggle to solve the problems inherent in collective action? A closer look at the events leading up to the Constitutional Convention and the creative process it spawned will reveal the thinking that gave birth to America's constitutional system.

THE ROAD TO INDEPENDENCE

Geographically, America was well situated to be the first nation to break with monarchy and embrace republicanism; distance limited Britain's capacity to govern the colonies—a problem that gained painful significance during the Revolutionary War. Beginning early in the colonial era, Britain had ceded to Americans responsibility for managing their own domestic affairs, including taxation. The colonists enjoyed this **home rule**, and the British found it agreeable as well. After all, Britain's first concern was to control America's foreign commerce, thereby guaranteeing itself a market for British manufactured goods and a steady supply of cheap raw materials. Thus for more than a century before independence the colonists had routinely elected their own leaders and held them accountable for local policies and taxes. Breaking with Great Britain may have been emotionally wrenching for many Americans, but unfamiliarity with self-governance was not a factor in their hesitancy to seek independence.

A Legacy of Self-Governance

The first colonial representative assembly convened in Virginia in August 1619. By about 1650 all of the colonies had established elective assemblies, which eventually gained the authority to initiate laws and levy taxes. The British appointed governors, colonial councils, and judges in most colonies, and some of these officials vigorously resisted the expansion of local prerogatives. But because the elective assemblies paid their salaries and funded their offices, these officers of the Crown found that they, too, had to accommodate popular opinion. The colonial experience thus taught Americans that a popularly elected legislature in control of the purse strings could dominate other governmental institutions. The next generation of leaders recalled this important and enduring lesson as they convened in Philadelphia to revamp the new nation's constitutional system.

In addition to experience in self-governance, the state assemblies supplied the nation with another vital resource: elected politicians experienced in negotiating collective agreements. As the vanguard of the independence movement, these politicians provided the nation with an era of exceptional leadership.

Americans also entered independence well versed in constitution writing. A royal charter or contract between the Crown and a British company or business entrepreneur had provided the foundation for most colonies. Later, the colonists themselves wrote constitutions, which they periodically revised. When in 1776 and again in

On March 5, 1770, British troops fired into a crowd of men and boys in Boston, killing five and wounding others. The massacre, depicted in this classic engraving by Paul Revere, gave the word *tyranny* new meaning. These and other events were instrumental in rousing colonial resistance to British rule on the eve of the American Revolution.

1787 the nation's leaders confronted the task of designing new government institutions, a written constitution was, not surprisingly, the instrument of choice.

Home rule may have had its benefits for the American colonies, but as training for self-governance it shortchanged the nation. As with the rest of its far-flung empire, Britain regulated all of its colonies' commerce and provided them with military security by means of its navy, the world's largest. Under this arrangement the colonies prospered and managed their own local affairs, but this ingrained free riding and gave them little experience in managing collective action. Britain had preferred to deal with the thirteen colonies individually rather than through some national assembly that might discover and pursue their common interests. Later, after the nation had declared its independence, politicians who had stridently resisted the Crown's incursions into their local authority found themselves incapable of addressing their collective problems as a nation. With nationhood, the free ride on Britain would end.

Home rule experienced its first strains during Britain's war with France in the 1750s. Known in America as the French and Indian War and in Europe as the Seven Years' War, this lengthy, multicontinent conflict drained both Britain's treasury and its military resources. Searching for assistance, Britain in 1754 summoned delegates from each of the colonies to a conference in Albany, New York, to invite their collective assistance in defending the western frontier against the French military and its Indian allies. Because six of the thirteen colonies failed to send delegates, this would-be first national assembly failed even before it convened.

Yet the Albany Congress produced the first serious proposal for a national government. One of Pennsylvania's delegates, Benjamin Franklin, already renowned throughout the country as the man who had tamed lightning, proposed a "Plan of the Union" that would have created a national government. The plan called for an American army to provide for the colonies' defense, a popularly elected national legislature with the power to levy taxes, and an executive appointed by the British king. (On learning of Franklin's plan, King George II declared, "I am the colonies' legislature.") But none of the colonial assemblies could muster much enthusiasm for Franklin's ideas. Why should they share their tax base with some dubiously mandated new governmental entity? And why should they undertake Britain's burden of providing for the colonies' security and overseeing trade? For them, free riding made eminent sense as long as they could get away with it. And they did get away with it; another decade would pass before Britain tried to force Americans to contribute to their defense. Only then did Franklin's proposal attract interest.

Dismantling Home Rule

France's 1763 defeat in the French and Indian War ended its aspirations for extensive colonization of America. The British, relishing their victory, had little idea, however, that the war would trigger events that would severely compromise Britain's claims in America over the next decade.

By the end of the war Britain was broke. With its citizenry already among the most heavily taxed in the world, the British government looked to the colonies to share in the empire's upkeep. At the time, the only British taxes on the colonies were duties on imports from outside the British Empire, designed less to raise revenue than to regulate commerce. To raise needed revenues, Britain decided to impose taxes. Moreover, to consolidate its power

In this eighteenth-century satirical drawing by a British artist, Bostonians gleefully pour tea down the throat of a customs official, who has just been tarred and feathered. In the distance colonists dump tea into Boston Harbor, just as they did in 1773 at the Boston Tea Party. And, lest one British misdeed go unnoticed, a symbol of the hated Stamp Act, passed in 1765, appears on the tree.

Britain began to violate home rule. Every revenue law the British government enacted during the decade after the French and Indian War contained provisions tightening its control over the internal affairs of the colonies.

The most aggressive challenge to home rule came in 1765 with passage of the Stamp Act.* This law imposed a tax on all printed materials, including legal documents, licenses, insurance papers, and land titles, as well as a variety of consumer goods, including newspapers and playing cards. (Proof of payment of the tax was the stamp affixed to the taxed document.) The tax had long been familiar to the British public, but Americans greeted it as a personal affront. It inflamed American public opinion, not so much because of the money extracted but because of the instruments used to extract it. Americans had paid taxes before, but they had been self-imposed, levied by the colonial assemblies to provide local services. Thus the American response, "No taxation without representation," was not simply the rallying cry of a tax revolt. In fact, Americans were not genuinely interested in representation in the British Parliament. Rather, the colonists were asserting home rule. A more accurate rallying cry would have been, "No taxation by a government in which we want no part!"

The colonial assemblies passed resolutions demanding the tax be repealed, and most sent delegates to a national conference, the Stamp Act Congress, to craft a unified response. For the first time they united against Britain by agreeing unanimously on a resolution condemning the tax. They could not agree, however, on a course of action.

The organized resistance of ordinary citizens was more successful.† Throughout the colonies local groups confronted tax collectors and prevented them from performing their duties. Over the next decade these scenes were repeated as Britain imposed a half-dozen new tax and administrative laws designed to weaken the colonial assemblies. Americans countered by boycotting British products and forming protest organizations, such as the Sons of Liberty, the Daughters of Liberty, and the more militant Committees of Correspondence. Vigilantism and public demonstrations overshadowed assembly resolutions.

---

*Earlier, the Sugar Act of 1764 had levied new duties on certain foreign imports and introduced new efforts to interdict Yankee smuggling to circumvent import duties. At the same time Parliament passed another inflammatory law, the Currency Act, which forbade the colonies from printing their own currency, thus requiring merchants to raise scarce hard cash to do business.

†"Nothing else is talked of," wrote Sally Franklin to her father, Benjamin, in London. "The Dutch [Germans] talk of the stompt act the Negroes of the tamp, in short every body has something to say." Mary Beth Norton et al., *A People and a Nation: A History of the United States* (Boston: Houghton Mifflin, 1990), 117.

Justly, the most famous of these demonstrations was the Boston Tea Party. No colony had chafed under Britain's new rules and import taxes more than Massachusetts, whose economy depended heavily on international trade and shipping. On a winter night in 1773 a group of patriots donned Indian dress and dumped 342 chests of tea owned by the East India Company into Boston Harbor to protest a new tax on Americans' favorite nonalcoholic beverage. Britain responded with the Restraining Acts and Coercive Acts, which closed the port of Boston to all commerce, dissolved the Massachusetts assembly, decreed that British troops in Boston must be quartered in American homes, and ordered that Americans charged with protest crimes and British soldiers charged with crimes against the colonists be sent to England for trial. Colonists viewed these last provisions as ensuring serious punishment for the first group and lax punishment for the second.

The Continental Congresses

When colonists elsewhere witnessed Britain's heavy-handed policies in Massachusetts, they recognized their own vulnerability. Without hesitation, then, they answered the call of Boston resistance leader Samuel Adams to assemble in the fall of 1774 at Philadelphia for what became the First Continental Congress. Each colony sent its leading professionals, merchants, and planters. These men had mostly known one another only by reputation, but at this meeting they would form a nucleus of national leadership for the next decade. Among them were the future nation's first presidents: George Washington, John Adams, and Thomas Jefferson.

The Continental Congress promptly passed resolutions condemning British taxes and administrative decrees. When the idea of creating a national government was raised, Franklin's plan of union, the only existing proposal for unification, was introduced and briefly but inconclusively debated. The most significant actions of the First Continental Congress were adoption of a Declaration of American Rights, which essentially reasserted home rule, and endorsement of an agreement to ban all trade with Britain until it rescinded the despised taxes and regulations. To enforce the boycott against the prospect of massive free riding, Congress called for the formation of local elective "committees of observation" in every county, town, and hamlet in the country. Soon many of these newly formed organizations began imposing patriotic morality with investigations of "treasonable" conversations and public rebukes of more ordinary vices. Earlier import boycotts had been modestly successful—enough to alter British policy—but with the capacity to identify and sanction potential free riders, the new boycott won almost total compliance.

The eight thousand or so members of these local committees provided a base for the statewide conventions that sprang up throughout the colonies when the British prevented the colonial assemblies from meeting. Unhampered by local British authorities, these conventions quickly became de facto governments. (When some colonies' assemblies were enjoined from meeting, they would adjourn to a local tavern and resume doing business as an unofficial provincial convention.) They collected taxes, raised militias, passed "laws" forbidding the judiciary from enforcing British decrees, and selected delegates to the Second Continental Congress, which met in Philadelphia in May 1775.

By the time the Second Continental Congress gathered, war had broken out. Spontaneous bloody uprisings in the spring of 1775 at Lexington and Concord in Massachusetts had provoked the state conventions to mobilize local volunteer militias and disarm suspected British loyalists. Events demanded concerted action, and the Second Continental Congress responded by acting like a national government. Congress had no legal authority to conduct a war effort, but throughout the colonies patriots desperately required coordination, and it was the only national institution available.

Congress first instructed the conventions to reconstitute themselves as state governments based on republican principles. Using their former colonial governments as a model, most states adopted **bicameral** (two-chamber) **legislatures**, and all created a governorship. Accustomed to difficult relations with the royal governors, the states severely limited the terms and authority of these newly minted American executives. This antiexecutive bias would persist and influence deliberations at the Constitutional Convention a decade later.

Then, acting even more like a government, the Second Continental Congress issued the nation's first bonds and established a national currency. It also authorized delegate George Washington to expand the shrinking Massachusetts militia into a full-fledged national army. (As if his colleagues had needed a hint, Washington attended the convention in full military dress of his own design.)

The Declaration of Independence

During its first year's work of creating states and raising and financing an army, Congress did not consider the fundamental issue of separation from England. But it was discussed on street corners and in taverns throughout the nation. In January 1776 the pamphleteer Thomas Paine published *Common Sense,* which moved the independence issue to center stage. Within three months 120,000 copies had been sold, and Americans were talking about Paine's plainly stated, irresistible argument that only in the creation of an independent republic would the people find contentment.

The restless citizenry's anticipation that Congress would consider a resolution of separation was realized in June when Virginia delegate Richard Henry Lee called for creation of a new nation separate from Britain. Congress referred his proposal to a committee of delegates from every region with instructions to draft the proper resolution. One member of this committee was a thirty-three-year-old lawyer from Virginia, Thomas Jefferson. Asked to draft a statement because of "his peculiar felicity of expression," Jefferson modestly demurred. This prompted the always-direct John Adams of Massachusetts to protest, "You can write ten times better than I can."[2]

Jefferson's qualifications to articulate the rationale for independence extended well beyond his writing skills. Possessing aristocratic tastes but democratic values, he never wavered from an abiding confidence in the innate goodness and wisdom of common people. "State a moral case to a ploughman and a professor," he once challenged a friend. "The former will decide it as well, and often better than the latter, because he has not been led astray by artificial rules."* In the end, Jefferson agreed to draft the resolution of separation.

---

*Whether drafting Virginia's first law guaranteeing religious freedom as a member of its House of Burgesses, revising Virginia's constitution, or founding the University of Virginia, Jefferson consistently engaged in activities liberating the inherent capacities of his fellow citizens. Joseph R. Conlin, *The Morrow Book of Quotations in American History* (New York: Morrow, 1984).

Jefferson concurred with the other delegates in many of the specific grievances itemized in the resolution he drafted, but for him the real rationale for throwing off British rule rested on the fundamental right of self-government. Such conviction produced this famous passage:

We hold these truths to be self-evident, that all men are created equal, that they are endowed by their creator with certain unalienable Rights, that among these are Life, Liberty and the pursuit of Happiness. That to secure these rights, Governments are instituted among Men, deriving their just powers from the consent of the governed. That whenever any form of government becomes destructive of these ends, it is the Right of the People to alter or abolish it, and to institute new Government. . . .

Jefferson's colleagues only made slight changes in this centerpiece of the **Declaration of Independence**, but they did amend his list of grievances. Foreshadowing the future conflict over race, Jefferson's indictment of Britain for introducing slavery into the colonies offended

In this 1782 British cartoon at the close of the Revolutionary War, Benjamin Franklin's diminutive, garden-variety snake, struggling to stay whole (see page 43), has become through unity a voracious "American rattlesnake," eager to consume British armies. "Two British Armies I have thus Burgoyn'd, And room for more I've got behind," it boasts. A sign posted on its rattle advertises ominously to British readers, "An Apartment to Lett for Military Gentlemen."

the sensibilities of slave-owning southern delegates. Thus at their insistence this grievance was stricken from the final resolution.* (The full text of the Declaration of Independence appears in the Appendix.)

In a solemn ceremony on July 4, 1776, each member of the Second Continental Congress signed the document. Rebelling against a colonial power with a huge occupation army was a dangerous enterprise. The conclusion of the Declaration—"we mutually pledge to each other our lives, our Fortunes, and our sacred Honor"—was no mere rhetoric.

AMERICA'S FIRST CONSTITUTION: THE ARTICLES OF CONFEDERATION

With the Declaration of Independence in hand, the delegates to the Second Continental Congress proceeded to "institute a new Government," as called for in the Declaration. Over the next several weeks they drafted and sent to the new states for ratification the nation's first constitution, the **Articles of Confederation**. Although not ratified until 1781, the Articles served as the nation's de facto constitution during the intervening war years.

As its name implies, the first American constitution created a **confederation**, a highly decentralized system in which the national government derives limited authority from the states rather than directly from citizens. Not only do the states select officials of the national government, but they also retain the authority to override that government's decisions.

The Articles transferred the form and functions of the Continental Congress to the new, permanent Congress, in which each state received one vote. Major laws required the endorsement of nine of the thirteen state delegations, while more fundamental changes, such as direct taxation, necessitated unanimous agreement to amend the Constitution. National authority was so restricted that the delegates saw little purpose for an executive branch or a judiciary. From time to time administrators might be required, but they could be hired as needed and directly supervised by the new Congress.

In adopting a confederation, the delegates sought to replicate the home rule they had lost in the 1760s. Clearly, after years of free riding under British rule, they were not yet willing to absorb the collective action costs associated with nationhood. Yet they also recognized that in declaring their independence they thrust upon themselves responsibility for supplying essential public goods—most important, defense and commercial markets—that Britain had provided under home rule. The same delegates who had pressed hardest for independence, knowing that it was likely to lead to war, were among those who most vigorously favored a confederation over a more centralized and powerful national government. Undoubtedly, the new nation's leaders still had a great deal to learn about the logic of collective action. But they would learn in time—the hard way. Their suspicion of national authority very nearly cost the fledgling nation its independence.

---

*Among the items deleted: "He [King George III] has waged cruel war against human nature itself, violating its most sacred rights of life and liberty in the persons of a distant people who never offended him, captivating them and carrying them into slavery in another hemisphere, or to incur miserable death in their transportation thither." In *Thomas Jefferson*, ed. Merrill D. Peterson (New York: Library of America, 1984), 21–22.

The Confederation at War

Faced with a war raging for over a year, the states, unwilling to give the national government sufficient authority to conduct the war, became chiefly responsible for recruiting troops and outfitting them for battle. The national military command, which answered to Congress, assumed responsibility for organizing the various state regiments into a single fighting force. In principle, Congress was assigned the role of coordinator. It would identify military requirements, assess the states, and channel their (voluntary) contributions to the army. Congress also was empowered to borrow money through bonds, but its lack of taxation authority made bonds a risky and expensive venture for the government, which had to offer high interest rates to attract investors.

The public's deep suspicion of government also prevented national officeholders from creating the administrative structures suitable for the new government's wartime responsibilities. John Adams even wanted to prevent Washington from appointing his own staff officers for fear that "there be too much Connection between them." Instead, he argued, Congress should select all officers so that these "officers are checks upon the General." Adams's appeal to the "proper Rule and Principle" stimulated serious debate, but he did not prevail in this instance. Adams was, however, more successful in other attempts to dilute executive powers.

The administrative vacuum sucked congressional committees into the daily affairs of requisitioning an army. These legislators struggled mightily, even heroically, to do their duty, but most were unskilled in administration and frequently unable to make timely decisions. In fact, the members of one committee expressed such a variety of views on the number of uniforms to be ordered that they were unable to come to a decision. The desperate plight of General Washington's army as the war continued attests to the naiveté and ineffectiveness of the confederation's structure. Thus the collective action problems described in Chapter 1 were evident in America's war effort: contagious levels of free riding and the reluctance of some states to contribute their fair share for fear that the other states would hold back (a classic prisoner's dilemma). Moreover, the undeveloped national administration provided fertile soil for equally debilitating free riding in the form of corruption.

Without the authority to play a more central role in administering the war, Congress responded to the quickly deteriorating military situation by decentralizing authority even further. Among other things, it passed resolutions instructing the states to supply their troops directly. Perhaps, some members reasoned, the states would be more forthcoming with support for their own sons in uniform. This scheme had the merit of converting a public good—military supplies that all state regiments could consume regardless of their state's contribution—into a more or less private good that linked the welfare of each state's troops to its legislature's effort. But the actual practice of thirteen states locating and supplying intermingled regiments scattered up and down the Atlantic seaboard presented a logistical nightmare. On hearing of it, General Washington caustically remarked that members of Congress "think it is but to say 'Presto begone,' and everything is done."

At the same time pressure mounted on various fronts, including within Congress itself, for Congress to assume greater authority to conduct the war.* Understandably, the military

---

*Ten years later these advocates of congressional authority would form the core group of nationalists, led by James Madison and Alexander Hamilton, pressing the nation for a new constitution.

commanders were the most outspoken in lobbying Congress and state governors for a "new plan of civil constitution."[3] General Washington advised Congress that an "entire new plan" providing it with the authority "adequate to all of the purposes of the war" must be instituted immediately. Washington's aide Alexander Hamilton, later one of the architects of the Constitution, showered members of Congress with correspondence urging them to grasp the emergency authority he claimed was inherent in the Articles. Without the "complete sovereignty" that could come only with an independent source of revenue, he argued, Congress would have neither the resources nor the credibility necessary to conduct the war. And, as the states' dismal performance had proved, if Congress did not take control, no one else could.[*]

The addition of the second major group—state officials—to the chorus for reform reveals the pervasiveness of frustration with the confederation. Although the confederation had sought to empower these officials above all others, many found themselves trapped in a classic prisoner's dilemma. They were prepared to sacrifice for the war, but only if they could be confident that the other states would also do their part. Moreover, many of their colleagues who had been outspoken champions of volunteerism were defeated in the 1780 elections by challengers calling for a strengthened national authority that could enforce agreements.

By the summer of 1780 some states were taking direct action. In August representatives of several New England states met and passed a resolution calling for investing Congress with "powers competent for the government." Several months later five northern states met at what is now known as the Hartford Convention to urge Congress to grant itself the power to tax. In a remarkable resolution the convention called for Congress to delegate to General Washington the authority "to induce . . . punctual compliance" from states that ignored their obligations to supply the army. The delegates realized that states would only cooperate (and end their prisoner's dilemma) under the threat of coercion.

Congress responded as best it could, but it labored under a constitution designed to frustrate national action. In 1781 Rhode Island, with less than 2 percent of the nation's population, vetoed a bill giving Congress the authority to levy taxes. Various administrative reforms were enacted but had to be watered down to win unanimous endorsement. Congress could not agree on how much independent authority to delegate to the executive offices it created. As a result, the offices had no authority, and their occupants served at the beck and call of the legislature's committees.

The tide turned after France, England's long-standing adversary, agreed to lend the Americans hard currency. By 1782 General Washington could write for the first time since the beginning of the war that his army was well fed, clothed, and armed. A reinvigorated American army and France's continued participation in the war presented Britain with the prospect of a far longer conflict. (France formally recognized American independence and agreed to support the United States unilaterally in 1778.) In October 1781 British troops, under General Charles Cornwallis, suffered defeat at Yorktown, Virginia, and Britain sued for peace. Thus the United States had somehow survived a war with an occupying army. In the jubilation of victory, however, momentum for political reform was lost.

---

[*]Hamilton also argued that Congress must delegate administration to "great officers of State—A secretary for foreign affairs—A President of War—A President of Marine—A Financier." In effect, he was calling for an autonomous national government with a legislature at its center and a separate executive branch.

The Confederation's Troubled Peace

Shortly after signing the peace treaty with Britain, the nation lunged toward new perils—indeed, to the point that many Americans and even more Europeans wondered whether the hard-won independence might still be lost in national disintegration. By 1787 American leaders were openly speculating about the prospect of Britain reasserting its authority over the barely united and internally divided states.

THE WAR-TORN ECONOMY. After six years of war, the nation's debt was staggering. Congress owed Americans about $25 million and foreign governments another $10 million. The most urgent concern was the back pay owed the army. In the spring of 1783 General Washington learned of a conspiracy forming among disgruntled officers to march on Congress. Greatly alarmed, he wrote his former aide Alexander Hamilton, now a member of Congress, that the army should be paid and "disbanded without delay." The army is "a dangerous instrument to play with," he warned ominously. Prudently, Congress followed Washington's advice.

Creditors who had supplied the troops formed another long line. But Congress was more successful in ignoring these unarmed claimants, some of whom eventually received partial payment from the states. Abroad, debts to Britain negotiated in the peace settlement and loans from European governments and private interests all had to be repaid before normal commercial relations with these countries could resume. In the face of so much debt, the national currency plummeted to approximately one-tenth of its prewar value.

The complexities of governing by confederation compounded the problem. Congress held the debt, but the states controlled the purse strings. As it had during the war, Congress prescribed annual state contributions to reduce the debt over twenty-five years. But no one expressed confidence that the states, having proven so unreliable in war, would step forward in peace to accept fiscal responsibility for the nation. With no enforcement mechanism in place the states again individually confronted a classic prisoner's dilemma: No state would contribute its share of the revenue so long as it suspected one or more of the other states might not meet its obligations. Congress faced two tough choices. It could try to penalize those states that reneged, or it could try to finance the debt on its own. The latter proved more feasible. Thus in the same bill that mapped long-term debt reduction Congress proposed a constitutional amendment giving the national government a source of direct revenue in the form of import duties. As in the past, however, the Articles' unanimous consent rule for amendments frustrated action. Unwilling to share the revenue from its already active port city of New York, the New York legislature killed this proposal.

TRADE BARRIERS AT HOME AND ABROAD. The nation's shaky finances were not helped by its trade problems, which also stemmed from the confederation's explicit reservation of all matters of commerce to the states. For example, Congress lacked the authority to negotiate credible trade agreements with other nations. European governments found this arrangement, in which trade agreements required the endorsement of each state's legislature, unwieldy. The national government also proved incapable of responding to discriminatory trade sanctions and other actions abroad. When the British and later the French closed their West Indies possessions to U.S. exports, the action threatened the fragile, war-torn economy that depended heavily on exports.

Economic relations among the states were nearly as unsatisfactory. States with international ports charged exporters from other states stiff user fees. New York victimized New Jersey; Virginia and South Carolina both extracted a toll from North Carolina. And each state minted its own currency. Some states, responding to political pressures from indebted farmers, inflated their currencies. Exchange rates fluctuated widely across states, rendering interstate commerce a speculative financial exercise.

To no one's surprise, many sectors of the economy clamored loudly for reform. The nation's creditors wanted a government able to pay its debts. Importers and the mercantile class desperately needed a sound currency and an end to capricious state policies toward other states' goods. The profits of southern tobacco and indigo growers depended wholly on open export markets, which only a national government could negotiate effectively. The need for a central authority that could create and manage a common market at home and implement a unified commercial policy abroad spurred diverse economic interests to call for a revision of the Articles of Confederation.

In the summer of 1786 Virginia made the first move, inviting delegates of other states to convene that fall in Annapolis, Maryland, to consider ways of strengthening the national government's role in commerce. Eight states named delegates, but when those from only five states showed up, the Annapolis convention adjourned after passing a resolution calling for another convention in Philadelphia nine months later. Thus the Annapolis convention earned a place in history by setting the stage for the Constitutional Convention in May 1787. Although the delegates had no reason to believe the next meeting would generate any better turnout, events during the intervening months, including **Shays's Rebellion**, galvanized interest and mobilized the states behind constitutional reform.

POPULAR DISCONTENT. In the economic depression that followed the Revolution, many small farmers lost their land and other assets. Markets were disrupted, credit became scarce, and personal debt mounted. The financial straits of small farmers spawned occasional demonstrations, but none so threatening as the one that erupted in the fall of 1786 in western Massachusetts, where taxes were especially onerous and the local courts unforgiving. Many farmers lost their land and possessions at the auction block, and some were even being hauled off to debtors' prison. The protest movement began with town meetings and petitions to the state legislature to suspend taxes and fore-closures. When their appeals failed to win much sympathy, these disaffected citizens found more aggressive ways to remonstrate their grievances. Under the leadership of Daniel Shays, a former captain in the Continental Army and a bankrupt farmer, an armed group composed mostly of farmers marched on the Massachusetts Supreme Court session in Springfield to demand that state judges stop prosecuting debtors. Shays's band was met by the state militia, but the confrontation ended peacefully after the magistrates adjourned the court.

In late January 1787 Massachusetts erupted once more, this time with enough violence to convince the states to convene in Philadelphia. Having learned that Shays planned an assault on a government arsenal in Springfield, delegates from Massachusetts appealed to the national government to send funds and troops. Once again unable to muster compliance among the states, Congress could offer neither troops nor money. A similar appeal to neighboring states proved no more productive. Finally, the state organized a militia (in part with private donations) that intercepted and repulsed Shays's "army" of about a thousand farmers outside the arsenal. Over the next several weeks some of Shays's men were captured, others dispersed, and the rebellion ended.

Had it been an isolated incident, even this event might not have persuaded state leaders of the need for a stronger national government. But Shays's Rebellion coincided with a wave of popular uprisings sweeping across the country. The same winter, two hundred armed farmers in Pennsylvania had tried to reclaim neighbors' possessions that had been seized by tax collectors. On the same day as Shays's defeat, these farmers rescued a neighbor's cattle from a tax sale. Virginia protesters, following the example of the insurgents in Massachusetts, burned down public buildings. Their favorite targets were jails and courthouses where tax and debt records were kept.

State legislatures, either intimidated by threats of force or genuinely sympathetic with farmers' demands, started to cave in under the slightest pressure from these constituencies. At times, these bodies' knee-jerk responses caused them to behave in ways more in keeping with revolutionary tribunals than with deliberative republican legislatures respectful of property rights. Throughout the country they summarily overturned unpopular court decisions, altered property assessments, and issued quickly devalued paper money, which they then forced creditors to accept as full payment of farmers' debts. One scholar offered this assessment: "The economic and social instability engendered by the Revolution was finding political expression in the state legislatures at the very time they were larger, more representative, and more powerful than ever before in American history."[4] Observing all this, the troubled James Madison of Virginia wrote his friend Thomas Jefferson in Paris, where Jefferson was serving as the states' ambassador: "In our Governments the real power lies in the majority, and the invasion of private rights...chiefly [arises]...not from acts of Government contrary to the sense of its constituents, but from acts in which the Government is the mere instrument of the major number of the constituents."[5] Madison's discomfort with arbitrary majority action guided his efforts and those of like-minded delegates throughout the Constitutional Convention.

Despite their defeat, the protesting farmers led by Daniel Shays won a number of reforms from the Massachusetts state legislature, which lowered court costs and exempted household necessities and workmen's tools from the debt collection process. The unintended impact of Shay's Rebellion on national reform was far more dramatic. It demonstrated that the confederation could not perform the most basic function of government—keeping peace.

SHAYS'S FORCES IN MASSACHU

To many observers, Shays's Rebellion represented a wildfire threatening to sweep the country into anarchy.[6] No matter how persuasive Hamilton, the beloved Washington, or any of the other **nationalists** were in promoting the cause of constitutional reform, it was Daniel Shays who offered the most compelling reason for states to send delegates to the Philadelphia convention. Ultimately, the states took the first steps toward true unification not in response to their collective dilemma, but rather out of a more fundamental concern with self-preservation. When they assembled in Philadelphia the next spring, delegates from all states except Rhode Island showed up.

DRAFTING A NEW CONSTITUTION

In their deliberations the fifty-five youngish, well-educated white males who gathered in Philadelphia in 1787 drew on their shared experience of war and its aftermath, but they did not do so reflexively or out of narrowly construed self-interest. They also were highly conversant in the ideas and theories swirling "in the air" during the Enlightenment, as the dominant intellectual current of the eighteenth century was known. Influenced by recent advances in science, scholars—and even America's politicians—sought through careful reasoning to discern the "natural laws" that governed economics, politics, and morality. The impact of these ideas was not merely a matter of their novelty and intellectual appeal, but also in how they illuminated Americans' experiences.

Thus the Constitution that eventually arose out of the convention was grounded in theories of politics, economics, and even science that were attracting attention at the time throughout Europe. The delegates cited dozens of contemporary and ancient philosophers during floor deliberations, often quoting them in their original language of Latin or French. Of these thinkers, several deserve to be singled out because their ideas are clearly discernible in the Constitution.

Philosophical Influences

Heading any list of influential Enlightenment thinkers is the English philosopher John Locke (1632–1704), whose brilliant writings on political theory and design of government read in some places as if the Framers were his sole audience. In 1690 Locke vigorously defended the still-novel idea of **popular sovereignty**—that is, citizens' delegation of authority to their agents in government, with the ability to rescind that authority.[7] This argument clearly influenced Jefferson's words in the Declaration of Independence. Moreover, Locke stressed individual rights and the limited scope of government authority. If Locke's ideas strike the modern student as unexceptional, it is because they are so thoroughly embedded in the U.S. Constitution and governmental system that they are taken for granted.

During the same era another Englishman, Sir Isaac Newton (1642–1727), established the foundations of modern mechanics and physics. His discovery of the laws of physical relations (such as gravity) inspired the Framers to search for comparable laws governing social relations. Evidence of Newton's influence can be seen in the Framers' descriptions of their design proposals to each other and later to the nation. Concepts such as "force," "balance," and "fulcrum" and phrases such as "laws of politics" and "check power with power" that seemed borrowed from a physics textbook were bandied about with great familiarity.

Perhaps more than anyone else, the French philosopher Charles, Baron de Montesquieu (1689–1755), supplied the Framers with the nuts and bolts of a design of government, particularly his classification of governmental functions and forms as legislative, executive, and judicial. Like Locke, Montesquieu championed limited government—limited not only in the nature of its authority but also in the size of the political community it encompassed. Thus during and after the convention opponents of reform invoked Montesquieu's case for the superiority of small republics as a powerful counterargument to those who advocated empowering the national government.

Finally, the Scottish philosopher David Hume (1711–1776) treated politics as a competition among contending interests, in much the same way that his fellow countryman Adam Smith described competition in the marketplace of an emerging capitalist economy. An ocean away, James Madison adapted Hume's arguments to his own purposes, much as Jefferson did Locke's.

America's founding leaders, though politicians, often behaved as if they were philosophers, carefully studying and even writing treatises on government. The most important is James Madison's three-thousand-word essay "Vices of the Political System of the U. States," which he drafted in the spring of 1787 after extensive research on ancient and modern confederations. (Madison had Jefferson scour Paris bookstores for source materials.) Madison circulated copies of his manuscript among fellow Virginians who would be attending the Philadelphia convention to prepare them for the reform proposal he was writing. Madison's sophisticated understanding of politics is apparent in a passage attributing the confederation's failure not to a moral breakdown of the citizenry but to the classic prisoner's dilemma embedded in faulty institutions: "A distrust of the voluntary compliance of each other may prevent the compliance of any, although . . . [cooperation is] the latent disposition of all."

Getting Down to Business

Most of the delegates representing their states in Philadelphia probably were unaware of the grand scope of the enterprise on which they were about to embark. Some undoubtedly assumed that the convention would simply return to the Annapolis agenda that sought to resolve commercial disputes at home and coordinate the states' commercial policies abroad. Others anticipated minor reforms of the Articles and were prepared to take the positions dictated by their state legislatures. But at least a few, most notably James Madison, were planning—indeed, plotting with others of like mind—to scrap the Articles of Confederation altogether and start over.

Sensing his fellow Virginian's hidden agenda, war hero Patrick Henry announced he "smelt a rat" and refused to join the delegation to Philadelphia. The Delaware legislature was similarly suspicious and instructed its delegates to oppose any scheme that undermined the equality of the states. Another small state, the ever-independent Rhode Island, boycotted Philadelphia altogether.

The convention opened on a rainy Friday, May 25, 1787. By near universal acclamation, the delegates elected General Washington to preside over the deliberations, and the convention began on a harmonious note. Madison sat at the front, where he could easily participate in floor debates and record the arguments of his colleagues.* The convention agreed to keep the proceedings secret to allow a frank exchange of views and to facilitate compromise. This decision also meant keeping the window shutters closed during one of the hottest summers in Philadelphia's history.

The Virginia and New Jersey Plans

On the first day of substantive business Madison and his nationalist colleagues sprang their surprise. Edmund Randolph, also from Virginia, introduced Madison's blueprint for a new constitution. In this revised constitution Madison favored those institutional design features more closely resembling parliamentary systems than those of the future American republic. In the **Virginia Plan**, as it came to be known, Madison appears to have been more concerned with fashioning an active national government, even if it imposed high conformity costs on the states. The Virginia Plan dominated floor debate well into July. Although few of its provisions survived intact in the final draft of the Constitution, the Virginia Plan succeeded in shifting the deliberations from patching up the confederation to considering anew the requirements of a national union.

The centerpiece of the Virginia Plan was a bicameral national legislature. Members of the lower chamber would be apportioned among the states by population and directly elected by the citizenry. The lower chamber would, in turn, elect the members of the upper chamber from lists of nominees supplied by the state legislatures. It also would elect the officers of the proposed executive and judicial branches (see Figure 2-1). Madison's intent was clear: only representatives, whose direct election by the people gave them special legitimacy in formulating national policy, would control the selection of the other officers of government.

To solve the nation's collective action problems, the Virginia Plan also gave the national government enforcement authority. It could make whatever laws it deemed appropriate and veto any state laws it regarded as unfit. If a state failed to fulfill its legal obligations, the national government could summon military force against it. This provision proved to be a tactical mistake because it inflamed opposition. In the meantime, the nationalists realized belatedly that military force would never be needed because the national government could directly implement its own policies and would no longer depend on the cooperation of the states.

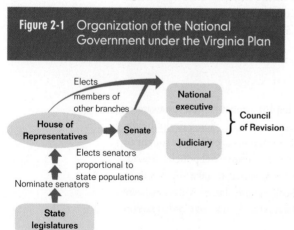

Figure 2-1 Organization of the National Government under the Virginia Plan

---

*Unable to fathom the purpose of certain provisions of the ancient constitutions he had examined in his preparation for the convention, Madison was determined not to leave future generations in the dark about the rationale of this new constitution. Thus he carefully recorded the business of the convention. *Notes on the Federal Convention* was discovered among Madison's papers after his death in 1837. The federal government paid his widow, Dolley, $30,000 for the papers and published them three years later. This discussion closely follows Madison's *Notes*.

With the states reduced to the status of junior partners, the national legislature would assume a standing comparable to that of the British Parliament. Madison did provide one check on this legislative dynamo: a Council of Revision, composed of the executive and certain judges, which could veto legislation. Its members, however, would be elected by the legislature. Thus skeptical delegates reasonably questioned how effective such a check could be. In any event, Madison proposed allowing Congress to override a council veto.

After Madison achieved early success in some preliminary floor votes, opposition, mainly from two sources, to his radical reforms solidified. Delegates representing the less populous states were understandably upset. They could easily calculate that they (and their citizens) would have far less representation under the Virginia Plan than they presently enjoyed with equal state representation and the one-state veto rule. Another bloc (mostly from small states as well) wanted stronger safeguards of state sovereignty. For these **states' rights** delegates, continued state participation in the selection of national officeholders was as important an issue as how legislative seats were to be apportioned.

Both groups coalesced around an alternative proposed by New Jersey delegate William Paterson, known as the **New Jersey Plan**. This late, hastily drafted response to the Virginia Plan was not as thoroughly thought through as Madison's proposal. It satisfied the requirements of its states' rights supporters, however, by perpetuating the composition and selection of Congress as it functioned under the Articles of Confederation and continuing to give each state one vote. But the New Jersey Plan broke with the Articles by giving Congress the authority to force the states to comply with its tax requisitions. This plan also allowed a simple majority vote to enact national policy rather than the supermajority required in the Articles. The New Jersey Plan thus eliminated the most objectionable features of the confederation. But its retention of a seriously malapportioned Congress representing the states rather than the citizenry did not come close to satisfying the demands of the nationalists.

Debate on the composition of Congress raged for weeks, with each side steadfastly and heatedly refusing to budge.* Stalemate loomed. As the meetings neared a Fourth of July recess, the delegates agreed to send the question of Congress—its selection and composition—to a committee with instructions to report out a recommendation after the break. Madison was not named to the committee.

The Great Compromise

The committee's solution was a Solomon-like compromise that split control of the legislature's two chambers between the large (House of Representatives) and small (Senate) states. The upper chamber, or Senate, would retain many of the features of Congress under the Articles of Confederation: each state legislature would send two senators to serve six-year terms. Madison's population-based, elective legislature became the House of Representatives. To sweeten the deal for the nationalists, who had rejected a similar compromise earlier in floor deliberations, the committee reserved to the House alone the authority to originate revenue legislation (see Figure 2-2).

---

*Madison's allies did make one significant concession, accepting an amendment that gave the states sole authority to select the members of the upper house. Thus the Senate began to assume its ultimate form. But the delegates from small states pressed for more: equal state representation in both chambers.

Figure 2-2 Virginia Plan, New Jersey Plan, and Great Compromise

Virginia Plan

★ Two-chamber legislature; representation based on state population

★ Lower chamber of legislature elected by the citizenry; upper chamber, executive, and courts elected by the lower house

★ Legislature can make any law and veto any state legislation

★ Council of Revision (composed of executive and court) can veto legislation, but legislature can override by majority vote

New Jersey Plan

★ Single-house chamber; equal representation for each state regardless of population

★ Legislature has same power as under Articles, with added authority to levy taxes and regulate commerce; can exercise supremacy clause over state legislation

★ Plural executive can be removed by legislature (on petition of a majority of states); courts appointed by executive

★ Supreme Court hears appeals in limited number of cases

Great Compromise

★ Two-chamber legislature, with lower chamber (House of Representatives) representation based on population and upper chamber (Senate) representation equal for every state

★ Authority to levy taxes reserved to the lower chamber

The unanimous agreement rule that had hobbled the confederation Congress was gone, replaced by a rule that wholly ignored states as voting entities and instead empowered a majority of each chamber's membership to pass legislation. Moreover, the delegates agreed to a broad list of enumerated or expressed powers, contained in Article I, Section 8, of the Constitution, that extended the authority of the national legislature far beyond that available to Congress under the confederation. These powers included the authority to declare war, maintain an army and navy, and borrow money. Another item on the list of new powers stood out: the authority "to regulate Commerce with foreign Nations, and among the several States." This **commerce clause** greatly expanded the new Congress's—and, in turn, the national government's—sphere of action. And another clause in Section 8 further compounded its impact. The Framers closed the long list of explicit powers with the following general provision: Congress shall enjoy the authority "to make all Laws which shall be necessary and proper for carrying into Execution the foregoing Powers, and all other Powers vested by this Constitution in the Government of the United States." This critical provision, called the **necessary and proper clause**, left the door open for a major expansion of Congress's legislative power and the nationalization of public policy during the twentieth century.[*]

Both defenders and critics of an activist federal government agree that all national policies affect interstate commerce in some way. Together these clauses have provided a rationale for enacting far-reaching national legislation, including federal laws against interstate kidnapping

---

[*] Chapter 3, Federalism, traces the nationalization of public policy via the necessary and proper clause. In addition to listing what Congress can do, the Constitution lists what it—and the states—cannot do. Article I, Section 9, restricts Congress from granting titles of nobility, spending unappropriated funds, suspending the writ of habeas corpus, passing ex post facto laws, levying income taxes (the Sixteenth Amendment ratified in 1913 rescinded this provision), and taxing state exports. Section 10 imposes restrictions on states, prohibiting them from conducting foreign policy (through entering into treaties or alliances or conducting war), printing money, passing laws undermining contracts, and imposing tariffs or duties on trade.

and bank robbery; regulations on agricultural production (covering even the growth of feed that never leaves the farm where it was grown); bans on racial and other discrimination in restaurants, hotels, and public transportation; laws against possession of guns near public schools; and thousands of other wide-ranging national policies.

The committee's proposal was adopted by a vote of 5–4, with the other states abstaining or absent. Opposition came uniformly from the nationalists who viewed the compromise as one-sided. Through the Senate a majority of the states could still prevail over national policy. But the nationalists also recognized that this was the best deal they could get. Because the preferences of the states' rights delegates were more closely aligned with those of the status quo, they could more credibly present the nationalist side with a take-it-or-leave-it proposition.

Now, more than two centuries later, the political logic of dividing representation in Congress between the citizens and the states no longer matches reality. The supremacy of the national government over the states was decided by the Civil War. Senators have been elected directly by the voters since adoption of the Seventeenth Amendment in 1913. Despite the new reality, the Senate—the institution that embodies the initial logic of states' rights—persists. Indeed, as noted in Chapter 1, once in place an institution tends to survive long after the circumstances that fashioned it in a particular form have changed beyond all recognition. Although it is difficult today to justify a system in which, for example, citizens of Wyoming count for sixty-five times as much as citizens of California in one chamber of the national legislature, Americans are stuck with it. Yet, while still badly malapportioned, the modern Senate has become as attuned as the House of Representatives to changes in popular sentiments (see Chapter 6, Congress).

Because the compromise plan substantially strengthened the national government's capacity for action, most nationalists except Madison reconciled themselves to it—at least initially. The man who during his lifetime was called "the father of the Constitution" maintained that ultimately the nationalists would prevail by letting the country stew a while longer under the Articles. Eventually he was talked out of that idea, but he remained profoundly disillusioned. Then, perhaps literally overnight, Madison scrapped the rest of the Virginia Plan and made what amounted to a 180-degree turn in his views on the proper relations among government institutions. A new, more strategic politician had emerged. Suddenly Madison expressed enthusiasm for a genuine separation of powers between the branches, with each side exercising **checks and balances** over the others. The reasoning behind his hurried reassessment might have gone something like this: if the state legislatures could corrupt the new Congress through their hold on the Senate, they also could corrupt the entire national government through Congress's power to select the officers of the other branches of government. The solution: insulate the executive and judicial branches and enlist them in containing any efforts by the states through the Senate to subvert national policy. Thus in early July, with the summer half over and the proceedings gathering momentum, Madison turned his attention to fashioning an independent executive and judiciary.

Designing the Executive Branch

Of all the delegates, Alexander Hamilton had shown the greatest enthusiasm for a strengthened, independent executive. His fixation on an executive elected for life, however, left him

CHECKS AND BALANCES IN THE CONSTITUTION

logic of politics

The Framers feared that a concentration of power in any one group or branch of government would lead to tyranny—that is, one group would gain enough power to dominate the government and strip other groups of their basic rights. Thus they devised in the Constitution something of a political game in which each of the three branches of government has some capacity to limit, or trump, the power of the other two.

This system of *checks and balances* largely originated with the French philosopher Charles, Baron de Montesquieu (1689–1755), who argued that the concentration of government power could be effectively limited by locating the several functions of government—legislative, executive, and judicial—in separate and independent institutions. Notice in the diagram that rather than defining "separation of powers" according to these functions, the Constitution described separate institutions *sharing* power. All three branches possess legislative, executive, and judicial authority.

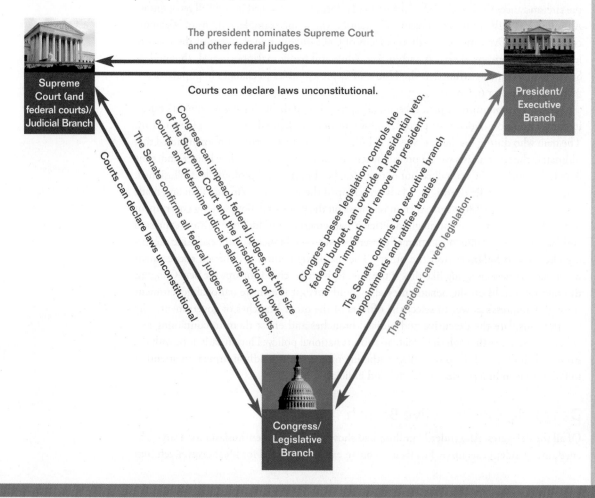

The president nominates Supreme Court and other federal judges.

Supreme Court (and federal courts)/ Judicial Branch

Courts can declare laws unconstitutional.

President/ Executive Branch

Congress can impeach federal judges; set the size of the Supreme Court and the jurisdiction of lower courts, and determine judicial salaries and budgets.

The Senate confirms all federal judges.

Courts can declare laws unconstitutional

Congress passes legislation, controls the federal budget, can override a presidential veto, and can impeach and remove the president.

The Senate confirms top executive branch appointments and ratifies treaties.

The president can veto legislation.

Congress/ Legislative Branch

The Framers, as do students of modern American government, considered how much military authority to grant the president and how Congress could constrain potential abuses of this authority. With Britain, Spain, and France controlling territories on America's borders, providing for the nation's security preoccupied the Framers. So, too, did an executive who might usurp power and turn the military against the other branches of government. Yet giving Congress the "power of the purse and the sword" clearly violated the accepted guiding principle of checks and balances. In the end the Framers accepted the limits of institutional design and hoped to produce presidents in the mold of George Washington.

so far on the fringe that he enjoyed little influence on the rest of the delegates as they turned their attention to this institution. His eloquent speeches were "praised by everybody . . . [but] supported by none," reported one candid delegate.

The delegates' lack of enthusiasm for an active, authoritative presidency is understandable. They had just finished dividing legislative authority into two coequal chambers with representatives and senators to be elected for different terms and from different constituencies. With each chamber able to block intemperate policies arising from the other, the Framers could more safely invest in them broad authority to make policy. Once the delegates dismissed the idea of a plural executive as impractical, the presidency no longer contained the internal checks that would have it control its excessive impulses.

This posed a serious dilemma for the convention. Even a casual survey of world history would turn up a panoply of absolute monarchs and other tyrants. Such a list supplied ample examples of the techniques arbitrary executives employed to exploit the citizenry and preserve their power. Indeed, all of the delegates had lived under an arbitrary executive's thumb. They despised King George III and his agents, the vilified colonial governors, who chronically were at odds with the colonial legislature over who had what authority. After the revolution the new states had overreacted by creating weak governors. Based on his brief experience as Virginia's wartime governor, Jefferson dismissed the office as a "cipher," a nonentity. In the end the only acceptable model of the new American president was, in the words of one historian, "sitting there in front of them . . . dignified, silent, universally admired and respected . . . impartial, honored for his selfless devotion to the common good, not intervening in, but presiding over, their councils—a presider, a *president*. The executive was to be—George Washington."[8]

The presence of a real-life example of an ideal executive presiding over the convention kept in view the kind of leadership the delegates sought to institutionalize, yet it does not appear to have made their task any easier. In the end, the delegates largely succeeded in fashioning an independent executive branch that might be incapable of abusing authority and might actually moderate excesses by an overreaching legislature. To achieve this, they designed several features. First, they limited the scope of presidential responsibilities and particularly the office's command authority. (The presidency of the twenty-first century might appear to belie their success. In Chapter 7 we will survey the evolution of the presidency and reconcile the modern with the early office.) Article II states, almost as an afterthought, that the president "shall take Care that the Laws be faithfully executed." Modern presidents sometimes assert that the **"take care" clause** allows them to undertake whatever actions the nation's well-being requires and is not expressly forbidden by the Constitution or public law. Yet, unlike Congress's expansive necessary and proper clause that bolsters their discretion in performing a long list of responsibilities, this mandate is not attached to any specific duty. Specifically, this new executive will appoint officers to fill vacancies in the executive department, receive and appoint ambassadors, negotiate treaties, serve as commander in chief of the army and navy, and periodically report to Congress on the state of the nation. The second design feature attached a legislative check, or veto, to each presidential duty. The Senate would confirm appointments and ratify any treaties (in this instance with a two-thirds vote) before they could take effect. Only Congress could declare war.

The third significant design feature was the **veto**, a negative action that would allow the executive to perform a "checking" function on the legislature. Unlike some constitutional executives, presidents cannot make policy or appropriate funds for programs, except as allowed in public laws. By requiring a supermajority vote of two-thirds of the members of each house to override a presidential veto, the Framers carved out an important role for the modern president in domestic legislation.

Over the next two centuries, the presidency became a much more consequential office, both in its duties and authority. But at least with respect to domestic policy, it has done so within a constitutional framework that has not changed. Most of the expansion has occurred through statutory provisions delegating policy responsibilities to the White House. If the Framers observed the president's role in domestic policy today, they might be shocked with what they found, but they would quickly recognize it as an extension of the office they envisioned.

One cannot be so confident that the Framers would come to the same assessment regarding the president's dominant role in foreign policy and national defense. Beginning with

World War II the United States became a leader in international affairs. Whatever advantages its status conferred, it also entailed numerous—well over a hundred—military actions. None began with Congress declaring "war," although all of the large-scale conflicts—Korea, Vietnam, and both Iraq wars, among others—found Congress passing resolutions backing the president's actions that initiated the conflict. Some analysts argue that contemporary international affairs and modern military technology have eclipsed the Constitution's capacity to prescribe appropriate authority and responsibilities available to the executive and legislature in modern wartime. In part the Constitution's limited and general language regarding foreign affairs has contributed to this uncertainty. During the George W. Bush presidency, administration and congressional views on the constitutional prerogatives for these branches during wartime diverged sharply at times. In Chapter 7 we will consider occasions during which White House officials have asserted that Congress has no role. Invariably the federal courts have had to resolve these constitutional disputes and have groped for answers along with the president and Congress. We take up these issues in detail later. The important point here is that the Constitution contains gaps—at times chasms—that have Americans more than two hundred years after the document was ratified asking fundamental questions about the appropriate role of Congress and the presidency. Much of the uncertainty occurs with subjects that Article II's creation of the presidency failed to resolve.

At the Constitutional Convention the delegates found that the only workable formula for agreement between the nationalists and states' rights advocates was to give both sides pretty much what they wanted, an approach that yielded the **Great Compromise**, and multiple routes for amending the Constitution. When the drafters turned to devising a procedure for electing the president, they returned to arduous committee deliberations and floor wrangling to find a compromise. This time Constitutional Convention politics produced arguably the most convoluted rules to be found in the Constitution: the workings of the **Electoral College**.

As a device, the Electoral College tries to mix state, congressional, and popular participation in the election process and in doing so has managed to confuse citizens for more than two hundred years. Each state is awarded as many electors as it has members of the House and Senate. The Constitution left it to the states to decide how electors are selected, but the Framers generally and correctly expected that the states would rely on statewide elections. If any candidate fails to receive an absolute majority (270) of the 538 votes in the Electoral College, the election is thrown into the House of Representatives, which chooses from among the three candidates who received the largest number of electoral votes. In making its selection, the House votes by state delegation; each state gets one vote, and a majority is required to elect a president (see Chapter 11 for more on the Electoral College). Until the Twelfth Amendment corrected the most egregious flaws of the Electoral College, votes for the president and the vice president were tallied side by side, resulting in a vice presidential candidate almost winning the presidency in the election of 1800.

Designing the Judicial Branch

The convention spent comparatively little time designing the new federal judiciary, a somewhat surprising development given that the Constitution gives the Supreme Court final jurisdiction in resolving differences between the state and national levels of government.

Why Women Were Left Out of the Constitution

Why is it that nowhere in the original Constitution or in the floor debates at Philadelphia are women mentioned? One reason is that the delegates to the Constitutional Convention, faced with the glaring deficiencies of the national government under the Articles of Confederation, were less concerned with individual rights than with making government more effective and establishing proper relations among the institutions they were creating. Early on, delegates agreed to allow the individual states to continue to decide which citizens should have the right to vote. Thus no one actually gained the right to vote in the Constitution.

Second, although it tacitly accepts franchise restrictions imposed by the states, the Constitution reads as though it was drafted to be as free of gender bias as eighteenth-century usage allowed. Throughout, the words *persons* and *citizens*, not *men*, appear. Eligibility to serve as a member of Congress, for example, begins with the statement "No Person shall be a Representative." Elsewhere: "The Citizens of each State shall be entitled to all Privileges and Immunities of Citizens in the several States." A few passages of the Constitution use the pronoun *he* (in each instance, however, the masculine pronoun refers back to a gender-free noun), but until

Susan B. Anthony

the twentieth century this referent was commonly employed and legally interpreted to include women. In

Armed with that jurisdiction and with the **supremacy clause** (Article VI), which declares that national laws take precedence over state laws when both properly discharge their governments' respective responsibilities, the Supreme Court emerged from the convention as a major, probably underappreciated, lever for expanding the scope of national policymaking.

States' rights advocates and nationalists did, however, spar over two lesser questions: Who would appoint Supreme Court justices—the president or the Senate? And should a network of lower federal courts be created, or should state courts handle all cases until they reached the Supreme Court, the only federal court? The convention split the difference over appointments by giving the president appointment powers and the Senate confirmation powers, and they left it to some future Congress to decide whether the national government needed its own lower-level judiciary. The First Congress exercised this option almost immediately, creating a lower federal court system with the Judiciary Act of 1789.

An important issue never quite resolved by the Constitutional Convention was the extent of the Court's authority to overturn federal laws and executive actions as unconstitutional—a concept known as **judicial review**. Although the supremacy clause appears to establish the this respect, then, women were not left out of the Constitution.

The third reason is that women's political rights simply had not yet become an issue. Absence of the issue, however, did not mean that women remained apolitical during the Revolution and the subsequent crisis in governance or that they failed to protest other aspects of their inferior legal standing. The ample evidence in private correspondence indicates that many women followed politics carefully. A few even published monographs that received wide circulation. One of the most famous correspondents of either sex during this era was Abigail Adams, the wife of John Adams and the mother of John Quincy Adams. Her numerous letters to her husband and leaders, such as Thomas Jefferson, exhibit a candor and insight that make them compelling to modern readers as well. To her husband, who was away attending the Continental Congress, she wrote, "In the new code of laws which I suppose it will be necessary for you to make, I desire you would remember the ladies, and be more generous to them than your ancestors. Do not put such unlimited power in the hands of husbands. Remember, all men would be tyrants if they could." This passage often has been celebrated as one of the first expressions of women's political rights in America. But, in fact, Adams was addressing various civil laws that allowed husbands to

confiscate their wives' property and made divorce all but impossible. Lack of a woman's rights in marriage—not suffrage—was the grievance of these early feminists.

Not until publication of Sarah Grimké's *Letters on the Equality of the Sexes, and the Condition of Woman* in 1838 and the Seneca Falls Convention declaration—"All men and women are created equal"—a decade later would women's suffrage be placed on the national political agenda. In 1869 Wyoming became the first state to add women to the voter rolls. Later in the nineteenth century, Susan B. Anthony of Massachusetts led a suffragist movement that claimed the right to vote under the Fourteenth Amendment and sought a constitutional suffrage amendment. In 1887 Congress defeated the proposal for the amendment, but the suffrage movement continued. President Woodrow Wilson (1913–1921) initially opposed the amendment, arguing that state action was more appropriate. But when protests grew into hunger strikes in 1918, he announced his support. The Nineteenth Amendment to the Constitution, guaranteeing women the right to vote, was ratified in 1920.

Source: Adapted from James Q. Wilson and John J. DiIulio Jr., *American Government: Institutions and Policies*, 7th ed. (Boston: Houghton Mifflin, 1998), 43.

Court's authority to review state laws, there is no formal language extending this authority to veto federal laws. Yet many of the Framers, including Hamilton, claimed that the Constitution implicitly provides for judicial review. Later in life Madison protested that he never would have agreed to a provision that allowed an unelected branch of government to have the final say in lawmaking. But in one of the great ironies of American history, Madison was a litigant in an early Supreme Court decision, *Marbury v. Madison* (1803), in which the Court laid claim to the authority to strike down any legislation it deemed unconstitutional.[9] In Chapter 9 we will return to this historic case and its profound effects on the development of the judiciary's role in policymaking.

Substantive Issues

In remapping federal-state responsibilities the Framers largely intended to eliminate the collective action dilemmas that had plagued states' efforts to cooperate under the Articles of Confederation. The states had to surrender some autonomy to the national government in order to eliminate the threat of free riding and reneging on collective agreements.

FOREIGN POLICY. Trade and foreign policy were at the top of the list of federal-state issues the Framers wanted the Constitution to solve. Shortly after the Revolutionary War, the states had found themselves engaged in cutthroat competition for foreign commerce. The Framers solved this dilemma by placing foreign policy under the administration of the president and giving Congress the explicit legislative authority to regulate commerce. As for common defense and security, the Framers placed those responsibilities squarely on the shoulders of the national government. The Constitution (Article I, Section 10) forbids any state from entering into a foreign alliance or treaty, maintaining a military during peace-time, or engaging in war unless invaded.

INTERSTATE COMMERCE. Relations among the states, a longtime source of friction, also figured prominently in the Framers' deliberations. As a result, Article I, Section 10, prohibits states from discriminating against each other in various ways. They may not enter into agreements without the consent of Congress, tax imports or exports entering local ports, print money not backed by gold or silver, or make laws prejudicial to citizens of other states.

The Framers balanced these concessions with important benefits for the states. The new national government would assume outstanding debts the states had incurred during the war, protect the states from invasion and insurrection, and guarantee that all states would be governed by republican institutions.

All these provisions of the Constitution are less well known than those creating and con-ferring powers on the several branches of government or the amendments known as the **Bill of Rights**. But the fact that Americans take them for granted reflects their success, not their irrelevance. With these provisions the Framers solved the most serious collective action dilemmas confronting the young nation, including trade. Taken together, the provisions to prevent states from interfering with commerce that crossed their borders established the essentials of a common market among the former colonies. As a result, the Constitution contributed vitally to the nation's economic development during the next century, not only through its directives on interstate commerce but also through the other trade and business-related provisions in Article I. One such provision prevents the government from passing laws impairing the obligations of private contracts; others mandate that the national government create bankruptcy and patent laws.

SLAVERY. Throughout America's history the issue of race has never been far removed from politics. It certainly was present in Philadelphia, despite some delegates' best efforts to prevent a regional disagreement on slavery from thwarting the purpose of the convention. But how could delegates construct a government based on popular sover-eignty and inalienable rights without addressing the fact that one-sixth of Americans were in bondage? They could not. Slavery figured importantly in many delegates' pri-vate calculations, especially those from the South. At several junctures, it broke to the surface.

The first effort to grapple with slavery was the most acrimonious and threatening. How should slaves be counted in allocating congressional representatives to the states? Madison had persuaded delegates to postpone this issue until they had finalized the design of the new Congress, but the issue soon loomed again. Trying to maximize their representation in the population-based House of Representatives, southern delegates insisted that slaves were undeniably people and should be included fully in any population count to determine representation. Northerners resisted this attempted power grab by arguing that because slaves did not enjoy the freedom to act as autonomous citizens, they should not be counted at all. In the end each side accepted a formula initially used to levy taxes under the Articles of Confederation, a plan that assigned states their financial obligations to the national government proportionate to population. Accordingly, the Constitution apportioned each state seats in the House of Representatives based on population totals in which each slave would count as three-fifths of a citizen.[*]

Later in the convention some southern delegates insisted on two guarantees for their "peculiar institution" as conditions for remaining at the convention and endorsing the Constitution in the ratification debates. One was the unrestricted right to continue importing slaves. The delegates from northern states, most of which had outlawed slavery, preferred to leave the issue to some future government. But in the end they conceded by writing into the Constitution a ban on regulation of the slave trade until 1808.[†] (A total ban on slave imports went into effect on January 1, 1808.) Late in the convention southerners introduced the Constitution's second slavery protection clause. It required northern states to return runaway slaves to their masters. After some delegates first resisted and then softened the language of the clause, the proposal passed.

Why did the delegations from the more numerous northern states cave in to the southerners? The handling of the slavery issue was likely another instance of intense private interests prevailing over more diffuse notions of the public good. Reporting to Jefferson in Paris, Madison wrote that "South Carolina and Georgia were inflexible on the point of slaves," implying that without the slave trade and fugitive provisions they would not have endorsed the Constitution. And since the southerners' preferences were secure under the Articles of Confederation, their threat to defect during the subsequent ratification campaign was credible. After launching anguished, caustic criticisms of southerners' demands during floor debates, the northerners cooled down and reassessed their situation. In the end, they conceded many of their antislavery provisions and adopted a more strategic posture that would allow them to gain something in exchange.

With neither side able to persuade the other to adopt its preferred position and yet with each effectively able to veto ratification, both sides began searching for a mutually acceptable alternative. Their first such attempt had produced the Great Compromise. This time

---

[*] The three-fifths rule had been devised under the Articles to resolve a sectional dispute over apportioning states' tax contributions according to population. At that time the northerners had a stake in recognizing the humanity of slaves—if slaves were people their numbers should be fully counted in apportioning tax obligations. Southerners had countered that, since they marketed slaves as property, slaves should be counted no more than any other property. After extended haggling, the groups agreed to add three-fifths of the number of slaves to a state's free population.

[†] The committee that drafted this language proposed that the ban on regulation end in 1800, but a coalition of New Englanders and southerners added eight years to the ban. Only Madison spoke out against extending the deadline. The delegates from Virginia, all of whom had owned slaves at one time or another, voted against extension.

LOGROLLING A CONSTITUTION

Many of the New England delegates who came to Philadelphia were frustrated by the nation's inability to conduct a coordinated commercial policy at home or abroad. Southerners, however, liked things pretty much the way they were, fearing that additional government controls might lead to taxes and regulations on their extensive agricultural exports to Europe. If the national government insisted, as in time it did, that a substantial share of exports must travel on U.S. ships, the Northeast (with its ports and shipping companies) would gain financially at the expense of southern producers. Consequently, the South had opposed giving the national government such commercial authority without the assent of two-thirds of both houses of Congress. This large supermajority would have given the South, in effect, a veto over any objectionable policy, and as a result no commercial provision would have been adopted. Southerners also were committed to warding off an antislavery measure that most northerners and their state legislatures were on record as supporting.

Consider the range of policy options before the delegates. We can rank the policy preferences of any individual delegate or group of like-minded delegates. Although northern delegates preferred an antislavery policy, they desired a strong commercial policy even more. We can illustrate their preferences for various policy combinations by assigning letters to the alternatives: a strong commercial policy, C; no commercial policy, c; proslavery, S; and antislavery, s. Northern delegates most preferred a strong commercial policy coupled with antislavery, followed by a strong commercial provision and an allowance for slavery, and so on.

Using letter combinations and the mathematical symbol for "is greater than," we can rank the northern delegates' preferences for possible policy combinations:

$$\text{Northerners: } Cs > CS > cs > cS$$

The South, on the other hand, preferred to maintain a proslavery policy and to defeat a commercial one. In floor debates at the convention, Southern delegates said they felt more strongly about maintaining slavery than about avoiding marginally more costly shipping. Using the same set of symbols, we can rank southern delegates' preferred policy combinations:

$$\text{Southerners: } cS > CS > cs > Cs$$

the solution took the form of a **logroll**—a standard bargaining strategy in which two sides swap support for dissimilar policies. In the end, New England accommodated the South by agreeing to two provisions: Article I, Section 9, protecting the importation of slaves until at least 1808; and Article IV, Section 2, requiring that northern states return fugitive slaves. In

Note that the North's most preferred combination of constitutional provisions—strong commercial institutions and a ban on the slave trade—was the least preferred combination in the South. And, conversely, the South's most preferred position was the least desired in the North. With their sincere preferences so opposed, frustrations mounted, as did the temperature of the rhetoric. Finally, each side realized that it could not win its most preferred combination of policies, and a search for a compromise solution began. Look carefully and locate the compromise package that each side found comparatively more attractive, bearing in mind that failure to reach agreement on these issues might well have endangered the success of the convention and left thorny issues unresolved during the ratification process. The compromise solution, CS, was a policy that combined strong commercial language and a provision permitting slavery. It took a while for the delegates to find it, but they did.

This solution took the form of a classic logroll. Instead of finding separate compromise policies on each issue, the delegates engaged in vote trading. To win its most important preference, each side conceded to the other its least important choice.

Finding a solution and implementing it are separate exercises that may be equally susceptible to failure. After all, each side must give up something important to win a concession in return. It is a situation ripe with the possibility of reneging, an instance of the classic prisoner's dilemma that always threatens cooperation. (We found such a situation in Chapter 1, where we discussed the classic prisoner's dilemma interrogation in the film *I Wake Up Screaming*.) And because delegates from each side appreciated the difficulty of having to return home and explain their agreement to an unpopular policy, the fear of reneging was real. New England delegates would have to justify writing slavery into the Constitution, while southerners would have to defend opening the door to dreaded commercial regulations.

To succeed, the logroll had to be consummated delicately and discreetly. In his record of the convention's proceeding, James Madison noted the careful language Charles Pinckney of South Carolina had used to signal to the other side that he and his southern colleagues were in agreement. "The true interest of the S[outhern] States is to have no regulation of commerce," said Pinckney, who then cited "the loss brought on the commerce of the Eastern States by the revolution" and the "liberal conduct [of those states] toward the views of South Carolina." Here, Madison inserted a footnote translating Pinckney's circumlocutions for future readers: by "liberal conduct," Pinckney "meant the permission to import slaves. An understanding on the two subjects of *navigation* and *slavery* had taken place between those parts of the Union."[1]

Logrolling is ubiquitous in all legislatures, whether they are constitutional conventions or student government committees. This form of strategic behavior is, in fact, essential for a society composed of many different and competing interests to transact its politics successfully. We will encounter numerous instances of it throughout this text. For a description of a less historic but no less curious logroll, see box "Porn for Corn" in Chapter 6.

---

1. Quoted in William Lee Miller, *The Business of May Next: James Madison and the Founding* (Charlottesville: University Press of Virginia, 1992), 135.

return, southern delegates dropped their opposition on an altogether different issue that was dear to the commercial interests of the northern states. Article I, Section 8, allows Congress to regulate commerce and tax imports with a simple majority vote (see box "Logrolling a Constitution," page 70).

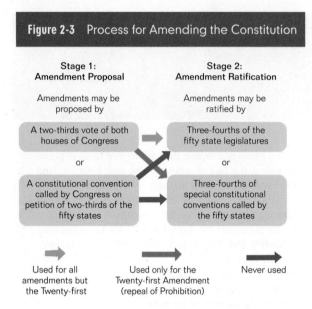

Figure 2-3 Process for Amending the Constitution

Stage 1:
Amendment Proposal

Amendments may be
proposed by

A two-thirds vote of both
houses of Congress

or

A constitutional convention
called by Congress on
petition of two-thirds of the
fifty states

Stage 2:
Amendment Ratification

Amendments may be
ratified by

Three-fourths of the
fifty state legislatures

or

Three-fourths of
special constitutional
conventions called by
the fifty states

Used for all
amendments but
the Twenty-first

Used only for the
Twenty-first Amendment
(repeal of Prohibition)

Never used

Amending the Constitution

In their efforts to provide a suitable means for amending the Constitution, the Framers broke new ground. (Amending the Articles of Confederation required the unanimous consent of the states, and the constitution creating the French republic in 1789 contained no amendment procedure whatsoever.) Perhaps the futility of trying to win unanimous consent for changing the Articles persuaded the Framers to find a more reasonable method for amending the Constitution, one that did not require a full convention like the Philadelphia convention. Yet they did not want to place the amendment option within easy reach of a popular majority. After all, some future majority frustrated by executive and judicial vetoes might try to change the Constitution rather than accommodate its opponents. So, again, the Framers solved the dilemma by imposing heavy transaction costs on changing the Constitution.

The concept of providing for future amendment of the Constitution proved less controversial than the amendment procedure itself. Intent on preserving their hard-won gains in the face of future amendment proposals, both the nationalists and states' rights advocates approached this matter warily. Delegates from small states insisted on endorsement of amendments by a large number of states, while the nationalists argued that the Constitution derived its legitimacy directly from the citizenry and that the citizens alone should approve any change. Unable to muster a majority for either position, the delegates again employed the formula of accepting parts of both proposals. As a result, the Constitution allows an amendment to be proposed either by a two-thirds vote of both houses of Congress or by an "application" from two-thirds of the states. Enactment occurs when three-fourths of the states, acting either through their state legislatures or in special conventions, accept the amendment (see Figure 2-3).

Since its ratification the Constitution has been amended twenty-seven times. In every instance Congress initiated the process, and in all but one case the state legislatures did the ratifying. (The Constitution and its amendments appear in the Appendix.) Six additional amendments—including the Equal Rights Amendment (see Chapter 4, Civil Rights)—were sent to the states but failed to win endorsement from a sufficient number. The paucity of near misses is deceiving, however. Each year dozens of amendments are proposed in Congress, but they fail to go any further either because they fail to attract the requisite two-thirds support in both chambers, or supporters foresee little chance of success in the states. During the 108th Congress (2003–2004), for example, members proposed amendments restricting marriage to a man and a woman; ensuring "God" is included in the Pledge of Allegiance; and providing a mechanism for Congress to replenish its membership should more than a quarter of its members be killed, as in a terrorist attack.

THE FIGHT FOR RATIFICATION

The seventh and final article of the Constitution spells out an important procedure endorsed by delegates in the final days of the convention: "The Ratification of the Conventions of nine States, shall be sufficient for the Establishment of this Constitution between the States so ratifying the Same." Everyone knew that this deceptively straight-forward provision was critical for the success of their enterprise. The delegates impro-vised by adapting the nine-state rule employed by the Articles for passing normal legislation, even though it was directed at the confederation's legislature and not the convention, and even though the Articles did not provide for amendment. And the ratification provision withdrew ratification authority from the state legislatures, which might have misgivings about surrendering autonomy, and gave it instead to elective special conventions. In sum, the delegates succeeded in a bit of legalistic legerdemain— appearing to conform to the requirements of the existing Constitution while breaking radically from it.

The Federalist and Antifederalist Debate

At the close of the convention, only three delegates refused to sign the Constitution. This consensus, however, is misleading; others who probably would have objected left early, and many prominent political leaders such as Virginians Patrick Henry and Richard Henry Lee had refused even to participate.

Over the next year every state but Rhode Island (it held out until 1790) elected delegates to state conventions that proceeded to dissect the Constitution and ponder its individual provisions. This was truly a time of national debate over the future of the country. As one observer noted, "Almost every American pen . . . [and] peasants and their wives in every part of the land" began "to dispute on politics and positively to determine upon our liberties."[10] On a lighter note, the *Boston Daily Advertiser,* responding to General Washington's call for public debate, admonished its readers: "Come on brother scribblers, 'tis idle to lag! The Convention has let the cat out of the bag."[11]

Delegates to the state conventions concentrated, predictably, on the concerns of their states and communities. Southern states carefully inspected each article for a northern avenue of attack on their "peculiar institution" of slavery. Finding none, all of the southern states except North Carolina lined up behind the Constitution. Constituencies and their delegates similarly aligned themselves for or against the Constitution according to its perceived impact on their pocketbooks. Small farmers, struck hard by declining markets and high property taxes after the war, had succeeded in gaining sympathetic majorities in many of the state legislatures. Thus they looked suspiciously on this attempt to shift fiscal policy to the national government.

Moreover, under pressure from small farmers, many state legislatures had printed cheap paper money (making it easier for the farmers to pay off their debts), overturned court deci-sions unfavorable to debt-laden farmers, and provided some with direct subsidies and relief. Thus these constituencies were reluctant to see their state legislatures subordinated to some more distant government that would assume control of critical activities such as currency and bankruptcy. The farmers failed to recognize, however, that the ascendancy of the national

With the New York ratification narrowly divided, proratification forces staged a massive rally. The parade was graced by a "ship of state," an already well-developed metaphor. At the time, New Yorker Alexander Hamilton was widely regarded as one of the Constitution's most effective sponsors.

government would benefit them by shifting public finance away from property taxes and toward import duties. Some northeastern merchants who foresaw this shift lobbied their delegates to oppose ratification.

In the public campaign for ratification these issues tended to be reduced to the rhetoric of nationalism, voiced by the **Federalists**, versus the rhetoric of states' rights, voiced by the **Antifederalists**. The divisiveness characterizing the Philadelphia convention thus continued. But the labels given the two sides were confusing. Although they consistently distinguished the Constitution's supporters and opponents, the labels confused the positions of these camps on the issue of federalism. Many of those who opposed ratification were more protective of state prerogatives, as the term *federalist* implies, than were many of the prominent "Federalists." Appreciating the depth of state loyalties, Madison and his colleagues early on tactically maneuvered to neutralize this issue by claiming that the Constitution provided a true federal system, making those seeking ratification Federalists. Their success in expropriating this label put their opponents at a disadvantage in the public relations campaign. One disgruntled Antifederalist proposed that the labels be changed so that Madison and his crowd would be called the "Rats" (for proratification) and his side the "Antirats."

Although in the end the Federalists prevailed and are today revered as the nation's "Founders," the Antifederalists included a comparable number and quality of proven patriots. Foremost among them was Patrick Henry, who led his side's counterattack. With him were fellow Virginians Richard Henry Lee, George Mason, and a young James Monroe, who would become the nation's fifth president under the Constitution he had opposed. Other famous outspoken opponents included Boston's Revolutionary War hero Samuel Adams and New York governor George Clinton.

In their opposition to the Constitution, the Antifederalists raised serious theoretical objections—ones that can still be heard more than two hundred years later. They argued that only local democracy, the kind found in small homogeneous communities, could approach true democracy. The United States, they asserted, already was too large and too diverse to be well ruled by a single set of laws. Turning their sights to the Constitution itself, the Antifederalists argued that a stronger national government must be accompanied by explicit safeguards against tyranny. Specifically, the Constitution needed a bill of rights—a familiar feature of most state constitutions. Some delegates to the convention proposed a bill of rights, but Madison and others had argued that it was unnecessary because the Constitution did not give the national government any powers that could be construed as invading the citizenry's rights. This argument, however, worked better at the convention than it did in the public campaign. The Antifederalists quickly realized they had identified a chink in the Constitution's armor and began pounding the issue hard. Even Madison's ally Jefferson wrote him from France insisting that individual rights were too important to be "left to inference." Suddenly on the defensive, Madison made a strategic capitulation and announced that at the convening of the First Congress under the new Constitution, he would introduce constitutional amendments providing a bill of rights. His strategy worked; the issue receded. In a sense, though, the Antifederalist strategy had worked as well. Madison kept his promise, and by 1791 the Constitution contained the Bill of Rights (see Table 2-1).

In June 1788 New Hampshire became the ninth and technically decisive state to ratify the Constitution. But Virginia and New York had still not voted, and until these two large, centrally located states became a part of the Union, no one gave the new government much chance of getting off the ground. But by the end of July both states had narrowly ratified the Constitution, and the new Union was a reality.

The Influence of *The Federalist*

Aside from eventually yielding a new constitution, the ratification debates fostered another national resource: eighty-five essays that were collected under the title *The Federalist*. Published under the shared pseudonym Publius in 1787–1788, the essays were written by Alexander Hamilton (who wrote the majority), John Jay (who wrote five), and James Madison (who arguably

TABLE 2-1	
The First Ten Amendments to the Constitution: Bill of Rights	
Amendment	Purpose
I	Guarantees freedom of religion, speech, assembly, and press, and the right of people to petition the government for redress of grievances
II	Protects the right of states to maintain a militia
III	Restricts quartering of troops in private homes
IV	Protects against "unreasonable searches and seizures"
V	Ensures the right not to be deprived of "life, liberty, or property, without due process of law," including protections against double jeopardy, self-incrimination, and government seizure of property without just compensation
VI	Guarantees the right to a speedy and public trial by an impartial jury
VII	Ensures the right to a jury trial in cases involving the common law (judge-made law originating in England)
VIII	Protects against excessive bail or cruel and unusual punishment
IX	Provides that people's rights are not restricted to those specified in Amendments I–VIII
X	Reiterates the Constitution's principle of federalism by providing that powers not granted to the national government are reserved to the states or to the people

wrote the best). In one of history's interesting twists of fate, Hamilton initially recruited fellow New Yorker William Duer to join the Publius team. His submissions were judged inadequate, however, and Hamilton turned to Madison. Duer, a professor at Columbia University, later found his appropriate medium in a highly successful American government textbook in which he introduced students to the already famous *Federalist* essays, to which he almost contributed. (Duer wrote a heartfelt dedication in his textbook to Madison, which is reproduced on page viii.)

Because their immediate purpose was to influence the delegates to the New York convention, where ratification was in trouble, the *Federalist* essays first appeared in New York City newspapers. At one point Hamilton and Madison were cranking out four essays a week, prompting the Antifederalists to complain that by the time they had rebutted one argument in print, several others had appeared. Reprinted widely, the essays provided rhetorical ammunition to those supporting ratification.[*]

Whatever their role in the Constitution's ratification, *The Federalist Papers,* as they are also called, have profoundly affected the way Americans then and now have understood their government. A few years after their publication, Thomas Jefferson, describing the curriculum of the University of Virginia to its board of overseers, declared *The Federalist* to be indispensable reading for all undergraduates. It is "agreed by all," he explained, that these essays convey "the genuine meaning" of the Constitution.

THE THEORY UNDERLYING THE CONSTITUTION

Two of Madison's essays, *Federalist* No. 10 and *Federalist* No. 51, offer special insights into the theory underlying the Constitution. (For the full text of both essays, see the Appendix.) In different ways, each essay tackles the fundamental problem of self-governance, which Madison poses in a famous passage from *Federalist* No. 51:

> If men were angels, no government would be necessary. If angels were to govern men, neither external nor internal controls on government would be necessary. In framing a government which is to be administered by men over men, the great difficulty lies in this: you must first enable the government to control the governed; and in the next place oblige it to control itself.

The last goal is tricky. *Federalist* No. 10 tackles the problem by both exploring the likelihood that tyranny by the majority would arise within a democracy and identifying a solution. It is a powerful, cogent argument grounded in logic. *Federalist* No. 51 deals with the delegation problem of keeping the citizenry's agents (that is, government officeholders) honest. The solution lies in pitting politicians against one another through the mutual vetoes embedded in the Constitution's separation of powers and checks and balances. This way, politicians can counteract each other's temptation to engage in mischief. Whatever their differences, these two essays can be read as following parallel paths—one at the societal level, the other at the governmental level—toward the same destination of a polity free from tyranny.

Federalist No. 10

Madison's first and most celebrated essay appeared in the November 24, 1787, issue of the New York *Daily Advertiser. Federalist* No. 10 responds to the strongest argument the Antifederalists could muster—that a "large Republic" cannot long survive. This essay borrows from the writings of David Hume, but over the course of a decade of legislative debate and

---

[*] Although they became famous, the *Federalist* essays, according to most historians, had a negligible impact on the outcome of the ratification process. Perhaps too many hard economic interests were in play for abstract arguments about the general welfare to do more than justify and dress up positions grounded firmly in self-interests. The New York convention shifted toward ratification only after New York City threatened to secede from the state if the vote went against ratification.

correspondence Madison had honed his argument to fit the American case.[12] Indeed, Madison had made the argument before—at the Constitutional Convention when defending the Virginia Plan in a floor debate.

The major task Madison sets out for himself in *Federalist* No. 10 is to devise a republic in which a majority of citizens will be unable to tyrannize the minority. Madison wastes no time identifying the rotten apple. It is **factions**, which he describes as "mortal diseases under which popular governments have everywhere perished." He defines a faction as "a number of citizens, whether amounting to a majority or minority of the whole, who are united and actuated by some common impulse of passion, or of *interest,* adverse to the rights of other citizens, or to the permanent and aggregate interests of the community" (emphasis added). Madison's factions appear to have many of the attributes of modern-day interest groups and even political parties.

Madison then identifies two ways to eliminate factions—authoritarianism and conformism—neither of which he finds

When James Madison was introduced with the accolade "Father of the Constitution," he frequently demurred, probably less from modesty than from disagreement with many of its provisions.

acceptable. Authoritarianism, a form of government that actively suppresses factions, is a remedy that would be worse than the disease. In a famous passage of *Federalist* No. 10 Madison offers an analogy: "Liberty is to faction what air is to fire, an aliment without which it instantly expires."

Conformism, the second solution, is, as Madison notes, "as impracticable as the first would be unwise." People cannot somehow be made to have the same goals, for "the latent causes of faction are . . . sown in the nature of man." Thus two individuals who are precisely alike in wealth, education, and other characteristics will nonetheless have different views on many issues. Even the "most frivolous and fanciful distinction" can "kindle their unfriendly passions," Madison observes, but most of the important political cleavages that divide a citizenry are predictably rooted in their life circumstances. In another famous passage the author anticipates by nearly a century Karl Marx's class-based analysis of politics under capitalism:

> But the most common and durable source of faction has been the various and unequal distribution of property. Those who hold and those who are without property have ever formed distinct interests in society. . . . A landed interest, a manufacturing interest, a mercantile interest, a moneyed interest, with many lesser interests, grow up of necessity in civilized nations, and divide them into different classes, actuated by different sentiments and views.*

---

* In an earlier version of this passage, delivered at the convention in defense of the Virginia Plan, Madison had added that those who owned slaves and those who did not had distinct and antithetical interests. He may well have omitted this reference to slavery here because it had proven controversial with southern delegates. After all, this is a public argument intended to persuade readers to support adoption of the Constitution.

If the causes of faction cannot be removed without snuffing out liberty, then one must control their effects. Madison identifies two kinds of factions—those composed of a minority of the citizenry and those composed of a majority—that have to be controlled in different ways. During the late eighteenth century, the ubiquitous problem of factional tyranny occurred at the hands of the monarchy and aristocracy, a "minority" faction, for which democracy provides the remedy. A minority faction "may clog the administration, it may convulse the society; but it will be unable to execute and mask its violence under the forms of the Constitution." Democracy, however, introduces its own special brand of factional tyranny—that emanating from a self-interested majority. In Madison's era many people— especially those opposed to reform—ranted that majority rule equaled mob rule. Thus supporters of the new constitutional plan had to explain how a society could give government authority to a majority without fear that it would trample on minority rights. Madison explained: "To secure the public good and private rights against the danger of . . . a [majority] faction, and at the same time to preserve the spirit and the form of popular government, is then the great object to which our inquiries are directed."

Parting ways with some of the leading political philosophers of his era, Madison dismisses direct democracy as the solution:

> [T]here is nothing to check the inducements to sacrifice the weaker party or an obnoxious individual. Hence it is that such democracies have ever been spectacles of turbulence and contention; have ever been found incompatible with personal security or the rights of property; and have in general been as short in their lives as they have been violent in their deaths.

So much for town meetings.

Madison contends that the republican form of government, in which elected representatives are delegated responsibility for making governmental decisions, addresses the tyranny of the majority problem in two ways. First, representation dilutes the factious spirit. Madison does not trust politicians to be more virtuous than their constituents, but he recognizes that, to get elected, they will tend to moderate their views to appeal to a diverse constituency. Here Madison subtly introduces his *size principle,* on which the rest of the argument hinges: up to a point, the larger and more diverse the constituency, the more diluted is the influence of any particular faction on the preferences of the representative.

A legislature composed of representatives elected from districts containing diverse factional interests is unlikely to allow a faction or a small coalition of them to so dominate the institution that it can deny rights to factions in the minority. This line of reasoning allows Madison to introduce a second distinct virtue of a republic. Unlike a direct democracy, it can advantageously encompass a large population and a large territory. As Madison argues,

> Extend the sphere, and you take in a greater variety of parties and interests; you make it less probable that a majority of the whole will have a common motive to invade the rights of other citizens; or if such a common motive exists, it will be more difficult for all who feel it to discover their own strength and to act in unison with each other.

In other words, their differences will pose a benign collective action problem. Any attempted collusion would confront such steep transaction costs that any efforts to engage in mischief would inevitably be frustrated.

Publicly reading the Constitution was a favorite activity at Tea Party rallies, as the movement's followers claimed the mantle of the American Revolution, and apparently of Captain America.

What has Madison accomplished here? He has turned the Antifederalists' "small is beautiful" mantra on its head by pointing out that an encompassing national government would be less susceptible to the influence of factions than would state governments: "A rage for paper money, for an abolition of debts, for an equal division of property, or for any other improper or wicked project, would be less apt to pervade the whole body of the Union than a particular member of it." A geographically large republic would encompass dispersed, diverse populations, thereby imposing serious transaction costs on their representatives in maintaining a majority coalition and minimizing the prospect of majority tyranny. Madison concludes: "In the extent and proper structure of the Union, therefore, we behold a republican remedy for the disease most incident to republican government."

Until the twentieth century, *Federalist* No. 10 attracted less attention than did some of its companion essays. Yet as the nation has grown in size and diversity, the essay has won new prominence for the prescience with which Madison explained how such growth strengthens the republic (see Map 2-1 on page 82). This Madisonian view of democracy often is referred to as **pluralism**. It welcomes society's numerous diverse interests and generally endorses the idea that those competing interests most affected by a public policy will have the greatest say in what the policy will be.

Federalist No. 51

By giving free expression to all of society's diversity, *Federalist* No. 10 offers an essentially organic solution to the danger of majority tyranny. *Federalist* No. 51, by contrast, takes a more mechanistic approach of separating government officers into different branches and giving them the authority to interfere with each other's actions. The authority of each branch must "be made commensurate to the danger of attack," Madison asserts. As for incentive: "Ambition must be made to counteract ambition. The interest of the man must be connected with the constitutional rights of the place." In other words, the Framers' efforts will have failed if future generations of politicians do not jealously defend the integrity of their offices.

Since popular election is the supreme basis for legitimacy and independence in a democracy, no constitutional contrivances can place appointive offices on an equal footing with elective offices. Madison explains:

> In republican government, the legislative authority necessarily predominates. The remedy for this inconvenience is to divide the legislature into different branches; and to render them, by different modes of election and different principles of action, as little connected with each other as the nature of their common functions and their common dependence on the society will admit.

Bicameralism is intended to weaken the legislature's capacity to act too quickly and impulsively, but even so it may not prevent the legislature from encroaching on the other branches. Madison offers the president's veto as a strong countervailing force and speculates that, by refusing to override the president's veto, the Senate might team up with the executive to keep the popularly elected House of Representatives in check. Madison even finds virtue in the considerable prerogatives reserved to the states: "In a compound republic of America, the power surrendered by the people is first divided between two distinct governments. . . . Hence a double security arises to the rights of the people. The different governments will control each other, at the same time that each will be controlled by itself."

Could this be the same James Madison who wanted to abandon the convention rather than agree to a Senate elected by the state legislatures, the same man who had wanted Congress to have an absolute veto over state actions? Madison's Virginia Plan had vested ultimate authority in a popularly elected national legislature, and this model of a legislature became the House of Representatives. So why is he commending a Constitution that severely constrains this institution's influence over policy?

Madison probably was playing to his audience.[13] *Federalist* No. 51 seeks to reassure those fence-sitters listening to Antifederalist propaganda that the Constitution would take a giant step down the short path to tyranny. After all, the Antifederalists were presenting the specter of a powerful and remote national government and, within it, the possible emergence of a *junta* composed of unelected senators and an indirectly elected president bent on usurping the authority of the states, undermining the one popularly elected branch of government (the House of Representatives), and ultimately subjugating the citizenry. Madison is countering with a portrait of a weak, fragmented system that appears virtually incapable of purposive action, much less of hatching plots. He must have grimaced as he (anonymously) drafted the passage extolling the Constitution's checks on his House of Representatives.

In summary, *Federalist* No. 10 conveys the theory of pluralism that guided the Constitution's chief architect; *Federalist* No. 51 explores how and why the governmental system that emerged from the political process in Philadelphia might actually work. Since these essays were written, Madison's insight into the operation of the Constitution has been largely borne out. As we shall see in Chapter 4, government policy sometimes fails to implement the preferences of national majorities for reasons he identifies in this famous essay.

Both the pluralism of competing interests and separated institutions have been judged less favorably by many modern students of American politics. With authority so fragmented, they argue, government cannot function effectively. And by adding a layer of institutional fragmentation on top of pluralism, the Framers simply overdid it. The result is an inherently conservative political process in which legitimate majorities are frequently frustrated by some minority faction that happens to control a critical lever of government. Furthermore, if the logic of *Federalist* No. 10 is correct, Americans do not need all of this constitutional architecture of checks and balances to get the job done.[14] Critics also point to the many other stable democracies throughout the world that function well with institutions designed to allow majorities to govern effectively. Would Madison have privately agreed with this critique? Probably so—after all, his Virginia Plan incorporated those checks and balances necessary to foster the healthy competition of factions and no more.

THE CONSTITUTION: BORN OF SWEET REASON OR POLITICS?

"America is a nation without a national government," one critic observed during the last days of the confederation, "and it is not a pretty sight." The Constitution was adopted to correct the problems inherent to localism. But rather than making a break with the past, as the nationalists had sought, the new Constitution simply veered in a somewhat more national direction. In the end, a century and a half of home rule, as well as the loyalty to state governments felt by those who had served successfully at that level, could not be denied. The new national government had to accommodate the states by allowing their participation in the selection of senators and reserving to them certain prerogatives and responsibilities.

It is deeply ironic that the kind of national pluralism Madison and his allies were trying to install already was at work at the convention, frustrating their success. Present were the contending interests that closely resembled the factions of *Federalist* No. 10. Large states competed with small over representation, the South pushed for constitutional protection for slaveholding, and the Northeast worked for favorable commercial regulations. The absence of a dominant majority faction meant intense bargaining resulting in shifting alliances that led to a novel, hybrid governmental system that is neither national nor confederative in nature. Many of the Constitution's provisions have no theoretical rationale; they are simply the hammered-out products of compromise. How does one justify the three-fifths rule, the malapportioned Senate, or the Byzantine procedures for electing a president, if not by explaining that each was born of political necessity? The Constitution is, in other words, a fine document arising not from the application of sweet reason but from politics. The document produced by the Constitutional Convention was a plan no delegate favored or could even have imagined on the opening day of the convention. It was, however, a plan that a substantial majority favored over the status quo and all could live with.

Map 2-1 The Shape of America's Population

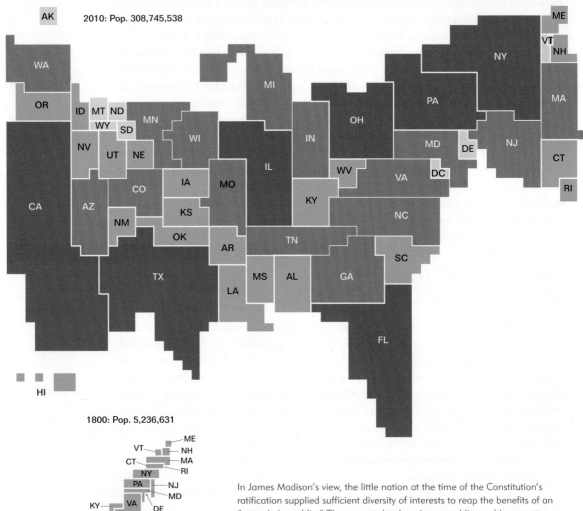

2010: Pop. 308,745,538

1800: Pop. 5,236,631

STATE POPULATION:

10,000,000+

5,000,000

1,000,000

200,000

In James Madison's view, the little nation at the time of the Constitution's ratification supplied sufficient diversity of interests to reap the benefits of an "extended republic." The present-day American republic would appear to satisfy *Federalist* No. 10's requirements even better. Writing to a friend forty years later, however, Madison worried that America would outgrow the Constitution. Projecting the nation's current rate of growth, he estimated that by 1930 it would become too crowded and too polarized between "wealthy capitalists and indigent laborers." He predicted that the United States would require a different constitutional system, one that was more like Britain's with its strong executive. The nation's history corresponded closely to Madison's prediction, as shown in the timing of the Great Depression, the calls for radical reform, and, in Franklin Roosevelt, the rise of the modern presidency.

Sources: U.S. Census Bureau and *The New York Times*.

Despite their efforts, Madison and the nationalists won only a partial victory with the launching of the Constitution; the nation still added up to little more than a collection of states. Nevertheless, America's political development since 1787 has seen the realization of many of the goals that eluded the nationalists at the Philadelphia convention. For example, by building the Constitution on the consent of the governed rather than endorsement by the states, the nationalists successfully denied state governments any claim that they could ignore national policy. Over the next several decades, however, state politicians unhappy with national policy routinely threatened to secede or to "nullify" objectionable federal laws. But none of these threats became a full-fledged constitutional crisis until the eleven southern states seceded from the Union shortly after Abraham Lincoln was elected to the presidency in 1860. With the Union victory in 1865, this threat to nationhood ended conclusively. A central government capable of forcing compliance was finally achieved by war. Yet, as we shall see in Chapter 3, Federalism, the nationalization of government authority remained limited by modern standards. Nowhere is this more evident than in the domain of civil liberties, the subject of Chapter 5.

But what about Madison's other goal of building a national society that could prevent majority factions from tyrannizing local minorities? The two-hundred-year history of governance under the Constitution has been one of gradual nationalization—so gradual, in fact, that the nation only recently realized Madison's aspiration. In slavery, segregation, and the disenfranchisement of southern black citizens, Madison's worst dreams were realized, and nearly two hundred years would pass before these citizens would achieve equality in civic life. Chapter 4 surveys this inglorious history to illuminate the weaknesses and limitations of the constitutional system. As Madison correctly predicted, the U.S. Senate proved to be an institutional barrier to quelling the threat of state-level tyranny of the majority. More importantly, the history recounted in Chapter 4 illuminates why and how citizens and politicians would find it in their interest to extend rights to disenfranchised members of the society.

TAKE A QUIZ

logic.cqpress.com

Test your knowledge of this chapter.

logic.cqpress.com

■ Key Terms ■

Antifederalists, 74

Articles of Confederation, 50

bicameral legislature, 48

Bill of Rights, 68

checks and balances, 61

commerce clause, 60

confederation, 50

Declaration of Independence, 49

Electoral College, 65

factions, 77

Federalists, 74

Great Compromise, 65

home rule, 44

judicial review, 66

logroll, 70

nationalists, 56

necessary and proper
    clause, 60

New Jersey Plan, 59

pluralism, 79

popular sovereignty, 56

Shays's Rebellion, 54

states' rights, 59

supremacy clause, 66

"take care" clause, 64

veto, 64

Virginia Plan, 58

Suggested Readings

Dougherty, Keith. *Collective Action under the Articles of Confederation.* New York: Cambridge University Press, 2001. Analyzes the Articles of Confederation and Shays's Rebellion with a keen eye toward identifying the historical circumstances that caused massive free riding to bring the young nation to a crisis.

Draper, Theodore. *A Struggle for Power: The American Revolution.* New York: Times Books, 1996. According to Draper, the Revolution represented the politics of self-interest rather than ideology. His account also examines the greater political context of the Revolution, in particular the long-standing conflict between the French and the British.

Kernell, Samuel, ed. *James Madison: The Theory and Practice of Republican Government.* Stanford, CA: Stanford University Press, 2003. This collection of essays by leading students of modern American politics compares Madison's political science and leadership strategies with current concepts and ideas, including those presented in Chapter 1. (Kernell's essay was spawned by issues encountered in reconciling *Federalist* Nos. 10 and 51 while writing this chapter.)

Ketcham, Ralph. *James Madison: A Biography.* Charlottesville: University Press of Virginia, 1990. An authoritative and highly readable biography of America's first political scientist.

Miller, William Lee. *The Business of May Next: James Madison and the Founding.* Charlottesville: University Press of Virginia, 1992. An absorbing account of the politics leading up to and at the Constitutional Convention. This history served as the chief source of the account reported in this chapter.

Norton, Mary Beth. *Liberty's Daughters.* Boston: Little, Brown, 1980. A systematic and persuasive assessment of the considerable behind-the-scenes contribution of women during the Revolution and the impact of the war on the transformation of family relationships.

Riker, William. *The Strategy of Rhetoric.* New Haven, CT: Yale University Press, 1996. A lively yet keenly analytical and systematic account of the Constitution's ratification as a political campaign.

Rossiter, Clinton. *1787: The Grand Convention.* New York: Macmillan, 1966. This classic portrayal of the Constitutional Convention remains the most readable and provocative treatment of the Framers at work in Philadelphia.

Wills, Garry. *Explaining America.* New York: Doubleday, 1981. An analysis of the logic and ideas of *The Federalist.* Few authors can match Wills's talent for rendering abstract concepts and ideas intelligible to the general audience.

Wood, Gordon S. *The Creation of the American Republic, 1776–1787.* New York: Norton, 1969. An indispensable intellectual history of the transformation of America from the Revolution through the adoption of the Constitution.

Review Questions

1. What steps were taken to construct a national government before the Articles of Confederation? What resulted from these steps?

2. How were decisions made under the Articles? What sorts of decisions were not made by the confederation? How did this system affect the war effort? How did it affect the conduct of the national and state governments once the war was over?

3. Why is the Electoral College so complicated?

4. How did the Framers balance the powers and independence of the executive and legislative branches?

5. What mechanisms for constitutional amendment were included in the Constitution? Why were multiple methods included?

3 Federalism

A registered marijuana grower under the Oregon Medical Marijuana Act, Jason Nelson, operated this elaborate cultivation system inside his Grants Pass, Oregon, home until he was charged with violating the federal ban on manufacturing marijuana.

- Is there a rationale for having some government services supplied locally, others by the states, and still others by the national government?

- Despite the Framers' efforts to keep the national government out of the states' business, was it

inevitable that so many policies once left to the states are now handled by the federal government?

- When elected officials from the states challenge national authority, what determines who will have the final say over policy?

On June 8, 2012, a jury convicted Jason Michael Scott Nelson, who was a registered medical marijuana grower under Oregon's state law, on federal charges of manufacturing marijuana. At his trial in a federal courthouse in Medford, Oregon, Mr. Nelson, the owner of a local bicycle shop, claimed that he was lawfully growing marijuana on behalf of four patients whose doctors had recommended it as a therapeutic treatment, in full accordance with the Oregon Medical Marijuana Act. That law, approved by the state's voters in 1998, allows for the cultivation, possession, and use of marijuana when doctors recommend it. The state's public health department has created a registry of the 54,280 patients and 2,090 physicians taking part in the program, and conducts criminal background checks on prospective growers like Mr. Nelson.[1]

Yet despite what Oregon voters have decided and what their state has done to assemble a complex cannabis bureaucracy, one central fact fouled Mr. Nelson's plans: growing and using pot remains illegal under federal law. Marijuana is classified as a Schedule I controlled substance, considered by Congress to have a high potential for dependency and no accepted medical use. No matter what a state does—and Oregon is one of the eighteen states that allow the medical use of marijuana—federal authorities can act to enforce federal laws. At the same time that states and cities have passed laws to regulate and tax pot dispensaries, federal Drug Enforcement Administration (DEA) agents have raided them. The conflict strikes at the very heart of questions of federalism. When should there be uniform policies governing all of the United States, and when should states be left on their own to settle contentious moral and political controversies? What sorts of issues can be resolved independently by states, and what issues spill across state borders, necessitating a federal response? When state and national powers collide, who should win?

The ultimate arbiter in controversies of American federalism is the U.S. Supreme Court, which has clearly sided with the national government on the issue of medical marijuana. The Court's ruling in the landmark 2005 *Gonzales v. Raich* case upheld the supremacy of the federal government in this part of the law, ruling that Congress's ban on pot cultivation and possession superseded state medical marijuana laws. That case stemmed from the arrest, by federal authorities, of Californian Diane Monson. When DEA agents and local sheriff's deputies descended on Monson's Oroville, California, home in 2002, they found six marijuana plants. While the sheriff's deputies were satisfied that she had her doctor's permission to smoke it to treat pain under the state's medical marijuana law, the DEA agents cited federal law and destroyed her plants.[2] Her case became a test not only of California's law but of state sovereignty and the reach of federal authority. After a Court of Appeal ruling backed Monson and California, the Supreme Court reversed it, ruling that the Constitution's commerce clause gave Congress the authority to regulate even homegrown pot because it was part of an interstate marijuana market. Surprising to some, the Court's most liberal justices all backed the DEA, while conservatives such as William Rehnquist and Clarence Thomas sided with Monson. Writing for this minority, Justice Sandra Day O'Connor called for restraints on federal power. She argued that the Court had gone too far in endorsing a uniform federal policy:

> This overreaching stifles an express choice by some States, concerned for the lives and liberties of their people, to regulate medical marijuana differently. If I were a California citizen, I would not have voted for the medical marijuana ballot initiative; if I were a California legislator I would not have supported the Compassionate Use Act. But whatever the wisdom of California's experiment with medical marijuana, the federalism principles that have driven our Commerce Clause cases require that room for experiment be protected in this case.

INTERACTIVE MAP

logic.cqpress.com

Explore a map of the policy patchwork of state marijuana laws.

O'Connor's dissent makes a classic **states' rights** argument. Consistent backers of states' rights have a philosophical commitment to the decentralization of authority, believing that it leads to greater governmental innovation and to a set of state policies that better represent the desires of each state's residents than a single, one-size-fits-all national policy. Yet proponents of federal power counter that the patchwork of policies created when states are free to do as they please makes it difficult to govern a nation where problems can spill over state lines as easily as Americans can drive across them. They point out that majority votes in states can often threaten the civil rights of minorities. The debate over exactly which powers should belong to the federal government and which are reserved to the states goes back to the very founding of the nation, as Chapter 2 illustrates. This conflict has been fought out in constitutional conventions, in courtrooms, and on battlegrounds of the Civil War. The idea of states' rights has been invoked by proponents of policies on both sides of the ideological spectrum. It is used as often to defend state gun control laws as it is to challenge the current federal preemption of many state abortion restrictions. Historically, states' rights arguments were wielded by the alcohol prohibition movement and, most shamefully, by defenders of slavery and the decades of state-sponsored racial segregation that soon followed slavery's abolition (see Chapter 4). Today, many social liberals argue that states should have the right to allow same-sex marriage, and that those marriages should be respected in other states. Arguments about the legitimacy of states' rights come down to the debate over whether state or national majorities should govern, and how far courts should go to protect the rights of minorities.

Even though the nation has grappled with these key questions of federalism for its entire history, the debate has never been completely resolved. The recent judicial battle over the constitutionality of President Obama's Patient Protection and Affordable Care Act, covered in greater depth in Chapter 7, was a fight over states' rights in which the national government won only a very limited victory. In realms such as medical marijuana, even a clear Supreme Court precedent leaves much legal murkiness. States have continued to pass medical marijuana laws since the *Gonzales v. Raich* decision. Colorado established an elaborate "seed to sale" tracking system using video surveillance to regulate and legitimize marijuana cultivation and distribution. Some local governments have banned pot dispensaries, while others have welcomed, regulated, and taxed them. As part of the Obama administration's shift in national drug policy, Attorney General Eric Holder in 2009 directed federal prosecutors to direct resources away from prosecuting "patients with serious illnesses or their caregivers who are complying with state laws on medical marijuana."[3]

In fact, Jason Michael Scott Nelson pointed to Holder's directive in his legal defense, arguing that it had entrapped him into growing medical marijuana. Jurors did not buy this defense, especially given the scale of Mr. Nelson's operation. No garden variety grower, he raised nearly one hundred 3-foot-tall plants under fifty-five water-cooled growing lights, and was caught attempting to ship 74 pounds of pot across state lines. It also did not aid his case that law enforcement officials seized three machine guns and two silencers when they searched his property. The bike shop owner was clearly breaking bad. While he may have been a state-registered grower, Mr. Nelson violated several federal laws and faced up to forty years in federal prison.

AMERICAN-STYLE FEDERALISM

In a federal system, the constitution divides authority between two or more distinct levels of government. For example, the system in the United States divides the national (federal) government and the states. **Federalism** is a hybrid arrangement that mixes elements of a *confederation,* in which lower-level governments possess primary authority, and **unitary government**, in which the national government monopolizes constitutional authority, as shown in Figure 3-1.

Before adopting a federal system in the Constitution, the nation experienced first a unitary government and then a confederation. The decision by the distant British government to impose a central, unitary authority to tax and administer the subordinate colonies precipitated the American War of Independence. After the war, the citizens of the newly independent states reacted to the colonial experience by rejecting unitary authority in favor of a confederation in which smaller state governments held ultimate power. But because the Articles of Confederation failed to give the national government any enforcement authority, the individual states could, and did, ignore legislation from Congress that they did not like. Consequently, the national government accomplished little.

---

* In this text and elsewhere, the terms *federal* and *national* are used interchangeably. This practice also characterized discussions leading to the formation of the Union. Any difference in usage was largely a matter of stress—that is, *federal* reflected the user's cognizance of the state elements also present in the national government. Hans Sperber and Travis Trittschuh, *American Political Terms* (Detroit, MI: Wayne State University Press, 1962), 148–149.

Figure 3-1 Comparing Three Systems of Government

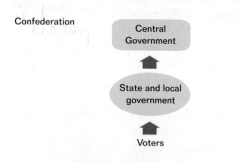

Unitary System

State and local government

Central Government

Voters

Authority is centralized with state and local governments administering authority delegated from central government. Examples: United Kingdom, France, and Japan

Federation

Central Government

State and local government

Voters

Authority is divided between central and state or local governments. Examples: Canada, United States under the Constitution

Confederation

Central Government

State and local government

Voters

Authority held by independent states and delegated to central government by consensus agreements. Example: United States under the Articles of Confederation

Across the world, unitary governments are far more common than federations and confederations combined. Under unitary systems, the lower-level governmental entities—such as counties and metropolitan districts in Britain and departments in France—are created by and ultimately dependent on the national government for authority and resources. Typically, the central government establishes national policies, raises money, and distributes it to the local units to carry these policies out. However deliberative and authoritative these subnational units may appear, they function largely as part of the administrative apparatus of the national government. A unitary government may decentralize its power by delegating some decisions and administration to a lower government entity, but even so the constitutional system remains unitary because the national government retains ultimate authority to alter or rescind this delegation.

In a federal system, however, a government has constitutional relations across levels, interactions that satisfy three general conditions:

- The same people and territory are included in both levels of government.
- The nation's constitution protects units at each level of government from encroachment by the other units.
- Each unit is in a position to exert some leverage over the other(s).[4]

The second condition, independence, is critical because it sets the stage for the third condition, mutual influence. The lack of independence rendered the national government impotent under the Articles of Confederation. With the states commanding a veto over the most important national legislation, the national government lacked the resources and authority to act independently of the states.

Occasionally, observers of American federalism refer to local governments as if they were a separate level in a three-tiered federal system. This characterization is inaccurate. Local governments, which include thousands of counties, cities, and *special districts,* such as school districts, water boards, and port authorities, are established by the states (see Table 3-1). They are not mentioned anywhere in the Constitution. In providing a limited range of government services, local governing bodies may pass laws, worry each year about balancing their budgets, generate revenue through taxes and fees, and spend public money through their own agencies, but these bodies do not exercise independent, constitutional authority. In a famous decision, Judge John F. Dillon concluded "that the great weight of authority denies *in toto* the existence, in the absence of special constitutional provisions, of any inherent right of local self-government which is beyond [state] legislative control." Dillon's Rule made it clear that local governments are mere "creatures of the state."[5]

State officials can and often do exercise their power to intervene in local affairs. They may determine matters as fundamental as the governing structures of cities, counties, and special districts, their taxation powers, and even their geographic boundaries. They can wield authority over local issues that are important to voters statewide, as New York's state legislature did in early 2008 when its members halted New York City mayor Michael Bloomberg's plan to charge an $8 toll to drivers entering Manhattan during rush hours. State officials, such as the Alabama legislature in its 1880 session, can also intervene in areas as trivial as "prohibiting the sale, giving away, or otherwise disposing of, spirituous, vinous, or malt liquors within two and one-half miles of the Forest Home (Methodist) church, in Butler county."

Even when metropolitan areas are ceded great discretion to decide local policies through state home-rule provisions, they remain the legal creations of states, which retain the authority to rescind or preempt local ordinances. Whereas the relations between the state and national governments are premised on separate constitutional authority and qualify as "federal," those between state and local governments are not and therefore can best be classified as "unitary."[6]

Evolving Definitions of Federalism

The three defining features of federalism, listed above, leave room for different kinds of relations

TABLE 3-1	
Numerous Governments Comprise America's Federalism	
National	1
State	50
County	3,033
Municipal	19,492
Township and town	16,519
School district	13,051
Other special districts	37,381
Total	89,527

Source: U.S. Census Bureau, *Statistical Abstract of the United States, 2010* (Washington, DC: U.S. Government Printing Office, 2010), Table 416.

New York City Mayor Michael Bloomberg's plan to charge a steep toll on all commuters entering Manhattan needed approval from the state legislature, just as many local government policies do. As this cartoon shows, his commuter tax was not well received by state legislators meeting in Albany.

Dual
- mutually
exclusive powers

Shared
- state & fed
jointly supply
services to citizens

between state and national governments. Two distinct forms of American federalism have been identified: dual and shared. **Dual federalism** is perhaps the simplest possible arrangement, leaving the states and the national government to preside over mutually exclusive "spheres of sovereignty." James Madison described this arrangement (and the intent of the Framers of the Constitution) in *Federalist* No. 45: "The powers delegated by the proposed Constitution to the Federal Government are few and defined. Those which are to remain to the State Governments are numerous and indefinite." For example, foreign policy and national defense are purely national concerns; matters that, "in the ordinary course of affairs, concern the lives" of the citizens are the responsibility of the individual states.

A second conception, called **shared** (or "cooperative") **federalism**, recognizes that the national and state governments jointly supply services to the citizenry. While each level of government has exclusive authority over some policy realms, state and federal powers intersect over many of the most important functions. Figure 3-2 gives examples of these areas of exclusive and shared authority.

Throughout American history, the nation's practices better resemble the overlapping arrangements of shared federalism rather than the neat divisions of dual federalism. In the early years of the nationhood, states exercised national authority on important matters. In the Civil War the Union forces assembled to put down the Confederacy were recruited and initially provisioned by the states. Only after the men joined the ranks of other states' enlistees did the federal government assume control.

Soon after that war, however, **nationalization** shifted the "indefinite" authority Madison assigned to state governments to the national side. Today, in fact, the national

Figure 3-2 The Constitutional Basis for "Dual" and "Shared" Federalism

National Government

Exclusive Powers
* Coin money
* Regulate interstate and foreign commerce
* Tax imports and exports
* Make treaties
* Make all laws "necessary and proper" to fulfill responsibilities
* Make war
* Regulate postal system

Powers Denied
* Tax state exports
* Change state boundaries
* Impose religious tests
* Pass laws in conflict with the Bill of Rights

Shared Authority
* Tax
* Borrow money
* Charter banks and corporations
* Take property (eminent domain)
* Enforce laws and administer a judiciary

State Governments

Exclusive Powers
* Run elections
* Regulate intrastate commerce
* Establish republican forms of state and local governments
* Protect public health, safety, and morals
* All powers not delegated to the national government or denied to the states by the Constitution

Powers Denied
* Tax imports and exports
* Coin money
* Enter into treaties
* Impair obligation of contracts
* Enter compacts with other states without congressional consent

Source: Adapted from Lee Epstein and Thomas G. Walker, *Constitutional Law for a Changing America: A Short Course,* 4th ed. (Washington, DC: CQ Press, 2009), Table III-1.

government has a hand in almost all policies that "concern the lives" of the citizenry. The most important expansions of national power are described later in this chapter. These include the New Deal policies of the 1930s and the Great Society programs of the 1960s, through which the federal government redesigned more limited state and local pension, welfare, and health care programs by providing most of the funding for them, designing a basic framework for each state to work through, and opening up eligibility to all qualifying Americans. In the past decade, the testing and funding provisions of the No Child Left Behind Act have sharply increased federal authority over the way local schools operate. The trend toward nationalization has not been entirely a one-way street. Both the Nixon and Reagan administrations pushed for a "New Federalism" by giving states more control over the implementation of some federal programs and grants, and Bill Clinton worked with Congress to increase state control over other federal policies through the "Devolution Revolution" of the 1990s. Currently, congressional Republicans led by House Budget Chair Paul Ryan have proposed giving states much more control over how to spend the federal grants that they receive to provide health care to their aged, disabled, and poor residents (though the plan would also dramatically cut the size of these grants). Yet these exceptions to the rule of ever-increasing federal power have occurred only with the willing agreement of federal leaders.

give states more control over fed grants

Overall, then, the United States has moved from Madison's dual federalism to a shared federalism in which federal officials generally decide how authority over intersecting state and federal policy areas should be divided. Indeed, the modern ascendancy of the national government surely would have amazed all (and horrified most) of the delegates to the Constitutional Convention. After all, protecting the states from encroachment by a stronger national government was, in the words of one nationalist delegate, "the favorite object of the Convention." All but a handful of the states' rights delegates were satisfied with the final product, and most of them later publicly advocated the Constitution's ratification. So why have their efforts to partition federal and state responsibilities into separate, self-contained spheres been so thoroughly eclipsed?

Part of the answer is that modern policy challenges and a political consensus that "the government" should provide more services and solve more problems than the Founders anticipated have made a joint, cooperative strategy across states and levels of government necessary. Pollution does not honor state boundaries; neither do unemployment, inflation, crime, greenhouse gases, methamphetamines, or irresponsible mortgage lenders. Then there is the Internet, which knows no boundaries whatsoever. National disasters such as Hurricane Katrina and the 2010 BP oil spill in the Gulf of Mexico affect areas far beyond the reach of floodwaters or oil slicks and require responses on a scale that no single state can provide. The increasing complexity of policy dilemmas and the growing interrelationship between American states have driven the move toward nationalization.

But political logic in tandem with the rules that govern the boundaries of American federalism are just as important in explaining the increasing involvement of the federal government in matters that, "in the ordinary course of affairs, concern the lives" of Americans. Federal officials have many incentives to increase federal power. Presidents are often rewarded when they bring state or regional policies into line with what their national constituency desires. Members of Congress can claim political credit when they work through the federal government to help their districts, and often draw on the immense national tax base to do so. When either logic leads to an expansion of federal authority that the states resist, the critical question becomes: Who gets to decide whether this expansion is legitimate? As the next section shows, the Constitution opened the door to nationalization by granting the federal government ultimate power to determine (within certain bounds) the extent of its authority over the states.

FEDERALISM AND THE CONSTITUTION

In countering Antifederalist alarms about an overly powerful national government, Madison cited two kinds of protections in the Constitution: first, the "structure of the Federal Government," referring mostly to the Senate; and second, explicit rules reserving important prerogatives to the states. Neither has proved an effective barrier to national action.

Transformation of the Senate

In the nineteenth century the equal representation of states regardless of population, combined with the selection of senators by state legislatures, gave the Senate the motive and the means to defend state prerogatives against national encroachment. The history of slavery reveals just how effective the institution was in this task. At first, some state legislatures were so possessive of the Senate and its members that they would pass resolutions instructing their senators how to vote on particular issues. Senators who failed to comply were asked to resign, and some did.[7] Even after this practice died out in the 1840s, most senators continued to regard themselves as agents of the state party organizations that controlled the state legislatures and elected them.

The real *coup de grâce* for the Senate as the bulwark of federalism came with ratification in 1913 of the Seventeenth Amendment, which mandated direct, popular election of senators. Amid persistent, widespread, and sometimes well-founded charges that senators bribed legislators to buy seats (and instances when divided state legislatures failed to agree on a nominee, leaving the state without representation for an extended period), a public consensus formed against indirect election of senators. Public pressure mounted to such an extent that more than three-quarters of state legislatures surrendered control and turned Senate selection over to popular election. The amendment, however, while targeting dysfunctional political practices, also knocked out an important prop of federalism because it removed senators' ties to the state legislatures. Today, the Senate is a central pillar of the national government. Senators may, incidentally, protect states' interests as they serve those of their constituents, but there are no guarantees. In fact, major extensions of federal authority have originated on the floor of the Senate, where more than a few of that chamber's members have cultivated a national constituency with an eye toward future presidential campaigns. Both Barack Obama and John McCain burnished their national credentials and launched their bids for the White House from the Senate, and members of the upper house made many of the key policy deals to pass the landmark pieces of legislation that characterized the early years of Obama's presidency.[8]

Constitutional Provisions Governing Federalism

The Constitution gives the national government at least as much responsibility for overseeing the integrity of the states as it does the states for overseeing the integrity of the national government. All but the original thirteen states entered the Union by an act of Congress; the national government defined the boundaries of territories, oversaw their administration, and eventually ushered them into the Union. Moreover, Article IV of the Constitution obliges the federal government to ensure that all states adhere to republican principles. While Congress may create new states, it cannot destroy an established state—say, by dividing it in half—without its consent. For their part, two-thirds of the states may petition Congress to convene a special constitutional convention to propose amendments. In these seldom-invoked provisions, the Constitution enlists each level of government to keep the other in check.

2/3 states for constitutional convention

Language distinguishing the authority and responsibilities of the states from those of the national government runs throughout the Constitution. In partitioning responsibilities, the Framers worked within a structure of dual federalism. Thus in three major sections of the Constitution they attempted to specify boundaries between the two levels of government. By understanding what these provisions sought but largely failed to do, we can better appreciate how America's governmental system has yielded to nationalizing forces.

THE SUPREMACY CLAUSE. The provision of the Constitution with the most profound implication for modern American federalism is the so-called supremacy clause in Article VI: "This Constitution, and the Laws of the United States which shall be made in Pursuance thereof [that is, in keeping with the principles of the Constitution] . . . shall be the supreme Law of the Land." Although this clause appears to give the national government license to do whatever it wants, the text actually contains an important qualifier: the national government enjoys supremacy, but only insofar as its policies conform to a Constitution that prohibits certain kinds of federal activities.[9] This qualifier restricted national authority throughout most of the nineteenth century. The original intent was simply to have the national government prevail over states when both governments were acting in a constitutionally correct manner. Thus the supremacy clause was framed to avoid impasses over jurisdiction rather than to cede authority to the national government. Over the next two hundred years, however, the sphere of legitimate national action expanded, allowing national policy to enter domains once occupied only by the states. Wherever the national government carved out new authority, it automatically became supreme.

Supremacy
- US > states when both have laws, US tops states
✳

THE POWERS OF CONGRESS. Article I, Section 8, lists the powers reserved to Congress. But these provisions have as much to do with federalism—that is, creating jurisdictional boundaries between the states and the national government—as they do with parceling out authority among Congress, the president, and the Supreme Court. After protracted deliberations in which many possibilities were considered, the Framers finally agreed to list in the Constitution a dozen or so **enumerated powers** that should be in the domain of the national government—specific authority that would enable the

Enumerated
- listed in Article I

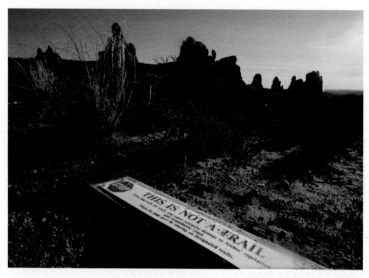

While the Constitution may guarantee that it is the supreme Law of the Land, constitutional battles today still address fundamental issues such as which governments—federal or state—reign supreme when it comes to land. In March 2010, Gov. Gary Herbert signed a bill authorizing Utah to use the power of eminent domain to seize federally owned lands in the state. Aimed at allowing oil and gas development in areas such as the one pictured here, which borders Arches National Park, Utah's move is considered a legal long shot at best. Still, the bill's passage reflects one state's frustration with a federal government that controls two-thirds of the land within Utah's borders.

government to address problems the states had not grappled with effectively under the Articles of Confederation. One example: even Antifederalists conceded that a national postal system made better sense than trying to stitch together thirteen individual state systems.

Recognizing that contingencies requiring a national response might arise in the future, the Framers added to Section 8 what is now known as the **elastic clause**. It allows Congress to "make all Laws which shall be necessary and proper for carrying into Execution the foregoing Powers."[10] This open-ended provision, whose interpretation later would undermine the restrictive purpose of the carefully worded list of enumerated powers, apparently escaped the attention of many of the delegates, since the convention accepted it with little debate. Later, the Antifederalists detected in it an opening for broad national authority, as did the generations of national officeholders who followed them. As the variety of economic transactions that directly involve interstate commerce has grown sharply over the past two centuries, so too has the sphere of policy over which the national government can claim some jurisdiction. Moreover, laws governing a broad variety of social relations that are only incidentally economic—such as racial discrimination in access to public accommodations and possession of handguns near public schools—have invoked the commerce clause to justify federal involvement in these longtime state responsibilities.

THE TENTH AMENDMENT. In the ratification debates Madison answered Antifederalist charges of impending tyranny by promising that once the new government was in place, he would immediately introduce a bill of rights (see Chapter 2). In view of the controversy surrounding federal power in the ratification debates, it is not surprising that many members of the First Congress insisted that the first ten constitutional amendments include protections for the states as well as for individual citizens.

The **Tenth Amendment** offers the most explicit endorsement of federalism to be found in the Constitution: "The powers not delegated to the United States by the Constitution, nor prohibited by it to the States, are reserved to the States respectively, or to the people." Yet, despite its plain language, the Tenth Amendment has failed to fend off federal authority. The powerful combination of the supremacy and elastic clauses reduces the Tenth Amendment to

Elastic = Necessary & Proper clause — created laws deemed "need"

The Constitution's Provisions for Federalism

Article I, Section 8, Commerce Clause TRADE

The Congress shall have Power . . . To regulate Commerce with foreign Nations, and among the several States, and with the Indian Tribes; . . .

Article I, Section 8, Elastic Clause Necessary/Prop

The Congress shall have Power . . . To make all Laws which shall be necessary and proper for carrying into Execution the foregoing Powers, and all other Powers vested by this Constitution in the Government of the United States, or in any Department or Officer thereof.

Article IV, Section 3, Admission of New States 2/3

New States may be admitted by the Congress into this Union; but no new State shall be formed or erected within the Jurisdiction of any other State; nor any State be formed by the Junction of two or more States, or Parts of States, without the Consent of the Legislatures of the States concerned as well as of the Congress.

Article IV, Section 4, Enforcement of Republican Form of Government Protection

The United States shall guarantee to every State in this Union a Republican Form of Government, and shall protect each of them against Invasion; and on Application of the Legislature, or of the Executive (when the Legislature cannot be convened) against domestic Violence.

Article VI, Supremacy Clause FED > STATE

This Constitution, and the Laws of the United States which shall be made in Pursuance thereof; and all Treaties made, or which shall be made, under the Authority of the United States, shall be the supreme Law of the Land; and the Judges in every State shall be bound thereby, any Thing in the Constitution or Laws of any State to the Contrary notwithstanding.

Tenth Amendment STATES

The powers not delegated to the United States by the Constitution, nor prohibited by it to the States, are reserved to the States respectively, or to the people.

Tenth = States' rights

little more than a truism: those powers not taken by the national government *do* belong to the states. About all that it offers critics of nationalization is lip service to the principle of states' rights.

Interpreting the Constitution's Provisions

The sweeping language with which the Constitution variously endorses national power and states' rights has given politicians easy openings to interpret the Constitution according to their own political objectives. Thus the Framers envisioned a Supreme Court that would referee jurisdictional disputes among the states and between states and the national government. Among the thousands of judicial decisions that have grappled with the appropriate roles of the national and state governments, one early Supreme Court ruling stands out for protecting the national government from incursions by the states. In 1816 Congress created a national bank that proved unpopular with many state-level politicians who preferred the state-chartered banks over which they exercised control. To nip this federal meddling into what it viewed as a state matter, Maryland levied a heavy tax on all nonstate-chartered banks. James McCulloch, an agent for the national bank in Baltimore, refused to pay the tax, and

CAN CONGRESS FORCE INDIVIDUALS IN ALL STATES TO BUY HEALTH CARE?

politics to policy

At the heart of one of today's most contentious policy controversies lies the age-old battle between the federal government and the states, waged through the reinterpretation of a venerable constitutional provision. In its 1824 *Gibbons v. Ogden* decision, the Supreme Court invoked the Constitution's commerce clause to give the federal government the power to prevent states from engaging in mutually destructive competition, and to open the door to federal involvement in many aspects of Americans' daily lives. Nearly two centuries later, U.S. District Judge Henry E. Hudson used the commerce clause to strike down a federal law regulating one of the most critical aspects of our daily lives, and opposed by many states. In December 2010, Judge Hudson's ruling threw out a key provision of President Obama's health care reform package. Hudson agreed with Virginia's attorney general that Obama and Congress did not have the authority to require all Americans to buy health insurance. The same constitutional clause that has empowered the federal government for so long was used by the states to check national power. When the Supreme Court upheld the health care law's constitutionality in 2012, it did not reverse Hudson's reasoning: the Court ruled that while an insurance mandate could not be justified by the commerce clause, it constituted a "tax" and thus fell under Congress's powers of taxation (see Chapter 7).

The policy that Judge Hudson struck down was itself an attempt to use a "command" tool (see Chapter 1) to solve a collective action problem. A completely free health care market can be plagued by the dueling incentives of its buyers and sellers. Insurance companies only want to cover people when they are healthy (and thus inexpensive to care for), but many people would rather pay for insurance only when they become sick. Each strategy is individually rational, but its unfettered pursuit could distort the market and cost lives. The health care reform legislation of 2010 set out to make both sides play fair by requiring universal coverage. It forced health insurers to cover anyone who could pay premiums, taking away their ability to deny coverage to those who are sick or have "preexisting conditions." Doing this alone would have set a dangerous temptation before young or healthy Americans: those who do not see the point in paying expensive premiums when they rarely go to the doctor might plan to buy insurance only when they get older or become sick, a free-riding strategy made easier because Obama's plan required insurers to then offer them coverage. To prevent such behavior, which would drive up the cost of insurance for everyone who was covered, the health care reform package mandated that all Americans buy insurance by 2014, using a command tool to prevent free riding.

WATCH A VIDEO

A Libertarian think tank argues that Congress has gone too far.

the two sides went to court. The historic decision *McCulloch v. Maryland* (1819) brought together the supremacy and elastic clauses and moved them to the forefront of constitutional interpretation.[11] Writing for the Court, Chief Justice John Marshall declared that because the national bank assisted Congress in performing several of its responsibilities enumerated in Article I, Section 8—namely borrowing money, levying taxes, and issuing a national currency—the elastic clause gave the national government the implicit authority to create the bank. In one of the most famous passages in Supreme Court opinion, Marshall enunciated this definitive constitutional doctrine:

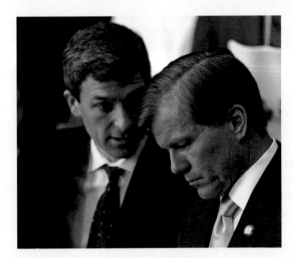

On February 12, 2010—even before the federal health care reform package became law—Virginia's House of Delegates passed the Virginia Health Care Freedom Act, which exempted Virginians from any federal mandate to purchase health insurance. Attorney General Ken Cuccinelli (left) appeared with Gov. Bob McDonnell as the governor signed the bill.

Leaders in many states whose voters opposed Obama's reform objected to this provision even before the package was passed, arguing that the federal government was overstepping the authority given to it by the commerce clause to regulate interstate commerce. Virginia's state legislature passed a law making it illegal to require mandatory health insurance for Virginians. The day after Obama signed the federal bill, Virginia's attorney general, Ken Cuccinelli II, filed suit against it. On his blog Cuccinelli argued, "It is unconstitutional because the federal government is claiming that the source of its power for imposing the mandate is the Constitution's Commerce Clause, which gives the federal government the power to 'regulate commerce among the several states. . . . ' We argue that if someone isn't buying insurance, then—by definition—he is not participating in commerce." Judge Hudson agreed, setting in motion the Supreme Court battle over a key provision of health care reform and an important facet of the ever-evolving balance of power between the federal government and the states.

Sources: Rosalind S. Helderman and Amy Goldstein, "Federal Judge in Va. Strikes Down Part of Health-Care Law," *Washington Post,* December 14, 2010; "Health Mandate Fight Hinges on Commerce Clause," National Public Radio, December 14, 2010; Ken Cuccinelli, "Why Virginia Is Suing the Federal Government over the New Health Care Law," accessed February 25, 2011, http://www.oag.state.va.us/FAQs/FAQ_Why_VA_Suing.html

Let the end be legitimate, let it be within the scope of the Constitution, and all means which are appropriate, which are plainly adapted to that end, which are not prohibited, but consistent with the letter and spirit of the Constitution, are constitutional.

Marshall iced the cake by removing the young national government from the purview of the states. Because "the power to tax involves the power to destroy," the supremacy clause implicitly exempts the federal government from state taxes.

Five years later, in 1824, the Marshall Court handed down another decision that must have appeared far less significant to contemporaries than it came to be regarded in the twentieth century. In settling a dispute between New Jersey and New York over each state's efforts to give a favored steam company a monopoly over shipping on the Hudson River, the Court held in *Gibbons v. Ogden* that neither state could control such a concession.[12] Only Congress possessed the authority to regulate interstate commerce.

In combination, these two cases created powerful precedents that would allow future national policy to develop free of the constraints of state prerogatives. Once the Court in *Gibbons* had sanctioned federal authority to regulate commerce, the supremacy clause gave the national government the authority to preempt the states in virtually all policies involving interstate commerce. Many traditional tasks of states, such as providing for public safety, enforcing fair advertising laws, and overseeing waste disposal, would slip easily into federal control via the commerce clause.

Congress is not the only branch of the federal government that has gained authority over policy areas once ruled by the states; the Supreme Court has also given itself the power to overrule state laws that it sees as inimical to the Bill of Rights or to a less explicit notion of "justice." Prior to the Civil War, the Bill of Rights was understood as applying only to the federal and not to state governments. The postwar passage of the Fourteenth Amendment, though, allowed later courts to use its due process clause (see Chapter 5) as a basis for striking down state laws that violated various explicit and implicit federal rights. The 1925 *Gitlow v. New York* ruling held that states could not abridge the free speech rights of their residents, while *Near v. Minnesota* (1931) applied the First Amendment's protections of a free press to the states. The door to intervention by the federal judiciary was opened more broadly by the 1937 *Palko v. Connecticut* decision, which held that states could not violate rights without which "neither liberty nor justice would exist." Based on this rationale, the Court held that a state prohibition on the use of contraceptives violated the inherent right to privacy of its residents (*Griswold v. Connecticut,* 1965) and then ruled that states could not impose strict limits on abortions like the Texas law struck down in *Roe v. Wade* (1973). Although federal courts sometimes recognize the limits of national power (see the Politics/Policy box on the individual health insurance mandate), by and large these cases demonstrate that the federal judiciary has often been as aggressive as Congress in expanding national authority over the states.

As national politicians sought over the years to expand their authority and responsibilities, they discovered that the wall between the federal government and the states was not as impregnable as most of the Framers had apparently supposed. The Constitution's provisions and language leave ample room for a variety of federal-state relations. Thus nationalization of public policy reshaped federalism largely unfettered by constitutional constraints and without triggering a constitutional crisis. Nationalization did not just happen, however. As many problems outgrew state borders, pressure usually built for a greater national role. But whether the federal government actually assumed responsibility remained—and still is—a political decision, reflecting as much the competition of interests as any objective rationale for national action. The buildup of antislavery sentiment in the northern states, which led to Abraham Lincoln's election in 1860, the South's secession, and the Civil War, remains the nation's most bitter and tragic conflict involving federalism. Yet while the war was nominally triggered by a dispute over the bounds of federal authority to abolish

■ LISTEN

Listen to the Supreme Court's oral arguments on health care and the Commerce Clause.

Congress takes control of many state jobs through commerce

slavery, it should be seen as a larger political and moral clash that broke down into military conflict rather than a battle over the principles of federalism.

THE PATHS TO NATIONALIZATION

Throughout the first half of the nineteenth century, the United States remained a nation of segmented communities whose commercial intercourse required minimal coordination across states. But as American workers began to produce more and more goods to be traded on distant markets, lawmakers began to shift their attention from strictly state and local matters to national problems and solutions. With growth, industrialization, urbanization, and the development of national

The Saturday Press

Vol. 1, No. 4   Minneapolis, Minn., Oct. 15, 1927   Price 3 Cents

A Direct Challenge to Police Chief Brunskill

Respectfully Submitted

In the *Near v. Minnesota* case, the U.S. Supreme Court held that the federal Constitution's First Amendment also preserved the freedom of the press from state incursion. Jay M. Near was the publisher of the *Saturday Press,* which accused Minneapolis's police chief and mayor of working with gangs that held a "deadly grip" on the city.

transportation and communication systems, the nation's appetite grew for public goods that outstripped the scope and resources of local communities and states.[13] In the early 1870s, for example, the farm states tried in vain to prohibit the railroads from engaging in rate discrimination and exorbitant charges. They finally turned to Washington for regulation, and in 1887 Congress obliged by passing the Interstate Commerce Act. A similar process spurred the federal government to enforce national food safety standards, enact antimonopoly laws, and undertake numerous other services.

The nationalization of public policy, which altered America's federal-state relations, was propelled by a rationale, or logic, that grew out of the requirements of collective action. Played out historically, the logic of collective action has assumed several forms. First Americans have at times decided collectively to adopt policies of such magnitude and scope that they outstripped the resources of states. The result has been a historic movement of large blocks of domestic policy from the state capitals to Washington. We soon will examine two important historical instances of this movement: Franklin Roosevelt's New Deal and Lyndon Johnson's War on Poverty.

Second, states have solicited federal intervention when they could not solve their problems by working together individually. Considering that the U.S. mainland is carved into forty-eight separate state jurisdictions, one can easily imagine a great variety of issues arising that require states' cooperation. And yet the Constitution prohibits formal interstate agreements (Article I, Section 10) in the absence of the national government's consent. Voluntary cooperation, by definition, holds the potential for reneging, particularly when serious, costly commitments are required. For that reason, following the 1906 San Francisco earthquake, which overwhelmed the capacity of California's state government to respond to $500 million in property damage and assist over 250,000 homeless residents, the states welcomed a national insurance policy against such disasters even though it meant surrendering control of disaster relief to federal agencies.

Finally, national majorities have increasingly insisted on federal involvement in what were formerly state and local matters. Sometimes mere expediency is at work as a national majority finds it easier to succeed in Washington than in each of the states. Similarly, companies with business around the country sometimes lobby for national regulations simply so that they do not have to deal with fifty different states' policies. On other occasions, the cause has been just and noble, as the history of civil rights policy in America shows. In asserting its authority to protect the rights of African Americans—from the Civil War in the 1860s to the civil rights laws a century later—the national government breached the separation of national from state spheres of control. Although the impact of civil rights on federalism has been profound, it is a subject with broad implications for all Americans and warrants separate consideration (see Chapter 4).

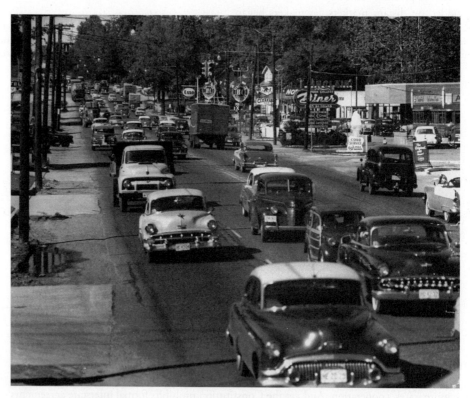

One major step toward nationalization that literally connected states was the building of the Interstate Highway System, now 46,837 miles long. Promoted by President Dwight D. Eisenhower in the 1950s, this massive public works project allowed people and products to move much more quickly within and across states, yet also imposed sharp costs on the small towns—such as the one pictured above, on the old U.S. Route 1 between Washington, DC, and Baltimore—that withered when they were bypassed by the new highways. Because decisions were made at the federal level, small-town residents who might have been able to influence their local or state governments had little say in the national policy.

Historic Transfers of Policy to Washington

President Franklin Roosevelt's New Deal, enacted in the 1930s, and President Lyndon Johnson's Great Society program, realized in the mid-1960s, represented two equally historic shifts toward nationalization. In addition to broadening the scope of federal responsibilities, these watershed programs followed the election of large national majorities to Congress from the president's party, with an apparent mandate to create a broad new array of collective goods.

Roosevelt's New Deal was a comprehensive set of economic regulations and relief programs intended to fight the Great Depression (1929–1940). The innovation of the New Deal stemmed less from the form of its policies than from their size and scope. During Roosevelt's first two terms (1933–1941), he and the huge Democratic majorities in Congress established economic management as one of the national government's primary responsibilities. Federal policy took two basic forms: regulating and financing (and with it prescribing) state action. Despite the continuing debate between present-day Republicans and Democrats over the proper division of federal and state responsibilities, no one has seriously proposed dismantling the framework of economic management constructed by the New Deal.

At the outset of the Depression, 40 percent unemployment rates were not uncommon in many communities. The states, responsible for welfare programs, had to reduce services to fend off insolvency. In the process, they also had to abandon people in need of help.* When the Roosevelt administration's offer to fund 90 percent of the costs for relief and new make-work programs finally came, the principle of federalism did not prevent state leaders from cheerfully accepting the help. All forty-eight states quickly signed up for the Works Progress Administration, Old Age Assistance, Civilian Conservation Corps, Social Security, and other federally sponsored public assistance programs. During these Depression years the dramatic growth in federal spending, coupled with corresponding reductions in funds at the state and local levels, provided evidence of the sharp shift from state to federal responsibility for social programs (see Figure 3-3).

Figure 3-3   Nationalization of Domestic Policy during the Depression

Percent of nonmilitary spending

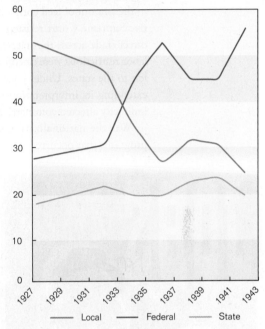

Local   Federal   State

Source: John Joseph Wallis, "The Political Economy of New Deal Fiscal Federalism," *Economic Inquiry* 29 (July 1991): 511.

Note: About half of the increase in federal spending in this figure took the form of direct financial support to indigent citizens.

---

* Unlike the federal government, most state governments are forbidden by their constitutions from enacting annual budgets that incur deficits. But while they may have to balance their budgets, most states can and do frequently borrow billions of dollars to build schools, roads, parks, dams, hospitals, canals, railroads, and other vital parts of their infrastructures.

To justify its unprecedented intervention in the economy, the Roosevelt administration invoked the commerce clause. Although demands for national regulation of the economy began modestly in the late nineteenth century, they reached a new level of intensity with the onset of the Great Depression. FDR's New Deal introduced regulations that touched virtually every aspect of the nation's economic life, from how securities were sold on Wall Street to the amount of feed corn a Kansas farmer could grow for his livestock. At first, a conservative Supreme Court resisted. Narrowly interpreting the commerce clause to include only direct trade across the states, the Court ruled that federal workplace policies such as child labor restrictions were unconstitutional because they regulated intrastate commerce, an area left to the states. Under great political pressure, however, the Court eventually relented by extending its interpretation of the commerce clause to include intrastate commerce that indirectly affected commerce across state lines.

Was the nationalization of authority over commerce and responsibility for welfare programs that occurred during the Depression inevitable? Perhaps if a different president had been elected in 1932, or if Congress has been unwilling to go along with Roosevelt's New Deal proposals, welfare and pensions might have remained entirely a state responsibility. Under different political circumstances, the Supreme Court could have resisted the pressure to expand its interpretation of the commerce clause. On the other hand, the scale of the economic devastation that the Depression wreaked may have made political upheaval a certainty and left only the federal government with the resources and flexibility to respond. Either way, the New Deal was certainly a critical juncture that set the United States further down the path of nationalization.

Another great wave of nationalization of domestic policy occurred in the mid-1960s. Elected in 1964 in an even larger landslide than FDR's 1932 victory, Lyndon Johnson and the overwhelmingly Democratic Congress launched a War on Poverty as part of their Great Society agenda. In 1964–1965 Congress passed more than a hundred new programs that would be carried out by states but funded (and controlled) through federal grants, spending over $5 billion. The largest of these was Medicaid, which provides health insurance to low-income families, senior citizens in nursing homes, and disabled Americans. Other traditional state and local responsibilities such as school funding, teacher training, urban renewal, and public housing became important federal responsibilities. As with the New Deal, these grants subsidized state programs that implemented national goals.

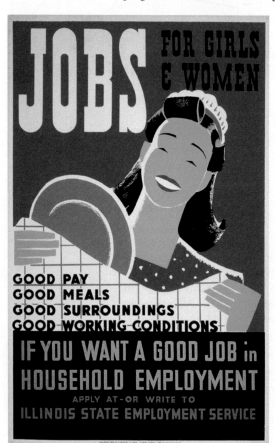

Franklin Roosevelt's New Deal included the federal Works Progress Administration, which among other employment opportunities promoted "Jobs for Girls and Women."

But all these grants came with strings attached. To qualify for funding, state and local authorities had to follow detailed programmatic guidelines prescribing how funds were to be spent. These strings greatly expanded the federal government's power, even over services such as schools that are still funded mostly by state and local governments. Because states now rely on the federal education grants that were created during the Great Society era, they have been forced to accept federal policy dictates such as the No Child Left Behind testing requirements in order to keep federal funds flowing (see box "No Child Left Behind: The Test of a Standardized Education Policy"). Without paying all of the costs of education, the federal government can still exert much control over it. Even while grant programs transfer money from the national to state governments, they often transfer authority back to Washington, DC.

Nationalization—The Solution to States' Collective Dilemmas

When modern state governments encountered the same collective action dilemmas that prompted their eighteenth-century counterparts to send delegates to Philadelphia, they solved these dilemmas in the same way—by shifting responsibility from the state to federal authorities. Every kind of collective action problem introduced in Chapter 1, from simple coordination to the prisoner's dilemma, has frustrated state action at one time or another and repeatedly required states to turn to Washington for help.

COORDINATION PROBLEMS. A nation composed of fifty states inevitably faces coordination problems—some dramatic, some rather mundane. Even when the states agree to cooperate, thereby allowing each to deal more effectively with a common responsibility, they may have difficulty figuring out precisely how to work together. For example, until 1986, the principle that each state administers its own driver's license laws appeared unassailable. But after heavy lobbying by state officials, Congress passed the Commercial Motor Vehicle Safety Act, which standardized state driver's licenses for interstate truckers and created a bureau within the Department of Transportation to centralize traffic violation records. What prompted federal intervention was the practice common among truckers of obtaining licenses in several states to maintain a valid license regardless of the number of traffic tickets accumulated. Centralized record keeping offered a far simpler solution to state coordination than requiring each state to update its records with those from every other state. Disgruntled truckers pointed to the new law as another example of interference by "heavy-handed Washington bureaucrats," but in fact it precisely fulfilled the states' request.

Even when the need for coordination is evident, there is no guarantee that the states will agree to shift this responsibility to Washington. In addition to the transaction costs of conforming to national standards, state politicians may worry that surrendering authority for one accepted purpose might lead the federal government to undertake less desirable policies. Such considerations are holding up agreement in Congress to strengthen national regulation of electrical transmission across the country. Every state exercises some regulatory control over its electricity industry. In an earlier era, when most utilities were

NO CHILD LEFT BEHIND

The Test of a Standardized Education Policy

politics to policy

The 2001 reauthorization of the 1965 Elementary and Secondary Education Act, now commonly known as No Child Left Behind, teaches two clear lessons about the ironies of American politics and federalism. When President Bush signed this act after it passed with strong bipartisan majorities in both houses of Congress, it appeared to be the culmination of his campaign pledge to be a uniter, rather than a divider, in Washington, DC. Today, it stands as perhaps his most controversial domestic policy initiative and has drawn fire from members of both parties in Congress. And while the inspiration for the act came from the education reforms that President Bush helped to pass when he was the governor of Texas, the extension of one state's approach to all the others led to the most far-reaching exercise of federal power over state and local schools in American history.

On his second day in office, President Bush began assembling the bipartisan coalition that he would need to pass No Child Left Behind by inviting Democratic senator Edward Kennedy to the White House. Surprisingly, the longtime liberal from Massachusetts and the Republican president found common ground in their shared goals of increasing funding for schools and narrowing the achievement gap between white and minority students. The act that they drafted together in 2001 provided billions of dollars more in federal aid to schools, but attached many strings to these funds.

Chief among the hundreds of new federal directives in the thousand-page bill was the requirement that states

administer standardized math and reading tests to all of their students, starting in third grade. Each state could develop its own tests, but the federal government got to

local monopolies with in-state generation and transmission, state-level policy made sense. Today, however, power flows through an extensive continental grid; residents of one state consume electricity from dozens of sources throughout the region. As demonstrated by a massive blackout that began with a minor power outage in Ohio but cascaded across the East Coast on August 13, 2003, state regulation no longer works. The question still being deliberated in Congress and the states is, can regulatory coordination be delegated to the Federal Energy Regulatory Commission (FERC) without surrendering state control over decide what happened when a school registered consistently low scores: financial sanctions would kick in, and students would be allowed to transfer. The new act traded the carrot of funding for the stick of sanctions and federal control. With the final vote coming just weeks after the September 11, 2001, terrorist attacks, members of Congress from both parties backed the compromise that Senator Kennedy and President Bush reached and passed No Child Left Behind by 381–41 in the House and by 87–10 in the Senate.

Soon after the act went into effect, though, it drew criticism from both sides of the aisle. Over the next few fiscal years, Democrats like Kennedy were disappointed that the amount of federal aid to schools did not grow as quickly as they anticipated. Teachers and parents worried that schools were turning into test-taking factories, focusing all of their attention on math and reading and simply "teaching to the test." Many states protested that the national regulations did not give them the flexibility to deal with their unique challenges. Arizona and Virginia asked for more time to teach English to students with limited proficiency before testing them in English. Utah's rural school districts have struggled to find teachers with college degrees in the subjects that they teach, as the act requires. Connecticut filed a lawsuit charging that the federal government must provide more funding to go along with the new directives.

With so many of their states in open rebellion against the national policy, fifty Republican members of Congress introduced legislation in 2007 that would have let states opt out of the No Child Left Behind testing requirements, without losing their federal funding. In March 2010, President Obama unveiled plans to update the act by preserving its emphasis on testing and accountability, but increasing state resources and giving states and schools more flexibility to meet their goals. While no major legislation has been passed to reverse No Child Left Behind, President Obama has effectively rewritten the law by granting states waivers from its requirements if they agree to a set of policies—including the promotion of charter schools and the use of test scores to evaluate teachers' performance—that his administration favors. Once again, the federal government has been able to exert great leverage over state education policy, even though it provides relatively little school funding.

Sources: Sam Dillon, "Battle Grows over Renewing Landmark Education Law," *New York Times,* April 7, 2007; Peter Baker, "An Unlikely Partnership Left Behind," *Washington Post,* November 5, 2007; Gail Russell Chaddock, "Obama's No Child Left Behind Revise: A Little More Flexibility," *Christian Science Monitor,* March 15, 2010; Lyndsey Layton, "Rethinking the Classroom: Obama's Overhaul of Public Education," *Washington Post,* September 21, 2012.

rates? (Nearly ten years after the blackouts of the Midwest and East Coast, members of Congress from the South and Northwest still have not agreed to new federal authority for fear that their cheap local electricity would chase market prices and drive up their local costs.)

RENEGING AND SHIRKING. In the nation's early years, states agreed to a course of common action but then failed to honor their commitments. The Constitution and

In this picture, a participant in the "Redneck Carp Tournament" swings at carp flying out of the Illinois River. This aggressive, voracious species of fish was imported by southern states in the 1970s to help keep wastewater treatment facilities clean, but Mississippi River flooding freed the carp to ravage the Missouri and Illinois Rivers (and their kayakers) throughout the 1990s. Five states situated on the Great Lakes have asked the U.S. Army Corps of Engineers to shut down the locks connecting Chicago's rivers to the lake to help fight the carps' spread. Illinois business leaders, though, fought the request, because in protecting the other states it would badly threaten Chicago's economy and flood control system. A federal court ruled in December 2010 that the locks could stay open, but the five Great Lakes states appealed the decision.

national laws solve many of these dilemmas by authorizing the federal government to take direct action in raising resources and administering policy. However, in certain situations national responsibility and jurisdiction is either undecided or allows the states a prominent role. Movements to reduce pollution and conserve natural resources, among the most pervasive and thorny challenges to effective collective action in recent years, have inspired innovative approaches enlisting federalism as a solution. Both problems qualify as tragedies of the commons, introduced in Chapter 1. No one wants to breathe polluted air, but without some mechanism to arrange and enforce agreements, everyone continues to pollute under the assumption that doing otherwise will not by itself clean up the atmosphere (that is, promote the public good or lead to the betterment of the "commons"). Coordinated national policies are necessary to solve this collective action problem, but they can sometimes emerge through state pressure. The clearest example of this comes from recent responses to the most pressing environmental concern of our era: climate change. Climate change presents a policy challenge that crosses state borders. Exhaust from the tailpipe of a California car can cause smog in the Los Angeles basin, but the carbon emissions can also trap heat in Earth's atmosphere and affect the global climate. Since many people are affected by the car's emissions, not just its driver, the environmental damage done represents an **externality**, an effect felt by more people than just the one who chose to cause it. When the federal government made little effort to combat greenhouse gas emissions, a group of states pushed America toward national action. California passed a landmark climate-change bill under Gov. Arnold Schwarzenegger's leadership, and was soon followed by fourteen states from Arizona to Maine. The federal government initially opposed the state laws, arguing that they could create a policy patchwork, but after Barack Obama's election, the Environmental Protection Agency (EPA) embraced California's tough fuel economy standards, making them the national standard by 2016. Though the first states to act may have worried about paying the full costs of environmental protection while other states shirked, the creation of a national policy to address the negative externality of greenhouse gas admissions solved this collection action problem.

Map 3-1   The United States' Carbon Footprint

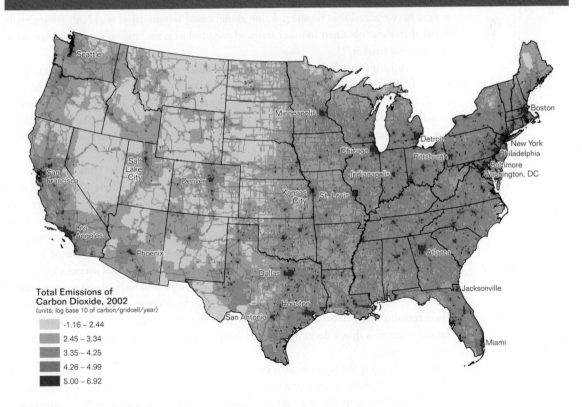

Total Emissions of
Carbon Dioxide, 2002
(units: log base 10 of carbon/gridcell/year)

-1.16 – 2.44
2.45 – 3.34
3.35 – 4.25
4.26 – 4.99
5.00 – 6.92

Source: Project Vulcan, Arizona State University. http://vulcan.project.asu.edu/GEarth/index.html.

Note: Released in 2008, this map displays America's "carbon footprint," the density of carbon dioxide emissions from sources such as power plants and automobiles as of 2002. While most carbon emissions come from urban areas, their impact on climate reaches throughout the country and indeed the world, a clear example of a negative externality that could be addressed by state or federal policies.

CUTTHROAT COMPETITION. Under the Articles of Confederation each state was free to conduct its own international trade policy. This arrangement allowed foreign governments and merchants to exploit competition among the states to negotiate profitable trade agreements. The losers were American producers and the states, which found themselves in a classic prisoner's dilemma. Their best strategy would have been first to agree among themselves on a single rate (to form a kind of cartel), and then to negotiate with Britain from a united front. But this approach would have required that none of the states break rank when the British offered to reward the first "defector" with an especially lucrative, sweetheart deal. Not wanting to be played for the sucker, all states underbid each other, or engaged in **cutthroat competition**. Searching for a solution, both nationalists and advocates of states' rights readily agreed at the Constitutional Convention that the states were best served by the national government assuming control in foreign affairs, including trade.

At various times cutthroat competition has prompted state officials to lobby Washington to prevent bidding wars. When the national government defended a 1937 federal minimum wage law before the Supreme Court, it reminded the justices that rather than usurping state prerogatives, Washington was actually serving the states: "State legislators . . . over a period of time have realized that no state, acting alone, could require labor standards substantially higher than those obtained in other states whose producers and manufacturers competed in the interstate market."[14]

Environmental regulation is another area in which the national government has taken action. To lure new business, states sometimes are tempted to relax their environmental standards to give them a competitive edge over their neighbors. Thus one state's strong environmental policies may expose it to other states' gamesmanship. As much as state officials like to complain about the policies of the EPA, the presence of national standards insulates environmental protection from cutthroat competition.

Competition among states can take other forms as well. Companies considering relocating facilities will strategically select two or three "finalist" sites in different states and then sit back and let them bid against one another by offering tax breaks or special services. Although the states generally would be better off if they could avoid this competition, none can afford to do so. Each state will raise its bid until the costs of subsidizing a new company through property improvements and reduced taxes exceed the expected economic benefits. States also face incentives to engage in a **race to the bottom** in social services by cutting back on things like the size of the monthly check a state pays to welfare recipients so that it will not become a "welfare magnet" that attracts the low-income residents of its neighbors. There remains much debate over whether or not states do indeed race toward the bottom,[15] but the incentives that a decentralized welfare policy creates to do so might harm society's most vulnerable.

Whether pitting the states against one another in a bidding war is a good thing depends wholly on whose interests are being served. By one recent estimate cities and states are paying about $40 billion annually in direct compensation, special services, and tax exemptions to lure and retain large employers.[16] Corporate executives seeking attractive concessions would understandably view any agreement among the states to avoid competition as unwelcome collusion. Alternatively, one could argue that these bidding wars represent a market mechanism establishing the true price of a project and hence promote efficiency.

Moreover, competition between states and performance comparisons may allow politicians across the country to discover which innovative solutions to common policy challenges actually work. The idea—that one state can experiment and, if successful, that other states and the national government may replicate it—presents a compelling justification for competitive federalism. Many state policy innovations have spread across the country. What is less certain is that the innovations that have been copied are always the most successful ones. In response to negative public opinion after Texas rated poorly in many national rankings of primary and secondary school test scores, politicians, including then-governor George W. Bush, made the state's low educational scores a political issue. During the next several years, educational expenditures increased significantly across Texas, as did, eventually, its test scores and national ranking. After he was elected president, Bush applied some parts of the Texas plan on a national scale through the No Child Left Behind legislation (see the Politics/Policy box on page 106). Opponents of this approach to education and critics of competitive federalism in general might ask how we know which parts of Texas's plan improved test scores and whether we can be sure that the nation copied a state's successful innovations rather than its failures.

The Political Logic of Nationalization

As countless political controversies teach us, promoters of a policy will sometimes try to shift it from the states to the national government because either they expect more sympathetic treatment in Washington or they find it easier than lobbying fifty state governments. National campaigns for legislation banning automatic weapons and handguns, regulating hazardous waste disposal, and mandating special education programs in public schools are instances in which "state" issues have been strategically shifted to Washington.

If a cause enjoys widespread national support, lobbying Congress is far more efficient than lobbying fifty state legislatures. After all, a single federal law can change a policy in all fifty states. In 1980 a mother whose teenage daughter was killed by a drunk driver formed Mothers Against Drunk Driving (MADD), which quickly mushroomed into a national organization with thousands of members. Initially, MADD pressed state legislatures for stiffer laws and higher drinking ages. And although all proclaimed their enthusiasm for removing drunks from the highways, those states with lower drinking ages had a financial interest in maintaining the status quo. Such states profited from underage customers who visited from neighboring states with higher legal drinking ages. As a result, variations in the states' drinking ages perversely encouraged some young people to take to the highways in search of alcohol.

In 1984 MADD took its case to Congress.[17] Few politicians proved willing to defend federalism against the movement to reduce drunk driving. In 1985 Congress passed legislation that instituted a simple, effective way to regulate drinking age laws. If a state failed to raise its drinking age to twenty-one in 1986, it would lose 5 percent of its federal highway funds. Failure to do so in 1987 would trigger a 10 percent deduction. All the states got the message and promptly raised the drinking age by 1988. They also brought suit in the Supreme Court, claiming extortion and federal intrusion into strictly state jurisdictions. The Court sided with the national government.[18]

Even those who do not desire national action sometimes invite it to avoid burdensome and varied regulations from each of the states. In recent years many state attorneys general

TAKE A SURVEY

logic.cqpress.com

■ Should gun control policy be decided in state capitols or in Washington, DC?

On Patriots' Day in April 2010, armed activists marched to demonstrate their right to bear arms in northern Virginia across the Potomac River from Washington, DC. Even though the Supreme Court's *District of Columbia v. Heller* decision struck down the District's handgun ban in 2008, gun control laws are still much stricter in the District than in Virginia. As a consequence, the activists did not march on the National Mall itself—the location of their protest was dictated by the nation's patchwork of gun control laws, itself a product of federalism.

have charged airlines with practicing illegal "bait and switch" advertising when they run local newspaper promotions for steeply discounted fares that few customers find available. The airlines, however, have successfully evaded state prosecution by persuading the Department of Transportation to assert its preemptive federal authority to regulate airline rates and advertising. Thus even businesses wanting to remain free of any government regulation may prefer to deal with one federal agency rather than having to fend off regulation attempts from fifty states.*

Perhaps the most compelling strategic reason for a group to prefer national over state policy is that the national arena may be the only place in which it can hope to prevail, especially when a policy is opposed in the community where it would need to be enforced. This situation characterized civil rights in the South during the 1960s, but virtually any domain of public policy where the state and national governments share responsibility is subject to

---

* Similarly, major software companies, including Microsoft and AOL, assembled in 2004 to respond to Utah's recently enacted law requiring any company loading cookies and other software onto a personal computer via the Internet to first obtain permission from the computer owner. With several other states poised to pass similar legislation, the software firms feared patchwork regulations would hamstring their capacity to innovate in this area. John Schwartz and Saul Hansell, "The Latest High-Tech Legal Issue: Rooting Out the Spy in Your Computer," *New York Times*, April 26, 2004.

this political maneuver. After increasing their majority in both the House and the Senate in the 2004 elections, Republicans opened the 109th Congress by promptly passing a law that moved most class-action lawsuits from state to federal court jurisdictions. Some state courts had earned reputations for favoring plaintiffs, which aggrieved Republican-supporting business groups and endeared them to Democratic-supporting trial lawyers' associations.

Perhaps no area of national policy has so thoroughly been reshaped by this dynamic than the extension of environmental protections at the expense of state and local constituencies. Protection of environmental resources can be costly—directly or indirectly—in lost jobs and business. Either way, local residents typically pay the bulk of the costs. Idaho ranchers worry that the reintroduction of wolves in the nearby national parks will endanger their sheep. The Navajos' coal-burning, electricity-generating plant in Arizona may blanket the Grand Canyon in dense fog, but they prefer the profits gained from selling electricity to a national market. The lumber industry in northern California and Oregon believes jobs will be imperiled if it must curtail the harvest of old-growth forest to protect the endangered spotted owl.

The rest of the country, by comparison, bears little of these costs. It can "afford" the appropriate environmental measures far better than can those whose livelihoods are adversely affected by them. Restoring the original ecology of Yellowstone National Park, maintaining a smoke-free Grand Canyon, and protecting an endangered owl are all desirable and essentially free public goods. Thus conflicts arising over the environment frequently pit local resource users (such as ranchers and developers) who bear the costs of environmental regulation against nationally organized environmental constituencies that do not.

Sometimes the reverse political process occurs as groups that lose at the national level seek smaller victories in those states where they enjoy majority support. A dramatic example is California's $3 billion initiative to fund stem cell research after George W. Bush's 2001 executive order limited federal support of this research. California's innovation in this area has now been replicated by stem cell research funds in many other states. Similarly, social conservatives, frustrated in their efforts to restrict abortion rights and validate school prayer at the national level, have lobbied state legislatures and sponsored petition drives to put these issues on state ballots. Table 3-2 shows the success of antiabortion groups in winning restrictive state laws since legalization of abortion in the Supreme Court's 1973 *Roe v. Wade* decision (see Chapter 5). Similarly, gun-control groups, unable to persuade Congress to adopt tougher handgun laws, have taken their campaign to the legislatures of sympathetic states. By 2007, twenty-eight states had passed laws mandating safety devices or other methods of keeping firearms away from children in order to prevent accidents. States and local governments that have passed even more stringent gun control laws may see them struck down, though, in the wake of the controversial 2008 *District of Columbia v. Heller* Supreme Court decision that overturned Washington, DC's handgun ban on the grounds that it violated the Second Amendment's right to keep and bear arms. In a 2010 decision, a 5–4 majority on the Court further confirmed that the Second Amendment provided a federal right to bear arms that states and local governments could not override with their own handgun bans.[19]

As James Madison emphasized in *Federalist* No. 10, states and the national government combine the citizenry's preferences into different groupings, with the result that the two levels of government may adopt different, even opposite, policies to address the same problem. Although Madison was prepared to take his chances with national majorities, whose decisions, he believed, would be moderated by the collective preferences of a broad, diverse nation, he

TABLE 3-2

Abortion-Rights Foes Secure State-Level Restrictions

Type of Policy	Explanation	Total Number of States
Abortion-specific informed consent	Prohibits abortion without the pregnant woman's "informed consent," which requires that she receive antiabortion lectures or materials approved by the state[a]	20
Antiabortion memorial	Requests that Congress ban abortion	25
Clinic violence	Prohibits violence toward or harassment of abortion clinics and workers	9
Conscience clause	Allows physicians not to provide abortions if they are opposed to abortion	36
Fetal disposal	Regulates disposal of aborted fetuses	11
Fetal experimentation	Prohibits experiments using material from aborted fetuses and bans abortions for the purpose of experimentation	30
Feticide	Outlaws killing of a fetus	10
Gag rules	Prohibit those working in state-run health care facilities from presenting abortion as an option to patients	18
Hospitals only	Stipulates that abortions only may be performed in hospitals	26
Insurance restrictions and bans	Permit restricted access only or prohibit insurance companies from including abortion in their health coverage	15
Mandatory counseling	Requires physicians to read a counseling "script" to any patient seeking an abortion	30
Medicaid ban	Eliminates federal funding of abortions	34
No wrongful life/wrongful birth policy	Prohibits lawsuits in which a person argues that he or she should not have been born (wrongful life) or parents allege that had they been informed correctly, they would have had an abortion (wrongful birth)	8
Parental consent or notification	Requires minors to obtain consent for an abortion from parents or the courts, or that a minor's parents be notified before an abortion is performed	44
Physician only	Stipulates that only licensed physicians may perform abortions	45
Post-viability	Establishes when viability occurs and regulates abortions after viability	30
Post-viability care	Requires postabortion care for a viable fetus	30
Public facilities	Bans the use of public facilities in performing abortions	6
Refusal clause	Allows physicians not to provide abortions if they are opposed to abortion	47
Reporting requirement	Stipulates that all abortions be reported to a state agency	20
Right to life	Makes it illegal to kill a fetus in the womb unless certain conditions are met and/or requires the physician to give any fetus born alive during an abortion a chance to live	12
Spousal consent	Requires the husband's consent for an abortion	9
TRAP (Targeted Restrictions on Abortion Providers) laws	Put restrictions on facilities that perform abortions	33
Waiting period	Specifies a period that must pass between the request for an abortion and the time the procedure is performed	26

Sources: Adapted from Deborah R. McFarlane and Kenneth J. Meier, *The Politics of Fertility Control: Family Planning and Abortion Policies in the American States* (New York: Chatham House, 2001), 94–95; and from Melody Rose, *Safe, Legal, and Unavailable?* (Washington, DC: CQ Press, 2007), 103–104.

a. "Informed consent" has a different meaning for other medical procedures.

also knew what we learned in our discussion of medical marijuana and federal environmental policy: that national majorities will at times impose costs on local constituencies. Thus federalism presents opportunities for two kinds of majorities—state and national—to pursue their interests in competition with each other. For better or worse, national majorities have the institutional resources to nationalize many policy questions that once were the exclusive domain of state majorities.

MODERN FEDERALISM

Early in the twenty-first century, the national government's primacy in setting domestic policy is secure, even in domains that once belonged exclusively to the states. Whether through outright takeover of a function or by selective financial inducements, Washington can pretty much dictate state policy when its policymakers are so inclined. Some observers find recent Supreme Court decisions beginning to fence in the federal government's ability to dictate policy. Even so, the shift has been modest and easily circumvented by an alternative strategy of financial inducements.

The National Government's Advantage in the Courts

Indicative of how far nationalization has shifted the balance of power, today's constitutional litigation over federalism typically concerns direct efforts by the federal government to regulate the activities of state and local governments and their employees. In *Garcia v. San Antonio Metropolitan Transit Authority* (1985) the Supreme Court approved the application of federal wage-and-hour laws to state and local employees. Writing for the majority, Justice Harry Blackmun dismissed the Tenth Amendment as too ambiguous to guide federal-state relations. But this was no great matter, he added, because the proper relations between the states and the national government were protected in other ways. The states' "sovereign interests," he wrote, "are more properly protected by procedural safeguards inherent in the structure of the federal system than by judicially created limitation on federal power." Because members of Congress come from the states, the majority opinion concluded, "the political process ensures that laws that unduly burden the States will not be promulgated."[20] Such an argument may have befitted federalism during the days when senators really were agents of their state legislatures, but, at the time of *Garcia v. San Antonio,* the Court had little basis for expecting the states' interests to win a sympathetic audience in Washington. Indeed, this decision illustrates just how much over the years the Supreme Court favored the national government in refereeing federal-state relations.

In recent years the Supreme Court has begun to take a more circumspect view of federal authority and has sought to preserve some semblance of state independence in federal-state relations. For example, in *United States v. Lopez* (1995) the Court narrowly decided in favor of a student who had been caught carrying a handgun onto campus in violation of the federal Gun-Free School Zones Act of 1990.[*] For the first time in many years the Court held that some "empirical connection" needed to be established between a law's provisions and its actual effect on interstate *commerce* before the national government could make policy

---

[*]The Gun-Free School Zones Act established a zone around public schools in which anyone caught having a gun was charged with a federal felony. *United States v. Lopez,* 514 U.S. 549 (1995).

that would supersede state policy in the traditional domains of state jurisdiction.[21] The Court first applied the *Lopez* rationale in 2000, when it overturned the 1994 Violence Against Women Act allowing female victims of gender-motivated violence to sue their attackers in federal court. Writing for a narrow majority, then–chief justice William H. Rehnquist argued that Congress had exceeded its commerce clause authority by intruding into state control of law enforcement. Unpersuaded by Congress's concerted effort to show that violence affected interstate commerce, Rehnquist responded, "Simply because Congress may conclude that a particular activity substantially affects interstate commerce does not necessarily make it so."[22] After applying this precedent in several decisions, however, the Court in 2005 rejected the *Lopez*-based argument that California's and nine other states' laws protecting the noncommercial cultivation of marijuana for personal, medical use prevent the federal government from enforcing national antidrug laws. However heartening recent small victories may be for defenders of states' rights, the medical marijuana decision reminds us that they have not seriously undermined the extensive authority nationalization has thrust on the federal government.

Preemption Legislation

Today the clearest and most unequivocal expression of nationalization's impact on public policy appears in the growth of **preemption legislation**—federal laws that assert the national government's prerogative to control public policy in a particular field. Preemption owes its existence to the supremacy clause and its frequent use to the nationalizing forces described earlier. Over the 150 years prior to the New Deal, Congress enacted 83 laws that in some way substituted federal policy for that of the states. From 1933 to 1969, 123 such statutes were adopted, and since 1969 twice that number.[23] If preemption were all that had changed federal-state relations, modern American federalism might still be described as dual. The national government's "sphere of sovereignty" would merely have grown at the expense of the states. But preemption accounts for only a small part of the impact of nationalization on federal-state relations. Generally, the jurisdictions of the states have not been curtailed so much as the national government has joined with the states in formulating policy. The result is the shared federalism described earlier in this chapter.

A cursory examination of trends in government growth during the twentieth century might raise the question of whether the impact of nationalization on reshaping modern federalism has been overstated here. Today states and localities employ more workers than ever before, their largest increases occurring since the nationalizing thrust of the New Deal (see Figure 3-4). Paradoxically, state governments have grown because of, rather than despite, nationalization. Just as the New Deal grafted national policy onto state administrations, much federal domestic policy continues to be implemented through the states instead of directly through the federal bureaucracy.

The national government has developed two ways—the carrot and the stick—to induce cooperation from the constitutionally independent states. The carrot consists of financial inducements, usually in the form of grants to states. The stick is regulation and mandates. Since the 1980s, chronic federal budget deficits have led national politicians to rely more heavily on the stick to achieve their policy objectives, and thus pass the costs on to the states.

preemption leg.
National govt's prerogative to control public policy

Figure 3-4 The Postwar Growth of Government Occurred at the Local Level

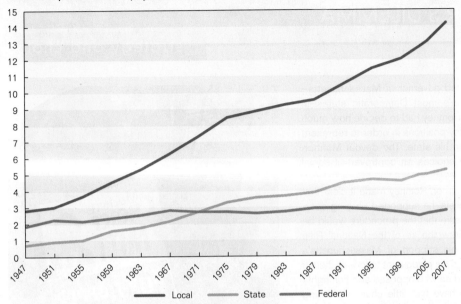

Number of public civilian employees (millions)

Legend: Local · State · Federal

Sources: For 1949, 1952, 1954, 1959, 1964, 1969–1988: U.S. Advisory Commission on Intergovernmental Relations, *Significant Features of Fiscal Federalism, 1990,* vol. 2 (Washington, DC: Author, 1990), 177; for 1989–1992: 1994, 151; for other years: U.S. Census Bureau, *Historical Statistics of the United States,* Series Y189–198 (Washington, DC: U.S. Government Printing Office, 1975), 1100; U.S. Census Bureau, *Statistical Abstract of the United States, 2000* (Washington, DC: U.S. Government Printing Office, 2000), Tables 524 and 525; U.S. Census Bureau, *Statistical Abstract of the United States, 2004* (Washington, DC: U.S. Government Printing Office, 2004), Table 453; U.S. Census Bureau, *Statistical Abstract of the United States, 2008* (Washington, DC: U.S. Government Printing Office, 2008), Table 448; U.S. Census Bureau, *Statistical Abstract of the United States, 2010* (Washington, DC: U.S. Government Printing Office, 2010), Table 450; U.S. Census Bureau, *Statistical Abstract of the United States, 2012* (Washington, DC: U.S. Government Printing Office, 2010), Table 461.

The Carrot: Federal Grants to the States

Although federal aid dates back to the Articles of Confederation, when the national government doled out public lands to the states, only during the last half-century have federal **grants-in-aid** become an important feature of intergovernmental relations. By one count, a mere handful of these programs that provide money to a state for a specific purpose existed before the New Deal; today they number in the hundreds. Typically these grants amount to more than just inducements for states to provide services that they otherwise might not be disposed to offer or could not afford. Rather, they give the national government opportunities to define these "state" programs with great specificity.

The exact structure of a grant can have an enormous impact on how much control the federal government exercises over the scope of state programs and even over the ideological direction in which policy is likely to move. Though it may seem like a bureaucratic detail, the

MITT ROMNEY AND AN AMBITIOUS GOVERNOR'S DILEMMA

strategy and choice

When he was elected governor of Massachusetts—one of the nation's most Democratic states—in 2002, Republican Mitt Romney had to decide how much he would adapt his policy positions in order to represent the left-leaning voters in his state. The devout Mormon faced especially tough choices on controversial social issues.

When he ran for governor, Romney made it clear that despite his personal beliefs, he supported keeping abortion legal in order to ensure that the procedure would be performed safely. He drew the ire of the National Rifle Association (NRA) for his support of Massachusetts's tight gun control laws and his pledge not to loosen them if elected. Indeed, a candidate who opposed abortion rights and gun control would have had little chance of being elected in the Bay State. As governor, Romney signed a universal health care plan and implemented same-sex marriage after the state supreme court ruled that gay and lesbian couples could not be denied the right to wed.

By making these difficult decisions, Romney succeeded in representing the views of the voters who sent him to Massachusetts's highest office. But when he set his sights on the White House, Governor Romney's liberal record on social issues presented a huge challenge to his new campaign. The voters that he now needed to impress, Republicans across the country in the 2008 presidential primaries, were much more conservative than the Massachusetts electorate. As it became clear that John McCain would capture most moderate Republicans, Romney sought to reestablish his conservative credentials. He urged Congress to amend the Constitution to ban gay marriage. He toured a gun show with representatives of the NRA. On the nation's most incendiary social issue, abortion, he described himself as pro-life and argued that states should be able to pass their own abortion laws. When he captured the Republican nomination in 2012, Romney attacked Barack Obama for passing a health care law that was, in many ways, modeled after the Massachusetts law that Romney had championed.

There are many reasons why Romney's presidential campaigns did not ultimately succeed, but surely the

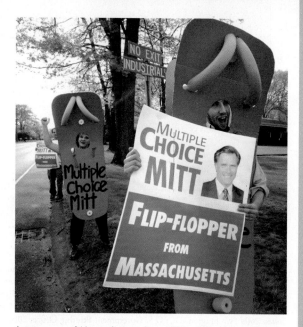

As governor of Massachusetts, one of the nation's most liberal states, Mitt Romney took moderate positions on issues such as immigration and gay rights. When he ran for president in 2008 and 2012, he first came under fire for these positions and then was accused of flip-flopping as he moved toward the right.

positions he took as Massachusetts governor created obstacles that he was not able to overcome with Republican primary voters and then with the national electorate. He faced the same dilemma that many ambitious governors do in a federal system: How far can you go to represent a state constituency if these positions are likely to alienate voters nationwide?

Sources: Joan Vennochi, "Romney's Liberal Shadow," *Boston Globe,* June 17, 2007; Scott Helman, "Romney Retreats on Gun Control: Ex-Governor Woos Republican Votes," *Boston Globe,* January 14, 2007; "Mitt Romney Says He Opposes Abortion: Switch Has Some Critics Asking Whether He Has a Philosophical Core," *Associated Press,* February 7, 2007.

difference between a **block grant** and a **matching grant** is crucial. When the federal government makes a block grant, it gives each state or local government an exact amount of money to spend for some purpose. If the state wants to do more in the policy area, it can, but the state's government must pay all the costs of this program expansion by itself. If state officials do not place a high priority on the policy area, they are free to spend less than the block grant, but all of the savings will stay in the federal treasury. States thus have little incentive to control their costs below the level of the block grant, and a huge disincentive to spend above it. They generally spend exactly as much as the block grant gives them, which effectively lets the federal government set state spending levels.

The logic and consequences of a matching grant work differently. With a matching grant, the federal government promises to provide matching funds, usually between one and four dollars, for every dollar that a state spends in some area. These blank checks, not surprisingly, often lead to major program expansions. A matching grant creates a "moral hazard," a situation in which people or groups behave differently, and often take more risks, when they do not have to pay all the costs of their actions.

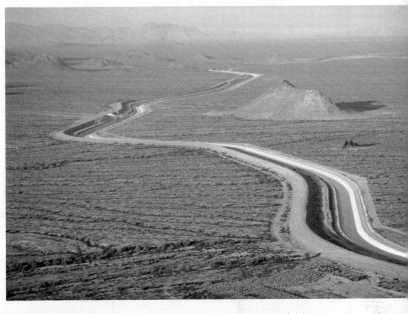

One type of federal policy expansion that generates little ideological debate is spending to help build water projects such as the Central Arizona Project, pictured above. Federal money has built massive dams and canals in the western states, helped to restore the Florida Everglades, eased the navigation of the Mississippi and many other rivers, and cleaned up environmental damage across the nation. These projects have broad bipartisan support, and the first time that Republicans and Democrats came together to override a veto during George W. Bush's presidency was in November 2007, when they overrode his veto of a $23 billion water project bill.

Consider the logic of Medicaid, the state health insurance program funded through federal matching grants. States are required to cover some of their poorest residents and provide a minimum number of health care services through Medicaid, but can choose to insure more people or pay for more services if they want. When a state's budget is flush and its leaders decide to expand Medicaid, a state that receives a $2-to-$1 federal match can cover an extra $300 million of services and spend only $100 million, because the federal government will pay the other $200 million. Its residents receive a lot of benefit, while its taxpayers assume little financial risk. This makes Medicaid expansion a relatively easy decision for state lawmakers. But when the state faces a budget crunch, the matching rate makes Medicaid cuts a bad deal. In order to save $100 million in state spending, state officials would have to trim Medicaid services by $300 million, leaving $200 million of federal grants on the table. This ensures a lot of pain for little gain, and explains why state and federal Medicaid spending has grown steeply over the past few decades. When states are not forced to pay the full costs of a new program, they take advantage of their blank checks to spend more and more federal money.

Why would the federal government ever give states a matching grant? National lawmakers have long realized the implications of this moral hazard for the growth of government. One

TABLE 3-3

How Many Federal Dollars Match One Dollar of State Spending?

State	Medicaid	Children's Health Insurance Program
Arkansas	$4.31	$4.25
California	$1.60	$1.86
Kansas	$2.30	$2.61
Mississippi	$5.61	$4.87
Montana	$3.54	$3.38
New York	$1.60	$1.86
New Mexico	$4.13	$3.99
Texas	$2.44	$2.46

Sources: These matching rates are from the 2010 fiscal year, reported in reports by the Kaiser Family Foundation ("Federal Medical Assistance Percentage (FMAP) for Medicaid and Multiplier") and Families USA (Federal Matching Rates for Medicaid and the State Children's Health Insurance Program [SCHIP]).

explicit rationale behind matching grants is that they can help capture the positive externality created when states care for the welfare and health care of their residents. Since Americans often move across state lines, these benefits—by ensuring that even those below the poverty line have received medical services and basic necessities—spill across the nation, and the grants help state lawmakers internalize the benefits that they create for their neighbors. According to Wallace Oates, a prominent theorist of fiscal federalism, matching grants should "be employed where the provision of local services generates benefits for residents of other jurisdictions."[24] Matching grants, because they can treat each state differently, ironically allow the federal government to equalize living conditions across states with radically unequal economies. Richer states receive smaller federal matches, and poorer states get larger matching grants, as Table 3-3 illustrates. The differences in these rates translate into billions more in federal dollars going to less affluent states.

Because matching rates incentivize higher state spending and redistribute money across the nation, they have become an issue of partisan contention. The Democratic-controlled Congresses that created and expanded Medicaid and welfare programs funded them through matching grants because they knew this financial arrangement would spur even the most conservative and cash-strapped states to spend freely on social services. When Republicans took control of Congress in 1994, they wanted to remove this moral hazard in order to restrain state and federal spending. After trying and failing to shift Medicaid to a block grant program in 1995, the Newt Gingrich–led Congress succeeded in block granting the Temporary Assistance for Needy Families program as part of a 1996 welfare reform deal with Bill Clinton. The ideological stakes of these battles over funding formulas were clear; both sides knew that government would grow more quickly under matching grants than block grants. The combatants also likely realize that shifting responsibility for funding a program from the national to the state governments dramatically changes who pays for it, as the Politics/Policy box on page 122 shows. These episodes illustrate once again that in fights over federalism, each combatant is usually more concerned with a policy goal than with shaping the proper relationship between national and state governments.

The Stick: Unfunded Mandates

Until the 1960s the only federal regulations applied to the states were those governing the routine reporting and accounting for grants.* Since then, Washington has relied increasingly on rules to pursue policy objectives. Not only are states required to administer policies they

---

* The one exception was the Hatch Act (1940), which sought to clean up corruption by preventing federal and state employees from engaging in a variety of partisan political activities.

might object to, but, adding insult to injury, the federal government may not even compensate the states for the costs of administration. One of the most controversial examples is the Education for All Handicapped Children Act of 1975, which requires states and school districts to offer prescribed, and in many cases costly, levels of special education for children with disabilities without providing more than a fraction of the funds needed to finance these mandated programs. Many school districts, as a consequence, find themselves strapped for resources and must curtail existing instructional programs to satisfy this federal mandate.

Crosscutting requirements are statutes that apply certain rules and guidelines to a broad array of federally subsidized state programs. Since the 1960s this device has been used widely to enforce civil rights laws. For example, the failure of any state to follow federal guidelines that prohibit discriminatory employment practices can result in prosecution of state officials as well as loss of grants. Another prominent area of crosscutting requirements is the environment. All state programs that include major construction and changes in land use must file environmental impact statements with the federal government.

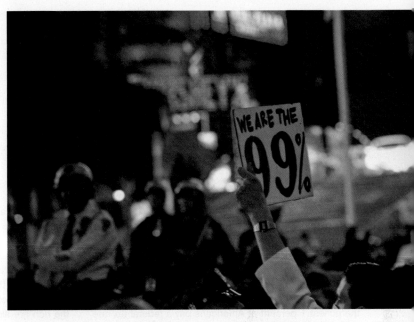

Occupy protesters focused on disparities between the nation's richest 1 percent and the other residents, a divide that is narrowed by federal tax structures but widened in the states.

Crossover sanctions are stipulations that a state, to remain eligible for full federal funding for one program, must adhere to the guidelines of an unrelated program. One example, mentioned earlier, is Congress's stipulation tying federal highway funds to state adoption of a minimum drinking age of twenty-one. Similarly, the Education for All Handicapped Children Act requires that a school district develop special education programs meeting federal guidelines to remain eligible for a broad variety of previously created grants-in-aid programs, including school construction and teacher-training subsidies.

National politicians frequently use crossover sanctions to influence state policies beyond their jurisdiction. In 1994 Sen. Patrick Leahy, D-Vt., proposed legislation banning the sale of soft drinks on public school campuses, and Sen. Dianne Feinstein, D-Calif., introduced a bill requiring that all students caught entering school with a handgun be suspended for a minimum of one year. Both bills provided for a cutoff in school aid funds if the districts failed to comply.

Direct orders are requirements that can be enforced by legal and civil penalties. The Clean Water Act, for example, bans ocean dumping of sewage sludge. In 1996, when the city of San Diego resisted a multibillion-dollar investment in a sophisticated sewage treatment facility that would alleviate the problem, the EPA brought suit in federal court to impose punitive financial penalties on the city.

WHO PAYS FOR GOVERNMENT? COMPARING STATE AND FEDERAL TAX BURDENS

politics to policy

One central fact of federalism that is seldom discussed but deserves serious contemplation is that shifting the responsibility for funding programs to the states also shifts the burden of paying for them to less affluent Americans, for better or worse. Most federal tax dollars are raised from income and payroll taxes, with higher earners paying a higher rate. This creates a progressive tax system, with the figure below showing that the richest 1 percent of Americans pay a federal tax rate that is five times as high as the rate paid by those whose incomes put them in the lowest 20 percent.

Yet states typically raise less of their money from income taxes—with Florida and Texas charging no income taxes at all. Instead, many rely on large sales and property taxes, which hit the poor harder because they spend so much of their money on housing and consumer purchases. This makes state taxes regressive, with poorer residents paying more cents on every dollar that

they earn to state governments than do the affluent. Some states are more regressive than others, as the figure below shows, but in all states those in the bottom 20 percent pay a higher tax rate than the top 1 percent. As a consequence, any shift in responsibility for health care or welfare services from the federal government changes who will pay the bill. To many, this is fair, because poor residents receive the bulk of these services, and because the rich are already paying such a high federal tax rate. To others, including the protesters who took to the streets during the 2011 Occupy movement, state tax structures represent an unfair advantage for the richest 1 percent.

Sources: Tax data are drawn from Citizens for Tax Justice, *America's Tax System Is Not as Progressive as You Think,* April 2011, and the Institute on Taxation and Economic Policy, *Who Pays? A Distributional Analysis of the Tax Systems of All 50 States,* 3rd ed., November 2009.

Certain federal laws allow the states to administer joint federal-state programs so long as they conform to federal guidelines—a practice known as *partial preemption.* If a state agency fails to follow the instructions of federal agencies, the state might lose control of the program altogether; alternatively, federal grants might be suspended via crossover regulations. Good examples of partial preemption regulations are state air pollution policies. Public law and the EPA set minimally acceptable standards, but enforcement of these standards rests mostly with state agencies.

Hardly any area of state policy is unaffected by federal regulations of one kind or another. A close look at the major federal laws listed in Table 3-4 reveals several interesting trends and characteristics. First, although federal grants were plentiful before the 1970s, few regulatory policies were in place. Second, since the 1970s the more coercive forms of regulation—direct orders and partial preemption—have been favored. Finally, the content of the policies reveals

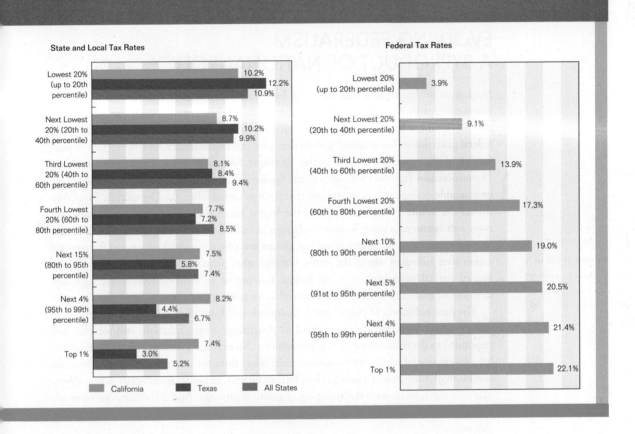

State and Local Tax Rates

	California	Texas	All States
Lowest 20% (up to 20th percentile)	10.2%	12.2%	10.9%
Next Lowest 20% (20th to 40th percentile)	8.7%	10.2%	9.9%
Third Lowest 20% (40th to 60th percentile)	8.1%	8.4%	9.4%
Fourth Lowest 20% (60th to 80th percentile)	7.7%	7.2%	8.5%
Next 15% (80th to 95th percentile)	7.5%	5.8%	7.4%
Next 4% (95th to 99th percentile)	8.2%	4.4%	6.7%
Top 1%	7.4%	3.0%	5.2%

Federal Tax Rates

Lowest 20% (up to 20th percentile)	3.9%
Next Lowest 20% (20th to 40th percentile)	9.1%
Third Lowest 20% (40th to 60th percentile)	13.9%
Fourth Lowest 20% (60th to 80th percentile)	17.3%
Next 10% (80th to 90th percentile)	19.0%
Next 5% (91st to 95th percentile)	20.5%
Next 4% (95th to 99th percentile)	21.4%
Top 1%	22.1%

the political processes that produced them. Federal regulation of the states is concentrated on civil rights and the environment—the two sectors in which national majorities are likely to be at odds with state majorities. The same policy disagreements also may explain why coercion is such a favored policy instrument today. Regulatory statutes compel states to administer policies they would spurn if federal regulations did not legally require their compliance.

When members of Congress pass a law that obligates the states to provide particular services, they are yielding to a temptation all politicians share: the desire to respond to some citizens' demands without being held responsible for the costs. In forcing the states to pay for a program, members are imposing costs for which they will not be held accountable. Like the grants process, mandates deprive state political representatives of their rightful decision-making authority. Of greater concern to fiscal conservatives, unfunded mandates increase government spending. In 1995 President Bill Clinton and the Republican Congress agreed to rein in future temptations to "spend" the states' revenues. The result was the Unfunded Mandates Reform Act, which required that new federal laws pay for the programs and regulations they imposed on the states. A 1998 study, however, found that the law was exerting minimal constraint on mandates.[25] Perhaps the temptation to respond to demands for services while avoiding costs overwhelms the ideologies of even conservative politicians. In any event, Congress has continued to enact preemptive and mandate legislation.

EVOLVING FEDERALISM: A BYPRODUCT OF NATIONAL POLICY

No feature of American government has been more dramatically transformed during the twentieth century than federal-state relations. Some of the most important contributions to this development have come through sudden bursts of national policymaking in which the federal government has assumed jurisdiction over and responsibility for large sectors of public policy once reserved to the states. President Roosevelt's New Deal response to the Depression and President Johnson's Great Society initiatives against poverty in America are two notable examples. It is instructive that both occurred when the Democratic Party controlled the White House and enjoyed the largest majorities in Congress ever seen in the twentieth century. In other instances, changes in federal-state relations have occurred more gradually and inconspicuously as interest groups and constituencies have pressed for national action after failing to win in the states. On still other occasions, the states themselves have invited federal participation to tap federal funding or to institute federal oversight and sanctioning authority to solve their own collective action problems.

The nationalization of public policy that proceeded from these causes did not arise from some grand design. Rather, it occurred as politicians sought solutions to problems and responded to the demands of their constituencies. No one had a stake in trying to rationalize intergovernmental relations or wrest authority away from the states. In this sense, then, the condition of modern federalism has had little to do with responses to collective action dilemmas and much to do with the interplay of political interests. And if the behavior of recent presidents and Congresses is any indication, federal-state relations will continue to evolve in this way.

In Chapter 4 we turn to a series of national decisions that even more dramatically refashioned federalism in America. The issue is civil rights for African Americans. The Civil War, Reconstruction, and the civil rights movement of the 1960s all required vigorous national action against entrenched state policies instituting slavery and, later, segregation. Southerners, recognizing that their positions on slavery and segregation were untenable, nevertheless sought to rationalize and defend their policies from the higher ground of federalism. The Confederacy's only president, Jefferson Davis, went to his grave steadfastly maintaining that the South's secession was not about slavery but about states' rights. Nearly a century later, Alabama governor George Wallace used the same rhetoric when confronted by federal officers seeking to enforce national laws and court orders. Because of the South's experience with civil rights, federalism came to be viewed as a hollow ruse that could be brushed aside without serious consideration whenever national action appeared necessary. Whether hollow or not,

TAKE A QUIZ

logic.cqpress.com

Test your knowledge of this chapter.

TABLE 3-4

Examples of Major Unfunded Mandates

Public Law	Kind of Mandate
Civil Rights Act of 1964 (Title VI) Prevented discrimination on the basis of race, color, or national origin in federally assisted programs.	Crosscutting
Age Discrimination in Employment Act (1967) Prevented discrimination on the basis of age in federally assisted programs.	Crosscutting
Clean Air Act Amendments (1970) Established national air quality and emissions standards.	Crosscutting, crossover sanctions, partial preemption
Occupational Safety and Health Act (1970) Set standards for safe and healthful working conditions.	Partial preemption
Endangered Species Act (1973) Protected and conserved endangered and threatened animal and plant species.	Crosscutting, partial preemption
Fair Labor Standards Act Amendments (1974) Extended federal minimum wage and overtime pay protections to state and local government employees.	Direct order
Education for All Handicapped Children Act (1975) Provided free, appropriate public education to all handicapped children.	Crossover sanctions
Hazardous and Solid Waste Amendments (1984) Reauthorized and strengthened scope and enforcement of the Resource Conservation and Recovery Act of 1976; established program to regulate underground storage tanks for petroleum and hazardous substances; required annual EPA inspections of state and locally operated hazardous waste sites.	Partial preemption
Asbestos Hazard Emergency Response Act (1986) Directed school districts to inspect for asbestos hazards and take the necessary actions to protect health and the environment; required state review and approval of local management response plans.	Direct order
Americans with Disabilities Act (1990) Established comprehensive national standards to prohibit discrimination in public services and accommodations and to promote handicapped access to public buildings and transportation.	Crosscutting, direct order
Clean Air Act Amendments (1990) Imposed strict new deadlines and requirements dealing with urban smog, municipal incinerators, and toxic emissions; enacted program for controlling acid rain.	Partial preemption
National Voter Registration Act (1993) Required states to provide all eligible citizens the chance to register to vote when they apply for renewal of their driver's license.	Direct order
Ban on Internet sales tax (rider on 1998 appropriations law) Placed a three-year moratorium on state sales taxes on Internet commerce and created a commission of state and industry representatives to recommend permanent policy.	Direct order
No Child Left Behind Act (2001) Established standards for performance of schools with frequent standardized testing required and prescribed levels of credentialed instructors.	Crossover sanction
Help America Vote Act (2003) Established standards and partially financed changes in voting procedures.	Direct order
Fair Minimum Wage Act (2007) Increased the federal minimum wage from $5.15 to $7.25 per hour by 2009.	Direct order
Internet Tax Freedom Act Amendments (2007) Extended the moratorium on states charging sales tax on Internet purchases until 2001.	Direct order

Sources: Advisory Commission on Intergovernmental Relations and various issues of *Congressional Quarterly Weekly Report* and *CQ Weekly.*

the concept of federalism will always be debated in American politics because the stakes of this fight are so high for policies critical to American life. "From the start," one scholar of the history of American federalism notes, "political opponents have fought about federalism because it affects who wins and who loses a particular fight."[26]

logic.cqpress.com

■ Key Terms ■

block grant,   119

cutthroat competition,   110

dual federalism,   92

elastic clause,   96

enumerated powers,   95

externality,   109

federalism,   89

grants-in-aid,   117

matching grant,   119

nationalization,   92

preemption legislation,   116

race to the bottom,   110

shared federalism,   92

states' rights,   88

Tenth Amendment,   96

unitary government,   89

■ Suggested Readings ■

Beer, Samuel H. *To Make a Nation: The Rediscovery of American Federalism.* Cambridge, MA: Belknap Press of Harvard University Press, 1993. Beer reviews the history of American federalism, its roots in traditional republican theory, and its modern evolution.

Berry, Christopher R. *Imperfect Union: Representation and Taxation in Multilevel Governments.* New York: Cambridge University Press, 2009. Berry looks at politics, public participation, and policy in the tens of thousands of special-purpose local governments and school districts that deliver critical services yet form nearly invisible layers of government within America.

Campbell, Ballard C. *The Growth of American Government: Governance from the Cleveland Era to the Present.* Bloomington: Indiana University Press, 1995. Another historical survey of nationalization that focuses almost exclusively on the national government.

Kettl, Donald H. *System under Stress: Homeland Security and American Politics,* 2nd ed. Washington, DC: CQ Press, 2007. This balanced look at federal, state, and local responses to the September 11, 2001, attacks examines the system-wide failures that led to the disaster—such as poor coordination among the nation's intelligence agencies—and assessing the consequences for the bureaucracy.

Lowry, William R. *The Dimensions of Federalism: State Governments and Pollution Control Policies.* Durham, NC: Duke University Press, 1992. A study of shared federalism in water pollution policy that finds a stronger state presence than is commonly assumed.

Peterson, Paul E., Barry G. Rabe, and Kenneth K. Wong. *When Federalism Works.* Washington, DC: Brookings, 1986. A thorough and authoritative study of modern federalism in America.

Skowronek, Stephen. *Building a New American State: The Expansion of National Administrative Capacities, 1877–1920*. New York: Cambridge University Press, 1982. A modern classic on the institutional conflicts involved in shifting the center of public policy from the states to Washington.

Wiebe, Robert H. *The Search for Order, 1877–1920*. New York: Hill and Wang, 1967. An authoritative, well-written historical survey of the nationalization of American life.

■ Review Questions ■

1. What are the main differences between unitary governments, confederations, and federal governments? Which type of government is most common?

2. Most of the Framers felt that the Constitution adequately protected the states against encroachment by the national government. How, then, did proponents of nationalization succeed in expanding the power of the national government?

3. When states encounter problems that cross state borders, why don't they just make formal agreements with each other to solve the problems? What happens in the absence of such arrangements?

4. Why would national majorities sometimes find it easier to work through the national government than through state governments? What are some examples of policy areas in which this strategy has been used?

5. What are the three main types of collective action problems faced by state governments? Give an example of each.

4 Civil Rights

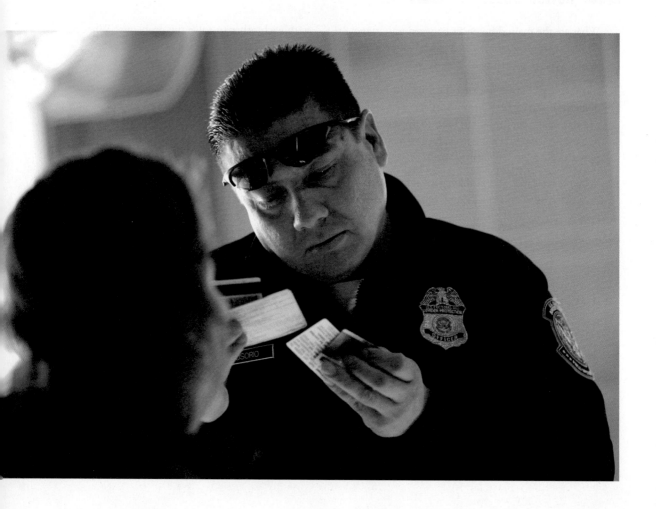

- How could a nation that embraced the Declaration of Independence's creed that "all men are created equal" condone slavery?

- Why would a majority in society ever seek to extend and protect the rights of its minorities in the face of huge costs—even those imposed by a tragic civil war?

- Does America's constitutional system impede or promote the cause of civil rights?

- Are "civil rights" generic, or do we define them differently across groups according to issues for which they seek protection?

All nineteen hijackers who coordinated, commandeered, and launched the September 11, 2001, attacks were Middle Eastern males. In the subsequent investigations, authorities found that other terrorist cell members implicated in the assaults were also Middle Eastern.

For the next five months, as federal agencies issued reports and advisories about terrorist threats, their communiqués frequently included mug shots of Arab suspects who allegedly were in the United States. Unavoidably, perhaps, government officials and ordinary citizens alike began to regard male Arab strangers with suspicion. This wariness took on more specificity as the Justice Department systematically interviewed twelve hundred male Middle Eastern visa holders in the United States; then–Attorney General John Ashcroft unveiled new procedures to expedite expulsion hearings for people who had overstayed or violated their visas; some pilots and flight crews refused to fly with "suspicious-looking" passengers (including, in one case, Rep. Darrell Issa, R-Calif., and, in another, a member of President George W. Bush's secret service). Critics of these measures charged discrimination and **racial profiling** (enlisting race or ethnicity as the primary criterion for identifying a suspect), starting a national debate over how government and airline officials should prevent the next terrorist attack, which nearly everyone thought was imminent.

One national survey taken soon after September 11 found that 58 percent of the public endorsed more intensive security checks for Arabs, while two-thirds supported "random stops" of people of Middle Eastern descent.[1] Arab American support groups and some local American Civil Liberties Union (ACLU) chapters opened "hotlines" for registering discrimination complaints. Civil liberties watchdogs argued that since only a tiny fraction of individuals posed a threat, treating with suspicion everyone who fit the Middle Eastern profile constituted discrimination.

The reaction to September 11 recalled the internment of Japanese Americans nearly sixty years earlier. After Japan bombed Pearl Harbor in 1941, the same fear of imminent attack— fueled by government alerts, air-raid drills, and other civil defense activities—gripped the

Shortly after the attack on Pearl Harbor, President Franklin Roosevelt began issuing executive orders that placed restrictions on Japanese Americans living on the West Coast. Eventually, more than 110,000 Japanese Americans—including native-born U.S. citizens—were removed to internment camps throughout the nation. The internees were given little time to dispose of their homes, businesses, or other property, causing financial ruin for many.

nation. Within months government officials in Washington spawned the plan—in hindsight, clearly unwarranted—to intern thousands of West Coast Japanese Americans in camps as far away as Arkansas for the duration of World War II.

The Transportation Department recalled this misguided relocation as it dealt with the September 11 crisis. To counteract charges of racial profiling in airport screening, which began in the aftermath of the terrorist attack, the department issued rules for airport and other security personnel that sought to balance protecting the public's right to security with preventing civil rights violations. The department prohibited screeners from giving travelers special attention based solely on their "race, color, national origin, religion, sex, or ancestry." Arab-looking males who spoke no English were to be screened no differently than other passengers, including, for example, elderly grandmothers who had their knitting needles confiscated by security guards.[2]

Critics of the policy countered that because dozens of known terrorists fit the same distinctive gender and ethnic profile, public officials are justified in using this information to identify hard-to-find suspects. One nationally prominent civil libertarian condoned racial profiling as "entirely appropriate," repeating former Supreme Court justice Robert Jackson's declaration that "the Constitution is not a suicide pact." In any event, observed one leading civil rights lawyer, it was expecting too much of screeners who must "make on the spot decisions about whom to detain and whom to question [to] disregard ethnicity."[3] The racial profiling debate will not be resolved anytime soon. Indeed, in 2010 it flared up again in a new arena of law enforcement—spotting and deporting illegal immigrants. The construction of a two-thousand-mile border fence from San Diego, California, into Arizona during the previous five years channeled increasing numbers of illegal border crossings along Arizona's unfenced border with Mexico. In April 2010 the public's frustration culminated in the passage of a local and highly popular but nationally controversial Arizona law requiring local law enforcement officers to check individuals' immigration status if, during the course of a legal stop for violation of traffic or other law, the officer reasonably suspects that the person is in the United States illegally.

The Arizona law raises issues of what civil rights, if any, *illegal* immigrants are entitled to. It also poses the question of how law enforcement officers could implement the law while *avoiding* racially profiling citizens of Hispanic descent. If, for example, the subject's dress, language skills, and general demeanor give the officer reasonable suspicion that the person is in the United States illegally, the law prescribes that the officer determine the individual's immigration status. If the person is unable to produce valid Arizona identification (such as a driver's license or nonoperating identification license) or a federally issued identification or alien registration document, the officer then should ask to see the individual's visa. If these papers are also unavailable, are out of date, or contain some other problem, the law enforcement officer must turn the individual over to the federal immigration service. Immediately, lawsuits were filed in federal court to block implementation of the law, and the U.S. Supreme Court ruled on the case in June 2012. Although the Court struck down other parts of the Arizona law as "preempted" by federal law, it let stand the key provision requiring local and state law enforcement officers to verify immigration status of individuals stopped for traffic violations and other minor offenses.[*]

New York City's mayor and police have been under attack for implementing an aggressive "stop and frisk" policy, ostensibly in order to combat the city's gun violence problem. Critics argue that the NYPD is racially profiling black and Latino youth. Out of almost seven hundred thousand stops in 2011, 87 percent of those stopped were black or Latino. City officials respond that they are not profiling but rather are only aggressively policing crime-infested neighborhoods.

With Hispanics comprising nearly a third of the state's citizenry, the new law virtually ensures repeated instances of ordinary citizens who have lost or left their driver's license at home being detained because they "look" illegal to the officer.

Well before the Arizona law and September 11 attacks, racial profiling had already become a controversial practice. Police departments from New Jersey to California were under investigation for stopping black motorists without cause. By the end of summer 2001, nine states had banned such practices. And in August the George W. Bush administration's Justice Department had launched a national investigation into the pervasiveness of racial profiling. Despite the apprehension of another attack, concerns with racial or ethnic profiling have continued

---

[*] A half-dozen other states used the Arizona law as a model for their own legislation to take direct action to enforce federal immigration laws. Since the Supreme Court issued its decision on the Arizona law, lower federal courts have upheld the "show-me-your-papers" provisions of laws in Alabama, Georgia, and South Carolina. Robbie Brown, "South Carolina: Federal Court Delivers Mixed Verdict on Immigration Measure," *New York Times*, November 15, 2012.

WATCH A VIDEO

logic.cqpress.com

■ Training
Arizona's
immigration
enforcement

to generate protective laws and enforcement practices. In 2003 the Justice Department issued guidelines for all federal officials to limit the influence of racial and ethnic information in searching for suspected terrorists. By 2005 twenty states had enacted some form of antiprofiling laws. Arguably, the controversies over airport screenings attracted careful scrutiny of racial profiling because past practices directed at African Americans had placed it on the national agenda. Prevailing opinion already held as suspect any use of profiling, placing on the defensive those who advocated it for ferreting out terrorists.

The controversies over airport screening and local enforcement of federal immigration laws remind us that civil rights established for one group apply to everyone. For many years, the term *civil rights* referred almost exclusively to the privileges of African Americans, and the history of civil rights in the United States concerned the emancipation of African Americans—first from slavery and then, in the twentieth century, from segregation. The legacy concerns the rights of everyone. The new federal laws, administrative practices, and agencies to secure the rights of African Americans became available to enforce the rights of "new" claimants. Voting rights laws authorizing Justice Department intervention against discriminatory practices in the 1960s were summoned by Hispanic voters fearing arbitrary rules, such as challenges of citizenship, that would disenfranchise them in the 2004 presidential election. The civil rights struggle of African Americans ends with all Americans changing their view of their own rights and privileges. In this respect, the debate over how closely airport screeners should consider the ethnicity and gender of passengers reflects prior debates over the civil rights of African Americans.

WHAT ARE CIVIL RIGHTS?

Throughout the nation's history, Americans have applied the terms **civil rights** and **civil liberties** to a variety of rights and privileges. Although they have sometimes been used interchangeably, *rights* and *liberties* do offer useful distinctions for organizing our discussion in this and the next chapter. We classify as civil liberties the Constitution's protections *from* government power, meaning the government *may not* take these freedoms—including the freedoms of speech, liberty, and the right to privacy—away. Typically, violations of these liberties occur when some government agency, at any level, oversteps its authority. Civil rights, on the other hand, represent those protections *by* government or that government secures on behalf of its citizens. The crucial difference is that civil rights require governments to act, whereas civil liberties are well served when government does nothing.[4]

In colonial times civil rights equaled "civic" rights—protections against arbitrary action by the distant British Crown. Although the term *civil rights* was not commonly used until the late 1760s, when colonial Americans rallied to the slogan "No taxation without representation," the colonists were clearly seeking these rights, including the right to vote and have their views represented in the British Parliament. Thomas Jefferson's eloquent statement in the Declaration of Independence that all governments must defer to humanity's "unalienable Rights" of "Life, Liberty and the pursuit of Happiness" gave the Revolutionary War its moral certitude.

Once they had gained their independence and established republican institutions, Americans turned from seeking protection from an arbitrary and distant government to looking for it from one another. In *Federalist* No. 10 James Madison explored whether a majority of citizens could use government authority to strip adversaries of their rights and thereby gain a permanent advantage. This prospect bothered leaders on both sides of the Constitution's ratification issue. For Madison and the other nationalists, the pluralism of a large republic provided the best insurance against such factionally inspired tyranny; as the number and diversity of groups increased, the likelihood that any one group could impose its will on another decreased. But Patrick Henry and others opposing ratification insisted on a bill of rights to further deter the new national government from usurping power. Along with voting (an issue the Constitution resolved by allowing the states to set voting requirements), virtually everyone's list of freedoms included freedom of speech, free assembly, and a free press.

Federalist 10

Modern-day "civil rights" encompass much more than these "civic" rights of political expression and participation. They also include safeguards against any effort by government and dominant groups in a community to subjugate another group and take unfair, mostly economic, advantage of it. Before the American Civil War, southern governments teamed up with white slave owners to configure state laws and institutions to legalize and preserve slavery. (In most southern states, for example, it was illegal for slave masters to free their slaves.) Many decades later, segregation in the South, also regulated by the states, dominated virtually all interpersonal contact between the races. Civil rights, then, also include the rights of individuals in their relations with one another: to live free from bondage and intimidation, to enter into contracts and own property, to have access to businesses that serve the public, and to enjoy equal educational opportunities.

THE CIVIL RIGHTS OF AFRICAN AMERICANS

In December 1997 Bill Lann Lee, a second-generation Chinese American, opened his acceptance statement as President Bill Clinton's acting assistant attorney general for civil rights by describing his post as "haunted by the ghosts of slavery, the Civil War, Jim Crow." He then proceeded to cite modern instances of racial, ethnic, and religious discrimination.[5] Indeed, as Lee knew and the history books describe, African Americans have been engaged in a two-hundred-year struggle for civil rights, spanning slavery to full citizenship. As we will see in this chapter and the next, the results have redefined the rights and liberties of *all* Americans.

The history of black civil rights provided a laboratory to test James Madison's ideas on democracy in America, laid out in his *Federalist* essays. Dominant white majorities throughout the South instituted slavery—and later segregation—to gain a permanent advantage over the black minority. And what is the solution to such tyranny? As Madison argued in *Federalist* No. 10, a diverse national community would be less inclined than state-level majorities to engage in tyranny and more likely to halt it.

The history of black civil rights follows Madison's script in another respect. The effort to secure civil rights rested less on making formal rules—which Madison noted had little impact on intemperate majorities—and more on configuring politics to allow society's competing interests to check one another. This chapter, as did Madison, recognizes civil rights in America as products of the political process. But the abuses of slavery and segregation endured for almost two centuries before the national majority struck out against local tyranny. The effect of institutions on democracy explains this disturbing situation. For one thing, the Framers rejected a national veto over all state laws, as Madison had repeatedly proposed. Public policy, such as public safety and regulation of elections, was left to state control, allowing slavery to flourish within the South.

African Americans faced two major obstacles in securing rights. First, the Constitution reserves important authority for the states, such as the power to determine voting eligibility. It also separates powers among the three branches of government, making it difficult for national majorities to control the federal government to the extent required to strike against tyranny in the states.

Madison's observation that government is controlled by "men" and not "angels" sums up the second obstacle to obtaining civil rights for African Americans. People do not engage in costly behavior without some expected return. Madison, recognizing that citizens and politicians alike act most forcefully when they have a personal stake in the outcome, believed that tyranny could best be avoided by empowering every faction to look out for its own interests. But what of a faction without the capacity to defend itself? This predicament is central to the nation's long ordeal over civil rights for African Americans. Indeed, politics based on self-interest in a fragmented constitutional system largely explains why it took so long to eradicate slavery, segregation, and other discrimination. Instead, the real question is why the civil rights of America's black population were ever addressed at all.

THE POLITICS OF BLACK CIVIL RIGHTS

The efforts to seek civil rights for African Americans took different forms at different times. Notably, in 1787 Benjamin Franklin convened an abolition society meeting in his home and invited delegates to the Constitutional Convention to attend. Throughout the antebellum era and during the Civil War, a small but persistent abolitionist movement forced the nation to face the discrepancy between the ideal of "Life, Liberty and the pursuit of Happiness" and the enslavement of 10 percent of its population. Emancipation shifted the issue from fundamental "life and liberty" rights to those of full citizenship.[*] Several years later the Fifteenth Amendment granted former slaves the right to vote,[†] but another century would pass before most could safely exercise this right. With civic rights secured, the dominant issue again shifted, this time to equal opportunity in the marketplace—particularly in education, employment, and housing.

---

[*] As late as 1858 Abraham Lincoln, in his famous Senate race debates in Illinois with Stephen Douglas, distinguished between citizenship rights based on equality and fundamental rights. He protected his flank by stating there was "no purpose to introduce political and social equality between the white and black races." But then, in one of the most progressive statements made by any elected officeholder of the time, he asserted: "There is no reason in the world why the negro is not entitled to all the natural rights enumerated in the Declaration of Independence. . . . I hold that he is as much entitled to these as the white man." Donald G. Nieman, *Promises to Keep: African-Americans and the Constitutional Order, 1776 to the Present* (New York: Oxford University Press, 1991), 43.

[†] This achievement stemmed in part from the Senate's insistence that the former Confederate states ratify the amendment as a condition of their reentry into the Union.

By and large, national majorities have over the decades consistently favored civil rights for African Americans, but only twice did they strike out forcefully against discrimination. The first time was Reconstruction after the Civil War; the second was the national attack on segregation in the 1960s. Why were rights advanced at these particular moments in American history and not at others? A look at the successes and failures will answer this question and illuminate the conditions under which national majorities are able to dictate national policy.

The Height of Slavery: 1808–1865

Late in 1807, with the Constitution's prohibition against the federal government's regulation of the slave trade about to expire, Congress passed a law ending the importation of slaves. Southern representatives in Congress, not yet aware that the rise of "King Cotton" would soon dictate a slave-centered, plantation economy, did not vigorously contest the new law. In fact, some probably anticipated that the restricted supply of new slaves might drive up the market value of their human property. Thus the nation took this first step toward eradicating slavery with deceptive ease. It would never be easy again.

Over the next decade slavery remained a side issue only because the northern and southern states carefully maintained regional balance in the Senate, thereby preserving the South's veto over national policy. This balance required matching states' entry—one slave state with one free state—into the Union. As we learned earlier, institutions created to achieve one goal can over time come to serve other purposes. Where equal apportionment of the Senate reassured small states that their interests would not be ignored in the new national government, by the 1820s this same rule guaranteed the South a veto over policy curtailing slavery. Many northern politicians found the practice objectionable, but did not press for its eradication against intransigent southerners for fear of fracturing fragile regional party alliances. Indeed, the North hoped that slavery would eventually wither away.

Do not look at the Negro.

His earthly problems are ended.

Instead, look at the seven WHITE children who gaze at this gruesome spectacle.

Is it horror or gloating on the face of the neatly dressed seven-year-old girl on the right?

Is the tiny four-year-old on the left old enough, one wonders, to comprehend the barbarism her elders have perpetrated?

Rubin Stacy, the Negro, who was lynched at Fort Lauderdale, Florida, on July 19, 1935, for "threatening and frightening a white woman," suffered PHYSICAL torture for a few short hours. But what psychological havoc is being wrought in the minds of the white children? Into what kinds of citizens

Between 1882 and 1950, 4,729 lynchings were reported in the United States. African Americans were the victims in about three-quarters of the cases. This 1930s NAACP poster graphically featured this tyrannical practice designed to intimidate the entire black population.

THE MISSOURI COMPROMISE. Then in 1819 the citizens of Missouri, most of whom had emigrated from the slave states of Kentucky and Tennessee, petitioned Congress for admission as a slave state. Instead of shriveling up, slavery threatened to expand beyond its southern borders, upset the balance, and ignite the nation. "Like a fire bell in the night," wrote a retired Thomas Jefferson, the political conflagration he foresaw "awakened and filled me with terror."[6]

After months of debate in Washington and throughout the country, Congress enacted the Missouri Compromise in 1820. The plan matched Missouri's entry as a slave state with Maine's as a free state, thereby maintaining the balance in the Senate between free and slave states. Moreover, the South agreed to accept Missouri's southern border as the northern boundary beyond which slavery could not extend in the future (see Map 4-1). The boundary at latitude 36°30' stretched to the end of the Louisiana Territory, where Spain's possessions began. Once again, slavery appeared to be fenced in. The compromise itself was a

Map 4-1   The Missouri Compromise and the State of the Union, 1820

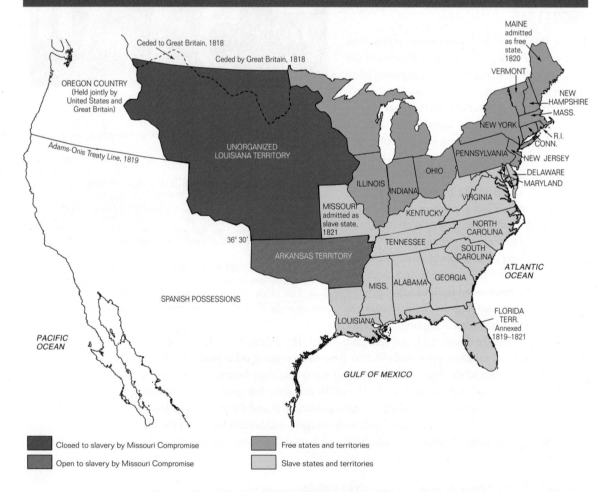

Source: Mary B. Norton et al., *People and a Nation: A History of the United States,* 2 vols., 5th ed. © 1998 Wadsworth, a part of Cengage Learning, Inc. Reproduced by permission. www.cengage.com/permissions.

classic "political" solution—one that was not entirely satisfactory to either side but that allowed agreement on a national policy applicable to the foreseeable future.

For the next decade or so this compromise worked. It began to unravel, however, as territories applying for statehood were not conveniently paired off as slave and free states. Gradually southern senators realized that, under the current formula, their ability to block national policy was doomed as more free than slave states joined the Union with continued westward expansion. Thus they began searching for an effective alternative to their Senate veto that would ensure continuation of the institution of slavery.

Meanwhile, the containment strategy also was losing favor in the North, where a small but highly vocal group of abolitionists had never accepted the compromise. More broadly, the abolitionist movement, under the banner of the Liberty Party, reminded the nation of its hypocrisy in condoning slavery. Although few voters endorsed its outright eradication, they were angry about slavery's territorial expansion.[*]

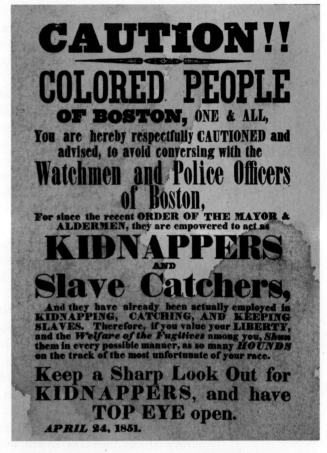

The Fugitive Slave Law of 1850 forced law enforcement authorities in both the North and the South to act as slaveholders' agents in seizing and returning their "property." As this broadside warned, even free African Americans were in danger of being seized and sent into slavery as unscrupulous law enforcement officials colluded with slaveholders in making bogus claims that these free citizens were actually runaway slaves.

THE WILMOT PROVISO AND THE COMPROMISE OF 1850. In 1846 David Wilmot, a Democratic representative from Pennsylvania, introduced a bill that would have gutted the compromise by banning slavery in the recently acquired territories. Wilmot denied any "squeamish sensitivities" or "morbid sympathy for the slave." Rather, he professed devotion to "the rights of white freemen . . . [and] white free labor."[7] Simply put, slave labor depressed wages for free, white workers. The Wilmot Proviso was introduced twice and passed the House of Representatives both times, but it made no headway in the evenly divided Senate. Still, the failure of Wilmot's proposal eventually led significant numbers of northern whites to recognize they had a stake in containing slavery.

By 1848 Wilmot's allies joined the abolitionists in the new antislavery Free Soil Party. Its election slate that year was headed by presidential candidate Martin Van Buren, who already had served one term as president, as a Democrat, in 1836. His 1848 campaign revolved

---

[*] After its recent war with Mexico, the United States had annexed territory in the Southwest, almost all of it falling into the slavery zone. Moreover, California was petitioning for statehood, and southerners were proposing that the 36°30' line be projected to the Pacific Ocean and California be split into one slave and one free state.

around a single issue: opposition to the extension of slavery on behalf of "free labor." The Free Soil Party managed to scare the two major political parties, the Democrats and the Whigs, by winning 10 percent of the national popular vote and finishing second in several states. Six years later the Free Soil Party joined a broader coalition against slavery's extension that called itself the Republican Party.

In 1850 the Missouri Compromise buckled under the weight of southern and northern grievances. Southerners had complained that runaway slaves who reached the North via the "Underground Railroad"—a network of abolitionists who hid slaves and provided them with transportation northward—were not being returned to their owners. At the same time, northerners were repulsed by slave auctions in Washington, DC, "within the shadow of the Capitol." But the compromise finally collapsed when California applied in 1849 for admission to the Union as a free state. If the South agreed to admit California, it would lose its ability to block legislation in the Senate. Ultimately the South did agree, but only in return for passage of the **Fugitive Slave Law** compelling northerners to honor southerners' property claims to slaves. Moreover, the new Compromise of 1850, introduced by aging Whig senator Henry Clay of Kentucky, allowed the residents of the territories to decide for themselves whether to apply for statehood as a slave or free state.

DRED SCOTT GALVANIZES THE NORTH. The South may have lost its Senate veto, but a few years later it would unexpectedly acquire a new one. In 1857 the Supreme Court delivered one of its most unfortunate decisions in *Dred Scott v. Sandford*.[8] With every justice writing a separate opinion, a 7–2 majority of the Court concurred that the federal government could not prevent slavery in the territories. The Herculean effort to legislate mutually acceptable policy over the previous half-century was undone in a single decision by the nine unelected justices. The mostly southern majority argued that the Constitution's Framers had never intended African Americans to be citizens. Consequently, African Americans enjoyed "no rights which a white man was bound to respect," and any federal law that interfered with the right of an individual to his property, including slaves, was unconstitutional. Sympathetic lower-court judges appeared ready to extend the logic of this argument and rule that state laws banning slavery also were unconstitutional. The specter of the whole nation being opened to slaveholding by judicial fiat galvanized the North. Campaigning vigorously on the slogan "Free Soil, Free Labor, Free Men," Republican candidate Abraham Lincoln won the 1860 presidential election. So too did so many fellow Republican congressional candidates that this young party took majority control of the House of Representatives and, in alliance with splinter parties, formed a narrow antislavery majority in the Senate. For the first time in American history, the president and a majority of both houses of Congress were aligned against slavery's extension.

Recognizing that the seemingly insurmountable transaction costs to effective majority action had finally and suddenly been swept away, the South did not wait to contest new antislavery policy in Congress. Once president-elect Lincoln announced that the national government would no longer tolerate "the minority [the South] over the majority," the southern states seceded, with South Carolina the first to proclaim its independence on December 20, 1860. By June 1861 ten more states had left the Union and established a new, confederation-style government. On April 12, 1861, the "Confederates" fired on Fort

THE EMANCIPATION PROCLAMATION

Emancipation of the slaves was born of war rather than politics, but its planning and implementation were nonetheless highly strategic. When read carefully, President Abraham Lincoln's Emancipation Proclamation, issued in the fall of 1862, appears to have been composed more with an eye to encouraging southern defections from the Confederacy than to emancipating slaves. Lincoln announced that slaves would be freed in those states that persisted with the rebellion. Slavery was to remain intact in the border states that had stayed in the Union, and even in those sections of the Confederacy that had fallen under Union control.

This policy exposed the president to the criticism that he had failed to free the slaves where he could and freed them where he could not. But by mapping emancipation this way, he prevented it from becoming politically divisive among the Union states (a few still allowed slave ownership), while simultaneously trying to drive a wedge into the Confederacy. Moreover, the rebel states might have to deal with slaves asserting their freedom. Not until the 1864 presidential campaign did Lincoln openly endorse the universal abolition of slavery.

In 1863 David Gilmour Blythe depicted a homespun Lincoln (his rail-splitter's maul is in the foreground) at work in his study writing the Emancipation Proclamation. Pushed to one side, unheeded, are the states' rights theories of John C. Calhoun and John Randolph. Instead, Lincoln rests his hand on the Holy Bible and heeds Andrew Jackson's call: "The Union Must & Shall Be Preserved."

Sumter, a federal garrison in Charleston harbor. The American Civil War had begun, a war that would claim more than six hundred thousand American soldiers dead and many thousands more maimed for life.

Thus the first half-century of racial politics in the United States closely followed Madison's prediction of tyranny in the states unconstrained by national majorities. In the South white majorities enlisted state authority to preserve slavery. They were aided and abetted by their agents in the Senate who, as Madison had warned, succeeded in frustrating national action. Only the decisive 1860 Republican electoral victory and the secession of the slave states from the Union gave the national majority sufficient control over government to enforce its preferences. Along the way, strategic politicians, including Wilmot and Lincoln, transformed a losing issue into a winning one by focusing narrowly on the territories and the interests of northern whites more concerned about their own welfare than the welfare of slaves. In the end, this appeal enabled these politicians to win control of the government and eventually eradicate slavery (see box "The Emancipation Proclamation").

Reconstruction: 1865–1877

In the five-year period from 1865 to 1870, slaves were formally emancipated (Thirteenth Amendment), granted citizenship (Fourteenth Amendment), and guaranteed the right to vote (Fifteenth Amendment). At the close of the Civil War, however, only a handful of Union states gave black citizens equal access to the ballot box. Some subjected African Americans to special criteria—such as proof of property ownership and literacy—that effectively disenfranchised most of them. Other northern states simply barred African Americans from voting.* For most states, then, freeing slaves and granting them full-fledged citizenship were two different things, and the latter was regarded as radical even by abolitionists. Militant abolitionist newspaper publisher William Lloyd Garrison concluded that, "according to the laws of development and progress," the franchise "is not practical."† So how did the Fifteenth Amendment manage to clear, with remarkable alacrity, the formidable hurdles of the amendment process?

The ability to count is invaluable to a politician. Shortly after the war ended in 1865, House Republican leader Thaddeus Stevens of Pennsylvania calculated the probable partisan makeup of Congress after the South returned to the Union. Taking into account that African Americans now counted as full rather than three-fifths citizens for apportioning congressional seats across the states, Stevens estimated that the South would gain thirteen seats over its prewar level. Moreover, with southern legislatures busily enacting laws, called **black codes**, that effectively prevented former slaves from voting (and thus from supporting the party of Lincoln), Stevens rightly suspected that all thirteen seats would be added to the Democratic column. Southerners, he noted, "with their kindred Copperheads [Democrats] of the North, would always elect the President [as well as] control Congress."[9] The outlook was bleak for the Republican Party. Even as Andrew Johnson of Tennessee, Lincoln's Democratic successor in the White House, planned for the South's rapid readmission to the Union, congressional Republicans were staring at possible defeat in the next national election. The Republican response was Reconstruction, whereby under the watchful eye of federal troops, the South would be transformed from a slave society into a free one in which African Americans would fully enjoy the privileges of citizenship. At least that was the plan.

---

* Of the eleven referendum votes held from 1865 through 1869 in eight northern states on constitutional changes to provide African Americans with the ballot, only those in Iowa and Minnesota in 1868 succeeded. The white voters of Illinois, Indiana, Pennsylvania, and New Jersey never voted on the issue, which may have indicated a higher intensity of racial prejudice in those states than in Connecticut, New York, and Ohio, where equal suffrage was defeated. LaWanda and John H. Cox, "Negro Suffrage and Republican Politics: The Problem of Motivation in Reconstruction Historiography," *Journal of Southern History* 33 (August 1967): 318–319.

† Another enemy of slavery who conceded that freedmen could not be transformed instantly into full citizens was Republican senator Charles Sumner of Massachusetts, who before the war had earned his abolitionist credentials the hard way by being severely caned by an enraged southern member of the House after a floor speech denouncing slavery.

THE FOURTEENTH AND FIFTEENTH AMENDMENTS. The Republicans' foray into political and social reconstruction began with the Fourteenth Amendment. It opens with a straightforward definition of citizenship that encompasses former slaves: "All persons born or naturalized in the United States, and subject to the jurisdiction thereof, are citizens of the United States and of the State wherein they reside." It then declares that no state shall "deprive any person of life, liberty, or property, without the due process of law; nor deny to any person within its jurisdiction the equal protection of the laws" (emphasis added). (Chapter 5 examines the full impact of the due process and equal protection clauses on the liberties of all Americans.)

Section 2 of the Fourteenth Amendment turns to the immediate business of Reconstruction. It reaffirms the constitutional prescription of apportioning seats in the House of Representatives according to a state's population, but then makes an exception: if a state fails to allow black males to vote in federal and state elections, the number of seats allocated to it will be reduced proportionately. A purely political calculation dictated the provision of additional seats only where the Republican Party stood a fighting chance of winning. The amendment was intended to protect two constituencies: African Americans in the South and the Republican majority in Washington, DC. After the war, as before, civil rights rode on the shoulders of partisan, self-interested politics.

But how did this skillfully crafted amendment gain the necessary support when new legislatures in the South were rejecting it by nearly unanimous majorities? The Republicans in Congress, enjoying veto-proof majorities and a recent landslide victory in the 1866 midterm elections, devised an ingenious plan to foil southern opposition. The First Reconstruction Act of 1867 disbanded the governments of the southern states (with the exception of Tennessee, which already had been readmitted to the Union), thereby voiding their votes against the amendment. It then replaced the state governments with five military districts, headed by generals and administered by more than twenty thousand northern troops. To ensure ratification once the state governments were reinstituted, the law bluntly extended the vote to all freedmen and withheld it from the white, rebel ex-soldiers. In Louisiana, where the racial composition of the adult male population was roughly evenly split, black voter registration soon doubled the registration of whites.* Then, putting one last nail in the Confederacy's coffin, Congress made readmission to the Union contingent on a state's ratification of the Fourteenth Amendment.

The narrow partisan purpose of Reconstruction is evident in what the Republican policy omitted. Abolitionists and black leaders pressed Congress for land reform and a degree of economic independence for slaves from their former masters. Instead, all that the freed slaves got from Congress was the ballot. Republican cabinet secretary Gideon Welles concluded cynically, "It is evident that intense partisanship rather than philanthropy is the root of the movement."[10]

Two years later congressional Republicans sought to make the black franchise inviolable by passing and sending to the states the Fifteenth Amendment. Quickly ratified, it simply states, "The right of citizens of the United States to vote shall not be denied or abridged by the United States or by any State on account of race, color, or previous condition of servitude."

---

*Similarly, in Alabama there were approximately twenty thousand more white than black men but forty thousand more black voters. C. Vann Woodward, *The Burden of Southern History* (Baton Rouge: Louisiana State University Press, 1968), 98–99.

Originally titled *The Clansman*, *The Birth of a Nation* is recognized as both one of the most important films in the development of American cinema and one of the most racist. D. W. Griffith's 1915 film was the first to use natural settings, night photography, original music, panning shots, moving cameras, and dozens of other innovations. It remains shocking today in part because it looks like a documentary. The blatant racism that depicted freed slaves as villains and the Ku Klux Klan as the salvation of humanity reveals the state of the nation's attitude toward African Americans at the time. It became a blockbuster hit, but not without severe criticism. President Woodrow Wilson described it as "like writing history with lightning. And my only regret is that it is all terribly true." Stung by the criticism, Griffith followed it with *Intolerance*, on the effects of bigotry and inhumanity. Though less famous, many critics consider it his greatest achievement.

RIGHTS LOST: THE FAILURE OF RECONSTRUCTION. Despite these efforts, Reconstruction's advancement of black civil rights proved temporary. Relying heavily on black support, Republicans dominated southern state legislatures for a few years, but white Democrats seized control of Tennessee and Virginia as early as 1869, and by 1877 all of the former Confederate states had reverted to white Democratic control. Once this happened, Reconstruction was doomed, and African Americans saw their newly acquired status as freed men and women slide back to near servitude.

Power slipped away from African Americans during these years for several reasons. Vigilante violence as a political resource erupted in the late 1860s. Murderous white rioters in New Orleans, Memphis, and other southern cities targeted politically active African

Americans and their white allies. In the countryside, the Ku Klux Klan, a secret society of white supremacist men, perfected intimidation through selective brutality.

Meanwhile, northern politicians' commitment to Reconstruction was waning. After many Republicans went down to defeat in the 1874 midterm congressional elections, apparently because of an economic recession, the new Democratic majority in the House of Representatives refused to appropriate funds to support the military forces that remained in the South. Northern constituents wanted their sons returned home. Congress passed additional laws to protect the freed slaves, but without serious enforcement provisions, they offered African Americans in the distant South little real support. With the rise of the Ku Klux Klan, accompanied by the rapid demobilization of the occupying Union Army, the trajectory of southern politics became clear.

Killed by the same short-term partisan considerations that gave birth to it, Reconstruction officially ended with the 1876 presidential election. The Democratic candidate, Samuel Tilden, came within one vote of an Electoral College majority, but in the disputed states of Florida and Louisiana both parties produced their own favorable vote counts. As a result, the election was thrown into the House of Representatives, where a Republican pledge to end Reconstruction induced southerners to break ranks and support the Republican candidate, Rutherford B. Hayes. In 1877 federal troops pulled out of the South, leaving African Americans at the mercy of their former masters.[11]

During the early post–Civil War years, therefore, the Constitution presented fewer barriers to majority rule than in any other period in American history. The Republican majority in Congress and the White House opted for a middle course of political reform. Rather than undertaking a massive social and economic reconstruction of the South, they limited Reconstruction to making the South Republican, thereby realizing the party's goal of remaining the nation's majority party and satisfying the interests of their constituents. Even so, local interests in northern congressional districts soon rose against this limited reconstruction. Twenty thousand war-weary northern soldiers remained in the South, and the government continued to assess high wartime taxes nationwide to achieve in the South what few white citizens anywhere would have tolerated in their own communities—the creation of a sizable black electorate. In the North voters no longer wanted to sacrifice to solve distant problems, and the Republican majority soon lost the will to act. Full citizenship for African Americans would wait one hundred years for the emergence of northern politicians whose constituencies favored intervention in race relations in the South.

The Jim Crow Era and Segregation: 1877–1933

In the 1890s **Jim Crow laws** (named after a popular minstrel show character of the era) were adopted throughout the South to disenfranchise black citizens and physically separate African Americans and whites. These laws institutionalized **segregation** of African Americans and whites in their access to schools, hospitals, prisons, public parks, restrooms, housing, and public conveyances. Indeed, hardly any government service or social interaction between the races was unaffected.

But to secure segregation the southern states had to prevent black citizens from voting, and so they did. By the end of the century all southern states constructed a maze of electoral laws that systematically excluded African Americans from civic life. One common device, the **white primary**, excluded African Americans from voting in primary elections. Because winning the Democratic primary in the solidly Democratic South was tantamount to winning the general election, this law effectively disenfranchised southern black voters. Another effective barrier was the **poll tax** levied on all registered voters, which typically had to be paid months before the election.

Perhaps the most notorious and effective legal barrier was the **literacy test**. Local white registrars would require prospective black voters to read and interpret arcane passages of the state's constitution. Few could satisfy the registrars' rigorous demands, and by 1910 less than 10 percent of black males were voting in the South. These restrictive laws also caught many poor and illiterate whites. Most states, however, provided **grandfather clauses**, which exempted from these registration requirements those whose grandfathers had voted before the Civil War.

Without the backing of the Supreme Court, the southern state legislatures would have found it harder to strip away black civil rights. The Court generally upheld segregation and disenfranchisement laws against challenges. Conversely, when federal laws extending rights to African Americans were challenged, the Court summarily overturned them. The Court based these decisions on a tortuously narrow reading of the Fourteenth and Fifteenth Amendments. Consider this passage from the Fourteenth Amendment: "No State shall make or enforce any law which shall abridge the privileges or immunities of citizens of the United States." The Supreme Court interpreted this clause to mean only that states could not abridge privileges conferred explicitly by the Constitution to the national government, such as unrestricted interstate travel and open navigation of rivers. The justices excluded state laws from the Bill of Rights' guarantees. Decades later, the Supreme Court would reject this interpretation of the Fourteenth Amendment and rediscover the broad national guarantees this clause provides.[*]

The *coup de grâce* came in 1896 when the Supreme Court, ruling in *Plessy v. Ferguson,* declared the South's Jim Crow laws and systematic segregation constitutional.[12] The case arose when shoemaker Homer Plessy, who was seven-eighths white (but still black, according to law), appealed his conviction for having violated Louisiana's segregation law by sitting in a "whites only" railroad car. The Court argued that the Fourteenth Amendment's guarantee of equal protection of the law referred only to "political" equality. If African Americans were socially inferior to whites, the Court reasoned, laws such as Louisiana's could reflect that inferiority so long as political equality was not compromised. The Court then ruled that government-enforced segregation of the races was constitutional as long as the facilities for African Americans and whites were equal. And apparently they were, the Court reasoned; after all, whites were prohibited from sitting in the black passenger car. With that ruling, the Court established nationally the **separate but equal doctrine**, which officially sanctioned segregation throughout the South for the next half-century. Dissenting justice John Marshall Harlan vigorously attacked the majority's reasoning in language that would provide a foundation for overturning the "separate but equal" doctrine a half-century later. Appearances of equality were a sham, he argued. "Every one knows that the statute in question had its origin

---

[*] Similarly, interpreting the Fifteenth Amendment, the Supreme Court held that state laws denying voting rights to African Americans were permissible unless they could be shown to be motivated by race. By applying the poll tax or literacy test to everyone, or even claiming to, the southern legislatures could satisfy the Court.

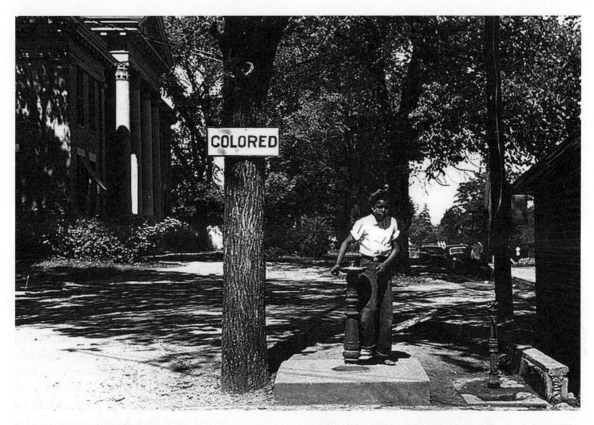

Until federal laws in the 1960s banned segregation in public accommodations, the doctrine "separate but equal" pervaded every aspect of social contact between the races throughout the South. The policy differed little from South Africa's dismantled apartheid system.

in the purpose, not so much to exclude white persons from railroad cars occupied by blacks, as to exclude colored people from coaches occupied by or assigned to white persons."*

Democratic Party Sponsorship of Civil Rights: 1933–1940s

From 1929 until 1933 the Republican Party presided over the worst depression in American history. Among the many victims of the economic hard times was the party itself. The Great Depression ended Republican dominance in national politics for the next fifty years. Ironically, while the rest of the nation was abandoning the Republican incumbent, Herbert Hoover, in favor of Democrat Franklin Roosevelt, most black voters were sticking with their party's ticket in the presidential election of 1932, despite being hit harder by the

---

*Why did a mostly Republican-appointed Supreme Court interpret the Fourteenth and Fifteenth Amendments in ways that negated Reconstruction? C. Vann Woodward reasonably conjectures that as Republican politicians reoriented their party toward rapidly emerging business constituencies, black civil rights became a low priority. See Woodward, *Reunion and Reaction: The Compromise of 1877 and the End of Reconstruction* (Boston: Little, Brown, 1966), 22–50.

Great Depression than any other group of Americans. (By 1936, however, three-quarters of African Americans supported Roosevelt's reelection.) Today, the appeal of mostly liberal Democratic politicians to black voters appears quite natural, requiring no special explanation. This partnership took nearly three decades to establish.

Both future partners first had to break enduring ties that pulled in opposing directions. The loyalty of black voters to the Republican Party grew out of emancipation and Reconstruction, and Democratic politicians had done nothing in the intervening years to prompt African Americans to question their partisanship. But their loyalty was rooted more in habit than reward and thus was susceptible to a Democratic appeal. For Democratic politicians, taking up the cause of African Americans was fraught with risk. Ever since its return to the Union, the South had provided the Democratic Party with the electoral base it needed to compete nationally. Northern Democratic members of Congress had long depended on the automatic victories of their southern colleagues to win majority control of Congress. Democratic presidential candidates could count on the South's large bloc of electoral votes; all they had to do was ignore segregation, just as their counterparts before the war had disregarded slavery.

THE NEW DEAL. Neither Franklin Roosevelt's winning electoral campaign in 1932 nor his "New Deal" to pull the nation out of the Depression overtly championed the cause of African Americans. Both did, however, alter political circumstances in a way that prompted black Americans and Democratic politicians to contemplate their mutual interests. When pressed, Roosevelt refused to battle southern Democratic senators for passage of popular antilynching legislation, privately citing his need for friendly relations with southern Democrats to enact his emergency economic policies.* Yet the New Deal's evenhanded treatment of the black community appealed to black voters. Many of its programs offered African Americans government assistance for the first time since Reconstruction. (Other programs, however, such as Social Security, excluded many low-income occupations that were disproportionately black.) Federal authorities investigated racial discrimination in relief aid distribution, especially prevalent in the South, and largely rooted it out. Roosevelt also appointed more than one hundred black administrators, some to prominent posts. Finally, the Justice Department rejuvenated its long-dormant civil liberties division.

Following the White House initiative, congressional Democrats added nondiscrimination language to a score of public laws creating federal programs. In 1941 Roosevelt issued an executive order banning employment discrimination in federal agencies, and he established the Committee on Fair Employment Practices to enforce nondiscrimination in defense-related industries. These measures, requiring that African Americans be treated as ordinary citizens, represented a major breakthrough for America's civil rights policy.

AFRICAN AMERICANS AND THE NEW DEAL COALITION. During the Roosevelt years, Democratic politicians continued to woo black voters, but from a sufficient distance to allow the Democratic Party to maintain its southern alliance. Nonetheless, hindsight

---

* While President Roosevelt had been reluctant to back federal antilynching and anti–poll tax legislation, many congressional Democrats introduced and championed hundreds of bills targeted at these and other civil rights issues. (The legislation repeatedly passed in the House of Representatives but, just as in the antebellum era, failed in the Senate, where the South held a greater share of the membership.)

reveals that subtle changes were under way in the political landscape, leading up to political realignment and the Democratic Party's embrace of black voters. In Washington twenty years of nearly uninterrupted Democratic control of both the presidency and Congress replenished the Supreme Court and lower federal judiciary with judges more sympathetic to civil rights claims. This laid the groundwork for an era of active judicial intervention against state laws enforcing segregation, particularly in public education.

More importantly, African Americans gradually shifted their party loyalties from the "party of Lincoln" to the "party of Roosevelt." The political transformation could not have been timed more propitiously for the Democratic Party, for hundreds of thousands of these potential new Democrats were migrating from the South, where they could not vote, to northern and midwestern cities, where solicitous Democratic political organizations eagerly registered and ushered them to the polls. The resulting demographic transformation of America's cities, recorded in Table 4-1, reflects the cumulative effects of several distinct forces.* For a century black sharecroppers and tenant farmers had been one of the least mobile population groups in the nation. But World War II (1939–1945) sent many young black males from the segregated Deep South into the armed services, where they were stationed in less racist, or at least less intimidating, communities. Other southern African Americans were lured north by relatively high-paying jobs in wartime industry. Still others followed after the war as farm mechanization rendered labor-intensive farming obsolete. Migration transformed these black citizens from political nonentities into pivotal voters.

TABLE 4-1

The Road to Political Power: African Americans Migrate North

	1930	1940	1950	1960	1970
All 12 SMSAs	7.6	9.0	13.7	21.4	30.8
New York	4.9	6.9	9.8	14.7	23.4
Los Angeles–Long Beach	5.0	6.0	9.8	15.3	21.2
Chicago	7.1	8.3	14.1	23.6	34.4
Philadelphia	11.4	13.1	18.3	26.7	34.4
Detroit	7.8	9.3	16.4	29.2	44.0
San Francisco–Oakland	4.9	4.9	11.8	21.1	32.7
Boston	2.9	3.3	12.3	9.8	18.2
Pittsburgh	8.3	9.3	18.0	16.8	27.0
St. Louis	11.5	13.4	5.3	28.8	41.3
Washington, DC	27.3	28.5	35.4	54.8	72.3
Cleveland	8.1	9.7	16.3	28.9	39.0
Baltimore	17.7	19.4	23.8	35.0	47.0

Source: Adapted from Leo F. Schnore, Carolyn D. Andre, and Harry Sharp, "Black Suburbanization, 1930–1970," *The Changing Face of the Suburbs,* ed. Barry Schwartz (Chicago: University of Chicago Press, 1976), 80. The figures were transposed to yield data on black percentages.

Note: Table shows the percentage of African Americans in central cities of the twelve largest Standard Metropolitan Statistical Areas (SMSAs).

Politicians seeking to win elections needed to adapt their appeals to their new constituents. Democratic state party conventions outside the South quickly adopted the civil rights cause on a variety of policy fronts. Invariably, many of these stances were unpopular with white voters, and not all state conventions wrote such planks into their platforms. Yet as early as the 1940s (see Figure 4-1) numerous state Democratic conventions ardently advocated civil rights.

---

*In Detroit, for example, the black population doubled from 8 percent in 1930 to 16 percent in 1950, and increased to 44 percent by 1970. Although Detroit had the most dramatic growth in black population, every major urban center throughout the nation experienced a similar trend. Edward G. Carmines and James A. Stimson, *Issue Evolution: Race and the Transformation of American Politics* (Princeton, NJ: Princeton University Press, 1989), Table 4-1.

Figure 4-1 Attention to Civil Rights in Nonsouthern State Party Platforms, 1920–1965

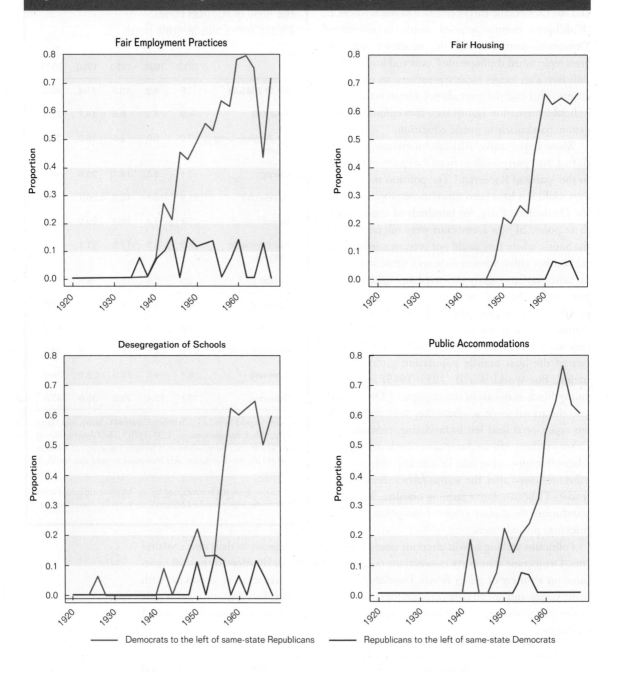

Source: Adapted from Figure 5 of Brian D. Feinstein and Eric Schickler, "Platforms and Partners: The Civil Rights Realignment Reconsidered," *Studies in American Development* 22, no. 1 (March 2008): 12.

Not until the growing Democratic commitment to civil rights received national expression from Congress and the presidency, where the electoral and governing coalition between northern and southern Democrats had prevented real advances in civil rights, would the fortunes of African Americans improve. The first crack in this coalition came in 1948, when Democratic president Harry Truman openly courted the black vote for reelection, even at the risk of alienating the South. A faltering, strike-plagued economy appeared to doom the unpopular president to electoral defeat. Desperately searching for a winning campaign plan, Truman's advisers proposed a novel strategy for the Democratic Party: "Unless there are real and new efforts . . . to help the Negro," stated one strategy memo, "the Negro bloc, which, certainly in Illinois and probably in New York and Ohio, *does* hold the balance of power, will go Republican." This strategy prompted President Truman in the 1948 election year to issue an executive order integrating the armed services and introduce legislation making Roosevelt's Committee on Fair Employment Practices a permanent agency. Truman's most important action was sponsoring a comprehensive civil rights bill, the first since the end of Reconstruction, that finally made racial lynching a federal crime, provided federal guarantees for voting rights, and prohibited employment and housing discrimination.*

At the Democratic Party's national convention in the summer of 1948, liberal northern Democrats pressed fellow delegates to adopt a strong civil rights platform. Southern delegates were outraged and bolted from the meeting. In the fall these "Dixiecrats," as they were called, ran their own candidate, Strom Thurmond, under the States' Rights Party banner and pulled several southern states' electoral votes away from the Democratic ticket (see Map 4-2). The defection reminded national Democrats that the South could be taken for granted only so long as the party left segregation alone. Despite losing this traditional stronghold, Truman won reelection.

The Truman administration's unsuccessful 1948 attempts to enact a civil rights law, like the defeat of the Wilmot Proviso a century earlier, presaged a later victory by identifying a political rationale for northern politicians to attack southern tyranny. With the New Deal, the Democratic Party attracted activist liberals and union leaders who were ideologically committed to civil rights. Like Republican abolitionists one hundred years earlier, their efforts made these activists important to their party, more than their numbers alone would attest.[13] But not until Democratic presidential candidates realized that the black vote might offset the potential southern losses did the party's politicians have a collective stake in advancing civil rights. Similarly, not until northern congressional Democrats discovered that speaking out against southern segregation won them the votes of the recent southern black migrants did a congressional majority committed to breaking up segregation coalesce.

Emergence of a Civil Rights Coalition: 1940s–1950s

The 1950s saw only modest advances in civil rights, but a new coalition—requiring renewed support for civil rights from the Republican Party and profound shifts within the Democratic Party, whose leaders historically had been hostile to the cause of African

---

*The legislation, predictably, died in the Senate, where southern members prevented it from coming to a vote.

Map 4-2   Truman Wins Presidency in 1948 Despite Dixiecrat Defection

		Electoral Vote		Popular Vote	
■	Truman (Democrat)	303	57.0%	24,179,345	50%
■	Dewey (Republican)	189	35.5%	21,991,291	45%
■	Thurmond (States' Rights Democrat)	39	7.5%	1,176,125	2%
	Wallace (Progressive)	0	0.0%	1,157,326	2%

Source: Presidential Elections, 1789–1996 (Washington, DC: CQ Press, 1997), 63, 115.

Notes: Numbers in parentheses are electoral votes. One electoral vote from Tennessee went to the States' Rights Democrat.

Americans—set the stage for success. Two landmark events of the 1950s stand out: the historic *Brown v. Board of Education of Topeka* decision and the Civil Rights Act of 1957.[14] Although important, both events proved more influential in identifying the issues and cleavages for the next decade than in yielding real gains in civil rights.

THE NAACP'S LITIGATION STRATEGY. In 1909 the National Association for the Advancement of Colored People (NAACP) began to represent black defendants throughout the South and to use the federal judiciary to challenge the legal structure of segregation. Although southern opposition in the Senate blocked legislative solutions, a decade of Roosevelt judicial appointments had recast the Supreme Court and many federal district and appeals courts with judges more sympathetic to the southern blacks' cause. One of its most important landmark victories during these early years came in 1944, when the NAACP persuaded the Supreme Court in Smith v. Allwright to throw out white primary laws.[15] The Court ruled that because race was the explicit criterion for discrimination, such laws violated the Fifteenth Amendment.

Nowhere in the South, however, was the electoral potential of the black vote close to being realized. Long-standing Supreme Court doctrine requiring that plaintiffs prove a law's discriminatory *intent* rather than simply demonstrate a bias in its *effect* frustrated the NAACP's efforts to dismantle other racial barriers. For example, in trying to eradicate the poll tax, which also disenfranchised poor whites, the NAACP could not satisfy the Court's tough requirements.

In the 1940s the NAACP launched a second line of attack against Jim Crow laws, this time targeting segregated public education. Since *Plessy v. Ferguson* in 1896, the federal judiciary had upheld segregation in the South, but the "separate but equal" doctrine proved to be an easy target. The soft underbelly of segregation was the word *equal*. Nowhere in the South did the separate facilities for African Americans equal those for whites.

The NAACP targeted the most blatant disparities. Since many states did not provide black graduate and professional schools and black residents were shut out of both public and private white facilities, the NAACP had a relatively easy time convincing the Court of the inequality of separating the races in education. In *Sweatt v. Painter* (1950) the Court unanimously agreed that the University of Texas could not stave off desegregation at its law school by instantly creating a black-only facility.[16] Then the NAACP successfully attacked segregated schools where separate facilities existed but were patently unequal in the education offered students. Less conspicuous forms of inequality were taken on next. In a 1950 decision the Court accepted the argument that intangible factors such as faculty reputation and alumni prestige contributed to educational inequality.

BROWN TRUMPS PLESSY. Having established that "separate but equal" could be unconstitutional, the NAACP directly attacked Plessy. The opportunity came in 1950 when Oliver Brown, an assistant pastor from Topeka, Kansas, violated local segregation laws when he tried to enroll his daughter, Linda, in a white neighborhood public school. Representing the NAACP, future Supreme Court justice Thurgood Marshall took up Brown's case, which four years later brought the pivotal Supreme Court ruling in *Brown v. Board of Education of Topeka*. Writing for a unanimous Court, Chief Justice Earl Warren argued that education is the foundation of good citizenship and thus constitutes "a right which must be made available to all on equal terms." Stipulating that racial segregation "generates a feeling of inferiority as to [black children's] status in the community that may affect their hearts and minds in a way unlikely ever to be undone," Warren concluded, "separate educational facilities are inherently unequal." With this 1954 ruling, Plessy, the principal legal prop of Jim Crow, crumbled.

The *Brown* decision, argued as a class-action suit on behalf of all citizens similarly denied access to white public schools, had broad legal ramifications. The next year the Court empowered lower federal courts to hear segregation cases and oversee the desegregation of public schools with "all deliberate speed."[17] Hundreds of school desegregation cases were filed in the federal courts in the decade after *Brown*.

At least symbolically, Labor Day 1957 was a watershed event in school integration. Elizabeth Eckford, textbooks in arm, and eight other black students were escorted through a hostile crowd into Little Rock's Central High School. The jeering student behind Eckford, Hazel Bryan, would later rue this moment when she became "the poster child for the hate generation, trapped in the image captured in the photograph." Later Bryan contacted Eckford to apologize, and subsequently they jointly participated in local racial tolerance workshops. The second photo was taken at the same site and by the same photographer on the fortieth anniversary of this historic moment.

Yet even this flurry of litigation did not end segregation. Efforts to implement *Brown* encountered all of the problems associated with enforcing judicial rulings. The decision was met by massive resistance across the South. Acting as if the nation were still governed by the Articles of Confederation, some state legislatures boldly asserted that public education lay beyond the national government's jurisdiction and that they would ignore the Court's "illegal" decision. When this bluff failed, state politicians devised more imaginative blocking tactics. In Virginia public schools were closed and "private" ones, created with state financing, opened in the vain hope that the new schools would be exempt from the *Brown* ruling. When these and other legal tricks were exhausted, state officials simply defied black parents and federal marshals sent to implement a desegregation ruling. The Supreme Court itself intervened in 1957, ordering the city of Little Rock, Arkansas, to enroll black students in all-white Central High School. When Arkansas governor Orval Faubus and school officials failed to comply, President Dwight Eisenhower sent in U.S. Army troops to escort black students to their new school.

The last bulwark of segregation's defense was tokenism—perhaps the most successful dilatory tactic of all. A school district would admit a handful of black students and then rush to federal court claiming compliance. The result would be another round of litigation during which further desegregation would be suspended. Civil rights lawyers may have won many cases during this era, but their clients had little success in gaining access to "whites-only" schools. In 1962, eight years after *Brown,* less than one-half of 1 percent of black students in the South were actually attending desegregated schools.

THE 1957 CIVIL RIGHTS ACT: REHEARSAL FOR THE 1960S. The year 1957 was ripe with political opportunity for the Democrats. With Republican two-term president Dwight Eisenhower ineligible for reelection in 1960, the Senate was full of ambitious Democrats grooming themselves for a presidential bid. John Kennedy of Massachusetts, Stuart Symington of Missouri, and Hubert Humphrey of Minnesota would later declare their candidacies and campaign actively in the 1960 presidential primaries. Other, less daring Senate colleagues could barely contain their aspirations for the top spot. Among them was Democratic majority leader Lyndon Johnson from Texas.

Daring or not, all would-be Democratic candidates had to appeal to a national constituency that now included substantial numbers of black voters in the large, vote-rich industrial states. For Johnson, a southerner, this requirement posed a serious problem. How could this Texan establish his credentials with African Americans and therefore be taken seriously by the northern Democratic Party leaders who controlled the nomination?

Johnson's vehicle into the national arena was the 1957 Civil Rights Act, which he introduced. This modest law allowed African Americans who felt their right to vote had been denied because of race to sue their state in federal court. But the prospect of expensive litigation and the provision that defendants—say, a local voter registrar—would be entitled to jury trials proved such formidable barriers that the NAACP and similar civil rights organizations filed suits designed only to establish widespread voting discrimination. To no one's surprise, few, if indeed any, black citizens gained the vote by virtue of this limited law.

The significance of Johnson's strategic sponsorship of the 1957 Civil Rights Act, then, lay more in what it represented politically than in any real gains it produced for African Americans. Southern senators, who wanted to boost Johnson's presidential bid over those of northern liberals Humphrey and Kennedy, strategically refrained from vigorous opposition and, in a few cases, abstained in the final floor vote. This message was reinforced by the passage of another, slightly less anemic, voting rights bill in the spring of 1960, only weeks before many of these senators headed for the Democratic presidential nominating convention. Although Johnson lost the Democratic presidential nomination to Kennedy, he won the consolation prize—the vice presidential nomination. And ever mindful of the black vote, Johnson and his colleagues oversaw enactment of yet another minority voting rights law during the summer before the 1960 presidential election.

With passage of the Civil Rights Act of 1957, the first civil rights law since Reconstruction, Democratic congressional leaders committed themselves to passing civil rights legislation. This and other early civil rights laws represented a transition, not so much for African Americans seeking full citizenship as for the Democratic Party.

Kennedy's narrow victory in 1960 reminded Democrats once again that winning the presidency without the South was virtually impossible. Even majority control of Congress would be jeopardized if more southern politicians decided—as a few in fact had—to disassociate themselves from northern Democrats and change parties. But even if the party accepted these risks and championed civil rights, it still lacked sufficient votes to enact the kinds of policies necessary to dismantle segregation. To jettison the party's southern wing by embracing civil rights and then fail to deliver on its commitment to the cause would constitute political suicide.

Yet during the 1960s Democratic presidents Kennedy and Johnson and their congressional colleagues broke with the South and committed the nation to an activist civil rights policy before it was politically expedient to do so. Why? Because doing nothing suddenly became the riskier strategy. A civil rights movement based on demonstrations and protest was generating a groundswell of support throughout the nation that the Democratic Party, which controlled Congress and the presidency, could not ignore. Failure to deal with this issue would have jeopardized the political relations of many Democratic politicians with their core supporters. Then, in the 1964 election, an event rarer than Halley's Comet occurred: the emergence of a *dominant* governing coalition in Washington. Not only did Democrats retain the presidency, but they also greatly enlarged their majorities in both chambers of Congress. Like a comet, this coalition did not last long, but while present it burned brightly. The result was half a decade of legislation followed by vigorous enforcement of laws dismantling segregation and voting discrimination. Finally, the national government had decided to finish the project of Reconstruction and assume responsibility for every citizen's civil rights.

The Civil Rights Movement: 1960s

Before the early 1960s, the civil rights movement, led by the NAACP, followed a strategy designed to influence judges more than politicians. This strategy had garnered some impressive court victories, but judicial successes had not translated into real gains in civil rights. Entering the 1960s, the civil rights movement took a new course—public protests directed against segregation and the authorities who administered it. Ultimately, the protests sought to influence public opinion and, in turn, Congress and the president.

This new course began in December 1955, when a black seamstress, Rosa Parks, boarded a city bus in Montgomery, Alabama. When Parks refused to surrender her seat to a white patron and move to the back of the vehicle, as the law required, she launched the historic Montgomery bus boycott, which became the model for later boycotts. In 1960 the first "sit-in" was held when several black college students in Greensboro, North Carolina, occupied seats in a local restaurant reserved for whites and refused to move until they were served or arrested.

Shifting strategy from litigation to mass demonstrations introduced collective action problems that had to be solved for the civil rights movement to succeed. Who would lead the movement in this new direction? Could the NAACP, an organization of lawyers—many of them white, nonsouthern volunteers—be expected to engage in, much less organize, massive civil disobedience? Disenfranchised black southerners did not have politicians—professionals in the art of solving collective action problems—to inspire and organize efforts to bring down Jim Crow through confrontation.

Ironically, segregation itself supplied the leaders who would press for its dissolution. Segregation in the South separated the races in all aspects of social organization: schools, churches, entertainment, hospitals, and professions; even cemeteries were segregated. Two largely parallel social groups coexisted in every community. Some black professionals—such as public school teachers—worked under the supervision of white-controlled institutions and would suffer serious repercussions if they challenged segregation. Other black professionals, however, served an exclusively black clientele and were fairly well insulated from white retribution: shop owners, morticians, and especially preachers—the latter were already well versed in organizing congregations and enjoyed credibility among those they would ask to make sacrifices. With control of scarce resources—skill at organizing and the trust of their congregations—and largely exempt of the potentially severe white reprisals, it is not surprising that black southern preachers participated in planning and coordinating demonstrations. Hundreds of them mobilized their congregations and coordinated with colleagues from other communities to generate large, effective demonstrations. The most important of these leaders, Rev. Martin Luther King Jr., was a Methodist minister. His organization, which during the next decade spearheaded demonstrations throughout the South, was appropriately named the Southern Christian Leadership Conference (SCLC).

Rosa Parks, whose refusal to move to the back of a city bus in December 1955 touched off the historic Montgomery, Alabama, bus boycott, is fingerprinted by Montgomery deputy sheriff D. H. Lackey. Her courageous act and subsequent arrest triggered massive demonstrations in the city and a boycott of local public transportation and white businesses. These events led eventually to the dismantling of local segregation policies and stimulated other acts of civil disobedience elsewhere.

King's strategy of nonviolent demonstrations and other forms of resistance may have been inspired by the Indian leader Mahatma Gandhi (1869–1948), but his political pragmatism was a page out of James Madison's playbook. Ultimately, King reasoned, rights would be won not in the courts through cogent argument but in legislatures through direct engagement with opponents whose interests were at stake. "Needless fighting in lower courts," King argued, is "exactly what the white man wants the Negro to do. Then he can draw out the fight."[18] If African Americans were to realize their rights, he knew they would have to claim them.

The first serious hurdle for the protest strategy was finding leaders who could bear the heavy transaction costs and personal risks, and who possessed the communication and organizational skills to mobilize a population inexperienced in expressing its grievances. The second problem, just as formidable, concerned the movement's followers. Specifically, would ordinary African Americans agree to demonstrate in the streets, boycott public transportation and white businesses, and confront local registrars bent on denying them their right to

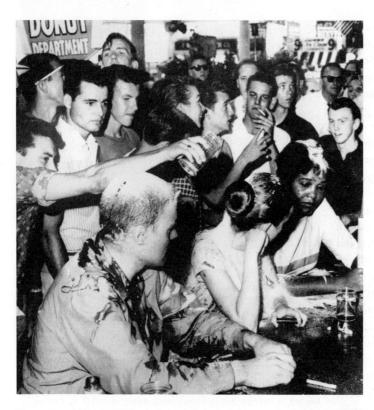

The scene is Jackson, Mississippi, where the local lunch crowd is drenching lunch counter demonstrators with mustard and ketchup. Such demonstrations occurred throughout the South in the 1960s. Most of the participants were local black and northern white college students.

vote? Many of these activities violated state and local segregation laws; participants would face a legal system administered by unsympathetic officials. More importantly, the vast majority of black southerners worked for white employers who would actively discourage participation. With these disincentives, many (perhaps too many) of those sympathetic with this new strategy might instead free ride.[19] A successful demonstration requires lots of people to voluntarily expose themselves to danger and other sanctions. Yet every individual knew that his or her participation would not make or break the demonstration. What would become of the civil rights movement if insufficient numbers answered the call to action?

History showed otherwise. Demonstrations began in earnest in 1960, and over the next six years almost 2,500 were held, with many receiving national news coverage.[20] In retrospect, the success of the movement is easy to understand. In addition to the nationally prominent clergy in SCLC headquarters, ministers with the professional and rhetorical skills to mobilize direct action ran most of the eighty-five local chapters throughout the South. Moreover, these local leaders enjoyed exceptional credibility with those whom they needed to motivate. When King and other SCLC leaders endorsed a boycott or some other action, the local chapters served as a focal point to coordinate a joint action. Without the organizational efforts of these local leaders, the movement would not have enjoyed such broadbased support.

The pivotal protest of spring 1963 in Birmingham, Alabama, forced the Democratic Party to commit to an aggressive civil rights policy and led directly to passage of the landmark Civil Rights Act of 1964.

THE BIRMINGHAM DEMONSTRATION. In early 1963 President Kennedy pleaded for patience from King and other leaders, arguing that Congress should enact his less controversial social programs before tackling segregation. Civil rights leaders suspected that Kennedy's real motivation was to keep the South in the Democratic column in the upcoming 1964 election. King and the other leaders had their own strategic reasons for impatience; demonstrations were turning violent, and events were only partially under their

Major Events in the Civil Rights Movement, 1955–1968

December 1955	African Americans in Montgomery, Alabama, begin boycott of city buses in protest of segregated seating.
September 1, 1957	Central High School in Little Rock, Arkansas, engulfed in turmoil as the governor calls out Arkansas National Guard to prevent enrollment of nine black students. President Dwight Eisenhower forced to send in federal troops to restore order.
February 1, 1960	Wave of "sit-ins" touched off across the South by four students in Greensboro, North Carolina, who are refused service at a segregated lunch counter.
May 4, 1961	"Freedom rides" begin as African Americans try to occupy "whites only" sections of interstate buses. U.S. marshals ultimately are called in to settle violent reaction to black efforts.
September 30, 1962	Federal troops are used to quell a fifteen-hour uprising by University of Mississippi students protesting the enrollment of a single black student, James Meredith. Two students are killed. (Televised live across the nation.)
April 1963	Demonstrations begin in Birmingham, Alabama. Local authorities use fire hoses and police dogs to disperse demonstrators.
August 28, 1963	March on Washington by more than two hundred thousand African Americans and whites. Rev. Martin Luther King Jr. delivers his "I Have a Dream" speech, and "We Shall Overcome" becomes the anthem of the civil rights movement.
September 1963	Demonstrations begin in St. Augustine, Florida, to protest the arrest and detention of seven students. African Americans boycott several northern schools in protest of de facto segregation. Four black children are killed in bombing of Birmingham, Alabama, church.
June 1964	Three civil rights workers, two white and one black, working to register black voters are killed in Mississippi. Murderers include sheriff's deputies.
July 1964	First in a wave of ghetto riots breaks out in New York City's Harlem.
January 1965	King organizes protest marches in Selma, Alabama. Marches end in violent attacks by police.
August 11, 1965	Ghetto riots erupt in Watts section of Los Angeles. Four thousand rioters are arrested; thirty-four are killed.
June 6, 1966	James Meredith suffers gunshot wound in march across Mississippi.
Summers 1966 and 1967	Riots and violent demonstrations occur in cities across the nation.
April 4, 1968	Martin Luther King Jr. assassinated in Memphis, Tennessee.

control. To keep the movement directed toward civil disobedience and peaceful protest, SCLC leaders needed to start producing results.

The selection of Birmingham as a protest venue reflected the broad strategic purpose of the demonstrations. Birmingham's segregation was no worse than in many other cities throughout the Deep South. But Birmingham had a notoriously intolerant local police chief, Eugene "Bull" Connor, known for rough treatment of civil rights demonstrators. He would provide a

Protesters parading down the streets of Birmingham, Alabama, in 1963 were bent on focusing national attention on their cause. The local police proved quite accommodating in demonstrating to the horror of television viewers throughout the nation the brutality with which segregation was enforced.

graphic display of the institutional violence that enforced segregation. As the nation watched on network television, Connor arrested and jailed two thousand marchers for not having a parade permit. The local law enforcement officers then resorted to police dogs and fire hoses to disperse peaceful demonstrators, including children barely old enough to go to school.

The Birmingham demonstrations succeeded when the city's business community agreed to negotiate with the protesters. But more important, the protesters created a national crisis that President Kennedy could not ignore. For years the monthly Gallup poll had asked its national sample of respondents to name the most important problem facing the country. Until the 1955 Montgomery bus boycott, civil rights never figured prominently in responses to this query. From April to July 1963, however, the percentage of respondents mentioning civil rights shot up from 10 to nearly 50 percent.

Suddenly, continued accommodation of southern Democrats imposed significant political costs on Kennedy. Failure to act might irreparably damage his reputation among black voters who might well provide a margin of victory in a reelection bid. These events, orchestrated by the civil rights movement, turned the president into a reluctant champion of its cause. Shortly after a televised address to the nation unveiling the new civil rights legislation, Kennedy invited movement leaders to the White House to plan a legislative strategy. The president explained to the group the bind he and the Democratic Party were in:

This is a very serious fight. The Vice-President [Lyndon Johnson] and I know what it will mean if we fail. I have just seen a new poll—national approval of the administration has fallen from 60 to 47 percent. We're in this up to the neck. The worst trouble of all would be to lose the fight in the Congress. We'll have enough trouble if we win; but, if we win, we can deal with those. A good many programs I care about may go down the drain as a result of this—we may go down the drain as a result of this—so we are putting a lot on the line.[21]

Democrats were about to commit to a strong civil rights program without having the means to succeed.[22]

THE DEMOCRATIC PARTY'S COMMITMENT TO CIVIL RIGHTS. On June 11, 1963, President Kennedy addressed the nation, proclaiming his full support for the aspirations of African Americans and announcing a major revision of the civil rights bill then before Congress. The courts would no longer determine violations; for the first time federal agencies could independently identify discrimination and impose remedies. Although this

For years Georgia senator Richard Russell (right) and other southerners had blocked civil rights legislation with the threat of a filibuster. New president Lyndon Johnson (left), however, was not deterred in his push for civil rights legislation. Here, two weeks after President John Kennedy's assassination, Johnson warns his Senate mentor to stand aside or be run down.

new proposal was far weaker than the sweeping civil rights reforms King and his colleagues had requested, they accepted it as a solid step in the right direction.

Five months later Kennedy was assassinated, and Vice President Johnson succeeded to the presidency. At the time, a strengthened version of the legislation, which had passed the House of Representatives on a bipartisan vote, was predictably stalled in the Senate. Southern senators did not have enough votes to defeat the legislation outright, but they were prepared to filibuster* it indefinitely.

Within a few days of assuming the presidency, Johnson addressed a joint session of Congress and a nationwide television audience to announce that a strong civil rights law would be the nation's memorial to the fallen president. This proclamation set the stage for a struggle in Washington. The outcome would make 1964 a year of historic successes for both civil rights and the Democratic Party.

THE 1964 CIVIL RIGHTS ACT. Once Johnson persuaded Senate Republicans to join northern Democrats in breaking the southern filibuster, the Senate promptly passed the

---

* The filibuster, allowing a minority of the Senate membership to delay floor consideration of legislation, is discussed more fully in Chapter 6.

THE 1964 CIVIL RIGHTS ACT AND INTEGRATION OF PUBLIC SCHOOLS

politics to policy

One of the most effective provisions of the 1964 Civil Rights Act authorized the Department of Health, Education, and Welfare to withhold federal grants from school districts that failed to integrate their schools. No longer could southern school boards hide behind token desegregation and endless visits to the federal courts. The effects were quick and dramatic: within a year more black children were admitted to formerly all-white schools than in the entire decade after the 1954 *Brown v. Board of Education of Topeka* decision. Within ten years over 90 percent of black children in the South were attending integrated schools.

Source: Gerald N. Rosenberg, *Hollow Hope: Can Courts Bring about Social Change?* (Chicago: University of Chicago Press, 1991), 50–51.

*Dashed line indicates missing data for 1967.

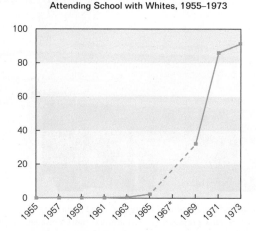

Percentage of All Southern Black Schoolchildren Attending School with Whites, 1955–1973

Civil Rights Act of 1964. This law, which was substantially stronger than the legislation President Kennedy introduced, authorized the national government to end segregation in public education and public accommodations (see box "The 1964 Civil Rights Act and Integration of Public Schools").

The Democratic administration's high-profile sponsorship of the civil rights law put forth civil rights as a decisive campaign issue in the 1964 presidential election. The Republican Party in Congress traditionally had been more supportive of civil rights than the Democrats, but in 1964 it began to veer sharply away from its long-standing support. At their national convention Republicans chose Barry Goldwater of Arizona as their presidential candidate, one of the few senators outside the South to oppose the 1964 civil rights bill. When the Democrats convened to nominate the incumbent president Johnson, they underlined the party differences on this issue by seating delegates who challenged segregationist Democrats and by selecting as Johnson's running mate Sen. Hubert Humphrey, a longtime vocal proponent of civil rights.

The outcome of the election was the largest presidential landslide in history. The Democrats also racked up huge majorities in the congressional elections. Goldwater won only five states in the Deep South and his home state of Arizona. With over 95 percent of black voters preferring Johnson, the Democratic and Republican Parties swapped constituencies in the South.[23] When the new Congress convened in 1965, northern Democrats dominated both chambers. Even some border states elected Democrats who were moderate supporters of civil rights and who were prepared to support national policies that would dismantle segregation. Finally, the sheer magnitude of the Democratic victory swamped the Constitution's separation-of-powers barrier to collective action. With the severe transaction costs of policymaking swept away, the Washington cognoscenti and ordinary voters alike sensed that the Johnson landslide would bring about an onslaught of civil rights legislation (see Map 4-3).

Map 4-3 The Key to Unlocking Black Voting Rights: Vigilant Administration of Civil Rights Laws

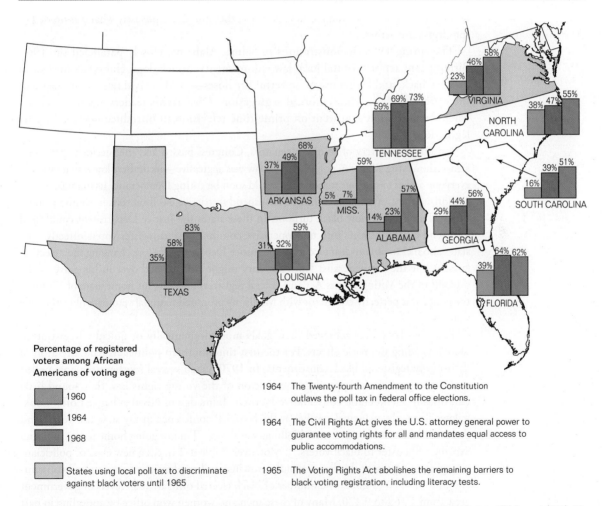

Percentage of registered voters among African Americans of voting age

- 1960
- 1964
- 1968

States using local poll tax to discriminate against black voters until 1965

1964 The Twenty-fourth Amendment to the Constitution outlaws the poll tax in federal office elections.

1964 The Civil Rights Act gives the U.S. attorney general power to guarantee voting rights for all and mandates equal access to public accommodations.

1965 The Voting Rights Act abolishes the remaining barriers to black voting registration, including literacy tests.

Source: Harold W. Stanley, *Voter Mobilization and the Politics of Race: The South and Universal Suffrage, 1952–1984* (Westport, CT: Praeger, 1987), 97. Copyright © 1987 by Harold W. Stanley. Reproduced with permission of ABC-CLIO, LLC.

THE VOTING RIGHTS ACT OF 1965. Every civil rights law enacted since 1957 addressed voting rights, but throughout much of the South black registration remained at low levels. Only 7 percent of eligible black citizens in Mississippi were registered in 1964; in Alabama the figure was 20 percent. Each of these civil rights laws had the same fatal flaw: they required individuals to prove discrimination in court. Black leaders thus pressed the White House to authorize federal agencies to guarantee the right to vote by taking over voter registration or directly supervising local officials, just as the 1964 Civil Rights Act authorized government action against segregation in education and public accommodations.

Responding to their pleas, President Johnson asked King and other leaders to "give the nation a chance to catch its breath" on civil rights. After all, African Americans would be well served, Johnson argued, by his Great Society programs in employment, education, and health care. But for movement leaders, Johnson's request asked too much. King and his colleagues knew that not since Reconstruction had such large, sympathetic majorities controlled both houses of Congress, yet from recent experience, they also knew precisely what was needed to spur legislative action.

The spring 1965 demonstrations in Selma, Alabama, closely paralleled the 1963 Birmingham actions. Brutal local law enforcement—attack dogs, club-wielding police on horseback, and liberal use of powerful fire hoses—yielded vivid television images of the official violence that enforced segregation. Civil rights leaders again succeeded when President Johnson went on prime-time television to introduce new civil rights legislation.

Ignoring the outcry of southern senators, Congress passed and the president promptly signed the Voting Rights Act of 1965. The law was aggressive—its drafters knew that virtually everyone added to the registration rolls would soon be voting Democratic. Its main provision authorized the Department of Justice to suspend restrictive electoral tests in southern states that had a history of low black turnout. In these states the Justice Department could (and did) send federal officers into uncooperative communities to register voters directly. The states also had to obtain clearance from the Justice Department before changing their election laws. While the Antifederalist Patrick Henry might have turned over in his grave at the thought of the Voting Rights Act and federal registrars entering his home state of Virginia, the policy was perfectly consistent with Madison's proposed national veto over objectionable state laws.

Few laws have ever achieved their goals more dramatically or quickly. Registration soared, yielding dramatic effects. For the first time southern politicians paid attention to their newly registered black constituents. In 1970, when several southern senators polled their colleagues about opposing an extension of the voting rights law, they found little enthusiasm. Democratic conservative Herman Talmadge of Georgia begged off: "Look, fellows, I was the principal speaker at the NAACP conference in my state last year." And South Carolina Democrat Ernest Hollings was direct: "I'm not going home to my state and explain a filibuster to black voters."[24] Moreover, Table 4-2 traces a new class of politicians emerging to represent this large, rapidly growing, and residentially concentrated constituency. From 1970 to 2002, the number of black elected officials at all levels of government grew from 1,469 to 9,470. Many of these men and women won office by appealing in part to white voters. In a real sense these many local officehold-ers paved the way for Barack Obama's success.

The 1965 Voting Rights Act was, then, a culminating achievement of the civil rights movement of the 1960s.

(For summaries of the 1965 law and other federal civil rights acts, see box "Key Provisions of Federal Civil Rights Legislation.") During the second half of the decade events began to change the way African Americans and whites looked at civil rights. In the summer of 1965 a two-week riot, in which thirty-four people were killed, exploded in the black neighborhood of Watts in Los Angeles. Over the next few summers similar riots would erupt in other cities. Late in 1965 the Vietnam War began to replace civil rights demonstrations on television news, and the vocal opposition of some civil rights leaders to the war sapped support in Washington. The next year Congress defeated a fair housing bill. (A somewhat weaker law was passed two years later, however.) Then, in 1968, King was assassinated in Memphis after leading a march supporting striking sanitation workers (see box "Major Events in the Civil Rights Movement, 1955–1968" on page 157). Riots erupted in cities throughout the nation. Shortly thereafter, "law and order" replaced civil rights as the mantra of political campaigns throughout the United States.

TABLE 4-2				
The Emergence of Black Politicians: A Result of the Surge in Black Voting				
Office	1970	1980	1990	2002
Members of Congress and state officials	179	365	465	671
City and county officials	715	2,807	4,481	5,749
Judges, sheriffs, and other law enforcement officers	213	528	769	1,081
Boards of education	362	1,214	1,655	1,969
Total	1,469	4,914	7,370	9,470

Source: Information supplied by the Joint Center for Political and Economic Studies, Washington, DC.

The Era of Remedial Action: The 1970s to the Present

The civil rights movement may have lost momentum, but the advances continued. Over the next thirty years, legislation (including the Fair Housing Act of 1968) shifted the responsibility for identifying and eradicating abuses from injured individuals and the courts to the federal bureaucracy. This redelegation of principal enforcement authority to the Department of Health, Education, and Welfare (HEW) made it much easier for federal agencies to administer civil rights policy. Rather than having to investigate and prove a specific discriminatory act that prevented African Americans from enjoying their rights, the government could focus instead on the "outcome" of local practices. The underrepresentation of African Americans on voter registration rolls and in apartment rentals, schools, employment, and the like was enough to establish a reasonable suspicion of discrimination, which the government could then remedy.

In the 1980s and 1990s civil rights enforcement moved beyond the South to include all government and private actions that yielded indicators of discrimination. A favorite target of federal investigators was schools. In fact, when these officials searched for evidence of discrimination in black versus white enrollment figures, they netted many schools outside the South where **de facto segregation** was in play. In these cases, the segregation was not mandated by law (**de jure segregation**), as it was in the South, but arose as a byproduct of former discriminatory housing laws that kept neighborhood schools segregated.* When the courts, the Department of Justice, and HEW decided jointly to force school districts to bus students to sometimes distant schools for the sake of integration, the measure produced waves of public protests. Indeed, busing proved to be one of the most contentious civil rights policies of the modern era, with public opinion surveys in the 1970s and 1980s showing it consistently to be one of the national policies most upsetting to Americans.

Note that the government found straightforward solutions for redressing discrimination in voting rights and schools: it enrolled black voters and redirected students to new schools. But what about past discrimination in employment? The government could not simply tell its own agencies or private businesses to hire an equal number of minorities. Instead, it resorted to **affirmative action**, a policy that requires any employers or government agencies that have practiced past discrimination to compensate minorities and women by giving them special consideration in their selection for employment and education. Affirmative action is most controversial when applied to government contracting, university admission rules to increase minority enrollments, and employment policies to promote minority presence and advancement in business and the professions. Early affirmative action efforts in the 1970s, rejected by both the federal courts and the American public, involved the use of **quotas**—that is, setting aside a certain share of admissions, government contracts, and jobs for those who suffered from past discrimination. In the most famous of these cases, *Regents of the University of California v. Bakke* (1978), the Supreme Court decided that, while creating a special admission pool for minority students might serve the laudable goals of attaining a diverse student body, the university medical school's approach violated the equal protection rights of white applicants.[25]

During the intervening decades the Supreme Court has decided numerous affirmative action cases without resolving the issue of preferential treatment beyond outlawing quotas. Virtually all of the tough cases that have reached the Court have been decided by a single vote, with the balance teetering in favor of or opposition to affirmative action according to the changing membership of the Court (see Chapter 9). Where in 1987 the Court ruled that sex could be considered along with other criteria in promotion decisions, and apparently could be done even without evidence of past discrimination, by 1995 it was prescribing "narrowly tailored" standards designed to achieve a "compelling government interest."[26]

In an effort to rectify the legacy of residential segregation for public education, during the 1970s the federal bureaucracy and courts adopted a policy of busing students to schools outside of their neighborhoods to achieve racial integration. For the next two decades school busing scored at or near the top of the list of policies most upsetting to the American public. As busing has declined in recent years as the judicially preferred remedy, so too has its status as a political issue.

The most recent decisions find the Court still grappling to identify acceptable avenues for favoring some applicants over others without using quotas. In 2003 it decided a pair of

---

* Until the Supreme Court ruled them illegal in 1968, *restrictive covenants* were commonly embedded in property deeds, preventing owners from selling the property to Jews and African Americans. *Jones v. Alfred H. Mayer Co.*, 392 U.S. 409 (1968).

Key Provisions of Federal Civil Rights Legislation

Civil Rights Act, 1957

Established U.S. Commission on Civil Rights to investigate the status of civil rights in the country. Made it a federal crime to attempt to prevent a person from voting.

Civil Rights Act, 1960

Increased sanctions against abridging or denying the right to vote. Permitted federal government to appoint "referees," under the jurisdiction of the courts, to register voters denied the right to vote by a pattern or practice of discrimination.

Civil Rights Act, 1964

Voting: By equating a sixth-grade education with literacy, the act made it more difficult to disenfranchise African Americans through literacy tests.

Public accommodations: Barred discrimination on basis of race, color, religion, or nationality in restaurants, service stations, theaters, transportation, and hotels with five rooms or more. Empowered attorney general to initiate suits.

Schools: Authorized attorney general to bring suit against segregated schools. Also permitted federal government to withhold funds from segregated schools.

Employment: Barred discrimination on the basis of race, color, religion, nationality, or sex in a range of employment practices. Established Equal Employment Opportunity Commission to enforce this provision.

Voting Rights Act, 1965

Permitted appointment, under Civil Service Commission, of voting examiners in place of local registrars

in all areas where less than 50 percent of those eligible to vote actually voted in the 1964 presidential election. Use of literacy tests and similar mechanisms suspended.

Age Discrimination in Employment Act, 1967

Prevented employment discrimination based on age for workers forty to sixty-five years old. Later amended to prevent mandatory retirement.

Fair Housing Act, 1968

Outlawed refusal to rent or sell housing on grounds of race or religion, but exempted citizens who rented or sold their homes without using a real estate agent.

Rehabilitation Act, 1973

Instituted affirmative action programs for employers to hire "qualified handicapped individuals" and barred discrimination solely on the basis of a disability.

Restoration of Civil Rights Act, 1988

Applied anti–sex discrimination standards to all institutions' programs if the institution received federal funding.

Civil Rights Act, 1991

Gave victims of intentional discrimination based on sex, religion, or disability the right to sue for monetary damages. (Victims of racial discrimination had had this right since a Reconstruction-era law.)

long-anticipated University of Michigan cases that had received apparently contradictory rulings at the appeals level. The Court's decisions reflected its own ambivalence over affirmative action; both were 5–4, and reached opposite results.[27] In the undergraduate case, the Court ruled that while diversity in higher education could be a "compelling interest," the university's assignment of one-fifth of the total points for admission on the basis of race was unconstitutional. The law school program, however, passed muster because race was merely

Abigail Fisher, a student denied admission to the University of Texas, took the school to court, charging that its policy of admitting any high school student ranking in the top 10 percent of his or her class precluded the need for an affirmative action policy.

one of the factors that the law school considered. But even that ruling provoked a vigorous dissent, and since then changes in membership have shifted the Court in a more conservative direction.[*]

Only nine years later, the Supreme Court in 2012 agreed to hear a case brought by a white student, Abigail Fisher, who was denied admission to the University of Texas. Fisher argued that because the University of Texas had a policy of admitting any high school student who ranked in the top 10 percent of his or her class, and because this policy resulted in the admission of substantial numbers of African American and Hispanic students, the university had already achieved its goal of "diversity." As a result, there was no need to consider race as a factor among the remaining group of discretionary admits (students who were admitted outside of the 10 percent plan). Some justices seemed sympathetic to this argument, and also frustrated with the university's inability to say whether, and when, a "critical mass" of minority students exists.[†]

The judiciary's collective ambivalence with affirmative action policy reflects national attitudes. Congress has been reluctant to take on the issue, its members perhaps recognizing the political problems it might face with the electorate were it to do so. Opinion surveys convey a public that mostly favors the principle of affirmative action while disapproving of almost every specific approach for achieving it. One national survey taken during the Court's deliberation of the Michigan cases found public opinion mostly running strongly against preferential treatment. When asked, "As you may know, the U.S. Supreme Court will be deciding whether public universities can use race as one of the factors in admissions to increase diversity in the student body. Do you favor or oppose this practice?" 65 percent registered opposition, and 26 percent registered support. Yet the same survey offered some endorsement of the Court's eventual decision. When asked if affirmative action were permissible to overcome past discrimination as long as it did not involve "rigid" quotas, 49 percent agreed compared to 43 percent who said the policy should be terminated.

READ MORE

logic.cqpress.com

See how the Court ruled in the *Fisher* case.

---

[*] Sandra Day O'Connor, the pivotal vote and author of the majority's opinion in the law school case, retired to be replaced by the distinctly more conservative justice Samuel Alito.

[†] See Amy Howe, "The *Fisher* Argument in Plain English," SCOTUSblog, October 10, 2012, www.scotusblog.com/2012/10/the-fisher-argument-in-plain-english/.

Beginning with passage of Proposition 209 by California voters in 1996, the political battle over affirmative action opened on a second front—the states. In a vote of 54–46 percent, Californians added language to the state's constitution banning the use of "race, sex, color, ethnicity or national origin as a criterion for either discriminating against, or granting preferential treatment to, any individual or group in the operation of the State's system of public employment, public education or public contracting." Unsurprisingly, those opposed to the proposition immediately went to court, but over the next five years most challenges were turned back, and 209's provisions changed the state's university admissions and hiring practices. In 1999 a similar referendum passed in Washington State, and in 2006 in the aftermath of the Supreme Court rulings, Michigan voters banned affirmative action and effectively undid the permissible affirmative action in the Court's decision. That same year the Florida legislature banned racial preference in university admissions. Among civil rights groups and their opponents, debate over the value and constitutionality of affirmative action continues today. Voters in five other states attempted to get similar measures on the ballot in November 2008, but in the end, enough signatures were gathered in only two states: Nebraska and Colorado. The measure passed in Nebraska but was narrowly defeated in Colorado.

THE LEGACY OF THE CIVIL RIGHTS MOVEMENT

Although race remained a prominent civil rights issue in the 1970s, the civil rights movement branched out to include women, the elderly, the disabled, homosexuals, and virtually every ethnic minority. The new directions of civil rights over the past several decades owe their progress, however, to African Americans' two-hundred-year struggle for civil rights. It paved the way politically for these new efforts, both in honing the techniques of demonstrations and protests and in creating a receptive audience in the news media and American public opinion. But most important, the black civil rights movement built a foundation of federal laws, judicial precedents, and administrative regulations that could be easily extended to other groups.

Equal Rights for Women: The Right to Vote

Long before abolitionists took up the cause of slavery, early feminists, later calling themselves **suffragists**, were campaigning for the vote. (Many early suffragists also were active in movements for prison reform, public education, temperance, and, above all, abolition of slavery.) These women viewed their cause as inextricably linked to full citizenship for African Americans in the "rising tide of prodemocratic sentiment."* Yet, despite their efforts, "sex" was excluded from the Fifteenth Amendment. Except for local school board

---

* During the colonial era, single property-owning women in New Jersey could vote. See Alexander Keyssar, *The Right to Vote* (New York: Basic Books, 2000); Judith Apter Klinghoffer and Lois Elkis, "The Petticoat Electors: Women's Suffrage in New Jersey, 1776–1807," *Journal of the Early Republic* 12 (1992): 159–193.

elections and liquor referenda in twenty states, women did not obtain the franchise until 1869, when the territory of Wyoming passed the first women's suffrage law.[28] In 1919, nearly a century after women organized and began promoting their cause, Congress sent the Nineteenth Amendment extending the right to vote to all women. The next year the amendment was ratified by the states.

Women, unlike African Americans, experienced little delay in implementing the right to vote. Although registration rates varied across states, women's rates approached three-quarters of men's within a decade after ratification. Over the next decade or so women were voting regularly at a rate only slightly below that of men.

From the late 1840s to the late 1860s, voting rights for African Americans and women tracked very different courses. Ironically, slaves had been liberated and handed the vote, while women, despite needing to traverse a much shorter distance, had progressed little toward gaining the franchise. (On two other issues—allowing inheritance and access to public education—the movement successfully revised many state laws.) Trying to account for the torpid pace of women's suffrage is risky. Even in an era before opinion polls regularly measured public sentiment, a comparison of the histories of blacks' and women's rights movements suggests political circumstances that extended voting rights for one group but not the other.

First, unlike the black vote, which contemporaries agreed would go directly to the Republicans, the women's vote appeared to confer little advantage to either party. Republicans found the black votes in the South particularly attractive since the former rebel states, poised to reenter the Union, would form a Democratic majority in Washington. Suffrage leaders Elizabeth Cady Stanton and Susan B. Anthony actively lobbied to include women in the Fourteenth Amendment and probably expected to succeed.[29] As Stanton famously declared, black suffrage opened the "constitutional door," and the suffragists intended to "avail [themselves] of the strong arm and the blue uniform of the black soldier to walk in by his side."* Their expectations were dashed when Republican leaders explicitly limited the amendment to male citizens. Claiming that including women would have endangered ratification, Republican politicians clearly viewed women's suffrage to be a costly issue.[†]

Without a compelling political advantage to be gained, few politicians—particularly the Republican majority in Congress framing the amendment—were prepared to absorb the heavy political costs of extending the vote to women. This is consistent with the history of suffrage. Enthusiasm for women's suffrage appears to have been concentrated among the urban, upper-middle class. Various other women's groups either opposed or ignored the

---

* See Ellen Carol Dubois, "Outgrowing the Compact of the Fathers: Equal Rights, Women's Suffrage, and the United States Constitution, 1820–1878," *The Journal of American History* 74, no. 3 (December 1987): 836–862, at 845.

† In one particularly heated exchange, Frederick Douglass—a former slave who had been present at the first national suffrage conference at Seneca Falls in 1848—argued that only when white women were "dragged from their houses and hung upon lamp-posts" would they have "an urgency to obtain the ballot equal to our own." Susan B. Anthony gave the withering response: "[I]f you will not give the whole loaf of suffrage to the entire people, give it to the most intelligent first." Mari Jo Buhle and Paul Buhle, *The Concise History of Woman Suffrage* (University of Illinois Press, 1978), 258.

issue. Unlike the black vote—desperately needed by Republicans if they hoped to retain control of Congress and the presidency after the rebel states were readmitted into the Union—the women's vote, especially given the narrow support base for this reform, conferred little political advantage to Republicans.[*]

Having lost out in the Reconstruction amendments, the women's movement set out to build national support. Yet, with only women remaining on the outside of the polling booth (at least formally), the movement no longer could cast its appeal in terms of universal suffrage. Now, women's suffrage became a women's issue and gave rise to two widely circulated and seemingly incompatible lines of arguments. Some proponents struck a conservative note. The more conservative line queried the inconsistency of denying women the vote when so many ill-informed and illiterate immigrant men were voting. The southern variant of this argument had the white women's vote diluting any chance of African Americans winning elections. At the other end of the ideological continuum, recasting the women's vote as a women's issue connected with a broader feminist platform. Denial of the franchise was simply emblematic of women's subjugation, a condition entrenched in the traditional family structure. Prominent women's issues today found their origins in the arguments of many late-nineteenth-century suffragists. These strongly held, incompatible views invariably competed for leadership of the movement. Whether these organizational weaknesses reflected or contributed to the failure of women's suffrage to win public support is difficult to say. As long as these fissures persisted the women's movement continued to attract supporters for various causes all along the ideological spectrum—including vocal pacifism during World War I—and it took nearly four decades to achieve the Nineteenth Amendment. Gradually, public support for women's suffrage increased, first in Wyoming in 1869 and over the next several decades in other, mostly western states. By 1919, fifteen states gave women the right to vote in at least some elections. Congress renewed consideration repeatedly from the mid-1880s until 1919, when with President Woodrow Wilson's strong endorsement, two-thirds of both the House and the Senate sent the Nineteenth Amendment to the states for ratification.

The Modern History of Women's Rights

The modern extension of subsequent civil rights guarantees to women clearly followed the civil rights movement. In fact, through a political miscalculation, sex discrimination was outlawed in the 1964 Civil Rights Act. Initially the legislation included language that covered discrimination based only on religion, national origin, and race. Southern opponents proposed and voted to add sex to this list, certain that it would decrease overall support for and ultimately defeat the civil rights bill. This strategy of weighing the

---

[*] Ironically, the difference in the partisan advantage between black and female vote extensions might well explain the historical differences in the success of these groups in exercising their newly won franchise. The reemergent Democratic Party throughout the South later systematically stripped the vote from ex-slaves with literacy tests, white primary laws, and poll taxes. Threatening no one, other than saloon proprietors, women exercised their franchise largely unhindered. Indeed, both political parties took credit for their newly won right and appealed for their support.

Victoria Claflin Woodhull was one of the most outspoken feminists of the late nineteenth century. The first woman to declare herself a candidate for the presidency, she also ran a brokerage firm and published a Marxist-tinged newspaper. In her 1871 keynote address to the National Woman Suffrage Association, Woodhull admitted her ultimate goal was the overthrow of the government, by treason if necessary. Her subsequent announcement that she practiced as well as preached free love lent credibility to opponents' claims that female suffrage would be the first step toward some brave new world.

legislation down with controversial provisions backfired, however, when Congress accepted their amendment and proceeded to pass the legislation.

The surprising legislative victory did not lead to immediate enforcement, however, even though the 1964 law created an enforcement mechanism—the new Equal Employment Opportunity Commission (EEOC)—authorized to investigate and file suits against racial discrimination in the workplace. With one early EEOC commissioner calling the sex discrimination policy "a fluke," the commission initially balked at enforcing the employment discrimination protections for women. But the agency revised its orientation after a successful political campaign focused national attention on employment discrimination against women.

The National Organization for Women (NOW) was formed in 1966 in direct reaction to the EEOC's refusal to enforce this provision. Organized along the same lines as the NAACP, NOW initially pursued a litigation strategy with mixed success. To establish a stronger legal foundation, NOW and other women's rights organizations dusted off the Equal Rights Amendment (ERA), which had been introduced in Congress in 1923 and every year thereafter with little fanfare and poor prospects. The amendment gave Congress the authority to implement the following statement: "Equality of rights under the law shall not be denied or abridged by the United States or by any State on account of sex."

Using many of the same tactics honed by the civil rights movement—demonstrations, televised appeals, Washington rallies, and intense lobbying—NOW and other feminist organizations won over a sympathetic public. The mostly male members of Congress were not far behind. After languishing for years, the ERA was sent to the states in 1972, and within the first year twenty-two of the required thirty-eight states voted for ratification. But then the amendment hit a brick wall with the abortion issue (discussed more fully in Chapter 5).[30] Thus instead of pitting men against women, as the Nineteenth Amendment had done earlier in the century, the ERA divided feminist and antiabortion women's groups. What began as an uncontroversial endorsement of women's rights—after all, the amendment's wording simply asserts that women enjoy the same rights as men—ended in strident, contentious rhetoric between opposing camps.* On June 30, 1982, the timetable for ratification expired, and the ERA became history.

---

* Public support waned. By 1981 less than half of all voters still endorsed the amendment in those states where it had not yet been ratified. Gallup poll cited in Jane Mansbridge, *Why We Lost the ERA* (Chicago: University of Chicago Press, 1986), 214.

Feminists may have lost the battle over the ERA, but they appear to have won the war. During the decades since the failed ERA campaign, national civil rights policy in areas of special concern to women has advanced steadily. In 1972 Congress enacted Title IX of the Higher Education Act, which prohibits funding for schools and universities that discriminate against women, including the size of their intercollegiate sports programs. When the Supreme Court in 1984 limited the law's coverage of private groups, ruling that it prohibited discrimination only in those programs of a private organization that directly benefited from federal funding, Congress responded by passing, over President Ronald Reagan's veto, a law that overturned the Court's decision.[31] And to send a message to the conservative Court, the Democratic majorities deliberately titled the new law the Restoration of Civil Rights Act of 1988.

Most significant developments in civil rights policy on employment practices have occurred during the past two decades, reflecting women's increasing presence in the workforce. However measured—whether by percentage of women in the workplace, or numbers of working mothers, or the share of women who are their families' primary breadwinner—the numbers indicate dramatic growth in women's workforce participation.

As employment issues increased, working women and their legal advocates discovered that the Civil Rights Act of 1964—just as some critics of the ERA had argued—offered ample legal protections for their discrimination claims. Though drafted principally to eradicate racial discrimination, the language of Title VII of that law is unequivocal in its provisions against sex discrimination in the workplace: "[It is] an unlawful employment practice for an employer . . . to discriminate against any individual with respect to his compensation, term, conditions, or privileges of employment, because of such individual's race, color, religion, sex, or national origin." During the last twenty years, as the Supreme Court has considered the merits of women's lawsuits charging sexual harassment by male supervisors, the Court has relied heavily on the 1964 provision to find that sexual harassment violates the federal civil rights law.

Congress further strengthened employment discrimination claims on various fronts. The Pregnancy Discrimination Act (1978) and the Family and Medical Leave Act (1993) prevent unfair firing and demotion during absences for childbirth and family medical emergencies. The Civil Rights Act of 1991 required employers to show that unequal hiring and compensation practices did not reflect gender discrimination and gave victims the right to sue for damages. In recent years gender has replaced race at the top of the civil rights agenda. The courts, Congress, federal agencies, and state legislatures devote a significant amount of time to policies governing relations between the sexes in the workplace.* Today, claims of sexual discrimination in hiring, pregnancy discrimination in retention and advancement, and harassment in the workplace constitute more than one-third of all complaints presented to the EEOC.[32]

---

*In 2009 Congress passed the Lilly Ledbetter Fair Pay Act to supersede a policy that sprung from a prior Supreme Court decision, which held that plaintiffs must file claims of pay discrimination within 180 days of the initial discrimination. In that case, Lilly Ledbetter learned as she was about to retire that her employer had for years been paying her male counterparts much more than it had been paying her. The Supreme Court threw out her case, but Congress amended federal law that set the deadline from the date of the most recent paycheck.

In February 2013, North Carolina began issuing driver's licenses with bright pink strips and "NO LAWFUL STATUS" to some illegal immigrants. Illegal, or undocumented, aliens enjoy fewer civil rights protections than do legal aliens and many states have taken measures to limit social services to them.

Rights for Hispanics

According to the U.S. Census Bureau, in 2009 the Hispanic population totaled 48 million, about 16 percent of the U.S. population.* Over the years Hispanics have experienced many of the same civil rights injustices endured by African Americans. As "national origin" became a protected rights category and as the Hispanic population has grown rapidly, so have the number of discrimination complaints. In many respects, Hispanics have successfully enlisted the legal, administrative, and judicial structures constructed to protect African Americans. Yet their civil rights concerns are also distinctive. The 2010 census figures indicate that slightly less than four in ten Hispanics are foreign-born, with most arriving from Mexico and Central America. Many lack the language skills to exercise their civic responsibilities in English. This introduces special civil rights issues associated with language and citizenship. Recognizing this problem early on, Congress passed the 1970 extension of the Voting Rights Act of 1965, requiring that ballots also be available in Spanish in those constituencies where at least 5 percent of the population is Hispanic.

Other recent government actions concerning language have been less accommodating, however. Whether from discrimination or the expressed difficulty of administering multilingual applications, a few states have adopted English-only laws mandating that most state business be conducted in English. When an applicant for an Alabama driver's license challenged the state's English-only law as a civil rights violation, a narrowly divided Supreme Court in *Alexander v. Sandoval* (2001) ruled that an individual could not challenge Alabama's regulation that all driver's license tests and applications be written in English. The 1964 Civil Rights Act allowed individual suits only in cases of "intentional discrimination." The law, according to the majority opinion, left to federal enforcement agencies the determination whether English-only rules had an inherently discriminatory outcome. The decision, in effect, turned this class of civil rights complaints away from the courts and to political and administrative institutions, and stimulated Hispanic efforts to influence national policy.

Illegal, or undocumented, aliens, who constitute a significant share of the Hispanic population, enjoy fewer civil rights protections than do legal aliens, who in turn enjoy less access

---

*African Americans and Asian Americans by comparison comprise 13.6 and 5 percent of the population, respectively. "U.S. Hispanic Population Surpasses 45 Million, Now 15 Percent of Total," U.S. Census Bureau Population Division, May 2008.

Map 4-4 High Concentration of U.S. Hispanics: A Guarantee of Political Influence

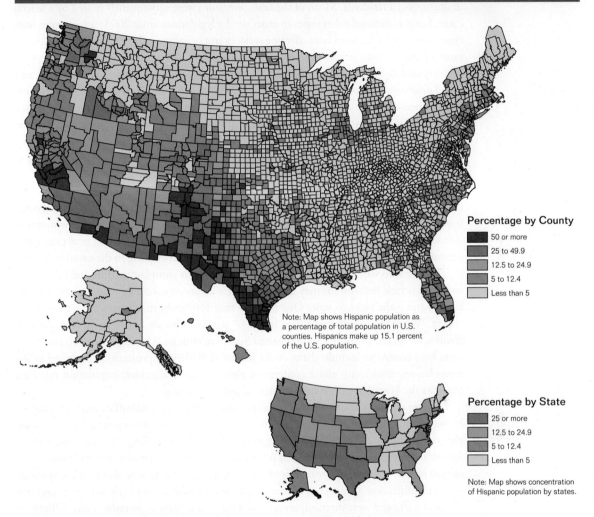

Percentage by County

- 50 or more
- 25 to 49.9
- 12.5 to 24.9
- 5 to 12.4
- Less than 5

Note: Map shows Hispanic population as a percentage of total population in U.S. counties. Hispanics make up 15.1 percent of the U.S. population.

Percentage by State

- 25 or more
- 12.5 to 24.9
- 5 to 12.4
- Less than 5

Note: Map shows concentration of Hispanic population by states.

Source: U.S. Census Bureau, Population Estimates, 2010. Internet release data: March 2011. Percentage by State as of 2009, U.S. Census Bureau Quickfacts.

Note: Map shows Hispanic population as a percentage of total population in U.S. counties. Hispanics make up 15.8 percent of the U.S. population.

to government than do citizens. The federal welfare reform law of 1996, for example, requires citizenship as a condition for obtaining food stamps and certain welfare benefits. Besides having limited rights, illegal aliens are unlikely to claim violations of rights they do have when doing so may draw attention to their illegal status and lead to their deportation. Employers who fail to pay minimum wage or provide mandated breaks potentially face stiff sanctions from both state and federal agencies. Yet illegal workers rarely report these abuses for fear that they might face deportation. As the number of illegal residents has swelled over the past several decades, many states—especially those that share a border with Mexico—have sought to stop providing social services to these individuals. In 1994 California voters overwhelmingly passed Proposition 187, a referendum denying government services to most undocumented residents. Much of the law's provisions were subsequently gutted by a federal court, but it stimulated other states to enact similar legislation. Since 2005 various states have enacted over one thousand laws affecting services and benefits available to immigrants. A few extend benefits, but the vast majority restrict services. In 2005 half the states enacted a total of thirty-nine laws affecting immigrants—largely in response to federal guidelines for grant-in-aid programs administered by the states. By 2012 virtually all the states were busy enacting immigration-related laws. Specifically, forty-four states placed 156 new laws (and more than a hundred resolutions) on the books altering government services for immigrants in some fashion. Moreover, as with the Arizona law criminalizing illegal status, many of these laws reflect state initiatives in response to concerns and preferences of their voters, instead of merely administrative adjustments to changing federal policies. As shown in Figure 4-2, the most active areas of policy that state legislation has addressed during the past several years has involved access to education, employment, and tightening access to driver's licenses and other forms of identification. As busy as state legislatures have been in these areas, the widespread election of Republicans in state government in the 2010 elections harbingered even more extensive legislation, including laws to detain those suspected of being in the country illegally.

The extent to which Hispanics succeed in having their complaints addressed by political and bureaucratic institutions may depend on their ability to maximize a fundamental political resource—the right to vote. One of every four foreign-born Hispanics is a naturalized citizen.* When this number is added to the 60 percent who are native-born, it means that about seven in ten Hispanics in the United States are citizens. Although the courts in recent years have tended to include aliens under federal civil liberties protections described in the next chapter, citizenship alone confers the right to vote. Therefore, population numbers overstate the Hispanic community's potential political power.

Another potential source of vote dilution comes out of voter identification laws adopted by twenty-one states in 2010. Prior to the 2012 election, many states passed laws that arguably made voting difficult for certain groups of people, including Hispanic and African American voters. Some laws required photo identification—such as a driver's license—but offered no easy way for the thousands of mostly minority citizens who do not drive to obtain photo identification. Other state laws reduced the time available for early voting in ways that minorities charged were discriminatory; still others made voter registration more difficult by eliminating same-day registration and/or limiting voter mobilization drives.[33] Despite a major controversy in Florida over extremely long waiting lines resulting from restricted early voting, in general the states' various voting law restrictions did not have an effect on the ultimate outcome of the election. To some degree, this was because of judicial intervention. In Pennsylvania, for example, a state court judge ruled that voters did not have enough time to obtain proper identification; he therefore prevented the photo identification law from taking effect before the election. However, because the U.S. Supreme Court previously upheld the right of states to require photo identification—generally speaking—as a justifiable protection against potential voter fraud[34], controversies over photo identification laws are

---

*To be eligible for naturalization, immigrants must have permanent resident visas for five years or, if married to a U.S. citizen, have lived in the country for three years.

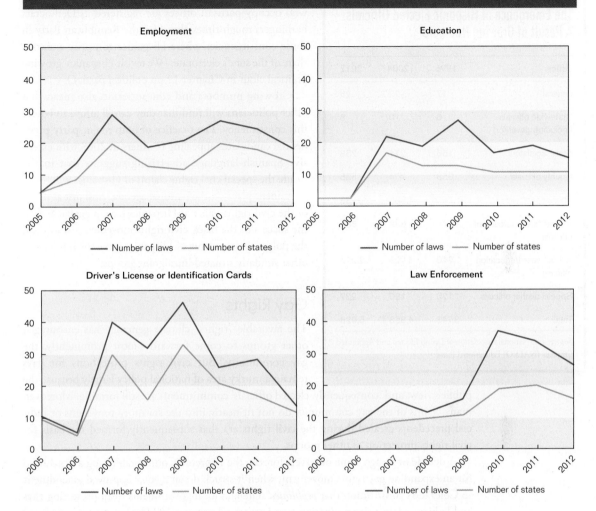

Figure 4-2   Growing Number of States Enacting More Laws Targeting Illegal Immigrants

Source: Annual Reports of National Council of State Legislatures.

certain to continue in future elections. Ultimately, civil rights groups remain concerned that these new laws will depress voting among poorer segments of the population, who will be less knowledgeable of the requirements and not have the necessary forms when they show up at the polls.

Despite the obstacles facing illegal aliens and other Hispanics, the long-term prognosis for Hispanic civic gains is bright. The population is growing rapidly (see Map 4-4), as are naturalization rates. Moreover, the population as a whole is quite young, with about 40 percent of Hispanics below voting age. As these young people, most of whom are native-born citizens, become eligible to vote, Hispanic electoral power is bound to surge. Finally, with the Hispanic population concentrated residentially, it ensures that a sizable number of office-holders will come from their ranks. Indeed, from 1996 to 2012 the number of elected

TABLE 4-3

The Emergence of Hispanic Elected Officials: A Result of Growing Numbers

Office	1996	2004	2012
Federal	17	22	26
Statewide officials (including governor)	6	10	8
State legislators	156	221	258
County officials	358	474	555
Municipal officials	1,295	1,585	1,738
Judicial/law enforcement officials	546	638	881
School board/education officials	1,240	1,723	2,225
Special district officials	125	180	237
Total	3,743	4,853	5,928

Source: The National Association of Latino Elected and Appointed Officials (NALEO) Educational Fund.

Hispanic officials increased from 3,743 to 5,928 (see Table 4-3). The fact that over 90 percent of these officials who occupy partisan offices are registered as Democrats harbingers tough times ahead for the Republican Party in those constituencies where Hispanics comprise a sizable share of the state's electorate. (We revisit Hispanics' growing political clout in Chapter 12 on political parties.)

Growing numbers and concentration also mean that other politicians will find that they can ill afford to ignore this constituency. The practice of both major-party presidential candidates appealing to voters in 2008 with extensive Spanish-language advertising suggests that in the future the special civil rights claims of Hispanics will find a prominent place on the national agenda. And just as many of the civil rights gains of Hispanics have piggybacked on the success of the black civil rights movement, so too will the policy achievements of Hispanics serve the interests of other similarly situated immigrant groups.

Gay Rights

The favorable "rights" climate generally has encouraged other groups to come forward—most prominently, the gay community. But civil rights protections for gays remain a murky area of national policy largely because the public's views and, consequently, elected officials' commitments are still forming. Moreover, many claims of the gay community do not fit neatly into the statutory provisions or judicial precedents created during the civil rights era that subsequently formed the basis for civil rights protection of other groups.

A decade or so ago some observers foresaw the Supreme Court establishing a beachhead for an expanding gay rights movement, when it struck down a voter-approved amendment to Colorado's constitution that *prohibited* state and local governments from protecting gays and lesbians against discrimination based on sexual orientation. The Supreme Court ruled that the amendment unconstitutionally denied gays equal protection, yet the Court did not actually confer any specific rights to gays. Nonetheless, by applying the critical Fourteenth Amendment to gay rights claims, *Romer v. Evans* made this group eligible for positive protections if state and local jurisdictions deemed them appropriate.[35] But in 1995 Congress voted down legislation that would have incorporated sexual orientation into existing employment rights laws. The next year it passed the Defense of Marriage Act (popularly known as "DOMA"), which not only rejects same-sex marriages but allows states to ignore these unions sanctioned in other states. More than symbolism was at stake in this law. By one count, over a thousand federal rights and benefits are available to married couples, including Social Security survivor's benefits, Medicaid eligibility, and estate tax exemptions or reductions.[36]

Despite these setbacks, the gay rights movement has celebrated some major successes. In 2009, Congress expanded federal hate crimes protections to individuals assaulted because of their sexual orientation. (The **hate crime** designation refers to those provisions of the criminal code that make illegal—or stiffen penalties for—violence directed against individuals, property, or organizations because of the victims' race, gender, national origin, or sexual orientation.) In 2010, Congress ended the military's "Don't Ask, Don't Tell" policy that permitted service by gays only so long as they did not disclose their sexual preference.

In addition, the gay rights movement has targeted laws at the state level. Currently, about thirty states and the District of Columbia extend hate crime protections to the gay community. However, the main field of political and legal pressure both for and

"There's nothing wrong with our marriage, but the spectre of gay marriage has hopelessly eroded the institution."

against gay rights concerns gay marriage. This controversial issue had been brewing in state and federal courts and in state legislative deliberations for over a decade before it burst into the national news early in 2004. The Massachusetts Supreme Court laid the groundwork late in 2003, when it ruled that a state law banning gay marriages violated Massachusetts's constitution. In 2008, the California Supreme Court similarly ruled that the state's ban on same-sex marriage violated the state constitution's equal protection provisions.

These sudden, mostly judicial changes in long-established policy were bound to trigger a reaction. Within weeks of the California decision, sponsors of an initiative to amend the California constitution to define marriage as the union of one man and one woman qualified for the 2008 election ballot. To the surprise of many, California voters—long thought of as among the most progressive in the country—passed the initiative by a margin of 52 percent to 48 percent. Numerous other states' referenda generated similar results. By the close of 2012, thirty-one states had passed laws or amended their constitutions to ban gay marriages outright. After years of hostility to gay marriage among voters, however, the 2012 election produced the first popular vote victories for the marriage equality movement when voters passed referenda in Maine, Maryland, and Washington. They joined the list of six states—Connecticut, Iowa, Massachusetts, New Hampshire, New York, and Vermont, along with the District of Columbia—where same-sex marriages had been approved by the courts or state legislatures. Another five states provide for civil union between same-sex partners (**civil unions** allow same-sex couples to receive many of the legal benefits of married couples, but without the "marriage" classification).

As states line up for and against gay marriage, the issue leaped from the states to the federal courts when in early 2012, the Ninth Circuit Court of Appeals ruled that California's constitutional ban on gay marriage is unconstitutional. Specifically, the court found that the equal protection clause—originally added to combat the unequal treatment of former slaves on the basis of *race*—prohibited the state of California from singling out same-sex couples,

INTERACTIVE MAP

logic.cqpress.com

Check out the differences in states' gay marriage policies.

taking away the right to marry from them *alone*. Then appeals courts in Boston and New York ruled that the DOMA similarly violated Fourteenth Amendment protections. In December 2012, the Supreme Court announced that it would take up appeals in both cases. The last decision from the Court on gay rights was *Lawrence v. Texas* (2003), in which the Court expanded gay rights by reversing a prior ruling and deciding that state antisodomy laws violated individuals' Constitutional privacy protections.[37] That opinion was authored by Justice Anthony Kennedy, who may be the critical vote in both the California case and the DOMA case.

Although those promoting gay marriage as a civil right have had limited success in altering the legal setting, they have been more successful in changing public opinion. Since the issue burst onto the national scene in the early 1990s, Americans have become increasingly receptive to the idea of same-sex marriage. In Figure 4-3 we find a significant liberalization of public opinion on gay marriage just as the American public has continued to become much more accepting of interracial marriage. In part opinions on gay marriage have changed. In

READ MORE

logic.cqpress.com

See how the Court ruled on same-sex marriage.

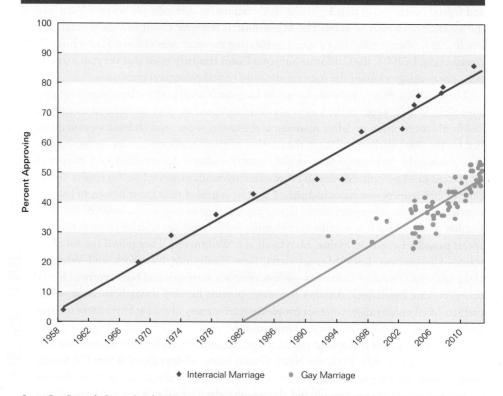

Figure 4-3 The Parallel Growth of Public Support for Interracial and Gay Marriages

Source: Pew Research Center, Social & Demographic Trends, "The Rise of Intermarriage," February 16, 2012, http://www.pewsocialtrends.org/files/2012/02/SDT-Intermarriage-II.pdf.

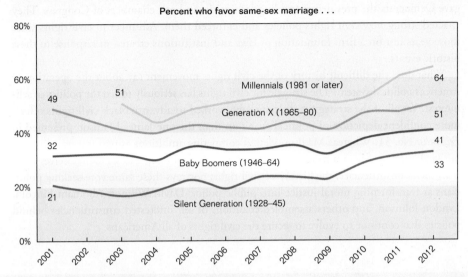

Figure 4-4 Support for Gay Marriage Differs across Generations

Percent who favor same-sex marriage . . .

Source: The Pew Forum on Religion and Public Life, Changing Attitudes on Gay Marriage, http://features.pewforum.org/same-sex-marriage-attitudes/slide2.php.

*Line labels indicate birth year of respondents.

2012 President Obama announced his own conversion from a preference to institute **civil unions** to full access to legal marriage. In Figure 4-4 we see that for every year since 2009 greater shares of Americans across every age cohort accept gay marriage. Equally consequential to changing minds is the changing composition of the population. The figure also shows younger people at every age cohort are more amenable to gay marriage than are their elders. As the composition of the electorate has changed, so too has public opinion.

CHALLENGING TYRANNY

This historical survey of civil rights in America reveals courageous men and women advocating for their fellow citizens who were suffering injustice. But this history also reveals that these efforts did not suffice. True to James Madison's observation in *Federalist* No. 10, the cause of civil rights is advanced only when a large national majority fully takes control of the federal government and challenges tyranny in the states. The politicians who assembled these broad national coalitions were keen political strategists. Abraham Lincoln and the Republican Party rode into office advocating "Free Soil, Free Labor, Free Men," not eradication of slavery. Nonetheless, their political success allowed them to conduct a costly and bloody war to preserve the Union and abolish slavery.

From the 1880s through the 1950s neither party could muster a majority even within itself, much less the government, on behalf of civil rights for African Americans.

Consequently, the cause languished, and generations of African Americans were doomed to lives marred by segregation's shameful regimen. Then, in the 1960s, the Democratic Party rode the crest of public opinion generated by the civil rights movement. The 1964 election gave Democrats the presidency and huge majorities in both chambers of Congress. They enacted strong new civil rights policies and enforced them. Advances in civil rights since those years rest on a firm foundation of laws and institutions created in response to these historic events.

What does the difficult history of the civil rights movement say about the operation of America's political system? The struggle for civil rights has seriously tested the politics of self-interest. Yet all of the strategic politicians who worked to advance black civil rights offer a more confident depiction of political ambition than the one James Madison presented in *Federalist* No. 51. Whereas Madison viewed competing ambitions as performing a limited, but vital, service of neutralizing politicians who might be inclined to serve themselves more than their constituencies, the history of civil rights portrays these same vote-seeking politicians as transforming moral justice into public policy. David Wilmot, Abraham Lincoln, Lyndon Johnson, and others assembled coalitions of self-interested constituencies behind policies that continue to evolve to secure the civil rights of all Americans.

● TAKE A QUIZ

logic.cqpress.com

Test your knowledge of this chapter.

logic.cqpress.com

▅▅ Key Terms ▅▅

affirmative action,   164

black codes,   140

civil liberties,   132

civil rights,   132

civil unions,   179

de facto segregation,   163

de jure segregation,   163

Fugitive Slave Law,   138

grandfather clauses,   144

hate crime,   176

Jim Crow laws, 143

literacy test,   144

poll tax,   144

quotas, 164

racial profiling,   129

segregation,   143

"separate but equal" doctrine,   144

suffragists, 167

white primary,   144

▅▅ Suggested Readings ▅▅

Anderson, Kristi. *After Suffrage.* Chicago: University of Chicago Press, 1996. Anderson assembles all of the available voting and registration data in providing a detailed and varied history of the entry of women into American politics.

Branch, Taylor. *Parting the Waters: America in the King Years, 1954–1963.* New York: Simon and Schuster, 1988; and *Pillar of Fire: America in the King Years, 1963–65.* New York: Simon and Schuster, 1998. These two installments of Branch's detailed political history of civil rights offer a wealth of instruction to students of politics and history alike.

Carmines, Edward G., and James A. Stimson. *Issue Evolution: Race and the Transformation of American Politics.* Princeton, NJ: Princeton University Press, 1989. Although these scholars use sophisticated statistical techniques, they offer an accessible and convincing account of the evolution of the Democratic Party among politicians and citizens as the party of civil rights.

Garrow, David J. *Bearing the Cross: Martin Luther King Jr. and the Southern Christian Leadership Conference.* New York: Morrow, 1986. An absorbing account of the rise of King from the Montgomery bus boycott to his assassination in 1968.

Keyssar, Alexander. *The Right to Vote.* New York: Basic Books, 2000. This highly readable history of the extension of voting rights in America has emerged as the authoritative source on the subject.

Oates, Stephen B. *With Malice Toward None: The Life of Abraham Lincoln.* New York: New American Library–Dutton, 1978. Our favorite Lincoln biography has two great virtues: Lincoln is shown to be a masterful politician, and the gradual emergence of emancipation as a wartime issue is described clearly.

■■■ Review Questions ■■■

1. What features of government did the southern states employ to prevent the eradication of slavery? What steps were necessary to remove the obstacles to emancipation?

2. What benefits did Reconstruction produce for former slaves? For northern whites? What benefits and which groups did Reconstruction "leave out," and why?

3. What party did most African Americans support prior to the 1930s, and why? Why did this change after the 1930s, and what was responsible for the change?

4. How did the civil rights demonstrations of the 1960s change the political calculations of Democratic politicians? How were the demonstrations planned strategically to increase pressure on politicians?

5. What challenges and opportunities do Hispanics face in their current civil rights efforts? How do these challenges differ from those blacks faced in their civil rights campaigns?

5 Civil Liberties

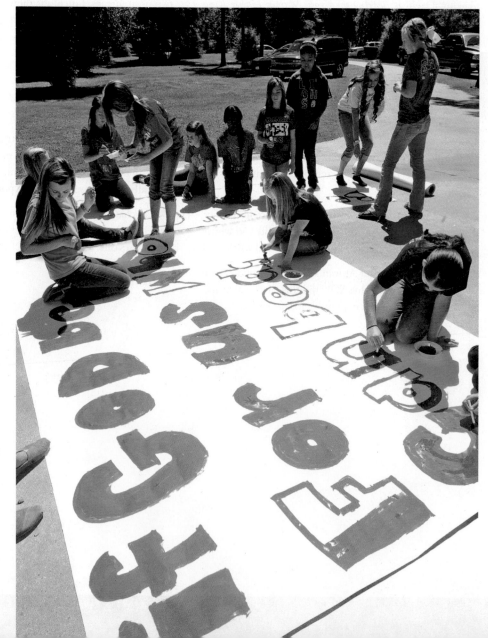

East Texas cheerleaders stirred constitutional controversy when they quoted Bible verses in the middle of a school football game. While the display was supported by some, it tests the Constitution's First Amendment protections of free speech.

- Has the existence of a formal Bill of Rights really secured the freedoms of Americans?

- Does the Supreme Court's primacy in this area of public policy imply that democracy requires an institution of unelected judges for its protection? What other ways of protecting civil liberties might there be?

- What roles, if any, do Congress, the president, and the states play in defining civil liberties?

- Since the Bill of Rights does not mention "right of privacy," how can the Supreme Court deem it to be a fundamental constitutional right?

Enlisting God for the Big Game

"If God is for us, who can be against us?" This is the question posed by the Apostle Paul in the New Testament, but also by a high school cheerleading squad in East Texas. The cheerleaders' use of biblical quotes on "run through" banners—the banners that the football players run through at the beginning of a game—is now the focus of a First Amendment battle. The Freedom From Religion Foundation complained that the cheerleaders' banners violate the First Amendment's restriction against the government's "establishment" of religion, while the cheerleaders claimed that the school board's attempt to prevent them from using religious language violated *their* First Amendment right to free speech. So far, a Texas State court judge has sided with the cheerleaders; they are allowed to continue using the banners, pending the ultimate outcome at trial. The school district claims that it is simply trying to be neutral, and to comply with existing Supreme Court law on the establishment clause.

Cell Phones

Cell phones are no longer just "phones." Instead, millions of Americans use their cell phones to send text messages, check their e-mail, take photos and videos, post on Facebook, and tweet on Twitter. As a result, an extraordinary amount of personal information and data is now stored on cell phones, and looking through someone's phone can tell you a lot about that person. Most people don't worry or even think about this possibility—until perhaps they lose their phone. But what happens when someone is arrested, even for a minor crime? Can the police search the entire contents of that person's cell phone, without a warrant?

This is the question facing many courts across the country, and so far, the decisions overwhelmingly favor law enforcement. The courts have allowed officers to search an arrestee's cell phone under "search incident to arrest," which means that the police do not need a warrant or have to make any separate showing that the contents on the phone are related to the alleged crime.

MTA Billboards

logic.cqpress.com

The MTA billboards generate controversy.

In September 2011, a woman named Pamela Geller submitted the ad shown on page 184 to the New York Metropolitan Transit Authority. Initially, the MTA denied her application due to the use of the word *savage*. However, after Geller sued, asserting her First Amendment right to free speech, a federal judge ruled that the MTA could not ban her message. As a result, the ad went up in New York subway stations in late September 2012.

Many New Yorkers objected to the ad, arguing that the language painted all Muslims as jihadists. Others worried that the ad would provoke *more* violence by extremists. In addition, copies of the ad were defaced by those who saw it as hate speech.

License Plates

Every week, millions of Americans go about their lives, driving to work, to school, perhaps to the pharmacy, or to the grocery store. But as law-abiding residents of cities such as San

Special cameras have the capacity to record thousands of license plates during a routine day, automatically sending the data to a dashboard computer and database. Ever increasing numbers of law enforcement departments are using this technology as are private firms that contract with auto repossession agencies. As this technology proliferates, the accumulated data on motorists' whereabouts introduces concerns over privacy.

Leandro, California, and Boston, Massachusetts, recently discovered, someone may be tracking their movements—by capturing their license plate numbers using automated readers. In some cases, patrol cars are using the readers; in other cases, it's a private company, such as a repossession business. But in either case, location data on your vehicle can be captured without your knowledge, stored—perhaps indefinitely—and later accessed by the police, despite the fact that you are not suspected of committing any crime. Civil liberties groups worry that this tremendous data-gathering enterprise goes too far, implicating both the Fourth Amendment's prohibition on unreasonable searches and seizures, and citizens' privacy interests.

NATIONALIZATION OF CIVIL LIBERTIES

Civil liberties claims—of all kinds—dominate today's newspaper headlines and lead television evening news programs, and for good reason. Occasionally an established freedom is being abridged. Arguably more common, however, a policy change expands personal liberties and extends established freedoms into new domains. Everyone prefers freedom to tyranny, but an expansion of civil liberties is often controversial. As the above cases illustrate, civil liberties claims frequently run up against the ardent preferences of a majority of the citizenry, the nation's legitimate security needs, or even the rights claims of others.

Civil liberties, though, have not always been so prom deliberations. At the end of the nineteenth century rea pers for more than a month to discover claims invok privileges as freedom of the press, speech, and religion tions would have struck the nineteenth-century public physician-assisted suicides, and abortions occurred in clandestine, and ultimately criminal, enterprises.

Civil liberties have emerged as a major part of the reasons. New technologies and modern lifestyles are vidual liberties into the public arena. Technological cations to medicine challenge established principles. an issue in 1996 when Congress passed the Commu ship of the Internet, or in 1997 when the Suprem tional.[1] The *real* issue was how existing standards medium in which juveniles could easily access sexu civil liberties issues are responses to cultural chang art, and politics.

Reining in Majorities

Over the past century, determination of national civil liberties policy has shifted from nearly the exclusive jurisdiction of states and communities to Washington. Previously, defendants' rights amounted to little more than what the local police and sheriff would allow. In many states local judges, prosecutors, and legal associations agreed that exclusively white (and mostly older) male jurors satisfied their standards of impartiality and that an attorney for indigent defendants represented an unneeded luxury. Local ministers tendered prayers to school principals, who handed them to teachers and students for morning recitations. Eventually, though, the national government assumed jurisdiction over defendants' rights and school prayer. With a new, expansive interpretation of the Constitution, the courts applied the Bill of Rights to state and local policies as well as national policy.

The histories of civil rights and civil liberties have much in common. Indeed, the constitutional amendments conferring full citizenship to recently freed slaves would later provide a rationale for the national government to enter the civil liberties arena. In both histories the judiciary played a pivotal role in denying or accepting the claims of an individual or group's rights over the objections of some local or national majority. But in other important respects, the history of civil liberties proceeds down a different path. As discussed in Chapter 4 the greatest advances in civil rights occurred when a national majority took up a minority's cause; so long as the national government continued silent, slavery and segregation were secure. The federal judiciary struck the first blows against segregation, but the rights of African Americans did not substantially improve until congressional majorities and presidents were prepared to stake their party's electoral fortunes on intervening directly against segregation and black disenfranchisement. In the end, civil rights required the sustained efforts of a national majority exerting the full force of the federal government. By contrast, advances in national civil liberties policy have frequently involved reining in majorities that assert their prerogatives over the objections of individuals and groups who did not wish to conform to prevailing social norms and rules. National policy protecting flag-burning demonstrators from incarceration, barring communal prayer at public school graduations, and preventing juries from hearing confessions from defendants before they were read their rights are just a few examples where recent civil liberties policy has frustrated the preferences of local and even national majorities.

The Bill of Rights Checks Majority Rule

Where the history of civil rights emphasizes the capacity of majorities to control policy, the history of civil liberties reminds us that the United States is a republic whose institutions are designed to temper the fleeting passions of majorities. The Framers well understood that civil liberties policy would at times check majority preferences; the First Amendment to the Bill of Rights intentionally begins with the emphatic and revealing language "Congress shall make no law," and covers six different areas of personal and political liberty. Unlike civil rights, civil liberties are a domain in which national majorities will be constrained in fixing national policy. This opening phrase also invited the Supreme Court to eventually define civil liberties, in part since the judiciary was designed to be insulated from popular pressures. Recognizing this fact, James Madison predicted that the courts "will consider themselves in a peculiar manner the guardians of [civil liberties]: they will be an impenetrable bulwark against every assumption of power in the legislative or executive; they will be naturally led to resist every encroachment upon rights."[2]

The Bill of Rights (see box "The Bill of Rights") was designed to limit the capacity of the government to impose conformity costs on those individuals and minorities whose

The Bill of Rights

Amendment I

Congress shall make no law respecting an establish ment of religion, or prohibiting the free exercis thereof; or abridging the freedom of speech, or of th press; or the right of the people peacefully to assem ble, and to petition the Government for a redress o grievances.

Amendment II

A well regulated Militia, being necessary to the secu rity of a free State, the right of the people to keep and bear Arms, shall not be infringed.

Amendment III

No Soldier shall, in time of peace be quartered in any house, without the consent of the Owner, nor in time of war, but in a manner to be prescribed by law.

Amendment IV

The right of the people to be secure in their persons, houses, papers, and effects, against unreasonable searches and seizures, shall not be violated, and no Warrants shall issue, but upon probable cause, supported by Oath or affirmation, and particularly describing the place to be searched, and the persons or things to be seized.

Amendment V

No person shall be held to answer for a capital, or otherwise infamous crime, unless on a presentment or indictment of a Grand Jury, except in cases arising in the land or naval forces, or in the Militia, when in actual service in time of War or public danger; nor shall any person be subject for the same offence to be twice put in jeopardy or life or limb; nor shall be compelled in any criminal case to be a witness against

[handwritten note: Bill of Rights is designed to protect individuals from government trying to take away rights]

[handwritten note: Anti-federalists]

[handwritten note: only change rights via Constitutional amendment]

...where the value in controversy shall exceed twenty dollars, the right of trial by jury shall be preserved, and no fact tried by a jury, shall be otherwise re-examined in any Court of the United States, than according to the rules of the common law.

Amendment VIII

Excessive bail shall not be required, nor excessive fines imposed, nor cruel and unusual punishments inflicted.

Amendment IX

The enumeration in the Constitution, of certain rights, shall not be construed to deny or disparage others retained by the people.

Amendment X

The powers not delegated to the United States by the Constitution, nor prohibited by it to the States, are reserved to the States respectively, or to the people.

views differ from those of the majority. By insisting that these first ten amendments be placed in the Constitution, the Antifederalist critics of ratification sought assurance that these rights could not be easily removed or abridged. Only if the majority was overwhelming and enduring could it absorb the high transaction costs required to modify these rights via a constitutional amendment. Thus the Supreme Court's authority to veto Congress and state governments on these policies places civil liberties under the protective purview of an institution intentionally insulated from the "popular passions" of the majority.

The generally clear and unequivocal language of the Bill of Rights also provides government officials with little latitude to relax its proscriptions. Yet no amendment has ever been judged absolute, and some are downright ambiguous. What precisely does the First Amendment clause "Congress shall make no law respecting an establishment of religion" really mean? Its narrow construction is unambiguous. Congress cannot "establish" a particular faith as the "official" religion of the country. Beyond that, the clause offers little guidance and has even fostered opposing interpretations of the relationship between church and state. Does it prevent a moment of silent prayer in public schools? Does it deny government transportation and textbook subsidies for children attending private, church-sponsored schools? Similarly, what does the Eighth Amendment's prohibition of "cruel and unusual" punishment mean, and of greater practical significance, who decides? Are the justices of the Supreme Court endowed with special insight on appropriate punishment? If not, should states' citizens decide the matter in their criminal statutes, as is largely the case today? If so, what did the Framers have in mind when they employed this language in the national Constitution?

Sometimes ambiguity arises from two or more clearly worded constitutional provisions that are directly opposed to each other. An example of a particularly thorny conundrum concerns how unregulated press reportage (a First Amendment right) undermines a criminal defendant's Sixth Amendment right to an impartial jury. Which value should prevail when press coverage introduces highly incriminating or biased information and opinions before the trial?

Other constitutional responsibilities, especially those concerning the country's collective security, may bring official actions into conflict with individual rights. The preamble to the Constitution charges the national government to "provide for the common defence," and Article II designates the president as "Commander in Chief." Does this presidential responsibility allow the government to restrict freedom of the press during times of war, as President Abraham Lincoln claimed, or to eavesdrop on defendant–attorney conversations, as the George W. Bush administration announced in the aftermath of the September 11 attacks? Whether liberties are competing with one another or with other parts of the Constitution, the Bill of Rights represents a Pandora's box of unanswered policy questions.

The absolute language of the Bill of Rights notwithstanding, civil liberties policy is essentially a line-drawing or boundary-setting activity separating what government actions are and are not permissible. At times all three branches of government, in grappling with an issue, disagree over the meaning of the Bill of Rights. In a series of rulings beginning in 1990, the Supreme Court started a protracted disagreement over a new standard for whether state and local laws impinged on protected religious practices. In *Employment Division v. Smith* the Court ruled that otherwise valid, neutral laws of general applicability (such as drug laws) that incidentally impinge on a particular religious practice do not violate the First Amendment's free exercise clause.[3] Seeking to blunt the impact of the decision, religious organizations of every persuasion that had been exempt from a wide variety of laws, ranging from antidrug statutes to zoning restrictions, lobbied Congress to enact a blanket law that would effectively exempt them from local regulations.

In 1993 Congress passed the Religious Freedom Restoration Act, which voided any law or regulation that "substantially burdened" religious practices if it could not be shown to serve a "compelling government interest . . . by the least restrictive means." In signing the new law, President Bill Clinton noted that it effectively reversed the Court's 1990 decision and in his judgment was "far more consistent with the intent of the Founders than [was] the Supreme Court." Four years later the Court ruled that Congress had overstepped its constitutional authority in applying the new law to the states (as opposed to the federal government) and struck down the act to that extent. The Court majority reminded Congress and the president that "[t]he power to interpret a case or controversy remains in the Judiciary."[4] Congress promptly reopened hearings and in 2000 enacted legislation making it harder for local governments to enforce zoning decisions against religious organizations. But the Supreme Court arguably still has the last word. Although it has declined to hear several cases involving the Religious Freedom Restoration Act in the past few years, each of the lower court's rulings allowed to stand in those cases has favored the government instead of the group claiming a violation of its First Amendment freedom of religion.* So, even in *not* deciding a case, the Supreme Court has been able to implement its policy preferences, despite attempts by Congress and the president to emphasize and restore religious freedom.

This rare demonstration of these institutions squaring off against each other contrasted with their usual practice of jointly defining current liberties and rights. The conflict also reconfirmed how the Constitution's language has permitted the modern Supreme Court to carve out a large role in formulating civil liberties policy. The judiciary's move to the forefront of civil liberties policy created a revolution in rights and liberties, an important theme of this chapter.

WRITING RIGHTS AND LIBERTIES INTO THE CONSTITUTION

The Constitution, as it emerged from the 1787 Philadelphia Convention, did not seriously address civil liberties. Late in the convention George Mason of Virginia had proposed prefacing the document with a bill of rights (many state constitutions already had one), but most delegates were skeptical about the need for such an addition.[5] (Mason subsequently cited this omission as the reason he turned against the Constitution's ratification.) The delegates reasoned that the solution to tyranny lay in correctly designed institutions that balanced interests through competition. Some delegates also feared that a list of rights in the Constitution might imply that the federal government had the authority to restrict the freedoms not expressly protected. Alexander Hamilton posed the question famously in *Federalist* No. 84: "Why declare that things shall not be done which there is no power to do? Why, for instance, should it be said that the liberty of the press shall not be restrained, when no power is given by which restrictions may be imposed?"

---

*In 2006 the Court did unanimously uphold application of the Religious Freedom Restoration Act against the *federal* government. *Gonzales v. O Centro Espirita Beneficiente Uniao Do Vegetal,* 546 U.S. 418 (2006).

Mason was not the only advocate of a federal bill of rights. Throughout the ratifying process Antifederalists rallied opposition by arguing vigorously that the new constitutional plan flirted with tyranny by omitting explicit protections for the citizenry. Recognizing a chink in their armor, Madison and fellow supporters of the Constitution conceded the point and agreed that after its ratification they would introduce at the first session of the new Congress the amendments required for a bill of rights.

The Constitution actually acquired civil liberties protections in several steps over a long period of time. The first step was inclusion of the Bill of Rights, which insulated citizens from interference by the federal government in a variety of areas. The second, taken more than seventy-five years later, after the Civil War, was ratification of the Fourteenth Amendment, which gave the national government the authority to protect the rights of former slaves. And in a third step, which occurred over the twentieth century and continues into the twenty-first, the Supreme Court interpreted the Fourteenth Amendment to apply the Bill of Rights to the actions of state and local governments. Judicial scholars commonly refer to this process as **incorporation**—that is, using the Fourteenth Amendment to make the Bill of Rights binding on *state* governments, not just the federal government. Thus, the nationalization of civil liberties has not only altered the balance of power between Washington and the states, but it has also dramatically expanded the range of protections offered by the Bill of Rights. The federal judiciary now plays an increasing role in this area of public policy.

The First Ten Amendments

In June 1789 James Madison, elected to the First Congress as a representative from Virginia, followed through on his earlier commitment to a bill of rights by introducing seventeen constitutional amendments. His letters indicate that he may even have been persuaded of the merit of having these government proscriptions stated explicitly. Writing to his friend Thomas Jefferson, Madison conjectured that constitutionally guaranteed rights "acquire by degrees the character of fundamental maxims of free Governments, and as they become incorporated with the national sentiment, counteract the impulses of interest and passion."[6]

Madison may have been won over to the Bill of Rights, but he steadfastly believed that the states and not the national government provided the most fertile soil for tyranny. Acting on that belief, one of the amendments he submitted to the First Congress limited state authority. It read: "No state shall infringe the right of trial by jury in criminal cases, nor the right of conscience, nor the freedom of speech or of the press." States' rights advocates, however, were suspicious. Madison's effort to restrain the states smacked of another "nationalist" ruse, and they struck it from the list of amendments sent to the states for ratification. Two years then passed before the required three-quarters of the states ratified the Bill of Rights. Although the Antifederalists lost the ratification fight, they salvaged a major political concession in the Bill of Rights, their chief legacy to future generations of Americans.

In 1833 states' righters secured a victory in a landmark Supreme Court decision that governed the Court's posture and removed civil liberties from the national agenda for nearly a century. *Barron v. Baltimore* concerned road repairs made by the city of Baltimore that caused a buildup of gravel and sand in the area of John Barron's wharf, impeding access of deep-bottomed vessels.[7] Barron sued the city of Baltimore for violating his constitutionally guaranteed property rights. Pointing out that the Fifth Amendment forbade the public "taking" of private property without "just compensation," Barron argued that this provision applied to the states as well as the federal government and, therefore, Baltimore owed him money.

The Supreme Court ruled unanimously against Barron, holding that the Bill of Rights restrained only the actions of the national government. The whole thrust of the Bill of Rights, the justices reasoned, was directed exclusively at federal power. In short, the federal courts could not alleviate the excesses of state and local governments. Handed down in an era of limited federal responsibilities, the ruling rendered the Bill of Rights virtually meaningless, for most citizens' quarrels were with their state governments. If a state's residents wanted the rights that Barron claimed, they should amend their state constitution, suggested the Court. The other option—to amend the U.S. Constitution to apply the Bill of Rights to the states—was left unsaid. Yet achievements on the civil liberties front continued, and instead of serving as the last word on the subject, *Barron* today is a historical relic, illustrating how Americans once regarded their rights and federal-state relations. Reflecting the low salience of civil liberties in the nation's civic discourse, an introductory American government textbook written ten years after *Barron* devoted fewer than 5 of its 332 pages to the Bill of Rights.[8] This would change with the doctrine of incorporation.

Incorporation via the Fourteenth Amendment

Among the several constitutional amendments proposed during Reconstruction was the Fourteenth—a text crammed with now-familiar phrases (see box "Fourteenth Amendment: Section 1"). Although the amendment, passed in 1868, was intended initially to protect former slaves by explicitly declaring that rights of citizenship were not subject to state controls, over time its sweeping language led other groups to seek its umbrella protections. Yet nearly a half-century of jurisprudence passed before the Supreme Court began to interpret the Fourteenth Amendment language as requiring the states to adhere to the national government's Bill of Rights protections.[9] One of the great ironies of American history is that while this amendment failed to achieve its immediate objective, a century later it extended the rights and liberties of all citizens in directions unimaginable to its authors.

The first sentence of the amendment provides for a unified national citizenship and thereby directly contradicts the Court's assertion in *Barron* that state citizenship and national citizenship are separate affiliations. The second sentence, in articulating both the **due process clause** and the **equal protection clause**, states flatly that *all* persons enjoy the same civil liberties and rights, which the states cannot deny "without due process of law" (that is, without following reasonable, legally established procedures), and which the states must apply equally to everyone. To the modern reader this

Fourteenth Amendment: Section 1

All persons born or naturalized in the United States and subject to the jurisdiction thereof, are citizens of the United States and of the State wherein they reside. No State shall make or enforce any law which shall abridge the *privileges or immunities* of citizens of the United States; nor shall any State deprive any person of life, liberty, or property, without *due process of law;* nor deny to any person within its jurisdiction the *equal protection of the laws* [emphasis added].

language seems plainly to say that states cannot violate the Bill of Rights, but in 1868 this broad interpretation of the Fourteenth Amendment continued to elude most readers—at least those on the Supreme Court.

In 1873 the Court rejected its first opportunity to incorporate the Bill of Rights into the Fourteenth Amendment. In the *Slaughterhouse Cases* a group of disgruntled butchers sued to invalidate a New Orleans ordinance that gave a single company a monopoly over all slaughterhouse business.[10] They based their appeal on the Fourteenth Amendment, arguing that the monopoly denied them the "privileges and immunities" (that is, the constitutionally protected rights) of citizens. The Court did not agree. By a 5–4 decision it ruled that the monopoly did not violate the Fourteenth Amendment because the amendment was intended to protect black citizens. Moreover, broad application of the amendment to state policy would "fetter and degrade the State governments by subjecting them to the control of Congress." With that decision, the Court effectively short-circuited any future development of the **privileges and immunities clause**; subsequently, lawyers trying to persuade the Court that the Fourteenth Amendment applied to the states targeted the due process provision that this decision did not address. Although plaintiffs in these cases consistently lost their arguments as well, most justices agreed that the due process clause might be construed to protect certain unspecified "fundamental rights."[11]

Some twenty-five years into the twentieth century, the Court gingerly began to incorporate into the Fourteenth Amendment those provisions of the Bill of Rights dealing with personal freedoms.[*] Only gradually, about the same time it was relinquishing its custodianship of laissez-faire capitalism, did the Supreme Court assume guardianship of civil liberties by applying piecemeal the various provisions of the Bill of Rights to state laws and practices (Table 5-1 shows the growth in the civil liberties docket of the Court). Through this process, called **selective incorporation**, civil liberties have been gradually "nationalized" (see Table 5-2). The Supreme Court first incorporated a provision of the Bill of Rights into the Fourteenth Amendment's due process clause in 1897, when it selected for incorporation the Fifth Amendment's ban on taking private property without compensation.

From the 1920s through the 1940s, the Court took up the First Amendment freedoms (speech, press, and religion), which remain the rights most carefully protected. At first, the justices viewed criminal rights as a special class for which incorporation did not apply.[†] But then, in the 1960s, the Court also covered most of the provisions of the Fourth, Fifth, and Sixth Amendments through the due process and equal protection clauses. Today, a third wave of advances in civil liberties may be forming as judges and politicians explore the right to privacy.

The Supreme Court's post-1925 incorporation decisions have served as precedents in guiding lower federal and state courts and, by offering new opportunities for litigation, have generated the dramatic growth in the civil liberties docket of the Court. Yet incorporation

---

[*] Throughout the nineteenth century litigants mostly contested property rights, not personal liberties. As a result, little case law on the subject accumulated.

[†] *Palko v. Connecticut,* 302 U.S. 319 (1937). At the same time, the Court also refused to assume federal jurisdiction over a double jeopardy case, finding that protection against double jeopardy was not as fundamental to "liberty" and "justice" as were the First Amendment guarantees.

TABLE 5-1

The Supreme Court's Civil Liberties Cases: A Major Share of Decisions

Civil Liberties Cases per Term			Civil Liberties Cases per Term		
Year	No.	%	Year	No.	%
1946	33	24	1981	47	32
1947	40	35	1982	54	35
1948	31	26	1983	66	43
1949	25	27	1984	62	44
1950	20	21	1985	69	45
1951	30	33	1986	69	45
1952	30	28	1987	56	39
1953	20	19	1988	59	42
1954	27	29	1989	61	47
1955	19	19	1990	40	35
1956	36	30	1991	38	35
1957	49	39	1992	40	36
1958	37	31	1993	35	40
1959	26	23	1994	30	36
1960	53	41	1995	28	37
1961	30	30	1996	30	37
1962	33	26	1997	31	35
1963	31	24	1998	23	29
1964	30	28	1999	39	53
1965	32	31	2000	32	44
1966	40	36	2001	31	40
1967	53	43	2002	25	34
1968	40	36	2003	35	47
1969	39	36	2004	32	42
1970	52	42	2005	36	45
1971	62	42	2006	26	37
1972	62	41	2007	26	38
1973	53	36	2008	26	34
1974	43	31	2009	35	46
1975	61	40	2010	45	59
1976	55	38	2011	36	54
1977	47	35			
1978	49	37			
1979	63	45			
1980	41	32			

Source: Adapted from Lee Epstein et al., *The Supreme Court Compendium: Data, Decisions, and Developments,* 5th ed. (Washington, DC.: CQ Press, 2012), Table 2-11 and Table 3-8. Updates provided by Lee Epstein.

Notes: In the table the term *civil liberties* encompasses the following issue areas: criminal procedure, First Amendment, due process, privacy, and attorneys. For 1995–2006, the totals on which the percentages are based do not include interstate relations cases. From 1946–1994, the Court heard fifty-five such cases, or an average of about one per term.

TABLE 5-2

Cases Incorporating Provisions of the Bill of Rights into the Due Process Clause of the Fourteenth Amendment

Constitutional Provision	Case	Year
First Amendment		
Freedom of speech and press	*Gitlow v. New York*	1925
Freedom of assembly	*DeJonge v. Oregon*	1937
Freedom of petition	*Hague v. CIO*	1939
Free exercise of religion	*Cantwell v. Connecticut*	1940
Establishment of religion	*Everson v. Board of Education*	1947
Second Amendment		
Right to bear arms	*McDonald v. Chicago*	2010
Fourth Amendment		
Unreasonable search and seizure	*Wolf v. Colorado*	1949
Exclusionary rule	*Mapp v. Ohio*	1961
Fifth Amendment		
Payment of compensation for the taking of private property	*Chicago, Burlington & Quincy R. Co. v. Chicago*	1897
Self-incrimination	*Malloy v. Hogan*	1964
Double jeopardy	*Benton v. Maryland*	1969
When jeopardy attaches	*Crist v. Bretz*	1978
Sixth Amendment		
Public trial	*In re Oliver*	1948
Due notice	*Cole v. Arkansas*	1948
Right to counsel (felonies)	*Gideon v. Wainwright*	1963
Confrontation and cross-examination of adverse witnesses	*Pointer v. Texas*	1965
Speedy trial	*Klopfer v. North Carolina*	1967
Compulsory process to obtain witnesses	*Washington v. Texas*	1967
Jury trial	*Duncan v. Louisiana*	1968
Right to counsel (misdemeanor when jail is possible)	*Argersinger v. Hamlin*	1972
Eighth Amendment		
Cruel and unusual punishment	*Louisiana ex rel. Francis v. Resweber*	1947
Ninth Amendment		
Privacy[a]	*Griswold v. Connecticut*	1965

Source: Adapted from Lee Epstein and Thomas G. Walker, *Constitutional Law for a Changing America: Rights, Liberties, and Justice,* 8th ed. (Washington, DC: CQ Press, 2013), Table 3-1.

a. The word *privacy* does not appear in the Ninth Amendment or anywhere in the text of the Constitution. In *Griswold* several members of the Court viewed the Ninth Amendment as guaranteeing (and incorporating) that right.

has occurred incrementally, case by case. Indeed, some provisions of the Bill of Rights are still not applied to the states: the Third Amendment prohibition against quartering soldiers, the Fifth Amendment provisions concerning grand jury hearings, the Seventh Amendment right to a jury trial in civil cases, and the Eighth Amendment right against excessive bail and fines. The states retain broad discretion in regulating these areas. Nonetheless, the accumulated precedents mean that Madison's vision of the national government as the ultimate guarantor of individual rights has largely been realized.

Judicial Interpretation

The incorporation of Bill of Rights provisions into the Fourteenth Amendment was a historic development in civil liberties, comparable to adoption of the Bill of Rights itself. As we have seen, incorporation occurred not through legislative mandate or the amendment process but through judicial interpretation. Once this was done, the Supreme Court could turn to the more substantive issue of whether particular state policies violated constitutional protections and, if so, what the remedies should be.

Supreme Court justices agree that as jurists they are obligated to interpret the Constitution as objectively as possible. Yet on any particular ruling they frequently disagree—sometimes sharply—over what an "objective" interpretation prescribes. A literalist, finding no language in the Constitution that protects burning of the U.S. flag, might conclude that the Bill of Rights does not defend this act. Another justice might view flag burning as a kind of political expression sufficiently close to speech and deserving of First Amendment protection.

All self-respecting judges believe that when they occupy the bench they must shed all of their personal preferences, ideologies, and partisanship. But evidence reveals that the personal and political ideologies of the nine justices on the Supreme Court are evident in almost every decision. Consequently, as justices come and go from the Court, judicial doctrine may change. Nativity scenes deemed objectionable and removed one Christmas may pass constitutional scrutiny and be reinstalled the next. Students of jurisprudence have long accepted that justices, like members of Congress and presidents, can be accurately classified as liberals and conservatives. As a result, trends in civil liberties tend to reflect the shifting ideological composition of the Court (see Figure 5-1).

The reality that justices do follow their ideological beliefs has the advantage of predictability, much appreciated by presidents who, in nominating these life-tenure officeholders, seek candidates who would continue to implement the president's political views, as if they were dutiful delegates, long after the president leaves office. By selecting and confirming nominees whose political values agree with their own, the White House and the Senate can seek to influence the course of judicial policy. Far from undermining democratic responsibility, judicial ideology allows elected officeholders to keep the judiciary from straying too far from the majority opinion in the nation.

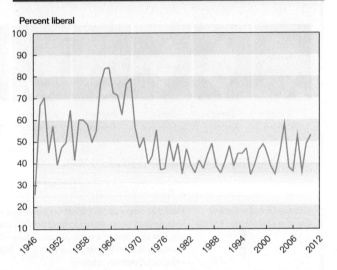

Figure 5-1 The Supreme Court's Shifting Ideology on Civil Liberties Cases

Percent liberal

Source: Adapted from Lee Epstein et al., *The Supreme Court Compendium: Data, Decisions, and Developments,* 5th ed. (Washington, DC: CQ Press, 2012), Table 3-8.

For example, the Supreme Court shifted in a conservative direction shortly after Republican Richard Nixon, elected president in 1968, started filling Court vacancies, and the trend continued even after he left office. Until Democratic president Bill Clinton made his first appointment in 1993, every justice was a Republican nominee. Chapter 9 examines this and other control mechanisms available to the elected branches to keep judicial policy from diverging sharply and potentially creating a constitutional crisis. Nowhere is this danger greater than in the delicate area of civil liberties, with its often polarizing effects on public opinion and its reliance on the Supreme Court to set national policy. (See Table 5-3 for cases in which the Roberts Court has, in decisions often with a bare majority of five justices, defined civil liberties for Americans.)

Major versus Peripheral Rights

This chapter focuses on the major rights in the Bill of Rights—that is, those that have been litigated heavily and developed in detail by the Supreme Court over the past two centuries. However, the rights given detailed treatment in this chapter are not the *only* rights in the Bill of Rights. There are other, more peripheral rights—meaning that their parameters have not been fully developed by the Supreme Court. These more peripheral rights include, for example, the right of assembly under the First Amendment and the Fifth Amendment's protection against having private property taken by the government without just compensation (known as the "takings clause").

TABLE 5-3

The Roberts Court: Five Justices Create a Conservative Tilt on Civil Liberties

| Ruth Bader Ginsburg | Elena Kagan | Sonia Sotomayor | Stephen Breyer | Anthony Kennedy | John G. Roberts Jr. | Samuel Alito | Antonin Scalia | Clarence Thomas |

5–4 Decisions* with Justices Alito, Kennedy, Roberts, Scalia, and Thomas Forming the Majority

Decision	Why the Decision Can Be Labeled "Conservative"
Citizens United v. Federal Election Commission (2010)	Held that corporations cannot be prohibited from using their general treasury funds to make independent expenditures to fund political speech, including speech that expressly advocates for the election or defeat of a particular candidate. Although labor unions benefit from this decision as well, the ruling is seen by many as a victory for "big business" and its influence on elections, at the expense of ordinary citizens.
Morse v. Frederick (2007)	Held that schools may prohibit student expression that can be interpreted as advocating illegal drug use. This decision tightened limits on student speech in public schools and moved further away from the Court's high-water mark of protection of student speech in *Tinker v. Des Moines*.
District of Columbia v. Heller (2008); *McDonald v. Chicago* (2010)	The Court in *Heller* held that the right "to keep and bear Arms" in the Second Amendment is an individual right not limited to service in a militia, and struck down Washington, DC's absolute ban on handguns. In *McDonald,* the Court held (through the doctrine of incorporation) that state and local governments were bound by the Second Amendment's restrictions, and therefore struck down a law in Chicago banning handguns. Both decisions were seen as a major defeat for gun control advocates.
Berghuis v. Thompkins (2010)	Held that a suspect must *unambiguously* waive his right to remain silent. In *Berghuis*, a suspect had remained mostly silent (with the exception of a few responses such as "yeah" or "no") for almost *three hours* of police questioning. However, near the end of those three hours, he responded to a question with an incriminating answer. The Court held that the suspect had thereby waived his right to remain silent under *Miranda v. Arizona*; in other words, his silence for the almost three hours prior to his incriminating statement did *not* count as an unambiguous invocation of his right to remain silent.
Gonzales v. Carhart (2007)	Upheld the nationwide ban on partial-birth abortions, saying the law that went into effect in 2003 does not violate a woman's constitutional right to an abortion. This decision limits the right to have an abortion as established in *Roe v. Wade*.

Note: Justice David Souter participated in the decisions during the 2007 and 2008 terms; his replacement, Sonia Sotomayor, in the 2010 decisions.

* In *Morse v. Frederick*, Justice Breyer did not join the *opinion* of the Court, but he did concur *in part* in the ultimate *judgment* of the Court. Justice Breyer argued that the Court could and should have decided the case on grounds other than First Amendment issues.

FREEDOM OF SPEECH

Amendment I: *Congress shall make no law . . .*
abridging the freedom of speech.

Freedom of speech is essential to representative government and the exercise of individual autonomy. But what exactly constitutes legitimate expression? And how does one balance free speech against other rights and claims?

Generally speaking, the Supreme Court has given a high level of protection to speech that is expressly political. However, there are limits to even this kind of speech. One of the most useful ways to make sense of the Court's free speech jurisprudence is to consider major categories of speech that are *excluded* from First Amendment protection. The sections that follow focus on two of the most controversial categories: speech that advocates illegal action and obscenity.

Speech that Advocates Illegal Activity

By the end of World War I in 1918, more than thirty states had enacted sedition laws aimed at pacifists, socialists, and communists—laws that forbade the advocacy of violence or other "unlawful" means to change the government (also known as "subversive" speech). Although the Court would wait until the *Gitlow* case in 1925 (discussed below) to incorporate the free speech clause of the First Amendment, it did seek to define the degree to which the *federal* government could regulate subversive speech. That opportunity arose in the 1919 case *Schenck v. United States*.[15] In mailings to men eligible for the military draft, Charles Schenck, general secretary of the Socialist Party in Philadelphia, argued that World War I was immoral; he urged draftees to resist. Schenck was convicted under the Espionage Act of 1917 for attempting to foment disloyalty and mutiny in the armed forces during time of war. Writing for a unanimous Court, Justice Oliver Wendell Holmes declared,

> The most stringent protection of free speech would not protect a man in falsely shouting fire in a theater and causing panic. . . . The question in every case is whether the words used are in such circumstances and are of such a nature as to create a *clear and present danger* that they will bring about the substantive evils that Congress has a right to prevent [emphasis added].

According to this legal test, if the government is unable to show that particular words demonstrate a "clear and present danger," the words are protected. The federal judiciary widely adopted Holmes's **clear and present danger test** to distinguish protected from unprotected expression. But the test did not ensure decisions that favored individual freedom. In Schenck's case, the Court ruled that his circulars did in fact constitute a legitimate danger, and affirmed his jail sentence.

In 1925 the Court finally decided that the First Amendment free speech clause applied to the actions of *state* governments.[16] The case was brought to the Court by Benjamin Gitlow, the leader of a radical faction of the Socialist Party who was arrested in New York City at the height of the Red Scare. Charged with advocating "criminal anarchy" through organized labor strikes, Gitlow was found guilty in a New York State court. In its review of his case, the

THE SUPREME COURT'S HISTORY OF PROTECTING UNPOPULAR SPEECH

politics to policy

In 1969 the Supreme Court ruled that freedom of speech allowed high school students in Des Moines, Iowa, to wear black armbands to school to express their opposition to the Vietnam War.[12] War protesters also began burning and otherwise desecrating the American flag. Court decisions protecting these highly unpopular acts soon followed. The defendant in *Texas v. Johnson* (1989) was a protester who burned an American flag outside of the 1984 Republican National Convention in Dallas, Texas.[13] Justice William Brennan, writing for the Court in a 5–4 decision, held that "if there is a bedrock principle underlying the First Amendment, it is that the Government may not prohibit the expression of an idea simply because society finds the idea itself offensive or disagreeable." The Court deemed the burning of the flag to be an expression of a political idea, and thus it was constitutionally sanctioned.

Shortly after the *Texas v. Johnson* decision, public opinion polls found that two-thirds of the American public favored a constitutional amendment protecting the flag. In response, Congress promptly enacted the Flag Protection Act of 1989, which, in less than a year, the Supreme Court struck down as unconstitutional.[14] The House of Representatives annually passes a resolution calling for a constitutional amendment prohibiting flag burning. On each occasion, the measure has failed in the Senate.

More recently, the Court considered the case of *Snyder v. Phelps*, in which members of the Westboro Baptist Church in Topeka, Kansas (led by Fred Phelps), protested at the funeral of Matthew Snyder, a soldier killed in Iraq. Similar to their messages at other military funerals, church members carried inflammatory signs that said "Thank God for Dead Soldiers," "God Hates Fags," and "You're Going to Hell." Unable to rid himself of this painful memory, Snyder's father sued Phelps, and in 2007 a Maryland jury awarded Snyder $10 million in damages for emotional distress and invasion of privacy. Although

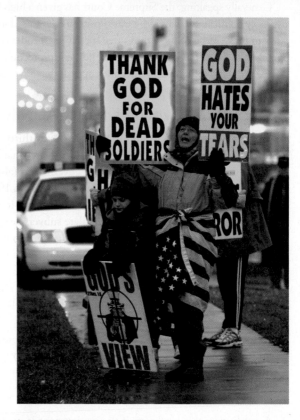

Margie Phelps, right, and other demonstrators from the Westboro Baptist Church in Topeka, Kansas, protest at the site of a memorial service for soldiers killed in combat. The church's protests at memorial services test the Constitution's First Amendment protections of free speech. The Supreme Court subsequently ruled that the protests are fully protected.

the vast majority of Americans no doubt sympathized with Snyder's father, on appeal the Supreme Court—in an 8–1 decision—held that the First Amendment fully protected these protesters' demonstrations at funerals.

Supreme Court ruled that states could not interfere with the "fundamental personal rights and 'liberties'" contained in the First Amendment. The Court thus established the Fourteenth Amendment's jurisdiction over the states, at least when it came to free speech. But, moving cautiously, the Court continued: "the State cannot reasonably be required to measure the danger from every such utterance in the nice balance of a jeweler's scale. A single revolutionary spark may kindle a fire that, smoldering for a time, may burst into a sweeping and destructive conflagration." So, despite the application of the First Amendment free speech clause to the states, Gitlow—like Schenck—went to prison.

Even during World War II and the conflicts that followed, the Court persisted in giving the government the benefit of the doubt during times of crisis. During the Korean War (1950–1953) the Court upheld the Alien Registration Act of 1940 by affirming the conviction of eleven top members of the American Communist Party for having advocated the violent overthrow of the government. After all, the government could not idly watch traitors hatch a rebellion, the Court argued. Indeed, Chief Justice Fred Vinson, in *Dennis v. United States,* adopted the interpretation of the clear and present danger test put forward by famed lower-court Judge Learned Hand; this interpretation is also known as the **clear and probable danger test**: "In each case [the courts] must ask whether the gravity of the 'evil,' discounted by its probability, justifies such invasion of free speech as is necessary to avoid the danger."[17] Although this test introduced the idea of probability or likelihood into the analysis (which in theory was more likely to protect the speaker), Dennis and his comrades suffered the same fate as Schenck and Gitlow.

Dissenting in *Dennis*, Justice Hugo Black wrote: "There is hope, however, that in calmer times, when present pressures, passions and fears subside, this or some later Court will restore the First Amendment liberties to the high preferred place where they belong in a free society." In 1969—twenty-four years after World War II ended—that is arguably what the Court did in the case of *Brandenburg v. Ohio. Brandenburg* involved not a Socialist or a Communist, but a member of the Ku Klux Klan. He was charged with violating the Ohio criminal syndicalism law, which among other things made it illegal to advocate crime and violence as a means of accomplishing political reform.[18] Brandenburg spoke at a televised rally in which he used racial slurs and warned that if the U.S. government continued to suppress the Caucasian race, "it's possible that there might have to be some revengeance [sic] taken." In a unanimous decision, the Court eschewed the clear and present danger test, and announced a new test: the government cannot forbid "advocacy of the use of force or of law violation" unless the advocacy is "directed to inciting or producing imminent lawless action and is likely to incite or produce such action." Although this formulation acknowledged the time element of the clear and present danger test by using the word *imminent,* it added two important ideas: first, the speaker must have the *intent* to incite others (the "directed to" language); and second, the illegal action must be *likely* to occur. These additions offer more protections to the speaker, by making the government's case harder to prove.

Although it took the Court several decades to settle on the appropriate test for government regulation of speech that advocates illegal activity (and although the test came far too late to protect individuals like Schenck, Gitlow, and Dennis), the *Brandenburg* test stands as an example of the Court's modern tendency to protect speech that the majority of Americans dislike or find offensive. (See the Politics/Policy box, "The Supreme Court's History of Protecting Unpopular Speech," on page 198 for further examples.)

CORPORATE FREE SPEECH

politics to policy

Prior to the Supreme Court's decision in *Citizens United v. Federal Election Commission,* federal law prohibited corporations and unions from using their *general treasury funds* to make direct contributions to candidates. It also prohibited them from using general treasury funds to make *independent expenditures* for speech that expressly advocated either the election or the defeat of a candidate (or speech defined as an "electioneering communication"). However, corporations and unions were allowed to establish political action committees, or PACs, which could receive contributions from individuals within a union or business and use the funds to support candidates and political causes (see Chapter 11).

In a 1990 case, *Austin v. Michigan Chamber of Commerce,* the Court upheld the prohibition on political expenditures by corporations and unions, citing the government's compelling interest in preventing "the corrosive and distorting effects of immense aggregations of wealth that are accumulated with the help of the corporate form and that have little or no correlation to the public's support for the corporation's political ideas."[1]

In 2010, in a 5–4 vote the Court reversed this policy. In *Citizens United,* the majority held that Congress cannot restrict political speech based on the speaker's corporate identity. In other words, Congress cannot single out corporations (and unions) and thereby discriminate on the basis of their identity (i.e., their identity as legal entities instead of individual human beings). The majority viewed the 2002 McCain-Feingold campaign finance law's attempts to regulate the speech of corporations as essentially viewpoint discrimination, based on not liking the *particular* speaker (and, therefore, that particular speaker's message). As a result, the majority held that the federal law at issue violated corporations' and unions' First Amendment rights.

SIPRESS

"If you prick a corporation, does it not bleed? If you tickle it, does it not laugh? If you poison it, does it not die?"

Justice Stevens's impassioned dissent (joined by Justices Breyer, Ginsburg, and Sotomayor) questioned the wisdom of the majority's equating the First Amendment rights of corporations with the First Amendment rights of individuals—a practice that, according to Justice Stevens, ignores the guarded skepticism with which the Framers viewed corporations and the fact that they conceptualized the First Amendment as protecting the free speech of individuals. As Justice Stevens derisively put it, "Under the majority's view, I suppose it may be a First Amendment problem that corporations are not permitted to vote, given that voting is, among other things, a form of speech."[2]

---

1. 494 U.S. 652, 660 (1990).

2. 558 U.S. ___ (2010); dissent at 33–34.

Sexually Explicit Expression

The First Amendment does not protect **obscenity**, whether expressed verbally, graphically, on the Internet, or on the conventional written page. The Supreme Court and law enforcement, however, have had problems defining obscenity and drafting objective standards that enable judges and police to distinguish the merely pornographic (sexually explicit) from the truly obscene. Until the 1950s obscenity was pretty much what local city officials, public librarians, postmasters, and movie censors said it was. In the meantime, the Supreme Court was adhering to an 1870s doctrine that designated as obscene any material inappropriate for children. Such a doctrine, however, required a variety of officials—from librarians to movie censors and even to beat cops—to judge what constituted obscenity. In one famous case in the 1930s, censorship found its way into a U.S. post office where a diligent postal official charged with enforcing the Comstock Act, which banned obscene material from the U.S. mail, presumably read and seized copies of James Joyce's novel *Ulysses,* claiming it contained "obscene" passages.

Despite these restrictive rules and practices, pornography flourished by the 1950s. Those charged with enforcing communities' moral codes were losing the war. Yet civil libertarians, including lawyers in the American Civil Liberties Union, were not happy either; obscenity policy allowed local officials to catch and prosecute the producers and consumers of pornography. Against this contentious backdrop, the Supreme Court reviewed obscenity policy in 1957 and issued a new doctrine in *Roth v. United States.*[19] The majority ruled that a work was obscene if it was "utterly without redeeming social importance" and, "to the average person, applying contemporary **community standards**, the dominant theme of the material, taken as a whole, appeals to prurient interests." With this language, the Court tried to thread its way between the conservative forces calling for tight local regulation of loose morals and the libertarians who sought to banish the concept of "obscenity" from jurisprudence. But every key word in the passage is ambiguous and subject to lenient or restrictive interpretation. Who decides the tastes of the "average person"? Which community's "standards"—a town's, a state's, or the nation's—should be applied? How much obscene material may a work contain before it "dominates" the work's theme? And how does one begin to define "prurient" in a way that would offer clear guidelines to those charged with enforcing obscenity laws?

Only as the Court answered these questions in later rulings did the full extent of the libertarian victory become clear. One of the most important follow-up decisions defined "community standards" as national standards, which is itself so vague that almost nothing could be deemed obscene.[20] Answers or not, these rulings propelled all federal, state, and local efforts to define and regulate pornography into federal court.

During the early 1970s an increasingly conservative Supreme Court began retrenching the "anything goes" doctrine of the 1960s. The reasons for the change in judicial policy came out of the changing political forces in Washington. Within five months of his inauguration in 1969, Republican Richard Nixon had made the first of the four Supreme Court appointments that would become available over the next two years. By 1973 the reconstituted Court was ready to formulate clearer and more stringent doctrine (and perhaps lighten its caseload). In the case of *Miller v. California* the Court shifted primary authority for obscenity policy back to the state—and, implicitly, to local—governments.[21] It reformulated the standard for obscenity: governments could ban and otherwise regulate those materials "which, taken as a whole, appeal to the prurient interest in sex, which portray sexual conduct in a patently offensive way, and which, taken as a whole, do not have serious literary, artistic, political or scientific value."

In the years since *Miller* many commentators, including members of the Court, have argued that this test still fails to offer adequate guidelines. Indeed, it remains unclear whether it improves upon Justice Potter Stewart's 1964 "I know it when I see it" definition of obscenity.[22] Yet returning the issue to the state level has greatly strengthened local authorities' hands in regulating a variety of sex purveyors such as massage parlors, topless bars, and pornographic book and video stores. And delegation to the states helped the Court clear its docket. Since adoption of *Miller* as its prevailing doctrine, the Court has decided less than a quarter of its obscenity cases in favor of First Amendment claims.[23]

Overall, then, the Court has struggled for decades to define obscenity in a way that balances individual liberty with prevailing norms of public decency and fosters consistent administration. This task might be impossible, especially with the onslaught of new media, such as the Internet. How can local standards apply when anyone can go to the local library and instantaneously call up on a computer a pornographic video from Copenhagen? The problem of the Internet has played out over the last decade in a back-and-forth between Congress and the Court. In 1996, Congress passed the Communications Decency Act, criminalizing the "indecent" and "patently offensive" online transmission of sexual materials accessible by children. However, in 1997, the Court struck it down, finding that in trying to protect youngsters from obscenity, the "vaguely worded" law would stifle adult access to protected speech.[24] In an attempt to remedy these deficiencies, Congress and President Clinton responded in 1998 with the Child Online Protection Act, which required websites to request some form of adult identification, such as a credit card, before offering their obscene or merely pornographic products. However, in a 5–4 ruling in 2004, the Supreme Court upheld a lower federal court's decision to issue a preliminary injunction barring enforcement of the act until after trial on its constitutionality. That came in 2008 when an appeals court held that the act was unconstitutional because, while the government has a compelling interest in protecting children, the provisions of the act were not *narrowly tailored* to that interest and certain provisions were impermissibly overbroad and vague. In refusing to hear the government's appeal, the Supreme Court essentially voided the law.

Despite these rebukes to Congress, the Court upheld the Children's Internet Protection Act of 2000, which, among other things, cut federal funding for public libraries that failed to implement Internet-filtering technology. The Supreme Court found this version more acceptable by a surprisingly clear-cut 6–3 majority.* Some justices reasoned that the censorship was modest in that libraries could remove the filter at the request of adult patrons. Moreover, libraries were not forced to participate; only if they accepted federal subsidies for their Internet services would the law apply. Still, given the ubiquity of the Internet, the constant concern of protecting children, and the primacy given to First

---

* *United States v. American Library Association,* 539 U.S. 194 (2003).

Amendment rights by the Court, this negotiation between Congress and the Court likely will continue.[*]

FREEDOM OF THE PRESS

Amendment I: *Congress shall make no law . . . abridging the freedom . . . of the press.*

An independent press is indispensable in maintaining a representative democracy. Without reliable information about the performance of officeholders, citizens would be hard-pressed to monitor their elected agents. Without the news media, politicians would find it difficult to communicate with their constituents and to keep an eye on each other. The role of the news media is so critical, in fact, we devote a full chapter to this "fourth branch" of government (see Chapter 14). The laws and judicial policy regulating the modern news media reflect the sweeping language of the First Amendment. We will take up the privacy of news sources, government censorship, and publication of classified information in Chapter 14. Here we consider conflicts between press freedom and individuals' privacy and defendant rights.

The Sixth Amendment guarantees that "the accused shall enjoy the right to . . . an impartial jury of the State." The importance of an impartial jury is obvious. As for a public trial, the history of the concept has less to do with prosecuting criminals than with preventing law enforcement officials from meting out arbitrary justice. By exposing the judicial process to public scrutiny, and, by implication, the press, the Framers intended to keep police, judges, and prosecutors in check.

In one famous trial, however, public scrutiny led to public chaos that threatened the defendant's right to a fair hearing. In 1954 Ohio osteopath Samuel Sheppard (whose case inspired the long-running television series and movie *The Fugitive*) was convicted of murdering his wife. His trial attracted almost as much news coverage as the O. J. Simpson trial some forty years later. Yet the Simpson trial, however tumultuous, was a model of judicial and press decorum compared with the Sheppard proceedings. The testimony of witnesses could not be heard at times because of the din from a courtroom packed with reporters. Moreover, the jurors, who were not sequestered, were exposed to the media circus throughout the trial. Order was eventually restored, but only years after Sheppard's imprisonment: in 1966 the Supreme Court found that the "carnival atmosphere" surrounding the trial had undermined Sheppard's right to a fair day in court, and it reversed his conviction.[25]

---

[*] Other recent examples of this negotiation are the cases of *Ashcroft v. Free Speech Coalition*, 535 U.S. 234 (2002), and *United States v. Williams*, 553 U.S. 285 (2008). In the first case, the Court struck down provisions of the Child Pornography Prevention Act of 1996 that included in the definition of child pornography computer-generated or virtual images of children (as opposed to actual images of real children). However, in the latter case, the Court upheld a provision of the PROTECT Act (passed in response to the adverse decision in *Free Speech Coalition*) that criminalized the offer to provide (e.g., to advertise or promote) child pornography, even if the images offered were computer-generated and thus not actually child pornography.

Does the *Sheppard* case require a uniform ban on the press in trials involving sensitive issues or famous defendants? Apparently not. In 1982 the Supreme Court overturned a Massachusetts law that excluded the public from trials of sex crimes involving victims under the age of eighteen.[26] Although it conceded the value of protecting an underage victim, the majority argued that the victim's welfare did not justify the mandatory exclusion of the public. Rather, the question of public access should be decided on a case-by-case basis.*

FREEDOM OF RELIGION

Amendment 1: *Congress shall make no law respecting an establishment of religion, or prohibiting the free exercise thereof.*

Although the First Amendment is best known for its free speech guarantees, it actually begins with freedom of religion. Many of the early colonies designated official churches, which believers and nonbelievers alike were forced to attend and support with their taxes (a practice that continued in some states even after independence). And yet, by the Revolution, America already was home to a great variety of religious denominations. In *Federalist* No. 10 Madison identified religious conflict as one of the issues bound to generate factional struggle.† In fact, Virginia's religious fights gave Madison the insight that factional conflict could provide a solid foundation for democracy. One of Madison's favorite observations on this score came from Voltaire: "If one religion only were allowed in England, the government would possibly be arbitrary; if there were but two, the people would cut each other's throats; but, as there are such a multitude, they all live happy and in peace."[27]

The religious freedom provision of the First Amendment prohibits Congress from passing any legislation "respecting an *establishment* of religion, or prohibiting the *free exercise* thereof" (emphasis added). But like the rest of the amendment, the **establishment of religion clause** and the **free exercise clause** at first applied only to actions of the federal government. In fact, some states retained laws discriminating against particular religions for years after the Bill of Rights was added to the Constitution.

Madison and Jefferson both subscribed to the frequently stated view that the First Amendment erects "a wall of separation" between church and state.‡ But theirs was merely one interpretation. Separation is not mentioned in the Constitution itself, and it has not been followed consistently by Congress or the Court. Nor can it be in many instances. Indeed, the Court has argued that tensions between the free exercise and establishment clauses may allow government to support religious institutions in various ways.

---

*A similar strain of judicial reasoning crops up in libel doctrine examined in Chapter 14.

†In private correspondence with Jefferson, Madison stated precisely the same argument in favor of religious diversity that he later would offer for factions. By letting a thousand denominations bloom, he reasoned, none would attract sufficient popular support to dominate the others.

‡Jefferson referred to a "wall of separation" between church and state in an 1802 letter written to the Danbury Baptist Association.

Establishment

Because the national government rarely had occasion to subsidize religious institutions or their ancillary activities during the nineteenth century, the first real establishment of religion decision did not come until 1899, when the Supreme Court allowed the federal government to subsidize a Catholic hospital that was open to all patients.[28] In 1947 the Supreme Court applied the due process clause to the establishment provision and thereby placed the states under the same restraints as those limiting the federal government.[29] As the Court entered this field of state policy, it found some states subsidizing parochial schools and others offering religious training in public schools. A 1960 survey of school districts revealed that 77 percent of schools in the South and 68 percent in the East were conducting Bible readings.[30] And throughout the nation most students accompanied the Pledge of Allegiance to the American flag with a prayer.

THE LEMON TEST. Over the years, most of the controversial policies triggering establishment arguments have concerned the various ways states have subsidized private schools. Tuition grants, textbooks, and school buses have all had their day in court. The most far-reaching of these cases was *Lemon v. Kurtzman* (1971), in which the Court specified three conditions every state law must satisfy to avoid running afoul of the establishment prohibition:[31]

1. The statute in question "must have a secular legislative purpose," such as remedial education.

2. The statute's "primary effect must be one that neither advances nor inhibits religion."

3. The statute must not foster "an excessive government entanglement with religion."

If any of these conditions are violated, the policy fails the *Lemon* **test**. The Court was trying mightily to construct clear doctrine, but with highly subjective criteria such as "primary" and "excessive" it succeeded better perhaps in describing how justices thought these issues through than in identifying to the states those policies that would satisfy the Court's interpretation of the "establishment" clause.

The problems inherent in applying *Lemon* soon became evident in the highly inconsistent decisions that followed its adoption. For example, sometimes the federal courts applied the test to dismantle nativity scenes on public property; at other times judges enlisted the same guidelines to approve official displays of nativity scenes as a celebration of the historic origins of Christmas.[32] The Supreme Court viewed prayers at school football games and convocation exercises as clear violations of the Constitution, but had no problem with the devotions that begin each day's business in Congress. In the judgment of one constitutional scholar, the vague, three-pronged *Lemon* test inspired judges to engage in reasoning "that would glaze the minds of medieval scholastics."[33]

TESTING A POLICY'S "NEUTRALITY." By the 1990s the Lemon test was fading from establishment decisions as the justices increasingly tested a policy's "neutrality." They used the **neutrality test** not so much to prevent favoritism among religious groups as to root out policies that preferred religious groups generally over nonreligious groups engaged in a similar activity. Tax credits for religious school tuition were permissible if they also were available for secular, private instruction. Religious organizations could meet on public school property as long as they observed the same access rules governing any other school club.

In 1994 the Supreme Court applied the emerging neutrality doctrine in *Board of Education of Kiryas Joel Village School District v. Grumet.*[34] A sect of Orthodox Jews in upstate New York persuaded the state legislature to carve out a new, publicly financed school district that would include only their community. Since students from that district who had no special needs already attended a private religious school, the new district would offer only special education classes for the community's disabled children. The Court ruled, however, that creation of this school district breached the rule of neutrality and was thus unconstitutional: "the district's creation ran uniquely counter to state practice, following the lines of a religious community where the customary and neutral principles would not have dictated the same result." Since then the Court has followed its neutrality rule in permitting public funding of mandated special education courses in parochial schools; in allowing state subsidies for some instructional materials in private schools, such as school computers and library resources; and in upholding as constitutional a school voucher program that allowed thousands of Cleveland, Ohio, students to attend religious schools.[35] This last decision in 2002 rekindled a hot political issue championed by President George W. Bush in the 2000 election but left out of his No Child Left Behind legislation in order to garner support for his education reforms. Now that the Court has removed this legal issue, vouchers may find renewed interest in Washington and many state capitals as a way of exposing public education to the discipline of market forces—that is, giving students and their parents the freedom to choose schools.

Just as the neutrality standard appeared to allow a host of subsidies for religious education, a 2004 Supreme Court decision made a critical distinction between funding religious institutions for their secular activities and funding religious training. The issue involved a college student in Washington State who received a state scholarship to help finance his undergraduate education. After he declared his intention to major in religious studies designed to train him to become a minister, however, the state withdrew the scholarship. This was standard practice in thirty-seven states at the time, and in a 7–2 opinion the Court found the state's decision appropriate.[36]

Although the Court continues to sustain the neutrality standard as the governing establishment doctrine, some question whether it has achieved the intended result. Critics charge that the Court has dismantled the chief barrier to expanded public subsidies for church-sponsored education, which some states have been eager to provide. Voters witnessed its door-opening effect when Republican candidate George W. Bush proposed during the 2000 campaign to federally fund "faith-based" social service programs. Bush couched his plan, which even won a tepid endorsement from his Democratic opponent, Al Gore, on the principle of neutrality, saying that the initiative would permit federal grants to church-affiliated social services and standardize eligibility requirements for all recipients.* A few years ago the prevailing *Lemon* test would have cast such a shadow over the constitutionality of such a policy that it probably would not have been seriously promoted by the president or deliberated by Congress.[37]

---

* Proving more controversial than screening of recipients was a Bush administration proposal in 2005 to allow religious organizations to base employment decisions on religion and for those employed to administer the federally subsidized programs.

Inspired by Cecil B. DeMille's 1956 film *The Ten Commandments*, the Fraternal Order of Eagles placed about two hundred of these granite structures at courthouses and other governmental buildings around the country. After four decades, these mostly ignored monoliths suddenly fueled controversy across the country as communities responded to a lower federal court ruling that the monuments were unconstitutional. In Texas, the ruling was ignored, landing this Austin monument in a Supreme Court case. The Supreme Court, in a fractured 4–1–4 decision (Justice Stephen Breyer concurred in the judgment but did not join the Court's opinion, and six of the justices wrote their own concurring or dissenting opinions), upheld the monument, but left little clear guidance for future establishment clause cases; the Court plurality explicitly did not apply the *Lemon* test, and instead relied on the "nature of the monument and our Nation's history." On the same day the Texas decision was handed down, the Court held 5–4 in a different case that displays of the Ten Commandments in county courthouses violated the establishment clause. Ironically, a marble statue of Moses holding these tablets adorns the façade of the U.S. Supreme Court building.

School Prayer and Bible Reading

None of the establishment issues has aroused more enduring enmity among religious conservatives than the Supreme Court doctrine banning prayer and Bible readings in public schools. This issue is, arguably, the only real wall separating church and state not yet breached by the Supreme Court. In *Engel v. Vitale* (1962) the Court ruled the following New York State–composed prayer unconstitutional: "Almighty God, we acknowledge our dependence on Thee, and we beg thy blessings upon us, our parents, our teachers, and our country."[38] The next year it invalidated Bible readings in public schools.[39]

Over the years these decisions and the later ones that bolstered them have angered many Americans. Indeed, neither a majority of the public nor those politicians who periodically ask for people's votes have ever been won over to the Supreme Court's point of view (see Figure 5-2). Congress has periodically considered a constitutional amendment allowing school prayer, most recently in 1998. Each time, however, proponents have attracted majority support in Congress but have failed to win the two-thirds support necessary to send an amendment to the states.[40]

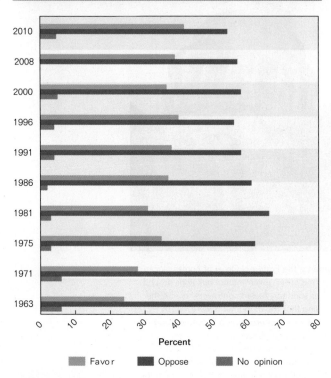

Figure 5-2 Americans' Disagreement with the Supreme Court on School Prayer

Percent

■ Favor   ■ Oppose   ■ No opinion

Sources: Gallup poll 1963, 1971; ABC News/*Washington Post* survey 1981, 1985 (September); all others, General Social Survey, National Opinion Research Center, University of Chicago.

Note: Question on school prayer: "The U.S. Supreme Court has ruled that no state or local government may require the reading of the Lord's Prayer or Bible verses in public schools. What are your views on this—do you approve or disapprove of the Court ruling?"

In the absence of a national policy alternative, states have continued to pass laws trying to circumvent or accommodate the federal courts, but with no success. In 1985, for example, the Court ruled unconstitutional an Alabama state law that mandated a moment of silence at the beginning of the school day.[41] Seven years later it found invocation and benediction prayers at graduation equally objectionable.[42] Moreover, in a throwback to the days of school desegregation in the 1950s and early 1960s, many local school districts throughout the South have simply ignored the federal courts' instructions on school prayer. Three years after the 1963 unequivocal banning of Bible reading, one study revealed that only one Tennessee school official of the 121 interviewed even bothered to claim compliance with the Court decision.[43] In 1997 a federal district judge found school prayers to pervade school life in Alabama despite the federal courts' efforts to forbid these practices. When the judge appointed a "monitor" to ferret out classroom violations of his order to end prayers, the Alabama governor denounced his action as tantamount to employing "secret police." Nearly 500 of the 636 students in the affected district, as well as students in other states, protested the judge's ban by walking out of class.[44] This is just one example of the judiciary's inability to enforce its own decisions, which is discussed more fully in Chapter 9.

Until recently school prayer seemed to be an exception to the rule that the Court's policy decisions do not stray far beyond the bounds of citizen opinion. In 2001, however, a federal appeals court turned away a challenge to a Virginia law permitting a moment of silence at the start of each class day in the state's high schools. And later in the year, the Supreme Court refused to review the decision, thereby letting it stand as state policy. So although it is safe to assume that these issues will remain contentious and that the judiciary will revisit them frequently, the courts might have found a way to accommodate the states and public opinion without seriously undermining the establishment clause.

Free Exercise

The case law delineating the free exercise doctrine is relatively clear and simple when compared with the tortured history of religious establishment cases. The doctrine's incorporation into the Fourteenth Amendment began on a spring day in 1938, when the Cantwells, a family of Jehovah's Witnesses, drove into New Haven, Connecticut, to proselytize their faith and solicit donations. Jehovah's Witnesses believe that each member of the church, as one of its ministers, is obligated to spread the gospel of salvation. Some local residents, however, objected to the Witnesses' intrusion on their privacy and called the police, who arrested the Cantwells for soliciting money door-to-door without a permit.

Ruling on this case in 1940, the Supreme Court decided for the first time that First Amendment protections of free exercise of religion were incorporated in the "fundamental concept of liberty embodied" in the Fourteenth Amendment. Connecticut's regulation of financial solicitation by religious groups, the Court ruled, represented an unconstitutional "censoring" of religion.*

What makes many free exercise cases difficult is that rarely is a particular religious practice specifically targeted by a law. Instead, many generally applicable laws—laws that are passed to solve some general societal problem, and are applied to everyone—interfere with some group's religious practice (such as rules requiring compulsory education up to a certain age). For years, when the Court was confronted with these situations, it generally asked whether the government had a compelling interest and then attempted to balance that interest against the degree of infringement on the individual's free exercise of religion.

This all changed with the Court's decision in *Employment Division v. Smith* (1990), involving two Native American church members who were dismissed from their drug coun-seling jobs for ingesting peyote (a hallucinogenic derived from cactus) as part of a religious ceremony.[45] When the state of Oregon denied their request for unemployment benefits, the church members sued the state for infringing on their free exercise of religion. In a surprising 5–4 decision authored by Justice Antonin Scalia, the Court ruled that otherwise valid, neutral laws of general applicability that incidentally impinge on a particular religious practice do not violate the First Amendment's free exercise clause, period; no compelling governmental inter-est need be shown. As discussed earlier in the chapter, Congress responded by passing the Religious Freedom Restoration Act, part of which has been upheld by the Court, and part of which has been found unconstitutional.

Still, as the Court reiterated in 1993, if a law is *not* neutral (in other words, if the law targets a specific religious practice), "it is unvalid unless it is justified by a compelling interest and is narrowly tailored to advance that interest."[46] As a result, the Court struck down a Hialeah, Florida, city ordinance after determining that the real purpose of the law was to stop the animal sacrifice performed by a Santeria church as part of a religious rite.

Both the free exercise and establishment issues spark competing rights claims that require careful balancing from courts. The problems are rooted in the language of the First Amendment. Does "free exercise" extend to behavior that imposes costs on the larger community—whether it be drug use, proselytizing, or disregard of local zoning ordinances? Does the prohibition against establishing a state religion cover moments of silence, church-sponsored school clubs, or overtly religious Christmas displays? As the Supreme Court's

---

* *Cantwell v. Connecticut*, 310 U.S. 296 (1940). The Court concluded that, "in spite of the probability of excesses and abuses, [religious] liberties are, in the long view, essential to enlightened opinion and right conduct on the part of citizens of a democracy." See Richard C. Cortner, *The Supreme Court and the Second Bill of Rights* (Madison: University of Wisconsin Press, 1981), 99–108, for a thoughtful review of this case.

wavering decisions reveal so clearly, there is no single "correct" answer to the questions raised by the First Amendment's guarantee of religious freedom. The courts, politicians, and public, then, have ample room to decide for themselves and thus disagree.

GUN RIGHTS

Amendment II: *"[a] well regulated Militia, being necessary to the security of a free State, the right of the people to keep and bear Arms, shall not be infringed."*

Until recently, the Second Amendment could have been placed in the category of peripheral rights—not because the right to own a gun is less important to many Americans than rights such as free speech, but because for over two hundred years, the Supreme Court interpreted the above clause as a collective good rather than a personal freedom. Easily the Second Amendment presents the most ambiguous language in the Bill of Rights. When Congress debated this amendment, the Revolution against the autocratic British regime was still a fresh memory. Indeed, the representatives expanded on this theme in the historically inconsequential Third Amendment banning the government from commandeering private homes to garrison troops. Most historians and judicial scholars have read the congressional deliberations and the wording of the amendment itself as guaranteeing the right of local militias to bear arms—a kind of collective good. What "good" it was intended to provide is somewhat vague. A modern reading and one preferred by pro-gun advocates has it represent the people's ultimate check against government tyranny. Yet a careful reading of the history suggests that the "State" refers actually to states' right to maintain a militia (a forerunner of the national guard) to counter insurrections such as the Whiskey Rebellion.

While the judiciary for decades consistently read the amendment as guaranteeing this limited collective right, this opinion had never wholly become a national consensus. And in fact, over the decades the collective good interpretation had rarely been litigated—perhaps as few as six cases in the first two centuries of the Republic.

Over the years a number of resourceful interest groups and elected officeholders have taken exception to this collective good interpretation. The National Rifle Association and others vigorously advanced the belief that the amendment guarantees an *individual right* to own a gun. Until 2008, the last word from the Court dated to 1939 in *United States v. Miller,* when the justices upheld registration of a sawed-off shotgun, using a rationale that seemed to deny an individual right.

This line of interpretation would change in 2008, however, when the Supreme Court issued its most important Second Amendment ruling to date: *District of Columbia v. Heller.* In a bitterly divided 5–4 opinion split predictably along conservative-liberal lines, the majority explicitly adopted the *individual* right interpretation of the Second Amendment. To do so it rejected the long-standing interpretation that the phrase "to keep and bear Arms" was limited to weapons used in military service.[47] Specifically, the Court held that Washington, DC's absolute prohibition of handguns used for self-defense in the home was unconstitutional under the Second Amendment. Two years later the Court issued another watershed Second Amendment ruling, holding that the Fourteenth Amendment incorporates the Second Amendment right announced in *Heller* to keep and bear arms for the purpose of self-defense.[48]

As a result, the Court struck down a Chicago law that effectively banned handgun possession by almost all private citizens who reside in the city. These two major decisions (with a bare five-member majority, consisting of the Court's conservative justices) have changed the political game when it comes to Second Amendment rights and have shifted the final word on gun rights from Congress, state legislatures, and municipalities to the Supreme Court.

In the short term, what this really means is that the *lower* federal courts are left to define the parameters of Second Amendment rights, without much guidance from the two Supreme Court decisions on the subject. As one appeals court judge mused, "there may or may not be a Second Amendment right in some places beyond the home, but we have no idea what those places are, what the criteria for selecting them should be, what [level] of scrutiny might apply to them, or any one of a number of other questions."[49] Indeed, in two recent decisions, different circuit courts reached very different conclusions concerning the right to carry guns not in the home—but in public, where there is the competing governmental interest in protecting its citizens. The Second Circuit upheld a New York State law that requires a person seeking a permit to carry a concealed weapon in public to demonstrate "proper cause" to do so, while the Seventh Circuit struck down an Illinois law that prohibits most people (with exceptions for law enforcement and hunters) from carrying a loaded, immediately accessible gun in public. It is likely that lower courts will continue to differ on the scope of the Second Amendment, until the Supreme Court decides to hear another gun rights case. By then, if the composition of the Court changes, the 5–4 support for individual gun rights could switch back to 5–4 support for the traditional collective right reading of the Second Amendment.

Even as the unclear judicial backdrop raises questions for politicians as to what gun control policies are available to them, they face even greater uncertainty on the political front. The series of mass killings at Columbine High School, Virginia Tech, Sandy Hook Elementary School, and a half-dozen others over the past decade has fueled a demand for action even as judges rein in policies designed to ward off gun violence. But what policies? In a national survey taken in early 2013, shortly after twenty-six children were killed in Sandy Hook, Connecticut, the Pew Research Center posed to respondents the major proposals for changes in gun control laws. Figure 5-3 reports the

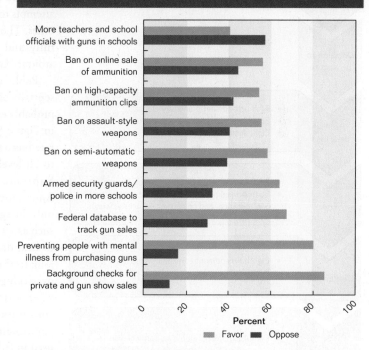

Figure 5-3 Public Support for Gun Policy Proposals

Source: Pew Research Center for the People & the Press, "In Gun Control Debate, Several Options Draw Majority Report," January 14, 2013, www.people-press.org/2013/01/14/in-gun-control-debate-several-options-draw-majority-support/.

Figure 5-4 The American Criminal Justice System

Stage	Governing Amendment
Reported or suspected crime	
Investigation by law enforcement officials	• Fourth Amendment search and seizure rights • Fifth Amendment self-incrimination clause
Arrest	• Sixth Amendment right to counsel
Booking	
Decision to prosecute	
Pretrial hearings	• Fifth Amendment grand jury clause • Sixth Amendment notification clause • Eight Amendment bail clause
Trial	• Fifth Amendment self-incrimination clause • Sixth Amendment speedy and public trial, jury, confrontation, and compulsory process clauses
Sentencing	• Eighth Amendment cruel and unusual punishment clause
Appeals, post-conviction stages	• Fifth Amendment double jeopardy clause

results of this survey. How far down the list new federal laws will extend, if any changes occur at all, remains to be seen.

CRIMINAL RIGHTS

"The history of liberty," remarked Supreme Court Justice Felix Frankfurter, "has largely been the observance of procedural safeguards."[50] Nowhere is this insight more applicable than to criminal rights. In fact, an article on world affairs in today's newspaper is highly likely to confirm Frankfurter's comment. Leaders in nondemocratic societies often throw their adversaries in prison on trumped-up criminal charges as an easy way of quelling the opposition.

But procedural safeguards remove the criminal process from politics and protect the individual citizen from the raw power of the state. The Framers had firsthand experience in this area: Britain had employed criminal statutes and prosecutions in its attempts to tighten its political control over the colonies. The wary drafters of the Bill of Rights carefully and systematically constructed barriers to arbitrary law enforcement.

Public safety and law enforcement are quintessentially state and local responsibilities. This fact probably explains why the Bill of Rights provisions in Figure 5-4 were among the last to be incorporated into the Fourteenth Amendment and applied to all levels of government. Until the 1960s the Supreme Court applied the Fourteenth Amendment's due process clause to defendants only in egregious instances of state misconduct, such as a 1936 case in which a suspect was tortured to near death before he confessed.[51] Clearly, for a long time a majority of the Court wanted to avoid overseeing the state criminal justice system. Even when it did accept the argument that a particular constitutional provision applied to the states, the Court hesitated to impose the rules and standards used in federal criminal cases.

The public has disapproved of the incorporation of criminal rights into the Fourteenth Amendment;

law-abiding citizens and their representatives tend to sympathize more with the victims of crime than with the accused. When a national survey asked Americans in 1972 whether the courts treat criminals "too harshly" or "not harshly enough," two-thirds said the latter. By 1994 this figure had risen to 85 percent, but perhaps reflecting the effects of more restrictive decisions in recent years and longer sentences, it dropped to 78 percent in 1996 and again to 64 percent in 2008.[52] Today criminal rights remain one of the most controversial aspects of modern civil liberties policy.

Elected officeholders have responded to these opinions and controversies by paying closer attention to the legal opinions of the men and women they are appointing and confirming to the federal judiciary. Although criminal rights have not been "unincorporated" or sharply curtailed, vigilant recruitment appears to have brought criminal rights court rulings into closer alignment with the preferences of the American public. As a consequence, Supreme Court decisions have on average become less supportive of criminal rights than they were during the 1960s, when major policy changes occurred in this field (see Figure 5-5). After the September 11 attacks led first to a sweeping new law, the USA PATRIOT Act of 2001, and shortly thereafter to numerous arrests and detentions of suspected terrorists and "enemy combatants," the federal judiciary initially looked away from most of the administration's practices to which it would clearly have objected in normal criminal cases. Since then, the courts have become increasingly circumspect. Since these decisions apply only to criminal rights in a national security context, we take them up separately after reviewing the established case law.

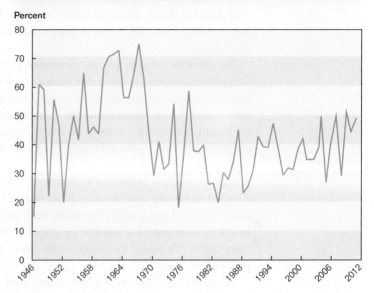

Figure 5-5 The Supreme Court's Criminal Rights Decisions in Favor of the Accused

Source: Lee Epstein et al., *The Supreme Court Compendium: Data, Decisions, and Developments,* 5th ed. (Washington, DC: CQ Press, 2012), Table 3-8.

Fourth Amendment: Illegal Searches and Seizures

Amendment IV: *The right of the people to be secure in their persons, houses, papers, and effects, against unreasonable searches and seizures, shall not be violated, and no Warrants shall issue, but upon probable cause, supported by Oath or affirmation, and particularly describing the place to be searched, and the persons or things to be seized.*

The Fourth Amendment is quite specific and detailed. At times efforts to determine what constitutes illegal searches and seizures and what remedies are available to defendants when police and prosecutors go too far have occupied much of the Supreme Court's time. Attempts to answer these two questions have generated two distinct sets of legal doctrine that continue to evolve with the changing ideological disposition of the Supreme Court and the ever-growing capacity of technology to unobtrusively monitor our behavior.

For centuries the principle was commonly asserted and eventually accepted that unless the police convinced a judge to give them a search warrant, the home was indeed a "castle" from which ordinary citizens could escape government intrusion. Indeed, colonists' vivid memories of British official intrusions at the advent of the Revolution probably guaranteed the Fourth Amendment's place in the Bill of Rights. Until recently the Supreme Court followed this principle—almost literally. The Court deemed out of bounds only police investigations that violated an individual's private *physical space*. Accordingly, the Court ruled that phone wiretaps performed without search warrants were legal and that any evidence obtained in this way could be introduced in a trial. The first real limitations on search and seizure "beyond the domicile" came not from the judiciary but from Congress, which, in setting up rules and administrative structures for regulating broadcast and telephone communications (the federal Communications Act of 1934), added language proscribing most police use of wiretaps.

Not until 1967 did the Supreme Court start expanding the domain of privacy and limiting police use of technology to conduct warrantless searches. Following accepted procedures, FBI agents placed a listening device outside the phone booth used by a suspected bookie, Charles Katz. They were rewarded with incriminating evidence that helped convict Katz. The case did not end there, however, because his lawyers challenged the wiretap, arguing that a telephone booth is a "constitutionally protected area." In *Katz v. United States* the Court agreed, breaking new legal ground in two respects.[53] First, the Court did not limit protections to discovery of physical evidence, and second, it indicated that even searches not involving "physical penetration" of an individual's space might be illegal.

Some have interpreted the *Katz* decision to say that whether the listening device is inside or outside the phone booth does not really matter. But in shattering the pane of glass, the Court opened a vast realm of possibilities, as reflected in the thousands of legal challenges and dozens of Supreme Court decisions that *Katz* spawned. For example, in 2001 the Court ruled that police cannot use a thermal imaging device to perform a blanket sweep of neighborhoods to look for basement marijuana fields.[54] This and other recent decisions have helped to clarify the Court's approach to search and seizure cases. The Court generally allows police searches and seizure of evidence without a warrant under the following circumstances:

- during a valid arrest (after all, the police must be sure those they arrest do not remain armed);
- when searching to ensure that evidence is not lost;
- when searching with the consent of the suspect;

- when the search occurs in "hot pursuit" of a suspect in the act of committing a crime;
- when seizing evidence that is in plain view; and
- when searching places other than residences that the Court has decided merit low protection (such as automobiles).[55]

Still, even the conservative-leaning Roberts Court has protected defendants' Fourth Amendment rights in two recent decisions. In one, the Court ruled unanimously that passengers in automobiles (in addition to the driver) are "seized" for Fourth Amendment purposes during a traffic stop, and can thus challenge the stop; in another, a closely divided Court strengthened Fourth Amendment protections for occupants who share their residences with others.[56]

One of the most difficult questions the Court has faced is what should be done with illegally obtained, incriminating evidence. The Court grappled with this question as early as 1914, when it decided that such material must be excluded from consideration by the trial judge and jury. But as late as 1949 the Court resisted incorporating this **exclusionary rule**, reasoning that if police act improperly, the accused person could complain to police superiors or file a private lawsuit (the main recourse provided by British law). Not until the early 1960s did an increasingly liberal Supreme Court, under the leadership of Chief Justice Earl Warren, turn to incorporation of criminal rights. In *Mapp v. Ohio* (1961) the Court finally extended the exclusionary policy to the states.[57] Unlike its decisions on obscenity or religious establishment, the Court's ruling on the exclusionary rule was clear and simple: improperly obtained evidence could not be admitted at any trial.

The Court majority must have believed it created an absolute standard. Over the next few years it and lower federal courts unflinchingly threw out improperly acquired evidence, no matter how incriminating. The public was outraged. But as membership on the Court became more Republican and more conservative, the seemingly absolute standard set down in *Mapp* became more ambiguous and flexible. In two 1984 cases the Court ruled that if law enforcement officers made a "good faith" effort to abide by established procedures, the evidence retrieved could still be introduced,[58] and in 2006, the Court ruled in a 5–4 decision that the exclusionary rule does not apply to evidence obtained after police failed to follow properly the "knock and announce" rule required by the Fourth Amendment.[59] The Court has also ruled that improperly acquired evidence is admissible if one could reasonably assume it would have been discovered anyway. (In the case on which this ruling was based, the evidence was the body of the murder victim, lying exposed in a field.[60])

While the exclusionary rule has been around for decades, modern technology is introducing new Fourth Amendment issues. In one of our opening cases, we found many courts willing to allow police to search one's cell phone contents incident to an arrest—without a warrant or any assertion that the evidence sought is related to the crime. However, the U.S. Supreme Court provided a small glimmer of hope for privacy-rights advocates in 2012, when it ruled unanimously that the police could not place a GPS tracking device on a suspect's vehicle without a warrant.[61] For four of the justices, the case seemed to turn on the fact that the vehicle was on private property at the time of placement. But others, such as Justice Alito, seemed to be concerned more broadly about expectations of privacy in the digital age, claiming that individuals did not expect that law enforcement would "secretly monitor and catalogue" their movements.[62] One thing is clear: this will not be the last case the Court decides involving modern technology and the gathering of electronic information about individuals. As we discuss later in the chapter, concerns about informational privacy are not limited to the Fourth Amendment context.

Fifth Amendment: Self-Incrimination

Amendment V: *No person . . . shall be compelled . . . to be a witness against himself.*

This protection applies not only to testimony in a trial but also to any statement made by a defendant awaiting trial. The principle against self-incrimination has been a bedrock of American jurisprudence. Only if granted immunity from prosecution, based on requested testimony, can an individual be legally compelled to testify. But what happens when defendants claim they were coerced or tricked into confessing?

PD 47   METROPOLITAN POLICE DEPARTMENT

Rev. 8/73 **WARNING AS TO YOUR RIGHTS**

You are under arrest. Before we ask you any questions, you must understand what your rights are.

You have the right to remain silent. You are not required to say anything to us at any time or to answer any questions. Anything you say can be used against you in court.

You have the right to talk to a lawyer for advice before we question you and to have him with you during questioning.

If you cannot afford a lawyer and want one, a lawyer will be provided for you.

If you want to answer questions now without a lawyer present you will still have the right to stop answering at any time. You also have the right to stop answering at any time until you talk to a lawyer.

WAIVER

1. Have you read or had read to you the warning as to your rights? _____

2. Do you understand these rights? _____

3. Do you wish to answer any questions? _____

4. Are you willing to answer questions without having an attorney present? _____

5. Signature of defendant on line below.

   _____

6. Time _____ Date _____

7. Signature of Officer _____

8. Signature of Witness _____

Reading this statement, or one very much like it, is standard operating procedure for police and sheriffs all across the country when making arrests.

Law enforcement officials have always preferred obtaining confessions to preparing for trials. The alternative, gathering evidence and building a case, can be time consuming and risky. As late as the 1960s, many police departments throughout the nation routinely induced confessions by beatings, threats, and severe deprivations. Moreover, "tricks of the trade," including placing codefendants in a prisoner's dilemma situation, induced some of the accused—even some who were innocent—to confess.

In 1964 the Supreme Court took the first step toward eradicating these abuses by applying the Fifth Amendment to the states.[63] It followed that decision with a controversial ruling two years later in *Miranda v. Arizona,* aimed at protecting suspects from self-incrimination during the critical time between arrest and arraignment.[64] In the *Miranda* case the Warren Court held that police custody is inherently threatening and that confessions obtained during that period can be admitted as evidence only if suspects have been advised of their constitutional right to remain silent. Moreover, defendants must be warned that what they say can be used against them in a trial, informed that they have a right to have a lawyer present for any statements (and that the state will provide an attorney if they cannot afford one), and told of the right to end the interrogation at any time.

In 1968, as part of a more encompassing crime law, Congress enacted legislation that sought to overturn *Miranda* by permitting all demonstrably voluntary confessions. Lawmakers intended the provision to return the judiciary's focus *to* the nature of the confession and *away* from strict adherence to the ***Miranda* rule**. For the next three decades, attorneys general and local prosecutors did not enforce this provision of the law, perhaps believing it to be unconstitutional. Then in 2000 a case involving the provision finally reached the Supreme Court. Arguing that the *Miranda* rule was a fundamental "constitutional principle," the Court held that Congress did not have the authority to change the *Miranda* decision.[65]

This does not mean, however, that the Court lacks the authority to change its own rule. In 2010, the Court issued three different decisions concerning *Miranda* rights, all of which lessen to some degree the protections under *Miranda*. Most significantly, the Court ruled that a suspect being interrogated must *unambiguously* invoke his or her right to remain silent under *Miranda*.

Sixth Amendment: Right to Counsel and Impartial Jury of Peers

Amendment VI: *In all criminal prosecutions, the accused shall . . . have the Assistance of Counsel for his defence.*

Defendants in any American courtroom can take comfort in the Sixth Amendment assurances that they are entitled to "a speedy and public trial, by an impartial jury of the State and district wherein the crime shall have been committed," a "compulsory process for obtaining witnesses in [their] favor," and "the Assistance of Counsel." The protections offered in this amendment have been subject to little controversy.

In 1932 the Supreme Court partially applied the Sixth Amendment to the states when it required them to provide all indigent defendants in capital cases (that is, those potentially involving the death penalty) with a lawyer. Full incorporation, however, had to wait until 1963, when Clarence Earl Gideon won one of the most famous decisions in Court history.[66] Gideon, a drifter, was accused of breaking into a pool hall. Unable to afford a lawyer, he asked the Florida trial judge for representation, but was turned down, convicted, and promptly sent to prison. There he became an inspiration for "prison lawyers" everywhere.

With classic David-versus-Goliath determination, Gideon researched the law and sent to the Supreme Court a handwritten petition claiming that his five-year prison sentence was unconstitutional because he had been too poor to hire an attorney and, as a result, had been required to defend himself.

Upon taking his case, the Court assigned Gideon a first-class attorney (and future Supreme Court justice), Abe Fortas, who successfully argued that Gideon's constitutional right to counsel had been denied. Indeed, the decision in *Gideon v. Wainwright* decreed that anyone charged with a felony must be offered legal representation. Later the Court expanded eligibility to include any defendant whose conviction might result in incarceration.[67]

More recently, the Court clarified that the right to have counsel at all "critical" stages of criminal proceedings includes the plea bargaining process, and extends not only to accepted guilty pleas, but to plea offers that lapse or are rejected. In a 5-4 opinion, Justice Kennedy pointed out that 97 percent of all federal prosecutions and 94 percent of all state prosecutions are the result of guilty pleas, and thus defendants are entitled to the protections of the Sixth Amendment throughout the process.[68]

In many conviction appeals the Sixth Amendment claim has turned from the availability of counsel to the adequacy of the defense that court-appointed attorneys provide. The appeals courts are reluctant to become closely involved with this part of the process, lest they find themselves asked to second-guess the defense whenever a guilty verdict occurs. Nonetheless, beginning with a 1984 case, the Court has prescribed that "counsel has a duty to make reasonable investigations or to make a reasonable decision that makes particular investigations unnecessary."[69] Evidence that the defense failed to perform at a minimal competence level offered the defendant grounds to request retrial. Generally, cases involving the death penalty have received the most careful appellate review.[70]

As for the Sixth Amendment's reference to juries and their procedures, the federal courts have largely allowed the states to determine jury size and whether unanimous agreement is required for conviction. However, the courts have concentrated on whether juries are adequately composed of the defendant's peers. Unrepresentative juries can arise in two ways: the pool of potential jurors is itself unrepresentative, or the selection process is biased. Until the 1960s African Americans in the South were effectively excluded from juries because jury pools were drawn from voter registration lists (see Chapter 4). When federal registrars signed up black voters, however, this discrimination was automatically dismantled.

Potential jurors may be rejected from service either for "cause" (arising from suspected prejudice) or as the target of a peremptory challenge. The latter, a pervasive practice in state and local courts, allows attorneys on both sides to reject a certain number of individuals without having to establish cause. Lawyers, seeking the most sympathetic jury possible, routinely exempt certain types of people depending on the nature of the case and the personal characteristics of the defendant. They may not, however, use their challenges to eliminate jurors on the basis of race or sex.

Eighth Amendment: "Cruel and Unusual" Punishment

> **Amendment VIII:** *Excessive bail shall not be required, nor excessive fines imposed, nor cruel and unusual punishments inflicted.*

The federal judiciary has been reluctant to define the Eighth Amendment's highly subjective phrase **"cruel and unusual,"** a reticence reflected by the Supreme Court in 2004 when it upheld the California "three-strikes" law, which sharply stiffens sentences for three-time offenders.[71] Instead, it has largely limited application of this amendment to death penalty cases. Until the 1970s the federal judiciary rarely intruded in state sentencing laws despite numerous opportunities to do so. Then, in 1972, the Supreme Court issued a stunning 5–4 decision in *Furman v. Georgia.*[72] The legal arm of the National Association for the Advancement of Colored People convincingly argued that the Georgia law allowing juries to determine whether to mete out the death penalty to a convicted murderer had led to large racial disparities in sentencing. African Americans convicted of murdering whites were far more likely to receive the death penalty than were whites convicted of the same crime. A close inspection of the 243-page decision, the longest in Court history, reveals that the majority declaration of the death penalty as "cruel and unusual" was not nearly so secure as it first appeared. Only three justices maintained that the death penalty inherently violates the Bill of Rights. The others who joined the majority took a narrow approach, citing discriminatory practices rather than questioning the death penalty itself as cruel and unusual.

Immediately the federal government and thirty-five states redrafted laws to deal with the Court's objection to Georgia's sentencing procedures. Some states tried to eliminate discrimination by mandating that certain heinous crimes carry an automatic death penalty. But these laws were later rejected under the Eighth Amendment as inherently arbitrary and because they did not allow consideration of mitigating circumstances in sentencing. The solution was found in a new Georgia statute that separated the conviction from the sentencing stage of the trial, allowing juries to weigh the particular crime and defendant and any mitigating and aggravating circumstances. In 1976 the 7–2 majority in *Gregg v. Georgia* proclaimed the new Georgia statute to be a "model" law, and the death penalty ceased to constitute cruel and unusual punishment.[73] Indeed, the Georgia solution appears to have become an acceptable option for the state governments that rewrote sentencing procedures shortly after the *Gregg* decision and for the prosecutors, judges, and juries that implement them. Numerous defendant appeals of faulty trial and sentencing procedures failed to win favor with the Court during the intervening years. However, in 2003 the Court rejected state laws authorizing judges to mete out the death penalty, holding that only juries can do so in deliberations separate from those establishing guilt.[74]

In other cases over the past ten years, the Court has found the following to be cruel and unusual punishment under the Eighth Amendment: the execution of defendants with "mental retardation"; the execution of juveniles; and the execution of a defendant who raped, but did not murder, a child. In addition, in 2009 the Roberts Court (with both Justice Roberts and Justice Kennedy in the majority) ruled that it violated the Eighth Amendment to sentence a juvenile to life in prison without the possibility of parole if the crime did not involve a murder. Despite these rulings from the Supreme Court finding violations of the Eighth Amendment in death penalty cases, more than 1,224 death sentences have been carried out since reinstatement of the death penalty in 1976, and as of October 2009, over 3,000 inmates were sitting on death row. About 38 percent of all executions since 1976 have taken place in Texas alone; its total of 460 executions far surpasses that of any other state. Both the escalation of executions in the mid-1990s and more recently the equally sharp decline (see Figure 5-4) have tracked

Figure 5-6 The Rise and Decline of the Death Penalty

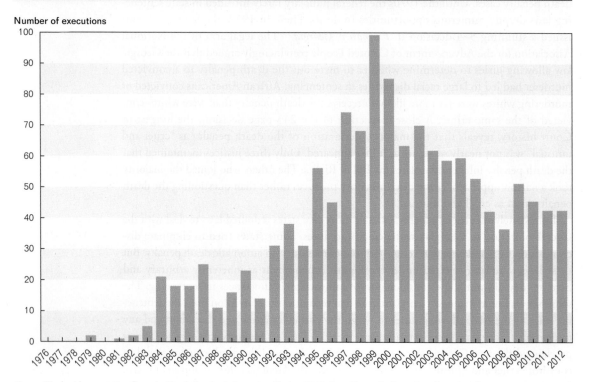

Number of executions

Source: Used with permission from the Death Penalty Information Center, 2013, http://www.deathpenaltyinfo.org/number-executions-state-and-region-1976.

trends in public opinion favoring capital punishment. Where in 1993 national survey respondents preferred the death penalty for murderers over life imprisonment by a 2–1 margin, a 2005 survey found the public evenly divided on this question. Nonetheless, acceptance of capital punishment appears well established both among the public and on the bench.

Time has shown that the rights of the accused are not always easy to appreciate or enforce. Criminal rights almost always trigger precarious balancing between the defendant's interest in fair treatment and the community's interest in punishing the guilty and maintaining social order. When a court frees a guilty person because of some technical glitch in the criminal justice system—such as from an improperly filled-out search warrant or an untimely prosecution—controversy erupts. Perhaps the morass of legal technicalities, as much as the other thorny issues described in this section, account for the delayed incorporation of criminal rights (see Table 5-4). By the late 1940s the Supreme Court had applied to the states the entire First Amendment—as well as the Fourth Amendment (without mandating the exclusionary rule)—but it hesitated until the 1960s to nationalize the remainder of the Bill of Rights.

TABLE 5-4

The Meandering Path of Criminal Rights

	Early	1960s and 1970s	Recent Developments
Search and seizure (Fourth Amendment)	*Wolf v. Colorado* (1949): Fourth Amendment applies to states but exclusionary rule not mandated.	***Mapp v. Ohio*** (1961): Improperly obtained evidence cannot be introduced at trial.	*United States v. Leon* (1984): Exclusionary rule not constitutionally protected but a means to deter police illegality. Allows good faith and inevitable discovery exceptions.
Non–self-incrimination (Fifth Amendment)	*Brown v. Mississippi* (1936): Outlaws confessions extracted by torture.	***Miranda v. Arizona*** (1966): Officers must inform suspects of their rights before interrogation.	*Illinois v. Perkins* (1990): For confessions heard by undercover police, the Court rules: "*Miranda* forbids coercion, not strategic deception."
Right to lawyer (Sixth Amendment)	*Betts v. Brady* (1942): Denies right to lawyer in state prosecutions where special circumstances do not apply.	***Gideon v. Wainwright*** (1963): Reverses *Betts,* guaranteeing all defendants charged with a felony a lawyer at trial.	*Ross v. Moffitt* (1974): Right to counsel is not required for discretionary appeals after conviction.
Double jeopardy (Fifth Amendment)		***Benton v. Maryland*** (1969): Forbids state reindictment of acquitted defendant.	*Heath v. Alabama* (1985): Double jeopardy does not apply across levels of government.
Capital punishment (Eighth Amendment)	*Louisiana ex rel. Francis v. Resweber* (1947): Death penalty not inherently "cruel and unusual" punishment.	***Furman v. Georgia*** (1972): "Arbitrary" sentencing process disallows death penalty.	*Baze v. Rees* (2008): Kentucky's lethal injection protocol (used by almost thirty other states) does not violate the Eighth Amendment.

Note: Cases in **bold** discussed in text.

PRIVACY

A right to privacy, unlike other civil liberties, is not explicitly stated in the Bill of Rights or elsewhere in the Constitution. Indeed, although an implicit "right of privacy" had been postulated by legal jurists as early as the 1890s, the Supreme Court did not explicitly recognize its existence until 1965.

But how could the Court "recognize" as constitutional a right that is nowhere mentioned in the Constitution? In 1965 the Court reasoned in *Griswold v. Connecticut* that Americans' guaranteed rights are not limited to those specifically identified in the Constitution.[75] Indeed, the Ninth Amendment says as much: "The enumeration in the Constitution, of certain rights, shall not be construed to deny or disparage others retained by the people." This amendment opened the door to unstated rights. Moreover, a reasonable reading of other amendments invites privacy into the Constitution's protected liberties. After all, what does the Constitution's guarantee of "liberty" mean if not privacy from state surveillance? Other explicit rights such as freedom of speech and assembly and the prohibitions against self-incrimination and unreasonable search and seizure require some measure of privacy if they are to be secure. These explicitly guaranteed rights form **penumbras**, or implicit zones of protected privacy rights on which the existence of explicit rights depends. For example, freedom of speech and a free press must include not only an individual's right to engage in these activities but also the right to distribute, receive, and read others' views. Without these other rights, the specific rights would be insecure.

Once identified, the right to privacy became subject to all the complexities of interpretation and enforcement associated with other civil liberties. But the overriding question was, in the absence of constitutional standards, what actions and practices are so personal or private that they should be shielded from interference by the government?

Childbearing Choices

The Supreme Court's attentiveness to privacy claims has largely been confined to an important but narrow domain of public policy: reproductive rights. In extending privacy in childbearing choices, the courts began not with abortion but with access to contraceptives. In 1961 Estelle Griswold, executive director of the Planned Parenthood League of Connecticut, opened a Planned Parenthood clinic, which dispensed contraceptives. Three days after the clinic opened, Griswold was arrested for violating an 1879 Connecticut law prohibiting the use of contraceptives. After losing her case in the state courts, the defendant appealed her test case in federal court. Not only did she win, but the Supreme Court decision, *Griswold v. Connecticut,* laid precedents that emboldened feminist and reproductive freedom groups to pursue abortion rights.

In 1972 Justice William Brennan's argument in *Eisenstadt v. Baird* bolstered the efforts of such groups: "[I]f the right of privacy means anything, it is the right of the individual, married or single, to be free from unwanted governmental intrusion into matters so fundamentally affecting a person as the decision to bear or beget a child."[76] One year later, in the landmark abortion rights decision *Roe v. Wade,* a Court majority ruled: "[T]he right of privacy, whether it be founded in the Fourteenth Amendment's concept of liberty . . . or . . . in the Ninth Amendment's reservation of rights to the people, is broad enough to encompass a woman's decision whether or not to terminate her pregnancy."*

Abortion rights in America did not begin with this historic and controversial decision; many states permitted abortion until the late nineteenth century. Moreover, in the ten years leading up to the *Roe* decision, eighteen states either relaxed or repealed their statutes prohibiting abortion. Thus the Court's nationalization in 1973 of a woman's right to terminate her pregnancy ended abortion's varying legality across the states.

This said, *Roe v. Wade* did not completely remove the states from abortion rights policy. This decision established that a woman's decision to end her pregnancy belongs within the protected sphere of privacy, but it did not wholly exempt abortion from government regulation. Rather, the Court ruled that in the interest of the mother's health and the "potential"

---

* But as Justice Byron White wrote in his dissent from the *Roe* decision, "the upshot is that the people and the legislatures of the fifty states are constitutionally disentitled to weigh the relative importance of the continued existence and development of the fetus, on the one hand, against a spectrum of possible impacts on the mother, on the other hand." *Roe v. Wade,* 410 U.S. 113 (1973).

life of the fetus, state governments could regulate abortions from the end of the first trimester of pregnancy to fetus viability (months four through six). Within the final trimester the states could forbid all abortions except those required "for the preservation of the life or health of the mother." In 1992 the Court backed away from the trimester standard, choosing instead the demarcating line of "viability" (which the Court did not define with precision) and substituted a more ambiguous "undue burden" criterion: prior to viability, states cannot ban abortions, but they can impose certain regulations on both the women who seek abortions and the doctors who perform them, as long as those regulations do not pose an "undue burden" on the woman's right to an abortion.[77] Waiting periods, counseling sessions, and parental consent were deemed constitutional as long as they did not place an undue burden on the abortion right.

Although *Planned Parenthood v. Casey* did amend the framework of *Roe*, the Court—in a plurality opinion co-authored by Justice Sandra Day O'Connor—was adamant that the essential holding of *Roe* remained. But a controversial decision in 2007 would call *Roe* into question. In 2003 Congress passed the Partial-Birth Abortion Ban Act, which prohibits very late-stage abortions. Although the Supreme Court in 2000 had struck down a Nebraska law that was almost identical to the federal law, in *Gonzales v. Carhart* (2007), the Court—in a 5–4 opinion authored by Justice Kennedy—accepted the federal limitations, despite the fact that the law did not contain an exception for the health of the mother (which the Court in *Roe* had said was required).[78] Notably absent from the Court that decided *Gonzales* was

now-retired Justice O'Connor, who had been replaced by the more conservative Justice Alito. Although *Roe v. Wade* has yet to be overturned, *Gonzales* may be a signal by the Roberts Court that it is open to doing so. Regardless, the controversy over abortion will continue to overshadow politics at all levels, whether reproductive rights remain largely a federal concern or are returned entirely to the states.

Indeed, abortion politics remains the subject of an intense political debate that takes many forms—confrontational demonstrations by the antiabortion movement, platform fights at presidential nominating conventions, and legislation both extending and voiding the *Roe* decision. Dozens of new state laws adjusting the boundaries of this privacy right (see Table 3-2, page 114) have been enacted and amended over the past decade. For example, at least

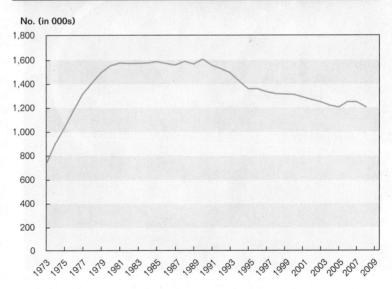

Figure 5-7 Abortions Are a Commonplace but Declining Form of Birth Control

No. (in 000s)

Source: Guttmacher Institute, "Trends in Abortion in the United States, 1973–2008" (New York: Guttmacher Institute, 2011); www.guttmacher.org/presentations/trends.pdf.

Note: By the end of 1970, four states had repealed their antiabortion laws, and eleven states had reformed them.

TAKE A SURVEY

logic.cqpress.com

■ You be the judge
on civil liberties.

ten state legislatures have passed laws requiring a woman seeking an abortion to have an ultrasound before the procedure is performed. Thirty-five years after *Roe,* abortion remains controversial. Every congressional and presidential candidate must declare his or her position on a woman's right to terminate a pregnancy. Confirmation hearings of federal judges invariably raise this issue as well, although the nominees dissimulate to avoid being pinned down in some future decision and, for some, to improve their chances for confirmation. Despite controversy, abortion is now established as a common form of birth control in America. As Figure 5-7 shows, the annual number of abortions has begun to decline, although the reasons are not altogether clear. It may simply reflect the decline of pregnancies among young, unmarried women over the same period.

The Brave New World of Informational Privacy

Although this chapter focuses on the protection of citizens from intrusions on liberty by the government, increasingly, circumstances arise that blur the line between gathering of information by government and that by third parties. The proliferation of e-mail, text messages, GPS technology, cloud computing, and smartphones and an explosion in the number of consumers who are conducting business online lead to concerns about (1) third parties who create and maintain massive online databases and (2) the extent to which the government easily can access that information. For example, employers, credit agencies, health providers, insurance companies, credit card companies, banks, and e-mail

Many users may not even be aware that so much digital information is being gathered when they are online. And, before the General Petreaus extramarital affair scandal in the fall of 2012 came to light, most Americans were unaware of how easy it is for the government to obtain e-mails from providers like Google—e-mails which most people assume are "private."

providers like Google all gather information on users, in ways that may be highly intrusive of individuals' privacy.

So why are the courts not flooded with suits charging the people who control these databases with invasion of privacy? Perhaps the long-standing judicial doctrine that information loses its privacy privilege once conveyed to third parties has discouraged claims. Or perhaps this area of civil liberties has simply failed to attract the kinds of group sponsorship typically needed to make strong cases and sustain them through the judicial system. But the biggest problem with regard to protecting informational privacy is that the law has trouble keeping up with changing technology. For example, the Electronic Communications Privacy Act was passed in 1986, well before most Americans knew what e-mail was. That law allows the government to obtain electronic communications that are over 180 days old without a warrant; only a subpoena is required. The Senate Judiciary Committee—led by Patrick Leahy, one of the authors of the 1986 law—recently approved a bill that would amend the law to give e-mail the same protection as physical documents stored in a person's house.[79] But despite the fact that Leahy expressed concern about the "growing and unwelcome intrusions into our private lives in cyberspace," there is no assurance that the bill will pass (particularly in light of opponents who argue that amending the 1986 law would make it harder for the federal government to gather evidence on alleged terrorists). In addition, even more proactive states such as California—which passed the first-of-its-kind Online Privacy Protection Act in 2003—will likely struggle to keep pace with changing technology. Finally, there is inherent tension between the idea of informational privacy and the reality that so many Americans voluntarily share personal, private details about their lives every day on the Internet. But as Justice Sotomayor stated in her concurrence in the GPS case: "[I]t may be necessary to reconsider the premise that an individual has no reasonable expectation of privacy in information voluntarily disclosed to third parties." In the end, individuals, legislators, and judges will need to reevaluate their ideas of privacy to match the realities of the digital age.

ASSESSING CIVIL LIBERTIES AS PUBLIC POLICY

At first, the nationalization of civil liberties in the Bill of Rights was not a popular idea. Madison's proposal to amend the Constitution to apply them directly to the states was handily defeated in Congress as those members sympathetic with the Antifederalists, who had insisted that civic freedoms be written into the Constitution, explicitly rejected the idea of extending them to the states.

READ MORE

logic.cqpress.com

Review the Supreme Court's civil liberties decisions for the 2013 session.

Only during the twentieth century, and gradually by incorporation, has the Bill of Rights come to be accepted as *national* policy that applies to every level of government. Yet states still formulate the rules that implement many of the rights guaranteed. For example, the Supreme Court allows states to determine the size of juries and level of agreement required to convict in state courts. Similarly, the states are free to decide the legality of physician-assisted suicide and have plenty of room to regulate the availability of abortions.

Civil liberties policy has developed on another front as well, one equally unimagined by its eighteenth-century sponsors. The members of Congress who drafted and deliberated these liberties and the state legislators who ratified them probably had in mind essentially "civic" rights: the right to dissent; to organize opposition; and, in extreme instances, to resist—essential bulwarks against the impulses of any intemperate majorities and tyrannical government officials. As we have seen, these rights have been broadened, in some instances dramatically, to create personal spheres of expression and privacy. This evolution is evident in modern case law on search and seizure, unconventional religious practices, nude dancing, the right to die, abortion, guns and property, and many other issues reviewed in this chapter.

Americans, however, do not see eye to eye on these matters. In fact, modern civil liberties number among the most divisive and unsettled issues facing the nation. None is more contentious than abortion rights. In the years since the 1973 *Roe v. Wade* decision, the issue has surfaced at every level of government, from neighborhood rallies and demonstrations to restrictive amendments in annual appropriations legislation in Congress. At times the intensity of disagreement even spills over into violence directed at the physicians who perform abortions and their clinics. Abortion, together with the other conflicting civil liberties issues on the modern scene—flag burning, school prayer, and assisted suicide, to mention a few—reminds us of the inherent fractious nature of public policy when it collides with personal behavior.

The modern Supreme Court's preeminent role in deciding these policies contributes to their controversy. Once, these issues resided exclusively in the political arena—that is, with state and local governments and with Congress. But as the Supreme Court carved out a larger role in these policies, its insulation from public opinion exposed its decisions to criticism and second-guessing. And, of course, its insulation has allowed it at times to issue highly unpopular decisions, such as its stance on flag burning and, during the 1960s, its restrictions on established law enforcement practices.

How does the image of a small number of unelected, life-tenured justices deciding public policy comport with the principles of democracy? Those who insist that majority rule must prevail in a democracy cannot justify the Court's having any role at all other than duties delegated to it by the democratic (that is, elected) branches of government. Others, however, may accept the authority of a national community to impose limits on itself and future majorities in making certain decisions. The elaborate rules to amend the Constitution are a prime example. Other limits can be found in the Bill of Rights. It removes various personal prerogatives and private behavior from casual government intrusion. The First Amendment opens with "Congress shall make no law . . . ," and the list of proscriptions continues throughout the ten amendments. Madison recognized at the outset that the Supreme Court was well designed to enforce these antimajoritarian rules. The Court's unelected, life-tenured members are well insulated from the "popular passions" that can run roughshod over personal freedoms. Moreover, the explicit prohibitions to congressional action create space for the Court to enter as the Constitution's guardian.

If a national majority wants to ban flag burning, it can wait for new justices to be appointed and hope they are sympathetic with its position, or it can try to pass a constitutional amendment. Both avenues promise a lengthy delay and high transaction costs for the majority with little guarantee of success.

Finally, still others may point out that the majority is not as frustrated in exerting its preferences as it might appear. Supreme Court justices are subject to many of the same social and civic influences as are ordinary citizens, and as these circumstances change, so might justices' opinions—in tandem with those of the citizenry. Two weeks after the September 11 attacks, Justice O'Connor observed without alarm, "We are likely to experience more restrictions on our personal freedom than has ever been the case in our country."[80] That these heightened restrictions may occur and be sanctioned in future judicial policy reflects not so much the compromise of principle in the face of reality as the fact that judicial doctrine includes provisions for balancing these elements. The phrase "compelling government interest," for example, allows evidence to inform doctrine and hence opens the way for doctrine to change with conditions.

Moreover, even though federal judges may not be elected, voters' preferences do not go unheard. While there are notable exceptions such as flag burning and prayer in public schools, Supreme Court policy rarely deviates far from public opinion. Perhaps surprisingly, this is true whether the decision is considered liberal or conservative. For example, in two recent surveys of Americans' constitutional attitudes, 70 percent of respondents said they would *oppose* a state law banning sex between people of the same gender (as did the Supreme Court when it struck down a Texas antisodomy statute in 2003), and 64 percent said that they agreed with *Roe v. Wade,* which established a woman's right to an abortion.[*] At the same time, 74 percent of respondents support banning abortions performed late in the term of a pregnancy, and 76 percent oppose banning ownership of a handgun. Public opinion on these two issues is in line with the Court's decision in 2007 to uphold the federal Partial-Birth Abortion Ban Act of 2003 and with the Court's recent Second Amendment decisions.[†] In sum, the Constitution provides many safeguards to ensure that this institution stays on track with national majorities—and the political branches of government that serve them—and to limit the Court's influence when it fails to do so. Civil liberties policy may consume much of the caseload of today's Supreme Court, but the nine-member Court acts knowing that its words are rarely the last.

Given the absolute language of the Bill of Rights, someone who is unfamiliar with the modern history of civil liberties policy might assume that it is settled policy. As we have seen here, however, civil liberties seem to be constantly changing. When judges come and go, they permit Court ideology to be brought into closer alignment with partisan control of the rest of the government. To the extent that citizens disagree on many of these civil liberties issues, so too will their elected officeholders and, in turn, the judges these politicians appoint. Other, more direct influences on the Court can be found in the efforts of organized interests as they sponsor clients and submit "friend of the court" briefs. And finally, ever-changing technology throws into question (and sometimes into confusion) civil liberties policies based on old realities. All of these forces guarantee that civil liberties policy, far from settled, as the Framers might have envisioned, will be continuously revisited and frequently revised.

TAKE A QUIZ

logic.cqpress.com

Test your knowledge of this chapter.

---

[*] Field Report, Constitutional Attitudes Survey, designed by Stephen Ansolabehere and Nathaniel Persily. Source: Private communication with Nathaniel Persily, November 2010.

[†] See also David G. Savage, "In Court of Public Opinion, U.S. Justices Mostly Get It Right," *Los Angeles Times,* October 16, 2010.

logic.cqpress.com

■ Key Terms ■

clear and present danger test, 197	establishment of religion clause, 204	neutrality test, 205
clear and probable danger test, 199	exclusionary rule, 215	obscenity, 201
community standards, 201	free exercise clause, 204	penumbras, 222
cruel and unusual, 218	incorporation, 190	privileges and immunities
due process clause, 191	*Lemon* test, 205	clause, 192
equal protection clause, 191	*Miranda* rule, 217	selective incorporation, 192

■■■ Suggested Readings ■■■

Carter, Stephen L. *The Culture of Disbelief: How American Law and Politics Trivialize Religious Devotion.* New York: Basic Books, 1993. A thoughtful argument against prevailing Supreme Court doctrine on the separation of church and state.

Hentoff, Nat. *Free Speech for Me . . . But Not for Thee: How the American Left and Right Relentlessly Censor Each Other.* New York: Harper Perennial, 1992. A highly original account of how political groups gain a political advantage through censorship.

Irons, Peter. *The Courage of Their Convictions.* New York: Free Press, 1988. Six case studies, including interviews with defendants who took their cases to the Supreme Court.

Lewis, Anthony. *Freedom for the Thought That We Hate: A Biography of the First Amendment.* New York: Basic Books, 2007. Although on balance Lewis is more comfortable with established free speech doctrine that embraces the marketplace metaphor, he does not consider it sacrosanct. Might hate speech and libel doctrines, among others, impose real cost on society? Once again, Lewis poses serious questions in a style and language appropriate for a general audience.

Winkler, Adam. *Gunfight: The Battle over the Right to Bear Arms in America.* New York: Norton, 2011. Excellent history of the evolution of the National Rifle Association and its role in promoting gun ownership as a personal freedom.

■■■ Review Questions ■■■

1. Through what individual steps did the Constitution acquire civil liberties protections?

2. How has individual liberty been elevated from a private local matter into a prominent national policy issue?

3. How has the role of national government differed in the development of civil rights policy versus that of civil liberties?

4. How did the Bill of Rights come to apply to states?

5. Do the states still have a role in defining civil liberties?

6 Congress

As the 112th Congress convenes on January 5, 2011, newly elected House Speaker John Boehner receives the gavel from his predecessor, now House Minority Leader Nancy Pelosi, symbolizing the dramatic power shift from the Democratic Party to the Republican Party effected by the 2010 midterm congressional elections. Pelosi no doubt looks considerably happier than she felt; Boehner's genuine joy was soon tempered by factional strife within his party's ranks. Both retained their offices in the 113th Congress (2013–2014).

- Why do members of the House and Senate follow complex, arcane rules and precedents in processing legislation even when such devices keep majorities from getting their way?

- Congressional incumbents rarely lose elections. Why, then, are they obsessed with the electoral implications of nearly everything they do?

- Why do members of Congress show such a strong inclination to be individually responsive but collectively irresponsible?

- Why have congressional party leaders become so much more powerful over the past thirty years?

Instead of celebrating with family and friends at home, members of Congress greeted the arrival of 2013 on Capitol Hill, struggling to reach agreement on legislation that would prevent draconian cuts in government spending and sharp increases in taxes for almost all American families in the new year. The spending cuts would be imposed by a law explicitly adopted by Congress in 2011 to force itself to act by making the alternative—huge automatic cuts in defense and discretionary domestic spending programs—intolerable. Taxes would increase because the large tax cuts enacted in 2001 and 2003 during the George W. Bush administration were scheduled to expire on December 31, 2012. Negotiations had dragged on during the "lame duck" session of the 112th Congress held after the 2012 elections, as President Obama and the Senate Democratic majority insisted that any deal to avoid these outcomes must raise revenues through higher taxes on the wealthiest Americans, while the House Republican majority rejected any tax increase and insisted on money-saving reforms of entitlement programs such as Medicare, Medicaid, and Social Security, which the Democrats in turn rejected. Unless the contending parties could resolve these fundamental differences, dire consequences were anticipated: financial pain for millions of Americans, higher unemployment, and a return to economic recession, not to mention universal scorn for a government incapable of governing.

Congress found itself in this unwelcome predicament for a variety of reasons: the growing ideological polarization of the congressional parties; the widening partisan divergence of their respective electoral bases in districts and states; the huge budget deficits produced by prior tax cuts, recession, feeble economic growth, and the expanding population of retirees drawing on the Medicare and Social Security programs; and divided party control of the federal government. It also stemmed from prior procedural choices and congressional indecision that kept putting off the day of reckoning.

The Bush tax cuts had been enacted under a special procedure called "reconciliation" that precluded a filibuster by the bill's Democratic opponents but also required that they have a fixed termination date, originally scheduled for December 31, 2010. Republicans had sought for years to make the cuts permanent but never had the votes. In late 2010, the Democrats, led by President Obama, agreed to extend the cuts for two more years in return for additional tax breaks for wage workers and extended unemployment benefits; at a time of sluggish economic growth and high unemployment, no one was eager to raise taxes. The extension ended December 31, 2012.

The spending cuts loomed because earlier congressional attempts to trim the deficit had failed. During the summer of 2011, the Republicans, who had won control of the House in 2010, sought to force Obama and the Senate Democratic majority to accept massive cuts in federal spending by refusing to raise the legal debt ceiling if they did not comply. Without a higher debt limit (which had been raised routinely for decades as necessary to accommodate spending already appropriated by Congress), the government would be unable to borrow enough money to pay all of its bills, threatening national and global economic turmoil. The administration was agreeable to some cuts but insisted on raising revenues—mainly by rescinding some of the Bush tax breaks enjoyed by wealthy individuals and corporations—as part of any deficit reduction package. Republicans adamantly refused to consider any revenue increases. In this round of chicken, both sides blinked, ultimately cutting a deal that raised the debt ceiling enough to ensure the government's borrowing capacity until early 2013, made much more modest spending cuts than Republicans had initially demanded, and raised no new revenues. The agreement also established a new bipartisan, bicameral committee of twelve that was supposed to come up with a comprehensive deficit reduction plan by November 2011. If that committee failed to come up with an acceptable proposal, large automatic spending cuts, technically called "sequestration," applied half to defense, half to domestic discretionary programs, would kick in on January 2, 2013, unless Congress and the president acted to prevent them. The committee could not agree on a plan, setting up the sequestration component of the so-called fiscal cliff that the country faced at the end of 2012.

The bargaining over action to avoid the fiscal cliff was complex because of ideological divisions within the parties as well as between them, posing major challenges to the president and the congressional party leaders. Obama had just won reelection promising to raise taxes on the rich while protecting social programs dear to Democratic constituencies. Many congressional Democrats strongly opposed any benefit-reducing changes in Medicare or Social Security that might be part of a grand bargain between the parties. Republicans were divided into a majority that refused on principle to vote for any tax increase ever—even the one for people earning over $1 million a year proposed by their leader, House Speaker John Boehner—and a minority willing to vote for higher taxes on the wealthiest taxpayers to avoid the global tax increases that would occur if the Bush tax cuts expired. A deal was finally reached in the Senate to restore the Bush tax cuts for all but the wealthiest individuals (those earning over $400,000 per year), extend unemployment insurance, and postpone sequestration for two months. It was enacted by a large margin, 89 for to 8 against, with majorities of both parties supporting it. In the House, however, most Republicans opposed the compromise, refusing to cast a vote to raise taxes for fear of offending their core constituents and inviting primary election challenges. But when the Senate's Democratic leader said the Senate would not reconsider any bill amended by the House, it was "take it or go over the fiscal cliff." Rather than risk the blame—and electoral punishment—for allowing that to happen, the Republican House leaders gave in and, in a

Congressman Paul Ryan, 2012 Republican vice presidential nominee, left, and Republican Senator Marco Rubio (Florida) exemplified the Republican split over whether to support a tax increase on the top 2 percent or let the Bush tax cuts lapse during the "fiscal cliff" showdown in December 2012. Ryan voted for the compromise and thus the tax increase, while Rubio voted against it. Both are potential candidates for the 2016 Republican nomination, inviting much speculation in the media about how this issue might affect their prospects.

rare move, allowed the bill to reach the floor for a vote even though a majority of the House Republicans opposed it. It passed at the very last moment, 257–167, with Democrats splitting 172–16 in favor, Republicans, 151 against to 85 for.

The action did not resolve the fiscal debate, however, for it simply delayed the hard choices to be made on the spending side for a couple of months. Moreover, the debt ceiling would again have to be raised at about the same time, opening the way to another showdown between the parties, with Congress again as the arena.

What do these events begin to tell us about Congress?

- The House and Senate occupy the center stage in national policymaking, although their power over legislation is not unalloyed, for the Constitution gives a share of legislative authority to the president.
- The congressional parties have become highly polarized along ideological lines, making it exceedingly difficult to resolve conflicts and make coherent policy when neither party has full control of the House, Senate, and White House.
- Electoral politics influences almost everything members of Congress do, collectively and individually.
- The majority party, through its leaders, directs and sometimes dominates the action in the House but less so in the Senate; the degree to which leaders exercise control depends, however, on how unified the parties are internally.

- The rules and organizational structures the House and Senate adopt have a deliberate and crucial effect on both the distribution of power and policymaking in Congress.
- It is always far easier to stop things from happening in Congress than to make things happen, and even the prospect of dire consequences from inaction does not guarantee action.

This chapter explores each of these themes while explaining how and why the House and Senate operate as they do. It also looks at how these institutions have evolved in response to the changing motives and opportunities, personal and political, of the politicians elected to them. Any such discussion must be prefaced, however, by a review of the constitutional design of Congress and the extensive powers granted it by the Framers.

CONGRESS IN THE CONSTITUTION

The basic structure of Congress is the product of the Great Compromise at the Constitutional Convention, described in Chapter 2. Balancing the demands of the large states for national representation against those of the small states for protection of states' rights, the Framers established in the Constitution a House of Representatives, with seats allocated by population and members elected by the citizenry, and a Senate composed of two members from each state chosen by the state legislature. Bicameralism (two houses) also resolved another dispute. Delegates to the convention disagreed about the appropriate degree of popular influence on government. But, using the bicameral structure, they were able to devise a mixed solution. Representatives would be "popularly" chosen in biennial elections held in even-numbered years. The two-year term was a compromise between the annual elections advocated by many delegates and the three-year term proposed by James Madison. Broad suffrage—the qualification for voting was to be the same as for the "most numerous Branch of the State Legislature" (Article I, Section 2)—and short tenure were intended to keep the House as close as possible to the people.

The Senate, by contrast, would be much more insulated from transient shifts in the public mood. Senators would be chosen by state legislatures, not directly by the voters. The term of office was set at six years, another compromise; terms ranging from three to nine years had been proposed. Continuity was ensured by the requirement that one-third of the Senate's membership stand for election every two years. The Senate could thus act as a stable, dispassionate counterweight to the more popular and radical House, protecting the new government from the dangerous volatility thought to be characteristic of democracies. As James Madison put it in *Federalist* No. 62, "The necessity of the Senate is . . . indicated by the propensity of all single and numerous assemblies to yield to the impulse of sudden and violent passions, and to be seduced by factious leaders into intemperate and pernicious resolutions." The Senate also incorporated remnants of state sovereignty into the new national government.

Qualifications for office also reflected the Framers' concept of the Senate as the more "mature" of the two chambers (*senate* is derived from the Latin *senex,* old man). The minimum age for representatives was set at twenty-five years; for senators, thirty years. Representatives had to be citizens for at least seven years; senators, for nine years. Both were required to reside in the state they represented. Representatives do not have to live in the districts they serve, but in practice they almost always do. These are the only qualifications for office specified in the Constitution. The property-holding and religious qualifications included in many state constitutions were explicitly rejected, as was a proposal to forbid a member's reelection to office after serving a term. The Articles of Confederation had included a reelection restriction, but the Framers thought it had weakened Congress by depriving it of some of its ablest members.

Washington's city planner, the young Frenchman Pierre L'Enfant, consulted the Constitution before placing the Capitol on the highest hill in the city. From 1825 to 1856 the Capitol lacked a large dome—the original low wooden dome is depicted here—causing L'Enfant to describe it as "a pedestal waiting for a monument."

Powers of Congress

As we saw in Chapter 2, the Constitution established a truly national government by giving Congress broad power over crucial economic matters. Article I, Section 8, authorizes Congress to impose taxes, coin and borrow money, regulate interstate and foreign commerce, and spend money for the "common Defence" and "general Welfare." Tacked on at the end of this list of specific powers is a residual clause authorizing Congress "to make all Laws which shall be necessary and proper for carrying into Execution the foregoing Powers, and all other Powers vested by this Constitution in the Government of the United States, or in any Department or Officer thereof." Accepted by many delegates as an afterthought, this **necessary and proper clause**—often known as the elastic clause because it "stretched" the powers of Congress—has proved to be the single most extensive grant of power in the Constitution, giving lawmakers authority over many different spheres of public policy (see Chapter 3). Indeed, it was under this authority that Congress banned discrimination in public accommodations and housing in the 1960s (see Chapter 4).

Congress was given significant authority in foreign affairs as well. Although the president is designated commander in chief of the armed forces, only Congress may declare war, raise and finance an army and a navy, and call out the state militias "to execute the Laws of the Union, suppress Insurrections and repel Invasions" (Article I, Section 8). The Senate was granted some special powers over foreign relations. In its "advice and consent" capacity, the Senate ratifies treaties and confirms presidential appointments of ambassadors.

The Senate also approves presidentially appointed Supreme Court justices and top executive branch officials. These powers reveal that, in part, the Framers viewed the Senate as an advisory council to the executive, modeled on the upper chambers of some state legislatures. But they also reflect the Framers' belief that the more "aristocratic" and insulated of the two houses would keep a steadier eye on the nation's long-term interests.

In distributing power between the House and the Senate, the delegates sought a proper balance of authority. One bone of contention was the power to raise and spend money. Some delegates wanted to give the House, as the chamber closer to the people, the exclusive authority to enact legislation to raise or spend money; the Senate would be allowed to vote on House bills but not amend them. The final compromise required merely that bills raising revenue originate in the House, with the Senate having an unrestricted right to amend them. The House was given no special mandate to initiate spending bills, but it has assumed that right by custom as an extension of its special authority over revenue bills.

Despite its many legislative powers, Congress does not have exclusive authority over legislation. The president may recommend new laws and, in emergencies, call Congress into special session. Most important, the president has the power to veto laws passed by Congress, killing them unless two-thirds of each chamber votes to override the veto.

[handwritten margin note: President can into special session / veto, 2/3 congressional override / Oveto]

The Electoral System

Two other choices made by the Framers of the Constitution have profoundly affected the electoral politics of Congress. First, members of Congress and presidents are elected separately. In parliamentary systems like those found in most European countries, government authority rests with the legislature, which chooses the chief executive (called the prime minister or premier). Thus voters' choices for legislators depend mainly on voter preferences for leader of the executive branch. In the United States, voters are presented separate choices for senator, representative, and president.

Second, members of Congress are elected from states and congressional districts by plurality vote—that is, whoever gets the most votes wins.* Some parliamentary systems employ **proportional representation**, which gives a party a share of seats in the legislature matching the share of the votes it wins on Election Day. For example, if a party's share of votes entitles it to eighty-five seats, the first eighty-five candidates on the party's slate go to parliament. The voters, then, choose among parties, not individual candidates, and candidates need not have local connections. Party leaders under this system are very powerful because they control parliamentary careers by deciding who goes on the list and in what order.

American legislators are elected from territorial units, not party lists. Parties do matter in congressional elections, and with rare exceptions, only major-party nominees have any chance of winning (see Chapter 12). But the parties do not control nominations. Almost all congressional nominees are now chosen by voters in primary elections—preliminary contests in which voters select the parties' nominees. Candidates thus get their party's nomination directly from voters, not from party activists or leaders.

Congressional Districts

After the first census in 1790, each state was allotted one House seat for every 33,000 inhabitants, for a total of 105 seats. Until the twentieth century the House grew as

---

*In the past, some states elected some or all of their U.S. representatives in statewide "at-large" districts. A 1964 Supreme Court decision, *Wesberry v. Sanders*, ended the practice by requiring that districts have equal populations. One state, Georgia, requires an absolute majority of votes to win general elections to Congress. If no candidate wins such a majority, a runoff election is held between the top two finishers.

population increased and new states joined the Union. Total membership was finally fixed at its current ceiling of 435 in 1911, when House leaders concluded that further growth would impede the House's work. Since 1911, states have both lost and gained seats to reflect population shifts between the decennial (ten-year) censuses. Changes in the sizes of state delegations to the House since World War II illustrate vividly the major population movements in the United States (see Map 6-1). States in the West and South have gained at the expense of the large industrial states in the Northeast and Midwest.

Map 6-1 Apportionment's Winners and Losers

Since 1950, the South and West have been gaining House seats at the expense of the Northeast and Midwest

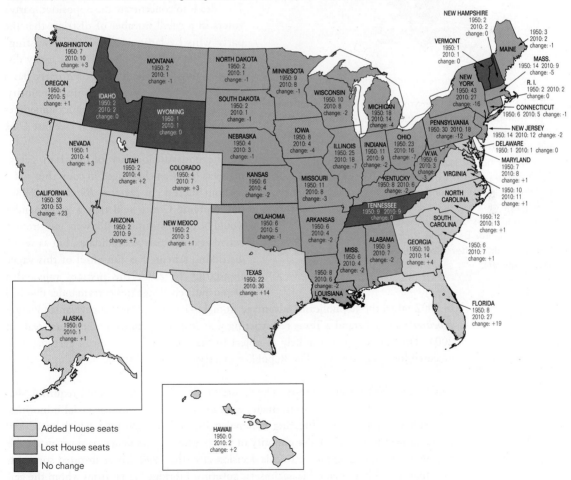

Source: U.S. Bureau of the Census, http://www.census.gov/prod/cen2010/briefs/c2010br-08.pdf.

Note: Alaska and Hawaii were not yet states in 1950.

The Original Gerrymander

The practice of "gerrymandering"—the extensive manipulation of the shape of a legislative district to benefit a certain incumbent or party—is probably as old as the Republic, but the name originated in 1812. That year, the Massachusetts legislature carved out of Essex County a district that historian John Fiske said had a "dragonlike contour." When the painter Gilbert Stuart saw the misshapen district, he penciled in a head, wings, and claws and exclaimed, "That will do for a salamander!" Editor Benjamin Russell replied, "Better say a Gerrymander"—after Elbridge Gerry, then governor of Massachusetts.

Federal law may apportion House seats among states after each census, but each state draws the lines that divide its territory into the requisite number of districts. In 1964 the Supreme Court ruled in *Wesberry v. Sanders* that districts must have equal populations.[1] In *Thornburg v. Gingles* (1986) the Court ruled that district lines may not dilute minority representation, but neither may they be drawn with race as the predominant consideration.[2] Within these limits states can draw districts pretty much as they please. If one party controls both the legislature and the governorship, it may attempt to draw district lines that favor its own candidates. The idea is to concentrate the opposition party's voters in a small number of districts that the party wins by large margins, thus "wasting" many of its votes, while creating as many districts as possible where one's own party has a secure, though not overwhelming, majority. Called **gerrymandering**, these tactics sometimes produce bizarrely shaped districts (see box "The Original Gerrymander").

The constitutionality of partisan gerrymanders has been challenged in court, but so far without success. In *Davis v. Bandemer* (1986) the Supreme Court held that a gerrymander would be unconstitutional if it were too strongly biased against a party's candidates, but as yet no districting scheme has run afoul of this vague standard.[3] In 2004 the justices rejected a Democratic challenge to a gerrymander that had in 2002 raised the Republicans' advantage from 11–10 to 12–7 in Pennsylvania (*Vieth v. Jubelirer*)[4] and let stand a Texas redistricting that cost the Democrats six House seats in 2004. Thus the Court is unlikely to object to the successful Republican gerrymanders executed for 2012 (see box "The Republican Gerrymander in 2012").

RACIAL GERRYMANDERING. The Court's 1986 *Thornburg* decision, requiring that legislative district lines not discriminate, even unintentionally, against racial minorities, was widely interpreted as directing mapmakers to design districts in which racial and ethnic minorities constituted a majority of voters wherever residence patterns made this feasible.[5] Attempts to conform to this decision after the 1990 census inspired some artistry that would have made Massachusetts governor Elbridge Gerry, from whom the gerrymander got its name, proud (see box "The Original Gerrymander"). For example, North Carolina legislators carved out two majority black districts (First and Twelfth)

Map 6-2 Acceptable and Unacceptable Gerrymanders

North Carolina, 1991, 1998, 2010

1991 version (rejected by the Supreme Court)

1998 version (accepted by the Supreme Court)

After the 2010 census (2012)

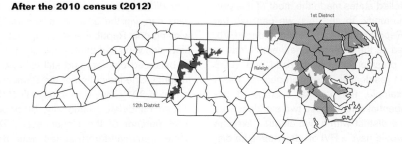

Sources: Congressional Districts in the 1990s: A Portrait of America (Washington, DC: Congressional Quarterly, 1993), 548; *Congressional Staff Directory* (Washington, DC: CQ Press, 1999); Congressional Districts, NationalAtlas.gov.

Note: North Carolina's First and Twelfth Districts were drawn to give the state its first black representatives in ninety-three years. First elected in 1992, the two black representatives were subsequently reelected; after the First District representative retired in 2003, she was replaced by another African American. Taking over from the Democrats in 2010, Republicans tweaked the district lines to create three overwhelmingly Democratic districts (First, Fourth, and Twelfth), leaving the other ten with narrower but comfortable Republican majorities.

that eventually came before the Court (see Map 6-2). The Court decided in 1993 that such irregular districts went too far,[6] and in 1995 that districts could not be drawn solely to benefit one race.[7] Thus the North Carolina districts (along with thirty-four districts in

THE REPUBLICAN GERRYMANDER IN 2012

strategy and choice

The Republican Party has long enjoyed an advantage House because its regular voters are distributed more efficiently across House districts than are regular Democratic voters. The advantage exists mainly because Democrats win a disproportionate share of minority, single, young, and gay voters who are concentrated in urban districts that deliver lopsided Democratic majorities. Loyal Republican voters are spread more evenly across suburbs, smaller cities, and rural areas, so that fewer Republican votes are "wasted" in highly skewed districts.

The Republicans' sweeping national victory in 2010 enabled them to strengthen this structural advantage by giving them control of the redistricting process in eighteen states with a total of 202 House seats. Democrats controlled the process in only six states with a total of 47 seats. (In twelve of the remaining states, the parties shared control; seven were redistricted by commissions, and seven were single-district states). Republican-controlled states made the most of this gerrymandering opportunity. To see this, we can use the *Cook Political Report's* Partisan Voting Index (PVI), which is computed as the difference between the average district-level presidential vote in 2004 and 2008 and the national presidential vote averages for these elections. For example, the national average of the Democratic presidential vote in these two elections was 51.2 percent, so a district with a two-election average of 54.2 percent would have a PVI of +3, whereas a district with an average of 48.2 percent would have a PVI of −3.

Republicans already held a considerable advantage by this measure before the 2012 redistricting, with 210 Republican-leaning districts (defined here as having a partisan voting index less than −2), compared with 175 Democratic-leaning districts (index greater than 2); the remaining 50 districts were balanced, with indexes between −2 and +2 (see the table in this box). After redistricting, there were eleven more Republican-leaning districts, five fewer Democratic-leaning districts, and six fewer balanced districts. This result was clearly intended; where Republicans controlled redistricting, the party gained sixteen favorable districts while the Democrats lost one and balanced districts were reduced by eleven.

Once the votes were counted, House election results matched district leanings with remarkable consistency. Only ten Democrats won Republican-leaning districts in 2012, and not a single Republican won in a Democratic-leaning district. The balanced districts were divided almost perfectly in half. If election results continue to reflect underlying district partisanship in this way for the rest of the decade, Democrats will find it very difficult to retake control of the House. Republicans can win the 218 seats required for a majority by winning only Republican-leaning seats, whereas Democrats can win all of the Democratic-leaning districts and all balanced districts and still fall four seats short of a majority. One indication of the Democrats' predicament is that in 2012 they won a majority of the votes cast for House candidates nationally, 50.5 percent, but only 46.4 percent of the House seats. The imbalance in some gerrymandered states was much greater; in Pennsylvania, Democrats won 51 percent of the vote but only 27 percent of the seats; in Michigan, they won 53 percent of the vote but only 36 percent of the seats. The Republicans' structural advantage in the distribution of their regular voters, enhanced by gerrymandering after

Control of Redistricting and Changes in District Partisanship, 2010–2012

Control of Redistricting		District Partisan Advantage		
		Democrat > 2	Balanced	Republican > 2
All Districts	2010	175	50	210
	2012	170	44	221
	Change	−5	−6	+11
Republican Control	2010	51	24	123
	2012	50	13	139
	Change	−1	−11	+16
Other Control	2010	124	26	87
	2012	120	31	82
	Change	−4	+5	−5
Election Results, 2012				
Democrat Won		170	21	10
Republican Won		0	23	211

Note: District partisan advantage is based on the *Cook* PVI; see text for a description.

the 2010 census, makes it likely that, like Barack Obama, any Democratic president elected in 2016 or 2020 can expect to face an entrenched opposition party in the House.

* David Wasserman, "Introducing the 2012 Cook Political Report Partisan Vote Index," *The Cook Political Report*, October 11, 2012, accessed at http://cookpolitical.com/house/pvi, October 15, 2012.

four other states) had to be redrawn. Modified twice before receiving final court approval, the districts had some of their rough edges smoothed off but retained all the earmarks of a painstaking gerrymander.

Unequal Representation in the Senate

The fifty Senate constituencies—entire states—may not change boundaries with each census, but they vary greatly in size of population. Sen. Dianne Feinstein, D-Calif., represents more than thirty-seven million people, while Sen. Mike Enzi, R-Wyo., has fewer constituents (570,000) than does the average U.S. representative (724,000). The nine largest states are home to 51 percent of the total U.S. population, while the smallest twenty-six states, with 52 percent of Senate seats, hold only 18 percent of the population. Unequal representation in the Senate sometimes matters politically. For example, Republicans held a Senate majority between 1981 and 1987 even though their candidates had received overall a smaller percentage of the popular vote than Democrats because Republican candidates won so many of the smaller states.[8]

Until 1913 senators were chosen by state legislatures. Most Americans had long since concluded that this method of selection was undemocratic and corrupting (between 1890 and 1905 charges of bribery shadowed Senate elections in seven different states).[9] But it took the reforming spirit of Progressivism at its peak to convince senators to agree to a constitutional amendment (the Seventeenth) providing for popular election.[10] As it turned out, they had little to fear from the change; senators have been about as successful in winning reelection as they had been in persuading state legislatures to return them to office.[*]

CONGRESS AND ELECTORAL POLITICS

The modern Congress is organized to serve the goals of its members. A primary goal for most of them is to keep their jobs. And since voters have the final say in their hiring and firing, a career in Congress depends on members winning the voters' endorsement at regular intervals. Reelection is not their only objective, but winning regular reelection is essential to everything else members want to achieve in office. Electoral imperatives thus shape all important aspects of congressional life.

Candidate-Centered versus Party-Centered Electoral Politics

The post–World War II era of Democratic majorities in Congress coincided with the emergence of a candidate-centered pattern of electoral politics. Similarly, the Republican

---

[*]A remaining democratic anomaly is the absence of representation of any kind, in the Senate or the House, for the 600,000 Americans who live in Washington, DC. Citizens living in the nation's capital do get to vote for three presidential electors, however. They also elect a nonvoting delegate to the House of Representatives (Eleanor Holmes Norton during the 113th Congress).

takeover of Congress in the 1994 midterm elections followed and reflected a resurgence of party-centered electoral politics that has continued since then, driven by the intense party competition for control of the House and Senate that has become the norm. Neither connection was accidental. During their era of dominance, congressional Democrats thrived on, and thus sought to encourage, a kind of electoral politics in which candidates operated largely as independent political entrepreneurs. Republican leaders, unable to win House majorities by playing the game this way (Republicans did manage to control the Senate from 1981 through 1986), sought in 1994 to have their candidates run more as a party team, emphasizing national issues and a common program of action. The strategy succeeded beyond their expectations. Thus in triumph the Republican majority, owing their newfound control to party-centered electoral politics, immediately moved to alter the House and the Senate, long shaped by the Democrats' candidate-centered electoral politics, to suit their own electoral and policy goals.

During the long period of Democratic majorities, members of both parties had won election to Congress, and stayed there, largely because of their own efforts. Most "recruited" themselves, organized their own campaigns, and raised their own campaign money. Party organizations and **political action committees (PACs)**—organizations that raise and distribute money for campaigns (see Chapter 13)— were ready to help, but not until campaigns had shown promise. "Promise" usually meant the candidate had won the primary election, gained some favorable media attention, and raised a substantial amount of start-up money—most of which often came from the candidate's own pockets.

Although congressional candidates ran under party labels for national offices, most congressional campaigns were personal and centered on local interests and values. National issues that did enter the campaign were given a local spin. Campaigns for reelection dwelled on the services, projects, and locally popular programs the incumbent delivered to constituents, making it possible for members to separate their electoral fates from those of their

Pete Sessions, R-Texas, announces to the Republican National Committee in September 2010 the launching of a 48-state "Fire Pelosi" bus tour. As chair of the National Republican Congressional Committee, responsible for recruiting and financing Republican House candidates, Sessions shared credit for his party's effective exploitation of the anti-Democratic political climate in 2010. Republicans gained 63 House seats to win a 242–193 majority—costing Pelosi her position as Speaker.

party's other candidates.[11] For example, between 1972 and 1992 House Democrats won victories in 45 percent of the districts that delivered majorities to Republican candidates in presidential elections (Republicans won in 12 percent of the much smaller number of districts that delivered majorities to Democratic presidential candidates).[12]

The local component of congressional elections had not always been so dominant. During much of the nineteenth century, party-line voting was far more common than it became later. Voters based their choices on the top of the ticket—the presidential candidates in presidential election years—and on the parties' platforms. Congressional candidates' fates were decided by national trends they could do little personally to shape or control. Changes in the laws regulating elections and parties around the turn of the century weakened parties and encouraged **ticket-splitting**—that is, voting for candidates of different parties for different offices.[13] The most important of these changes were the introduction of primary elections for choosing the parties' nominees and the secret ballot (see Chapter 12). Still, party conflicts over national policy, most notably the political battles over President Franklin Roosevelt's New Deal, continued to inject a strong national component into congressional elections until the 1950s. As the New Deal controversies faded, however, the party coalitions built around them fractured under the stress of divisive new issues, most prominently civil rights, the Vietnam War, and social issues such as abortion and the environment. Party lines became blurred, and party loyalty among voters declined.

The Advantages of Incumbency

Congressional incumbents both exploited and abetted the loosening of party ties. The decline in party loyalty among voters offered incumbents a chance to win votes that once would have gone routinely to the other party's candidate. Members could expand their electoral base by emphasizing individual character, legislative performance, and constituency services, encouraging voters to use such criteria in deciding how to vote.[14] Realizing that the growth of candidate-centered electoral politics worked to the advantage of incumbents willing to build a personal following, members of Congress voted themselves greater resources for servicing their states and districts—that is, higher allowances for staff, travel, local offices, and communication. These allowances are now worth more than $1.2 million per legislator in the House and up to three times as much per senator, depending on the population of the state represented.[15]

Electoral data demonstrate the success of these efforts. The average share of votes won by House incumbents increased from 61 percent in the 1940s and 1950s to 67 percent in the 1980s; estimates of the value of incumbency, measured in the extra share of votes a candidate typically received by running as an incumbent, rose from 1–2 percentage points to 8–10 percentage points over the same period. The proportion of incumbents winning more than 60 percent of the vote grew even more steeply, from as low as 41 percent in 1948 to as high as 88 percent in 1988.[16] Incumbent reelection rates also have generally been higher since the mid-1960s, although some years, notably in the early 1990s and 2010, have been exceptions. Even before the 1960s House incumbents were winning reelection very consistently; their overall success rate since World War II exceeds 92 percent.

In the earlier period, incumbents were successful largely because they represented districts that voted consistently for one party's candidates. From the mid-1960s through the 1980s, they became much more successful in winning in districts where their party did not have a natural majority. Since then, incumbents have continued to win at high rates, but to an increasing extent because they represent districts with electorates that favor their parties' candidates, incumbent or not. The changing ability of congressional candidates to win against the partisan grain—measured by their ability to win a state or district their party's presidential candidate lost—is illustrated in Figure 6-1. Both House and Senate candidates were unusually successful in winning seats in the other party's presidential territory in the 1970s and 1980s, but such victories have since become rarer and were particularly scarce in 2012. This trend reflects the growth in party-line voting discussed in Chapter 12 and reflects a decline in the ability of incumbents (and other candidates) to separate themselves from their party's collective fate. In particular, electoral fortunes of congressional candidates are increasingly tied to those of their presidential candidates; the correlations between the vote shares won by presidential candidates and

Figure 6-1   States and Districts Delivering Split Outcomes in Presidential and Congressional Contests, 1952–2012

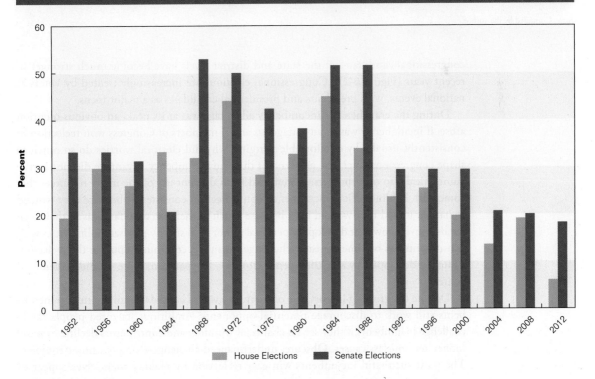

Sources: Compiled by authors.

Figure 6-2   The Correlations Between the Presidential and Congressional Votes at the District and State Levels Have Become Very High

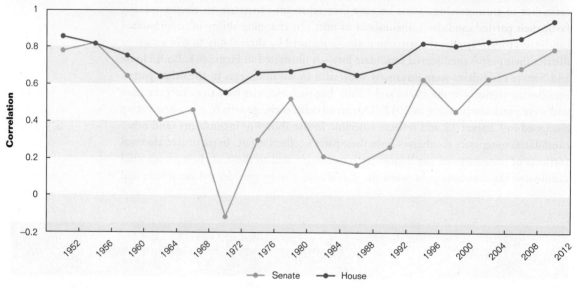

Source: Compiled by the author.

congressional candidates at the state and district levels have become much stronger in recent years (Figure 6-2).* Congressional elections are increasingly treated by voters as national events, with presidents and presidential candidates as a major focus.

During the era when the incumbency advantage was at its peak, an obvious question arose: if incumbency was so advantageous and if members of Congress won reelection so consistently, usually by comfortable margins, why did electoral worries do so much to shape congressional life? The answer was that the incumbency advantage did not accrue automatically to officeholders; it stemmed from diligent use of the many resources that come with holding office. Incumbents won reelection consistently because they worked so hard at it, and they worked hard because much of their electoral fate was in their own hands.[17] Even now that developing personal rather than strictly partisan political ties with constituents has become a greater challenge, members continue to pursue the reelection strategies developed by an earlier generation in a less partisan, more candidate-centered context.

Despite the growing importance of party, individual candidates still matter, so incumbents still work to discourage potential opponents. Ambitious, talented people rarely challenge incumbents if they see no chance of winning; and contributors decline to waste money on hopeless causes. Obscure, underfinanced challengers simply cannot compete. The most successful incumbents win easy reelection by making themselves appear so

---

*Correlations take values from 0.0 (no relationship at all) to 1.0 (a perfect relationship).

invincible that no qualified opponent is willing to take them on.[18] But an image of invincibility is not invincible. It is vulnerable to unexpected events, such as the House bank scandal that provoked a storm of outrage from the press and public and led to the largest turnover of membership in fifty years in 1992, or the strong national partisan tides that emerged in 1994, 2006, and 2010. Such events demonstrate why members of Congress—even those with long records of past electoral success—are right to worry about reelection. The strength of the Republican tide in 1994 surprised nearly everyone on Capitol Hill, as Republicans succeeded in turning long-simmering public anger over the Clinton administration, economic and social conditions, and congressional malfeasance against Democratic candidates for both national and local offices. Thirty-four Democratic House incumbents, including Speaker Thomas Foley of Washington, were defeated. Republicans suffered in turn in 2006 through widespread disaffection with President Bush and the Iraq War and from ethics scandals besetting some congressional Republicans. Four years later, high unemployment and unhappiness with the Obama administration cost fifty-two Democratic incumbents their House seats, two-thirds of the defeats coming in districts the Democrats had won in 2006 and 2008. Anti-Washington sentiments even touched Republican incumbents in 2010; two Republican senators were defeated in primary elections by candidates preferred by the party's zealously conservative Tea Party wing, and a third Republican senator met the same fate in 2012.* Members of Congress, then, inhabit a world fraught with far more electoral uncertainty than their wins/losses record would lead one to believe. An easy victory against feeble

---

* In 2010, one of the two, Lisa Murkowski, R-Alaska, managed to win reelection as a write-in candidate; Richard Lugar, R-Ind., a thirty-six-year Senate veteran, lost his primary in 2012.

Until the 1890s, Americans voted with paper ballots supplied by party workers or printed in newspaper advertisements. The voter simply took the ballot to the voting desk and publicly submitted it. On this 1876 ballot for the Republican ticket of Rutherford B. Hayes and his vice presidential running mate, William Wheeler, the voter voted for all Republicans from president down to the lowly register of deeds. Because this method of voting made ticket-splitting so difficult, the success of congressional candidates was tied to the fortunes of their party's presidential candidate.

opposition in one election carries no guarantee of success against a talented and well-financed challenger in the next. And even if a state or district is safe for the incumbent's party, primary election challenges from candidates representing ideological factions within the party remain a threat.

CONSTITUENT SERVICE. Recognizing that they hold their jobs at the sufferance of sometimes-fickle electorates, members of Congress are highly responsive to their constituencies. Decisions on legislative issues are shaped by the potential need to explain and defend them in future campaigns.[19] Most members also spend a great deal of time back home, keeping in touch and staying visible. They solicit and process **casework**, requests from constituents for information and help in dealing with government agencies. A lost Social Security check? A bureaucratic mix-up over veterans' benefits? A representative or senator is ready to help. Some requests—and services—go well beyond the expected. One constituent tried to get his senator to intercede with the head of the state university's board of regents to raise the C grade his son received in a political science course.[20] The senator did not comply, but electoral logic makes it hard to resist almost any opportunity to please people back home.

VULNERABLE SENATORS. Although senators engage in many of the same constituency-building activities as representatives, they have not been as successful in keeping their jobs. Since 1946 their overall rate of reelection, 79 percent, has left them three times more likely to lose their seats than House incumbents. But because senators face reelection only one-third as often, tenure in office tends to even out between the chambers. Overall, though, Senate election outcomes are more variable than House outcomes; in the postwar era, incumbent reelection rates have been as low as 55 percent (1980) and as high as 97 percent (1990). Even when Senate incumbents do win, their margins of victory tend to be narrower than those of representatives. Why do Senate incumbents win less consistently and typically by narrower margins? First, because states (other than the seven with only one representative) are more populous and diverse than congressional districts, most senators are unable to develop the kinds of personal ties to constituents that many representatives cultivate. Second, states are more likely than congressional districts to have balanced party competition; a much smaller share of states than districts are securely in either party's pocket. Third, Senate races attract a larger proportion of experienced, politically talented, well-financed challengers. Fourth, states usually fit media markets—formed by cities and their suburbs reached by local TV and radio stations and newspapers—better than House districts, making it easier for challengers to get out their messages. Senators receive far more attention from the news media than representatives, but so do their opponents. Representatives may be largely ignored by journalists, but this vacuum leaves them freer to shape the information that does reach constituents. And finally, senators are more readily associated with controversial and divisive issues, and they do not have the pressure of a two-year election cycle to keep them attuned to the folks back home. All these things contribute to making senators more vulnerable than representatives to defeat by challengers.

National Politics in Congressional Elections

The resurgence of party-centered campaigning since 1994 has strengthened the national component of congressional election politics, but even during the heyday of locally focused, candidate-centered elections, national forces continued to have a palpable effect on electoral fates. In midterm elections the president's party almost always loses congressional seats, but the size of its losses depends in part on the performances of the national economy and the president. Losses tend to be fewer when the economy is booming and the president is popular, greater when the economy or the administration's popularity sags. Thus, for example, congressional Democrats suffered in 1994 from, among other things, Bill Clinton's low job approval ratings and voters' doubts about the economy. In 1998, by contrast, Clinton's approval rating stood nearly twenty points higher than it had in 1994, and the economy was in its best shape since the 1960s. As a result, the Democrats broke precedent by actually gaining House seats. Similarly, George W. Bush's leadership in the war on terrorism produced high approval ratings in 2002 that helped his party achieve small gains in the House and Senate; with Bush's ratings twenty-five points lower in 2006, Democrats picked up enough seats to take control of both chambers.* In 2010 high unemployment, public dissatisfaction with the direction of the economy, and Barack Obama's mediocre approval ratings cost the Democrats sixty-four House and six Senate seats.

As the 1994, 2006, and 2010 elections showed so dramatically, members of Congress cannot always dissociate themselves from their party's fate, so they retain a personal stake in their party's public image as well as the public standing of the president. Nor can they separate themselves from Congress itself, though incumbents frequently try to do so. Individual members remain far more popular than Congress collectively, but they still suffer at the ballot box when the public's normally mild hostility toward Congress becomes intense, at least if one party controls both chambers and thus absorbs all the blame. Individual members cannot do much about such sentiments by themselves, so they concentrate on activities such as casework, in which their individual efforts can make a difference.

Representation versus Responsibility

Different electoral processes produce different forms of representation. In a party-centered electoral process, for example, legislators represent citizens by carrying out the policies promised by the party (or parties in multiparty systems) winning a majority of seats. Legislators know they will be held responsible by voters for their party's performance in governing, so ensuring the success of their party and the government takes top priority.

---

* Clinton's 66 percent job approval rating in 1998 was the highest for any president at a midterm election since Gallup began measuring the percentage more than fifty years ago; Bush, with 63 percent approving, came in second (matched by Ronald Reagan in 1986). Partly as a consequence, the 1998 and 2002 midterm elections were only the second and third since the Civil War in which the president's party gained House seats (the other was the 1934 contest). By 2006, Bush's approval rating had fallen to 38 percent, and Democrats picked up thirty-one House seats and six Senate seats. Gary C. Jacobson, "Referendum: The 2006 Midterm Congressional Elections," *Political Science Quarterly* 122 (Spring 2007): 1–24.

[handwritten margin notes: "Logrolling - I'll vote for this if you vote for mine." and "Pork Barrel - $$ to State, Candidate center"]

The candidate-centered electoral process that flourished during the long period of Democratic control prior to 1994 gave members of Congress far more incentive to be individually *responsive* than collectively *responsible*. Trends since then have reduced but by no means eliminated this imbalance, which is a primary source of Congress's collective action problems. For example, electoral logic induces members to promote narrowly targeted programs, projects, or tax breaks for constituents without worrying about the impacts of such measures on spending or revenues. Recipients notice and appreciate such specific and identifiable benefits and show their gratitude at election time. Because the benefits come at the expense of general revenues (money supplied by the taxes that everyone pays), no one's share of the cost of any specific project or tax break is large enough to notice. Thus it makes political sense for members of Congress to pursue local or group benefits that are paid for nationally even if the costs clearly outweigh the benefits. Conversely, no obvious payoff arises from opposing any particular local or group benefit because the savings are spread so thinly among taxpayers that no one notices.

The pursuit of reelection therefore makes *logrolling*—a legislative practice in which members of Congress offer reciprocal support to each other's vote-gaining projects or tax breaks—an attractive strategy (see Chapter 2). But this situation creates a classic prisoner's dilemma. When everyone follows such an individually productive strategy, all may end up in worse shape politically when shackled with collective blame for the overall consequences. Spending rises, revenues fall, the deficit grows, government programs proliferate, and the opposition attacks the logrolling coalition—in practice, the majority party—for wastefulness and incompetence. Individual responsiveness leads to collective irresponsibility.

Democratic candidates suffered across the board in 2010 as voters turned against the aggregate consequences of collective irresponsibility: a government they perceived as too big, too expensive, and too inept. To demonstrate that they were different, the triumphant Republicans promised to shrink government, cut taxes, and change how the government operates. In particular, many pledged to abstain from earmarks—items individual members routinely insert into spending bills or revenue bills providing special benefits to their states, districts, and campaign contributors. Although earmarks account for less than one-half of 1 percent of federal spending, they are easy targets of public criticism—a list of "**pork barrel**" projects they finance always turns up some of dubious worth*—and are especially scorned by the Republican Party's very conservative Tea Party wing, so forgoing earmarks was thought to have considerable symbolic importance. If Congress does permanently abandon the practices of earmarking and pork-barreling, it will be a remarkable transformation. Most members are convinced that delivering such local benefits pays important electoral dividends. A comment by Michele Bachmann, R-Minn., a leading voice of the Tea Party faction, suggests that symbolism will not trump more practical considerations: "Advocating for transportation projects for one's district does not in my mind equate to an earmark."[21]

---

*According to the C-SPAN Congressional Glossary, *pork barrel* came into use as a political term in the post–Civil War era. It comes from the plantation practice of distributing rations of salt pork to slaves from wooden barrels. When used to describe a bill, it implies the legislation is loaded with special projects for members of Congress to distribute to their constituents back home as an act of largesse, courtesy of the federal taxpayer.

SURPRISING SUCCESS

The Tax Reform Act of 1986

politics to policy

Although its instinct is to do the opposite, Congress sometimes can find a way to enact policies that impose costs on specific groups to produce benefits shared by many people. For example, the Tax Reform Act of 1986 eliminated a host of special tax favors to reduce tax rates for everyone. Although the law was a popular idea pushed by Republican president Ronald Reagan and embraced by Democrats who did not want their party left defending "special interests," its success nonetheless depended heavily on the procedural strategies of congressional leaders. The package was assembled behind closed doors without recorded votes so no member could be blamed personally for eliminating any particular tax break. It then came to the floor of the House under a modified closed rule that allowed only three specific amendments to be offered (see section "Making Laws" for an explanation of closed rules). Some powerful members whose support was deemed essential received special concessions in the form of breaks for specific taxpayers in their states or districts—with support for the bill set as the minimum price for any concession. Among other taxpayers, sports facilities in New Jersey (the Meadowlands complex), Miami (Joe Robbie Stadium), and New Orleans (the Superdome) received special treatment.

In the Senate, which does not use closed rules, the bill's principal sponsor, Sen. Bob Packwood, a Republican from Oregon, won agreement that amendments on the floor had to be revenue neutral—that is, any change producing a tax benefit to some group had to be offset by increased taxes on another group. This agreement prevented the kind of logrolling among proponents of special tax breaks that would have unraveled the package.

Members of both houses had to go on record as for or against a substantial cut in taxes for a large majority of taxpayers. Because members were given no opportunity to do any behind-the-scenes favors for the myriad special interest groups that traditionally have feasted at tax-writing time, they could not be blamed for not doing the favors. By agreeing to tie their own hands, then, members were able to solve the acute collective action problem that tax bills always present. In the end, the bill's success took most seasoned observers of Congress by surprise, illustrating how uncommon such an outcome is.

Sources: R. Douglas Arnold, *The Logic of Congressional Action* (New Haven, CT: Yale University Press, 1990), chap. 8; Jeffrey H. Birnbaum and Alan S. Murray, *Showdown at Gucci Gulch: Lawmakers, Lobbyists, and the Unlikely Triumph of Tax Reform* (New York: Vintage, 1988).

The same logic that encourages logrolling makes members of Congress hesitate to impose direct costs on identifiable groups to produce greater, but more diffuse, benefits for all citizens. For example, laws designed to clean up the environment for everyone impose direct costs on industrial firms, such as the expenses incurred in installing antipollution equipment. The cost of compliance is clear to every firm affected, but the benefit of any firm's investment is diffused across so many people that few are likely to know of it. Members of Congress, then, fear retaliation from the losers without a compensating increase in support from the winners. Congressional majorities have found ways to get around this problem. One tactic is to delegate authority to bureaucratic agencies or state governments, letting them take the heat (see Chapter 8). Another is for legislative leaders to frame the lawmaker's choice in a way that highlights credit for the general benefits while minimizing individual responsibility for the specific costs.

More broadly, the trick is to make the electoral payoffs from disregarding special interests to benefit a broader public outweigh the costs. One essential ingredient is that the issue be important (or potentially important if an opponent raises it in a future election campaign) to many voters. A challenge for legislative leaders is to frame the decision on an issue in a way that forces members to put themselves on the record for or against the issue's general benefits without having an opportunity to amend or modify the policy to serve narrower interests. Meeting this challenge requires skillful manipulation of congressional procedures. In addition, leaders may have to buy off the most powerful potential opponents with special concessions or side deals (see box "Surprising Success: The Tax Reform Act of 1986," which describes a classic example of successful execution of the strategy described here).

WHO SERVES IN CONGRESS?

The people who win seats in the Senate and House are by no means "representative" of the American people in any demographic sense. Almost all members have graduated from college; 37 percent have law degrees. Next to law, business is the most common prior occupation. A large majority are professionals of one kind or another; only a handful have blue-collar backgrounds. Most have served in lower elected offices. The true vocation of the average member is, in fact, politics.

Women and racial minorities continue to be underrepresented in Congress, though their numbers have been increasing (see Figures 6-3 and 6-4). In 1961 only three African Americans and twenty women held House or Senate seats; by 1981 the number of black members had grown to seventeen, while only one more woman had been added. Growth continued to be slow until 1992, when the number of African Americans and Hispanics in the House increased sharply after the 1982 Voting Rights Act amendments had been interpreted to require states to maximize the number of "majority-minority" districts when drawing new district lines. The 1992 election also saw women candidates and campaign donors mobilized in unprecedented numbers in response to an event widely publicized in 1991: the insensitive handling by an all-male Senate committee of sexual harassment charges made by college professor Anita Hill against Supreme Court nominee Clarence Thomas. Women also represented a change from politics as usual in a year when that was what most voters wanted.

After the 2012 elections the Senate included twenty women, three Hispanics, two Asian Americans, and one African American[22]; the House included eighty-one women, forty-one African Americans, twenty-five Hispanics, and eight Asian Americans. The congressional parties differ sharply in diversity. In the 113th Congress (2013–2014), for the first time ever women and ethnic minorities make up a majority (53 percent) of the House Democratic membership; in contrast, white men comprise 90 percent of the Republican House membership. Sixteen of the twenty women Senators are Democrats, although half of the six ethnic minority Senators are Republicans. All seven openly gay or bisexual members of Congress are Democrats. Congress remained overwhelmingly white and male for so long because white males predominated in the lower-level public offices and private careers that are the most common stepping-stones to Congress. As women and minorities have continued, albeit slowly, to assume a larger share of state and local offices and professional careers in law and business, their representation in Congress has continued to rise as well.

Figure 6-3 Women in Congress: Higher Numbers but Still Underrepresented

Sources: Norman J. Ornstein, Thomas E. Mann, and Michael J. Malbin, *Vital Statistics on Congress 1997–1998* (Washington, DC: CQ Press, 1998), 40; data for 1998–2012 compiled by the authors.

Figure 6-4 Congress Has Grown More Diverse but Has Yet to Mirror the Electorate

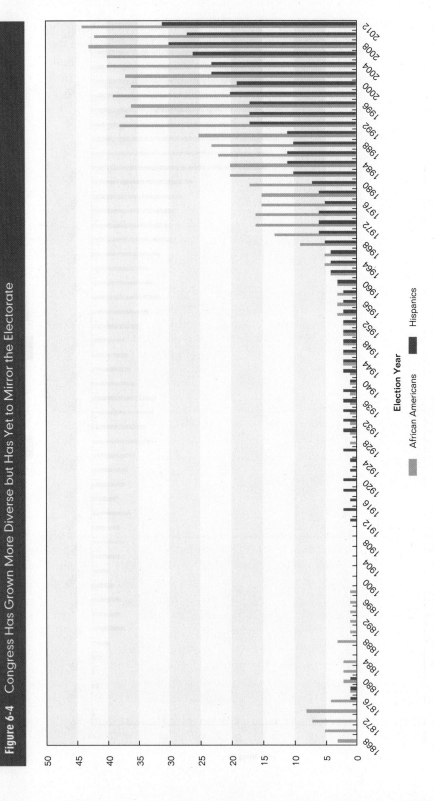

Election Year

African Americans   Hispanics

Sources: Norman J. Ornstein, Thomas E. Mann, and Michael J. Malbin, *Vital Statistics on Congress 1997–1998* (Washington, DC: CQ Press, 1998), 38–39; data for 1998–2012 compiled by the authors.

The gender and racial makeup of Congress makes a difference. For example, black members led the fight for sanctions punishing South Africa for its apartheid system in the 1980s. And the influx of women has made Congress far more attentive to issues of sex discrimination and sexual harassment.[23] The stark differences in diversity between the Republicans and Democrats elected to the 113th Congress may also contribute a demographic dimension to the growing ideological polarization of the congressional parties (discussed later in this chapter).

THE BASIC PROBLEMS OF LEGISLATIVE ORGANIZATION

The Constitution established a basic framework for a national legislature, but today's Congress is the product of more than two centuries of institutional development. Although the House and Senate have evolved into highly complex institutions with remarkably elaborate and arcane rules, procedures, and customs, a logic underlies this sometimes bewildering complexity. To understand how Congress reflects the diverse and conflicting needs and intentions of its members, one must understand what representatives and senators want to accomplish and what obstacles they have to overcome to achieve their goals.

The delegates in Philadelphia created and empowered a national legislature—on paper at least; it was up to members of Congress to make the words into an institutional reality. To exercise the powers conferred on them by the Constitution, the House and Senate had to solve some basic problems: how to acquire information, how to coordinate action, how to resolve conflicts, and how to get members to work for common as well as personal goals. As these problems have become more acute over the years, members of Congress have scrambled to adapt the institution to cope with them more effectively while recognizing that every solution raises problems of its own. The challenges that spurred members to develop the modern Congress fall into two classes: problems besetting the House and Senate as organizations and problems arising from the competing individual and collective needs of members.

The Need for Information

Legislation is only as effective as the quality of knowledge underlying its inception. For example, a legislator cannot regulate the stock market sensibly without knowing how the market works or attack environmental pollution effectively without knowing how pollution is produced. As the United States has become more and more complex—socially, economically, and technologically—and the activities of the federal government have expanded, the informational demands on Congress have grown enormously.

Congress has responded with a solution common to the problem of performing complex social tasks efficiently: division of labor and specialization. The division of labor has given rise to the committee and subcommittee systems, large personal and committee staffs, and specialized research agencies that characterize the modern Congress. Specialists are able to develop a deeper understanding of their domains. By becoming specialists themselves or by drawing on the knowledge of other specialists, members of Congress can make better-informed decisions, and Congress, in turn, becomes a more effective institution. To provide the chamber with expertise, members must invest a lot of time and effort in mastering an area of specialization (as we learned earlier, public goods are more attractive in their

House Democratic women gather together on the steps of the U.S. Capitol. A record seventy-seven women were sworn into the House for the 113th Congress, fifty-three Democrats (26 percent of the Democratic membership) and twenty-four Republicans (10 percent of the Republican membership).

consumption than in their production). Congress compensates members who master an area of specialization and supply specialized information with enhanced influence in their area of expertise. For example, unparalleled mastery of health care issues has made Rep. Henry A. Waxman, D-Calif., the most influential House Democrat by far in this important policy area. One problem, however, is that specialists may dominate policymaking in their domains, shutting out the broader viewpoints of other members. Thus the efficiencies gained by a division of labor are paid for by diminished participation in policymaking outside one's specialty.

Coordination Problems

As noted in Chapter 1, any group of people trying to act in concert faces coordination problems. Coordination becomes more difficult—and necessary—the greater the group's workload and the more elaborate its division of labor. As the volume and complexity of Congress's work have grown, so has its need for traffic management: dividing up the work, directing the flow of bills through the legislative process, scheduling debates and votes on the floor. Coordination problems of this kind usually are solved by a group giving one or several of its members the authority to coordinate—that is, take on the role of "traffic cop." In Congress party leaders serve this function; but procedures also shape policy. Control over the agenda—deciding what gets voted on when—is a powerful legislative weapon. For example, a majority of House members probably would have preferred to censure rather than impeach Bill Clinton, but the Republican House leaders refused to allow a vote on censure, leaving a vote for impeachment as the only alternative to letting the president off completely. (Had they allowed a vote on censure, Clinton probably would have avoided impeachment and trial in the Senate.) Members thus sacrifice a measure of their autonomy in return for the gains in efficiency that come from delegating agenda control to party leaders.

Resolving Conflicts

Legislation is not passed until the majorities in both houses agree to its passage. The rich pluralism of American society guarantees that resolving conflicts is a fundamental task of any institution that reflects America's diversity. Agreement requires successful politicking: getting people who are pursuing divergent, even conflicting, ends to take a common course of action. Even when there is a consensus on ends, Congress often must resolve disagreements about means. During the 108th Congress (2003–2004), for example, almost all members agreed that a major overhaul of intelligence gathering was needed to combat terrorist threats, but leaders had to reconcile competing ideas about what should replace the current system in order to reform intelligence. Disagreements that divide the parties fundamentally can be extremely difficult to resolve, as the account of the struggle over taxes and spending during the 112th Congress at the beginning of this chapter attests.

Many of Congress's rules, customs, and procedures are aimed at resolving or deflecting conflicts so it can get on with the business of legislating. For example, when representatives speak on the floor of the House, all remarks are officially addressed to the Speaker, making it less likely that debates will degenerate into personal confrontations. More substantively, members delegate the task of building legislative coalitions to party leaders, who hold such positions by virtue of their demonstrated skills at negotiating legislative deals. The political parties in Congress themselves serve as ready-made coalitions. Party members agree on matters often enough to adopt a common label and to cooperate routinely on many—but by no means all—of the matters that come before the House and Senate. The presence of ready-made coalitions resolves many conflicts in advance, reducing the transaction costs of negotiating agreements on legislation. The price, however, is loss of autonomy to the party and of authority to leaders: individual members incur greater conformity costs because they cannot always do what is politically best for themselves rather than their party.

Collective Action

Everyone who wins a seat in the House or Senate wants to belong to a well-informed, effective legislature capable of fulfilling its constitutional mandate. Moreover, senators and representatives run under party labels and so have a stake in their party's reputation. But all of them have personal interests as well: winning reelection or advancing to higher office by pleasing constituents and campaign contributors, enacting pet policies, and attaining influence and respect in Washington. The problem is that what members do to pursue individual goals—tax breaks for local firms, special projects for their constituents, maintaining their ideological purity by rejecting compromise—may undermine the reputation of their party or of Congress as a whole. The tension between individual and collective political welfare—the standard prisoner's dilemma—pervades congressional life. Congress has responded to the problem by developing devices such as the committee system that give members individual incentives to work for collectively beneficial ends. As noted, members who contribute to Congress's performance by becoming well informed about issues in their subcommittee's jurisdiction are rewarded with preeminent influence over policy in that area. Others listen to them, and they are given a chance to take personal credit for particular pieces of legislation.[24]

Transaction Costs

In trying to meet its many challenges, Congress must cope with another pressing problem: high transaction costs. These costs, as noted in Chapter 1, are literally the price of doing politics—the time, effort, and bargaining resources (favors to be exchanged) that go into negotiating agreements on action in the absence of agreement on the purposes of the action. Because many of the transaction costs involved in building legislative coalitions are unavoidable—such as the conflicts to be ironed out, compromises to be arranged, and favors to be traded—Congress has organized itself to reduce other transaction costs. One way is the use of fixed **rules** to automate decisions. For example, the **seniority rule,** by routinely allocating first choice in committee chairs, offices, and committee assignments to majority party members who have served longest, reduces the time and energy members would otherwise put into competing for these valued positions. Another way is to follow precedent; battles over legislative turf, for example, are minimized by strict adherence to precedent in assigning bills to House committees. The pressing need to reduce transaction costs explains, then, why Congress does its work within an elaborate structure of rules and precedents. Absent these devices, transaction costs can be high. An example was the Senate's struggle to reach agreement on procedures for Bill Clinton's impeachment trial in 1998. Presidential impeachment trials (fortunately) occur so rarely that few usable rules or precedents were available. Like any attempt to reduce transaction costs, following precedent or seniority can have its own downside, for it inevitably increases the power of some members at the expense of others. Rules are never politically neutral.

Time Pressures

The pressure to avoid unnecessary transaction costs is intensified by the ticking clock—both within the one-year session of Congress and over the two-year tenure of each Congress. The chief source of Congress's authority is its power of the purse over government revenue raising and spending. But if it fails to enact a federal budget in some form each year (or session), large portions of the federal government have to shut down, as happened in late 1995 when the Republican Congress and Democratic president played a high-stakes game of chicken over the budget that resulted in two partial government shutdowns before the Republicans gave in. As budgets have grown larger, broader in scope, and, in recent years, more hotly contested, Congress often has found it difficult to enact them on schedule. Thus it has continued to tinker with the budgetary process. Other legislation has to pass through all the hurdles (outlined later in this chapter) within the two-year life of a Congress. Bills in the pipeline but not enacted by the end of the second session of one Congress must be reintroduced in the next Congress.

The organization and rules of the House and Senate have evolved over two centuries through the accumulation of solutions deliberately chosen to overcome the pressing challenges just described (as well as, of course, to serve the immediate political needs of the majority then in power).[25] Because its membership substantially exceeds that of the Senate, the House experiences organizational problems more acutely than does the Senate. Senators can get away with looser organization and retain more individual autonomy and equality simply because there are fewer of them. Their counterparts in the House, to solve their coordination problems, have to follow stricter rules of procedure and tolerate greater control by leaders.

ORGANIZING CONGRESS

To preserve the House and Senate as the powerful legislative bodies envisioned in the Constitution, members of Congress have had to devise means to overcome the formidable barriers to effective collective action discussed in the previous section. The crucial institutional structures they have created to exercise, and therefore preserve, Congress's power in the federal system are the party and committee systems.

The Parties

Decisions in the House and Senate are made (with a few important exceptions) by majority vote. Majorities not only enact bills but also set rules, establish procedures, choose leaders, and decide how to organize their respective houses. This reality creates powerful incentives for members of Congress to join and maintain durable coalitions—that is, political parties (for a broader analysis of the logic of party formation, see Chapter 12). What individual members give up in freedom to go their own way is more than made up for by what they can gain by cooperating with one another.

Parties do not arise through spontaneous, voluntary cooperation, however. Like other coalitions, political parties are formed when people recognize it is in their best interests to cooperate despite their disagreements. Party coalitions are assembled and maintained by party leaders. But leaders cannot lead without effective means to resolve conflicts, coordinate action, and induce members to cooperate when they are tempted to do otherwise. Members, in turn, must sacrifice independence by conceding some authority to party leaders. Yet as we noted in Chapter 1, when a group delegates authority to a leader to achieve coordination and reduce transaction costs, it risks incurring conformity costs and agency losses.

Members of Congress, aware of the risks, relinquish autonomy only so far as necessary, which accounts for the notable differences in the evolution of party leadership between the House and Senate as well as the changes over time in the power of House and Senate leaders.[26]

DEVELOPMENT OF CONGRESSIONAL PARTIES. Parties began to form in the first session of the First Congress. A majority of members in the House favored the program for national economic development proposed by Alexander Hamilton, President George Washington's secretary of the Treasury, and worked together under his leadership to enact it. James Madison, a member of the House, and Thomas Jefferson, the secretary of state, led the opposition to what they saw as an unwarranted expansion of federal activity. Recognizing the obvious—that, to prevail, they needed more votes in Congress—Madison's followers sought to increase their numbers by recruiting and electing like-minded men to the House.

These "factions" soon had names—Hamilton's Federalists and Jefferson's Republicans (later called Democratic-Republicans and then Democrats)—and party competition was under way. (See Chapter 12 for a fuller account of these developments.)

When the House and Senate divided into parties, congressional and party leadership merged. Formal leadership was established more quickly and more powerfully in the House because, as it was the larger and busier body (the Senate's legislative role was decidedly secondary in the early Congresses), its collective action problems were more acute. Elected by the reigning majority, the **Speaker of the House** became the majority's leader and agent. Speakers were given the authority to appoint committees, make rules, and manage the legislative process on the majority party's behalf.

Joseph Cannon was the last of a generation of powerful Speakers of the House of Representatives. During his tenure as Speaker of the House, "Uncle Joe" swatted many an opponent. Too many of his victims were fellow Republicans, however, and in 1910 thirty-six of them joined with Democrats in the historic revolt that dismantled the strong Speaker system and decentralized House administration.

SPEAKER OF THE HOUSE. Centralized authority reached its peak under Thomas Brackett "Czar" Reed, a Republican from Maine, who served as Speaker in the Fifty-first (1889–1890), Fifty-fourth (1895–1896), and Fifty-fifth (1897–1898) Congresses. Reed appointed all committees and committee chairs, exercised unlimited power of recognition (that is, decided who would speak on the floor of the House), and imposed new rules that made it much more difficult for a minority to prevent action through endless procedural delays. He also chaired the Rules Committee, which controlled the flow of legislation from the other committees to the floor of the House.

Although denounced by his opponents as a tyrant, Reed could not have amassed so much power without the full support of the Republican House majority. They were willing to delegate so much authority for two reasons. First, disagreements within the Republican Party were, at the time, muted; no important faction thought its interests could be threatened by a powerful leader allied with a competing faction. Second, service in the House had not yet become a career. The average member served only two terms. Indeed, in some places the local party organizations that controlled nominations enforced a two-term limit so that more of the party's stalwarts could enjoy the honor of serving in Congress. Without long-term career prospects and accustomed to party discipline, most members had little reason to object to strong leadership.

But once these conditions no longer held, the House revolted. Republican Speaker Joseph Cannon of Illinois (served 1903–1911) made the mistake of offending the progressive faction of the Republican

Party that had emerged since Reed's day; he denied its members committee chairs and opposed the policies of the progressive Republican president, Theodore Roosevelt. In response, the Republican insurgents formed an alliance with Democrats who voted in 1910 to strip the Speaker of his power to appoint committees and chairs, forced him off the powerful Rules Committee, and limited his power of recognition. The increasingly career-oriented membership filled the power vacuum with a more decentralized and impersonal leadership structure, making seniority the criterion for selecting committee chairs. By weakening the Speaker, House members in effect chose to tolerate higher transaction costs to reduce their conformity costs.

The degree of consensus within a party continues to affect how much authority party members are willing to delegate to party leaders. In the 1970s, for example, the Democrats strengthened the hand of the Speaker. He was given the authority to nominate all the Democratic members of the Rules Committee and to appoint temporary committees and special legislative task forces to deal with complex or controversial bills. At the same time, the Democratic Caucus (the organization of all House Democrats) reasserted its authority over committee organization, appointments, rules, and chairs. Once committee chairs became subject to election by secret ballot in the caucus, they lost much of the autonomy they had enjoyed since the New Deal.

Democrats could afford to strengthen their party's capacity to act collectively because the ideological distinctiveness of southern Democrats had been undermined by the in-migration of northerners, industrial development, the movement of conservative whites from the Democratic into the Republican camp, and the Voting Rights Act of 1965, which brought black voters into southern Democratic electorates. A more cohesive Democratic Party saw smaller potential conformity costs in centralizing authority and faced an assertive Republican president, Ronald Reagan, and from 1981 through 1986 a Republican-controlled Senate. By the 1990s congressional Democrats were more unified than they had been in decades.[27]

Republicans granted even more authority to their leaders when they took over the House in 1995. Unified by the party's Contract with America, House Republicans made Newt Gingrich the most powerful Speaker since Cannon. At his behest, the Republican Conference (the Republican counterpart of the Democratic Caucus) ignored seniority in appointing committee chairs, ratifying without dissent the slate proposed by Gingrich. The Speaker also had a strong say in all the committee assignments, which he used to reward loyal junior members, and was given control of the House Administration Committee, which supervises management of the nonlegislative business of the House. The new majority party also adopted a rule limiting committee chairs to three two-year terms, reducing anyone's opportunity to build an independent committee domain. House Republicans gave their leader an unusually strong hand to overcome their coordination and other collective action problems because they believed that keeping their promise to act on every item in the Contract with America within one hundred days of taking office was crucial to their and their party's future electoral fates.

By 1997, however, House Republicans' unity had frayed badly, and one faction mounted a quickly aborted attempt to depose the Speaker. Gingrich hung on until Republican members, angry at the party's losses in the 1998 midterm election, forced him to resign—a pointed reminder that party leaders, as the majority's agents, are subject to dismissal if they do not satisfy their principals. Gingrich's eventual replacement, Dennis Hastert of Illinois, assisted by the hard-line tactics of Tom DeLay, first as majority whip, then as majority leader, was able to maintain a high level of party unity, notably keeping his narrow but overwhelmingly conservative House majority together in support of the George W. Bush administration's legislative proposals. Leading the Democrats in opposition to the Bush administration during the 110th Congress (2007–2008) and in alliance with the Obama administration during the 111th Congress, Speaker Nancy Pelosi presided over the most unified Democratic team in at least fifty years. Her leadership was crucial to Obama's major legislative victories on economic stimulus, health care reform, and economic regulation legislation. The Republican majority under her successor, John Boehner, also sought to present a highly unified front on the House floor, although Boehner sometimes found it hard to resolve intraparty disputes between the party's conventional conservatives and its larger, more radically antigovernment conservative faction associated with the Tea Party. For example, this faction's intransigence left him no choice but to allow the bill crafted by the Senate and the Obama administration to avoid the fiscal cliff in 2012 to reach the House floor for passage with mostly Democratic votes, breaking an unwritten rule that any legislation not supported by a majority of the House majority party will not be brought up for a vote. In sum, Congress is subject to what political scientists have labeled **conditional party government**, meaning that the degree of authority delegated to and exercised by congressional party leaders varies with—is *conditioned by*—the extent of election-driven ideological consensus among members.[28]

Increased Partisanship

The decline and resurgence of congressional partisanship since the 1950s is evident in Figure 6-5. The proportion of "party unity" votes—those on which the party majorities took opposite positions—has increased since the 1970s (although more steeply and uniformly in the Senate than in the House). More importantly, as the party coalitions have become more homogeneous, the proportion of representatives and senators of both parties who vote with their party's majority on these party unity votes has risen steadily and was about 15 percentage points higher during the three most recent administrations than it was during the Nixon-Ford administration. The House vote on the impeachment of Bill Clinton in December 1998 epitomized this trend; 98 percent of House Republicans voted for at least one article of impeachment, while 98 percent of House Democrats voted against all four articles. Despite the bipartisan support for President George W. Bush's response to the al-Qaeda attacks of September 11, 2001, party unity on votes that split the parties reached their highest levels in the postwar era in both houses during his administration, only to be topped during the first Congress of the Obama administration.

As the congressional parties became more unified, they also became more polarized along ideological lines. The ideological gap between the two parties in both houses of Congress has widened appreciably since the 1970s (see Figure 6-6). Republicans grew, on average, steadily more conservative. Democrats became more liberal as their party's conservative southern members were gradually replaced in Congress by Republicans, leaving the remaining southern Democrats ideologically more similar to other congressional Democrats. Ideological polarization thus helped to unite the parties internally, separate them from each other, and strengthen party leaders. It also made life harder for the dwindling number of ideologically moderate members.

Figure 6-5 Rising Party Unity in Congress

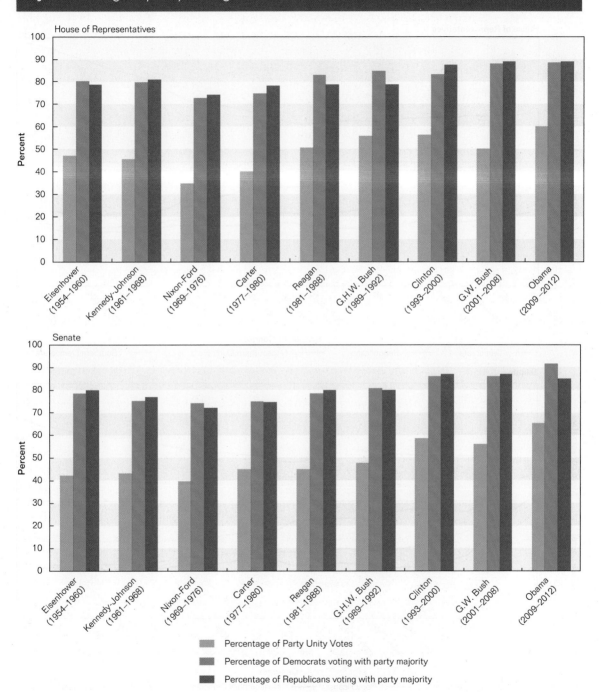

Source: CQ Weekly, January 3, 2011, 37; and http://library.cqpress.com/cqweekly/document.php?id=weeklyreport113-000004207218&type=hitlist&num=0&.

Note: Party unity votes are those votes on which party majorities took opposite positions.

Figure 6-6 The Widening Ideological Gap between the Parties

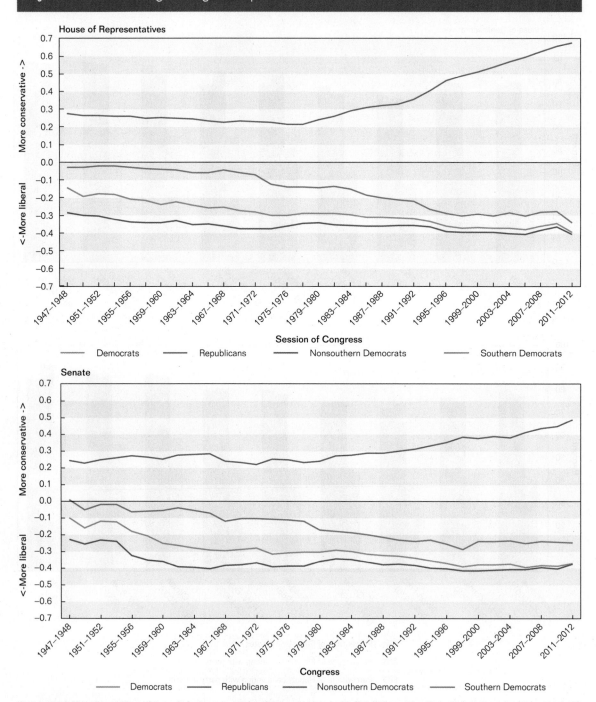

Sources: Keith T. Poole and Howard Rosenthal, *Congress: A Political-Economic History of Roll Call Voting* (New York: Oxford University Press, 1997). We thank Keith T. Poole for data updated through 2010.

PARTY ORGANIZATION. The majority party in the House is led by the Speaker of the House, whose chief assistants are the **majority leader** and the **majority whip** (see Table 6-1 for a list of major-party offices and organizations in the House and Senate). The structure of the minority party, the Democrats in the 113th Congress (2013–2014), is similar to that of the majority party but without the Speaker; the minority leader is its head. The party whips head up the whip organization— the members who form the communication network connecting leaders with other members—whose purpose is to help solve the party's coordination problems. (The term *whip* comes from Great Britain, where the "whipper-in" keeps the hounds together in a pack during a foxhunt.) In addition to these official party committees, the Rules Committee is, in effect, an instrument of the majority party.

Party members give House party leaders resources for inducing members to cooperate when they are tempted to go their own way as free riders (for example, by breaking ranks on roll-call votes to enhance their own electoral fortunes at the expense of their party's collective reputation for effective governance). These resources mainly take the form of favors the leaders may grant or withhold. For example, party leaders have a strong voice in all committee assignments (officially the province of the Steering Committees); Speaker Boehner used this influence prior to the 113th Congress (2013–3014) to strip four Republicans of their plum committee assignments for bucking his leadership too flagrantly and as a warning to other potentially disloyal members.[29] Leaders also control the legislative agenda. Because a place on the agenda is a scarce resource, scheduling decisions determine the fates of many bills. Leaders also choose how much of their own time, energy, and organizational resources to devote to each legislative proposal. In the past, they have also controlled access to pork, routinely using earmarked projects to win support of wavering members. Boehner's 2011 pledge to ban earmarks—assuming he sticks with it—thus deprives him of an important customary bargaining resource.[30] Party leaders can also help with reelection campaigns, especially the fund-raising component. Party leaders are therefore in a position to make it easier (or more difficult) for members to attain positions of influence, shape policy, and win reelection.

House party leaders are members' agents, however—not their bosses. They do not hire and fire party members; voters do, and so voters come first. Members, then, choose the style of leadership they believe will best serve their goals. Party leaders, who are elected or reelected to their positions at the beginning of every Congress, are thoroughly, if informally, screened. They are members who have been around for a long time and whose styles, abilities, and flaws are well known. In the pre-Gingrich decades when Democrats held a majority of seats, they chose

---

TABLE 6-1

Party Committees and Leaders in Congress

House of Representatives

Republicans	Democrats
Speaker	
Majority Leader	Minority Leader
Majority Whip	Minority Whip
Conference (all Republicans)	Caucus (all Democrats)
Steering Committee	Steering Committee
Policy Committee	Policy Committee
National Republican Congressional Committee	Democratic Congressional Campaign Committee

Senate

Democrats	Republicans
President Pro Tempore	
Majority Leader	Minority Leader
Assistant Majority Leader (Whip)	Assistant Minority Leader (Whip)
Conference (all Democrats)	Conference (all Republicans)
Policy Committee	Policy Committee
Steering and Outreach Committee	National Republican Senatorial Committee
Democratic Senatorial Campaign Committee	

Note: Table covers the 113th Congress (2013–2014).

leaders, such as Thomas "Tip" O'Neill of Massachusetts (majority leader 1973–1977), who were experts on procedure rather than policy and who cared more about building successful coalitions than about achieving specific legislative goals. But when the Republicans took over the majority in 1995, Speaker Gingrich, as we saw earlier, pursued—with the full support of Republican members—a legislative agenda much more policy and ideologically focused than those undertaken by the Democratic Speakers before him. This has since become the norm for Speakers of both parties.

For the minority party in the House, legislative leadership is normally less crucial because the party's legislative role has usually been modest. When the party balance is very close, minority leaders can sometimes influence legislation by forming alliances with more moderate members of the majority party, although this has happened rarely in recent Congresses (the fiscal cliff vote was the only instance during the 112th Congress). When the majority enjoys a wider margin, minority leaders choose between two strategic options: cooperating with the majority, and thus exerting some influence but getting little credit, or opposing and attacking the majority to position their party for future electoral battles. The minority leaders' dilemma is sharpened when a president of their party sits in the White House, because the president has to cut deals with the majority to accomplish anything at all. As former minority whip, Gingrich managed to lead Republicans to majority status by abandoning a strategy of accommodation in favor of harsh partisan confrontation. Subsequently, Democratic minority leaders Richard Gephardt and then Nancy Pelosi sought to retake the House (and win the Speakership) through energetic campaigning and fund-raising on behalf of Democratic candidates, an effort crowned with success in 2006. In the 111th Congress (2009–2010) Republican minority leader John Boehner led his party's resolute opposition to the Democrats' legislative initiatives and ended up as Speaker in the next Congress.

PARTIES AND PARTY LEADERS IN THE SENATE. Over the years the Senate has been slower than the House to develop formal leadership positions, and senators have never delegated as much authority to their leaders as have representatives. Senators initially saw themselves as ambassadors from sovereign states, and as such could accept no less than equal rights with one another. In the years since, they have retained wide freedom of individual action because, with its smaller size, the Senate is able to get by without elaborate procedural shackles.*

---

*The Senate began with twenty-six members and did not reach one hundred until 1959; the House already had exceeded one hundred members by 1793.

Under the Constitution, the vice president is the presiding officer of the Senate. The designated **president pro tempore** presides when the vice president is absent. But neither office has a real leadership role—after all, the vice president, who seldom presides, is not chosen by the Senate, and the president pro tempore, as the Latin term suggests, is formally a temporary position. In fact, in the first few Congresses a new president pro tempore was elected every time the vice president was away. In practice, no one led the Senate during the pre–Civil War period.

Parties formed in the Senate almost from the start, but party members were little inclined to delegate authority. The party caucuses did not take full control of committee appointments until 1846, after which they avoided intraparty conflicts over committee control by resorting to a strict seniority rule. Not until the end of the nineteenth century did senators concede the means to enforce party discipline—on procedural matters only—to party leaders.

President pro tempore is now, by tradition, the majority member with the greatest Senate seniority. In the 106th Congress (1999–2000), ninety-six-year-old Strom Thurmond, a South Carolina Republican first elected to the Senate in 1954, filled the position. In the 112th Congress (2011–2012), the office was held by Daniel Inouye (D- Hawaii), then eighty-six. After Inouye's death in December 2012, the office went to the relatively youthful Patrick Leahy (D-Vt.), seventy-one. Leahy is third in line of presidential succession after Vice President Joseph Biden and House Speaker John Boehner.

The positions of majority leader and minority leader were not formalized until 1913.

The power and influence exerted by Senate leaders have depended largely on their personal political skills and the extent of intraparty divisions. Lyndon Johnson, who led the Senate Democrats from 1953 until resigning to become vice president in 1961, exercised extraordinary influence over the Senate through skillful persuasion and manipulation. The resources at his disposal were no greater than those of other Senate leaders, but he used them to greater effect. Although no majority leader has since matched Johnson's fire or authority, others, such as Bob Dole, a Kansas Republican (served 1985–1987, 1995–1996), and George Mitchell, a Maine Democrat (served 1989–1995), have been skillful and effective majority leaders.

Party leadership in the Senate is more collegial and less formal than in the House. The minority party has greater influence in the Senate because so much of that body's business is conducted under **unanimous consent agreements** negotiated by party leaders. These agreements, which can be killed by a single objection, might govern, for example, the order in which bills are considered and the length of debate allotted to them. However, the majority party in the Senate is still at a considerable advantage because its leader strongly shapes, if not fully controls, the Senate's agenda. Hence the switch in party control to the Democrats in January 2007 portended more than simply a reshuffling of offices. Unanimous consent agreements serve as only the most extreme examples of the general rule: the capacity of House and Senate party leaders to lead depends largely on the willingness of party members to follow.

Although intense partisan rivals, Democrat Harry Reid, Senate majority leader (left), and Republican Mitch McConnell, Senate minority leader, confer regularly on procedural matters. The Senate's rules make it easy for a disgruntled minority to block action, so like it or not, Reid has to accommodate McConnell, just as Reid had to be accommodated when Republicans held the majority before 2007.

OTHER GROUPS IN CONGRESS. Although parties are by far the most important of Congress's coalitions, members have formed dozens of other groups. Some are explicitly ideological (Republican Study Committee, Progressive Caucus, New Democrat Coalition, Blue Dog Coalition, Tea Party Caucus). Others are based on demographics (Black Caucus, Hispanic Caucus, Asian Pacific American Caucus, Caucus for Women's Issues). Bipartisan groups form around shared regional interests (Northeast-Midwest Coalition, Western Caucus, Appalachian Caucus) and economic concerns (Steel Caucus, Automotive Caucus, Wine Caucus, Biotechnology Caucus). Other groups focus on specific issues (Pro-Life Caucus, Pro-Choice Caucus, Human Rights Caucus). No fewer than thirty foreign countries enjoyed the attention of a congressional caucus in the 112th Congress.

Such groups give members better access to information and allies on issues that are of special concern to them (or their constituents) and that do not fit neatly into regular party or committee categories. The groups reflect the value of ready-made alliances in a system where success depends on building majority coalitions.

The Committee Systems

The committee systems of the House and Senate are the second organizational pillar upholding the institutional power of Congress in the federal system. Although committee power has at times been used to frustrate party majorities and leaders, committees are ultimately subject to the majority party, and the committee and party systems are closely integrated and mutually dependent. House committees, like House party leaders, are more powerful than their counterparts in the Senate, again reflecting the need for tighter organization in the larger body.

EVOLUTION OF CONGRESSIONAL COMMITTEES. The first Congresses delegated authority to committees sparingly. Instead, the House would turn itself into a Committee of the Whole (sitting as a committee, the House operates under a more flexible set of rules), frame a piece of legislation, elect a temporary committee to draft the bill, then debate and amend the bill line by line. After reassuming its guise as the House, it would vote on final passage.

From the start, this process was intolerably cumbersome. One early member, Fisher Ames of Massachusetts, likened it to trying to make a delicate etching with an elephant's foot.[31] Thus the House began to delegate more and more work to permanent committees. Ten were in place by 1809, twenty-eight by 1825. Transaction costs were further reduced by having committee members appointed by the Speaker rather than elected. As the Speaker emerged as leader of the majority party, appointments became partisan affairs, and choice committee assignments became rewards for party loyalty and bargaining chips in campaigns for the Speakership.

The Senate was slower to set up permanent committees. Despite their smaller numbers and lighter workload, senators also found they were spending too much time on electing a new committee to draft each bill, and the Senate began to accumulate **standing committees**—those that exist from one Congress to the next unless they are explicitly disbanded. The initial twelve were established in 1816; by 1841 there were twenty-two. The Senate also was slower to delegate legislative action to committees and has never gone as far in this direction as the House. After the Senate's parties assumed the right to make committee assignments, seniority became the criterion for selecting committee chairs: the office was awarded to the majority party member with the longest term of service on the committee. Reducing transaction and conformity costs, the seniority rule avoided two unwelcome alternatives: election, which would have led to divisive, time-consuming intraparty squabbles, and appointment by party leaders, which would have given the leaders more power than senators thought desirable or necessary.

TYPES OF COMMITTEES. The standing committees of the House and Senate embody Congress's division of legislative labor. Standing committees have fixed jurisdictions (that is, they always deal with the same legislative topics) and stable memberships, both of which facilitate specialization. Once appointed, a member in good standing (that is, one who has not flagrantly annoyed party leaders) can expect to keep the seat unless his or her party suffers large electoral losses. Party ratios on committees generally match party ratios in the House and Senate. A House party with a narrow overall majority usually gives itself somewhat larger committee majorities, and it always accords itself extra seats on the most important committees. The job security associated with standing committees gives committee members both the motive and the opportunity to become knowledgeable about policy issues under their committee's jurisdiction. Expertise brings influence—other members defer to the judgment of committee experts they trust—and therefore a chance to make a real difference in at least one area of national policy.

Although committee membership is generally stable, changes occur when legislators seize the opportunity to move up to the committees deemed more important and desirable than the others. At the top of the heap in both chambers are the money committees—the Ways and Means and the Appropriations Committees in the House, the Finance and the Appropriations Committees in the Senate—because their activities are so central to Congress's main source of power in the federal system, its control over the budget. The House and Senate Budget Committees share some of this prestige. Seats on the Senate Foreign Relations and Judiciary Committees also are in demand because of the Senate's special authority over treaties and diplomatic and judicial appointments. In the House the powerful Rules Committee, which controls the flow of legislation from committees to the floor, is especially attractive. Among the least desirable committees are those dealing with the internal administration of Congress, particularly its members' ethics; many members feel uncomfortable sitting in judgment on their colleagues.

COMMITTEE ASSIGNMENTS. Assignments to committees are made by party committees under the firm control of senior party leaders and are ratified by the party membership.

Members pursue committee assignments that allow them to serve special constituent interests as well as their own policy and power goals. For example, the Agriculture Committees attract members from farm states, and the Armed Services Committees attract members from regions with large military installations.

Because party leaders want to keep their followers in office, they are responsive to arguments that a particular assignment will help a member win reelection. Moreover, when members are assigned to the committees that best serve their personal and political interests, they will take committee work more seriously, making a larger contribution to their party's overall performance. The danger is that committees may become stacked with members whose views do not represent those of their party's majority. By and large, party leaders have managed to avoid this problem by judicious distribution of assignments, especially to the committees whose jurisdictions are most important to the party. A party's committee members are, like party leaders, the party's agents, and party majorities use their ultimate control over committee assignments to keep their agents responsive to the party's desires.[32]

Most committees are divided into subcommittees, many of which also have fixed jurisdictions and stable memberships. Like full committees, subcommittees encourage specialization and, at the same time, reward members who develop expertise with special influence over their own small pieces of legislative turf. Both committees and, in the Senate, subcommittees come with staffs of experts to help members do their work. Most committee staffers report to committee and subcommittee chairs; the ranking minority committee members control a much smaller set of staff assistants.

In addition to the standing committees, Congress also forms special, select, joint, ad hoc, and conference committees. In theory, most **special committees** and **select committees** (the terms are interchangeable) are appointed to deal with specific problems and then disappear. A good example was the House's Select Committee on U.S. National Security and Military/Commercial Concerns with the People's Republic of China, appointed in 1998 to investigate technology transfers to China and disbanded a year later after issuing a 1,016-page report detailing the loss of military secrets to that country and recommending steps to stop it. However, some special and select committees sometimes last through many Congresses—for example, the Senate's Special Committee on Aging has been around since 1961.

JOINT COMMITTEES. These are permanent committees composed of members from both chambers; the committee leaderships rotate between the chambers at the beginning of each newly elected Congress. **Joint committees** gather information and oversee executive agencies but do not report legislation. One joint committee (Library) oversees the Library of Congress, the U.S. Botanic Garden, and public statuary; another (Printing) oversees the U.S. Government Printing Office and the arrangement and style of the *Congressional Record*, which publishes all of the speeches and debates on the floors of the House and Senate. In the House the Speaker occasionally appoints **ad hoc committees** to handle bills that are particularly sensitive (congressional pay raise legislation, for example). **Conference committees** are appointed to resolve differences between the House and Senate versions of bills (see section "Making Laws" in this chapter). The committees of the 113th Congress are listed in Table 6-2.

COMMITTEE POWER. A century ago House committees were dominated by the Speaker, who appointed committee members and chairs. The revolt against Speaker

TABLE 6-2

The Committees of the 113th Congress

House of Representatives	Party Ratio	Number of Subcommittees	Senate	Party Ratio	Number of Subcommittees
House of Representatives			**Senate**		
Standing Committees			*Standing Committees*		
Agriculture	29R:19D	6	Agriculture	12D:9R	–
Appropriations	30R:21D	12	Appropriations	16D:14R	12
Armed Services	37R:28D	7	Armed Services	13D:12R	6
Budget	22R:18D	–	Banking, Housing, and Urban Affairs	12D:10R	5
Education	25R:18D	4	Budget	12D:10R	–
Energy and Commerce	31R:24D	6	Commerce, Science, and Transportation	13D:11R	7
Ethics	5R:5D	–	Energy and Natural Resources	12D:10R	–
Financial Services	34R:31D	5	Environment and Public Works	10D:8R	6
Foreign Affairs	28R:27D	6	Finance	13D:11R	–
Homeland Security	20R:14D	6	Foreign Relations	10D:9R	9
House Administration	6R:3D	–	Health, Education, Labor and Pensions	12D:10R	–
Judiciary	23R:13D	5	Homeland Security and governmental Affairs	9D:7R	4
Natural Resources	26R:21D	–	Indian Affairs	8D:6R	–
Oversight and government Reform	23R:13D	5	Judiciary	10D:8R	7
Rules	10R:4D	2	Rules	10D:8R	–
Science, Space, and Technology	22R:17D	5	Small Business and Entrepreneurship	10D:8R	–
Small Business	13R:11D	5	Veterans' Affairs	8D:7R	–
Transportation and Infrastructure	33R:27D	6	*Select Committees*		
Veteran's Affairs	14R:11D	4	Select Committee on Ethics	3D:3R	–
Ways and Means	24R:16D	6	Select Committee on Intelligence	9D:7R	–
Select Committees			Special Committee on Aging	11D:9R	–
Permanent Select Committee on Intelligence	12R:9D	–	Joint Economic Committee	6D:4R	–

Cannon in 1910 effectively transferred control over committees to committee chairs, who, under the altered rules, owed their positions to seniority, not loyalty to their party or its leaders. By the 1950s both chambers were run by a handful of powerful committee chairs who could safely ignore the wishes of party majorities. Conservative southern Democrats, continually reelected from one-party strongholds, chaired the most powerful committees and cooperated with Republicans to thwart policies supported by a majority of Democrats, especially in the area of civil rights. The most notorious example was Howard W. Smith, a segregationist Virginia Democrat who used his position as chair of the House Rules Committee during the 1950s to stop civil rights bills. The rules allowed chairs to run committees like dictators, and some of them did.

In 1959 frustrated younger liberals formed the Democratic Study Group (DSG) to take on the conservative Democrats, hoping that they could make up in numbers what they lacked in institutional clout. Over the next decade the DSG grew large enough to take over and revitalize the Democratic Caucus. The most important changes occurred after the 1974 election, when the public reaction to the Watergate scandal brought seventy-four new Democrats, eager for action and disdainful of seniority, into the House. At their instigation, the Democratic Caucus adopted a rule that forbade any individual from chairing more than one committee or subcommittee; this way, many more members could enjoy this privilege. Committee members and the caucus, rather than chairs, assumed control over committee rules, budgets, and subcommittee organization. Committee nominations were transferred from Democrats on the Ways and Means Committee, who had held this authority since the revolt against Cannon, to the caucus's own new Steering and Policy Committee.*

The caucus itself elected committee chairs by secret ballot (secrecy removed the threat of retaliation). In 1975 the caucus actually deposed three committee chairs, all elderly southern conservatives, underlining the new reality that the party's majority, not seniority, would now have the final say in who runs committees.

These changes produced a more fragmented and decentralized committee system in which fully half of the Democrats in the House chaired a committee or subcommittee. Although members benefited individually, they found it more difficult to act collectively. The simultaneous strengthening of the Speaker's authority, described earlier, logically complemented these changes. The party leaders may have found the task of coordination more difficult, but they also were given more tools (for example, control of nominations to the Rules Committee) to carry it out. The net effect was a strengthened party capacity for collective action and a decline in the power of conservative Democrats.

The new Republican majority that took over the House in 1995 revised committee rules to ensure that the legislative agenda outlined in its Contract with America would move swiftly to enactment. The new rules gave committee chairs greater control over subcommittees by authorizing them to appoint all subcommittee chairs and control the work of the majority's committee staff. But committee chairs themselves now had to report to the Speaker and were limited to three consecutive terms (six years) as chair. All these changes gave the Republican majority more control over its committees than any House majority had exercised since the early years of the twentieth century. Returning to power in 2007, Democratic leaders dropped the term limits and generally followed seniority in choosing committee chairs but maintained the tighter controls over committee assignments. In 2011 the new Republican House majority reinstituted term limits but otherwise chose chairs according to seniority.[33]

JURISDICTION. In the House, does international trade policy fall within the jurisdiction of the Energy and Commerce Committee or the Foreign Affairs Committee? Should education programs for veterans be handled in the Senate by Veterans' Affairs or by Health,

---

*The Steering and Policy Committee was subsequently split into a Steering Committee, which retained the authority to make committee assignments, and a separate Policy Committee.

Education, Labor, and Pensions? Where does something like homeland defense, which affects virtually every aspect of American life—transportation, energy infrastructure, international trade, the administration of justice, national defense—fit? Moreover, such technical issues are overlaid with political agendas. Committees and subcommittees compete for jurisdiction over important policy areas, but the supply of legislative turf is always insufficient to meet the demand. Thus it is not surprising that the House and Senate have altered the number and jurisdictions of their committees from time to time; nor is it surprising that such changes have been highly contentious.

Within Congress, the constant pressure to multiply standing committees and subcommittees arises out of the increasing complexity, volume, and scope of legislative business and members' desires to serve as committee and subcommittee chairs, especially now that Congress is populated by career politicians seeking their own pieces of the action. Inactive committees are hard to kill off. For example, the Senate maintained a Committee on Revolutionary Claims (requests for payment of bills incurred during the American Revolution) until 1920, when it pruned its standing committees back from seventy-four to thirty-four. Many of the disbanded committees had not met in years, but their chairs clung to them because committees came with staff and office space. The cutbacks were achieved only by giving individual senators their own clerks and offices.

Since the 1920s the House and Senate have trimmed their committee systems several times, notably in the Legislative Reorganization Act of 1946, which sharply reduced the number of standing committees in both chambers (from thirty-three to fifteen in the Senate, from forty-eight to nineteen in the House). The act also rearranged committee jurisdictions to reduce the overlap and confusion and to make the House and Senate systems more similar. Reductions were achieved by consolidation, however, so many former committees simply became subcommittees. The most recent committee changes occurred in 1995, when the victorious House Republicans abolished three standing committees and made other modest alterations in committee jurisdictions.

The political problem with trying to distribute committee jurisdictions more sensibly is that changes redistribute power and upset long-established relationships among committee members, administrative agencies, and interest groups. Nevertheless, Congress must rationalize jurisdictions occasionally, or the emergence of new issues will lead to turf battles, overlapping jurisdictions, uneven workloads, and confusion. For example, homeland security policy is so multifaceted that by one count, eighty-eight congressional committees and subcommittees, which included as members every member of the Senate and all but twenty representatives, held jurisdiction over one or more of its components.[34] Outsiders (and a few insiders) advocated the creation of new committees in both houses to handle the new Department of Homeland Security's nominations, budget, and legislation and to oversee its operation. As one former deputy defense secretary put it, "If they don't create a separate oversight committee in the House and Senate, there's never going to be a functioning department. You can't create a new department if all the elements of the new department keep going back to their old bosses."[35] But members of Congress relinquish jurisdiction over important matters with great reluctance, and homeland security was no exception. Congress established the new department in 2002, but the House and Senate did not form new standing committees on homeland security until 2005. Powerful leaders of existing committees resisted giving up jurisdiction—and not only out of pure self-interest, for they could plausibly argue that the deep fund of experience and expertise, both of members and of staff, regarding the department's diverse component agencies (see Chapter 8) held by their old committee overseers might be lost if a new committee took full jurisdiction over them. The result could be enfeebled congressional oversight.[36]

Party leaders sometimes cope with the problem of multiple jurisdictions by using **multiple referrals**—that is, sending bills, in whole or piece by piece, to several committees at the same time or in sequence. For example, a banking reform bill introduced in the House in the 102nd Congress (1991–1992) went first to Banking, Finance, and Urban Affairs, then to Energy and Commerce, then to Agriculture, then to Judiciary, and finally to Ways and Means.[37] In recent Congresses, about 20 percent of all bills and 34 percent of major bills have been subject to multiple referrals in the House.[38]

THE MONEY COMMITTEES. The "power of the purse" has inspired the most contentious jurisdictional fights. In the earliest years of government, revenue and spending bills were handled by Ways and Means in the House and Finance in the Senate. Then, during the 1860s, the spending power was transferred to a separate Appropriations Committee in each house to help deal with the extraordinary financial demands of the Civil War. Other committees in both houses later broke the Appropriations Committees' monopoly on spending, and by 1900 authority over national finances was spread among nearly twenty House and Senate committees. In the House this devolution of authority was not such a great impediment to action when powerful Speakers dominated the chamber, but a few years after the revolt against Cannon the Republican House majority underlined its commitment to parsimony by restoring the Appropriations Committee's monopoly. The Senate followed suit in 1922.

Since then, legislative spending has been a two-step process in each chamber. In the first step the committee with jurisdiction over a program *authorizes* expenditures for it, and in the second the Appropriations Committee *appropriates* the money—that is, writes a bill designating that specific sums be spent on authorized programs. The sums appropriated need not and often do not match the amounts authorized because more spending may be authorized than the appropriators, concerned with the total size of the budget, are willing to appropriate. For some important programs expenditures take the form of **entitlements,** which designate specific classes of people who are entitled to a legally defined benefit. Social Security and Medicare payments and military pensions are examples. Congress must spend whatever it takes to cover those who are eligible for entitlements—unless it changes the eligibility standards or the amounts to which the eligible are entitled.

After 1921 the money committees took on the institutional task of protecting congressional majorities from the collective damage that the pursuit of individual electoral goals threatened to impose. In the House the powerful Appropriations Committee used its authority to keep members' desires for locally popular projects (such as dams, highways, and harbor improvements) and programs (such as housing, urban renewal, and police equipment) from pushing up taxes or deficits to politically intolerable levels. Tax legislation emerging from Ways and Means was routinely deemed ineligible for amendment to prevent a scramble for revenue-draining tax breaks for local firms or well-connected interests.

BUDGET REFORM. By the early 1970s the ability of the money committees to enforce collective self-control had been seriously eroded. The committee reforms weakened committee leaders, and a move toward congressional "openness"—doing more business in public—made it harder for individual members to resist the temptation to promote locally popular projects of dubious worth. At about the same time, President Richard Nixon used his authority to impound—refuse to spend—some of the funds authorized and appropriated by Congress to subvert the spending priorities of its Democratic majorities. In 1972, for example, he refused to spend $9 billion in clean-water funds and terminated many agricultural programs.[39]

R&B musician John Legend and actress Kerry Washington testify before a House Appropriations Committee hearing on "Funding for the Arts" in 2008, providing a livelier spectacle—and getting more media attention—than the more typical parade of bureaucrats requesting funding for their agencies' programs.

Nixon even impounded appropriations passed over his veto. His actions posed fundamental challenges to the House and Senate as institutions as well as to their Democratic majorities.

Congress responded with the Budget and Impoundment Control Act of 1974. The act subjected presidential impoundment authority to strict congressional control. More important, it revamped Congress's budgetary process with the goal of making impoundment unnecessary. Among other things, the act established a Budget Committee in each chamber to oversee the coordination of taxing and spending policies. It also instituted procedures and timetables for setting budget targets, supervising the committees' decisions on revenues and spending, and reconciling the tax and spending bills enacted by Congress with the targets. The system was designed to compel members to vote on explicit levels of taxation, expenditures, and deficits, thereby taking direct responsibility for the fiscal consequences of the many separate decisions made during a session.

Despite Congress's good intentions, the reformed budget process proved entirely incapable of preventing the huge budget deficits produced by budget politics during the Reagan and Bush administrations of the 1980s and early 1990s. Orderly budgeting fell victim to the intense partisan conflict between the Republican presidents and congressional Democrats over budget priorities. Presidents Ronald Reagan and George H. W. Bush sought to keep taxes low, congressional Democrats to protect popular domestic spending programs. Since both low taxes and spending for popular programs proved politically irresistible, the budget was left unbalanced. No amount of reform, then, could have prevented the massive budget deficits of the 1980s and early 1990s because nothing can force Congress to follow the rules it makes for itself. Procedures are chosen to produce desired outcomes; when the rules stand in the way of desired outcomes, members can always find ways around them.[40]

Attempts to reduce the deficit by procedural devices failed repeatedly until both sides developed the political will to support a precarious agreement. The negotiations that produced the Budget Enforcement Act of 1990, a package of tax increases and program cuts designed to reduce the projected deficit by some $500 billion over five years, exemplified budgeting under divided government. It consisted of improvised deals worked out in charged, high-level negotiations between the president and congressional leaders. Congress and the administration, both under Democratic control after the 1992 elections, made further inroads into the deficit in 1993 with another round of tax increases and spending cuts intended to reduce the deficit by another $500 billion between 1994 and 1998.

Still, the budget did not come into balance, requiring yet another round of budget confrontations and negotiations, stretching from 1995 to 1997—and this time between a Republican Congress and a Democratic president. The agreement became possible when the booming economy produced a bonanza of tax revenues, making it much easier to accommodate the desires of both sides. By 1998 the economy had produced so much in new tax revenues that the budget was in surplus, and budget politics turned, temporarily, to the happier task of choosing among tax cuts, additional spending for government programs, or paying down the national debt. But a slowing economy put the squeeze on resources in 2001, and revenues were further reduced by major tax cuts enacted at the behest of the George W. Bush administration. As spending rose with the cost of homeland security and the wars in Afghanistan and Iraq, deficits returned. The severe recession that began in late 2007 and lasted for the next eighteen months, combined with the Obama administration's package of tax cuts and spending programs intended to revive economic growth, produced huge budget shortfalls and made deep spending cuts the primary objective of congressional Republicans in 2011. Democrats, meanwhile, wanted new tax revenues to balance the cuts, leading to a series of showdowns, including the high-level negotiations to avoid the fiscal cliff in late 2012, which largely ignored the formal budget process. Inevitably, partisan politics will continue to dominate the budgeting process, and the formal budget rules will guide the action only insofar as they do not prevent congressional majorities from doing what they want.

Congressional Staff and Support Groups

In addition to relying heavily on its committee system, Congress has sought to cope with its expanding workload by adding staff (see Figure 6-7) and specialized research agencies. Staff doubled between the mid-1950s and the late 1970s (with most of the growth in personal staff); the numbers then remained stable until 1995, when House Republicans reduced House committee staffs by 30 percent. The cuts, however, left them with much larger committee staffs than they had had when House Republicans were in the minority; the staffers who lost their jobs were all on Democrats' payrolls.

Personal staff assistants manage members' offices in Washington and back in the state or district. They also draft bills, suggest policy, prepare position papers, write press releases, handle casework for constituents, deal with lobbyists, and negotiate with other staff on their boss's behalf. Almost any political or legislative chore short of casting formal votes in committee or on the floor can be delegated to staff assistants. Committee staffs are deeply involved in all legislative activities; they organize hearings and investigations, research policy options,

Figure 6-7 Expanding Congressional Staff

Number of employees

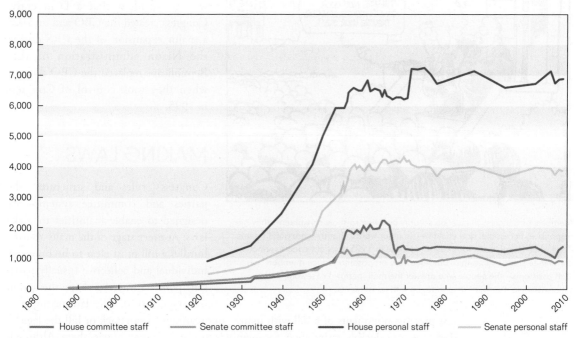

House committee staff — Senate committee staff — House personal staff — Senate personal staff

Source: Norman J. Ornstein, Thomas E. Mann, and Michael J. Malbin, *Vital Statistics on Congress 2012* (Washington, DC: Brookings, forthcoming), Tables 5-1 and 5-5.

attend to legislative details, and negotiate with legislators, lobbyists, and executive branch officials on behalf of the party faction on the committee that employs them.

Members receive additional help in gathering and processing information from several specialized congressional agencies. The Government Accountability Office (GAO) audits and investigates federal programs and expenditures, probing for waste, fraud, and inefficiency. The Congressional Research Service (CRS) gives Congress access to a highly professional team of researchers. The Congressional Budget Office (CBO), created as part of the 1974 budget reforms, provides Congress with the economic expertise it needs to make informed fiscal decisions and to hold its own in conflicts with the president's Office of Management and Budget (see Chapter 7). Among its tasks are economic forecasting and economic policy analysis. Although CBO was mainly designed to serve the collective institutional needs of Congress, it also serves members individually; it will, on request, provide analyses to let members know how various budget alternatives would affect their home states and districts.

By using the expert advisers within committee staff and congressional support agencies, members of Congress do not have to take the word of experts from the executive branch or interest groups, who cannot always be expected to impart unbiased information. Although

Members of Congress pursue job security by trying to show constituents they are responsive, accessible, and effective—in other words, that they are good agents. Thus when Republicans took over the House in 1995, they cut congressional committee staffs by one-third but rejected a proposal to reduce members' personal staff assistants—the people who answer the mail, perform casework, and otherwise help members keep in touch with constituents.

officially bipartisan, the support agencies are the most valuable to the majority party in Congress when the other party controls the executive branch. Indeed, it was no accident that a Democratic Congress created the CBO and initiated a major expansion of the CRS during the Nixon administration or that Republicans replaced the CBO director when they took control of Congress in 1995.

MAKING LAWS

Congress's rules and structures—the parties and committee systems—are designed to enable majorities to make laws. At every stage of the many routine hurdles a bill must clear to become law, individual and collective (usually partisan) political interests shape the action (see Figure 6-8). The lawmaking process presents opponents of a bill with many opportunities to sidetrack or kill the legislation. It is considerably easier, then, for members to stop bills than to pass them. Although Congress quickly bypasses regular legislative procedures in emergencies,* and party leaders now regularly circumvent normal procedures when trying to enact important and controversial bills, an examination of these procedures completes the picture of how ordinary legislative politics is supposed to work.[41]

Introducing Legislation

Only members may submit legislation to the House or Senate. Many proposals originate outside Congress—from the executive branch, interest groups, constituents—but they must have a congressional sponsor to enter the legislative process. The process itself is largely routine and routinely political. Some bills carry (informally) their authors' names; the Bipartisan Campaign Reform Act of 2002 is informally known as the McGain-Feingold Act after Reps John McCain, R-AZ, and Russell Feingold, D-WI. The America Invents Act, a patent reform bill enacted in 2011, is better known as the Leahy-Smith Act after its

---

* For example, within three days of the attacks of September 11, 2001, Congress passed a joint resolution (PL 107-40) authorizing the president "to use all necessary and appropriate force against the nations, organizations, or people that he determines planned, authorized, committed, or aided the terrorist attacks." Congress also passed a major antiterrorism bill (PL 107-56) on October 25, a little more than a month after President Bush had requested it.

principal sponsors Sen. Patrick Leahy, D-Vt., and Rep. Lamar Smith, R-Texas. Even whole programs may be named after their authors. For example, the government helps college students finance their educations through Pell grants, named after Democrat Claiborne Pell of Rhode Island, who championed the program when he was in the Senate. Personal credit for what is, after all, a collective act of Congress (one vote is never sufficient and rarely necessary to accomplish anything) is a valuable commodity. Proponents of bills try to line up cosponsors both to build support (by sharing credit) and to display it (increasing the chances for legislative action). Most important bills are introduced in the House and Senate at the same time so the chambers can work on them simultaneously.

The parties and the president (with the cooperation of congressional friends) also use legislative proposals to stake out political positions and to make political statements. Presidents regularly submit proposals they knew are "dead on arrival" to establish a record that their party could run on in the future. Members of Congress routinely do the same.

Assignment to Committee

After a bill is introduced, it is assigned a number (preceded by *H.R.* in the House, *S.* in the Senate) and referred to a committee. Even the number assigned can make a political point. In 2011 House Republicans gave top billing (*H.R.* 1 through 5) to proposals aimed at repealing or gutting the health care reform legislation enacted a year earlier. Most bills are routinely assigned to the appropriate committee; complex bills are often referred to several committees, and controversial bills are occasionally handled by temporary ad hoc committees appointed for that single purpose. The Speaker makes the nonroutine decisions in the House, manipulating the committee process to ensure more friendly or expeditious treatment of legislation important to the majority party. In the Senate party leaders negotiate agreements to settle disputed referrals.

Once a bill has been referred to a committee, the most common thing that happens next is: nothing. Most bills die of neglect—and are meant to—in committee. Many more bills are introduced than members have time to deal with—more than ten thousand in a typical two-year Congress. Some bills are introduced "by request," meaning the introducer was doing someone—a constituent or campaign contributor—a favor by offering the bill but has no further interest in its fate. Bills introduced by the minority party to score political points or embarrass the majority are deliberately buried. Like party leaders, committee chairs and their allies strive to avoid situations in which their party

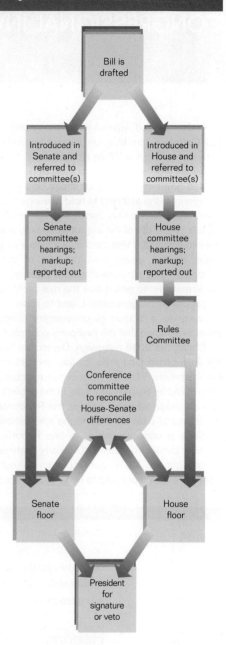

Figure 6-8 How a Bill Becomes a Law

- Bill is drafted
- Introduced in Senate and referred to committee(s)
- Introduced in House and referred to committee(s)
- Senate committee hearings; markup; reported out
- House committee hearings; markup; reported out
- Rules Committee
- Conference committee to reconcile House-Senate differences
- Senate floor
- House floor
- President for signature or veto

CONGRESSIONAL INVESTIGATIONS

Under divided government, the party controlling Congress has to share lawmaking power with the party controlling the White House, and the party's more ambitious legislative goals are likely to be frustrated. But divided government does not impair Congress's powers of oversight—the authority to hold hearings and investigations, issue subpoenas compelling testimony from individuals in and out of the executive branch, and generally pry into any matter that catches a member's eye. Indeed, under divided government the use of this authority becomes more attractive for both partisan and institutional reasons: to embarrass the rival party by exposing its supposed misgovernment, and to assert Congress's authority as a branch of government coequal to the executive branch that the rival party controls.

During the 2006 campaign, Democrats had criticized the Republican Congress for lax oversight of the Bush administration. With the Republican members' electoral fates linked by shared party label to the public's evaluation of the president and his policies, the Republican leaders' reluctance to draw attention to the administration's shortcomings is understandable. As one Republican House member candidly observed, "Our party controls the levers of government. We're not about to go out and look beneath a bunch of rocks to try to cause heartburn."[1] But

protecting the administration led to accusations that the Republican Congress had given up its constitutional status as a coequal branch of government. Democrats could thus claim the constitutional high road while pursuing investigations that promised significant partisan payoffs.

After the 2006 elections, recognizing that the president and Senate Republicans would limit what they could accomplish legislatively, the victorious Democrats immediately initiated a series of investigations targeting the administration and its officials. Targets for investigation reflected the Democrats' pent-up demand for "accountability" in the executive branch—treatment of prisoners at Guantánamo, secret wiretaps, firings of U.S. attorneys, misuse of intelligence to justify the Iraq War. In the first one hundred days, the House alone held at least one hundred hearings. Few of these hearings and investigations led to legislation, but Democrats hoped they would expose the administration's alleged misgovernment and become grist for election campaigns in 2008. The administration fought back through assertions of executive privilege (see Chapter 7) and stalling in response to committees' demands for documents.

Four years later, it was the Republicans' turn to pepper the now-Democratic White House with subpoenas.

---

colleagues might have to cast potentially embarrassing votes. If the committee decides on further action, the bill may be taken up directly by the full committee, but more commonly it is referred to the appropriate subcommittee.

Hearings

Once the subcommittee decides to act, it (or the full committee) may hold hearings, inviting interested people—from executive agencies, from interest groups, from academia, from almost anywhere—to testify in person or in writing about the issue at stake and proposals to deal with it. In a typical recent two-year Congress, the Senate held about 1,200 hearings;

Darrell Issa, R-Calif., incoming chair of the House Oversight and Government Reform Committee, who had once declared Obama "one of the most corrupt presidents in modern times" (he later apologized, saying the president was not personally corrupt), immediately drew up a list of targets for inquiries: "the release of classified diplomatic cables by WikiLeaks; recalls at the Food and Drug Administration; the role of Fannie Mae and Freddie Mac in the foreclosure crisis; the Financial Crisis Inquiry Commission's failure to identify the origins of the meltdown; as well as business regulations and alleged corruption in Afghanistan."[2] Other new Republican committee chairs planned to investigate "the Justice Department's civil rights division, the radicalization of Muslims in the United States, homeland security grant money and air cargo and port and chemical plant security."[3] Like the Democrats before them, Republicans aimed to expose and perhaps rectify real problems and mistakes, but also to score political points and embarrass the administration with an eye to the 2012 elections, as in the House hearings on the fatal security lapses in Benghazi, Libya, on September 11, 2012. And like the Bush administration before it, the Obama administration was quick to

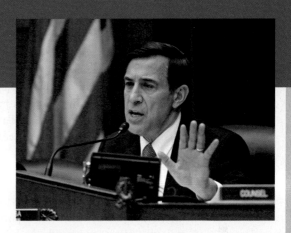

On becoming chair of the House Oversight and Government Reform Committee in 2011, Darrell Issa, R-Calif., initiated a wide-ranging agenda of investigations into alleged government malfeasance. His most pointed investigation, conducted in October 2012, focused on security failures prior to the September 11, 2012, terrorist attack in Benghazi, Libya, that killed Ambassador J. Christopher Stevens and three other Americans—mistakes that Republicans promoted as a campaign issue against Barack Obama.

invoke "executive privilege" whenever possible to avoid revealing sensitive or embarrassing information.

1. Zachary Roth, "Investi-gate," *Washington Monthly,* June 2006.

2. Philip Rucker, "Incoming GOP Chairmen Have a Long List of Issues to Investigate," *Washington Post,* January 4, 2011.

3. Ibid.

the House, about 2,300. Hearings may be orchestrated to make a record for (or against) a particular proposal, to evaluate how a program is working, or simply to generate publicity—for committee members as well as issues. Committees can investigate almost anything, including the White House or Congress itself. The White House is especially likely to be targeted when controlled by the congressional majority's rival party (see box "Congressional Investigations"). Senate committees also hold hearings to evaluate judicial, diplomatic, and senior administrative appointments.

Hearings also provide a formal occasion for Congress to monitor the administration of the laws and programs it enacts. The heaviest duty falls on the Appropriations subcommittees in the House, for government agencies have to justify their budget requests to these panels every year. Congress often is criticized for shirking its duty to oversee the administration of laws. After all, if carried out, comprehensive oversight would be a tedious, time-consuming, politically unrewarding chore. Instead, members of Congress set up administrative procedures that give affected interests an opportunity to protest damaging bureaucratic policies and decisions. In this way, members can confine their oversight to those areas of administration where the political stakes are demonstrably high. Members operate more like firefighters than police, waiting for fire alarms to go off before taking action rather than patrolling the streets looking for crime.[42] By relying on people affected by administrative decisions to alert it to problems, Congress, in effect, puts a big bumper sticker on bureaucrats that says, "How am I driving? Call 1-800-Congress" (see Chapter 8).

Reporting a Bill

If the subcommittee decides to act on a bill (and often it does not), it marks it up—that is, edits it line by line—and reports it to the full committee. The full committee then accepts, rejects, or amends the bill. With the exception of important and controversial bills, committees usually defer to subcommittees; otherwise, they lose the benefits of a division of labor.

Much of the coalition building that produces successful legislation takes place as subcommittees and committees work out the details of bills. No one wants to waste time on a bill that has no chance of passing—unless political points could be scored, as when House Republicans voted more than thirty times during the 112th Congress for legislation repealing Obama's health care reforms knowing full well that, even in the unlikely event that any such bill got through the Democrat-controlled Senate (none did), Obama was certain to veto it.[43] If a bill cannot attract solid support from at least the majority party committee members (and perhaps minority party members as well), its chances on the House or Senate floor are slim indeed. But if amendments, compromises, and deals can build a strong committee coalition for a bill, its chances on the floor are very good. The committee system, then, also divides the labor of coalition building.

The written report that accompanies every bill reported out of committee is the most important source of information on legislation for members of Congress not on the committee and for other people in government, including the agencies and courts that have to implement and interpret the law once it is passed. These reports summarize the bill's purposes, major provisions, and changes from existing law. They also summarize the arguments for and against the bill.

Scheduling Debate

When a committee agrees to report a bill to the floor, the bill is put on the House or Senate calendar—a list of bills scheduled for action. Each chamber has different calendars for different types of bills. In the House noncontroversial bills are put on the Consent Calendar (public bills) or Private Calendar (bills concerning individuals) to be passed without debate. Such bills also may be dealt with expeditiously under a suspension of the rules, which waives almost all of the formalities to allow swift action. Most legislation passed by the House follows one of these routes.

Controversial or important bills are placed on the Union Calendar (money bills) or House Calendar (other public bills). The committee reporting such bills must ask the Rules Committee for a rule, a resolution that specifies when and how long a bill will be debated and under what procedures. The rule may permit amendments—changes in wording—from the floor (**open rule**), only certain amendments (**restricted rule**), or no amendments (**closed rule**). A rule may also specify the order in which amendments are considered, thereby stacking the deck to favor particular outcomes. Majority party leaders use restricted or closed rules to keep unwanted amendments off the agenda, both to protect their party's members from casting embarrassing votes and to keep legislative packages from unraveling. Closed rules help to solve the majority's prisoner's dilemmas; many proposals that would not be enacted piece by piece because different members would defect on different sections can pass if they are voted on as packages. As partisan competition became more intense during the 1980s, Democratic House leaders used restricted or closed rules to maintain control of the floor agenda. Republicans objected strenuously but, after taking over in 1995, resorted to restrictive rules themselves to prevent Democrats from hindering the Republicans' promised speedy action on proposals set forth in the Contract with America (see Table 6-3).

TABLE 6-3

The Growth of Restrictive Rules in the U.S. House

Congress	Total Rules Granted	Open Rules		Restrictive Rules	
		Number	Percent	Number	Percent
95th, 1977–1978	211	179	85	32	15
96th, 1979–1980	214	161	75	53	25
97th, 1981–1982	120	90	75	30	25
98th, 1983–1984	155	105	68	50	32
99th, 1985–1986	115	65	57	50	43
100th, 1987–1988	123	66	54	57	46
101st, 1989–1990	104	47	45	57	55
102nd, 1991–1992	109	37	34	72	66
103rd, 1993–1994	104	31	30	73	70
104th, 1995–1996	151	86	57	65	43
105th, 1997–1998	142	72	51	70	49
106th, 1999–2000	184	93	51	91	49
107th, 2001–2002	112	41	37	71	63
108th, 2003–2004	128	33	26	95	74
109th, 2005–2006	138	24	17	114	83
110th, 2007–2008	159	23	15	136	85
111th, 2009–2010	95	0	0	95	100
112th, 2011–2012	144	14	10	130	90

Source: Roger H. Davidson and Walter J. Oleszek, *Congress and Its Members,* 13th ed. (Washington, DC: CQ Press, 2012); and *Survey of Activities of the House Committee on Rules for the 112th Congress* (Washington, DC: U.S. Government Printing Office, 2013).

Note: Democrats claim that Republicans misclassified rules in the 104th–106th Congresses, thereby overstating the frequency of open rules.

The longest speech in the history of the Senate was made by Strom Thurmond of South Carolina. Thurmond, a Democrat who later became a Republican, spoke for twenty-four hours and eighteen minutes during a filibuster against passage of the Civil Rights Act of 1957. This display of stamina was no fluke; in 2002 at the age of ninety-nine Strom Thurmond finally decided to retire from the Senate.

Democrats did the same to ensure enactment of their "100-Hour Agenda" after taking over in 2007.

If the Rules Committee holds hearings on a rule, interested members may express their views on the legislation. After hearings, a bill may be granted a rule, or it may be denied a rule entirely, at least until the originating committee has revised it to the Rules Committee's satisfaction. Once the Rules Committee grants a rule, it must be adopted by a majority vote on the floor. When floor action on a bill is constrained by its rule, a House majority has, in fact, consciously chosen to constrain itself. Sometimes the House kills a bill by voting against the rule rather than against the bill itself. In 1994, for example, the House rejected a rule for a bill to elevate the Environmental Protection Agency to cabinet status because the bill did not require the new department to consider the economic costs and benefits of new environmental regulations. The House's action killed the legislation.

In 2001 Republican House leaders tried to kill a campaign finance reform bill they strongly opposed by proposing a rule so unacceptable to the bill's proponents that they joined in voting the rule down. When the Republican leaders refused to act further on the bill, its supporters eventually got it out of Rules through a **discharge petition**, which brings a bill directly to the floor without committee approval when signed by a majority of House members (218). This discharge petition was a rare success; since 1967, only twelve such petitions have received the required 218 votes.*

The Senate has no equivalent of the House Rules Committee or, indeed, any rules limiting debate or amendments. Thus the leaders of both parties routinely negotiate unanimous consent agreements to arrange for the orderly consideration of legislation. Unanimous consent agreements are similar to a rule from the House Rules Committee in that they limit time for debate, determine which amendments are allowable, and provide for waivers of standard Senate procedures.

Without a unanimous consent agreement, there is no limit on how long senators can talk or on how many amendments they can offer. Individuals or small groups can even **filibuster**—hold the floor making endless speeches so that no action can be taken on the bill or anything else—to try to kill bills that the majority would otherwise enact. And breaking a filibuster is difficult. Under Senate rules an extraordinary three-fifths majority of the Senate

---

*Ultimate success is even rarer for discharged bills. Since 1910, when the procedure was first instituted, only three bills brought to the House floor via discharge have become law: once in 1931, once in 1960, and again in 2002, when Congress passed the Shays-Meehan campaign finance reforms.

membership (sixty votes) is required to invoke **cloture**, which allows a maximum of thirty additional hours of debate on a bill before a vote must be taken.

Conservative southern senators used filibusters most notoriously in their rear-guard action against civil rights laws a generation ago, but senators of all ideological persuasions now use the tactic. In fact, filibustering has become much more common in recent years and was especially rife after Republicans lost control of the Senate in 2007 (see Strategy and Choice box, p. 288). During the 111th Congress (2009–2010), Democratic majority leader Harry Reid, facing a Republican minority bent on obstructing Barack Obama's legislative agenda, filed 139 cloture motions, of which 91 came to a vote and 63 received at least sixty votes, thus ending debate and opening the way to a final vote. In the post-election "lame duck" session in December 2010, a successful cloture motion led to the repeal of the "Don't Ask, Don't Tell" policy, allowing gays to serve openly in the military, but the attempt to end debate on the DREAM Act of 2010, which would have opened a path to citizenship for undocumented immigrants who had come to the United States as children and had graduated from college or served in the military, fell short, winning only fifty-five votes. Even the threat of a filibuster can stop action on legislation because Senate leaders dislike wasting time on bills not likely to pass. With filibustering now so routine—more than half of the major legislation considered by the Senate in recent Congresses has been subject to filibusters and other delaying tactics[44]—the new reality is that the support of sixty senators is needed to pass any controversial piece of legislation except the budget resolution, which is protected from filibusters by a special rule.

In addition to permitting filibusters, the rules allow individual members to tie the Senate up in knots by refusing to concur with unanimous consent agreements aimed at facilitating the chamber's work. Senators, then, must depend on mutual restraint and bipartisan cooperation to get their work done. When cooperation breaks down, the Senate is immobilized. Senators thus buy lower conformity costs at the price of higher transaction costs.

Debate and Amendment

In the House the time for debate is divided equally between the proponents and opponents of a bill. Each side's time is controlled by a floor manager, typically the committee or subcommittee chair and the opposing ranking member. If amendments to a bill are allowed under the rule, they must be germane (pertinent) to the purpose of the bill; extraneous proposals, known as **riders**, are not allowed. Debate on amendments usually is restricted to five minutes for each side. The House often debates bills as a Committee of the Whole because, acting in the guise of a committee, the House is less encumbered by formal procedures. For example, for the Committee of the Whole, a **quorum**—the number of members who must be present for the House to act officially—is 100 rather than the usual majority of 218, and a member chosen by the Speaker wields the gavel. The House must revert back to itself, however, to vote on legislation.

Floor debates do not change many minds because, jaded by experience, politicians are rarely swayed by one another's eloquence. Debates are for public consumption: to make arguments that members will use to justify their votes to constituents and others; to shape public perceptions through the media; to guide administrators and courts when they apply and interpret the legislation; to stake out partisan positions; to show off. More important, formal floor debates serve to legitimize policy. Whatever deals and compromises went into building a legislative coalition, whatever the real purposes of its supporters, they have to make a case that the proposed action will serve the public interest. The opposition has equal time to argue against the action. Occasionally public justification assumes historic proportions, such as in 1991 when ninety-four senators and more than three hundred representatives took the floor to explain their positions on U.S. intervention in the Persian Gulf.

Floor action does more to shape legislation in the Senate than in the House. Because unanimous consent is required to limit Senate debate (except when cloture is used to end a filibuster), members are free to spend as much time as they like debating a bill. Unlike in the House, few conflicts are resolved in Senate committees or subcommittees; senators do much more legislating on the floor, offering amendments or complete alternatives to the bill reported by the committee. Senate amendments need not even be germane; important bills are sometimes passed as amendments—or riders—to completely unrelated bills. For example, in 1994 when the Senate passed a bill elevating the Environmental Protection Agency to cabinet status—the same bill the House killed by voting down the rule—it also inserted into the text an amendment that would have reauthorized the 1974 Safe Drinking Water Act. Unrestrained floor debate is the fullest expression of the Senate's individualistic, participatory ethos. It also provides a prominent forum for the articulation of any social interest that catches the fancy of even one senator.

The Vote

Members of Congress are ever alert to the political implications of votes on important bills. The fate of legislation often is decided by a series of votes rather than a single vote. For example, opponents of a measure may propose "killer" amendments, which, if passed, would make the bill unacceptable to an otherwise supportive majority; in 2002 House Republican leaders tried to kill campaign finance reform with this tactic. In addition, opponents may move to recommit the bill—that is, to send it back to committee for modification or burial—before the final vote. And on occasion, members may try to straddle an issue by voting for killer amendments or to recommit but then voting for the bill on final passage when these moves fail. Sophisticated observers have little trouble picking out the decisive vote and discerning a member's true position, but inattentive constituents may be fooled.

How do members of Congress decide how to vote? Political scientist John Kingdon sought to find out by asking them. They revealed that, along with their own views, the opinions of constituents and the advice of knowledgeable and trusted colleagues have the strongest influence on their decisions. Often members are aware of what their constituents want without anyone having to tell them. At other times they rely on letters, phone calls, faxes, e-mails, text messages, editorials, and polls to get a sense of what people think. Even on issues on which constituency opinion is unformed, members try to anticipate how constituents would react if they were to think about the issue. The idea is to cast an *explainable vote*, one that can be defended publicly if it is brought up by a challenger in some future campaign. This is not always easy, for a vote that is explainable to the strong partisans who vote in primary elections may not be explainable to the broader, more moderate voters needed to win the general election, and vice versa. Not every vote has to please the people who hire and fire members of Congress, but too many "bad" votes can expose a member to the charge of being out of touch with the folks back home.[45]

In general, members have reason to listen to anyone who can supply them with essential information: political information about how constituents and other supporters will view their actions and technical information about what the legislation will do. They also have reason to weigh the views of anyone who can help or hinder them in winning reelection, advancing their careers in Washington, and having an impact on policy. Constituents' views count the most because they have the most direct control over members' careers, but the views of interest groups, campaign contributors, and party leaders also shape decisions, especially on issues of little concern to constituents.

Most constituents know and care little about most of the issues on which members vote. The minority of the public that does pay attention varies from issue to issue. The relevant constituency opinions are those held by people who care, pay attention, and are not securely in the other party's camp, for their support will be affected by how the member handles the issue. In other words, the politically relevant interests on most issues are special interests. For that reason, in Congress intense minorities often prevail over apathetic majorities. One example: opponents of gun control, led by the National Rifle Association, have stopped or weakened gun control legislation many times over the years despite widespread public support for stronger regulation of firearms. Even the recent rash of deadly school shootings has not yet changed this political equation.

Trusted colleagues strongly influence voting decisions because legislators cannot possibly inform themselves adequately about all the matters that require a vote. They depend instead on the expertise of others, most often members of committees (usually from their own party) with jurisdiction over the bills outside their own specialties. Members say that lobbyists, executive branch officials, party leaders, congressional staff, and the news media influence their decisions much less than do constituents and colleagues. Groups representing special interests are deeply involved in congressional policymaking, but their direct influence is not strongly felt at this point in the legislative process; effective groups work through constituents and colleagues (see Chapter 13).

How influential is the president when the votes are finally cast? Occasionally presidents have been able to win against the odds by persuading wavering members of their party to stick with the team or by cutting special deals with pivotal members. For example, in 1993 President Clinton's successful appeals to party loyalty were crucial to his razor-thin budget victories (218–216 in the House, 51–50 in the Senate, where Vice President Al Gore's vote broke a tie); no Republican in either chamber would support the budget because it included tax increases. Essential, too, were the bargains made to modify the bill to satisfy reluctant Democrats.[46] On most votes, however, the administration's wishes are by no means paramount. Thirty-four House Democrats voted against Obama's signature health care reform bill in 2010, for example.

The same is true of the wishes of party leaders. Senate leaders exert little formal influence at this or any other stage of the legislative process. House leaders use their much more formidable powers at earlier stages and through control of the agenda. The majority party's leaders may, if they wish, do much to frame the choices that House members face. But their job is to construct legislative packages that party members are comfortable supporting. If they are successful, no persuasion is necessary. If they fail, few members are likely to put party loyalty ahead of constituents' views except under the most intense pressure and on the party's most important bills.

THE ORIGIN AND EVOLUTION OF THE SENATE FILIBUSTER

strategy and choice

Nothing is more emblematic of the Senate's special character than the filibuster—the ability of a minority of senators to block action on legislation or presidential appointments by extending debate, holding the floor until the majority gives up or grows to a supermajority that wields the sixty votes now necessary to adopt a cloture motion, which terminates debate and allows the Senate to proceed to a vote on the matter. Ironically, this hallowed practice originated more by accident than by design. Between 1789 and 1806, the Senate's rules included a motion "to move the previous question," which if adopted by a simple majority, ended debate and compelled a final vote on the matter at hand. When the rules were revised that year, the previous question motion was dropped because it was rarely used and did not seem necessary for the Senate to do its business. Three decades then passed before a Senate minority bent on obstruction found it could exploit the absence of any formal procedure for ending debate by conducting a filibuster.

From 1806 until 1917, a single senator could block action by refusing to end debate. That year, under strong pressure from President Woodrow Wilson and a public appalled that twelve antiwar senators had successfully filibustered a bill to arm U.S. merchant ships threatened by German submarines, the Senate adopted Rule 22, which allowed a two-thirds majority to invoke cloture. Cloture was made a bit easier in 1975 when the required majority was reduced to three-fifths of the Senate's membership (sixty).

Before the 1970s, filibusters were rare, but their use has since increased dramatically, producing the "sixty-vote Senate" for presidential appointments or bills other than budget resolutions, which may not be filibustered. Why this increase? One reason is that majorities no longer forced filibusterers to exhaust themselves speaking round the clock in order to hold the floor. Growing demands on senators' time—for travel back home and raising campaign money as well as for managing their formidable legislative workloads—made them reluctant to adopt such a time-consuming strategy of attrition.

Instead, senators in opposition to the filibusters now fight them with cloture motions, which minimize the filibusters' expense as they no longer shut down other Senate business. This low cost makes the filibuster an attractive option for individual senators bent on extracting legislative concessions as well as killing legislation. The filibuster has also become a standard weapon of partisan warfare in an increasingly polarized Senate, epitomized by its use in the 111th Congress (2009–2010) as a key component of the Republicans' strategy of root-and-branch obstruction of Barack Obama's legislative agenda.

At various times, both Republican and Democratic Senate majorities have contemplated curbing or eliminating the filibuster by a simple majority vote (fifty-one), a move dubbed the "nuclear option" because it would escalate partisan conflict to total war. There is little question that a majority could legally do so. But none has, and the filibuster survives for several reasons. First, the next election could turn a majority into a minority, and while in the majority, senators have been willing to absorb the transaction costs imposed by a filibustering minority as the price of avoiding more severe conformity costs in future Congresses in which they might be in the minority. That is, senators tolerate obstruction in order to retain the right to obstruct. Second, minorities have avoided pushing obstruction to the point where the majority becomes sufficiently angry and frustrated to risk the fallout from using the nuclear option. Third, that fallout would be heavy; an infuriated Senate minority has a variety of options beyond the filibuster for frustrating and harassing the majority.

The issue came up again at the beginning of the 112th Congress (2011–2012) and was resolved in a manner illustrating the balance of considerations that tend to restrain both sides. The reduced Democratic majority (down to fifty-three from fifty-nine in the previous Congress) would certainly find it more difficult to invoke cloture, but their reduced numbers and the reality that they had to defend twenty-three of the thirty-three Senate seats up for election in 2012 left

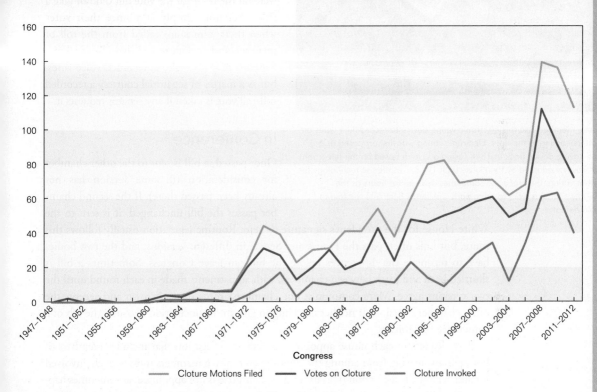

160

140

120

100

80

60

40

20

0

1947–1948 1951–1952 1955–1956 1959–1960 1963–1964 1967–1968 1971–1972 1975–1976 1979–1980 1983–1984 1987–1988 1990–1992 1995–1996 1999–2000 2003–2004 2007–2008 2011–2012

Congress

—— Cloture Motions Filed   —— Votes on Cloture   —— Cloture Invoked

Source: http://www.senate.gov/pagelayout/reference/cloture_motions/clotureCounts.htm.

their hold on majority status shaky. This did not seem a propitious moment to curb minority rights, and a proposal to make cloture easier won only twelve Democratic votes. Instead, Majority Leader Harry Reid, D-Nev., reached a "gentlemen's agreement" with Minority Leader Mitch McConnell, R-Ky., in which Reid foreswore the "nuclear option" and McConnell promised to do the same were he to become majority leader in 2012. McConnell also offered to limit filibustering on "motions to proceed" to legislation and nominations. And Reid agreed to refrain from blocking Republican amendments via procedural tricks. But both sides eventually accused

the other of reneging, and at the beginning of the 113th Congress Democrats again contemplated limiting filibusters, at least on motions to proceed, by a simple majority vote, but in the end made only minor adjustments. Thus the filibuster survived once more.

Sources: Gregory Koger, *Filibustering: A Political History of Obstruction in the House and Senate* (Chicago: University of Chicago Press, 2011); Sarah A. Binder and Steven S. Smith, *Politics or Principal? Filibustering in the United States Senate.* (Washington, DC: Brookings, 1997); Brian Friel and Niels Lesniewski, "Senate Limits 'Holds,' Keeps Filibuster," *CQ Weekly,* January 31, 2011, 260.

House members use this electronic voting device to record their votes on matters coming to the floor. Electronic voting was first proposed as a time-saving device back in 1848 (using a system based on the telegraph) but was not adopted by the House until 1973. Despite the technology for instant voting, the process is sometimes delayed for hours as the majority's leaders work to bring party dissidents back into the fold to avoid defeat.

In the House unrecorded voice votes may be cast, but at the request of at least twenty members a recorded **roll-call vote** is taken. When voting by roll call, members insert a small plastic card into one of the more than forty stations scattered about the House floor and press a button for "yea," "nay," or "present" (indicating they were on the floor for the vote but did not take a side). Senators simply announce their votes when their names are called from the roll of members rather than record them by machine. Senators may also take unrecorded voice votes, but as a matter of senatorial courtesy a recorded roll-call vote is taken if any senator requests it.

In Conference

Once passed, a bill is sent to the other chamber for consideration (if some version has not already been passed there). If the second chamber passes the bill unchanged, it is sent to the White House for the president's signature or veto. Routine legislation usually follows this route, but bills often pass the House and Senate in different versions, and the two bodies have to reconcile the differences before the bill can leave Congress. Sometimes a bill is shuttled back and forth between chambers, with adjustments made in each round until the two versions agree. More commonly, one chamber simply drops its own and accepts the other chamber's version. If neither is willing to give in, reconciliation becomes the job of a conference committee.

Party leaders in each house appoint a conference delegation that includes members of both parties, usually from among the standing committee members most actively involved for and against the legislation (if a conference committee is not appointed, as sometimes happens, the bill dies). The size of the delegation depends on the complexity of the legislation. The House delegation to the conference handling the 1,300-page Clean Air Act amendments of 1990 consisted of 130 representatives from eight different committees. The Senate got by with a delegation of nine from two committees. But the relative size of the delegations is not important, for each chamber votes as a separate unit in conference, and a bill is not reported out of conference to the House and Senate until it receives the approval of majorities of both delegations.

Conference committees are supposed to reconcile differences in the two versions of a bill without adding to or subtracting from the legislation. In practice, however, they occasionally do both. Conference committees generally exercise the widest discretion when the two versions are most discrepant. Once conferees reach agreement on a bill, they report the details to each chamber. A conference report is privileged—that is, it can be considered on the floor at any time without going through the usual scheduling process. The divisions of opinion in conference committees normally reflect the divisions in the chambers they represent, so majorities assembled in conference can usually be reproduced on the House and Senate floors. If both chambers approve the report, the bill is sent to the president.

Sometimes one or both chambers balk and send the conferees back to work, perhaps with instructions about what to change. If differences cannot be reconciled, the bill dies. This outcome is unusual, however; when a proposal has attracted enough support to make it this far and members face a choice to take it or leave it, they usually take it. This situation strengthens the hands of the committees that originally reported the legislation because the conference delegates are normally drawn from these committees and the conference gives them a chance to have the last word.

To the President

Upon receiving a bill from Congress, the president has the choice of signing the bill into law; ignoring the bill, with the result that it becomes law in ten days (not counting Sundays); or vetoing the bill (see Chapter 7 for more information on the veto process). If Congress adjourns before the ten days are up, the bill fails because it was subject to a **pocket veto** (the president, metaphorically, stuck it in a pocket and forgot about it). When presidents veto a bill, they usually send a statement to Congress, and therefore to all Americans, that explains why they took such action.

Congressional override of a presidential veto requires a two-thirds vote in each chamber. If the override succeeds, the bill becomes law. Success is rare, however, because presidents usually can muster enough support from members of their own party in at least one chamber to sustain a veto. When a head count tells presidents that an override is possible, they hesitate to use the veto because the override would expose their political weakness. Of the 487 regular vetoes cast between 1945 and 2012, only 51 were overridden. Presidents also exercised 310 pocket vetoes, none of which could be overridden, over the same period.[47] Presidents often prevail without having to resort to a veto because members of Congress are reluctant to invest time and effort in legislation that will die on the president's desk. The exception is when congressional majorities want to stake out a position on a prominent issue to score political points. The veto, then, is a major weapon in the presidential arsenal; presidents can threaten to kill any legislative proposal they find unsatisfactory, usually leaving Congress with no choice but to cut presidents in on deals.

A Bias against Action

Emerging from this review of the process and politics of ordinary congressional lawmaking is one central point: it is far easier to kill a bill than to pass one. Proponents of legislation have to win a sustained sequence of victories—in subcommittee, in committee, in Rules (in the House), in conference, on the floors of both chambers (repeatedly), and in the White House—to succeed. To do this supporters of a bill have to assemble not one but several majority coalitions. Opponents need win only once to keep a bill from going forward. The process imposes high transaction costs, conferring a strong bias in favor of the status quo.

UNORTHODOX LAWMAKING. The majority party can easily find its legislative agenda frustrated by the minority party when ordinary legislative procedures are followed. As party divisions in Congress have intensified and minority obstruction has become more common over the past three decades, majority party leaders have improvised unorthodox procedures to enact legislation. In the House, these include designing complex special rules to structure debate and amendment to minimize the minority's influence, bypassing or overriding committees to draft bills directly, rewriting legislation in conference committee after it has passed the floor, and combining separate bills into huge omnibus packages that leave members the choice of accepting all or getting nothing. In the Senate, the minority party has probably contributed most to deviations from orthodoxy through the unbridled use of the filibuster, compelling leaders to negotiate supermajority coalitions of at least sixty votes to act on controversial issues. Majority Senate leaders have responded with procedural strategies designed to minimize the damage. In dealing with important and controversial legislation, unorthodox procedures have in fact become the congressional norm.[48]

Unorthodox lawmaking requires a heavy investment of leaders' resources—time, energy, and favors—reflecting the high transaction costs incurred in getting Congress to act collectively on issues that provoke strong disagreement. Only a limited number of measures can receive such treatment, thus enhancing the status quo bias of legislative politics. Proposals that fall along the wayside can always be revived and reintroduced in the next Congress, however. Indeed, it is not at all unusual for many years to elapse between the initial introduction of a major piece of legislation and its final enactment. Proposals for national health insurance had been on the congressional agenda intermittently for more than sixty years before the landmark Patient Protection and Affordable Care Act finally passed in 2010. Defeats are rarely final, but neither are most victories; the game is by no means over when a law is enacted. The real impact of legislation depends on how it is implemented by administrators and interpreted by the courts (see Chapters 8 and 9). And laws always are subject to revision or repeal by a later Congress. That victories or defeats almost always are partial, and conceivably temporary, contributes a great deal to making politics—cooperation in the face of disagreement—possible. Politicians recognize that taking half a loaf now does not mean they cannot go for a larger share in the future.

EVALUATING CONGRESS

Americans hold contradictory views about their national legislature. In the abstract, most people approve of the Constitution's institutional arrangements. Any proposals for change advanced by constitutional scholars and reformers are ignored by virtually everyone else. And Americans generally like their own representatives and senators, who always receive substantially higher approval ratings from constituents than does their institution (although their individual standing does suffer when Congress is especially unpopular). Most incumbents win reelection even when the public professes to be thoroughly fed up with national politics and the politicians of one or both parties. But Congress as it operates and its members as a class are rarely appreciated, and it is unusual for a majority of Americans to approve of its performance (see Figure 6-9).

The public's typical disdain for Congress reflects the low repute garnered by politicians as a class. Habitual contempt for politicians arises from the nature of politics itself. Americans use politics as a vehicle for social decisions even when they share no consensus about the best

Figure 6-9 Congress Rarely Receives High Marks from the Public

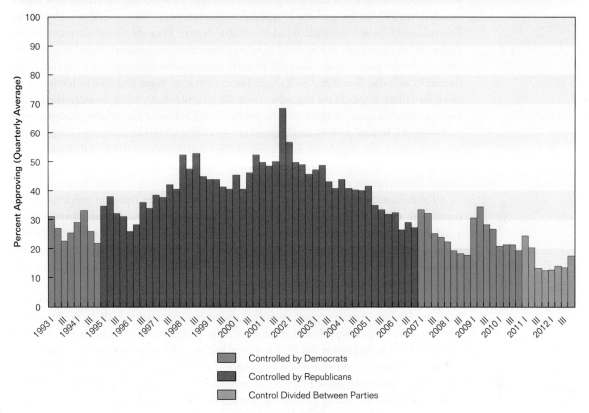

Controlled by Democrats

Controlled by Republicans

Control Divided Between Parties

Note: Compiled by authors from 756 surveys conducted by 14 commercial and media polling organizations.

course of action. Politics, then, inevitably requires compromises and trades, the results of which leave no one fully satisfied. The alternative to compromise—stalemate—is often equally scorned by a public more inclined to view legislative gridlock as a product of partisan bickering than of intractable conflicts among legitimate values, interests, and beliefs. In reality, Congress's difficulty in deciding on a budget, reforming the health care system, or dealing with an array of social problems (poverty, education, job loss) reflects the absence of any public consensus on what should be done about these issues. The only consensus is that national leaders, when failing to act, have not done their job.

Congress's poor reputation also arises from the very nature of pluralism. In pluralist politics, adamant minorities frequently defeat apathetic majorities because the minorities invest more of their political resources—votes, money, persuasive efforts—in getting their way. Indeed, the ability of pluralist systems to weigh the intensity of preferences as well as to count heads is viewed as a major advantage because it means that groups tend to win when they care most and lose when they care least. But it also means that "special interests" often win out over general interests, leaving members of Congress perpetually open to the charge of violating the public trust.[49]

■ **DATA UPDATE**

logic.cqpress.com

View the most recent numbers on public approval of Congress.

Congress's reputation also suffers from recurrent ethics scandals, including those involving such powerful leaders as Democratic Speaker Jim Wright (forced to resign in 1989 over a shady book deal); Republican Speaker Newt Gingrich (fined and reprimanded in 1997 for lying to the House Ethics Committee); Ways and Means chair Dan Rostenkowski (jailed for mail fraud in 1996); Senate Finance Committee chair Bob Packwood (resigned in 1995 to avoid expulsion for sexual harassment); Republican House majority leader Tom DeLay (resigned in 2006 under indictment for violating campaign finance laws); and Rep. Charles Rangel, former chair of Ways and Means (censured in 2010 for failure to pay taxes and other financial irregularities). More broadly, the House bank overdraft scandal of 1992 and the publicity that followed about other congressional perks—gyms, beauty parlors, and limousines—fueled widespread scorn for Congress and helped Republicans overthrow forty years of Democratic rule in 1994, and diverse scandals, several involving members' relationships with convicted lobbyist Jack Abramoff, helped Democrats to victory in 2006.

All of these sources of public disdain for members of Congress represent conditions to be coped with rather than problems that can be solved. Senators and representatives cannot avoid making political deals, representing conflicted publics, or paying special attention to intensely held views. And not all of them will resist the many opportunities for corrupt self-dealing that come with the job. Thus members of Congress as a class are never likely to be revered by the public for any length of time.

Still, approval of Congress does vary in response to how it seems to be doing its job. The public prefers bipartisan agreement to partisan bickering; cooperation with the president over conflict between the branches; and, most of all, successful government policies. For example, in early 1998, on the heels of the 1997 balanced budget agreement between Clinton and the Republican Congress and against a background of a booming stock market and unemployment and inflation rates down to levels not seen since the 1960s, public approval of Congress in the Gallup poll reached 57 percent, up nearly thirty points from its low in 1992. But when Congress engaged in a highly partisan battle over impeaching Clinton for perjury and obstruction of justice in his attempt to cover up his sexual dalliance with a White House intern, its level of public approval fell sharply.

Evaluations of Congress became dramatically more positive in the wake of the al-Qaeda attacks on the United States in September 2001. The approval rating reached a record high of 84 percent a month after planes hit the World Trade Center and the Pentagon. With Congress itself under apparent biological attack from anthrax disseminated through the mail (its source was later found to be domestic and unrelated to the September 11 attacks) and displaying bipartisan resolve in supporting the Bush administration's initial proposals to combat terrorism, Congress-bashing went suddenly out of fashion. The distinction in the public mind between Congress as a revered constitutional invention and as a bunch of politicians doing the messy and often unsightly work of politics dissolved for a brief time, and Congress was included in the surge of patriotic affection for the symbols of American democracy the attacks had inspired (see Chapter 10). Soon, however, the public's view of Congress resumed its normal shape; within a year approval of Congress had fallen below 50 percent, and by the 2006 midterm election it was down to 25 percent. Public regard for Congress rose briefly after the Democrats' takeover but slumped back down into the low 20s as the economy fell into a deep recession during the final year of the George W. Bush administration and did not improve during the economic difficulty of Obama's first term. During the past decade, intense partisan conflict has been far more common than bipartisan cooperation, so a large majority of the public has found fault with Congress most of the time. The battles over taxes and spending during the 112th Congress provoked the lowest approval ratings of Congress ever recorded.

Despite all its faults, perceived and real, the U.S. Congress remains the most powerful and independent legislature in the world. It has retained its power and independence for both constitutional and institutional reasons. The Constitution not only granted the House and Senate extensive legislative powers, but also provided the basis for electoral independence from the executive. Congress's formal legislative powers and electoral independence would have been of little avail, however, had members not created effective institutional devices for acquiring information, coordinating action, managing conflict, and discouraging free riding. By developing the party and committee systems and securing the assistance of numerous staff and specialized research agencies, members of Congress have given themselves the organizational means to carry out, and thus to retain, their constitutional mandate. But their task is rarely easy nor the way smooth, for the Madisonian system that Congress epitomizes erects formidable barriers to collective action, and the range and complexity of contemporary political conflicts continually test Congress's fundamental ability to do politics successfully.

TAKE A QUIZ

logic.cqpress.com

Test your knowledge of this chapter.

logic.cqpress.com

Key Terms

■ Suggested Readings ■

Arnold, R. Douglas. *The Logic of Congressional Action.* New Haven, CT: Yale University Press, 1990. Explains how congressional leaders can manipulate the rules to overcome electorally induced free riding when they want to enact policies that impose short-term or concentrated costs to achieve longer-term or diffuse benefits.

Cox, Gary W., and Mathew D. McCubbins. *Legislative Leviathan: Party Government in the House.* Berkeley: University of California Press, 1993. Lucid explanation of the logic that undergirds the House party organizations; makes a strong case that congressional parties are more powerful than most observers have assumed.

Davidson, Roger H., Walter J. Oleszek, and Frances E. Lee. *Congress and Its Members.* 12th ed. Washington, DC: CQ Press, 2010. Thorough, authoritative text that is especially good at explaining rules and procedures.

Dodd, Lawrence D., and Bruce I. Oppenheimer. *Congress Reconsidered.* 10th ed. Washington, DC: CQ Press, 2013. Offers historical and theoretical perspectives on congressional change and an up-to-date discussion of the contemporary Congress.

Fenno, Richard F., Jr. *Home Style: House Members in Their Districts.* Boston: Little, Brown, 1978. Fenno's close personal observation of House members' interactions with their constituents produces a wealth of insights about how representation actually works.

Jacobson, Gary C. *The Politics of Congressional Elections.* 8th ed. New York: Longman, 2012. A comprehensive look at congressional elections.

Kaiser, Robert G. *An Act of Congress: How America's Essential Institution Works, and How it Doesn't.* New York: Knopf, 2013. A fascinating and up-to-date case study of how a bill (the Dodd–Frank Wall Street Reform and Consumer Protection Act of 2012) became a law.

Mayhew, David R. *Congress: The Electoral Connection.* New Haven, CT: Yale University Press, 1974. Classic analysis of how electoral incentives shape almost every aspect of congressional organization and behavior.

Rohde, David W. *Parties and Leaders in the Postreform House.* Chicago: University of Chicago Press, 1991. Explains the decline and resurgence of party unity in the House over the past several decades, paying special attention to how the reforms of the 1970s fostered greater partisanship.

Sinclair, Barbara. *Unorthodox Lawmaking: New Legislative Processes in the U.S. Congress.* 4th ed. Washington, DC: CQ Press, 2011. Explains how and why Congress has increasingly ignored its own standard legislative procedures to get its work accomplished.

■ Review Questions ■

1. How do the differences between the House and the Senate reflect the competing interests of small and large states?

2. How does the electoral system established by the Constitution differ from that of other parliamentary democracies?

3. What constraints are placed on states when they draw districts for congressional elections? How can parties give their members an advantage through districting?

4. Why does the House have stricter rules and greater leadership control than does the Senate? How do these differences affect the day-to-day operation of the chambers?

5. If members are elected by majorities from their districts, why do interest groups sometimes prevail, even in conflicts with majority opinion?

7 The Presidency

Bill Clinton and Barack Obama.

- What happened historically to transform the president from the "chief clerk" of the government (Abraham Lincoln's job description) to a formidable politician whose preferences must be taken into account?

- All modern presidents seek the public's support for their policies. But does their ability to sway public opinion really help them in dealing with other politicians in Washington, and if so, how?

- Does the growth of the "institutional presidency" risk transforming America's executive into an isolated, imperial office?

((If you send me legislation that does not guarantee every American private health insurance that can never be taken away, you will force me to take this pen, veto the legislation, and we'll come right back here and start all over again." Immediately, the members of Congress and other guests assembled to hear President Bill Clinton's 1994 State of the Union address stood up and applauded with apparent enthusiasm. To most news reporters and perhaps to most viewers, the president's statement affirmed the opinion that he was on track to win comprehensive health care reform. Democrats held their largest majorities in the House of Representatives and the Senate since the 1970s (by eighty-two and fourteen seats, respectively). The president appeared poised to give the legislation's passage his full attention. Despite an advertising campaign against the administration's plan launched months earlier by the health care industry, the American public still solidly backed the president's program. One national poll taken the week of Clinton's address found the respondents saying they favored "President Clinton's plan to reform health care" by a margin of 57 to 38 percent, the same margin of public support recorded shortly after Clinton had unveiled his legislation the previous September.[1] To key congressional Democratic leaders, however, the president's veto rhetoric represented a serious miscalculation, one they later concluded killed any chance of reform that year.[*]

The conditions his threat imposed for a minimally acceptable bill took off the table various compromise measures that enjoyed broader support. Unable to muster much enthusiasm for the administration bill among his Democratic colleagues, Senate Majority Leader George Mitchell fashioned a compromise bill designed to command sufficient support to avoid both a filibuster from Senate Republicans and a veto from the president. He did not come close to getting even a majority of the fifty-seven Democrats to agree, let alone the sixty senators required to prevent a filibuster. In late August, Mitchell announced that health care reform was dead for the remainder of the 103rd Congress. The president's plan never came to a vote in either chamber of Congress. In that fall's election Democrats lost fifty-four House seats

---

[*] President Clinton later agreed with the assessment that his statement had been a serious tactical miscalculation.

and nine Senate seats, which in both instances surrendered control of the chamber to Republicans. Comprehensive health care reform fell off the agenda for nearly fifteen years.

The political postmortems found many reasons for failure.[2] The debate over whether the plan would have worked continued long after the legislation had been discarded. Some senior Democratic senators on key committees derided the one-thousand-page bill as so complicated as to be unfathomable. For many Americans, the plan's complexity sowed uncertainty and confusion over what the reform meant for their own health care, with which most were well satisfied. In late fall of 1993 the health care industry unveiled a coordinated television campaign in which "Harry and Louise," a typical middle-class American couple, sat at their kitchen table worrying that the Clinton plan would ruin their health care coverage. President Clinton was slow to respond. Many fellow Democratic politicians accused him of going AWOL at critical moments when the opposition campaign was in full swing and public support began to crack. In selling the reform to the public, the administration could not expect help from Democrats in Congress. Within weeks of Clinton's 1994 State of the Union all-or-nothing veto threat, public support turned decisively against the administration's plan. By mid-February, the 58 percent support from late January had dropped to 46 percent and would remain at or below that level for the rest of the year.

These failures of execution followed a more fundamental flaw that provided lessons for future politicians. To prevent the plan from being hijacked by the well-heeled pharmaceutical and health services industry or torn asunder by partisans measuring each provision against their rigid ideological yardsticks, the president tried an end run. He created a task force composed of hundreds of policy experts and headed by the first lady, Hillary Clinton. This group met in secret for months, occasionally summoning doctors, insurers, hospitals, and others for information but excluding them as well as members of Congress and groups representing consumers from the plan's formulation. Even if no legislator viewed it as an ideal plan, President Clinton calculated, a majority of both chambers would prefer it to the present system. In effect, he gambled that the best bet for passage involved short-circuiting the highly charged political process that had doomed even modest health care reforms in the past.

The task force's private deliberations throughout the summer of 1993 superficially resembled another summer-long, secret deliberation that had a mandate to revamp institutions. The delegates at the Constitutional Convention spent a sweltering summer in 1787 sequestered behind closed shutters in Philadelphia hammering out a new national government. A critical ingredient present at this Convention but missing from the Clinton task force was the full participation of the legitimate stakeholders in devising a reform. The Convention's delegates were the agents of their states and the key interests in their states, where Clinton's health reform task force was principally composed of policy wonks. The president could shut out of his task force those who had a vested stake in the outcome, but in doing so, he only strengthened their resolve to press their case with the public and Congress, which would, of course, have final say.

Like every Democrat since Franklin Roosevelt, Barack Obama won the 2008 presidential election with a promise to create a national health care system. The election also strengthened the party's control of the House and Senate. For the first time since the debacle in 1994, Democrats held unified control of the government and were poised to tackle their party's legacy issue. Moreover, health care had become a more serious and costly national problem. Nearly a seventh of the nation's gross domestic product was tied up in health care costs. As the new president and his political advisers plotted strategy, they went to school on Clinton's

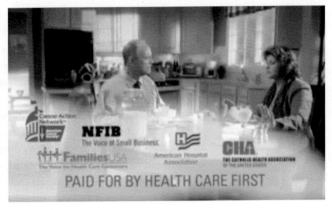

The first Harry and Louise ads exploited the pervasive ambivalence of many Americans, who agreed that a better national health care policy was needed but who also were satisfied with their own health coverage. Nearly twenty years older (and approaching Medicare coverage), Harry and Louise decide it is time fix the health care system.

experience. Indeed, they seem to have decided on a simple course: "Whatever Bill Clinton did, do the opposite."[3] Rather than send Congress a fully formed plan, Obama would only outline the basic contours of reform and leave it to Congress to flesh out the policy. It must, the president insisted, include all Americans, provide coverage regardless of previous health problems, and use the existing structure of private health insurance and health maintenance organizations (HMOs) as the foundation for reform.

Immediately, seven House and Senate standing committees went to work, and soon, several very different kinds of national health care reforms emerged.[*]

The House Ways and Means Committee began sweating the details of a single-payer system—that is, a government health care administration along the lines of the systems in Canada and most of Europe—as either a full replacement or supplementary service to private insurance and HMO care. Meanwhile, in the Senate, with Republicans threatening to filibuster any direct government provision of health care services, Finance Committee chair Max Baucus undertook private discussions with his committee's moderate Republican senators to graft universal coverage onto the existing care system. The numerous reform ideas blossoming during the summer of 2009 sowed their own confusion as the public heard about one plan progressing through Congress, then another that was altogether different. This opened the door for outlandish claims by those opposed to any reform. The 2008 Republican vice presidential nominee, Sarah Palin, spotted what she branded as "death panels" designed to withhold lifesaving care from the elderly. One national survey found 30 percent of respondents (and 47 percent of Republicans) believing that these death panels were, indeed, embedded in the reform legislation.[4]

With reform momentum flagging, Obama reentered the deliberations by convening closed-door negotiations with industry trade associations, among them health care providers, hospitals, pharmaceutical companies, and doctors, as well as the service workers' union. Members of Congress were conspicuously absent. In negotiations with the administration, the industry agreed to support reform that would generate billions of dollars in savings in

---

[*] The relevant standing committees were the House's Education and Labor; Budget; Energy and Commerce; and Ways and Means and the Senate's Finance; Budget; and Education, Labor and Pensions.

exchange for comprehensive care based on the existing system and without the numerous cost-containing regulations circulating in Congress. In announcing the agreement, President Obama cheerfully noted that these groups would kick in millions for a national advertising campaign to win passage of the final plan that came out of Congress. Harry and Louise returned to the airwaves clamoring for reform. Of course, the reform would now have to conform to the contours of an agreement that differed in key ways from legislation that was currently under various committees' consideration.*

Even had German statesman Otto von Bismarck never observed, "To retain respect for sausages and laws, one must not watch them in the making," someone—perhaps many some-ones—would have had this epiphany during the summer of 2009. In the wake of Obama's industry summit, House Democrats insisted that they would bring a bill to conference that contained cost controls and guaranteed affordable care, even if that required a government backup program. Meanwhile, the few Republicans in the Senate who had taken tentative steps toward a Democratic-led reform retreated to the opposition. With Democrats holding sixty seats—the bare minimum to ward off a Republican filibuster—Senate Majority Leader Harry Reid tried to close ranks. But Senate Democrats who represented states as diverse as California and Nebraska could only agree on a plan after heavy bouts of horse trading. When Reid announced that the Senate had agreed to a $100 million amendment to the health care bill to subsidize Nebraska's participation in expanded Medicaid costs—quickly dubbed the infamous "Cornhusker Kickback"—everyone in Washington knew that it was the price Sen. Ben Nelson had levied in return for his support of the bill.†

During the summer, Gallup recorded the lowest levels of public confidence in Congress in thirty-five years. Consider the irony that, at the moment when Congress was passing argu-ably the most important social legislation since the New Deal, only 12 percent of the American public judged it to be doing a good job.[5]

As the summer recess approached, no plan emerged that could command bipartisan sup-port. By fall, many returned from recess shocked by their encounters with constituents at town meetings. A few vulnerable Democrats from marginal districts lost their appetite for any health care reform. Party members in both chambers accused the president of failing to educate the public and to lead fellow Democrats toward legislation they could rally behind and end the disarray. One Democratic leader's aide confided to a reporter his reading of the White House strategy: "[L]et the Congress duke it out through the legislative process, and then come in at the end and finish the deal."[6] By the close of 2009 this hands-off strategy was no longer viable. Congressional Democrats began openly clamoring for Obama to become more engaged in helping the House and Senate settle on a single plan and promote it with the public. None wanted to walk the party line for a bill that was not going anywhere, while aspiring Republican candidates back in their districts were climbing over one another to win their party's nomination for the promising 2010 midterm election.

---

* These included controls on hospitalization costs and giving government the ability to elicit competitive bids on prescription contracts.

† The public's collective disgust included many Nebraskans, who expressed themselves directly in letters and phone calls and in the senator's plummeting poll numbers. Senator Nelson would lamely claim he knew nothing of the deal and announced he would oppose the amendment in the floor vote. Subsequently, he announced oppo-sition to the bill itself, but in the end supported it.

Early in 2010 Obama launched a public relations campaign to remind the public of the benefits of reform and to prod Democrats—mostly in the Senate—to pass a final bill. When the policy was finally cobbled together through legislative maneuvers that prevented Senate Republicans a chance to filibuster, every Democrat greeted the final vote passing the bill with a combined sense of relief and dread. Their fears proved fully justified. Eight months later sixty-seven House Democrats surrendered their seats to Republicans. Only the fact that comparatively few Senate Democrats were up for reelection in 2010 narrowly prevented that chamber from falling to Republicans as well.

We have told these two stories in some detail because together they offer insights into the prospects of presidential leadership. They share essential features that make comparison possible but involve fundamentally different legislative strategies that press us to look for explanation beyond personalities and the specific features of the histories. Both involved Democratic presidents asking Democratic-controlled Congresses for a comprehensive health care reform. Where Clinton's bill never came to a vote, the misnomer "Obamacare" was enacted. But here too the case studies offer striking similarities. Both ended in a Democratic debacle in the next election. Moreover, with the main provisions of the new health care law kicking in after 2013, its fate ultimately rested on Obama's reelection in 2012.

What do these cases tell us about the modern presidency? For starters, no one in Washington or the country questioned the appropriateness of presidential leadership for orchestrating major changes in national policy. Congress is ill suited by virtue of its membership and bicameral organization to solve all of the coordination puzzles that major alterations of public policy require. Clinton sensed this when he tried to solve the collective action problem by converting the policy into a simple, binary choice: his reform or the status quo.

But defining Congress's decision in this way requires that the president control its agenda, a feat a few presidents have managed to achieve and then only briefly. The industry's massive television advertising campaign opposing the Clinton plan simply made a presidentially structured choice politically unpalatable even to the president's own party's legislators. President Obama approached his Democratic Congress from the opposite direction: launch a reform debate and sign whatever new policy springs from the legislative mill (recall the sausage metaphor). If the result did not vindicate Clinton, it certainly reveals what motivated Clinton to pursue his wrongheaded course.

Ironically, both sets of policies and political outcomes might have ended better for these presidents and their partisan allies had either president fully implemented his stated intentions of educating the public on the necessity and specifics of the policy as it wended its way through Congress. Both approaches required lengthy development of the final legislation, during which time the president was unable to promote its still uncertain provisions. This delay did not deter opponents, though, who could claim all sorts of unattractive qualities to the emerging plan. Moreover, each president became distracted by other pressing issues. So by the time a final bill was unveiled neither president gave it the kind of public relations blitz that the public had come to expect and that the president's partisans depended on in order to cover their unpopular votes. In executing their health care strategies, both Clinton and Obama, two political leaders accustomed to generating a favorable public response, took their leadership for granted. As a result, neither served as a focal point to rally supporters and coordinate decisions among the disparate points of view that populate Congress.

The Patient Protection and Affordable Care Act signed into law by President Obama remains more an aspiration for providing health care for all Americans than a fulfillment. It contains no public option (government-provided health care), and administration of its many complex provisions remains unknown until the plan is fully implemented in 2014.

In the end President Obama was able to sign the Patient Protection and Affordable Care Act, and in 2012 it withstood a series of court challenges that had its fate hang on a single vote in the Supreme Court (see box "Chief Justice Roberts Stands Alone," page 406). But Obama, like Clinton, stumbled badly in leading Democratic legislative majorities to a policy that had been party creed ever since FDR had removed it from his Social Security proposal in 1933. Perhaps health care in twenty-first-century America was too big and too complicated for systematic, comprehensive reform. Or perhaps these lapses in leadership by two skilled politicians raise broader questions about the capacity of modern presidents to lead national policy, particularly domestic policy. Perhaps Clinton's and Obama's shortcomings are endemic to the institution. That is to say, maybe the problem is not an unsolvable health care puzzle, but modern presidents simply do not possess the resources adequate to the task of turning national policy in new directions. In the next section we argue that the failure of the presidency as an institution to guarantee its occupants easy leadership is rooted in the office's constitutional legacy.

THE HISTORICAL PRESIDENCY

The trick in designing an energetic presidency lies in avoiding a Napoleon, an ambitious individual who would use the temporary advantages conferred by a national crisis to permanently alter the constitutional order. By rejecting a plural office, the Framers accepted the proposition that, unlike the bicameral legislature, the executive would contain none of the internal checks provided by institutional design (described in *Federalist* No. 51) or factions (*Federalist* No. 10). The Constitutional Convention delegates finally solved the dilemma by giving the executive enough resources for coordinating national responses during emergencies but insufficient authority to usurp the Constitution. They achieved this objective—at least to the satisfaction of the majority that enacted Article II—by withholding certain executive powers, such as broad and easily invoked emergency powers that executives in other presidential systems have sometimes employed to get the upper hand over their political opponents. Power gravitates toward the office during moments of national urgency, but it does not involve suspension of other governmental actors' constitutional prerogatives. It remains confined to dealing with the emergency, and it dissipates as the crisis recedes or the government's response appears to fall short.

During the Republic's first century, presidents typically assumed a small role as a governmental actor. Their accomplishments were mostly limited to their responses to wars, rebellions, and other national crises. In fact, early presidents played a larger role in conferring

Introduced by their member of Congress in return for past political support, job seekers, hats in hand, approach the president for positions in his administration.

benefits to their political parties. On a day-to-day basis, filling vacancies in a growing federal bureaucracy consumed most of nineteenth-century presidents' time. Throughout the century, all federal employees—from the secretary of state to the postmaster in Cody, Wyoming—were appointed directly by the president or one of his agents. Large chunks of presidents' daily calendars were devoted to interviewing job seekers, listening to their party sponsors, and signing appointment letters. And because party colleagues in Congress and national party committees expected their nominees to be appointed, presidents could derive little political advantage from the appointment authority. Rather, it was a thankless task, befitting a clerk. "For every appointment," President Grover Cleveland observed ruefully, "I make one ingrate and ten enemies." Presidents took special care, however, in naming their cabinets. After all, these department heads represented important factions and interests within the president's party that had to be served if the president hoped to win renomination and election and enjoy his party's full support in Congress.

The Era of Cabinet Government

Nineteenth-century Congress routed all matters related to administration and policy through the appropriate department secretary. When a president had a question about a

The Republican Congress passed the 1867 Tenure of Office Act to prevent President Andrew Johnson, elevated to office after President Lincoln's assassination, from ending Reconstruction by removing key administration officials without Senate confirmation. When Johnson ignored the law and dismissed his war secretary, the House of Representatives quickly impeached him, and the Senate came within a single vote of removing him from office.

policy, needed clarification on complaints or rumors about an agency head's performance, or sought advice on whether to sign or **veto** a bill, he consulted his cabinet. Indeed, the nineteenth-century department heads composing the cabinet routinely performed much of the work now carried out by the president's staff.

Clearly, a strong cabinet did not necessarily make for a strong president. Cabinet appointees, who were resourceful, independent, and frequently ambitious politicians, could not be expected to subordinate their own welfare and that of their department to the needs of their titular leader. An adviser to President Warren G. Harding may have only slightly exaggerated a basic truth in remarking, "The members of the cabinet are the president's natural enemies."[7] Thus a pattern of intersecting interests characterized president-cabinet relations: presidents selected their department heads for their political assets, such as their influence with a particular wing of their party in Congress or with the electorate (see box "Lincoln and His Cabinet"). Those who joined the cabinet, however, were likely to pursue their own political and policy objectives and, perhaps incidentally, the president's (if indeed he harbored any). The result was a partnership based not on loyalty but on reciprocity: cabinet members helped the president achieve his limited political goals, and, by their cabinet appointment, he afforded them opportunities to pursue their agendas.

The modern cabinet has lost much of its luster as an attractive office—that is, one with real political clout. Control over policy and even of department personnel has gravitated to the Oval Office. Consequently, whereas ambitious politicians in the nineteenth century saw a cabinet post as a stepping-stone to the White House, modern politicians are more likely to view a stint in the cabinet as a suitable conclusion to a career in public service.

Parties and Elections

A paramount concern for nineteenth-century politicians was winning control of the White House. After all, whichever party captured the presidency won control of several hundred thousand federal patronage jobs. Moreover, in this patronage era before election reforms guaranteed voters privacy and an easy opportunity to split their votes among the parties' slates of candidates, the party that won a state's presidential contest almost invariably gained control of all the other state and local offices on the ticket. (For an example of the nineteenth-century, party-supplied ballot, see page 247.) As a result, the political party that carried the presidency almost always took control of Congress as well.

Presidential candidates were the engines that pulled the party trains. A look at the coverage of the president and Congress by daily newspapers in Cleveland, Ohio, from 1824 to 1876 reveals just how specialized the president's role was during this era (see Table 7-1). In

LINCOLN AND HIS CABINET

strategy and choice

Upon taking office in 1861, Republican president Abraham Lincoln confronted a nation threatening to dissolve. He also had to contend with a weak, young Republican Party composed of politicians who only recently had coalesced for the sole purpose of defeating the majority Democratic Party. To keep the party coalition together, Lincoln filled his cabinet with Republican leaders, even some of his rivals for the presidency.[1] Secretary of the Treasury Salmon Chase and Secretary of State William Seward, Lincoln's principal rivals for the presidential nomination, strongly disliked each other, but their support within the party and Congress kept both in Lincoln's cabinet.

Other cabinet officials of lesser stature but with impeccable political credentials were Pennsylvania's corrupt party boss and senator Simon Cameron, who was forced to resign the post of secretary of war, and Maryland Republican Party leader Montgomery Blair, who oversaw the patronage-rich Post Office Department. Blair's presence in the cabinet proved critical as he muscled the Maryland state legislature to defeat narrowly a motion calling for Maryland to secede from the Union.

Perhaps the most formidable cabinet member of all was the brusque Edwin Stanton, Cameron's replacement as secretary of war and a leader of the "war Republicans" in Congress. At times this gave him a

veto over policy. "Stanton and I have an understanding," Lincoln wrote a friend. "If I send an order to him which cannot be consistently granted, he is to refuse it. This he sometimes does."[2] Thus by surrendering control over large blocks of the executive branch to these self-interested, strong-willed politicians, President Lincoln succeeded in keeping the fragile Republican majority in Congress behind the unpopular Civil War.

---

1. David Herbert Donald, "Lincoln, the Politician," in *Lincoln Reconsidered: Essays on the Civil War Era* (New York: Random House, 1956).

2. David Herbert Donald, *Lincoln* (London: Jonathan Cape, 1995), 334.

---

total coverage (measured in column inches) presidents (or presidential candidates) moved to center stage in presidential election years and receded into the background during midterm election years, when they were not on the ballot. In 1840, 98 percent of all stories were centered on the president, and only 2 percent dealt with Congress. Ten years later, in a midterm election year, nearly the opposite was true. Unlike today, when presidents dominate the television network evening news, in the nineteenth century they received little media coverage outside of presidential election campaigns. Congress, not the government's chief clerk, held the spotlight.

TABLE 7-1

Nineteenth-Century Newspaper Coverage of Presidents: Heavy Only in Presidential Election Years

Election Year	Percentage of Political News Devoted to	
	President	Congress
1824 (presidential)	43	57
1830 (midterm)	40	60
1840 (presidential)	98	2
1850 (midterm)	16	84
1860 (presidential)	76	24
1870 (midterm)	19	81
1876 (presidential)	70	30

Source: Samuel Kernell and Gary C. Jacobson, "Congress and the Presidency as News in the Nineteenth Century," *Journal of Politics* 49 (November 1987): 1016–1035.

Note: Percentages based on total column inches devoted to Congress (including members and committees) and the president (including cabinet and presidential candidates) by daily newspapers in Cleveland, Ohio, 1824–1876.

At the national party nominating conventions, presidential candidates usually were valued a great deal more for their widespread popular appeal and willingness to distribute patronage according to party guidelines than for their policy pronouncements.[*]

As a result, candidates with little experience in government frequently enjoyed an advantage over established politicians who might be associated with a particular faction of the party or who, as officeholders, had taken controversial positions on divisive national issues. National military heroes—Andrew Jackson, Zachary Taylor, and Ulysses S. Grant, and a number of generals who were nominated but lost—made fine presidential candidates. But for most of those who won, leadership ended on Election Day when their glorified "clerkship" began.

What, then, does the nineteenth-century presidency say about the role of the modern president? If the Constitution thrusts command authority on the office, its first century of occupants failed to notice. Yet the nineteenth-century experience is not wholly divorced from the circumstances in which modern presidents find themselves. Even then, the singular character of the office gave presidents a competitive advantage over other national politicians in attracting the public's attention. Their capacity to serve as a focal point—coordinating the efforts of state parties during national elections and occasionally in mobilizing the nation for war—offers a glimmer of national leadership that would shine far brighter in the next century.

THE MODERN PRESIDENCY

By any measure the national government grew dramatically throughout the twentieth century.[†] After World War I the United States somewhat reluctantly became a global power requiring presidents' increased attention to foreign relations. On the domestic front, the national government and presidential responsibilities grew at a similar pace. As noted in Chapter 3, large domains of services, once reserved exclusively for states and local communities—or set beyond the purview of all governments—came to be funded and regulated from Washington via an extensive network of grants-in-aid programs to the states.

Consider some of the myriad programs that make up modern agricultural policy. The U.S. Department of Agriculture (USDA) offers farmers a broad assortment of services from planting to marketing crops. The Occupational Safety and Health Administration (OSHA)

---

[*] There were, however, a few "litmus test" issues such as the tariff, and during moments of national crisis the president's policy preferences would suddenly matter a great deal—consider Lincoln's position on slavery in the territories in 1860.

[†] Recall from Figure 1-2 the rapid growth of government revenue during the early twentieth century after the adoption of the income tax.

regulates the working conditions of farmhands, the Environmental Protection Agency (EPA) regulates the use of pesticides, the Securities and Exchange Commission (SEC) regulates the farm commodities markets, and the USDA and Food and Drug Administration (FDA) inspect the sanitation of food processing and distribution facilities. Every other sector of the modern marketplace similarly involves a pervasive federal presence. (In the next chapter we will systematically survey the growth of the federal bureaucracy and the problem this inevitably poses for elected officials in trying to translate constituents' demands into policy.) The point for us here is simply that the modern presidency is itself the cumulative product of the changing place of Washington in national and world affairs. As a matter of course, legislation creating or revamping programs assigns presidents statutory authority to oversee and even make changes in policy and administration that serve the program's mission. Even Congresses controlled by the opposition party routinely assign presidents broad discretion to administer policy.*

They have little choice since the Constitution designates to the president "take Care that the Laws be faithfully executed." Moreover, the president appoints the executives who administer the departments, agencies, and courts. The president's executive responsibilities spill over to legislative initiative as Congress seeks guidance in creating annual budgets and periodically reauthorizing and revamping programs and bureaucracy.

Of more recent origin, but just as important in defining the modern office, has been the emergence of **divided government** as the normal state of affairs in Washington. It pits a president against an opposition party that controls one or both chambers of Congress. A kind of zero-sum game often follows, as each side profits from the other side's failure. For most of American history, party control was unified across the legislative and presidential branches. The winning presidential candidate customarily pulled his party's congressional candidates into office on his electoral coattails. Table 7-2 shows that from 1920 until the first postwar election in 1946, divided government appeared only once (1931–1932), when Democrats won control of the House of Representatives, which ushered in a long-standing Democratic dominance of national politics in the next election. Of the thirty-three Congresses since then, however, twenty have experienced divided party control. (Chapter 12, Political Parties, considers the various causes for this development.)

And how do modern presidents deal with an opposition Congress? As relations with Congress become uncooperative, presidents necessarily rely more heavily on their constitutional and other unilateral resources. Vetoes and threats to veto may become critical assets in forcing the legislature to pay attention to the president's preferences. Presidents have also responded to an opposition Congress by pulling decisions into the White House. This includes heavy reliance on executive orders, centralized administration, and broad assertions of executive privilege. Moreover, presidents carefully screen department and agency appointments to ensure that administrators will remain responsive to them and resist the pull of the opposition Congress.

---

*There is some evidence that they do so with strings attached. One study found opposition-controlled Congresses write longer laws on average as they try to anticipate efforts by unsympathetic administrations to suborn or redirect the policy. David Epstein and Sharon O'Hallaran, *Delegating Powers* (New York: Cambridge University Press, 1991).

TABLE 7-2

The Growth of Divided Government, 1920–2012

Election Year	President	House of Representatives	Senate
1920	R (Harding)	R	R
1922	R (Coolidge)	R	R
1924	R (Coolidge)	R	R
1926	R (Coolidge)	R	R
1928	R (Hoover)	R	R
1930	R (Hoover)	D	R
1932	D (Roosevelt)	D	D
1934	D (Roosevelt)	D	D
1936	D (Roosevelt)	D	D
1938	D (Roosevelt)	D	D
1940	D (Roosevelt)	D	D
1942	D (Roosevelt)	D	D
1944	D (Roosevelt)	D	D
1946	D (Truman)	R	R
1948	D (Truman)	D	D
1950	D (Truman)	D	D
1952	R (Eisenhower)	R	R
1954	R (Eisenhower)	D	D
1956	R (Eisenhower)	D	D
1958	R (Eisenhower)	D	D
1960	D (Kennedy)	D	D
1962	D (Kennedy)	D	D
1964	D (Johnson)	D	D
1966	D (Johnson)	D	D
1968	R (Nixon)	D	D
1970	R (Nixon)	D	D
1972	R (Nixon)	D	D
1974	R (Ford)	D	D
1976	D (Carter)	D	D
1978	D (Carter)	D	D
1980	R (Reagan)	D	R
1982	R (Reagan)	D	R
1984	R (Reagan)	D	R
1986	R (Reagan)	D	D
1988	R (G. H. W. Bush)	D	D
1990	R (G. H. W. Bush)	D	D
1992	D (Clinton)	D	D
1994	D (Clinton)	R	R
1996	D (Clinton)	R	R
1998	D (Clinton)	R	R
2000	R (G. W. Bush)	R	D*
2002	R (G. W. Bush)	R	R
2004	R (G. W. Bush)	R	R
2006	R (G. W. Bush)	D	D**
2008	D (Obama)	D	D
2010	D (Obama)	R	D
2012	D (Obama)	R	D

* Democrats gained control of the Senate after Vermont senator James Jeffords switched from Republican to independent (voting with the Democrats) in May 2001, breaking the 50–50 tie left by the 2000 elections.

** The Senate had forty-nine Democrats, forty-nine Republicans, and two independents.

The following sections assess modern presidential leadership against the backdrop of a more modest constitutional office. For purposes of discussion we distinguish these opportunities for leadership across several spheres of government action: conduct of international affairs, administration of federal programs, and legislation. In the first sphere, the Constitution endows presidents with special advantages in deciding national policy. The administrative presidency is on less firm constitutional ground, but the sheer work of government has led to ever-increasing delegations of authority and responsibility for running the government. The president's legislative leadership remains the most subject to political circumstances and, as we found in the introduction, to the president's skills as a politician.

The President as Commander in Chief and Head of State

With several major European powers occupying territory bordering the United States, and frequently at war with one another, national security and foreign affairs were special concerns of delegates to the Constitutional Convention. The young nation's dismal record in international relations under the Articles of Confederation moved all but the most fearful delegates to shift this responsibility to the presidency. On the home front, the domestic uprising in 1786 by disgruntled Massachusetts farmers led by Daniel Shays, and the contagion of unrest that it spawned in the other colonies, exposed the Confederation's inability to provide national security.

THE COMMANDER IN CHIEF. The Constitution declares the president to be **commander in chief** of the nation's armed forces. The notion of putting the military under the control of a single individual was difficult for the Framers. One troubled convention delegate proposed limiting the military to no more than five thousand troops, provoking General George Washington to quip sarcastically that the Constitution also should limit invading armies to three thousand.[8] His point made, the Framers settled on a different kind of check on the president's powers as commander in chief: only Congress can declare war.

History and recent experience alike demonstrate that Congress's war declaration authority does not resolve the problem of a president taking the nation into war. Presidents often commit troops and engage in hostilities and then go to Congress for authority to continue. We saw this dynamic at work in the aftermath of the September 11 terrorist attacks. For all practical purposes, the public and Congress gave the president a blank check to fight terrorism. Hardly anyone in Washington or the country second-guessed the president's decision to invade Afghanistan in search of Osama bin Laden. A year and a half later, Bush still retained the initiative in winning a Democratic Congress's grudging endorsement to invade Iraq. Presidents acting in this sequence can set Congress's agenda for a choice to continue the conflict or desist in such a way that places the legislature in a severe bind. Calls to pull back are branded as abandoning the troops in the field. Even when America's invasion of Iraq was found to have been based on faulty evidence and the conflict was going badly, the Democratic-controlled Congress in 2007 could not collectively bring itself to cut off, or even curtail, funding for the troops.

American history is replete with instances of the president's ability to make the first move and thereby frame Congress's choice to either accept or reject the president's actions. In reality, the legislature may have little choice but to ratify the president's decisions. Within six months of the Confederate firing on Fort Sumter in 1861, President Abraham Lincoln suspended the writ of *habeas corpus* that prevented the Union Army from detaining civilians suspected of spying or even of just publicly opposing the war effort. He did not consult Congress before acting. Lincoln also approved a naval blockade of southern ports, extended voluntary military enlistment to a period of three years, increased the size of the army and navy, and authorized the purchase of materials, all without congressional sanction or even appropriation. Later, Lincoln justified his actions to Congress by relying exclusively on his authority as commander in chief: "The executive found the duty of employing the war power, in defense of the government, forced upon him. Whether strictly legal or not," he added, these measures "were ventured upon . . . trusting, then as now, that Congress would readily ratify them."[9]

One need not look hard to find modern analogues. After the Democratic majority took control of Congress in 2007, it sought through a variety of measures to wind down the war in Iraq. After several false starts, Congress finally agreed to attach a rider to a supplemental funding bill for the Iraq War that tied funding to a timetable for withdrawal. President Bush promptly vetoed it and demanded a bill with no strings attached. As the date approached when existing funds for the war were projected to be depleted, the Democratic Congress and Republican president engaged in a game of chicken. To outsiders Congress appeared to hold the upper hand; if it did nothing, the American military would grind to a halt. Washington's political elite knew from experience that this prospect would, in fact, force Congress to back down in the face of withering criticism that its inaction would hamstring the ability of troops in the battlefield to defend themselves. Shortly after a failed attempt to override the veto, Congress capitulated and gave the president the funds he requested. That the president can take a military action and, with troops in the field, effectively oblige Congress to support it represents a conundrum that Congresses have struggled with throughout the history of the Republic.

Congress's exclusive authority to declare war has, in most respects, become a hollow check on the president's commander-in-chief initiative. Neither the Korean War (1950–1953) nor

Figure 7-1 Near-Continuous Military Engagement since the End of the Cold War

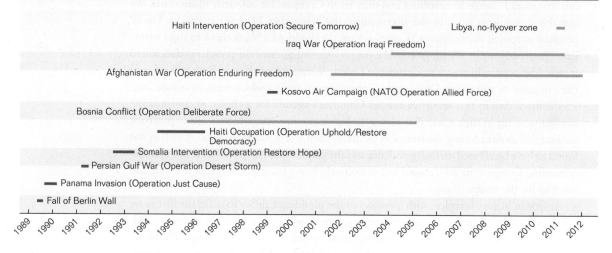

Sources: Adapted from a timeline by Dow Jones, Inc. (1999); and www.pbs.org/wgbh/pages/frontline/shows/pentagon/etc/cronagon.html.

Note: End of conflict demarked by end of casualties. Colored bars indicate that military personnel and/or peacekeeping forces were still deployed as of April 2011.

the Vietnam War, which began over a decade later, was ever formally declared. In 1973 Congress sought to carve out new authority for itself by approving the **War Powers Act** over President Nixon's veto. The law requires the president to inform Congress within forty-eight hours of committing troops abroad in a military action. Moreover, the operation must end within sixty days unless Congress approves an extension. But neither the law's constitutionality nor its effectiveness in limiting the president's military authority has ever been tested. Presidents have continued to commit the military without informing Congress—witness Ronald Reagan's 1983 invasion of Grenada, George H. W. Bush's 1992 deployment of U.S. troops to Somalia as part of a United Nations (UN) peacekeeping force, Bill Clinton's commitment of American forces in the North Atlantic Treaty Organization's 1999 action against Yugoslavia, and Barack Obama's 2011 participation in the UN's creation of a "no fly" zone over Libya. In fact, since 1989 U.S. armed forces have been almost continuously engaged somewhere in the world (see Figure 7-1). Although members of Congress may question presidents' policies, Congress as an institution has not challenged presidential authority to order an extended military engagement without a declaration of war.*

After all, does Congress really want to unwittingly strengthen the resolve of the nation's enemies and further endanger troops in combat, as opponents of such a policy would claim?

Where presidents can change a policy unilaterally, they gain the opportunity to exercise agenda control over Congress's choices. Although unanticipated by the Framers, who sought

---

*As a result, Congress sometimes finds itself presented with a presidential *fait accompli.* In 1907, for example, a startled Congress learned that President Theodore Roosevelt had sent the entire U.S. fleet on a two-year world cruise intended to impress other nations, especially Japan, with the U.S. resolve to play an active role in world affairs.

to have Congress set the president's agenda by having it present bills to the president for his up or down "vote" (that is, the veto), the president's capacity to take the initiative is embedded in the institutional design of the executive and legislative branches.

HEAD OF STATE. The Confederation government, consisting of little more than a legislature, also found it difficult to transact foreign affairs. Even routine duties, such as responding to communications from foreign governments, proved to be an ordeal. To promote commerce, the states tried to fill this vacuum, but European merchants and governments were able to pit one state against another in a ruinous competition for markets and trade. The Framers discerned that a single executive would enjoy an inherent advantage over Congress in conducting foreign policy. With some misgivings, then, they provided the president with broader authority to transact diplomatic affairs than they were willing to allow on the domestic front.

From the outset, President George Washington interpreted the Constitution's provision "to receive Ambassadors and other public Ministers" to mean that he alone could decide whether the United States would recognize a new government and, accordingly, "receive" its ambassadors. The howls of protest in Congress that greeted this interpretation were echoed in the Capitol a century and a half later when President Harry Truman recognized the state of Israel.

The most important constitutional limitation on the president's leadership in foreign affairs is the requirement that a two-thirds majority of the Senate ratify treaties. At times, the Senate has rebuffed a president's leadership by rejecting a treaty negotiated by the White House. Perhaps the most famous exercise of the Senate's ratification authority occurred at the close of World War I, when that chamber rejected the peace treaty that contained provisions for President Woodrow Wilson's brainchild, the League of Nations. Overall, however, this reservation of authority has proven less consequential than the Framers probably assumed.

To sidestep treaty rejections, presidents sometimes negotiate **executive agreements,** which are exempt from Senate ratification. Unlike treaties, which require ratification from two-thirds of the Senate's membership, executive agreements are simply statements of understanding between the administration and a foreign government. They are frequently employed to implement a broader agreement contained in a treaty, but also occasionally to achieve in practice a policy to which Congress would never agree or that it would rather keep private. During the Vietnam War, Congress discovered that President Lyndon Johnson created a number of executive agreements tendering foreign aid funds to countries that kept token forces in Vietnam.[10]

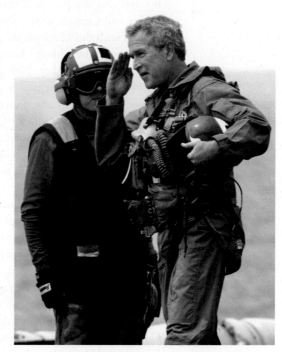

In May 2003, President Bush landed his fighter jet on the aircraft carrier USS *Abraham Lincoln* with a massive "Mission Accomplished" banner draped across the ship. His arrival was chronicled by all the major broadcast and cable outlets and print media photographers. Widely proclaimed by admirers and critics alike as the "mother of all photo opportunities," cable news networks devoted the rest of the day's airtime to replaying the magnificently choreographed images.

However, executive agreements cannot supersede U.S. law. Congress can pass laws that remove these agreements, and the courts may judge them to violate the Constitution or existing law and void them. But in most instances executive agreements remain "in force" as long as the parties find their interests well served by them. Because they can be changed easily, executive agreements, not treaties, constitute the primary instruments for conducting relations with other countries.

The President as Chief Executive

The Framers' deep ambivalence about the kind of executive they wanted is reflected in Article II's rambling provisions for the office. Compared with Article I's detailed development of the structure and powers of Congress, Article II is long on generalities and short on details. It begins by stating, "The executive Power shall be vested in a President of the United States of America." Instead of proceeding to define this power, the article abruptly shifts to a lengthy description of the means of election, qualifications for office, succession procedure, and compensation.

Not until Section 2 does the Constitution confer meaningful administrative authority. It states that the president may appoint the officers of government "by and with the Advice and Consent of the Senate"—that is, by a majority confirmation vote. Yet, not content with this check on the president's discretion, the Framers immediately qualified this authority by adding, "but the Congress may by Law vest the Appointment of such inferior Officers, as they think proper, in the President alone, in the Courts of Law, or in the Heads of Departments." Section 2 is more revealing in what it leaves unsaid about the president's administrative powers. At the outset, it declares simply that from time to time the president may "require the Opinion, in writing, of the principal Officer in each of the executive Departments." Then, as if the office's sketchy appointment and administrative authority fully equipped presidents, the Constitution, in Section 3, admonishes the president to "take Care that the Laws be faithfully executed" ("**take care**" **clause**; see also Chapter 2).

But where does the Constitution enumerate the administrative tools presidents need to carry out this mandate? Conspicuously missing is any provision for executive departments or their administrative heads, who later would constitute the president's cabinet. Perhaps the Framers should be applauded for leaving the structure and work of administrative departments wholly to the discretion of future Congresses, to be determined in pace with the nationalization of public policy. This omission, however, precluded careful consideration of the administrative controls suitable to this new executive. Had the Framers actually created at least some of the easily anticipated "inferior officers" alluded to in the Constitution, more explicit administrative authority might have emerged as well. The Framers could have given the president the authority to propose budgets, oversee spending, supervise personnel, and even countermand administrative decisions. These were, after all, among the familiar routine duties of eighteenth-century executives, just as they are for present-day senior administrators, including the president. Instead, in leaving the creation of the "several departments," the Framers also gave that body the authority to define the president's role as chief executive.

By giving the president full discretion to decide when to stop working through the UN and to invade Iraq, Congress assumed a measure of responsibility for the war's outcome.

Given the conspicuous absence from the Constitution of any real administrative authority for the president, it was by no means obvious that the growth of the national government would enhance the president's control over public policy. Congress could have kept the president at bay, as it often did in the nineteenth century, by insisting that executive agencies report directly to congressional oversight committees. But as the obligations of government mounted, oversight began to tax Congress's time and resources and interfere with its ability to deliberate new policy. So instead of excluding the chief executive from administration, Congress found its interests best served by delegating to the White House a sizable share of administration and, necessarily, the policy discretion that goes with it. The fact that the same political party generally controlled both the legislative and executive branches during the first half of the twentieth century, when the growth of government and the delegation of responsibilities to the president were being established, made it easier for Congress to transfer administration to the president. Given the scale of growth in the number and variety of federal programs during the twentieth century, Congress really had no practical alternative.

DELEGATION. By delegating to the president and the appointed executive branch the discretion to decide how best to implement and adjust policy to achieve its objectives, Congress shares a substantial amount of its lawmaking powers with the president. As early as 1950, a survey found that over 1,100 public laws delegated discretionary authority to the White House.[11] If such a survey were undertaken today, the number would, of course, be far larger.

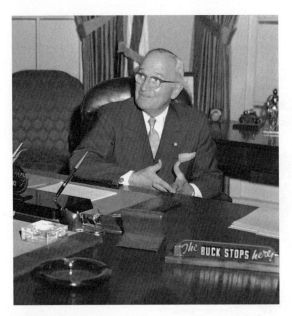

Contemplating the shock that his successor, General Dwight Eisenhower, would experience in the Oval Office, President Harry Truman remarked, "He'll sit here and he'll say, 'Do this! Do that!' And nothing will happen. Poor Ike—it won't be a bit like the Army. He'll find it very frustrating."

In writing public laws Congress can choose to delegate more or less rulemaking authority to the president. If it opts for too little, it freezes policy until the next act of Congress and may leave in place rigid programs that fail to respond to changing conditions. If, however, Congress delegates too much discretion to the executive, it may surrender control over important implementation decisions that could alter the intent of the legislation. In 1980 Congress erred in that direction when it passed the Paperwork Reduction Act, designed, as its name implies, to reduce the forms clogging the federal government and irritating citizens. When the U.S. Department of Health and Human Services proposed a survey of Americans' sexual practices to better understand and combat the AIDS epidemic, President Ronald Reagan, acting on his delegated power to implement the law, invoked the act to stop the department from printing the surveys.

At times, Congress delegates not from programmatic necessity but to gain political advantage. When legislators agree on the goals of a bill but disagree on its specifics, they may deliberately swath its intent in vague language— thereby delegating broad authority to the executive branch—to secure majority support. At other times, members of Congress may find political advantage in delegating to the president broad responsibility for policies that might have politically unattractive outcomes. In such instances, legislators "pass the buck" and hope to avoid blame. In the 1970s, for example, the principle that endangered species should be protected aroused far less controversy than any particular plan to achieve it. To avoid negative repercussions, Congress delegated to the U.S. Fish and Wildlife Service the discretion to establish criteria for classifying species as "endangered" and "threatened." Years later, when the service listed the northern spotted owl as a threatened species and limited the logging industry's access to Oregon's old-growth forests, the industry vented its anger at the agency and President George H. W. Bush—not at Congress. Not only did members of Congress escape retribution, but they also won some credit for subsequently softening the economic blow by passing a law that permitted timber companies to harvest fallen trees.

As indispensable as the executive office is for administering the panoply of government programs, the president is a tricky agent for Congress to delegate to. It is, after all, a separate branch of government largely insulated from congressional control. Congress does not hire, nor can it easily fire, this agent. And because of the threat of a veto, Congress might find its hands tied when trying to alter how a policy is administered or to rein in a president determined to take a program in a direction different from the one Congress intended. Moreover, with presidents separately elected and frequently representing a different political party than the one that controls Congress, presidents will rarely if ever view their role as Congress's dutiful agents. "Let anyone make the laws of the country, if I can construe them," President William Howard Taft once remarked.[12] A legislature that delegates too much discretion to a president may find that it surrendered control.

EXECUTIVE ORDERS. Until the twentieth century, presidents found themselves ill equipped to intrude into administrative practices and thus rarely did so. Instead, Congress exercised oversight of the bureaucracy by assigning its committees and subcommittees jurisdictions that matched those of the federal departments. Presidents stayed in the background and, except during national crises when they acted on their authority as commander in chief, seldom contested congressional control over the executive departments. To the degree that the presidents of that era sought to influence policy, they generally did so informally through their political appointees who ran agencies and departments. They also, on occasion, issued formal instructions called **executive orders**. An executive order has the force of law until the president or a successor retracts it, Congress nullifies it, or a federal court rules it violates either the Constitution or some federal law. The government did not begin retaining and cataloguing executive orders by publishing and assigning them consecutive numbers until 1907; by spring 2013 presidents had issued over 13,700 executive orders. In 2001 President Bush relied on his inherent authority when he issued an executive order creating the White House Office of Homeland Security, which would "develop and coordinate the implementation of a comprehensive national strategy to secure the United States from terrorist threats or attacks."* A month after twenty school children and six adults were gunned down in Newtown, Connecticut, President Obama issued nineteen executive orders designed to tighten administration of current laws, train first responders, and examine new gun control measures.

The vast majority of executive orders arise from the authority and responsibilities explicitly delegated to the president by law. Most frequently they are enlisted to establish executive branch agencies, modify administrative rules or actions, change decision-making procedures, and give substance and force to statutes (see box "Presidents Making Policy: Executive Orders Address a Variety of Issues"). For example, the Pendleton Act of 1883 inaugurated the civil service system for federal employees by converting about 10 percent of the federal workforce from political patronage positions to merit appointments based on examinations (see Chapter 8). This law also authorized the president to issue executive orders extending the civil service system to other classes of workers. Over the next half-century, presidents signed executive orders that shifted hundreds of thousands of employees from political patronage positions into the civil service system.

A much smaller class of executive orders is based not on some explicit congressional delegation but on presidents' assertions of constitutional authority. Not until the twentieth century did presidents begin seriously to entertain the notion that the "take care" clause might give them more authority than their predecessors had claimed. Early-twentieth-century president Theodore Roosevelt was the first to subscribe to this expansive view of the office. "The most important factor in getting the right spirit in my administration," wrote Roosevelt, reflecting on his term, "was my insistence upon the theory that the executive power was limited only by specific restrictions and prohibitions appearing in the Constitution or imposed by Congress in its constitutional powers."[13]

In 1974 President Richard Nixon decided that some appropriations already signed into law no longer squared with his policy to fight inflation by reducing government spending. So

---

* Subsequently, the president asked and received legislation establishing Homeland Security as a full-fledged department.

Presidents Making Policy

Executive Orders Address a Variety of Issues

February 1998	Applied the patient's "bill of rights" to all federal health programs. Created a White House council to coordinate efforts to fix the Y2K (year 2000) problem.
May 1998	Extended federal workforce affirmative action guidelines to cover sexual orientation.
June 1998	Directed federal agencies to avoid any action that would degrade the condition of coral reef ecosystems within U.S. waters.
November 2002	Delegated to attorney general authority to detain undocumented Caribbean aliens at Guantánamo Bay until admission is decided.
March 2003	Confiscated blocked funds held in U.S. banks by Iraqi banks and government agencies for eventual disbursement to Iraqi people.
June 2004	Directed the Small Business Administration and the Veterans Affairs and Commerce Departments to create centers for faith-based initiatives to expand participation of religious organizations in their grants programs.
April 2006	Blocked property of persons in connection with the conflict in Sudan's Darfur region.
July 2007	Interpreted the Geneva Conventions Common Article 3 as applied to a program of detention and interrogation operated by the CIA.
January 2009	Revoked Executive Order 13440 (July 2007) and ensured lawful interrogations in compliance with Geneva Conventions.
June 2012	Exempted from deportation young people who entered the United States illegally with their parents.
January 2013	Improve incentives for states to share information with the background-check system for gun purchases.

Note: All executive orders are listed in the following government website: www.archives.gov/federal-register/executive-orders/.

he *impounded* previously appropriated money by instructing the Treasury Department to withhold funds from the agencies responsible for implementing the programs. Disbursement of appropriated funds is quintessentially an executive action, but it is also a policy decision the Constitution explicitly delegates to Congress. Can the president legally withhold funds? Members of Congress howled in protest, and the agencies in line to receive the funds went to various federal district courts to force the president to release impounded funds. Before the president relented, several federal district courts ruled for the plaintiffs in lawsuits challenging President Nixon's actions. After extensive negotiations with the White House, Congress subsequently enacted the Budget and Impoundment Control Act of 1974, severely limiting the president's power to freeze spending without congressional consent.

BUDGETING. Presidents carry out one of their most important "clerical" tasks when they formulate and send to Congress the annual budget for all federal programs. Yet budgeting also offers them an opportunity to set the spending priorities of the federal government. In fact, this authority exists because Congress long ago insisted that presidents assume responsibility for the government's bookkeeping. Until the 1920s, agencies sent their budget requests directly to the House Appropriations Committee, which held hearings, determined appropriations, and passed them on to the chamber for a vote and then over to the Senate for its consideration. During this process, no one formally solicited the president's views. But when the flow of department and agency budgets began to congest the legislative process, Congress in 1921 passed the Budget and Accounting Act, which gave the president responsibility for compiling budgets from the executive departments and submitting them to lawmakers as a single package. With this act Congress found itself strengthening the president's role in national policymaking.

The president's annual budget, submitted to Congress on the first Monday in February, culminates months of assembling and negotiating requests from the agencies to bring them into conformity with the White House's policy goals and proposed spending ceiling. Some years, the president's budget has sailed through Congress with minimal changes. Other years, Congress has ignored the president's proposals and written a wholly "congressional" budget, daring the chief executive to veto it. As we will see later in the chapter, presidential and congressional budgets can differ so much that compromise becomes a test of political will.

The president's budget provides Congress with valuable technical and political information. Running into hundreds of pages, it supplies congressional committees with economic forecasts, projected tax revenues, baseline spending estimates for each department broken down by program, and other essential information for devising spending and taxation legislation. Politically the budget represents the president's "opening bid" in negotiations over how much the government should spend on particular programs and where the revenue will come from. From the early 1980s until the late 1990s, annual deficits forced politicians in both branches to concentrate on spending cuts or tax increases, unpalatable either to the beneficiaries of retrenched programs or to taxpayers. When the president made the first move in his budget, Congress could shed some of the political costs associated with trimming popular programs. This does not mean, however, that presidents have an easy time with Congress. Some years a president submits a budget, and it is accepted with only minor tinkering. At other times Congress mostly ignores the president's proposal. In 1984 a prominent Democratic chair of a House budget committee tersely pronounced Republican Ronald Reagan's budget to be "DOA" (dead on arrival). Whether presidents can take advantage of their formal agenda-setting opportunities to shape public policy depends on Congress's receptivity to their recommendations. In 1997 President Bill Clinton turned the tables on Congress. He sent to Capitol Hill a budget that targeted savings on Medicare but shied away from identifying cuts to achieve the savings. The Republican-controlled budget committees first denounced and later pleaded with administration officials to pinpoint where they would like the cuts to be made. The president had effectively passed the buck. Congress, facing the next deadline on the budget calendar, was forced to increase premiums and reduce benefits to bring the program's finances into conformity with the blueprint for balancing the budget.

CENTRALIZED ADMINISTRATION. During the late 1930s the office's growing role and the sheer amount of work that accompanied it led to the development of the **institutionalized presidency**, in which a set of offices and staff were created to assist the president. The staff would continue to grow in number and scope of activity. The responsibilities and resources available to modern presidents certainly set them apart from their nineteenth-century predecessors or any figure imagined at the Constitutional Convention.

Through delegation, Congress has "pushed" work toward the presidency—and, with it, not only considerable discretionary authority but also responsibility. In 2010 an accident spilling millions of barrels of oil into the Gulf of Mexico sent reporters to the White House within hours to find out what the government was planning to do about it. Presidents have responded by creating procedures to ensure that department and agency heads, most of whom owe their office to the president's appointment, fully take the president's views into account. Given the peripheral role of the nineteenth-century president, rerouting the flow of information and decisions proved no mean feat.

Theodore Roosevelt, who succeeded assassinated president William McKinley in 1901 and then went on to win the 1904 election, dedicated himself to refashioning the executive branch and exerting control over administration. In 1902 he issued an executive order prohibiting all federal employees from communicating with Congress, "either directly or indirectly, individually or through associations, to solicit an increase of pay or to influence or to attempt to influence in their own interest any other legislation." His handpicked successor, William Howard Taft, extended the so-called **gag rule** to cover "congressional action of any kind" and barred workers from responding to congressional requests for information except as authorized by their department heads.[14] Moreover, these choices placed the president at the forefront of efforts to propose future policy changes.

In 1939 Franklin Roosevelt approached the same goal, but somewhat differently and with greater success. Citing his statutory responsibility to prepare the annual budget, the president, through an executive order, required that all department communications to Congress that could affect future budgets first be cleared as consistent with the president's policy by the Bureau of the Budget (the predecessor to today's **Office of Management and Budget**, or **OMB**). Unlike the gag rule, Roosevelt's order has endured, and today **central clearance** is a standard procedure for agency officials heading to Capitol Hill to give testimony.[15] The clearance procedure has strengthened the president's hand in national policy, but not because it prevents agencies from communicating to Congress their policy differences with the president. (In fact, Congress can easily probe agency representatives when they testify at congressional hearings.) Rather, it stops officials from casually expropriating the president's endorsement for their legislative initiatives. Central clearance also alerts the White House early to attempted end runs in which an agency might seek more money and statutory authority than the president favors.[*]

---

[*] Yet Congress may curb even this administrative prerogative. For example, in 1982, during a Republican administration, House Democrats pushed a law through Congress that prevented the OMB from revising or delaying submissions of certain mandated agency reports to Congress. Morton Rosenberg, "Congress's Prerogative over Agencies and Agency Decisionmakers: The Rise and Demise of the Reagan Administration's Theory of the Unitary Executive," *George Washington Law Review* 57 (January 1989).

In the third and more recent case, the president enlisted the mechanisms of central clearance for quite a different purpose. Elected in 1980 on a promise "to get the government off the backs of business," President Reagan, upon entering office, issued an executive order instructing all federal agencies to submit any new regulations or rules to the OMB for a cost-benefit analysis. The reduced heft of the *Federal Register,* which lists proposed regulations, offers evidence of his success at curbing new rules; between 1980 and 1987 it shrank from eighty-seven thousand pages a year to fewer than fifty thousand.[16] Angered by this mechanism to block enforcement of various laws, the Democratic-controlled House voted to cut off funding for the OMB agency that administered regulatory reviews. The Senate entertained legislation to reorganize this presidential agency and subject the officer who administered oversight to Senate confirmation. After negotiations, Congress and the White House informally agreed that the OMB would relax its clearance rules and Congress would withhold legislative action.

In these cases, the further the presidents reached, the stronger the resistance from those whose own prerogatives were invaded by the innovation. The gag rule lasted less than a decade, and although both forms of central clearance introduced by Franklin Roosevelt and Ronald Reagan have become accepted procedure, they are exercised within negotiated bounds and are subject to numerous legislated exceptions. Congress has signaled clearly that a president who seeks to extract too much control from these practices is likely to lose them.

UNITARY PRESIDENCY. When presidents try to extend their influence unilaterally by issuing controversial executive orders—as with Nixon's impoundment orders—opponents are quick to charge that the chief executive is trying to turn the office into an **imperial presidency**, an elected monarch with a retinue of aides to do his bidding. Rarely is this label fair. The expectations of the American people and government officials for modern presidents exceed the explicit authority delegated in the Constitution. During George W. Bush's administration the president and vice president invoked a novel theory of presidential authority that they referred to as the **unitary executive**.

According to this argument, the Framers gave presidents far more command authority than past presidents and those who dealt with them had appreciated. With respect to administration, the unitary executive holds that presidents may remove all subordinates in the executive branch; they may also direct these subordinates to take a particular action; and, finally, they can veto any objectionable actions, including those mandated by Congress. If the unitary executive doctrine were to prevail, the president presumably could rescind any of the thousands of specific mandates, requirements, and obligations that federal law places on the heads of federal departments and agencies. After all, as Antonin Scalia, a Supreme Court justice and big fan of the unitary executive, argued in a decision, "It is not for us to determine, and we have never presumed to determine, how much of the purely executive powers of government must be within the full control of the President. The Constitution prescribes that they *all* are."*

In hundreds of **signing statements**—statements that he would attach to the legislation as he signed it into law—President Bush took exception with various provisions as encroaching

---

*In the same decision, Scalia repeated the blanket authority he reads the Constitution as endowing the president with: "The executive Power shall be vested in a President of the United States. . . . This does not mean *some* of the executive power, but *all* of the executive power." *Morrison v. Olson,* 487 U.S. 654, 705 (1988).

on his executive responsibility and declared that he reserved the prerogative not to enforce them, although in only one instance did he clearly follow through with his threat to sign and ignore a provision.*

During the 2008 presidential campaign President Obama took Bush to task for his numerous signing statements. But during Obama's first term he too issued signing statements—albeit significantly fewer—hinting a nonenforcement of certain provisions. In signing the Defense Authorization Act of 2013 Obama singled out restrictions in the bill on transferring detainees out of military prisons in Afghanistan and Guantánamo Bay, Cuba. He signed the bill but then claimed he had the constitutional power to override the limits.[†]

After more than two centuries of governance under the Constitution, we are still arguing over which branch or level of government has what power to make national policy. Bush's frequent invocation of his unilateral authority in signing statements reminds us that these are not inconsequential, pedantic, scholarly debates. Nor do they concern some narrow band of discretion falling in the interstices between the branches' otherwise clearly defined jurisdictions. Rather, Congress and the president continue to contest a broad swath of government authority. The persistence of such disagreements over two centuries reflects in part the presence of ambiguous boundaries separating the jurisdictions of the several branches. As we found in Chapter 2, the Framers understood that the trick in designing durable institutions included leaving to future generations of leaders to define at the margins the responsibilities and prerogatives of the several branches.

And, of course, divided party control of Congress and the presidency, which has become the normal state of affairs in the modern era, installs officeholders who have a vested interest in probing these boundaries. During the long historical era when the same party controlled both branches (see Table 7-2), the division of authority between the branches had little significance. With divided control, the zero-sum game over policy and votes in the next election motivates politicians to probe the law and precedents for opportunities to prevail over the other side both on policy and on politics. Congress enjoys certain advantages in this contest, such as attaching riders to appropriations bills forcing funds to be spent on or withheld from particular programs and voiding recently adopted regulations. Many executive orders and signing statements are issued for the same purpose—to control the policy in the face of disagreement from the legislature.

The President as Legislator

The Constitution gives presidents only a modest role in the legislative arena. They may call Congress into special session (little used, since the modern Congress is nearly always in session) and, most important, veto laws passed by Congress. Presidents also are called on to

---

* One clear instance occurred in 2008, when, citing the unitary executive, Bush instructed the secretary of homeland security to withhold a congressionally mandated report on the number of complaints filed by citizens who felt that some action by the department had violated their civil rights. See Charlie Savage, "Administration to Bypass Reporting Law," *New York Times,* October 25, 2008.

† Specifically, he said, the provision "could interfere with my ability as commander in chief to make time-sensitive determinations about the appropriate disposition of detainees in an active area of hostilities." If it operates "in a manner that violates constitutional separation of powers principles, my administration will implement it to avoid the constitutional conflict."

report "from time to time" to the legislative branch on the state of the Union.
Yet as we found in the introduction to
this chapter, modern presidents are legislative dynamos. If major changes in
policy are to occur, they will invariably
involve the president's early sponsorship and promotion.

The adage coined by President
Franklin Roosevelt that "the president
proposes, Congress disposes" aptly
describes an important aspect of modern presidential leadership—one that
the Framers did not envision when
they placed the president at the end of
the legislative process, where he passively accepts or rejects bills sent from
Congress for his signature. However,
the growth in the president's administrative duties has ensured that
Congress will give a chief executive's
legislative proposals serious consider-

President Obama's gun control announcement in January 2013, streamed live,
allowing customers at a busy gun shop to listen in.

ation. As noted above, Congress begins deliberating the all-important annual budget only
after the president has submitted spending and taxation proposals for the next fiscal year,
with planned expenditures broken down for each federal agency. More generally, lawmakers expect the president to advise them about problems with current policy and administration and to recommend adjustments to improve performance. Presidents—and their
appointees who administer federal agencies—enjoy an informational advantage, inherent
in all delegation, that may also give them an advantage when proposing legislation. At
times, presidents can improve their chances of legislative success by selectively withholding
information from legislators who prefer some policy they oppose. In a variety of ways,
modern presidents' central role in administration ensures them a major role in the legislative process. Consequently, about 90 percent of presidents' initiatives are considered by
some congressional committee or subcommittee.[17]

In assembling support for their legislation, presidents begin with their party allies in
Congress. These men and women have a stake in their party leader's success, but this does
not mean they will bow before the president's wishes. Members of Congress must, after
all, attend to the interests of their constituents. Presidents cultivate the support of fellow
partisans in Congress in many ways designed to strengthen members' standing back
home. These include advocating spending on programs and public works (such as highways and water treatment plants) for a district or state, appointing a member's congressional aide as an agency head, and visiting a lawmaker's district to generate local
enthusiasm and financing for the next reelection campaign. (President Bill Clinton's
prowess as a party fund-raiser is described in Chapter 12, box "The President as Party
Coordinator.") Moreover, politicians in the White House and the two chambers of

Congress follow the dictates of different electoral calendars. Consequently, presidents routinely confer with their party's congressional leaders to determine which issues and stances attract support and to decide when to schedule presidential initiatives. The president's fellow partisans in Congress, conversely, do what they can to support their leader. Their shared party label might cause voters' assessments of the president's success to affect their own fortunes in the next election.

Mutual accommodation requires effort, but the incentives for the partisans from the president's party in Congress and the White House to cooperate are powerful. In President Clinton's last year in office, Democrats supported his publicly stated position in roll-call votes 89 percent of the time in the Senate and 73 percent in the House. Impressive statistics, to be sure, but during his first year in office, Clinton's successor, George W. Bush, managed to do even better, enjoying fellow Republican support at 94 percent and 86 percent of the time in the Senate and House, respectively.

None of these incentives to cooperate is present in the president's relations with legislators from the opposition party. Indeed, opposition partisans in Congress correctly recognize that the president's legislative success might very well debit their vote count in the next election. Although no one wants to be perceived by voters as blocking the chief executive's initiatives for narrow partisan advantage, opposition party members have a stake in defeating the administration when they disagree with its policies and in co-opting credit for passage of those initiatives with which they agree. As a consequence, opposition members' roll-call votes on average line up with the president's position less than half the time. The absence of a single Republican vote for the health care bill in 2010 represents an extreme instance of a long-standing pattern.

One implication of the shared political stakes of fellow partisans in Congress is that when presidents find their party in majority control of the House and the Senate, they have excellent prospects for passing their legislative agenda. Twice during the twentieth century presidents enjoyed huge majorities in both chambers. The legislative floodgates opened, and a broad array of new social policies poured out of Congress. The first set of programs, known as the New Deal, occurred in the early 1930s as President Franklin Roosevelt and congressional Democrats sought to ameliorate the Great Depression. The second, which we have already encountered in Chapter 4, was President Lyndon Johnson's Great Society policies during the mid-1960s.

Conversely, during divided government, when the president confronts congressional majorities with different policy preferences and an opportunity to tarnish the president's standing with voters, several perverse political outcomes may occur. On issues where the political parties differ sharply, neither side will be willing to compromise, and in the resulting **gridlock** the government accomplishes little and may even come to a halt. This chapter later examines a classic case of gridlock, the budget confrontation between President Clinton and the Republican Congress that briefly padlocked most federal agencies in the fall of 1995. Another kind of gridlock will occur when both sides recognize a policy problem that entails an unpopular solution. As the 112th Congress assembled in January 2011, the Republican-controlled House of Representatives and Democratic Senate and White House faced a number of tough decisions: a widening budget deficit, a depleting Social Security fund, and soaring Medicare and Medicaid costs. Each side's fear that it would be maneuvered into a stance where the public would hold it responsible for an unpopular solution made each reluctant to make the first move.

THE VETO. Perhaps the president's most formidable tool in dealing with Congress is the veto. The Framers, ever alert to opportunities to introduce "checks and balances," were already familiar with the concept of an executive veto, exercised by most state governors. Unlike the president's administrative powers in Article II, Section 2, the veto authority is defined quite precisely by the Constitution. (See section "Making Laws" in Chapter 6, where the place of the veto in the legislative process is described in detail.) Over the past half-century, presidents have averaged fewer than ten vetoes a year. The record belongs to Republican president Gerald Ford. Although he served less than one full term (from August 1974 until January 1977), Ford vetoed sixty-six bills (see Figure 7-2). In the 1976 election he campaigned on his veto record, claiming that only a Republican in the White House would stand between hard-earned taxpayer dollars and the "spendthrift" Democratic Congress. Only twelve of Ford's vetoes were overridden, even though the Democrats commanded large majorities in both the House and the Senate. Thus Ford won many of the battles, but he lost the war—the election.

The Framers frequently referred to the veto as a "negative"—an appropriate characterization of this inherently conservative instrument. The veto allows presidents to block Congress, but unlike the **line-item veto** authority forty-three state constitutions give their governors, the president must veto the whole bill.*

Moreover, unlike most negotiating settings where each side must agree to a joint outcome, Congress acts first. That vetoes are reactive—a response to "take it or leave it" proposals from Congress—limits a president's ability to shape policy.

Especially when dealing with an opposition Congress, presidents often enlist their veto authority. The veto offers presidents a clear, self-enforcing means of asserting their preferences.

---

* In 1996 Congress enacted the Line Item Veto Act allowing the president, within five days of signing a bill into law, to reject spending provisions and tax breaks that affected fewer than a hundred persons or entities. Congress could repass these provisions with a simple majority vote, but the president could veto them as well, requiring Congress to override with a two-thirds vote. A couple of years later the Supreme Court, in a 6–3 decision, struck down the line-item veto as violating the Constitution's separation of powers doctrine.

Figure 7-2 Presidential Use of the Veto

Sources: Calculated by the authors from The American Presidency Project, "Presidential Vetoes," http://www.presidency.ucsb.edu/data/vetoes.php.

Moreover, as Alexis de Tocqueville first observed in 1836, the public nature of the veto—frequently boosted by accompanying messages—enhances it as "a sort of appeal to the people," which modern presidents have not been shy about invoking whenever they discern public backing for their stands.[18] Earlier we noted that the Framers carefully tailored the president's veto authority to achieve a couple of seemingly contradictory goals: to install a check capable of stalling legislative abuses while continuing to deny the executive the unilateral authority that, throughout history, had proven so injurious to the welfare of ordinary citizens. The veto, with its strong but exclusively negative quality, seemed to meet both objectives. The Framers failed to appreciate fully how a skilled politician in the White House could use the threat of this endgame option to manipulate Congress's expectations about the likely result of alternative legislative packages, and thereby insert his policy preferences into legislation at an early stage of the process.

The record of presidential-congressional relations under modern divided party control of government indicates that the Framers were only partly correct. The veto certainly does not allow presidents to dictate policy, but it does normally require Congress to take into account the president's preferences as legislation is written. Lawmakers need concede only the minimum number of provisions necessary to present the president with a bill more attractive to the administration than the status quo, or the current policy. Whether the veto offers the president great or little influence over public policy often depends on how close the White House's priorities are to the status quo compared with the priorities of Congress. (To understand how the "take it or leave it" option allows Congress to ignore the president's veto on some occasions but not others, see box "The Veto Game.")

Presidents might be the last to vote, and then only to accept or reject a piece of legislation, but this does not mean that they will passively await the choice Congress presents them. Facing an opposition Congress, modern chief executives do all they can to break out of the Constitution's "take it or leave it" bind. Here presidents sometimes find the threat to veto legislation useful. They commit in advance to veto a bill if it fails to include or omit certain provisions. To be effective, a veto threat must be credible—that is, presidents must convince those they wish to persuade that they are not bluffing and will actually follow through if Congress does not accommodate them. This strategy requires that the threat be explicit and leave the president little wiggle room. Moreover, it must be public—the more public the better—so that presidents will incur political embarrassment by backing down. Ronald Reagan is famous for his "make my day" and "line drawn in the sand" announcements in which he insisted that Congress give him legislation that reflected his preferences or suffer a veto. Of course, such announcements may be costly, so presidents do not issue them casually. Bravado stands against popular bills can backfire immediately in an adverse public response. In such instances Congress will be sure to pass the threatened bill in order to elicit the veto and remind voters just where the president stands. Heading into the 1992 presidential election the Democratic Congress passed the highly popular Family and Medical Leave Act despite President H. W. Bush's veto threat. He promptly vetoed the bill. So, what did Congress do? It changed the language slightly and passed it again and forced yet another veto.

And tying one's own hands to gain credibility entails risks. Presidents cannot change their position without hurting themselves politically. As a result they rarely do. But whenever presidents ponder such a move, they invariably remember when George H. W. Bush accepted the Republican presidential nomination in 1988 by declaring, "Read my lips: no new taxes." Several years later, during a funding crisis that threatened to shut down the federal government, Bush relented and agreed to the Democratic Congress's demand for a tax increase. Immediately, politicians and the press howled that the president had lied to the American public. Republican consultant and television pundit Ed Rollins declared it "the most serious violation of any political pledge anybody has ever made."[19] During the 1992 campaign Bill Clinton ran ads showing the rousing convention pledge and questioning whether Bush could be trusted. Exit surveys found a quarter of all Clinton voters and a fifth of all who supported third-party candidate Ross Perot citing the broken promise as a reason for their vote.[20]

Even so, modern presidents threaten vetoes frequently. President Clinton averaged fifty-five threats per year during his six years (1995–2000) when Republicans controlled the House and Senate.* Similarly, in his last Congress, a contentious two years with Democratic majorities in both the House and the Senate, President Bush issued numerous threats.

WATCH A VIDEO

logic.cqpress.com

George H. W. Bush gives his "Read my lips, no new taxes" speech.

---

*The Clinton average represents the combined tally from several sources: *CQ Weekly,* the OMB's "Statements of Administration Purpose," and AP wire stories. One study over a longer time frame found that 90 percent of presidents' veto threats extracted concessions from Congress. Charles Cameron, *Veto Bargaining* (New York: Cambridge University Press, 2000), 188.

Having campaigned in 1988 on the slogan "Read my lips: no new taxes," President George H. W. Bush was hunted down by reporters in 1990 after he conceded a tax increase in negotiations with congressional Democrats. When reporters caught the president jogging one morning and baited him with his contradiction, he yelled, "Read my hips." In the national news story that followed, the president's response was reported as an expression of his disregard for his promises.

MOBILIZING PUBLIC OPINION. Until the early twentieth century, presidents routinely satisfied their constitutional obligation (Article II, Section 3) to report on the state of the Union by conveying their messages to Congress by courier. There, an officer of Congress read the presidential communiqué inaudibly to an inattentive audience more interested in socializing after a long adjournment. Today, however, sophisticated broadcast communications have transformed the **State of the Union address** into a televised "prime-time" opportunity for presidents to mold public opinion and steer the legislative agenda on Capitol Hill. The influence presidents derive from this event depends in large part on the susceptibility of politicians in Washington to the political breezes presidents can stir up in the country.

The nationally televised State of the Union address is today simply the most prominent instance of a strategy of **going public**—that is, engaging in intensive public relations to promote the president's policies to the voters and thereby induce cooperation from other elected officeholders in Washington. Presidents and members of Congress share constituencies. If presidents can win the public's backing for themselves and their policies, opponents in Congress may fear voters' reprisals in the next election. Understanding this reality, popular presidents frequently exploit their ability to grab the public's attention and generate favorable news coverage for their legislative initiatives. If they succeed in rallying public support for their policies, they may force the accommodation of a Congress otherwise indifferent or opposed to the president's ideas.

Evidence suggests that presidents view going public as a viable alternative to negotiating with the opposition on Capitol Hill. As a Clinton aide explained to reporters who were complaining about the heavy travel schedule, "Clinton has come to believe that if he keeps his approval ratings up and sells his message as he did during the campaign, there will be greater acceptability for his program. . . . The idea is that you have to sell it as if in a campaign."[21] Immediately after Senator Jeffords's defection in 2001 cost Republicans control of the Senate, reporters asked President Bush's chief of staff, Andrew Card, how the president would respond. Card replied that Bush might have to switch strategies and "use the bully pulpit a little more . . . to get [his legislation] moving."*

(Originating with President Theodore Roosevelt's characterization, "bully pulpit" refers to the advantageous position afforded the office for rallying public support.)

Perhaps at no time did governing and campaigning so meld together as in early 1999, when the Senate deliberated President Clinton's removal from office. With the charged impeachment proceedings serving as an uninviting backdrop for the annual State of the Union address, many members of Congress publicly and privately advised Clinton to cancel or postpone the event. Ignoring this advice and Republicans' chilly reception in the audience, Clinton delivered a critically acclaimed speech. Then, instead of dutifully retreating to the White House to await the Senate's verdict, he immediately took his legislative program on the road. During the next three weeks he logged nineteen separate appearances outside Washington. By going public at this unlikely moment, Clinton drew the contrast between his attentiveness to the "business of the American people" and the Republican Senate's preoccupation with the impeachment trial, which a majority of the public opposed.

In the aftermath of reelection President Bush used his 2005 State of the Union address to launch a "Sixty Stops in Sixty Days" blitzkrieg around the country to build a grassroots campaign for a massive overhaul of Social Security. His appearances were accompanied by extensive television advertising by the Republican National Committee and business groups supporting his privatization proposal, as well as by various groups opposed to his reforms. In pursuing this strategy Bush outdid Clinton by engaging Congress with unprecedented levels of travel to telegenic settings, speeches to appreciative audiences, and targeted television commercials.

If asked to name a president whose addresses drew a warm response from the American public, many would think first of Franklin Roosevelt, whose nationally broadcast radio addresses, known as "Fireside Chats," rallied the American public during the Depression

---

* Card added, "This experience is one that obviously we wish we didn't have to live through." Other Bush advisers elaborated that the president might travel to states of vulnerable Democratic senators to pressure them to back his policies. "When you have a coalition-style government," explained one aide, "you have to use the bully pulpit to change the terms of the battlefield." Dana Milbank and Amy Goldstein, "Bush to Pursue Unaltered Agenda," *Washington Post,* May 26, 2001.

THE VETO GAME

logic of politics

The veto game begins with the president and Congress at odds over a change in government policy (the status quo). If the two sides can agree on a change, a new policy will be created. If they continue to disagree and the president vetoes Congress's preferred policy, there is no change, and the status quo prevails. (It is assumed the congressional majority is too small to muster the two-thirds support needed for a veto override.) Within this context, three scenarios are possible:

Scenario 1: The president and Congress have sharply different policy preferences.

This scenario depicts the simplest situation—and the only one that might actually end in a veto. Congress passes legislation changing the status quo. The president prefers the status quo, refuses to compromise, and simply vetoes the new legislation Congress has passed.

Anticipating this outcome, Congress may not even bother to create the legislation. When President Ronald Reagan (1981–1989) announced early in his first term that he would welcome legislation weakening certain provisions of the Clean Air Act, environmentalists in Congress knew that any attempt to strengthen the law during his tenure was doomed to failure. For the next eight years, then, the House Commerce subcommittee dealing with the environment occasionally held hearings but did not take action. The president's tacit veto trumped any real efforts to strengthen policy.

Scenario 2: Congress favors a more drastic change in policy than does the president.

In Scenario 2 both Congress and the president want a change in the status quo, with Congress favoring a greater change than does the president. If Congress passes a law incorporating its preferences, the president will veto the bill since the administration favors the status quo more than the change Congress advocates. Nevertheless, Congress does not have to capitulate and precisely meet presidential demands. It only has to alter the original legislation enough to make the proposed policy marginally more attractive to the president than the status quo. Since the president's policy preferences are better served by signing than vetoing, the bill will become law.

When President George H. W. Bush (1989–1993) announced he would welcome a modest strengthening of the Clean Air Act, he shifted the game from Scenario 1 to Scenario 2. By stipulating early the provisions the bill would have to contain to win his signature, including a ceiling of $20 billion in new federal obligations, he was trying to signal precisely where the compromise

and World War II. Others might recall John Kennedy's speeches and live press conferences. Of recent presidents, Reagan and Clinton scored well in public relations. From this list of specialists in presidential rhetoric, we might conclude that nothing much has changed over the past half-century. An examination of the number of times presidents have gone public, however, reveals a different picture. We can easily discern the steady growth in public relations undertaken by the White House in the rising number of presidential speeches and days devoted to political travel.

should be. The Democrats immediately went to work on new legislation, but they did not confine themselves to the changes the president had proposed. After all, they only had to provide him with a bill that he found marginally more attractive than current policy. In the end, the Democratic House and Senate passed a stronger bill than the president had wanted, and Bush reportedly spent almost the full ten days vacillating between a veto and a signature. Finally, Bush pronounced the legislation barely acceptable and signed into law the 1990 revision of the Clean Air Act. The president's temporizing and carping reflect how well congressional Democrats squeezed all they could from the president.

Scenario 3: The president favors a more drastic policy change than does Congress.

In Scenario 3 the president and Congress swap places. The president favors a greater policy change than does Congress. Congress wants to change public policy as well, but by far less than does the president. Thus Congress can confidently pass its preferred legislation and expect the president to sign it since the bill goes further in meeting the president's goal than does the status quo. In this situation the

veto is worthless; Congress's preferences are enacted into policy.

In 1983 President Reagan sent Congress a budget calling for a 10 percent increase in defense spending. The Democratic-controlled House agreed to only a 4 percent increase. When asked about the lower figure at a news conference, the president hinted that he might have to veto such a bill. The Democrats, however, quickly turned the tables. On hearing of Reagan's comment, a Democratic leader retorted that the president had better be careful, for the next time the House might just lower the increase to 2 percent! President Reagan grudgingly signed the 4 percent increase.

More often than not, presidents who find themselves in this position are liberals promoting new social programs. Perhaps this finding accounts for the comparatively infrequent use of the veto by Democratic presidents (see Figure 7-2).

These simple illustrations of veto policies reveal much about the role of the veto in presidential leadership. In the first instance, the veto allows the president to single-handedly preserve the status quo. In the second, it prescribes the kind of compromise that allows both sides to agree. In the third, the veto proves worthless in pushing Congress where it does not want to go.

Today presidents devote a great deal of their time and energy, and the efforts of more than a quarter of their staff, appealing directly to the American people for support for themselves and their policies. Though appearing on prime-time television is the most dramatic way of going public, presidents rely on this method sparingly, holding their major television addresses in check (see Figure 7-3). They know they will lose the public's attention if they go to this well too often. During the energy crisis of the late 1970s, Jimmy Carter informed a consultant that he was about to give yet another nationally televised

A familiar scene: a president meeting with representatives of a core constituency. In this instance President Obama addresses the 2009 convention of the AFL-CIO, the nation's largest labor organization.

speech—the fifth!—on the crisis and the need to conserve energy. Backed with polling data, the consultant dissuaded him from doing so, arguing that the public had stopped paying attention to him.*

Since the Carter years, the continued growth of cable and satellite service has eroded presidents' capacity to enlist television to go public. In the 1960s, when viewers had few choices other than NBC, CBS, and ABC, these networks would agree to suspend commercial programming and broadcast the president's address. They even used the same camera feeds; consequently, viewers had little recourse other than the apparently drastic alternative of turning off the television, which, as audience ratings suggest, very few did. Since 1970 the proportion of American households that subscribe to cable and satellite television has grown from 7 percent to over 90 percent, and the number of cable channels has multiplied dramatically. Viewers have more alternatives to watching a presidential speech than ever before. Now, of course, they need only reach for the remote to choose among dozens of viewing options. Figure 7-4 illustrates one result of this profusion of

---

*Several decades earlier, Franklin Roosevelt had made a similar point in private correspondence: "The public psychology . . . [cannot] be attuned for long periods of time to the highest note on the scale. . . . People tire of seeing the same name, day after day, in the important headlines of the papers and the same voice, night after night, over the radio." Douglass Cater, "How a President Helps Form Public Opinion," *New York Times Magazine,* February 26, 1961, 12.

Figure 7-3 Presidential Addresses: Going Public More Often

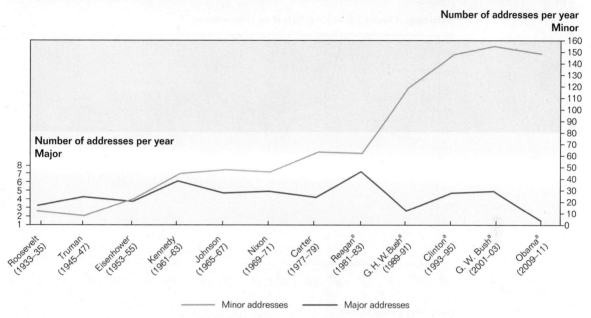

Number of addresses per year
Minor

Number of addresses per year
Major

——— Minor addresses　　——— Major addresses

Sources: Data for Roosevelt, Truman, Eisenhower, Nixon, and Carter are from William W. Lammers, "Presidential Attention-Focusing Activities," in *The President and the American Public,* ed. Doris A. Graber (Philadelphia: Institute for the Study of Human Issues, 1982), Table 6-1, 152. Data for Kennedy, Johnson, Reagan, G. H. W. Bush, Clinton, and G. W. Bush are from the *Public Papers of the Presidents* series. See also Samuel Kernell, "The Presidency and the People: The Modern Paradox," in *The Presidency and the Political System,* ed. Michael Nelson (Washington, DC: CQ Press, 1984), 242.

Note: Data reflect yearly averages. To eliminate public activities inspired by concerns of reelection rather than governing, only the first three years have been tabulated. For this reason, Gerald Ford's record of public activities during his two and one-half years of office has been ignored. Data on President Obama's first three years in office was calculated by Samuel Kernell and Josh Benjamin using www.whitehouse.gov/briefing-room/speeches-and-remarks.

a. Includes television addresses only.

choices—a sharp reduction in the share of households that tune into the president's annual State of the Union address.*

Mindful of the limitations of television, presidents communicate with voters in other ways. They take their messages to the public through appearances at graduation exercises, union conferences, and conventions held by trade and professional associations, where they can address the concerns of particular constituencies. Figure 7-3 reveals that these less visible, minor addresses have provided increasingly attractive vehicles for presidential communication: Reagan, Carter, and Nixon used them, on average, four times more often than did

---

*Aware that when viewers change channels, they often do not return for the rest of the evening, the big three television networks have increasingly balked at surrendering airtime to presidents for national addresses. The first instances of outright refusal occurred in the 1980s, when President Reagan encountered network resistance to his request for airtime on two separate occasions. In June 1992 the networks denied President George H. W. Bush a time slot for an evening press conference, and six of President Clinton's appearances (through January 1998) failed to attract full network coverage.

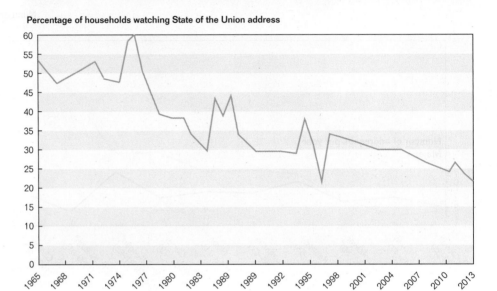

Figure 7-4 The Impact of Cable Television on the President's Audience

Percentage of households watching State of the Union address

Source: Nielsen Media Research.

Note: Data reflect Nielsen ratings for State of the Union addresses delivered from 1965 through 2013.

Truman, Roosevelt, and Hoover. George H. W. Bush managed to double the already high frequency of these targeted addresses; during his first three years in office he made, on average, a minor address every three days. Clinton did Bush one better; he delivered a minor address nearly every other day during his first three years in office. George W. Bush began his term with a barrage of public speeches, probably to gain the public's acceptance after a delayed, litigated election victory despite receiving fewer popular votes nationally. He was campaigning for his education reform proposals in Florida during the September 11, 2001, terrorist attacks. Abruptly, his schedule of minor addresses to targeted constituencies yielded to national appeals for unity in combating terrorism at home and in Afghanistan. But within several months the president resumed his public relations strategy, and by the end of his third year Bush had far eclipsed President Clinton's record of appearances.

Presidential foreign and domestic travel, typically undertaken for different political purposes, has increased significantly in the past half-century (see Figure 7-5). President Dwight Eisenhower's 1959 "goodwill tour" around the world is generally recognized as the first international presidential travel for which favorable publicity appeared to be the primary consideration. Subsequent presidents have favored the idea as well. Presidents Carter and George H. W. Bush, who enjoyed their greatest policy successes in foreign affairs, traveled extensively. By the end of his third year in office, Bush was so conspicuously absent due to overseas travel that his critics—especially his opponent in the next election, Bill Clinton—found a large segment of the public agreeing with them that the president was not paying enough attention

Figure 7-5   Going Public Involves More Presidential Travel

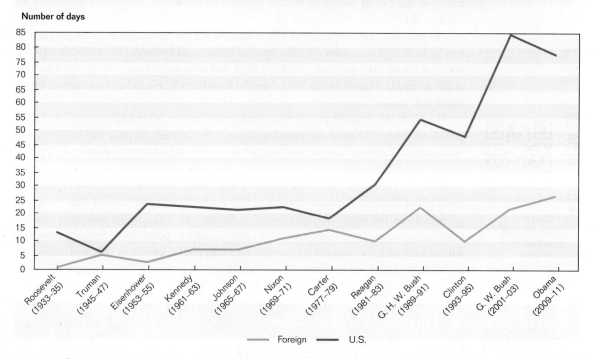

Number of days

Foreign —— **U.S.**

Sources: Data for Roosevelt, Truman, Eisenhower, Nixon, and Carter are from William W. Lammers, "Presidential Attention-Focusing Activities," in *The President and the American Public,* ed. Doris A. Graber (Philadelphia: Institute for the Study of Human Issues, 1982), Table 6-5, 160. Data for Kennedy, Johnson, Reagan, G. H. W. Bush, Clinton, and G. W. Bush are from the *Public Papers of the Presidents* series. See also Samuel Kernell, "The Presidency and the People: The Modern Paradox," in *The Presidency and the Political System,* ed. Michael Nelson (Washington, DC: CQ Press, 1984), 244.

Note: Data reflect yearly averages. To eliminate public activities inspired by concerns of reelection rather than governing, only the first three years have been tabulated. For this reason, Gerald Ford's record of public activities during his two and one-half years of office has been ignored. Data on President Obama's first three years in office was calculated by Samuel Kernell and Josh Benjamin using www.whitehouse.gov/schedule.

to solving the economic recession at home. Under pressure to focus on domestic issues, Bush postponed a trip to Asia in late 1991, saying that he had stayed home to keep tabs on the Democratic Congress.

Clinton had a special reason for his heavy travel schedule around the country: with third-party candidate Ross Perot in the race, Clinton had won the 1992 election with just 43 percent of the popular vote. By the 1996 election Clinton had averaged a visit to California, with its fifty-four electoral votes, every six weeks. Just as a precarious victory had motivated Clinton to travel, it also spurred his successor, George W. Bush, who eked out an Electoral College (and Supreme Court) victory despite winning half a million fewer popular votes than did his Democratic opponent, Al Gore. Much of his frenetic travel schedule in 2002 was directed at raising record-shattering campaign contributions (see box "The President as Party Coordinator" in Chapter 12) for Republican Senate candidates. By the end of his third year, President Bush logged nearly a third of his days in office traveling somewhere in the United States or abroad. If anyone thought this frenetic travel was an anomaly, they need only consider President Obama's travels. His first two years nearly match Bush's averages, and 2011 found him on the road continuously in pursuit of a billion-dollar pot of campaign contributions for Democratic campaigns (including his own) in 2012.

The president's capacity to shape public opinion and mobilize support for his policies will vary by issue, by the responses of other opinion leaders, and by the public's established preferences on issues. On each score President Bush had a far easier time rallying the American public to invade Afghanistan in 2001 than did President Obama in building support for his health care reform.

The president's leadership of public opinion also rests on the public's appraisal of him as president. When an unpopular president issues public appeals, citizens will be inclined to ignore him and suspect base motives for his appeal. Long-term trends in presidents' approval ratings display the present-day public as less enthusiastic with all politicians who occupy the Oval Office. Presidents begin their terms on *honeymoon* with the public, as a significantly greater share of survey respondents applaud the president's early performance than one would guess based on the recent election results (see Figure 7-6). These initial periods of goodwill have become increasingly short-lived. One reason is partisan polarization. Survey respondents who identify with the opposition party quickly swing to disapproval, as indicated in the large spread in partisans' job performance evaluations shown in Figure 7-6. Consequently, when

Figure 7-6 Partisan Polarization and Presidential Approval

Percentage

—— Percentage point difference in performance rating between president's and opposition party's identifiers
—— Overall percentage approving the president's job performance

Source: Adapted from presidential approval ratings found at http://www.ropercenter.uconn.edu.

presidents speak to the public in national addresses, they find themselves increasingly preaching to their choir of like-minded partisans.[22]

Everything we have considered thus far about the emergence of the modern presidency implies vastly more work and activity than was envisioned by the Framers. As government programs have grown, Congress has delegated to the chief executive significant responsibility for managing the large bureaucracy and ample discretion for adapting policy to changing circumstances. Modern presidents aspire to be more than administrators, of course, and whether in lobbying Congress or in communicating to the public, they depend heavily on staff to help them do their work. Consequently, the emergence of modern presidential leadership has been accompanied by the steady development of a larger, more complex staffing system.

The Institutional Presidency

As an organization the presidency began modestly. When President Washington summoned his secretary to help him with correspondence, Thomas Jefferson walked through the door with pen and paper. With such quality, who needs quantity? By the early 1800s the number of staff working in and around the White House was fewer than a dozen, of whom two or three were clerks who spent most of their time copying letters, receiving visitors, and running errands.[23] When Franklin Roosevelt entered the White House more than 130 years later, the president's staff had grown to about fifty, most "**detailed staff**" from another government agency sent over to lend the White House a hand.[*] (Agencies were happy to loan the president staff, since it ensured them inside information of what the president was up to.) Despite the heavier workload associated with overseeing the executive branch departments, the presidency remained undeveloped as an institution. It remained an informal working group whose daily assignments were personally managed by the president.

In 1937 the President's Committee on Administrative Management, also known as the Brownlow Committee, concluded its detailed analysis with "the president needs help." Likening the president to the chief executive officer of a large corporation, Louis Brownlow, one of a new breed of progressive public administration reformers, called for the creation of an organization dedicated to helping the occupant of the Oval Office become the administrator that modern governance required. If the president was indeed the government's CEO, as Brownlow claimed, he needed the same kinds of authority, expertise, and information modern corporate executives had at their fingertips. The president needed a professional staff.

The recommendations in the **Brownlow report** ignored the fact that the Constitution withholds from the presidency the kinds of authority CEOs typically enjoy in running their businesses. The chief executive's constitutional predicament was not lost on Congress, however. When a delighted President Roosevelt forwarded Brownlow's recommendations to Capitol Hill for enactment, he was rebuffed. Many in Congress, still angry over FDR's ill-fated attempt to pack the Supreme Court (described in Chapter 9), refused to act on the

---

[*] And, at least in a few instances, to keep tabs and report back to the agency what the president was doing. The FBI and War Department were large contributors to the president's staff before the White House had its own.

report's recommendations. Not until two years later, with the world edging toward the precipice of war, did Congress agree to a reduced form of Brownlow's staffing proposal.

Thus the institutional presidency was born. Christened the **Executive Office of the President (EOP)**, it housed five "new" presidential agencies, two of which were and remain significant assets: the Bureau of the Budget (precursor to the present-day Office of Management and Budget, or OMB) and the **White House Office**, the president's personal staff system.[24] These new resources proved vital to FDR, who frequently bemoaned his inability to elicit advice from and give orders to the departments except through the cabinet secretaries. In frustration, he sometimes compared himself to "a power plant with no transmission lines." His enlarged staff would allow him to keep tabs on the daily business of the departments and agencies. The Brownlow report called for the creation of an office—soon to be called the White House Office—comprising six loyal "Assistants to the President," who would serve the president with "a passion for anonymity." (When President Roosevelt read this phrase, he reportedly chuckled and quipped that such an animal does not exist in Washington.)

It is fitting that a separate presidential staff would arise during Roosevelt's presidency. More than the growing workload underwrote this development. Fearful that many of the cabinet departments would subvert the plethora of New Deal programs, the president persuaded Congress to create an array of relief agencies outside the standing bureaucracy.*

This arrangement gave the president greater control over its policies, but at a heavy cost of having personally to manage decisions that would otherwise have been delegated to professionals in the bureaucracy. Moreover, he suspected that Democratic state politicians throughout the South and West were less enthusiastic with the New Deal than were some Republicans. Consequently, he broke from standard party routines of relying on these politicians for filling various New Deal programs' state administrative positions in favor of appointees—even Republican appointees—who genuinely supported his policies. This separation of presidents' interests from the interests of other politicians in their party has become ever more pronounced over the decades. One can reasonably view the institutional presidency, as one political scientist aptly described it, as a "presidential branch of government separate and apart from the executive

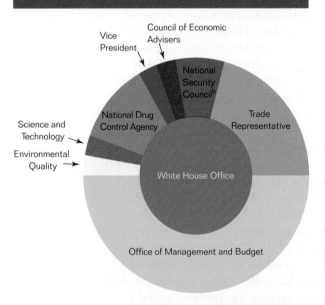

Figure 7-7 Organization of the Executive Office of the President[a]

Source: Figure adapted from Bradley Patterson, "Key to the Organization Chart of the Obama White House Staff," Summer 2009, http://whitehousetransitionproject.org/resources/briefing/SixMonth/Patterson%20-%20OBAMA%20WHITE%20HOUSE%20STAFF.pdf.

a. Area proportionate to number of senior assistants. Offices concerned with residence, security, and administration of the White House are excluded.

b. NSC includes the Homeland Security Council; does not include staff "detailed" from agencies.

*The Works Progress Administration (WPA) was not housed in the Department of the Interior and over time vied with that department's Public Works Administration for funding and projects.

branch," which "sits across the table from the executive branch . . . and imperfectly attempts to coordinate both the executive and legislative branches in its own behalf."[25]

Over the years the Executive Office of the President has housed those agencies the president or Congress would like to keep in the shadow of the White House. Typically, the dozen or so agencies that make up the acronym world of the modern EOP work much more closely with the president and the White House Office staff than they do with each other.*

In performing classic staff functions, either these agencies gather information—from the departments and agencies (**National Security Council**, or **NSC**), Congress (OMB), or the broader policy environment (Council of Economic Advisers and Council on Environmental Quality)—or they help to maintain the organization itself (Office of the Vice President and Office of Administration). With no programs to administer, the presidential bureaucracy does not require a field staff outside of Washington.

The largest and most important of the presidential agencies is the OMB. Staffed by accountants, economists, and tax lawyers, the OMB creates the annual federal budget, monitors agency performance, compiles recommendations from the departments on **enrolled bills** (bills that have been passed in identical form by both houses of Congress and presented to the president for his signature), and performs central clearance over agencies' communications with Congress. Another important agency within the EOP is the NSC. Its statutory responsibility appears modest: to compile reports and advice from the State and Defense Departments and the Joint Chiefs of Staff and to keep the president well informed on international affairs. Yet the national security adviser, who heads this presidential agency, has at times assumed a role in conducting foreign policy that is close to that traditionally associated with the secretary of state. The president's OMB director and national security adviser spend as much time working with the president as do any cabinet secretaries or other staff advisers.

The White House Office has grown in both number and complexity. What began as a small, informal group of half a dozen aides has evolved into a large, compartmentalized, multilayered bureaucracy. Richard Nixon assembled the largest staff, at almost 660. It probably would have continued to grow had the Watergate scandal that drove him from office not sent some Nixon aides to federal prison and turned the size of the White House staff into a campaign issue. Moreover, Congresses since then, most controlled by opposition parties, have reined in staff growth through budgets and legislative language limiting the president's ability to borrow staff from other agencies.

The present-day White House staff has leveled off at about 450 full-time positions. In large part the growth of staff follows the ever-expanding responsibilities of presidents, but it also springs from modern leadership strategies. Approximately a third of the staff attend to some aspect of public relations—travel, speeches, tending the press, and cultivating support among various constituencies. Similarly, as presidents have steadily centralized tasks that once were performed by their allies in the departments and agencies, they have added staff. Reputedly, no more than three or four of President Truman's aides ever dealt with vetting presidential appointments. Today, recruitment of appointees for the departments and federal judiciary is done almost exclusively from within the White House by a team of several dozen assistants.

■ WATCH A VIDEO ▶

logic.cqpress.com

Richard Neustadt describes President Truman's staffing arrangement in an earlier generation of small staffs.

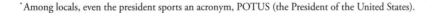

* Among locals, even the president sports an acronym, POTUS (the President of the United States).

In the early years small White House staffs were informally organized according to tasks and the working styles of the presidents. Franklin Roosevelt and Harry Truman favored a collegial organization in which they personally supervised their aides. Roosevelt resisted the notion of fixed staff assignments; throughout his term only his press secretary, appointments secretary, and counsel had well-defined duties and routines. FDR fostered competition by giving an aide projects that duplicated another aide's assignment. The staff were well aware of this practice, and therein lay its effectiveness. Aware that the president might already have been briefed on a subject, or soon would be, FDR's aides undertook their assignments with special diligence, not to be outdone. Not only were they thorough; they resisted the temptation to slant their reports to promote or nix a course of action according to their personal preferences. Through staff competition Roosevelt largely solved the "dependency" problem that afflicts all principals who rely on agents for information and advice.

Truman preferred more cooperative relations among his staff. He conducted a meeting each morning with ten to twelve of his "senior" staff to receive reports and give out assignments. Later presidents tried to emulate FDR's and Truman's collegial management styles, but as staffs grew, later presidents found themselves devoting inordinate time to managing individuals whose positions were created to help the president get through the day. President Jimmy Carter was the last president to try to run the White House staff informally, but it proved so frustrating that he abandoned it in favor of an organization administered by a chief of staff. Perhaps reflecting his military background, President Eisenhower had introduced the more orderly and hierarchical organization headed by a chief of staff. His assistants had fixed routines, job titles, and middle-level supervisors. Whatever its advantages in clarifying day-to-day responsibilities and relieving the president from personally having to manage his agents, it rendered the president heavily reliant on and vulnerable to his chief and other staff judging what actions he should take or which policies he should embrace.[*]

The chief of staff has become a fixture in the White House. More broadly, specialists performing specific routine tasks have replaced yesterday's agents who depended on the president for assignments. Reflecting the more sophisticated division of labor, aides are recruited for specific offices and job titles according to their experience at different tasks. With several exceptions the **chief of staff system** has more to do with imposing a chain of command than with clarifying responsibilities and shielding the president from having to micromanage the staff's routine activities (see Figure 7-8).[†]

Presidents commonly cut through the structure by creating informal working groups and more visible task forces. An increasingly favored practice involves assigning senior aides with special authority to coordinate policy development across the departments and agencies and other EOP offices. President Obama designated a number of these policy "czars" who caught the attention of members of Congress and the news media because of their lofty political credentials. When the president announced the appointments of former Senate majority leader Thomas Daschle to head his health reform effort and former EPA head Carol Browner

---

[*] On many issues Eisenhower's chief of staff instructed White House aides that if an issue could not be reduced to a single page, it was not ready for the president's consideration.

[†] When a new aide joins the White House Office, she or he is presented an organization chart identifying who does what and where.

to oversee energy and environmental policy, every Washingtonian sensed that they would not be ordinary White House aides. Rather, they would carry the president's clout in their dealings with others who shared policy responsibilities in this domain.

With its clear organizational lines, fixed assignments, and loyal and enthusiastic employees, one might think the White House staff system should run like a well-tuned engine. The facts, however, belie this naive expectation. Every recent president has experienced serious staffing problems that have erupted into public controversy, if not scandal. Many aides are motivated as much by interest in advancing a particular cause or policy agenda as by a desire to serve the president. This tendency is reinforced by outside pressures as key constituencies lobby for one of their own to be on the staff. "Everyone in the White House has a constituency," complained senior Reagan aide Michael Deaver.[26] In 1978 a Carter aide who sided with his Jewish constituency's opposition to the sale of reconnaissance jets to Saudi Arabia called a press conference and resigned in protest.[27] More often, staff will discreetly "leak" to the press information supporting their preferences. (The strategy of White House leaks is taken up more fully in Chapter 14.)

Most of the president's staff come to Washington lacking the experience that will serve them best in their new positions. Typically, they arrive at the White House fresh

H. R. Haldeman, chief of staff to President Richard Nixon, became entangled in the presidentially directed Watergate cover-up. After federal indictment in 1973, his boss asked him to resign his White House post, which he dutifully did. Haldeman subsequently served a brief prison term over this affair. In retirement he reflected on "the lessons of Watergate" in numerous public interviews and a memoir.

from the presidential campaign, a setting that rewards behavior that may be counterproductive once the candidate becomes president. For example, rather than seek compromise on a controversial policy with members of Congress, campaign aides in the White House might wrongly advise their president to stand firm on constituency commitments and appeal for public support, even when reasonable accommodations are available.

Some staff members view their positions at the White House as way stations to lucrative careers. These aides may have a greater stake in the outcomes of decisions and making their mark on policy than in respecting the integrity of the organization's procedures designed to inform presidents and advance the presidential agenda. As staff members compete with others inside and outside the White House for influence, the tenets of orderly organization can crumble. Consequently, staff turnover is high, and by the beginning of the second term, if there is one, the staff has been largely reconstituted with fresh appointments and reorganized assignments. In selecting aides and organizing the staff system, modern presidents are confined to working within a hefty organization that is largely beyond their personal supervision. For them, solving the dependency problem involves giving access to as many aides and points of view as they can accommodate.

Figure 7-8 The Organization of the Obama White House[a]

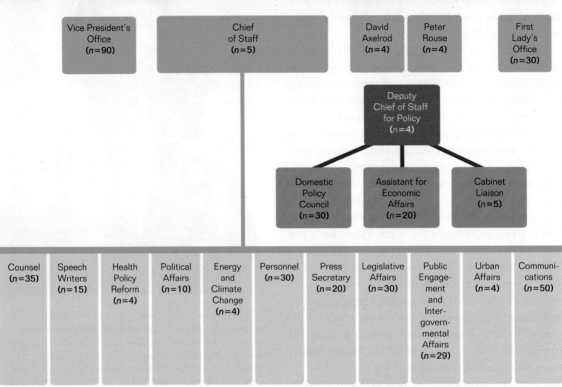

Source: Figure adapted from Bradley Patterson, "Key to the Organization Chart of the Obama White House Staff," Summer 2009, http://whitehousetransitionproject.org/resources/briefing/SixMonth/Patterson%20-%20OBAMA%20WHITE%20HOUSE%20STAFF.pdf.

a. Records and housekeeping offices omitted. Staff numbers are approximate.

PRESIDENTS AS STRATEGIC ACTORS

Through delegation and the successful assertion of authority, modern presidents are thoroughly enmeshed in the administration of the government's vast bureaucracy. Aided by an elaborate presidential staffing system, their day-to-day activities fully realize the Constitution's job description: "The executive Power shall be vested in a President of the United States." The modern presidency enjoys far more responsibility and authority, a much bigger and more expert staffing system, and a greater capacity to speak to the public than the Framers could possibly have imagined. Yet presidents still do not sit at the controls and pull the levers of government. The fundamental dilemma facing U.S. presidents remains: they have too little authority to satisfy the expectations for their performance. George W. Bush's flirtation with the unitary executive—a doctrine that could have endowed him with stronger command authority—ended ignominiously as he became unpopular in the nation and ignored in the Congress. Recent events proved the doctrine to be a chimera as fleeting as the power derived from politics.

In part this dilemma reflects the intractability of many of the problems modern presidents must deal with. After the September 11 attacks showed how easily commercial aircraft could be turned into weapons, the president and Congress responded with a series of public laws, executive orders, and administrative regulations costing billions of dollars and inconveniencing all travelers. Subsequent inspections of aviation security found that the new systems were far from achieving a safe commercial aviation system. The disparity between expectations and performance reflects the reality of politics. The office remains tethered to its limited constitutional mandate, and the Constitution intentionally tilted power relations among the branches toward Congress, as befitting a democracy. Particularly in an era of divided party control of government, presidents rarely find other politicians in Washington rushing to fulfill their requests. Except for moments of national crisis, presidential success remains problematic and depends today, as in the past, on the president's talent as a politician.

Abraham Lincoln, whom historians generally rank as America's greatest president, frequently referred to his job as "chief clerk." Everyone, he complained, needed him to do something for them. Their ranks included job seekers wanting patronage appointments, generals seeking more troops and supplies, and members of Congress requesting his endorsement—or at least his signature—for their pet legislation. In his classic treatise *Presidential Power and the Modern Presidents,* Richard E. Neustadt argues persuasively that despite sharp expansion of statutory authority and the dramatic growth in the institutional resources we have presented in this chapter, the modern presidency still confronts a dilemma of leadership.[28] The demands of the office continue to exceed the resources available to incumbents to meet them. As a consequence, whether a new president will emerge a leader and actually shape national policy or recede into the more passive routines of clerkship remains uncertain and, for every president, a problem to be resolved. Whether a chief executive succeeds in converting his "clerkship" responsibilities into real leadership has less to do with the authority of the modern office than with the president's political skill. Whether the politician in the White House recognizes the opportunities offered by this setting and is able to take full advantage of them is an altogether different matter.

logic.cqpress.com

Test your knowledge of this chapter.

---

logic.cqpress.com

▬ Key Terms ▬

Suggested Readings

Cohen, Jeffrey. *The Presidency in the Era of 24-Hour News.* Princeton, NJ: Princeton University Press, 2008. Although based on sophisticated statistical techniques, the research reported in this book is full of insights on the effects of the transformation of the news industry on modern presidential communications.

Kernell, Samuel. *Going Public: New Strategies of Presidential Leadership.* 3rd ed. Washington, DC: CQ Press, 1997. The author develops more fully the argument summarized here that modern presidents are more inclined than were their predecessors to engage in public relations in seeking influence in Washington.

Neustadt, Richard E. *Presidential Power and the Modern Presidents: The Politics of Power from Roosevelt to Reagan.* 4th ed. New York: Free Press, 1990. This volume is *the* classic statement of the leadership predicament confronted by all presidents. Originally published in 1961 and in print ever since, the book is a touchstone for anyone aspiring to understand the American presidency.

Woodward, Bob. *Obama's Wars.* New York: Simon and Schuster, 2010. Once again Woodward gained access to nearly everyone in writing a breezy but informative insider's account of military policymaking in the Obama administration.

Review Questions

1. What are the powers granted to the president in the Constitution? What are the nonconstitutional sources of presidential power? When were these sources of power first tapped?

2. What are executive orders? Executive agreements? What are the president's alternatives to using them?

3. How did the presidency of the 1800s differ from that of today? In particular, how did the president's interactions with his party and his cabinet change over time?

4. What are the trade-offs between the collegial and chief-of-staff models of presidential staff organization?

Which model seems to have predominated with recent presidents?

5. What is "going public"? What specific tools or resources are available to the president when he chooses to use this strategy?

6. How has the rise of cable and satellite television affected the president's ability to communicate with the public?

7. Why don't members of Congress go public as often as the president does? Why doesn't the president use this tactic on every issue?

8 The Bureaucracy

A U.S. Border Patrol agent at the memorial service for Agent Brian Terry, who was killed in a firefight along the U.S.-Mexico border in December 2010. At the scene of the shootout were two AK-47 assault rifles, which the Bureau of Alcohol, Tobacco, Firearms and Explosives had lost track of through the disastrous "Operation Fast and Furious."

- Who controls the bureaucracy? The president? Congress? The courts? No one?

- How can the government grow while the bureaucracy shrinks?

- Why do efforts to make government agencies more accountable lead to the proliferation of red tape?

- How can elected officials design formal and informal mechanisms to oversee the implementation of laws by millions of unelected bureaucrats?

After U.S. Border Patrol Agent Brian Terry was killed in a December 2010 shootout with suspected border bandits in the desert near Nogales, Arizona, grief over this tragedy turned into shock when two of the assault rifles found at the scene were traced back to a secretive but now infamous project known as "Operation Fast and Furious." The two AK-47s had originally been sold by the hesitant owner of a Glendale, Arizona, gun store acting on instructions from agents of the Bureau of Alcohol, Tobacco, Firearms and Explosives (ATF). The ATF then tracked these and thousands of other guns sold from shops in Arizona, hoping to trace them to Mexican drug cartels. Yet many of the weapons escaped surveillance, smuggled to other states and across the border.

Forty of the guns wound up in the Ciudad Juárez, Mexico, arsenal of Jose Antonio Torres Marrufo, the Sinaloa cartel's top enforcer known as "The Jaguar."[1] Two more were recovered at the scene of the slaying of a Mexican state attorney general's brother, a discovery that U.S. agents initially sought to hide from the Mexican government.[2] All told, 797 firearms—less than half of those sold through this operation—were recovered on both sides of the border, including 195 that had been used in crimes or intercepted by police in Mexico.[3]

What was the ATF, a large federal **bureaucracy** tasked with a difficult and high-stakes job, hoping to accomplish through Fast and Furious, and how did it go so terribly wrong? The plan was devised by agents in the ATF's Phoenix office who knew how American guns were getting to Mexican cartels. Since the United States requires criminal background checks before a gun can be purchased in a store, a "straw buyer" with a clean record would walk into a gun shop and buy high-powered weaponry, sometimes many guns at a time. (There is no federal law against selling multiple assault rifles—even hundreds of them—to a single buyer, even if he or she seems suspicious.) The straw buyer would then turn around and sell the guns to someone else, who'd sell them to a drug cartel. Encouraging gun store owners to make these sales, ATF agents videotaped suspicious purchasers and then attempted to follow the guns as they made their way to a cartel or another criminal group. That meant being patient, watching the guns pass from owner to owner in order to build a case against the cartel leaders in whose hands they eventually ended up. But these many steps created more chances for AK-47s and other assault weapons to fall through the cracks and into the hands of criminals without being tracked, increasing the risks that the operation would enable rather then fight crime.

Not everyone in the ATF bureaucracy thought this was a good idea. One agent in the Phoenix office recalled, "We voiced our concerns quite vocally to the point of yelling, screaming. We were overridden."[4] Top field agents and administrators maintained that this sting operation represented cutting-edge law enforcement until Border Patrol Agent Terry's death made it clear that the risks inherent in the project had become reality. The ATF, hampered by weak gun control laws and low levels of staffing, failed to monitor where many of the guns were until they wound up in a crime scene. The firearms spread too quickly outside of southern Arizona for the local agents there to monitor them, and they slipped past the U.S.-Mexico border from New Mexico and Texas. After Terry's murder, an unnamed law enforcement source admitted to a journalist, "My worst fear was that they would be used in a homicide of a Mexican military official or a Mexican police official. It crossed my mind that they would be used against U.S. forces, but I didn't think it would happen this soon."[5] John Dodson, an ATF agent who had worked on the operation, was also haunted by its bloody aftermath. "With the number of guns we let walk, we'll never know how many people were killed, raped, robbed," he said. "There is nothing we can do to round up those guns. They are gone."[6]

The high-profile failure of Operation Fast and Furious provides a dramatic illustration of the challenges faced every day by a federal bureaucracy charged with tasks as mundane as delivering the mail and as critical as defending the nation from a terrorist attack. Accomplishing either of those tasks requires the coordinated actions of thousands upon thousands of federal employees, each an expert in a specialized job but needing to work in concert with others. Conducting their operations requires a hierarchical structure that can pass along vital information to top administrators, without leaking key data. What's more, the frequent need for secrecy within a chain of command often makes it hard for lawmakers at the top of both the executive and legislative branches to oversee how a bureaucracy implements the legislation that they pass. In the immediate wake of Agent Terry's killing, Congress wanted to learn about Operation Fast and Furious and find out who was in charge of, and thus accountable for, its failure. Who was overseeing this bureaucracy run amok?

Answering that question was a challenge in itself, with separate investigations devolving into a bitter partisan struggle. In Congress, there was unanimous, bipartisan agreement that this was a massively bad idea. When it became clear that ATF Acting Director Kenneth Melson received weekly briefings on the project and even asked for access to the live feed from video cameras installed in gun shops to monitor purchases, he resigned. But this did not end the long and partisan fight between congressional Republicans and the Obama administration over whether the president or his cabinet knew what was happening in Arizona.

To find out, Chairman Darrell Issa's House Committee on Oversight and Government Reform demanded internal documents from the ATF and the Justice Department. Attorney General Eric H. Holder Jr. refused to provide them, arguing that the release of the 1,300 pages of subpoenaed documents would harm law enforcement operations. When Holder testified before Congress, stating both that he was not aware of the operation and that he had not discussed it with President Obama, Republicans in the House called for Holder to resign and threatened impeachment. After President Obama claimed that the documents were protected from release by executive privilege, Issa's committee voted along party lines to recommend that the full House rule Holder in contempt of Congress.[7] The House voted in June

■ WATCH A VIDEO

The debacle of "Operation Fast and Furious"

2012, largely along partisan lines, that Holder was in contempt of Congress, the first time in American history that such a vote had ever been cast against a sitting member of a president's cabinet.[8] Later that year, a congressional report found responsible five ATF agents, ranging from Acting Director Melson to the agent in charge of the Phoenix field office where the operation was carried out.[9] A 471-page report by the Justice Department's inspector general faulted some Justice Department officials for not raising red flags about the operation when they signed off on wiretaps, but "essentially exonerated" Attorney General Holder.[10] Presidents and cabinet members can never be aware of every detailed operation of the government they head, even when bureaucratic failure comes with such a great cost.

When Mexican officials seized this arsenal of Jose Antonio Torres Marrufo, the Sinaloa cartel's top enforcer, in Ciudad Juárez, they found forty weapons purchased in the United States under Operation Fast and Furious.

The tragic tale of Operation Fast and Furious shows how bureaucracy—a seemingly dry subject—holds high stakes and poses tough problems for American government. Though not clearly envisioned by the Framers, the diverse departments, agencies, bureaus, commissions, and other units of the executive branch that encompass the bureaucracy are necessary to turn political choices into policy realities. Government would cease to function at all without bureaucrats. Yet the many millions of individuals who carry out this work each have their own career goals, policy preferences, and human frailties that sometimes get in the way of government working well.

The challenges faced by a bureaucratic system are multifaceted. Scholars Anthony Bertelli and Laurence Lynn phrase one of them simply: "While citizens and their representatives expect public managers to 'get the job done,' significant aspects of 'the job' that public managers are supposed to accomplish are often ambiguous. These unelected officials must decide what the law, circumstances, and common sense require of them in given situations. Once they have exercised their best judgment, it is all too common for these same citizens and their representatives . . . to say to an offending public manager, 'No, that's not the job we wanted you to do.'"[11] When bureaucrats go far beyond the bounds of what the public wants, as in Operation Fast and Furious, they risk upsetting the balance that Alexander Hamilton laid out in *Federalist* No. 70, contrasting the need for "energy in the Executive" against the need for "safety." And when politicians seek to constrain bureaucrats, they run into the problem laid out by sociologist Max Weber in 1919. After observing the highly professionalized German bureaucracy, Weber noted how hard it was for generalist politicians to keep tabs on expert bureaucrats, who possessed information that lawmakers and the public did not.

All of these challenges are different facets of the basic dilemma of delegation, made more difficult by the fact that American bureaucracy forms the second of two layers of delegation.

The American people delegate power to make their collective decisions to elected officials. These lawmakers then hand over power to enforce and implement these decisions to the unelected bureaucrats whom they employ. Bureaucrats—ranging from cabinet secretaries to social workers to teachers to Drug Enforcement Administration agents—both serve and exert authority over the public. Enabling bureaucrats to understand what the public and lawmakers desire, and ensuring that they deliver it, is a constant and crucial challenge.

Though the Framers were largely silent on the design of American bureaucracy, the solution to this dilemma of delegation is built into our Constitution: our system of separated powers provides distinct checks on the bureaucracy. The executive branch employs all of these unelected officials, directing them through the thousands of top administrators who are appointed by the president. Congress attempts to control those who implement the laws that it passes, both through the power of its purse strings and through oversight of administrative activities. The courts provide a vital check by upholding both administrative law and constitutional principles, forcing the bureaucracy to follow standardized processes and protecting against the tyranny of the majority. Highlighting how deeply connected the Federalists' system of separated powers is to the operation and legitimacy of the bureaucracy, the title of Bertelli and Lynn's book characterizes American administrators as *Madison's Managers*.

THE DEVELOPMENT OF THE FEDERAL BUREAUCRACY

The Framers viewed the executive as the necessary source of "energy" in government, but questions of administration received remarkably little attention at the Constitutional Convention, and the Constitution itself said little about how the executive branch was to be organized. As we saw in Chapter 7, it did authorize the president, with the advice and consent of the Senate, to appoint ambassadors, Supreme Court justices, heads of departments, and other senior executive branch officials. Congress was left with the task of establishing executive departments and determining how they would be staffed.

Through American history, Congress has created executive branch agencies with authority to implement the laws it passes, and presidents have necessarily delegated their executive chores to numerous subordinate agents. In the nation's earliest years these agents delivered the mail, collected customs duties (taxes on imported goods) and excise taxes (on alcohol and luxuries), prosecuted violations of federal laws, and managed relations with foreign nations. Surely the Framers did not envision anything like today's 184,000-member Department of Homeland Security or the rest of the federal establishment, comprising some two thousand departments, bureaus, agencies, and commissions, which employ some 2.9 million nonmilitary personnel. But then they could not have anticipated the proliferation of demands for collective action that the next two centuries of social, economic, and technological change would provoke. A product of these demands, the modern bureaucracy also mirrors in a very direct way the pluralistic nature of American politics and society. Every new agency has been brought into being by a unique configuration of political demands and forces. Reflected in each agency's mandate and organization is the attempt of a successful policy coalition to preserve its victory through institutional design. The remarkable variety of arrangements adopted to administer government policies is largely a product of the endless search by Congress and the White House for ways to maximize the potential political benefits and minimize the potential political costs each time they decide to exercise and delegate their authority. The end product is the extravagantly diverse collection of entities that now compose the federal bureaucracy.

Modest Beginnings: The Dilemma of Delegation

From the beginning, Congress was wary of delegating too much power to the executive. The colonial experience with the king's governors and other royal officials was too fresh. But members of Congress also knew that delegation was unavoidable; the Continental Congress's attempt to make all administrative decisions through congressional committees had proven quite impractical. Delegate John Adams, for one, "found himself working eighteen-hour days just to keep up with the business of the 90 committees on which he served."[12]

With these experiences in mind, the First Congress began its work on the executive branch by reestablishing the departments that had existed under the Articles of Confederation: Treasury, Foreign Affairs (quickly renamed State after Congress decided to assign the department some domestic duties), and War. Congress also authorized the hiring of an attorney general to give the president and department heads legal advice. The larger departments were soon subdivided into more specialized offices, later called bureaus. For example, by 1801 the Treasury Department was dividing its work among units headed by a commissioner of revenue, who supervised tax collection; a purveyor in charge of buying military supplies; and an auditor who, among other duties, oversaw the operation of lighthouses. The Treasury Department also included a General Land Office to deal with the sale of public lands.[13]

Congress readily agreed that each executive department should be headed by a single official responsible for its operations. There was far less consensus, however, about whether department heads were accountable to Congress or to the president. As noted earlier, presidents appointed senior officials, but appointments were subject to senatorial approval (see Chapter 7). Could presidents, then, dismiss officials without the consent of the Senate? The First Congress gave the president the sole right of removal, but only narrowly; Vice President John Adams cast the tie-breaking vote in the Senate.[14] The issue came up again during the Jackson administration (1829–1837) and later during Reconstruction (1865–1877) before it was finally settled in the president's favor: officials held their jobs at the pleasure of the chief executive. Nonetheless, many lower-level federal jobs such as local postmaster were, by the time of the Adams administration (1797–1801), effectively controlled by Congress. When the president turned to members of Congress for advice on appointments in their states and districts, they had quickly come to expect that it would be followed.

The dismissal controversy was one of many instances in which Congress faced the familiar dilemmas of delegation. The advantages of delegating authority to a unified executive that could energetically and efficiently implement laws were clear. But so was a potential drawback: executives might also pursue ends contrary to those desired by congressional majorities. Recognizing this drawback, Congress leveraged its authority to establish executive branch agencies and set their annual budgets as a way to balance the president's power.

The executive struggled with the same dilemma. Even the skimpy government of the Federalist period (1789–1801) was too large to be managed by the president and his cabinet secretaries without delegating authority to subordinate officials. Thus the executive also faced a standard principal–agent problem: how to ensure that agents acting ostensibly on its behalf would faithfully carry out official policies. As the nation has grown and the range of federal activities expanded, so has the challenge of keeping appointed officials responsive to elected officials, just as elected officials are, in their turn, supposed to be responsive to the citizenry. As we will see in this chapter, the various ways in which the government has tried to meet this challenge have had enduring consequences for the modern bureaucracy.

The Federalist Years: A Reliance on Respectability

For many decades the federal government had few responsibilities, and so it was small. In fact, George Washington (1789–1797) had so few staff that he occasionally called on his cabinet chiefs to take dictation, making them secretaries in a less exalted sense.[15] Yet Washington and his successors still had to deal with the problem of delegation, heightened during the Republic's early days by long distances and primitive communications between the nation's capital and the states and cities where federal policies were administered.

During this period most federal government workers, laboring far from their bosses in the capital, were occupied with delivering the mail and collecting duties and taxes. The potential for corruption was considerable. President Washington believed that popular support for the young national government depended on honest and competent administration. Thus he sought to appoint civil servants of character and ability who were respected by their communities—in other words, men of superior education, means, family, and local reputation. The problem of delegation was to be met, in the first place, by choosing the right sort of people as agents. Other techniques also were used to ensure honest administration. Officials sometimes were required to post bonds of money or property that they would forfeit if they failed to perform their duties. Customs and alcohol tax collectors received a share of the proceeds from the sale of goods they seized from smugglers, giving them a financial incentive to detect and thwart smuggling. Heavy fines were imposed for giving or taking bribes.[16]

President Washington's efforts to establish an honest, competent federal civil service largely succeeded. Although presidents remained free to dismiss officials at will, an informal custom of tenure during good behavior emerged and remained in place until the 1820s. Indeed, it was not uncommon for officials to pass positions on to their sons or nephews.[17] This practice, consistent with Federalist notions of government by respectable gentlemen, was contrary, however, to the democratic spirit that eclipsed Federalist views during the early decades of the nineteenth century.

Democratization of the Civil Service: The Spoils System

The most prominent spokesman for this democratic spirit, President Andrew Jackson, argued that public offices held as, in effect, private property would "divert government from its legitimate ends and make it an engine for the support of the few at the expense of the many." Moreover, "the duties of all public officers are, or at least admit of being made, so plain and simple that men of intelligence may readily qualify themselves for their performance."[18] In other words, when it comes to governing, "no experience is necessary." Jackson thus advocated **rotation in office**; an official would serve in a position for a short, fixed period, then move on to something else, perhaps in government, but more often returning to private life. (The norm of rotation in office was also commonly practiced in Congress for much of the nineteenth century, an informal forerunner of the modern term limits movement discussed in Chapter 15.) The Jacksonian idea was to democratize the civil service along with the rest of the political system.

The democratic ideal of rotation in office meshed with the practical need of party organizations to reward the activists they relied on to mobilize the expanding mass electorate (see Chapter 12). Who better deserved appointment to public office than the men who had proved their mettle by helping their political party to triumph? Debating this issue in 1835, Sen. William Marcy, a New York Democrat, ensured himself a place in the history books by celebrating "the rule, that to the victor belong the spoils of the enemy,"[19] and giving the **spoils system**— the practice of the winning party dispensing government jobs—its name. Once government jobs became a primary resource for maintaining party machines, members of Congress developed an even keener interest in influencing appointments to federal offices in their states and districts.

Ironically, rotation in office and the spoils system, meant to democratize administration, led instead to its bureaucratization. Bureaucratic organization arises when leaders try to solve the huge problems of coordination and delegation raised by many forms of large-scale collective action. Max Weber, the German sociologist, delineated more than a century ago the characteristic features of bureaucratic institutions[20]:

President Andrew Jackson's campaign to democratize public administration led to the distribution of government jobs to loyal party workers. This depiction of Jackson astride a gluttonous hog makes it clear that the "spoils system," as this practice came to be called, was by no means universally celebrated.

- a hierarchical structure of authority in which commands flow downward and information flows upward (for coordination and control);
- a division of labor (to reap the advantages of specialization in taking on complex tasks);
- a consistent set of abstract rules regarding what is to be done and who is to do it (for coordination among specialists, control over subordinates, and uniformity of action in each position regardless of who holds it);
- impersonality, treating everyone in the same category equally regardless of who they are as individuals (for consistency and impartiality);
- a career system, with appointment and advancement by demonstrated merit, and often considerable job security (to create incentives for loyal and effective performance); and
- specified goals toward which the collective action is aimed (unlike, for example, economic markets, in which individuals and firms have goals—making money—but the market as a whole does not).

The model bureaucracy is, in short, a purposive machine with interchangeable human parts designed to facilitate collective action (coordinating relevant actors, discouraging free riding, and enforcing cooperative agreements) while enabling principals to control agents. Centralized control is exercised over large numbers of people performing complex social tasks, greatly amplifying the power of whoever sits at the apex of the hierarchical pyramid. The classic example is an army, with its clear chain of command from the five-star general at the top down to the lowliest private at the bottom. Most modern business corporations, government agencies, and even spiritual enterprises such as the Roman Catholic Church also have organized themselves bureaucratically for more effective central control over collective pursuits. But whatever its advantages, bureaucratic organization imposes heavy conformity costs on both bureaucrats and the people they deal with in return for reducing transaction costs and agency losses (see Chapter 1).

American bureaucracies, like American political parties, arose more from expedience than from conscious design. The Jacksonian Democrats had no intention of erecting new bureaucratic structures, but the spoils system created administrative problems that begged for bureaucratic solutions. With its widespread rotation in office, the spoils system was fraught with the dangers of incompetence and corruption. Jackson, no less than Washington, sought honest, efficient government, recognizing that the continued success of his party depended on delivering it. Jobs thus became more specialized and clearly defined so that novices could quickly master and perform them. Administrative jurisdictions and responsibilities were spelled out in greater detail to avoid confusion and conflict among people who would be in office only for a short time. Hierarchies became more formal and elaborate, with new procedures designed to monitor and control agents who had no long-term stake in how they performed their jobs. Officials kept meticulous records of their actions, which were subject to audit by a separate set of specialists. Government became more impersonal.[21]

The complex arrangements needed to ensure control quickly bred the kind of **red tape**—labyrinthine procedures, layers of paperwork (in quadruplicate!), demands for strict adherence to form—for which bureaucracies are legendary. In 1836, for example, the House Ways and Means Committee blamed the Treasury Department's excessive workload on an accounting system that required the concurrence of no fewer than five officers—the treasurer, the auditor, the comptroller, a secretary, and the registrar—for all receipts of funds and expenditures. "The result of the reciprocal checks here established," the committee noted, "is that no money can be received or paid out without the agency of these five separate offices, involving the labor of one or more clerks in each."[22] When senior officials place the desire to monitor agents ahead of efficiency (in this case by arranging for them to monitor each other), chronic bureaucratic sluggishness is the inevitable result.

Civil Service Reform

Under Jackson, the federal administration did not become fully bureaucratized in the Weberian sense; rotation in office precluded the development of government service as a career with job security and advancement based on merit. Only after the Civil War

(1861–1865) were calls from citizens and reformers to adopt this additional component of bureaucracy finally heard. The emerging industrial economy raised administrative problems that a civil service composed of short-term amateurs was poorly suited to address. More important, financial scandals, particularly during Ulysses S. Grant's administration (1869–1877), fueled attacks on the spoils system and prompted political support for civil service reform.[23] Perhaps the most dramatic incident was the exposure of the Whiskey Ring, a massive conspiracy of revenue collectors and whiskey distillers to evade taxes, which, when exposed, led to 230 indictments and the resignation of one member of Grant's cabinet. Civil service reformers also exploited their pivotal positions as leaders of a swing constituency in an era of close two-party electoral competition.

On July 2, 1881, Charles Guiteau, upset at being rejected for a patronage appointment, assassinated Republican president James A. Garfield in a Washington train station. Garfield died on September 19, 1881. The public uproar over the incident galvanized support in Congress for civil service reform.

Defenders of the old system did not give up easily, however, and reforms that protected officials from political firing and imposed merit criteria for hiring and advancement were extended gradually. The most compelling argument for reform was the assassination of President James Garfield in 1881 by a demented job seeker incensed at having lost a chance for a patronage appointment. The ensuing revulsion against the spoils system led in 1883 to passage of the Pendleton Act, the basis of the modern civil service. The act itself put only 10 percent of federal jobs under the merit system, but it authorized the president to extend coverage by executive order. Presidents from Grover Cleveland onward did exactly that, although, ironically, for the crassest of partisan motives. Each president about to relinquish office to the opposition party extended civil service protection to thousands of his own patronage appointees. By the time Franklin Roosevelt became president in 1933, 80 percent of federal workers were included in the merit system.[24]

The merit system bred its own set of agency problems, however. Rotation in office may have left the government short on experience and efficiency, but it had kept officials in close touch with ordinary citizens and responsive to the elected politicians who appointed them. Some proponents of a professional civil service naively thought it would turn government agencies into efficient, politically neutral tools subject only to the will of policymakers in Congress and the White House. Career bureaucrats, however, inevitably develop their own personal and institutional interests, and the rules designed to protect them from political retaliation make it difficult to punish them for shirking or incompetence. They become the reigning experts in their bureau's procedures and policy domains, magnifying the problems of hidden action (principals unable to observe what agents are doing) and hidden information (agents knowing things that principals do not) inherent in principal–agent relationships (see section "Delegation" in Chapter 1). Moreover, they can easily develop perspectives quite different from people outside of government. Organized into unions, bureaucrats form a potent political force. These problems are compounded by a Constitution that compels Congress and the president to share, and compete for, control over administration; the agents can play their multiple principals against one another. The political attempts to come to terms with these problems are responsible for much of the complexity and diversity of the administrative units added to the federal government over the past century.

AN EXPANDING GOVERNMENT

DATA UPDATE

logic.cqpress.com

Explore an interactive timeline on the growth of the civil service over time.

Despite dramatic changes in *how* the government operated after Jackson, *what* it did changed very little. The number of federal officials grew along with the population, but they continued to perform the same limited set of tasks assigned during the Federalist period: collecting duties and taxes, delivering the mail, disposing of public lands in the West, granting patents, managing relations with foreign nations and Native Americans, and maintaining a small army and navy. The federal establishment began small and stayed that way for decades because most Americans wanted it that way. Cheap, limited government was part of the democratic creed professed by disciples of Thomas Jefferson

---

Figure 8-1 Changes in Federal Civilian Employment

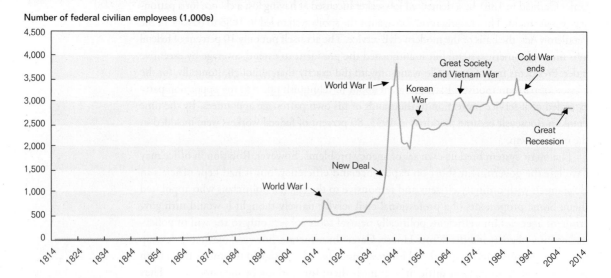

Sources: Harold W. Stanley and Richard G. Neimi, *Vital Statistics on American Politics, 1999–2000* (Washington, DC: CQ Press, 2000), 259–256; data for 1999–2011 from U.S. Office of Personnel Management, *Federal Civilian Workforce Statistics, Employment and Trends,* bimonthly release.

and Jackson, and any attempts to expand the federal domain met firm resistance in Congress.

After the Civil War, however, the federal government began expanding its activities and personnel, and that trend, with a few exceptions, has continued to the present day. As Figure 8-1 reveals, federal employment grew steadily but not very steeply (except during World War I) from the 1870s until the New Deal period (1933–1941), when the rate of growth began to increase. World War II produced a dramatic surge in the size of the federal workforce that was only partially reversed afterward. The number of civil servants continued to trend upward until 1990, then underwent steady decline until the onset of the war on terrorism. As a proportion of the population, the federal workforce has actually been shrinking since the 1950s (see Figure 8-2). The federal government has not been shrinking in any other sense, however; politicians have found many ways to expand the government's activities without expanding its workforce.

Government could only grow if Congress and the president were willing to delegate authority to new agencies. Historically, the most common reasons for delegating authority have been to handle large-scale administrative tasks, to exploit expertise, to avoid blame for unpopular decisions, to make credible commitments to stable policy, or to deal with crises demanding swift, coordinated action. Varying goals have inspired varying degrees of delegation as well as different organizational strategies for limiting potential agency losses (see Chapter 1). Political battles arising from conflicting goals within Congress and between Capitol Hill and the White House have also done much to shape and reshape bureaucratic institutions.

Figure 8-2   Federal Civilian Employment Compared to the U.S. Population

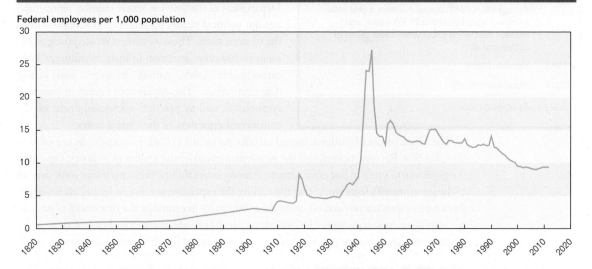

Federal employees per 1,000 population

Sources: 1921–1961: calculated by authors from Harold W. Stanley and Richard G. Neimi, *Vital Statistics on American Politics, 1999–2000* (Washington, DC: CQ Press, 2000), 259–260 and 355; U.S. Office of Personnel Management, *Federal Civilian Workforce Statistics, Employment and Trends,* bimonthly release; Bureau of the Census data at www.census.gov/compendia/statab/cats/population.html.

TABLE 8-1

Origin of Cabinet-Level Departments

1789	War, State, and Treasury (the attorney general, a part-time appointee, sat in on cabinet meetings as well)
1798	Navy (split off from War)
1849	Interior
1870	Justice (Office of the Attorney General was established in 1789 and elevated to department status in 1870)
1889	Agriculture (established in 1862 but not elevated to cabinet status until 1889)
1903	Labor (established as the Bureau of Labor in Interior in 1884; achieved cabinet status as the Department of Labor and Commerce in 1903; split from Commerce in 1913)
1903	Commerce (established as part of the Department of Labor and Commerce; split from Labor in 1913)
1947	Defense (combined War, Navy, and new Air Force Departments; initially called the National Military Establishment; renamed Defense in 1949)
1965	Housing and Urban Development
1966	Transportation
1977	Energy
1979	Health and Human Services (formerly Health, Education, and Welfare, 1953–1979)
1979	Education (established as a free-standing subcabinet department in 1867; placed in Interior a year later; eventually ended up in Health, Education, and Welfare, from which it split when it was raised to cabinet status)
1988	Veterans Affairs
2002	Homeland Security

Source: Compiled by the authors.

The Cabinet

Agencies that rise to the department level and gain a seat in the president's cabinet receive no special powers or privileges. Presidents can and do invite whomever they wish to serve in their cabinets, regardless of whether they head a department. For example, Lisa P. Jackson, administrator of the Environmental Protection Agency, and Ron Kirk, U.S. Trade Representative, enjoyed cabinet-level status during the first Barack Obama administration. Over the years, however, political entrepreneurs have fought vigorously to confer departmental status on the agencies that administer policies affecting their constituents. They do this in part for a leg up in the competition for scarce resources and in part for symbolic recognition of the political centrality of their concerns. Each addition to the roster of cabinet-level agencies represents and helps to sustain the political triumph of a particular coalition. The history of the cabinet thus provides a concise, if incomplete, picture of the succession of social and economic interests that have become powerful enough to command this level of political recognition (see Table 8-1).

THE EARLIEST DEPARTMENTS. Until 1849, Treasury, State, Navy, and War stood alone as cabinet-level departments. They were joined that year by the Department of the Interior, whose creation represented a major political victory for members of Congress from the western states. These westerners wanted the government to pay more attention to their constituents' concerns: public lands, natural resources, and Native American affairs. The department's creation provided symbolic as well as practical acknowledgment of the continental expansion of the United States.

The Department of Justice achieved cabinet status in 1870 after Congress, in response to the Civil War, Reconstruction, and the problems created by the growth of industry, expanded the government's role in law enforcement. Among other things, the department took over all of the government's legal work, thereby ending the expensive practice of letting each department hire its own lawyers and allowing the ruling party to centralize the processing of patronage appointments of judges, U.S. attorneys, and U.S. marshals. The head of the Justice Department, the attorney general, has been a key political figure in most administrations.[25]

CLIENTELE AGENCIES. The Departments of Agriculture (1889), Labor (1903), and Commerce (1903) represented a new type of government agency altogether. Unlike the existing departments, which served general social purposes, each of the new departments was established to serve the particular clientele indicated by its title: farmers, labor unions, and business. In seeking cabinet-level status, these constituencies were represented by sophisticated interest groups, which lobbied intensely on behalf of their clients (organized labor successfully insisted on the separation of "its" department from Commerce in 1913). In granting their wishes and supporting department budgets, members of Congress could claim credit for the continuing flow of benefits they provided to an important set of constituents.

One of the original four cabinet-level departments, the Treasury Department takes on tasks that range from advising the president on economic policy to the literal printing of money. Here Treasury Secretary Timothy Geithner, who took a lead role in negotiations with Congress over the "fiscal cliff" in late 2012, appears on a Sunday morning news show to press the administration's case.

The demand for such clientele agencies reflected the emerging national market economy and the Industrial Revolution's legacy of increasingly distinct economic interests. With the advent of the new industrial economy, information became a valuable resource. Thus in their early years all three departments devoted an important part of their work to gathering and disseminating the kinds of technical information needed by their clients. The Department of Agriculture helped farmers by sponsoring experiments; collecting, testing, and distributing new plants and seed varieties; and gathering crop and market statistics. Labor settled industrial disputes and looked out for workers' welfare, but also conducted economic research through its Bureau of Labor Statistics. Commerce sought to make American business more prosperous and competitive internationally by, among other activities, gathering and publishing commercially useful data. The Census Bureau, which, besides counting heads every ten years, produces detailed information on the domestic economy and foreign trade, came under its jurisdiction.

THE MILITARY ESTABLISHMENT. The Department of Defense (1947) was a legacy of the Second World War and the emergence of the United States as an international superpower. Until World War II the United States had maintained a modest military establishment, except in times of war. Indeed, until the twentieth century state militias were the main sources of trained soldiers for wartime duties; the colonial experience had convinced Americans that large standing armies were tools of oppression. In 1796 the American army numbered 3,300, climbing to only 16,200 by the eve of the Civil War. During the war it expanded to more than 1 million, but a few years later it was back under 25,000. The army grew to 3.7 million during World War I but fell to 214,000 in 1920 and to 135,000 by 1932. Shifts in naval strength were less dramatic but followed a similar pattern.[26]

In the summer of 1997 federal workers moved into Washington's newest federal building, the largest to be built in half a century. According to one estimate, it contains as much space as a 150-story skyscraper. With great irony (and perhaps some hypocrisy), the new structure was named after Ronald Reagan, a politician who bashed the bureaucracy with special zeal.

The enormous military machine assembled to fight World War II—8.3 million soldiers, a 2,800-ship navy, an air corps of 2.4 million personnel, and 80,000 planes—also quickly shrank after 1945, but it remained much larger than in the prewar period. With the onset of the Cold War, it was expected to remain large indefinitely.[27] For U.S. military and civilian leaders, World War II was instructive: only with a unified command of all military forces could the government coordinate the land, sea, and air operations essential for modern warfare. In 1947 Congress, acting on this knowledge despite considerable resistance (the navy in particular resented losing full-fledged departmental status), combined the army, navy, and air force into a single, cabinet-level National Military Establishment, headquartered in a five-sided building in northern Virginia, across the Potomac River from Washington, DC. The department was renamed Defense two years later (to avoid the unfortunate acronym NME, "enemy"). From then on, the Pentagon became the symbol of the large, expensive military responsibilities assumed by the United States as a world power.*

EXTENSION OF THE FEDERAL DOMAIN. Established in 1979, the Department of Health and Human Services (HHS) embodies another major transformation in the government's role. HHS, like its predecessor, the Department of Health, Education, and Welfare (HEW), is an umbrella department containing numerous social welfare agencies and programs that have their roots in the New Deal and its aftermath. The establishment of HEW in 1953 by a Republican administration and Congress was a pivotal political statement: the Republicans had finally accepted the legitimacy of the federal government's expanded role in providing for the economic welfare of Americans; their party would not repeal the New Deal but only manage it more efficiently. The creation of HEW also was a Republican effort to reduce the autonomy of officials appointed by the Democrats during the New Deal.

---

*The Pentagon's symbolic status made it a target of al-Qaeda terrorists, who crashed a hijacked airliner into its west wall on September 11, 2001. The terrorists' original objective was probably an even more potent symbol, the White House, with the Pentagon chosen as a secondary target when the pilot could not locate the presidential mansion. R. W. Apple Jr., "After the Attacks: The Trip Back; Aides Say Bush Was One Target of Hijacked Jet," *New York Times,* September 13, 2002, A1.

The next three departments also consolidated expansions of the federal domain while making pointed political statements. The Department of Housing and Urban Development (HUD) embodied the commitments of the Kennedy and Johnson administrations to reviving inner-city neighborhoods and solving urban housing problems. HUD also was linked to the civil rights movement. President John F. Kennedy campaigned for the department in part so he could appoint Robert C. Weaver as its head, thereby seating the first African American in the cabinet. It was President Lyndon Johnson, however, who finally made the appointment after he convinced Congress to authorize HUD in 1965.

The new Department of Transportation became home to all the agencies established piecemeal over the years to promote different forms of transportation: highways, air carriers, railroads, sea transport, and, later, urban mass transit. These agencies often had worked at cross purposes—for example, the agency responsible for locating new highways would labor in ignorance of the plans of the agency responsible for locating new airports. President Johnson proposed the department's creation in 1966 to improve coordination of plans and policies for the various interlocking transportation modes. Congress agreed, but only after carefully limiting the department's authority over federal spending for transportation projects. Members were not about to reduce their own influence over a domain so rich in "pork."

The Department of Energy embodied another effort to coordinate policy, this time for types of energy (coal, oil, natural gas, atomic, hydroelectric, geothermal, solar). Its establishment in 1977 was President Jimmy Carter's political response to the energy shortages of the early 1970s and a declaration of his administration's commitment to assuring the nation of adequate supplies of the energy essential to modern American life.

THE SYMBOLISM OF CABINET STATUS. The creation of the Departments of Education in 1979 and Veterans Affairs in 1988 was almost entirely symbolic. By pushing through the legislation that established a cabinet-level Department of Education, Carter kept his promise to the teachers' groups whose support had been crucial to his bid for the White House. The elevation of the Veterans Administration to the Department of Veterans Affairs and to cabinet status was, among other things, a belated symbolic bow to veterans of the long, contentious Vietnam War as well as an effort by the Republican Reagan administration to woo the veteran vote. Neither department came with much in the way of new programs. Education took over programs and bureaus from HEW and other agencies; Veterans Affairs continued to do what it had done as an independent executive agency. Symbolism, then, played a major role in the creation of both departments. Proponents of the departments also hoped that cabinet status would strengthen each department's interests in the battle for government's limited resources, including the president's attention. But symbolism has its drawbacks. Until George W. Bush made education a centerpiece of his 2000 presidential campaign, Republican leaders had regularly sought to dismantle the Department of Education out of hostility to its largely Democratic clientele.

THE DEPARTMENT OF HOMELAND SECURITY. The terrorist attacks of September 11, 2001, inspired the latest addition to the cabinet, the Department of Homeland Security (DHS). President Bush's initial response to the manifest failures of the agencies responsible for preventing such horrors was an executive order establishing a White House Office of Homeland Security, to be headed by former Pennsylvania governor Tom Ridge and charged with coordinating domestic preparedness and counterterrorism among some fifty federal agencies. Despite widespread recognition that an office lacking an independent budget or statutory authority would not be able to overcome congressional and bureaucratic resistance to any sweeping redistribution of authority and resources, the president resisted congressional pressure to create a new cabinet-level department until his staff could work out, in secret, a detailed plan for the department that satisfied the administration's ambitions. The result was a motion, unveiled on June 6, 2002, that was immediately recognized as the most far-reaching government reorganization since the formation of the Department of Defense more than fifty years earlier.

The DHS combined twenty-two agencies having at that time more than 180,000 employees and budgets totaling more than $33 billion, with most resources taken from eight of the existing cabinet departments (see Table 8-2). The diverse agencies that were absorbed into DHS reflect the wide range of potential terrorist targets. They included, for example, the Coast Guard and Transportation Security Administration (both from the Department of Transportation), the Immigration and Naturalization Service (from the Department of Justice), the Animal and Plant Health Inspection Service (from the Department of Agriculture), the Nuclear Incident Response Team (from the Department of Energy), the Federal Computer Incident Response Center (from the General Services Administration), and the Secret Service and Customs Service (both from the Department of the Treasury). DHS did not, however, absorb any of the major agencies dealing with intelligence (the FBI, CIA, or NSA) whose lapses of analysis and coordination were the focus of the post–September 11 investigations.

As is the case with all bureaucratic agencies, the structure and authority of DHS reflect its political origins. Experts had for years recommended reorganizing the government to better address the emerging terrorist threat, but congressional and bureaucratic resistance prevented any change until the need for it was so shockingly demonstrated. The attacks had put the United States on a war footing, and the president's constitutional primacy in defense matters, backed by the public's focus on terrorism, forced Congress to concede unprecedented, sweeping authority over the organization of a cabinet-level agency. Most significantly, the administration won the authority to write its own personnel rules for the department and, if it chose, to ignore protections previously enjoyed under collective bargaining agreements by the many unionized employees in affected agencies. In wartime, the president's national security rationale for reducing transaction costs in managing homeland security policy trumped Congress's normal reluctance to risk higher conformity costs and agency losses by broad delegations of authority to the president.

The DHS is now behind only Defense and Veterans Affairs in number of personnel, although other departments have much larger budgets, notably Treasury, which pays the interest on the public debt, and HHS, which administers the Medicare program (see Table 8-3). Altogether, the executive branch departments account for about 63 percent of the civilian government workforce and about 80 percent of the more than $3.7 trillion the federal government spends annually. The rest is accounted for by a host of agencies that, for a variety of calculated political reasons, have been placed outside the mainline departments.

TABLE 8-2

Nearly Two Dozen Agencies Move to Homeland Security

The Agency's Former Departmental Home	Agencies Now in the Department of Homeland Security			
	Border and Transportation Security	Emergency Preparedness and Response	Science and Technology	Information Analysis and Infrastructure Protection
Justice	Immigration and Naturalization Service Center for Domestic Preparedness	Domestic Emergency Support Team National Domestic Preparedness Office (FBI)		National Infrastructure Protection Center
Treasury	U.S. Customs Service Federal Law Enforcement Training Center			
Agriculture			Plum Island Animal Disease Center	
Transportation	Transportation Security Administration			
General Services Administration	Federal Protective Service			Federal Computer Incident Response Center
Health and Human Services		Chemical, Biological, Radiological, and Nuclear Risk Assessments		
Energy		Nuclear Incident Response Team	Lawrence Livermore National Laboratory Environmental Measurements Laboratory	National Infrastructure Simulation and Analysis Center Energy Security Program
Defense			National Bio-Weapons Defense Analysis Center	National Communications System
Commerce		Integrated Hazard Information System		Critical Infrastructure Assurance Office
Independent agencies		Federal Emergency Management Agency		
Other	The Coast Guard (from Transportation), the Animal and Plant Health Inspection Service (from Agriculture), and the Secret Service (from Treasury) report directly to the department secretary.			

Source: White House, reprinted in *CQ Weekly*, November 16, 2002, 3002.

Noncabinet Agencies

The expansion of the federal government has not been confined to cabinet-level executive departments. Since the Civil War, Congress and the president have created an additional set of administrative bodies to make and carry out national policy. Most fall into one of

Projected Cabinet Department Staff and Budget Outlays: 2013 Budget

Department	Personnel (thousands)	Budget (billion dollars)
Agriculture	92.3	154.4
Commerce	42.0	9.8
Defense	756.8	691.3
Education	4.3	54.9
Energy	16.4	32.5
Health and Human Services	71.5	944.9
Homeland Security	188.9	56.4
Housing and Urban Development	9.4	42.0
Interior	69.8	13.1
Justice	118.6	40.8
Labor	17.4	70.0
State	32.5	31.5
Transportation	57.9	81.0
Treasury	111.8	539.9
Veterans Affairs	306.6	139.6

Source: U.S. Office of Management and Budget, Analytical Perspectives, *Budget of the United States Government, Fiscal Year 2013*, 120, 452.

three general categories: independent executive agencies, regulatory commissions, and government corporations.

INDEPENDENT EXECUTIVE AGENCIES. Executive agencies are placed outside departments for one of several reasons, all political. Presidents promoting new initiatives that demand quick action may want to avoid placing bureaucratic layers between them and the responsible agency. For example, President Kennedy kept his cherished Peace Corps out of the stodgy and unsympathetic State Department. When the Soviet Union launched its space vehicle Sputnik in 1957, the National Aeronautics and Space Administration (NASA), established in 1958, was the administrative response. Its status as an independent executive agency reflected both the space program's urgency and the politicians' desire to keep it in civilian hands. NASA proved to be a brilliant organizational success, fulfilling President Kennedy's audacious dream of landing a man on the moon by 1969. Agencies also may report directly to the president to enhance the agency's prestige; the Environmental Protection Agency (EPA), a candidate for cabinet status during the Clinton administration, is an example. In keeping with the president's role as commander in chief, the directors of National Intelligence, the U.S. Arms Control and Disarmament Agency, and the Selective Service System all report directly to the president. Their independent status is intended, in part, to keep important defense-related activities—intelligence gathering, arms control negotiations, and the draft—under predominantly civilian control.

The independent executive agencies, as organizations, look much like the divisions within regular executive departments. They typically are headed by presidential appointees, subject to Senate approval, who serve "at the pleasure of the president"—meaning the president can dismiss them at any time. One example is the Social Security Administration, which has a budget larger than any cabinet-level department except HHS ($881.7 billion in 2013) and was part of HHS until 1995. The Veterans Administration was an independent executive agency before it was elevated to the Department of Veterans Affairs in 1988. The United States Information Agency was also independent until 1997, when Republican Jesse Helms of North Carolina, chair of the Senate Foreign Relations Committee, insisted that, for economy's sake, it be put under the State Department.

INDEPENDENT REGULATORY COMMISSIONS. Unlike the independent executive agencies, independent regulatory commissions are designed to maintain their independence from the president and the executive departments. Congress adopted the commission form of administration to cope with new problems of delegation. The emergence after the Civil War of an industrial economy with a national market gave rise to economic dislocations and disputes on a scale too wide to be managed, as in the past, by local authorities. As a result, the railroads and the steel, oil, and banking industries became targets for national regulation. But Congress could not and did not want to do the regulating itself; the issues were too many, too technical, too dynamic, and too fraught with political conflict. The regulatory commission represents Congress's attempt to hedge against the potential political costs of delegation by restricting the influence of presidents and party politics on regulatory decisions. Table 8-4 lists the most important independent regulatory commissions.

Typically, independent regulatory commissions are run by boards of commissioners (usually five in number) who conduct their decision making by majority rule rather than by single directors. The commissioners are appointed by the president, with the consent of the Senate, to serve fixed, staggered terms of no fewer than five years. Terms are staggered so presidents cannot stack the deck in their favor by new appointments; terms of five or more years ensure that service exceeds any single presidential term. In most cases the president cannot dismiss appointees without cause—evidence of some sort of malfeasance—and therefore cannot simply replace commissioners whose decisions are displeasing. Appointments are bipartisan, with no party permitted to have more than a one-vote majority. In theory, this keeps presidents from stacking the agency with their own partisans, but in practice, they always can find someone in the other party who shares their regulatory goals.

On occasion Congress does give the president greater than normal authority over regulatory bodies. Some agencies are governed by commissioners who serve at the president's pleasure. Other regulatory agencies, such as the Food and Drug Administration and the Occupational Safety and Health Administration, are ordinary bureaus housed in executive departments and subject to the normal executive authority. Congress is not without means

TABLE 8-4

Independent Regulatory Commissions

Agency	Year Established	Term of Service	Service at President's Discretion?
Federal Reserve System (Fed)	1913	14	No
Federal Trade Commission (FTC)	1914	7	No
Federal Deposit Insurance Corporation (FDIC)	1933	6	No
Federal Communications Commission (FCC)	1934	7	No
Securities and Exchange Commission (SEC)	1934	5	Yes
National Labor Relations Board (NLRB)	1935	5	No
Federal Maritime Commission (FMC)	1961	5	No
Equal Employment Opportunity Commission (EEOC)	1965	5	Yes
National Transportation Safety Board (NTSB)	1966	5	Yes
Postal Rate Commission (PRC)	1970	6	No
Consumer Product Safety Commission (CPSC)	1972	7	No
Commodity Futures Trading Commission (CFTC)	1975	5	No
Federal Election Commission (FEC)	1975	6	No
Nuclear Regulatory Commission (NRC)	1975	5	No

Source: Compiled by the authors.

INSULATING THE FED

logic of politics

Sometimes the task given an independent regulatory commission is such a hot potato that members of Congress, the president, and even lobbyists maintain a hands-off policy. When the task is the sensitive one of setting a nation's economic course, the logic of insulating the commission from political pressures makes imminent sense. The Federal Reserve System, popularly known as the Fed, is the most independent and powerful of the regulatory commissions. Its main responsibility is to make monetary policy.

The decisions handed down by the Fed influence the country's supply of credit and level of interest rates, which in turn affect the rates of inflation, unemployment, and economic growth. During periods of economic recession and high unemployment, the Fed buys securities from banks, increasing the banks' reserves so that they have more money to make loans. Interest rates then fall, stimulating investment that leads to faster economic growth and job formation. This makes everyone happy. When a booming economy and low unemployment bring (or sometimes even threaten) inflation, the Fed puts on the brakes by selling securities, which reduces the supply of money banks can lend, thereby raising interest rates. Profits fall, investment declines, the economy slows, and some people may lose their jobs. This does not make everyone happy.

Members of the Fed's board of governors are appointed by the president, with the Senate's approval, to a single fourteen-year term; they can be removed only for cause (evidence of wrongdoing). The board's chair, who dominates its deliberations and is appointed for a renewable four-year term, is one of the most influential people in government. During the long economic expansion and stock market boom of the 1990s, the financial community scrutinized Chairman Alan Greenspan's every comment for omens about the future of interest rates, and every hint of an increase brought a sharp (but often temporary) drop in the price of stocks and bonds. When the economy later slowed after September 11, 2001, and stock prices tumbled, the Fed began reducing interest rates in an effort to stave off recession, cutting them eleven times in 2001 alone. In 2004, as signs of economic recovery set off inflation worries, the Fed began raising rates again. Rising interest rates contributed to a crisis in the housing market, forcing up mortgage costs while the price of houses was

Alan Greenspan (right) congratulates his successor, Ben Bernanke.

falling. Large financial institutions lost billions of dollars when many homeowners, especially those with variable-rate mortgages, could no longer meet their mortgage payments on houses now worth less than what they owed on them. It was left to Ben Bernanke, Greenspan's successor appointed in 2006, to deal with the financial fallout of the housing meltdown in 2008 by pumping $540 billion in loans into the money market funds in an attempt to unfreeze the credit market.

Presidents sometimes complain about the Fed's decisions, but they do not really desire greater control over the Fed because they do not want responsibility for its decisions. Neither does Congress, which even allows the Fed to finance itself through its own investments. Politically insulated, the Fed is left alone to take the heat for the painful steps sometimes needed to protect the nation's economy. Nonetheless, the Fed is usually careful to accommodate the fiscal policies of the president and Congress. Even when the president and Congress are genuinely unhappy with the Fed's actions, they dare not do much beyond grumbling about it because any real action to curb the Fed might spook the financial markets.

Source: Jeffrey E. Cohen, *Politics and Economic Policy in the United States* (Boston: Houghton Mifflin, 1997), 215–221.

for keeping these agencies at least as responsive to it as to the president, but sometimes Congress chooses not to use the tools at its disposal. A major reason for delegating authority to an independent agency is to avoid direct responsibility for unpopular decisions. In 1887 Congress set up the now-defunct Interstate Commerce Commission to regulate the railroads in part because any decision made about shipping rates would likely anger some politically potent interest. The Postal Regulatory Commission takes the heat for increases in postage rates. The most striking case, however, is the Federal Reserve Board, which makes decisions of enormous consequence for the entire economy (see box "Insulating the Fed"). In this case and in others, the agency's independence helps to insulate the president and Congress from the political fallout from unpopular decisions, explaining why both have been willing to accept this form of administration.

Over the years, the government's regulatory reach expanded in roughly three waves. The first, which swept in during the late nineteenth and early twentieth centuries as government sought to cope with a rapidly expanding national market economy, was regulation of the railroads (Interstate Commerce Commission), trusts (Federal Trade Commission), and monetary system (Federal Reserve System). The second, also economic in focus, occurred during the 1930s as part of the Franklin D. Roosevelt administration's response to the Great Depression. The government assumed responsibility for, among other things, the integrity of the banking system (Federal Deposit Insurance Corporation), the stock market (Securities and Exchange Commission), and labor relations (National Labor Relations Board). The third wave occurred during the 1960s and 1970s as a growing network of activist organizations lobbied successfully for federal protection of consumers (Consumer Product Safety Commission), motorists (National Transportation Safety Board), the environment (Environmental Protection Agency, Nuclear Regulatory Commission), and civil rights (Equal Employment Opportunity Commission).

The third wave did the most to expand the scope of regulation (see Figure 8-3). The dramatic growth in regulation during the 1970s, as measured by the number of pages in the *Federal Register* (which publishes all new administrative rules that have the force of law), was followed by a drop in the 1980s after the deregulation of the transportation and telecommunications sectors and the 1981 arrival of the Reagan administration, which was ideologically hostile to regulation. The Clinton administration clearly was not, and regulatory activity expanded once again during the 1990s before leveling off during the more antiregulatory George W. Bush administration. The regulatory climate continues to shift in response to real-world events. The banking crisis of 2008 (see box "Reregulating Finance") and the BP oil spill in the Gulf of Mexico in 2010 (see box "The Capture of the Minerals Management Service," page 387) served as forceful reminders of how costly lax regulation can be, sparking new bursts of regulatory action.

Variations in the structure, duties, and procedures of independent regulatory agencies, as with all other government agencies, stem from the politics of their creation. Agencies embody the objectives, strategies, and uncertainties of the coalitions that bring them into being. Because the interests making up these coalitions have diverse objectives, agencies often are given potentially incompatible missions. For example, the ICC was supposed not only to regulate railroads in the public interest but also to ensure they remained profitable. Interests opposed to regulation sometimes lose the battle over creating an agency but win the war by strangling it with "fragmented authority, labyrinthine procedures, mechanisms of political

Figure 8-3 The Growth of Federal Regulation

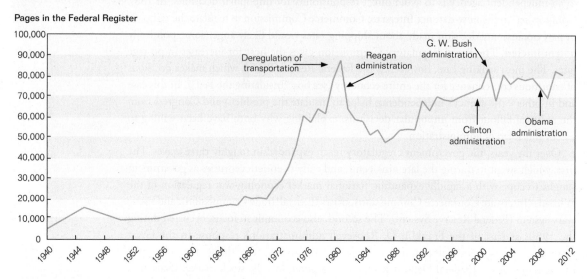

Pages in the Federal Register

Sources: Harold W. Stanley and Richard G. Neimi, *Vital Statistics on American Politics, 2003–2004* (Washington, DC: CQ Press, 2003), 266; data for 2003–2009 compiled by author from the *Federal Register* for that year.

intervention, and other structures that subvert the bureaucracy's performance and open it up to attack."[28] In other words, unresolved political conflicts may be built into an agency's structure, where they will continue to play themselves out in a new venue.

INDEPENDENT GOVERNMENT CORPORATIONS. When Congress puts the government in the business of delivering the kinds of services usually provided by private corporations, it sometimes imitates the corporate form of administration as well. Like private corporations, government corporations are typically run by a chief executive officer, or CEO, under the supervision of a board of directors or commissioners and chosen in the same manner as members of regulatory commissions. Government corporations can buy and sell property, lend and borrow money, and sue or be sued like any other business. Congress, however, may put any constraints it chooses on their organization or activities.

Besides the U.S. Postal Service, the most important of the government corporations are the Tennessee Valley Authority (TVA) and the National Railroad Passenger Corporation, or Amtrak. The TVA was created in 1933, during the New Deal, to develop electric power, water transportation, and agriculture in the Tennessee Valley area, which at the time was poor and economically backward. Amtrak, launched in 1970, represents Congress's effort to maintain intercity rail passenger service, which had been dying out for want of investment and from competition from air, bus, and auto travel. The U.S. Postal Service actually predates the Constitution; it was established in 1777 by the Second Continental Congress. Known then as the Post Office Department, it was for much of its history the largest government agency

REREGULATING FINANCE

politics to policy

Regulators have a tough time keeping up with something as dynamic and complicated as the modern financial system. Rules adopted in the 1930s to regulate banks and the stock market became increasingly obsolete during the postwar period, as ingenious financiers created new, highly profitable instruments of finance and exchange. From the 1970s onward, old regulations were gradually set aside, blurring the lines between savings banks, investment banks, insurance companies, and Wall Street firms. Meanwhile, a thriving, unregulated trade in complex and often opaque financial instruments going by such names as "credit default swaps" and "collateralized debt obligations" developed alongside the more familiar, regulated markets for stocks and bonds. In the 2000s, investment firms using such devices created hundreds of billions of dollars in bonds, based directly or indirectly on home mortgage obligations that suddenly became worthless when housing prices collapsed and millions of overextended homeowners couldn't pay their mortgages. Fearing an implosion of credit markets indispensable to the whole economy, the federal government intervened in 2008 with the Troubled Asset Relief Program (TARP), which provided $700 billion to rescue some giant financial firms and General Motors from impending insolvency. TARP achieved its purpose of stabilizing the credit markets, and taxpayers are likely to recoup a large portion of the $700 billion. The action, however, was very unpopular, not only because it bailed out the very firms whose greed and incompetence had contributed to the crisis, but also because it did not prevent the worst recession since the Great Depression.

The financial crisis and its dire economic consequences made it politically imperative that something be done to prevent a recurrence. The end result was the passage in July 2010 of the Wall Street Reform and Consumer Protection Act, the most sweeping overhaul of financial regulation since the 1930s. The act created a new federal Bureau of Consumer Protection to protect borrowers from predatory lenders; a Financial Stability Oversight Council to monitor and, if necessary, intervene to mitigate risks to the financial sector of the kind that produced the 2008 meltdown; and a Federal Insurance Office, to monitor the insurance industry. It also gave new regulatory authority to the Federal Reserve Board (see box on page 366), the Securities and Exchange Commission, and the Commodity Futures Trading Commission.

The legislation, which would affect the profits of Wall Street firms, banks large and small, and diverse businesses involved in loaning to consumers, passed only after nearly two years of aggressive lobbying and contentious debate on how best to prevent or manage future financial crises. As a major item on President Obama's agenda, the bill received little Republican support on final passage (three votes each in the House and the Senate), reflecting the highly polarized atmosphere prevailing in Washington. Its enactment ended neither the debate nor the lobbying, for as always Congress necessarily delegated much of the detailed rulemaking to the regulatory agencies. As the *New York Times* reported the day it passed, "the same groups that fought to shape the legislation—bankers and business groups, consumer advocates and trade unions—already have turned their attention to the rulemaking process, seeking a second chance to influence outcomes."[1] Completion of this detailed work will take years. Meanwhile, Wall Street's financial wizards can be counted on to conjure up profitable new credit instruments that will keep federal regulators scrambling to catch up.

---

1. Binyamin Appelbaum and David M. Herszenhorn, "Financial Overhaul Signals Shift on Deregulation," *New York Times*, July 15, 2010.

delivering the most familiar government service. It also was a major source of congressional patronage during the heyday of patronage-based party politics in the latter decades of the nineteenth century (see Chapter 12). But politics did not promote efficiency or innovation in the postal service, and by the post–World War II economic expansion, the system's inadequacies had become quite evident. The agency was radically reorganized as a government corporation in 1970.

INDIRECT ADMINISTRATION. Over the past sixty years federal spending in real (inflation-adjusted) dollars has increased by 670 percent, and federal programs and activities have mushroomed. Yet the federal workforce has scarcely grown at all (see Figure 8-1, page 356); in fact, as a proportion of the population (and total labor force) it has been falling for more than fifty years (see Figure 8-2, page 357). How can this be? The answer, as we saw in Chapter 3, is that many federal policies and programs are administered by someone else: state governments, private contractors, and grant recipients. State governments administer such major social welfare programs as Medicaid and Temporary Assistance for Needy Families. State and local agencies also carry out some of the federal government's regulatory work, such as enforcing air pollution rules and occupational health and safety standards. By delegating administrative duties to state and local government agencies, Congress can add programs, which voters like, without increasing the federal bureaucracy, which voters do not like.

The federal government also provides grants to private nonprofit organizations and to state and local governments to implement programs. For example, the Department of Education's programs for Indian education, special education, library construction, vocational education, and adult education are all carried out by nonfederal organizations funded by grants dispensed by the department. Nonfederal institutions, including universities, research laboratories, and think tanks, administer more than 80 percent of the federal government's scientific research funds.[29] The government also contracts with private companies for a countless variety of goods and services. The Department of Energy, for example, uses contractors to operate nuclear weapons plants; NASA uses contractors to load the space shuttle and to pick up its reusable engines after liftoff.[30] By one recent count, 1,931 private companies had contracts to work on counterterrorism programs in the United States. Contracts and grants thus provide another way for the federal government to take on more tasks without hiring more personnel. For politicians, the payoff can be significant. They can claim credit for reducing the size of the federal bureaucracy without reducing popular programs and services.

Indirect administration is not without political risks to principals. During investigations in 2004 into the abuse of prisoners held by the American military at Abu Ghraib prison outside of Baghdad, Iraq, senior members of Congress discovered that the accused abusers included some private contractors hired by the Defense Department to conduct interrogations.[31] Later, the activities of a private firm handling security for the State Department created another political stir symptomatic of the problems created by the administration's extensive use of private contractors in Iraq and Afghanistan (see box "Outsourcing War").

Because much of the government's work is performed by someone other than federal bureaucrats, a head count of federal personnel drastically understates the government's true size. According to one authoritative estimate, in 2005, in addition to the federal civilian workforce of 1.9 million, full-time equivalents of 7.6 million employees worked under federal contracts; 2.9 million held jobs created by federal grants; 767,000 worked for the Post Office; and 1.44 million served in the armed forces, for a total federal workforce of 14.6 million.[32] Add the estimated 4.6 million in state and local positions created by federal mandates, and the total reaches 19 million.[33]

BUREAUCRACY IN ACTION

Who are the bureaucrats? The people who staff the myriad federal agencies by and large contradict the stereotypical image of "bureaucrat" prevalent in American popular culture. Accused variously of being inordinately "inflexible, rule-bound, cautious, impersonal, haughty, fearful, deceptive, alienated, or secretive," the reality disclosed by empirical research suggests, if anything, the contrary.[34] Moreover, the federal civil service mirrors the American population far more accurately than, say, Congress. Thirty percent are minorities, matching the overall population; 45 percent are women. Their range of skills matches that of workers in the private sector, as does their dedication to their jobs. Their views on most public or personal issues are indistinguishable from the views of other citizens—except that they place a higher value on civic participation and commitment to democratic values. Contrary to popular belief, civil servants generally perform their jobs as well as or better than people doing the same work in the private sector. Most, in fact, want to be good "agents," responsive to elected officials and supportive of the missions assigned to their agencies.[35] The federal bureaucracy displays numerous and sometimes severe shortcomings, to be sure, but these cannot be fairly blamed on the civil servants staffing the institutions. The vast majority spend their days managing programs and delivering services that most people would regard as essential to modern life: working to ensure the safety of food, drugs, consumer products, the workplace environment, and the transportation system; delivering the mail and keeping order in the nation's vast electronic communications systems; providing monthly retirement and unemployment checks to the millions of Americans who depend on them; attending to the needs of veterans; pursuing criminals and defending the nation from foreign enemies; and protecting the natural environment and responding to disasters, natural and man-made. The list could go on for pages. We tend to take such services for granted, paying attention only when something goes wrong, but we would certainly notice if they stopped.

Bureaucratic Culture and Autonomy

In theory, bureaucratic agencies are subject to the authority of Congress, the president, and the courts, but bureaucrats are by no means always kept on a short leash; some agencies operate with substantial autonomy, while others are carefully monitored by their multiple principals. The ability of agencies to expand their autonomy—that is, to use their discretionary authority as they think best—depends on a variety of circumstances, not the least of which are the political skills of individual bureaucrats.

It is neither surprising nor necessarily a bad thing that government agencies strive for autonomy. During long service in agencies, people develop a strong sense of what their

OUTSOURCING WAR

logic of politics

On September 16, 2007, guards employed by Blackwater USA, a private firm hired by the State Department to provide armed security for its employees in Iraq, opened fire in a Baghdad square, killing seventeen civilians and wounding eighteen others. The guards claimed they had been fired on and were simply defending themselves; Iraqi witnesses said the action had been unprovoked. An FBI investigation found no evidence of an attack on the guards and determined that at least fourteen of the seventeen deaths were entirely unjustified.[1] The Iraqi government was outraged and moved to ban Blackwater from operating in the country but quickly lifted the ban when the United States made it clear that, without Blackwater's services, American diplomats could not leave the heavily protected "Green Zone." The State Department did not try to justify the guards' action, but it did defend its use of private firms to provide its security. The U.S. ambassador to Iraq, Ryan Crocker, testifying before a Senate committee on the issue, put it this way: "There is simply no way at all that the State Department's Bureau of Diplomatic Security could ever have enough full-time personnel to staff the security function in Iraq. There is no alternative except through contracts."[2]

Plainclothes military contractors took an active part in firefights during the Iraq and Afghanistan wars, suffering

casualties alongside U.S. troops. These contractors were wounded in an attack in the Logar province of Afghanistan in 2011.

The same could be said of the American war efforts both in Iraq and in Afghanistan. The estimated 160,000 employees working for private contractors in Iraq in 2007 actually outnumbered the American military personnel there. In 2011, more civilian contractors than American soldiers died in Afghanistan.[3] In addition to providing security, they performed such vital functions as transporting food,

agency is supposed to do and how it is supposed to do it—that is, they absorb its **bureaucratic culture.** Political scientist James Q. Wilson defines an organization's culture as its "persistent, patterned way of thinking about the central tasks of and human relationships within [the] organization. Culture is to an organization what personality is to an individual. Like human culture generally, it is passed on from one generation to the next. It changes slowly, if at all."[36]

Bureaucrats imbued with their agency's culture come to dislike interference from outsiders ignorant of the problems, practices, and political environment the bureaucrats know so intimately. They also tend to value their agency's programs and services more highly than outsiders might and thus seek the resources and the freedom to carry out their missions in fuel, and ammunition for the U.S. forces. Proponents claim that outsourcing such services saves money; its critics argue that the savings are mythical but the costs in lost accountability are real.[4] The Blackwater incident, the Abu Ghraib prison scandal, and criminal investigations into alleged corruption in multibillion-dollar procurement contracts highlight the problems inherent in delegating key functions on this scale under chaotic conditions. Monitoring agents is always problematic, but all the more so when the people responsible for the monitoring are in short supply and distracted by more pressing duties. As Shay D. Assad, the director of defense procurement and acquisition policy, put it, "in a combat environment, we didn't have checks and balances we should have in place, so people who don't have ethics and integrity are going to be able to get away with things."[5]

The broader issue of how to prevent massive agency losses has become increasingly acute as the total spent by the government through contracts and grants has grown to more than $500 billion per year. For example, when the Pentagon more than doubled the volume of goods and services it purchased from the private sector between 2001 and 2006, it found itself without the staff and expertise needed to oversee the contracts and had to hire private companies to do the supervisory work. "In some instances, businesses that had won multibillion-dollar contracts were later awarded additional contracts to supervise their own performance."[6] This is obviously not a recipe for effective control of agents.

---

1. David Johnston and John M. Broder, "FBI Says Guards Killed 14 Iraqis without Cause," *New York Times,* November 13, 2007, A1.

2. Peter Grier and Gordon Lubold, "Private Security in Iraq: Whose Rules?" *Christian Science Monitor,* September 20, 2007, at www.csmonitor.com/2007/0920/p01s05-wome.html, accessed December 21, 2007.

3. Rod Nordland, "Risks of Afghan War Shift from Soldiers to Contractors," *New York Times,* at http://www.nytimes.com/2012/02/12/world/asia/afghan-war-risks-are-shifting-to-contractors.html?_r=0, accessed December 7, 2012.

4. Peter W. Singer, "Sure. He's Got Guns for Hire. But They're Just Not Worth It," *Washington Post,* October 7, 2007, at www.brookings.edu/opinions/2007/1007militarycontractors.aspx, accessed December 21, 2007.

5. Eric Schmitt and Ginger Thompson, "$6 Billion in Contracts Reviewed, Pentagon Says," *New York Times,* September 21, 2007, A1, at www.nytimes.com/2007/09/21/washington/21contract.html?pagewanted=print, accessed December 21, 2007.

6. Josh Rogin, "The Hidden Cost of a Buying Spree," *CQ Weekly,* July 23, 2007, 2168.

---

the way they believe is best. On the whole, then, there is nothing undesirable about having agencies staffed with people who have a strong sense of professionalism and confidence that their work is important and that they know best how to do it. A nation would not want its military officers, for example, to think any other way. The problem is that the very conditions that give an agency high morale and a strong sense of mission may encourage it to seek independence from political control.

The development of distinctive bureaucratic cultures and missions also inhibits cooperation between agencies. The FBI's traditional mission, for example, has been to catch and punish lawbreakers, so it has come to value the kind of information that can be used to convict criminals in public court. The CIA is charged with secretly monitoring potential foreign

The U.S. Forest Service, which maintains the nation's 152 national forests, enjoys a reputation for professionalism and independence. The agency has achieved this standing despite the fact that 90 percent of its revenue traditionally comes from logging permits. A less professional organization might favor logging and forget conservation. Controlled burns are routinely employed by the U.S. Forest Service to maintain healthy forestlands and prevent massive fires that would endanger nearby private property.

enemies and thwarting their plots, so it resists any release of information that might eventually expose its informers or methods. The two agencies also operate under very different sets of legal constraints imposed by Congress in response to actual or imaginable abuses of power. Hence even after September 11 the FBI and CIA have remained reluctant to share information, and getting them to cooperate in other ways has remained difficult.

For similar reasons, the integration of the DHS's disparate bureaucratic components, each imbued with its distinctive bureaucratic culture, into an institution capable of coping with the huge range of tasks needing coordinated attention if the United States were to be made secure from terrorist attack has proven a daunting task. The legislation creating DHS provided for a year of transition to get the department up and running, but the process has taken years to complete. Experts on mergers and acquisitions from the private sector—people who had overseen huge corporate acquisitions at General Electric, Hewlett-Packard, and Lockheed Martin—had to be solicited for advice, for no one else had experience with reorganization on such a grand scale.[37]

Bureaucrats as Politicians

As partisans of their agencies and missions, bureaucrats are necessarily politicians. Indeed, the Weberian notion of civil servants who act as neutral instruments for implementing the policies chosen by their elected superiors has never taken hold in the United States. Agency officials operate in a world of competition for scarce resources, often intense conflicts among interests and values, and multiple bosses (principals). Scholars have proposed a variety of motives, in addition to the desire for autonomy, that might account for bureaucratic behavior. These motives include a quest for larger budgets, more subordinates, and greater authority; the chance to do some good; a preference for a stable, predictable environment; and the opportunity for career security and advancement. But whatever the goals, they can be achieved only through politics: mobilizing supporters, gathering allies, negotiating mutually beneficial deals with other politicians, keeping in touch with people whose cooperation is needed, and adapting to the realities of power.

The political environment of most government agencies is occupied by the House and Senate members of the subcommittees handling agencies' authorizing statutes and budgets, the committee and subcommittee staff, the political appointees who head agencies, the White House (especially its Office of Management and Budget), the interest groups affected by agency activities, and the federal courts. Occasionally, the news media and the broader public also show up on the radar screen. Bureaucrats' most important political relationship is usually the one with Congress, as it controls the organization, authority, budgets, and staffing—in fact, the very existence—of departments and bureaus. Although presidential appointees rarely stay in their agencies more than a few years, members of Congress and senior committee staff are in for the long haul, as are the interest groups that play an important role in Congress's political environment. Keeping Congress happy often means keeping interest groups happy.

Politically astute bureaucrats carefully cultivate members of Congress and their staffs. The principle is simple, though following it is sometimes far from simple: do things that help members to achieve their goals and avoid doing things that have the opposite effect. Along the way, establish a reputation for competence and frugality. No one whose job relies on voters is going to defend bureaucratic ineptitude or malfeasance.* Keeping in touch, usually through congressional staff, also is crucial. Politicians and bureaucrats live in an uncertain, ever-changing world. Good information is a scarce and therefore valuable commodity (see Chapter 6). Information about their own activities is one political resource bureaucrats have in abundance. A regular exchange of intelligence helps both sides anticipate consequences and reduces the incidence of unpleasant surprises. Shrewd bureaucrats are responsive to informal suggestions as well as legislative mandates; they can take a hint. In short, bureaucrats prosper by convincing their congressional

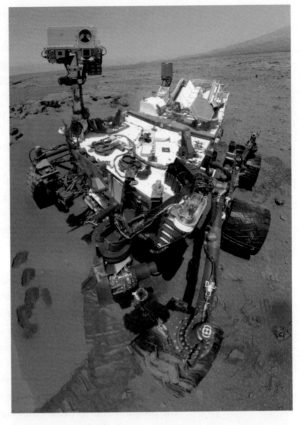

The National Aeronautics and Space Administration runs the U.S. space program, an expensive program ($18.2 billion in 2013) that has no direct impact on the lives of most Americans. To win support, NASA encourages the public to share in the excitement of space exploration by offering spectacular pictures and detailed information on websites devoted to each of its missions. This image is from NASA's Curiosity rover, which landed on Mars in August 2012 and fired a laser, "turning a small Martian rock into ionized, glowing plasma."

---

* Just the opposite; for example, congressional outrage went into overdrive when, six months after the attacks of September 11, 2001, the Immigration and Naturalization Service (INS) sent word to the Florida flight school where two of the terrorists had been trained that the terrorists' student visas had been approved. The agency had granted approval the previous summer, before the attacks, but "backlogs and antiquated computers" had delayed delivery, and the INS had failed to recheck what was in the pipeline. Elizabeth A. Palmer and John Godfrey, "Sensenbrenner Leading the Charge for Immediate INS Overhaul," *CQ Weekly,* March 16, 2002, 705.

principals that they are good and faithful agents—never an easy task where hidden action and hidden information abound.

The survival of bureaucrats, like that of other politicians, also depends on having an appreciative constituency. Some agencies acquire organized constituencies at the moment of birth—the interests who lobbied them into existence. Others have to organize supporters themselves. An early secretary of commerce, for example, helped to found the U.S. Chamber of Commerce. Many of the groups that now lobby on behalf of programs for the physically disabled, the mentally ill, and other disadvantaged people were brought into being through the efforts of government officials in social service agencies (for other examples, see Chapter 13).[38] Agencies that service politically feeble clienteles—such as the Bureau of Prisons (federal criminals) and the Agency for International Development (foreign countries)—inevitably suffer in the struggle for political attention and resources. Government agencies also try to cultivate broad public support, and most have public relations offices devoted to publicizing their activities.

Savvy bureaucrats design and manage their programs in ways that enhance political support in Congress. If feasible, programs produce widely distributed local benefits even when their main purpose is to generate diffuse national benefits. For example, defense spending buys a diffuse national good—protection from potential enemy nations—but also helps the local economies where the money is spent. Aware of this aspect of military procurement, Pentagon officials protect weapons programs by making sure weapons components are produced in as many states and districts as possible.[39]

Bureaucrats also target benefits to key members of Congress. For example, from 1965 through 1974 a disproportionate share of grants for water and sewer facilities under a program administered by HUD went to the districts' subcommittee members who dealt with the program and to those conservatives who otherwise might have voted against it.[40] To sweeten such deals, bureaucrats make sure members of Congress take credit when local projects or grants are announced. They also try to stay in close touch with the organized interests active in their policy domains to anticipate and possibly head off political problems. The interest groups, for their part, naturally want to maintain cordial relations with "their" agencies as well.

Bureaucratic Infighting

Agencies with different missions, clienteles, skills, and ideologies compete for influence, authority over policy, control of implementation, and resources. A striking example was the bitter infighting between the State and Defense Departments over guidance of policy toward the war in Iraq, when Defense Secretary Donald Rumsfeld took a hawkish position early on while Secretary of State Colin Powell urged more caution. When President George W. Bush decided to wage a preemptive war in Iraq opposed by most of America's traditional allies, this represented an internal victory for Rumsfeld and the neoconservative intellectuals on his staff. Bureaucratic infighting also takes place within organizations. Many military professionals, for example, were unenthusiastic about the nation-building role they were assigned in Iraq. The armed forces are organized, equipped, and trained to fight wars, not to police cities, manage public works, or install democratic institutions. Thus they did not share their civilian bosses' ambition to control the process of rebuilding Iraq. Indeed, strong disagreements between civilian and military leaders are routine; in July 2010, General Stanley McChrystal, U.S. commander in Afghanistan, had to resign after comments from his staff highly critical of civilian administration officials, including Vice President Joe Biden and Obama's national security adviser, were reported in *Rolling Stone*.[41]

WHO CONTROLS THE BUREAUCRACY?

The more things elected representatives want the government to do, the more discretionary authority they must give to administrators. The proliferation of government agencies and programs during the New Deal and afterward has led critics to charge that Congress has abdicated its authority to the president, to an out-of-control bureaucracy, or to the clients the agencies serve.[42] The charges deserve to be taken seriously. Congress, in fact, has delegated a wide range of tasks, often with only the vaguest guidelines on how authority is to be exercised. In 1914, for example, Congress authorized the Federal Trade Commission to enforce laws against "unfair methods of competition . . . and unfair or deceptive acts or practices" without defining what these methods, acts, or practices were. At times, government agencies and programs have served private interests almost exclusively; the history of the Department of Agriculture is littered with examples. Regulatory commissions have sometimes served as the handmaidens of the interests they are supposed to regulate in the public interest. Until the mid-1970s, for example, the Civil Aeronautics Board fought valiantly to protect the major airlines from competition. Congress often pays little attention to what its bureaucratic agents are doing, as administrative oversight is not a high priority (see Chapter 6). However, congressional majorities have found many ways in which to delegate authority without abdicating control. Legislators are fully aware of principal–agent dilemmas (though they do not think of them in those terms) and have strategies to cope with them.

These strategies can be placed into two general categories, named by political scientists Mathew McCubbins and Thomas Schwartz: "police patrols" and "fire alarms." In **police patrol** oversight, Congress works hard to directly monitor whether agencies are implementing laws faithfully and efficiently. When engaging in this type of work, members of Congress and their staffs investigate a sample of executive branch activities to detect and fix any deviations from legislative goals and, as bureaucrats notice that they are being watched, discourage future deviations. In **fire alarm** oversight, Congress designs procedures that allow interest groups and ordinary citizens to raise an alarm when something has gone wrong. Courts, agencies, and legislators can then solve problems that have been detected by interested parties. While Congress itself may rush to the scene when a fire alarm is pulled, it leaves the monitoring of bureaucracies to those who have the highest stakes in their operation. This saves lawmakers a great amount of effort, while still allowing them to correct bureaucratic drift.

McCubbins and Schwartz argue that Congress conducts oversight primarily by setting up fire alarm mechanisms. Too much time can be wasted on police patrols where there is no crime, and the violations detected through patrols—which include investigative hearings, scientific studies, and field observation—may be so minor that no voters care about them. By contrast, when Congress enables fire alarm oversight by requiring agencies to make public reports and take comments on the rules that they would like to adopt, it exerts no effort on its own. When something goes wrong enough for the public to complain, Congress can come to the rescue and win the gratitude of voters. "Instead of sniffing for fires," McCubbins and Schwartz observe, "Congress places fire-alarm boxes on street corners, builds neighborhood fire houses, and sometimes dispatches its own hook-and-ladder in response to an alarm."[43] While this section shows that legislators engage in both types of oversight, fire alarms probably accomplish the most. Ironically, for rational reasons, Congress delegates to others much of the task of overseeing the agencies to which it has delegated power.

Methods of Congressional Control

Congress operates from a position of overwhelming strength in its relationship to administrative agencies. It creates and empowers them by ordinary legislation, and it can eliminate or change them in the same way. Most agencies require new budget appropriations every year to continue functioning. Congress also has a say in who is appointed to head departments and bureaus. Indeed, some programs are set up with the explicit understanding that a particular individual will or, in some cases, will not be chosen to run it. Any president who wants an agency to thrive will choose appointees who can get on well with the agency's handlers in Congress. Bureaucratic agents recognize that, at some level, the very existence of their agency (and jobs) depends on at least the toleration of their congressional principals even when the principals seem to be paying no attention to what they are doing.

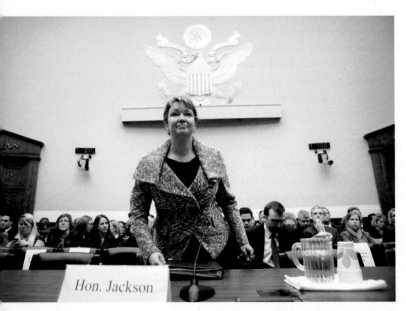

Congress routinely uses hearings to call executive branch officials on the carpet when the majority party objects to what their agencies are doing. With much of the House Republican caucus skeptical that human activity is warming up the planet, the Environmental Protection Agency's plans to curb greenhouse gas emissions immediately became a target. Here, Lisa P. Jackson, head of the EPA, prepares for grilling by the House Energy and Commerce Committee's Energy and Power subcommittee in February 2011.

Congress uses a variety of methods to keep its bureaucratic agents in line. Among them are the sorts of costly activities that are most often part of police patrol oversight:

- **Hearings and investigations,** in which bureaucrats are called before subcommittees to explain and defend their decisions, and outsiders are sometimes invited to criticize them. Most agencies must testify annually about their activities before the House Appropriations subcommittee that has jurisdiction over their budgets.
- **Mandatory reports,** in which Congress requires executive agencies, even the president, to report on programs. For example, under an antidrug bill passed in 1986 the

president is required to submit a report every March 1 on whether certain nations where illegal narcotics are produced or transshipped have "cooperated fully" with U.S. efforts to stem the drug traffic. Countries not certified as cooperating face a cutoff in U.S. aid.

- **Legislative vetoes,** which allow one or both houses of Congress (sometimes even individual House and Senate committees) to veto by majority vote an agency's policy proposals. Although the Supreme Court in 1983 declared the legislative veto unconstitutional because it violates the separation of powers, Congress continues to enact legislative vetoes, and agencies continue to send decisions to Congress for prior approval, knowing that Congress has other sanctions at its disposal if they do not.*

- **Committee and conference reports,** which often instruct agencies how Congress expects them to use their "discretion." Though not legally binding, bureaucrats ignore such instructions at their peril.

- **"Limitation riders,"** attached to appropriations bills, which forbid an agency to spend any of the money appropriated on activities specified by Congress in the rider (used to block agencies from issuing regulations opposed by Congress, among other things).[44]

- **Inspectors general,** with independent offices (outside the normal bureaucratic chain of command) in virtually every agency, who audit agency books and investigate activities on Congress's behalf.

- The **Government Accountability Office,** with a staff of more than five thousand, which audits programs and agencies and reports to Congress on their performance.

Congress can also guard against agency losses by putting a time limit on delegations of authority. For example, the expanded wiretap and surveillance authority included in the USA PATRIOT Act's broad grant of new powers to investigate and detain suspected terrorists enacted after September 11 was set to expire automatically by the end of 2005 unless Congress extended it. As former House majority leader Dick Armey explained, "We gave the Justice Department a huge increase in power" but with an expiration date "on the theory that would make them more responsive to oversight."[45] Congress extended the act's authority, slightly modified, in 2006.

A variety of *procedural devices* also are available to Congress for monitoring and controlling bureaucrats. Congress may not have the capacity to specify *what* bureaucrats are to do, but it can tell them *how* they have to do it. The broadest procedural requirements are found in the Administrative Procedure Act of 1946 (APA), which covers all rulemaking by government agencies unless an agency's legislative authorization specifies otherwise.

Congress normally regulates by delegating broad grants of authority to regulatory agencies and letting them fill in the details by making rules. These rules have the force of law,

---

* Nothing prevents Congress from passing legislation contrary to Supreme Court rulings, and Congress can have its way as long as it does not depend on the courts to enforce compliance. One scholar notes: "An agency might advise the committee: 'As you know, the requirement in this statute for committee prior-approval is unconstitutional under the Court's test.' Perhaps agency and committee staff will nod their heads in agreement—after which the agency will seek prior approval of the committee." Louis Fisher, in *Extensions,* a newsletter of the Carl Albert Congressional Research and Studies Center (Spring 1984): 2.

just as if Congress itself had enacted them. When an agency wants to make a rule, it first must give public notice in the *Federal Register*, outlining the proposed rule, disclosing the data and analysis on which it is based, and inviting written comments from the public. Public hearings may be held as well. The agency then responds to public comments, often in staggering depth, providing a comprehensive record of how and why the rule was promulgated and, upon occasion, making modifications in the final rule. This process creates the rulemaking record that will be needed to justify the agency's decision if it is challenged in federal court.

These procedures serve several purposes. For one thing, they make rulemaking a public act, observable by members of Congress and anyone else—often, the interest groups who recognize how critical rulemaking is in their issue areas—who may be interested. They also give members of Congress and agency officials advance notice of the political fallout that any particular regulation would produce, allowing them to avoid political trouble. When the Federal Trade Commission proposed rules in 1982 requiring more complete disclosure of funeral costs and used car defects, undertakers and used car dealers protested loudly. Members of Congress, who were quickly reminded just how many undertakers and used car dealers they had in their districts and how influential they were, forced the agency to back down.[46] In other words, the APA sets up a fire alarm mechanism that alerts members of Congress when delegated authority is being exercised in a way that might hurt them politically. In effect, it recruits interested outsiders to monitor the activities of bureaucratic agents on Congress's behalf.

When it chooses, Congress can fine-tune procedures to guarantee a desired balance of interests in regulatory policymaking. For example, the National Environmental Policy Act of 1969 requires federal agencies, as well as many other public and private entities, to consider what effects all major undertakings (construction projects, landfills, dredging schemes, and so forth) might have on the environment and to prepare environmental impact statements specifying the environmental effects of proposed projects and their alternatives. The act also gives private citizens legal **standing** to bring suit in federal court to challenge the adequacy of impact statements and, indirectly, the proposals they were intended to justify. Standing enables environmental groups and their lawyers to enforce compliance through the courts, ensuring that environmental interests will not be ignored. When Congress granted standing, it was setting up a fire alarm for environmental lawyers to pull.

How, then, do we reconcile this picture with news clips of members of Congress portraying themselves as enthusiastic bureaucracy bashers on the principle that "no politician ever lost votes by denouncing the bureaucracy"?[47] They are, in fact, the principal architects of the bureaucracy, and its design generally suits the political purposes of the congressional coalitions that create and sustain its various components. It is no accident that the division of responsibilities among agencies in the executive branch tends to mirror the division of legislative turf in the congressional committee and subcommittee systems. This is not to say, however, that Congress has exclusive control over the administration of agencies. The president and the federal courts also have a major say, and Congress itself is subject to pressure from interest groups, the media, and constituents on how it deals with administrative issues. Moreover, the fragmented political system can give agencies considerable room to maneuver in pursuit of their own ends.

The President and the Bureaucracy

The president, who as the chief executive is charged by the Constitution with seeing that the laws are faithfully executed, sits officially atop the bureaucratic hierarchies of the executive branch. The heads of departments and other executive agencies and their immediate subordinates—the undersecretaries, assistant secretaries, and bureau chiefs—serve at the president's pleasure, as do members of some of the governing boards, commissions, foundations, institutes, and public corporations that make up the rest of the executive branch. With their duty to implement laws, power to appoint senior government officials, and other congressionally conferred grants of authority, presidents have enormous administrative responsibilities. The institutional realities, however, impose formidable barriers to presidential influence—let alone control—over the sprawling federal bureaucracy.

THE POWER OF APPOINTMENT. Presidents pursue their policy goals by appointing senior officials loyal to them and their ideas. For example, Ronald Reagan's appointment in 1981 of conservatives Anne Gorsuch Burford to head the Environmental Protection Agency and Michael Connolly as general counsel to the Equal Employment Opportunity Commission resulted in sharp reductions in these agencies' regulatory activities.[48] Congress, however, may not be content to sit on the sidelines, and presidents may find their influence diluted. Indeed, if enough members of Congress oppose the objectives of the president's appointees, they can force the agency back into line. Both Burford and Connolly eventually resigned under heavy congressional and public criticism for failure to carry out their agencies' mandates.

Sonia Sotomayor is sworn in to answer questions about her hotly contested judicial philosophy and be grilled by members of the Senate Judiciary Committee in July 2009. When Sotomayor's confirmation came up for a floor vote, her answers were enough to satisfy the nine Republicans who voted along with fifty-nine Democrats to confirm her to the Supreme Court.

American presidents enjoy much stronger appointment powers than other chief executives: the U.S. president appoints more than four thousand officials, whereas leaders in France, Britain, and Germany appoint one to two hundred.[49] Yet appointments can come at a cost. The agencies within the U.S. government with the greatest percentage of presidential appointments tend to perform more poorly than agencies with a higher ratio of career civil servants.[50] What's more, when an agency run by presidential appointees fails, as the Federal Emergency Management Agency (FEMA) did during Hurricane Katrina, the public can hold the president personally accountable. FEMA was run by more appointees than other agencies, and headed by Michael Brown, whose prior experience consisted primarily of running the International Arabian Horse Association. After what was widely viewed as FEMA's incompetent management of Katrina's aftermath, Brown resigned, saying "I think it's in the best interests of the agency and the best interest of the president."[51]

SENATORIAL APPROVAL. Presidential appointments require Senate approval, and senators make the most of their authority. Rarely does the full Senate reject a nominee, but it is not unusual for an appointment to be withdrawn after an unfavorable committee vote or, earlier, after unfavorable publicity during a hearing on the appointment. In 2009 President Obama had to withdraw his first nomination for HHS secretary as it emerged that the nominee owed back taxes, and the president lost his first choice for commerce secretary when the nominee became the subject of a federal investigation (later dropped). Many nominations are not even made because presidents anticipate Senate opposition and decide the fight is not worth the political resources it would take to win. Senators also use the approval process to extract promises from appointees about what they will or will not do in office, further limiting administrative discretion. Seeking Senate approval in 2007, Michael Mukasey, George W. Bush's nominee to replace Attorney General Alberto Gonzales, who had resigned after months of harsh criticism for politicizing the Justice Department and for his role in setting the administration's policies on torture and surveillance, had to promise that he would resign if asked by the White House to violate the law or the Constitution. His confirmation was nearly derailed when he ducked the question of whether the technique of simulated drowning called "waterboarding" used to interrogate suspected terrorists constituted torture, but after declaring that he personally found the procedure "repugnant," he was confirmed on a 53–40 vote.[52]

Presidents have sometimes used "recess appointments" to appoint officials the Senate has refused to ratify. The Constitution allows the president to make temporary appointments of officials normally requiring Senate confirmation without Senate approval while the Senate is in recess (Article II, Section 2). Recess appointments expire at the end of the Senate's next session, and thus may last for as long as nearly two years. The Senate can block this ploy by remaining in pro forma session during break periods, such as the customary two-week Thanksgiving and five-week Christmas breaks. As long as a member officially gavels the Senate open and then gavels it closed at least once every four days—a process that takes only a few seconds—the Senate is formally in session and no recess appointments can be made. In December 2007 the Senate used this strategy to prevent George W. Bush, who had already made 171 such appointments during his presidency, from making any more.[*]

In addition to the Senate, the president may have to satisfy the clientele groups that care intensely about who heads "their" agency or risk alienating them and weakening the agency. Thus the secretary of labor requires the nod of the AFL-CIO, at least if the president is a Democrat; the chair of the Federal Reserve Board must measure up on Wall Street; and the head of the National Institutes of Health needs the respect of the academic and research communities. Clientele groups of the president also may benefit from the appointments process, because presidents often use appointments as symbolic payoffs to important factions in their party's electoral coalition. Recent presidents have taken pains to assemble administrations that recognize the racial, gender, and geographic diversity of the nation. For example, Obama's twenty-two cabinet-level appointees included six

[*] Henry B. Hogue, "Recess Appointments: Frequently Asked Questions," Congressional Research Service, January 9, 2012, www.senate.gov/CRSReports/crs-publish.cfm?pid=%270DP%2BP\W%3B%20P%20%20%0A; and Paul Kane, "The Fastest Gavel in the Senate," New York Times, December 31, 2007, A13.

women, three Latinos, three Asian Americans, and two African Americans. Presidents also take care to ensure that their party's various ideological factions are acknowledged and represented. In making appointments for any reason, however, the president also must weigh competence; policy expertise may not be essential, but no president wants to be embarrassed by appointees too ignorant or unskilled to manage their agencies' business (such as FEMA head Michael Brown).

Some presidents, notably Ronald Reagan and George W. Bush, have tried to ignore other criteria in order to stack their administrations with personal or ideological loyalists, but with incomplete success. Sheer numbers pose a serious problem. Because presidents are responsible for filling more than four thousand positions, they must rely on the advice of others and an imperfect screening process to fill most of the slots. They also must accept the fact that most appointees will be total strangers to them. In short, the president, as principal, can make only limited use of the power of appointment to guard against political losses.

Once appointed, even initially loyal officials tend, as Richard Nixon's chief domestic aide famously put it, to "go off and marry the natives," becoming agents of their departments or bureaus instead of the president. Political appointees typically serve short terms—about two years—and often are unfamiliar with the rules, programs, and political relationships of the organizations they lead. To avoid disastrous mistakes, let alone to achieve anything positive, they need the candid advice and active cooperation of permanent civil servants. In return, they can offer effective advocacy of their agency's interests in the battles waged over programs and resources within both the administration and Congress.[53] In doing so, they may come to identify with the success of their agency rather than with that of the president, and thus pursue more programs and larger budgets—or defend programs and budgets from cuts—without regard for how their agency fits into the administration's overall program. Department and bureau heads also wield powers delegated directly to them by Congress, allowing them to bypass the president and further promote their independence from the president and their dependence on Congress.

MECHANISMS FOR PRESIDENTIAL SUPERVISION. In an attempt to gain some control over the far-flung activities of the federal bureaucracy, presidents have built up their own supervisory bureaucracy in the Executive Office of the President (analyzed more fully in Chapter 7). The president's primary control instrument is the Office of Management and Budget, which oversees agency budgets and rulemaking and assembles the annual budget for all government agencies that the president is required to submit annually to Congress. The budget process allows presidents to emphasize their own priorities and policy goals. When Congress ignores presidents' recommendations—which it frequently does—presidents may use the veto to nudge that recalcitrant legislative body closer to their own budget preferences, as President Bush did with considerable success after the Democrats took control of Congress in 2007 (see Chapter 7).

For bureaucrats, favorable treatment in the president's budget is worth pursuing—so they have an incentive to keep the White House happy. But this inherently political relationship works two ways: the White House is much more likely to get its way if it can persuade political appointees and permanent civil servants that their best interests are served by doing what it wants. Because presidents do not hold undisputed authority over

Presidents seek to control bureaucrats in realms as seemingly innocuous as the regulation of movie theater popcorn. When White House Deputy Chief of Staff Nancy-Ann DeParle got wind that the Food and Drug Administration was considering a proposal forcing theaters to post nutritional information for buttered popcorn—which can contain more calories than two Big Macs!—as part of President Obama's national health care reform, she worried that it would be lampooned as an extreme example of nanny state intrusion into our daily lives. DeParle called the FDA Commission, which President Obama had appointed in 2010, and after chilly conversation the FDA backed down.[56]

the executive branch, bargaining or indirect manipulation through mobilized interest groups or congressional allies is often more effective than issuing orders.[54]

By constitutional design, presidents enjoy special authority over agencies involved in diplomacy and national defense, and this authority is greatly magnified in times of national crisis. Moreover, public support for presidents is highest in such moments, so opposition to presidential demands carries unusually high political risks. President George W. Bush, like his predecessors, did not hesitate to use this institutional and popular wartime advantage to assert control over policy and institutions. Congress quickly complied with the president's request for legislation authorizing him "to use all necessary and appropriate force against the nations, organizations, or people that he determines planned, authorized, committed, or aided the terrorist attacks on the United States that occurred September 11, 2001."* He also won an extraordinary degree of authority to shape and run the DHS as he saw fit and a remarkably free hand on almost every aspect of the Iraq War. Pushing the limit, the administration had demanded total discretion in deciding how to spend $60 billion of the $78.5 billion supplemental appropriation for the war. Secretary of Defense Rumsfeld said flatly that "whatever is put forward by the Congress by way of money will be expended in a way that the president decides it should be expended."[55] Congress refused to go that far but agreed to give the president full discretion to allocate $15.7 billion of the total appropriated. Even after the Democrats assumed control of Congress in 2007 on promises to end the war in Iraq, Bush got his way on funding for the war by reframing the issue as one of supporting American troops rather than financing an unpopular war. The Bush administration also sought to extend the broad authority enjoyed by the president in his role as commander in chief to other executive functions, continuing the struggle with Congress for control of the bureaucracy that has been part of American politics since the first Congress.

The Courts and the Bureaucracy

The third main branch of government, the judiciary, also shares authority over the bureaucracy. The United States inherited the English common law principle that the government, no less than individual citizens, is bound by law. Under this principle, a dispute between the government and a private individual over whether the government is acting according to law—that is, a statute duly passed by Congress and signed by the president—comes before the courts as a normal lawsuit. The judge treats the government as any other party to a lawsuit, granting it no special status whatsoever. This tradition has strongly influenced

---

*This broad antiterrorism package (PL 107-56), enacted at the behest of the administration, passed 357–66 in the House, 98–1 in the Senate during the last week of October 2001.

the development of American administrative law. Judicial review of administrative deci-sions is taken for granted; regulatory commissions and agencies have, from the beginning, been constrained by the courts' defense of individual rights.

Expansion of the government's regulatory activities, particularly during the New Deal, put a host of bureaucratic agencies in the business of making rules and applying them—that is, agencies were authorized to make general rules, just like a legislature, and to adjudicate indi-vidual cases under them, just like a court. Federal courts maintained appellate jurisdiction over both sets of activities, hearing appeals on rules as well as their enforcement, and court decisions gradually imposed a set of procedural standards that Congress eventually codified in the Administrative Procedure Act of 1946.

Under the APA, any agency dealing with individual cases like a court must act like a court—that is, it must hold hearings conducted by neutral referees (now called admin-istrative law judges). Parties may be represented by counsel, with written and oral testi-mony and opportunities for cross-examination. Decisions handed down by the agency must be issued in writing and justified on the evidence in the record. Those decisions that violate these procedures can be challenged and overturned in federal court. An agency that wants its judgments sustained must carefully follow the rules of administrative due process.

Over the years the federal courts have come to interpret the APA as requiring almost as much procedural care in making rules as in deciding cases. Courts have elaborated on and formalized the APA's notice and hearings requirements and now insist on a comprehensive, written justification backed by a complete record of all information and analysis that went into an agency's decision. The APA allows courts to invalidate rules only if they are "arbi-trary and capricious," which would seem to give agencies wide latitude. Yet in the 1960s and 1970s the courts used judicial review "to create and impose on agencies a huge body of administrative law which was so complex and demanding that it allowed judges to strike down new agency rules whenever they pleased."[57] The courts were particularly interested in highly contentious, highly technical areas of regulation: the environment, health, and safety. Soon regulatory agencies adapted, however, by overwhelming the courts with reams of data and analysis, both to convince the judges they had made the most scientifically defensible choice and to make it more difficult for judges lacking technical expertise to say otherwise. The courts have since backed off a bit, but they still play a major role in shaping regulatory decisions.

Congress may, of course, rewrite the law if the courts invalidate rules that solid House and Senate majorities want to see implemented, and it may also alter the courts' jurisdiction over administrative matters. Yet any change must negotiate the usual congressional obstacle course, which, as we saw in Chapter 6, is by no means easy, particularly if the president pre-fers the courts' position. Congress does rectify both judicial and administrative decisions it does not like, but only under major provocation.

Iron Triangles, Captured Agencies, and Issue Networks

The politics of program administration gives agency staff, members of Congress, and organized interest groups powerful incentives to form mutually beneficial alliances to manage policy in their areas of specialization. When successful, these alliances become

iron triangles: narrowly focused subgovernments controlling policy in their domains, out of sight or oversight of the full Congress, the president, and the public at large. The classic examples operated in the areas of agriculture, water, and public works, where the active players enjoyed concentrated benefits—projects benefiting private interest groups, budgets and programs for administrators, and electoral support for congressional sponsors from grateful beneficiaries.[58] The broader public, excluded from the process, paid the diffuse costs.

Similarly, the politics of regulation allows the regulators to be "captured" by the very interests they are supposed to regulate. Once Congress establishes a regulatory agency in response to some threat to public welfare—whether it be railroad monopolies, dangerous or quack medicines, or impure processed food—the agency's dealings are with the very industries it should be regulating. Because industries have an enormous economic stake in how they are regulated, they become the primary source of political pressure on the regulators. Ironically, the regulated sectors also are the primary repository of the expertise—information and personnel—agencies need. Add to this the routine legislative mandate that the agency maintain the economic health of the industries it regulates, and the story is complete: regulators become the allies, if not agents, of the sector they regulate. At times, for example, the Food and Drug Administration (FDA) catered to drug companies; the Interstate Commerce Commission (ICC) ended up at the beck and call of established firms in the trucking industry; and the Civil Aeronautics Board (CAB), as noted earlier, protected the major airlines from competition. The story of the Minerals Management Service (see box "The Capture of the Minerals Management Service") serves as a reminder that capture is by no means a thing of the past.

In reality, though, iron triangles and captured agencies survive only as long as the costs they impose on everyone are small enough to avoid attracting serious attention from political entrepreneurs in Congress or the White House who may be scouting for popular issues to champion. For example, the CAB and the ICC no longer exist; the former was abolished in 1985, and ten years later the latter, by then more than one hundred years old, was finally put to rest. The marketplace now governs the sectors they once regulated. In the early 1960s one congressional coalition forced the FDA to impose much tougher standards for proving the safety and efficacy of new drugs. The 1990s, however, saw another coalition compel it to ease up again on the ground that delays in approval of new drugs also hurt the public health.

Members of Congress learned from these experiences and designed new regulatory procedures to prevent the capture of agencies such as the EPA (see the discussion of "standing" earlier in this chapter). The proliferation of self-proclaimed public interest groups in the 1960s also changed the political environments of many agencies, leaving them no option but to negotiate a far more complex, open, and conflict-ridden configuration of political forces (see Chapter 13). Thus scholars now talk of policy domains shaped by **issue networks**—amorphous, ever-changing sets of politicians, lobbyists, academic and think-tank experts, and public interest entrepreneurs such as Ralph Nader—rather than iron triangles.[59]

Agencies adapted. The Department of Agriculture now pays attention to nutrition and other consumer concerns as well as to the needs of agribusiness. Today's EPA considers the economic as well as environmental effects of its decisions. But agencies do not always find it

THE CAPTURE OF THE MINERALS MANAGEMENT SERVICE

logic of politics

On April 20, 2010, BP's Deepwater Horizon drilling platform exploded, unleashing a gusher of oil deep in the Gulf of Mexico that ultimately produced the largest oil spill in history. The vast ecological and economic damage inflicted by the disaster put the spotlight on the Minerals Management Service (MMS), a bureau in the Department of the Interior charged with overseeing offshore drilling operations as well as managing leases for, and collecting royalties from, oil and gas production on federal lands. Investigators from the Interior's inspector general's office found an agency with all the signs of having been "captured" by the industry it was supposed to regulate. The revolving door—MMS inspectors coming from and returning to the industry—as well as shared experience in the industry fostered a cozy relationship between agency and industry officials. As the Lake Charles, Louisiana, district manager told investigators, "Obviously, we're all in the oil industry. We're all from the same part of the country. Almost all of our inspectors have worked for oil companies on these same platforms. They grew up in the same towns. Some of these people they've been friends with all their lives."[1] Employees in the district office had accepted numerous gifts, including hunting and fishing trips, golf tournaments, crawfish boils, football tickets, shotguns, and other favors from drilling company representatives. Some inspections of drilling platforms were of questionable rigor, with drilling company employees allowed to fill out the inspection forms themselves. One inspector who had previously worked for a drilling company conducted inspections of its platforms—none of which

detected any noncompliance—while he was negotiating a return to the company in a new position.

This was not the first time the MMS had come under fire for taking favors from energy companies. A 2008 investigation of its Denver office found that MMS employees had shared drugs and sex with company representatives as well as accepted gifts and free holidays.[2] Resignations and felony convictions followed, but the agency was left intact. In 2010, however, an administration less friendly to the industry than its predecessor was in office, and the Gulf oil spill and the Louisiana investigation led to the reorganization and renaming of the MMS to the Bureau of Ocean Energy Management, Regulation, and Enforcement (BOEMRE). Its three missions were split into three separate agencies: a Bureau of Ocean Energy Management (for negotiating leases), a Bureau of Safety and Environmental Enforcement (overseeing drilling operations), and an Office of Natural Resources Revenue (collecting royalties). Whether these agencies avoid capture will depend on the kind of bureaucratic culture they develop and the level of scrutiny they receive from Congress, the White House, and the news media.

---

1. Office of the Inspector General, U.S. Department of the Interior, *Investigative Report: Islands Operating Company, et al.*, March 31, 2010.

2. Charlie Savage, "Sex, Drug Use, and Graft Cited in Interior Department," *New York Times,* September 11, 2008.

easy to adapt because new missions may go against the culture of an agency. For example, the U.S. Army Corps of Engineers, which for two centuries had been damming rivers, dredging harbors, and draining wetlands, was not eager to make cleaning up toxic wastes and protecting threatened ecosystems a high priority. But when the political environment changes, government agencies have little choice but to change as well.

BUREAUCRATIC REFORM: A HARDY PERENNIAL

Every modern president has viewed the federal bureaucracy as a problem that needs fixing. The Clinton administration's effort focused on improving the delivery of bureaucratic services. Vice President Al Gore headed the administration's National Performance Review, which sought ways to "cast aside red tape"; encourage entrepreneurial administration that "put customers first"; decentralize authority to "empower those who work on the front lines"; and, in general, produce "better government for less" with a reduced workforce.[60] Not to be outdone, the Republican House freshmen elected in 1994 sought not merely to reinvent government but also to disinvent it. House Republicans proposed abolishing the Departments of Commerce, Energy, Education, and Housing and Urban Development, terminating many of their programs and bureaus and distributing the remainder to other departments. The George W. Bush administration tried another tack, proposing in 2001 to shrink government and increase efficiency by expanding "competitive sourcing" (letting firms in the private sector bid against government agencies for contracts to deliver government services) to include jobs currently performed by 425,000 civil servants, about one-fourth of the total federal workforce. Barack Obama took up the bureaucratic reform theme in his 2011 State of the Union address, promising to send Congress a proposal "to merge, consolidate, and reorganize the federal government in a way that best serves the goal of a more competitive America."[61]

Both the Republican and Democratic initiatives were imbued with political logic. Making government work like a business that depends on keeping customers happy has obvious appeal. So does getting rid of obsolete, wasteful programs and agencies and using competition to increase efficiency. Yet despite some success in improving the performance of several agencies and reducing the number of federal employees, the Clinton administration's goal of an efficient, customer-friendly bureaucracy remained largely unfilled. And House Republicans, though slashing some agency budgets and terminating a few programs, failed to eliminate any major agency, let alone whole cabinet departments. By 2003 the Bush administration's target for competitive sourcing had been reduced to 103,000 jobs in the face of congressional resistance and new, post-9/11 realities.[62] The fact is that the federal bureaucracy is hard to reform and still harder to prune because its actions and structure have a political logic of their own.

The Logic of Red Tape

Red tape does not flourish by accident. It proliferates because it helps principals control and monitor their agents (the goal of the APA) and helps agents demonstrate to their principals that they are doing their jobs correctly. Many rules and procedures are adopted to ensure fair or at least equal treatment of each citizen by preventing unaccountable, arbitrary behavior. For example, federal agencies procuring goods and services from the private sector are bound by an elaborate set of requirements imposed on them by Congress.

Even after the Federal Acquisition Streamlining Act of 1994 simplified the rules, especially for relatively small purchases, the *Federal Acquisition Regulation,* which spells them out, still runs to more than five thousand pages. Bureaucrats have a strong incentive to follow the rules, for there is only one safe answer—"I followed the rules"—when a member of Congress asks pointedly why a favorite constituent did not get the contract.[63] By the same logic, bureaucrats like to have rules to follow. Detailed procedures protect as well as constrain bureaucrats, so red tape is frequently self-imposed.

Empowering bureaucrats on the front lines of service delivery may increase efficiency and even customer satisfaction, but it also may make it easier for bureaucrats to go astray. Each time an agency does so, Congress tends to write more elaborate procedures and add another layer of inspectors and auditors to keep it from happening again. Thus *red tape often springs directly from Congress's desire to control administration.* As a result, although Congress rails against red tape in general, it views with suspicion attempts to reduce the controls that generate it. Successful efforts at easing controls could reduce congressional ability to monitor and influence administration, a risk congressional majorities have been reluctant to accept, especially when the other party holds the White House.

Reformers seeking bureaucratic efficiency may also run into several other problems. Efficiency stems from using resources in a maximally productive way, so any assessment of efficiency must be based on measures of output. The output of many agencies defies measurement, however. Diplomats in the State Department are supposed to pursue the long-term security and economic interests of the nation. How do we measure their "productivity" in this endeavor? Complicating matters even more, agencies sometimes are assigned conflicting objectives. Is the Internal Revenue Service supposed to maximize tax compliance, requiring tough enforcement, or customer service, requiring flexible, sympathetic enforcement? Effective enforcement and effective customer service are not the same thing.

Because an agency's degree of success in accomplishing its vaguely defined ends is often impossible to measure, bureaucrats focus instead on outputs that can be measured: reports completed, cases processed, meetings held, regulations drafted, contracts properly concluded, forms filled out and filed. These means become the ends because they produce observable outputs for which bureaucrats can be held accountable. The result is yet more red tape. The notorious bureaucratic focus on process rather than product arises from the reality that, unlike private businesses, government agencies have no "bottom line" against which to measure the success or failure of their enterprise.

The Bureaucratic Reward System

Conflicting goals and the lack of a bottom line hardly inspire the creative, "entrepreneurial" government envisioned by the Clinton-Gore National Performance Review. Entrepreneurs take risks proportionate to prospective rewards. Civil servants, by contrast, seldom profit personally from their attempts to make agencies more productive or customer-friendly. And if bold new approaches end in failure, they can count on being blasted in the media and in Congress. Bureaucrats are famously cautious for a good reason: a mistake is much more likely than a routine action to set off a fire alarm in Congress. If an alarm does sound and the routine was followed, the routine, rather than the bureaucrat, gets the blame.

The merit system rewards conscientious, long-term service; it does not encourage entrepreneurial risk taking. Congress could, of course, decide to give agency managers more authority to hire, promote, reward, redeploy, or fire staff personnel on the basis of their performance. But doing so would mean reducing the civil service protections put in place for well-considered political reasons: to avoid a partisan spoils system and to preserve congressional influence over administration.

The Clinton and Bush administrations' plans for reforming government inevitably included proposals to reduce bureaucratic waste and improve policy coordination by consolidating overlapping agencies and programs. Every president since Franklin Roosevelt has sought to do the same. And of course, it is easy to find examples of duplication, confused lines of authority, and conflict among the government's multifarious activities. Basic scientific research, for example, is funded by the National Science Foundation; the National Institutes of Health; the Departments of Energy, Agriculture, and Defense; and NASA. The National Park Service, the Forest Service, the Bureau of Land Management, and the U.S. Fish and Wildlife Service all manage public campgrounds. Responsibility for developing water resources is spread over five separate agencies. The government has programs to keep tobacco farming profitable and to discourage smoking. One agency subsidizes the lumber industry by building logging roads into national forests; another tries to curb it to protect endangered species. And the list could go on.

This duplication would all seem senseless if government pursued a coherent set of interrelated goals, but it does not. Government pursues overlapping, conflicting, or disconnected goals in response to the diverse demands Americans place on it. Each agency, and each program, reflects the coalition of forces that brought it into being and that now form its political environment. Different coalitions want different things and design different administrative institutions to get them.

In short, then, the problem of bureaucracy is not bureaucracy but politics. It is not impossible to reform, reinvent, streamline, or shrink the administrative leviathan, but it is impossible to do so without changing power relationships among interests and institutions. Deregulating the bureaucracy and empowering frontline bureaucrats would make agencies more efficient, but it also would make them less accountable to elected officials. Consolidating and rationalizing bureaucratic authority would reduce duplication, confusion, and expense, but it also would create losers whose interests or values would no longer enjoy undivided institutional attention. America's bureaucracy is disjointed because the political views of its people are fragmented. Bureaucrats face the challenging task of meeting the expectations of courts, Congress, and the president because our Constitution separates political power. Our nation's bureaucracy is characteristically American, reflecting the pluralistic politics and Madisonian institutions that shape all facets of our government.

TAKE A QUIZ

logic.cqpress.com
Test your knowledge of this chapter.

logic.cqpress.com

■ Key Terms ■

bureaucracy,   347

bureaucratic culture,   372

committee and conference reports,   379

Federal Register,   367

fire alarms,   377

Government Accountability Office,   379

hearings and investigations,   378

inspectors general,   379

iron triangles,   386

issue networks,   386

legislative vetoes,   379

limitation riders,   379

mandatory reports,   378

police patrols,   377

red tape,   354

rotation in office,   352

spoils system,   353

standing,   380

Suggested Readings

Bertelli, Anthony M., and Laurence Lynn Jr. *Madison's Managers: Public Administration and the Constitution.* Baltimore: Johns Hopkins University Press, 2008. Combines political theory with political economy to show how American bureaucracy is both constrained and legitimized by the system of separated powers.

Gormley, William T., Jr., and Steven J. Balla. *Bureaucracy and Democracy: Accountability and Performance.* 2nd ed. Washington, DC: CQ Press, 2012. The factors that ultimately lead to bureaucratic successes and shortcomings, with a focus on accountability.

Lewis, David E. *The Politics of Presidential Appointments: Political Control and Bureaucratic Performance.* Princeton, NJ: Princeton University Press, 2008. Explains why some agencies have more appointees than others and how this affects bureaucratic performance.

Light, Paul C. *Thickening Government: Federal Hierarchy and the Diffusion of Accountability.* Washington, DC: Brookings, 1995. How and why bureaucratic layers have multiplied and how this affects accountability and effectiveness.

Seidman, Harold. *Politics, Position, and Power: The Dynamics of Federal Organization.* 5th ed.

New York: Oxford University Press, 1998. How politics shapes bureaucratic organizations and practices.

Shapiro, Martin. *Who Guards the Guardians? Judicial Control of Administration.* Athens: University of Georgia Press, 1988. A lucid and informative account of court–agency relations since the New Deal.

Skowronek, Stephen. *Building a New American State: The Expansion of National Administrative Capacities, 1877–1920.* Cambridge: Cambridge University Press, 1982. Classic account of the development of the modern American bureaucracy, focusing on the civil service, the army, and agencies regulating the economy.

Waterman, Richard W. *Presidential Influence and the Administrative State.* Knoxville: University of Tennessee Press, 1989. Case studies from the Nixon, Carter, and Reagan administrations of presidential efforts to implement policies via the bureaucracy.

Wilson, James Q. *Bureaucracy: What Government Agencies Do and Why They Do It.* New York: Basic Books, 1989. If you read only one book on the bureaucracy, it should be this one.

Review Questions

1. Why is a bureaucracy necessary? What are the general characteristics of bureaucracies as set forth by Max Weber?

2. What powers does the president have over the bureaucracy? What powers does Congress have over the bureaucracy? Why would political actors ever choose to exercise less control over a bureaucratic actor?

3. How were members of the bureaucracy selected in George Washington's time? In Andrew Jackson's

time? In Barack Obama's time? How do the ways in which bureaucrats get their jobs relate to their performance once in office?

4. How can the rules or procedures Congress establishes for bureaucratic agencies affect how those bureaucracies do their jobs?

5. If everybody hates "red tape," why does it still flourish? Why might bureaucrats themselves prefer to have detailed rules governing some of their actions?

9 The Federal Judiciary

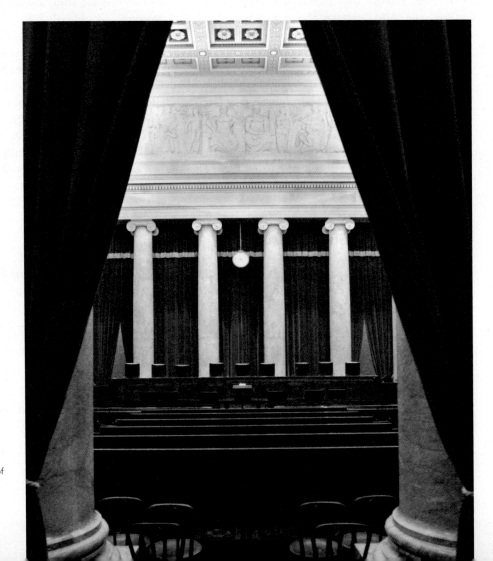

The Supreme Court of
the United States,
Washington, DC.

- Should nine unelected justices have the authority to nullify state and national laws enacted by elected representatives?

- Since all federal judges are appointed for life and are independent of one another, how can the federal judiciary be expected to dispense justice consistently and equitably?

- Is the judiciary truly, as Alexander Hamilton argued in *The Federalist,* "the least dangerous branch" of government?

- In what ways is the judiciary susceptible to the same pressures of politics and national opinion that affect the elected branches?

- If the Supreme Court "guards" the Constitution, then who guards the guardians?

By 1800 the national leaders who led the nation through the Revolution and adoption of the Constitution divided into two warring camps: the ruling Federalist Party, led by John Adams and Alexander Hamilton, who advocated a vigorous national government, and the Democratic-Republican opposition, led by Thomas Jefferson and James Madison, who favored less federal activity. Once allies, these two groups now despised and feared one another. Each believed that the future of the Republic rested on its party's victory in the presidential election of 1800. Consequently, that year's electoral campaign was one of the bitterest in American history.

Both sides indulged in negative campaigning, but the Federalists excelled at it; they attacked Jefferson as the devil incarnate. In political pamphlets and letters to the editor, the Federalists called Jefferson an "infidel" and "atheist," a darling of the French Revolution who favored the use of the guillotine, a proponent of majority rule (and thus apt to destroy the republican Constitution), a philanderer, and—perhaps the ultimate insult for a politician—a "philosopher." The author of one pamphlet added that Jefferson was not even a very good philosopher—barely adequate for a college professor but certainly not for a president. The attack finally dredged the bottom in charging that Jefferson had written a "textbook" on American government that promoted abstract ideas and "hooted at experience."

Toward the end of the campaign both sides sensed that Jefferson could not be stopped, but neither anticipated the magnitude of the Democratic-Republican victory. Not only did the party walk away with the Electoral College vote, but it also took control of Congress. It was not clear who had been elected president, however, because of a quirk in the Constitution's rules that caused votes cast for a party's vice presidential candidate to be counted as if they were cast for the presidential candidate. As a result, when Jefferson and his running mate, Aaron Burr, ended up with the same number of electoral votes, they found themselves tied for the presidency. The apparent tie triggered a constitutional provision requiring the election to be decided by the House of Representatives, still controlled by the outgoing Federalists.*

During the weeks between the election and the House vote, rumors of conspiracies swirled across the nation. Would the Federalist Congress ignore the Constitution's technical glitch and ratify Jefferson's victory, or would it exploit the opportunity to deny the White House to this so-called free-thinking radical? One scenario had the Federalists contriving a tie vote in the House, thus taking the presidential election beyond circumstances anticipated by the Constitution. Another had President Adams stepping down at the end of his term and Secretary of State John Marshall assuming caretaker control of the executive branch until a new presidential election could be called.† And yet another option, which clearly lay within the Constitution's provisions and was perhaps more seriously considered, had the Federalists electing Burr president as the lesser of two evils.‡ None of these options appeared feasible, however. Thus, after weeks of strategizing and perhaps a little soul searching, the Federalist Congress ratified the nation's choice, and Jefferson became the third president of the United States.

Had power not transferred peacefully in this first real test of the new Republic, the election of 1800 might have weakened the Constitution permanently. Failure here would have put the Constitution's integrity in doubt and left future politicians with a prisoner's dilemma of deciding whether to abide by the rules or reneging before the other side could. But the Federalists did not capitulate altogether. Their risky fallback strategy triggered a different kind of constitutional crisis with the unanticipated outcome of reconfiguring power among the branches of government, in particular the Supreme Court.

SETTING THE STAGE FOR JUDICIAL REVIEW

As they prepared to leave office, the Federalists passed the Judiciary Act of 1801. The law, designed to protect the Constitution against perceived Democratic-Republican schemes, sharply increased the number of district and appeals courts and conveniently created new judgeships for aspiring Federalists.§ The partisan purpose of this last-minute reform was evident in the provision that shrank the size of the Supreme Court from six members to five. Intended to take effect after President Adams filled the current chief justice's vacancy and a sitting member left the Court, this feature of the law would have denied the new Democratic-Republican administration the right to appoint a justice for a long time, if

---

* The Twelfth Amendment corrected this problem in 1804.

† Evidently, Marshall seriously considered his elevation. He reportedly promoted it as "legal" among colleagues, and one biographer spotted Marshall's pen in anonymous newspaper endorsements of this option. On hearing of this plot, Virginia's Democratic-Republican governor and future president, James Monroe, warned vaguely that force would be enlisted to remove Marshall, Virginian or not. Donald O. Dewey, *Marshall versus Jefferson: The Political Background of* Marbury v. Madison (New York: Knopf, 1970), 42–43.

‡ In the end, though, Burr proved to be Jefferson's ideal running mate; he scared many Federalists even more than did the radical from Monticello. Burr later took up dueling and assumed imperial aspirations—raising "soldier of fortune" armies to seize western territories from the French and create his own country.

§ Article III of the Constitution gives Congress the power to establish lower federal courts.

ever. Moreover, President Adams nominated and the Senate quickly confirmed outgoing secretary of state John Marshall as the new chief justice.

At this point, the story turns from the grand drama of contending partisan armies to a soap opera about the personal foibles and ambitions of politicians. President Adams needed help processing the flurry of last-minute Federalist judicial appointments and so asked his new chief justice to stay on briefly as secretary of state. According to Jefferson, Adams was still signing appointment commissions at nine o'clock the evening before his departure from office. Apparently, in the rush, Marshall left on his desk a stack of signed and sealed justice of the peace commissions for the District of Columbia, five-year positions created to reward loyal Federalists. The next day Marshall, as chief justice of the United States, delivered the oath of office to the new president, his archrival, Thomas Jefferson.

Later, on discovering or being advised (the lore is inconsistent on this point) that some of the commissions had not been delivered but were lying around the office, Jefferson ordered that they be withdrawn. These commissions were the least of the Federalists' worries, however.

After the inauguration the Democratic-Republicans derided the judiciary as a "hospital of decayed politicians" and made clear their intention to repeal the Judiciary Act as soon as their Congress opened the following December. In a letter Jefferson expressed his party's senti-ment: the Federalists "retired into the Judiciary as a strong hold . . . and from that battery all the works for republicanism are to be beaten down and erased by fraudulent use of the con-stitution."[1] In his message to the new Congress, Jefferson's intent was also clear: "The judi-ciary system of the United States, and especially that portion of it recently erected, will of course present itself to the contemplation of Congress." Indeed, in private, and apparently unbeknownst to Jefferson, some nervous Federalist politicians were urging their recently appointed judges to ignore the new Congress until the Marshall Court could come to their rescue. The convening of Congress promised an epic partisan battle in which the Democratic-Republicans controlled the presidency and (narrowly) both chambers of Congress, while the Federalists directed the federal judiciary.

But could Congress legally abolish courts and thereby remove life-tenured judges? More precisely, could Democratic-Republicans in Congress somehow be prevented from eliminat-ing the Federalist-created judgeships? With repeal of the Judiciary Act imminent, Federalist politicians urged Marshall to defend the party's bulwark by voiding any such repeal legisla-tion. This strategy presupposed, of course, that the Supreme Court possessed the authority, known as **judicial review**, to rule acts of Congress unconstitutional. Judicial review appears to have been implicitly provided in Article III of the Constitution, debated at the Constitutional Convention with some Framers assuming that the final wording of Article III included it but others—most notably, James Madison—arguing that it did not, and brought up again, more hotly, at various states' ratifying conventions. Nearly everyone appears to have accepted that the Constitution's supremacy clause (Article VI) allows the Supreme Court to exercise judicial review and veto *state* laws that trespassed on federal jurisdiction or violated the Constitution. But whether this unelected branch enjoyed authority comparable to the veto power of Congress and the president was altogether different—could the Supreme Court declare an act of Congress unconstitutional?

On February 3, 1802, by a 16–15 vote, the Senate repealed the Judiciary Act and elimi-nated the Federalist judgeships. All but one Democratic-Republican voted for repeal, and all Federalists voted against it. The House passed the repeal bill a month later, with only a single

Democratic-Republican holdout, and Jefferson promptly signed it into law.* The Supreme Court had already decided that it would not or could not resist repeal, but Jefferson and his allies did not learn this until the Court's next session, in 1803.

On March 2, 1803, the long-anticipated showdown over the repeal of the Judiciary Act ended badly for the Federalists as the Court ruled in *Stuart v. Laird* that Congress had the authority under Article III to reorganize the judiciary.[2] The Federalist barricade had been dismantled; the Democratic-Republican victory was complete. The Federalist Party would never again win control of the presidency or either chamber of Congress. Chief Justice Marshall had not caved in, however. The young Constitution had survived the election of 1800, the partisan confrontation surrounding the Judiciary Act, the Federalists' late-night machinations on the eve of Jefferson's inauguration, and the Democratic-Republicans' resolute resistance. As important as the peaceful, albeit difficult, transfer of government control was for the nation's future, it was followed by a comparably significant, and eventually better known, judicial event. Six days before the *Stuart* decision, the Marshall Court delivered another ruling that at the time was largely ignored as a toothless partisan maneuver. Subsequently, however, the *Marbury v. Madison* decision would come to be appreciated for establishing the Court's "coequal" status among the branches of the American government.

William Marbury and several other Federalists who had been denied their eleventh-hour justice of the peace commissions nearly two years earlier appealed to the Supreme Court for redress. They asked the Court to issue a **writ of mandamus**, a judicial instruction to a government officer—in this instance Secretary of State James Madison—to perform his duty and deliver the commissions. Based on the facts of the case, *Marbury v. Madison* did not seem the ideal vehicle for establishing "new" authority for the Court: the issue bordered on the trivial, and Chief Justice Marshall was himself deeply entangled in the dispute. His oversight as secretary of state, after all, had caused the problem in the first place. Moreover, a casual inspection of Marshall's options suggests that *Marbury* was a terrible case for a weak Court to face because it presented an apparent no-win situation. On the one hand, if the Court decided in favor of Marbury and ordered Madison to deliver the commissions, Marshall could reasonably assume that its decision would be ignored. (No administration official had even bothered to appear before the Court to defend Jefferson's decision to withdraw the commissions.) There was even talk in the Democratic-Republican press of impeaching the justices if they decided in Marbury's favor. Such a ruling, then, jeopardized the long-term health of the federal judiciary. On the other hand, if Marshall ruled against Marbury, the Court would appear to be kowtowing to the Democratic-Republicans and confirming the judiciary's subordinate position. Faced with this dilemma, Marshall found an ideal solution that not only extricated the Court from its predicament but also established an important principle for the future.

In ruling on the case, Marshall asked three questions: First, does Marbury have a right to the commission? Second, do the laws of the United States afford him a remedy? Third,

---

*To avoid colliding immediately with the Court, Congress then suspended the Court's schedule for the next thirteen months. This move not only eased the dismantling of the eliminated courts but also prevented the Court from continuing the partisan battle while Congress was out of session.

is the appropriate remedy a writ of mandamus issued by the Supreme Court? Marshall's affirmative answer to the first two questions boded well for Marbury. However, Marshall answered no to the third question, concluding that the Supreme Court did not have jurisdiction to hear the case.

While dismissal by a court for lack of jurisdiction was nothing novel, Marshall's *reasoning* would have far-reaching consequences for the balance of power between the Court and Congress. Marshall's argument was as follows: Article III of the Constitution explicitly lists cases that are within the Supreme Court's original jurisdiction,* and a writ of mandamus is not one of them. Article III of the Constitution does not give Congress the power to *add* to the Court's original jurisdiction. Because the Judiciary Act of 1789 attempted to add a writ of mandamus to the Court's original jurisdiction, the act conflicts with the Constitution. In such a conflict, either the Constitution is superior to ordinary laws or it is on the same level as ordinary laws (and therefore may be altered when the legislature desires to change it). If the Constitution is not superior, then it would be a meaningless check on the powers of government. If, however, the Constitution is superior to ordinary laws, "then a legislative act contrary to the constitution is not law." Marshall then delivered the conclusion that solidified the Court's power of judicial review: because the Constitution is the supreme law of the land, acts of Congress that conflict with the Constitution are unconstitutional and, thus, void. In one of his most famous statements, Marshall wrote: "It is emphatically the province and duty of the judicial department *to say what the law is.*"[3] By refusing to hear the case, Marshall backed away from a confrontation he could not win and simultaneously asserted new judicial authority.

Marbury v. Madison did not immediately strengthen the Court's power in its relations with the president or Congress. After all, Marshall's ruling did not require that the other political actors do anything to affirm the Court's newfound authority. It required only that the Court refuse to act in Marbury's behalf. The *Marbury* decision is a testament to Marshall's strategic political skills, as Jefferson and the Democratic-Republicans remained confident that the Federalist bench had at last been tamed.[†]

However, the Court's ruling in *Marbury* proved to be one of the most important Supreme Court decisions in its history. It provided a precedent that the other branches' actors did not repudiate (after all, the Court upheld Secretary of State Madison's action) and a rationale for the Court's broad authority to declare acts of Congress (and of the president) unconstitutional. This expansive vision of judicial review remained untested for nearly half a century, until the Court decided to enlist it in the infamous *Dred Scott* case. However, the Court's success in overturning key parts of the Missouri Compromise of 1820 had little to do with the other branches' acquiescence to its claimed authority and a lot to do with a sympathetic

---

*Cases of original jurisdiction are those that can be brought directly to the Supreme Court, without going to some lower court first.

†Although the Supreme Court left *Marbury* alone for much of the nineteenth century, there is evidence that early on it was accepted as legal dogma. *Marbury* was cited numerous times by lower courts and in lawyers' arguments. Whenever Jefferson encountered these citations, he objected. As late as 1823 he griped to one of his Supreme Court appointees, "This case of Marbury and Madison is continually cited by bench & bar, as if it were settled law, without any animadversion on its being *merely* an obiter dissertation by the Chief Justice." Letter from Jefferson to Justice William Johnson, June 12, 1823, cited in Dewey, *Marshall versus Jefferson*, 145 (emphasis added).

John Marshall (1755–1835) had never sat on the bench before his installation on the Supreme Court. Moreover, his legal education was limited to reading Blackstone's *Commentaries* with his father and to three months of lectures by George Wythe at the College of William and Mary in 1780. Marshall's formidable powers of reasoning and leadership in unifying his colleagues behind unanimous decisions were complemented by an amiable disposition and "some little propensity for indolence."

president in office and a Congress so riddled with internal disagreement that it could not nullify the ruling.

Over time, however, the other branches affirmed the Court's power of judicial review. When in 1895 the Supreme Court declared unconstitutional a federal law that taxed income derived from property, Congress implicitly conceded the Court's authority and turned to the laborious amendment process, eventually passing the Sixteenth Amendment.[4] Eighty years later another case testing and affirming judicial review arose. In *United States v. Nixon* the Supreme Court rejected President Richard M. Nixon's claim that the Watergate tapes were protected by executive privilege, and ordered him to surrender the tapes to a special prosecutor. President Nixon largely complied, notwithstanding a mysterious eighteen-minute gap during a critical Oval Office conversation. Whether his compliance reflected heartfelt acceptance of the Court's power of review or recognition that balking would lead quickly to impeachment does not matter. The Supreme Court prevailed in asserting judicial review over actions of the executive.

While the discussion on separation of powers later in the chapter makes clear that Congress and the president nevertheless sometimes refuse to abide by the Court's decisions, their general acknowledgment of the Court's power of judicial review has enhanced the Court's power vis-à-vis Congress and the president to a level that was not foreseen in 1803 when *Marbury v. Madison* was decided.

THREE ERAS OF THE COURT'S JUDICIAL REVIEW

The Supreme Court's exercise of judicial review has varied substantially across different decades. Between 1790 and 1860, portions of only two federal laws were declared unconstitutional. The frequency with which the Court struck down acts of Congress and presidential executive orders remained low throughout the late nineteenth century, but as Table 9-1 shows, it surged during the 1920s and 1930s. The exercise of judicial review then receded to nineteenth-century levels over the next two decades, but in the 1960s an activist Court once again scrutinized federal and state laws alike. This ebb and flow of the Court's intrusion into the decisions of Congress and the president have marked the three eras in the modern Court's development.

In each of these three eras, the most important cases that came before the Court embodied particular unresolved questions about the interpretation of the Constitution. These questions first concerned nation–state authority, then government regulation of the economy, and finally civil rights and liberties. As the controversy surrounding each issue developed, the federal judiciary confronted an upwelling of cases in which it asserted its preferences over those of other national, as well as state, officials.

Nation versus State

During the first and least active of these issue eras (from the Founding to the Civil War), the judiciary's most significant cases probed the unresolved jurisdictional boundaries between the national and state governments. Under Marshall's leadership, the Court generally favored national authority when it conflicted with states' rights. Reasoning that the national government had been approved directly by the citizenry in special ratification conventions, Marshall maintained that the national government's legitimacy was both independent of and superior to that of the individual states and concluded that the power of judicial review applied to the actions of state governments. As the rulings in the following historic cases illustrate, during the nineteenth century, the Court's major policy decisions frequently turned on the question of the federal government's authority vis-à-vis the authority of the states.

MCCULLOCH V. MARYLAND AND NATIONAL SUPREMACY. One of Marshall's historic decisions on national supremacy came in 1819 in *McCulloch v. Maryland,* a case that was, like *Marbury,* rooted in party conflict.[5] When in power, the Federalist Party created a nationally chartered bank and appointed party members to administer it. Showing their displeasure, several Democratic-Republican–controlled state governments, including Maryland's, sought to tax the national bank out of existence. In the *McCulloch* decision, Chief Justice Marshall, speaking for the Court, issued the famous declaration that "the power to tax involves the power to destroy." Thus, state taxation of federal property or its activities was unconstitutional. But first Marshall dealt with an even more fundamental issue. The state argued that in the absence of any provision in the Constitution explicitly authorizing Congress to charter a national bank, the national government had exceeded its authority. Marshall responded that the necessary and proper clause (Article I, Section 8) gave Congress a broad mandate to use "all means which are appropriate" to carry out any of its explicitly enumerated powers, as long as the means are plainly adapted to achieve such enumerated power(s) and not otherwise constitutionally prohibited. In *McCulloch,* the enumerated powers at issue included the power to levy and collect taxes, borrow money, and regulate commerce. Because the establishment of a national bank was an appropriate means plainly adapted to such enumerated powers, the Court rejected Maryland's argument that Congress had overstepped its constitutional bounds. The practical result in the case was that federal authority trumped state authority. In *Dred Scott,* decided thirty-eight years later, that result was reversed.

TABLE 9-1

The Supreme Court's Willingness to Declare State and Federal Laws Unconstitutional

Years	Federal	State and Local
1790–1799	0	0
1800–1809	1	1
1810–1819	0	7
1820–1829	0	8
1830–1839	0	3
1840–1849	0	10
1850–1859	1	7
1860–1869	4	24
1870–1879	7	36
1880–1889	4	46
1890–1899	5	36
1900–1909	9	40
1910–1919	6	119
1920–1929	15	139
1930–1939	13	92
1940–1949	2	61
1950–1959	4	66
1960–1969	18	151
1970–1979	19	195
1980–1989	16	164
1990–1999	24	62
2000–2009	15	36
2010–2011	3	4
Total	166	1,307

Source: Lawrence Baum, *The Supreme Court,* 11th ed. (Washington, DC: CQ Press, 2013), Table 5-2, 163.

Note: Table shows the number of federal and state and local laws declared unconstitutional by the Supreme Court. The Court has always been more willing to exercise judicial review over the states than to apply the doctrine in striking down federal laws.

DRED SCOTT V. SANDFORD AND STATES' RIGHTS. Despite its Federalist leanings, the Marshall Court could not permanently establish the explicit powers of the state and national governments. Marshall died in July 1835, and at the end of that year President Andrew Jackson selected Roger B. Taney to serve as the next chief justice. Jackson favored Taney largely because of his advocacy of states' rights, and, true to his reputation, Chief Justice Taney led the Court away from the national supremacy doctrine Marshall had crafted. Taney's effort culminated in *Dred Scott v. Sandford* (1857), which, as we found in Chapter 4, brought the nation to the brink of a civil war by claiming that African Americans were not citizens under the Constitution.[6] In addition to ruling that escaped slaves in the North had to be returned to their owners, Taney's majority opinion held that federal laws outlawing slavery north of the Mason–Dixon line (for example, as set in the Missouri Compromise) unconstitutionally infringed on settlers' territorial rights to self-government and private property.*

The overwhelming public outcry against Taney's reasoning left the Court—an unelected branch of government—seriously discredited. *Dred Scott v. Sandford* took on issues that were too important and divisive to be settled by judicial fiat. In the end, after politics failed, the enduring problems of states' rights and slavery could only be settled by war rather than by legislation or litigation. The defeat of the Confederacy in the Civil War signaled a decisive triumph for federal over state government.

After the Civil War, the Fourteenth and Fifteenth Amendments were ratified, and Congress passed laws that committed the Court to review state laws that ran counter to national statutes. The Court was not bound to support the federal government in every dispute, but it was obliged to devote more attention than ever before to policies emanating from the lower levels of government. Thus after 1860 the decisions striking down state and local laws increased markedly (see Table 9-1). Oliver Wendell Holmes Jr., one of the most distinguished Supreme Court justices of the early twentieth century, observed, "I do not think the United States would come to an end if we lost our power to declare an Act of Congress void. I do think the union would be imperiled if we could not make that declaration as to the laws of the several States."[7]

Regulating the National Economy

The major issue during the second era of judicial review, from the end of the Civil War to the 1930s, was the government's regulation of the economy. Although the Civil War had settled the supremacy issue in favor of the national government, the actual scope of government powers at both levels remained uncertain. With the rapid industrial expansion after the war, Washington, DC, and state capitals alike came under increasing pressure to regulate monopolies and to provide new services to the citizenry. Most such demands were brushed aside, but some, such as the call to regulate the railroads, proved politically irresistible. Invariably, whenever a state or, infrequently, the national government enacted a regulatory policy, it quickly found its way onto the docket of an unsympathetic Court.

---

*The opinion in *Dred Scott v. Sandford* was only the second time the Court had overruled an act of Congress. Considering that in the first instance, *Marbury,* the Court had merely asserted its authority but did so in such a way as to avoid reversing the president's action, the *Dred Scott* decision may represent the real, if inauspicious, beginning of judicial review of acts of Congress.

THE PRIMACY OF PROPERTY RIGHTS.

By the late nineteenth century, a constitutional tradition had developed that shielded business from economic regulation. The Framers considered the right to private property to be fundamental, and equated it with liberty. Indeed, it was the economic problems caused by the Articles of Confederation—namely, its failure to prevent state raids on property rights—that brought the delegates together in Philadelphia in the first place. Marshall shared the Framers' commitment to property, and during hard economic times the Court vigilantly protected the integrity of contracts against state efforts to annul them on behalf of debtors. Marshall wrote in one decision, "[T]he people of the United States . . . have manifested a determination to shield themselves and their property from the effects of those sudden and strong passions to which men are exposed."[8]

Congressional attempts to curb child labor by taxing the items produced were repeatedly rebuffed by the Supreme Court in the early twentieth century.

After the Civil War the Court generally maintained its historical sympathy for property rights. The Fourteenth Amendment was adopted in 1868 to protect newly freed slaves from the repressive actions of the former Confederate states. The amendment said, in part, that no state shall "deprive any person of life, liberty, or property, without due process of law." As we saw in Chapter 4, the nineteenth-century Supreme Court discovered little basis in the due process clause to shield African Americans from disfranchisement and segregation. It did, however, find ample justification for protecting railroads and other businesses from regulation. To invoke the due process clause, the Court defined corporations as "persons."

The Supreme Court did not deliver a pro-business decision in every case, however. It consistently upheld state prohibitions against the sale of alcohol and occasionally affirmed state regulation of business when the public interest was at stake.[9] But this last criterion, "public interest," is ambiguous, and it prevented the Court from settling on a consistent doctrine. Consequently the states continued to test the boundaries of permissible regulation, and the early-twentieth-century federal courts were inundated with these cases.

The Court's track record in work-hour regulation is one example. In *Lochner v. New York* (1905) the Court struck down a New York law restricting the work hours of bakers to a maximum of ten hours a day or sixty hours a week.[10] Laws "limiting the hours in which grown and intelligent men may labor to earn their living," the majority declared, "are mere meddlesome interferences with the rights of the individual." Three years later, however, the Court upheld an Oregon statute limiting the workday of female workers.[11]

During the 1920s the Supreme Court became decidedly more conservative on economic issues, and with unprecedented vigor struck down laws regulating business in state after state. Figure 9-1 shows a steady rise in the number of economic measures overturned under the due

Figure 9-1 Changing Caseload of the Supreme Court by Decade

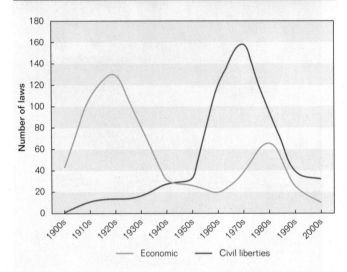

Economic ——— Civil liberties

Source: Lawrence Baum, *The Supreme Court,* 11th ed. (Washington, DC: CQ Press, 2013), Figure 5-1, 174.

Note: Figure shows the number of economic and civil liberties laws (federal, state, and local) overturned by the Supreme Court by decade. Civil liberties category does not include laws supportive of civil liberties.

process clause, reaching a peak of 133 from 1920 to 1929.[12] These decisions won the Court the enmity of many elected officials who found that the justices obstructed their efforts to respond to the demands and needs of their constituents.

After the great stock market crash of 1929, the nation plummeted into a deep economic depression. State and federal governments responded with numerous emergency economic reforms, many of which the Court narrowly affirmed. Yet, as the Great Depression lingered on and the government intervened more substantially in the economy, the Court majority consistently ruled against regulation. From 1934 to 1937 the Court, still made up of justices who had been appointed before the Depression, struck down twelve statutes enacted during President Franklin D. Roosevelt's first term. These included laws creating emergency relief programs, controlling the production of coal and basic agricultural commodities, regulating child labor, and providing mortgage relief, especially to farmers.

A NATIONAL CONSENSUS AND THE COURT'S ABOUT-FACE. Earlier, the Civil War had ended slavery and rendered moot the *Dred Scott* decision. In this era of economic turmoil, resolution of the impasse between the Supreme Court and the elected branches of government required a direct confrontation. Shortly after his landslide reelection in 1936, President Roosevelt proposed a plan for revamping the judiciary. Its most consequential and controversial provision allowed the president to appoint an additional Supreme Court justice for every sitting justice over the age of seventy. Ostensibly the **Court-packing plan** would alleviate the backlog of cases on the Court's docket. With the opportunity to name as many as six new justices to the high bench, its real purpose was obvious—to give Roosevelt a Court majority sympathetic to his New Deal programs. Public reaction to the idea was generally negative, and the legislation failed in Congress, despite its lopsided Democratic majorities. Ultimately, however, victory went to Roosevelt. With a 5–4 decision in a case about regulating wage and working conditions in Washington State, the Court began to uphold the same type of economic regulations it had been rejecting for the past two years.[13]

The Court's about-face started when one justice began to favor federal economic assistance. Justice Owen Roberts's famed "switch in time that saved nine" allowed the Court to bend to the emerging national consensus that recovery required the government's active management of the economy. In the years after the Court-packing crisis, President Roosevelt sealed the Court's retreat from economic policy by filling vacant seats on the bench with appointees who were committed to the New Deal. He had many opportunities: between 1937 and 1941, seven members of the Court either died or retired. Only Roberts and Harlan Fiske Stone, whom Roosevelt raised to chief justice, remained. The justices, now more in tune with the elected branches' thinking about the federal government's role in the economy, began to pay attention to a different set of issues—civil rights and civil liberties. But whether the Court was dealing with the economy or civil rights, one thing became clear in the post–New Deal era: the Court's rulings shifted power dramatically to the federal government and away from the states. In the end, the dramatic conversion of the Supreme Court's agenda and its view of federal power came not through institutional reform, as

might have been expected. Rather, it resulted from the replacement of retirees with a new generation of jurists in closer agreement with the president and Congress. Below we will see that the power to appoint like-minded judges is an important tool with which presidents influence the federal judiciary's policies, and that even for the *unelected* branch, politics matters.

The Rise of Civil Rights and Civil Liberties

The third era of judicial review began in earnest in the 1940s. During this period the Court's concern was the relationship between the individual and government. We surveyed the broad scope of this new direction in Chapters 4 and 5; here we are interested in why the Supreme Court went in this particular direction.

A number of historical reasons for this development have been proposed, and all of them may be true. After abandoning a role to say what does and does not fall within Congress's authority to regulate interstate commerce, the federal judiciary found that much of its previous agenda of cases had been cleared. Some legal historians have suggested that the Supreme Court then strategically turned to a field where it could act unconstrained by the separation of powers system: the rights of individuals. The Court initially opened the door when it incorporated free speech rights through the Fourteenth Amendment, and other individual rights soon followed. In particular, incorporation benefited criminal defendants, who were then poised to make myriad claims that the Bill of Rights protected them from arbitrary actions by state and local law enforcement officials. Arising at the same time, as we found in Chapter 4, legal forces were assembling in the National Association for the Advancement of Colored People and elsewhere to challenge segregation and disenfranchisement in the federal courts. In sum, the confluence of historical forces sent new kinds of cases to the Supreme Court at a moment it was receptive to a fresh set of issues over which it could comfortably assert its authority.

A Fourth Era? Reasserting Judicial Review and a Return to States' Rights

One common factor in the previous two eras was the Court's broad interpretation of Congress's power to regulate activity under the commerce clause. When the Supreme Court finally got pushed on board President Roosevelt's economic policies during the late 1930s and early 1940s, it did so by largely surrendering to Congress and the presidency responsibility for deciding what constituted "interstate commerce." In one of the most important laws of the civil rights era, Congress passed the Civil Rights Act of 1964 that barred segregation and discrimination in all forms of public accommodations. Citing its authority to regulate interstate commerce, Congress sought to prevent the "disruptive effect" of racial discrimination on interstate commerce. The Supreme Court agreed, thereby giving the federal government authority to regulate what might seem like purely local commerce—renting a hotel room, serving customers at restaurants, transportation services, and the like.[14] More generally, the broadly defined commerce clause gave the federal government authority to regulate virtually all commerce—much of it formerly under the exclusive jurisdiction of *state* governments. And with the exception of a few lone dissenting justices here and there, this expansive view of the commerce clause held for decades.

But things would start to change with the arrival of a more conservative Supreme Court led by Chief Justice William H. Rehnquist. Rehnquist—originally appointed by Richard Nixon—was elevated to Chief Justice by another Republican president, Ronald Reagan. In addition, Reagan was able to appoint three other justices who, as it turned out, were sympathetic to reining in the power of the federal government over the states. These four justices—Rehnquist, O'Connor, Scalia, and Kennedy—joined with Justice Clarence Thomas, a George H. W. Bush appointee, to decide a 1995 case that marked the arrival of the fourth era of assertive judicial review. In *United States v. Lopez*—for the first time in almost sixty years—the Court struck down legislation as exceeding Congress's powers under the commerce clause.[15] In a 5–4 decision written by Chief Justice Rehnquist, the Court held that gun possession in a school zone was not economic activity that could substantially affect interstate commerce. Five years later, with the same Republican-appointed justices in the majority, Chief Justice Rehnquist penned another 5–4 decision that made clear *Lopez* was not a fluke. In *United States v. Morrison*, the Court struck down part of the Violence Against Women Act as beyond the scope of Congress's commerce clause power on the ground that gender-motivated crimes of violence were not in any sense "economic activity."[16]

Underlying these decisions was the five-member majority's concern that the federal government had gone too far and encroached on areas that traditionally should be left to state governments. Thus, the Rehnquist Court was in effect rebalancing the power relationship between the federal and state governments. The current Supreme Court led by Chief Justice Roberts has signaled that it will follow the groundwork laid by the Rehnquist Court. In its most high-profile decision to date, five members of the Court (in a majority opinion written by Chief Justice Roberts) held that Congress did not have the authority under the commerce clause to force individuals to purchase health insurance. Although the law was upheld by a different five-member majority under Congress's taxing power (see the box on page 406), the

Roberts Court continued the trend of scrutinizing and limiting the federal government's power under the commerce clause.

In sum, this era's Supreme Court enlists its judicial review prerogative broadly. This can be easily seen in Table 9-1 by the comparatively large number of federal and state laws invalidated. The modern Court's assertiveness has placed it in position as the political system's chief referee keeping the political institutions in their proper orbits. In 1998 the Court struck down Congress's attempt to give the president a line-item veto (see Chapter 7). In 2001 it unanimously rejected an appeals court ruling that Congress delegated too much regulatory discretion to the Environmental Protection Agency (EPA) and, in effect, unconstitutionally abdicated its authority. And in 2008 the Court rejected President George W. Bush's executive order that Texas must retry a Mexican citizen convicted in a death penalty case because he had not been given the opportunity to consult with the Mexican consulate, as required by the World Court. Without explicit authorization by public law, the president's authority was insufficient to act alone. In these and other cases the Supreme Court acted as a disinterested third party applying the rule book—that is, the Constitution—to keep those officeholders who compete over public policy in their proper constitutional roles.

In another less controversial but important respect, the present-day judiciary's referee role has motivated it to be deeply involved in the administration of national policy. A much greater share of the judicial branch's caseload involves overseeing the bureaucracy's performance in relation to its statutory responsibilities and limitations. Whenever the EPA issues a new pollution standard, there is a fair chance that an affected party will sue the agency, claiming that it exceeded its authority. The Court must determine whether the agency conformed substantively and procedurally to its statutory responsibilities and guidelines. In many other cases, the Court simply decides what the law says. Bankruptcy law protects retirement funds from liens by creditors. Does this include 401(k) savings accounts that can be withdrawn at any time but with a penalty before the individual reaches a certain age? Yes, the Court answered in 2005. Then, for the next session, it considered whether Social Security disability payments were similarly protected.[17] By one count well over half the Court's decisions interpreting public laws from 2000 through 2011 took the form of statutory interpretation compared to just over a quarter that were decided on constitutional questions.[18] At times, the Court will even recommend changes in the law that will produce the intended results and resolve conflicting laws and ambiguous delegations of authority to the bureaucracy.[19]

In many instances the modern federal judiciary acts as an extension of the bureaucracy. When the federal government believed that software giant Microsoft violated antitrust laws, it could not, unlike governments in many other countries, directly penalize the company. Antitrust laws required that the government sue Microsoft; have a judge and jury decide if the charges were true; and, if so, formulate an appropriate penalty. On many other occasions public laws place the federal courts at the end of the administrative process to hear appeals from private parties who argue that an agency's administrative regulation or other action exceeded its authority.

THE STRUCTURE OF THE FEDERAL JUDICIARY

The United States has several hundred federal courts, but only the Supreme Court is explicitly mentioned in the Constitution's Article III. The Framers knew more would be needed,

CHIEF JUSTICE ROBERTS STANDS ALONE, AND PUTS HIS STAMP ON "THE ROBERTS COURT"

politics to policy

Scholars often refer to different eras of the Court by the name of the Chief Justice who served during that time. As discussed in Chapter 5, the era in the 1960s in which the Court expanded the rights of criminal defendants is known as "the Warren Court." "The Rehnquist Court" will be known in part for rebalancing the relationship between the federal government and state governments.

In the spring of 2012, as the Supreme Court was preparing to decide the constitutionality of the Patient Protection and Affordable Care Act (also known as "Obamacare"), John Roberts had been Chief Justice for fewer than seven years. The highest-profile decision of "the Roberts Court" so far was *Citizens United*, discussed in Chapter 5. That decision was predictably 5–4, with the Court's conservative justices striking down sections of a bipartisan campaign finance reform law. In President Obama's State of the Union address in 2010 (just weeks after the Court's decision) he did something unusual for a sitting president: he openly and directly criticized the Court for their decision. This criticism was not just unusual, but awkward; six of the justices (including Chief Justice Roberts) were sitting in the chamber, just steps away from the president.

This backdrop made the Court's pending decision on the constitutionality of the Patient Protection and Affordable Care Act all the more intriguing. Heightening the stakes was the fact that presidents since Teddy Roosevelt had tried to pass health care reform, and some, like Bill Clinton, had suffered political bruises in the process. And here stood Barack Obama, who could say he was the first to actually get it done. Would the Court's conservative justices undo President Obama's signature legislative achievement? Would this case provide further evidence–along with *Citizens United*–that the Roberts Court was nakedly partisan just like the elected branches?

Most assumed that the answer to those questions lay in the hands of one justice: Anthony Kennedy, the swing vote on the Court. Few–including the other eight justices–could have predicted that the real wild card would be Chief Justice Roberts. At the conference in which the justices voted, there were four votes to affirm, four votes to reverse. Chief Justice Roberts spoke last, and

but unable to agree whether to create a separate federal judiciary or have the state courts oversee the initial trials and lower-level appeals, they agreed to defer the decision and let Congress create "inferior" courts as necessary. Congress promptly did so in the Judiciary Act of 1789. Of the various types of courts Congress has created over the years, those of most interest here are **constitutional courts**, which are vested with the general judicial authority outlined in Article III.* (See Figure 9-2.) These lower-level courts, designed to

---

* The nonconstitutional courts are classified as legislative courts. They are created by Congress under Article I and fulfill some special purpose; their judges are appointed by the president for fixed terms. Examples are the U.S. Court of Military Appeals, the U.S. Tax Court, and bankruptcy courts.

indicated that Congress had exceeded its powers under the commerce clause in creating the individual mandate. He then assigned himself the draft opinion.[†] The implication of course was that he would be drafting the majority opinion *striking down the law*.

In the end, Chief Justice Roberts did write the majority opinion. And he did side with the four conservative justices in holding that Congress did not have the power to pass the act under the commerce clause. But the shock was that the other part of his majority opinion *upheld* the Patient Protection and Affordable Care Act and its controversial individual mandate under Congress's power to tax. On that issue, he was the lone conservative who sided with the four "liberal" members of the Court.

What did this unique vote mean for the legacy of the Roberts Court? Much like Chief Justice John Marshall in *Marbury v. Madison*, Justice Roberts was able to avoid some unpalatable political consequences. If he had sided with Scalia, Thomas, Alito, and Kennedy in striking down the entire law, the

Roberts Court's reputation would have been politicized beyond repair. The legacy of the Roberts Court might have been the institution's damaged legitimacy. And overturning the Court would have likely become an issue in the upcoming presidential campaign. On the other hand, had the Court upheld the law under the commerce clause, Roberts would have been roundly criticized by fellow conservatives as undoing the work of his predecessors in redefining the commerce clause.

Perhaps the brilliance of Roberts's unique vote is that he made *neither* side completely happy, yet in the long term he enhanced the Court's credibility. As the chief justice stated the matter in his majority opinion, "Members of this Court are vested with the authority to interpret the law; we possess neither the expertise nor the prerogative to make policy judgments. Those decisions are entrusted to our Nation's elected leaders, who can be thrown out of office if the people disagree with them. It is not our job to protect the people from the consequences of their political choices." Justice Roberts sent a clear message, not to the president or Congress, but to the American people: if you don't like the Patient Protection and Affordable Care Act, take it up with the political branches, not the Court.

---

[*] Jeffrey Toobin. *The Oath: The Obama White House and the Supreme Court* (New York: Doubleday, 2012).

[†] When the chief justice is in the majority, he can assign the opinion to himself, or to another justice.

handle litigation, exercise the same power of judicial review available to the Supreme Court. In this sense the entire federal judiciary serves as agents of the Supreme Court. The lower federal courts weigh the merits of a case against prescribed Supreme Court doctrine and presumably arrive at approximately the same decision the Supreme Court would have rendered had it heard the case.

As we have seen, Congress delegates work to specialized committees and sizable staffs to deal with the myriad issues and policies it handles. Similarly, the modern presidency includes a large retinue of highly specialized White House staff and an Office of Management and Budget (OMB) to monitor the hundreds of executive branch agencies. As with these other institutions, the Supreme Court's effectiveness also rests on delegation—in this case, on

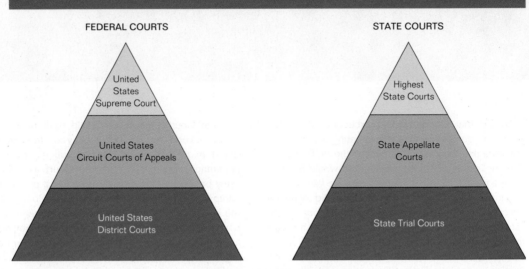

Figure 9-2 The Structure of the Federal and State Court Systems

FEDERAL COURTS

- United States Supreme Court
- United States Circuit Courts of Appeals
- United States District Courts

STATE COURTS

- Highest State Courts
- State Appellate Courts
- State Trial Courts

In both the state system and the federal system, most cases begin at the bottom of the pyramid, in trial courts. Parties who lose at the trial level can usually appeal their case. In the federal system, a litigant appeals to the appropriate Circuit Court of Appeals, and in the state system, a litigant appeals to the appropriate state-level appellate court (although some states do not have courts at this level). At the top of the pyramid in the federal system is the U.S. Supreme Court, which has discretion over most appeals. At the top of each state's pyramid, there is also a court with ultimate authority to hear appeals; most are called the "Supreme Court" of that particular state.

persuading the lower federal judiciary, by the strength of its opinions, to implement its policies.

Jurisdiction of the Federal Courts

As almost every American law school student immediately learns, federal courts are courts of *limited* jurisdiction. The precise scope of federal court jurisdiction is not, in fact, so simple, which accounts for the semester-long law school courses devoted to this subject. Generally speaking, federal courts are authorized to hear two types of cases: those concerning "federal questions" and those involving citizens of different states. Among other things, federal question jurisdiction includes questions of U.S. constitutional law, such as the various civil liberties claims reviewed in Chapter 5. Or, more commonly, this jurisdiction involves the judiciary's interpreting and applying federal statutes in criminal and civil cases. For example, the Justice Department successfully sued Microsoft in federal court for engaging in monopolistic practices. The second major type of federal jurisdiction concerns cases where states or citizens of different states sue each other. The reasoning here is that a citizen of State A who is sued by a citizen of State B in State B might not be treated fairly by a court in State B.*

---

*Federal statutory law also imposes the requirement that the amount at issue between citizens of different states must be more than $75,000.

Jurisdictional questions can be complicated by the fact that state courts also have jurisdiction over federal civil claims, unless Congress has given federal courts *exclusive* jurisdiction over certain kinds of federal cases, which it often does. Moreover, defendants can invoke "removal jurisdiction" to transfer a case filed from state court to federal court if the case could have originated there. As a practical matter, the vast majority of cases that can be heard in federal court usually will be heard in federal court instead of state court. In addition, a criminal defendant who has been convicted under a state criminal law in state court, but who feels that his federal constitutional rights have been violated, can appeal his case to the U.S. Supreme Court—although the defendant is generally required to first "exhaust" his appeals through the state court system. For example, the defendant in the seminal case of *Miranda v. Arizona,* after losing his appeal to the Supreme Court of Arizona, successfully appealed to the U.S. Supreme Court, which determined that the defendant's Fifth Amendment rights against self-incrimination had been violated.[*]

The Supreme Court's Delegation

The federal judiciary is organized as a three-layered pyramid. At its base are ninety-four **district courts** staffed by approximately 590 active judges.[†] Every state has at least one district court, and the three largest states—California, New York, and Texas—have four. District courts are trial-level courts, and (with some exceptions) most cases in the federal system must start there. If one of the parties is not satisfied with the outcome of a case at the district court level, this party must appeal the case to one of the U.S. Courts of Appeals. There are currently thirteen **courts of appeals**, administered by approximately 158 active judges (see Table 9-2). Eleven separate geographic regions, or "circuits," cover the fifty states; a twelfth is assigned to the District of Columbia (see Map 9-1). The thirteenth, called the U.S. Court of Appeals for the Federal Circuit, has a nationwide jurisdiction and deals mostly with specialized federal law such as patent and trademark law. Usually sitting as three-judge panels, courts of appeals review district court decisions.

The Supreme Court is the court of final appeal. Under its appellate jurisdiction, the Court may hear cases appealed from the lower federal courts or directly from the highest state courts when an important constitutional question is in dispute. Through these channels, the Court receives the bulk of its work. Article III also gives the Court original trial court jurisdiction in all cases "affecting Ambassadors, other public Ministers and Consuls, and those in which a State shall be Party." This constitutional quirk required the Supreme Court in 1998 to hear a dispute between New York and New Jersey over which state "owned" Ellis Island, which is located at the mouth of the Hudson River. Original jurisdiction cases always have accounted for a small part of the Court's work—only about 160 cases in two hundred years.

The Supreme Court depends heavily on the lower courts behaving like loyal agents in deciding thousands of cases annually. The Court's lofty position at the apex of this

---

[*] Finally, federal courts also have jurisdiction under federal law to hear *habeas corpus* petitions. Although a discussion of the complicated topic of *habeas corpus* is beyond the scope of this chapter, the basic idea is that a criminal defendant in state court may file an action in federal court, alleging that the state's incarceration violates the Constitution or other federal law.

[†] The most recent figure is for 2010, and does not include vacancies or pending nominees. In addition, over 350 senior judges at the district court level preside over a reduced caseload.

Map 9-1 The Federal Judiciary

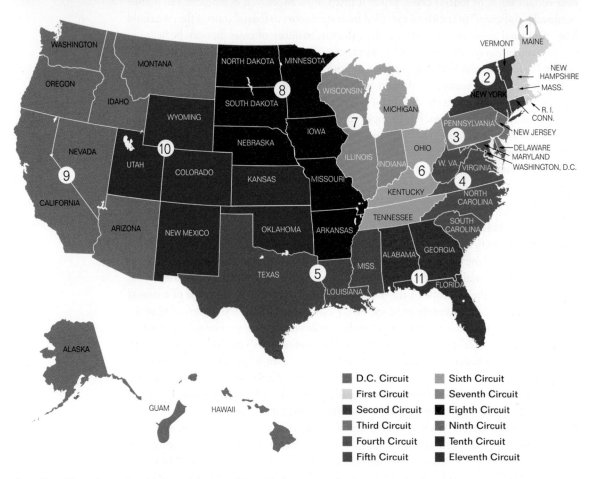

- D.C. Circuit
- First Circuit
- Second Circuit
- Third Circuit
- Fourth Circuit
- Fifth Circuit
- Sixth Circuit
- Seventh Circuit
- Eighth Circuit
- Ninth Circuit
- Tenth Circuit
- Eleventh Circuit

Source: United States Courts, Court Map, www.uscourts.gov/Home.aspx.

pyramid of federal courts suggests a command over the subordinate courts' policies that in fact does not exist. Contrary to the clean lines of authority implied by the organizational structure, the judicial system is anything but a tightly supervised hierarchy. Rather, it is a decentralized organization, physically dispersed across the nation and administered at every level by independent, life-tenured judges. Unlike the presidency, which delegates oversight of the bureaucracy to OMB, or the House and Senate, which delegate responsibility for drafting legislation to committees, the Supreme Court wields few administrative controls over the lower courts. Thus, successful implementation of the Supreme Court's policies is not guaranteed and depends greatly on the degree to which the justices concur in a course of action and on how clearly they communicate it to their colleagues throughout the judiciary.

The Limits of Internal Control

If the Supreme Court truly sat atop a hierarchical organization, it would enjoy a far different relationship with the district and appeals courts. Like the CEO of a major corporation or a cabinet secretary, it would routinely supervise and give orders to its subordinate agents. Motivated by the knowledge that making the wrong choice might result in an unfavorable merit review, demotion, or even dismissal, subordinates would defer to their principal and seek guidance. None of these techniques to keep subordinates on the right track is available to the Supreme Court in steering decisions from the district and appellate courts. Instead, the life tenure of judges, which insulates the judiciary from the other branches, also insulates judges from each other.

Only Congress can remove a federal judge, and then only for serious offenses—not for incompetence or policy disagreement with the Supreme Court. Moreover, the Supreme Court cannot distribute the caseload to the lower courts; the distribution of cases depends on geographical jurisdictions created by Congress and, to some extent, litigants' choice of courts.

The Supreme Court also may have difficulty enforcing implementation of its decisions in the lower courts. Outright resistance to Supreme Court decisions by lower-court judges is unusual but does occur. Declaring that the Court "erred," an Alabama federal judge in 1983 upheld prayer in the public schools, in spite of the Court's prohibition of the practice.[20] In a capital punishment case in 1993 an appellate judge kept granting a stay of execution despite the Supreme Court's rejection of the defendant's appeal. When a lower court disregards a directive, the Court has several options available. It may hear the case a second time, rebuke the lower-court judge, issue a writ of mandamus ordering the lower-court judge to take a specified action, or assign the case to a different court. Because all such alternatives are costly in terms of the time and monitoring required, they illustrate the limits of Supreme Court control, though they also ensure that the Court will ultimately prevail if it feels sufficiently strongly on an issue.

More commonly, policy differences occur when lower-court judges take advantage of ambiguities arising from the particular facts of a case or in the language of Supreme Court doctrine to avoid complying with the higher court's preferences. This is precisely what happened in the aftermath of *Brown v. Board of Education*.[21] When the Court ordered public schools to desegregate with "all deliberate speed" instead of setting a deadline, it unwittingly invited segregationist federal judges throughout the South to move at a snail's pace.

Yet the Supreme Court is not helpless. It can reverse lower-court decisions when it disagrees; even the threat of reversal often deters deviations from Court doctrine. After all, a reversal represents a "defeat" for a judge, and those who suffer frequent reversals may damage their reputations. A poor reputation, in turn, alerts judges higher up to scrutinize their judgments carefully for incompetence or noncompliance with established precedents. Fearing reversal, most judges strategically temper their rulings to conform sufficiently with established doctrine, and thus to withstand litigants' efforts to persuade an appeals court or the Supreme Court to review the rulings.

Nonetheless, reversal remains an imperfect sanction. Some judges may be willing to risk a few reversals to defend strongly held views and to force other courts to reconsider current policy. In addition, given the Supreme Court's ability to control the number of cases it hears on appeal—a very small percentage of all cases actually appealed—most circuit court judges realize that the probability of the Court reviewing their decisions is very low. However, a

TABLE 9-2		
The Federal Judiciary: Number of Judges		
Court	Circuit	District
D.C. Circuit	11	15
1st	6	29
2nd	13	62
3rd	14	61
4th	15	56
5th	17	83
6th	16	62
7th	11	47
8th	11	42
9th	29	112
10th	12	39
11th	12	69
Federal Circuit	12	–

Source: Administrative Office of the U.S. Courts.

Note: Current as of December 2011, including vacancies.

circuit court, like the liberal Ninth Circuit Court of Appeals in the West, can press its luck a bit too much. Over the past decade the Supreme Court has overturned the Ninth Circuit's judgments at more than twice the rate of the other appeals courts, and about half of these reversals brought a frequently divided Supreme Court into unanimous agreement.[*] As a result, the present Supreme Court monitors this wayward delegate closely. About one-third of all cases the Court reviews originate in this circuit, again about twice the share one would expect.

JUDICIAL DECISION MAKING

The pyramid shape of the court system accurately portrays the realities of the modern federal judiciary, at each level of which the caseload continues to mount. As alluded to above, the huge docket of the judicial branch means that the risk of reversal may not be so great. In fiscal year 2011, over 289,000 new cases were filed in the federal district courts, and over 55,000 new cases were filed in the circuit courts of appeals. The Supreme Court, in contrast, decides fewer than 100 cases annually, or about 1 percent of the appeals it receives. For example, in the 2010 term, 7,857 cases were filed in the Supreme Court, but only 86 cases were argued.[22] These numbers reveal that the intermediate, appeals level of the judiciary, not the Supreme Court, oversees the district courts' compliance with prevailing doctrine. As long as the appeals courts' judgments agree with the policies of the Supreme Court, the latter is free to act as a "general staff or selective formulator of policies."[23]

Selecting Cases

In 1925, when the number of appeals began to grow at an alarming rate, the Supreme Court persuaded Congress to change the rules granting access to a hearing by the Court. Over the years these rules have been strengthened in favor of giving the Court greater discretion to choose the cases it reviews. Instead of having a right to "their day in court," litigants must file a **writ of certiorari** requesting that the Court order a lower court to send it the records of the trial in question. With this device, the Supreme Court gained control over its caseload since the vast majority of the cases arrive by this route. Indeed, the Court has managed to cut in half the number of cases it hears annually, despite a six-fold increase in the number of requests.

---

[*] In one reversal in 2011, the unanimous Court, clearly exasperated, overruled a three-judge panel with a cryptic opinion: "The Court of Appeals offered a one-sentence conclusory explanation. That decision is as inexplicable as it is unexplained. It is reversed." David G. Savage, "High Court Restores Rape Conviction," *Los Angeles Times,* March 22, 2011.

Discretionary control over its caseload solved only part of the Court's problem, however. From the eight thousand or so certiorari requests it receives each year, how does the Court decide which one hundred (or fewer) to review? In small, intimate work settings members need not delegate agenda control in order to coordinate their decisions. The Supreme Court's **rule of four** provides that when four justices support hearing a case the certiorari petition is granted.[24] Although this rule protects the prerogatives of individual justices, it does so at a cost to each member of having to cull through a mountain of petitions. Unlike congressional and presidential staffs numbering in the thousands, the Supreme Court is served not by a large bureaucracy to help it sort through that mountain and find cases that satisfy its criteria, but instead by a small retinue of law clerks. Each justice is permitted to hire up to four clerks, usually graduates of the country's most prestigious law schools, who spend a year or two at the Court. Most justices retain clerks who agree with them ideologically in the hope that they will read certiorari petitions the same way the justice would. Justice Clarence Thomas described his dependence on clerks as "mates in a foxhole."[25] Others have enlisted clerks who differ in their political views. This taxes the justice to some degree since he or she must view recommendations from these clerks with a measure of circumspection. On the other hand, this arrangement is well suited to give the justice a preview of the kinds of arguments other justices are likely to make.*

READ MORE

■ *logic.cqpress.com*

Cases the Supreme Court has granted certiorari during its next term.

This 1885 *Puck* magazine cartoon calls for Congress to relieve the Supreme Court's congested docket. Relief would come later with reforms giving the Court the writ of certiorari.

---

*It also offers the justice an opportunity to triangulate the opinions of his or her clerks in figuring out whether a case best suits the justice's interests. If one assumes that clerks are no different from anyone else in Washington in advancing some policies over others, judges are always exposed to the possibility that a clerk will promote a case that advances his or her point of view more than it does the justice's. If the justice can sample different points of view, he or she has a better prospect of determining whether it is a case the justice would like to hear.

Because the opportunity to hear cases is limited, justices take a hard, strategic look at each petition before promoting it to their colleagues. Do the facts of the case allow the Court to arrive at a "clean" decision that will guide the lower courts? More important, will the justice's preference stand a chance of garnering the five votes necessary to win if the case is heard on its merits? If not, a justice who otherwise would want to hear a case may pass on it for fear of allowing the majority to establish even more firmly a policy he or she opposes.[26] Thus, deciding whether to hear a case is itself a major decision—and one fraught with political strategy. After all, as Chief Justice William Rehnquist acknowledged, "There is an ideological division on the Court, and each of us has some cases we would like to see granted, and on the contrary some of the other members would not like to see them granted."[27] And because justices want to weigh in on cases in which they think the lower courts have made an error, cases granted certiorari have a good chance of being overturned. In a typical year almost two-thirds are.

RESOLVING LOWER-COURT DISAGREEMENTS. Recognizing that the Court has a strong stake in maintaining standards and coherence within this highly decentralized organization, justices look for cases they can use to resolve ambiguities and conflicting lower-court decisions. One recent example discussed in Chapter 5 is whether the government's attachment of a GPS tracking device to a vehicle constitutes a search under the Fourth Amendment. The Seventh and Ninth Circuits previously had held that such action was not a search, but in 2012, the Supreme Court unanimously affirmed the D.C. Circuit's judgment that it was a search. In this and on numerous other issues, contradictory policies reflecting different ideological preferences of judges percolate up the judicial pyramid.

Chief Justice William Rehnquist, who served as a law clerk for Justice Robert Jackson (served 1941–1954), meets with his clerks to discuss pending cases.

TAKING CUES FROM OTHERS. In selecting cases for resolution, the justices economize by paying close attention to what others tell them. In addition to hearing from the plaintiff (or prosecutor in criminal cases) and defendant, the Court allows interested groups not party to the litigation—interest groups, businesses, and government agencies, among others—to submit *amicus curiae* (friend of the court) briefs arguing that a certiorari petition should be granted or denied. Just as interest groups testify before Congress in hearings, business, government, nonprofits, and other interest groups "testify" before the Supreme Court in these briefs. Of all the interested parties, the most important and prolific is the federal government itself.

Through the office of the **solicitor general**, the administration lets the Court know which cases it thinks are important.

The anecdotal record has long acknowledged that the presence of *amicus curiae* briefs from prestigious sources increases a case's chances of being accepted by the Court. One systematic analysis of the Supreme Court's decision to grant or reject certiorari found that the solicitor general—the chief attorney for the U.S. government—supported a hearing in about half of the cases the Court accepted.[28] And in controversial cases—defined as those cases in which lower courts disagreed or various groups had filed *amicus curiae* briefs on both sides of the issue—the Court's decision to hear a case followed the solicitor general's recommendation more than 95 percent of the time.

At first glance, these figures suggest that the solicitor general acts as the Court's agenda setter. A more subtle process is probably at work, however. The government and interest groups tend to promote those cases they think will attract the Court. In this way, they actually help the Court separate wheat from chaff and identify those decisions that most deserve the Court's attention. In lieu of an extensive bureaucracy to process nearly eight thousand cases, the Court has informally and effectively delegated some of this work to outside agents. When they sound an alarm, the Court pays attention.*

Doctrine: Policymaking by the Court

Congress passes laws, courts make doctrine. Both are public policy, but they take very different forms. A public law typically assigns responsibility and appropriates money to a federal agency to achieve certain stated policy goals. A judicial policy decision, by contrast, typically states a rule or doctrine. In rendering decisions the Court prescribes guidelines for district and appeals judges to apply when trying similar cases. These guidelines are considered **judicial doctrine** that lower-court judges carefully weigh. Not only does judicial doctrine make their jobs easier; it also provides valuable information for estimating how far lower courts can diverge from the Supreme Court's preferences before being reviewed and overturned.

Judicial doctrine assumes two forms: procedural and substantive. **Procedural doctrine** governs the specific ways in which the lower courts should do their work. **Substantive doctrine**, more akin to policymaking, guides judges on which party in a case should prevail. Sometimes the two doctrines clash, such as when the Court decides to change current policy— for example, a search-and-seizure doctrine—but in doing so, it repudiates existing methods or procedures that the lower courts have dutifully followed.

PROCEDURAL DOCTRINE. Like the managers of other decentralized organizations, the Supreme Court has sought to exercise control and to cope with its ever-growing caseload by establishing standard operating procedures prescribing how lower federal courts should decide cases. The most important such doctrine, *stare decisis* (Latin for "let the decision stand"), directs the lower courts, as well as the Supreme Court itself, to follow established precedent in deciding current cases. Generally precedents are earlier decisions that established

---

* And were they to abuse this influence by overtly calling attention to cases that they would like the Court to hear, but that do not really require its attention, they would find their legal briefs carrying less weight with the Court.

a new substantive doctrine. Consider *Griswold v. Connecticut,* the case that established the implicit right of privacy (see Chapter 5). Especially at the appellate stages of a case, the plaintiff's and the defendant's lawyers invoke precedents that support their positions. To the extent that they follow *stare decisis,* the lower courts find it easier to extend the Supreme Court's preferences. This, in turn, frees the Court to monitor closely those decisions that fail to follow precedent or are otherwise unresolved.

Even when followed conscientiously, *stare decisis* cannot strictly determine the outcome of many cases; new and unusual circumstances arise for which existing doctrine offers little guidance. Or the doctrine may be ambiguous, perhaps reflecting uncertainty or disagreement among members of the Court over what the policy should be. Or, as happens frequently, the facts of a case may bring two doctrines into conflict. The ability to interpret doctrine and apply precedents to specific cases is an important skill. Among other things, a judge must decide whether a specific precedent applies to a particular case. Some judges develop strong reputations for writing convincing opinions that influence the way other judges think about comparable cases—that is, their opinions assume value as precedent.

Other procedural doctrines identify who may initiate cases in federal court and under what circumstances. Only litigants who are directly and adversely affected by the disputed action have the right, or **standing**—that is, sufficient personal stake in the outcome to bring the case to court (see also Chapter 8). Similarly, the Court long ago established the principle that the judiciary would not rule on moot (otherwise resolved) or hypothetical issues. Do presidents have the authority to impound appropriated funds? The only way to find out is for a president to impound money and have someone file suit. Though at times highly inconvenient to other actors, this doctrine prevents the judiciary from becoming embroiled in hypothetical issues. But in the federal sentencing debacle, this doctrine trapped the Court into deciding a state-level case emphatically while remaining mute on virtually identical circumstances in federal sentencing rules. Yet another important procedural doctrine establishes a boundary of federalism within the judiciary: only those cases in the state courts that raise a constitutional question at the outset—such as a civil liberty protected by the Bill of Rights—may be appealed to the federal judiciary after a loss in the state courts.

After inflaming white southerners with the Court's ruling in *Brown v. Board of Education* in 1954 and other groups throughout the country with liberal civil liberties rulings, Chief Justice Earl Warren became a target of a grassroots impeachment campaign. In this 1963 photo he accepts impeachment literature while passing picketers. No Supreme Court justice has ever been removed by impeachment.

SUBSTANTIVE DOCTRINE. As the Supreme Court selects and decides cases, it is less interested in simply "seeing justice done" in a particular instance than in identifying standards and general characteristics of cases

JUDICIAL ACTIVISM

politics to policy

Judicial activism is a term often associated with "liberal" decisions by the courts. Commonly, it arises when a judge issues a ruling that broadens the conventional view of civil and criminal rights. In Chapter 5 we reviewed the activism of the Warren Supreme Court, which throughout the 1960s dramatically expanded the rights of criminal defendants. Activism also applies to instances in which a court intervenes beyond simply ruling whether legislation or, more commonly, implementation by a government agency violates the Constitution or some federal statute. Decisions described as activist are typically those in which a court actually prescribes how a policy needs to be changed or implemented to satisfy the judge's opinion of what is required for it to comply with the Constitution or some federal statute.

The term *activist*, objectively speaking, can be ascribed to judges who make decisions that can be categorized as either liberal or conservative. In other words, when judges are accused of being activists and substituting their policy views for those of elected officials or government agencies charged with implementing policy, the substantive outcome may be conservative. Here are two recent decisions—one conservative, one liberal—that have attracted the *activist* label.

District of Columbia v. Heller (decided in 2008) is a prime example of an activist decision that is also conservative. In *Heller*, the Supreme Court decided that the Second Amendment's right to bear arms was not a group right, but rather an individual right. This decision can be characterized as activist because, as law professor and dean Erwin Chemerinsky explains, the Court "both ignored precedent and invalidated a law adopted by a popularly elected government."[1] Furthermore, the decision is viewed by gun control advocates as conservative because the five members of the Court in the majority were interpreting the Second Amendment in a way that made it harder for the elected branches of the federal government (and, as the Court held in a subsequent case, state governments) to regulate guns and, therefore, to address the consequences of violent crimes committed with guns.

By contrast, a recent decision that could be classified as liberal activism is one in which the Supreme Court upheld the decision by a three-judge district court ordering the state of California to reduce its prison population by approximately forty thousand inmates.[2] The lower court's order was the culmination of both a ten-year-old case and a nineteen-year-old case in which the plaintiffs alleged that California's overcrowded prisons failed to provide constitutionally adequate medical care and mental health care to prisoners. Although the district court noted that federal courts must proceed with caution when intervening in a state's affairs, the judges ultimately determined that the courts had no choice but to step in, and the Supreme Court agreed that the action was necessary to remedy the violation of prisoners' constitutional rights. The Supreme Court's decision can be seen as activist because the federal courts arguably are substituting their judgment for the judgment of the elected branches of the state of California. The decision also can be characterized as liberal because the court is protecting the constitutional rights of prisoners—a class of people not generally favored by conservatives, who are known for being "tough on crime."

---

1. Erwin Chemerinsky, "The Supreme Court Gun Fight: A Case of Conservatism. A Case of Conservative Activism," *Los Angeles Times*, June 27, 2008.

2. See *Brown v. Plata*, 131 S.Ct. 1910 (2011).

that will allow a decision to be applied to government policy as well as to future cases. In the *Miranda* decision discussed in Chapter 5, the Court set out clear police procedures for protecting defendants against self-incrimination. Today thousands of local law enforcement jurisdictions follow the *Miranda* guidelines as a standard operating procedure when making an arrest.

Some issues lend themselves better than others to this form of policymaking. One issue that did not was obscenity. The Supreme Court agonized for years over how to define obscenity, one of the few kinds of speech that does not enjoy First Amendment protection. As noted in Chapter 5, the effort led one exasperated justice to exclaim, "I know it when I see it!" As a result these cases continued to be decided inconsistently across the nation's state and federal district courts and required the appeals courts and Supreme Court to devote considerable attention to reconciling decisions and clearly defining obscenity.

Although the ideology of judges matters most at the higher levels where doctrine is made, current doctrine often leaves judges with abundant discretion in the lower courts. Aside from the conventional liberal-conservative distinction that applies to many cases, judgments also vary according to the way a judge views his or her role on the bench. A judge who in the absence of a clear violation of the Constitution or established doctrine will defer to the policies emanating from the elected branches is commonly described as exercising judicial **restraint**. Those who change doctrine to conform with their view of the Constitution in a changing society are exercising judicial **activism**. In modern political debate, the term *activist* has often been used pejoratively to describe a judge who seeks to substitute his or her policy views for the views of the legislature. The Warren Court during the 1960s was widely regarded as activist in that it reopened and changed doctrine in many areas of civil rights and civil liberties. During this era activism and liberalism were used more or less interchangeably in the news media to describe judges and their decisions. However, in the present era, with most of the activist views of the Warren Court solidified as established policy, activism is just as likely to be found among judges favoring a conservative policy agenda. Thus, as the box on page 417 further explains, the term *activist* can apply to either a conservative or a liberal justice.

Deciding Doctrine

Every Supreme Court decision contains two elements essential to creating doctrine. The first is the vote that decides the case in favor of one of the parties. The second is the opinion, a statement or set of statements in which the majority explains the rationale for its decision in a way that creates doctrine (that is, makes policy) and the minority, if there is one, articulates why it dissents.

A unanimous Court decision, simply because it is less likely to be reversed in the future, creates more compelling precedent than does a case decided by a 5–4 vote. After the justices express their views on a case and vote tentatively on the outcome in a private conference, the chief justice (if voting with the majority) assigns one of the majority the task of drafting an opinion.* The task is not insignificant; the author of an opinion voices the majority position and, in doing so, strongly influences the shape of that judicial policy.

Once the majority opinion is drafted, it often undergoes prolonged internal bargaining as the writer tries to persuade the other justices that its legal arguments are correct. The author of the opinion generally writes to maintain the decision's core support as well as appeal to

---

* If the chief justice is in the minority, the most senior associate justice in the majority assigns the opinion.

dissenters who might be converted. In 1954 Chief Justice Earl Warren used his considerable powers of persuasion to coax reluctant justices to abandon their disparate, and strongly held, positions on school desegregation and forge a unanimous opinion against segregation in *Brown v. Board of Education.*

Successful persuasion has its costs, however. Generally, to persuade colleagues to maintain or shift their positions, the drafter must change the opinion's language and perhaps blur its message, allowing each member of the majority to find language in the opinion with which he or she can agree. Thus reluctant justices joined Warren's opinion in *Brown* on the condition that he not specify a time schedule for school desegregation. The consequences, we found in Chapter 4, were considerable. The failure to set a deadline allowed southern school boards to delay by first resisting and then engaging in token desegregation and tying up enforcement with litigation. The price of broad support among the justices may be vague, imperfectly enforced doctrine.

The prevalence of closely divided decisions—containing numerous opinions—is a modern development (see Figure 9-3). The rationale on which an opinion is based may be more consequential for future cases than for the decision itself. Because all justices wish to influence future decisions, each has an interest in opinion writing. A justice who disagrees with the

Figure 9-3   Number of Dissenting and Concurring Opinions

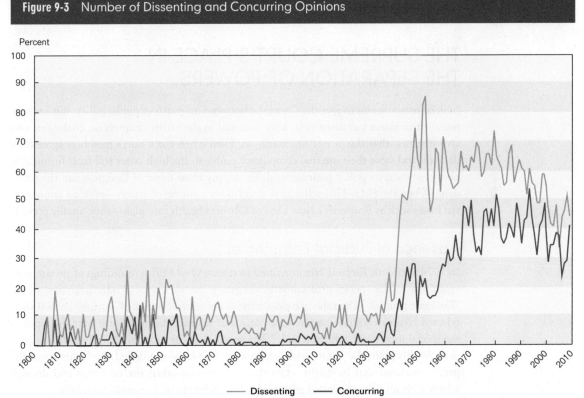

Source: Lee Epstein et al., *The Supreme Court Compendium: Data, Decisions, and Developments,* 5th ed. (Washington, DC: CQ Press, 2011), Table 3-2 and Table 3-3.

majority of the Court may elect to explain why in a **dissenting opinion**. A justice who has unique reasons for supporting the majority may choose to write a **concurring opinion**. Concurring and dissenting opinions allow justices to provide their interpretations of what the majority opinion means. Although only the majority opinion counts as the Court's final decision in any given case, dissenting and concurring opinions may nonetheless influence reactions to the majority's position, by lower-court judges, or by a future Supreme Court revisiting the policy.

Until passage of the Judiciary Act of 1925, which gave the Supreme Court greater control over its caseload, the Court decided far more cases than it considers today. Obligated to review many lower-court decisions with which it agreed, the Court before 1925 produced a large number of unanimous opinions. As the Supreme Court has freed itself to focus on cases that contain important, unresolved policy issues, the proportion of controversial cases has risen dramatically, and thus there are higher numbers of concurring and dissenting opinions.

Two other influences contributed to this rise in opinion writing. First, the Court stopped contesting the authority of Congress and the president to regulate economic activity and began applying the Bill of Rights to state—not just federal—actions. That the justices would not march in unison toward this new body of judicial doctrine is not surprising. The second influence has been the rise of divided party control of government—a pattern whose effects on the presidency were examined in Chapter 7. An important result of this political development has been an ideologically more heterogeneous Supreme Court.

THE SUPREME COURT'S PLACE IN THE SEPARATION OF POWERS

Judicial review seems to give the Court the last word on much of public policy. But we have found throughout our discussion, both here and in the earlier chapters on civil rights and civil liberties, that this is not necessarily so. Even when the Court's members agree on a decision and solve their internal compliance problem, the high court still faces formidable obstacles when its policy preferences differ sharply from those of Congress and the president. When the elected branches have decided on a course of action—even on controversial issues such as Roosevelt's New Deal or Obama's health care plan—they usually prevail.

Absence of Judicial Enforcement

In 1974 President Richard Nixon refused to release Oval Office recordings of private conversations to the special prosecutor investigating the variety of misdeeds known as the Watergate scandal. When the two sides went to court, the Supreme Court, by an 8–0 vote, rejected Nixon's claim of executive privilege and instructed him to turn over the tapes to the special prosecutor, which he did.[29] The contents of the tapes led directly to his resignation. At this point the Court's role largely ended. Had Nixon defied the Court—and the press speculated that he might—Congress would have taken the next step and decided whether his refusal constituted grounds for impeachment and removal from office.

The absence of enforcement authority has allowed Congress and the president at times to ignore Supreme Court rulings. As President Andrew Jackson famously remarked on learning that the Court had ruled his policies regarding removing Cherokee Indians from their land unconstitutional,[30] "They made their decision. Now, let them enforce it." Jackson ignored the decision and forced the Cherokee to give up their lands in return for land west of the Mississippi River. Many died on the trek later known as the Trail of Tears.

The Court's inability to enforce its decisions is strikingly apparent in the failure of *Immigration and Naturalization Service v. Chadha* (1983) to end legislative practices that Congress and presidents have long found useful. In *Chadha* the Court declared the one-house legislative veto unconstitutional (see Chapter 8), upsetting procedures established by Congress and the executive branch.[31] The case itself concerned a minor issue, the deportation of a man who had overstayed his student visa, but its implications were potentially far-reaching for policymaking. The legislative veto dates back to 1932, when Congress and the president agreed to provisions that since then have been included in more than two hundred public laws, including the War Powers Act. These provisions allow either one or both houses of Congress to pass a resolution to reject an agency's action. Although *Chadha* technically voided this mechanism, the executive departments still abide by these legislative vetoes. And Congress and presidents have good reasons for favoring this approach that allows Congress to delegate lawmaking discretion to the executive branch without surrendering ultimate control. A bureaucrat is free to design a policy within broad guidelines, but if it drifts too far away from the legislature's intent, Congress can rescind it by passing a resolution. Presidents realize that Congress is more willing to relax control when it knows it can easily reassert its preferences if it disagrees with the bureaucracy's implementation of a policy. By continuing to honor these statutory provisions, designed to create more flexible principal–agency relations, the elected branches have colluded informally to "overrule" the Supreme Court's verdict on the unconstitutionality of the legislative veto.[32]

Constitutional and Statutory Control

Several provisions of the Constitution equip Congress and the president with the power to rein in the Supreme Court when they disagree with its decisions. Article III allows Congress to set the jurisdiction of the Court and to create lower courts. The Constitution is silent on the size of the Supreme Court, which means the Framers implicitly gave this authority to Congress. During the nineteenth century, Congress did, in fact, add to and subtract from the number of justices, but since 1869 the number has been set at nine. At times, when one of the political parties has captured control of the White House and Congress, it has expanded the size of the lower judiciary as a way of creating vacancies that can be filled with sympathetic judges.[33] The net effect of this practice is to bring the judiciary into closer alignment with changes in national opinion.

When all else fails, Congress may move to amend the Constitution (Article V). The Fourteenth Amendment's declaration that "all persons born or naturalized in the United States . . . are citizens of the United States" was designed to invalidate the Court's claim in *Dred Scott v. Sandford* that African Americans cannot be U.S. citizens. After repeated failures to persuade the Supreme Court that the Constitution does not forbid an income tax, Congress sent to the states the Sixteenth Amendment legalizing the personal income tax once and for all. The states ratified it in 1913.

The historical rarity of congressional attempts to amend the Constitution does not mean they are altogether irrelevant to the relations between the elected branches and the judiciary. The recurrence of these attempts reminds justices that they cannot long impose a radically different interpretation of the Constitution without triggering a reaction from the elected branches. In 1937 President Roosevelt lost the Court-packing battle but won the war in preventing the Supreme Court from overturning any more of his New Deal economic recovery policies. The conservatives on the Court confronted the stark reality of the superior authority of the elected branches, and so they nimbly began undoing precedents they had asserted only a few years before. Shortly thereafter, the Four Horsemen—the apocalyptic nickname given to the conservative justices who voted in unison against Roosevelt's policies—left the bench and were replaced by justices sympathetic to New Deal economic policies.

Legislative responses to disagreeable Supreme Court interpretations to public laws are, by contrast, straightforward and routine. One study found that from 1967 through 1990 Congress averaged a dozen new laws a year explicitly designed to reverse or modify a federal court ruling. Moreover, about half of all Supreme Court decisions that involved interpretation of federal law became the specific subject of congressional hearings. And another study found that from 1954 through 1990 Congress passed new laws to reverse 41 of 569 Supreme Court decisions voiding state or federal laws in some way.[34]

One area in which congressional oversight has been especially rigorous is civil rights. In 1980 the Supreme Court ruled on violations of the 1965 Voting Rights Act. To obtain a ruling on whether the electoral rules diluted the political impact of a racial minority, the plaintiff had to demonstrate that the laws not only had an adverse "effect" but also were enacted with the "intent" to discriminate.[35] Because some of the local laws in question had been on the statute books for a half-century or more, proving intent was sometimes impossible. In 1982, when Congress renewed the Voting Rights Act for another seven years, it added language stating that plaintiffs need only demonstrate vote dilution—such as shifting from district to at large elections and gerrymandering (see chapter 6)—to challenge local electoral laws. In 1991, with the enactment of new civil rights laws, Congress overrode nine Supreme Court decisions.

Department of Justice

The Department of Justice assumes primary law enforcement responsibilities for the federal government, and houses many well-known agencies such as the Federal Bureau of Investigation, the Drug Enforcement Administration, and the Bureau of Alcohol, Tobacco, Firearms and Explosives. In addition, the Department of Justice is by far the most frequent and most important litigant in the federal court system, where it is the primary representative of the federal government. Indeed, the structure of the department parallels that of the federal courts, giving it the power (and efficiency) to press for legal action at all levels of the federal court system. The head of the department, the **attorney general** of the United States, can select cases and choose to file in courts where the Justice Department is most likely to win and create precedent for its legal position on an issue.

The department includes the U.S. attorneys, one for each of the ninety-four federal judicial districts. Presidential appointment and department supervision guarantee that U.S. attorneys serve as dutiful agents as they choose cases and enlist the court system to implement administration policy. In 1996, after a number of black churches had been firebombed,

President Bill Clinton announced a special effort to find and prosecute the culprits. Over the next six months, several cases were
prosecuted in federal court. Conversely, in the same year when
California passed an initiative intended to legalize the use of marijuana for medicinal purposes, the U.S. attorneys stayed clear of
prosecution, despite the Justice Department's warning that possession of marijuana remained a federal crime. In January 1998
the Clinton administration changed its policy. It moved in federal
court to shut down the California marijuana clubs where members met to use the drug for purportedly medical purposes.[36]

These and other instances of Justice Department litigation acting as an instrument of administration policy reflect a level of
responsiveness from U.S. attorneys uncharacteristic of other government agencies. U.S. attorneys depend on the attorney general
and the White House for their job security. The capacity of these
officials to embarrass the administration by investigating and filing criminal charges and civil suits against other government officials led Franklin Roosevelt, and all of his successors, to resist
efforts to insulate U.S. attorneys with civil service protections.

Judicial Recruitment

The Constitution provides that all federal judges shall be nominated by the president with the "Advice and Consent" of the
Senate (Article II, Section 2). Traditionally, the president has
deferred on district court nominations to the preferences of
the senators from the state in which the court is located.
Appointments to the courts of appeals and Supreme Court,
however, tend to be more presidential and less collegially reliant
on the Senate's "advice" than are lower-court appointments. In
fact, judicial nominations represent the veto game in reverse (see
box "Senate Confirmation: Another Kind of Veto Game," page

By the time Attorney General Alberto Gonzales
appeared before the Senate Judiciary Committee in
July 2007 for yet another grilling, he looked haggard.
If so, he had good reason to be. The Senate's hearings
commenced five months earlier with sworn testimony
and sympathetic questioning of fired U.S. attorneys
Carol Lamm, David Iglesias, John McKay, and H. E.
"Bud" Cummins (and others). The intervening months
had produced a steady flow of damaging Senate
revelations, unflattering news coverage, and
weakening support among Senate Republicans.

426). The president nominates, and the Senate accepts or rejects. As with the legislative
veto, this shared responsibility provides politicians in these institutions with their best
chance to influence the policies flowing from the federal judiciary. Moreover, it guarantees
that the president and Senate will carefully consider the nominee's political views. From the
earliest days of the Republic, the president and Congress have appreciated the merits of
appointing like-minded colleagues to the federal judiciary. As we saw in the opening of this
chapter, the outgoing Federalists understood this as early as the 1790s, when they stuffed as
many of their partisans as possible into this branch before vacating the presidency and
Congress. Two hundred years later, so too did George H. W. Bush and Bill Clinton, each of
whom appointed members of their own parties 90 percent of the time. As a result, the partisan division of the roster of active judges resembles that of Congress.

In picking judicial nominees, presidents and Senate sponsors also have a stake in selecting
individuals with strong professional credentials. Most nominees, for example, are practicing

attorneys or sitting judges. Other things being equal, quality appointees will more effectively represent the president's views on the high bench. Moreover, less-than-stellar résumés may open the way for senatorial and other opponents who can claim to disapprove of the nominee not because they disagree with his or her views but because of a desire to appoint only the best-qualified candidates with impeccable records. In early 1970 Nixon selected G. Harrold Carswell. Senate Democrats successfully attacked Carswell's lackluster career in his state's court system. There should be room for mediocre justices, argued Sen. Roman Hruska of Nebraska, Carswell's exasperated Republican supporter, because "all Americans, even the mediocre members of society, deserve to be represented" on the Court. But this argument failed to persuade the majority of the Senate. In 2005 President George W. Bush's Supreme Court nominee, Harriet Miers, knew she was in trouble when both liberal Democrats and conservative Republicans found some of her positions on issues troubling. Within a month of careful scrutiny her intellectual credentials and experience for the position had been effectively impugned, and the president withdrew her nomination.

PRESIDENTIAL APPOINTMENTS. Historically, nominations to the district courts have concerned the senators from the state where the court is located more than the president. Consequently, modern presidents delegate the task to those senators in a practice known as **senatorial courtesy**—one of the last vestiges of the patronage era of American politics. Because the courtesy of such appointment power is extended only to senators of the president's party, this practice largely explains why every administration's nominations are so heavily skewed in favor of judges from that party.

Presidents traditionally have taken greater personal interest and enjoyed more discretion in filling vacancies to the appeals courts. Senatorial courtesy has never formally applied to these appointments, probably reflecting the greater policy importance of these judges as well as the impracticality of vetting a nominee with all of the senators from those states encompassed by the court. Nine western states, for example, fall within the jurisdiction of the Ninth Circuit Court of Appeals.[37] Presidents have generally relied on the Department of Justice to screen candidates for the courts of appeals.

Nominees to the Supreme Court, the highest federal tribunal, receive the full attention of the president, the Senate, and the many constituencies whose interests are affected by judicial decisions. A president's impact on the composition of the Court depends on the frequency with which vacancies arise—something over which the president typically has no influence. But vacancies do occur, and every recent president, except Jimmy Carter, has had via appointments to Supreme Court vacancies (see Table 9-3) an opportunity to shape the future direction of judicial policy.

When a vacancy occurs at any level of the federal judiciary, the president enlists several criteria in choosing a nominee. Understandably, in appointing an individual to

TABLE 9-3

Number of Supreme Court Appointments Available to Recent Presidents

President	Number of Supreme Court Appointments
Kennedy (Dem., 1961–1963)	2
Johnson (Dem., 1963–1969)	2
Nixon (Rep., 1969–1974)	4
Ford (Rep., 1974–1977)	1
Carter (Dem., 1977–1981)	0
Reagan (Rep., 1981–1989)	3
Bush, G. H. W. (Rep., 1989–1993)	2
Clinton (Dem., 1993–2001)	2
Bush, G. W. (Rep., 2001–2009)	2
Obama (Dem., 2009–2010)	2

a lifetime position of such importance, presidents try to guess how the nominee will vote on the controversial issues of the day—especially those that concern the president's supporters. Yet predicting a future justice's votes has at times proved to be a highly unreliable science. One never knows how the particulars of a case will affect a justice's thinking. Also, suddenly insulated from political pressure, elected officeholders who join the Court may shed political positions that had more to do with their roles as representatives than with their sincere preferences.

One way of reducing uncertainty is to select nominees from the president's party—and, in fact, more than 90 percent of all nominees to the Supreme Court have shared the president's party affiliation. Another is to interview potential nominees carefully and subject their work to intensive examination. Sandra Day O'Connor, for example, was interviewed twice by administration officials and once by President Reagan before he announced her nomination to the Supreme Court.

Presidents also may regard a vacancy as an opportunity to reward a political ally or personal associate. President Franklin Roosevelt appointed Alabama senator Hugo Black to the Court in recognition of Black's strong support for the New Deal and the Court-packing plan. Few anticipated that this Alabama politician, who had once belonged to the Ku Klux Klan, would become one of the Supreme Court's most ardent civil libertarians. But perhaps the most famous example of all of a justice surprising the appointing president occurred in President Dwight Eisenhower's nomination of Earl Warren, the governor of California, to serve as chief justice, reportedly as a reward for the crucial support Warren's delegation provided for Eisenhower's nomination at the 1952 Republican convention. Eisenhower later regretted his choice of Warren as well as that of another justice, William Brennan, who along with Warren proved too activist and liberal for Eisenhower's taste. Asked if he had made any

Obama with Elena Kagan, and then with Sonia Sotomayor. Obama appointed both Elena Kagan and Sonia Sotomayor to the U.S. Supreme Court. Sotomayor was the first Hispanic woman appointed to the Court.

SENATE CONFIRMATION
Another Kind of Veto Game

Under the Constitution the president nominates candidates to the federal judiciary, and the Senate confirms or rejects them. This sequence reverses the veto game described in Chapter 7 in which Congress proposes legislation and the president either endorses or vetoes it. In this game it is the Senate that confronts a "take it or leave it" decision that limits its opportunity to shape the result. When the White House and Senate are controlled by the same political party, the two sides cooperate informally to identify candidates both can support. As a consequence, nominees rarely encounter difficulty or delay in confirmation. Under divided government, however, the opposition party's rejection of the president's candidates—either outright or by inaction—has become increasingly commonplace as the Senate has tried to insinuate its preferences into judicial nominations. How, then, can compromise occur when divided government threatens to stall the nomination process?

President Bill Clinton's dealings with the Republican Senate demonstrated two possible solutions. Clinton accommodated the Senate by nominating moderate judges whose views were acceptable to its conservative majority. An alternative solution was to assemble a "package" of nominees that would allow Republicans to identify some appointments in exchange for confirmations of others. President Clinton had been reluctant to do this, however, largely because Republicans wanted conservative jurists, who were bound to stir up heated opposition from some of Clinton's core constituencies.

Nonetheless, in 1999 Sen. Orrin Hatch, R-Utah, chair of the Senate Judiciary Committee, persuaded the president to negotiate such a deal. Entering mid-June with seventy-two vacancies in the federal judiciary and forty-two Clinton nominations awaiting Senate action, Hatch's committee had yet to conduct its first confirmation hearing for 1999. In the meantime, Hatch was promoting Republican Ted Stewart, conservative head of Utah's Department of Natural Resources, for a vacancy to the federal district court in Salt Lake City. With a wink and a nod, Hatch suggested that were Clinton to nominate Stewart, the committee would go to work processing the president's pending nominees.

For nearly two months President Clinton had hesitated. If he agreed, the Senate might clear dozens of pending nominees. But then he would lose the opportunity to fill the Utah vacancy with someone who shared

mistakes as president, Eisenhower, it is widely reported, responded, "Yes, two, and they are both sitting on the Supreme Court."[38]

Presidents also may use appointments to buttress and build political alliances. Historically, an appointee's region of origin was an important criterion. More recently, presidents have focused on the religion, sex, and race of nominees in an effort to build support with constituencies who might reward having one of their own appointed to the Supreme Court. Just as Louis Brandeis broke the anti-Semitic barrier to the Court earlier in the century, Thurgood Marshall was the first African American on the Court, and Sandra Day O'Connor the first woman. That O'Connor was a conservative appointed by a Republican (Reagan) suggests that presidents can make these symbolic gestures to constituencies without jeopardizing their policy goals.

SENATE CONFIRMATION. Once the president has named someone to fill a judicial vacancy, the Senate Judiciary Committee schedules confirmation hearings so that it can his views on environmental policy. Worse, the president might anger environmentalists who adamantly opposed Stewart's nomination and had been publicly pressuring Clinton to reject Hatch's overture. Clearly the Stewart nomination would be costly, and the president had to be sure he would get something in return. But could he assume that Hatch would, or even could, safely usher many of his nominees to their seats on the federal bench?

The deal with Hatch represented a political minefield. How many pending nominees would Republicans allow through the committee in exchange for Stewart? Once Stewart's name was sent up, would Hatch, who had urged the president's removal during the impeachment trial earlier in the year, renege and play the president as a sucker? A successful deal required the president and Hatch to navigate around a potential prisoner's dilemma. Beyond this, Clinton had to wonder about the fate of his nominees on the Senate floor even with the committee's endorsement. Republican Senate majority leader Trent Lott already had groused that Hatch's committee had been too generous with Clinton's nominations over the years. Would Stewart sail

through confirmation while the Republican Senate (perhaps with Hatch's private complicity) refused to bring the president's nominees to a vote?

In mid-June the president decided time was running out and he had to make a move. In a phone conversation Hatch and Clinton agreed to proceed in small, cautious steps that would allow each to avoid a potential double cross. The president discreetly initiated the routine FBI check and submitted Stewart to the American Bar Association for its assessment. In return, the Senate Judiciary Committee on June 17 held its first hearing on eight of Clinton's judicial nominees. Two weeks later the deal finished up when the president announced his intent to nominate Stewart, and Hatch announced his committee's goal to clear for a Senate vote at least ten of Clinton's pending nominees.

During the 107th Congress (2001–2002) the tables were turned as Republican president George W. Bush sent judicial nominations to an unresponsive Democratic Senate. That the two sides failed to achieve a compromise of the kind just described is testament to the difficulty of solving this class of prisoner's dilemmas.

make a recommendation to the full chamber. When the same party controls the presidency and Senate, these nominations sail through the chamber with only cursory examination. But when the opposition controls the Senate, as has happened in about half of the Congresses over the past half-century, the process of scrutinizing the nominee often becomes highly political and slows to a crawl as the opposition majority becomes—to use its characterization—"highly deliberative." Although only eight Supreme Court nominees were rejected (or withdrew their doomed nominations) during the twentieth century, five of these have occurred since 1964 when Republican presidents tried to get judicial conservatives past a Senate controlled by Democrats.

Toward the end of a president's first term, the opposition-controlled Senate becomes so deliberative that nothing much happens until the senators learn the identity of the next president. In 1996, a presidential election year, the Republican Senate set a record in confirming none of President Clinton's nominees for the appellate court and only seventeen for the district court. Two years later, with the president facing possible removal from office, the Senate confirmation process halted once more. In fact, not until mid-June 1999 did Senate confirmation hearings resume, and then only after President Clinton and Senate Judiciary Committee Republicans cut a political deal. In the past, the election of a new president normally has thawed the freeze on Senate confirmations, but perhaps as retribution for the Republican majority's treatment of Clinton, George W. Bush's nominations mostly languished during his first term. Politically, the cadre of chronically pending appointments festered party divisions as interest groups mobilized their force for and against Clinton's and then Bush's nominees. With the increased number of Republican senators after the 2004 election, the issue came to a head. In danger of losing any opportunity to filibuster objectionable nominations, the Democrats in the Senate agreed to let some of Bush's blocked appointees be confirmed by the Republican majority.* During the summer of 2008, with President Bush's tenure nearing an end and little prospect of confirmation by the Democratic-controlled Senate, the president submitted a single nomination to fill one of the forty-seven vacancies on the federal district and appeals courts. Even with a near filibuster-proof majority in the Senate, President Obama fared little better during his first two years. And by the middle of Obama's fourth year as president, he had *fewer* conformations and *more* vacancies compared to both Clinton and George W. Bush at the same point in their presidencies.[39] In part, Obama's paltry success in his first two years reflected the more pressing business of dealing with the recession and passing a national health care reform that dominated Senate business. But an increase in Senate seats by Republicans in 2010 meant that Republicans could use the same dilatory tactics at the end of Obama's first term that were employed by the Democrats at the end of George W. Bush's presidency. In June 2012, the Republicans invoked the "Thurmond Rule," which refers to an opposition party's decision to block further confirmations of appeals court nominees during an election year.[40] By Election Day 2012, only two of the twenty-six individuals nominated by Obama in the first half of 2012 had been confirmed, and thirty-four nominees still awaited confirmation.†

The confirmation "veto" offers an opposition-controlled Senate more influence than the generally small number of rejected nominees would indicate. Presidents, calculating the prospects of defeat of a nominee, usually forgo the battle and potential embarrassment of defeat and opt for someone whom the administration and the Senate find acceptable. Whatever the Senate's indirect influence, one can reasonably conclude that partisanship and ideology represent primary considerations in nomination and confirmation of federal judges. Because judges do in fact make policy, it is fitting that the president and Congress take their ideology into account and understandable that they would prefer judges who agree with their own political views.

TURNOVER AS THE SOURCE OF SHIFTING JUDICIAL IDEOLOGY. With few exceptions, judges appointed by Democratic presidents tend to vote in a liberal direction,

---

* As a result the number of vacancies had shrunk to forty-four by June 2005, less than half the number during the period when the opposition party controlled the Senate.

† Statistic compiled by the authors based on publicly available data from the Administrative Office of the U.S. Courts, retrieved on November 7, 2012.

and those appointed by Republican presidents tend to be conservative.[41] Consequently, when one party dominates the presidency, the cumulative impact of new appointments on the ideological complexion of judicial policy can be great. As Republicans returned to the White House in 1953 for the first time in two decades, they encountered a Supreme Court wholly appointed by Democrats Roosevelt and Truman. But by the time President Eisenhower had left office in 1961, his five appointees constituted a "Republican" majority of the membership. Since then, Republican presidents have appointed twice as many justices as Democrats. The trend toward Republican control of the White House has also shifted the Supreme Court in a distinctly more conservative direction.

Toles © 2000 The Buffalo News. Reprinted by permission of Universal Press Syndicate. All rights reserved.

A variety of evidence reveals the indirect impact of presidents on the direction of policy coming out of the judiciary. As discussed above, the justices appointed by Republican presidents Reagan and George H. W. Bush, who ushered in the "Fourth Era," had a dramatic impact on the balance of power between the federal government and state governments. In other areas of law, however, Justice Sandra Day O'Connor—a Reagan appointee—often served as the pivotal swing vote between the Court's liberal and conservative factions during the years when Rehnquist was chief justice. When she retired in 2006 and was replaced by the more conservative Samuel Alito, the median opinion of the Supreme Court shifted sharply to the right.*

Although three other new members have joined the Court since August 2005 (Chief Justice Roberts, Justice Sotomayor, and Justice Kagan), in each of those cases the new justice largely shared the same ideology as the justice he or she replaced. However, with Alito's replacement of O'Connor, a more conservative justice took the place of a less conservative one. As a result, this one replacement has caused the entire Court to shift to the right. In addition, because Alito can be counted on as an ideological conservative, Justice Anthony Kennedy has taken O'Connor's place as the swing vote in many cases. Because Justice Kennedy is more conservative than Justice O'Connor, the close decisions are now more likely to break 5–4 in the conservative direction.

One high-profile example of this conservative shift is the Court's decision in *Citizens United v. Federal Election Commission,* discussed in Chapter 5. In that 5–4 decision, the Court held that corporations cannot be prohibited from using their general treasury funds to

---

*According to some judicial scholars, Alito is one of the most conservative justices to serve on the Court in the past seventy years—ranking third behind only current justice Clarence Thomas and former chief justice William Rehnquist. Adam Liptak, "Court under Roberts Is Most Conservative in Decades," *New York Times,* July 24, 2010.

Figure 9-4 Presidential Imprint on the Federal Bench

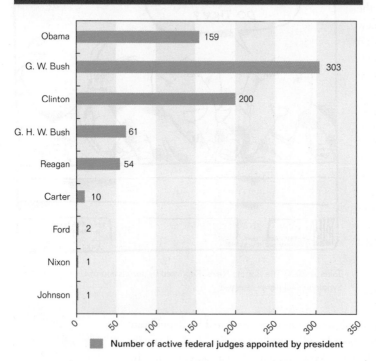

Obama — 159
G. W. Bush — 303
Clinton — 200
G. H. W. Bush — 61
Reagan — 54
Carter — 10
Ford — 2
Nixon — 1
Johnson — 1

Number of active federal judges appointed by president

Source: Personal correspondence with Alliance for Justice, November 2012.

make independent expenditures to fund political advertising for candidates and causes. But that decision—with Justice Alito in the majority—overturned a prior decision in which O'Connor voted with the majority.[*]

The effect of presidential appointment and Senate confirmation in steering the judicial branch on the same ideological course as elections move the executive and legislative branch is relatively easy to follow in the turnover of the small Supreme Court. Less evident is the fact that even appointments to the lower levels of the federal judiciary shift judicial policy in a direction favored by the elective officeholders who nominate and confirm them. Research scoring the ideological stance of federal district judges' decisions finds that even though their opinions are constrained by the appeals courts and Supreme Court above them, they still manage to favor the ideological preferences of the president who appointed them. In Figure 9-4 each set of judges appointed by a Democratic president on average scored more liberal than any set of judges appointed by a Republican president.

The presence of correlation between the ideological views of federal judges and the party of the president who appointed them should bother only naïve observers who believe there is embedded in the Constitution clear answers to the myriad of complex issues that reach the judiciary for resolution. The Framers, we found in Chapter 2, intentionally spurned comprehensive prescriptions in appreciation of their ignorance about what the future held. Keying appointments to identifiable preferences of potential nominees offers the primary mechanism for keeping the judicial branch from taking public policy in some perverse direction that elective leaders could not abide. The fact that these judges are appointed for life, however, means that at any given moment, the collective preferences of the judiciary may be significantly different from those politicians who occupy Congress and the White House. This introduces the potential for conflict between the branches, with one of them asserting that it has the last

---

[*] In addition to signaling an ideological shift, there are other reasons that *Citizens United* may be a defining decision for the Roberts Court. Although the Court enjoyed relatively high ratings from the American public for decades, its favorability rating reached a new low of 52% in April 2012 (down from 64% in April 2009—before *Citizens United*). "Supreme Court Favorability Reaches New Low," Pew Research Center for the People & the Press, May 1, 2012.

word. The insulation of judges from public opinion leads to a legitimate question: who guards the guardians?

WHO GUARDS THE GUARDIANS?

The question that arose in Chapter 5 rears its perplexing head again here: How appropriate is it that unelected, life-tenured judges can decide on the constitutionality of acts of Congress? This arrangement does violate the democratic principle of majority rule, but it met the Framers' broader concerns that they create a balanced political system in which competing interests check one another. Majorities, we saw in *Federalist* No. 10, are just as capable of exploiting their control of government to pursue their own interests and take advantage of the powerless as are kings and other unelected rulers. Through the Constitution's separation of powers and checks and balances, the Framers appear to have planned for the judiciary to be part of the Constitution's balancing act.

But does not judicial review's seemingly absolute authority violate the republican principle of balance as much as it does the democratic principle of majority rule? Who is to guard this guardian? The constitutional amendment process offers one certain way to countermand the Court's ruling of unconstitutionality, but the process is difficult and thus rarely employed. The Constitution also empowers Congress to alter the size (and therefore the ideological complexion) of the Court as well as change its jurisdiction, but these ploys have been attempted even less frequently. Perhaps the rarity with which Congress has resorted to these difficult constitutional remedies reflects its ability to achieve adequate responsiveness through easier and less controversial means.

This chapter has identified several subtle sources of limitations on the absoluteness of judicial review. To enforce its policies, the judiciary depends on the compliance of other institutions. In the face of concerted opposition—whether from school districts bent on segregation or Congress and presidents wanting to preserve a legislative veto—the Court may have a difficult time changing public policy. Moreover, Congress can effectively nullify an adverse judicial decision by writing a new public law that addresses the Court's concern or achieves the same goal in a somewhat different way. The Supreme Court may rule that Congress cannot order local sheriffs to administer federal gun control procedures, but the ruling does not prevent Congress from tying such compliance to the eligibility of states and their communities for federal grants.

On close inspection, the federal judiciary appears to lack the kinds of internal resources that would allow it to be a powerful, autonomous policymaker. The limited veto authority offered by judicial review, the huge caseload, the lack of enforcement authority, and even the life tenure of its members reveal it to be an organization ill designed to formulate and implement public policy. Finally, the fact that presidents nominate federal judges and the Senate must confirm them ensures that the judiciary will not long stray far from the mainstream of opinion. The Court's decisions, just like those emanating from the other branches, come and often go; rarely are they final. In sum, the doctrine of judicial review has worked because it does not foreclose effective responses from the other branches. This is, of course, the principle we have found throughout our inquiry to lie at the core of America's republicanism.

■ TAKE A QUIZ

logic.cqpress.com

Test your knowledge of this chapter.

Key Terms

activism, 418

amicus curiae, 414

attorney general, 422

concurring opinion, 420

constitutional courts, 406

court of appeals, 409

Court-packing plan, 402

dissenting opinion, 420

district courts, 409

judicial doctrine, 415

judicial review, 395

procedural doctrine, 415

restraint, 418

rule of four, 413

senatorial courtesy, 424

solicitor general, 415

standing, 416

stare decisis, 415

substantive doctrine, 415

writ of certiorari, 412

writ of mandamus, 396

Suggested Readings

Brest, Paul, and Sanford Levinson. *Processes of Constitutional Decisionmaking.* 3rd ed. Boston: Little, Brown, 1992. A detailed introduction to the structure and function of the federal court system emphasizing the important policymaking opportunities enjoyed by lower-court judges.

McCloskey, Robert, and Sanford Levinson, eds. *The American Supreme Court.* 2nd ed. Chicago: University of Chicago Press, 1994. A comprehensive historical account of the development of the Supreme Court as a political branch of government.

Rosenberg, Gerald N. *The Hollow Hope: Can Courts Bring about Social Change?* Chicago: University of Chicago Press, 1991. One of the few books to carefully examine the effects of Court decisions on public policy.

Toobin, Jeffrey. *The Nine: Inside the Secret World of the Supreme Court.* New York: Random House, 2007. A highly readable account of recent politics on the Supreme Court, including "insider" stories on decision making among the nine distinct personalities on the bench.

Woodward, Bob, and Scott Armstrong. *The Brethren: Inside the Supreme Court.* New York: Simon and Schuster, 1979. Not only highly readable, but generally regarded as an accurate fly-on-the-wall report of the inner workings of the Supreme Court.

Review Questions

1. How does the Supreme Court's ability to delegate tasks compare with those of the other branches?

2. Why is the judiciary regarded as the "least dangerous" branch of government?

3. What features of the Court make it appear undemocratic?

4. How does the Court enforce its decisions on lower courts? On the executive and legislative branches?

5. How do executive branch attorneys influence the Court's agenda?

10 Public Opinion

President Barack Obama signs into law the Patient Protection and Affordable Care Act in 2010.

- Do policy advocates try so hard to move public opinion because people's views are so easy to manipulate or because they are so difficult to manipulate?

- Polls often present conflicting evidence about the public's opinions on political issues. When can we believe polling results?

- How can stable and coherent public opinion arise from a population that often is uninformed about basic political facts and lacks consistent political views?

- To what extent does public opinion determine public policy?

- How accurately can we predict Americans' political views by knowing their age, race, sex, religion, or education?

During his successful 2008 campaign for the presidency, Barack Obama promised to overhaul the health care system. It was a popular promise; rising health care costs and unemployment rates were swelling the ranks of the uninsured, and most Americans seemed ready to let the federal government take responsibility for making sure that everyone had access to adequate health services. But when Obama and his Democratic allies in Congress sought to fulfill his campaign promise, they met resolute resistance from Republican minorities in the House and Senate and prevailed only after months of intense political maneuvering. As the reform package worked its way through the legislative labyrinth, it became increasingly unpopular, and by the time the President signed the bill into law, more Americans opposed it than favored it.

Did the Democratic administration, by its action, simply ignore public opinion? Or did it assume that unhappiness with its reforms rested on misinformation that would be dispelled once they were in place? Did ordinary citizens actually have meaningful opinions on the issue, or were their expressed views just the echoes of slick propaganda campaigns mounted by self-serving special interests with a financial stake in the outcome? Did Republican attacks on the administration's proposals reflect sincere policy differences, or were they designed to erode public support for reform in order to hand Obama a major political defeat? That the answer to all these questions may be yes introduces us to the crucial but complicated role of public opinion in American politics.

Polls published around the time of Obama's initial election in 2008 portrayed a public in which 76 percent believed the system needed fundamental changes or complete rebuilding, 63 percent described the health care system as in crisis or with major problems, 84 percent thought the risk of losing a job and thus health insurance was a serious problem, and 55 percent worried about not being able to afford health care. Majorities also seemed to support a greatly expanded government role in health care: 54 percent agreed that "it is the responsibility of the federal government to make sure all Americans have healthcare insurance," 51 percent said they favored "the government paying for all necessary medical care for all Americans" (36 percent were opposed), and 62 percent favored "the U.S. government guaranteeing health insurance for all citizens, even if it meant raising taxes."[1]

So the public was ready for a major overhaul along the lines of the Obama administration's proposal, which through a complex mix of federal rules, mandates, subsidies, taxes, and new administrative mechanisms would expand coverage to almost all Americans? Not exactly: on average, in eighty-five surveys taken between July 2009 and the bill's passage on March 23, 2010, 47 percent opposed Obama's plan, while only 40 percent favored it.[2] Most of the separate parts making up the complicated legislative package were popular: majorities favored requiring insurance companies to cover preexisting conditions and to continue to cover people who become sick, providing subsidies so that poor families can buy insurance, raising taxes on high-income families, and requiring employers to provide health insurance to workers, with subsidies for small businesses. The broad goal of universal coverage also enjoyed widespread support. However, most people opposed placing new limits on Medicare reimbursements and requiring everyone to buy health insurance (to prevent free riders who would not buy insurance until they were sick or injured) and enforcing this requirement through fines.

Despite supporting the majority of its parts, most people did not see the whole package of changes as improving their own health care coverage, even if they believed it would improve the health care delivery system more generally. Moreover, most Americans thought the reforms would increase health care costs and taxes, add to the federal deficit, and hurt the economy.[3] Many were also worried about greater government involvement in the health care system; in a survey taken shortly after it became law, 65 percent thought the health care bill "will expand the government's role in the health care system too much." Nonetheless, in the same survey, 51 percent also thought "that it did not go far enough in regulating the health care industry," including, somewhat illogically, 47 percent of those who thought it expanded government too much.[4] More generally, large portions of the public—35 to 56 percent, depending on the specific question and survey—admitted confusion about the bill and its likely consequences, although confusion did not prevent most of them from offering an opinion on it. According to the polls, then, majorities of Americans thought there was a health care crisis but were satisfied with their own health care arrangements, favored most of the main features of Obama's reform package separately but not together, and wanted the government to guarantee health care for all but balked at giving it the authority and means to do so.

Polls were not the only source of information on public opinion, to be sure. Members of Congress received countless letters, e-mails, phone calls, and faxes from constituents. Interest groups with a major stake in the health care system—doctors, hospitals, insurance companies, labor unions, large corporations, small-business owners, drug manufacturers, AARP, and many, many more—bombarded Congress with their conflicting versions of what "the people" wanted.

As the debate heated up, interest groups spent millions of dollars on propaganda aimed at bringing people to their side, for none of the players in the politics of health care reform treated public opinion as settled. Although it is true that opinion polls taken around the time of the 2008 election found widespread support for a major overhaul of the health care system, this consensus did not guarantee public backing for any particular reform. The administration's

Republican opponents focused public attention on the costs rather than the benefits of reform and gained ground by playing on the public's skepticism that the government could do anything right. The Patient Protection and Affordable Care Act became law on March 23, 2010, without a single Republican vote for it in either chamber. Enactment did not settle the issue, which remained a major point of contention between congressional candidates in the 2010 midterm elections. In the months after enactment, the public remained almost evenly divided on the reforms, although only about 37 percent favored outright repeal rather than giving the law a chance to work or tweaking it with additional legislation.

By the last week of October 2012, well into Barack Obama's second campaign for the presidency, the number of people who favored outright repeal of the law had grown by six points to 43 percent,[5] but likely 2012 voters placed it sixth on the list of important issues facing Congress—well behind various economic and budgeting issues, Medicare, Social Security, and education.[6] The low popularity and salience of the Patient Protection and Affordable Care Act, along with the fact that President Obama's opponent in 2012, Mitt Romney, enacted a similar plan in Massachusetts as governor, meant that there was very little discussion of health care reform during the 2012 general election campaign. The issue, however, *was* a focal point of the Republican nominating contest in the winter of 2012—as Michele Bachmann, Herman Cain, Newt Gingrich, and Rick Santorum all pledged to repeal "Obamacare" (their name for the Patient Protection and Affordable Care Act) on "day one" in the Oval Office. Rick Perry, who also ran for the GOP nomination, went so far as to refuse to implement parts of the policy as governor of Texas. He stated his reasons in a letter to the Obama administration in which he called the legislation a "power grab" by the federal government that would find "no foothold" in Texas. Perry had done his homework—public opinion on whether it is the responsibility of the federal government to see to it that everyone has health insurance is widely divided by party identification. Only 12 percent of Republicans think this responsibility lies with the federal government while 67 percent of Democrats think so. Interestingly, independents split relatively evenly, with 41 percent agreeing with the Democratic position and 48 percent siding with the Republicans.

Because the act's various provisions kick in at different times and it will not take full effect until 2018, public attitudes are sure to continue to be in flux until people's own experiences, rather than the biased projections of partisan supporters and opponents, come to inform their opinions. As we will see later in this chapter, public opinion tends to move in response to real conditions rather predictably.

READ MORE

logic.cqpress.com
Rick Perry's letter to Kathleen Sebelius.

WHAT IS PUBLIC OPINION?

The effort that went into probing (through countless polls) and shaping (through public statements and advertising campaigns) opinion during the political battles over health care reform attests to the importance of public opinion's role in American politics. To understand this role, we must first consider an elementary question: What is public opinion? The simplest definition, proposed more than fifty years ago by the eminent political scientist V. O. Key Jr., is that **public opinion** consists of "those opinions held by private persons which governments find it prudent to heed."[7] According to this definition, every government, democratic or otherwise, has to pay attention to public opinion in some fashion. Democracies differ from other forms of government in terms of which private persons governments find it prudent to heed (potential voters and those who can sway potential voters) and the main reason it is prudent to do so (an election is coming). In the United States basic constitutional guarantees—regular elections, broad suffrage, freedom of speech and press, freedom to form and join political organizations—allow citizens to express their views freely and compel government leaders to take the public's opinions into account if they want to keep their jobs. These guarantees also make it both possible and essential for political leaders and policy advocates to try to shape and mobilize public opinion on behalf of their causes.

The origins of these guarantees predate the Constitution, and American public opinion has from the beginning been treated as a political force to be alternatively shaped, mollified, or exploited. The object of the *Federalist* was to sway educated public opinion in favor of the Constitution, but national ratification was secured only when its proponents bowed to the widespread public demand that a bill of rights be added (see Chapter 2). In the first years of the Republic, leaders of the nascent parties quickly established newspapers to promote themselves and their policy proposals and to attack the ideas and character of their opponents.

Effects of the Fugitive-Slave-Law.

An artist's passionate denunciation of the Fugitive Slave Law shows four black men being shot down by a white posse, with captions citing *Deuteronomy* ("Thou shalt not deliver unto the master his servant which has escaped from his master unto thee") and the Declaration of Independence ("We hold that all men are created equal") to underline the evil and injustice of the law and the "institution" it was designed to sustain.

The highly partisan press they created continued to give form and voice to public opinion throughout the nineteenth century. Ever mindful of the public's concerns, ambitious politicians routinely sought to squeeze political advantage from whatever issue excited the people, be it hysteria about the supposed machinations of secret societies, which led to brief success for the Anti-Masonic Party in the 1830s, or hostility to Irish Catholic immigrants, which did the same for the American or "Know-Nothing" Party in the 1850s (see Chapter 12).

The leaders of movements dedicated to the abolition of slavery, prohibition of alcoholic beverages, suffrage for women, and the end of the spoils system (see Chapters 8, 12, and 13) labored mightily to mold public opinion (through pamphlets, speeches, demonstrations, sermons, editorials, magazines, novels, and plays) and then to serve as agents for its political expression. Any incident that inflamed public sentiment was fair game for exploitation. Enforcement of the Fugitive Slave Law, for example, led to incidents that regularly outraged northern communities, helping abolitionists to win converts and silence opponents. Then, as now, interest group entrepreneurs sought to mobilize public opinion as a weapon in the policy wars, threatening electoral retaliation against leaders who refused to support their cause.

Modern efforts to measure, shape, and exploit public opinion have spawned two linked industries: scientific polling and public relations. The first is devoted to sounding out the public on an endless array of issues, and the other to marketing ideas, policies, and politicians. Before the advent of scientific polling, politicians gauged public opinion haphazardly, relying on information supplied by editorials, pamphleteers, local leaders, spokespersons for social causes, party activists, and sometimes even less conventional sources. According to one member of Congress who served in the 1930s, "This might sound odd, but myself and many other members of Congress that I knew, used to get a lot of ideas on how the general public felt by reading the walls in bathrooms in towns and cities that we were in."[8] Self-selected, perhaps angry, with axes to grind, such sources were of doubtful reliability. Even open expressions of public sentiments, such as marches, rallies, and riots, could not be taken at face value because they said nothing about the views of the majority who had stayed home. Not until well into the twentieth century was **scientific polling** developed as a tool for systematically investigating the opinions of ordinary people.

MEASURING PUBLIC OPINION

The basic techniques developed to measure public opinion accurately are simple in concept but often difficult to carry out in practice: select a random sample of the population of interest, ask the people in the sample some appropriate questions about their views, and count up their answers. The larger the sample, the more closely the sample's answers will approximate the answers the pollster would get if the entire population could be asked. As the sample gets larger, however, the rate of improvement in accuracy declines; it makes little sense to use a sample size larger than 1,200–1,500 people unless the outcomes of interest are divided by extremely small margins close to 50 percent. With numbers in the 1,200–1,500 range, researchers can be confident that, nineteen times out of twenty (95 percent of the time), the sample's division on a typical question will fall within 3 percentage points of the entire population's division. This is called the poll's margin of error, the maximum of which can be quickly approximated by dividing 1 by the square root of the total number of people in the sample. For example, if 45 percent of the respondents in a poll of 1,500 people say they approve of the president's job performance, chances are nineteen in twenty that the interval from 42 to 48 percent (45 percent plus or minus 3 points) covers the actual level of approval throughout the whole U.S. population. In order to reduce that interval to plus or minus 2 percentage points on either side of the sample estimate, a researcher would have to bear the cost of interviewing 1,000 more people—an increase of two-thirds the sample size to get a reduction of one-third in the margin of error. Strange as it may seem, a sample of 1,500 mirrors a population of 250 million just as accurately as it would a population of 10,000. Notice that the approximate formula for the margin of error does not require knowledge of the size of the entire population; it requires only the size of the sample.

A truly random sample of any population is rarely feasible, however, because there is no single directory where everyone is conveniently listed and so can be given a perfectly equal chance of being selected, which is what strict random sampling requires. Even as telephone landlines are vanishing from the population, most commercial polls are conducted over the phone using random-digit dialing, so they do not reach the 2 percent of the population without telephones of any kind, and if they are only dialing landline exchanges, they do not reach roughly a third of the population that has only wireless phone services.[9] For example, the National Health Interview Survey conducted by the Centers for Disease Control and Prevention estimates that nearly six in ten adults between the ages of twenty-five and twenty-nine live in a cell phone–only household. The comparable share of senior citizens is 8.5 percent. Adults in mobile-only households also tend to rent their home/apartment as opposed to owning, live outside the Northeast, live at or near poverty levels, and be of Hispanic ethnicity. These characteristics are likely to be correlated with political attitudes, which means missing these people systematically may yield a survey with biased results.

Even for sampling methods that cover the entire population of interest, not everyone selected is willing to answer questions, and people who refuse differ systematically from the people who answer the pollster's questions (on average, refusers have less money, education, and political knowledge—also things that correlate with political attitudes). Methods have been developed to adjust for these problems—most often, weighting the responses of people in underrepresented demographic categories more heavily than the responses of those in overrepresented categories—but they work imperfectly, so no poll is completely free of the biases they introduce.

Another potential problem with interpreting polls lies in the questions, which respondents may not always understand or may answer incorrectly—by, for example, offering an instant opinion on an issue they have never thought about before. Even the most carefully designed question is subject to some measurement error because the fit between the words and concepts used in questions and how people actually think about issues is never perfect. Properly conducted polls with well-designed questions are nonetheless far less subject to distortion than any other method of measuring public opinion (see box "Straw Polls," which describes some pitfalls of alternative techniques for measuring public opinion).

From modest beginnings in the 1930s, opinion polling has grown into a vast industry producing an endless stream of information about the public's views on almost any conceivable matter. Every president since Jimmy Carter (1977–1981) has had an in-house pollster taking regular readings of the public's pulse. George W. Bush, who claimed to disdain polls,

Straw Polls

Newspapers and magazines had taken "straw polls" for a hundred years before the advent of scientific polling. The term refers to tossing straws in the air to see which way the wind is blowing. The *Harrisburg Pennsylvanian* sponsored the first known newspaper poll in 1824, correctly predicting that Andrew Jackson would win the popular vote in the presidential election. The polling techniques varied, but all allowed respondents to select themselves to be participants in the poll. Sometimes readers were invited to clip facsimile ballots from the paper, fill them out, and send them in, or they were mailed postcards that they were asked to complete and return.

The *Literary Digest*, a popular magazine, had used the postcard method successfully to forecast the presidential winner in every election from 1920 to 1932. In 1936 it again sent out ten million postcard ballots to names and addresses taken from telephone books, voter registration lists, club rosters, and lists of automobile owners and mail-order customers. The returned cards split 57 percent for Alf Landon, the Republican candidate, to 43 percent for Franklin Roosevelt, the Democratic president running for a second term. On Election Day Roosevelt defeated Landon, 62 percent to 38 percent, winning every state but Maine and Vermont.

How did the *Literary Digest* get it so wrong? First, its sample was badly biased for an election that, unlike the previous contests, divided the electorate strongly along economic lines. During the Great Depression, telephones and cars were luxuries that many Americans could not afford; those who could afford them were far more likely to favor Landon and the Republican Party. Second, the respondents selected themselves. Only 22 percent of those who were sent the postcard ballot responded. The kinds of people who respond to mail surveys are not typical; they tend to have more education, more money, and more ardent political views. Finally, the postcards were sent out too early (September) to pick up any late-breaking trends. Meanwhile, the fledgling Gallup poll, following more sophisticated sampling principles based on the science of probability (and drawing on a much smaller sample), accurately predicted Roosevelt's landslide victory.

Modern professional polls mainly avoid the pitfalls of straw polling, but the resort to nonscientific sampling is still common. The White House reports mail counts ("the mail is running 5 to 1 in favor of the president's position"); members of Congress claim to know the public mind from responses to questionnaires inserted into their newsletters. But not all nonrandom sampling is nonscientific. As response rates to traditional phone polls drop into single digits and the Internet and mobile platforms continue to replace existing modes of communication, new methods are developing that use the science of statistics to construct samples that *represent* the population without being *randomly drawn* from the population.

nonetheless maintained access to an estimated $1 million worth of public opinion research annually.[10] Barack Obama, described by his press secretary as "way too busy to sit around looking at polls," had access to more than $4 million in polling services via the Democratic National Committee during his first eighteen months in office.[11] And in the 2012 presidential election, the two major party candidates spent $39.7 million on polling services—with the Obama campaign outspending the Romney campaign on polling by three to one. Even a candidate or leader who has no intention of yielding to public opinion needs to learn about what people are thinking in order to understand them and persuade them to follow.

Efforts to shape and channel public opinion have grown apace. As presidents have become more reliant on grassroots public support for winning policy battles, the line between campaigning and governing has blurred. Early in 1997, when campaign-weary news reporters asked Clinton's press secretary why the president maintained such a heavy travel schedule even after winning reelection, he replied, "Campaigns are about framing a choice for the American people. . . . When you are responsible for governing you have to use the same tools of public persuasion to advance your program, to build public support for the direction you are attempting to lead."[12] George W. Bush followed suit, crisscrossing the country to, in his words, "gin up support" for his ten-year, $1.6 trillion tax cut in 2001 and repeating this tactic in 2005 in an unsuccessful attempt to rally a skeptical public behind his proposal to privatize part of Social Security. Barack Obama did the same in an unsuccessful campaign to boost public support for his health care proposals.

The president has no monopoly on the "tools of public persuasion." Virtually all large modern institutions—government agencies, political parties, corporations, universities, foundations, religious bodies, and so on—employ public relations specialists whose job is to present the organization in the best possible light. Interest and advocacy groups of all kinds issue reports and exposés, publish newsletters and magazines, jostle for space on the op-ed pages of newspapers, and promote their causes through ads in the mass media. Groups both opposing and supporting Bush's proposed changes in Social Security sought to sway the public to their side with expensive mass advertising campaigns, as did rival interests competing to shape or prevent Obama's health care legislation.

Institutions also promote the *expression* of public opinion. Pollsters articulate public opinion by the very process of measuring it. A 1997 survey on issues raised by the threat of global warming discovered that 60 percent of Americans were apparently willing to pay an additional twenty-five cents per gallon for gasoline to reduce hydrocarbon emissions, a level of support that came as a surprise to people on both sides of the policy debates.[13] Policy advocates routinely take polls hoping to demonstrate that the people are on their side, and they do not always resist the temptation to choose questions that will elicit the "right" responses, a subject discussed later in the chapter. Organized efforts to mobilize citizens to write, call, protest, or otherwise express their views to political leaders also are common. The banking industry, for example, got many of its customers to protest vigorously when in 1998 the Federal Deposit Insurance Corporation (FDIC) proposed a regulation requiring banks to monitor their customers' transactions and report to federal agents any activity that might indicate money laundering. More than two hundred thousand comments arrived by e-mail, virtually all of them opposing the regulation, and the FDIC quickly backed down.[14] Firms specializing in organizing or, according to their critics, counterfeiting outpourings of "grassroots" sentiment are now available for hire by anyone.

Modern techniques for molding or measuring public opinion have contributed to the nationalization of American politics. Earlier strategies for gauging and shaping opinion depended on institutions such as newspapers and party organizations whose primary focus was local. The relevant publics were those of specific cities, towns, counties, and, to a lesser extent, states; national opinion emerged only as an aggregate of diversely measured local opinions. The advent of scientific polling has made it possible to measure and therefore to treat public opinion as a national phenomenon. National polls probe issues of national concern, raising their visibility in the minds of politicians, the news media, and the public alike. Organized efforts to shape public opinion have taken on national dimensions as well. To be sure, politicians who hold their jobs by the grace of local electorates maintain an abiding interest in local opinion (ask any member of Congress), but the institutional forces that shape local opinion have themselves become national in scope.

Finally, albeit unintentionally, the work to measure and shape public opinion has helped individual citizens to act collectively. Individual expressions of opinion to influence public policy are subject to the standard free-rider problem, because it is exceedingly unlikely that any single person's message will make a difference. But polls and mobilization campaigns can produce collective expressions of opinion that politicians ignore at their peril. And for most people, participation in a quick poll is relatively cost-free, especially as survey research firms figure out how to let people take polls on their mobile phones and computers while preserving the scientific properties of the sample.

THE ORIGINS OF PUBLIC OPINION

Public opinion attracts all this attention because of its effect on political behavior, most notably voting, which is the main, sometimes the only, political act of the great majority of ordinary citizens. Like the vote, public opinion has its political effect as an aggregate phenomenon, but also like the vote, it is no more than the sum of its individual parts. To make sense of public opinion, we need to understand the basis of individual opinions.

Attitudes

Where do the individual opinions that collectively constitute public opinion originate? Most scholars who study public opinion believe that expressed opinions reflect underlying attitudes. Basically, an **attitude** is "an organized and consistent manner of thinking, feeling, and reacting with regard to people, groups, social issues, or, more generally, any event in one's environment."[15] An attitude thus combines feelings, beliefs, thoughts, and predispositions to react in a certain way. For example, a person's attitude toward the Republican Party might include feelings ("I trust the Republicans"), beliefs ("the Republican Party is against high taxes"), and an inclination to answer "Republican" to a pollster's question about which party handles the economy better. When invited to state opinions or cast votes, people respond in ways that express the underlying attitudes evoked by the choices they face.

Individuals differ widely in the attitudes they bring to bear on political choices. Some people have an elaborate set of informed, organized, internally consistent attitudes that allow them to understand, evaluate, and respond to almost any political phenomenon that catches their attention. Such people are unusual, however. Most people have more loosely structured sets of political attitudes, not necessarily consistent with one another or well informed by facts and concepts. And some people's attitudes are so rudimentary that they offer little guidance in making sense of or responding to political phenomena. People also differ in how strongly they hold attitudes. Some are intensely partisan—the "rock-ribbed Republicans" and "yellow-dog Democrats" (who would vote for a yellow dog if it were a Democrat) of political lore (for further discussions of partisan attitudes, see Chapters 11 and 12). Others maintain attitudes that are far more tentative and open to modification by new information or ideas. Individuals thus vary widely in how they form opinions and make political choices, and the forces that shape public opinion work in different ways on different people.

Ideologies

Elaborately organized sets of political attitudes often take the form of political **ideologies**. In theory, ideologies promote consistency among political attitudes by connecting them to something greater, a more general principle or set of principles. In practice, ideologies often combine attitudes linked more by coalitional politics than by principle. The ideological labels commonly used in American politics are *liberal* and *conservative.* Over time, the meanings of these labels change, reflecting shifts in the clusters of issue positions adopted by rival sets of political leaders, who, like other people centrally involved in politics, routinely use ideological categories to simplify the complexities of political life.

In American politics today, **liberals** typically favor using government to reduce economic inequalities, champion the rights of disadvantaged groups such as racial minorities and women, and tolerate a more diverse range of social behaviors. They prefer a smaller defense establishment and usually are less willing to use military force in international politics. They believe that the rich should be taxed at higher rates to finance social welfare programs. **Conservatives** distrust government and have greater faith in private enterprise and free markets, but they are more willing to use government to enforce traditional moral standards. They favor a larger military and more assertive pursuit of national self-interest. Conservatives advocate lower taxes, particularly on investment income, to stimulate growth and to restrict the government's capacity to finance social welfare programs. But these two sets of attitudes are by no means the only logical ways to combine political views. For example, some people are libertarians, who prefer to minimize government regulation of both social and economic behavior and oppose any military involvement except direct defense of U.S. territory. But these two standard combinations approximate current party alliances, with most liberals in the Democratic Party and most conservatives in the Republican Party. In the December 2011 Cooperative Campaign Analysis Project's baseline survey, only 11 percent of Democrats described themselves as ideologically conservative and only 2.5 percent of Republicans called themselves liberals.

Although *liberal* and *conservative* are used constantly in public discussions of politics and are familiar to everyone active in politics, these terms do not guide the political thinking of most citizens, nor do the opinions most people express fall neatly into one ideological category or the other. When asked to place themselves on a scale from very liberal to very conservative, a little more than half the people classify themselves as liberals or conservatives; of the rest, about 23 percent locate themselves in the middle, and another 24 percent do not place themselves at all.[16] Those who do locate themselves on the scale tend to take positions on issues that are consistent with their chosen location, but a substantial minority takes positions inconsistent with it. About half the adult population can apply the terms *liberal* and *conservative* correctly to political issues and figures, but only about one in five uses these terms spontaneously to explain their own opinions on parties and candidates.[17] Ideological labels may be indispensable to politicians and pundits, but most citizens get by without them and feel no obligation to be consistently liberal or conservative.

Adopting a liberal or conservative pattern is not the only way people organize their political attitudes. Some studies suggest that a person's political attitudes reflect a small number of **core values**, such as individualism, support for equal opportunity, moral traditionalism, or opposition to big government. A favorable attitude toward Republicans might reflect the values of individualism and opposition to big government. Attitudes that arise from the same core value will be in harmony, but because most people maintain more than one, attitudes also can conflict.[18] Psychologists have found that people are uncomfortable holding inconsistent attitudes and tend to modify one attitude or the other to reduce inconsistency when they become aware of it, mitigating, in the technical jargon, cognitive dissonance. Often, however, people remain blissfully unaware of inconsistencies among their attitudes, keeping them in separate mental compartments so they are not brought to mind at the same time by political figures and events. A citizen who dislikes "big government" but favors stricter regulation to protect consumers, workers, and the environment is by no means unusual.

Partisanship

For most Americans, the political attitude that shapes opinions and organizes other political attitudes most consistently is their disposition toward the political parties. A large majority of Americans are willing to identify themselves as Republicans or Democrats and respond to political questions accordingly. Party identification is subject to varying interpretations, but they are complementary rather than mutually exclusive. The researchers who developed the concept in the 1950s viewed party identification as a psychological phenomenon. People who were willing to label themselves Democrats or Republicans identified with the party in the same way they might have identified with a region or an ethnic or religious group: "I'm a New Yorker, an Irish Catholic, and a Democrat." The party preference was, literally, an element of an individual's personal identity, either rooted in powerful personal experiences (best exemplified by the millions who became Democrats during the Great Depression) or learned, along with similar identifications, from family and neighborhood. So interpreted, identification with a party was thought to establish an enduring orientation toward the political world. Voters might defect if they had strong enough reactions to particular candidates, issues, or events that ran counter to their party identification. But once these

Families often pass on partisan identities to their children, just as they pass on religious and ethnic identities or a passion for the hometown sports teams. Usually the process is informal and unconscious, but such products as these T-shirts are available to parents who don't want to leave anything to chance.

short-term forces were no longer present, the influence of party identification would reassert itself, and they would return to their partisan moorings. For most citizens, only quite powerful and unusual experiences would inspire permanent shifts of party allegiance.[19]

Another interpretation emphasizes the practical rather than psychological aspects of party identification. People think of themselves as Democrats or Republicans because they have found, through past experience, that their party's politicians are more likely than the politicians of the other party to produce preferred results. Past experience is a more useful criterion than future promises or expectations because it is more certain. Party cues are recognized as imperfect, and people who are persuaded that a candidate of the other party would deal more effectively with their concerns vote for that candidate. If cumulative experience suggests that politicians of the preferred party are no longer predictably superior in this respect, the party preference naturally decays.[20] According to this interpretation, partisanship can change gradually in strength or direction without the psychological upheaval associated with revising one's personal identity.

But, again, these interpretations are not mutually exclusive. A party might be just a shorthand cue for some voters, but a source of personal identity for others. Cumulative practical experience with leaders and policies might well strengthen or weaken an individual's sense of psychological identification with a party. Conversely, gut feelings about the parties may simply be the brain's efficient way of storing the results of cumulative experiences, providing a shortcut to action (deciding how to vote or to evaluate political actors and events) without further cognitive effort. However interpreted, party remains for a large majority of voters a default cue: unless there is a compelling reason to do otherwise, Americans interpret political phenomena in ways that favor the preferred party. For example, after George W. Bush was finally awarded Florida's electoral votes and thus the presidency in December 2000, 85 percent of self-identified Republicans thought that he had won fair and square, 11 percent that he had won on a technicality, and 3 percent that he had stolen the election. However, among self-identified Democrats, only 18 percent thought that he had won fair and square, 49 percent that he had won on a technicality, and 31 percent that he had stolen the election.[21] Reactions to Bill Clinton's impeachment in 1998 also were sharply partisan: nearly two-thirds of self-identified Republicans wanted him impeached and convicted, while about 85 percent of Democrats did not.[22]

Such partisan discrepancies are not exceptional; indeed, responses to political actors and events have become increasingly polarized along party lines over the past thirty years. Reactions to George W. Bush and Barack Obama are illustrative. Bush entered the White House in 2001 with the widest partisan difference in job approval of any newly elected president since polling began more than fifty years ago (in no small part because of the partisan battles over the Florida vote count). Democrats rallied to his side in the upsurge of national solidarity inspired by the terrorist attacks of September 11, 2001 (see Figure 10-1), but the gap soon began to widen again. Among Republicans, Bush's approval rating stayed very high, while among Democrats it began a steady decline, briefly interrupted by reactions to the successful military phase of the Iraq War in April 2003 and the capture of Saddam Hussein in December 2003. By the fall of 2004, the gap between the parties' identifiers had widened to an average of more than seventy-nine percentage points, an all-time high. Similar differences appeared in the distribution of responses to questions on almost anything having to do with the Bush administration and its policies. Partisan reactions to Barack Obama have been almost as polarized, but with the party positions switched. His signal policy initiative, health care reform, drew support from an average of 71 percent of Democrats but only 12 percent of Republicans.[23] In his first year in office, an average of 88 percent of Democrats and only 23 percent of Republicans approved of his performance. The 65-point spread is the largest of any president's first term—and evaluations of Obama only became more polarized as his term played out.[24]

Party identification, like other attitudes, affects beliefs as well as opinions. Attitudes introduce bias into perceptions and interpretations of political information because people tend

Figure 10-1   Partisan Attitudes Strongly Influenced Evaluations of Presidential Performance

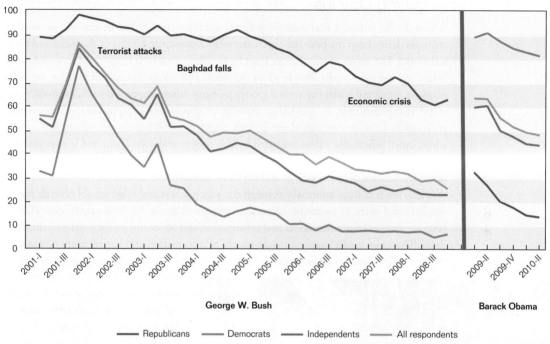

Percentage approving (quarterly averages)

George W. Bush   Barack Obama

———— Republicans   ———— Democrats   ———— Independents   ———— All respondents

Sources: CBS News/*New York Times* and Gallup polls.

to pay more attention and give more credence to sources and information that confirm rather than challenge their beliefs. For example, a 2004 study found that Republicans outnumbered Democrats in conservative radio commentator Rush Limbaugh's audience more than seven to one, while Democrats outnumbered Republicans among viewers of Michael Moore's anti–George W. Bush documentary *Fahrenheit 9/11* by more than five to one.[25] And although postwar searches of Iraq turned up neither weapons of mass destruction (WMDs) nor evidence that Saddam Hussein had been involved in terrorist attacks against the United States, millions of Americans continued to believe the contrary because it neatly fit their view of the dictator. Not surprisingly, Republicans, backing the war and the Bush administration, were much more likely than Democrats to express these beliefs.* Similarly, people with negative opinions of Barack Obama were much more likely than others to believe the thoroughly discredited claim that he was foreign born and thus ineligible to be president (still today about 30 percent of Republicans say he is foreign born).[26] In general, the more ambiguous

---

*An April 2004 CBS News/*New York Times* poll found that 73 percent of Republicans, but only 33 percent of Democrats, believed Iraq had possessed WMDs; a June 2004 poll from the same source found that 52 percent of Republicans, compared to 33 percent of Democrats, thought Saddam Hussein had been personally involved in the September 11, 2001, attacks. See http://pollingreport.com/iraq.htm.

the situation, the more prior attitudes such as party identification shape beliefs; the Florida vote count is a classic example, for to this day no one can conclusively say who really won.

Acquiring Opinions

Where do the attitudes that underlie political opinions come from? In one way or another, attitudes derive from the practical experience of growing up and living in the social and political world. The menu of possibilities is set by families, schools, friends, opinion leaders of all kinds, and the mass media. People adopt the values and beliefs that pay off in some way—for example, confirming identity with a group, pleasing others important to them, making the world comprehensible, or validating material or psychological aspirations. Children who grow up in families that talk about politics adopt political beliefs and values, just as they adopt other beliefs and values imparted by the people who raise them and whose approval they value. Schools reward the learning of political knowledge and values through the study of the Declaration of Independence and the Constitution or the conduct of classroom elections; they also teach politics informally through the way teachers and other school officials resolve conflicts and exercise authority. Later, peer groups—friends, fellow students, coworkers—become sources of political ideas and information and of incentives for paying attention to them. The news media supply a steady stream of information and commentary designed to shape people's thinking about politics. And even entertainment programming about politics (Aaron Sorkin's *The West Wing* or *The Newsroom*) can convey political ideas to unsuspecting viewers. Books, movies, and television shows impart political values in ways that engage people's emotions as well as their intellects. Movie offerings run the gamut from the classic and idealistic *Mr. Smith Goes to Washington* and *All the President's Men* to the more cynical *JFK* and *Primary Colors*. **Political socialization**, as the process of acquiring political attitudes is known, takes place during childhood and young adulthood, but new experiences can alter attitudes at any stage of life. People who are out of work for the first time, or run the bureaucratic maze of paperwork and regulations necessary to start a small business, or see how much the government takes out of their first paycheck, or try to keep a toxic waste incinerator out of their neighborhood may well revise their

In 2012, the HBO television network premiered Aaron Sorkin's latest series *The Newsroom* about a fictional cable news network, Atlantis Cable News. The show is unique among political dramas in that its story lines center on real political events from the not-so-distant past. The 2013 season, for example, contains an episode on how the Atlantis team, led by anchor Will McAvoy (played by Jeff Daniels), covers the 2012 presidential election. The show celebrates the cast's work ethic and patriotism in the face of corporate and commercial pressures that constrain their ability to report the news as they would like to present it to their audience.

attitudes toward government and politics in light of their new experiences. When political attitudes do not "work," when they no longer seem to give adequate guidance for understanding and acting, we change them.

Although attitudes are certainly influenced by personal experiences, they are by no means dominated by them. For example, most people base evaluations of the president's economic performance on their beliefs about the national economy, not on their own family's economic fortunes. Large majorities say the health care system is in crisis even though their own medical arrangements are satisfactory. The perception that public schools are failing or crime is rampant creates a potent political issue even when most people are satisfied with their own local schools or feel safe in their neighborhoods. Indeed, when people rely solely on their own circumstances to make

After nearly five decades away from their country, Cuban exiles have never forgotten their homeland or abandoned public rallies as a means of reminding the American public and politicians of their cause. Here, they toss a giant sculpture of Fidel Castro's head into a garbage truck in a mock burial ceremony held in 2006. The sculpture was originally intended for display in New York's Central Park, but the Miami Cubans convinced the artist who created it to let them destroy it instead.

political judgments, it often is because they are unaware of what is happening more broadly and so have no other information to go on. Because politics is primarily about the provision of collective goods, and ordinary citizens can achieve political ends only through collective action, it is logical that political opinions would reflect attitudes arising more from collective than from personal experiences. For example, people can be unemployed for any number of reasons, but whatever the reason, their economic future is brighter when unemployment stands at 5 percent rather than 10 percent, and it therefore makes sense to use national rather than personal unemployment to judge the president's management of the economy.

Widely shared experiences give rise to the political ideas and opinions that are advanced by the various agents of political socialization. The experiences of slavery, segregation, and continuing racial prejudice have given many African Americans a view of politics that leads them to express greater support for government programs aimed at integrating schools, workplaces, and neighborhoods than is typical among whites. Millions of working people who were helped by Franklin Roosevelt's New Deal during the Great Depression developed an abiding loyalty to the Democratic Party. Some experiences fix political thinking for generations; it took a hundred years for white southerners to move beyond political attitudes forged in the Civil War and Reconstruction. Collective political attitudes and beliefs of this sort are grounded in experience, but not necessarily direct experience. Rather, they arise from how families, politicians, journalists, historians, storytellers, songwriters, moviemakers, and artists interpret events. Such interpretations offer socially based cues to "appropriate" attitudes for people who identify with a group but have not themselves shared its formative experiences. Conflicting attitudes arising from competing versions of experience underlie much of the diversity of political opinions both within and between social groups.

Information

Generally, people tend to develop more complex, richly informed attitudes only when the payoff is greater than the cost of doing so. Individuals raised among politically active people, or who spend more years in school where they are exposed to political concepts and information, or whose jobs put them in touch with political affairs on a regular basis, are more likely to develop elaborate and well-informed political views, because they can do so without conscious effort. Most people, however, live in social settings where political ideas, events, and personalities are far down on the list of things their families and peers talk or care about, so they have neither the opportunity nor the incentive to develop informed, sophisticated political attitudes on their own. Because people are "cognitive misers," reluctant to pay the cost of acquiring information that has no practical payoff, the opinions they express on issues often appear to be both uninformed and unstable.

Numerous polls have found the public to be surprisingly ignorant of basic political facts, concepts, and issues. A sampling of questions illustrating typical levels of public information on political matters is shown in the box "The Public's Political Knowledge." The percentages listed reveal that large majorities know some basic facts about the presidency and can identify major political figures such as the vice president and their state's governor. Smaller majorities know something about government institutions, such as the Supreme Court's authority to rule on the constitutionality of legislation or the president's power to appoint federal judges, and they understand basic political facts such as which party is more conservative. But more detailed policy questions and lower-level political figures go unnoticed by most of the public. In August 2012, the Pew Research Center asked people questions about the candidates and the presidential campaign, which had been waging for nearly a year and on which nearly a billion dollars of advertising had been spent. Among registered voters about to cast ballots in the election, only 40 percent knew that Republicans had a majority in the House of Representatives and only 39 percent knew that John Roberts was chief justice of the Supreme Court. People did a little better on characteristics of the candidates—60 percent knew that Massachusetts was the state that Romney once governed, and 75 percent correctly identified Illinois as the state Obama represented in the U.S. Senate.

The box also reveals that knowledge of political facts varies with the availability of free information about them. One source of free information on items in the list is the basic high school civics course. But people are most aware of leaders and events on the front page and the nightly television news. Less newsworthy figures and issues go largely unrecognized. The difference in recognition of Newt Gingrich (60 percent) and his successors Dennis Hastert (10 percent) and Nancy Pelosi (74 percent) during their respective terms as Speaker of the House is instructive. Although all three held the same formal position, Gingrich, as point man for the Republican "revolution" initiated in 1994, attracted far more attention from the news media than Hastert, so more people could identify him. Nancy Pelosi, celebrated as the first woman ever to serve as Speaker and a major figure (and Republican target) in health care reform politics, became even more prominent than Gingrich.

TAKE A SURVEY

logic.cqpress.com
News Quiz: It's not all about the 2012 campaign.

The Public's Political Knowledge

- 95 percent knew the length of the president's term (1989)

- 89 percent knew the meaning of veto (1989)

- 84 percent identified Dick Cheney as the vice president (2004)

- 76 percent knew the Democrats had a majority in the House of Representatives (2007)

- 75 percent knew it took a two-thirds vote to override a presidential veto (2006)

- 74 percent could identify Nancy Pelosi as Speaker of the House (2010)

- 73 percent identified the governor of their state (1989)

- 71 percent knew the Republicans are the more conservative party (2012)

- 66 percent knew whether Obama won their home state in 2008 (2012)

- 62 percent knew Tony Blair was prime minister of Great Britain (2004)

- 57 percent knew which party had a majority in the Senate (2012)

- 55 percent knew that David Petraeus was commander of U.S. forces in Afghanistan (2010)

- 52 percent knew each state has two U.S. senators (1978)

- 52 percent knew what the Fifth Amendment is (1989)

- 46 percent knew that the first ten amendments are called the Bill of Rights (1989)

- 30 percent knew that the term of a U.S. representative is two years (1978)

- 28 percent knew that John Roberts was chief justice of the Supreme Court (2010)

- 25 percent could identify both senators from their state (1989)

- 25 percent knew that the term of U.S. senators is six years (1991)

- 20 percent could name two First Amendment rights (1989)

- 19 percent knew David Cameron was prime minister of Great Britain (2010)

- 2 percent could name two Fifth Amendment rights (1989)

Sources: The 2004 and 2008 entries are from the American National Election Studies; 2006 data are from the 2006 Congressional Election Survey of the Center on Congress of Indiana University; 2007 and 2010 data are from the Pew Research Center for the People and the Press; 2012 data are from the Cooperative Campaign Analysis Project; other entries are from Michael X. Delli Carpini and Scott Keeter, *What Americans Know about Politics and Why It Matters* (New Haven, CT: Yale University Press, 1996).

Ignorance does not necessarily prevent people from expressing opinions; pollsters can get as many as one-third of the people they interview to offer opinions on entirely imaginary issues.[27] Uninformed opinions are not very stable, however. The same person asked the same question at different times may well give different answers. When a sample of citizens was asked in both January and June 1980 whether the United States should take a more cooperative or more confrontational stance toward the Soviet Union, only 45 percent gave the same answer both times, even though 30 percent would be expected to do so if they simply answered randomly both times.[28]

Answers may be affected by even ostensibly minor changes in question wording. Public support for the Iraq War, for example, varied systematically according to how polls questioned it. People asked whether the United States "had made the right decision" in going to war were consistently the most supportive, whereas those asked whether "the result was worth the cost in American lives" were consistently the least supportive. The difference averaged about ten percentage points (and more than fifteen points during 2003 and 2004, when the war was still relatively popular).[29] Similarly, in surveys taken during 2009 and 2010, on average, 60 percent of Americans said "no" when asked whether the Afghanistan war had been a mistake, 53 percent said "yes" when asked if it had been the right decision, 49 percent said it was "worth the cost," but only 45 percent said they "favored" the war.[30]

Because wording can influence responses, poll questions are sometimes formulated to elicit maximum support for the views advocated by their sponsors. But even legitimate pollsters need to be careful about how their choice of words affects results—one reason why they asked so many different questions in probing public support for the wars in Iraq and Afghanistan. Sophisticated users of polling data recognize that polls always provide a *mediated* take on public opinion and pay close attention to the details of sampling and question wording when interpreting them.

Framing

Social scientists have argued for years about whether unstable survey responses mean that many people's expressed opinions are not anchored in relevant attitudes or that survey questions are too crude to gauge attitudes accurately.[31] Although there are elements of truth in both views, the most important source of instability in a person's expressed opinions is probably **ambivalence**. Particular issues may evoke attitudes and beliefs that pull in opposite directions. When that happens, the response to a pollster's questions depends on which considerations come to mind first and seem most weighty. And that depends on the context: recent events, reference to particularly potent symbols or images (such as the mention of American lives or Saddam Hussein in questions about the Iraq War), or questions that have come earlier in the survey.

Some people might believe the poor deserve government help, but they also might detest welfare cheats. Thus these people might well respond differently if asked about their views on "government programs to help the poor" rather than "welfare programs" (see box "Public Opinion and Welfare Reform," page 466). They also might respond differently depending on whether earlier questions brought to mind hungry kids or welfare queens. Or they might respond differently depending on whether last night's TV documentary focused on homeless families or welfare scams. In other words, their responses are shaped by the considerations most recently brought to their attention because they think of them first.[32] The context frames the question, and the frame determines which attitudes govern the response.

Framing explains how both the mass media and political campaigns can affect people's expressed political opinions. The messages sent by the media and the candidates do not have to change underlying attitudes to change expressed opinions. All they have to do is frame the issue in a way that draws out one response rather than the other. For example, one experimental study found that tolerance for public rallies by the white supremacist Ku Klux Klan was significantly lower when framed by a television news story as a public order issue than when it was framed as a free speech issue.[33] Other studies have shown that the content of TV news programs affects the standards people use to evaluate presidents; people who have watched stories about a particular problem give greater weight to the president's performance on *that* problem when forming their overall evaluation of his performance.[34] Simply by covering some issues and ignoring others, the news media help

WATCH A VIDEO

logic.cqpress.com
See the
"Stretch" ad on
Mitt Romney.

FRAMING MITT ROMNEY

On August 2, 2012, Barack Obama's campaign released an ad called "Stretch." The point of "Stretch" was to continue the months-long effort to frame Mitt Romney as a wealthy venture capitalist who destroyed more jobs than he created during his time at Bain Capital. The ad asks listeners to compare themselves to Mitt Romney on two dimensions—income and taxes:

> You work hard, stretch every penny, but chances are you pay a higher tax rate than him: Mitt Romney made twenty million dollars in 2010, but paid only 14 percent in taxes—probably less than you.

> Now he has a plan that will give millionaires another tax break and raises taxes on middle-class families by up to two thousand dollars a year. Mitt Romney's middle-class tax increase: he pays less; you pay more.

How did members of the Obama campaign decide this was a productive way to frame their opponent? They looked at public opinion data during the Republican primary, when Romney's Republican challengers were using this same line of attack on Romney—and they likely noticed an interesting pattern. For example, in January 2012, a representative sample of Americans were asked how well they thought the phrase "personally wealthy" described Romney (and Obama, too). Forty-five percent said they thought the phrase described Obama "very well," but the comparable number for Romney was 72 percent. When asked how well phrases like "cares about people like me" or "cares about the wealthy" described each candidate, an interesting pattern was revealed. Half of the survey respondents thought Obama could be described as caring about people like them (41 percent thought this for Romney), and just about half thought Obama could also be seen as caring about the wealthy. But 89 percent (almost everyone!) thought the phrase "cares about the wealthy" described Romney "very" or "somewhat well." And the correlation between

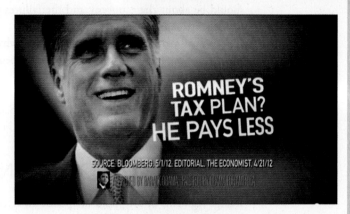

people who thought Romney was personally wealthy and those who thought he could be seen as caring about the wealthy was .6, which is quite high for items that have such lopsided distributions. The corresponding correlation for Obama was only .18. The Obama campaign saw an opening. If it continued what Romney's Republican challengers started in January, framing Romney as personally wealthy, the campaign could underscore a fundamental difference between the two candidates that benefited Obama and hurt Romney.

Once Romney became the de facto Republican nominee, the Obama campaign aired an ad called "Firms" that used a recording of Romney singing "America the Beautiful" while a voiceover announcer said Romney "had millions in a Swiss bank account and in tax havens in the Bahamas and the Cayman Islands." They continued this line of attack all through the summer. By August, and the Republican convention in Tampa, Florida, the share of people who thought the phrase "cares about people like me" described Romney somewhat or very well had dropped to 34 percent—and the gap between him and Obama on this evaluation had grown. Whether due mainly to his personal constraints and characteristics or to his opponent's relentless attacks exploiting his personal wealth, Romney had been framed as a candidate who cared about the wealthy more than the middle class—and, for most Americans, more importantly, more than "people like them."

to define the political agenda (see Chapter 1), influencing which considerations are in the foreground when citizens make political judgments; in technical terms, they **prime** their audience to use particular frames in responding to political phenomena. Election campaigns, as we see in the next chapter, set out not to change people's political views but to bring to the forefront attitudes that favor their candidates. In the 2008 presidential campaign, John McCain tried to leverage his military experiences and make national security and foreign policy important considerations because voters gave him and his party superior marks in these domains. Barack Obama sought to convince Americans that their vote should be about the economy and the failures of the Bush administration, frames that strongly favored the Democratic side.

From this perspective, we can understand why the answers to pollsters' questions about the value of the wars in Iraq and Afghanistan seem inconsistent. Different questions evoked different frames, putting different beliefs and attitudes into play. Americans responded more positively when asked about the rightness of the decision, bringing to mind U.S. intentions and perhaps the evils of Osama bin Laden and Saddam Hussein, than when reminded of the deaths of American soldiers and other costs of the wars.

IS PUBLIC OPINION MEANINGFUL?

If large segments of the public are politically ignorant, hold inconsistent views, and can be manipulated by varying the words or context of questions, how can public opinion play its assigned role in democratic politics, which is to guide and constrain elected agents? The answer is that, despite the deficiencies uncovered by survey research, public opinion continues to play a crucial and effective part in American politics because a variety of formal and informal political institutions give it shape and force. And public opinion is meaningful because, although individual opinions may be badly informed and unstable, **aggregate public opinion**—the sum of all individual opinions—is both stable and coherent.

Stability of Aggregate Public Opinion

The evidence for the stability of aggregate public opinion is impressive. When there is no obvious reason to expect significant change, the distribution of opinion tends to be highly stable. One study examined more than a thousand policy questions asked in identical form at least twice in surveys conducted between 1935 and 1990. In a majority of cases there was no appreciable change in the distribution of public responses between surveys, and nearly half of the changes that did occur were modest. On some questions, aggregate public opinion has followed a stable trend for several decades. Figure 10-2 illustrates the consistency of aggregate public opinion on whether the government is spending too little on health care. The figure shows a gentle upward trend with little year-to-year volatility from 1972 to 2008, and then, corresponding to public discourse about the Patient Protection and Affordable Care Act and its passage in 2010, the percent of people saying we are spending "too little" on protecting the nation's health drops to levels previously seen in the mid-1980s. Even this remarkable piece of legislation did not shift opinion on spending for health care outside of its previously observed range.

Figure 10-2   Public Opinion on Health Care Spending: Too Little

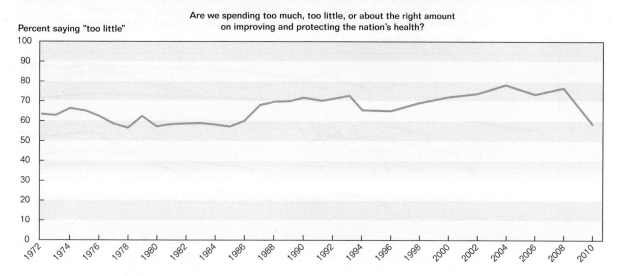

Source: General Social Survey, National Opinion Research Center, University of Chicago.

Typically, when substantial changes in the distribution of public opinion occur, they reflect intelligible historical trends or responses to changed conditions.[35] For example, the public's expressed willingness to vote for presidential candidates without regard to race, religion, and sex has grown steadily over the past several decades as public policy and public sentiment turned against discrimination on these dimensions, although Mormons face some lingering prejudices, and atheists and gays need not apply (see Figure 10-3). Support for greater spending on national defense rose in the late 1970s and early 1980s, responding to crises in Iran and Afghanistan and President Ronald Reagan's leadership on the issue, but then declined once the government had increased military spending. Shrinking defense budgets during the 1990s eventually led to greater public support for higher defense spending, even before the terrorist attacks of September 11, 2001. But by 2004, after a large increase in the defense budget and amid growing disillusion with the Iraq War, public opinion had turned against higher defense spending once again (see Figure 10-4). In aggregate, then, public opinion appears both consistent and intelligible.[36]

Other studies have detected broad cyclical changes in public opinion across a range of issues, with opinion swinging back and forth between liberal and conservative "moods." The inevitable shortcomings of both the liberal and conservative approaches to government eventually make the opposition's ideas more attractive. Experience with conservative policies moves public opinion in a liberal direction, while experience with liberal policies makes the public more conservative.[37] For example, the liberal expansion of the welfare state in the 1960s under Lyndon Johnson eventually led to the conservative tax revolts of the late 1970s and early 1980s and the election of Reagan, a conservative Republican, as

Figure 10-3 Growing Acceptance of Women and Minorities as Presidential Candidates

If your party nominated a generally well-qualified person for president who happened to be [Catholic, black, Jewish, a woman, an atheist, a homosexual, Mormon], would you vote for that person?

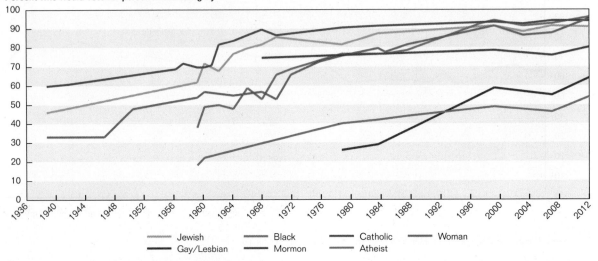

Source: Gallup, "The Presidency," www.gallup.com/poll/4729/Presidency.aspx.

Figure 10-4 Public Opinion on Defense Spending, 1960–2012

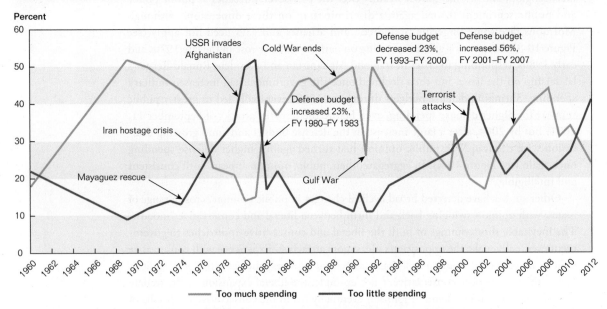

Sources: Harold W. Stanley and Richard G. Niemi, *Vital Statistics on American Politics, 1999–2000* (Washington, DC: CQ Press, 2000), Table 3.22; data for 2000–2003 from Polling Report, www.pollingreport.com/defense.htm#Military; data for 2004–2012 from the Roper Center, www.ropercenter.uconn.edu.

president. The growing economic inequalities produced by the policies of Reagan and his successor, George H. W. Bush, revived, at least temporarily, public support for government programs to improve the economic well-being of the less affluent, helping to elect Bill Clinton. Changes in mood bring about changes in policy, as candidates more in tune with the new mood win office and many of the holdovers adapt to survive. After Reagan's victory in 1980, congressional Democrats had to adapt to stay in office, and they did—by joining Republicans to cut income taxes and social welfare spending. Similar changes are being negotiated in the Republican Party after the 2012 election. Increased turnout by Latino voters (who also increasingly broke for Barack Obama) in this election has caused Republicans to examine their policies on immigration and deportation. Similarly, the party took note as marriage equality (in terms of same-sex marriage) was legalized in Maine, Maryland, and Washington State and small-quantity sales of marijuana were legalized in Colorado and Washington State.

Aggregate opinion also varies in coherent ways over the shorter term. The president's level of public approval typically varies from month to month with economic conditions and international events. The two Bush presidencies offer striking examples. The senior Bush's level of approval in the Gallup poll reached what was then a record 83 percent in early 1991 in appreciation of his skillful handling of the Gulf War, but continuing high unemployment and slow economic growth over the next eighteen months, along with Bush's seeming inattention to the problem, brought it down to 32 percent. George W. Bush's approval ratings had been stuck in the low 50s for months until the September 2001 terrorist attacks. His forceful response to the crisis and the strong upsurge of national unity provoked by the attacks rallied virtually all Americans to his side, driving his approval ratings to record levels—up to a remarkable 92 percent in one national poll. It thereafter began a steady decline, briefly interrupted by the triumphant early days of the Iraq War and Saddam Hussein's capture eleven months later, eventually dipping below 30 percent as disillusion with the Iraq War and bad economic news sapped the president's support among all but Republican loyalists (see Figure 10-1, page 447). Barack Obama's approval numbers have been relatively resistant to shifting economic and international events; even the killing of Osama bin Laden produced only a five-point bump in May 2011. At two other points there were somewhat steeper decreases in approval: from early May through August 2009, and in June and July 2011. Both appear connected to economic uncertainty, including increases in unemployment in 2009 and stock market convulsions during the difficult debt ceiling negotiations in 2011. Most other presidents have experienced greater peaks and valleys in their approval ratings in their first terms. Obama's approval rating looked much like one might expect given the chronic economic challenges he faced: initial popularity in the "honeymoon" after he was inaugurated, which was then gradually eroded by Americans' persistent pessimism about the economy and the overall direction of the country. **Aggregate partisanship**—the proportion of poll respondents labeling themselves Republicans or Democrats—also shifts with changes in economic conditions, political events, and presidential approval. Popular presidents presiding over growing economies and successful foreign policies enhance their party's strength among voters; failed policies, foreign and domestic, undermine it.[38] As a whole, then, public opinion does not move erratically or unintelligibly. When it is not stable, its movements can usually be explained by real-world events and circumstances.

Opinion Leadership

How can stable and coherent public opinion arise from unstable and incoherent individual opinions? Part of the answer lies in the aggregation process itself. When survey responses are added together, **measurement errors** (from the mismatch of survey questions with the attitudes they are supposed to measure) and random individual changes tend to cancel one another out; therefore, the average remains the same if circumstances remain the same. The more important part of the answer lies in the division of labor between the minority of the public that is attentive and informed and the much larger majority that is neither. A small segment of the public forms opinions by paying close attention to political events and issues. The uninformed and inattentive majority routinely free rides when forming opinions by taking cues from members of this attentive segment. In aggregate, public opinion is given rationality and coherence by these **opinion leaders**.[39]

Opinion leadership arises naturally as people respond to different incentives. The widespread ignorance of political facts and issues does not mean that most Americans are dunces. Indeed, in an important sense political ignorance is rational. It takes time and energy to become informed. Political issues and processes often are exceedingly complicated, and even the most devoted student of politics cannot hope to master them all. Most citizens, on most political questions, receive no tangible payoff from becoming better informed. People are unlikely to improve either U.S. policy or their own lives by developing a better understanding of the Israeli-Palestinian conflict. The same goes for health care policy. Better information holds no promise of a better outcome because the views of any single individual are so unlikely to be decisive. It makes sense to gather information about options when we get to make the decision (what kind of car to buy), but not when our influence on the choice is effectively nil (what kind of helicopters the Marines should buy).

Suppose we do want to participate in politics, if only in a small way, by voting or by responding to a public opinion poll. Or suppose friends are discussing politics. To join in, we need to adopt some positions on the issues. But how do we know which side of an issue to favor, and why, without investing the time and effort to learn about it? If we are like most people, we rationally free ride on the efforts of others, following the cues given by people we consider informed and whose biases we know. They may be people we know personally— friends, relatives, or coworkers who pay special attention to politics; community activists; or leaders in our places of worship. They may be public figures—political leaders, TV or radio personalities, and newspaper columnists. Organizations such as the Sierra Club, the Roman Catholic Church, and the U.S. Chamber of Commerce may be sources of cues. Thus instead of learning about an endless variety of complicated political issues, all we have to learn is whose attitudes reliably match or contradict our own and then follow their cues. Their biases need not match ours for the cues to be useful; sometimes we can determine what we are for by noting who is against it, and vice versa. In effect, we avoid incurring information costs by delegating opinion formation to (we hope) reliable agents chosen for that purpose.

Cognitive shortcuts of this sort are available because interested people and groups have a stake in gathering and disseminating political information. Some folks find politics as fascinating as others do baseball and enjoy being recognized by friends as political mavens. But most people who traffic in political information do so to pursue their power and policy goals more effectively. The activities and biases of information specialists usually reflect their institutional roles. Tobacco company officials need to know every-thing that is said about the dangers of secondhand smoke to counter these claims and defend corporate profits. The American Cancer Society's staff seeks out and publicizes information emphasizing the damage tobacco does to the nation's health and health care budgets. Think tanks such as the American Enterprise Institute (conservative) and the Center for American Progress (liberal) sponsor research and issue reports designed to further their ideological agendas. Newspaper columnists and radio talk show hosts are paid to express opinions on political issues. Professional politicians and those with political ambitions also need to master issues and be prepared to discuss them. A pluralist political system breeds—and depends on—opinion leaders of many kinds.

The sources of opinion leadership differ from issue to issue, as does the audience for policy. Many political issues go unnoticed except by distinct **issue publics**—subsets of the population who are better informed than everyone else about an issue because it touches them more directly and personally. Farmers pay attention to farm programs; retired people (and their doctors) keep tabs on Medicare policy; research scientists monitor National Science Foundation budgets and rules. Citizens committed to a moral cause, such as protecting animal rights, banning abortion, or protecting civil liberties, form issue publics for policies affecting their cause. Most policy domains are of concern only to issue publics, so it is usually their

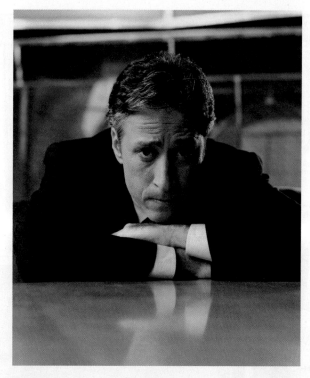

The popularity among young adult viewers of Jon Stewart's nightly parody of TV network news, *The Daily Show with Jon Stewart* on the Comedy Central cable channel, has made the comedian a genuine if reluctant opinion leader. The ironic finding by a poll taken during the 2004 presidential campaign that Stewart's viewers were better informed than people who watched only regular network or cable news programs or read newspapers is no doubt more the result of self-selection in his audience than of his program's raw informational content.

opinions, not mass opinion, that matter to politicians. Together, opinion leaders and issue publics are the main conduits of public opinion in a pluralist political system. They apply most of the routine pressures felt by government officials engaged in the day-to-day making of public policy on the countless matters dealt with by the federal government. By the same token, their interest makes them the targets of most organized attempts to sway and mobilize public opinion for political ends.

Aggregate public opinion, then, is given its coherence and focus by opinion leaders, typically based in institutions, whose knowledge, ideas, proposals, and debates define the positions and options from which ordinary citizens, acting logically as cognitive misers, adopt their expressed views. This conclusion does not mean that public opinion is routinely manipulated by self-serving elites (although there is no shortage of attempts to do so); pluralist competition usually denies any particular opinion leader a monopoly. Opinion leaders maintain their leadership status only if people choose to follow them. During the 2012 Republican primaries, even Republican voters accepted the framing of Mitt Romney as

©2010 Harry Bliss. Distributed by Tribune Media Services, Inc.

www.harrybliss.com

4/26

"Mr. President, the people have spoken ...
and they're not making <u>any</u> sense."

personally wealthy and "out of touch" (see box "Framing Mitt Romney," page 453), while simultaneously rejecting the media's framing of the GOP primary as the search for "anyone but Romney."

The aggregate stability of popular views reveals that, in an often confused and poorly articulated way, people do have a real basis for the opinions they express. They respond to opinion leaders not randomly but in ways that are consistent with the values and notions about politics they have accumulated during their lives. Cognitive shortcuts would be of no value if they did not bring people somewhere near the destination they would have reached by taking the longer path.[40] Agents can be fired; opinion leaders, therefore, lead by expressing the political sentiments of those who follow them. This is why politicians, who are fully aware of how fickle and poorly informed people's expressed opinions may be, still think twice about going against the polls. Aggregate opinion is meaningful, and aggregates are what count when a politician is running for reelection or trying to get a bill passed.

For this reason, public opinion, at least as measured by polls, is regularly if not invariably found to influence public policy. One summary study concluded that public opinion significantly affected public policy in three-quarters of the fifty-two possible instances examined in thirty separate research studies; the more prominent the issue, the more likely public opinion was to be influential.[41]

THE CONTENT OF PUBLIC OPINION

Political opinions reflect people's underlying values and beliefs about how the world works. This fact is no less true of second- or third-hand opinions—those derived, respectively, from one other person or from an opinion leader through another person—than of original opinions, which are formed through personal experience. This is because core values and beliefs influence people's choice of cue-givers (recall who listens to Rush Limbaugh and who to Michael Moore). Americans share a broad consensus on basic political values that puts real limits on what is politically possible. Yet within these bounds, Americans find plenty on which to disagree. Consensus on the basics makes politics—defined here as reaching agreement on a course of common, or collective, action despite disagreement on the purposes of the action—*possible;* disagreement within this general consensus makes politics *necessary.*

Consensus on the System

Opinion polls find that almost every American supports the institutional underpinnings of modern democracy: the right of every citizen to vote; the freedom to speak, write, and work with others for political goals; the right to due process and equal treatment by courts and other government agencies. Although each of these principles was once controversial (see Chapters 4 and 11), opposition to them has now virtually disappeared from public life. Large majorities also favor a capitalist economy, defined as one in which businesses are privately owned, free markets allocate goods, people choose their own occupations, and incomes depend on the market value of services rendered. No one with serious aspirations to political leadership attacks democracy or free enterprise.

When it comes to the practical application of these abstract values, however, consensus breaks down. When a poll taken in 1940 asked a sample of Americans, "Do you believe in freedom of speech?" 97 percent said yes. When those who answered yes were asked, "Do you believe in it to the extent of allowing fascists and communists to hold meetings and express their views in the community?" 76 percent said no. In 1940, the year these questions were posed, war was raging in Europe, and both fascism and communism loomed as serious threats. But even in calmer times, many people who say they favor First Amendment rights would deny them to people with unpopular views. Polls taken in the mid-1970s found 82 percent agreeing that "nobody has the right to tell another person what he should or should not read," but also 50 percent agreeing that "books that preach the overthrow of the government should be banned from the library."[42] A 2007 survey found Americans were divided on the question of whether "freedom of speech should . . . extend to groups that are sympathetic to terrorists," with 50 percent saying it should, and 45 percent saying it should not.[43] When the abstract value of free expression comes up against the more tangible matters of national security or social order, free expression does not always come out on top. It is therefore important to note that free speech and other democratic values find stronger support among the minority of Americans who specialize in politics; those who play the political game are more supportive of its rules.[44] When the George W. Bush administration proposed "Operation TIPS," a program to recruit transportation workers, utility crews, letter carriers, and other private citizens to report suspicious activities to the government as part of the war on terrorism, members of Congress from both parties objected and quickly passed a law killing the program.

Other basic political values are also hedged. Large majorities say they favor free enterprise and dislike government meddling in the economy, but majorities just as large back laws regulating businesses in order to protect the environment or the health and safety of workers and consumers. Again, people who pay more attention to politics are more likely to recognize the implications of one position for another and to offer more consistent sets of opinions. But almost everyone holds political values and beliefs that clash. Forced to choose, people have to consider trade-offs; sometimes political conflict and compromise even occur right in our own heads.

At one level, the values of democracy and capitalism are not compatible. Democracy treats people as equals and permits majorities to rule. Capitalism extols liberty, not equality. It distributes its rewards unequally and leaves crucial economic decisions (what products to produce, what jobs to offer, where to build factories) in the hands of individuals and private corporations,

Majorities of Americans value free enterprise, job opportunities, cheap and abundant energy, and an unobtrusive government, but majorities also value clean air and water, the continued survival of wild creatures in their natural environments, and some measure of protection from market risks. The tension among such competing values—symbolized here by endangered polar bears on the Arctic National Wildlife Refuge, a fragile environment holding substantial oil deposits—creates personal as well as political dilemmas, especially when the price of gasoline skyrockets.

whose goals are profits. The fear that democracy would bring economic ruin by allowing popular majorities to despoil the wealthy minority was a central motive behind the Constitution's elaborate avoidance of direct popular rule. But the fear proved to be groundless because Americans have come to make sharp distinctions about the kinds of equality they consider appropriate. Just about everyone favors political equality. Support for equal opportunity is at least as strong: statements such as "everyone in America should have an equal right to get ahead" and "children should have equal education opportunities" are accepted almost without dissent when posed in opinion polls.[45] Americans have also come to support equal pay for equal work and generally to oppose discrimination against any class of persons (women, racial minorities, and gays) in the workplace.

Very little popular support exists, however, for mandating equal outcomes. Asked whether, under a fair economic system, all people would earn about the same or people with more ability would earn higher salaries, 7 percent chose the first option, 78 percent the second.[46] Nor is there much support for affirmative action programs intended to remedy past discrimination against women or racial minorities by putting them first in line for jobs and school admissions. When asked whether "ability determined by test scores" or special treatment "to make up for past discrimination" should govern decisions on jobs and college admission, overwhelming majorities choose test score ability (although vaguer forms of affirmative action are generally supported—question wording is highly consequential in this area).[47] The result is that Americans, renowned since Alexis de Tocqueville's day for their egalitarian social and political values, tolerate huge—and growing—differences in wealth and well-being among individuals and groups.

Politicians: A Suspect Class

Americans approve overwhelmingly of the U.S. political system and its symbols; pride in the Constitution and the flag are nearly universal. They are normally far less pleased, however, with the people they elect to run the system. Criticizing the government is a national pastime with a pedigree longer than baseball's, but the public's distrust of government and its practitioners deepened markedly over the last half of the twentieth century. Figure 10-5 traces the public's varying cynicism about government through a set of questions that have been asked repeatedly in the biennial American National Election Studies and occasionally

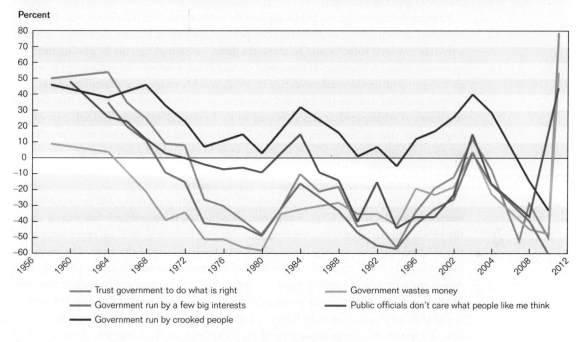

Figure 10-5 Americans' Varying Cynicism about Government

Percent

Legend:
— Trust government to do what is right
— Government run by a few big interests
— Government run by crooked people
— Government wastes money
— Public officials don't care what people like me think

Sources: American National Election Studies, CBS News/*New York Times* and Gallup polls.

Note: The entries are the percentage of respondents expressing confidence in government minus the percentage expressing a lack of confidence in government on each question. The questions are:

1. How much of the time do you think you can trust the government in Washington to do what is right—just about always, most of the time, or only some of the time? ("Always" or "most of the time" minus "some" or "none of the time.")

2. Do you think that people in government waste a lot of money we pay in taxes, waste some of it, or don't waste very much of it? ("Some" or "not much" minus "a lot.")

3. Would you say that the government is pretty much run by a few big interests looking out for themselves or that it is run for the benefit of all? ("Benefit of all" minus "a few big interests.")

4. Please tell me if you agree or disagree with this statement: Public officials don't care what people like me think. ("Disagree" minus "agree.")

5. Do you think that quite a few of the people running the government are crooked, not very many are crooked, or hardly any of them are crooked? ("Hardly any" or "not many" minus "quite a few.")

in other surveys. More than in the 1950s and 1960s, Americans in recent years have been inclined to believe that public officials are crooked and that the government wastes tax money, cannot be trusted to do what is right, is run by a few big interests for their own benefit, and does not care about ordinary people.

The most common explanation for these trends is that the conflicts over civil rights and the Vietnam War in the 1960s, followed closely by the Watergate scandal that drove a president from office (note the sharp drops in 1974), led to a more critical press and a disillusioned public. Confidence revived somewhat with the economy in 1984, but later problems, including a stagnant economy during the George H. W. Bush administration

(1989–1993), large federal budget deficits, assorted political scandals, high crime rates, and a pervasive sense that the United States was moving in the wrong direction, kept public distrust of government high.

One result was widespread public support for measures to curb politicians: term limits for legislators, constitutional amendments compelling Congress to balance the budget, national referenda in which voters would be allowed a direct say in making laws by putting them on a national ballot. A large part of the appeal of Ross Perot, who won 19 percent of the vote as an independent presidential candidate in 1992, was his image as a champion of political reforms intended to make elected officials more accountable to ordinary people. Any popular sentiment as widespread as this is bound to find political sponsors. Indeed, part of the Republicans' strategy for taking control of Congress in the 1994 elections was a promise to act on constitutional amendments to impose term limits and a balanced budget. The confidence measurements reached a low point in 1994, evidence of the anger at government that Republicans both fanned and exploited to win Congress.

Confidence in government rebounded with the booming economy and balanced federal budget during the second Clinton administration but still remained far below what it was in the 1950s. This trend continued through the first year of George W. Bush's presidency until the al-Qaeda attacks on the United States effectively reframed the issue. The events of September 11, 2001, and their aftermath had an immediate and dramatic effect on how Americans responded to polling questions about their government and its leaders. Not only did Bush's approval rating shoot to record highs, but so did approval of Congress (84 percent in one poll, topping the previous high of 57 percent) and congressional leaders. The proportion of respondents who said they trusted the government in Washington to do what is right "almost always" or "most of the time," which had been below 45 percent in every poll since the Watergate scandal in 1974 and had fallen as low as 18 percent in the early 1990s, jumped to 56 percent. The sharp rise in expressed support for government and its leaders reflected a radical change in the context in which people thought about these questions. Under deadly attack from shadowy foreign enemies, Americans rallied behind their government as the defender and institutional embodiment of American democracy. For a brief time, politicians and other government officials enjoyed the kind of broad public support normally reserved for such national symbols as the flag and the Constitution. Moreover, the attacks were a forceful reminder of the need for a government capable of organizing and sustaining collective action in pursuit of that most fundamental of public goods, security from foreign attack. In this context, the ordinary annoyances and frustrations people associate with government and politics became decidedly secondary.

This mood did not, however, survive the reemergence of politics as usual and the increasingly bitter partisan differences provoked by the Iraq War and other Bush administration decisions. By 2008, amid deep public discontent with the war, the economy, and the overall direction of the country, cynicism again dominated Americans' views of their elected leaders. And the first four years of the Obama administration, beset by stubbornly high unemployment, rising budget deficits, and increasing U.S. casualties in Afghanistan, did little to stop the trend. Further, in late 2011, ratings agencies downgraded the nation's credit score for the first time in history. One agency, Standard & Poor's, accompanied its downgrade with a strong critique of the political brinksmanship in Congress that prevented the government from increasing its debt ceiling, saying that this style of politics renders the U.S. government "less stable, less effective, and less predictable" in managing its finances. The widespread belief that the government couldn't be trusted to do anything right was growing—a CBS/*New York Times* poll in October 2011 revealed that 89 percent of Americans thought the government could only be trusted some of the time (and many said none of the time). Only 10 percent said it could be trusted most of the time or just about always.

Public Opinion on Issues

Popular agreement on the fundamentals of representative democracy does not translate into agreement on every important policy area. In each of three broad domains—the economy, societal morality, and foreign policy—the central issues have consistently generated wide divisions of opinion. It is crucial to understand how these differences split the public because these factions form the raw material from which political leaders try to construct majority coalitions. When the public is divided in different ways on different issues and lacks consensus on which are most important, strategies for assembling and maintaining party coalitions become more difficult to conceive and execute.

ECONOMIC ISSUES. Although Americans believe fundamentally in capitalism, almost no one believes that private businesses should be completely unregulated or that the things people value should be allocated exclusively by an unfettered free market. Political conflict occurs over how far the government should go in regulating business and redressing market-driven economic and social inequalities. Historically, the trend has been toward an ever-larger government role in managing economic affairs, with notable expansions in the 1930s under Franklin Roosevelt's New Deal policies, in the 1960s with Lyndon Johnson's Great Society programs, and in the 1970s with new laws to protect consumers and the environment (see Chapter 8). Today, government action to enhance economic welfare usually enjoys broad public support. At the same time, people are less than enthusiastic about paying the costs of "big government" in the form of higher taxes and greater bureaucratic regulation. Programs that serve the middle class attract the most support; programs that serve the poor are on shakier political footing.

More specifically, large majorities typically support stable or increased government spending for programs that serve (or will eventually serve) nearly everyone: Social Security (pensions for the disabled or retired), Medicare (medical care for retirees), and unemployment insurance (cash for people laid off from jobs). Social Security is so popular that politicians call it "the third rail of American politics—touch it and you are dead" (referring to the high-voltage rail from which subway trains draw their power). George W. Bush's 2005 campaign to whip up support for reforming the program implicitly acknowledged the danger; the president spent months traveling the country telling audiences that Social Security needed a major overhaul to remain fiscally sound without mentioning that, absent major tax increases that Bush had ruled out, the overhaul would have to include substantial cuts in promised future benefits. Other individual government programs designed to improve health and welfare also command broad support—with a few revealing exceptions (see box "Public Opinion and Welfare Reform," which lists some typical poll results and illustrates how such opinions can affect major policy decisions).

PUBLIC OPINION AND WELFARE REFORM

politics to policy

The public is broadly supportive of major social spending programs—except those that evoke the wrong frames. Consider the public's responses to the following question: "Should spending on the following programs increase, decrease, or stay the same?"

	Increase	Stay the Same	Decrease
Social Security (2011)	41%	46%	11%
Medicare (2011)	48	39	14
Improving and protecting health (1993)	74	18	8
Public schools (2008)	74	19	5
Welfare (2008)	26	42	30
Aid to poor people (2008)	60	31	7
Food stamps (2000)	16	51	33
Nutritional aid to poor people, formerly food stamps (2011)	34	38	25
Solving problem of the homeless (1996)	58	31	11
Aid to college students (1996)	53	38	9
Child care (2008)	56	34	7

Note: Percentages may not add to one hundred due to rounding.

Only a tiny minority wants the government to spend less on Social Security, health, the public schools, college loans, child care, and the homeless than it is already spending. Programs whose names evoke the wrong symbols, however, enjoy much less support. Here, for example, 30 percent would reduce spending on "welfare," and only 26 percent would increase it, although 60 percent would increase spending on "aid to poor people"—overlooking the fact that welfare *is* aid to poor people. This is a clear example of framing. Most Americans think government should help the poor, but the word *welfare* conjures up images, however unfair, of lazy people living off the sweat of the taxpayers. Charity is a virtue, but so is self-reliance, and poverty issues can be framed in terms of either one.

Images and frames do matter. In 1996 the Republican Congress sent Bill Clinton a welfare reform bill that cut back on federal assistance to poor people. Among other things, the bill imposed a time limit on welfare eligibility for the first time since the adoption of the original assistance program in the 1930s. It also slashed the food stamp program, which apparently shares welfare's negative connotations (see the entry for food stamps in the table). Most congressional Democrats opposed the bill, but, facing reelection, Clinton signed it anyway because it was widely supported by a public that had applauded his previous campaign promise to "end welfare as we know it."

Sources: The 1993 data are from the General Social Survey, reported by Robert S. Erikson and Kent L. Tedin in *American Public Opinion,* 5th ed. (Boston: Allyn and Bacon, 1995), 89; 1996, 2000, and 2008 data are from the 1996, 2000, and 2008 American National Election Studies; 2011 data are from CNN/Opinion Research Corporation poll March 11–13, 2011.

By and large, Americans seem to support a wide range of economic and social welfare policies that commonly are classified as liberal. But when it comes to principles, as opposed to programs, Americans are much more likely to think of themselves as conservatives. Majorities also agree with conservative politicians who say that taxes are too high, that the government wastes a lot of money, that bureaucrats are too meddlesome, and that people ought to take care of themselves rather than depend on government handouts.

SOCIAL AND MORAL ISSUES. Politics is about the distribution of goods, which can be moral as well as material. The great struggles to abolish slavery, achieve votes for women, prohibit alcohol, and end racial segregation were driven largely by moral rather than economic considerations. Today social and moral issues produce some of the most heated political controversies. Questions about abortion, religion in public life, and the rights of women, ethnic and racial minorities, immigrants, and gays make up an important part of the political agenda. These issues raise conflicting considerations that are difficult to reconcile, not only between opposed groups but also for individuals in their own minds.

In modern times abortion is the best known example. Since the Supreme Court handed down its *Roe v. Wade* ruling in 1973, thereby overturning state laws making abortions illegal, the abortion issue has become a defining one for a whole political generation. Groups with starkly opposing positions have dominated the public debate. At one extreme are those who want the law to forbid abortion as murder; at the other are those who object to any restriction on a woman's right to have an abortion. Neither of these positions commands a majority, although more favor no restriction (35 percent in 2012) than favor a total ban (15 percent). For most people (47 percent), the answer is "It depends."[48]

Aggregate public opinion on abortion is both highly stable and acutely sensitive to how the issue is framed. Figure 10-6 shows the trends in responses to one set of questions posed regularly in polls since 1965. After an initial increase in support for legalized abortion (coinciding with *Roe v. Wade*), aggregate opinion has changed little. Large majorities think abortion should be legal if the pregnancy resulted from rape or would endanger the woman's health or if there is a strong chance of serious birth defects. The public is much more evenly split on whether abortion for financial or family reasons should be legal. Other variations in the question wording produce a similar spread.

Unlike the activists on both sides, most Americans are torn on the issue. Majorities agree that "abortion is murder" (57 percent)[49] and "morally wrong" (51 percent)[50], but they also think that a woman should be allowed to have an abortion if she wants to and her doctor agrees to it (51 percent),[51] and oppose a constitutional amendment outlawing abortions (70 percent). Perhaps the best expression of the average person's view is summed up by an option offered by one poll on the issue: "I personally feel that abortion is morally wrong, but I also feel that whether or not to have an abortion is a decision that has to be made by every woman for herself"; 78 percent agreed.[52]

Abortion is the kind of issue that defies political resolution because the wide disagreement on values leaves little space for agreement on action. It generates intense feelings among minorities on both sides who tolerate nothing less than full support for their position. Intense feelings are, moreover, far more prevalent among political activists (some of whom are activists *because* of their intense feelings), and they are most common among the minority that would forbid abortion entirely. Ordinary citizens are much less certain about how the issue should be resolved and remain uncomfortable with either extreme. Thus exploitation of the issue politically is a delicate undertaking. In running for president in 2008, John McCain had to maintain a firm "pro-life" position to attract support from conservative Christians, many of whom were Republicans primarily because the party was committed to banning abortion,

Figure 10-6 Public Support for Abortion Rights: Dependent on the Reason for the Abortion

Percent

— If the woman's own health is seriously endangered by the pregnancy

— If she becomes pregnant as the result of a rape

— If there is a strong chance of a serious defect in the baby

— If the family has a very low income and cannot afford any more children

— If she is not married and does not want to marry the man

— If she is married and does not want any more children

Sources: Harold W. Stanley and Richard G. Niemi, *Vital Statistics on American Politics 2003–2004* (Washington, DC: CQ Press, 2003), Table 3-16; General Social Survey, 2006–2010.

without leading uncommitted moderates to worry that "choice" would immediately be threatened if he were to win. In 2012, Mitt Romney balanced these demands by changing his once pro-choice position to a pro-life stance.

Americans take conservative positions on most other social issues, but in practice their views are often balanced by considerable respect for individual freedom. Formal prayer in public schools, banned by Supreme Court decisions in the early 1960s, receives widespread public support. Likewise, majorities take strong "law and order" positions, favoring capital punishment for murderers and opposing the legalization of drugs such as marijuana and cocaine. In 2006, half of Americans favored a constitutional amendment that would permit Congress to outlaw burning the American flag as a form of political protest.[53] Few support unrestricted access to pornography. Social conservatism grew during the 1990s as problems of crime, drug abuse, single-parent families, and welfare dependency became the focus of political attention. Yet the public was leery about using government to impose traditional moral standards on private citizens. A recent example, however, suggests Americans may be adopting more tolerant attitudes on some social questions. In May 2012, President Obama announced that his thinking about gay equality had changed, and he now supported the position that same-sex couples should be allowed to legally marry. *USA Today* and Gallup asked Americans whether they approved or disapproved of the president's new position. Mirroring public opinion on the issue, 51 percent approved, although partisans were as usual split, with 71 percent of Democrats approving and 74 percent of Republicans disapproving (53 percent of independents approved).*

FOREIGN POLICY. During the 2004 and 2008 election campaigns, issues of foreign policy, particularly regarding the war in Iraq, shared a small bit of the spotlight with the national economy. In light of the war's controversial justification and growing cost in American life and treasure, this was not at all surprising. But it was unusual. Except when Americans are dying overseas, foreign policy issues tend to be remote from everyday experience, and few people pay sustained attention to foreign affairs. In such relatively quiet times, public opinion on foreign policy is particularly responsive to opinion leadership. The president is the most important opinion leader on foreign policy, but presidential influence varies according to whether other opinion leaders—rival

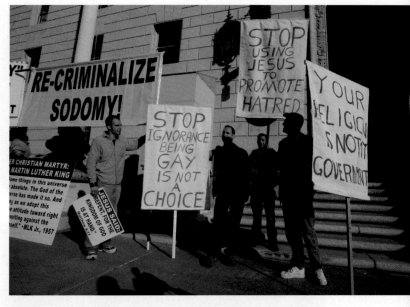

The abstract ideal of equal rights is widely shared by Americans, but its application is often vigorously disputed. Here, supporters and opponents of gay marriage mount competing demonstrations outside the California Supreme Court, which was hearing arguments in March 2008 on the constitutionality of a voter initiative that banned gay marriage in 2000. The California Supreme Court overturned the ban, prompting yet another initiative on the 2008 California ballot, which passed narrowly, 52–48. It, too, was overturned by a federal appeals court in February 2012. On December 6, 2012, the U.S. Supreme Court announced it would hear this California case.

politicians, foreign policy experts, and news commentators—agree or disagree with the White House.[54] Since World War II large majorities have supported an active international role for the United States, but backing for particular policies has been much more variable.

Until the breakup of the Soviet Union at the end of 1991, the Cold War conflict between the United States and the Soviet Union framed both public and elite thinking on foreign affairs. The avowed U.S. objective of "containing" the Soviet Union to prevent the expansion of communism enjoyed broad public acceptance, but the public did not agree on all of the actions taken in the name of containment. Both the Korean and Vietnam Wars lost popular support as casualties mounted.[55] Later, majorities opposed proposals by the Reagan and Bush administrations to give military assistance to the Nicaraguan contras in their civil war against the avowedly socialist Sandinista government. In all of these cases, public divisions reflected in a direct way the divisions among opinion leaders. In general, opinion on whether to take a tougher or more conciliatory approach to dealing with the Soviets varied with U.S. perceptions of Soviet behavior; events such as the Soviet invasion of Afghanistan in 1979 to prop up a threatened communist regime made a tougher line more popular, whereas arms control agreements and

---

* As of this printing, there are nine states (plus the District of Columbia) in which gay marriage is offered. Fourteen states in total recognize same-sex unions or partnerships, and thirty-seven expressly limit marriage to opposite-sex couples.

A decade after the attacks of September 2001 and the start of wars in Iraq and Afghanistan, a unique study by the Program for Public Consultation asked Americans to consider arguments for and against cutting military spending.[57] Most people (76 percent) thought the national defense budget should be cut—with an average reduction of about 20 percent. Interestingly, one of the areas people slated for small cuts was funding for special forces. These highly trained special operations forces (Green Berets, Army Rangers, Delta Operators, and Navy SEALs, as well as elite aviators, Marines, and even special canine units) undertake covert missions against terrorist groups and elite or irregular forces. It was a team of special forces operators (a Navy SEAL team) that killed Osama bin Laden in the spring of 2011. Survey respondents recommended a 10 percent cut to special forces, while recommending support for conventional ground forces be cut by 23 percent. Across all areas, Democrats cut more than Republicans, but in terms of support for special forces, independents recommended an increase in funding for these operators.

summit meetings between the United States and the Soviet Union during the Cold War years made conciliation more popular.[56]

National leaders reached no new consensus on a guiding framework for U.S. foreign policy during the post–Cold War era of the 1990s, so neither did the public. The war against Iraq to liberate Kuwait in 1991 attracted widespread public support even before its stunning success because Iraq's invasion threatened the U.S. economy (by putting the Persian Gulf oil supply at risk) and America's closest ally in the region, Israel. But the Clinton administration had great difficulty building popular support for policies aimed at resolving conflicts in Somalia, Bosnia, Haiti, and Kosovo, partly because the administration itself was vague about what was at stake for the nation in these conflicts and partly because other opinion leaders opposed the administration's policies.

Drift and division on foreign policy issues ended almost instantly with the assaults on the World Trade Center and the Pentagon in 2001. Foreign policy issues became, tragically, anything but remote. The Bush administration moved immediately to direct virtually all of its foreign policy resources to mounting a multifaceted war on terrorism. Leaders in both parties overwhelmingly supported the administration's initial actions, and so did the public; in October 2001 polls, nine of ten Americans said they backed the ongoing military action against the terrorist organizations and the Taliban government in Afghanistan (see Figure 10-7). A large majority was even willing to accept several thousand U.S. casualties if that was what it took to succeed.[58] With the United States itself in harm's way, little opinion leadership was at first necessary; indeed, any leader who did not support a vigorous, conspicuous response would have been badly out of step with mass opinion. But after the initial rout of the Taliban in Afghanistan with the fall of Kandahar and the Battle of Tora Bora in December 2001, the administration's shift of focus to Iraq was not so uniformly applauded. That war became less popular over time as citizens and leaders divided increasingly along party lines over the wisdom of the invasion, especially after a major premise of the war, that Iraq possessed WMDs, was discredited (see Figure 10-8). The war in Afghanistan consistently attracted greater popular support and was less divisive than the war in Iraq, although both eventually provoked unusually wide partisan divisions. Majorities in every partisan category backed the Obama administration's decision to expand U.S. troop levels in Afghanistan to combat the resurgent Taliban in 2009, but as American casualties mounted and the war dragged on with few signs of progress, support continued to slide. Rather than sharing a consensus, on foreign policy the public is increasingly

Figure 10-7   Popular Support for the War in Afghanistan

Percent supporting war

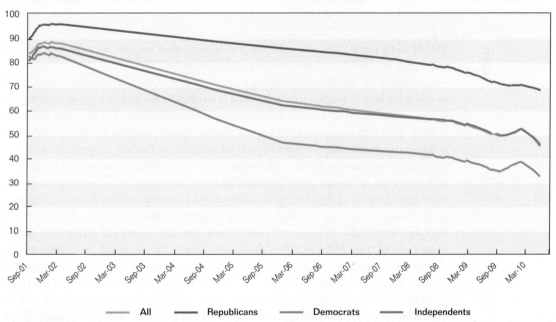

Source: Smoothed trend of 102 ABC News/*Washington Post,* CBS News/*New York Times,* CNN, ANES, *Time,* Gallup, Fox News, *Los Angeles Times,* NBC News/*Wall Street Journal, Newsweek,* Pew, and Quinnipiac polls.

Figure 10-8 Popular Support for the War in Iraq

Percent supporting war

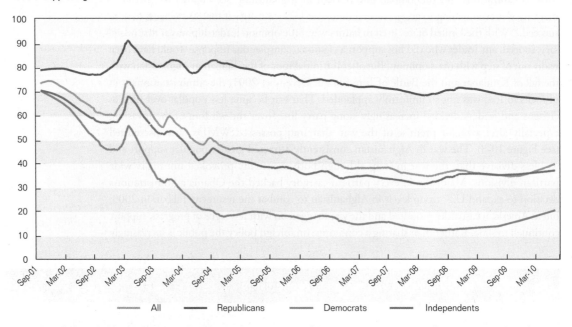

Source: Smoothed trend of 731 ABC News/*Washington Post*, CBS News/*New York Times*, CNN, ANES, *Time,* Gallup, Fox News, *Los Angeles Times*, NBC News/*Wall Street Journal, Newsweek,* Pew, and Quinnipiac polls.

divided along party lines, not only over the ongoing wars but also over the legitimacy of preemptive wars and the value of working with allies or the UN.

Few contest the necessity of combating terrorism to protect the U.S. homeland, but a decade later there has been little agreement on how best to accomplish this goal. In some sense, living with the threat of terrorism has become the "new normal" for most people. Ten years after the attacks in 2001, most Americans think the United States is "neither winning nor losing" the war on terror—a pattern that does not differ by party identification or Tea Party support. But simultaneously, most people also say that the increased security and surveillance measures have not gone too far in restricting Americans' civil rights and that the actions taken by the government are "just about right" in terms of their level of intrusiveness and inconvenience. Finally, nearly 80 percent of Americans, across party and Tea Party support, agree that the country has not yet recovered from the events of the "9/11 Decade"—the attacks, the wars in Iraq and Afghanistan, and the global financial crisis. Almost a fifth of the country believes the nation will "never recover" from these events.[59] Luckily, or unluckily, depending on how you look at it, the survey measuring these attitudes happened to be in the field in May 2011 when Barack Obama announced the United States had found and killed Osama bin Laden. Somewhat surprisingly, but consistent with the modest bump in the president's approval rating discussed earlier, the death of bin Laden did not alter Americans' attitudes about winning the war on terror or recovering from the 9/11 Decade. Living with the threat of terrorism is America's new state of "normal."

EFFECTS OF BACKGROUND ON PUBLIC OPINION

People's opinions on specific issues reflect the knowledge, beliefs, and values they have acquired over their lifetimes. The public's diverse points of view often represent differences in background, education, and life experiences. When polling data are analyzed, these differences show up in the way opinions vary with demographic characteristics such as race, ethnicity, gender, income, education, region, religion, and age. Politicians pay close attention to group differences because they determine feasible coalition-building strategies.

Race and Ethnicity

The sharpest differences of opinion between major groups in U.S. politics occur between African Americans and whites, and the biggest gap is on issues related to race. Unlike in the past, a large majority of white Americans now reject segregation and support equal opportunity for all races, but they disagree with African Americans on what, if anything, should be done about the lingering effects of racial discrimination. A 2003 survey asked respondents if they favored or opposed "affirmative action programs for racial minorities." Seventy percent of African Americans but only 44 percent of non-Hispanic whites said they supported such programs. In the same survey, 49 percent of African Americans but only 22 percent of whites thought that race should be taken into account in college admissions to promote "diversity."[60] African Americans also are more likely than whites to favor greater government action to provide jobs, health care, and other government services. But they are less supportive of defense spending and foreign wars; according to a February 2008 Gallup poll, 87 percent thought the Iraq War had been a mistake.[61] Finally, 44 percent of African Americans oppose the death penalty for murder, compared with only 16 percent of whites.

These contrasting views reflect the profoundly different perceptions and life experiences of African Americans and whites in American society. African Americans, along with numerous other minority groups—Hispanics, Native Americans, and Asian Americans of diverse national origins—share a history of discrimination based on race; many have experienced discrimination firsthand. Whites tend to think that legal equality has now been achieved and that any special effort to overcome the effects of past discrimination is unfair. African Americans also tend to have lower incomes than whites and so are typically more favorably disposed toward government efforts to improve economic welfare. Their greater propensity to oppose the death penalty reflects skepticism, based on bitter historical experience, about the fairness of the criminal justice system toward black defendants.

On all of these issues, the views of African Americans are closer to the positions taken by the Democratic Party, and African Americans vote overwhelmingly Democratic. As a result, they are a crucial part of the Democratic coalition. Only twice since World War II has the Democratic presidential candidate won more of the white vote than the Republican candidate (Lyndon Johnson in 1964 and Bill Clinton in 1996); every other Democratic victory (Harry Truman in 1948, John Kennedy in 1960, Jimmy Carter in 1976, Bill Clinton in 1992, and Barack Obama in 2008) has depended on huge majorities among African Americans to offset narrower Republican majorities among whites. African Americans also

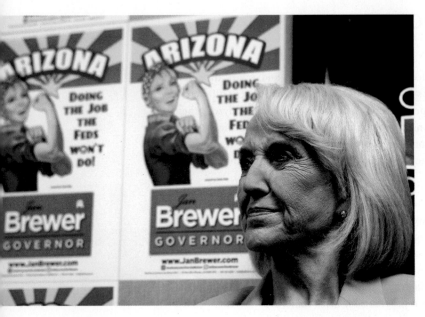

In 2010, the Arizona state Senate passed the Support Our Law Enforcement and Safe Neighborhoods Act, the broadest and strictest anti–illegal immigration measure in recent U.S. history. Arizona governor Jan Brewer signed the bill into law. In June 2012, the U.S. Supreme Court upheld one provision of the law and overturned three others providing a partial victory for Gov. Brewer and for President Obama, who sued Arizona to keep the law from taking effect. By striking down the portions they did, the justices, citing the supremacy clause of the Constitution, said states could not overstep the federal government's immigration enforcement authority. By upholding the portion it did, the court said it was proper for states to partner with the federal government on immigration enforcement. Public opinion polls consistently show Arizonans to be supportive of the legislation (64 percent)[63] while Latino voters in Arizona wholly oppose the law (81 percent).[64]

gave Al Gore his popular plurality in 2000, awarding him more than 90 percent of their votes.* Not surprisingly, they voted for Barack Obama, the first African American to run for president on a major-party ticket, almost unanimously.[62] Obama also inspired extraordinarily high turnout among black voters, which contributed to his victories in some important swing states.

Other minority groups show distinctive patterns of issue opinion and voting behavior, but in most instances these patterns reflect the group's economic status rather than particularly ethnic views. Hispanics tend to have lower incomes and so favor more extensive government services and the Democratic Party; Asian Americans tend to have higher incomes and so are economically more conservative and more Republican than Hispanics. But there are enormous differences within these broad categories in the ethnic backgrounds and economic status of subgroups. Hispanics include Cuban Americans, Puerto Ricans, Mexican Americans, immigrants from the nations of Central America, and people whose roots in the Southwest go back centuries. Asian Americans include people of Korean, Japanese, Chinese, Vietnamese, Philippine, and Laotian extraction, some further divided into different eras of immigration and regions of origin.

Generalizing about group opinions is risky, although one pattern seems to hold: ethnic minorities do express strong and distinctive political views on issues directly affecting their groups. Cuban Americans are deeply concerned about U.S. policy toward Cuba. Opposed to any softening of the official U.S. hostility toward Cuba's communist government, Cuban Americans favor Republicans, who generally take a harder line against the dictatorship. Mexican Americans are far more likely than other groups to oppose the denial of public education and health care to undocumented immigrants, a view that brings them closer to the Democrats.

Gender

On most kinds of issues, the sexes think alike, but on some things they do not. Women are consistently less inclined than men to support the use of violence in foreign and domestic

---

*According to *American National Election Study, 2000,* Gore won 91 percent of the black vote; the Election Day exit polls put the figure at 90 percent.

policy. For example, they are more likely to oppose military involvement in foreign conflicts, to support arms control negotiations, and to back gun control, and less likely to demand the death penalty for murderers.* The differences between the sexes on such issues can be quite large, twenty percentage points or more. By smaller margins, women have more favorable attitudes toward social welfare spending and regulations designed to protect the environment, consumers, and children.[65] The reasons for these differences are still a matter of debate. What is known is that they have created a "gender gap" in recent electoral politics, with women more supportive than men of the Democratic Party and its candidates, and men more supportive of Republicans. In 2008 Barack Obama's vote ran about seven percentage points higher among women than among men; unmarried women are especially likely to favor Democrats and account for most of the difference between the sexes.[66]

It is interesting to note that women and men do not differ much on sex-related issues. Both show high levels of support for women and men having an equal role in society and politics; the sexes do not differ in distribution of opinions on abortion.

Income and Education

The politicians who designed the Constitution thought the most enduring political conflicts would pit the poor against the rich. Surveys find abundant evidence that opinions differ among income classes, but the differences are modest compared with those found in most other modern industrial nations. People with lower incomes are more inclined to support spending on government services helpful to people like them: Social Security, student loans, food stamps, child care, and help for the homeless. People with higher incomes are notably less enthusiastic about government spending on social programs or taxing higher incomes at higher rates. Economic self-interest easily explains these differences: people getting more of the benefits tend to see greater merit in social programs than do those paying more of the costs.

On noneconomic issues, however, higher-income groups tend to be more liberal than lower-income groups. This difference has less to do with income than it does with education. People in higher-income groups tend to have more years of formal education, and the more education people have, the more likely they are to take the liberal side on issues such as abortion, gay rights, equality of the sexes, freedom of speech, and minority rights.

Religion

Religion has played an important role in American political life since the founding of the first colonies. A large majority of Americans profess a religious affiliation, and more people belong to religious groups than to any other kind of organization. Religious beliefs shape values, including many of the values people pursue through political action. The movements to abolish slavery, prohibit alcohol, extend civil rights to African Americans, end the war in Vietnam, and ban abortion have all been strongly imbued with religious ideals.

Differences in religious beliefs often underlie differences in political opinions. Not surprisingly, religious beliefs influence opinions on more social issues than economic issues. People

---

* In April 2003, 53 percent of men compared to only 41 percent of women favored preemptive war against countries that might attack the United States. See CBS News/*New York Times* poll, April 11 -13, 2003, http://cbsnews.com/sections/opinion/polls/main500160.shtml.

Despite the fact that the Constitution mandates a separation of church and state, religion and politics come together more often than people realize. When states give employees days off for religious observances or when government scholarships are given to students at colleges affiliated with specific churches, people have argued the separation of church and state is violated. In January 2012, the Freedom From Religion Foundation erected this billboard off Route 295 in Warwick, Rhode Island. The foundation placed its first billboard in Madison, Wisconsin, in 2007 and since then has placed 695 billboards in 61 American cities.

who are secular (no religious preference), Jewish, or members of one of what scholars call the mainline Protestant denominations, such as Episcopalians, Presbyterians, and Congregationalists, tend to be more liberal on social issues. Evangelical Protestants, such as Southern Baptists and Pentecostals, tend to be very conservative. Roman Catholics, who form the largest single denomination, fall in between, but only on average; a wide variety of social views are supported by various organizations within the Catholic Church. Regardless of religious affiliation, the more active people are in religious life, the more socially conservative they are likely to be.

Beginning with the Reagan administration, the Republican Party has made a concerted effort to win the support of evangelical Protestants and other religious conservatives, with a good deal of success. Although the country as a whole was split down the middle between Bush and Gore in 2000, white voters of the religious right went for Bush, 80 percent to 18 percent.[67] Aware of this fact, Bush's 2004 reelection campaign made a special effort to organize get-out-the-vote drives through their churches. Even in 2008, when economic issues were far more salient than social issues, white, born-again Christians gave McCain 74 percent of their votes.[68] Christian conservatives have become so large and active an element in the Republican coalition that they now dominate the party organization in many states. In 2012, white, born-again Christians made up slightly more than a third of the Republican primary electorate. These voters supported Rick Santorum and other candidates who dropped out early in the timeline like Michele Bachmann and Rick Perry over Mitt Romney (only 20 percent favored Romney) for the party nomination. Republican primary voters who believed abortion should always be illegal were almost twice as likely to support Santorum over Romney for the nomination. Many people thought this meant that Romney's path to the nomination would be challenging, but while these groups are vocal and dedicated, they are a relatively small component of the GOP primary electorate—at least compared to those who do not identify themselves as born-again Christians and think abortion should be legal at least some of the time. The risk for the party is that when the media frame it as a place where these groups dominate the process, affluent and educated social liberals who would otherwise be attracted by Republican economic policies may become alienated from the party.

Other Demographic Divisions

Other demographic divisions of opinion are worth noting. Younger voters tend to be more liberal than their elders on social and economic issues; they are, for example, much more supportive of gay marriage. City dwellers are more liberal than residents of suburbs, small towns, or rural areas. People living near the coasts or in the upper Midwest tend to be more liberal than people living in the South, the plains, or the mountain states, particularly on cultural issues. The red state–blue state division made so much of in recent presidential elections reflects this culturally based regional divide. White southerners once stood out starkly from the rest of the population in their opposition to racial integration, but the gap has almost entirely disappeared.

Differences of opinion among major social groups constitute the raw material of electoral politics. Candidates and parties trying to win elections have no choice but to piece together coalitions out of the material at hand. The more affluent voters tend to be economic conservatives but social liberals; voters with more modest incomes combine economic liberalism with social conservatism. Social issues have given Republicans a wedge to split the Democratic coalition by appealing to the social conservatism of voters who, on economic issues, think like Democrats. And Democrats have countered by using issues such as abortion rights and gun control to woo highly educated voters (particularly women) whose economic interests place them closer to the Republicans. Because there are more voters with modest than with ample incomes, Democratic candidates usually like campaigns to focus on economic issues, while Republican candidates want to talk about "family values" and law and order.

Republican presidential hopeful former Pennsylvania Senator Rick Santorum speaks at the Tabernacle Baptist Church, in Coralville, Iowa, on Sunday, December 11, 2011, just a few weeks before the Iowa caucuses. Nearly 60 percent of Iowa Republican caucus-goers identified themselves as born-again Christians or Evangelicals.

PUBLIC OPINION: A VITAL COMPONENT OF AMERICAN POLITICS

The vast network of organizations engaged in measuring or trying to influence public opinion attests to its crucial influence in American politics. But the complexity of the network also underlines the reality that public opinion's influence is rarely simple or unmediated. Individual opinions become public opinion only when aggregated, and organizations and leaders do the aggregating. Polling organizations reveal and express public opinion even as they measure it. Politicians and other policy advocates give it shape, focus, and force through their efforts to persuade and activate citizens to support their causes. The mass media report and interpret the collective political experiences that become the material basis for individual opinions. Opinion leaders provide the cues that the rationally ignorant majority uses as shortcuts to

TAKE A QUIZ

■ *logic.cqpress.com*

Test your knowledge of this chapter.

forming its opinion. Individual opinions, although rooted in personal values and experiences, are both shaped by and expressed through leaders and institutions.

Leaders and institutions do not, however, control public opinion. People choose which leaders to follow and which messages to heed according to the values and beliefs they accumulate over a lifetime. Their assessments of parties, issues, candidates, and other political phenomena, derived from personal observations and life experiences as well as from families and friends, retain a strong practical component, reflecting real interests and needs. For most people, basic political orientations, whether reflections of ideologies, a few core values, or simple party preferences, are quite resistant to change. The raw individual material that goes into the construction of public opinion is not particularly malleable, and neither, therefore, is aggregate opinion. Candidates, policy advocates, and anyone else whose political goals require public support (or at least acquiescence) have little choice but to work within the formidable if often hazy constraints imposed by public attitudes. They succeed, if at all, by framing the choice favorably rather than by changing minds. This is clearest in the electoral context, which is the subject of the next chapter.

logic.cqpress.com

■■■ Key Terms ■■■

aggregate partisanship, 457	core values, 444	opinion leaders, 458
aggregate public opinion, 454	framing, 452	political socialization, 448
ambivalence, 452	ideologies, 443	prime, 454
attitude, 443	issue publics, 459	public opinion, 437
cognitive shortcut, 458	liberals, 444	scientific polling, 439
conservatives, 444	measurement errors, 458	

■■■ Suggested Readings ■■■

Asher, Herbert. *Polling and the Public: What Every Citizen Should Know.* 7th ed. Washington, DC: CQ Press, 2007. A nontechnical primer for citizens who wish to become smarter, more critical consumers of polls and the media stories that report them.

Brody, Richard R. *Assessing the President: The Media, Elite Opinion, and Public Support.* Stanford, CA: Stanford University Press, 1991. The public's rating of the president is shaped by the economy, international crises, political scandal, the news media, and politicians.

Clawson, Rosalee A., and Zoe M. Oxley. *Public Opinion: Democratic Ideals, Democratic Practice.* Washington, DC: CQ Press, 2008. This introduction to public opinion links normative theory to empirical research.

Norrander, Barbara, and Clyde Wilcox. *Understanding Public Opinion.* 2nd ed. Washington, DC: CQ Press, 2002. These essays highlight the diversity of approaches to explaining public opinion.

Page, Benjamin I., and Robert Y. Shapiro. *The Rational Public.* Chicago: University of Chicago Press, 1992.

Mass public opinion responds in reasonable ways to national political events and experiences.

Sniderman, Paul M., and Edward G. Carmines. *Reaching Beyond Race.* Cambridge, MA: Harvard University Press, 1997. A cleverly designed survey using computer-assisted telephone interviews examines what white Americans say about race when they face no risk of appearing racist.

Stimson, James A. *Public Opinion in America: Moods, Cycles, and Swings.* 2nd ed. Boulder, CO: Westview Press, 1999. Broad trends in public opinion on a wide range of policy issues, or public "moods," both shape and reflect broad trends in national policy. At the most general level, government policies do respond to public preferences.

Zaller, John. *Nature and Origins of Mass Opinion.* New York: Cambridge University Press, 1992. Four simple axioms about how people respond to political information generate a rich variety of models of how public opinion shifts in response to events and to elite persuasion.

Review Questions

1. How have modern techniques for molding and measuring public opinion contributed to the nationalization of American politics?

2. Do voters think in terms of ideologies? Are voters' attitudes generally consistent? If not, what explains the inconsistency?

3. Since aggregate opinion is simply the combination of all individual opinions, how can it be more stable and coherent than individual opinion?

4. Who are opinion leaders? Why might typical individuals rely on the statements or positions of these opinion leaders in forming their own opinions? What are the limits on how much these opinion leaders can control public opinion?

5. In which areas does the American public agree or disagree on basic political values and policies? How does this agreement or disagreement make politics possible or necessary?

Voting, Campaigns, and Elections

November 4, 2008

November 3, 2010

Elections invite ordinary citizens to choose leaders and register their opinions on how they have performed. Democrat Barack Obama's decisive victory in the 2008 presidential election reflected widespread unhappiness with the Republican administration of George W. Bush. Two years later, amid continuing high unemployment, doubts that the government's policies had helped the economy, and the growing deficits the policies produced, Obama's party took, in his words, "a shellacking" in the midterm congressional elections. In 2012, despite the still sluggish economy, Obama convinced a majority of Americans to give him a second term.

November 6, 2012

- If Americans cherish the right to vote, why do so many neglect to exercise it?

- Why is political party identification, which many Americans discount, still the best single predictor of how people will vote?

- If attentive and informed voters are likely to be turned off by negative advertisements, why do campaigns pour so much money into running them?

- Does the American system of campaign finance facilitate or undermine democratic accountability?

Voters delivered sharply different verdicts in each of the federal elections held in 2008, 2010, and 2012. In 2008, the Democrats had enjoyed a decisive victory. Their presidential candidate, Barack Obama, won a larger share of the popular vote than any Democrat since Lyndon Johnson in 1964, defeating John McCain, 52.9 percent to 45.7 percent. They also added 21 House seats and 6 Senate seats to the majorities they had won in 2006, giving them 257–178 and 59–41 advantages, respectively, in the two chambers.* The 2010 election erased all of their House gains from 2006 and 2008 and more, with Republicans gaining a net 63 seats to win a 242–193 majority, their best showing since 1946. Republicans also picked up 6 Senate seats. Like 20 of the 32 previous federal elections held since World War II (see Table 7-2, page 310), the 2010 midterm election yielded divided government— the White House and at least one house of Congress controlled by different parties—and a highly acrimonious partisan stalemate that left major national economic and fiscal problems to fester. The American public hated the stalemate and the acrimony, but in 2012, after months of saturation campaigning, with more than $6 billion spent on persuading them to do otherwise, voters ended up endorsing the political status quo. Barack Obama won reelection, 51.1 percent to 47.2 percent for his Republican rival, Mitt Romney. Democrats gained a net 2 Senate seats to increase their majority to 55–45; Republicans easily retained control of the House, although their majority was reduced by 6 to 234–201.

The electoral processes that produced these results differed in important respects. Both 2008 and 2012 were presidential election years, but 2010 was not. When the White House is at stake, the primary and general election contests for president dominate the political stage. In 2008, for the first time since 1952, no sitting president or vice president was running, and both parties engaged in lively primary election seasons. The Democrats' choice quickly narrowed down to two candidates, either of whom would represent a historical first: Hillary Clinton would be the first woman, or Barack Obama would be the first African American, to win a major-party presidential nomination. Obama won a narrow victory

---

*The 59-seat Democratic majority included two senators who ran as independents but voted on organizational matters with the Democrats; two independents are also included in the Democrat's 55-seat majority after 2012.

through superior organization and a strong appeal to younger voters. In the Republican contest, John McCain began the primary season mired in third place in the polls but managed to pull off a remarkable come-from-behind victory to become, at 72, the oldest first-time presidential nominee (see Chapter 12). He then chose a young, charismatic, and largely unknown woman, Alaska governor Sarah Palin, as his vice presidential running mate—only the second woman ever to be nominated for the office.

The nation McCain and Obama competed to lead was deeply unhappy with its current regime. George W. Bush's approval ratings languished in the mid-20s, the lowest of his presidency. An overwhelming majority of Americans were dissatisfied with the direction of the country.[1] The ongoing war in Iraq was a factor, but the main source of such widespread dissatisfaction was the economic crisis, triggered by the steep decline in housing prices that began in late 2006. The turmoil eventually spread to the credit and stock markets, wiping out major financial institutions and reducing Americans' wealth by trillions of dollars. By fall 2008, the nation was already heading into the worst recession since the Great Depression of the 1930s.

The economy came to dominate electoral politics, to the great advantage of Obama and other Democratic candidates. In every election, each side tries to persuade voters that the issues that the public thinks it handles better than its rival are the issues that should determine their votes. The Democratic Party's customary advantage on economic issues was even greater than usual under the conditions prevailing in 2008. With his military background, McCain's strength was foreign policy, but the financial crisis forced him to focus instead on economic issues, which were not his strong suit. It also made it harder for McCain to avoid partisan association with the Bush administration and therefore to counter Obama's most potent theme, that a McCain presidency would be equivalent to a third Bush term.

Presidential elections are as much about candidates as about issues, and so the personal characteristics of the candidates were a central focus of both campaigns. The McCain campaign emphasized his heroism as a prisoner of war in Vietnam and his image as a patriotic man of honor and an independent-minded maverick. It also sought to raise doubts about Obama's character and associations, attacking him for empty eloquence, "palling around with terrorists,"[2] and embracing socialism. The idea was to raise enough uncertainty about Obama that voters would see him as too risky a choice, regardless of what they thought of McCain's Republican associations. Obama was careful always to praise McCain's wartime heroism while portraying him as unaware and out of touch with the economic struggles of ordinary Americans. Obama's main goal, however, was to convince voters, the vast majority of whom knew nothing about him at the start of the campaign season, that he was qualified to be president. He sought to do so by displaying a mastery of the issues and their connections to voters' lives and by projecting a steady, calm, and disciplined image through the lengthy primary and general election season as voters were getting to know him.

In the end, voters opted for change over experience. Unhappiness with Bush and the economy also gave Democratic congressional candidates a potent campaign issue that they exploited with great success. The election gave Democrats full control of the federal government for the first time since 1994—and also full responsibility for dealing with a deep recession and the two troublesome wars in Iraq and Afghanistan.

Two years later, in 2010, voters again opted for change, but this time Obama and the Democrats were the victims. With the help of Democratic majorities in the House and Senate, Obama had pushed through a huge economic stimulus package targeting the recession, initiated comprehensive reforms of the nation's health care system, and signed a major redesign of financial regulation aimed at preventing a repeat of the financial meltdown that had made the recession so severe. These legislative achievements made the 111th Congress among the most productive in many years and were fully consistent with promises Obama made during his successful campaign for the White House. Obama also kept his campaign pledge to wind down the United States' involvement in Iraq and to reallocate American forces to confront the resurgent Taliban in Afghanistan. In short, Obama had done what he might reasonably believe he had been elected to do. Yet a majority of Americans remained unhappy with the state of the nation and its politics, and Obama's approval ratings had dipped below 50 percent by the beginning of his second year in office. The main reason was that, despite successful

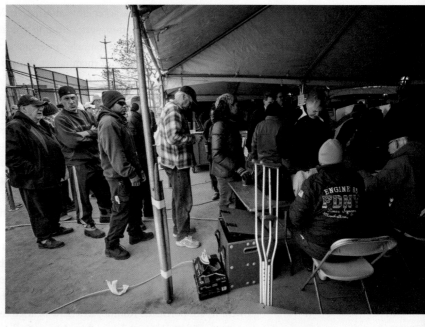

Long lines at the polls are common in urban areas during presidential elections, but many voters in New York faced additional problems in 2012 when the devastating storm Sandy deluged the area just before the election. These voters in Far Rockaway wait patiently to vote in tents set up as emergency polling sites.

efforts, initiated by Bush but continued by Obama, to rescue the financial system (and Chrysler and General Motors), and despite Obama's huge economic stimulus package, the economy did not rebound vigorously enough to keep unemployment from rising to 10 percent and remaining near that level through the midterm elections. The administration's economic policies almost certainly kept the recession from getting much worse, but as a campaign theme, the counterfactual (how much more severe the recession would have been without these actions) did not carry much force against the reality of a painfully slow recovery, and most Americans came to see the administration's economic policies as ineffective or even harmful.[3] Thus they also objected to the sharp increase in the federal budget deficit that these policies necessarily produced.

Health care reform was also politically problematic, for its immediate political effect was to polarize the public and inspire the upsurge of populist conservatism and intense hostility to Obama that were manifest in the Tea Party movement. Attacking Obama with the same accusations of "socialism" used by the McCain-Palin campaign in 2008, Tea Party conservatives reenergized the Republican Party and made the president and his policies the focus of congressional campaigns across the country. A majority of independents also opposed Obama's health care reform and consequently disapproved of Obama's performance in office. Independent voters, whose support had been essential to Democratic victories in 2006 and 2008, thus favored Republicans in 2010, and this was a major source of Republican congressional gains.

The results of the 2010 election led to two years of intense, unproductive partisan conflict especially on budget issues. Unable to reach agreement on actions to attack the unemployment problem or to address the sharp increase in the federal deficit occasioned by the deep recession, the president and Congress effectively left it up to the voters to decide which side should prevail. The weak economy clearly left Obama vulnerable, but to exploit that vulnerability, the

Republicans had to offer an acceptable alternative. Mitt Romney, in his second campaign for the Republican nomination, was a leading candidate from the start. To be nominated, however, he had to persuade the staunch conservatives who dominate the Republican caucuses and primaries that he was one of them rather than the moderate he had seemed to be while serving as governor of Massachusetts. It was not easy, and over the course of the primary season, he ran behind a succession of more conservative Republicans (first Rick Perry, then Herman Cain, then Newt Gingrich, then Rick Santorum) in straw polls of Republican voters. Romney disposed of each of these rivals, using his superior financial resources to advertise their various political liabilities and to persuade most Republicans that he had the best chance of defeating Obama. To do so, he staked out positions on economic and social issues that were considerably more attractive to conservative Republicans than to the more moderate voters he would need in the general election. (See Chapter 12.)

This helped Obama, for presidents seeking reelection in bad economic times cannot succeed without changing the subject.[4] His campaign needed to make the election something other than a referendum on Obama's economic management, for most Americans thought the economy was in bad shape and disapproved of Obama's handling of it. Thus the Obama campaign labored to frame the choice as one between two distinct candidates and partisan visions of the future rather than a referendum on the administration's record on jobs and growth. Its ads portrayed Romney as a hard-hearted capitalist who reaped millions from deals that eliminated American jobs, stashing his profits in overseas banks to avoid taxes. They also painted Romney and his party as far out of the mainstream on such issues as abortion, women's rights, and immigration reform. The campaign succeeded in changing the subject for enough voters to keep the weak economy from ending Obama's presidency, attracting large majorities of women (especially unmarried women) and minorities to offset Obama's deficit among white males.[5] The "Great Recession" was central to electoral politics for three successive elections, but in 2012, it no longer determined the outcome.

In both 2008 and 2010, then, the American electorate delivered a powerful message of discontent with the status quo, reallocating power in Washington and thereby initiating major changes in the direction of national policy. In 2012, in contrast, the message was mixed, and the status quo prevailed. However, that outcome had profound consequences for the direction of national policy, for it ensured that Obama's signal legislative achievements—the overhaul of the heath care system and financial regulations—would not be quickly undone.

The reversals of partisan fortunes registered in these three elections offer a vivid illustration of how elections link public opinion and government action in the United States. Elections enable ordinary citizens, in aggregate, to reward or punish elected officials for their performance in office and to influence national policy by selecting or replacing leaders according to their actions or proposals. Elections not only prompt elected officials to take voters' views into account when they make policy choices but also provide a reason for citizens to think about and form opinions on issues and candidates. For candidates and their parties, these opinions serve as the raw material of electoral politics. As we saw in Chapter 10, Americans are divided on a broad range of political issues. Often, the divisions do not form consistent patterns; different groups come together on different issues. The challenge for each candidate or party is to find ways to persuade voters of disparate and often conflicting views to agree on a common action, which is to vote for their side. Building coalitions—getting people to agree on an action in the absence of agreement on the purposes of the action—is what pluralist politics is all about, and it is as fundamental to electoral politics as it is to governing. The challenge for voters is to figure out which candidate or party will best serve their interests and represent their values. The way voters, candidates, and parties attempt to meet these challenges is the subject of this chapter. To begin, however, we need to examine the logic of elections and their historical development in the United States.

THE LOGIC OF ELECTIONS

Democracy in America is representative democracy. James Madison, in defending the Constitution in *Federalist* No. 10, adopted the term *republic* to emphasize the distinction between democracy as eighteenth-century Americans saw it and the proposed new system:

> The two great points of difference between a democracy and a republic are: first, the delegation of the government, in the latter, to a small number of citizens elected by the rest; secondly, the greater number of citizens, and greater sphere of country, over which the latter may be extended.

The sheer size of the new nation made self-government by direct democracy impossible (imagine the transaction costs). If the American people were to govern themselves at all, they would have to do it indirectly through the delegation of their authority to a small number of representative agents. But delegation raised the unavoidable danger, immediately acknowledged by Madison, that these agents might use their authority to serve themselves rather than the people they are supposed to represent: "Men of fractious tempers, of local prejudices, or of sinister designs, may, by intrigue, by corruption, or by other means, first obtain the suffrages [votes], and then betray the interests of the people."

As noted in Chapter 1, any delegation of authority raises the possibility of agency loss. Whenever we engage someone to act on our behalf, we face the risk that they will put their interests ahead of ours. Worse, it is often difficult to tell whether they are faithful agents because we cannot see what they do or know why they are doing it. The problem of delegation has no perfect solutions. One effective, if *imperfect,* solution adopted by representative democracies is to hold regular, free, competitive elections. Elections ameliorate the delegation problem in several ways. First, they give ordinary citizens a say in who represents them. Second, the prospect of future elections gives officeholders who want to keep (or improve) their jobs a motive to be responsive agents. And third, elections provide powerful incentives for the small set of citizens who want to replace the current officeholders to keep a close eye on representatives and to tell everyone else about any misconduct they detect.

Elections do not guarantee faithful representation; indeed, many Americans today do not feel faithfully represented (see Figure 10-5, page 463), even though the United States holds more elections for more public offices than any other nation in the world. But the absence of regular, free, competitive elections does make it unlikely that ordinary citizens will be represented at all. Competitive elections in which virtually all adult citizens are eligible to vote are the defining feature of modern democratic governments.

THE RIGHT TO VOTE

The practice of selecting leaders by ballot arrived in North America with the first settlers from England. So, too, did the practice of limiting suffrage. Every colony imposed a property qualification for voting, and many denied the franchise to Catholics, Jews, Native Americans, and freed black slaves. Women were rarely allowed to vote.

Many of these restrictions survived the Revolution intact; only about half of the free adult male population was eligible to vote at the time the Constitution was adopted. The story since that time has been the progressive, if sometimes frustratingly slow, extension of the franchise to virtually all adult citizens (defined as people who have celebrated their eighteenth birthdays) not in prisons or mental institutions. Every expansion of suffrage had to overcome both philosophical objections and resistance rooted in the mundane calculations of political advantage. The triumph of (nearly) universal adult suffrage reflects the powerful appeal of democratic ideas, combined with profound social changes, the struggles of dedicated activists, and the perpetual scramble of politicians for votes.

Wider Suffrage for Men

The property qualifications and voting restrictions brought over from England in colonial times reflected the basic social realities there. Most adults were poor, illiterate, and dependent;

Nineteenth-century itinerant American artist George Caleb Bingham sometimes depicted local campaign scenes. In fact, Bingham was as much politician as painter. An ardent supporter of Whig candidate William Henry Harrison in the 1840 presidential election, Bingham gave speeches and painted banners. He also was elected to the Missouri legislature (on his second attempt) and later served as state treasurer. In *The County Election* citizens line up to declare their votes publicly. Although the painting offers a stylized image of democracy in early America, the inebriated voter toward the end of the line being helped to the poll serves as a reminder that this painter-politician also had the sensibilities of a realist, to be expected of someone who once had been narrowly defeated for election.

George Caleb Bingham; *The County Election,* 1852; oil on canvas.

they were servants, tenants, hired hands, or paupers. Members of the upper-class minority—a well-born, prosperous, and educated elite—took for granted their right to govern. They were not about to risk the existing social order, which served them so well, by extending voting rights to people whose interests might be better served by changing it. The trip across the Atlantic took some of the bite out of the property qualifications. Land was easier to acquire and far more evenly distributed in the colonies than in England, so a larger proportion of adult males qualified to vote. In the more fluid colonial communities, property restrictions often were enforced laxly if at all. By the revolutionary period any "respectable" man—meaning white, Protestant, and gainfully employed—was, in practice, allowed to vote in many places.[6]

The Revolutionary War exerted a powerful influence on the demands to enlarge the franchise. The rallying cry against England of "no taxation without representation," initially a demand for home rule, also implied that anyone who paid taxes should have the right to vote. Men who risked their lives in the fight for independence felt entitled to full political citizenship regardless of wealth. More important and more long-lasting, the ringing pronouncements in the Declaration of Independence that "all men are created equal" and enjoy unalienable rights to "Life, Liberty, and the pursuit of Happiness" and that governments derive "their just powers from the consent of the governed" left little ground for denying voting rights to any citizen.

Still, universal suffrage for (white) men was not fully achieved until the 1840s in the wake of the triumph of Jacksonian democracy. The rear guard defense of suffrage restrictions rested on traditional arguments: people without a stake in the social order should not have a voice in governing it. If every man were allowed to vote, the votes of those dependent on the wealthy for their livelihoods—employees, tenant farmers, servants, and apprentices—would be controlled by their patrons, enhancing the power of the rich. If, to avoid such untoward influence, a secret ballot were used, the more numerous poor might support unscrupulous demagogues promoting schemes to redistribute wealth. The argument for limiting suffrage boiled down to this: only the independent and virtuous were fit to govern, and the best evidence of independence and virtue was being a property-holding, white, Protestant male.

Gradually, however, this view lost ground to the argument for political equality implicit in the Declaration of Independence, and opposition to universal male suffrage became a political liability. The more democratic the electorate, the more politically suicidal it was to oppose more democracy. The French observer Alexis de Tocqueville noted with his usual clarity:

> There is no more invariable rule in the history of society: the further electoral rights are extended, the greater is the need of extending them; for after each concession the strength of the democracy increases, and its demands increase with its strength. . . . Concession follows concession, and no stop can be made short of universal suffrage.[7]

Suffrage for Women

As Tocqueville correctly observed, the democratic logic that justified giving the vote to all white men did not stop there; it also nurtured demands that all adult citizens, regardless of race or sex, be eligible to vote. For more than a century, race, sex, and the institution of slavery interacted to complicate suffrage politics. The women's suffrage movement grew directly out of the antislavery movement, sharing its underlying ideals and some of its activists. Suffragists felt betrayed when the Civil War amendments (formally, if not in practice) enfranchised the

SHALL WOMEN VOTE?

No, They Might Disturb the Existing Order of Things

The campaign to give women the right to vote was fueled by the hope that their presence in the electorate would improve the moral tone of political life. This 1909 cartoon, captioned "Shall Women Vote? No, they might disturb the existing order of things," suggests that the existing order was thoroughly corrupt and thus ought to be disturbed.

newly freed black men but not white or black women. The largely successful effort by white southerners to purge blacks from the electorate after the end of Reconstruction (see Chapter 4) raised a major barrier to giving women the vote. Southern whites opposed any action that might focus national attention on repressive local electoral practices. As one Mississippi senator candidly put it in the 1880s, "We are not afraid to maul a black man over the head if he dares to vote but we can't treat women, even black women, that way. No, we'll allow no woman suffrage. It may be right, but we won't have it."[8]

The resistance to women's suffrage was gradually overcome by a combination of social change—the expansion of education for both sexes, the entry of women into the workforce outside the home—and political need. Western territories (later states) were the first to grant women the right to vote, not because places like Wyoming and Utah were hotbeds of radical democracy but because women were expected to vote for "family values" in raw frontier communities. The campaign for suffrage sometimes took on nativist overtones, proposing to use women's votes to uphold Anglo-Saxon civilization; indeed, many suffragists did not object to the literacy tests, poll taxes, and other devices designed to keep the "wrong" sorts of people out of the electorate. As women's suffrage grew at the state and local levels, politicians competing for women's votes naturally supported further expansion. Once party politicians sensed an irresistible trend, they scrambled to make sure their side was not stigmatized for standing in the way. Only southern Democrats held out to the bitter end; the defense of white supremacy trumped everything else.[9] The Nineteenth Amendment to the Constitution, adopted in 1920, finally guaranteed women everywhere the right to vote.

Suffrage for African Americans, Young Americans

Despite ratification of the Civil War amendments, the effective extension of the vote to blacks and other minorities came much later, again as a result of social changes and the political incentives they produced. The story, crowned by the landmark Voting Rights Act of 1965, is told in Chapter 4.

The most recent expansion of voting rights—the Twenty-sixth Amendment (1971), which lowered the voting age of citizens to eighteen years—also was a political move, one provoked by the Vietnam War. The idea appealed to antiwar activists because young people were so prominent in their movement. Politicians who supported the war also endorsed the amendment because it enfranchised the troops fighting in Vietnam, most of whom were under the age of twenty-one. The movement echoed the logic advanced after the Revolutionary War that those who risk their lives on the battlefield ought to have a voice in governing the nation they are defending.

Consider, though, what consequences did *not* ensue from the formal expansions of suffrage. The propertyless did not despoil the propertied; hence the conformity cost most dreaded by defenders of limited suffrage never materialized. Votes for women did not immediately transform electoral politics in any measurable way: no distinctive pattern of women's voting was evident until the 1980s, following a steep increase in the proportion of single working women in the electorate. The only discernible consequence of granting eighteen-year-olds the right to vote was a decline in the percentage of those eligible who turn out to vote. The Fourteenth and Fifteenth Amendments did not prevent a century of racial discrimination at the polls. Only the Voting Rights Act quickly and effectively achieved its goals of increasing African American voting in states practicing discrimination. The democratic idea has yet to reach its logical limits, however. Some activists have proposed enfranchising children and noncitizen residents, even those illegally in the United States.[10] In contemporary America, "no taxation without representation" implies a remarkably inclusive franchise.

WHO USES THE RIGHT TO VOTE?

Most Americans agree that the right to vote is the very essence of democracy. On Memorial Day and other holidays the nation honors the soldiers who have fought and died for that privilege. If the right to vote is so valuable, then, why do millions of Americans choose not to exercise it?

It might seem paradoxical that many people who think that the right to vote is worth dying for do not bother to go to the polls. But this reality is not paradoxical at all: it is inherent in the logic of elections. The benefits of elections—in both the broad sense of maintaining democratic accountability and in the narrower sense of electing a preferred candidate—are collective benefits. People enjoy these payoffs even if they have not helped to produce them by voting. It makes perfect sense for citizens to insist on the right to vote, for it gives leaders a reason to care about people's interests, opinions, and values. But it makes equal sense not to bother voting if the only purpose in voting is to influence leaders. After all, the likelihood that any single vote will influence anyone or anything is minute. Totaled up, votes are decisive; individually, they count for next to nothing. Why, then, spend the time and energy required to go to the polls if individual participation, or its absence, makes no difference in the outcome of the election? The real question is not so much why millions of Americans do not vote, but why millions of Americans forgo free riding and *do* vote.

The same logic applies to gathering information about the competing candidates and parties if a person chooses to vote. There is no point in investing time, energy, or money in becoming better informed about electoral options because the payoff for casting the "right" vote—for the candidate who would, in the voter's view, do the best job—is for all practical purposes nil. If there is no real chance that a vote will be decisive, it is of no consequence whether the vote is right or wrong. Ignorance, like abstention from voting, is rational.

Followed to its logical conclusion, this line of reasoning would lead to the collapse of electoral politics and thus to the collapse of democracy: no voters, no accountability, no

TABLE 11-1

Influences on Voter Turnout

	Presidential Elections	Midterm Elections
Demographic Characteristics		
Income	15.8	4.6
Education	16.6	27.0
Age	29.0	25.7
African American	−4.4	−8.5
Mexican American and Puerto Rican	−5.7	−9.3
Lives in southern state	−16.3	−9.8
Lives in border state	−6.1	−8.4
Social Involvement		
Years in community	10.7	23.3
Church attendance	15.1	10.2
Homeowner	.7.5	5.5
Currently employed	2.1	
Psychological Characteristics		
Internal efficacy	2.9	
External efficacy	10.6	8.2
Evaluation of Parties and Candidates		
Strength of party identification	10.6	17.5
Affect for a party	11.4	
Cares which party wins presidential election	6.4	
Cares which party wins congressional elections		20.7
Affect for a presidential candidate	5.6	
Mobilization by Parties and Campaigns		
Contacted by a party	7.8	10.4
Close presidential election	3.0	
Gubernatorial election	5.0	
Open House seat		3.7
Unopposed House seat		−4.0
Toss-up House election		6.0
Legal Organization of Elections		
Voter registration closing date	−5.6	
Literacy test (African Americans)	−16.0	
Poll tax (African Americans)	−10.2	
Periodic registration (African Americans)	−11.6	
Voting Rights Act (African Americans)	26.4	
Voting Rights Act (whites)	19.5	

Source: Steven J. Rosenstone and John Mark Hansen, *Mobilization, Participation, and Democracy in America* (New York: Macmillan, 1993), 130–131. Copyright © 1993 by Macmillan Publishing Company. Reprinted by permission of Pearson Education, Inc.

Note: Data for presidential elections cover 1956 through 1988; data for midterm elections cover 1974 through 1986. Table entries are the differences in turnout rates between the highest and lowest values taken by each variable, controlling for the effects of the other variables. For income, it is the difference between people in the highest (top 4 percent) and lowest (bottom 16 percent) of five income groups; for education, it is the difference between people with some college and people with no more than an eighth-grade education. For age, it is the difference between the oldest and youngest citizens. Party affect is measured by the absolute value of the sum of positive comments about the first party and negative comments about the second minus the sum of positive comments about the second party and negative comments about the first (responses to questions about what respondents liked and disliked about the parties); affect toward presidential candidates is measured equivalently. The voter registration closing date indicates the number of days prior to the election that one can last register to vote. Voting Rights Act is coded 1 if respondent lived in a state covered by the Voting Rights Act in 1986 or 1972; 0 otherwise.

consent of the governed. In practice, however, these free-rider problems are overcome, but they are overcome quite imperfectly and in ways that have important consequences for how American democracy actually works.

The share of eligible voters who go to the polls has varied widely over American history (turnout patterns are traced in Chapter 12). The most important change in the past half-century was the sharp decline in voter turnout between 1968 and 1972. Since then, an average of only about 58 percent of the eligible electorate has bothered to register and vote in presidential elections; even the hotly contested 2012 presidential race inspired a turnout of only 58.7 percent.[11] Variations in turnout pose the questions we address in this section: Who votes, why, and to what effect? Why do turnout rates vary, and does it matter?

Individual Factors Affecting Turnout

A great deal of research has gone into figuring out who votes, who does not, and why. The state of the art in this endeavor is still represented by the work of political scientists Steven J. Rosenstone and John Mark Hansen; their findings are partially summarized in Table 11-1.[12] The entries in the table indicate the difference a particular factor makes in the likelihood of voting (with the effect of the rest held constant). For example, other things being equal, turnout in midterm elections (when people vote for senators and representatives but not the president) is twenty-seven percentage points higher for the most educated as compared with the least educated. In presidential elections turnout among the oldest citizens is twenty-nine points higher than it is among the youngest citizens.

Age and education have the strongest influence on voting, but many other things affect turnout as well. African Americans and Hispanics are less likely to vote (taking all other factors into account), as are people who live in southern states or states bordering the South. People with deeper roots in their communities (longer-time residents, homeowners, church members, and people with jobs) are more likely to go to the polls, as are individuals with greater confidence in their own ability to understand and engage in politics (internal efficacy, as it is known in political science) and in their ability to influence the decisions of government (external efficacy). Turnout also is higher among people with stronger partisan views and electoral preferences and those who live in areas with active parties and competitive campaigns. Finally, turnout is higher where legal barriers to registration are lower.

Why is sex missing from this list of influences on voting? Other things being equal, the voting rates for men and women are about the same. Also absent are measures of trust in government and beliefs about government responsiveness; the cynical and distrusting are as likely to vote as everyone else. This point contradicts a popular explanation for the decline in participation between the 1960s and 1990s—that it resulted from the dramatic increase in public cynicism and mistrust since 1960.[13]

The explanation for these patterns is straightforward. Voting and other forms of political participation, such as contributing money or time to campaigns, writing letters to elected officials, and attending political meetings, incur costs but produce benefits. People participate when they can meet the costs and appreciate the benefits. Those with money, education, experience, free time, and self-confidence find it easier to meet the costs; those with a greater psychological stake in politics—from a concern with issues, a sense of obligation to carry out their duties as citizens, or a strong interest in parties or candidates—receive greater benefits (also mainly psychological) from participation. Voting, therefore, is rational for the millions of individuals who derive personal satisfaction from going to the polls. Expressing themselves through voting outweighs the typically modest cost of casting a ballot.

Institutional Factors Affecting Turnout

Differences in participation cannot be explained completely by individual differences in resources and psychological involvement, however. The institutional context—for example, variations in registration laws—affects turnout equally. The more onerous the registration requirement, the higher the cost of voting. In the decades after the Civil War, southern states adopted devices such as poll taxes, literacy tests, and the requirement that voters reregister periodically to discourage African Americans from voting. In many cases, these practices discouraged poor whites from participating as well. But after the Voting Rights Act of 1965 banned literacy tests and authorized the Justice Department to oversee voter registration in states with a history of flagrant racial discrimination, voting among African Americans (and whites) increased sharply. Still, the effects of old practices linger on. Even with the end of formal and informal restrictions on voting and the advent of two-party competition in their region, southerners are notably less likely to vote than are Americans who reside elsewhere. Schemes to skew the electorate for political advantage are by no means a thing of the past. Prior to the 2012 election, more than a dozen states adopted a requirement that voters show a picture ID at the polls, raising the cost of participation for poor and minority voters, who are less likely to possess driver's licenses or passports. They are also more likely to vote for

The elderly vote. Free time, a distaste for taxes, and dependence on government retirement programs render the elderly a highly vigilant, issue-oriented electorate whom politicians approach with some fear and great care.

Democrats, and all but one of the state governments that adopted this requirement were controlled by Republicans.

Social circumstances also play a crucial part in stimulating turnout. Social connections create personal incentives to participate when, for example, coworkers take note of who is performing their citizen's duty to vote (and who is wearing the "I voted" sticker). These connections also provide plenty of free information through casual conversation touching on politics. Even more significant, however, are the deliberate efforts of political activists of all kinds to get people to vote. Often, people participate because they are asked, a fact that has never been a secret to politicians. The desire to win elections has inspired extensive efforts by candidates, parties, interest groups, and other campaigners to get their potentially free-riding supporters to show up at the polls. The massive and effective turnout efforts mounted by the Obama campaigns in 2008 and 2012 are cases in point.

The assorted demographic and institutional influences on voting produce an electorate in which wealthy, well-educated, older white people are overrepresented and the poor, uneducated, young, and nonwhite are underrepresented. Unequal resources are only part of the reason. The other is that people with social advantages are more likely to be mobilized by parties, interest groups, and campaign organizations. Political leaders deploy their scarce resources efficiently, targeting the people who are cheapest to reach and likeliest to respond. In other words, they go after people like themselves (educated and relatively affluent), people already organized and identified by membership in voluntary associations, and people whose social characteristics already incline them to participate. "Thus," in the words of Rosenstone and Hansen, "the pressures that political leaders face to use their own resources most effectively build a class bias into their efforts to mobilize."[14] It takes an extraordinary effort backed by abundant organizational resources, such as that undertaken by the Obama campaign in 2012, to counteract this tendency.[15]

Variations in Turnout over Time

If these factors explain variations in participation among individuals, what accounts for variations in turnout over time? More specifically, why did turnout decline from an average of about 68 percent in 1952–1968 to about 55 percent in 1992–2000 before rising above 58 percent again in the three most recent presidential elections? (See Figure 12-3, page 540.) The initial decline was especially puzzling to scholars because voter registration laws were eased and educational attainment rose over the period—two trends that should have increased turnout. But they did not do so because their effects were more than offset by contrary trends. Rosenstone and Hansen's analysis of the forces contributing to changes in turnout is summarized in Table 11-2.

Easier registration and increased formal education had a positive effect on turnout, but other changes had the opposite effect. For example, extending the franchise to eighteen-year-olds reduced the turnout percentage by enlarging the pool of eligible voters with the age group least inclined to vote—citizens younger than twenty-five.

TABLE 11-2

Sources of the Decline in Voter Turnout between the 1960s and 1980s

Change	Effect on Percentage Change in Turnout between 1960s and 1980s	Percentage of Total Decline in Turnout
Easing of voter registration laws	+1.8	
Increased formal education	+2.8	
A younger electorate	−2.7	17
Weakened social involvement	−1.4	9
Declining feelings of political efficacy	−1.4	9
Weakened attachment to and evaluation of political parties and their candidates	−1.7	11
Decline in mobilization	−8.7	54
Net change in voter turnout	−11.3	100

Source: Steven J. Rosenstone and John Mark Hansen, *Mobilization, Participation, and Democracy in America* (New York: Macmillan, 1993), 215. Copyright © 1993 by Macmillan Publishing Company. Reprinted by permission of Pearson Education, Inc.

Note: The first column lists the net contribution of each change in electoral conditions to changes in the turnout rate between the 1960s and 1980s; the second column indicates the proportion of the total change in turnout over this period accounted for by each factor.

Turnout also declined because fewer people had deep community roots, felt politically efficacious, or felt strongly about parties and candidates.

The major reasons for the decline, however, were institutional: a decline in **mobilization** by parties, candidates, and groups such as labor unions. Fewer people were voting in part because fewer people were being mobilized—that is, being asked to vote by activists working for parties or candidates. Most candidates and parties have replaced labor-intensive door-to-door campaigns with money-intensive television and direct-mail campaigns. Moreover, because media campaigns are so expensive, parties and others concentrate scarce resources on the tightest races, thereby reducing attempts to mobilize voters in less competitive races. The fading of the civil rights movement diminished efforts to get African Americans to register and vote. The decline of the labor movement eroded the unions' traditional grassroots campaigning, though in recent elections labor leaders have sought, with some success, to reverse this trend. When the competing presidential campaigns invested heavily in grassroots activities to get out the vote in 2004, 2008, and 2012, turnout was significantly higher. In short, turnout rates are directly affected by the activities of political entrepreneurs pursuing offices or policies. When their goals, tactics, and resources change, so does the level of electoral participation.[16]

THE MOTOR VOTER LAW

logic of politics

Tens of millions of eligible Americans do not bother to vote in national elections. This rampant free riding inspires chronic editorial hand-wringing and numerous projects for boosting turnout. Any attempt to raise turnout through legislation, however, automatically becomes a partisan issue. Politicians believe, despite evidence to the contrary, that higher turnout favors Democrats.[1]

The National Voter Registration Act of 1993, popularly known as the motor voter law, is a case in point. Enacted over Republican opposition, the law requires states to allow citizens to register to vote when applying for or renewing their driver's licenses, to register by mail, or to receive mail registration forms and assistance in filling them out at state welfare offices. It also forbids states to purge voters from the rolls for failing to vote. The purpose of the bill is to increase turnout by making registration easy—in other words, by reducing the cost to the citizen.

Republicans attacked the proposal in Congress and later in the courts as, in the words of Republican senator Paul Coverdell of Georgia, "a classic example of a bully government placing an extreme financial burden on our states."[2] Their real concern, however, was not the unfunded mandate (see Chapter 8), but the prospect of hordes of new Democratic voters. Ironically, the law's effect so far has favored Republicans; the regions with the largest increases in registration under the law have been Republican strongholds in the South and West.

The motor voter law added millions to the voter rolls, and analysts suggest that it has the potential to increase turnout by as much as ten percentage points.[3] But voting participation was actually lower in the presidential (1996 and 2000) and midterm (1998) elections held after the law took effect than in the two comparable elections immediately before (1992 and 1994). Many of the new registrants apparently did not immediately begin voting, indicating that the cost of registering was not what was keeping them from the polls. The increases in turnout for the three most recent presidential elections, especially among young voters, may have been facilitated by the law, but intensive registration campaigns and strong feelings aroused by the competing presidential candidates probably had more to do with it.

---

1. Benjamin Highton and Raymond E. Wolfinger, "The Political Implications of Higher Turnout" (paper presented at the annual meeting of the American Political Science Association, Boston, September 3–6, 1998).

2. Alan Greenblatt, "Court Rejects 'Motor Voter' Case, But the Battle Isn't Over," *Congressional Quarterly Weekly Report*, January 27, 1996, 232.

3. Benjamin Highton and Raymond E. Wolfinger, "Estimating the Effects of the National Voter Registration Act of 1993," *Political Behavior* 20 (June 1998): 79–94.

The decline in voting turnout after the 1960s was much more pronounced among those whose participation is most dependent on outside stimulation: the poorest and least educated citizens. In general, the smaller the electorate, the greater its upper-class bias. Logically, a biased electorate should produce biased policy because politicians naturally cater to the people whose votes control their futures. In times of tight budgets, for example, Congress has been more willing to cut social welfare programs benefiting poor people (food stamps, job training programs, and aid to families with dependent children) than to cut social welfare programs benefiting the politically active middle class (Social Security and Medicare). Even so, the systematic evidence suggests that the policy preferences of voters and nonvoters are usually not very different and that few, if any, election results would change if every eligible person voted.[17] Such evidence has not, however, kept policies designed to raise turnout from provoking partisan squabbles (see box "The Motor Voter Law").

How Do Voters Decide?

Casting a vote is making a prediction about the future—that electing one candidate will produce a better outcome in some relevant sense than electing another candidate. To make such a prediction, a voter has to choose the standards for "better" and "relevant" and then determine which candidate best meets the standards. These choices are made under conditions of considerable uncertainty, and because the likelihood of casting a decisive vote is so tiny, people find it makes little sense to put much effort into acquiring information that might reduce uncertainty. Thus they economize by using simple cues as cognitive shortcuts and by relying heavily, if selectively, on the free information delivered by the news media, campaign advertising, opinion leaders, and their own experience to inform their predictions.

Past Performance and Incumbency

One way to predict the future is to look at the past. Voters may treat an election as a referendum on the incumbent's or majority party's performance in office. Has the current agent done an adequate job of serving the voters' values and interests? One simple rule is to vote for incumbents who have performed well. The question then becomes, performance on what? The answer depends on the office, the circumstances, and what the voter considers important. Presidents seeking reelection often are held accountable for the national economy—the rates of inflation, unemployment, and economic growth. Economic problems probably cost Jimmy Carter and George H. W. Bush their jobs, while a strong economy contributed to Ronald Reagan's reelection in 1984 and to Bill Clinton's in 1996. The question famously posed by Reagan captures this standard: "Are you better off now than you were four years ago?" Presidents also may be reviewed for their conduct of foreign policy. Dwight Eisenhower's success in ending the war in Korea helped ensure his reelection in 1956; Carter's inability to obtain the release of the U.S. diplomats held hostage by Iran damaged his reelection chances in 1980. George W. Bush's reelection hinged in good part on how voters weighed his response to the September 11, 2001, attacks, particularly his decision to invade Iraq. The performance of representatives and senators, by contrast, is often measured by their success in providing services and projects for their states and districts or in casting acceptable votes in Congress (see Chapter 6). But some voters hold the president's party as a whole responsible, casting their congressional votes according to how well they think the administration has governed.

■ DATA UPDATE

logic.cqpress.com

Presidential and Senate elections are often won by the same party in many states.

Endorsements by well-known interest groups give voters cheap and reliable cues about the policy inclinations of candidates. Here, Vice President Dick Cheney accepts the gift of a fancy flintlock rifle from leaders of the National Rifle Association (President Kayne Robinson, right, and Vice President Wayne LaPierre, left), an unmistakable signal to voters on either side of the gun control issue that the 2004 Bush-Cheney ticket stood with the NRA against greater regulation of firearms.

Voters unhappy with President Bush and the Iraq War took it out on congressional Republicans in 2006; similarly, voters objecting to President Obama, his policies, and the sorry state of the economy punished Democratic candidates for Congress in the 2010 midterm elections. In both cases, the president's party lost majority control of the House and, in 2006, the Senate as well.

Assessing the Issues and Policy Options

How can voters assess performance efficiently? Personal experience supplies a good deal of politically relevant information. Looking for a job, shopping at the supermarket, or trying to get a mortgage to buy a house teaches people about unemployment, inflation, and interest rates. Taking out a student loan or applying for veterans' benefits teaches something about government programs. Millions of retired Americans are keenly aware of the size of their monthly Social Security checks. The threat of a military draft certainly raised the political consciousness of college-age Americans during the Vietnam War. Those without direct experience with certain issues learn about them through the news media. For example, crime became a bigger public issue in the 1990s than it had been a decade earlier—even though the crime rate had actually declined—because of the greater emphasis the news media put on it. And, of course, Americans needed no direct personal experience of terrorist attacks and the Iraq War for these events to shape their judgments of George W. Bush's fitness for reelection in 2004.

Another strategy for predicting which candidate will be the more satisfactory agent is to compare the future policy options each represents. By the positions they take on issues, by their overall ideological stances, or by their party affiliations, candidates offer choices among alternative national policies. Which policy positions matter? The answer depends on the voters and current circumstances. For voters with strong views on abortion, any difference between candidates on this issue may be enough to settle their choice. **Single-issue voters** also coalesce around causes such as gun control (its most adamant opponents) and environmental protection (its most adamant proponents). Instead of a single issue, other voters may consider bundles of issues, choosing between, say, the expectations of lower taxes and more generous social spending. The times also may determine which issues become important to voters. Civil rights became critical in the 1964 election when the Republican candidate, Sen.

Barry Goldwater of Arizona, voted against the Civil Rights Act of 1964. What to do about Vietnam dominated voter opinion while American soldiers were fighting there. Similarly, the wisdom of invading Iraq was central to voters' deliberations in 2004. Iraq was expected to be the central issue again in 2008, but with the collapse of housing prices, frozen credit markets, a plummeting stock market, and a looming recession, the economy overwhelmed all other issues. In 2010, a critical issue for many voters, most conspicuously those who sympathized with the Tea Party movement, was the growth in federal government spending and activism during the Obama administration, issues that continued to play a major role in 2012.

Voter Cues and Shortcuts

The news media and the campaigns supply plenty of free information about candidates' positions on the issues and policy promises. But voters cannot take the information at face value, for candidates have an incentive to misrepresent themselves to win votes. Voters can deal with this problem by taking cues from opinion leaders (see Chapter 10). In electoral politics, opinion leadership is often formalized through endorsements from organizations and individuals. A candidate supported by the NARAL Pro-Choice America, the Reverend Jesse Jackson, or the Sierra Club is certain to have rather different policy objectives from one endorsed by the Christian Coalition, the National Rifle Association, the National Taxpayers Union, or the Tea Party Express.

Voters also make predictions based on the candidates' personal characteristics. One set of personal considerations includes qualities such as competence, experience, honesty, knowledge, and leadership skills. Another set includes characteristics such as sex, race, ethnicity, age, and place of residence. The rationale for such criteria is straightforward. Voters cannot anticipate all the problems and issues that will come up after the election, nor can they easily monitor the behavior of their elected officials. Much of what these agents do is out of public sight, and much of the information they act on is unknown to their constituents. Under these circumstances, using personal criteria makes a great deal of sense. A candidate's demographic features give voters clues about his or her personal values. Voters feel that people who are like them in some tangible way are more likely to think and act as they would in the same circumstances. As an African American, Barack Obama faced the challenge of convincing a majority of voters that, although he may not look like them, he nonetheless understood their needs and values and would thus be an effective agent for them. His rival in 2012, Mitt Romney, with a fortune estimated to be worth $230 million, struggled to persuade voters of modest means that he could nonetheless feel their economic pain. A candidate's competence, background, and character give clues about how far he or she can be trusted to do the right thing even when no one is watching.

The most important information shortcut voters use to make predictions is the **party label**. A large majority of voters continue to take their cues from the parties, even though popular attitudes toward parties as institutions tend to range from indifference to outright hostility.[18] The party label provides useful information for both **performance voting** (voting for the party in control, or "in-party," when one thinks the government is performing well; voting for the "outs" when one thinks the party in charge is performing poorly) and **issue voting** (the typical positions of Republicans and Democrats differ in predictable ways on many issues). Most voters drastically simplify their electoral evaluations and decisions by developing a consistent bias in favor of the candidates of one of the major parties, making the party label the most influential "endorsement" of all.

The Power of Party Identification

As the best single predictor of the vote in federal elections, **party identification** is a central focus of modern electoral research (see Chapter 10). Since the 1950s a biennial survey, the American National Election Studies, has asked scientifically selected samples of the American public a set of questions probing the strength and direction of their partisanship. Respondents are first asked, "Generally speaking, do you usually think of yourself as a Republican, a Democrat, an independent, or what?" Those who answer "Democrat" or "Republican" are then asked, "Would you call yourself a strong Democrat (Republican) or a not very strong Democrat (Republican)?" Those who answer "independent" or something else are then asked, "Do you think of yourself as closer to the Republican Party or the Democratic Party?" Answers to these questions locate respondents on a seven-point scale: strong Democrats, weak Democrats, independents leaning Democratic, pure independents, independents leaning Republican, weak Republicans, and strong Republicans. This scale serves as the standard measure of party identification.

Party identification has proven to be a strong predictor of the vote in any election in which candidates run under party labels. In 2012, for example, about 9x percent of the strong partisans voted for their own party's presidential candidate; weaker partisans tended to be less loyal but still strongly favored their party's candidate, while independents split their votes, giving Romney a modest majority. In general, the weaker a survey respondent's partisanship, the more likely he or she was to vote for a minor-party candidate (see Figure 11-1).

Figure 11-1 Party Identification: A Strong Predictor of the Presidential Vote

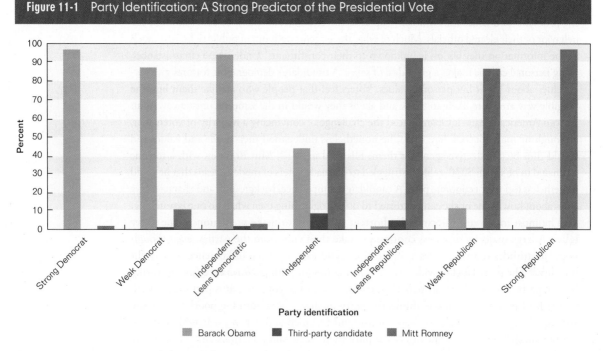

Source: 2012 Cooperative Congressional Election Study

Figure 11-2 Partisan Voting in Presidential Elections

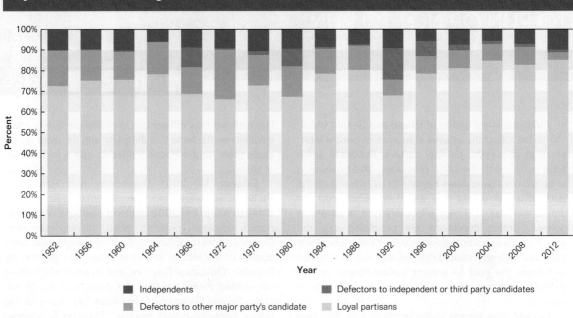

Source: 1952–2008: Amercian National Election Studies; 2012: Cooperative Congressional Election Study.

The connection between party identification and vote choice varies over time but is always quite powerful. Figure 11-2 shows that in elections from 1952 through 2012, typically about three-quarters of presidential voters were self-identified partisans supporting their party's candidate. Their portion of the electorate has been growing since the 1970s, reaching its highest levels yet in 2004 (84.5 percent), 2008 (82.9 percent), and 2012 (85.3%). The proportion defecting to the opposing party's candidate ranged from 7.6 percent to 24.1 percent, and the proportion voting for independent or third-party candidates varied from less than 1 percent to 15.3 percent. Usually, less than 10 percent are pure independents who claim to favor neither party. Still, there are enough independents and partisan defectors to keep party identification alone from determining who wins or loses elections.

ELECTION CAMPAIGNS

If voters are short of information and uncertain about their choices, the candidates and their allies are only too happy to help them out. Experienced campaigners are fully aware of voters' reliance on free information and cognitive shortcuts, and they concoct strategies for winning votes accordingly. Each campaign emphasizes selected facts and cues aimed at getting at least a plurality of voters to the polls. The choice among strategic options depends on what the candidate and campaign staff believe will work in this contest in this year with this electorate. Campaigns are intensely pragmatic, opportunistic affairs, highly variable because they must adapt to circumstances that are highly variable—the office in question,

TO RUN OR NOT TO RUN

strategy and choice

Variations in the quality of House and Senate candidates reflect the rational strategies of people interested in successful political careers. Politically ambitious people with the skills, resources, and experience to be effective candidates hesitate to try to move up the political ladder unless they are likely to succeed, for defeat will stall, and may effectively end, a career in politics. Unless conditions are promising—say, the incumbent is in political trouble or the seat is open—the strongest potential candidates will stay out of the race and leave the field to weaker candidates for whom defeat will be less costly to their already unpromising careers.

As politicians decide to run or not to run, they also gauge the national partisan breezes. A strong economy, the absence of party scandal, or a president who enjoys the public's support might tilt the election toward the president's fellow party members, while the opposite conditions will shift the political winds toward the out-party's candidates. Because quality candidates have career investments to protect, more will come forward when national conditions are favorable to their side. Moreover, because the presence of quality candidates greatly affects the election outcome, their anticipated responses will tend to reinforce and magnify the effect of national conditions on congressional elections. The

figure shows how differences in challenger quality affect election results. Note that the party with the most quality challengers for the House tended to gain a larger share of seats.

Entering fall 2001 Democratic and Republican Party officials were busy trying to entice quality candidates to run in the 2002 midterm elections. With economic indicators pointing mostly toward recession, Democrats were optimistic that they might take back control of the House and strengthen their grip on the Senate. "On Labor Day, we had them exactly where we wanted them," recalled the director of the Democratic Senate Campaign Committee. "We were talking Social Security. It was nirvana." Then on September 11 the terrorist attacks on the World Trade Center and the Pentagon totally changed the national agenda. Suddenly potential challengers in both parties found it unseemly to tout their partisan aspirations for political office. At the same time, many of the mostly Republican incumbents who had been leaning toward retirement announced that they would do their patriotic duty and serve another term. Knowledgeable observers from both political parties concluded that the terrorist attacks and subsequent events deterred many quality Democratic candidates and limited the party's prospects in the 2002 elections.

whether the contest is a primary or general election, and current political events and issues. Nonetheless, all competitive campaigns have features in common because they face many of the same challenges.

The Basic Necessities: Candidates and Messages

The basic necessities of any campaign are a candidate, a message, and a way to inform voters about both. A **candidate** is a person who can be portrayed as sufficiently qualified and trustworthy for the job. Achieving this status is not as simple as it sounds. Members of the

Challenger Quality: A Factor in Party Success

In House elections the party with the most quality challengers has tended to win a larger share of House seats.

Relative Challenger Quality and House Seats Swings, 1946–2012

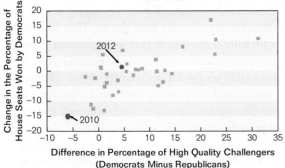

Source: Data compiled by the authors.

Note: Data points represent House elections from 1946 through 2012.

The political climate in 2006 was far different. The unpopularity of the Bush administration and the Iraq War was apparent well before the election (see Chapter 10), encouraging vigorous Democratic challenges and discouraging potentially strong Republican candidates from taking on Democratic incumbents. Anticipating a favorable national tide, Democratic operatives, candidates, and contributors positioned themselves to exploit it. As a result the Democrats picked up thirty Republican seats while losing none of their own.[1] Effectively exploiting similarly favorable national conditions in 2008, the Democrats picked up another twenty-one House seats. The tide turned decisively in 2010, when popular unhappiness with the economy and the general direction of the country promised a banner year for Republicans. The result was the largest Republican advantage in challenger quality and the party's largest gain in House seats for the entire period. In 2012, in contrast, the Democrats' modest advantage in challenger quality was echoed by an equally modest increase in House seats, a gain of eight over 2010.

1. Gary C. Jacobson, "Referendum: The 2006 Midterm Congressional Elections," *Political Science Quarterly* 122 (Spring 2007): 1–24.

House of Representatives often run unopposed because no one is willing to take them on in the primary or general election. Even more often, members run against candidates so lacking in political experience, talent, temperament, or background that voters do not consider them seriously as viable choices. Sometimes, although less frequently, senators are equally lucky: Sen. Jim DeMint of South Carolina, for example, was opposed in 2010 by a candidate who raised no money, did almost no campaigning, and was under federal indictment on an obscenity charge.[19] Guess who won?

Because potential candidates think strategically, the quality of House and Senate candidates varies with their prospects for success. The smaller the chances of winning, the less likely the talented and ambitious are to run (see box "To Run or Not to Run"). Presidential contests usually attract plenty of political talent, but even the pool of presidential candidates may be affected by expectations: when President George H. W. Bush seemed unbeatable in 1991 after the Gulf War triumph, some prominent Democratic presidential prospects decided not to run, leaving room for Arkansas governor Bill Clinton, a relative unknown, to move to the front of the pack.

GETTING OUT THE MESSAGE. The **message** is the answer to the voter's question: why should I vote for this candidate rather than another? It tells voters why, in their terms, this particular candidate is their best choice. Messages are shaped by candidates' theories about the political beliefs, perceptions, values, and responses of different segments of the electorate. Uncertainty is so pervasive and good information about voters so valuable that campaigns invest heavily in research—if they can afford it.

Presidential campaigns can afford it, and they employ the full range of research techniques. They run hundreds of opinion surveys and conduct numerous **focus group** sessions in which a small number of ordinary citizens are observed as they talk with each other about political candidates, issues, and events. Presidential campaigns use focus groups to test their general themes as well as the specific advertisements promoting those themes. They monitor the effects of campaign ads and events with daily tracking polls that sample citizens' views on a continuing basis to measure changes in responses. In 1988 there was nothing accidental about the Bush campaign's relentless attacks on the Democratic opponent, Michael Dukakis, for being "soft on crime." Nor was it simple intuition in 1992 that made Clinton's campaign manager, James Carville, put up the now-famous sign reminding himself and the rest of the staff of their campaign's most powerful theme: "the economy, stupid." Nor was there anything mysterious about Clinton in 1996 endlessly repeating the vow to protect "Medicare, Medicaid, education, and the environment," or about George W. Bush choosing to define himself as a "compassionate conservative" in 2000 and as the nation's shield against terrorism in 2004, or in Barack Obama's effort to tie John McCain to Bush's unpopular legacy in 2008, or in the 2012 Obama campaign's depiction of Mitt Romney as a cold-hearted capitalist with retrograde social views. In each case the campaign's research told it that these messages were winners.

These examples illustrate something else about campaign messages: they are chosen opportunistically. Slow economic growth during the administration of George H. W. Bush handed the Clinton campaign in 1992 a powerful, ready-made theme, and the campaign really would have been stupid not to make the most of it. This holds for the Romney campaign in 2012 as well; its strongest argument for replacing Obama was lingering high unemployment. Clinton's questionable candor about his draft record, experimentation with marijuana, and alleged extramarital adventures handed the Bush campaign its central message: Bill Clinton was too untrustworthy to be president. Bob Dole took advantage of the aura of scandal permeating the first Clinton administration to make the point again in 1996. By embracing "compassionate conservativism," the younger Bush sought to attract moderate swing voters weary of the Democratic administration but repelled by the hard-line conservatism displayed by congressional Republicans. Bush also vowed repeatedly to "uphold the honor and dignity of the office" of president, a not-so-subtle appeal to voters disgusted by Clinton's behavior. Imagine how different the 2004 campaigns would have been had the terrorist attacks of September 2001 never occurred, or how different the 2008 campaigns would have been had the economy been booming and had Bush been popular.

The same opportunistic strategy is applied to congressional races. The House bank scandal (see Chapter 6) gave House challengers a powerful message for their 1992 campaigns: vote the self-serving deadbeats out of office. The controversial hearings in 1991 over the nomination of Clarence Thomas to the Supreme Court provided another stick. Anita Hill's accusations that Thomas sexually harassed her were handled clumsily by a committee of middle-aged men, who, many women thought, "just didn't get it." The result was that a candidate's sex became an important shorthand cue for many congressional voters in 1992, who thus elected nineteen additional women to the House (raising the total at the time to forty-seven) and four to the Senate (for a total of six).

Candidates work hard to convey the message that they do "get it," that they understand and care about the concerns of their fellow citizens. Like other job seekers, candidates prepare glowing résumés highlighting their credentials, experience, and accomplishments. But they also try to show that, regardless of their backgrounds, they share some common ground with voters of all sorts. Patrician Yale graduate George H. W. Bush advertised his fondness for pork rinds and bass fishing to connect with ordinary folks during his campaign in 1988. Clinton's impromptu saxophone jams showed that he could be just one of the gang. It is a robust appetite for votes, not food, that leads candidates to eat bagels and lox at a corner deli in a Jewish neighborhood in the morning, black-eyed peas at an African American church at lunch, and green chili enchiladas at a Mexican American fiesta in the evening. The implicit message is empathy: "Though I may not be one of you, I appreciate your culture and understand your special needs and concerns, so I can serve effectively as your agent."

Professional campaign strategists are an integral part of every serious national campaign and often continue to provide political advice to the winner. None has been more prominent in this role than Karl Rove (shown here at a fundraiser for his new PAC), hailed as a political genius for his strategic and tactical planning of Bush's successful campaigns in 2000 and 2004 but loathed in some (Democratic) quarters for alleged duplicity and dirty tricks. In 2012, Rove headed two independent PACs that raised and spent nearly $300 million on behalf of Mitt Romney and selected Republican congressional candidates. Like Romney, most candidates he backed lost, including ten of the twelve Senate hopefuls, tarnishing, at least temporarily, Rove's star.

Actions intended to symbolize a candidate's concerns do not always work as planned, however. In 1972 the Democratic candidate, Sen. George McGovern of South Dakota, displayed his ignorance rather than appreciation of Jewish culture when he ordered milk to go with his kosher hot dog while campaigning in a Jewish neighborhood in Queens, New York. Handed a tamale while campaigning among Mexican American voters in San Antonio in 1976, Gerald Ford took a vigorous bite out of the inedible cornhusk wrapper, a gaffe that made all the network news broadcasts. During the 1988 presidential campaign, Michael Dukakis reaped widespread ridicule, not enhanced credentials on defense issues, when news broadcasts showed him peering out dolefully from under an ill-fitting helmet while riding on an army tank.[20] In 2012,

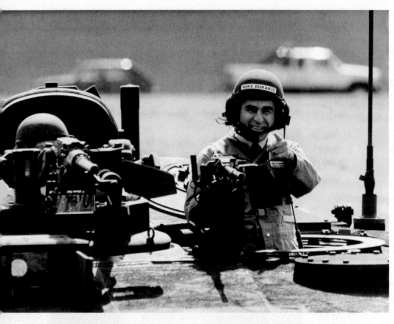

Despite the potential for embarrassment, candidates find it hard to resist donning unusual costumes as they pursue media attention while campaigning around the country. In 1988, Democratic presidential aspirant Michael Dukakis sought to burnish his credentials as a prospective commander in chief by donning a helmet and riding in the machine gunner's spot in an army tank. Unfortunately for him, the event produced visuals that had the opposite effect, making Dukakis the butt of countless jokes and cartoons.

Mitt Romney expressed his enthusiasm for the U.S. auto industry by telling a Detroit audience, "I drive a Mustang and a Chevy pickup truck. Ann [his wife] drives a couple of Cadillacs," inadvertently reinforcing the Democrats' depiction of him as an out-of-touch millionaire. In each instance, the action conveyed a message subverting the one intended. Campaign advisers may want to display their candidates as all things to all people, but the human material often proves recalcitrant.

Acquiring and maintaining a public image appropriate to the office sought is a particular challenge for presidential candidates, who are subject to intense scrutiny by both their opponents and the news media over many months of campaigning. Most presidential primaries now take place so early in the election year—two-thirds of the states had selected convention delegates for one or both parties by the end of March 2012—that campaigns begin shortly after the midterm election, if not earlier. In years with crowded primary fields (at one time eight Democrats and seven Republicans were officially in the race for the 2008 nominations; eight Republicans contested the 2012 caucuses and primaries) aspirants have to fight for attention and to make sure that they, rather than their opponents or skeptical reporters, shape their public images. Candidates blessed with famous names (in 2000 George W. Bush, governor of Texas and son of a former president, and Elizabeth Dole, holder of cabinet positions in the Reagan and George H. W. Bush administrations, president of the Red Cross, and wife of the 1996 Republican candidate, Bob Dole; in 2008 Hillary Clinton) and ample money (in 2000 Bush; in 2004 Howard Dean and John Kerry; and in 2008 Barack Obama, Hillary Clinton, and Mitt Romney; Romney again in 2012) enjoy a distinct advantage in these endeavors, but front-runners also become all the other candidates' favorite targets, and the candidate with the most money doesn't always win the nomination, as Dean learned in 2004 and Romney learned in 2008.

Televised debates are another special challenge for presidential candidates trying to convey the message that they are right for the job. For clear front-runners, especially those not fully comfortable in front of television cameras, the risks of damaging missteps during a debate outweigh the potential gains from winning it. But the media and public now expect debates, so there is no graceful way to avoid them. For challengers and candidates behind in the polls, the nationally televised debates offer a chance to share equal billing with the leader and to make up lost ground before the largest audiences of the campaign. Independent candidate Ross Perot, for example, made the most of his opportunity in 1992, stealing the first debate from Bush and

Clinton with his folksy style, populist rhetoric, and handmade charts, thereby giving his candidacy a major boost.[21] Usually, however, independent and minor-party candidates are excluded; Ralph Nader and Pat Buchanan protested vigorously but fruitlessly when they were kept out of the debates in 2000 on the ground that their support in preelection polls was too low to make them viable candidates and thus eligible to participate. Only Obama and McCain shared the debate stage in 2008; Obama, looking younger and calmer than his better-known opponent, was the consensus winner of all three of their debates, giving his candidacy an important boost. Ironically, Obama's first debate with Mitt Romney in 2012 nearly derailed his reelection bid; Romney's forceful performance and Obama's lackluster responses turned an Obama lead into a tie in the preelection horse-race polls and made the final weeks of the campaign touch-and-go.

Debates demand considerable preparation—cramming and rehearsal—as much to prevent embarrassing lapses in knowledge and misstatements as to score points. Predictably, the leading candidates focus on avoiding mistakes and tend to stick with their tried-and-true campaign themes while deflecting their opponents' efforts to shake things up. Running behind in 1996, Bob Dole

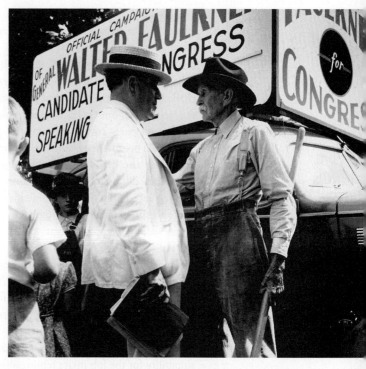

Campaigning for Congress in 1938 in Crossville, Tennessee, Walter Faulkner followed the standard practice of his day: passing through towns and hamlets, attracting an audience with loudspeakers attached to his car, and "pressing the flesh." Photograph by Dorothea Lange from her Farm Security Administration series.

went on the attack, charging Clinton with destroying Americans' faith in their government: "[Y]ou have thirty-some in your administration who have been investigated or in jail or whatever, and you've got an ethical problem. . . . I'm not talking about private, we're talking about public ethics."[22] Clinton countered with a neat (and no doubt prepared) variation on the "Medicare, Medicaid, education, and the environment" theme, declaring loftily that "no attack ever created a job or educated a child or helped a family make ends meet. No insult ever cleaned up a toxic waste dump or helped an elderly person."[23] In 2008 McCain was primed to counter Obama's argument that a McCain administration would equal a third Bush administration: "I am not President Bush," he said during their third debate. "If you want to run against President Bush, you should have run four years ago."

In 2000 the George W. Bush campaign initially seemed reluctant to schedule debates, fearing that Bush might show to disadvantage against the experienced and thoroughly informed Al Gore. As it turned out, they need not have worried. Gore had trouble finding the middle ground between appearing too overbearing and seeming too passive. Voters found him more articulate and better informed, but Bush appeared more likeable. More important, in the eyes of Republicans and enough independents, if by no means all voters, Bush seemed sufficiently knowledgeable and coherent to qualify for the presidency. In other words, the Bush campaign won the "expectations game" played out in the media prior to the debates by keeping expectations low enough that Bush's performance could be seen as "surprisingly" effective. Mitt Romney won the expectations game in his first debate with Obama in 2012, but mainly because Obama's performance fell so far below expectations. Like Obama, presidents Ronald Reagan, G. H. W. Bush, and G. W. Bush faltered in their first scheduled debate, perhaps because sitting presidents are unaccustomed to direct, hostile face-to-face challenges to their policies and performance. All four were better prepared for subsequent debates, and all but G. H. W. Bush won reelection.

Debates rarely cover new campaign ground, but they remain popular among the media and public because they show the presidential candidates up close under sustained pressure. They may also help frame the choice in clear terms for voters. In 2004, for example, the candidates' differences on the wisdom of the decision to invade Iraq came out starkly in the debates: repeatedly, Bush defended his choice as an integral part of the war on terrorism, while Kerry attacked it as a dangerous and unnecessary distraction from it. In 2008 the debates underlined the generational and temperamental contrasts between the two presidential aspirants as well as their stark differences on plans to deal with the economic crisis. Obama and Romney offered clearly contrasting views on the government's role in the economic and social lives of Americans in 2012. Candidates for the House and Senate occasionally participate in debates, but incumbents often duck debates to deny their obscure opponents free publicity and the opportunity to upstage them.

NEGATIVE CAMPAIGNING. Campaign messages emphasizing one candidate's personal suitability for the job invite rebuttals from the other side. **Negative campaigning**, pointed personal criticism of the other candidate, is thus a normal if sometimes ugly component of the electoral process—and an effective one. As one Democratic consultant explained: "People say they hate negative campaigning. But it works. They hate it and remember it at the same time. The problem with positive is that you have to run it again and again to make it stick. With negative, the poll numbers will move in three or four days."[24] Campaign professionals distinguish between accurate comparative ads that highlight differences between the candidates (fair) and strictly personal attacks of dubious accuracy or relevance (unfair), although voters may not always appreciate the distinction. Negative ads exploit voters' uncertainty inherent in the delegation of authority to powerful agents. Research suggests that negative ads do inform people about the candidates but also make them less enthusiastic about voting for any particular candidate.[25]

As negative campaigns have proved effective, candidates have sought to erect defenses against them. In 1988 Bush campaign adviser Lee Atwater created a series of attack ads that succeeded in branding Dukakis, who began the campaign unfamiliar to most voters, as a far-out liberal, soft on crime and weak on defense. Four years later, Clinton's strategists, determined to prevent a similar fate for their candidate, organized a rapid response team that blanketed the news media with forceful rebuttals of every charge made by Bush or his supporters, often on the same day charges were made. They also replied swiftly to negative television ads. For example, within forty-eight hours of the broadcast of a spot criticizing Clinton for his tax record while governor of Arkansas, the Clinton campaign produced, tested with a focus group, revised, and aired its own spot that included some text from the Bush ad with "UNTRUE" stamped across it.[26] The idea was to counter negative messages before they could sink in. The wisdom of this strategy was apparent in 2004, when John Kerry was evidently hurt by his slow reaction to charges from a group calling itself the "Swift Boat Vets and POWs

for Truth" that had mounted an independent campaign harshly assailing his
Vietnam service. In 2008 the McCain campaign's attempt to portray Obama as someone who, as Sarah Palin put it in her stump
speech, "pals around with terrorists" was
forcefully countered by the Obama campaign (and by Obama himself during the
third debate), and most Americans came to
regard the charge as unfair.[27] One common
explanation for Romney's loss in 2012 was
his campaign's ineffective response to ads
broadcast in swing states during the spring
and summer, when many voters were just
getting to know him, attacking him as a
greedy venture capitalist, indifferent to the
fates of people working for the companies
he made a fortune buying, restructuring,
and selling.

Negative or not, campaign ads are rarely
subtle, for their targets are the rationally

Negative campaign ads are a staple, if often deplored, component of
presidential campaigns. The most effective ones take advantage of a
candidate's mistakes. Here, the Republican National Committee reminds voters
of a statement Barack Obama made at a fund-raiser in San Francisco in 2008
to underline its claim that he is an elitist who looks down on ordinary middle
Americans. Notice the cable car in the background to remind voters of the
connection to San Francisco, a city known for its social liberalism.

ignorant, marginally involved voters who have not already made up their minds—not the
informed political sophisticates or the confirmed partisans for whom the information provided by campaigns is superfluous. As one campaign consultant put it:

> The voters have a lot more important things on their minds than political campaigns. . . .
> Most of the people we are trying to reach with our message don't think about [cam-
> paigns] at all until late October. They don't read all the news magazines, the *Wall Street
> Journal,* and two local dailies. They don't watch CNN and C-SPAN. They watch "Wheel
> of Fortune," and they think about politics and campaigns less than five minutes a week.[28]

Simplicity, repetition, exaggeration, and symbolism (images of home, family, neighborhood, and flag) are therefore the staples of campaign advertising. Accuracy is not a priority;
as Romney's chief pollster put it, "we're not going to let our campaign be dictated by fact
checkers."[29]

In the end a successful campaign comes down to several basics. Its goal is to win a majority of votes, not every vote. Planners begin by using past voting records, polling, and telephone or door-to-door canvassing to figure out who is certain to support the candidate, who
is up for grabs, and who is certain to support the opponent. The central clue here, at least for
general elections, is the voter's party identification. The campaign is designed to appeal to the
first two groups but especially to the second—particularly if, as is usually the case, the first
does not amount to a majority. Campaign staffs find out where the swing voters live, what
they care about, and what their mood and concerns are this year. The most sophisticated
operations also now use the reams of commercially available data on individuals' characteristics, values, and tastes to "microtarget" specific campaign messages to the most susceptible.
Campaign strategists work to frame the choice—establish what the election is about—in a

way that underlines their candidate's strengths and plays down his or her weaknesses. In doing so, they develop a simple, coherent campaign theme that explains both why the candidate should be elected and why the opponent should not. Finally, they repeat the theme ad nauseam to reach the crucial late-deciding voters who pay almost no attention to politics. None of these things, however, can be accomplished without money.

The Other Necessity: Campaign Money

No matter how qualified the candidates are or how powerful their message, neither will count for much if voters never hear about them. Thus the third requirement of a competitive campaign is an effective way to communicate with voters. For most of America's history, party organizations and newspapers were the chief conduits for political propaganda. Parties organized marches, rallies, and picnics; supplied the speakers; did the door-to-door canvassing of potential voters; and distributed pamphlets, broadsides, and posters bearing the campaign message. The campaign itself was a team affair, agitating for the election of all of the party's candidates, although the spotlight usually was on the top of the ticket.

After World War II, however, patronage-based party organizations declined, and television gained popularity as a campaign medium (see Chapter 12). As a result, parties gradually lost their central role in campaigns, to the point that by the 1960s campaigns had largely become the province of individual candidates and their personal organizations. Candidates had to assemble their own campaign teams, raise the funds, hire the consultants and technical specialists, and design and execute their own individual campaign strategies, sometimes with the help of their national or local party organizations but often without it.

All of these activities cost money. Modern campaigns for federal office are unavoidably expensive. There is simply no way for most candidates to organize and plan a campaign, do research, develop and package a message, and get that message out to potential voters on the cheap. Genuine electoral competition that gives voters a choice of agents and gives the winners an incentive to remain faithful (lest they be replaced) requires that candidates raise and spend money—lots of it. In 2012, for example, the 132 House candidates in highly competitive elections—defined as races in which the winner received 55 percent or less of the major-party vote—spent on average more than $2 million each. Senate candidates in competitive races typically spend much more, although the total varies with the size of the state's population. The record was broken in 2012 when Democratic challenger Elizabeth Warren spent more than $41 million defeating Scott Brown, R-MA, who spent almost $35 million. On a per-voter basis, however, the most expensive 2012 campaign was in Montana, where incumbent Democrat Jon Tester and challenger Denny Rehberg spent nearly $22.8 million courting the state's 481,600 voters, more than $47 each. Presidential campaigns are in a class by themselves, with total expenditures exceeding $2 billion in 2008 and again in 2012.

REGULATING CAMPAIGN MONEY. Currently, all of the money spent on major campaigns for federal offices comes from private sources.* Privately financed elections inevitably raise two related problems for American democracy. First, democracy demands political

---

*Federal matching funds are available for presidential candidates, but serious candidates now refuse them to avoid the spending limits they must adhere to if they accept the money.

equality: one person, one vote. But because money is distributed unequally, its role in electoral politics threatens democratic equality. Second, privately financed elections raise the suspicion that elected officials will serve as agents of their contributors rather than of their constituents. The dilemma, then, is that meaningful elections require money, but the pursuit of money can subvert the very purpose of elections.

Efforts to resolve this dilemma through regulation have generally failed. Prior to the 1970s, campaign money was effectively unregulated. Congress had, from time to time, passed limits on contributions and spending, but the limits were easily circumvented and never enforced. This casual attitude toward campaign money faded with the spread of candidate-centered campaigns and the rise of broadcast campaigning, both of which quickly drove up costs. Higher costs accelerated not only the demand for campaign money but also the fear that the winners would favor contributors over constituents.

Congress's response was the Federal Election Campaign Act of 1971 (FECA), extensively amended in 1974. FECA provided partial public funding for presidential campaigns and required full public reporting of and strict limits on all contributions and expenditures in federal elections. It also established a Federal Election Commission to enforce the law and to collect and publish detailed information on campaign contributions and expenditures. The Supreme Court, in *Buckley v. Valeo* (1976), upheld the reporting requirements and contribution limits (to prevent "corruption or the appearance of corruption") but rejected spending limits on the ground that they interfered with political speech protected by the First Amendment.[30] Presidential candidates, however, could be required to abide by spending limits as a condition of receiving public funds for their campaigns. Also in *Buckley* the Court overturned, again on First Amendment grounds, ceilings on how much of their own money candidates could spend on their campaigns and on how much anyone could spend to agitate for or against candidates independently of candidates' campaigns.

Concerned that spending limits were choking off traditional local party activity in federal elections, Congress liberalized FECA in 1979, amending the act to allow unrestricted contributions and spending for state and local party-building and get-out-the-vote activities. A 1996 Court decision gave party organizations the right to unfettered independent spending as well.[31] Funds for these activities were commonly called **soft money**, as contrasted with the "hard money" raised and spent under FECA's limitations. When the unregulated soft money contributions to party committees ballooned, soft money became the favorite target of campaign finance reformers, and in March 2002 Congress passed the Bipartisan Campaign Reform Act (BCRA), which among other reforms prohibits parties from raising or spending soft party money for federal candidates. Aided by the high emotions generated by the presidential race, the parties countered by raising vastly increased sums of hard money, and many former soft money donors redirected their contributions to so-called 527 committees (named after the section of the tax code dealing with them) and to 501(c) committees ("charitable" groups under the tax code who can finance campaigns if they maintain the fiction that they are merely informing voters, not advocating the election or defeat of particular candidates). Such committees together spent about $500 million on independent campaigns for—or, more often, against—the presidential candidates in 2004 and another $400 million in 2008 (see box "Soft Money Finds a New Home"). BCRA's attempt to limit independent campaigning by such groups was struck down by the Supreme Court in 2007. The Court went further

Broadly speaking, campaign finance now operates through two parallel systems. Money going directly to candidates or parties is subject to limits on the size of contributions and full public disclosure of sources.* Presidential candidates who accept public funds also must observe spending limits, though McCain was the last candidate who did so (and for the general election only). But in the other system, money raised and spent outside of the parties' and candidates' campaigns is not subject to limits or, in some forms, disclosure of contributors. In practice, this means that any citizen who wants to invest any amount of money in campaign activities can find a legal way to do so, and anonymously at that. NON SEQUITUR © 2012 Wiley Ink, Inc. Dist. By UNIVERSAL UCLICK. Reprinted with permission. All rights reserved.

in 2010, overturning precedent to invalidate any restriction on independent campaign spending by any organization, including corporations and labor unions, on the ground that groups enjoyed the same First Amendment protections as individuals.[32] The effect of these decisions is evident in the growth of nonparty independent expenditures in congressional elections, which grew from $54 million in 2006 to $120 million in 2008, to $279 million in 2010, and to nearly $500 million in 2012. With at least $667 million spent on the presidential race, total spending by independent groups in 2012 exceeded $1 billion.*

THE FLOW OF CAMPAIGN MONEY. Although the proponents of the original FECA had hoped to rein in the cost of campaigns, the flow of campaign money has continued to outpace inflation. Total funding from all sources for the general election campaigns for president rose from $453 million in 1996 to $676 million in 2000, $1.3 billion in 2004, and more than $2 billion in 2008 and 2012. Spending in House and Senate campaigns also has continued to grow since FECA took effect, rising by averages of about 9 percent in House elections and 12 percent in Senate elections (in inflation-adjusted dollars) from one election year to the next. In 2012 the average House campaign spent about $1.2 million, and the average Senate campaign about $9.0 million. Both supply and demand have driven campaign spending up. The supply of contributions continues to grow because the stakes represented by elections are so great. Decisions made by the federal government affect every aspect of American economic and social life, so there is no shortage of incentives for trying

---

*In the 2012 federal elections, individuals could give no more than $2,500 per candidate per campaign, with primary, runoff, and general election campaigns treated as separate campaigns. Nonparty political action committees are limited to $5,000 per candidate per campaign. Parties may give no more than $5,000 to a House candidate and $43,000 to a Senate candidate. The $2,500 individual contribution limit also applies to presidential primary candidates; presidential candidates who accept public funds for the general election may not accept any other direct contribution to their campaigns. Contributions from foreign sources are illegal in all federal elections. The individual and party contribution limits are indexed for inflation; the PAC limit of $5,000 is not.

SOFT MONEY FINDS A NEW HOME

politics to policy

The story of how campaign finance reform led to the flood of "soft money" in presidential election campaigns, and how reforms aimed at stemming the flood merely rechanneled it, exemplify the partisan conflicts, dilemmas, and unanticipated consequences that vex campaign finance policy. With their party in debt after the 1968 election, congressional Democrats embraced reform proposals that would limit campaign spending and finance presidential campaigns with public funds. Republican opposition to these reforms collapsed in the wake of the Watergate scandal, in which campaign finance abuses had figured prominently. After Richard Nixon resigned in August 1974 to avoid impeachment, his successor, Gerald Ford, who like Nixon opposed public financing of campaigns, reluctantly agreed to sign the Federal Election Campaign Act (FECA) amendments, conceding that "the times demand this legislation."

Use of the new system in the 1976 elections exposed an unanticipated problem. To meet spending limits, the presidential campaigns focused on mass media advertising to take advantage of its efficiencies and maintained tight central control of all other campaign activity to avoid violating the law. State and local parties had little chance to participate, and the absence of the familiar paraphernalia of grassroots campaigns—bumper stickers, lapel buttons, yard signs—was widely noted and lamented. To preserve a role for local parties and grassroots activists in presidential campaigns, Congress in 1979 amended FECA to permit state and local parties to raise and spend money on party building, voter registration, and get-out-the-vote activities. No limits were placed on contributions or expenditures for these purposes, and, until the law was amended again in 1988, the sums involved did not even have to be reported to the Federal Election Commission. These funds were nicknamed "soft money" to distinguish them from the tightly regulated "hard money" governed by the public funding system.

Permissive interpretations by the Federal Election Commission and the federal courts of what constituted "party building" allowed presidential candidates to raise and spend unlimited sums under the legal fiction that they were merely helping to fertilize the grassroots. Consequently, presidential campaign finance became almost as wide open as it had been before the reforms of the 1970s. For years, partisan disagreements kept Congress from reforming the system, but finally in 2002, scandals surrounding the collapse of energy giant Enron, a generous donor of both hard and soft campaign money to both parties, induced majorities in both houses to pass the Bipartisan Campaign Reform Act (BCRA) despite strong opposition from Republican leaders. Among other things, BCRA banned soft money contributions to the parties, completely depriving them of this source of funds.

But soft money did not disappear. Tax-exempt groups organized under regulations in section 527 of the revenue code can raise unlimited money to spend on voter mobilization, issue advocacy, and almost any other campaign activity as long as they refrain from expressly advocating the election or defeat of a federal candidate and do not coordinate their activities with parties or candidates. In response to BCRA, most large soft money donors shifted to supporting 527 committees, whose financial participation in federal elections jumped from $151 million in 2002 to $405 million in 2004. With the Supreme Court's 2010 decision in *Citizens United v. Federal Election Commission* tossing out all limits on independent spending, including campaigns paid for out of corporate and union treasuries, the total spent independently on federal campaigns by parties and PACs reached an estimated $1.3 billion in 2012.

Sources: Dollar Politics, 3rd ed. (Washington, DC: Congressional Quarterly, 1982), 8–24; Frank J. Sorauf, *Inside Campaign Finance* (New Haven, CT: Yale University Press, 1992), 147–150; Steve Weissman and Ruth Hassan, "BCRA and the 527 Groups," in *The Election after Reform: Money, Politics, and the Bipartisan Campaign Reform Act*, ed. Michael Malbin (Lanham, MD: Rowman and Littlefield, 2006); and http://reporting.sunlightfoundation.com/2012/return_on_investment, accessed November 12, 2012.

to influence who gets elected and what the winners do in office. In recent elections, intense competition for control of Congress as well as the White House has also stimulated heavier investment in campaigns. And demand is continually keeping pace with supply. Candidates' appetites for campaign funds continue to grow because the cost of developing an effective message and getting it out to voters continues to climb.

House and Senate spending averages mask the huge variation in the amounts available to individual congressional candidates or spent on their behalf. Some candidates raise and spend millions, while others have to make do with almost nothing. A select minority of races attract heavy independent spending; the rest are largely ignored. These differences result from strategic choices made by contributors, candidates, parties, and independent committee entrepreneurs. Congressional candidates in search of campaign contributions can tap four basic sources: individuals, political action committees (PACs; discussed in detail in Chapter 13), their own pocketbooks, and party organizations. House candidates typically receive about 55 percent of their funds from private individuals and get about 35 percent from PACs; another 7–8 percent comes out of their own pockets. Senate candidates raise relatively more from individuals (about 60 percent) and less from PACs (about 20 percent). Direct party contributions amount to only about 1 percent of candidates' funds, but the parties also help out with significant amounts of **coordinated** and especially **independent campaign spending**. Party committees make coordinated expenditures on behalf of candidates for activities such as polling, producing ads, and conducting research on the opposition; the totals are, however, limited by law.* Independent party expenditures are not limited and go for campaign activities (mainly advertising) that are not supposed to be coordinated in any way with the candidate's campaign; such expenditures grew explosively after BCRA closed the parties' soft money loophole and now account for a significant share of total spending in competitive contests. In 2012, for example, the twenty-two Senate candidates in the eleven most hotly contested races were supported by an average of $2.6 million in independent party spending; the comparable figure for the eighty-nine most competitive House candidates was $653,000. The congressional parties also help their candidates by encouraging their incumbents in safe seats to pass some of the money on to needier candidates; many incumbents have also formed so-called leadership PACs to supply funds to fellow partisans. Thus, although House and Senate campaigns are still primarily candidate-centered in their activities and messages, the national parties have a far larger role in financing them than they did when FECA was adopted back in the 1970s.

All types of contributors and independent spenders, with the possible exception of the candidates themselves, distribute their funds strategically. They avoid wasting resources on hopeless candidacies, preferring instead to put their money behind their favorites in races they expect to be close, where campaigning and therefore campaign spending might make a difference. Contributors also favor likely winners whose help they might need after the election. In practice, then, congressional incumbents, usually safe—or, at worst, in tight races for reelection—have the least trouble raising campaign funds. How much they actually acquire depends in good part on how much they think they need; the safer they feel, the less they raise and spend.

---

*In 2012 coordinated expenditures by federal and state committees were limited to $91,200 in House races; limits for Senate races depend on the state's population and ranged up to $5.2 million (California).

Figure 11-3 Incumbent versus Challenger: Campaign Spending in Contested House Elections

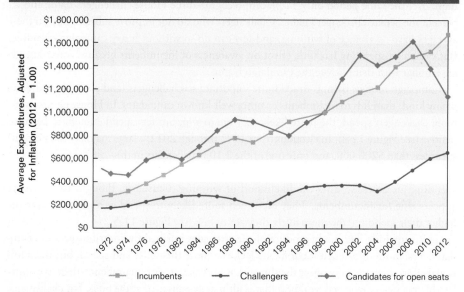

Source: Compiled by the authors from Federal Election Commission data.

Does it matter how much candidates are able to raise and spend? It matters only to the degree that a lack of money prevents candidates from getting their messages out to voters. Campaign money has little to do with the results of general elections for president. The presidential candidates' campaigns always are at least adequately financed, and huge sums of additional money are now spent by party organizations and independent committees on the candidates' behalf. Add to this the abundant free information the media transmit about presidential candidates, and the balance of resources makes little difference. What matters is how voters respond to the competing campaign messages.

Campaign money does matter in presidential primaries, in which rationally ignorant voters cannot rely on party labels as default cues and so need to know something about the candidates. Well-known candidates have a leg up, but lesser-known contenders, to have any chance at all, need to get the attention of voters, which almost always requires spending substantial sums of money. Held in January at the beginning of the primary season, the Iowa caucuses and New Hampshire primary once gave unknowns such as Jimmy Carter (1976) and Bill Clinton (1992) an opportunity to parlay relatively inexpensive early successes into fund-raising bonanzas for later primaries (see Chapter 12). But with so many states now holding primaries in February and March, candidates have little time to exploit unexpected success and cannot compete effectively without raising a great deal of money before the election year begins.

In House and Senate races, money—specifically, the lack of it—is frequently decisive. Typically, half of Senate incumbents and 70–80 percent of House incumbents win by default because their opponents spend too little money to make a race of it. Voters tend to reject candidates they know nothing about in favor of those they recognize. In the elections held from 1980 through 2008, an average of 92 percent of House voters and 96 percent of Senate voters recognized the incumbent's name. Awareness of the challengers was much less common; over the same period only 54 percent recognized the House challenger's name and 77 percent the Senate challenger's name. Challengers who do not improve substantially on these averages have no chance of winning, and few can do so without heavy campaign spending. But campaign spending has little effect on awareness of incumbents because voters already are familiar with them before the campaign begins.[33]

Campaign money, then, is much more important to challengers (and obscure candidates of any kind) than it is to incumbents or other well-known candidates. In House elections the more challengers spend, the more likely they are to win, but few spend enough to be competitive (see Figure 11-4). In elections from 1992 through 2012, a large majority (60 percent) spent less than $200,000, and only one of the 2,103 challengers in this category was successful (he defeated an incumbent under federal indictment who later served time in prison). As spending increases, so does the likelihood of winning. Curiously, though, the opposite appears true for incumbents. They are much more likely to spend at high levels, yet the higher their spending, the more likely they are to lose (see Figure 11-5).

This surprising fact is a byproduct of the strategies pursued by contributors and candidates. The more threatened incumbents feel, the more they raise and spend, but the additional effort does not fully offset the threat that provokes it. For incumbents, then, spending lavishly is a sign of electoral weakness that is ultimately registered at the polls. For challengers, higher spending is a sign, as well as a source, of electoral strength. Challengers with better

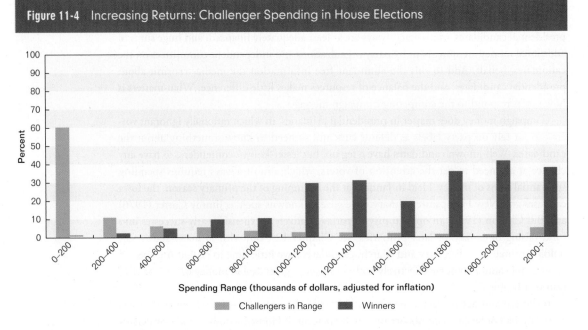

Figure 11-4 Increasing Returns: Challenger Spending in House Elections

Challengers in Range   Winners

Source: Compiled by the authors from Federal Election Commission data, 1992–2012.

Figure 11-5 Heavy Campaign Spending: The Sign of a Weak Incumbent

Spending Range (thousands of dollars, adjusted for inflation)

■ Percentage of Incumbents whose spending fell in range
■ Winners as a percentage of incumbents within spending range

Source: Compiled by the authors from Federal Election Commission data, 1992–2012.

prospects (attractive candidates with potentially effective messages) are able to raise more money; and the more they spend, the more professional their campaigns, the more voters they reach, and the more support they attract. Challengers do not have to outspend incumbents to win. Indeed, only 20 percent of the successful House challengers in the past decade spent more than the incumbents they defeated; on average, they spent $873,000 less. They simply have to spend enough to make their case. When both candidates spend enough money to mount full-scale campaigns, the content of the campaigns, not the balance of resources, determines the outcome.

HOW ARE CAMPAIGN FUNDS SPENT? Once candidates have raised campaign money, they have to decide how to spend it, unless, like many congressional incumbents, they face such feeble opposition that they are free to pass it on to other candidates, donate to party committees, or stash it away for some future contest. No one is certain about the most effective way to use scarce campaign resources. The most commonly expressed view is that "half the money spent on campaigns is wasted. The trouble is, we don't know which half."

Because a fundamental goal of every campaign is to reach voters with the candidate's message, the largest expense is advertising, with television and radio ads leading the way. Senate campaigns make heavier use of broadcast advertising, while House campaigns use more "persuasion mail." The reason is efficiency. Media markets in large metropolitan areas may include as many as thirty House districts (Greater New York). Thus House candidates opting for broadcast advertising have to pay for a station's entire audience, not just that fraction living in the target district. Mailings, by contrast, can be targeted precisely to district residents.

Still, House campaigners with enough money often use television even where it is inefficient because it is the only way to reach many potential voters and avoids the risk of campaign brochures being tossed out as "junk mail."

Only a small proportion of spending goes for traditional campaigning—speeches, rallies, soliciting votes door-to-door, and shaking hands at the factory gate. Yet these activities remain a major part of every campaign because candidates hope to extend their impact far beyond the immediate audience by attracting news coverage. Campaigns display considerable imagination in coming up with gimmicks that will gain free media exposure; indeed, campaign professionals work so hard for it that they prefer to call it "earned" media. One particularly brave House challenger even traveled with a large pig to underline his opposition to the incumbent's "pork barrel politics" (see Chapter 6). What local TV station could resist the visuals? Another tactic is running paid ads designed to provoke controversy. The ensuing news coverage then spreads the message to an audience much larger than the one originally exposed to the ad.

In pursuing favorable news coverage, presidential campaigns are in a class by themselves. Indeed, modern presidential campaigns are basically made-for-TV productions. Candidates tolerate grueling travel schedules, participate in countless carefully staged events, and compose pithy "sound bites"—short comments designed to be excerpted for broadcast, such as George H. W. Bush's "read my lips: no new taxes" promise in 1988—to get their messages on the news and out to the voters. The celebratory postconvention bus tour taken by the Clintons and Gores in 1992 is a successful example; it brought out large, exuberant crowds, generating a good deal of positive media coverage both nationally and in the states visited. Presidential candidates also exploit soft news and entertainment shows. In recent elections, both parties' candidates have made multiple appearances on television's talk and comedy shows, chatting with Oprah Winfrey and Regis Philbin, joking with David Letterman and Jay Leno, trading stories with Larry King. In 2008, Sarah Palin went on *Saturday Night Live* to joke with Tina Fey, who had been parodying her in the comedy show's sketches, while John McCain went on Letterman's show to stop the needling Letterman had been giving him for having canceled an appearance a few weeks earlier. The campaigns take these events seriously, for these shows reach audiences who do not otherwise pay much attention to political news. Barack Obama continued the tradition in 2012, chatting with Jon Stewart and hitting all of the major late-night talk and entertainment shows, but Mitt Romney largely avoided such uncontrolled venues.

When it comes to media coverage, the rich get richer, and the poor get ignored. The best-funded campaigns (for president or hotly contested Senate seats) get the most attention from the news media. Poorly funded candidates may be desperate for news coverage because they cannot afford to buy airtime, yet the very fact of their poverty makes them look like sure losers and therefore not worth covering. Campaigns that must depend on the news media to get their messages out invariably fail.

A large share of congressional campaign funds pays for expenses not directly connected to reaching voters. One study found that nearly a quarter of the money spent went into overhead—staff salaries, office and furniture rental, computers and other equipment, telephone calls, travel, legal and accounting services, and the like. Every serious campaign now also supports a website designed to attract volunteers and contributors as well as to get out the campaign's message. Fund-raising is another major expense, particularly for Senate candidates, who spend 20 percent of their money on just raising more money. Because of their larger

■ WATCH A VIDEO

logic.cqpress.com

Sarah Palin and Tina Fey place each other in a 2008 *Saturday Night Live* skit.

constituencies, Senate candidates usually have to raise bigger sums than House candidates do, but FECA contribution limits compel them to raise it in the same-size chunks.

WHERE ARE PRESIDENTIAL CAMPAIGN FUNDS SPENT? Presidential candidates invest heavily in television advertising, the most efficient way to reach an electorate of more than one hundred million people. In recent elections the campaigns have together spent hundreds of millions of dollars on television time. Decisions about where to spend the money are dominated by the design of the Electoral College (see box "The Electoral College: Where the Big States Hold the Cards"), which encourages a strategy of focusing on states with large numbers of electoral votes that are not securely in one party's camp rather than on the national electorate. Whoever wins the most popular votes in a state, except for Maine and Nebraska, gets all of its electoral votes no matter how narrow the margin of victory.* The object of a presidential campaign, then, is to piece together enough state victories to win at least 270 electoral votes.

When the election is expected to be close, the obvious strategy is to concentrate on states that polls indicate could go either way, and to ignore entirely states that seem locked up by either side. For example, in 2012, the campaigns focused on a narrow set of so-called battle-ground states that preelection surveys suggested were seriously in play. Both candidates invested heavily in the largest of these states—Florida (29 electoral votes), Pennsylvania (20), Ohio (18), and initially Michigan (16; the Romney campaign ceded Michigan early in the fall)—and they also campaigned intensively in the medium-sized swing states, including Virginia (13), North Carolina (15), Wisconsin (10), and Colorado (9). With the national balance so close, even states with few electoral votes got attention if polls suggested they were in doubt: Nevada (6), Iowa (6), and New Hampshire (4). The vast majority of the more than one million TV campaign ads were broadcast in battleground-state media markets. Visits from the presidential and vice presidential candidates were also heavily concentrated in these states; Ohio received the most visits from both Romney (51) and Obama (22).[34] States not on the battleground list were generally ignored; had they depended on the campaigns for information, California's eighteen million registered voters would scarcely have known a presidential election was taking place. In the end, Obama won ten of the eleven battleground states, losing only North Carolina, to win a comfortable 332–206 electoral college victory despite winning the national vote more narrowly, 51.1 percent to 47.2 percent for Romney.

Money and Elections: Policy Issues

Perhaps now it is clearer why the dilemma noted at the beginning of this discussion of campaign money is so thorny. Elections are supposed to keep agents responsive by making them compete with other would-be agents for the votes needed to win and hold their jobs. This does not mean that every election must be hard fought, but it does require agents to antici-pate serious competition if they serve their constituents poorly. Serious electoral competition is expensive, though, because informing voters about alternatives is so expensive. These costs are met by gathering large sums of money from people and groups whose values and interests may differ from those of voters. This practice raises the suspicion that elected officials will be

---

*In Maine and Nebraska the electoral vote can be divided if one congressional district votes for a candidate who loses statewide.

The Electoral College

Where the Big States Hold the Cards

The Constitution's formula for allocating electoral votes to each state is simple: number of senators + number of representatives = number of votes in Electoral College. This formula heavily favors the populous states, which not only have a lot of electoral votes, but, following a rule adopted by all states except Nebraska and Maine, award all their state's electoral votes to the candidate receiving the most votes. This winner-take-all rule means that California with its 55 electoral votes, Texas with 38, and New York and Florida with 29 each, carry the most electoral weight. Based on the 2010 census, the ten most populous states in the nation control 256 out of the 270 electoral votes needed to elect a president. By contrast, the thirteen least-populous states have only 46 electoral votes—fewer than those held by the largest state, California.

The largest states do not necessarily see the most action, however, because some of them are reliably in one party's column. In recent elections, California and New York have been safely Democratic, while Republicans have had a lock on Texas. White House hopefuls plan their campaign stops accordingly, heavily crisscrossing those vote-rich states that are not firmly in one party's hands—such as Florida, Ohio, North Carolina, and Virginia in 2012—at the expense of the vote-poor states and those not considered in play.

An ongoing criticism of the Electoral College system is that a candidate can win a plurality of the popular vote nationally but still not be elected because of failure to gain a majority in the Electoral College. This happened to presidential candidates

Andrew Jackson in 1824, Samuel J. Tilden in 1876, Grover Cleveland in 1888, and Al Gore in 2000. Jackson and Cleveland succeeded, however, in their next runs for the office. More typically, the electoral vote merely exaggerates the margin of victory of the winner of the popular vote. In 1992, for example, Bill Clinton won 43.3 percent of the popular vote but 68.7 percent of the electoral vote; Barack Obama won 52.6 percent of the popular vote but 67.7 percent of the electoral vote in 2008, and 51.1 percent of the popular vote but 61.2 percent of the electoral vote in 2012. The 2000 and 2004 elections, however, proved exceptions to the rule. In 2000, George W. Bush's share of the popular vote (47.8 percent) nearly equaled his slice of the electoral vote (50.4 percent); the two figures were equally close in 2004, when Bush won 50.7 percent of the popular vote and 53.2 percent of the electoral vote.

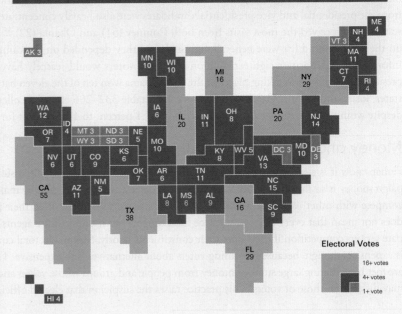

The States in Proportion to Their Electoral Votes, 2012–2020

Source: Compiled by authors.

more responsive to financial supporters than to voters, undermining the purpose of elections and, eventually, democracy. The evidence for the claim that campaign money buys influence and that elected officials ignore voters to please donors is actually quite tenuous (see Chapter 13). But no one denies that money buys **access**, or a politician's ear.

Still, the news media and self-proclaimed public interest lobbies have convinced most Americans that campaign donations buy, in addition to White House hospitality and golf dates with congressional leaders, specific policy favors. The democratic dilemma posed by the campaign finance system has grown more acute with the rise in campaign spending, and major changes in the system are proposed in Congress after every election. In 2002, nearly three decades after the adoption of FECA, reformers succeeded in enacting BCRA, but it did little to resolve the fundamental problems. Some popular reform proposals are based on a misunderstanding of electoral politics. For example, most Americans are convinced that campaigns have become too expensive and would like to impose ceilings on campaign spending. But if the goal is competitive elections, the greater problem is that a large number of campaigns are too poorly funded to give voters even a modestly informed choice. Moreover, unless the spending limits are quite high, they will help incumbents at the expense of challengers (see Figures 11-4 and 11-5, pages 514 and 515).

Another reform suggested would democratize congressional campaign finance by forbidding large donations and banning PACs, forcing candidates to finance their campaigns with small contributions from private individuals. This reform runs aground on a standard freerider problem, however. Because a candidate's victory benefits all who desire it whether or not they contribute to the campaign, and because no single small contribution will affect the outcome or buy access to the victor, it is impossible for most candidates to raise enough money in small donations to conduct a competitive campaign. Recognizing this fact, reformers have proposed a standard solution: financing campaigns with tax dollars. In their view, elections untainted by special-interest contributions are a public good that citizens should compel themselves to purchase just as they pay for national defense. The precedent is the system for financing presidential campaigns (ignoring, for the moment, independent spending and the candidates' option to stay out of the system).

For many who support the idea, publicly financed congressional elections have another advantage: candidates could be required to accept spending limits in return for public funds for their campaigns. But again, unless the limits are high enough, this scheme would hurt challengers, reducing electoral competition. Yet if every campaign gets enough money to be truly competitive, the system will be expensive, with tens of millions of tax dollars spent on many candidates who have no serious prospects of winning. Moreover, any method of public finance would have to accommodate primary elections and third-party or independent candidacies. So far, the idea of extending public funding to congressional candidates has made little headway because the public does not support the move. Opponents have succeeded in characterizing public funds as "welfare for politicians," a frame that combines two widely unpopular referents.

The ultimate barrier to a more egalitarian campaign finance system, however, is the First Amendment as currently interpreted by the Supreme Court. Even if campaigns were fully funded by tax dollars and private contributions to candidates prohibited, people and organizations would remain free to spend all the money they could gather on independent campaigns supporting or attacking candidates. Moreover, we can be certain that many of the people and groups who now send dollars to candidates would merely redirect their funds

Sheldon Adelson   Linda McMahon

Spending huge sums on electoral politics doesn't guarantee victory. In 2012, billionaire casino owner Sheldon Adelson spent more than $70 million in support of Republican presidential candidates, $20 million for Newt Gingrich in the primaries, and the rest for Mitt Romney in the general election.[35] Both lost, as did all six congressional candidates Adelson backed. Another wealthy loser was Linda McMahon, who spent $50 million of her wrestling empire fortune in 2010, and another $49 million in 2012, trying to win election to the Senate from Connecticut, both times receiving less than 44 percent of the vote.

into independent campaigns if the law closed off other avenues of participation. Because no one believes that the justices will change their minds anytime soon, some reformers have proposed amending the Constitution to allow Congress to impose "reasonable" spending limits on everyone. House minority leader Richard Gephardt sponsored such an amendment in 1997; it went nowhere then, and its prospects haven't improved since.

Despite widespread agreement among politically active people that the campaign finance system is flawed in one way or another, fundamental changes are unlikely because there is no consensus on what would count as an improvement or how to achieve it. Even reining in soft money, a minor change, took an extraordinary effort. Larger changes likely will come only in the form of ever more inventive campaign finance practices. But this is not necessarily a bad thing: if the campaign finance system is far from egalitarian, it remains remarkably pluralistic. People espousing a wide variety of interests and values take part in financing campaigns, and no single point of view predominates. Promising candidates with potentially effective messages usually can find financial allies, and therefore elected officials can anticipate electoral trouble if they get out of touch or out of line with the people who elected them. Money is important because candidates need it to reach voters, but the voters still have the last word.

THE LOGIC OF ELECTIONS REVISITED

Despite all the problems with U.S. elections, they work remarkably well to preserve American democracy. Regular, free, competitive elections guard the nation against the dangers that inevitably arise when citizens delegate authority to governments. Elections allow citizens, as principals, to pick their agents and to fire and replace those whose performance falls short. The threat of replacement provides elected officials with a powerful incentive to listen to their constituents. Elections also create incentives for entrepreneurs and organizations to solve the free-rider and coordination problems that beset citizens acting as collective principals. Aspiring leaders and their political allies compete for votes by keeping an eye on officials and informing citizens about their shortcomings, paying the information costs that individual citizens would not rationally pay. Similarly, by getting out the vote on Election Day they turn citizens who might otherwise rationally abstain from casting a ballot into voters. They also bear much of the cost, through polling and focus groups, of keeping track of what citizens want from their agents in government, again making up for the lack of rational incentives for individual political expression. But all of these activities cost money, and the campaign finance system presents its own set of agency problems that are not easily solved.

Elections also induce candidates and campaigns to help solve the massive coordination problem faced by millions of voters trying to act collectively to control or replace their agents. By offering competing frames for a voting decision, they clarify and focus the electoral choice to the point where rationally ignorant voters can manage it. Candidates' opportunistic choice of issues puts voters' concerns on the agenda and helps make election results intelligible: in 2012, for example, a crucial issue really *was* the appropriate strategy for invigorating the economy and bringing down the deficit. When candidates form relatively stable coalitions with other would-be leaders—that is, combine into political parties—they narrow the choices to a manageable number, often as few as two. Indeed, party labels simplify voters' choices across offices and over a series of elections. They also allow voters to hold elected officials collectively responsible for their performance in office. In other words, elections create strong links between public opinion and government action. But they do so only because politically ambitious people have found that it serves their own purposes to engage in the activities that forge the links. One durable institutional byproduct of political ambition pursued under American electoral rules, the party system, is the subject of the next chapter.

TAKE A QUIZ

logic.cqpress.com

Test your knowledge of this chapter.

logic.cqpress.com

■ Key Terms ■

access,   519

candidate,   500

coordinated campaign
  spending,   512

focus group,   502

independent campaign
  spending,   512

issue voting,   497

message,   502

mobilization,   493

negative campaigning,   506

party identification,   498

party label,   497

performance voting,   497

single-issue voters,   496

soft money,   509

▬ Suggested Readings ▬

Abramson, Paul R., John H. Aldrich, and David W. Rohde. *Change and Continuity in the 2012 Elections.* Washington, DC: CQ Press, 2014. The 2012 elections provide the context for exploring basic voter behavior and post–World War II political patterns.

Campbell, Angus, Philip E. Converse, Warren E. Miller, and Donald E. Stokes. *The American Voter.* Chicago: University of Chicago Press, 1976. First published in 1960, this seminal survey-based study of American voting behavior presents the classic psychological theory of party identification. It is still essential reading for every student of American politics.

Downs, Anthony. *An Economic Theory of Democracy.* New York: Harper and Row, 1957. The seminal theoretical work explaining how electoral and party politics reflect rational strategies of candidates and voters.

Fiorina, Morris P. *Retrospective Voting in American National Elections.* New Haven, CT: Yale University Press, 1981. Survey-based study supporting the Downsian theory of party identification as a running tally of positive and negative experiences with the parties' performance in government.

Lupia, Arthur, and Mathew D. McCubbins. *The Democratic Dilemma: Can Citizens Learn What They Need to Know?* New York: Cambridge University Press, 1998. The answer, according to the theory and experimental evidence reported in this book, is a clear yes; despite "rational ignorance," people use freely available cues to make reasoned choices among candidates.

Miller, Warren E., and J. Merrill Shanks. *The New American Voter.* Cambridge, MA: Harvard University Press, 1996. Sequel to *The American Voter,* with an emphasis on generational changes in patterns of turnout and partisanship since the New Deal.

Niemi, Richard G., and Herbert F. Weisberg. *Controversies in Voting Behavior.* 4th ed. Washington, DC: CQ Press, 2001. Sixteen important journal articles that collectively give the reader a good feel for contemporary debates on voter behavior, from voter turnout to campaigns to the party system.

Popkin, Samuel L. *The Reasoning Voter: Communication and Persuasion in Presidential Campaigns.* 2nd ed. Chicago: University of Chicago Press, 1994. How voters use "gut reasoning" and information shortcuts to decide how to vote in primary and general elections for president.

Popkin, Samuel L. *The Candidate: What It Takes to Win—and Hold—the White House.* Oxford University Press, 2012. The three things presidential campaigns have to accomplish to win, and why what got you there won't keep you there when you run for reelection.

Rosenstone, Steven J., and John Mark Hansen. *Mobilization, Participation, and Democracy in America.* New York: Macmillan, 1993. The most prominent and intractable question in American politics is why voting turnout has declined over the past thirty years. Rosenstone and Hansen offer the closest thing we have to an answer that is actually supported by evidence.

Vavreck, Lynn. *The Message Matters: The Economy and Presidential Campaigns.* Princeton, NJ: Princeton University Press, 2009. What matters is not just the state of the economy, but how candidates and campaigns react to it, that determine who wins presidential elections.

▬ Review Questions ▬

1. What are the potential problems with delegating authority to representatives in government? How do elections help reduce these risks?

2. What benefits do people get from voting? Which of these benefits do they still receive if they personally do not vote?

3. Voting, in effect, makes voters choose between a future governed by candidate A and one governed by candidate B. Most voters can't predict the future. What tools allow voters to make these predictions of future performance?

4. What are the main differences between modern campaigns and those of the patronage-based party organizations of the past? Why are campaigns more expensive now?

5. Where does the money required to finance these modern campaigns come from? What are the legal limitations on campaign spending? How has the passage of bans on "soft money" changed these limitations?

12 Political Parties

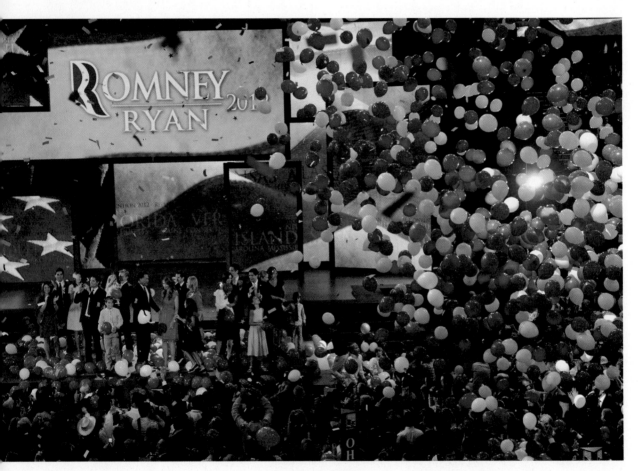

National conventions display party politics in its most colorful and distilled form. Here, Mitt Romney is greeted with unrestrained enthusiasm by delegates to the 2012 Republican National Convention.

- Why does a nation as diverse as the United States sustain only two major parties?

- If the first generation of leaders elected under the Constitution rejected political parties on principle, why did they create them anyway?

- Today national party conventions merely certify the winners of primary elections instead of choosing the presidential nominees, as they did in the past. So why do the parties continue to hold these gatherings?

- Ninety percent of Americans claim they always vote for the person best suited for the job, regardless of party. Why, then, is party-line voting so prevalent, and why are partisans so polarized?

In his 2008 election night victory speech, Barack Obama declared, "In this country, we rise or fall as one nation, as one people. Let's resist the temptation to fall back on the same partisanship and pettiness and immaturity that has poisoned our politics for so long." His sentiments echoed those of his immediate predecessor, George W. Bush, who promised in his 2000 campaign a bipartisan approach to governing that would end the fierce partisan bickering of the Clinton years. "I have no stake in the bitter arguments of the last few years," he said in his acceptance speech at the Republican National Convention. "I want to change the tone of Washington to one of civility and respect." At the end of the bitterly partisan 2012 campaign, both Obama and his Republican rival Mitt Romney were again promising to reach across a partisan divide that had only grown wider and deeper during Obama's first term. In making such vows, they sought to align themselves rhetorically with the disdain for parties and partisanship that is endemic in American popular culture. More than 90 percent of Americans claim they always vote for the candidate they think is best suited for the office, regardless of party.[1] Typically, more than half tell pollsters that the two major parties "do such a poor job that a third major party is needed."[2] Most Americans usually say they prefer that control of government be divided between the parties rather than monopolized by one party.[3] Some political scientists and other observers have concluded from such responses that parties no longer matter much to voters.[4] Yet the same electorate, supposedly so hostile or indifferent to parties, has, in elections since 2000, cast the most consistent party-line votes for president since modern election polling began more than sixty years ago. According to a national exit poll taken the day of the 2012 election, 92.5 percent of self-identified partisans voted for their own party's presidential candidate, and only 6.5 percent defected to the opposition, the highest level of party loyalty ever recorded in an exit poll.[5] House and Senate electorates have also displayed historically high levels of party-line voting in recent elections; a record 93.5 percent of partisans reported a party-line House vote in the 2012 exit poll. Moreover, wide partisan divisions immediately emerged after these elections, with popular evaluations of the winners more sharply divided along party lines than for any other newly elected or reelected president.[6] Entering the White House on the heels of the most partisan (and disputed) election in living memory, Bush's pledge to be "a uniter, not a divider" proved ephemeral. Despite the huge upsurge in national unity that followed the September 11 attacks, the election that returned Bush to the White House in 2004 turned out to be even more intensely partisan than the one that first put him there. By the end of Bush's second term as president, in 2008, partisan divisions in Washington were far wider than they had been before he took office, and Americans' assessments of his administration were the most polarized along party lines ever recorded—until Obama's first term (see Chapter 10).

Barack Obama was no more successful in bridging the partisan divide. Despite the fact that he appointed three Republicans to his cabinet, held meetings with congressional Republicans during his first months in office, and actively sought bipartisan support, Republicans in both houses voted almost unanimously against his major initiatives to stimulate the economy and restructure the health care system. The public also split decisively along party lines on these issues; divisions between Obama's Democratic supporters and Republican opponents in Congress accurately reflected the divisions between their respective electoral coalitions back home.[7] By the time he sought reelection in 2012, partisans were even more divided in their evaluations of his performance than they had been for Bush; in the Gallup polls taken during October and November 2012, an average of 90 percent of Democrats approved of Obama's job performance, compared to only 8 percent of Republicans.

Clearly, reports of the parties' demise no longer match reality. Indeed, anyone who looks at how people vote and evaluate politicians, who wins elections, and how the nation is governed would have to conclude that the two major parties rarely have been healthier. A large majority of voters are willing to identify themselves as Republicans or Democrats, and, of these partisans, a very large majority vote loyally for their party's candidates (see Chapter 11). Rarely does a candidate win state or federal office without a major-party nomination; as of 2012, forty-nine of the fifty state governors and all but 2 of the 535 members of Congress were either Democrats or Republicans.* Moreover, party remains the central organizing instrument in government (see Chapter 6).

The wide gap between people's opinions about and behavior toward political parties has deep roots in American history. None of the politicians who designed the Constitution or initially sought to govern under it thought parties were a good idea—including the very people who unwittingly created them. Even in their heyday in the latter part of the nineteenth century, parties never lacked articulate critics or public scorn. Still, parties began to develop soon after the founding of the nation and, in one guise or another, have formed an integral part of the institutional machinery of American politics ever since. The chief reason for their longevity is that the institutions created by the Constitution make the payoffs for using parties—to candidates, voters, and elected officeholders—too attractive to forgo. American political parties represent the continuing triumph of pure political expedience.

Although expedience explains the existence of the parties, the activities that maintain them contribute to successful democratic politics in unforeseen ways. Indeed, the unintended consequences of party work are so important that most political scientists agree with

---

*Two independents served in the 113th Congress (2013–2014): Sen. Bernard Sanders of Vermont and Sen. Angus King of Maine. Of the 7,296 citizens serving in state legislatures in 2012, only 31 (0.4 percent) were neither Democrats nor Republicans.

E. E. Schattschneider, who said that "[p]olitical parties created democracy and [that] modern democracy is unthinkable save in terms of parties."[8] Parties recruit and train leaders, foster political participation, and teach new citizens democratic habits and practices. Beyond that, they knit citizens and leaders together in electoral and policy coalitions and allow citizens to hold their elected agents collectively responsible for what the government does. They also help to channel and constrain political conflicts, promoting their peaceful resolution. Finally, parties organize the activities of government, facilitating the collective action necessary to translate public preferences into public policy (see Chapters 6 and 7). In short, political parties make mass democracy possible.

This chapter examines the origin and development of national parties in the United States and explains what parties are, why and how they were invented, and how they have evolved.

Scholars have proposed a variety of formal definitions of **political party**. Two of the most prominent stand in clear contrast to one another (except in their conventional sexism). Edmund Burke, an eighteenth-century British politician and political philosopher, defined a party as "a body of men united for promoting by their joint endeavors the national interest, upon some particular principle in which they are all agreed."[9] Anthony Downs, in his modern classic *An Economic Theory of Democracy,* defined a party as "a team of men seeking to control the governing apparatus by gaining office in a duly constituted election."[10] Although rhetorical references to principle are a staple of party politics, the American parties have displayed a shared appetite for public office a good deal more consistently than they have for the pursuit of shared principles.

THE CONSTITUTION'S UNWANTED OFFSPRING

The Constitution contains no mention of political parties. During the nation's founding, parties were widely considered to be dangerous to good government and public order, especially in republics (see box "No One Wanted to Party"). In such an intellectual climate, no self-respecting leader would openly set out to organize a political party.

The pervasive fear of parties reflected both historical experience and widely held eighteenth-century social beliefs. Factional conflict brought to mind the bloody religious and political wars of England's past and the internal strife that destroyed the republics in ancient Greece and Rome and, later, the city-states of Renaissance Italy. Society was viewed ideally as a harmonious whole, its different parts sharing common interests that all wise and honest authorities would dutifully promote. (Pluralism, though implicit in James Madison's defense of the Constitution in *The Federalist,* was not yet on the intellectual horizon.) People in authority saw themselves as agents acting on behalf of the whole community; any organized opposition was therefore misguided at best, treasonous at worst. Accepting the same perspective, rivals justified their opposition by imagining that those in power were betrayers of the community's trust. When the leaders of the new government took the steps that led to the creation of the first political parties, they did not expect or want party competition to become a permanent feature of American politics. Rather, their aim was to have the common good—their version, naturally—prevail and their opponents consigned to oblivion. The first parties were created as temporary expedients.

No One Wanted to Party

In the early years of the United States, conventional wisdom inveighed against political parties. Benjamin Franklin spoke out against the "infinite mutual abuse of parties, tearing to pieces the best of characters."[1] In *Federalist* No. 10 James Madison called them a species of "faction," which, by definition, holds intentions "adverse to the rights of other citizens, or to the permanent and aggregate interests of the community." George Washington used his Farewell Address to "warn . . . in the most solemn manner against the baneful effects of the Spirit of Party, generally,"[2] and his successor, John Adams, averred that "a division of the republic into two great parties . . . is to be dreaded as the greatest political evil under our Constitution."[3] Even Thomas Jefferson once declared, "If I could not get to heaven but with a party, I would not go there at all."[4]

---

1. Richard Hofstadter, "The Idea of a Party System," in *After the Constitution: Party Conflict in the New Republic*, ed. Lance Banning (Belmont, CA: Wadsworth, 1989), 20.

2. Nobel E. Cunningham, ed., *The Making of the American Party System: 1789 to 1809* (Englewood Cliffs, NJ: Prentice Hall, 1965), 16.

3. Hofstadter, "The Idea of a Party System," 20.

4. Richard Hofstadter, *The Idea of a Party System: The Rise of Legitimate Opposition in the United States, 1780–1840* (Berkeley: University of California Press, 1970), 123.

Expedient they were, but temporary they were not. Disdained by almost all, parties nonetheless flourished. The First Amendment's guarantees of freedom to speak, write, and assemble ensured that party activities would be legal. Beyond that, the framework of institutions established by the Constitution created powerful incentives for undertaking the activities that created and sustained parties. The design of the Constitution also had a profound effect on the *kind* of parties that developed. The party system has changed in important ways over the years as political entrepreneurs have adapted parties to new purposes and opportunities, but the basic features that reflect the constitutional system have reappeared in every period.

Incentives for Party Building

The political incentives that spawned parties are transparent. In any system where collective choices are made by voting, organization pays. When action requires winning majorities on a continuing basis in multiple settings, organization is absolutely essential. The Constitution's provisions for enacting laws and electing leaders therefore put a huge premium on building majority alliances across institutions and electoral units. Parties grew out of the efforts of political entrepreneurs to build such alliances and to coordinate the collective activity necessary to gain control of and use the machinery of government.

TO BUILD STABLE LEGISLATIVE AND ELECTORAL ALLIANCES. The first American parties appeared in Congress when leaders with opposing visions of the nation's future began competing for legislative votes. Passing legislation requires majority support in the House and Senate. Any leader wanting to get Congress to act has to identify enough supporters to make up a majority, arrange a common course of action, and then get supporters to show up and vote. To control policy consistently, then, legislative leaders found it advantageous to cultivate a stable group of supporters, forming durable alliances that sharply reduced the transaction costs of negotiating a winning coalition on each new proposal. Since lawmaking powers are shared by three institutions—the presidency, the House, and the Senate—the value of alliances that cross institutional boundaries was also obvious.

Given the diversity of American society, it is impossible for stable alliances of any appreciable size to be built solely on shared interests or values. Rather, alliances are, by necessity,

Both major parties are coalitions with internal divisions over policy and ideology that often threaten to pull them apart. Desire for majority status, however, provides a powerful incentive for party factions to hang together despite their disagreements.

coalitions: participants have to agree to cooperate on action even though they have different, even conflicting reasons for doing so. Holding diverse coalitions together takes continuing political effort, for participants cooperate only as long as it serves their purposes. The sustained organizational effort needed to keep legislative coalitions working in harmony produces legislative parties.

Organized competition for votes in Congress leads directly to organized competition for votes in congressional elections. Coalitions vying for majority status need to recruit like-minded candidates and work to elect them; successful legislative alliances in Washington depend on successful electoral alliances in the states and districts. The organizational work required to negotiate and maintain electoral alliances expands legislative parties into electoral parties.

The presidential selection rules also offer powerful incentives for building electoral alliances across districts and states. The Constitution assigns selection of the president to the Electoral College or, if no candidate wins a majority of electors, to the House of Representatives. Many early observers expected the House to make the choice most of the time, believing that sectional jealousies would keep a majority of electors from uniting behind a single candidate. In fact, sectional rivalries and the competing ambitions of the larger states were constant sources of political friction. The incentives embodied in the rules for selecting the president provide a powerful counterweight to sectionalism, however. If an alliance can recruit and elect people pledged to one candidate in enough states, it can win the presidency.

The alternative is to stack the House of Representatives with enough supporters to make the alliance's choice prevail should no candidate win a majority in the Electoral College. In either case, the problem is to sustain cooperation among numerous politicians, often with competing purposes and interests, across great distances. To the degree that the effort succeeds, the result is a national party organization.

TO MOBILIZE VOTERS. No matter how well organized, electoral alliances fail if they cannot get enough people to vote for their candidates. The competition for votes motivates alliance leaders to attract voters and get them to the polls on Election Day. In the early days of the Republic, electioneering followed traditional forms. The custom of political deference to one's "betters" had by no means died with the Revolution. The natural agents of a harmonious society were thought to be its most prominent and successful members, and a community's interests were assumed to be safest in the hands of those with superior breeding, education, and experience in public affairs. Restrictions on suffrage were common (see Chapter 11). Those who could vote made their preferences known orally and in public, a practice that encouraged deference to the local gentry. The elections themselves were decided largely on a personal basis; contests, if they arose, were between individuals backed by their personal followers. In such circumstances, open pursuit of political office was thought to be unseemly, and campaigns had to be conducted on the sly, through friends and allies. This is not to say that election campaigns were unknown; after all, the techniques of soliciting support and rounding up votes had been known for centuries because elections had been held for centuries. But they were techniques designed for small communities with even smaller electorates that, for the most part, took their cues from local worthies.

After the adoption of the Constitution, property and other qualifications for (white male) voting were progressively reduced or eliminated, and the egalitarian spirit of the frontier gradually eclipsed the habits of deference, even in the older states. As the size of the electorate increased, so did the task of identifying and attracting supporters and getting them to show up at the polls. Whoever could win over these new voters would enjoy a distinct political advantage. The networks of leaders and activists assembled to mobilize electoral support became the first party organizations.

TO DEVELOP NEW ELECTORAL TECHNIQUES. Once organized, electoral parties initiated new relationships between voters and elected leaders. The personal appeals and services that candidates had used to win the support of their neighbors since colonial times did not disappear, but they were, by themselves, inadequate for reaching a much larger, dispersed, and anonymous electorate. Party organizers turned to mass communications—newspapers, pamphlets, public letters, and printed speeches—designed to excite voters with emotional appeals on issues. The temptation to press hot buttons was irresistible when campaigns sought to persuade politically unsophisticated and uninvolved people that they had a stake in the election and a compelling reason to vote. Anyone trying to mobilize citizens to vote also has to overcome the electorate's tendency to free ride, for a party's victory is a collective good that people get to enjoy whether or not they vote (see Chapter 11). Since the beginning, then, much of the work of campaigns has been aimed at overcoming, by one means or another, the free-rider problem.

TO USE PARTY LABELS AND ENFORCE COLLECTIVE RESPONSIBILITY. Voters need a way to distinguish among candidates, and party labels offer a serviceable shorthand cue that keeps voting decisions cheap and simple—as long as the labels are informative. The more accurately a candidate's party label predicts what he or she will do in office, the more useful it is to voters and the more voters will rely on party cues in making their choices. In addition, the more voters rely on party cues, the more valuable party labels are to candidates. Would-be leaders adopt one of the existing political identities to benefit from the electorate's cue-taking habits. Local candidates join national party alliances even though local political divisions may have no logical relation to the issues that national parties fight about.

Once they have adopted the party label, however, politicians have a personal stake in maintaining the value of their party's "brand name," which may impose conformity costs by requiring the subordination of their own views and ambitions to the party's welfare and reputation. Party labels allow voters to reward or punish elected officials as a group for their performance in office. If voters do not like what the government is doing and want to "throw the rascals out," they have an easy way to identify the rascals: they are members of the majority party. The threat of collective punishment gives the majority party a strong incentive to govern in ways that please voters. Parties, then, developed into three-part systems connecting (1) the *party in government,* an alliance of current officeholders cooperating to shape public policy; (2) the *party organization,* dedicated to electing the party's candidates; and (3) the *party in the electorate,* composed of those voters who identify with the party and regularly vote for its nominees.[11]

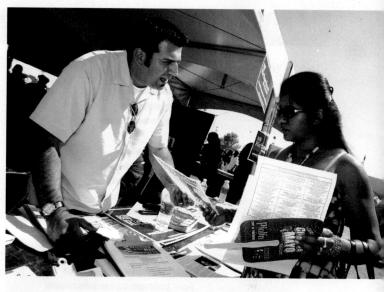

Registration and "get out the vote" drives are among the oldest party strategies in America. At election time the national Democratic Party organizes these drives among those core supporters who tend to participate in relatively low numbers—among them, Hispanics and African Americans. These efforts were crucial to Barack Obama's reelection victory in 2012.

Basic Features of the Party System

Parties emerged, then, not because anyone thought they were a good idea but because the institutional structures and processes established by the Constitution made them too useful to forgo. Their obvious value to elected leaders competing for political goods, to candidates competing for office, and to voters in search of cognitive shortcuts to voting decisions guaranteed that parties' practical virtues would be rediscovered by every political generation. Parties have not always taken the same form, to be sure; there is more than one way to arrange for collective action in American politics. But certain features reappear in every historical party system because they reflect the basic constitutional structure of American government. These features include competition between two major parties made up of decentralized, fragmented party coalitions that are maintained by professional politicians.

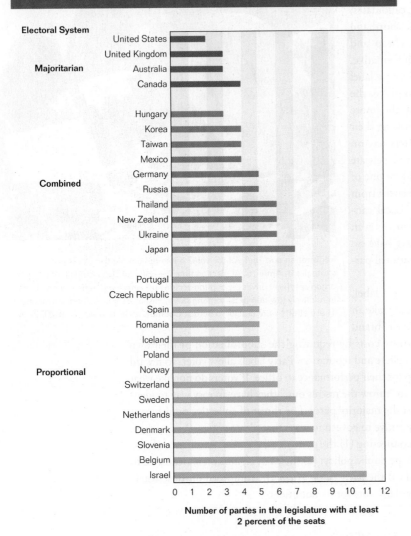

Figure 12-1 Type of Electoral System Determines Number of Parties

Sources: Pippa Norris, *Electoral Engineering: Voting Rules and Political Behavior* (New York: Cambridge University Press, 2004), 87; and *The Europa World Year Book 2004* (London: Europa Publications, 2004).

TWO-PARTY COMPETITION. During the first few Congresses, national leaders gradually divided into two major camps, initiating a pattern of two-party competition that has continued, with a few temporary exceptions, to this day. Americans tend to think of a **two-party system** as normal, but most modern democracies have more than two parties (see Figure 12-1). It is, in fact, remarkable that a people continually divided by region, religion, race, and ethnicity, not to mention social beliefs and economic interests, could fit into as few as two major political camps. But this pattern has continued for a compelling reason. In any election where a single winner is chosen by plurality vote (whoever gets the most votes wins), there is a strong tendency for serious competitors to be reduced to two because people tend to vote strategically. If their favorite party's candidate has no chance to win, they turn to the less objectionable of the major-party candidates who does have a chance to win (see box "Third-Party Blues"). This tendency is so strong that scholars have given it the status of a law, known as Duverger's law, named after the French political scientist who articulated it.[12] Office seekers, aware of this pattern, usually join one of the two competitive parties rather than pursuing office as independents or third-party nominees.

This logic is sufficiently compelling that, at most, only an election or two is required after the disruption of old party alliances and the appearance of new party coalitions for voters to narrow the viable choices down to two. In horse racing terms, to survive, a party must win or place; a third-place show is no better than out of the money. Competition for survival, not to mention victory, puts strong pressure on party leaders to assemble broad coalitions, extending the party's hand to the voters ready to give up on their first choice. Any idea promoted

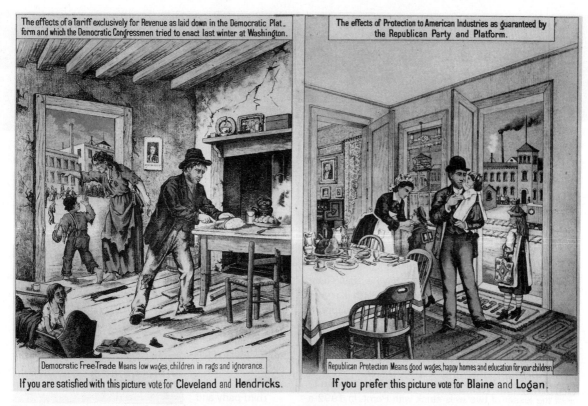

The effects of a Tariff exclusively for Revenue as laid down in the Democratic Plat form and which the Democratic Congressmen tried to enact last winter at Washington.

The effects of Protection to American Industries as guaranteed by the Republican Party and Platform.

Democratic Free-Trade Means low wages, children in rags and ignorance.

If you are satisfied with this picture vote for **Cleveland** and **Hendricks**.

Republican Protection Means good wages, happy homes and education for your children.

If you prefer this picture vote for **Blaine** and **Logan**.

This 1884 Republican poster explains to voters why they should vote Republican. High tariffs supported working families because they kept products made by cheap foreign labor out of the country. With protection, the factories hum (compare smokestacks), food is on the table, and mom does not yell at the kids. Note also the prominence given party labels during the nineteenth century.

by a third party that proves to be popular with voters is subject to poaching by one, or some-times both, of the established parties maneuvering to co-opt the disaffected. Thus incentives to expand electoral coalitions also help to reduce the number of parties to two.

Elections in the United States have almost always been winner-take-all affairs, so the rules have continually worked to reduce the viable options to two. An alternative kind of electoral system—**proportional representation**, under which a party receives legislative seats in proportion to its share of votes—is used in many European democracies. This system helps to preserve smaller parties because votes for their candidates are not wasted (hence the proportional systems listed in Figure 12-1 produce an average of 6.5 legislative parties), but it has never been tried in the United States on any significant scale. Once two-party competition was in place, both parties had a stake in preserving electoral rules that discriminate against third parties. State legislatures controlled by the major parties, for example, erected legal hurdles to getting on the ballot and banned **fusion tickets**, which allow minor parties to boost their votes by nominating candidates also nominated by major parties.

Strictly speaking, the winner-take-all logic applies only within a given electoral unit (a single congressional district or state, for example); it does not require that the same two

THIRD-PARTY BLUES

logic of politics

Third-party and independent candidates have a hard time with the winner-take-all electoral system. Even with considerable popular backing, these candidates may get few votes if their supporters believe they cannot win and vote instead for one of the major-party candidates. For example, many voters who preferred independent Ross Perot in 1992 but believed—correctly—that he could not win, voted for Bill Clinton or George H. W. Bush in an effort to keep their least favorite candidate from winning. By arguing that "a vote for Perot is a vote for Bush," the Clinton campaign attracted Perot supporters whose top priority was replacing Bush. The Republicans made a variation of this pitch—"a vote for Perot is a vote for Clinton"—to voters who preferred Perot to Bush but Bush to Clinton. Only voters whose disdain for both major-party candidates exceeded their desire to elect the lesser of two evils stuck with Perot. In 1992 a surprising 19 percent of the voters did so, but Perot's vote dropped to 8 percent in 1996, and his successor as the Reform Party candidate, Pat Buchanan, won less than 1 percent in 2000.

In the end, then, only those third parties (or independent candidates) that manage to supplant one of the two reigning parties as a viable option in voters' minds gain rather than lose support from strategic voters. The last time this occurred on a national scale was 1856, when the Republicans surged ahead of the Whigs, who were fatally split over the slavery issue.

Third-party and independent candidates can be influential despite their electoral futility, however. Ralph Nader, candidate of the Green Party in 2000, gave George W. Bush the presidency. Had he not been on the ballot in Florida, any plausible redistribution of the ninety-seven thousand votes he received would

parties face each other in every electoral unit. But for purposes of electing a president, the entire United States works as a single electoral unit. The contest for the presidency became so central to electoral politics that it shaped party competition for lesser offices as well.

DECENTRALIZED, FRAGMENTED PARTY COALITIONS. Another reason the two-party pattern endures is that federalism fragments the political system. Historically, national parties have been assembled from diverse state and local political factions concerned chiefly with the vibrant politics of their states, counties, or cities. The decentralized policymaking system allowed these local parties to work together to elect national leaders while going their own way on matters closer to home. National leaders could maintain diverse, unwieldy coalitions because many of the factions within them had little contact with one another except when choosing the party's presidential candidate. Indeed, since the beginning have given the state to Al Gore (most of Nader's support came from liberals who preferred Gore to Bush). Nader immediately became the exemplar of the dangers of "wasting" a vote, and when he ran again in 2004 his national vote total dropped from 2,882,995 (2.74 percent) to 443,830 (0.37 percent), and he was not a factor. Nor was he a factor in 2008, winning only 0.54 percent.

Sometimes potentially formidable third-party candidates decline to run to avoid playing the spoiler. In

polls taken at the beginning of 2012, Libertarian Ron Paul, when matched against Barack Obama and Mitt Romney, was preferred by as many as 21 percent of registered voters. Most of his support came at Romney's expense, and his decision not to run on the Libertarian Party ticket or as an independent gave the Republican candidate a much better chance of winning.

Even when independent and third-party candidates do not affect the outcome, the policies and ideas they promote may survive them through adoption by one, sometimes both, of the major parties. For example, many of the regulatory innovations sought by the Populist Party in the 1890s became part of the Democrats' New Deal after 1932. George Wallace's 1968 campaign theme of law and order soon found its way into many Republican campaigns. And the legislative term limits advocated by Perot ended up in the Republicans' 1994 "Contract with America." Third-party movements thus contribute to the policy agendas of the major-party coalitions even as the winner-take-all electoral system continues to deny third-party candidates public office.

the major parties have been diverse, unwieldy coalitions, ready to fly apart unless carefully maintained. Skillful management and the compelling need to hold these factions together for any chance at office have usually, but by no means always, kept the parties from self-destructing.

PROFESSIONAL POLITICIANS. At the time the Constitution was adopted, political leadership was the prerogative of successful and prominent men who viewed service in public office as a temporary duty that fell to members of their class. As organization became essential to winning public office, political power flowed into the hands of people with the skills to build networks of party workers, manage alliances of local leaders, and mobilize voters on Election Day. Personal wealth, education, and status were still advantages, but they no longer were essential. Of those attracted to party politics, many were ambitious

From the 1940s to the 1970s the Democratic Party balanced northern presidential nominees with southern vice presidential nominations to appeal to the divergent political views of Democratic voters in these regions, especially on the race issue. Despite the sometimes bitter relations between the candidates and their staffs, in 1960 Massachusetts-born John Kennedy was compelled to team up with Texan Lyndon Johnson to strengthen his bid for the South. An August 1960 campaign stop in Amarillo, Texas, was one of their few joint appearances. In fact, most of the time these candidates ran separate campaigns in different parts of the country, with little coordination between them. At the bottom of the photo is Lyndon Johnson's wife, Lady Bird Johnson.

people who latched onto the party as a vehicle for personal advancement; opportunism made no small contribution to the emergence of political parties.

Eventually the variety and frequency of elections generated by the multilayered federal system made party management a full-time job in many places. To maintain the electoral machinery, party managers had to attract resources and reward the efforts of party workers. Thus **patronage**—jobs, offices, government contracts, business licenses, and so forth—grew in importance. By the 1840s, when they were fully developed, parties had become ends in themselves to the thousands of local politicos who depended on them, one way or another, for their livelihood. That dependence ended in the late nineteenth and early twentieth centuries, however, when reforms largely destroyed the patronage-based party organizations. Today, full-time professionals manage the parties, and the activists are mainly amateurs who volunteer their time.

THE DEVELOPMENT AND EVOLUTION OF THE PARTY SYSTEMS

The historical development of parties reveals how they were shaped by politicians' strategic reactions to the opportunities and challenges posed by the Constitution. Scholars have identified a sequence of five (possibly now six) distinct historical party systems. Each system derives its special characteristics from its era's society, economy, and technology, as well as the goals and tactics of political leaders. But common strategic responses to ongoing institutional incentives unite them all.

The first party system (1790–1824) illustrates the logic that led to the creation of national parties. Institutional innovation in the second party system (1824–1860) set parties on their basic organizational course. The full flowering and then decline of party machines under Progressive assault characterized the third (1860–1894) and fourth (1894–1932) party systems. Each of these systems also was defined by its distinctive pair of rival coalitions, but the

Figure 12-2 American Political Parties

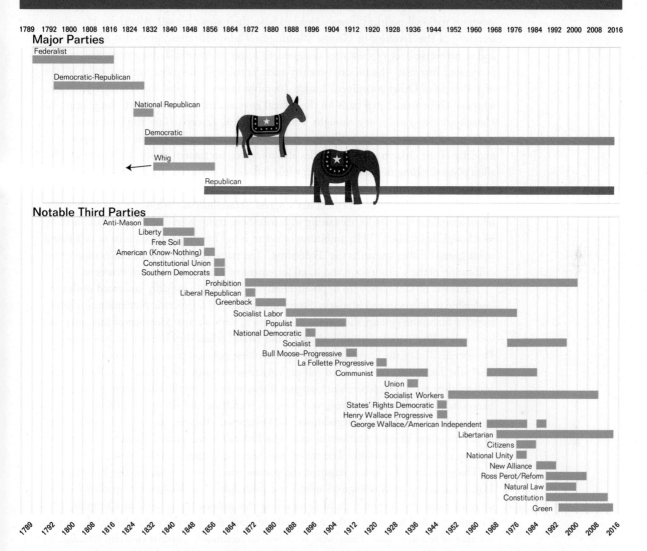

1789 1792 1800 1808 1816 1824 1832 1840 1848 1856 1864 1872 1880 1888 1896 1904 1912 1920 1928 1936 1944 1952 1960 1968 1976 1984 1992 2000 2008 2016

Major Parties

Federalist
Democratic-Republican
National Republican
Democratic
Whig
Republican

Notable Third Parties

Anti-Mason
Liberty
Free Soil
American (Know-Nothing)
Constitutional Union
Southern Democrats
Prohibition
Liberal Republican
Greenback
Socialist Labor
Populist
National Democratic
Socialist
Bull Moose–Progressive
La Follette Progressive
Communist
Union
Socialist Workers
States' Rights Democratic
Henry Wallace Progressive
George Wallace/American Independent
Libertarian
Citizens
National Unity
New Alliance
Ross Perot/Reform
Natural Law
Constitution
Green

1789 1792 1800 1808 1816 1824 1832 1840 1848 1856 1864 1872 1880 1888 1896 1904 1912 1920 1928 1936 1944 1952 1960 1968 1976 1984 1992 2000 2008 2016

Sources: Congressional Quarterly's Guide to U.S. Elections, 5th ed., Vol. 1 (Washington, DC: CQ Press, 2006). Updates provided by Rhodes Cook and the authors.

Note: Throughout U.S. history there have been more than 1,500 political parties. For this chart Congressional Quarterly editors have selected those parties that achieved national significance during presidential election years. The spaces between the rules on this chart indicate the election year only. For example, the Constitutional Union Party and the Southern Democrats were in existence for the 1860 election only and were gone by 1864. Similarly, the Green Party first fielded a presidential candidate in 1996.

coalitional nature of American parties is clearest in the creation and erosion of the party coalitions of the fifth party system (1932–?). The party coalitions have changed enough since the 1950s to suggest that a sixth party system is now in place, although there is no consensus on its date of origin.

The First Party System: The Origin of American Parties

The American party system was born in the first few Congresses as leaders with opposing views on national political issues sought to have their views prevail. Alexander Hamilton, secretary of the Treasury in George Washington's administration, proposed an ambitious and controversial set of measures designed to foster economic development and to give propertied interests—financiers, wealthy merchants, and manufacturers—a stake in the new Republic. Other prominent leaders, notably James Madison and Thomas Jefferson, who saw no constitutional basis for the federal government doing any such thing, opposed Hamilton's program. They thought Hamilton's ideas favored New England over other regions and threatened the well-being of the small farmers and tradesmen who made up a majority of the citizenry. The two sides also disagreed on foreign policy: Hamilton and his allies wanted strong ties with England, while Jefferson's group leaned toward France.

Hamilton's pursuit of votes in Congress led him to create what was, in effect, a legislative party. Although he was not a member of Congress, "Hamilton was involved much in the manner of a modern floor leader, caucusing with members, trying to round up votes, and helping to schedule legislation."[13] His ambitious effort to enact his proposals led him to cultivate a stable group of allies known as the "Federalists." The name derived from its earlier support for ratification of the Constitution and its endorsement of a strong national government.

Members of Congress who opposed Hamilton's policies gradually coalesced under the leadership of Jefferson and Madison. Protesting the alleged aristocratic pretensions (or intentions) of Hamilton's group, they styled themselves as Republicans. Members of this party also were called Democratic-Republicans until the 1820s, when they became known simply as Democrats. Today, the Democratic Party is the oldest political party in the world.

As the Federalists continued to roll up legislative victories, the Democratic-Republicans realized they needed more votes in Congress if they were to prevail. That meant getting more like-minded people into Congress, which meant recruiting and electing candidates. Because senators were chosen by state legislatures, the Democratic-Republican national leaders began to pay attention to state elections as well. The Federalists recognized the same realities and reached the same conclusions. The two groups began to compete in elections.

The presidential election required the parties' attention as well, for the Federalists—Hamilton, acting in Washington's name, and John Adams as Washington's successor—had demonstrated the importance of controlling the presidency as well as Congress. The Constitution had left it up to the states to decide how to select their presidential electors. A number of selection procedures were tried—most commonly popular election, selection by the state legislature, or some combination of the two. In 1800, for example, five of the sixteen states chose electors by popular vote, and state legislatures made the choice in the others. The Framers expected the electors to be prominent local men who would deliberate with others from their states before deciding how to cast their votes.[14]

Challenging Adams for the presidency in 1800, Jefferson and his Democratic-Republican allies realized that these deliberations could be circumvented if they recruited and elected a majority of electors pledged to support Jefferson (see Chapter 9). By reaching out to local political leaders who were potential electors and to the growing mass of voters who chose the electors and state legislators, Jefferson successfully patched together an alliance of state and local factions, which led to a historic victory for his Democratic-Republicans and the ousting of the Federalists. In another innovative maneuver intended to rally voters to their cause, the Democratic-Republicans wedded organization to a controversial issue. They attacked the Alien and Sedition Acts, enacted by the Federalists in 1798 to stifle political criticism, as a frontal assault on republican government itself.* Their tactics were adapted to an expanding electorate:

> Party spokesmen . . . exploited every available agency of mass communication: official papers such as petitions against governmental measures, public circular letters from congressmen to their constituents, newspapers, pamphlets, handbills, private letters which circulated among leading figures, and personal contacts and word-of-mouth communications.[15]

It is no accident that the Democratic-Republicans did the innovating: the history of party building is largely a story of the "outs" finding new ways to become the "ins." The losers then imitate successful innovations. The Federalists tried with uneven success to duplicate the Democratic-Republicans' organizational efforts. They were hampered, however, by their nostalgia for deferential politics—the feeling that "better" people like them were by right the natural leaders—which left them uncomfortable making popular appeals to an increasingly egalitarian electorate.

With the designation of competing slates of electors pledged to support specific presidential candidates, the candidates replaced individual electors as the objects of the voters' decisions. The practice of pledging therefore went a long way toward democratizing the choice of president. In doing so, it strengthened the president's hand within the constitutional system as an executive chosen by the people and beholden to them, not other politicians.

The first parties were by no means the elaborate national organizations that emerged a generation later. One eminent historian has characterized them as "loose collections of provincial interests. . . . Highly local, evolving from rivalries within towns and cities, counties and states, they appealed to an electorate without firmly anchored, hereditary loyalties."[16] Both parties' coalitions were unstable, lacking even uniform names. In fact, any loyalty felt by politicians or voters did not extend much beyond the immediate issue or election.

When their pro-British leanings put them on the wrong side in the War of 1812, the Federalists faded as a national force. In the aftermath of the party's collapse, politicians and informed observers hoped that party competition—and therefore parties—would disappear. The idea that organized opposition would or should be a permanent part of American national politics was still unorthodox. Nevertheless, the first parties accurately presaged future developments.

The Second Party System: Organizational Innovation

By the second decade of the nineteenth century the Democratic-Republicans had eclipsed the Federalists nearly everywhere. James Monroe crushed the Federalists' last presidential

---

*The Sedition Act, for example, imposed fines and imprisonment on anyone convicted of publishing "any false, scandalous and malicious writing" bringing the president, Congress, or U.S. government into disrepute. Ten editors and publishers—all Democratic-Republican supporters of Jefferson—were convicted under the statute; on becoming president, Jefferson pardoned them all. See Jeffrey B. Morris and Richard B. Morris, *Encyclopedia of American History,* 7th ed. (New York: HarperCollins, 1996), 147.

nominee in 1816 and was reelected without significant opposition in 1820. The Monroe years were so lacking in party conflict that the period was dubbed the Era of Good Feelings. But the end of party conflict did not mean the end of political conflict; it only meant that political battles were fought within the remaining party. Without the need for unity to win national elections, party networks fell apart. Personal and factional squabbles reemerged to replace party conflict in most states. One immediate consequence was a dramatic falloff in voter participation in presidential elections: turnout among eligible voters dropped from more than 40 percent in 1812 to less than 10 percent in 1820—eloquent testimony to the parties' crucial role in mobilizing voters (see Figure 12-3).

Party competition revived with a fight for the presidency. Under the first party system, the parties' congressional **caucuses** (members assembled with their allies to make party decisions) nominated presidential candidates—a natural development because electoral competition began as an extension of party competition in Congress. This method became a problem, however, when the Federalists dissolved, leaving almost everyone in Congress a nominal Democratic-Republican. With one party so dominant, whoever picked its nominee effectively picked the president. The caucus, then, could have its way as long as there was a general consensus among its members on the nominee, as in the case of Monroe. Without a consensus, the caucus lost influence and legitimacy.

Figure 12-3 Voter Turnout in Presidential and Midterm Elections, 1789–2012

Sources: Jerrold G. Rusk, *A Statistical History of the American Electorate* (Washington, DC: CQ Press, 2001), Tables 3-3 and 3-5. Data for 1998–2012 are from Michael P. McDonald, "Turnout Tables," http://elections.gmu.edu/voter_turnout.htm.

In 1824, after Monroe, no fewer than five serious candidates—all of them Democratic-Republicans—sought the presidency. The congressional caucus nominated William Crawford, who came in third in the electoral vote and dead last in the popular vote. Andrew Jackson, hero of the Battle of New Orleans in the War of 1812, won the most popular and electoral votes but a majority of neither. John Quincy Adams came in second, and House Speaker Henry Clay came in third in popular votes but fourth in the Electoral College. (The remaining candidate, John C. Calhoun, withdrew early and was elected vice president instead.) Because no candidate received a majority of electors, the election was thrown into the House of Representatives. There, Clay gave his support to Adams, who, upon taking office, made Clay his secretary of state—and, hence, the heir apparent to the White House, since Adams was the fourth president in a row who had previously served as secretary of state.

Jackson's supporters were outraged that a "corrupt bargain" had denied "Old Hickory" his rightful place in the White House. In the midst of that outrage a shrewd New York politician, Martin Van Buren, recognized the opportunity to build a new political coalition. Believing that a national party along the lines of the old Jeffersonian coalition would have the best chance of containing the most explosive issues of the day, particularly slavery, Van Buren put the case for such a party like this:

> Political combinations between inhabitants of the different states are unavoidable & the most natural & beneficial to the country is that between the planters of the South and the plain Republicans of the north. The country has once flourished under a party thus constituted & may again. It would take longer than our lives (even if it were practicable) to create new party feelings. . . . If the old ones are suppressed, geographical divisions founded on local interests or, what is worse prejudices between free and slave holding states will inevitably take their place.[17]

With Jackson as the focal point, Van Buren assembled a political network that became the Democratic Party. Central committees set up in Washington and Nashville, Jackson's hometown, promoted the formation of state organizations, which in turn promoted Jackson clubs or committees in towns and counties. Aided by a nationwide chain of newspapers established to support the cause, Van Buren and Jackson used this organizational pyramid to spread propaganda that kept Jackson and the "wrong" done him in the public consciousness. Local politicians, recognizing Jackson's popularity as a vehicle for their own ambitions, rallied voters with meetings, marches, barbecues, and hickory pole raisings.[18]

Supporters of President Adams had no choice but to put together a network of their own. Adams detested parties and had sought during his administration to build a coalition that incorporated all factions of the old Democratic-Republican and Federalist Parties. He did nothing himself to cultivate electoral allies. Yet his backers, in the process of nominating electors and candidates for other offices and working to get people to vote for them, created what amounted to an Adams party. As one historian has put it, "just by standing for reelection Adams brought a national party into being."[19]

NATIONAL CONVENTIONS. Jackson's smashing victory in 1828 was, among other things, a powerful lesson in the value of political organization. The 1832 election, which he also won handily, featured the first **national party conventions**.* The national convention was promoted as a more democratic alternative to the discredited congressional caucus, allowing much broader popular participation in making presidential nominations. But it also was an eminently practical device for solving problems of conflict and coordination that stand in the path to the White House. The convention was the occasion for assembling, and later refurbishing, the national party coalition. It provided a forum for doing the politicking that convinced diverse party factions to agree to rally behind a single presidential ticket—without necessarily agreeing on anything else. It also was a giant pep rally, firing up the party troops for the contest to come.

The Democrats held a national convention again in 1836, this time to nominate Van Buren as Jackson's successor. Meanwhile, Jackson's leading opponents, including Henry Clay and Daniel Webster, organized themselves as the Whig Party, a name borrowed from British political history that had come to symbolize opposition to royal tyranny, which "King Andrew" Jackson's opponents were fond of alleging. A fractious coalition promoting national development but united primarily by their hostility to Jackson, the Whigs did not hold a national convention but instead attempted to divide and conquer by running three regional candidates. Their plan was to combine their strength behind the strongest candidate in the Electoral College or, failing that, to throw the election into the House.

When that strategy flopped in 1836, the Whigs turned to a ploy that won the party its only two presidential victories: nominating a popular military hero without known political coloration and obscuring party divisions by not writing a platform. The Whig nominee in 1840 was William Henry Harrison, hero of the Battle of Tippecanoe (fought against a confederation of Native American tribes in 1811) and extolled as a rough-hewn man of the people. He defeated Van Buren in a contest that moved party competition to an entirely new level—but whether higher or lower is still a matter of debate.

The 1840 campaign extended organized two-party competition to every state in the nation, framing not only the contest for president but also competition for offices at all levels of government. Competition inspired unprecedented efforts to involve and mobilize ordinary voters, turning political campaigns into the most exciting spectacles the era offered. As one historian of the period observed:

> Those tens of thousands of men and women who attended the mammoth Whig festival at Nashville in 1840; those untold millions who carried torches, donned uniforms, chanted slogans, or cheered themselves hoarse at innumerable parades and rallies; those puffed-up canvassers of wards, servers of rum, and distributors of largess; and all those simple folk who whipped themselves into a fury of excitement and anxiety as each election day approached, were thrilling to a grand dramatic experience, even a cathartic experience. There was no spectacle, no contest, in America that could match an election campaign.[20]

In effect, the parties solved the problem of free riding endemic to mass electorates by making participation exciting and fun. One sign of their success was a dramatic increase in

---

*Actually, the Anti-Masonic Party had held a convention in 1831, and Jackson's loosely organized opponents, calling themselves National Republicans, had convened a small national gathering that year as well. But the Democratic convention that met in Baltimore to renominate Jackson in 1832 is considered the original full-scale national party convention.

turnout (see Figure 12-3, page 540). In 1824 only 27 percent of the eligible electorate (adult white males) bothered to vote in the presidential election. When Jackson was elected in 1828, turnout rose to 55 percent, and it stayed at about that level for the next two presidential contests. In 1840 fully 78 percent of the eligible voters took part. More striking evidence of the crucial role of parties—and party competition—in making mass democracy a reality could scarcely be imagined.

Participation in the hoopla surrounding the presidential contest bred strong feelings of party loyalty among many voters. The emotional ties and bonds of loyalty developed in the heat of battle became powerful forces to keep the parties intact even when the inevitable strains that beset such diverse coalitions threatened to break them up.

THE SPOILS SYSTEM. Parties on the rise always attract opportunists. The politicians who flocked to Jackson's banner or joined his Whig opponents were not, for the most part, altruists; rather, they carried on the party work because they were ambitious for an office or other favors. These motives are neither surprising nor appalling. Parties pursue a collective good: victory for their candidates and policies. All who prefer the winner benefit from the party's victory whether or not they contribute to it. Thus, without some prospect of private reward for party activists as well, the free-rider problem would have left parties stillborn. The men who worked to elect Jackson or Harrison took as their right the spoils of victory— mainly government jobs but also contracts to supply goods and services to the government or special projects from which they might profit.

The pursuit of political spoils, which came to be known as the spoils system (see Chapter 8), intensified party competition and put a heavy premium on winning. For better or worse, party entrepreneurs proved themselves willing to rise above principle if that was the price of winning. On the positive side, putting victory ahead of principle made parties open and inclusive. For a time, broad national coalitions helped manage the dangerous intersectional conflict over slavery and other divisive issues. The high stakes also inspired imaginative efforts to mobilize the first mass electorate in history. On the negative side, the desire to win contributed to corruption, moral myopia regarding slavery, and public cynicism about the honesty and motives of politicians. In either case, the Democrats and Whigs of the second party system set the pattern for the future: every successful American party has cared more about winning elections than about furthering a consistent set of principles.

Indeed, principled conflict is often a threat to party coalitions. Established party politicians put unity first because their careers depend on it, but voters have no such stake and may care very deeply about the positions a party takes on controversial issues. The Whigs and the Democrats built coalitions around differences on economic policy. The Whigs favored a national bank, high tariffs to protect U.S. manufacturers, and federally sponsored public works; the Democrats rejected the bank and the activist economic role it implied and advocated low tariffs to benefit farmers. Both parties had northern and southern wings and so were badly split by the slavery issue. Leaders tried to keep slavery off the political agenda, but, as feelings intensified, this proved impossible. When the extension of slavery became the dominant national issue, the coalitions that formed the second party system fell apart. For the first and only time in U.S. history, a third party emerged to supplant one of the two dominant parties.

The Third Party System: Entrepreneurial Politics

The Republican Party, organized in 1854 as a coalition of antislavery forces, is unusual only in the success of its challenge to the two-party establishment. Third parties have arisen time and again, but most have failed to attract enough of a following to become more than obscure refuges for the disaffected. On a few occasions, however, third parties have managed to shake up the system, leaving notable traces in party politics long after they have disappeared. The Anti-Masonic Party and the American (Know-Nothing) Party are examples from the pre–Civil War era (see Figure 12-2). Both sprouted in periods of economic distress and social crisis, originating as antiparties—movements of "the people" against corrupt and compromising party regulars. As soon as they showed a capacity to win elections, however, they attracted opportunists seeking to jump-start political careers.* For some ambitious men, the protest party was a way station to a position of leadership in a major party. Anti-Masons joined the Whigs; Know-Nothings joined the Republicans.

The Republican Party was organized in opposition to the Kansas-Nebraska Act (1854), which overturned limits on the extension of slavery to the territories enacted earlier in the Missouri Compromise of 1820 and the Compromise of 1850. It drew leaders and followers from two earlier antislavery parties as well as the Know-Nothings, antislavery Whigs, and dissident Democrats. Its adopted name laid claim to the mantles of both the Jeffersonian Republicans and the National Republicans who had backed Adams against Jackson.

Although founded on the slavery issue, the Republican Party was by no means a single-issue party. It also appealed to business and commercial interests (elements of the old Whig coalition) by promising a protective tariff and a transcontinental railway and to farmers by promising free land for homesteading. On only its second try the party elected a president, Abraham Lincoln. His victory over divided opposition in 1860 triggered the South's secession from the Union and then the Civil War, from which the Republicans emerged as the party of victory and union. For the next generation the party sought to retain its ascendancy by appealing variously to patriotism, national expansion, and laissez-faire capitalism and by distributing pensions to Civil War veterans and protective tariffs to manufacturers.

The end of Reconstruction in 1876 restored local control to white southern politicians (see Chapter 4) and left the newly revived Democratic Party an equal competitor for national power. Democrats benefited from overwhelming majorities in the South, where whites despised the Republicans as the party of the enemy and African Americans were largely disenfranchised. The Democrats also had pockets of strength in the West, in the border states (heavily settled by southerners), and among immigrant groups in urban northern areas (especially German Lutherans and Irish Catholics).

PARTY MACHINES. Party organizations reached their peak of development during the third party system. Patronage—jobs, contracts, development rights, zoning favors—generated by the rapid growth of industrial cities provided the capital; party entrepreneurs

---

*The Anti-Masonic Party elected two governors and won fifty-three House seats during the 1830s; seven governors, five senators, and forty-three House members were elected on the Know-Nothing ticket during the 1850s.

provided the management. The classic **party machines** were built on simple principles of exchange: party politicians provided favors and services to people throughout the year in return for their votes on Election Day. They found an eager market for their offerings among the growing population of poor immigrants whose basic needs—shelter, food, fuel, jobs, and help in adapting to a new and bewildering country—were far more pressing than any concern for party programs or ideologies. One such party politician was George Washington Plunkitt, who, thanks to such exchanges, thrived during the heyday of New York City's Tammany Hall Democratic machine at the turn of the twentieth century (see box "The Wisdom of George Washington Plunkitt").*

The late-nineteenth-century party machines represented the culmination of trends reaching back to the Jacksonian era. Politics had become a full-time profession for thousands of individuals. Those who took it up were mostly "men of slender social distinction, whose training came not from the countinghouse or the university, but from the street gang, the saloon, the fire department, the political club."[21] Winning local elections was the paramount goal of party professionals; issues, programs, and candidates (national as well as local) mattered only insofar as they could help or hinder that goal. National parties were contentious alliances of local party organizations competing for patronage. Votes were sought wherever they were available by whatever means worked.

THE PROGRESSIVE ATTACK. Party machines were regularly attacked as corrupt and inefficient and party politicians as incapable of imagining, let alone implementing, solutions to the many problems created by the growth of large industry and national markets. Reformers, working almost entirely from within the two-party system, sought to destroy the party machines by depriving party leaders of the capacity to reward followers. Eventually, they succeeded. The most important changes were introduced during what is now called the **Progressive Era**—the decades just before and after the turn of the twentieth century, overlapping the end of the third party system and the beginning of the fourth. The most important reforms were the civil service, the Australian ballot, and primary elections.

After passage of the Pendleton Act in 1883, reformers began to replace the spoils system with a civil service system in most jurisdictions. Under the spoils system, the winning party filled appointive government jobs with its faithful workers, firing everyone who had not worked for the ticket. The civil service system turned government jobs into professional careers. Appointment and advancement depended on merit (typically, performance on a competitive examination), not political pull, and civil servants could not be fired except "for cause"—failing to do their jobs or committing crimes (see Chapter 8). As more government jobs were brought under civil service, the rewards for party work shrank, reducing the number of party workers.

---

* The most powerful Democratic faction in New York City for nearly a century was commonly referred to as "Tammany Hall." The name reflected its origins in the Society of Saint Tammany, named after a legendary Delaware Indian chief. Founded in 1789 as a patriotic fraternal and charitable club, it had become by the 1840s the club of choice for leading Democratic politicians, and by the 1860s "membership in Tammany and leadership of the Democratic organization were so parallel as to be interchangeable." Tammany Hall was the "wigwam" where the club met. See Arthur Mann, "Introduction," in *Plunkitt of Tammany Hall,* ed. William L. Riordan (New York: Dutton, 1963), xii–xiii.

The Wisdom of George Washington Plunkitt

There's only one way to hold a district: you must study human nature and act accordin'. . . .

To learn real human nature, you have to go among the people, see them and be seen. I know every man, woman, and child in the Fifteenth District, except them that's been born this summer—and I know some of them, too. I know what they like and what they don't like, what they are strong at and what they are weak in, and I reach them by approachin' at the right side.

For instance, here's how I gather in the young men. I hear of a young feller that's proud of his voice, thinks he can sing fine. I ask him to come around to Washington Hall and join our Glee Club. He comes and sings, and he's a follower of Plunkitt for life. Another young feller gains a reputation as a baseball player in a vacant lot. I bring him into our baseball club. That fixes him. You'll find him workin' for my ticket at the polls next election day. . . . I rope them all in by givin' them opportunities to show themselves off. I don't trouble them with political arguments. I just study human nature and act accordin'. . . .

* * *

What tells in holdin' your grip on your district is to go right down among the poor families and help them in the different ways they need help. I've got a regular system for this. If there's a fire in Ninth, Tenth, or Eleventh Avenue, for example, any hour of the day or night, I'm usually there with some of my election district captains as soon as the fire engines. If a family is burned out I don't ask whether they are Republicans or Democrats, and I don't refer them to the Charity Organization Society, which would investigate their case in a month or two and decide they were worthy of help about the time they are dead

George Washington Plunkitt dispensing advice from the New York County Courthouse bootlack stand.

from starvation. I just get quarters for them, buy clothes for them if their clothes were burned up, and fix them up until they get things runnin' again. It's philanthropy, but it's politics, too—mighty good politics. Who can tell how many votes one of these fires brings me? The poor are the most grateful people in the world, and let me tell you, they have more friends in their neighborhoods than the rich have in theirs.

* * *

Another thing, I can always get a job for a deservin' man. I make it a point to keep track of jobs, and it seldom happens that I don't have a few up my sleeve ready for use. I know every big employer in the district and the whole city for that matter, and they ain't in the habit of saying no to me when I ask them for a job.

Source: William L. Riordan, ed., *Plunkitt of Tammany Hall: A Series of Very Plain Talks on Very Practical Politics* (New York: Dutton, 1963), 25–28.

Another reform associated with the Progressive Era was the secret ballot. Prior to the 1890s each party produced its own ballots (listing only its candidates), which were handed to voters outside the polling place (see Chapter 7). Because party ballots were readily distinguishable, voters could not keep their choices to themselves or easily vote a **split ticket**—that is, vote for candidates of different parties for different offices—for this required manipulating several ballots. The system invited corruption and intimidation; party workers could monitor voters and reward or punish them accordingly. Thus between 1888 and 1896, 90 percent of the states adopted the **Australian ballot**, named for its country of origin. The new type of ballot, still in use today, was prepared by the government, listed candidates from all parties, and was marked in the privacy of a voting booth. This change made it much more difficult for parties to exchange favors for votes because it left no (legal) way for the party to know if voters had kept their side of the bargain.

With adoption of the Australian ballot, the government became involved in party nominations, for someone had to determine officially which parties and names would be listed on the government-produced ballot. Laws were passed to regulate party nominating conventions and, later, to allow a party's voters to nominate candidates through **primary elections**. Strong party machines were still able to dominate primaries, but as party organizations were weakened by other changes, primaries deprived them of a crucial political resource: the ability to control access to elective public office by controlling nominations.

Progressives advocated, and in many places achieved, other reforms intended to detach local politics from national politics on the ground that "there is no Republican or Democratic way to pave a street" (forgetting that Democrats and Republicans may have different priorities in deciding whose streets to pave or who gets the paving contract). At the local level, elections were made officially "nonpartisan" and held separately from federal elections. States also adopted laws requiring would-be voters to register before Election Day (to reduce the possibilities of fraud) and to pass literacy tests (unlike the old party-produced ballots, the Australian ballot could be used only by literate voters). Professional city managers were hired to run cities like business corporations, and urban services were "taken out of politics" by putting them under the control of independent boards. At the national level a constitutional amendment, ratified in 1913, took the choice of U.S. senators from the state legislatures and gave it to the voters, eliminating the party politics that had governed the selection of senators.

Although ostensibly aimed at rooting out corruption and cleaning up electoral politics, progressive reforms also were designed to enhance the political clout of the "right" kind of

OFFICIAL SAMPLE BALLOT
General Election ★ November 6, 2012 ★ Flagler County, FL

THIS SAMPLE BALLOT IS FOR INFORMATIONAL PURPOSES ONLY. IT IS NOT FOR VOTING!

Kimberle B. Weeks
Supervisor of Elections

The advent of the Australian ballot allowed voters to pick candidates across parties. With whole-party tickets at an end, candidate-centered campaigns began their ascendency.

people—educated middle- and upper-middle-class folks like the reformers themselves—at the expense of poor urban immigrants and their leaders "of slender social distinction." Stricter voter registration laws discriminated against the poor and uneducated. Literacy tests had the same effect and were used widely in the South to disenfranchise African Americans and sometimes poor whites.

Progressive reforms were adopted to varying degrees in almost every state. And on the whole they worked, weakening or destroying party machines and preventing their resurrection. Where the progressive agenda was most fully achieved, parties became little more than empty shells, existing mainly to help the state government administer elections. Until 1989, for example, official party organizations in California were not even allowed to endorse candidates in primary elections. Vigorous party organizations did survive, though, in some places, often for many years. For example, a tightly controlled Democratic machine ran Chicago until the 1970s. Over the long run, however, progressive reforms deprived state and local party organizations—the basic building blocks of national parties—of much of their political power.

THE CONSEQUENCES OF PROGRESSIVE REFORMS. These changes had several important consequences for electoral politics. First, turnout declined. Tighter registration laws, the Australian ballot, and literacy tests discouraged voting. With fewer jobs and favors to reward the party workers, fewer people were willing to do the work that wedded voters to the party and brought them to the polls. According to Figure 12-3, from the Civil War to the 1890s about 80 percent of the eligible electorate voted in presidential elections. By the 1910s turnout had fallen to around 60 percent. It fell further when women were enfranchised in 1920 and the number of eligible voters doubled. It has not risen much above 60 percent in any election year since. Many women initially ignored politics as "men's business," and women's turnout levels—which today surpass men's—took a half-century to pull even. Turnout declined most among poor and uneducated people, the very citizens most dependent on parties for incentives to vote. (For more on turnout, see Chapter 11.)

The reforms also began to shift the focus of electoral politics from parties to candidates. When party organizations controlled nominations and voters chose between whole party tickets, political careers were bound tightly to parties. With the advent of the Australian ballot and primary elections, these bonds weakened. Candidates could win nominations with or without the party's blessing by appealing directly to voters; they could campaign separately from the party's team because voters could now split their tickets more easily. The full flowering of candidate-centered electoral politics had to await the development of new communication technologies—mainly television and computerized direct mail—but the seeds were planted by the progressive reforms.

By altering the incentives to perform party work, reforms also contributed to changes in the demographics and goals of party organizations. Traditional party organizations were built on material incentives attractive to working-class people; consequently, parties concentrated on winning elections to keep the material benefits flowing. As their resource base shrank, patronage-based parties were supplanted by party organizations made up of middle-class people inspired by nonmaterial incentives—devotion to a particular candidate, issue, or ideology—people for whom a party victory was often less important than the success of their preferred candidate or issue positions.

Paradoxically, the Progressive Era left the Republicans and Democrats organizationally weaker but more entrenched than ever in the political system. Once considered private groups, parties were now treated by the law in many states as essentially public entities charged with managing elections. Regulations tended to privilege the two major parties and discriminate against new parties and independent candidates. Moreover, the advent of primary elections encouraged dissidents to work within the established parties because outsiders could now compete for control of the party's machinery and name. Why should malcontents buck the long odds against winning under a new party label when they could convert an established party to their cause? Thus, for example, conservative Christian activists, inspired by their opposition to *Roe v. Wade* (see Chapter 5), took over the Republican Party apparatus in many states, and soon their positions on social issues such as abortion and gay rights became the party's official positions. Similarly, the antigovernment Tea Party activists mounted their insurgency within the Republican Party rather than setting up a party of their own (see Chapter 11). No new party has come close to challenging either of the major parties since the nineteenth century, but those parties have suffered some convulsive changes as the result of challenges from within.

The Fourth Party System: Republican Ascendancy

From the end of Reconstruction in 1876 until 1894, the third American party system settled into place, and the Republicans and Democrats competed on nearly even terms. In 1896 the Democrats reacted to a severe economic downturn by adopting the platform of the People's Party, or Populists, a party of agrarian protest against high railroad rates and the gold standard, whose first presidential candidate had won five states in 1892. The Democrats nominated for president William Jennings Bryan, a candidate with strong Populist sympathies. Bryan and the Democrats proposed, among other economic innovations, to make silver as well as gold a monetary standard. The silver standard would increase the money supply, easing interest rates and therefore the pressure on debtors, which included most farmers and westerners. The Republican campaign persuaded many urban workers that the Democrats' proposals threatened their livelihoods ("sound" money backed by gold was the backbone of the financial system that sustained the industrial economy) and so converted them into Republicans. The reaction to the agrarian takeover of the Democrats left the Republicans with a clear national majority for the next generation; the new alignment is commonly designated the fourth party system.

The Republican Party ultimately lost its ascendancy to the Great Depression. Having taken credit for the prosperity of the 1920s with policies highly favorable to financial institutions and industrial corporations, the Republicans and their president, Herbert Hoover, were saddled with the blame for the economic devastation and high unemployment that followed the 1929 stock market crash. Franklin Roosevelt, the Democratic candidate, defeated Hoover in the 1932 election. Roosevelt's New Deal solidified a new coalition of interests that gave the Democrats a popular majority. Despite the coalition's slow demise since the 1960s, the Democratic Party has retained that majority—sometimes barely—to this day.

President Franklin Roosevelt and his allies assembled the Democrats' New Deal coalition from remarkably diverse segments of American society. In this 1936 photo Roosevelt chats with members of one group served by New Deal policies, North Dakota farmers who have received drought relief grants.

The Fifth Party System: The New Deal Coalition

Nothing illustrates the diversity of American party coalitions more strikingly than does the **New Deal coalition**, which brought together Democrats of every conceivable background. It united white southern segregationists with northern African Americans (few southern African Americans could vote), progressive intellectuals with machine politicians, union members and their families with the poorest farmers, Roman Catholics with Southern Baptists. These diverse groups agreed on only one thing—electing Democrats—while having very different reasons for wanting to do so.

Some were attracted by Roosevelt's New Deal policies, which, in tackling the Depression's devastation, radically expanded the federal government's responsibility for, and authority over, the economic and social welfare of all Americans. The Wagner Act of 1935, known as organized labor's "bill of rights," cemented union support. Public works programs pulled in poor and unemployed citizens, including northern African Americans (who until then favored the party of Lincoln), and provided patronage for urban machines. Farm programs appealed to distressed rural voters. Progressive intellectuals applauded the federal government's expanded role in attending to the economic welfare of citizens. The adoption of the Social Security and unemployment insurance systems earned the gratitude of working people whose economic insecurity had been so painfully exposed by the Depression.

Other groups were part of the Democratic coalition by tradition. Conservative southern whites were still expressing political identities forged in the Civil War. Roman Catholics, already disproportionately Democratic (a tinge of anti-Catholic nativism was a legacy of the

DON'T FORGET WHO GOT YOU THERE, CHAMP...

GOP

TEA PARTY

DAVE GRANLUND © www.davegranlund.com

Republicans' Know-Nothing heritage), had become overwhelmingly so in 1928, when the party chose Al Smith, the first of their faith to be nominated for president by a major party. They remained in part because the Democrats kept their pledge to repeal Prohibition. As a movement, Prohibitionism was largely Protestant, with clear anti-Catholic and anti-immigrant overtones. Jews in the cities of the East and Midwest also had supported Smith, in reaction to the rural and small-town Protestant bigotry his candidacy had provoked, and stayed with the Democrats under Roosevelt, an early and staunch enemy of Nazi Germany.

The opposing Republican coalition was a smaller, inverted image of the Democratic coalition: business and professional people, upper-income white Protestants, residents of smaller towns and cities in the Northeast and Midwest, and ideological conservatives. It was united by what it opposed: Roosevelt's New Deal programs and the greatly enlarged federal bureaucracy they engendered (see Chapter 8), which Republicans excoriated as unconstitutional, unwise, and un-American.

EROSION OF THE NEW DEAL COALITION. The complexities of coalition politics aside, national electoral competition during the New Deal period was organized around a single question: Are you for or against the New Deal? As long as that was the question, the New Deal alignment held. But when new issues became the focus of electoral politics, the Democratic coalition began to unravel. The Republicans enabled new issues to shape electoral politics by finally recognizing that the major New Deal programs were there to stay; a party in search of a national majority cannot cling forever to losing positions. When they finally regained the White House in 1952 (using the old Whig ploy of nominating a military hero, General Dwight Eisenhower), it was on a promise not to repeal the New Deal but to administer its programs more frugally. Once that question was settled, other issues could come to the fore.

The first and most important of these issues was civil rights for African Americans (discussed in detail in Chapter 4). As the Democrats became the party of civil rights, white southerners began to depart. At about the same time, the war in Vietnam also split the Democrats, largely along the fault lines of class. The party machine politicians and labor leaders whose blue-collar constituents supplied most of the soldiers generally supported the war, as did most southern Democrats. Opposition was led by liberal intellectuals and was most conspicuous on elite university campuses. New controversies over the bounds of acceptable social behavior deepened the split as sexual freedom, pornography, abortion, women's rights, and gay rights became the stuff of politics.

Traditional Democratic constituencies also were divided over new economic initiatives. The Great Society programs enacted during Lyndon Johnson's presidency (1963–1969) lacked the broad appeal of the New Deal. The major New Deal programs—Social Security, unemployment insurance, and Medicare (a New Deal–type program, although not enacted until 1965)—serve politically active majorities. Great Society programs—housing subsidies, school nutrition programs, Head Start, food stamps, and Medicaid—serve a politically apathetic minority: the poor. For many working-class and middle-class Democrats, the New Deal was for "us," but the Great Society's War on Poverty was for "them." The costs of these programs weighed more heavily as economic growth slowed in the 1970s, increasing opposition to taxes. A new issue—environmental protection—also posed dilemmas for Democrats, pitting blue-collar jobs (or recreation activities) against the aesthetic and health benefits sought by middle-class environmentalists.

The Republicans, although less diverse than their rivals, could not avoid some serious divisions of their own. The conservative and moderate wings struggled for dominance from the New Deal period until the 1980s. Conservatives took over the national party in 1964, nominating one of their own, Sen. Barry Goldwater of Arizona, for president. Goldwater's vote against the Civil Rights Act of 1964 endeared him to southern segregationists but alienated moderates in his own party, as did his hostility to the core New Deal programs. His overwhelming defeat left the party temporarily in tatters. It quickly recovered, however, by taking advantage of the deep divisions within the old Democratic coalition to win five of the next six presidential elections.

Republican candidates since Richard Nixon have built winning coalitions by combining affluent economic conservatives (and, in 2010, antigovernment Tea Party enthusiasts) with middle-class and working-class social conservatives, particularly from what is called the Christian Right. To attract economic conservatives, the Republicans declared war on taxation, regulation, and welfare; to win over social conservatives, they offered law and order, patriotism (opposition to the Vietnam War left Democrats vulnerable here), and "traditional family values," defined to mean a ban on abortion, promotion of prayer in public schools, and opposition to same-sex marriage. But this coalition is not much more united than its Democratic counterpart. Many affluent economic conservatives are not attracted to the Christian Right's social agenda, and many social conservatives of modest means remain reluctant to expose themselves to the mercies of an unfettered free market.

CHANGING THE RULES. Divisions within the parties' electoral coalitions during the 1960s were played out in intraparty battles that reshaped the parties as organizations. One major result was the progressive-style reform of presidential nominations. The Democrats' nominating practices had fallen into disrepute because many southern delegations were

Battles between Vietnam War demonstrators and the Chicago police outside the 1968 Democratic National Convention caused a revolt in the convention, culminating in the removal of the Chicago mayor, Richard J. Daley (pictured left, with fist raised), as a delegate. Not only did the last of the party machine mayors depart, but the turmoil also stimulated the party to install reforms that have dramatically altered the way the political parties nominate their presidential candidates.

discriminating against black voters just recently activated by the civil rights movement. It was the Vietnam War, however, that triggered wholesale reform. When those Democrats opposed to American involvement in Vietnam sought to nominate an antiwar candidate in 1968, they found the diverse, arcane state procedures for selecting delegates to the national nominating convention a formidable barrier. Only fifteen states held primary elections, and in some of them support in primaries did not translate into convention delegates. Presidential primaries were merely venues for candidates to show party bosses how electable they were. Because party leaders chose the delegates in most states, leaders from the larger states dominated the convention. In Pennsylvania, for example, the antiwar candidate, Sen. Eugene McCarthy, won 72 percent of the primary votes, but Vice President Hubert Humphrey got 80 percent of Pennsylvania's convention delegates.

In 1968 the convention was still the quadrennial coming together of diverse and fractious state party organizations that it had been since the 1830s. Most party regulars were, by habit, loyal to their president, Lyndon Johnson, and his anointed successor, Vice President Humphrey. Meeting in Chicago, the Democrats nominated Humphrey while antiwar protests filled the streets outside the convention hall. When the demonstrations got out of hand, they were violently suppressed by the Chicago police on the orders of Mayor Richard J. Daley, boss of the strongest surviving party machine and a major Humphrey backer. The party's internal divisions, dramatized by the riots and exposed to the world on national television, doomed the Democratic ticket and led to the election of Richard Nixon as president.

PRIMARY ELECTIONS AND CAUCUSES. To repair the Democratic coalition and restore the convention's legitimacy, a party commission (the McGovern-Fraser Commission) drew up a new set of criteria specifying that convention delegations had to be chosen in a process that was "open, timely, and representative." The state parties could comply in one of two ways. They could hold a primary election, the outcome of which would determine at least 90 percent of the state's delegation. Or they could hold local party caucuses open to all Democrats, who would select delegates to a meeting at the county, congressional district, or state level. These delegates would in turn elect delegates to the national convention. The easiest option was the primary, and most state parties have adopted it. In 2008 Democratic primaries were held in thirty-seven states; the rest selected delegates via caucuses. In 2012, with no serious challenge to Obama's renomination, Democratic presidential primaries were still held in thirty-three states.

In another change, the winner-take-all method of allocating delegates went out the window. Instead of awarding all of a state's delegates to the top vote getter, the new rules allocated delegates proportionally to candidates according to the share of votes they received in the primary or the caucus. To meet the "representativeness" standard, delegations had to include more minorities, women, and young adults. Because most elected officeholders were white males over thirty, these rules meant that many of them could no longer attend the convention.*

The Democrats' delegate selection rules created a whole new ball game. Previously the party's supreme plum, its presidential nomination, had been conferred by party leaders, who sought to pick a winner who would be obligated to them and therefore send presidential favors their way. Moreover, they wanted a candidate who would help the whole party ticket on Election Day. Now the nomination goes to the candidate who can best mobilize support in primary elections. If party leaders are to exercise any influence in this process, they must do it by delivering endorsements and electoral resources to their favorite before and during the primary season.

The new process may be "fairer," as intended, but it has threatened other party goals, namely winning and governing. In some years, the candidate who most excites the activist minority who show up for primary elections (turnout is typically 20 to 30 percent of eligible voters) was not even the best vote getter among Democrats generally, let alone the broader electorate. For example, Sen. George McGovern, the 1972 nominee, was the choice of anti-war Democrats but no one else; he won only 38 percent of the general election vote, the worst showing for a Democrat since the New Deal realignment.

The system also allows outsiders with tenuous links to other Democratic leaders to compete. Jimmy Carter, an obscure one-term governor of Georgia, won the nomination and then the White House in 1976 but found it nearly impossible to work effectively with his party in Congress. Carter's lack of experience in the ways of Washington, and his lack of political ties to its movers and shakers, clearly handicapped his administration (see Chapter 7).[22] Responding to such problems, the Democrats altered their rules several more times to give party regulars more influence in the selection process. Prominent elected officials—governors, senators, and representatives—are now automatically among the convention delegates. These so-called **super-delegates** accounted for 823, or 19 percent, of the 4,257 votes at the Democrats' 2008 convention. Because Barack Obama led Hillary Clinton by only 137 votes among delegates allocated through the primaries and caucuses, the superdelegates effectively determined the choice of candidate for the first time. Most of them sided with Obama after the final primaries in June, assuring him of the nomination. Had they instead handed the nomination to Clinton, they would have outraged Obama supporters and split the party badly, a potential downside evidently overlooked when the party added superdelegates to the mix.

The nomination process enables the parties to solve the coordination problem posed by competing presidential aspirants. Sometimes party elites do the coordinating; if they can reach broad agreement on which candidate to support, they can be decisive, as the

---

*The Republican Party also adopted primary elections as the basic method of choosing delegates but allows states to maintain a winner-take-all process; Republican candidates competed in thirty-seven state primaries in 2012.

nomination of George W. Bush in 2000 illustrated. Bush initially faced a crowded field of twelve candidates, but by the beginning of the delegate selection process (the Iowa caucuses on January 24), six had dropped out, and by early February only Sen. John McCain remained a serious rival. Bush swept away the competition by persuading the Republican Party establishment, elected officials and campaign donors alike, that his candidacy offered the best chance of returning the White House to Republican control. Bush was acceptable to all factions of the party, from affluent "country club" Republicans to religious conservatives, emerging as the consensus solution to the party's problem of coordinating Republican opposition to Democratic nominee Al Gore.

Leaders are not the only partisans who can coordinate the choice of presidential nominee. In 2004 it was the Democrats who attended the Iowa caucuses on January 19 who effectively organized the nomination of Bush's opponent. Prior to the caucuses, Democrats across the country were divided on whom they wanted to challenge the president, with six candidates getting significant support in polls; Vermont governor Howard Dean led but was preferred by only a quarter of Democratic voters. By giving John Kerry the nod over Dean and the other candidates (with 37 percent of the vote), Iowa Democrats signaled their belief that he was the party's strongest prospect to defeat Bush. Kerry got an immediate boost in the national polls, which was reinforced by his victory in New Hampshire eight days later. By mid-February, Kerry had become the Democrats' consensus favorite and had locked up the nomination.

John McCain performed a similar feat in 2008. His national support soared after his performance in the January primaries in New Hampshire, Michigan, South Carolina, and Florida, and he subsequently sewed up the nomination by winning 61 percent of the delegates at stake in the primaries held in twenty-one states on February 5.

Democratic voters had a much more difficult time settling on their candidate in 2008 (see Figure 12-4a). Hillary Clinton led in national polls for all of 2007 but could not add to her numbers. Barack Obama's early victories in Iowa and South Carolina transformed the contest into a two-person race with him as the leading candidate, but Clinton came back in New Hampshire and did well in some later primaries, and ordinary Democrats remained almost evenly divided until the end of the primary season in June. Clinton's effort to overcome Obama's early delegate lead was seriously hampered by the party's proportionality rule. For example, she won 52 percent of the vote in California's primary to Obama's 43 percent, but she got only 55 percent of the delegates to his 45 percent.

The 2008 presidential nomination process in both parties left no doubt that party allocation rules matter. McCain won 46.7 percent of the votes cast in all Republican primaries and ended up with 72.9 percent of the delegates; Obama won a larger share of the votes cast in his primaries (47.3 percent) but a smaller share of his party's delegates (53.2 percent). Hillary Clinton actually won a larger share of total votes cast in all Democratic primaries than Obama (48.0 percent) but ended up with fewer delegates (44.6 percent) because of Obama's showing in the states holding caucuses.

Mitt Romney's road to the Republican nomination 2012 was considerably rockier than the road of Bush in 2000 or McCain in 2008. His record as a relatively moderate governor of the liberal state of Massachusetts was a serious handicap in appealing to Republican primary voters, who tend to be very conservative (the primary electorates of both parties typically over-represent the parties' respective ideological extremes). Although he was among the front-runners from the start of the campaign, he faced a cyclical series of challenges from more conservative candidates. Over the course of the primary season he found himself behind in

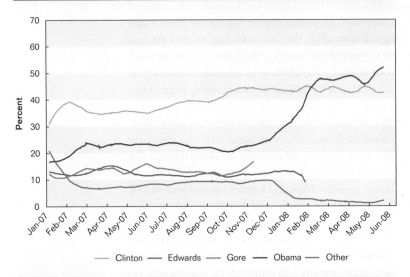

Figure 12-4a Democratic Nomination Preferences, 2007–2008

Clinton — Edwards — Gore — Obama — Other

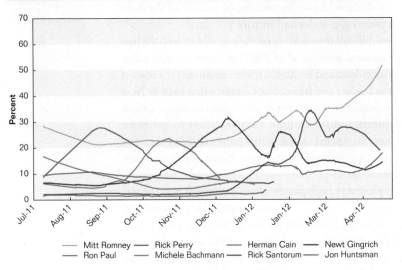

Figure 12-4b Republican Nomination Preferences, 2011–2012

Mitt Romney — Rick Perry — Herman Cain — Newt Gingrich
Ron Paul — Michele Bachmann — Rick Santorum — Jon Huntsman

Sources: www.pollingreport.com/wh08dem.htm, accessed June 15, 2008, and http://www.pollingreport
.com/wh12rep.htm, accessed July 27, 2012.

the polls to Texas governor Rick Perry, then to entrepreneur and talk show host Herman Cain, then to former House Speaker Newt Gingrich, and finally to former Pennsylvania senator Rick Santorum (Figure 12-4b). Romney overcame each of these challenges by portraying himself as a "severe conservative" and adopting issue positions consistent with that portrayal while using his superior financial resources to publicize the various political liabilities of his opponents. He eventually won over most conservative Republicans by convincing them that he would be the strongest candidate against Barack Obama, but his efforts to woo them made it harder for him to moderate his positions to attract the more centrist swing voters in the general election.

THE CONVENTIONS EVOLVE. Now that primaries and caucuses effectively determine the parties' nominees, the purpose and meaning of national conventions have changed. Conventions were once venues for state and local party leaders to renegotiate their complex coalitions and to choose a torchbearer around whom the troops could rally. Now, delegates belong to candidates, not party officials. Conventions no longer choose the party's candidate; caucus activists and voters in primaries do. The focus is less on renewing the party coalition and rallying the faithful and more on presenting an attractive image and message to citizens watching the action at home on television. In 2000, for example, the Republicans sought to present a friendlier, more inclusive, and more moderate face than they had displayed in 1992 and 1996. In place of the hard-line conservatives who had defined the party's image in the 1990s, prime-time speakers included a stream of Republican

African Americans, Hispanics, and women of all ethnic backgrounds. An openly gay Republican representative was even given the podium, although he was allowed to speak only on foreign policy. The message of moderation and inclusiveness and the nominee's espousal of a "compassionate conservatism" were designed to make the party more attractive to groups with whom it had been relatively unpopular in recent years—women, minorities, and moderate swing voters. In 2004 the Democratic convention that nominated John Kerry emphasized his heroic action as a young naval officer in Vietnam. Featured prominently were sailors who had served with him on the "swift boats" that patrolled the Mekong Delta. The idea was to convince voters that Kerry had the qualities of leadership and courage necessary to combat international terrorism, attempting to counter the inevitable Republican charge that a Democratic president would be insufficiently zealous in defending the nation.

In 2008 both parties' conventions became venues for patching up party divisions arising from the bruising primary season as well as for trumpeting the candidates' central campaign themes for the fall (see Chapter 11). Barack Obama sought to unite the Democrats behind his candidacy by giving his defeated rival Hillary Clinton a prominent speaking role in return for her enthusiastic endorsement, hoping to soften the disappointment of Democrats who had been eager to nominate and elect the first woman to the White House. John McCain sought to unite the Republicans by wooing social conservatives, most of whom had not supported his candidacy, by choosing one of them, Gov. Sarah Palin of Alaska, as his running mate. Both efforts were largely successful.

As in 2000, the 2012 Republican convention featured a roster of speakers far more diverse than the party's actual composition,* partly to convince voters that not all its leaders were wealthy white men like its nominee, partly in recognition of demographic trends that would eventually enfeeble the party if it could not expand its appeal to an increasingly diverse American electorate. The convention's most memorable moment, however, was the unscripted monologue by the flinty eighty-two-year-old actor Clint Eastwood addressed to an empty chair representing Barack Obama. The Democrats sought to use their 2012 convention to revive Obama's sagging support among voters who had responded to his message of "hope" in 2008 and to remind them what they had not liked about the previous Republican administration, an assignment taken up most enthusiastically and effectively by former president Bill Clinton, a prime-time speaker at every Democratic convention since 1988.

These efforts serve as a reminder that conventions are still crucially important to parties, reassembling the party coalitions for the fall campaign as well as showing voters what sorts of people make up the party and what groups and causes they champion. A display of party unity still matters, not merely to energize activists, its earlier purpose, but to convince the public that the party has its act together and can be trusted to govern.

A party's self-display at its national convention is not without risk, as both parties have had more than one occasion to discover. Party activists often hold more extreme views on the issues of the day than do ordinary party voters, who may question whether the party actually represents their values and interests. The problem is illustrated in the box "Voters versus Party Activists in 2008: Differences of Opinion," which compares the views of voters who identify

logic.cqpress.com

Clint Eastwood debates an empty chair at the 2012 GOP National Convention.

---

* According to Pew surveys taken during the first half of 2012, 87 percent of Republican Party identifiers are non-Hispanic whites, compared to 61 percent of Democratic identifiers. They are also older on average than Democrats or independents; see http://www.people-press.org/2012/08/23/a-closer-look-at-the-parties-in-2012, accessed October 17, 2012.

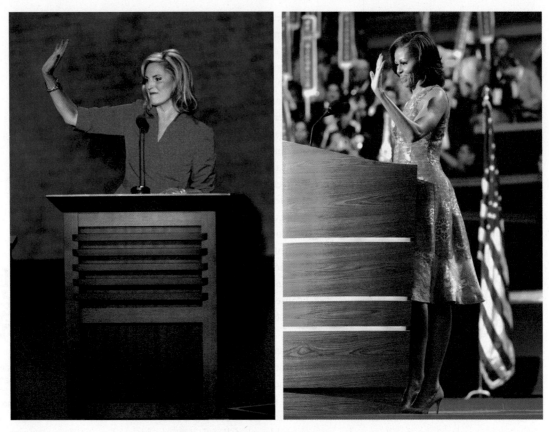

Each party's 2012 convention featured an eloquent speech by the candidate's wife designed to soften and humanize her husband's image; the campaigns thus deftly exploited the fact that both wives were viewed more favorably and had broader appeal than their husbands.

themselves as Republicans or Democrats with the respective parties' convention delegates in 2008. On almost every question the opinions of convention delegates are more sharply divided than those of their parties' voters; on average, the respective delegations' responses differ by about sixty percentage points. On a few issues, delegates' views are also quite distinct from the views of party supporters (Democrats on abortion; Republicans on health care policy). It is easy to understand why many voters would see the Republicans as too conservative and the Democrats as too liberal to represent their views reliably. However, the responses show that ordinary Democratic and Republican voters differ on many issues as well, particularly on the Iraq War, health care policy, and same-sex marriage. The average difference in responses among the parties' voters is about thirty-eight percentage points.

No similar study was conducted in 2012, but a survey of convention delegates from ten competitive states found huge party differences in beliefs about economic policy. For example, 99 percent of the Democrats considered the administration's bailout of the auto industry a success, whereas 90 percent of Republicans said it was a mistake. Two-thirds of the Democrats but only 1 percent of Republicans said the main source of the federal deficit was insufficient revenue; more than 90 percent of Republicans blamed entitlements such as Medicare and Social Security, compared to 5 percent of the Democratic delegates.[23]

Voters versus Party Activists in 2008

Differences of Opinion

	Democratic Delegates	Democratic Voters	Republican Voters	Republican Delegates
1. Ideology: Liberal	43%	48%	5%	0%
Moderate	50	34	30	26
Conservative	3	16	63	72
2. The United States did the right thing in taking military action in Iraq.	2	14	71	80
3. Prefer health coverage for all and higher taxes to lower taxes leaving some without health coverage.	94	90	40	7
4. Protecting the environment is more important than developing new sources of energy.	25	30	9	3
5. Gun control laws should be made more strict.	62	71	32	8
6. Illegal immigration is a very serious issue.	15	36	63	58
7. Same-sex couples should be allowed to marry legally.	55	49	11	6
8. Abortion should be generally available to those who want it rather than under stricter limits or not permitted.	70	43	19	0
9. The condition of the economy is good.	2	7	40	57
10. The 2001 Bush tax cuts should be made permanent.	7	34	62	91

Source: CBS News/*New York Times* polls, July–August 2008, www.cbsnews.com/htdocs/pdf/RNCDelegates_issues.pdf and www.cbsnews.com/htdocs/pdf/RNCDelegates_who_are_they.pdf, accessed September 2, 2008.

Note: Percentage indicates the proportion of each group that agreed with each numbered statement.

CONSEQUENCES OF FRACTURED ALIGNMENTS. When issues arise that split the existing party coalitions, partisan identities weaken, and the party label may not provide the information voters want. The fracturing of the New Deal alignments in the 1960s and 1970s and the difficulty party politicians faced in reconstructing stable coalitions around new issues reduced the importance of party cues to voters, who became less certain about which political camp to identify with. The consequences of this breakdown were abundantly evident in election and polling results.

Party-line voting declined, and ticket splitting increased. As we saw in Figure 11-2 (page 499), party-line voting in presidential elections declined between the 1950s and the 1970s. The same was true of House and Senate elections during this period: the proportion of voters who were party loyalists fell by more than ten percentage points. Ticket splitting increased

Figure 12-5 Split-Ticket Voting

Percent Voting a Split Ticket

■ Between presidential and House candidates
■ Between Senate and House candidates

Sources: For 1952–2004 and 2008, American National Election Studies; for 2006, 2010 and 2012, Cooperative Congressional Election Study.

Note: Data not available for 1954 and 1962.

sharply over the same period (see Figure 12-5). Clearly, party identification lost some of its influence on the vote as the New Deal coalition unraveled.

VOTERS BECAME MORE INDIFFERENT TO THE PARTIES. Political scientist Martin Wattenberg analyzed responses to four decades (1952–1992) of survey questions asking people what they liked and disliked about the parties. He found that, over time, the net sum of voters' comments about the parties became increasingly neutral (an even partisan balance of likes and dislikes) mainly because a growing share of respondents had nothing good or bad to say about either party.[24] In 1952 far more voters gave responses that, when summed up, favored one of the parties than gave responses that were evenly balanced between the parties; by the 1970s neutrality was as common as partisan bias.

WITH VOTERS SUBSTITUTING PERSONAL CUES FOR PARTY CUES, THE ELECTORAL ADVANTAGE ENJOYED BY CONGRESSIONAL INCUMBENTS GREW. Incumbents got greater mileage from their name recognition advantage and assiduous delivery of services to constituents when fewer voters automatically rejected them because of their party affiliation. (For details, see section "The Advantages of Incumbency" in Chapter 6, pages 244–248.)

THE ELECTORATE BECAME MORE VOLATILE. The Democrats' presidential vote dropped by twelve million between 1964 and 1968; the Republican vote dropped by fifteen million between 1984 and 1992. In House contests partisan vote swings became more variable across districts, making election results less predictable from one election to the next.[25]

INDEPENDENT AND THIRD-PARTY CANDIDATES INCREASED THEIR TAKE. Between the beginning of the New Deal in 1932 and 1964, no minor-party or independent candidate received more than 3 percent of the vote. Between 1968 and 1996, three candidates in four races exceeded that margin: George

Wallace (14 percent in 1968), John Anderson (7 percent in 1980), and Ross Perot (19 percent in 1992, 8 percent in 1996).

DIVIDED PARTISAN CONTROL OF GOVERNMENTS BECAME COMMON. American voters now regularly divide control of the White House and Congress between the parties (see Table 7-2, page 310). Do they do it on purpose? Certainly, moderate voters might prefer **divided government** because it allows each party to block the other's more extreme proposals and forces both parties to compromise when making policy.[26] People who simply distrust politicians also might prefer to have the parties in a position to check one another. Despite this logic, there is little evidence that many people deliberately split their votes to achieve moderate policies or to make "ambition counteract ambition." Divided government is more likely a byproduct of voters applying different criteria for different offices, responding to the specific options in each contest, or making tradeoffs among their incompatible preferences (for low taxes but generous middle-class entitlements, for less regulation but more protection from environmental and market risks).[27] But even if few people deliberately vote for divided government, most are happy when they get it. For example, in 2008, a year when voters gave the Democrats unified control of the federal government, 52 percent of respondents in the American National Election Studies said they preferred to have the presidency and Congress split between the parties, while only 21 percent preferred to have one party control both branches (the rest said it did not matter).

MEDIA AND MONEY. The weakening of party influence on voters was hastened along by technological changes and the growing availability of campaign resources—money, skill, activists—from sources other than political parties. The most important technological innovation was the advent of television as a campaign medium, but newer technologies, such as computerized direct mail, mass-produced campaign videos, and now the Internet, have contributed as well. The electronic media have made parties less essential to candidates and voters alike. Ross Perot was able to conduct a surprisingly successful campaign in 1992 with no party at all behind him. (He did not organize the Reform Party until 1995.) Voters informed by the news media as well as by the candidates' electronic campaigns are offered cheap cues other than party labels to guide their decisions. News coverage of elections, not to mention campaign advertising, focuses on individual candidates and largely ignores parties, thus inviting voters to do the same.

The technology of modern campaigns is expensive, driving up the demand for campaign funds. The proliferation of candidate-centered campaigns also has driven up costs because such campaigns cannot operate with the economies of scale enjoyed by candidates working as a party team, communicating a common message, and sharing the cost of consultants, specialists, and advertising. But these changes would not have happened had the supply of money not risen to meet the demand. It did so because a growing economy provided the funds for people to invest in politics, and the expanding role of the government in their lives and businesses gave them more reasons to do so.

THE REVIVAL OF THE PARTIES: A SIXTH PARTY SYSTEM?

Despite the forces working against parties, and despite the public's doubts about the value of parties in general, the Democratic and Republican Parties continue to dominate electoral politics. Indeed, the evidence in Figure 12-5 indicates a revival of partisanship among voters over the past two decades, with ticket splitting falling to levels last seen in the 1960s; voters have also become steadily less likely to express neutral (rather than positive or negative) views of the major parties since 1980.[28] Parties have survived for the same reasons they came into being: elected officials, candidates, and voters still find them indispensable.

Partisanship Endures

Although fewer voters think of themselves as staunch partisans than was the case forty years ago, most people are still willing to call themselves Democrats or Republicans, and significantly, party affiliation remains the single best predictor of how people will vote. The distribution of partisan identities from 1952 through 2012, shown in Figure 12-6, is surprisingly stable despite the dramatic political events that occurred within that period. The proportion calling themselves independents has grown, but most independents are actually closet partisans leaning toward one of the parties and supporting its candidates as consistently as do weak partisans.[29] The proportion of "pure" independents grew from 6 percent in 1952

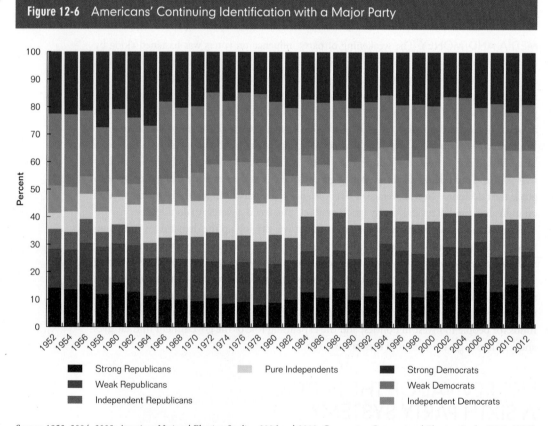

Figure 12-6   Americans' Continuing Identification with a Major Party

Legend:
- Strong Republicans
- Weak Republicans
- Independent Republicans
- Pure Independents
- Strong Democrats
- Weak Democrats
- Independent Democrats

Sources: 1952–2004, 2008: American National Election Studies; 2006 and 2010: Cooperative Congressional Election Study; 2012: ANES 2010–2012 Evaluations of Government and Society Study, February 2012 survey.

to 15 percent in 1976, but has since fallen to an average of about 11 percent during the past two decades. Because self-described independents are less likely to vote, their usual share of the electorate is actually closer to 7 percent. The proportion of strong partisans (of both parties) declined between the 1950s and the 1970s but has since rebounded.

Party Differences

Voters may not think much of parties, but large majorities still admit to a party preference and use parties to guide their voting decisions. They do so because, despite the divisions within the party coalitions and regardless of how they feel about the parties, the party labels still carry valuable information about candidates (see box "2012 Party Platforms"), continuing to provide the cheap, shorthand cue so useful to rationally ignorant voters. Indeed, more people think party labels offer clearer guidance now than at any time since 1952; over the past thirty years, the proportion of Americans seeing important differences in what the parties stand for has grown from about half to three-quarters (see Figure 12-7).

In general, Republicans tend to favor a smaller, cheaper federal government; they advocate lower taxes, less regulation of business, and lower spending on social welfare. They would be more generous only to the Defense Department. Democrats are more inclined to regulate business on behalf of consumers and the environment and are more supportive of

Figure 12-7 Americans Increasingly See Important Differences in What the Republican and Democratic Parties Stand For

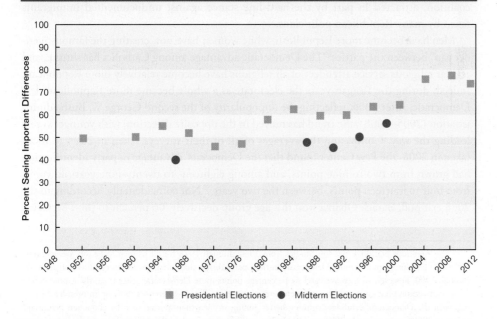

Sources: 1952–2008: American National Election Studies; 2011: ANES 2010–2012 Evaluations of Government and Society Study, spring 2011 survey.

government programs designed to improve domestic welfare; they would spend less on national defense. Democrats are more concerned with "fairness" and equality, Republicans with letting free enterprise flourish. Republicans would ban abortion and gay marriage and allow official prayer in public schools; Democrats would not. Not all candidates adhere to their party's modal positions; some Republicans support freedom of choice on abortion, and some Democrats advocate large defense budgets. But the party label continues to distinguish candidates from one another on many issues with considerable accuracy. In Congress party divisions are sharper and clearer now than they have been since the nineteenth century (see Chapter 6). As the predictive accuracy of party labels has grown in recent decades, so has the usefulness—and therefore use—of party cues.

Changes in the Party Coalitions

The party coalitions of the 2000s still retain strong traces of the New Deal alignment (for example, lower-income voters are still more likely to be Democrats; higher-income voters, Republicans), but they have undergone several crucial changes since the 1960s. In the 1950s white southerners were overwhelmingly Democratic, but they responded to the civil rights revolution—and the Republicans' "southern strategy" to exploit the discontent civil rights aroused—by moving gradually but steadily into the Republican camp. A solid majority of white southerners now identify themselves as Republicans. African Americans favored Democrats even before the 1960s, but the magnitude of the Democratic advantage more than doubled in the 1960s, has remained huge ever since, and was reinforced by Obama's two candidacies. Latino voters, representing a growing share of the electorate, have also become an important component of the Democratic coalition, attracted in part by the hard-line stance against undocumented immigrants taken by many Republican politicians.

Men have become more Republican, while women have not, creating the famous "gender gap" between the parties.* The Democratic advantage among Catholics has shrunk, and regular religious service attendees of all religions have become relatively more Republican. Indeed, during the Reagan years the electorate as a whole became more Republican, less Democratic. After 2004, reflecting the unpopularity of the second George W. Bush administration (2005–2008), the trend has moved in the opposite direction, with younger voters leading the way. Comparing the averages of all of their surveys taken in 2004 to those taken in 2008, the Pew Center found that the Democrats' advantage in party identification had grown from two to nine points, and among eighteen- to twenty-nine-year-old voters from four to fourteen points, between the two years.[30] Not coincidentally, according to the 2008 exit poll, Barack Obama won this age group decisively, 66 percent to John McCain's

---

*The American National Election Studies from 1964 through 1978 found women to be, on average, only about two percentage points more Democratic in their partisanship than men. In studies conducted from 1980 through 1990, however, women averaged six percentage points more Democratic; since then, the gender gap in party identification has grown to about eleven percentage points. These differences show up in presidential voting, with the Democratic candidate running better among women than among men by about ten percentage points in 2000, seven points in 2004, and five points in 2008. For a general discussion of the gender gap in party identification, see Warren E. Miller and J. Merrill Shanks, *The New American Voter* (Cambridge, MA: Harvard University Press, 1996), 141–145.

32 percent.[31] Most younger voters stuck with Obama in 2012, giving him 60 percent of the vote to Mitt Romney's 44 percent.[32]

The changes in the party coalitions have been extensive enough to suggest that a sixth party system is now in place. Because the changes occurred gradually and at different times, the new system's starting date is unclear: some analysts propose 1968, while others say 1980 or 1984. Whatever the timing, the most salient difference between the current and New Deal party systems is the Republican Party's increased strength, exemplified by its winning majorities in the House and Senate in six straight elections (1994–2004), unprecedented since the fourth party system, and its retaking of the House in 2010, erasing the Democratic gains of 2006 and 2008.

The Republicans' competitive status is threatened, however, by demographic trends. The Republican coalition includes a disproportionate share of white (87 percent), male, older, religiously active, and socially conservative people, all shrinking portions of the electorate. The Democratic coalition is younger, is more female, and includes a much larger share of minority voters (38 percent), including Latinos, the fastest growing segment of the electorate.[33] Younger voters tend to be more secular and socially liberal and are likely to remain so as they age. Mitt Romney's inability to attract more young, nonwhite, secular, and female voters was widely viewed by Republican analysts as a sign that their party faced long-term decline if it did not expand its appeal beyond its current, diminishing base. Party leaders will no doubt try to do this—while fighting over the appropriate strategy—for pursuit of majority status has always shaped and reshaped the American parties.

A second distinctive feature of the current party system is that partisan differences on issues and policy are wider and deeper than they were during the New Deal party system. The widening ideological divide between the parties in Congress over the past several decades (see Figure 6-5 on page 263) has been echoed, to varying degrees, at all levels of the party system. In general, the more actively engaged Americans are in politics, the more polarized along party lines they have become. Partisan differences in ideology and policy have widened the most among political professionals and the amateur activists who contribute to campaigns, put up yard signs, work for candidates, and encourage their friends and neighbors to vote for their side. To a lesser extent, partisan polarization has also increased among people whose participation is limited to voting; it has not increased only among the politically inactive and uninvolved.[34] Scholars still debate whether Americans as a whole have become more polarized in their opinions on political issues, but there is abundant evidence that they have responded to the clearer cues issuing from the more polarized political class by sorting themselves more consistently into the party that best fits their own political beliefs and preferences.[35] People who call themselves conservatives and express conservative opinions on policy issues are much more likely to identify as Republicans, and self-identified liberals and people holding liberal policy views are more likely to identify as Democrats, than was the case a few decades ago.

The sorting process has been gradual; it has been most noticeable among conservative southern whites, but it is by no means confined to them. Figures 12-8a and 12-8b illustrate one of its consequences: the Republican coalition, predominantly conservative from the start, has grown substantially more so. In the most recent decade, a majority (52 percent) of Republicans have categorized themselves as conservative or extremely conservative, up from 34 percent in the 1970s; the proportion placing themselves somewhere right of center has grown from 63 percent to 76 percent. Meanwhile, the Democratic center of gravity moved

READ MORE

logic.cqpress.com

The Republican Party assesses how to widen its appeal.

2012 Party Platforms

These excerpts from the 2012 Democratic and Republican platforms reveal some of the differences between positions typically held by the parties. But few voters learn of these differences by reading the platforms. Rather, they learn about the parties' positions through political news and campaign advertising.

	Democrats	Republicans
Abortion	The Democratic Party strongly and unequivocally supports *Roe v. Wade* and a woman's right to make decisions regarding her pregnancy, including safe and legal abortion, regardless of ability to pay. We oppose any and all efforts to weaken or undermine that right.	[W]e assert the sanctity of human life and affirm that the unborn child has a fundamental individual right to life which cannot be infringed. We support a human life amendment to the Constitution. . . . We oppose using public revenues to promote or perform abortion and will not fund organizations which advocate it.
Energy	We can move towards a sustainable energy-independent future. . . . That means an all-of-the-above approach to developing America's many energy resources, including wind, solar, biofuels, geothermal, hydropower, nuclear, oil, clean coal, and natural gas. . . . Democrats support . . . building a clean energy economy by extending clean energy incentives that support American businesses and American jobs.	[W]e will not pick winners and losers in the energy marketplace. . . . We will let the free market . . . determine the industry outcomes. . . . We will end the EPA's war on coal. . . . We support . . . opening the coastal plain of the Arctic National Wildlife Refuge (ANWR) for exploration and production of oil and natural gas. . . . We are committed to approving the Keystone XL Pipeline and to streamlining permitting for the development of other oil and natural gas pipelines.
Guns	We . . . will preserve Americans' Second Amendment right to own and use firearms. We believe that the right to own firearms is subject to reasonable regulation. . . . We can focus on effective enforcement of existing laws, especially strengthening our background check system, and we can work together to enact commonsense improvements—like reinstating the assault weapons ban and closing the gun show loophole—so that guns do not fall into the hands of those irresponsible, law-breaking few.	We uphold the right of individuals to keep and bear arms This also includes the right to obtain and store ammunition without registration. We support . . . allowing those with state-issued carry permits to carry firearms in any state that issues such permits to its own residents. We oppose legislation that is intended to restrict our Second Amendment rights by limiting the capacity of clips or magazines or otherwise restoring the ill considered Clinton gun ban.
Same-Sex Marriage	We support marriage equality and support the movement to secure equal treatment under law for same-sex couples.	We reaffirm our support for a Constitutional amendment defining marriage as the union of one man and one woman.
Income Tax	[W]e are committed to extending the middle class tax cuts for the 98 percent of American families who make less than $250,000 a year, and we will not raise taxes on them. . . . The Democratic Party opposes efforts to give additional tax cuts to the wealthiest Americans at the expense of the middle class and investments in our future.	[W]e propose to . . . Reform the tax code by reducing marginal tax rates by 20 percent across-the-board in a revenue-neutral manner; eliminate the taxes on interest, dividends, and capital gains altogether for lower and middle-income taxpayers; end the Death Tax; and repeal the Alternative Minimum Tax.
Global Warming	The national security threat from climate change is real, urgent, and severe. The change wrought by a warming planet will lead to new conflicts over refugees and resources; new suffering from drought and famine; catastrophic natural disasters; and the degradation of vital ecosystems across the globe. That is why, in addition to undertaking measures to . . . promote efficiency, clean energy, and renewable sources of power here at home, the President . . . [has] worked to build an international framework to combat climate change.	[Not mentioned]

	Democrats	Republicans
Health Care	We believe accessible, affordable, high quality health care is part of the American promise, that Americans should have the security that comes with good health care, and that no one should go broke because they get sick. . . . [W]e enacted landmark reforms that are already helping millions of Americans, and more benefits will come soon.	Republicans are committed to [Obamacare's] repeal. . . . We support legislation to cap non-economic damages in medical malpractice lawsuits. . . . Individuals with preexisting conditions who maintain continuous insurance coverage should be protected from discrimination . . . [G]overnment must promote Health Savings Accounts and Health Reimbursement Accounts to be used for insurance premiums.
Iran	The President is committed to using all instruments of national power to prevent Iran from acquiring nuclear weapons. . . . The President's early offer of engagement with Iran—quickly rebuffed by the regime—allowed the United States to expose Iranian intransigence and rally the international community as never before. . . . As a result, Iran is now increasingly isolated and the regime faces crippling economic pressure.	Iran's pursuit of nuclear weapons capability threatens America, Israel, and the world. That threat has only become worse during the current Administration. A continuation of its failed engagement policy with Iran will lead to nuclear cascade. In solidarity with the international community, America must lead the effort to prevent Iran from building and possessing nuclear weapons capability.
Social Security	[W]e will find a solution to protect Social Security for future generations. We will block Republican efforts to subject Americans' guaranteed retirement income to the whims of the stock market through privatization. We reject approaches that insist that cutting benefits is the only answer.	While no changes should adversely affect any current or near-retiree, comprehensive reform should allow younger workers the option of creating their own personal investment accounts as supplements to the system.
Immigration	Democrats are strongly committed to enacting comprehensive immigration reform . . . that brings undocumented immigrants out of the shadows and requires them to get right with the law, learn English, and pay taxes in order to get on a path to earn citizenship. We need an immigration reform that creates a system for allocating visas that meets our economic needs, keeps families together, and enforces the law . . . President Obama and the Democrats fought for the DREAM Act, legislation ensuring that young people who want to contribute fully to our society and serve our country are able to become legal residents and ultimately citizens.	[W]e oppose any form of amnesty for those who, by intentionally violating the law, disadvantage those who have obeyed it. . . . We will create humane procedures to encourage illegal aliens to return home voluntarily . . . State efforts to reduce illegal immigration must be encouraged, not attacked. . . . The double-layered fencing on the border, . . . never completed, must finally be built. . . . [F]ederal funding should be denied to universities that provide in-state tuition rates to illegal aliens. . . . [W]e support English as the nation's official language.
Voter Identification	The Justice Department has . . . prevented states from implementing voter identification laws that would be harmful to minority voters. Democrats know that voter identification laws can disproportionately burden young voters, people of color, low-income families, people with disabilities, and the elderly, and we refuse to allow the use of political pretexts to disenfranchise American citizens.	[W]e applaud legislation to require photo identification for voting and to prevent election fraud, particularly with regard to registration and absentee ballots. We support State laws that require proof of citizenship at the time of voter registration to protect our electoral system against a significant and growing form of voter fraud.

Sources: Adapted from 2012 Democratic and Republican platforms at http://www.gop.com/wp-content/uploads/2012/08/2012GOPPlatform .pdf and http://assets.dstatic.org/dnc-platform/2012-National-Platform.pdf

left, although the Democratic Party remains a broad center-left coalition in which self-identified liberals are still a minority. Since the 1970s, the proportion of Democrats locating themselves left of center has increased from 36 percent to 48 percent, but the modal location of Democratic identifiers continues to be "middle of the road." The advent of sharply polarized, nearly evenly balanced party coalitions has ratcheted up electoral competition for federal offices, spurring the development of various national party organizations.

Modern Party Organizations

On paper the modern Democratic and Republican Parties might be depicted as pyramidal organizations. Each party's sovereign body is its national nominating convention, which officially elects the national party chair and ratifies the states' selections to the party's national committee (the Republican National Committee or the Democratic National Committee). The national committee, with at least two members from each state, is charged with conducting the party's affairs between national conventions and hiring and directing a large

Figure 12-8a Ideology of Republican Party Identifiers, by Decade

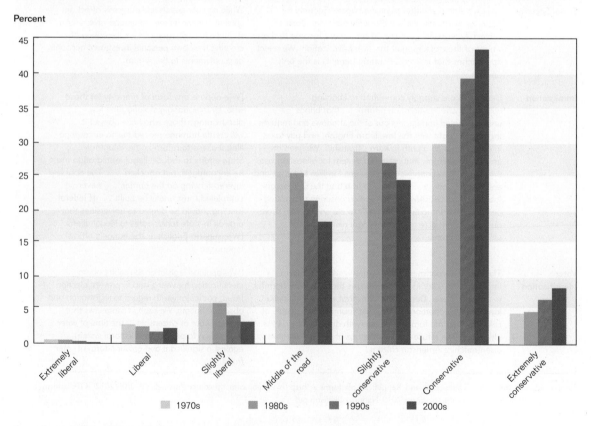

Source: American National Election Studies.

Figure 12-8b Ideology of Democratic Party Identifiers, by Decade

Percent

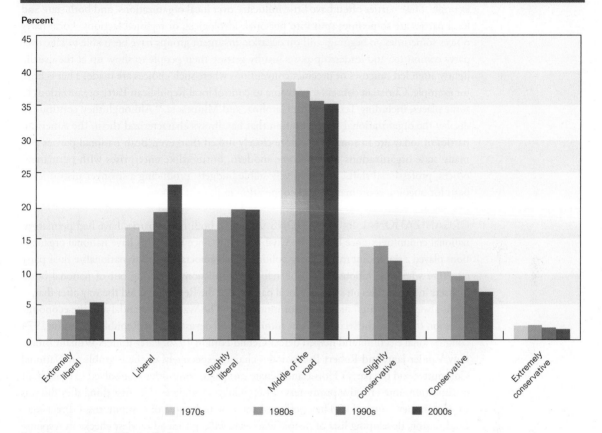

Extremely liberal · Liberal · Slightly liberal · Middle of the road · Slightly conservative · Conservative · Extremely conservative

■ 1970s ■ 1980s ■ 1990s ■ 2000s

Source: American National Election Studies.

professional staff. Below the national committees are the state committees and chairs, which oversee the committees representing congressional and state legislative districts and counties. Further subdivisions would include diverse township, city, ward, and precinct committees, also with formal leaders, some chosen by caucuses, some in primary elections.*

CONTROL. In reality, however, the national parties are far from hierarchical organizations, and at most levels they are controlled by elected politicians, not party officials. The national party's chair is always the choice of the party's presidential nominee, and the national committee's primary task is to win or retain the presidency, although attention is given to other forms of party building between presidential contests. House and Senate candidates have their own separate national campaign organizations—all under the control of their respective party's congressional leaders (see Chapter 6).

---

* Party organization at the state and local levels is highly varied, reflecting differences in historical development, local custom, and state law. Moreover, in many places the formal party units are joined by a diverse set of party clubs, caucuses, factional organizations, and allied interest groups that also participate in party politics.

Elected officials also usually control state parties, which are in no way subordinate to the national parties; governors are frequently the most powerful figures in their state parties, for example. State parties often have little influence over local organizations, and both state and local parties are sometimes split into personal, ideological, or regional factions. Local party offices sometimes go begging, and on occasion insurgent groups have been able to take over party committee and leadership posts just by getting their people to show up at the usually lightly attended caucuses or precinct conventions where such choices are made. That is how, for example, Christian conservatives came to control local Republican Party organizations in some places, including Texas, South Carolina, and Minnesota.[36] Although they continue to display the organizational fragmentation that has always characterized them, the American parties of today are in some ways more closely linked than ever. Both national parties and many state organizations have become modern, businesslike enterprises with permanent offices, professional staffs, and relatively stable budgets, producing a stronger institutional basis for ongoing coordination and cooperation in pursuit of power.

ORGANIZATIONAL INNOVATIONS. Although both major parties have had permanent national committees since before the Civil War, only since the 1970s have national organizations played a significant role in party politics. The Democrats began to nationalize their party structure when the various post-1968 reform commissions operating out of national headquarters imposed rules on state and local parties. But the Republicans led the way after that.

As always, the "outs" did the major innovating. The Watergate scandal and the economic recession that beset the second Nixon administration devastated the Republicans in the 1974 congressional elections and helped defeat Gerald Ford in 1976. Party leaders William Brock, Guy Vander Jagt, and Robert Packwood—chairs, respectively, of the Republican National Committee and the party's House and Senate campaign committees—resolved to build their organizations into effective promoters of Republican candidates. The first thing they did was to raise money—lots of it. They perfected the new technique of computerized direct-mail fund-raising, developing lists of people who were willing to send modest checks in response to regular solicitations to create a steady source of income for the party. Their growing success during the early 1980s, when they were raising 80 percent of their money through the mail-in checks averaging less than $30, is documented in Figure 12-9.

With the money coming in, the Republicans enlarged their organization staff and began to provide a host of services to their candidates. Today they help candidates for federal office raise money, comply with campaign finance regulations, design polls, set up websites, research opponents' records, put together lists of voters to contact, and design campaign strategy. They contribute a good deal of money directly to candidates' campaign war chests. In some years, they have conducted national campaigns for the entire party ticket. Republican candidates also are helped indirectly by the money and training the national party has contributed to state and local Republican organizations across the nation to strengthen the party at the grass roots. In addition, the campaign committees stepped up efforts to identify, recruit, and train effective candidates for Congress and, in some instances, for state offices as well.[37]

The Democrats were shocked into a similar effort to expand the services offered by their national party committees when in 1980 they lost both the White House (to Ronald Reagan) and their Senate majority. They played catch-up in fund-raising until 2008, when they outspent the Republicans for the first time (see Figure 12-9). Contrary to expectations, the ban

Figure 12-9 Growth of Party Spending in Federal Elections

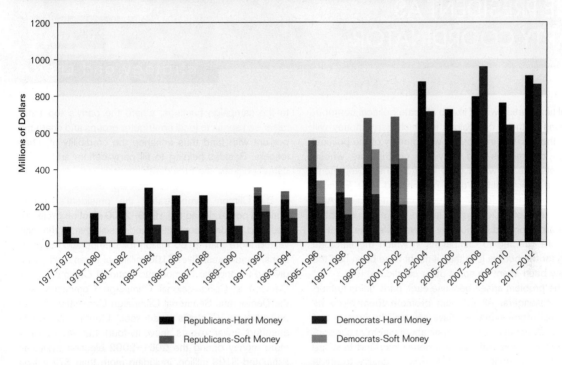

Source: Federal Election Commission (1978–1998) and Center for Responsive Politics (2000–2012).

Note: Before 1991 the Federal Election Commission did not require parties to report soft money spending; after 2002 soft money was banned.

on soft party money enacted in 2002 (see Chapter 11) did not put them at further disadvantage, as they were able to make up much of the difference by raising more hard dollars. Republicans, too, vastly increased their take of hard money, and between them, the parties raised $1.59 billion for the 2004 federal election campaigns, $1.75 billion for the 2008 campaigns, and more than $2.09 billion for 2012 campaigns. Instead of transferring soft money to state parties to help federal candidates as they had in the past, the Hill committees simply switched to spending hard money on independent campaigns (separate from the candidates' campaigns) in the most competitive congressional races. Spending of this sort exceeded $253 million in 2012, up from a mere $2.9 million in 2002.[38] The president remains the preeminent fund-raiser for his party, as Bill Clinton, George W. Bush, and now Barack Obama have so amply demonstrated (see box "The President as Party Coordinator").

Although modern parties continue to play a major financial and organizational role in electoral politics, they have clearly lost the near-monopoly they had on campaign resources until the mid-twentieth century. Candidates, rather than parties, are the focus of campaigns; the party's activities are aimed at helping individual candidates compete more effectively, not at promoting the party. According to political scientist John Aldrich, "A new form of party has emerged, one that is 'in service' to its ambitious politicians but not 'in control' of them

THE PRESIDENT AS PARTY COORDINATOR

strategy and choice

Political parties would like to allocate political contributions to those campaigns in which party money will have the greatest impact. So would many of the political action committees and individual contributors whose interests ride on which party controls the government. Despite their common goal, parties and their financial supporters face a formidable coordination problem. As a result, tens of millions of dollars in campaign contributions are allocated inefficiently in every election. That is, they are directed to campaigns in which the electoral bang for the buck is less than it might have been had the money been spent on some other candidate.

The problem arises because each party fields numerous challengers. All of them promote themselves as potential winners, but few have any realistic prospect of victory. Donors are left uncertain about whom to support. Presumably, party officials are better informed than are individual contributors, but they may be unable to guide potential donors effectively or prevent the inefficient distribution of resources produced by candidates busily trying to amass large campaign war chests. In the competition for donations, the most skilled fund-raisers are incumbent officeholders, precisely those politicians whose election is often least dependent on additional money. To the degree they succeed, they divert money from those who need it most—the party's competitive challengers. Yet a party official who intervenes to try to redirect money from the party's incumbents to its challengers will soon join the ranks of the unemployed.

So what can parties do? Two things: first, they can raise as much money as possible for themselves by assuring donors that they will spend it wisely. As shown in Figure 12-9, both have partially succeeded in these efforts. Another strategy is for the party to send its president

to the campaign hustings, where the party's top fund-raiser can speak to local contributor groups and share the podium with (and thus enhance the credibility of) challengers. Besides helping to fill party coffers and candidates' pockets, the president's appearances show other donors where to invest their campaign dollars.

Bill Clinton demonstrated the president's unique drawing power during the 1999–2000 election cycle. He attended, by one count, 295 fund-raising events that harvested more than $160 million for Democratic congressional candidates. Over $100 million of these funds were divided among the Democratic National Committee, the Democratic Congressional Campaign Committee, and the Democratic Senatorial Campaign Committee. Not to be outdone, Clinton's successor, George W. Bush, attended fewer events (seventy-four) but raised even more money during the 2001–2002 election cycle, an estimated $193 million, including more than $72 million for the party's three main national campaign committees.[1] During his tenure as a two-term president, Bush personally raised nearly $1 billion for his party, its candidates, and his own reelection.[2] Barack Obama continued the tradition, headlining more than 250 fundraising events during his first term in office.

---

1. Mark Knoller of CBS Radio News kindly supplied these figures. For a fuller analysis of Clinton's financial signaling during the 2000 election cycle, see Gary C. Jacobson, Samuel Kernell, and Jeffrey Lazarus, "Assessing the President's Role as Party Agent in Congressional Elections," *Legislative Studies Quarterly* 29 (May 2004): 159–184.

2. Deb Riechmann, "Bush Still Raking in Cash for GOP," *USA Today*, August 15, 2008, http://usatoday30.usatoday.com/news/washington/2008-08-15-1495881878_x.htm.

---

as the mass party [of the past] sought to be."[39] Outside groups also now participate much more extensively in campaigning for (or more often against) candidates, mainly as auxiliaries of the parties; such groups spent hundreds of millions of dollars on independent campaigns during the 2010 and 2012 elections (see Chapter 11).

EXPEDIENCY PERSISTS

American parties developed and continue to endure because they have proven so useful to politicians and voters attempting to act collectively within the institutional framework established by the Constitution. The federal system offers powerful incentives for organizing and expanding both legislative and electoral coalitions—that is, political parties—to win and exercise political power. For one thing, it rewards political entrepreneurs who can organize collective action across government institutions and electoral arenas. For another, it prompts voters to use party labels to simplify their decisions, giving politicians a reason to cooperate with party leaders to maintain the value of the party's "brand name."

Although the party coalitions have shifted periodically in response to new national issues and conflicts, leaving five—perhaps six—identifiable party systems, the basic pattern of competition between two broad, usually fractious coalitions persists. The two-party system arises from strategic voting in the winner-take-all competition for the presidency (and for all other federal offices as well) and has been strengthened by laws (mandating, for example, primary elections) that treat the parties as official components of the electoral machinery. Party coalitions remain fractious because party entrepreneurs pursuing majorities must combine diverse groups that are neither natural allies nor disposed to pay high conformity costs for the sake of the party. But these coalitions persist because party organizations remain decentralized, mirroring the decentralized institutions of American federalism.

Progressive Era reforms, followed by the development of new technologies of communication after the Second World War, weakened traditional party organizations and ended their monopoly control of campaigns, but parties continue to play a central role in electoral politics. Despite their expressed disdain for parties, voters still rely heavily on party cues in making their decisions because party labels continue to provide useful, cheap information about candidates. Party entrepreneurs, for their part, have simply redesigned party organizations to operate more effectively in today's media-based, largely candidate-centered electoral arena. They are walking down the trail blazed by Jefferson and Van Buren, and for the same reason: to elect those who share their views so that they may shape public policy to their liking.

TAKE A QUIZ

logic.cqpress.com

Test your knowledge of this chapter.

logic.cqpress.com

■■■ Key Terms ■■■

Australian ballot,   547

caucuses,   540

divided government,   561

fusion tickets,   533

national party conventions,   542

New Deal coalition,   550

party machines,   545

patronage,   536

political party,   527

primary elections,   547

Progressive Era,   545

proportional representation,   533

split ticket,   546

superdelegates,   554

two-party system,   532

▄▄ Suggested Readings ▄▄

Aldrich, John H. *Why Parties? The Origin and Transformation of Party Politics in America.* Chicago: University of Chicago Press, 1995. An astute theoretical and historical analysis of American parties that deepens and extends the approach taken in this text.

Chambers, William Nesbit, and Walter Dean Burnham, eds. *The American Party Systems: Stages of Political Development.* 2nd ed. New York: Oxford University Press, 1975. Fascinating historical essays on American party development. The essay by Eric L. McKitrick explaining how partisan politics helped Abraham Lincoln and how its absence hurt Jefferson Davis during the Civil War is especially instructive.

Cohen, Jeffrey E., Richard Fleisher, and Paul Kantor, eds. *American Political Parties: Decline or Resurgence?* Washington, DC: CQ Press, 2001. Historical and contemporary materials explore changes in American parties and analyze party weaknesses, the reasons for revitalization, and the responsibilities of parties in a democracy.

Levandusky, Matthew. *The Partisan Sort: How Liberals Became Democrats and Conservatives Became Republicans.* Chicago: University of Chicago Press, 2009. Details how Americans have increasingly sorted themselves into the political party that best fits their ideological and policy preferences, contributing to the growth in party polarization over the past several decades.

Mayhew, David R. *Placing Parties in American Politics.* Princeton, NJ: Princeton University Press, 1986. To understand why some states developed strong party organizations and others did not, read this book.

Mayhew, David R. *Electoral Realignments: A Critique of and American Genre.* New Haven, CT: Yale University Press, 2002. As its title suggests, the idea of periodic party realignments of the kind discussed in this chapter is examined and questioned in this book.

Polsby, Nelson W. *Consequences of Party Reform.* New York: Oxford University Press, 1983. According to Polsby, the consequences have not been good.

Riordan, William L., ed. *Plunkitt of Tammany Hall.* New York: Dutton, 1963. According to the subtitle, "a series of very plain talks on very practical politics, delivered by George Washington Plunkitt, the Tammany Philosopher, from his rostrum—the New York County Court House bootblack stand." Includes a good introductory essay on nineteenth-century party machine politics.

Sundquist, James L. *The Dynamics of the Party System,* rev. ed. Washington, DC: Brookings, 1983. Highly detailed study of historical party realignments; for those who prefer complex stories to simple ones.

▄▄ Review Questions ▄▄

1. Where did U.S. parties first arise? Why did they prove necessary in this setting? Why did parties spread from there to other areas of politics?

2. Why do third parties tend to do so poorly in U.S. elections? Why do such parties do so much better in other democracies?

3. How has the nomination process for party candidates changed over time? If national conventions no longer decide on the party's presidential nominee, why are they still held?

4. How do party activists differ from rank-and-file voters of their party? What consequences does this difference have for American politics?

5. How and why have the parties become more polarized on ideology and issues over the past several decades?

13 Interest Groups

Car dealers like this one have joined together to lobby government through the National Automobile Dealers Association, an interest group with a grassroots membership of eighteen thousand small businesses spread across every political district in the country. In 2010 this self-professed "Main Street" group won a key exemption from federal oversight in Congress's financial reform bill, while lobbyists representing Wall Street's biggest interests lost out.

- Are interest groups a necessary evil in any political system that allows the freedom of speech and assembly, or do they play a valuable democratic role?

- As the number of interests represented in Washington has grown, have they become more or less powerful?

- Free riding should doom "public interest" lobbies. Why do so many emerge and thrive nonetheless?

- Most lobbyists are paid advocates of special interests. Why should politicians believe anything they say?

- Are lawmakers who accept campaign contributions from a political action committee "bought and sold" by that interest group?

As Congress considered financial reform legislation to tighten regulations on Wall Street in the spring of 2010, "K Street" mobilized as it rarely had before. This Washington, DC, address has become synonymous with the lobbying firms that represent America's biggest and most powerful interests, ranging from doctors' and hospital associations to oil and pharmaceutical corporations to the megabanks whose multibillion-dollar derivative trading enterprises were directly threatened by the bill before Congress. Bank lobbyists swarmed Capitol Hill after the chair of the Senate Agriculture Committee, Sen. Blanche Lincoln, proposed a crackdown on trading derivatives, the complex financial instruments that many blamed for the global financial crisis of 2008. A total of 1,500 lobbyists, bank executives, and other interested parties visited Lincoln's committee in the weeks leading up to a key hearing.[1]

To their shock and dismay, many of these Washington insiders found the doors of power closed to them. "We're on the outside, knocking on the window and saying, 'Hey, listen to us just a little bit,'" complained a senior executive at one of the nation's biggest financial institutions. A lobbyist representing Wall Street in Washington worked for six months on the bill in the hopes of securing thirty-minute meetings with senators or their staffs.[2] With unemployment still high and the public still furious at Wall Street bankers, committee members could not afford to be seen as under the thumb of K Street interests. Senator Lincoln, in the political fight of her life in Arkansas, needed to show her constituents that she could be tough on big business, using the bill as a centerpiece of her reelection campaign.

In its journey through the legislative process, the bill had to withstand a "lobbying juggernaut," with nearly $600 million spent by the finance sector to soften it.[3] Some portions of the bill, such as the most aggressive approach that Senator Lincoln had advocated, were weakened. But it nonetheless dramatically increased regulation on derivatives and other risky trading, and established a new federal consumer protection bureau aimed at stopping lending abuses. Its passage by narrow margins in the House and Senate that summer represented a policy landmark as well as a historic political defeat for Wall Street and K Street.

Yet one interest group emerged victorious from this battle over banking, with its business granted an explicit exemption from oversight by the consumer protection bureau. Car dealerships, which broker hundreds of billions of dollars' worth of automobile loans, won the exemption despite calls from consumer advocates to place them under the new federal regulations just like other brokers. The key to their victory was a lobbying strategy that played to their political strengths.[4] They followed Congress's lead in the rush to bash Wall Street and relied on their grassroots network rather than only on Washington lobbyists. Portland, Oregon, auto dealer Ed Tonkin, the trade group's president, argued, "The public wants Congress to focus on Wall Street bankers, not Main Street auto dealers."[5] They trumpeted opinion polls, claiming that voters were on their side, and brought dealers and their employees to testify and meet with legislators. They played the role of the underdog, even though the National Automobile Dealers Association has spent $10 million on lobbying since 2008. With eighteen thousand auto dealerships spread out in congressional districts across the country, they found many doors open to them. With populist rhetoric, an unblemished image, and strategically located members working to their advantage, auto dealers were the rare financial interest that emerged from financial reform unscathed.

Looking at who lost and who won in this policy fight with billion-dollar stakes teaches valuable lessons about the role of interest groups in our nation. **Interest groups** are omnipresent in American politics, but not omnipotent. Lobbyists may show up everywhere in Washington, DC, but they by no means dictate what goes on there. Part of why we see interest groups being so active is that they need to work so hard for the opportunity to make their pitch to elected officials and to be heard over the cacophony of competing voices. Large, well-heeled lobbies have suffered shocking defeats, while smaller groups have won surprising victories. The enduring power of the electoral connection that ties lawmakers to voters can explain why they may sometimes ignore powerful lobbyists, while the logic of collective action shows why there is often lobbying strength in small numbers.

Although the dynamics of interest group power vary from time to time and group to group, their presence on the political scene remains a constant. Interest groups and lobbying are inevitable and, indeed, essential components of modern democratic politics. They also are a continual source of problems for democracy. The American political system could not function without the endlessly busy work of organized interests and their representatives trying to sway policy in their favor. Yet there has never been a time in American history when they have not been under attack from one quarter or another as threats to democracy itself. This chapter looks at why interest groups are both essential and problematic.

THE LOGIC OF LOBBYING

The logic of lobbying is transparent. People who want to influence government decisions that affect their lives and welfare quickly recognize the advantages of banding together with others of like mind and asking astute and powerful friends to help out. Governments, for their part, have good reason to welcome **lobbying**, defined as appeals from citizens and groups for favorable policies and decisions. Even officials in blatantly nondemocratic governments find life considerably easier if they have the support, or at least the acquiescence, of the governed (as any parent knows). Such officials cannot estimate the costs and benefits of alternative actions without having some idea of how people will react to their initiatives. All governments also need the information, political as well as technical, that people and organizations outside the government are in the best position to provide—for a price. Elected officials, looking to keep their jobs, try to accommodate the people who command valuable electoral resources—votes, money, organizational structures, and skills. And always and everywhere, at least a few government officials have been willing to trade favors for personal "gifts" of every imaginable sort.

Modern politics also breeds professional **lobbyists**. For the same reason they hire lawyers to represent them in court, people hire agents who are specialists to represent them before legislatures and executive agencies. Like courts, modern legislatures and bureaucracies are complex institutions bound by arcane rules, procedures, and customs. People wanting these institutions to act on their behalf are more likely to succeed if they are represented by agents who understand how the institutions work and enjoy warm personal friendships with the key institutional players.

Lobbying as a profession thus emerged with modern representative government and has flourished with the growing scope and complexity of government activities. Figure 13-1 shows that lobbying is now the most costly route through which interest groups attempt to influence government. This figure reports the total amount that all groups—whether they were political action committees or simply collections from individuals—spent on campaign contributions to congressional candidates in recent election cycles, compared with lobbying expenditures. As you can see, even though campaign contributions are the most frequent source of citizen concern about government being "bought and sold," they are merely the tip of the influence iceberg. Interest groups spend billions more every cycle on lobbying than they do on campaign contributions. This shows that interest groups value their K Street representation as much as they worry about who represents voters on Capitol Hill.

This comparison, along with the billions of dollars devoted to both lobbying and campaign contributions, also raises concerns about the legitimacy of interest groups and lobbyists. Their very presence, not to mention any political success they may achieve, raises the suspicion that "special interests" win at the expense of the "public interest." Even people who deny that the public interest can be defined objectively—as do many modern political scientists—often argue that successful lobbying

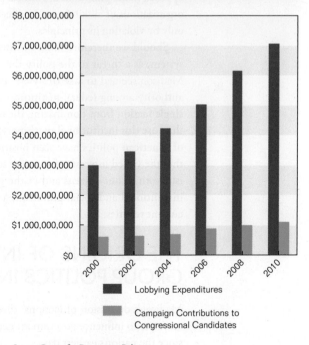

Figure 13-1 Lobbying Expenditures Dwarf Campaign Contributions to Congress

Source: Center for Responsive Politics.

subverts the basic principles of democratic equality and majority rule. Groups vary widely in wealth and in how readily they can be organized for collective action, creating marked imbalances in the representation of social interests. Moreover, policy gridlock and political paralysis in the face of pressing national problems are commonly blamed on the cacophony of competing interests. For these reasons, organized political interests have been attacked and criticized as long as they have existed.

James Madison, with his usual cogency, captured the dilemma posed by politically active groups in his famous discussion of factions in *Federalist* No. 10. For Madison, factions were by definition pernicious, pursuing selfish aims contrary to the rights of others or to the public interest. As such, factions were, in Madison's view, a major threat to popular government: "The instability, injustice, and confusion introduced into the public councils" by the "dangerous vice" of faction "have, in truth, been the mortal diseases under which popular governments have everywhere perished." (The full text of *Federalist* No. 10 appears in the Appendix.)

Why, then, not just get rid of factions? Madison's answer was that factions could be eliminated only by "destroying the liberty which is essential to [their] existence . . . [or by] giving every citizen the same opinions, the same passions, and the same interests." He found the first cure "worse than the disease" because popular government is supposed to protect liberty; he found the second impossible: "as long as the reason of man continues to be fallible, and he is at liberty to exercise it, different opinions will be formed."

Practically speaking, then, to maintain the freedoms specified in the First Amendment—to speak, publish, assemble, and "petition the Government for a redress of grievances"—a political system must tolerate factions even though they may be, as by Madison's definition, opposed to the public good. Political parties, interest groups, lobbyists, and peaceful political organizations of all kinds are, in effect, licensed by the Constitution and can be suppressed only by violating its principles.

Should we therefore think of interest groups only as a necessary evil in a free political system, as a threat to the polity that needs to be contained through institutional design? Madison seemed to take this view, and as we saw in Chapter 2, his solution was to divide authority among federal institutions. This fragmentation of authority would prevent any single faction from dominating the others. The wide variety of competing interests could then use this institutional machinery to thwart each other's selfish designs. Later observers of American politics have seen positive value in the groups that work energetically to further the varied interests of so many segments of our diverse society, celebrating the pluralism both of our citizens and of the groups representing them. Both approaches focus on institutional and social pluralism, a key characteristic of America's political history and current realities.

THE ORIGINS OF INTEREST GROUP POLITICS IN AMERICA

Madison's discussion of factions, though abstract, was anything but academic. Organized attempts to influence government decisions have been an integral part of American politics since the nation's earliest days.

The Colonial Era

Merchants, manufacturers, and ethnic and religious minorities during the colonial era actively sought favorable policies from the authorities in London as well as from colonial governors and assemblies. By the middle of the eighteenth century, such groups had developed most of the techniques of persuasion still used today. Colonial interests submitted petitions to the government, hired agents to "handle the delicate work involved in extracting concessions from ministers and lesser bureaucrats," examined the voting records of legislators to identify prospective supporters, organized letter-writing campaigns, reminded legislators that a group's supporters were among their constituents, and formed logrolling coalitions with other interests.[6]

American interests and their British allies learned to cultivate parliamentary leaders as well as draft legislation and slip it into an opportune spot on the parliamentary calendar. They also bombarded members of Parliament with information and arranged for expert testimony. Such insider lobbying—direct appeals to lawmakers for policy support by narrowly focused interests—has been a familiar part of legislative politics in Anglo-American democracies ever since.

The eighteenth century also witnessed the invention of the **public interest lobby** and the tactic of appealing to the general public for support of an outsider group's goals. The chief innovator was the English radical John Wilkes, whose Bill of Rights Society promoted a general cause—the expansion of suffrage—rather than defending any particular interest. Disdaining the customary methods of friendly persuasion, the Wilkesites attacked government officials.[7] Similar organizations appeared in the colonies, the best known of which was the Sons of Liberty. Among other subversive activities, this group threw the Boston Tea Party.

By the time of the American Revolution, a wide variety of politically active groups had emerged: merchants' societies, chambers of commerce, religious sects, organizations pushing radical causes, groups interested in local improvements, ethnic associations, insurance societies, clubs with social and intellectual aspirations, workers' organizations, and military and professional associations. Delegates to the Constitutional Convention, many of whom had served in colonial state legislatures, were so accustomed to being lobbied that they agreed to meet behind locked doors and to keep their deliberations secret until after the convention was over. No official record was kept "lest word of their intentions leak out and they become beset by a horde of citizens seeking to advance their own interests."[8] This was by no means the last time the public interest was best served by letting negotiations proceed out of the public eye.

The Early Republic

As Madison had anticipated, the American political system allowed "factions" to flourish. Political parties emerged almost immediately (see Chapter 12). Of the many coordinated efforts made to shape government decisions in the early decades of the Republic, most were directed at state and local governments, since at that time they made most of the decisions important to citizens. By the 1830s organizations of all kinds formed an integral part of American life. French visitor Alexis de Tocqueville noted with astonishment the abundance

Joseph Keppler, one of the most popular political cartoonists of his day, pays tribute to the "Bosses of the Senate." By 1889 the Senate was known as the millionaires' club. The presiding officer was a Wall Street banker, and its principal members represented the oil, lumber, railroad, insurance, silver, gold, utility, and manufacturing interests. Note that the "People's Entrance" is "closed." This cartoon could run in a newspaper today, since a 2009 analysis published in *Roll Call* found that fifty senators had net worths of more than one million dollars.

and variety of organized groups in the United States: "In no country in the world has the principle of association been more successfully used, or applied to a greater multitude of objects, than in America. . . . There is no end which the human will despairs of attaining through the combined power of individuals united into a society."[9]

Because most of these groups that Tocqueville observed sought to achieve their ends without involving the government, they were not what we would call political interest groups, but many did have explicit political aims. Examples were the American Anti-Slavery Society (founded in 1833); the National Trades Union (1834), which lobbied for a ten-hour workday*; and the American Temperance Union (1836), which lobbied for a halt to the sale of alcoholic beverages, or prohibition. Like Madison, Tocqueville thought that such associations could be dangerous to public order and good government, but his observations convinced him that voluntary groups were essential to an egalitarian social and political system.[10] Later observers were not so sure. During the years of national expansion—geographic and industrial—after

---

*Employers of this era could demand as much work time as their employees would tolerate. People desperate for employment put up with workdays of twelve to fourteen hours—sometimes even more during the lengthy days of summer.

But Their Mothers Still Loved Them

1841. Historian James Silk Buckingham defined *lobbyists* as "agents, selected for their skill in the arts of deluding, persuading, and bribing members of legislative bodies."

1856. Poet Walt Whitman dismissed "lobbyers" as "crawling serpentine men, the lousy combings and born freedom sellers of the earth."

1873. A reporter for *The Nation* depicted the professional lobbyist as "a man whom everybody suspects; who is generally during one half of the year without honest means of livelihood; and whose employment by those who have bills before a legislature is only resorted to as a disagreeable necessity."

1875. Novelist John William De Forest in his novel *Honest John Vane* let out all the stops: "Men of unwholesome skins, greasy garments, brutish manners, filthy minds, and sickening conversation; men who so reeked and drizzled with henbane tobacco and cockatrice whisky that a moderate drinker or smoker would recoil from them as from a cesspool; men whose stupid, shameless boasting of their briberies were enough to warn away from them all but the elect of Satan . . . [and] decayed statesmen, who were now, indeed, nothing but unfragrant corpses, breeding all manner of vermin and miasma."

1888. Everit Brown and Albert Strauss's *Dictionary of American Politics* offered this definition: "*Lobby, The*, is a term applied collectively to men that make a business of corruptly influencing legislators. The individuals are called lobbyists. Their object is usually accomplished by means of money paid to the members, but any other means that is considered feasible is employed."

Source: Margaret Susan Thompson, *The "Spider Web": Congress and Lobbying in the Age of Grant* (Ithaca, NY: Cornell University Press, 1985), 54–57.

the Civil War, the scope of the federal government's activities expanded enormously, and so did the activities aimed at shaping its decisions. Among the most visible were those undertaken by the newly emerging large-scale industrial corporations and trusts. The methods of their political agents, exposed by a generation of journalists and social critics known collectively as "muckrakers," tainted lobbying with an evil reputation it has never fully lived down (see box "But Their Mothers Still Loved Them").

Citizens outraged by political corruption formed new associations to agitate for reform. Over time, these groups succeeded in reorganizing government at all levels and rewriting the rules of electoral and party politics (see Chapters 8 and 12). These changes were part of a larger collection of innovations—child labor and wages-and-hours laws, regulation of railroads and other large-scale business enterprises, women's suffrage, the income tax—that were adopted during the late nineteenth and early twentieth centuries, a period historians now label the Progressive Era (see Chapter 12). The impetus for these innovations, as well as a good deal of the resistance to them, came from interest groups of every description.

One of the most remarkable, if temporary, successes was achieved by the Anti-Saloon League, which engineered the adoption of the Eighteenth Amendment. It prohibited the sale of alcoholic beverages in the United States from 1919 to 1933, when the amendment was repealed. The league's leaders, Purley Baker and Wayne Wheeler, were among the most astute politicians of their day. They put together an organization led by paid professional staff and supported by monthly subscriptions as well as large donations from wealthy benefactors. Tactically, the league concentrated on electoral politics with the simple goal of defeating "wets" and electing "drys" (politicians who favored a prohibition on alcohol sales). It monitored legislative votes and demanded written pledges from aspiring candidates who wanted the league's support and did not have track records on the issue. The league did not care whether candidates themselves drank; it cared only how they would vote on legislation restricting liquor sales. It established the value of its support by mobilizing sympathetic voters (largely through Protestant churches) and persuading them to cast votes based exclusively on the liquor issue: wets were punished at the polls.[11]

Labor unions—groups of workers who agree to negotiate jointly with their employers, and who pay dues to support their collective goals—have played an enormously important role in American politics for the past century. Union leaders have used a portion of these dues to help fund the campaigns of sympathetic candidates, and union members are often the primary foot soldiers making phone calls and knocking on doors to mobilize voters as Election Day approaches. Two "unions of unions," the American Federation of Labor and Congress of Industrial Organizations (AFL-CIO) and the Service Employees International Union (SEIU), are arguably the most powerful forces on the left today and key allies of the Democratic Party. Their union-backed candidates are frequently opposed by politicians supported by business groups, such as the U.S. Chamber of Commerce and the National Federation of Independent Business. These groups donate through their political action committees and rely on their members, who are often prominent constituents in legislative districts, to lobby lawmakers.

The groups that had so impressed Tocqueville in the 1830s had been largely local and short-lived. By the twentieth century, however, large-scale organizations like the national labor and business groups just mentioned began to proliferate. They turned into constant fixtures in campaigns, and their representatives began to take up permanent residence in Washington, DC, and in state capitols. Interest group activity became an industry unto itself, which is now centered in K Street in Washington but reaches everywhere that key policy decisions are made. Americans now have a permanent organizational base to attend to their political interests, whether these interests happen to be protecting the right to bear arms, the right to make reproductive choices, or the right to surf (see box "Mobilizing a Wave of Protest"). Interest groups are now an institution in American politics, potent and enduring.

The Pluralist Defense of Interest Groups

With the emergence of stable political associations as major players in national politics, scholars began to study interest groups. One result was the first systematic defense of their legitimate role in a modern democracy. The case was made most fully by political scientist David Truman in his influential book *The Governmental Process,* published in 1951.[12] Truman viewed the proliferation of political interest groups as a natural and largely benign consequence of economic development. These groups formed spontaneously whenever shared interests were threatened or could be enhanced by political action. Modern industrial society, characterized by an ever more elaborate division of labor, became awash in interests and therefore in interest groups. As society became progressively more fragmented and variegated, so did the universe of associations.

Because groups were free to organize and participate in an open political system, the political process balanced competing interests, just as James Madison had promised. If established groups advocated policies that threatened the interests of other citizens, the threatened would organize to defend themselves. Demands provoked counterdemands, and so policies embodied the numerous compromises and trade-offs necessary for building winning coalitions within and between political institutions. Aware that overreaching would stir opposition, established groups prudently moderated their demands. Thus unorganized interests constrained active groups even when they were not represented by lobbies of their own.

Truman and other pluralist scholars also emphasized that the American political system was particularly conducive to pluralist politics. Its decentralized structure offered numerous points of access—political parties; congressional committees and subcommittees; the courts; the enormous variety of federal, state, and local governing agencies—where groups could bid for favorable policies. It also provided a set of political actors—elected officials—whose purposes were served by building broad-based coalitions and defending widely shared values. In this idealized conception, pluralist politics created a policy balance that reflected both the distribution of interests in society and the intensity with which they were pursued. Widely shared interests weighed in heavily because elections make numbers count; intensity entered the equation because the people who care the most about an issue are those most inclined to organize and act.

Clearly, then, this view of American pluralism did not embrace the customary disdain of "special interests." Rather, interest groups were regarded as essential and valuable participants in the democratic politics of a modern industrial society. Without their participation, policy would be made in far greater ignorance of what citizens actually wanted from their government.

As a description of reality, this sunny conception of pluralism was open to some obvious criticisms. No one doubted that organized groups often were important political players; this was not at issue. But it was also undeniable that the groups most visibly active in politics did not, by any stretch of the imagination, form a balanced cross section of economic or social interests. Some interests, such as those of large industrial corporations, seemed to be vastly overrepresented; other interests, such as those of migrant laborers and the unemployed, were not represented at all. "The flaw in the pluralist heaven," as political scientist E. E. Schattschneider put it, "is that the heavenly chorus sings with a strong upper-class accent."[13] The power and resources possessed by lobbyists tend to reflect the power that the groups they represent have in society. This compounds the inequalities present in the nation. Observers who are not swayed by Truman's defense of interest group pluralism worry that the close connections between K Street and Capitol Hill allow the affluent and informed to use the machinery of government for their narrow benefit while unorganized groups go unheard.

The Problem of Collective Action

A subtler but equally important explanation for the observed bias in group representation lies in the way the incentives for collective action and the barriers to organization vary across different types of groups. The explanation, developed by the economist Mancur Olson in *The Logic of Collective Action* (1965), begins by pointing out that classical pluralists such as Truman were mistaken in assuming that people would form interest groups spontaneously to promote or defend shared interests.[14] Someone has to take on the work of organizing the group and finding the resources to keep it going. And to succeed, organizers

MOBILIZING A WAVE OF PROTEST

The Surfrider Foundation Saves the "Trestles" Surf Spot

politics to policy

W hat does it take to motivate Americans not merely to join an interest group but to work actively to achieve its goals? One interest group discovered how to organize and motivate a set of individuals previously known for their disorganization, stubborn individualism, and political apathy, winning a huge policy victory as a result. The Surfrider Foundation, allying with other environmental organizations and taking on a state bureaucracy and labor unions, managed to get thousands of Southern California surfers out of the waves and into the energetic political activism that saved the Trestles surf spot.

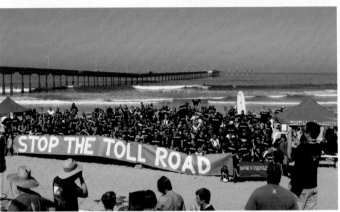

After its founding in 1984 as a nonprofit dedicated to preserving the quality of oceans and beaches, the Surfrider Foundation won a series of legal victories but struggled to establish itself as a grassroots force. Surfrider members who cared enough to pay nominal dues to the organizations were not as eager to lobby their legislators or walk the campaign trail on behalf of friendly candidates. California's waves, after all, are excellent in the weeks leading up to Election Day. Realizing that they needed to demonstrate their mass support in order to obtain real political power, Surfrider's leaders began to build local networks all across the country, from Long Island to Maine to Texas to Lake Michigan, that grew into seventy chapters with fifty thousand members. Then a California transportation agency's plans to build a toll road through the state park containing the world-class Trestles surf spot gave Surfrider the opportunity to flex its newfound grassroots muscle.

One key to mobilizing Surfrider members was that the toll road threatened something important to their daily lives; many surfed, bodyboarded, or swam on a daily basis, and most had visited the iconic Trestles break. Surfrider had also assembled an organizational structure that allowed its members to quickly mobilize in response to the plans to build a six-lane toll road. With links to legal and scientific experts, they knew how to challenge the plans and could work through their local chapters to buttress this challenge. Focused on one achievable goal, members could see how writing to their representatives and taking part in protests could yield concrete gains. Add to this the fact that "Save Trestles" bumper stickers and T-shirts became status symbols along the West Coast, and all of the elements for a successful mobilization were in place.

Surfrider demonstrated the power of its grassroots campaign when 3,500 protesters attended the critical hearing held by the California Coastal Commission in February 2008. This was the largest crowd in the commission's thirty-six-year history, with its executive director marveling, "I've never seen anything like this." Of course, labor union members who supported construction of the six-lane road also attended, but the commission voted 8–2 to kill the proposed project. The Surfrider Foundation had shown that it could call thousands of its members to action to save a historical break, and likely hit the surf to celebrate.

Source: Terry Rodgers, "Toll Road Proposal Voted Down," *San Diego Union-Tribune,* February 7, 2008.

have to overcome a standard collective action problem: most political interest groups pursue collective goods that, by definition, all group members will enjoy whether or not they help to provide them. Rational self-interest could lead to universal free riding, dooming the organization and the effort unless some way is found around this difficulty.

This collective action problem poses more of a challenge to some interests than others, Olson pointed out, with the scale of the group and the stakes of its involvement in public policy determining whether its members are likely to work together toward their common goal. These factors help us understand why, for instance, there is no powerful lobby working on behalf of airline passengers, while airlines themselves are well organized and influential. First, small groups are easier to organize than large groups. Most of us fly at one time or another, and everyone who flies is annoyed at having to pay an extra fee to check a bag or eat lunch. But it would be very difficult to sign every passenger up as a dues-paying member of a group dedicated to passing a law prohibiting these fees. The transaction costs involved in bringing together a handful of airlines to oppose such a law are much lower than the costs of building an association of millions of passengers. For the small community of airlines, free-rider problems are less severe, since free riders—in this case, airlines that do not contribute to an industry-wide lobbying effort—are more readily detected and subject to pressure to cooperate in defending the industry. Second, interests with a great deal at stake in a policy domain are more readily organized for political action than are people with little at stake. (Airline fees are a minor annoyance to all of us, but they are a source of billions of dollars in much-needed revenues for airlines.) When prospective costs or benefits of a policy are large, so are incentives to invest in political action. When the support for a group is a mile wide but only an inch deep, as it is for airline passenger rights, coordination becomes difficult, and the potential for political power often goes unfulfilled.

Group size and stakes often are inversely related, compounding the bias. For a few fortunate groups, a single member might have enough at stake to justify paying the entire cost of pursuing the group's collective interests. ExxonMobil, for example, might find it profitable to invest in lobbying for repeal of price controls on gasoline even if it has to pay the entire cost of producing a benefit that would have to be shared with all gasoline producers (a small group—just ten companies control 79 percent of U.S. domestic refining capacity). By contrast, many widely shared, diffuse collective interests will be poorly represented if those who share them behave rationally and remain free riders.

This analysis may explain why lobbies representing narrow economic interests predominate in Washington, but it raises a new question: Why are there nonetheless so many vigorous lobbies claiming to speak for widespread, diffuse interests? Indeed, one of the most striking changes in the interest group universe over the past three decades has been the proliferation of organizations claiming to represent millions of citizens devoted to some version of the "public interest." How have the leaders of public interest groups, which have broad public support but are seemingly too large and focused on issues with stakes that are too low in order to organize effectively, solved the collective action problem that should have doomed them?

One reason behind the proliferation of public interest groups is that some people who care passionately about an issue do not act like coldly rational calculators. They are willing to contribute to groups espousing causes they care about without worrying about whether their

THE POLITICAL POWER OF SMALL NUMBERS

While Mancur Olson's 1965 book *The Logic of Collective Action* may have been the first academic work to lay out the organizational advantage conferred on a small group with intense interests, he was not the first to recognize it. Representative Clem Miller, a young congressman from California's north coast, saw exactly this logic at play when he compared the lobbying efforts of two agricultural groups in 1959. Both groups, the walnut growers and the poultrymen, faced economic collapse as record production levels drove prices so low that small farmers were taking a loss on every nut or egg that they sold. Lawmakers were sympathetic to the plight of each type of farmer. Both groups lobbied Congress for relief. Only one, though, won political action, and the secret to its success lay in its size and concentration of interests.

Because walnut growers had bumper crops in both 1958 and 1959, their nuts and foreign imports flooded the market to drive down prices. All walnut farmers faced an economic problem. Organizing the industry to ask for solution, though, was relatively easy. Walnut farming was concentrated in California, and the independent growers had already organized themselves into associations that

effectively reduced their numbers. "The walnut industry is well organized," Congressman Miller observed. "This is easy to understand. One marketing cooperative controls seventy per cent of the state's productive." Instead of asking for help with disparate voices, the small network of marketing associations worked together in unison. They laid the groundwork for a successful lobbying effort by coordinating grassroots efforts in much that same way that the "main street" car dealers did, detailed in this chapter's opening vignette. "Each California

contribution will make any appreciable difference. **Moral incentives**, the personal satisfactions of active self-expression, trump the economist's concept of rationality for the countless concerned citizens who send checks to groups pursuing environmental protection, a ban on abortion, political reform, same-sex marriage or its abolition, animal rights, and a host of other social causes. These groups did not arise spontaneously through the action of concerned citizens; most were put together by enterprising activists supported by charitable foundations, wealthy individuals, or the government itself. Yet many are sustained by dues and small contributions from a large number of private citizens.

But another important route to organizing public interest groups recognizes that many of us do act rationally, and provides concrete benefits to those who join. Many of the most successful organizations circumvent the collective action problem by offering **selective incentives**— benefits that can be denied to individuals who do not join and contribute. The American congressman received a personal, carefully reasoned, five-page letter," Congressman Miller recounted. "Quite properly, the group worked through the congressman in whose district the association offices and many growers are located." The growers then hired a lobbyist who identified a solution—the government could buy surplus walnuts for school lunches, using the tariffs collected on imported nuts—and traveled to Washington to press their case. After making allies of their representatives, the farmers stood with members of Congress to demand that the Secretary of Agriculture take action. Under withering political pressure, he eventually complied.

Though no less needy or sympathetic, the poultrymen won no such governmental assistance. At first glance, this seems surprising because so many chicken farmers spread across the nation petitioned Congress for help. Independent poultrymen, who did not work through marketing associations, were being driven to bankruptcy by an oversupply of eggs and meat produced by new, bank-financed industrial farms. The sector was thus split internally. It did not help the cause that poultrymen came from many different states whose legislators were not as used to working together as the California congressional delegation. After a loose confederation agitated for a committee hearing, more than two hundred chicken farmers descended on Washington, DC, and testified for two days about their plight. Yet despite numbers that dwarfed the walnut growers, they never hired a lobbyist to help press their case in a strategic fashion. They came and left congress without proposing a concrete solution. "All of the men were active poultrymen who had to get back to their flocks," Miller pointed out. "Who was going to coordinate policy between New Jersey, California, Alabama, Wisconsin, Georgia, and Kansas? The answer from them was, 'No one.'" Without a single voice to carry the ball, even the impassioned testimony of so many farmers led nowhere. Congress passed a weak resolution, and the many poultrymen suffered.

Source: Clem Miller, "The Walnut Growers and Poultrymen," in *Member of the House: Letters of a Congressman*, edited by John W. Baker (New York: Charles Scribner's Sons, 1962).

Automobile Association (AAA), an interest group founded in 1902 to push for the construction of more roads, actively lobbies Congress on issues such as vehicle safety, car theft, and gasoline prices. But for the vast majority of members, joining AAA is a way to get roadside assistance, maps, and discounts at motels. By offering these selective benefits, the group solved a collective action problem similar to the one faced by airline passengers. Other massive lobbies have followed the same path. Attorneys become members of state bar associations in order to practice law, physicians join the American Medical Association to qualify for malpractice insurance and to receive the association's journal, and farmers seek membership in the American Farm Bureau Federation to receive the assistance of county farm agents. Groups that initially attract members by providing them with individual benefits may invest some of their resources in pursuing collective benefits through political action. The largest interest group in the United States by far—AARP—was formed to market insurance to senior citizens and thrives by providing members with a variety of selective benefits. Indeed, to a remarkable extent the interest groups that now throng the nation's capital are offshoots of organizations that fulfill many goals of their members extending far beyond political action but are politically powerful nonetheless.

CONTEMPORARY INTEREST GROUPS

The exact dimensions of the present-day interest group universe are unknown, but it is an expanding one. According to one estimate, the number of lobbying organizations more than tripled between the 1960s and the 1990s; a subsequent analysis indicated a further doubling between 2000 and 2005.[15] The website Lobbyists.info, an authoritative directory of interest groups and lobbyists, lists approximately twenty-two thousand lobbyists serving a host of corporations, labor unions, trade and professional associations, political action committees, and advocacy groups, including lawyers registered as lobbyists, public relations consultants, and think tank staff. In addition to the active lobbying organizations sponsored by private sector organizations, government entities—states, cities, counties, and their agencies—are behind much lobbying activity. No fewer than 168 California government bodies employ Washington, DC, representatives. So do more than three hundred colleges and universities, 148 Native American tribes, sixteen ethnic groups, and more than one hundred religious organizations.[16] More than twenty-seven thousand individuals are registered as lobbyists with Congress, and more than one hundred thousand Washingtonians are employed somewhere in the lobbying industry.[17] Like other industries, lobbying has its ups and downs. When congressional Republicans and President Obama frequently deadlocked over policy after the 2010 elections, lobbying firms took a financial hit because of the policy slowdown. "Historically, when you look at the third and fourth quarter of election years, we've been down," explained an executive with Patton Boggs, DC's largest lobbying firm. In election years, he added, "you have a reduced number of legislative fights that occur in the third and fourth quarter."[18]

Most advocacy groups also are the creatures of preexisting institutions. From abolition to temperance to civil rights to nuclear disarmament to the "right to life," churches and synagogues have provided a stable institutional base for organizing movements pursuing social and political change. Most of the self-designated public interest groups that have proliferated in recent decades initially were financed by patrons—philanthropic foundations, corporations, wealthy individuals, or the government itself—and many depend on continuing subsidies for significant parts of their budgets. The interests of welfare recipients, the mentally ill, children, and the homeless do not lack advocates, even though such groups themselves are not organized for collective action. Their causes have been taken up by lobbies representing the social service professionals (mostly government employees) who run the programs that serve these groups. Political campaigns can spawn lobbying groups. After the 2012 presidential election, a group of President Obama's key advisers formed a tax-exempt advocacy group, "Organizing for Action," that aimed to turn the president's electoral coalition into a grassroots advocacy network (and to do so more successfully than its 2009 incarnation, "Organizing for America"). The group leased the sophisticated voter data sets and outreach software that the Obama campaign had developed, essentially becoming an extension of campaign itself. In the vast realm of organized interests in America, there are even groups that

WATCH A VIDEO

logic.cqpress.com

Can "Organizing for Action" turn the Obama campaign into an interest group?

The Cetacean Lobby

While its goals and tactics are certainly unique, the Sea Shepherd Conservation Society has much in common with other public interest groups. It is led by a charismatic, if controversial, political entrepreneur. To fund its activities, it relies on large donations from wealthy individuals as well as dues from a small but passionate base of members. And it has taken advantage of the new media masterfully to raise its profile and expand its mass support, through the television show *Whale Wars*.

After his radical tactics got him kicked out of Greenpeace, the environmental group that he helped to found, Paul Watson organized Sea Shepherd to stop the hunting of minke whales and endangered fin whales carried out by the Institute of Cetacean Research. The institute, which despite its subsidy from the Japanese government produces little actual research and instead sells the meat of the whales it catches, complains that Sea Shepherd tactics of confronting whaling ships violate international law and endanger its crews. This notoriety has attracted the support of many rich and famous animal rights activists, including Las Vegas magnate Steve Wynn (who

helped the Sea Shepherds buy a submarine) and *Price Is Right* host Bob Barker (who donated funds to purchase the ship that bears his name). Most effectively, this interest group has capitalized on the primary "advance" in television—reality shows—by starring in the Animal Planet show *Whale Wars*. Every week, interested viewers can watch the Sea Shepherds confront the Japanese whaling fleet with their unique form of radical civil disobedience, practiced by a crew that makes up for its maritime inexperience with an immense reservoir of outrage.

claim to speak for the whales and mount civil disobedience campaigns to stop them from being hunted (see box "The Cetacean Lobby").

Not every group depends on outside assistance for its resources. Prominent public interest groups such as Common Cause, Public Citizen, and the Public Interest Research Group (PIRG) are financed principally by membership dues and small donations, as are many of the large environmental lobbies, such as the Sierra Club, the National Audubon Society, and the Wilderness Society. These and other organizations have taken advantage of modern computer technology to solicit and maintain a mass membership and donor base through Internet and direct-mail appeals to current and prospective supporters. Because they depend mostly on moral incentives—persuading people to invest in collective goods despite the temptation to free ride on the efforts of others—their memberships and budgets fluctuate with circumstances. They tend to grow when opponents run the government and shrink when sympathetic politicians are in power (see box "The Blessings of Adversity").

 WATCH A VIDEO

logic.cqpress.com

Turning the Obama campaign into an interest group.

Why Have Interest Groups Proliferated?

Several interacting factors have contributed to the rapid proliferation of interest groups since the 1960s. For one thing, the *social ferment* initiated by the civil rights movement and continued by the Reagan-era conservative and right-to-life movements has inspired and

THE BLESSINGS OF ADVERSITY

strategy and choice

Voluntary organizations that survive on dues and small contributions from a mass membership often do best when the political climate is the most unfavorable. Such groups solicit most of their members and raise most of their money through direct-mail appeals, which are most effective when they invoke threats that make people angry or fearful enough to leave off free riding and join up or send another check. As one practitioner put it, "You've got to have a devil. If you don't have a devil, you're in trouble."[1] Devils are easier to find when power is in enemy hands. Thus, for example, membership in the National Rifle Association (NRA), a group adamantly opposed to any kind of gun control, grew rapidly during Democrat Jimmy Carter's administration (1977–1981), peaked in the early 1980s, then drifted downward from 1984 though 1991 when pro-gun Republicans Ronald Reagan (1981–1989) and then George H. W. Bush (1989–1993) sat in the White House. NRA growth revived with the election of gun control advocate Bill Clinton in 1992, then fell off again after the Republicans took control of Congress in 1995. But after the 1999 shootings at Columbine High School in Colorado (two students killed twelve school-mates and a teacher and injured twenty-three other people before committing suicide), proposals for stricter gun laws gained momentum, and in response NRA membership rose sharply to reach its highest level ever in 2000. After George W. Bush defeated gun control advocate Al Gore that year, NRA membership began to tail off,[2] but in the eighteen days after the 2012 Sandy Hook elementary school shooting, the organization reported that its rolls swelled by one hundred-thousand new members. During the policy negotiations over gun control in the wake of the killings, the NRA told reporters that "our goal is to get to 5 million before this debate is over."[3]

For environmental groups the pattern was inverted. They received an enormous boost from the Reagan and Bush administrations. Their best (if unwitting) recruiters were James Watt, Reagan's first secretary of the interior, and Anne Gorsuch Burford, head of the Environmental Protection Agency, who made no apologies for putting private economic interests ahead of environmental protection. The Sierra Club's membership rose from 181,000 in 1980 to 364,000 in 1985 and to 650,000 in 1992, and its budget more than quadrupled (from $9 million to $40 million). The National Audubon Society grew by 50 percent, adding 200,000 members to its rolls during the Reagan-Bush years, and other major environmental groups also grew rapidly. After 1992, however, with an environmentalist safely in the White House, membership in most of these groups stabilized or fell off, and by 2000 the Sierra Club was down to 550,000 members. But George W. Bush's victory that year threw environmentalists on the defensive once again, rallying against what its publications portrayed as his administration's multipronged assault on environmental values. By 2004 the Sierra Club had raised its membership to 757,000 and its budget to more than $95 million.

1. Jeffrey M. Berry, *The Interest Group Society* (Boston: Little, Brown, 1984), 84.

2. Kelly Patterson and Matthew M. Singer, "The National Rifle Association in the Face of the Clinton Challenge," in *Interest Group Politics,* 6th ed., ed. Allan J. Cigler and Burdett A. Loomis (Washington, DC: CQ Press, 2002), 60–65; Kelly Patterson, personal communication, July 28, 2004.

3. Katie Glueck, "NRA: 100,000 New Members After Sandy Hook Shooting," *Politico*, January 10, 2013.

instructed the stream of organizations that agitated for social change. Some led the opposition to the war in Vietnam; others asserted the rights of women, gays, Native Americans, Hispanics, Asians, and people with disabilities. Environmental and consumer groups emerged, along with the antiabortion and conservative Christian movements and animal rights organizations. Today, the Occupy movement, the Tea Party and mass movements on both sides of the immigration, and same-sex marriage debates have galvanized sizable segments of society. The list could (and no doubt will) go on. Organizers of **social movements**—amorphous aggregates of people sharing general values and a desire for social change—quickly imitate successful innovations, and each new group has been able to draw on the experience of its predecessors.

The clientele for such groups has come from a *growing and increasingly well-educated and affluent middle class,* people with a surplus of money or time to invest in causes that excite their moral imaginations strongly enough to discourage free riding. *Technological innovations*—e-mail appeals, campaigns run via Facebook or Twitter, and "microtargeted" mail that uses consumer databases to identify those who

Organized in 2009 as a reaction to President Obama's economic stimulus, bank bailout, and health care policies, the "Tea Party" is a set of loosely confederated interest groups that have given voice to populist anger across the nation. Various state and local Tea Party groups mobilized their members at town hall meetings, at marches on Washington, and in Republican primaries to nominate Tea Party loyalists in the 2010 and 2012 elections.

would likely support a movement and tailor a message to their concerns—have made it easier and cheaper than ever before for entrepreneurial leaders to establish and maintain organizations that have a large number of geographically scattered and socially unconnected members.

Successful groups inspire *opponents* as well as imitators. Corporate and business leaders whose interests were threatened by the political gains of environmental and consumer groups organized to defend themselves. Legislation that added to their regulatory burden and threatened the bottom line was a powerful stimulus to political action by industries and firms. Business leaders also sought to beef up the intellectual case for their side by financing think tanks* dedicated to promoting conservative ideas and policies—among them the Hoover Institution, the American Enterprise Institute, the Heritage Foundation, and the Cato Institute.[19]

The most important part of the dynamic behind the expanding interest group universe, however, has been the *encouragement of the federal government itself.* In addition to stimulating the organization of business interests, the growing scope of government activity has encouraged the proliferation of organizations in the nonprofit and public sectors:

---

* *Think tank* is the common term for an organization that employs or sponsors professional intellectuals to study issues of public policy and to prepare books, reports, newspaper essays and opinion pieces, magazine articles, and speeches promoting their conclusions. Most, though not all, adhere to some identifiable ideology that reflects the values and interests of their sponsors.

The growth, during the twentieth century, of public schools, parks and forest preserves, agricultural research stations, public hospitals, and social welfare agencies of all kinds stimulated the creation of numerous professional associations made up of the providers of these new public services. *These groups often were created at the suggestion of public officials who realized the political value of organized constituents working to promote their programs from outside of government* [emphasis added].[20]

Prominent examples include private business groups such as the U.S. Chamber of Commerce and the Business Roundtable, which were created under the leadership of secretaries of commerce in, respectively, the Taft and Nixon administrations; the American Farm Bureau Federation, which developed from a network of official advisory committees to the U.S. Department of Agriculture's county agents; and the National Organization for Women (NOW), a leading feminist organization. Indeed, the women's movement itself was jump-started by the government. In the early 1960s the Kennedy administration sponsored legislation that encouraged the creation of a commission on the status of women in every state. Later, the state and federal governments funded a series of conferences on women's issues. In 1966 some delegates to the annual meeting of state commissioners on the status of women, frustrated by how their position as government officials limited their ability to take political action, sought a voice by founding NOW, which could work outside government.[21]

The federal government also has contributed to the proliferation of interest groups through the tax code. Many groups qualify as nonprofit organizations, which are exempt from most taxes, and donors may deduct contributions to some kinds of nonprofit groups from their taxable income. The government also subsidizes the mass mailings of nonprofit groups through special postal rates. These organizations do face some restrictions on their political activity, however; they may educate, but they are not supposed to lobby openly or to engage in partisan electoral politics. The philanthropic foundations that fund many advocacy groups are themselves creatures of tax policy; rich people and families put their assets into foundations as a legal way to avoid income and inheritance taxes. Administrations also subsidize some politically favored organizations by hiring them to conduct studies or carry out specific projects. Groups thrive in good part because public policy has encouraged them to do so.

Finally, although discussions of pluralist politics commonly assume that government programs emerge in response to interest group demands, in reality it often is the other way around: interests (and interest groups) arise *in defense of government programs.* Typically, groups benefiting from government programs get organized and active only after the programs are in place. For example, most of the potent groups defending the interests of elderly people emerged after the enactment of Social Security (1935), Medicare (1965), and the Older Americans Act of 1965; AARP did not become the eight-hundred-pound gorilla of American politics until these programs were already in place to defend.

With or without the deliberate instigation of government officials, new policies create constituencies ripe for organization. People who adapt their plans to existing policies (on tax credits for capital investments, for example) develop a stake in continuation of the policies. And it is easier to mobilize people to defend what they already have than to pursue the more doubtful prospective benefits they do not yet enjoy—that is, the threat of loss is a more powerful spur to action than the hope of gain.[22] In general, the more the government does, the more incentives it creates for organized political action.

Fragmentation and Specialization

The expanding interest group universe also reflects the fragmentation of old interests and the growing division of labor among groups sharing the same broad goals. New organizations form when new issues pull old groups apart; increasingly complex issues and fragmented policy processes force groups to specialize in order to be effective. Meanwhile, as links between diverse problems have become more transparent, a wider range of organized interests has pushed into formerly isolated issue domains.

Farm policy, for example, was for many years the exclusive domain of the farm bloc, an alliance composed of a handful of interest groups (most notably the American Farm Bureau Federation), U.S. Department of Agriculture officials, and members of Congress from the farm states who sat on the agriculture and appropriations committees and subcommittees. Together, they formed a classic iron triangle that dominated federal agriculture policy (see Chapter 8). Today, more than two hundred organizations attempt to shape agricultural policy in a far more diffuse policy environment. Commodity groups (representing, for example, growers of wheat, cotton, corn, soybeans, rice, sugar beets, and peanuts, as well as producers of milk, honey, beef, chicken, and wool) have been joined by groups concerned with nutrition, sustainability, food safety, international trade, "locavore" eating habits, farm credit, food processing and distribution, environmental quality, and the welfare of rural residents. A study of 130 of these groups found that only one in six pursued a broad agenda; the rest addressed only a narrow range of policy issues in their chosen niches.[23] The participants are far too many and diverse to form anything resembling the stable, exclusive iron triangle of old.

The growth of federally sponsored medical research has also spawned a variety of specialized lobbying organizations. Various bodily organs (heart, lungs, brain, kidneys, eyes) as well as diseases (HIV/AIDS, diabetes, epilepsy, cystic fibrosis, arthritis, lupus) have their own advocacy groups. Cancer research is promoted not only by the American Cancer Society, but by groups specializing in its various forms (breast, prostate, ovarian, leukemia, lymphoma). Associations lobby for more investment in curing birth and developmental diseases (spina bifida, cystic fibrosis), maladies of youth (sudden infant death syndrome) and age (osteoporosis), and mental as well as physical illnesses (bipolar disorder, autism, alcoholism). All want the health research budget to grow, but each also works to expand the share devoted to its particular specialty.

Specialization responds not only to changes in the external environment but also to organizational imperatives. To survive, an interest group must convince its individual or institutional backers that their continued investment is worthwhile. To do so, it must distinguish itself from similar outfits competing for the same constituency by showing that its contribution is unique. Some have done so spectacularly, with either high-profile events (such as the Susan G. Komen Race for the Cure walk to fight breast cancer) or famous spokespeople (such as the Michael J. Fox Foundation for Parkinson's Research). Most groups survive by staking an exclusive claim to leadership and expertise on a particular subset of issues. To avoid mutually destructive poaching, potential competitors for the same constituency reach informal accommodations, deferring to each other's issue turf. Opponents do not threaten an interest group's health; indeed, as we saw earlier in this chapter, powerful opponents often invigorate a group. A group is in the greatest danger from similar groups appealing to the same supporters. This problem makes the formation of coalitions tricky. Groups often have to form alliances to succeed politically, but to be submerged in a coalition threatens the loss of a group's special identity. Thus many groups are

Michael J. Fox, actor, Parkinson's disease patient, and founder of the Michael J. Fox Foundation for Parkinson's Research, confers with Senator Orrin Hatch on Capitol Hill as they jointly advocate for passage of a bill that would fund stem cell research into this and other diseases. Groups successfully pressuring Congress to devote more resources to combating "their" disease have inspired imitators, making this strategy increasingly common.

reluctant to participate in coalitions and join them only on a temporary basis for specific purposes.[24] Nonetheless, groups with common interests—and no fear of losing their separate identities—do sometimes form new groups that are, in effect, standing coalitions. More than a few of the organizations listed in *Washington Representatives* are coalitions of other groups that are themselves representatives of institutions. There is even a National Association of Business Political Action Committees (NABPAC), representing 132 business political action committees (PACs) that themselves represent corporations and trade associations. NABPAC advises its members on PAC management, fund-raising, and candidates, and testifies in defense of PACs in congressional hearings on campaign finance legislation.

WHAT DO INTEREST GROUPS DO?

What do all these interest groups spend their time doing? For most, the first objective is not political influence but simple survival. Interest group leaders keep their organizations in business by cultivating and retaining patrons willing to pay the bills or supply other essential resources. This activity not only absorbs a great deal of time and energy but also strongly shapes a group's political activity. Organizations that survive on small contributions from a mass membership, for example, have no choice but to focus on the issues that continue to generate contributions. Common Cause, which initially advocated a broad range of civic reforms, has spent much of its time in recent decades agitating for campaign finance reform because the issue always tops the list when members are surveyed at membership renewal time.

Lobbying groups that represent corporations and trade associations have to pass muster with executives or boards of directors who may have only a shaky understanding of political realities. As a result, group leaders may spend as much time explaining government to their patrons as they do explaining their patrons' interests to government officials. They also may spend more time engineering a consensus among patrons on what the group's policy goals should be than pursuing the goals themselves. For example, "representatives of the Peanut Growers Group . . . spent considerably more time agreeing on what they would contest in the 1985 farm bill than they did working to get it."[25] In short, interest group leaders and their constituents are involved in a principal-agent relationship, with all the familiar problems and challenges such relationships pose (described in Chapter 1 on page 32). On a more mundane level, group officials must manage their offices—hiring and firing, assigning work, keeping staff productive and content. All of this activity adds up; interest group officials spend a good deal of their time just keeping the organization going.

Insider Tactics: Trafficking in Information and Cultivating Access

Interest groups have proliferated in Washington, DC, in part because the federal government's expanded activities affect almost everything that people care about deeply, giving them plenty of reasons to defend or extend their interests. But to do so they first must know when and how their interests are at stake, not always a simple matter in a world of complex issues and processes. Meanwhile, political decision makers, facing the same complex and uncertain world, are always hungry for information about the potential consequences of different courses of action. The informational needs of politicians and interest groups create a basis for mutually beneficial exchanges. The importance of these exchanges was confirmed when officials from a representative sample of 175 organizations with Washington offices were asked to specify their most important activities: exchanging and presenting information topped the list, shown in Table 13-1.[26]

The information provided by interest groups is inherently suspect,

TABLE 13-1

What Lobbying Groups Say They Do

Activity	Percentage Engaging in Activity
1. Testifying at hearings	99
2. Contacting government officials directly to present the group's point of view	98
3. Engaging in informal contacts with officials—at conventions, over lunch, and so forth	95
4. Presenting research results or technical information	92
5. Sending letters to members of the group to inform them about its activities	92
6. Entering into coalitions with other groups	92
7. Attempting to shape the implementation of policies	90
8. Talking with people from the media	89
9. Consulting with government officials to plan legislative strategy	86
10. Helping to draft legislation	85
11. Inspiring letter-writing or telegram campaigns	84
12. Shaping the government's agenda by raising new issues and calling attention to ignored problems	84
13. Mounting grassroots lobbying efforts	80
14. Having influential constituents contact their members of Congress	80
15. Helping to draft regulations, rules, or guidelines	78
16. Serving on advisory commissions and boards	76
17. Alerting members of Congress about the effects of a bill on their districts	75
18. Filing suit or otherwise engaging in litigation	72
19. Making financial contributions to electoral campaigns	58
20. Doing favors for officials who need assistance	56
21. Attempting to influence appointments to public office	53
22. Publicizing candidates' voting records	44
23. Engaging in direct-mail fund-raising for the group	44
24. Running advertisements in the media about the group's position on issues	31
25. Contributing work or personnel to electoral campaigns	24
26. Making public endorsements of candidates for office	22
27. Engaging in protest demonstrations	20

Source: From a survey of interest groups reported in Kay Lehman Schlozman and John T. Tierney, *Organized Interests and American Democracy,* copyright © 1985. Reprinted by permission of Pearson Education, Inc., Upper Saddle River, New Jersey.

of course, for, as government officials realize, it is intended not merely to inform but also to persuade. Thus much of what goes on between lobbyists and government officials is aimed at establishing sufficient trust to permit mutually beneficial exchanges of information. For example, lobbyists spend a lot of their time just keeping in touch with the government officials—members of Congress, congressional staff, bureaucrats—who deal with their issues so they can know when their interests are at stake. Much of their work lies in responding to proposals or actions, and early warning of a proposed action often is essential to an effective response. Lobbyists also gather intelligence by regularly reading newspapers, blogs, and more specialized publications and talking to other lobbyists as well as to government officials. Keeping in touch facilitates cordial relations with the officials they might do business with someday. People are more inclined to listen to friends than to strangers, but even mere acquaintance makes it easier to interpret, and therefore take into account, a lobbyist's pitch. Indeed, just being visible is important: "*You have to be seen.* Even if the legislators don't know who you are, if they see you often enough, they'll start to feel you belong."[27]

When an issue of concern to an interest group does arise, information is central to persuading government officials to act. Decision makers need two related types of information: technical and political. The Environmental Protection Agency cannot carry out its mandate, and Congress cannot legislate clean air or water, without a great deal of technical information on the dangers of, say, greenhouse gases. Many important policy questions are fiendishly complex; government officials, wishing to avoid disastrous, costly mistakes, welcome any information that reduces uncertainty and the likelihood of nasty surprises. Knowing this, interest groups provide volumes of technical information designed to show that their preferred course of action will produce superior results and that policies they oppose will fail, cost too much, or produce new disasters.

Political information tells politicians how voters are likely to react to alternative policies. Lobbyists, not surprisingly, take pains to point out that the actions they favor will please a politician's supporters and the actions they oppose will have the opposite effect. Whenever possible, they carefully frame proposals in terms consistent with prevailing currents of public opinion. They may conduct scientific public opinion polls to demonstrate support for their side or artfully craft a communications strategy to put the best possible spin on their client's position. Following the attacks of September 11, 2001, many lobbyists repackaged their policy pitches as ways for Congress to fight terrorism by doing everything from drilling for oil in Alaska to reestablishing telecommunications monopolies to including California-grown dates in the food packages air-dropped into Afghanistan during the holy month of Ramadan.

Since politicians know that lobbyists are advocates, when can they trust a lobbyist's information? Only when both sides expect to have a continuing relationship. Rational choice analyses of many games show that when they are repeated over and over, the players have far greater incentives to cooperate with one another and to be truthful and straightforward in their dealings. Lobbying is, in this way, like a repeated game. A lobbyist who needs to stay in a politician's good graces on a continuing basis must maintain credibility or go out of business. If information turns out to be misleading or inflicts political damage, its source will never be heeded again.

Lobbyists do have ways of increasing the credibility of their messages. One reason they arrange for scientists or scholars to testify at congressional committee hearings is to back technical claims with evidence from more neutral sources. Testimony also allows groups to put their cases into the public record that will later guide the interpretation of laws by courts and administrative agencies. Because arranging testimony is costly for a lobbyist, it demonstrates to members of Congress that the group represented really does care about the issue under discussion. Testimony also is a way for lobbyists to show the people who pay their bills that they are doing their jobs. Often the same representatives of a group show up at the same subcommittee hearings and give the same testimony year after year, not because they expect to be effective but because the activity fits their job description. They are sustaining the organization, if not the cause.

The credibility of political information is enhanced when a group mobilizes its constituency as a part of the lobbying effort. Supportive letters, e-mails, phone calls, telegrams, and faxes from the districts of key members of Congress reinforce the impression that a favorable vote is in their best interests. A representative or senator who is skeptical of messages coming from some hired gun in Washington may be convinced by evidence that some constituents care enough to put time and effort into sending the same message. This is why the automobile dealers who fought for an exemption from the financial reform bill of 2010 were so successful, as we saw in this chapter's introduction. They were able to mount a significant grassroots campaign for the exemption in every congressional district, relying on dealership owners and their employees, rather than slick K Street lobbyists, to carry the message directly to their representatives. The dealers won because they could call upon a political resource that Goldman Sachs and other Wall Street banks fighting the bill did not possess. Lobbying by informing requires *access,* the professional lobbyist's indispensable stock in trade. Persuasive information does no good if it does not reach decision makers. Politicians grant access to people who can help them achieve their own goals. These people are the representatives of politically important interests in their constituencies, the supporters who help finance their campaigns, the men and women who have provided valuable information or assistance in the past—in other words, the people who can help them do what they want to do more effectively. Indeed, successful lobbying is political persuasion in its purest form: a lobbyist must get people to do what he or she wants them to do by convincing them that the action serves their goals.

Legislators and other government officials always have more things to do than they have time to do them. An interest group can encourage a sympathetic politician to spend time on its issue by making it cheaper (in time and staff resources) for the politician to do so. (See Table 13-1, page 597, for some of the things lobbying groups can do to help politicians.) By helping officials plan legislative strategy, assemble legislative coalitions, draft legislation, organize hearings, and write rules and regulations, lobbyists will not so much change minds as activate politicians already on their side by reducing the politicians' cost of getting involved.

Interest groups also can make the jobs of regulators and other bureaucrats easier. Congress usually writes general legislation, leaving decisions on the detailed rules and regulations up to the administrative agencies. The Administrative Procedure Act of 1946 requires that all such proposed rules and regulations be published in the *Federal Register* before they are promulgated and that public hearings be held on them if anyone objects (see Chapter 8). An important task of many group officials is to monitor the *Federal Register* for proposed rules that might affect their group's interests and to provide research and testimony in opposition or support.

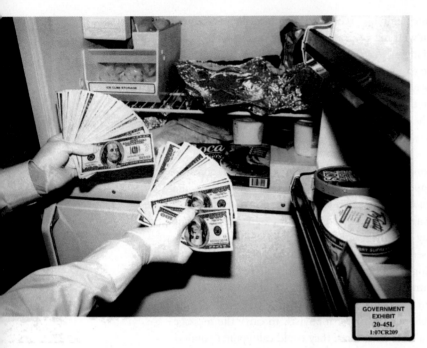

GOVERNMENT
EXHIBIT
20-45L
1:07CR209

In pursuing insider influence, lobbyists do not always forgo illegal inducements, and politicians do not always resist the temptation to accept them. Bribery scandals are thus a recurring if relatively infrequent feature of political life in Washington, DC. One-time high-powered lobbyist Jack Abramoff wound up in jail for fraud and corrupting public officials, and former Republican Rep. Bob Ney resigned his seat in 2006 and went to prison because of his association with Abramoff. In 2009 former Democratic Rep. William Jefferson was convicted on eleven counts of corruption, in a case that featured the discovery of $90,000 in cash in the freezer of his Washington, DC-area home.

For their part, regulators, hoping to avoid writing rules that get shot down by appeals to the courts or Congress, keep in touch with politically potent groups in the sectors they regulate. Often the relationship is formalized through the creation of advisory groups representing the relevant private interests, which can be consulted on a continuing basis. About one thousand such groups exist, including the Interagency Committee on Smoking and Health of the U.S. Department of Health and Human Services and the U.S. Department of Agriculture's Burley Tobacco Advisory Committee.[28] Again, the benefits are mutual. On the one hand, the interests represented on the advisory group have permanent access to decision makers, so their views are guaranteed a hearing. On the other hand, the regulators can get an early reading on the likely reaction to their proposals and maintain a conduit to the groups whose interests they affect. Interest group officials, sitting on the inside, develop a greater appreciation for technical, legal, and political grounds for regulatory decisions and may end up lobbying their own members to accept them.

Interest groups also can be valuable to bureaucrats as allies in dealing with the elected officials who control their budgets. During the Cold War, for example, all three branches of the military mobilized civilian support groups to help fight the battles in Congress and, more important, with each other, for a larger share of the defense pie. The Navy League, Air Force Association, and Association of the U.S. Army lobbied vigorously for the programs and weapon systems sought by their respective services and against those of rival services. Each organization enjoyed the financial support of the defense contractors who proposed to build the weapons systems they advocated.

Outsider Tactics: Altering the Political Forces

The **insider tactics** just described depend on personal access to government officials and work through mutually beneficial exchanges between lobbyists and politicians. The **outsider tactics** employed by interest groups do not require any personal contact with politicians and may take the form of implicit or explicit threats—real pressure—rather than offers of reciprocally helpful exchanges. The strategy is to persuade politicians to act as the group desires by altering the political forces they feel obliged to heed.

One common tactic is use of the mass media to shape public opinion. The Center for Responsive Politics tries to generate support for its campaign finance reform proposals by assembling and publicizing reports on campaign contributions and spending. Think tanks regularly hold press conferences to bring attention to research reports on public issues. The Children's Defense Fund assembles and publicizes reports on childhood poverty to encourage public pressure on Congress to spend more on programs for poor children. Other groups try to get the media to buy their version of the public interest on, for example, the danger from pesticides or the incidence of breast cancer so that the threat of bad publicity will hang over the heads of politicians who oppose their demands.

Demonstrations—picketing, marches, sit-ins—are another time-honored outsider device. The principal techniques, around for centuries, were used by antislavery groups, suffragists, and prohibitionists, but they were perfected in their contemporary form by civil rights groups in the 1950s and 1960s and have since been widely imitated by a host of social movements. Demonstrations are intended to focus public attention on the cause. Freedom marches in the South brought the issue of segregation—and the brutality of its defenders—into the homes of Americans everywhere through the then-fresh medium of television (see Chapter 4). Demonstrations also may show the breadth of support for a cause. In the early 1970s opponents of the Vietnam War amassed hundreds of thousands of demonstrators in Washington, DC, for this purpose. Beginning in the late 1990s, protesters at World Trade Organization meetings and other top economic summits have engaged in vigorous, anarchic, and puppet-filled activities. Civil disobedience—sit-ins and other demonstrations that openly violate the law—dramatizes the intensity of commitment; it is difficult to ignore a cause for which large numbers of people are willing to go to jail. Finally, demonstrations foster group solidarity—shared work and risk are powerful bonding agents—and thus may strengthen the

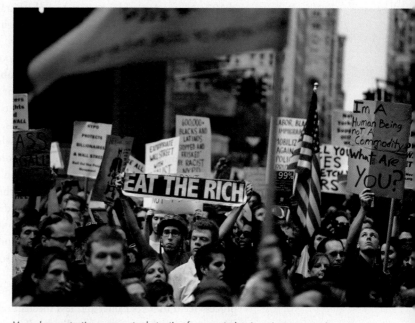

Mass demonstrations are a staple tactic of groups trying to get government leaders to pay attention to their issue. Throughout 2011, the Occupy movement staged some of the most energetic, sustained demonstrations in a generation, taking over public parks first near Wall Street and then across the nation to protest against economic inequality and corporate power. Along with the Tea Party movement, which came from the diametrically opposite pole of the political spectrum, Occupy heralded a new era of movement politics in America. Yet because Occupy avoided traditional lobbying techniques and hierarchical organization—indeed, because most of those camping out were fundamentally opposed to such traditional routes to influence—the group's ultimate impact remains uncertain.

TAKE A SURVEY

Which movement
reshaped
American
politics?

organization. Demonstrations are used most often by groups that do not enjoy insiders' access. They have become so familiar in Washington, DC, that, unless they are extraordinary in some way, the news media pay little attention to them.

Reports, news conferences, and demonstrations aimed at putting issues on the agenda and compelling government officials to do something about them depend on media attention. If the news media ignore them, they fail. Private interests that wish to publicize their views without the uncertainties of relying on free coverage may, if they can afford the cost, buy advertising. After its disastrous oil spill in the Gulf of Mexico, BP spent more than $93 million on the television, newspaper, and radio "Making It Right" public relations campaign designed to demonstrate all that the company was doing to help the Gulf Coast recover. Of course, this campaign itself backfired, as members of Congress from affected areas attacked BP for spending money cleaning up its image instead of their beaches and fisheries.

Insider and outsider strategies are not mutually exclusive, and groups may use either or both, depending on circumstances and opportunities. The health insurance industry employs top Washington professionals for its day-to-day insider lobbying, but in 2009–2010 it adopted outsider tactics to fight Barack Obama's health care reform package. Most organizations, however, tend to specialize in one strategy or the other. Groups with money and expertise whose issues are narrow or nonconflictual usually take the insider route. Large groups whose issues are conspicuous and contentious are more likely to operate from the outside, relying on **grassroots lobbying**, mobilizing members to send messages that reiterate the group's demands to their senators and representatives. For example, when the National Rifle Association wants to prevent new restrictions on firearms, its members shower Congress with letters, e-mails, faxes, and phone calls supporting its position. The intended message is that people who care enough to write on an issue care enough to vote for members of Congress according to their stance on the issue. A rough rule of thumb is that the amount of attention that elected officials pay to these sorts of communication is directly proportional to the amount of thought and effort that real voters put into them. Members of Congress discount patently stimulated mail—that is, hundreds of identically worded letters—that may count for less than a handful of spontaneous, original messages. Indeed, some supposedly grassroots efforts, particularly those run by firms specializing in the business, are so patently artificial that they are dismissed as "Astroturf campaigns."

This is not news to the organizations that use this tactic, so some contrive to make the process seem more personal and less mechanical. Some groups provide appropriate letters that vary in wording, typeface, and styles of stationery; others ask members to use their own words but to emphasize suggested themes. Members may be urged to write in longhand, even to use colloquial grammar, to make messages appear more authentic.

Outsider tactics differ from insider tactics because they impose real pressure, even threats—sometimes veiled, sometimes not—pushing politicians to act in ways they otherwise would prefer not to. Politicians, then, are far more resentful of outsider lobbying tactics than of insider ones. Any student who has interned in a Capitol Hill office has seen the reaction when an interest group mounts a campaign to jam the legislator's phone lines for the day with calls from irate constituents, many of whom may not be well versed in the pros and cons of a policy. Indeed, such tactics can backfire when overdone; the pose of "standing up to pressure" has its political attractions, after all.

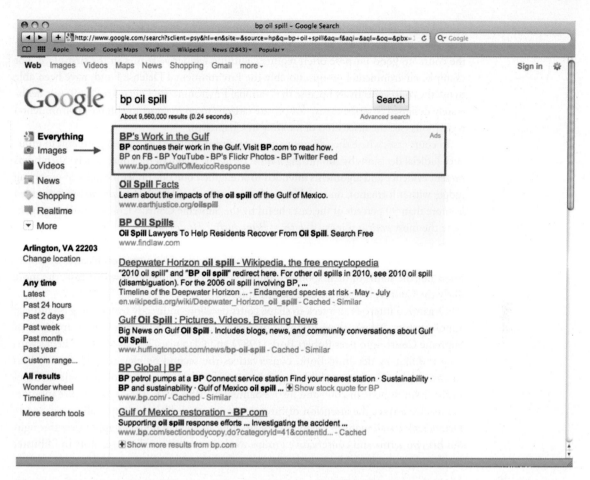

After an explosion of one of its Gulf Coast rigs led to the massive oil spill in 2010, BP had to control both environmental damage and the damage to its own image. The company spent more than $93 million on its "Making It Right" advertisement campaign, and purchased sponsored links that appeared first on Google and Yahoo searches for the term *oil spill*. No interest wants the kind of publicity that BP received during the spill, but the ability to communicate directly with consumers and voters gave it the chance to tell its version of the story.

Litigation

One tactic that is equally available to insiders and outsiders is litigation. Interest groups snubbed by lawmakers or regulators may seek redress in court, challenging hostile laws or regulations. This strategy is especially attractive to groups that can rest claims on constitutional rights and that do not have the political clout to influence elected politicians. During the 1940s and 1950s, when many black citizens were effectively denied the right to vote and there was only limited public sympathy for their cause, civil rights groups used the courts extensively (see Chapter 4). People in jail or accused of crimes, unpopular religious minorities, and groups on the political fringe—none of whom is likely to be championed by officials who depend directly on voters for their jobs—have all found redress in court. But then so have General Motors, Philip Morris, and Microsoft. Despite the notable court victories of some groups on the margins of society, large corporations with deep pockets make the most frequent and effective political use of litigation.

Although about one-third of the Washington representatives of interest groups are lawyers, only a small proportion of interest groups list litigation as their predominant activity. Using the courts to good purpose often requires winning legislative battles in the first place. For example, environmental groups, notably the Environmental Defense Fund, have been able to use the courts effectively because the National Environmental Policy Act (1969) was deliberately designed to make it easy for private citizens to go to court to enforce environmental regulations (see the discussion of *standing* in Chapter 8).

In court cases where they do not participate directly, interest groups may attempt to influence judicial decisions by submitting *amicus curiae* or "friend of the court" briefs. Such briefs present evidence and arguments intended to strengthen one side under the guise of supplying judges with information on social facts relevant to the decision. Today, *amicus* briefs are filed in more than 90 percent of the cases heard by the Supreme Court.[29] Controversial cases generate the most *amicus* filings; *Webster v. Reproductive Health Services,* an important abortion rights case decided in 1989, attracted seventy-five *amicus* briefs signed by hundreds of organizations.[30] Court decisions seem to be affected by neither the numerical balance of *amicus* briefs nor the status of their sponsors, but the more briefs submitted with a case, the more likely the Court is to hear the case (see Chapter 9).

Organized interests also seek to shape court decisions indirectly by lobbying on judicial appointments. Nearly three hundred groups joined the battles over Senate approval of Supreme Court nominees Robert Bork (1987) and Clarence Thomas (1991), liberals winning the first by derailing Bork, conservatives the second by elevating Thomas.[31] Less extensive but still vigorous lobbying campaigns faced off over the nominations of Chief Justice John Roberts in 2005 and Justice Samuel A. Alito Jr. in 2006. Lower court appointments also attract the attention of interest groups, with liberal groups calling on Senate Democrats to stall many of George W. Bush's appeals and circuit court appointees throughout his two terms and conservative groups working with Republican senators to filibuster many judges appointed by Barack Obama at the beginning of his administration.

Electoral Politics and Political Action Committees

Both outsiders and insiders use electoral politics to influence elected officials, but insiders offer electoral help, while outsiders more commonly threaten electoral harm. Groups unhappy with current policy always can try to replace the current decision makers with friendlier ones by recruiting and financing challengers, but this tactic is used mainly by partisan or ideological organizations. For example, GOPAC, chaired by Georgia Republican Newt Gingrich from 1986 to 1995, when he became House Speaker, nurtured the political careers of many of the Republican freshmen elected to the House in 1994. EMILY's List, a group dedicated to recruiting and training pro-choice women to run for office, has played an important role in many campaigns since the early 1990s. More typically, though, groups monitor and publicize the voting records of elected officials on their key issues. The idea is to identify friends and enemies so that campaign contributors and voters sympathetic to the group know which politicians to reward and which to punish (see box "The Return of the Dirty Dozen"). Interest groups act most conspicuously in electoral politics, however, through PACs.

As noted in Chapter 11, modern election campaigns are unavoidably expensive. Candidates who are not independently wealthy have to rely primarily on private individuals and PACs to pay the bills. In their modern form, PACs are a creation of the Federal Election

THE RETURN OF THE DIRTY DOZEN

strategy and choice

During the 1970s an environmental lobby, Environmental Action (EA), compiled and publicized a list of the "Dirty Dozen," twelve members of Congress who supposedly had the worst environmental records (according to EA's standards). The group shrewdly targeted members who were vulnerable as well as objectionable. In elections from 1972 through 1980, twenty-four of the fifty-two who made the list (some more than once) were defeated—a striking record when compared with the greater-than-90-percent success rate of incumbents during the period. A consultant who worked on the campaigns claimed that the tactic "was very effective at making congressmen think twice about certain votes. There were numerous examples of members of their staff calling and saying, 'Is the congressman close to being on the list?' or 'Is this vote going to be used to determine the list?'"[1]

The group's later campaigns were less successful as it ran out of vulnerable targets, and it faded away. But another environmental alliance, the League of Conservation Voters (LCV), revived the tactic for the 1996 election and has since used it with considerable success. In elections from 1996 through 2010, more than 60 percent of the members of Congress were targeted as the Dirty Dozen.[2] Like EA, LCV deliberately targeted close races where its investment—including $12.5 million in independent expenditures during this period[3]—had a reasonable chance of paying off. Its goals were both to defeat objectionable candidates and to demonstrate the perils of opposing environmental interests. The tactic's potential was underlined by the reaction of Bob Dornan, a former representative trying in 1998 to recapture the California district he had lost in 1996, to being listed. The flamboyant conservative, with a career LCV environmental support score of about 10 on a 100-point scale, said, "In my heart, I'm a Greenpeace kind of guy."[4]

ABOUT   ISSUES   MEDIA   STATES   ELECTIONS   ACT   SCORES

LEAGUE OF CONSERVATION VOTERS

ELECTIONS

2012 DIRTY DOZEN

LCV's trademark Dirty Dozen program targets candidates for Congress — regardless of party affiliation — who consistently vote against clean energy and conservation and are running in races in which LCV has a serious chance to affect the outcome. Since 1996, more than 80 percent of the Dirty Dozen have been defeated. Check back regularly for new additions to the 2012 Dirty Dozen. Click here to view the 2012 State-Level Dirty Dozen candidates.

THE DIRTY DOZEN

ANN MARIE BUERKLE	DAN BENISHEK	DAN LUNGREN
HOUSE : New York 24	HOUSE : Michigan 01	HOUSE : California 07
DENNIS REHBERG	FRANCISCO CANSECO	GEORGE ALLEN
SENATE : Montana	HOUSE : Texas 23	SENATE : Virginia
HEATHER WILSON	JOE WALSH	JOSH MANDEL
SENATE : New Mexico	HOUSE : Illinois 08	SENATE : Ohio
LINDA MCMAHON	MITT ROMNEY	TIM HOLDEN
SENATE : Connecticut	PRESIDENT :	HOUSE : Pennsylvania 17

Paid for by the League of Conservation Voters, www.lcv.org., and not authorized by any candidate or candidate's committee.

2. *League of Conservation Voters,* http://www.lcv.org/elections/dirty-dozen/ (October 12, 2012).

3. *League of Conservation Voters,* www.lcv.org/campaigns/2006-campaigns.html (February 2, 2008).

4. *League of Conservation Voters,* http://lcv.org/dirtydozen/callahan_poststmt.htm (June 3, 1999).

1. Bill Keller, "The Trail of the Dirty Dozen," *Congressional Quarterly Weekly Report,* March 21, 1981, 510.

Figure 13-2 The Growth of PACs

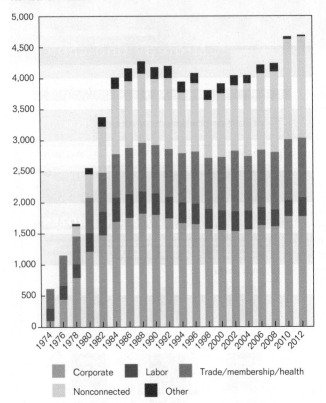

Number of PACs

Corporate Labor Trade/membership/health
Nonconnected Other

Source: Compiled by the authors from Federal Election Commission data.

Campaign Act of 1971 (FECA; as amended in 1974). FECA encouraged groups to form PACs by clarifying their legal status and specifying rules under which they could legitimately participate in financing campaigns; it also put the financial activities of PACs on the public record. To qualify as a *multicandidate committee* (the legal term for a political action committee), a PAC must raise money from at least fifty people and contribute to at least five candidates. The maximum contribution is $5,000 per candidate per campaign, which means, in effect, $10,000–$5,000 each for the primary and general election campaigns (plus another $5,000 if there is a primary runoff in states where one is required when no candidate wins more than half the votes cast). By contrast, individuals may contribute only $2,400 per candidate per campaign.

GROWTH OF PACS. The number of PACs grew dramatically in the first decade after FECA was enacted but then leveled out at about four thousand in the mid-1980s and has remained near that level since then (see Figure 13-2). PAC contributions to candidates grew in a similar fashion, increasing by 375 percent between 1974 and 1986 (see Figure 13-3). Thereafter PAC contributions grew only modestly until 2000, when the bitter legacy of impeachment politics and the closely fought battle for control of both houses of Congress inspired a new surge of PAC spending, which continued to grow through 2008. The sharp increase in PAC activity during FECA's first decade and the continuing financial importance of PACs since then are at the center of a lively controversy, for PAC generosity raises an obvious question: What do PACs get in return for their contributions? Indeed, assaults on the legitimacy of interest groups now focus commonly on PACs.

The term *PAC* is applied to a diverse set of organizations. The categories of PACs used by the Federal Election Commission (FEC) in reporting financial activities—labor, corporate, corporation without stock, cooperative, trade/membership/health, and nonconnected—merely hint at the variety.* Some amount to little more than an entrepreneur with a mailing list; others are adjuncts of huge corporations or labor unions. Some pass out millions of

---

*The first two PAC categories, labor and corporate, are self-explanatory, as is the minor category of corporations without stock. Cooperatives, another minor category, are special economic entities owned by their members, such as the dairy cooperatives run by groups of dairy farmers. The trade/membership/health category includes PACs representing trade, business, and professional associations. Nonconnected PACs have no separate organizational sponsor; the category includes a wide variety of ideological and single-issue groups.

dollars in every election cycle; others exist only on paper. Donations may be made at the sole discretion of the PAC director or only after extensive input from the PAC's contributors. The goals of some are immediate, narrow, and self-interested; others pursue long-term objectives based on broad ideological visions. Most PACs just give money, but a few also provide campaign workers, offer endorsements (who would not want to be regarded as a "friend of small business"?), produce advertising, advise on campaign strategies, get out the vote, and recruit and train candidates.

Upon which candidates do PACs choose to bestow these gifts? When they pursue the short-term goal of access to those in control of Washington's policy machinery, PACs will shift their contribution patterns as control of Congress shifts. In the years before 1994, when the Democrats controlled Congress, many business-oriented PACs supported incumbent Democrats who seemed certain to be reelected, switching to Republican challengers only when their prospects looked extraordinarily promising. Although most business groups are closer to Republicans ideologically, they were reluctant to risk loss of access by offending Democratic incumbents when they ran for Congress. The short-term pursuit of access to Democrats was at odds with the long-term goal that these business groups had of aiding Republicans who were more sympathetic to their requests. When Republicans took control after 1994, the short- and long-term goals of business PACs were more easily reconciled. Republican leaders threatened retaliation against PACs that continued to support Democrats.[32] As New York representative Bill Paxon, chair of the National Republican Congressional Committee, put it,

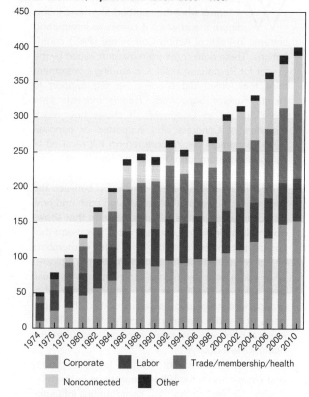

Figure 13-3 The Increase in PAC Contributions

Millions of dollars, adjusted for inflation (2006 = 1.00)

Corporate Labor Trade/membership/health
Nonconnected Other

Source: Compiled by the authors from Federal Election Commission data.

> Our members have felt they were carrying the legislative water for many of these groups who then gave their money to the other side. It's very difficult for me to argue that people should open their arms to those who are embracing their opponents. I certainly am not going to embrace someone who's constantly stabbing me in the back. We're making sure that the members know who's wielding the knife.[33]

Thus whereas in the four elections between 1988 and 1994 Democrats received an average of 54 percent of corporate PAC contributions to House candidates, in the four subsequent elections Democrats received an average of only 34 percent. In 2007, the first year after the Democrats resumed control of the House, their share went back up to 49 percent.[34]

What, Exactly, Do PAC Contributions Buy?

While numbers never lie, it is always tricky to interpret what the numbers like those in this figure mean when it comes to interpreting patterns in Political Action Committee (PAC) contributions. These data come from a report issued by the Center for Responsive Politics, a leading government think tank, titled *Big Labor Gave Big Support to Health Reform Supporters, Health Interests Lent More Support to Opponents*. It shows how much members of Congress who supported or opposed 2010's landmark health care reform bill received in contributions from labor PACs and from health care industry groups.

The figure shows a clear correlation between the source of a representative's campaign cash and how he or she voted on this bill, a correlation that shows up on bill after bill in Congress. Does this mean that campaign contributions "buy" the votes of members of Congress? Did the supporters of Obama's plan—all of whom were Democrats—back it simply because they relied so heavily on the support of the labor groups who advocated its passage? Did the opponents of health care reform, nearly all Republicans, oppose it in order to court contributions from the health care industry?

One interpretation of the link between money and votes answers both these questions in the affirmative, contending that PAC contributions influence the votes of legislators who are bought and sold to the highest bidder. In this view, PAC contributions buy votes in Congress. Another view, though, holds that lawmakers are unlikely to shift their positions on such a high-profile, hotly contested issue as health care reform, and instead posits that representatives are able to raise large sums of money from a PAC because they have already taken clear positions on the side of that interest. In this view, PAC contributions are aimed at helping friendly candidates win office.

The PACs that work for the interests of labor or business groups have broad ideological agendas. Their goal is to maximize the number of seats held by people sympathetic to their views, changing policies by changing representatives rather than by

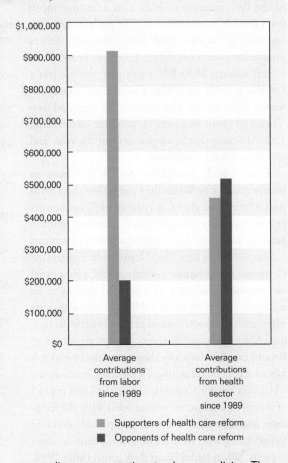

Supporters of health care reform
Opponents of health care reform

persuading representatives to change policies. Thus they support both incumbents and promising challengers, often concentrating their resources on the closest races in which their contributions will do the most good. The PACs of groups that want to buy as much access as possible—or even attempt to buy votes—will focus their money only on incumbents, especially those in the safest seats. Exploring the complex patterns that link levels of competition to PAC contributions can tell us what interest groups think they are buying. Simply observing a correlation between money and voting behavior, on the other hand, is insufficient evidence to indict lobbyists or lawmakers.

Some PACs also conduct independent campaigns for or against specific candidates, a practice that has become increasingly common in recent elections. For a campaign to be independent, it must not coordinate its activities with the candidate's campaign. The law does not limit independent expenditures, but they must be reported to the FEC. In the 2008 campaign cycle, for example, 146 PACs spent a total of $135 million on independent campaigns for or against particular House, Senate, and presidential candidates. Although the size of independent PAC expenditures is unlimited, PACs are still required to raise the funds for these expenditures in small chunks, putting a functional limit on what they will be able to raise and spend. The landmark *Citizens United v. Federal Election Commission* decision, handed down by the Supreme Court in 2010, removed even this constraint. By a 5–4 margin, the Court held that independent spending by corporations and by unions was speech protected by the First Amendment and thus could not be prohibited or limited. Instead of having to work hard to raise money for its PAC and then spend PAC money on an independent campaign, a corporation or union can now use money directly from its treasury to fund political advertisements on behalf of or in opposition to a candidate. With the funding floodgates opened, independent expenditures rose to $220 million with a month still to go in the 2010 campaigns, nearly doubling the 2008 figure even though the White House was not at stake.[35] So-called super PACs emerged, such as one named American Crossroads that raised more than $24 million from corporations and individuals to spend on behalf of conservative candidates in the midterm elections. Although it also empowers labor groups on the left, the *Citizens United* decision again raises the specter that the unequal distribution of wealth in society will directly translate into a distribution of interest group power that favors the most affluent voters on each side of the ideological spectrum.

PAC INFLUENCE. How does PAC activity affect public policy? According to one view, PACs corrupt the entire legislative process, giving citizens "the best Congress money can buy" because members vote with an eye more to the interests of their PAC donors than to those of their constituents or the nation. Proponents of this view say that PAC contributions buy votes and policy, period.[36] The evidence usually offered for this charge, however, is largely circumstantial or anecdotal. An investigative reporter or a campaign reform lobby such as the Center for Responsive Politics reveals that members supporting legislation desired by some interest groups—milk producers, used car dealers, physicians, the banking industry, and the National Rifle Association are examples—got more campaign money from PACs representing the group than did members who opposed the legislation.

Such evidence is inconclusive, however. PAC officials counter that they are merely helping to elect legislators who share their own conception of the public interest. It would be bizarre indeed if PACs distributed money randomly to friend and foe alike; no one should expect them to be that careless. The fact is, no simple matching of contributions to roll-call votes (recorded votes cast on the floor of the House or Senate) or other activities can prove that PACs buy influence. More careful scholarly studies have found that PAC contributions are driven almost entirely by party, ideology, and state or district interests and exert, at most, only a modest effect on a legislator's decisions. On issues that attract little public attention and do not divide members along party or ideological lines, votes appear to reflect, in a modest way, prior PAC contributions. But these are rare issues indeed. Despite the many tales of members who vote to please financial backers or who demand money from lobbyists in return for help, there is little reliable evidence that policy is being bought wholesale by special interests.[37]

This is not to say, however, that PAC contributions do not have other effects on some members of Congress. Both members and PAC officials admit that, at minimum, contributions ensure access—a necessary if not sufficient condition for insider influence. Doors are open to lobbyists representing groups who have supported members' campaigns. Furthermore, roll-call votes are by no means the only important decisions shaping legislation. Crucial choices are made before bills reach the floor, but little is known about how PACs influence the preliminary stages of the legislative process. One study did find, however, that PAC contributions stimulated committee activity on behalf of the PAC's legislative goals.[38] Interest groups are not likely to put much time, energy, and money into PAC activities without some perceived legislative payoff.

Still, there are some formidable barriers to PAC influence. Many important issues generate conflicts among well-organized interests, giving members access to PAC money no matter which side they take and thus freeing them to take whatever side is consistent with their personal or district preferences. Given the variety of sources of campaign money available to incumbents—private individuals and parties as well as the thousands of PACs—most should have little difficulty financing campaigns without putting their principles on the block. Again, the representation of such a vast array of interests through PACs buttresses David Truman's pluralist defense of interest groups. Furthermore, the point of campaigns is to win elections, not raise money. Campaign contributions are a means to an end—winning votes and elections—not the end in themselves. For incumbents, the marginal return on campaign spending is small; the prospective value, in votes, of even the maximum PAC contribution ($10,000) is tiny. Thus it makes no sense for a member, to please a PAC, to take a stand that produces even a small net loss of voter support. The sentiments of a member's constituents, when they can be estimated, far outweigh campaign contributions in determining roll-call votes.

Finally, one fact, often overlooked, is that members of Congress are in a much stronger position to influence PACs than PACs are to influence them. Like other forms of lobbying, the activities undertaken by PACs are largely defensive. They ignore invitations to fund-raisers held by legislators at their peril because they risk losing access and putting the interests they represent at a competitive disadvantage. Yet for politicians, granting access is relatively cheap; it does not promise action—it promises merely the opportunity to be heard. Groups are thus "awash in access but often subordinate in influence."[39] PACs that cannot afford to say no or to offend members by funding their challengers are scarcely the powerhouses of legend.

It is important to remember that PACs are not themselves lobbying organizations, though lobbyists sometimes organize PACs to try to bolster the political clout of the interest groups they represent. In fact, PACs form a relatively small, quite specialized part of the interest group universe, and only a small portion of the money spent to influence politics passes through them. Most politically active interest groups do not form PACs at all. Rather, they use one or more of the other methods described in this chapter to influence politics. If PACs were to be abolished tomorrow, interest group politics would continue unabated.

INTEREST GROUP POLITICS: CONTROVERSIAL AND THRIVING

The charges levied against PACs are only the most recent variation on the enduring theme that special interest lobbies subvert democracy and trample the public interest. Scholarly critics of mid-twentieth-century interest group politics emphasized two faults. The first was captured by Schattschneider's oft-quoted observation, noted earlier, that in the pluralist paradise, "the heavenly chorus sings with a strong upper-class accent"—that is, group representation is biased in favor of wealthy corporations and affluent individuals. The second was that rampant pluralism had let private interests hijack public authority. The mutually advantageous iron triangles formed by interest groups, agencies, and congressional subcommittees allowed special interests to dominate their policy domains. Agencies established to protect the public were soon captured by the very interests they were supposed to be regulating.

As we saw in Chapter 8, few observers today fret about iron triangles or captured agencies. The rise of public interest groups and the fragmentation of the interest group universe, as well as the ability of legislators to learn from past mistakes, broke up the iron triangles and liberated (or eliminated) the captured regulatory agencies. Public interest groups kept the spotlight on agencies and changed the political equation by promising political benefits (good publicity, a reputation as the defender of citizens) to elected officials who pursued the groups' versions of the public interest and by threatening political damage to those who did not. Organizational fragmentation undermined old accommodations: the more than two hundred organizations active in agricultural policy, for example, cannot form stable, autonomous alliances with agencies and legislators.[40] Changes in the way Congress operates also contributed to the breakup of iron triangles. During the 1970s, the legislative process became more open and permeable, committee and subcommittee autonomy declined, and influence over policy became more widely distributed. There were simply too many potential players for stable subgovernments to persist. Since then, the growing legislative dominance of party leaders has proven equally inhospitable to them.

The demise of iron triangles, however, has not ended the criticism of pluralist politics. The charge of class bias remains plausible. Business organizations and other groups representing well-heeled interests still account for the largest share of lobbying expenditures by far (see Figure 13-4). Even public interest groups represent largely upper-middle-class clienteles— well-educated people with enough discretionary income to indulge in expressive contributions to causes they deem worthy. The interests of poor people, welfare mothers, and the homeless may be represented, but only through the financial contributions of the more affluent people and organizations presuming to speak for them.[41]

Although iron triangles no longer reign, the proliferation of groups that contributed to their demise has created problems of its own. The clamor of competing groups is blamed for **policy gridlock.** With more active players, policy advocates find it harder to assemble winning coalitions. And with so many groups capable of vigorously defending themselves, some observers argue that it is impossible to initiate any change that imposes concentrated costs to achieve general benefits even if the benefits greatly outweigh the costs.[42]

Examples of policy gridlock are plentiful. The long battle to reduce the budget deficits during the 1980s and 1990s (and resumed with vigor in the 111th Congress, 2009–2010) is

Figure 13-4 Business Dominates Lobbying Expenditures

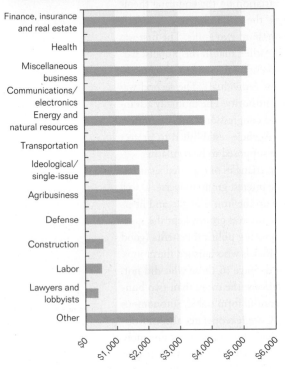

Lobbying expenditures in 1998–2012
(in millions of dollars)

Source: Center for Responsive Politics at http://www.opensecrets.org/lobby/top.php?indexType=c, October 12, 2012.

one. Although nearly everyone pays lip service to the ideal of a balanced budget, every spending program and every tax break is defended by organized beneficiaries, while deficit reduction, a diffuse collective good, inspires far less active organized support.

Yet if interest group politics produced only gridlock and maintenance of the status quo, then we would not have seen the passage of landmark health care and financial reform legislation in 2010. Both were stridently opposed by a multitude of interest groups, but the public spotlight shining on the issues and the active arm-twisting done by President Barack Obama and then–House Speaker Nancy Pelosi made siding with constituents or party leaders a better payoff for legislators than siding with potential contributors. And, of course, there were influential interest groups on both sides of these bills, ready to back in the next election the lawmakers who stood with them. If our rich ecosystem of interest group politics did not allow major policy shifts, then the airline, telecommunications, and trucking industries would never have been deregulated; tax reform would have failed in 1986; major deficit-reduction packages would not have been enacted in 1990, 1993, and 1997; and Medicare would not have been overhauled in 2003. Interest groups may shape but rarely stifle progress on the biggest issues facing lawmakers.

The health care bill demonstrated that a president claiming a policy mandate and legislative leaders using every trick up their sleeves are still the primary forces in the policy process. Specialized, fragmented groups are dependent on members of Congress or White House officials to build and lead legislative coalitions. Legislators control access, an essential commodity that is in ever-greater demand because of the growing number of interest groups. As the real insiders, members of Congress are in the best position to know when particular interests are likely to be at stake—crucial information for lobbyists facing a political world fraught with uncertainty. Moreover, opposing groups often simply cancel one another out, leaving politicians free to pick and choose among interests according to their own personal or partisan beliefs. There are some obvious and important exceptions—not many elected officials are willing to cross AARP, for example—but most interest groups exercise little clout individually. Collectively, however, they remain enormously influential, for they are the main source of the technical and political information that shapes public policy.

Although James Madison would be astonished at the proliferation of organized "factions" in contemporary American politics, he also would be the first to acknowledge the logic behind this development. The rules and institutions established by the Constitution, adapted to a drastically transformed society and economy, have made interest groups both inevitable and essential. Government distributes scarce goods and values, creating incentives for citizens to influence its decisions. Acting on their First Amendment rights, citizens exercise their freedom to combine forces and act together to pursue their interests and values through politics. The wider and the greater the impact of government decisions, the more diverse and intense is the level of interest group activity. Moreover, the more government does, the more officials need to know about the potential consequences of their choices. Elections make political information essential; complexity makes technical information essential. Modern American government could not function without the information supplied by organized interests.

Yet Madison also would be the first to recognize that factions continue to raise serious problems for American democracy. The interest group universe, though remarkably large and diverse, favors some interests at the expense of others. The resources needed to gain influence—money, access, and expertise—are distributed very unevenly. And some groups are able to overcome the barriers to collective action more easily than others. Narrow private interests thus often enjoy an advantage over broader ones.

These problems are somewhat mitigated by electoral incentives; candidates for public office rationally champion widely shared values and interests whether or not these have wealthy or well-organized advocates. The advent of many lobbying groups dedicated to some moral vision of the public good also has mitigated the problems just described. The institutional and social pluralism Madison thought would cope adequately with the "mischiefs of faction" has grown ever more luxuriant, embracing more groups that are more highly specialized and linked in increasingly complex ways. This change has raised the specter of hyperpluralism and policy gridlock, but interest groups can only stop action on the biggest problems when there is no popular consensus behind a single solution. Congress and the president find it difficult to balance the budget not simply because special interests defend every spending program and every tax break but also because there is no popular consensus on what combination of spending cuts and tax increases should be made to balance it (or, indeed, that balancing the budget is the most important goal of government). The conflicts among organized interests mirror, and sometimes crystallize, divisions and uncertainties prevalent among Americans. To paraphrase the comic strip character Pogo, we have met the special interests, and they are us.

logic.cqpress.com

Test your knowledge of this chapter.

logic.cqpress.com

Key Terms

■■■ Suggested Readings ■■■

Browne, William P. *Private Interests, Public Policy, and American Agriculture.* Lawrence: University Press of Kansas, 1988. A thorough case study of modern interest group politics. It focuses on the agricultural sector and shows how the proliferation of interest groups has transformed the once-cozy politics shaping farm policies.

Cigler, Allan J., and Burdett A. Loomis. *Interest Group Politics.* 7th ed. Washington, DC: CQ Press, 2007. A collection of contemporary essays that examine the development of organized interests and recent changes in interest group politics. The book covers such topics as the Internet as an organizational tool, the political role of corporate lobbyists, and interest groups and gridlock.

Lowi, Theodore J. *The End of Liberalism: The Second Republic of the United States.* 2nd ed. New York: Norton, 1979. A vigorous scholarly polemic arguing that private interest groups have taken control of bureaucratic agencies, allowing special interests to dominate policymaking and thereby subvert democracy.

Moe, Terry M. *The Organization of Interests: Incentives and the Internal Dynamics of Interest Groups.* Chicago: University of Chicago Press, 1988. A critique and revision of Mancur Olson's seminal argument in *The Logic of Collective Action,* which asserts that political

entrepreneurs and nonmaterial incentives often are able to solve the free-rider problem.

Nownes, Anthony J. *Total Lobbying: What Lobbyists Want (and How They Try to Get It).* Cambridge: Cambridge University Press, 2006. A recent analysis of the activities that lobbyists engage in, combined with in-depth interviews with lobbyists that reveal their goals and strategies.

Olson, Mancur. *The Logic of Collective Action: Public Goods and the Theory of Groups.* Cambridge, MA: Harvard University Press, 1965. A classic analysis of how the free-rider problem hampers organization for voluntary collective action and how the problem can be overcome.

Schlozman, Kay Lehman, and John T. Tierney. *Organized Interests and American Democracy.* New York: Harper and Row, 1986. A thorough account of Washington-based interest groups in the early 1980s. It concludes that the huge increase in the number of groups has not changed the balance of group power, for groups representing business interests still far outnumber their opponents.

Walker, Jack L., Jr. *Mobilizing Interest Groups in America: Patrons, Professions, and Social Movements.* Ann Arbor: University of Michigan Press, 1991. Emphasizes the role of patronage by government agencies and private foundations in organizing interests for collective political action.

■■■ Review Questions ■■■

1. What sorts of benefits do politicians receive from lobbyists? If these groups are so beneficial, why do citizens view them with such suspicion?

2. What actions has the government taken to foster interest groups? How do governmental policies themselves create potential interest groups?

3. How do "insider" and "outsider" lobbying tactics differ? What situations favor the use of each? When might an interest group choose to enlist litigation as it tries to influence policy?

4. What do political action committees (PACs) get in return for their donations to candidates? What evidence exists that such contributions are corrupting our political system?

5. How will the Supreme Court's *Citizens United v. Federal Election Commission* decision shape the role of interest groups in federal elections? Are there ways to reconcile the protection of First Amendment rights of interest groups with concerns about their influence over elections and policy?

14 The News Media

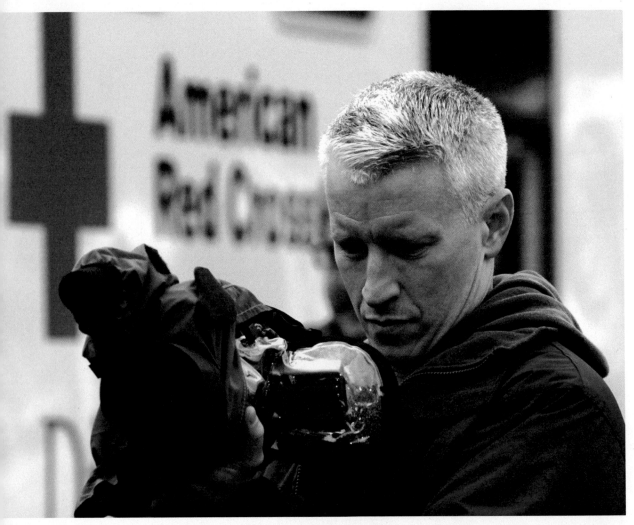

CNN correspondent Anderson Cooper shoots live footage at the site of the 2006 Sago mine disaster. The reporting of Cooper and others on the scene reflected what they saw unfolding in front of them, which led many in the press to conclude erroneously that the claim from family members—that twelve miners were alive—was true. In fact only one miner survived. Both the *Washington Post* and the *New York Times* got the headline wrong. As did Cooper on CNN, initially.

- What role does the news media play in a democracy? Are current news organizations fulfilling this role?

- In the United States, news is the product of private, profit-seeking businesses. How does this weaken or strengthen its value to citizens in monitoring their elected officials?

- Is the news an objective "mirror reflection" of what happens in the world, or is it a subjective collection of stories?

- How has digital technology altered the operations, profitability, nature, and influence of the news? What does the future hold for legacy products like daily print newspapers?

It was near dawn on January 2, 2006, when a methane gas explosion in the Sago mine, about an hour south of Morgantown, West Virginia, threatened the lives of twenty-nine miners. Sixteen escaped immediately, but thirteen men were trapped thousands of feet below the earth's surface, their state unknown. The trapped miners had enough oxygen in small respirators to sustain them for an hour, and they had been trained to find pockets of air and seal themselves off from carbon monoxide if necessary. While the mining company and state officials assembled rescue crews, it would be hours before any of them entered the mine, and even then, progress was painstakingly slow. Twenty-four hours after the explosion, the rescue teams were less than halfway down the mine. It was impossible to know where the thirteen miners were and how they fared.

Word of the explosion quickly spread through the nearby town of Buckhannon, and media—both local and national in television, audio, and print, traditional and online—arrived. They waited for word on the thirteen miners for more than forty hours before reporting, just before midnight on January 3, that one man was found dead but twelve were alive somewhere in the mine. Despite the odds, all indications from the scenes outside the Sago mine were that a miracle had happened. Church bells rang out at the Baptist church across the street, where family members were waiting, and ambulances sped to the mine's entrance.

Reporters and editors at print newspapers across the country hurried to get the story into their papers' morning editions. The *Washington Post* headline proclaimed, "12 Found Alive in W. Va. Coal Mine." And in the *New York Times,* "12 Miners Found Alive 41 Hours after Explosion." CNN's Anderson Cooper had been on the scene for days reporting the tragedy and providing wall-to-wall coverage for the twenty-four-hour news channel. He was reporting from a street corner near the Sago Baptist Church, where family members were gathering, when he learned that the miners were alive. Near the end of the segment, Cooper announced, "I'll tell you when the church bells started ringing, I mean, we knew something was going on." He then concluded the segment with these words: "We know now that twelve miners have been found alive somewhere . . . an optimistic note was expressed by the governor. We are anticipating a press conference at any moment now . . . It is truly a remarkable moment."

The problem was, none of that was true.

No press conference followed Cooper's segment, at least not for many hours, and when official word came, it was not the word reporters anticipated. Cooper stayed on the air until the wee hours of morning, finally signing off around 4:00 a.m. after covering the first official press conference held by the governor and mining officials since word came of the rescue. At 3:15 a.m., state and mining officials told reporters that only one miner had been found alive and the others were dead. They had first learned this from rescue teams around midnight and had confirmation from emergency medical teams just before 3 a.m. Around the country many newspapers replated their front pages, called back their delivery trucks, and reprinted the paper to change headlines from bold announcements of "12 Alive" to devastating versions of "Chaos at mine: 12 Dead." For some papers, like the *Washington Post* and the *New York Times*, it was too late—the correct version of the story would appear only on their webpages.

How did the nation's top media outlets get the story so wrong?

Coverage of the Sago mine tragedy raises fundamental questions about journalistic norms and the demand-driven nature of twenty-four-hour news that defines media culture in the twenty-first century. A closer look at CNN's coverage on the night Sago rescue teams found the miners reveals important examples of high-quality attempts at reporting and corroboration in real time, but also of the pressures of investigating a story on live TV with the whole world watching. Put simply, Cooper reported what he was seeing—reflecting the events like a mirror in real time on live TV—and despite several attempts to find evidence for the claims that the miners were alive, in the end, Cooper made an inference that they were alive based on what he saw happening in front of him. Here is what happened:

- Near 11:00 p.m. on Tuesday night, one miner was found dead near the cart that transported the men into the mine. The cart was empty—the men had taken their lunch pails, their oxygen masks, and everything else they had with them and left the cart.
- The governor made an official statement of this information to the families at Sago Baptist Church and to the media in the press center. News of the empty cart was interpreted as hopeful, since it meant the remaining miners may have found a collection of breathable air and built a wall to keep bad air out, as they had been trained to do.
- Near 11:45 p.m. rescue workers found the other twelve men behind a plastic wall they built to keep poisonous fumes out. All but one were dead. The rescue team radioed to the command center at the top of the mine that twelve men were found, one alive. The transmission had to clear eleven thousand feet and several relay stations to reach the command center. Rescue workers wore oxygen masks, making the transmission of the message even more difficult.
- State officials and mining officials in the command center listening over a loudspeaker believe they heard a message that said twelve men were found, *all* alive. They erupted in celebration as they awaited additional confirmation from the rescue team, which was moving toward a "fresh air" substation where masks could be removed and better communication would be possible.
- An unknown person or persons privy to the information from rescue workers used a cell phone to tell other mine employees and members of the missing miners' families that word had come that the remaining twelve miners were alive and that they would be bringing them out of the mine soon.

- Family members at Sago Baptist Church spread the news quickly among themselves. The governor was with them and heard the news too. Someone ran to the bell tower and rung the bells. Family members rushed outside hugging, crying, and screaming, "They're alive! They're alive!" The governor rushed to cross the street to the mine to confirm what he heard, and as he left the church, he flashed a "thumbs up" sign to those gathered outside the church (including some reporters) saying something about "miracles."
- The emergency dispatcher contacted the ambulance coordinator on site to say that the rescue team found the remaining men and they may need transport for as many as twelve miners. The ambulance driver asked if the men are alive. The dispatcher said, "as far as I know." Ambulances left the staging area and headed to the mine's entrance.

As these events unfolded on the night of January 3, Anderson Cooper was on air reporting live from the scene. Early on, he is skeptical of the reports he is receiving, but as word spreads and other CNN correspondents on scene share their observations, Cooper's qualifying statements, such as "if it turns out to be true," fall by the wayside. The next day, amidst accusations of rushing to put false information on the air, Cooper defended himself and his reporting. "We have to rely on the facts as we gather them, all the sources we have access to. We were tightly controlled physically . . . no officials came to talk to us. There's only so much you can do."

Journalists at Sago, covering a breaking news story and under pressure to get information out quickly, were misled to the inference that the miners were alive by believing that the secondhand information provided by an unknown man at the church was buttressed by primary source evidence, *by what they saw with their own eyes*: a church with bells ringing, full of celebratory family members that included the governor, who flashed the thumbs-up sign as he left the revelry, telling people to believe in miracles, as ambulances rolled to the mine's entrance. These are the things they saw! How could it not be true that the miners were found alive? Seeing these things, it turns out, is quite separate from believing and knowing one of the *many* things that this string of evidence might imply. With more time, without the pressure of live television or a midnight press deadline, reporters might have stopped to ask themselves what was missing from this list of evidence, like an official confirmation from the mine or the state, or reports from local hospitals on the condition of the miners in their care—or simply that none of the evidence before them was firsthand evidence and that all of it could have been predicated on the same faulty rumor.

What should CNN, Anderson Cooper, or the scores of other journalists who reported that twelve miners in the Sago mine were alive have done in the face of the celebrating families, a smiling governor, and ringing church bells? What would you have done? Without the luxury of time, the choices shrink. Sago is a tough case; surely much of the blame lay with mining officials who, once they learned of the erroneous leak to family members and media, decided *not* to issue a contradictory statement of any kind until the emergency medical teams confirmed the condition of *all* twelve miners, which left most families celebrating for three hours before learning their loved ones had died. But in the era of continuous, live news coverage, on cable TV and the Internet, every step of the news process is being done faster and in real time—and because of these pressures, reporters may be tempted to rely on one another's judgments about what is happening as informational shortcuts. Whether we call the reporting

READ MORE

logic.cqpress.com

Read the full transcript of Anderson Cooper reporting live from the Sago mine.

at Sago a "mistake" because reporters got it wrong by not waiting for official confirmation or merely a real-time reflection of what was happening on the ground at the scene, there's no doubt that the modern media environment has permanently challenged and perhaps even changed the standards of reporting, especially relative to where they were decades ago.

This digital revolution is only the most recent development in a long, steady stream of innovations in mass communications technology that have periodically transformed the news media. Each change made the news more widely available to more consumers. News has also become more engaging, with most technical advances enhancing the news report, first with engraved images, then with photographs, sound, and moving images, and now with an interactive relationship between news producer and consumer via the Internet. Marketplace competition for consumers' attention is a key driver of these innovations, prompting news providers to embrace new communications technologies as they try to get an edge on their competitors. The result is news that is cheaply and easily available to everyone. The speed and ubiquity with which today's news is produced demands a vigilant consumer who can sort through what is being presented as evidence and decide how much weight it deserves. The implications of this for citizenship, politics, and government are surely important—but it is too soon to tell exactly what they are.

DEVELOPMENT OF THE NEWS BUSINESS

The **news media** are the organizations that gather, package, and transmit the news through some proprietary communications technology. To characterize the news media as businesses does not discredit their integrity as suppliers of vital civic information. To the contrary, the influence of profit seeking has been in some respects highly democratic. Especially since the introduction of mass circulation and advertising, the news media have been in continual competition to increase the audiences for their product. The national broadcast networks, newspaper chains, public television and radio programs, twenty-four-hour cable news shows, and news blogs—even Twitter—all reflect the press's entrepreneurial tradition.

The following history explores the evolution of production technology, business organization and practices, audience characteristics, and regulatory environments that have continuously transformed America's news media.

The Economics of Early Newspapers

While editors of colonial newspapers shared the same desire to maximize profits that now drives modern media corporations, the constraints facing their businesses were quite different from what they are today. In colonial times almost no one earned a living solely by publishing the news. Instead, most early newspapers were run by people in related businesses, such as print shop owners and postmasters, who ventured into the news business because their marginal printing and delivery costs made newspaper publishing a viable sideline.[1] Still, producing newspapers in the colonial era was an extremely expensive undertaking. In fact, high unit costs—the costs of transmitting a news product to each consumer—characterized journalism in the United States until the mid-nineteenth century. Some of these costs stemmed from the nation's poor communications and transportation infrastructure. It was not unusual for newspapers to feature "breaking news" that had occurred two months earlier. (Compare that with the streaming news banners supplying viewers with instant poll responses to the 2008 presidential candidates' remarks during televised debates.)

Perhaps the main source of high unit costs was the time-consuming, labor-intensive printing process. Every page had to be composed (in reverse) from individual pieces of metal type. And the act of printing a single impression on paper with a wooden, hand-cranked press required thirteen separate steps. The best printers of the day could manage to print only 240 impressions an hour. The printing process itself was characterized as "physically demanding work, repetitive and often dreary, usually carried on in uninviting, foul-smelling (urine was the preferred substance for soaking the leather covers of inking balls), and poorly lighted surroundings."[2]

By the mid-1770s approximately twenty-five weekly newspapers were serving the colonies. Some, such as the *Massachusetts Spy,* helped to whip up public support for independence; others opposed the notion. But this era's most significant medium of political communication was the pamphlet. During the Revolution Thomas Paine's famous pamphlet, *Common Sense* (1776), became an instant best-seller: more than 120,000 copies were sold in its first three months. Eventually more than a half-million copies were published.[3] The pamphlet was the preferred medium for good reason. More durable than newspapers, it could (much like used college textbooks) be passed easily from reader to reader. Where sufficient demand existed, in fact, commentaries or reporting that first appeared in a weekly paper—as with the *Federalist* essays—would be republished in pamphlet form to allow wider circulation.

With the emergence of the Federalist and Democratic-Republican parties in the 1790s, commercial concerns redirected newspapers toward politics. Almost immediately the parties launched newspapers wherever they competed in order to advance their particular vision for the Republic. Objective reporting had little place in these partisan organs. Instead, their pages advocated party platforms, promoted candidates, and attacked the opposition.[4] These party-sponsored newspapers did not attract large audiences. According to one estimate, during the first few decades of the Republic the number of subscribers held steady at approximately four thousand, most of whom were likely voters, already committed to a party.[5] The laws of supply and demand could not be defied for the long term, however; the papers had to be subsidized by the parties. And, when possible, party politicians turned to the government for subsidies in the form of printing contracts or appointment of newspaper editors as local postmasters.

The union of press and party politics was fully realized during the administration of Andrew Jackson (1829–1837). Three of the five members of Jackson's group of close advisers (identified in the press as his "kitchen cabinet") were seasoned journalists, including Postmaster General Amos Kendall, whom the opposition press dubbed "Jackson's lying machine." Jackson also developed a close relationship with Francis Blair, editor of the *Washington Globe,* with whom he exchanged government printing contracts for favorable news. In fact, Jackson appointed fifty-seven editors to patronage positions, primarily as postmasters or customs agents. This unrestrained use of the spoils of victory led even some of Jackson's supporters to worry that placing so many editors on the public payroll might compromise freedom of the press.

Thus, during the early days of the Republic, newspaper publishers came to serve as the agents of the party politicians who hired and fired them. Readers were more or less incidental to this relationship, except that publishers needed sufficient numbers of subscribers to justify the party's financial support. These publishers' real principals were the politicians who recruited and financed them. Publishers knew that if their papers lacked sufficient partisan fervor, their sponsor might withdraw its subsidy. Moreover, the government subsidy also might disappear if the party lost the election. Consequently, the newspapers championed their party as if their survival depended on it—because it did. In sum, within a couple of decades of ratification of the First Amendment, the notion that the "free press" would guard the citizenry's liberties against the designs of ambitious politicians had been replaced by dedicated partisan boosterism.

The changeable fortunes of political parties in election years provided a poor foundation for building a business. Many editors probably wanted to extricate themselves from the grip of their partisan principals, not so much to justify the Framers' faith in the press as to place their small businesses on a more secure financial footing. Somehow they would have to break their financial dependence on political parties.

The Rise of the Penny Press

While parties were generally interested in communicating only with the party faithful, businesses had an incentive to reach a larger audience, thereby generating revenue and attracting advertisers. But increasing market size depended on lowering prices, and that in turn depended on lowering unit costs. Until some cheaper, less labor-intensive way to print newspapers could be found, these small businesses would be locked into low readership and party subsidies.

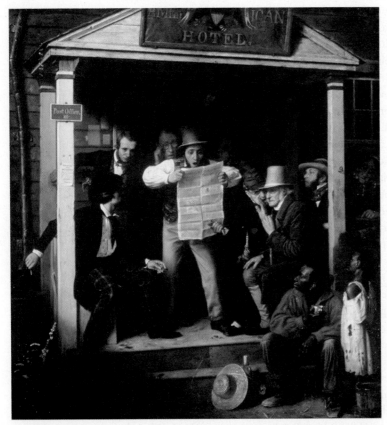

Baltimore artist Richard Caton Woodville's War *News from Mexico* (1848) depicts the singular role of newspapers in informing the citizenry during this era. Note that women and African Americans, neither of whom could vote, remain interested, if peripheral, participants in the scene.

Liberation began in the 1830s with the adaptation of steam power to printing and the development of faster, more reliable cylinder presses. These two technologies introduced dramatic economies of scale, allowing publishers to sell papers more cheaply, increase their audiences, and, in the process, split away from party sponsorship (see Figure 14-1). The *New York Sun* was the first paper to enlist this new technology, but not until several years later, when the *Sun*'s competitor, the *New York Herald*, hit the newsstands, was the full potential for cultivating a mass readership realized.

The *Herald* sold for a penny, while most of the competition was still wedded to six-cent, limited

Figure 14-1 The Rise and Decline of Newspapers

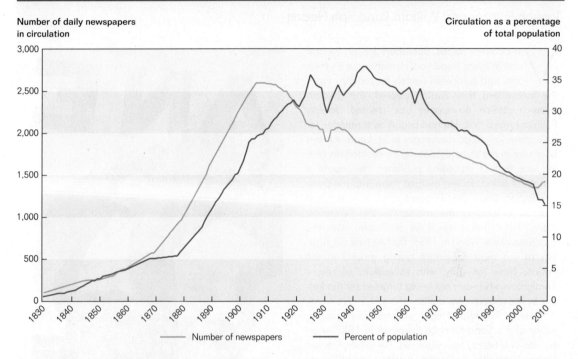

Number of daily newspapers
in circulation

Circulation as a percentage
of total population

— Number of newspapers   — Percent of population

Sources: The data for 1830 and 1840 are taken from Michael Schudson, *Discovering the News: A Social History of American Newspapers* (New York: Basic Books, 1978), 13–14; for 1850–2000, Harold W. Stanley and Richard G. Niemi, *Vital Statistics on American Politics, 2005–2006* (Washington, DC: CQ Press, 2006); for 2008, "Survey of Statistics" online, Bureau of the Census, Table 1099; and for 2009, Harold W. Stanley and Richard G. Niemi, *Vital Statistics on American Politics, 2011–2012* (Washington, DC: CQ Press, 2011), Table 4.2.

editions. Soon the *Herald*'s readership was twice that of its nearest competitor, and advertising revenues soared. The success of the "penny press" depended on more than price, however.* To attract new readers, the *Herald* and the dozen imitators that soon surfaced in the nation's largest markets expanded the realm of the news to include human interest stories and coverage of crime, business, and social events. Not only did these topics squeeze out space devoted to party politics, but editors muted their partisan affiliations in order to appeal to a broader audience.† To supply copy for newspapers' expanded coverage—particularly coverage of the

---

*Several contemporaneous social changes also aided the rise of the penny press. Sidney Kobre identifies these factors as the growth of cities, the modernization of transportation, the rise of a larger working class, the onset of mass production of consumer items, and increases in literacy, among others. Sidney Kobre, *The Development of American Journalism* (Dubuque, IA: William C. Brown, 1969), 208.

†In the first edition of the *Herald,* its publisher, John Gordon Bennett, a longtime Democratic Party functionary who had clashed with others in the party, denounced allegiances to all political parties and political principles. He claimed that the *Herald* would support no party or faction. Instead, he said, it would concentrate on reporting the news "stripped of verbiage and coloring." Michael Schudson, *Discovering the News: A Social History of American Newspapers* (New York: Basic Books, 1978), 22.

The Megapublishers

Joseph Pulitzer and William Randolph Hearst

Via different routes, publishers Joseph Pulitzer and William Randolph Hearst came to New York and competed fiercely for readers. From the innovations their rivalry fostered, the modern mass-circulation newspaper was created. Joseph Pulitzer arrived first. He had begun as a reporter for a German-language newspaper in St. Louis. After a brief stint in the state legislature, he decided his calling was that of crusading publisher. He bought a couple of ailing dailies, merged them into the present-day *St. Louis Post-Dispatch,* and demonstrated that by expanding the market to the "common man," large dailies could be profitable. With the purchase of the *World* in 1883, Pulitzer took his strategy to the most important testing ground in the nation, New York City, with its millions of recent immigrants who were not being targeted for marketing by the mainstream dailies.

William Randolph Hearst was named managing editor of the San Francisco Examiner in 1887 when he was only twenty-four years old. His father, George Hearst, a wealthy California investor and U.S. senator, had owned the newspaper for seven years. Eight years later, in 1895, the younger Hearst bought the New York Journal and challenged the World.

For a while, Hearst (like Pulitzer) became infatuated with holding public office. He served in the House of Representatives for two terms but gave it up to dedicate himself to "yellow journalism." Hearst's insatiable political ambition and megalomania were captured by actor, writer, and producer Orson Welles in his 1941 classic film Citizen Kane (see photo).

Both men used their newspapers to promote causes. Hearst's paper, like the man, was more flamboyant and erratic in its commitments. His political views vacillated from the radical left to the radical right. When he boosted Franklin Roosevelt for the Democratic Party nomination in 1932, he did so vigorously and with hyperbolic praise; his ardor was repeated a few years later when he turned against Roosevelt. Pulitzer, by contrast, employed his editorial pages (as well as the news articles themselves) to promote consistently liberal causes. Freedom of speech, personal liberty, and the excesses of "money power" were the staples of his commentaries.

In 1912 Pulitzer, in a bequest to Columbia University, established annual awards for achievements in journalism and letters. The coveted Pulitzer Prize is awarded annually on the recommendations of an advisory board at the Columbia School of Journalism.

war with Mexico—the *Sun* joined with several dozen other papers to create the Associated Press (AP). It remains the dominant wire service today, and is increasingly enlisted as newspapers cut back their overseas and Washington news bureaus.

Competition for a mass readership became even more intense at the end of the nineteenth century. Screaming headlines and sensational stories tempted newsstand browsers. Critics of these devices, many of whom worked for competing papers, derided these papers as "**yellow journalism**"—a reference to the yellow ink in which the comic strips, especially the nightshirt-clad Yellow Kid in Joseph Pulitzer's *New York World,* were printed.[6] These criticisms impressed publishers around the country less than did the huge circulations and profits megapublishers like Pulitzer and William Randolph Hearst were accumulating (see box "The Megapublishers: Joseph Pulitzer and William Randolph Hearst"). From 1870 to 1900 the circulation of the nation's daily newspapers grew from roughly two and a half million to more than fifteen million. By 1904 there were twelve million readers of Sunday papers.

Publishers of established successful newspapers in one city often tried to repeat their success elsewhere. The result was the emergence of the great modern newspaper chain. Building on the success they enjoyed after launching the *Detroit Evening News* in 1873, the brothers James and E. W. Scripps owned nine daily newspapers by 1900 and twenty-two by 1910. But it was Hearst who built the largest chain. By 1935 he owned twenty-four dailies and sixteen

In 1898 William Randolph Hearst's *New York Journal* stirred war fever with its unsubstantiated charges that the Spanish had destroyed the U.S. battleship *Maine* in a Cuban harbor.

Sunday newspapers from New York to Los Angeles. Indeed, at one point he could boast that nearly one in four Americans read one of his papers.[7]

Like Hearst, newspaper publishers and editors discovered that their freedom from party control enabled them to influence public opinion and, in turn, national politics. And few were reluctant to assume their weighty civic responsibility as opinion leaders. The transformation of newspapers into instruments of mass communication meant that politicians frequently found themselves genuflecting to powerful editors and publishers. Some rising stars in the news industry, in fact, tried to exploit their influence on public opinion by running for elective office. The most famous instance arose in 1872, when New York publisher Horace Greeley won the Democratic Party's nomination for president. The power of the media was not lost on incumbent Republican Ulysses S. Grant, who welcomed another newspaper publisher, Henry Wilson, to be his running mate.

In many ways the period between 1883 and 1925 was the golden age of newspapers. They essentially held a monopoly over mass communication in the growing urban markets; national political news was reported in their pages or not at all. Moreover, the publishers and editors who ran the chains relished the power their monopolies conferred. Reflecting the

[handwritten margin notes: muckraking — exposure of scandals, corruption, injustices — 19th C. Progressive]

interests of a mass market, these newspapers took a decidedly populist slant on America's national civic life at a time when few other institutions did. Corporate greed, government abuse, and **muckraking** exposés of the rough edges of capitalism on the lives of ordinary Americans won the papers a large audience. Even cartoon protagonists—among others, the syndicated Happy Hooligan and the Katzenjammer Kids cartoon series—were lower-class, immigrant urchins.[8] The most vivid demonstration of this medium's willingness to exercise its power came in 1898, when the Pulitzer and Hearst chains declared war on Spain. Shortly thereafter, Congress issued an official declaration of war. During the heat of jingoistic propaganda, the sales of the two New York papers soared to one and a half million copies a day. Citing the inflammatory rhetoric, one critic of the fighting dubbed the venture "Mr. Hearst's War." The prime minister of Spain echoed this sentiment when he ruefully remarked that newspapers in America apparently had more power than did the national government.[9]

Over the past half-century the extensive power of newspapers has eroded substantially. One need look no further than the declining circulation figures to appreciate the extent to which consumers have substituted first radio, then television, and more recently the Internet for newspapers. In 1920, the year of the first commercial radio broadcast, about 2,400 daily newspapers dotted the nation with a circulation encompassing 31 percent of the population. By 2006 the number of dailies had declined by 60 percent, and the daily news circulation shrank to almost half the 1920 share. With the loss of their monopoly on the news, the formidable publisher barons—the Pulitzers and Hearsts—disappeared from the political landscape.

The Emergence of Radio and Television

In 1920 Westinghouse launched the nation's first commercial radio station, KDKA, in Pittsburgh. Within a few years five hundred stations were broadcasting to an audience of two million. By 1930 just over 40 percent of all households owned radios.[10] Despite its advantages, radio initially had little to do with civic affairs. During its first decade, most radio news consisted of brief on-the-hour announcements, which the newspapers welcomed because they believed readers would then turn to them for the "whole story." By the early 1930s, however, radio was beginning to take advertising dollars away from the papers. In 1933 the newspaper association organized a news boycott of radio. No longer could radio networks draw news from the papers or the AP wire service, which the newspaper industry effectively controlled. The boycott collapsed quickly, however, under pressure from advertisers and independent broadcasters. Within several years, the print industry's efforts to keep radio broadcasting out of the news business was history.[11]

For several decades radio threatened to eclipse newspapers as the primary news medium. As early as 1940 *Fortune* magazine reported that most respondents to its reader survey claimed to get their news mainly from the radio. President Franklin D. Roosevelt noted the rapid growth of radios as a common household appliance and strategically used radio communication during his presidency. In 1933 shortly after his inauguration he went on the air nationwide to announce a brief "bank holiday" (closing) and emergency legislation to bolster the banks' solvency. The size of his audience and the outpouring of support prompted the president to deliver more national radio addresses. Altogether he delivered thirty "fireside chats." In Figure 14-2, which is taken from archival material found in Roosevelt's Oval Office files, we can see the extent to which the radio audience swelled over a five-year period, from

Figure 14-2   FDR Radio Audience Ratings, 1936–1941

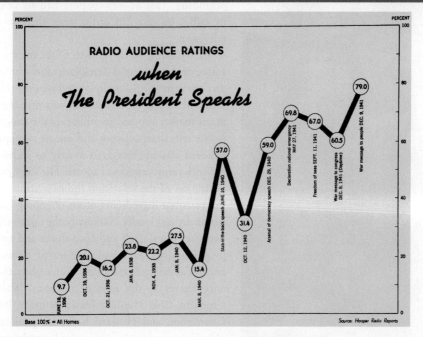

This chart, found in President Roosevelt's office files, depicts the early development of mass audiences in presidential communications.

Source: Hooper Radio Reports; Courtesy of Franklin D. Roosevelt Presidential Library.

1936 to 1941. Of course, the last rating of 79 percent of all households came after Japan's attack on Pearl Harbor and the U.S. entry into the Second World War.*

Throughout World War II Roosevelt's fireside chats and regular news broadcasts kept the American public informed about the war's progress. Today, radio remains a significant but distinctly secondary source of news. Rather, the medium has found a special niche in the talk radio format—particularly in syndicated and call-in programs with a conservative slant on public affairs. One 2004 study found national and local conservative talk programs totaled forty thousand broadcast hours a week throughout the country, compared to only three thousand for liberal talk shows.[12]

Although television technology was developed by the 1930s, the television broadcast industry did not take root until the close of the war in 1945 as national production turned from weapons to consumer goods. The 1950s witnessed astonishing growth as the public embraced television as an essential home appliance. From 1950 to 1960 the television audience exploded from six to sixty million viewers, more than 88 percent of U.S. households.[13] By the end of the 1960s the penetration of televisions into America's

---

*Note the small discrepancies between the numbers of homes tuned into Roosevelt's addresses and the percentages of households actually owning radios in Figure 14-3. They suggest that everyone owning a radio listened to FDR's fireside chats. In fact, more households are reported listening than actually owning a radio. Although these small differences could easily reflect differences in measurement, they are consistent with the anecdotal evidence that neighbors gathered around the radio to hear the president.

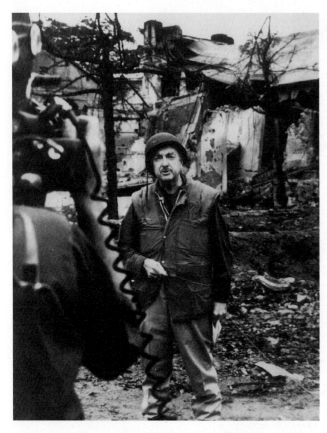

On location in Vietnam in the aftermath of the Tet Offensive in 1968, CBS anchor Walter Cronkite broke from the standard of objective journalism when he concluded his report with the judgment that the war would end in a stalemate. At the same time, our military leaders were privately concluding that the severe casualties inflicted on the Vietcong and North Vietnamese forces constituted a decisive victory for the United States. Nonetheless, Cronkite's assessment confirmed the numerous news images, and one month later U.S. president Lyndon B. Johnson announced he would not seek reelection.

homes was nearly complete. Households with television outnumbered those with indoor plumbing. Just as newspapers had to adapt to radio, so too did radio with the rise of television.

Contributing to the growth of the television audience was the rapid development of a broadcast infrastructure—locally owned stations affiliated with one of three national networks. Each major market also had an affiliate of the national public television network and one or two independent stations relegated mostly to showing network reruns and local sports. The early concentration of the television industry contained the essential ingredients of an oligopoly both nationally and locally. Nationally, the three major networks dominated audience shares and news programming. This was the era of network anchors as national celebrities. With nightly audience shares in the tens of millions, Walter Cronkite, Chet Huntley, David Brinkley, John Chancellor, and Howard K. Smith projected objectivity and authority as guides to current events. For many Americans the nightly evening network news became their chief source of news.

But as with every other news technology reviewed here, market dominance is never permanent. Even at the peak of network television in the early 1980s, when 42 percent of the television audience regularly tuned into one of the three evening network news programs, cable was on the horizon. Over the next two decades cable and satellite, which initially served a largely rural niche

market that lay beyond clear over-the-air broadcast signals, would take away a large chunk of the networks' market share in all programming areas, including news. In 1970 less than 10 percent of viewers received cable. Over time, as cable providers began to invest heavily in laying lines into urban and suburban markets, they began offering substantially more channels to lure new subscribers. Where in 1970 the average subscriber had seven channels available, by 2000 this subscriber enjoyed over sixty-three options.[14] Cable providers' strategy of innovation and marketing succeeded. Today, the share of television households subscribing to cable or comparable satellite services is just short of 90 percent.

Broadcast Technology Introduces Regulation

The advent of radio not only introduced a major new player to a news industry; it exploited a commons—the airwaves—that drew government into the regulation of the news for the first time. During the early 1920s hundreds of stations came on the air, creating massive congestion problems across the broadcasting spectrum. Stations overcrowded desirable spots on the radio dial, causing signal interference and threatening to reduce this new medium to an unintelligible Tower of Babel. Broadcasters acting individually could not solve this classic tragedy of the commons. Soon, they accepted that the airwaves were a public good instead of their private property. The solution was to establish a government commission that could license stations to occupy a particular spot on the bandwidth. Since the airwaves belonged to the public, the Communications Act of 1934 reasoned that in return for their exclusive licenses, broadcasters must "serve the public interest, convenience and necessity." Although the law explicitly prohibited government censorship, it did not precisely define what the mandate to serve the public interest entailed. Responsibility for interpreting and implementing Congress's legislative intent was given to a new independent agency (see Chapter 8), the Federal Communications Commission (FCC).

Millions of Americans—with RCA television—will see history as it is made at the two National Political Conventions.

Look before you vote — with Television

As political leaders step up to speak, you're right with them on the platform. This year, television joins press and radio as a "political reporter" in Philadelphia at the Republican Convention, June 21, and the Democratic Convention, July 12.

The Candidate will be televised as he looks into the camera – talks to the people, face to face. His appearance, smile, gestures, combine with his voice to complete the transmission of personality. You have a new chance to know your man!

Important as any in history, the 1948 political conventions will be covered from start to finish by keen-eyed RCA Image Orthicon television cameras. Highlights and sidelights, all will be seen. And what the television camera catches will be sharp and clear on the screens of RCA Victor home television receivers...

Today, 40,000,000 Americans are within easy reach of daily television programs.

Television as an aid to good

citizenship and to the formation of an enlightened public opinion is only one way in which developments from RCA Laboratories serve the Nation and its people. Advanced research is part of any instrument bearing the name RCA or RCA Victor.

When in Radio City, New York, be sure to see the radio, television and electronic wonders at RCA Exhibition Hall, 36 West 49th Street. Free admission. Radio Corporation of America, RCA Building, Radio City, N. Y. 20.

This 1948 ad for RCA televisions promised a new day for democracy. We voters just need to see and size up the candidates for ourselves.

The 1934 law also instituted the **equal time** provision, which required stations to provide equal access to candidates for office. And by lodging this authority in an independent agency, they removed it as a resource for some future political party. Over the years, another prominent FCC policy, called the **fairness doctrine**, required that stations devote a share of their airtime to public affairs programming, and that they do so in a manner that is balanced and equitable. In 1987 the FCC dismantled this rule on the theory that it caused stations to shy away from examining political issues for fear of violating some regulator's view of fairness. This policy appears to have been correct, for shortly afterward talk radio with a political slant blossomed across the nation. Much of the public and many members of Congress have recently expressed interest in restoring some form of the fairness doctrine, but with the rapid spread of broadband Internet as an alternative, wide-open source of political expression, the issue may soon become moot.

In local media markets many newspaper publishers frequently sought to recapture advertising revenue lost to television by buying a local station. They were, after all, already producing news copy, and with over 40 percent of stations' profits typically coming from local news programming, newspaper publishers viewed acquisition of a local station as an easy extension of their business. In 1975 this strategy had become disturbing to an FCC concerned with reductions in the variety of available news sources. The agency adopted a regulation banning cross-ownership in markets where it had not already occurred. Under the new rules a newspaper could not control a local television station in the same market served by the newspaper.*

The Digital Revolution: Internet and Mobile

As televisions were taking hold in American households in the 1950s, the electronic computer was emerging on the scientific scene in labs and universities around the world. In 1969, the first point-to-point message between remote computers was sent from University of California–Los Angeles computer science professor Leonard Kleinrock's lab in Boelter Hall to Douglas Engelbart's lab at the Stanford Research Institute (SRI) in Menlo Park, California. With the transmission of the word *login* (successful on the second try!) what we think of as today's Internet was born. A decade or so later, the development of protocols to link multiple networks together were standardized and the concept of a worldwide web of computers was introduced. By the early 1990s commercial Internet service providers began to emerge, and by 1995 the Internet, which began as an idea funded by government and research entities, was fully commercialized. A private good became a public good, but not one people could use by free riding—they would have to pay some cost. Just how the public would get to access this collective good would take coordination among government agencies, research scientists, and the business community. This web of networks was uncharted territory, and without some mutually agreed-upon paths its use and development would be wildly inefficient.

In the early days, most people accessed the World Wide Web from a computer connected to the Internet through an analog telephone line. The transmission of data was accomplished using a device called a modem—a "*mo*dulator-*dem*odulator" that translated between analog and digital signals. Connectivity was slow, but progress was fast. In 1985, the FCC opened up unused portions of the digital broadcast spectrum for commercial use, and soon, a group of engineers and businesspeople came together to solve a basic collective action problem facing the industry: if commercial enterprises were going to leverage the connectivity of the World Wide Web, they had to make devices that could connect to the Internet and even connect to one another from anywhere; in other words, they all agreed on the goal, but they needed to agree on the path to that goal. The fruits of this work (see box "Wi-Fi Brings Together Government, Entrepreneurs, and Researchers to Solve Coordination Problems") are what we today call Wi-Fi technology, and in 1999 Apple computer put a Wi-Fi adapter in each of its new laptops, ushering in a new era of Internet connectivity. Continued cooperation between government entities and technology researchers and companies has resulted in subsequent advances in connectivity, particularly among mobile networks. The first commercially available mobile phones to connect to the Internet were launched in the late 1990s in Europe and Asia.

---

*In 2007 the FCC "relaxed" this ban on newspaper/broadcast cross-ownership in some of the largest media markets. In many communities the newspaper industry has fallen on hard times. Some newspaper publishers argued that adding a television station was the only way they could keep their newspapers afloat. However, these relaxed rules are being challenged in the courts.

By 2001, Americans were able to read their e-mail and surf the Web on their mobile phones—changing the way we access, interact, and react to the news forever. As with the other transitions to newly emerging technologies, news on the Web has changed the industry, particularly for newspapers. As more and more people read newspapers on their connected devices, the number of people who actually read the physical newspaper has declined steadily. Advertising losses from classifieds (which moved to the Internet on websites like Craigslist and eBay) and declining rates for display ads (due to decreased subscriptions) are forcing newspapers in America to reinvent their business models. Unfortunately, a large part of the reinvention has been the downsizing of newsrooms, with losses coming across the board including editors and reporters.

The first e-mail was sent from this computer on the UCLA campus to a computer at Stanford. The growth of such rapid-fire communication over the World Wide Web significantly changed the ways in which information is shared.

An Ever-Changing News Media

As a business, the news industry has been continuously transformed by technological advances as competing producers have sought a greater share of their potential market. The trend clearly points toward ever-expanding access to greater amounts of information. In this respect, market competition has provided a collective good in offering more people easier access to a greater variety of news. The history of the news in the United States has always been a story of change, which makes it especially instructive to present-day students, since the news media—indeed, the nature of news itself—continue to change rapidly. From the early days of the Republic, when several dozen weekly and a few daily newspapers delivered the national news, to today, when mobile and online sites routinely receive millions of visits, the history of the news media is essentially market responses to changing communications technology. As a new technology made mass communication easier and cheaper—that is, reduced the unit cost, the cost of distributing a news item to a consumer—those who produced the news either adapted, left the market, or assumed a subordinate rank. To a great degree the changes have been cumulative. The modern newspapers, themselves heirs of the penny press, are undoubtedly financially in decline because of the loss of ad revenue caused by the Internet, but they are likely to endure into the foreseeable future because their brands are strong—and consumers associate them with high-quality news product. New communications technology does not drive an old technology out of business, but instead forces these suppliers to more carefully target their audience and

greater share of markets due to technology → greater variety

WI-FI BRINGS SECTORS TOGETHER TO SOLVE COORDINATION PROBLEMS

strategy and choice

Wi-Fi, the short-range wireless broadband technology that so many of us rely on, is the result of surprising cooperation among telecommunication regulators, business entrepreneurs, and engineers. It started in 1985 when the Federal Communications Commission opened up several bands of the wireless spectrum (900 MHz, 2.4 GHz, and 5.8 GHz) for use without a government license. Initially, wireless equipment makers developed their own proprietary methods of operating on the newly opened bands. This meant that equipment from one vendor could not talk to equipment from another—limiting the potential uses of wireless technology, and decreasing each company's potential sales. Competitors soon realized that through cooperating with one another to set a standard method of wireless connection, they could all potentially benefit. The market was essentially suffering because of the chaos surrounding wireless connectivity.

Researchers from NCR Corporation and Bell Labs worked with the Institute of Electrical and Electronics Engineers (IEEE) to define the wireless connectivity standards. The IEEE committee, called 802.11, worked for many years to minimize conformity costs across the various vendors with interests in the market. The final set of standards was not in keeping with every company's preferences, but was acceptable to 75 percent of the committee members. Transaction costs may have been high, but the committee managed to keep conformity costs relatively low.

Engineers started building wireless connectors to meet the standards, and companies started making compatible devices. By 2000, the technology was standardized and named "Wi-Fi," and Apple Computer was offering Wi-Fi adapters on all of its iBooks. Today, Americans own countless devices that connect to the Internet using Wi-Fi technology, including televisions, cameras, phones, computers, and even cars.

The story of Wi-Fi demonstrates clearly that cooperation among government agencies and competing businesses can create a market—and a highly profitable one at that. All the market needed to flourish was someone to help the various actors coordinate their behavior.

tailor their news accordingly. Television news scooped afternoon newspapers, leading the industry to consolidate around the morning daily. Radio lost its general news audience only to find a new, secure niche in talk radio. On the whole, innovation in mass communications has resulted in a dramatic expansion of news as a consumer product in a highly competitive marketplace.

Thinking of news as a product in a competitive market helps account for the alacrity with which this industry has embraced innovations in communications technology. As previously noted, in addition to reduced unit costs, most of the new technologies have presented consumers with news that comes in a more attractive, lifelike package. Newspapers introduced photographs in the late nineteenth century; radio captivated the public with live sound; television initially offered anchors Edward R. Murrow and John Cameron Swayze reading news reports and interviewing public figures; the invention of Tri-X film in the 1950s allowed

Blogs and User-Generated Content

Blogs have come a long way since they hit the digital scene in 1997. No longer just a collection of personal diaries, blogs today span all topics and all points of view—from personal musings to high-quality reporting from journalists at legacy newspapers. Blogs have changed the publishing industry, aspects of public relations, politics, the entertainment industry, and journalism.

As of this printing, Technorati estimates the most popular blog on the Web is *The Huffington Post* (www.huffingtonpost.com), which has over one thousand authors and covers topics from the Academy Awards to presidential elections. It was founded in 2005 and in 2012 became the first digital media outlet in the United States to win a Pulitzer Prize for its original coverage about wounded veterans.

In an interview in *Wired* magazine in 2007, *Huffington Post* president and editor-in-chief Arianna Huffington called bloggers the "pit bulls of journalism" and credited their persistent nature for bringing important stories to light. Bloggers' openness helps break through the media clutter to illuminate important issues and is changing the way traditional journalism engages readers, she said. "Blogging at its best is deeply personal, and once readers get used to that kind of connection to a writer, it's hard for them to accept anything less."

Bloggers have influenced and continue to influence politics and journalism in important ways. In 1998, Matt Drudge's news aggregator, the Drudge Report (www.drudgereport.com), scooped *Newsweek's* Michael Isikoff by suggesting an inappropriate relationship existed between President Clinton and a White House intern. The story became known to Americans as the Monica Lewinsky scandal and led to the impeachment of President Bill Clinton. Similarly, various blogs claim credit for bringing to light (and to the mainstream media) the questionable provenance of the documents on which Dan Rather, the CBS evening news anchor, based his reporting during the 2004 presidential election when he questioned the service of President George W. Bush in the Texas Air National Guard. The documents were later determined to have come from people who lied about their origins and several CBS News employees lost their jobs.

Blogs have changed the media in another important way by providing the opportunity for consumers to insert information directly into the news stream. Through comment sections on blogs, readers are able to connect not only with bloggers and journalists, but also with one another. Sometimes these public connections help solve coordination problems by serving as a focal point for people with the same interests who previously had a hard time finding one another. The downside of consumer-generated content in the news stream, however, is that it becomes difficult to separate good reporting and truth from opinion and polemics.

correspondents in the field to report on camera; the introduction of satellite technology allowed live reports from anywhere on earth (and beyond); and finally, cable brought viewers many more news options, including some—like C-SPAN and ESPN—that specialize in in-depth coverage of a narrow range of news. The Internet is capable of distributing news from anywhere, whatever its format, to every computer or mobile device connected to the Web. And the Internet empowers a new, broad class of consumers—namely, those motivated to set up a website—and turns them into *producers,* allowing them to join the news media. This includes politicians. In March 2011, after the United States launched cruise missiles and airstrikes against the regime of Libya's Moammar Kadafi to create a no-fly zone that would protect Libyans trying to overthrow Kadafi, President Obama explained the military action in a nationally televised address. Immediately, critics responded, not with news conferences, but by posting their own videos. Sen. Rand Paul, R-Ky., went on YouTube to challenge the constitutionality of the action.

NEWS AS A CONSUMER PRODUCT

One might think that easier access to news and information, combined with the population's steadily increasing educational attainment, would convert the United States into that elusive, ideal democratic polity in which fully informed citizens elect representatives who enact enlightened public policy. Not so. Students of journalism and communications are quick to point out some potentially troubling trends that accompany truly mass communications. The proliferation of alternative media gives viewers the opportunity to opt out of consuming political information altogether. Even for those who are attentive to news, the profusion of programming choices may allow consumers to select those sources that they find most congenial with their political views, thus reinforcing preexisting beliefs instead of providing new information. These consumer trends portend not-so-welcome behaviors by the media in order to retain and grab people's attention—more sensationalized headlines and faster production of the news are just two of the consequences of our current media environment that make both the production and the consumption of news challenging. But recent evidence suggests people are responding. A report by the Pew Research Center's Project for Excellence in Journalism shows that among people interested in news, the ease of accessing media means more time spent reading, watching, and listening to trusted legacy media sources. In a crowded marketplace, consumers are looking for trusted brands, not just brands they like.

How the News Is Produced: Content and Form

Walter Lippmann, a newspaper columnist and co-founder of *The New Republic*, worried about democracy and its future. Writing in the 1920s, he saw a particular role for journalism in fostering democracy, and he had concerns about whether he and his colleagues were up to the task. He wrote, in *Liberty and the News,* that "[t]he news of the day as it reaches the newspaper office is an incredible medley of fact, propaganda, rumor, suspicion, clues, hopes, and fears. And the task of selecting and ordering that news is one of the truly sacred and priestly offices in a democracy. For the newspaper is in all literalness the bible of democracy, the book out of which a people determines its conduct." Lippman's vision of the press was one of sifting through the propaganda, rumor, fact, and fear to emerge with "the news"—the information that a good citizen needed to know to function in democracy.

This vision of the press requires a sophisticated cadre of both journalists and citizens that is perhaps unrealistic, but it is surely the aspiration of high-quality news operations to fulfill this role, or perhaps an even greater role in the connected twenty-first century—to enable people to be citizens of the world in which they live. But while Lippmann saw the challenges to journalism center on honing the craft of reporting, today's challenges are more complicated. Competition for news audiences, the twenty-four-hour news cycle, and the Internet have brought about structural changes to the news business that would surely make Lippmann shudder.

News organizations are businesses. And businesses have to make money or they cease to exist. While it may seem important to a functioning democracy to have a fully operational, high-quality press in place, news organizations exist independently from government in America and are, for the most part, profit-seeking operations. Most of the profits come from advertisers who want to expose audiences to their products. Because of this, news outlets do everything they can to attract and keep an audience.

SENSATIONALIZATION. One of the easiest ways to do this is to give the members of an audience what they want, which may be very different from what they need. As information outlets expand, on cable, the Internet, satellite radio, and even social networking sites like Facebook and Twitter, the need to give audiences what they want (so they will tune in and come back) grows. And often, to attract audience attention, producers and editors package the news in more sensational ways—whether that means bigger, bolder, more salacious headlines or vitriolic exchanges on air.

Some cable news outlets admittedly have an overt political slant to appeal to a particular segment of the population. The slant comes out in the selection of which news to report and how it is reported. Charges of **media bias** go back as far as the era of the partisan press, but it is a fairly recent phenomenon for broadcast news. When the three broadcast networks dominated the market, they bunched together in the political middle like candidates pursuing the median voter. If any of them had adopted a distinctly partisan or ideological slant on the news, the wayward network would have forfeited a share of the available audience, placing it at a competitive disadvantage for viewers and advertising. So, they all delivered pretty much the same news and garnered roughly the same audience ratings.

With the proliferation of competitive cable news channels, the situation changed. When the Fox News channel started out, CNN already dominated this second-tier news market. Rather than match the product of its larger, more established competitor, Fox sought to appeal to a segment of the market that was dissatisfied with its news options. For years conservatives, especially conservative Republicans, had viewed the national media as biased in favor of liberal causes and points of view.* Discerning an opportunity to gain a profitable market niche by differentiating its product from that of CNN and the broadcast networks, Fox News introduced a conservative slant by hiring conservative news anchors and loosening traditional constraints on editorializing while presenting the news. And it created energetic, combative talk shows propounding conservative views. In 2008 a third of self-classified "conservative Republican" survey respondents said they wanted to see their viewpoints presented in the news rather than news with "no point of view." Only 15 percent of independents preferred a point of view in their news. The share of self-proclaimed "liberal Democrats" wanting news that expressed their views resembled the preferences of their polar opposites: 31 percent preferred news with a liberal slant.

Fox's business strategy worked. About half of conservative viewers say they regularly go to Fox for news, compared to less than a fifth of the self-identified liberal audience.[15] By 2002

---

*Consequently, in 2008 it came easy for Republicans at their national convention to chant a refrain of "media bias" directed at the mainstream television news producers for questioning the credentials and preparation of Sarah Palin, the virtually unknown governor of Alaska, when John McCain tapped her to be his running mate.

Fox was winning larger audiences than its cable competitors. As President George W. Bush's public approval ratings and support for his party declined, however, so too did Fox's audience shares. Emboldened and consistently scoring third in the cable news rating game, MSNBC switched strategy by hiring openly partisan, Democratic-boosting pundits to ride the new political crest; it succeeded—albeit modestly when compared to Fox—in gaining market share, mostly at the expense of CNN.[16]

SPEED. Another way modern news outlets try to attract audiences is by being the place to go for breaking news. In other words, they want to be first. But, they also want to be right. It does an outlet no good to be quick to publish or broadcast stories that are always incomplete or wrong. This is what makes the Sago mine story important. Many outlets, rushing so as not to be left behind, ended up running headlines that needed to be reprinted or were just flat-out wrong. The tension that reporters, editors, and producers felt while reporting on Sago illustrates the often-inherent incompatibility of trying to be *both* first and right.

READ MORE

logic.cqpress.com

Review the complete nine principles of journalism.

REPORTING. Increased competition has given rise to many different forms of news programming and presentation. The Pew Research Center's Project for Excellence in Journalism convened a nationwide conversation among journalists that resulted in a statement of nine principles of journalism. Two of those principles are worth noting: (1) that journalism is in essence a discipline of verification and (2) that its practitioners must maintain an independence from those they cover. About the principle of verification:

> Journalists rely on a professional discipline for verifying information . . . a consistent method of testing information—a transparent approach to evidence—precisely so that personal and cultural biases would not undermine the accuracy of their work. The method is objective, not the journalist. Seeking out multiple witnesses, disclosing as much as possible about sources, or asking various sides for comment, all signal such standards. This discipline of verification is what separates journalism from other modes of communication, such as propaganda, fiction or entertainment.

And about independence:

> Independence is an underlying requirement of journalism, a cornerstone of its reliability. Independence of spirit and mind, rather than neutrality, is the principle journalists must keep in focus. While editorialists and commentators are not neutral, the source of their credibility is still their accuracy, intellectual fairness and ability to inform—not their devotion to a certain group or outcome.

READ MORE

logic.cqpress.com

Check out the *New York Times'* ethics code in full.

Verification and independence are cornerstones of journalistic integrity and ethics. As news organizations produce more programming and fill more web space, the levels of verification, independence, and reporting may vary. News programming that is aimed at entertaining the audience while providing some information on timely, important topics are often referred to as "infotainment"—a combination of information and *talk shows*

entertainment. These shows or websites are typically low on reporting—that is, they have very little verification, and the host or writer is rarely independent from the topic or guests on the program. Some people refer to **infotainment** news platforms as "soft" news programming, as opposed to news produced through the craft of reporting, which is often called "hard" news. While soft news contains less reporting, it may be more engaging and entertaining. In fact, work by political scientists Matt Baum and Sam Kernell shows that for people who are not that interested in public affairs or current events, soft news programming—and even programming like *The Daily Show* or *Saturday Night Live*, which are almost pure entertainment programs—can prove highly informative. The downside, however, is that it also provides more opportunities to mix argument and assertion in with fact and verification, leading to more shouting matches.

The effects of competition, sensationalization, speed, and the proliferation of infotainment programming have taken their toll on the press and the news business as a whole. In 2011 and 2012, the Pew Research Center asked Americans to rate the believability, objectivity, and accuracy of thirteen news outlets. Sharp increases over the last several years suggest that audiences are attuned to what is happening to the news business. Nearly two-thirds say that stories in the news are often inaccurate, and more than three-quarters say that new outlets tend to favor one side of the political debate over the other. Still, however, people say that the news sources *they* use, as opposed to news in general, are more likely than not to get things right. And even more reassuring for the press is the fact that people trust the information they get from the media more than information they get from any other public source—including the federal government and the president.

On average, though, only 56 percent of survey respondents thought the press was believable—down fifteen points from a decade ago. Over the last decade, every news outlet's rating suffered double-digit drops. Overall, Americans trust the press less than they did a decade ago. Of national news programs, the CBS show *60 Minutes* fares the best in terms of believability with 64 percent giving it a believable rating. See Table 14-1 for the full set of ratings.

The trends have a partisan tilt to them, too. Today, only Fox News is rated positively by at least two-thirds of Republicans (among national outlets in the survey). A decade ago, only one of the outlets was *not* rated positively by this many Republicans (NPR). The differences by party are presented in Table 14-2.

TABLE 14-1

Believability of News Organizations

How much can you believe each?	% Positive	% Negative	% Can't Rate
Local TV news	65	35	5
60 Minutes	64	35	10
ABC News	59	41	7
Wall Street Journal	58	41	19
CNN	58	42	6
CBS News	57	43	6
Daily newspaper you know best	57	43	8
NBC News	55	44	5
NPR	52	47	21
MSNBC	50	50	10
The New York Times	49	50	19
Fox News	49	51	8
USA Today	49	51	17

Note: The survey had an *N* of 1,000. Ratings for each news organization are based only on those who could rate it.

Source: Pew Research Center for the People and the Press, July 19–22, 2012, http://www.people-press.org/2012/08/16/further-decline-in-credibility-ratings-for-most-news-organizations/#current-believability-ratings.

TABLE 14-2

News Organizations' Credibility Ratings by Party, 2002–2012

% giving each a positive believability rating	Republicans						Democrats					
	2002	2004	2006	2008	2010	2012	2002	2004	2006	2008	2010	2012
60 Minutes	74	61	58	61	60	51	85	77	73	79	77	81
ABC News	67	54	58	55	53	43	80	73	69	72	76	77
CBS News	70	53	49	48	51	45	80	71	65	68	71	77
CNN	72	64	58	55	48	40	84	83	73	79	78	76
Daily newspaper you know best	63	52	54	61	58	49	73	59	64	70	71	65
Fox News	76	71	76	75	77	67	67	55	51	51	43	37
Local TV News	72	54	61	70	67	68	72	67	65	68	71	70
MSNBC	70	56	50	52	46	32	80	75	65	74	79	69
NBC News	68	57	56	51	51	41	82	72	71	75	77	74
The New York Times	–	50	43	41	40	37	–	70	62	70	76	65
NPR	63	44	53	50	51	48	64	63	60	68	69	59
USA Today	70	57	54	55	48	50	70	65	59	59	64	54
Wall Street Journal	86	65	67	66	67	57	75	67	66	68	68	65

Source: Pew Research Center for People and the Press, July 19–22, 2012, http://www.people-press.org/2012/08/16/further-decline-in-credibility-ratings-for-most-news-organizations/#current-believability-ratings.

Where People Get Their News

After local TV news, which provides information on weather and sports, broadcast network TV news is still the most popular place to get news for most Americans. An average of 22.5 million people watch ABC, CBS, or NBC News each night. On average, another 13.1 million people tune in for the networks' morning shows. *PBS NewsHour*'s average viewership is roughly 1 million viewers, putting it on par with various cable news programs.

Nielsen Media Research reports that at any given time on a typical evening, 3.3 million people (on average) are watching cable news. The most popular cable news outlet is Fox News, which has dominated the market for ten years despite seeing steady declines in viewership for the last two years. In 2011, Fox averaged 1.9 million viewers in prime time. By comparison, CNN averages roughly 654,000 viewers in prime time. Despite the popularity of cable news among a certain portion of the population, the Pew Research Center's Project for Excellence in Journalism (PEJ) reports that more people tune in to watch the broadcast evening news on NBC, ABC, or CBS than to watch all of cable news in prime time, on all channels, combined.

Second to TV, radio is the most popular source of news for most Americans. But PEJ reports that digital and mobile options are growing. Nearly 40 percent of people say they listen to Pandora or Spotify regularly, and 11 percent of people who own cell phones say they do this in the car instead of listening to the AM/FM radio (these data come from eMarketer). For the first time in years, NPR listenership dropped.

Americans are now fully in the digital and mobile age. PEJ reports that more than three-quarters of U.S. adults own a laptop or desktop computer, almost half own a smartphone, and nearly 20 percent own a tablet. Surprisingly, half of cell phone users and more than half of tablet owners use their devices to access the news; and when they do, they are visiting well-known, legacy news outlets like the *New York Times* or CNN, and they are staying longer and coming back more often than when digital news meant reading only on a laptop or desk-

Republican Party volunteers check their smartphones for polling results on Election Night 2012. While mobile platforms have widened and deepened people's experience with news, they still tend to refer to trusted sources for their information rather than announcements on sites like Twitter.

top computer. People's experience with the news is widening and deepening because of mobile platforms, but they are remaining loyal to their trusted brands for news. Very few people actually get their news by following the recommendations from friends or acquaintances on Facebook and Twitter.

Of all media platforms, traditional newspapers are suffering the most as we embrace the digital revolution, even though they are a destination site for readers of news on mobile devices. In 2011, PEJ estimates that print advertising revenues were down approximately $2.1 billion, or 9.2 percent. Online advertising was up, but the losses in print ads outweighed the gains by a ratio of about ten to one. Most newspapers are making ends meet largely through cutting.

As they have moved their content online, hundreds of papers have constructed pay walls as a way to prevent free riding. Why would people pay for the paper to be delivered to their front door if they could read it for free online in a format they quite frankly were coming to prefer? How to combat this classic free-riding problem continues to prove challenging to papers. The *New York Times* instituted a metered model in 2011 that allows online readers access to the landing page of each section and the paper's homepage, plus twenty articles each month, before being asked to pay a fee to continue to access the news on the site. In March 2012, the *Times* dropped the number of articles to ten free each month. Pay walls may help soften the fall-off from ad revenues, but it seems most industry leaders know this is not the solution to the revenue problems facing newspapers.

Figure 14-3 shows the rise and fall of people's usage of various media outlets over time. The graph, by political scientist Michael J. LaCour, labels the eras of rising media trends as print during the period when newspapers are growing and dominate the news market; broadcast, which represents the rise of broadcast television; post-broadcast for the period

Figure 14-3 The Rise and Fall of Media Environments, 1820–2010

Source: Newspaper, radio, and television data from U.S. Census Bureau. Internet households and mobile subscription data from World Bank. Cable TV data from Television Bureau of Advertising. Data are percent of households with each type of media by year, except for Mobile, which is percent of adult population. Graph by Michael J. LaCour, 2013.

ushering in cable television; and digital, which represents the Internet and mobile technologies. Notice that nearly every household in America has a radio, a television, and at least one mobile connected device. Many households have some form of cable or satellite television, but fewer than that have access to the Internet in the house (although they have a mobile device that may or may not be able to surf the Web). Even a third of American households have broadband Internet connectivity. The one declining line is for newspapers, whose circulation has plummeted to pre–turn-of-the-twentieth-century levels.

How the Media Influence Citizens

The plethora of news products raises complex questions about how and how well the American public learns about politics. Years ago, news choices were much more limited. For most individuals, the news consisted of the morning newspaper and one of the network nightly news programs. Everyone received similar doses of information at the same time. Now that news is ubiquitous, Americans enjoy far greater latitude in deciding what news to consume and when. What does the increasing abundance of news imply for the average citizen trying to make sense of politics in Washington?

POLITICAL POLARIZATION. One might think that the profusion of news across the spectrum of political ideology would result in a better-informed citizenry. Moreover, as consumers sample a variety of viewpoints, they might become more tolerant—or at least more sophisticated—in appreciating alternative points of view on controversial issues. Neither result is necessarily true. The main effect appears to lie in giving consumers the latitude to select news producers according to their assessment of their reliability. Moreover, the multitude of news choices allows consumers to avoid information that contradicts their prior beliefs. Hence, the profusion of news via cable television and the Internet might contribute to the trend toward partisan and ideological polarization (see Chapter 12) among those who are interested in politics.

GOING NEWSLESS. Choices will reflect differences in lifestyles and interests, and citizens may consume more varied amounts and news content than ever. Or, paradoxically, they may consume less. The same communications technologies that are broadening the availability of news are even more actively expanding the range of entertainment options. With so many choices, fewer citizens today may be tuning into news and current affairs programming than in the past.

If Lippmann were here today looking at the modern news environment, what would he say? That there is more news would likely please him, but that its quality as the gatekeeper of important information varies would no doubt displease him. In their book, *Blur,* Bill Kovach and Tom Rosenstiel write that the famous American news anchor and reporter, Edward R. Murrow, worried in the 1960s that truth was always at a disadvantage in the broadcast environment because it took time. Paraphrasing Winston Churchill, Murrow said, "A lie can go around the world while the truth is still getting his pants on"—an observation more apt today than it was decades ago when Murrow anchored the news.

News producers, from journalism professors to corporate owners, fondly refer to themselves as occupying the "fourth branch of government," perhaps envisioning their role as the gatekeepers Lippmann conjured up in his mind. We turn now to an evaluation of how this oversight branch is faring in the digital age of media.

NEWS MEDIA AS THE "FOURTH BRANCH"

The collective action problems citizens face in monitoring their elected leaders require some type of coordinating mechanism to solve. When citizens succeed in finding this mechanism, their politicians will be motivated to serve their constituency faithfully, or they will run the risk of defeat in the next election. In other contexts (most notably in political control of the bureaucracy), gaining access to information is no small task. Agents inherently enjoy an informational advantage over the principals they serve. They are quick to disclose information that places their performance in a favorable light and to conceal that which damages their reputations. We have already examined one solution the Framers devised to counteract the information deficit—frequent elections. Presumably, the Framers expected that ambitious challengers coveting the incumbent's office would ferret out incompetence and malfeasance in office.* But when challengers fail to perform due diligence on this score, or when there are no challengers, the press fills the void.

The early appearance of a free press in the First Amendment, which occupied—then as now—a special status within the Bill of Rights, is not happenstance. Both proponents and opponents of the Constitution's ratification agreed that the press had been crucial in mobilizing public protests and boycotts and coordinating the colonies' efforts during the early days of the independence movement. Recognized as a bulwark against tyranny, no one objected to including freedom of the press alongside freedom of speech and religion. Thomas Jefferson explained to a friend his rationale for listing it at the beginning of his proposed Bill of Rights: "The basis of our government being the opinion of the people, the very first object should be to keep that right."† In sweeping language, the First Amendment constructs a wall between the government and the press: "Congress shall make no law . . . abridging the freedom of speech, or of the press." Journalists are understandably inclined to see this provision as establishing a "fourth branch" of government charged with monitoring and reporting the self-interested actions of politicians in the other branches.

Despite the apparent consensus behind the principle of freedom of the press, the practices of the new government initially went in the opposite direction. The First Congress sent the Bill of Rights amendments to the states for ratification; the Fifth Congress passed the Sedition Act in 1798. It expressly forbade any criticism of the president and Congress, both controlled by the Federalist Party, that contained "any false, scandalous and malicious writing . . . to bring [government officials] . . . into contempt or disrepute or to excite against them . . . the hatred of the good people of the United States." After passage, the John Adams administration promptly arrested twenty-five people and convicted eleven, mostly newspaper editors aligned with the emerging Democratic-Republican opposition. The resulting political uproar contributed to the Federalist debacle in the 1800 election from which it never recovered. The newly installed President Jefferson pardoned all convicted under this act, and the new Democratic-Republican–controlled Congress passed resolutions of apology and

---

* Even opponents of the Constitution's ratification endorsed frequent elections but charged that the Framers did only a half-hearted job in installing the safeguards of elections. With the campaign slogan "Tyranny begins where annual elections end," Patrick Henry hammered ratification advocates on the grounds that elections were too infrequent.

† In a favorite, often-quoted passage of journalists, Jefferson added with customary rhetorical flare, "were it left to me to decide whether we should have a government without newspapers or newspapers without a government, I should not hesitate a moment to prefer the latter." But with the accumulated bruises that accompany public life, Jefferson came to despise the partisan press. During his long retirement at Monticello, Jefferson prided himself on never picking up a "putrid" newspaper and turning to poetry instead. Meanwhile, down the road at Montpelier, his longtime political partner James Madison spent his retirement (he outlived all of the Constitution's other Framers) poring over news from Washington and firing off letters to the editor to correct wrongheaded news and opinions.

compensation. The real lesson of this early test came with the disastrous political consequences of blatantly breaching press freedom.*

In the modern era public policy has buttressed the news media's independence. First, the idea that the press should be fair is left to the marketplace to address, at least where print journalism is concerned. Lawsuits by disgruntled candidates charging unfair treatment from the local press have always fallen on deaf ears in the courts. Hypothetically, anyone can start a newspaper, and certainly, anyone can set up a website or a blog. During the modern era the courts have extended the First Amendment's categorical language in two important areas of journalism that have served to insulate news producers from government censorship and intimidation. These concern government efforts at prior restraint and the press's exposure to libel and slander laws.

Prior Restraint

When a government seeks to *prevent* the publication and dissemination of written and recorded speech, it is exercising **prior restraint**. Beginning with a 1931 decision, the Supreme Court has consistently taken a dim view of this form of censorship.† Perhaps the most famous application of this doctrine occurred in 1971 when the *New York Times* and other newspapers announced their intent to publish the *Pentagon Papers,* an immense, top-secret compilation of U.S. government decisions and information about the Vietnam War.[17] The Nixon administration won an injunction against publication in a district court with the argument that publication would undermine national security at a moment when the war was still raging. In striking down the lower court's decision to suspend publication, the Supreme Court emphasized its four-decades-old precedent: "any system of prior restraints of expression comes to this Court bearing a heavy presumption against its constitutional validity." In other words, the government had to demonstrate—and in this case had failed to do so—that publication of the documents would damage national security. Today this presumption lives on, and prior restraint is rarely permitted, except in "troop-ship" circumstances, when a news report threatens to endanger the lives of American soldiers by publicly disclosing their position.

Slander and Libel

A similar strain of judicial reasoning crops up in libel doctrine. (This covers both written—**libel**—and spoken—**slander**—forms of false and malicious information that damages another person's reputation.) Civil litigation involving private citizens follows well-established standards of what constitutes libel and appropriate monetary damages,

---

* The most famous of those arrested was Vermont newspaper editor Matthew Lyon, who won election to Congress while in jail awaiting trial. In the deadlocked election of 1800 decided in the House of Representatives, Lyon casts the decisive vote for Thomas Jefferson.

† The case establishing this doctrine is *Near v. Minnesota,* 283 U.S. 697 (1931). Jay Near was the editor of a small Minnesota newspaper who used his paper as a forum for vilifying Jews and politicians. After a state judge ordered him to stop publication, Near challenged the state law that allowed local courts and law enforcement to shut down a "malicious, scandalous, and defamatory newspaper, magazine, or other periodical." In enunciating new doctrine, the Court did acknowledge that national security might sometimes require government censorship.

Twenty-first Century Media:
Mediums Change, but the Craft Endures

There's no doubt technology is changing the way news is made, produced, and consumed, but how different is the actual act of reporting in the Internet age? To find out, we went to three of the nation's top political reporters and interviewed them about the changing nature of their job.

Mark Barabak:
The Craft of Journalism

Mark Z. Barabak is one of America's top political reporters. He wrote his first political story in the late 1970s, when he was just sixteen years old, and he's been practicing the craft of journalism, in one way or another, ever since. Barabak has reported from forty-eight states, covering nine presidential elections, Capitol Hill, the White House, and one of only two successful gubernatorial recall elections in our nation's history. In his thirty-five years as a reporter, he has seen a lot of technological changes, but none greater than the development of the Internet and its impact on the production and consumption of news.

■ WATCH A VIDEO

logic.cqpress.com

Mark Barabak talks about behind-the-scenes reporting on a story.

Washington Post reporter Dan Balz always looks for a compelling story.

Barabak acknowledges that digital technology has made some aspects of reporting easier, citing the ability to research, view, and read primary sources from any connected device or to watch video sources on websites such as YouTube. But he also stresses that the things that made reporters great in the 1960s and '70s are the same things that make reporters stand out today. "The craft," he says, "is still the craft."

What Barabak is getting at is that in the era of Internet and cable news a scoop has been redefined to mean beating another reporter online or on the air by a matter of seconds. But reporter's careers, Barabak warns, are not elevated by getting a breaking news story out thirty seconds before another reporter. The kind of reporting that propels careers to greatness, he says, is the kind that results in having something *no one* else has—an angle that no one else has seen, or an analysis that no one else has thought of. How does a reporter get this kind of exclusive content? The answer may surprise you. "It takes relationships to break stories," Barabak says. "Trust and relationships.

These are the things a reporter's career is built on." Despite the ubiquity of information available online, the news business is still very much a people business.

Barabak admits, though, that there are important ways technology is changing the news. In a world of unlimited information, trusted sources of news are becoming more valuable in his view, not less. "What I do, what journalists do—take a huge amount of information, synthesize, and present it in a cogent and clear fashion—is more important than ever." Perhaps because of this, Barabak is not worried about the future of newspapers in the digital age. "People have been saying that newspapers are dying my whole career," he recalls. He worries a bit about the economics of it but not enough to give him great pause. "If you're a newspaperman, you live with the uncertainty," he concludes.

Dan Balz: A Cut Above the Norm

Dan Balz has covered nine presidential elections for the *Washington Post* and is one of America's great political journalists. In 2011 the White House Correspondents' Association awarded him the Merriman Smith award for excellence in his coverage of the president under the pressure of imminent deadline. Balz has had many front-page stories, despite the tremendous amount of competition for the paper's most coveted spot. Speaking about the real estate under the paper's masthead, Balz says, "Those stories that make it do so because the news is compelling and exclusive."

A front-page story at the *Post* gets scrutinized at the highest levels—going all the way to the paper's executive and managing editors. "Some front-page stories sail onto the page," Balz reports. "Others get surgery because they don't quite measure up in some way but are of enough import to justify the extra work." Qualities that increase a story's chance of making it to the top spot include having a fresh or original angle and writing that is a "cut or two above the norm," he says.

Front-page stories have always gotten more attention than stories inside the paper, but the pressure to be fast and first online is changing these editorial standards. The Internet operates as a fast-paced environment and brings a palpable competition to stay abreast of breaking news, "even," Balz adds, "if it is not all that compelling."

Balz's impression of the Internet is an "insatiable beast" that results in stories sometimes being written in great haste. The demand for speed, he says, "can sometimes mean mistakes that would be caught under normal circumstances slip by." But, he cautions, "if there are people who take the attitude that mistakes on the Web can be cleaned up and therefore aren't as bothersome as mistakes in the print edition, they are a distinct minority."

Jeff Zeleny: Big Fish, Big Pond

Jeff Zeleny graduated from the University of Nebraska in 1996 with degrees in journalism and political science. Since then he has traveled to all fifty states, six continents, and more than three-dozen countries. Only five years after graduating from college, Zeleny won a Pulitzer Prize for his work with colleagues at the *Chicago Tribune.* As national political correspondent for the *New York Times,* he traveled around the world with President Obama. In the spring of 2013, Zeleny made the move to TV news when hired by ABC News as senior Washington correspondent. In very little time, he has proven himself to be one of the nation's top political reporters.

Jeff Zeleny is senior Washington correspondent for ABC News and lives in the nation's capital.

What advice does Zeleny have for college students who want to become journalists or for young reporters starting out? "There's no substitute for good reporting," he says. "The digital age and the fast-paced world of Twitter have not eliminated the need to knock on doors and talk to voters." In fact, Zeleny thinks today's chaotic media environment actually *elevates* the need to connect with real people in real communities—and to listen to them. "I am always amazed at what I learn from just listening," he says.

Zeleny's advice to young reporters is simple: be a big fish in a small pond. Starting out at the *Des Moines Register* and covering the Iowa caucuses made Zeleny a young, go-to "big fish" during the Iowa caucuses in 2000. When the national media arrived in Des Moines, Zeleny was there to help them connect with Iowa insiders and political elites. He might have started out as a big fish in a small pond, but today he's a big fish in any pond. With dozens of bylines on the front page of the *New York Times* in 2012, Zeleny is writing American politics into history. Does he worry that new forms of media are diminishing the demand for high-quality reporting? Not too much. "The media may have changed," he says, "but the craft of journalism remains just that, a craft."

but when one party is a newspaper and the other a public figure—such as a politician, televangelist, or movie star—an altogether different doctrine kicks in. Simply stated, public figures largely forfeit legal recourse to protect their reputation. Not only must injured individuals prove that the story was false; they must also prove that the news producer acted with "malice" by publishing the damaging story it knew to be false. This test raises the bar of proof so high that politicians and other public figures stand little chance of winning in court.[18] Presumably, because the press is free from any real threat of being sued, it will feel less constrained in seeking and speaking truth to politics. Critics charge that such a high threshold of proof gives news media free rein to distort public figures' actions and motives.

NEWS AS THE PRODUCT OF POLITICS

From 1962 until his retirement in 1981, Walter Cronkite anchored the *CBS Evening News.* During his tenure, public opinion surveys repeatedly found him to be one of the most trusted persons in the country. When Cronkite matter-of-factly closed each broadcast with his signature statement, "And that's the way it is," the American public believed him. But is news reporting ever a simple, objective "mirror image" of reality? Americans are accustomed to thinking about news—especially television news—in this way. But Anderson Cooper's reflection of reality that night near the Sago mine earned him criticism from his peers in the news business, not praise. Perhaps it is more accurate and suggestive to think about news less as an objective record and more as a particular *representation* of facts and events.

Most political news does not actually claim to report events. One careful content analysis of two major newspapers found that barely 1 percent of politics-related news stories did so. Instead, almost all of the examined news derived from political talk intended to attract public notice. A quarter of all stories came from interviews, and another 42 percent came from press conferences and news releases. Altogether, individuals and organizations engaged in talk or discourse of some kind contributed two-thirds of all sources of political news.[19]

Political talk assumes many forms—from official declarations to press releases to "off the record" conversations with a reporter over lunch. Politicians undertake these activities because they are important to political success. As naturally garrulous as elected officeholders may appear on camera, political purpose lies behind all of their efforts to make news. They may be simply trying to garner favorable publicity or to build public support for their position on some issue. Frequently the ultimate target of their efforts is not the public but other politicians in Washington. But whatever the strategy underlying their public utterances, they must in every instance persuade a reporter that what they have to say is worth transmitting to an audience.

Earlier chapters noted some of the many news-making activities undertaken with specific purposes in mind—activities such as the publication of the *Federalist,* interest groups' creation of websites and newsletters for their members, the selection of Birmingham and Selma as sites for major civil rights demonstrations, campaign advertising, and the staging by presidents of bill-signing ceremonies in the White House Rose Garden. In each of these

President Theodore Roosevelt has been generally credited with introducing the trial balloon to the presidency. He would try out an idea on a reporter, but if it backfired he would deny the story and denounce the reporter. In these early days of White House correspondents, the president held the advantage in the relationship.

instances, someone—James Madison in one instance, the Reverend Martin Luther King Jr. in another—made news in order to influence the preferences of the public and, ultimately, the positions of other leaders.

The great majority of political news derives more from what people are *saying* than from what they are *doing,* but this does not necessarily diminish its status as news or its value to the audience. Much of what specialists and officials have to say is invaluable to a public trying to make sense of a particular set of facts or group of actions. For example, a scientist publishes a paper offering a new explanation for climate change; the chair of the Federal Reserve Board interprets the latest economic indicators at a congressional briefing; the head of a local housing agency announces a critical shortage of shelters for the homeless. In deciding to portray the gravity of a problem and in selecting the information to disclose—including whether to disclose it at all and when—these experts and officials are using the news media to achieve some political purpose.

Unlike television commercials produced by inspired Madison Avenue copywriters or academic journal articles hammered into submission by solitary professors, political news does not spring forth as the product of a single actor or set of collaborators. Rather, it is the

When Mark Felt revealed (and *Washington Post* reporter Bob Woodward confirmed) that he was Deep Throat in May 2005 it ended over three decades of continuous speculation. Felt was the second in command at the FBI and headed its day-to-day operations, which gave him direct access to hundreds of FBI interviews investigating the Watergate burglary. Suspecting complicity in the break-in and subsequent cover-up in the leadership of the Justice Department and White House, Felt claimed he had no alternative to spurring investigation through news leaks. Shortly before his tenure as Deep Throat, Felt had become embittered with the Nixon administration after being passed over as J. Edgar Hoover's successor at the Bureau.

joint product of two sets of independent actors—politicians and the news media—frequently competing with one another to define the story. As they engage each other in an enterprise of news making, they do so to achieve different and frequently incompatible goals. Politicians seek to influence the course of political events. Not surprisingly, they want news stories to cast them and their positions on the issues in the most favorable light. Those in the business of reporting and producing the news must keep a keen eye on their audience's interest in the proposed story and the willingness of their readers or viewers to rely on their coverage over that of a competitor. Reporters find it pays to demonstrate independence from their political sources and not simply pass along what politicians would like the public to know. The relationship between politicians and reporters, then, reflects a tension between reciprocity and competition.

Occasionally, unhappiness over the other side's performance erupts publicly in charges and countercharges. Politicians typically complain that the news media are biased and uninformed; reporters may charge that they, or the news, are being manipulated.

When politicians participate in news making, they usually have two audiences in mind: the public and fellow politicians. Although elected officeholders are always on the lookout for ways to improve the public's estimate of their service, much of their news-making activity is really an attempt to communicate with other politicians. The reason is simple: public statements often capture their colleagues' attention and force a response when a private communication will not. In 1993 the leader of the Congressional Black Caucus called a press conference to declare that just because almost all of its members were Democrats, President Bill Clinton should not take for granted the caucus's support for his proposed welfare reforms. Surely the caucus had said this repeatedly to the president and his staff, but by going public they placed him on notice that disregarding their views might damage his support with the African American community. Similarly, when a president threatens publicly to veto legislation nearing a floor vote in Congress, the threat gains credibility by having been publicized. If Congress were to pass the legislation anyway and a veto were not forthcoming, the president would damage his reputation both on Capitol Hill and with the public. Recognizing this to be the case, legislators regard public threats more seriously than threats conveyed privately.

Every elected politician in Washington has a press secretary on staff to generate favorable news about the boss. The president's press secretary probably has the biggest job of them all, befitting the importance of public opinion to modern presidential leadership. The institutions within which these politicians serve offer them numerous occasions to generate favorable news. Members of Congress can, among other things, conduct public hearings, publicly state their issue positions on the floor of their chamber in front of C-SPAN's cameras, and insert speeches and press releases into the *Congressional Record*. Every time a president steps outside the White House, he is trailed by the White House press corps, which looks for a story in a presidential speech, an appearance in an elementary school classroom, or even a foray into a department store to shop. In late 2009 President Obama and his advisers knew that presidential travel and media appearances on long-form talk shows ensured the network television coverage required to keep health care reform in the news and on the minds of a reluctant Congress. In one week's time the president was on *60 Minutes, Late Show with David Letterman*, and five Sunday talk shows. Members of the White House press corps, who literally go everywhere with the president unless the "lid is on" (and assurances are made to them that no news will be made in their absence), could conclude little other than health care reform was the most important topic in the nation at that time.

One venerable news strategy employed by politicians to transact politics with one another is the **trial balloon**. A politician "floats" a policy or some other idea with a reporter on the condition that the source of the story remain anonymous. If the story containing the proposal elicits a favorable response from others in Washington, the politician then publicly announces the proposal. Presidents often float trial balloons by persuading a member of Congress to propose a policy, allowing the president to gauge the political breezes before committing to a course of action.

Another discreet news-making strategy equally available to presidents, members of Congress, and lesser government officials is the news **leak**. This political term, first listed in Noah Webster's American dictionary in 1832, refers to giving strategically consequential information to the news media on the condition that its source not be identified by name. The "leaker" may be seeking to influence the public, other politicians, or both. The most common leaks involve a source revealing something good about itself or bad about someone else.[20] More than simply scoring points, the most important leaks force an action or a response from others in Washington. Arguably, the most famous leaker in American history was "Deep Throat," who continuously provided news reporters at the *Washington Post* leads for investigating the June 1972 break-in at Democratic headquarters at the Watergate Hotel. Later, as revelations mounted, a special Senate committee began conducting a formal, nationally televised investigation. Deep Throat continued his news leaks, leading Senate investigators to new and productive avenues of inquiry into the Watergate scandal, ultimately ending in Richard Nixon's resignation from the presidency and the sentencing of numerous White House aides to federal prison.

An interesting variant that appeared more than once during the massive leaking that accompanied the Clinton White House sex scandal was the "inoculating" leak. Independent counsel Kenneth Starr, who was investigating the affair between President Clinton and White House intern Monica Lewinsky, denied serving as the source of leaks and then blamed Clinton's staff. He chided White House aides for peremptorily releasing

The Dicey Game of Leaks

Protecting the anonymity of sources has long been a cherished right of the news industry. Some argue that extending such a guarantee to a source—say, a government official, such as Mark Felt (also known as Deep Throat), who is leaking information revealing the participation of other government officials in a lie—represents the highest service this "fourth branch of government" can perform for the public. Generally, leaks also make for great stories that attract large consumer interest. But leaks do not necessarily speak truth to politics. What happens when government officials anonymously leak information, including false information, in order to gain some political advantage over other politicians? Are news reporters being manipulated by government officials who benefit by remaining anonymous while spinning stories to their advantage or attacking those who disagree with them? Or are reporters—men and women who are proud of their savvy pursuit of a scoop—in cahoots with the politicians in order to break a stunning story?

All of these questions were raised by the Valerie Plame scandal, which showed that the use of "leaking" sources can be a very dangerous political game. In February 2002, the Central Intelligence Agency sent former diplomat Joe Wilson to Africa to investigate whether Iraq had purchased uranium from Niger. Wilson's subsequent report back to the CIA concluded that the sources documenting such a purchase were not credible. Almost a year and a half later, Wilson wrote an op-ed piece in the *New York Times* in which he criticized President George W. Bush's continuing reference to the African uranium purchase to make his case for the invasion of Iraq. Eight days later Wilson's wife, Valerie Plame—a career CIA operative—was "outed" in the *Washington Post* by veteran syndicated columnist Robert Novak,

who referred to his sources merely as "[t]wo senior administration officials."

The firestorm that followed centered on two questions: Who were these anonymous officials who leaked Plame's identity to the press—effectively ending her career, endangering field operatives, and possibly violating a criminal law in the process—and was the purpose of the leak to retaliate against her husband for criticizing the Bush administration?

It would take three years and the appointment of a special prosecutor, Patrick Fitzgerald, to answer the first question. Novak's sources included Karl Rove, President Bush's close friend and senior adviser, and Richard Armitage, then–assistant secretary of state. But the biggest controversy centered on special prosecutor Fitzgerald's questioning of Judith Miller, a reporter for the *New York Times* who researched but never actually wrote a story about Joe Wilson and the administration's response to his claims. In the end, Miller spent twelve weeks in jail for refusing to reveal her source—who turned out to be Vice President Dick Cheney's chief of staff, I. Lewis "Scooter" Libby, who was later convicted of perjury for his role in the Plame affair. Miller and her paper claimed that the "freedom of the press" allowed her to shield sources from revelation, even when crimes were involved. Federal courts recognize a vague, weak shield right by insisting the investigators first pursue other avenues to the information. But unlike many states that have passed strong shield laws that protect journalists from having to testify about their sources in court, the Supreme Court has never agreed that the "freedom of the press" implies this professional freedom. Eventually, the Miller case turned from a professional *cause célèbre* to a sordid instance of a journalist abetting a vengeful government official's effort to ruin someone's career.

unfavorable information in order to minimize any future damage when the news became public. The president's lawyer, David Kendall, vigorously challenged Starr's assertions, arguing that the independent counsel's office had waged an ongoing campaign of leaks and then placed blame on the president.[21] Virtually every administration in recent decades has at one time or another become entangled in a major scandal or conflict that was begun or fueled by leaks. In its eight years, President George W. Bush's administration had to deal with several major controversies based on leaked information. In the Valerie Plame scandal (see box "The Dicey Game of Leaks"), White House aides were finally exposed as leaking information that revealed the identity of a CIA operative in a vendetta directed at her husband, a diplomat who had recently criticized the administration in a newspaper op-ed essay.

News Producers: Reporters and Their News Organizations

Both the broadcast and print news outlets rely heavily on the talents of their reporters and correspondents, who work directly with politicians and other sources in uncovering stories and following leads. Sometimes a close relationship with a source will allow the reporter to scoop a story for his or her news organization or gain an exclusive interview. In their own words, reporters often say their job is about relationships with people who will give them the information they need.

The role of reporter is so pivotal to making news that a professional creed has grown up around the job, setting its members apart from others who work in the news business. Reporters make the initial decisions about the newsworthiness of a story and may play the chief role in defining the context or framework within which the story will be eventually reported. Within their organizations, reporters may act as a story's sponsor; "selling" a story to the editor is a venerable challenge and a source of journalistic pride.

THE BEAT. Both newspapers and broadcast media cover the regular sources of important stories in a systematic fashion by permanently assigning reporters to certain venues, traditionally called **beats**. At the national level, regular news beats include the White House, Congress, the Supreme Court, the State Department, and the Pentagon. Moreover, during political campaigns reporters are assigned to cover each of the major candidates. At the White House reporters receive much of their information at the daily briefings conducted by the president's press secretary. In fact, nearly all government agencies and senior officials have press staffs responsible for providing the media with information. More often than not, these are the agents who initiate "news" by issuing a statement or talking with a reporter. Beginning with the Afghanistan War, the military began taking reporters beyond briefings and embedding them in military units, in part to avoid a credibility gap and engender sympathetic coverage (see box "The Military's Media Strategy").

The beat system has several important implications for news. Because news organizations rely on a continuous flow of stories, beat reporters routinely file dispatches every day or so, regardless of their newsworthiness. The president is a favorite subject for daily reporting; a national news broadcast almost always mentions the president, even if only to report what movie was screened over the weekend in the White House theater. Recognizing reporters' need for material, the office of the White House press secretary supplies them with self-serving stories and ample photo opportunities.

If a particular government agency is not on a beat, it is less likely to generate news. In the late 1980s a major scandal was uncovered at the Department of Housing and Urban Development in which an undersecretary awarded government subsidies and consulting contracts as political favors. Although the scandal involved many clear violations of the law and millions of dollars, the story first broke in an obscure trade journal devoted to housing issues. The national newspapers and networks had not assigned a correspondent to regularly monitor HUD, but this specialized journal had. Beats allow news organizations to work efficiently because their agents in the field can specialize in particular sectors of the government. But they also steer the news toward sometimes trivial events while missing more important ones.

Another implication of the beat system is that reporters for rival publications and networks tend to write about the same limited range of events. Moreover, while on the beat they are in daily contact with other correspondents from other news organizations whom they tend to regard more as colleagues than competitors. The White House press corps consists of members of an organized club that has been in continuous operation for over a half-century. Given the close proximity in which reporters on the same beat work, news reports emanating from a particular beat tend to be similar across newspapers and even across the news media—Twitter, a favorite way for national journalists to communicate, has only exacerbated this tendency. Occasionally these social dynamics create a conspicuously narrow or skewed representation of an event. On such occasions, critics charge reporters with practicing **pack journalism**, in which journalists follow the same story in the same way because they talk to one another while reporting and read each other's copy for validation of their own reporting or interpretations.

SELECTING THE NEWS. To accommodate the various limitations in carrying capacities, how much news they can deliver, the news media must exercise discretion in allocating time and space to news stories. The media employ various criteria in deciding which stories to include in their papers and broadcasts. The first criterion is the authority and status of the source. Like no other politicians, presidents command the front pages and lead stories. Far behind are the Senate and its *members*, who edge out their counterparts in the House of Representatives.[22] Another consideration, according to some media observers, is the number of "talking heads," which may help to explain why the Senate rates more highly than does the House. The rest of Washington is normally relegated to coverage by the wire services (Associated Press and Reuters) to which newspapers subscribe; these reports may or may not make the inside pages of the nation's newspapers.

A second criterion for running a story is its level of controversy: conflict and disagreement are preferable to consensus. As journalists attempt to sell stories to editors and news organizations compete with each other, the news media often create controversy where it does not exist. In early 1995 Speaker Newt Gingrich dressed down the press corps for refusing to cast a bipartisan meeting with President Clinton in a favorable light. After Gingrich announced that the recently elected Republican Congress looked forward to working constructively with the Democratic president, a reporter asked, "What do you think it [bipartisanship] will break down over?" Gingrich retorted, "You just heard the leaders of the Republican Party say that

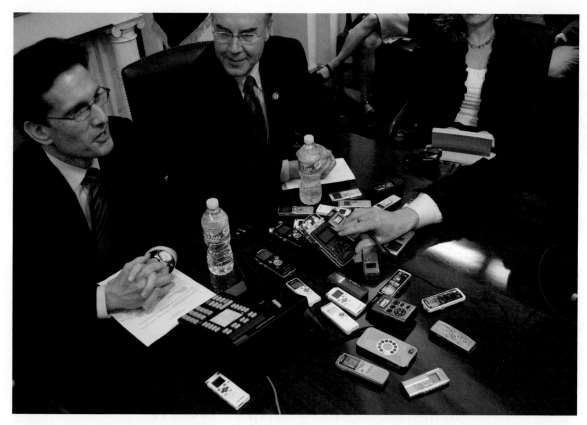

Pack journalism without the pack. This has become a familiar scene at Washington press briefings, leading more than one newsmaker to threaten to bring in a recorder and let it conduct the conferences with the other recorders.

the Democratic president today had a wonderful meeting on behalf of America; we're trying to work together. Couldn't you try for twenty-four hours to have a positive, optimistic message as though it might work?"[23]

A third criterion, closely related to the second, is negativity—bad news is preferred to good news. Economic downturns attract greater coverage than does rising prosperity. Similarly, the news media find far more to criticize than to praise in politicians' performances. Presidents cry foul more than most, though Congress fares little better.[24] In 1993, when asked pointedly in a press conference why he thought his popularity had dropped fifteen percentage points in only two months, President Clinton quickly shot back, "I bet not five percent of the American people know that we passed a budget . . . and it passed by the most rapid point of any budget in 17 years. I bet not one in 20 American voters knows that because . . . success and the lack of discord are not as noteworthy as failure."[25] The systematic evidence on this issue suggests that presidents' complaints are not far off the mark. One study, which scored every evening network news statement about the last four presidents during the first year of their administration, found that all, on average, received negative press. Only President Obama narrowly gained more favorable than unfavorable news during any three-month period, and he managed it only during his first quarter in office.[*]

To the extent that reporters and their editors actively filter and interpret messages in a way that favors conflict over consensus and bad news over good, the news media do not serve as a strictly neutral conduit for the flow of civic information to their intended audience. Some media critics charge that in selecting which messages to communicate and in slanting the content, news organizations inject a pernicious bias. Such charges are more abundant than is the evidence supporting them. Nonetheless, survey research finds respondents generally claiming to detect a media bias. Indeed, partisans on opposite sides of numerous issues believe that their views are not receiving fair coverage. In recent years "media watch" organizations have proliferated to keep a sharp eye out for press bias against their particular point of view. They are quick to sound an alarm, and in doing so they put pressure on news organizations to give their side more "balanced" (that is, more sympathetic) coverage. Organizations undertake these costly exercises because they believe that news influences voters and ultimately national policy.

There's some evidence that they are right—to a point. A landmark set of experiments done in the 1980s found that readers and watchers of news were influenced by what the press covered in a very specific way: it shaped what they thought *about,* not what they *thought.* Media researchers call this **agenda setting** when it relates to issues or topics and **priming** when it relates to the criteria with which we evaluate candidates or elected leaders. The press have the power to shape people's priorities, but not to persuade them or change their attitudes about issues or politicians.[26]

STRATEGIC RELATIONS BETWEEN POLITICIANS AND REPORTERS

Politicians have long enlisted the cutting-edge communications technology of their age. The **franking privilege** gave nineteenth-century members of Congress free access to the postal system, and it is still embraced by their present-day counterparts. Rare is the modern congressional staff without a resident webmaster. In 2012, Republican presidential nominee Mitt Romney first announced selection of his vice presidential running mate not at a press conference but via a digital message to people who had downloaded his campaign "app." And in 2008, after a rough introduction to the national media, Sarah Palin got media coverage by refusing to give reporters interviews, but telling them she would make statements "on the record" using Twitter. The result of this was that when she tweeted something, which she did judiciously, everyone covered it. It was, in many ways, a brilliant strategy—it kept her from having to do live interviews, while still keeping her in the news. When Jessica Pellien, CNN's national political reporter, asked at a forum in 2010 when Sarah Palin would disappear

---

[*] Even during the first quarter of 1991, when the Gulf War lifted George H. W. Bush's Gallup poll approval rating to a record-setting 88 percent, the president still barely managed to win mostly favorable coverage. The network news sound-bite data for this analysis were generously provided by the Center for Media and Public Affairs.

from the media scene, the answer of course was obvious to everyone but the reporters in the room. She would no longer be a feature of the news environment when reporters stopped reporting on every one of her tweets! She was controlling her relationship with the press very effectively.

The average politician has trouble getting his or her message to voters because he or she attracts too little news coverage and direct communication is far too expensive. To address this problem, most politicians "buy" as much direct communication as they can afford and chase as much news attention as their skills and positions of authority permit. To that end, many politicians have perfected techniques of generating favorable coverage. Presidents, for example, have appreciated for years that foreign travel and visits to disaster sites engender favorable news reports, although Mitt Romney's foreign trip in the summer of 2012 proved that this wasn't necessarily true for challengers. And as President George W. Bush demonstrated by his delayed response to Hurricane Katrina, failure to rush to the scene of disasters can engender the public's enmity. So, in 2012 when Hurricane Sandy hit the New Jersey and New York shoreline, few were surprised to find the president on the scene immediately, even though the election was only about a week away.

Television viewers crave visual images, and savvy politicians have learned how to create irresistible ones. In the 1950s anticommunist witch-hunter Sen. Joseph McCarthy always appeared with loose sheets of paper that he could wave at any live camera and claim contained his list of 205 or 81 or 57 (the number changed daily) known communists in the State Department.[27] Civil rights leaders in the 1960s realized that by confronting southern segregation through often-violent television images of segregationists in action, they could validate their claims of racism to the rest of the nation. The movement's success with highly telegenic passive resistance continues to inspire the media strategies of those who protest to advance a cause.

In many respects, relations between politicians and reporters have not changed much since the early days of the Republic, when a newspaperwoman spotted President John Quincy Adams skinny-dipping in the Potomac and threatened to scream if he came out of the water before giving her an interview on his policy toward the state banks.[28] (Adams had been hiding in the White House, hoping to avoid public statements on the issue.) This amusing scene is a reminder of the tension inherent in the relationship between politicians and reporters. If they could, each side would exploit the other since each possesses (and would prefer not to surrender) something the other needs. The politician needs sympathetic access to voters, and the reporter requires information that makes for a good story. Both are, in some sense, costly to obtain. No working journalist wants to appear to be a publicist for some politician. And the conveyed information that best serves the politician's purposes will rarely coincide with that good story coveted by the reporter. President Adams clearly thought no story at all would best suit his purposes, but the intrepid reporter caught him in an unguarded moment. This obstacle to cooperation is precisely what the Framers had in mind when they placed protection for the press immediately after freedom of speech in the First Amendment. Anyone suspicious of the concentration of government authority should applaud the wariness with which the press and politicians deal with one another.

THE MILITARY'S MEDIA STRATEGY

strategy and choice

During the Civil War, a newspaper correspondent tried to acquit himself with Union general William Tecumseh Sherman by saying that he simply sought to report the truth. Sherman instructed him to take the next train out of town: "The truth, eh? No sir! . . . We don't want the enemy any better informed than he is. Make no mistake about that train." Until recently military authorities could aspire to control news from the front. As long as the military could manage the news effectively, it could prevent useful information from falling into enemy hands, and it could bury failures and promote sympathetic coverage. The first Persian Gulf War, in 1991, was probably the last conflict in which the military could hope to "contain" news reports from the front.

The relations between the military and the news media during the Afghanistan and Iraq Wars displayed features similar to the relations between politicians and the news media. Advancing communications technology liberated journalists from transmission centers, removing them from military oversight and censorship. Hundreds of journalists roamed Afghanistan, unescorted and unconfined. At times, American soldiers found themselves approaching not the enemy but swarms of network and freelance reporters representing news media from all over the world. As one officer remembered

An embedded journalist, left, communicates with his newsroom during an attack near Baghdad as U.S. Marines take up positions around the capital.

ruefully, soon after a firefight with the Taliban forces in a remote village, reporters from Al Jazeera, the Arab television news network, showed up to conduct live interviews and transmit graphic images of civilian casualties while the American soldiers looked on. As war approached in March 2003, a small army of print and broadcast journalists descended on Iraq equipped with satellite phones and video transmission backpacks. General Sherman's

CONCLUSION: POLITICIAN–PRESS RELATIONS THEN AND NOW

Veteran newspaper reporters sometimes wax nostalgically about the "good old days" when the print journalists ruled the news and worked closely with politicians on the basis of mutual trust and profit. The "good old days" probably never were as rosy as hindsight allows, but a look back at politician–press relations in an earlier era during the 1930s and 1940s does reveal much more relaxed and mutually satisfactory interactions than one finds today. It was an era in which news about national politics was dominated by a small number of Washington correspondents who had organized themselves policy of banishing the news media from the front was simply no longer viable.

Communications technology in the field and news programming at home were combining to pull the public into the war as never before. One news editor summed up the military's emerging news dilemma: "[T]he Pentagon can't keep information from people, like it did so well in the first Persian Gulf War. That's clearly going to be a losing game now." The Pentagon realized, as it planned the invasion of Iraq, it would also need a media strategy. Its novel plan took the form of **embedding** more than six hundred journalists (as many as eight hundred, by one estimate) to military units. Within general guidelines requiring the withholding of information that might be useful to the Iraqi military commanders, who were reputed to be avid fans of U.S. cable news channels, reporters were free to interview soldiers and file reports from the field whenever they liked.[1] Moreover, embedded slots were not limited to American journalists; even Al Jazeera was awarded a half-dozen positions. Most assessments have concluded that the military's strategy was a brilliant stroke of political generalship.

But soon rivalries broke out between the military services as each discovered that these embedded journalists were writing inspiring stories of heroism and success. Each service viewed favorable publicity as a key ingredient in its annual budget battles with the other services. Some of America's generals enjoyed candid on-camera interviews and did not hesitate to use their network appearances to disclaim responsibility for any failure. Jostling for reporters and the media limelight became intensely competitive. By most accounts, during the early days of the invasion the army was a big winner in numbers of both reporters and favorable stories filed with news bureaus. The navy attracted almost 150 embedded reporters, no small share of the total. But much to the chagrin of the admirals, the Pentagon instituted a news blackout as the ships launched their missile attacks. An undersecretary of defense tried to smooth over ruffled feelings: "The contributions of every service are going to be well known. We are a combined arms team nowadays."

---

1. The U.S. military was discovered in late 2004 to have planted a false story with CNN in order to fool the enemy. Mark Mazetti, "PR Meets Psy-Ops in War on Terror," *Los Angeles Times*, December 1, 2004.

professionally to reduce cutthroat competition. These Washington fixtures cultivated close, frequently chummy relations with the comparatively few politicians who actively sought to influence the news.

Then as now, the president was at the center of the news media's attention. During his years in the White House, Franklin D. Roosevelt (1933–1945) conducted 998 biweekly press conferences with a regular group of White House correspondents. The president used these "family gatherings," as he called them, as occasions to make significant announcements. Reporters favored press conferences because they created a level playing field and limited competition for stories. They came to the Oval Office expecting hard news that would secure them a byline on the front page of the next day's paper. "[Roosevelt] never sent

Shortly after the 1962 California gubernatorial election, the defeated Richard Nixon held what was then termed his "last press conference." There he made bitter reference to his treatment by the press, saying they "would not have Nixon to kick around anymore."

reporters away empty-handed," reminisced one veteran, adding that correspondents "are all for a man who can give them several laughs and a couple of top-head dispatches in a twenty-minute visit."[29] In return, the correspondents gave Roosevelt and his New Deal full and generally sympathetic coverage.

Throughout our inquiry into the logic of American politics, we see that collective action generally involves two or more actors successfully solving a prisoner's dilemma. Each participant has to agree to forgo some short-term advantage, pay some cost, or accept risk that the other side will break an agreement in order to secure a more attractive outcome through cooperation. Institutions create settings that bring these actors together and ensure that any agreements will be honored. Thus far, we have examined how governmental institutions allow politicians to engage in mutually profitable exchange by solving this dilemma. Here, a more informal institution, Roosevelt's biweekly open press conferences, regulated by the ground rules of hard news and no favoritism, allowed the president and the press to cooperate to achieve their separate goals. Both sides, then, got what they needed from their long-standing relationship. Two key elements of the setting that allowed this relationship between the president and the press corps to succeed in overcoming each side's temptation to exploit the other was the community's stability and small size. The president served as an authoritative and routinely available source for more than a dozen years, a long enough time for a trust relationship to develop, where each party knew the other intimately.

The Washington, DC, of today contains a far larger, more diverse population of news producers (see Figure 14-4). They compete as much with each other as with politicians in ferreting out stories. One could sense this emerging reconfiguration as early as 1961, when President John F. Kennedy conducted his first press conference on live prime-time television. Network news bureaus relished their newfound access to the press conference and quickly turned Roosevelt's "family gathering" into a media event. Veteran news reporters understandably despised the intrusion of network cameras, likening it to "making love in Carnegie Hall."[30] Derision toward modern television-based journalism remains commonplace (to learn why, see box "The Shrinking Presidential Sound Bite"). The problem print correspondents had with television journalism ran deeper, though. The television cameras reported stories instantly. With television, print coverage became nearly obsolete.

Today's freewheeling marketplace of politicians and reporters is a far cry from the cartel-like setting that permeated politician–press relations during Roosevelt's time. Today many more politicians engage in political talk, trying to attract the attention of an increasingly diverse news media. By one count, more than ten thousand government officials in Washington, DC, alone are involved in press and public relations on a daily basis. The number of trade associations and other interest groups seeking to influence public opinion easily surpasses this number. The greatest barrier to successful media exposure is the sheer volume of competing news stories chasing media outlets on any given news day. This is now coupled with the sheer volume of news outlets producing news on any given day.

Television competed with newspapers for audiences and advertisers and, consequently, for the attention of presidents and other politicians. Now, the Internet potentially wields the same impact. "An item can emerge on an Internet Web site," complained a former network correspondent, "worm its way into a late-night comedian's act, appear as a topic on the morning radio show, and catapult onto the pages of the *New York Times*—all within the space of a few hours."[31] The medium of Internet communication is ill suited for the cultivation of cozy politician–press relations. Rather, it is conducive to the flourishing of a prisoner's dilemma between reporters and government officials, one that arises from competition and manipulation.

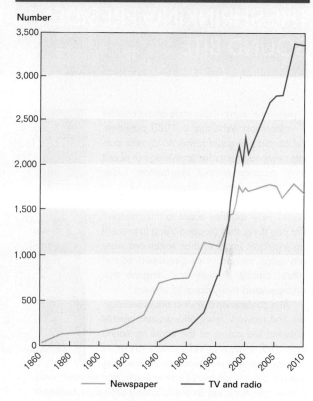

Figure 14-4 Growth of Congressional Press Corps

Source: Harold W. Stanley and Richard G. Niemi, *Vital Statistics on American Politics, 2011–2012* (Washington, DC: CQ Press, 2011), Figure 4-1.

Note: Press corps members are those correspondents entitled to admission to the Senate and House press galleries and radio and television galleries. Prior to 1986, the number of press corps members was recorded approximately every ten years.

Some students of the news media attribute the modern era's strained relations between politicians and the press to the widespread suspicion among reporters that presidents will lie to them whenever it serves their interest and they think they can get away with it. Veteran journalists point to two specific events—Vietnam and Watergate—as critical in fostering a pervasive and enduring **credibility gap**. Charges of presidential manipulation became daily occurrences during the Vietnam War, which took place largely on Lyndon Johnson's watch. Before the credibility gap had much chance to dissipate, the Watergate scandal broke, and eventually, through the persistent efforts of reporters, President Nixon was forced to resign in 1974. The most recent rendition of Washington correspondents protesting that they were duped was the Bush administration's campaign of false claims about the imminent threat of Saddam Hussein's chemical, biological, and nuclear weapons of mass destruction in order to justify an invasion of Iraq. In the aftermath of September 11, 2001, and with the United States at war in Afghanistan, the national press adopted a largely uncritical stance toward these claims. Vietnam, Watergate, and the Iraq War—all

THE SHRINKING PRESIDENTIAL SOUND BITE

strategy and choice

Politicians' survival depends on successful adaptation. Whereas in 1968 presidential candidates could speak on camera during news segments for an average of about forty seconds without interruption, today they should consider themselves lucky to achieve the average allotment of nine seconds.[1] How did they adapt to this change? For one thing, they stopped trying to present an argument (most of their sentences were too long). Instead, they developed **sound bites**, catchy phrases and slogans that encapsulated their appeal to viewers.

At a conference of former press secretaries and network news officials, participants debated the cause of the shrinking sound bite. Did politicians increasingly prefer to engage in empty sloganeering, or were they adapting to a news media less willing to give them airtime? These questions led to the following exchange between former *NBC Nightly News* anchor John Chancellor and President Jimmy Carter's press secretary, Jody Powell:

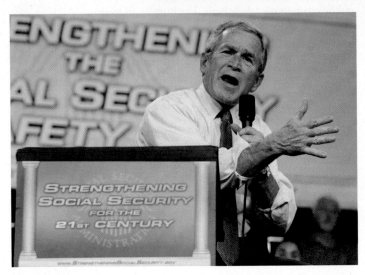

Chancellor: I think television reporters out in the field—when presented with pre-packaged, pre-digested, plastic-coated phrases and with no opportunity to question a president—want to get something that isn't just pre-packaged and pre-digested, and that's why you are getting a more contentious kind of reporting in the twenty seconds at the end of the spot. I had an argument with [CBS correspondent] Tom Pettit during the 1988 election, and I said, "Why is it that all of our correspondents end their pieces with some little snippy, nasty saying? Why don't they just say, 'And tomorrow the president goes to Cleveland.'" And Pettit says, "It wouldn't come out that way. They would say, 'Tomorrow the president goes to Cleveland and no one knows why.'" . . .

So you compress the political propaganda on the one hand, or increase the reactive hostility on the other hand, and that's what a minute-and-a-half television spot is today. I think both sides are probably equally responsible for it, but I think that the politicians started it.

Powell: I will just raise a logical question. Assuming that there are other things to do in a White House . . . now and then, . . . why would you go to all of the trouble to [package the president's message] if you did not find yourself faced with a situation in which it's the way to deal with it? . . . Are we supposed to believe that one morning ten, fifteen years ago somebody in the Johnson White House or the Nixon White House . . . woke up and said, "We don't need to do this, but just for the hell of it, why don't we create this whole structure here about going out on the road and doing that sort of thing?" Or rather perhaps it was a reaction—maybe intelligent, maybe unwise, maybe in the public interest, maybe not— . . . to a set of circumstances which they saw and said, "We've got to do something."

Source: Daniel C. Hallin, *The Presidency, the Press, and the People* (La Jolla: University of California Extension, 1993).

1. Daniel C. Hallin, "Sound Bite News: Television Coverage of Elections, 1968–1988," in *Do the Media Govern? Politicians, Voters, and Reporters in America*, ed. Shanto Iyengar and Richard Reeves (Thousand Oaks, CA: Sage, 1997), 57–65.

falling within the professional careers of many of today's news editors and senior reporters—have conditioned reporters to greet all White House claims with a suspicion of duplicity. Yet even without these major press failings, a credibility gap would probably still color the politician–press relationship. It is embedded in the tension between the preferred news story of reporters and that of politicians. In the absence of institutions designed for their mutual benefit, such as Roosevelt's "family gatherings," the news media's relationship with politicians is likely to remain one of mutual suspicion.

TAKE A QUIZ

logic.cqpress.com

Test your knowledge of this chapter.

logic.cqpress.com

Key Terms

agenda setting, 654

beats, 651

credibility gap, 659

embedding, 657

equal time, 629

fairness doctrine, 629

franking privilege, 654

infotainment, 637

leak, 649

libel, 643

media bias, 635

muckraking, 626

news media, 620

pack journalism, 652

priming, 654

prior restraint, 643

shield laws, 650

slander, 643

sound bites, 660

trial balloon, 649

"yellow journalism," 625

Suggested Readings

Ansolabehere, Stephen, Roy Behr, and Shanto Iyengar. *The Media Game: American Politics in the Television Age.* New York: Macmillan, 1993. A brief overview of news and politics, this book offers especially useful treatments of the news and information in election campaigns and reports experiments in media effects on public opinion.

Baum, Matthew A. *Soft News Goes to War.* Princeton, NJ: Princeton University Press, 2003. This book successfully resolves two inconsistent findings in public opinion research: a public expressing less interest in foreign affairs than in previous times but scoring as well informed as in the past. Baum presents persuasive evidence that many who shun formal news do, nonetheless, become informed via "soft" news entertainment programs.

Davis, Richard, and Diana Owen. *New Media and American Politics.* New York: Oxford University Press, 1998. A thorough survey of the various "new media," this volume also compares modern communication technologies with traditional media, noting their respective effects on political knowledge and awareness.

Hamilton, James T. *All the News That Is Fit to Sell.* Princeton, NJ: Princeton University Press, 2004. An economist examines modern television programming practices as a product of business strategies. A surprisingly readable book in which the author explains the decline of traditional news and the rise of infotainment.

Iyengar, Shanto, and Richard Reeves, eds. *Do the Media Govern? Politicians, Voters, and Reporters in America.* Thousand Oaks, CA: Sage, 1997. This fine anthology combines social science research with journalistic introspection. Taken together, these essays offer a comprehensive survey of scholarship on politics and the news media.

Kovach, Bill, and Tom Rosenstiel. *Blur: How to Know What's True in the Age of Information Overload.* New York: Bloomsbury Press, 2011.

■ Review Questions ■

1. How do market forces make political news more "democratic"? Have market forces played the same role in press coverage throughout American history?

2. Why did newspaper editors accept party subsidies in the early Republic? What motivated these same editors to give up the subsidies later? Why didn't they give them up earlier?

3. How did the rise of newspaper chains affect the political influence of the press? What ultimately eroded the political power of these chains? How and why has the influence of newspapers continued to decline today?

4. How and why do politicians seek to manipulate the news? What strategies do they use to generate beneficial coverage?

5. What resources do politicians have that might allow them to "go around" the press and communicate with the public directly? In general, how successful are these attempts?

15 The Prospects for Institutional Reform

Comedian Stephen Colbert campaigns for the super PAC that he created, "Americans for a Better Tomorrow, Tomorrow." These new campaign finance organizations, which can raise and spend unlimited sums of money to influence elections, have been the target of reformers' attempts to shine further light on their donors and even to ban them through a constitutional amendment. Yet reformers with a sense of humor may have enjoyed reading the Colbert super PAC's filing to the Federal Election Commission, which reported that he had raised $1,023,121 and included an appendix, stating, "Yeah! How you like me now, F.E.C? I'm rolling seven digits deep! I got 99 problems but a non-connected independent-expenditure only committee ain't one!"

- Since Americans generally believe that the United States is the most successful democracy in history, why are there so many movements to reform it?

- How does the power given to states in the U.S. federal system allow them to experiment with reforms, and how likely is it that successful innovations will spread to the national government?

- Can citizens trust elected officials—who by definition have been winners at the game of politics—to set its rules in a way that will be fair to all players?

- Is it too hard to change the structure of government in the United States, or too easy?

For advocates of campaign finance reform, the battle to pass the "DISCLOSE Act" through Congress in July 2012 might have seemed like déjà vu all over again. Struggling against partisan politics and a Senate filibuster, they were losing a battle that they thought they had won a decade earlier. The bill, an acronym for "Democracy Is Strengthened by Casting Light On Spending in Elections Act of 2012," would have required independent groups that spend money on politics to disclose the names of any contributors who gave them more than $10,000. While it had majority support in the Senate, the bill lacked the backing of the supermajority required to close debate, falling victim to the same filibuster that had defeated a similar bill in 2010. With Democratic authors and only a few Republican cosponsors, the measure divided members along party lines, and a companion bill was bottled up in the Republican-controlled House. Knowing that the act was dead, its supporters held a midnight vigil for the legislature and bemoaned the consequences of a campaign finance system with contribution limits that were easy to evade and disclosure requirements easy to avoid. Laying the blame on the opposing party, Democratic Senate Majority Leader Harry Reid railed that "[p]erhaps Republicans want to shield a handful of billionaires willing to contribute nine figures to sway a close presidential election. If this flood of outside money continues, the day after the election 17 angry old white men will wake up and realize they've just bought the country."[1]

The partisan divisions and institutional hurdles facing the DISCLOSE Act mirrored the obstacles that campaign finance crusaders finally overcame with the passage of the Bipartisan Campaign Reform Act (BCRA). Also known as "McCain-Feingold" for the two senators—Republican John McCain and Democrat Russell Feingold—who championed it, that bill had been stalled by Senate filibusters and partisan splits in the House for session after session until it finally won passage in 2002.

Yet that victory, like many for reform movements in American politics, was neither complete nor permanent. The BCRA attempted to block hundreds of millions of dollars in political spending that had flowed into American elections during the 1990s. Ever since the Supreme Court's 1976 *Buckley v. Valeo* decision announced that spending money on politics

During the congressional debate over the DISCLOSE Act, advocates of the measure argued that it would reveal the secret sources of campaign spending, while opponents warned that it would have a chilling effect on speech if donors faced intimidation.

was necessary to exercise free speech, and thus that spending could not be limited, reformers worried that viewing money as speech would benefit the richest interests. The Court allowed Congress to limit direct contributions to political candidates, a system of limits on contributions, but opened up other avenues for so-called soft money (contributions of an unlimited size) to influence elections. These avenues included money raised by political parties in massive chunks, as well as spending by interest groups on advertisements that were aired suspiciously close to elections. While well-heeled donors could not give vast sums of money directly to candidates, they were allowed to make big donations to parties or to spend money independently of campaigns ("independent expenditures") but nonetheless aimed at boosting the electoral chances of the candidates they backed. Campaign finance groups worried that these kinds of contributions could be just as corrupting as money given straight to candidates, and that a system with uncapped political donations tilted the playing field in favor of moneyed interests.

The McCain-Feingold reforms were aimed squarely at these sorts of contributions, banning soft money donation to parties and electioneering advertisements that independent groups aired within a month of a primary contests or two months of a November general election. They were also aimed at fixing a disruption of the fundamental "principal-agent" relationship underlying American democracy. If politics is the relationship between principals (voters) and agents (politicians), then allowing another group—wealthy donors—to make such large contributions that they can effectively control the actions of politicians disrupts the electoral connection that ties politicians to voters. BCRA prohibited these unlimited contributions, whether from private industry or from unions, from rich Republicans or from rich Democrats, and eventually won enough bipartisan support to pass out of Congress. President George W. Bush signed the bill in March 2002, though he did so reluctantly in a quiet ceremony. "The American electorate will benefit from these measures to strengthen our democracy," President Bush noted in a press release that day, but he also noted that "the bill does have flaws. Certain provisions present serious constitutional concerns."[2]

Advocates of free speech, ranging from Republican lawmakers to the American Civil Liberties Union, agreed, and soon filed suit against the BCRA. In modern politics, they argued, spending money to air one's views broadly was necessary to exercising the freedom of speech, and elections were the time in which airing political speech was most important. Although the BCRA survived an early court challenge, the Supreme Court's 2010 *Citizens United* decision struck down its ban on spending by independent groups during elections, allowing corporations and unions to spend unlimited sums of money on this type of speech. In his opinion, Justice Anthony Kennedy wrote that "political speech must prevail against laws that would suppress it, whether by design or inadvertence." He further argued that the First Amendment "has its fullest and most urgent applications to speech uttered during a campaign for political office."

With that decision, the campaign finance regimen constructed by the BCRA regime had been effectively dismantled, and money flowed through new routes into the 2010 and 2012 campaigns. Groups spending independently of candidates purchased nearly a billion dollars' worth of political advertising in the 2012 election cycle, with $809 million of that sum spent on negative advertisements attacking a candidate. Almost half a billion dollars of this was spent by the 857 "super PACs" created in the wake of the *Citizens United* decision, groups that combined funds from wealthy donor organizations into sophisticated advertisement campaigns.[3] Even more worrying to reformers was spending by 501(c)(4) organizations, groups that relied on a part of the Internal Revenue Service tax code to spend money on politics but keep the names of their donors anonymous. These were the sorts of contributions that the DISCLOSE Act aimed at revealing, but its failure left them secret.

Defeated in the Supreme Court, stymied in Congress, and enraged by the creative political consultants who set up 501(c)(4) groups, campaign finance advocates turned to a Hail Mary attempt at reform: amending the Constitution. Multiple groups are collecting signatures to pass an amendment declaring that political money is not speech, overturning the *Citizens United* decision. Nine state legislatures have passed resolutions calling for the amendment,[4] and President Obama has suggested that he favors it.[5] Yet the road to a constitutional amendment in America is arduous, even more difficult than getting a bill past a Senate filibuster or defending it in the courts. Both parties would have to favor the amendment and remain united, a collective agreement that could easily fall apart if one side thought that it could gain an electoral advantage by reneging on the deal. The campaign faces long odds, by virtue of the design of our political system. The impediments to change that are built into U.S. institutions have seemed to trap this reform just when its advocates argue that it is most needed.

Casting campaign finance reform in these terms ties them to the themes replayed throughout this book. All reforms are proposed solutions to some collective action problem, but they may themselves create new collective action problems, or move us too far on the continuum between imposing transaction costs (in this case, by opening the door to corruption) and imposing conformity costs (by infringing upon free speech). Reforms may attempt to solve collective action problems, but the process of reform itself faces many of these same problems. Changing American political institutions, it should come as no surprise, is neither simple nor easy.

Mitch McConnell talks about the First Amendment and political money.

Robert Reich
argues for a
constitutional
amendment.

TOWARD A MORE PERFECT UNION?

Americans revere the Constitution and memorize its preamble, but often try to amend it. We salute the flag, yet debate whether we should require everyone to pledge allegiance to it or prevent anyone from burning it. Although the vast majority of our citizens view our leaders and government as legitimate—even after bitterly contested elections—few of us question the legitimacy of attempts to improve our governing institutions. It is a characteristic paradox of our political creed that we celebrate our nation's democracy as the greatest in world history, while constantly considering what reforms* might move us toward a more perfect union.

Hard polling numbers demonstrate the exceptional patriotism of Americans as well as the reasons why efforts to change the nation are regarded as patriotic. In a recent international survey, 94 percent of Americans answered that they were proud of their country, a figure that easily surpassed the levels of national pride found in large European countries. Sixty-five percent of Americans would be willing to fight for their country in a war, which again rose far above the levels measured in France, Germany, Great Britain, Italy, and Spain. But when Americans were asked how satisfied they are with their democracy, 28 percent said they were "not very satisfied," and 7 percent were "not at all satisfied."[6] Many of those who are proud of the United States and willing to fight for it are not completely contented with the way the government works, a dissatisfaction that gives rise to many fervent, patriotic reform movements.

That does not mean, of course, that the American governmental system makes the process of reform easy. Satisfied with their work, the Framers constructed the Constitution so that a momentary flash of popular passion would not undo it. After the passage of the Bill of Rights, a mere seventeen amendments have been added to the Constitution, a testament more to the deliberate obstacles built into the amendment process than to a lack of reform ideas.

Worried that those unhappy with the new government would soon press for yet another constitutional reform, the Framers intentionally placed high transaction costs—the investments of time, effort, and resources needed to reach collective decisions—on attempts to change the American political system. In the states, where the Framers worried less about constitutional revisions, proponents of reform have faced fewer barriers, many reform experiments have been launched, and a few have spread across the country. Yet changing the rules of politics and policymaking at the federal level remains difficult. Perhaps this reflects the pride of Americans in their nation, but the resistance to change that is woven into American political institutions can also be viewed as a consequence of collective action dilemmas. The collective action problems that inspire reform efforts also confront campaigns for change with new problems. Before they begin their battles, disparate reform groups must settle on a single proposed solution, a dilemma in itself. Once the fight is joined, collective action problems pose further obstacles to organizing a movement, assembling a broad coalition, and winning in the multiple political arenas that have authority over the structure of government.

The strategic incentives that politicians face also play into the process of reform. Although not every change in the way U.S. government works is initiated by an elected official, it is nearly always necessary to secure the sponsorship or at least the grudging acquiescence of

---

*We use the term *reform* here to denote any proposed change to U.S. governing institutions, while remaining agnostic about whether particular reforms would improve the operation of American politics or harm it.

politicians for anything to happen. This inescapable fact could be an impenetrable barrier against changes to the status quo. After all, elected officials by definition succeeded under the old rules of the game. While those on the losing side of politics often want to change the rules, the winners generally have the power to set the rules. This logic does not, however, dictate stasis in American institutions.

Because democratic competition makes it uncertain who will hold power after the next elections, electoral pressures open three clear routes to reform. First, those in government often yield to calls for reform because they wish to maintain their popularity and win again. Politicians may even find future political advantage in reform. As Chapter 4 discussed, leaders opposing slavery in territories won widespread support from white voters worried about having to compete with slave labor. Some of the Republicans who promoted Reconstruction, the most ambitious constitutional reforms since Philadelphia in 1787, did so to stave off the specter of Democratic congressional majorities once the rebellious southern states were readmitted to the Union. In a second rationale for reform, elected officials who fear that they may soon lose their offices have an incentive to change the rules so that they will still have some influence once they are on the outside of the power centers. Third, when politicians fail to forecast the political tides and are swept out of office, new leaders brought in by the surge may want to secure reforms before their power also washes away. Even though the strategic incentives politicians face make changes to the system that elected them less likely and more complicated, they do not rule out reform entirely.

The logic of American politics, then, both creates problems that need to be solved and places profound obstacles in the way of any proposed solution. It is a formula for incrementalism, for continual skirmishing over the important narrow details of the political system within a lasting consensus over its broad shape. Revolutionary change is unlikely, while persistent tweaking is certain.

This chapter tells the stories of both successful and failed reforms, viewed through the lens of the collective action framework. It maps the path to change, highlighting the many roadblocks as well as a few opportunities to accelerate change. It then focuses on four areas of proposed reform, viewed as solutions to the four major collective action problems identified in the introduction. To solve their *coordination problems,* political parties have employed various methods—today, they have often settled on the direct primary—to focus the support of their adherents on a single candidate. When voters want more turnover among politicians, but hesitate to sacrifice the seniority that their representative has built up while other districts keep their incumbents, they deal with their *prisoner's dilemma* by supporting **term limits**. Because individual citizens are tempted to *free ride* in a democracy by not making the effort to cast a ballot, reformers have made various attempts to boost turnout. Finally, presidents have sought line-item veto powers in order to stop members of Congress from writing budgets that deliver spending to each of their districts while turning the overall budget into a *tragedy of the commons.*

Each story demonstrates the trade-offs between solving an old problem and creating a new one, as well as the strategic dilemmas faced by political actors who care both about reforming the political process and about advancing their own policy goals and political careers. Reformers often draw upon the tool kit of institutional design described in the introduction to this book, proposing changes that can be evaluated according to the transaction and conformity costs that they impose. When would-be reformers do settle on an idea, the narratives illustrate, their campaigns for change must overcome both collective action problems and the institutional impediments built in by the Framers. To implement change, reformers can harness the energy and ingenuity of a nation whose citizens are as engaged in the operation of their democracy as any people in the world. Combined, these obstacles and opportunities make changing American politics difficult yet not, as our rich history of reform shows, impossible.

THE BARRIERS TO INSTITUTIONAL CHANGE

How difficult it is to reform U.S. institutions depends on how fundamental and broad an intended reform will be. The sturdiest barricades are built around the Constitution, which is amended only rarely and with great effort. Changing the statutes that govern the everyday operations of the national political system is less difficult, but still no easy task. Facing these daunting prospects, many reformers begin at the state level, pushing for change with a more limited geographic scope in the hope that their ideas will then spread across the country.

Amending the Constitution

Amending the Constitution may be the toughest task in American politics. It has been accomplished only seventeen times in the past two centuries, a rate of less than one amendment per decade. This is no accident. To ensure that their work at the Constitutional Convention not be undone quickly or foolishly, the Framers placed formidable barriers in the way of a proposed change. They required amendments to gain support from multiple layers of government so that neither the states nor the federal government could impose new rules upon each other. They used supermajority voting rules to prevent narrow coalitions from making broad changes. All in all, they stacked the deck against any faction that wished to rewrite the rules.

The obstacles that the Framers put in the way of reform can be thought of as transaction costs imposed on anyone attempting an amendment. The first impediment in the most viable path* toward amending the Constitution is the requirement that any proposal receive the support of two-thirds of the members of both houses of Congress. This means that a reform movement must first gain a congressional sponsor, a politician convinced that leading this difficult fight will be a wise use of time and political capital. The sponsor must then lobby committee and floor leaders in both houses to convince them that holding hearings and a vote on the proposal is worth the investment of scarce time on their agendas. While it is difficult even to secure a vote on a proposed amendment, the supermajority rule makes this vote tougher still to win. Except in rare circumstances in American political history, getting two-thirds support in both houses requires bipartisan agreement, and it has always necessitated building a coalition across much of the American ideological spectrum. Backers of an amendment may have to bargain with reluctant legislators, compromising on critical details of the language. It certainly entails a major organizational effort, backed

---

*As described in Chapter 2, an amendment can also be proposed if two-thirds of the states petition Congress to call a constitutional convention. The fact that this route has never been taken is testimony to the high transaction costs—and unclear payoffs—associated with it.

While the obstacles that the Founders put in place make amendment of the *actual* Constitution quite difficult, the Web makes a *virtual* rewrite of the Constitution very easy. In 2012, Slate.com invited both legal scholars and its readers to propose their favorite reforms, an inventive attempt at "fixing" the Constitution through crowdsourcing.

by displays of public support that promise that the proposed amendment has a good chance of winning eventual ratification.

The recent history of a proposed constitutional ban on flag burning shows that even when an effort to amend the Constitution is well organized and popular, securing enough votes in Congress is no easy trick. As discussed in Chapter 5, the 1989 Supreme Court case that struck down a Texas ban on flag desecration led to a widely supported effort to place the ban in the Constitution. The proposed amendment soon gathered the necessary two-thirds majority in the House of Representatives. Yet senators, perhaps because their longer terms insulate them against electoral forces, have been less supportive. In the run-up to the 2006 elections, the proposed amendment failed on a 66–34 vote, one short of the necessary Senate supermajority. A poll taken at the time showed that it was favored by a 56 to 40 percent margin among American adults, a level of support that is perhaps not high enough to ensure ratification by the states if and when it clears the hurdle of the U.S. Senate.[7]

This second stage of the process—ratification—also comes with high transaction costs. To ratify an amendment proposed by Congress, three-fourths of the state legislatures must support it (or, in the path taken only in the Twenty-first Amendment's ratification, special conventions called by three-fourths of the states must back it). Essentially, the proponents of an amendment must surmount the hurdles that they overcame in Congress thirty-eight more times, winning majority votes in states with diverse political cultures and different forms of legislative organization. Broad national support is no guarantee of victory at this stage. As Chapter 4 details, the Equal Rights Amendment received overwhelming support in Congress and quickly won victories in many state legislatures across the country. But six years after its ratification drive began, the ERA stalled with support from thirty-five states, agonizingly close to victory but caught up in state political debates over abortion rights. Because constitutional amendments must succeed in varied political venues and often over an extended period of time, many reform campaigns that begin with overwhelming support eventually fail.

Yet the Framers' barriers are not the only roadblocks to reform; anyone wishing to change the U.S. political system must also solve collective action dilemmas. First, all those who agree that the old system is broken must coordinate on the way to fix it. If reform leaders can agree, motivating their followers becomes the next challenge. One clear problem that anyone trying to turn a popular idea into a well-organized movement needs to overcome is the incentive that sympathetic supporters have to free ride. Voters may be open to an idea, but unwilling to contribute money to a ratification campaign or spend their own time rallying support for it. They may simply sit on the sidelines and wait for someone else to exert the effort, because political reforms rarely promise a huge payoff to all of their many backers. Various political entrepreneurs have organized membership groups to overcome this problem by gathering together citizens who care deeply about one area of reform, winning some notable successes. Direct legislation leagues in many states were key in importing the initiative process from Switzerland and spreading it across the United States in the early twentieth century. Today, groups like Common Cause and the League of Women Voters push for "good government" reforms such as campaign finance laws, and the contributors to U.S. Term Limits have successfully enacted and maintained term limits on many state legislators. Still, these groups face the constant challenge of keeping their members active and engaged on issues that have little concrete impact on most people's daily lives. If the support for change is a mile wide but an inch deep, we can expect little to happen.

This logic may have doomed the most recent attempt to remove the Constitution's requirement (Article II, Section 1) that the president be a "natural born" citizen. To most modern Americans, this provision adopted at the time of the Founding may seem anachronistic, and there are few apparent reasons to prevent naturalized citizens from running for the office. But while an amendment to eliminate this qualification for office might ultimately succeed, no organized group has a strong incentive to campaign for such an amendment. One moment of hope for this cause came after Arnold Schwarzenegger, who was born in Austria but became a U.S. citizen in 1983, was elected governor of California. A group of supporters capitalized on his early popularity by running a few television ads in his home state advocating the change, and Sen. Orrin Hatch introduced a constitutional amendment that would allow it.[8] Yet the movement quickly fizzled, and the proposed amendment has gone nowhere. No narrow group has an incentive to push for it, and the vast numbers of voters who might support it have every incentive to free ride.

A final barrier to change is erected by American voters, who often hesitate to take the fundamental and universal step of amending the Constitution, even when an idea seems personally appealing. Public opinion on the issue of gay marriage illustrates this tendency. In a 2004 national poll, 55 percent of Americans said that they felt same-sex marriage should be illegal. Yet when they were asked about a constitutional ban on gay marriage, only 38 percent said they would support it, while 58 percent preferred to leave the issue up to the states.[9] The American public can be reluctant to alter their foundational document even for momentarily popular causes.

Combined, these forces create a **status quo bias** in U.S. political institutions. The system fundamentally favors a continuation of its current design, making deviation from the basic blueprint difficult. Building stability into political institutions is reasonable, since they are intended, among other things, to stabilize power relationships and to make deals durable enough for people to make them in the first place. Much the same appraisal can be made for other mature democracies, but this bias is abnormally strong for the U.S. political system, with its separated branches and comparatively weaker political parties. It is not automatically a conservative bias, placing as many obstacles in the path of efforts to enact term limits (usually favored by conservative voters) as it does in the way of campaign finance reforms (backed most strongly by liberals). Rather, it is a bias against adopting new institutions and in favor of preserving old ones, regardless of their ideological tenor.

Enthusiasm about Arnold Schwarzenegger, who is not a "natural born citizen," prompted some supporters to call for a constitutional amendment that would allow immigrants who had become citizens to run for the nation's highest office (following in the footsteps of George W. Bush, pictured with Schwarzenegger in this photo). Yet because no organized group has a direct stake in pushing hard for this reform, it met the same quiet end as many other apparently popular ideas for amending the Constitution.

Reforms That Stop Short of Constitutional Change

This status quo bias still exists, though not as strongly, for the rules that govern American politics but are not so fundamental as to be enshrined in the Constitution. Changing a statute, a regulation, or an internal rule of Congress can be easier than amending the Constitution, with fewer steps required and less reluctance expected from voters or legislators. This does not mean, however, that reformers can simply scale down their ambitions to ensure their success. The system's typical checks and balances apply here, especially those possessed by the judicial branch. The fundamental dilemma is that if reformers stop short of amending the Constitution, those charged with interpreting the Constitution can stop a reform in its tracks.

As Part II of this book demonstrated, anyone who has an idea for a bill faces considerable difficulties convincing Congress to turn it into a law, pressuring the president to sign it, and lobbying the federal bureaucracy to implement it in a particular way. Nothing in this process is simple, with the legislative and executive branches able to put a check on radical policy change. Still, compared with amending the Constitution, the obstacles to passing a statute are much less imposing; congressional vote thresholds are lower, and states need not give their assent. The key difference, though, is the additional check possessed by the judicial branch. Even if a law is passed by Congress and signed by the president, federal judges may throw it out—or invalidate some portion of it—by ruling that it is unconstitutional.

The intervention of the judicial branch occurs frequently in American politics. As we have seen, two key parts of the BCRA reforms have been thrown out by the Supreme Court. The underlying basis for these decisions was the reasoning, set forth in the 1976 *Buckley v. Valeo*

Supreme Court decision, that political spending represents an exercise of constitutionally protected speech. This famous case not only established an important precedent; it also (as Chapter 11 shows) invalidated half of the victories that had seemed to be won by the major campaign finance reform law passed just two years before.

The 1974 amendments to the Federal Election Campaign Act together formed a comprehensive approach to constraining the influence of money on American politics by setting limits both on the amount of money that candidates could raise and on the sums that candidates and their allies could spend. In *Buckley*, the Supreme Court upheld the caps on contributions, but not on spending. Under the Court's interpretation, candidates were allowed to spend as much as they could raise, millionaire candidates were free to give their campaigns unlimited sums, and interest groups could spend money for or against candidates so long as they acted independently. In the words of a leading campaign finance expert, "Congress's grand scheme of regulation was savaged."[10] Although reformers appeared to win a major victory by passing the 1974 amendments in the wake of the Watergate scandal, half of their statutory changes disappeared as Supreme Court justices assumed their roles as interpreters and defenders of the Constitution.

Federalism as an Opportunity for Reform

One more avenue to reform—blocked by fewer obstacles, but reaching fewer people—is opened by America's federal system. The states serve as key **laboratories for reform**. States control their own governing structures, providing their citizens the opportunity to change politics on a smaller scale and giving everyone else the chance to observe the effects of a reform without risking it themselves. Activists have seized upon this opening just as political observers have celebrated the patchwork of policy that it can create. In a famous passage from his 1932 *New State Ice Co. v. Liebmann* decision, Supreme Court Justice Louis Brandeis wrote, "It is one of the happy incidents of the Federal System that a single, courageous state may, if its citizens choose, serve as a laboratory and try novel social and economic experimentation without risk to the rest of the country."

Reformers have won many victories when they experiment first with the political system of one state and then seek to spread their ideas across the country. As Chapter 4 noted, the national struggle to give women the right to vote won its first victories in the states. Suffragists, the well-organized groups led by women such as Elizabeth Cady Stanton and Susan B. Anthony, first secured the franchise in the territory of Wyoming in 1869. They found much success in the West, where women received the right to vote in Colorado (the first state success) in 1893, and in Utah, Idaho, and then Washington over the next two decades. This piecemeal approach to reform then spread eastward, putting ever more pressure on Congress to pass the women's suffrage amendment that had been introduced each session for decades. The House and Senate finally passed the proposal in 1918, and when the Nineteenth Amendment was ratified two years later, the national government had followed the states in allowing women to vote.

Not every reform that begins its journey in the states sees national success. In the early twentieth century, many western states and a few others began America's experiment with direct democracy by giving citizens the right to initiate legislation by petition, throw out laws written by legislators, and recall elected officials. These reforms have remained popular in the states that adopted them—and, as the box on page 676 shows, served as springboards to further reform—but their spread slowed down greatly after 1918. Only five states have enacted direct democracy measures since then, and the idea has never gained serious traction at the federal level. Legislative term limits are also an idea that, after an initial rapid proliferation across the country, have not been adopted widely and are clearly stalled at the national level. Not surprisingly, the states can sometimes be a graveyard for reforms as well. In many ways, this makes sense. At the heart of Brandeis's reasoning is the idea that experiments can go awry, and that voters in other states and the nation as a whole can judge whether or not a vanguard reform is worth replicating in their government. Federalism provides an opportunity for reforms to succeed—and to fail.

FOUR STORIES OF REFORM AND COLLECTIVE ACTION

Despite all the obstacles in the way of changing our political system, the American people have often fought to overcome them. Some of these reform movements have transformed our democracy, most have gone nowhere, and many have met with partial success. Nearly all of them can be thought of as attempts to draw upon the apparatus of the Framers' tool kit, described in Chapter 1, to solve collective action problems. Our introductory framework can also be used to evaluate the impact of these changes to determine whether or not they truly deserve to be judged "reforms."

Candidate Nominations: Parties Solving Their Coordination Problems

Whenever an office comes open that the parties compete for in American politics, there is no shortage of people willing to stand as their party's standard bearer. We live in—as one book on candidate emergence put it—*The United States of Ambition.*[11] But this abundance of volunteers creates a dilemma. How do the parties focus their electoral supporters on just one candidate, instead of seeing their coalition fracture into many small groups backing each ambitious contestant? In the language of collective action, parties and their members face a coordination problem. Even when all of the voters in a party want to see one of its candidates win office, they face the challenge of figuring out which one has the most support and cooperating with each other to cast all of their ballots for the chosen standard bearer. In a large-scale democracy such as the United States, party adherents cannot coordinate their action through personal communication; some sort of institutional solution is needed.

Over our nation's history, parties have experimented with three different solutions to this coordination problem. All of these methods of designating a formal party nominee are examples of *agenda control,* one of the design mechanisms introduced in our first chapter's description of the Framers' tool kit (pages 25–33). In each of them, some portion of a party's membership helps set the agenda of options available to general election voters. This solves the coordination problem by focusing all of the party's electoral resources on one nominee, so that party members do not waste their votes by working at cross-purposes. But it comes at the clear

DIRECT DEMOCRACY AS A SPRINGBOARD TO FURTHER REFORM

logic of politics

After turn-of-the-century Progressive reformers pushed for direct democracy provisions to take power out of the hands of state legislatures, their victories eased the way to future reforms. One of these provisions, the citizen initiative now allowed in twenty-four states, gives anyone the power to propose new laws. Of course, successful initiatives are authored far more often by interest groups than by everyday citizens. It takes organizational might in order to collect enough signatures to put an initiative on the ballot and to fund the campaign for its passage. But even though initiatives do not simply amplify the "voice of the people," they offer someone other than current elected officials the chance to enact new laws.

This is especially helpful to reform causes when a new law directly threatens the interests of lawmakers. The path to legislative approval is quite difficult for laws like term limits, which throw officeholders out of office when their time is up, or campaign finance regulations that make it harder for politicians to raise money. By opening up another route for such proposals, the initiative process greatly improves their chances of becoming law. One example of a reform that was stifled in the legislature, but which succeeded through direct democracy, is Colorado's "Give a Vote to Every Legislator" (GAVEL) amendment. Before this initiative passed in 1988, the majority party ruled the state legislature with an iron fist, able to kill bills in committees without taking a vote and to keep them from reaching the floor of either house. Minority party members complained, but it should come as no surprise that majority leaders stifled their reform proposals in the legislature. Things did not change until a coalition of twenty-three interest groups—many of which were at odds with the Republican majority—put the GAVEL initiative on the ballot. It passed by a 72 to 28 percent margin, stripping the majority party of its ability to control the legislative agenda.

Without the initiative process, such a change would have been next to impossible in Colorado. Across the states, recent research has shown, direct democracy has eased the way to the adoption of limits on how much anyone could contribute to legislative candidates or to parties. And as the map illustrates, states with initiative provisions have been much more likely to pass term limits on their legislators. Voters in nearly every state that allows initiatives backed term limits, although courts in four of these states later invalidated the measures. Where reform groups lacked the ability to go directly to the ballot, term limits almost never succeeded. In only three states did legislators vote to limit their own terms. In two of these, Utah and Idaho, they did so facing the pressure of planned initiatives, and later repealed their term limits before they took effect. Louisiana's is the only legislature that has term limited itself in the absence of direct democracy provisions.

Sources: John Straayer, *The Colorado General Assembly,* 2nd ed. (Boulder: University Press of Colorado, 2000); John Pippen, Shaun Bowler, and Todd Donovan, "Election Reform and Direct Democracy: Campaign Finance Regulations in the American States," *American Politics Research* 30, no. 6 (2002): 559–585.

Note: There are six states in which term limits passed but were subsequently either overturned by courts (Massachusetts, Oregon, Washington, and Wyoming) or repealed by legislatures (Idaho and Utah). Only in Oregon, from 1998 through 2001, did limits go into effect by removing veteran members before the limits were overturned.

price of giving tremendous power to those with authority to set the agenda, and it imposes less obvious costs as well. This brief history of the various reforms made to the way that American parties choose their nominees—a story told more thoroughly in Chapter 12—considers the different types of costs brought by attempts to solve the coordination problem.

States That Have Imposed Term Limits and That Allow Citizen Initiatives

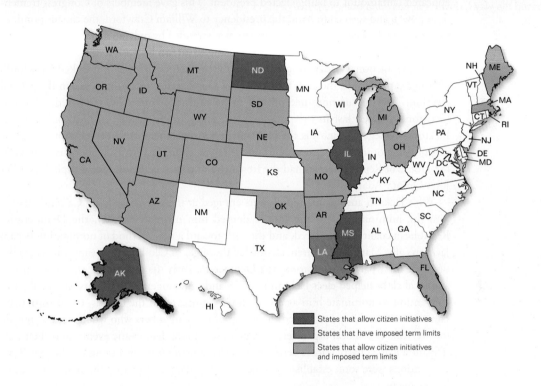

States that allow citizen initiatives

States that have imposed term limits

States that allow citizen initiatives and imposed term limits

This map is adapted from the list of term limit laws compiled by the National Conference of State Legislatures and available at www.ncsl.org/programs/legismgt/about/states.htm. It includes all states that initially passed term limits, even if those limits have since been repealed by legislatures or invalidated by courts. It is also adapted from the list of states with citizen initiatives compiled by the Initiative and Referendum Institute and available at www.iandrinstitute.org/statewide_i&r.htm.

The first method devised to nominate presidential candidates, an innovation that the Federalist and the Democratic-Republican Parties used in the early years of the Republic, was the congressional caucus. To coordinate the behavior of their voters, party leaders elected to Congress would pick a presidential nominee. This imposition of elite authority over mass action comes quite close to being a command solution, one in which a single actor is given dictatorial power to command the actions of others. It leads to coordination, to be sure, but it also imposes high conformity costs—the sacrifices that come with having to abide by the decisions of others—by forcing voters in a party to back a nominee whom they did not choose. By placing this crucial decision in the hands of a congressional caucus, party leaders also deprive themselves of the opportunity to test the mass appeal of potential nominees.

These twin flaws—the perceived illegitimacy of elite authority in the young democracy and the caucus's lack of responsiveness to public sentiment—contributed to the downfall of the caucus system after the presidential election of 1824. Since the Democratic-Republican Party had grown dominant by this time, securing the party's nomination appeared tantamount to being elected president. This gave members of Congress tremendous power, and seemed to hand the presidency to William Crawford, the caucus nominee that year. Yet the February 14, 1824, caucus was attended by only 66 members of Congress, with the remaining 195 representatives refusing to attend because they supported one of many other factional leaders who aspired to the presidency that year but lacked Crawford's plurality support.[12] In the end, four powerful Democratic-Republicans ran in the general election. The caucus nominee proved to be ordinary voters' least favored option as Crawford finished last in the popular vote. The plurality leader, in both popular and Electoral College voting, was the charismatic retired general Andrew Jackson. Congress misjudged popular sentiment, but because no candidate won a majority outright, the House of Representatives had the final say and coalesced behind second-place finisher John Quincy Adams.

With Jackson and his many followers enraged at the way that "**King Caucus**" denied him the nomination and the House denied him ultimate victory, the Democratic-Republican coalition splintered, and the shift toward a new method of nomination began. Jackson's ally, Martin Van Buren, channeled the anger of Old Hickory's supporters into the first true mass party organization, the Democratic Party. Its pyramid of state committees and local clubs helped elect Jackson in 1828 and came together in the first national party convention to nominate him again in 1832. Compared to the caucus, the **nominating convention** ostensibly broadened the group of party members who would set the agenda for everyone else. Local organizers attended these more democratic events, and their participation helped party leaders better gauge the public support for various candidates. Party conventions were soon established in nearly every state, completing the rebellion against King Caucus.

Yet while the convention system was initially "regarded as a great triumph for the plain people over the aristocracy," in the words of one contemporary scholar, soon "[c]onditions developed that were so intolerable as to arouse indignation and protest."[13] Put in terms of the collective action framework, as the century wore on and some parties transitioned from mass organizations to tightly controlled machines, conventions veered toward again becoming "command" solutions to the coordination problem. This occurred because party conventions were private functions, initially unregulated by government. The seemingly democratic mechanism of the convention was open to manipulation by the party organizations that maintained complete control over its operation. For many decades, bribery at a state convention did not constitute a legal offense, and the delegates, selected

CAUCUS CURS in full YELL, or a WAR-WHOOP to saddle on the PEOPLE, a PAPPOOSE PRESIDENT.

After losing the battle for the presidency in 1924, Gen. Andrew Jackson won his war against the caucus system of nomination and ultimately won the office that he felt "King Caucus" and Congress had denied him. In this contemporary cartoon, Jackson is shown battling the "caucus curs."

in local primaries or caucuses, were not guaranteed the right to vote by ballot. Party machines and bosses could dictate nominees, and "[b]oth sneaks and sluggers were employed as the occasion dictated."

The current system of nomination used in the United States—choosing candidates through a primary election or, less frequently, a caucus attended by everyday voters—came as a result of the Progressive Era crusade against corrupt conventions. Turn-of-the-century Progressive leaders were sincerely outraged by the control that party bosses exerted over conventions, but they also saw that the old system stifled their own political ambitions. They recognized that a direct vote by party members, organized and regulated by government,

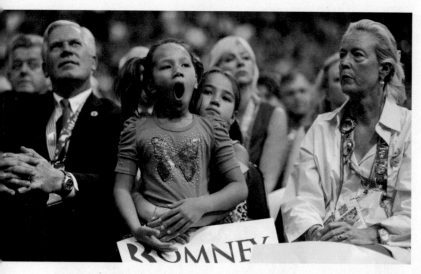

Presidential nominating conventions used to be dramatic, high-stakes events as the vote to pick the nominee stretched long into the night. Today, they are made-for-television spectacles planned to boost the campaign of a nominee chosen many months before, and they sometimes bore even those attending them. Here, seven-year-old Emma Maginn yawns while listening to speeches at the 2012 Republican National Convention.

could clean up corrupted nominations while at the same time improving their own chances of winning a nomination. "Fighting Bob" La Follette's Progressives led Wisconsin in jettisoning the convention and replacing it with the nation's first mandatory primary in 1903, which in turn helped nominate La Follette and many of his allies. By the time that California adopted the primary in 1909, and then elected Progressive Hiram Johnson to office the next year, a total of fifteen states required primaries.[14] By midcentury, every state had adopted primaries or caucuses to nominate candidates for state and federal office, providing an infrastructure that became ever more important in nominating presidential candidates through the 1960s and 1970s.

Today, parties use primaries for nearly all state and national nominations. While the details of who can vote in them and how ballots are structured vary in critically important ways, the collective action implications of all these systems can be analyzed together. Compared with the congressional caucus, with conventions, or with the systems that most European nations use to give party leaders power over nominations, a primary is much further removed from a command solution. Party members, at least those who care to participate in a primary, set their own agenda for the general election. This democratization of the process also provides a useful gauge of all candidates' popularity. Still, primary elections do impose some conformity costs. In 2008 primary voters who were energized by Hillary Clinton's campaign had to support Barack Obama if they wanted a Democrat to win in November, just as followers of Mike Huckabee and Mitt Romney were forced to unite with John McCain's backers in hopes of securing a Republican victory.

The major challenges that primary campaigns create come through the transaction costs that they impose. State and local governments spend millions of dollars to administer primary and caucus elections, the financial cost of keeping them fair and open. Candidates themselves often spend far more to compete in these contests, and the "money primary" that this creates can tilt the system toward favoring those who are able to raise large sums or to fund their own campaigns. Finally, if party elites in conventions or legislative caucuses pick nominees with an eye toward winning in the general election, then selecting them instead through a primary imposes an ideological transaction cost on nominees. Primary candidates have to take positions outside of the political center to please the party faithful, while those seeking to please party leaders would have an incentive to position themselves as the most moderate, electable candidate. While none of these are convincing arguments to justify a return to the nominating systems of the past, they do point out that a party's current solution to its coordination problem brings with it collective action trade-offs.

Term Limits as a Way Out of the Prisoner's Dilemma

Legislative term limits are an ancient idea—practiced in Athenian democracy and advocated by Aristotle—that has been revived in modern America. Term limits mandate turnover in a legislature, preventing representatives from running for reelection after they have held office for a specified period of time, typically six or eight years. These limits universally enforce a preference that many voters have for a government run by temporary servants whose tenure is cut short, no matter how well or poorly they serve the public. Because they intentionally sever the electoral connection between voters and their representatives, term limits can be thought of as a solution to one collective action problem that leads to another dilemma.

For voters wishing to be represented by a series of new legislators who bring fresh perspectives into office but don't stay there long, term limits provide a way out of the prisoner's dilemma that they face. Suppose a voter in one district has this preference. He can voice it by voting against his incumbent legislator once she has served a few terms in office. But during her tenure, this legislator has probably built up seniority on a committee, a reputation within the legislature, and the lawmaking experience necessary to deliver policies that the voter desires and certainly some special projects for the district. Voting the incumbent out would sacrifice all of these advantages. Another voter in a neighboring district might also favor turnover in the abstract, but faces the same concrete quandary. Both voters would like to elect someone new to office, but each worries that the other will defect from this plan and continue to vote for the current legislator. If either voter stands on principle and votes against the incumbent, his neighbor could reap the rewards of reelecting the only legislator in the area with much seniority, who could then deliver the lion's share of special projects to the district. In the end, both will probably play it safe, keep their incumbents in office, and grumble.

This is the crux of a prisoner's dilemma; neither voter can risk choosing his most preferred option because he will suffer when the other voter reaps the rewards of deviating from this strategy. The potential path out of it follows the common pattern of solutions to prisoner's dilemmas. Term limits use the power of governmental command to bind all voters together in regularly dumping their incumbents, ensuring that no district can defect to build up its legislator's seniority and influence. They coerce cooperation, once a majority of voters across the political system decide that they want turnover for turnover's sake.

Thinking about term limits this way provides a reasonable response to one argument often made against them. Politicians ranging from former California Assembly Speaker Antonio Villaraigosa to fictional *West Wing* President Josiah "Jed" Bartlet have asserted that "[w]e have term limits, and they are called elections."[15] Certainly, voters in a district can use elections to limit the terms of their own incumbents, but this amounts to unilateral disarmament if voters in other districts do not follow suit. Voters in some districts will use elections to maintain senior legislators in office and keep their interests influential, unless there is an enforceable agreement to limit everyone's term.

Of course, the language of collective action was rarely used by the modern campaign for term limits that began in the late 1980s. During this decade, dissatisfaction with Congress and state legislatures mounted in the wake of a number of scandals, but the voters—perhaps because they faced the prisoner's dilemma—kept reelecting their own incumbents at high rates. Groups of activists across the country saw an opportunity to take advantage of the public's momentary "throw the bums out!" mood to push for a reform that had been enacted in the Athenian legislature and in the first American Congress under the Articles of Confederation. Legislative term limit proposals came from a liberal group in the state of Washington and from conservative activists everywhere else.

Initially, many of these were grassroots groups run by people like Oregon health club owner Frank Eisenzimmer, who led the drive to pass his state's "LIMITS: Let Incumbents Mosey into the Sunset" initiative in 1992 (see box "The Health Club Owners Who Changed Oregon Politics"). Very soon, however, a national group dubbed U.S. Term Limits professionalized the movement, spending money raised from conservative donors on initiative campaigns in many states. Their efforts met with considerable success. Twenty states imposed term limits on their legislators between 1990 and 1996. At the time, the movement seemed poised for national success as well. Some state laws contained provisions limiting the number of terms for which members of the U.S. Congress from these states could serve. George Will, a prominent national political commentator, published *Restoration: Congress, Term Limits and the Recovery of Deliberative Democracy* in 1992, and the "Contract with America" that Republican congressional candidates pledged to in 1994 called for a vote on federal term limits.

Since that time of promise for term limit proponents, however, very little has gone right. When the constitutional amendment that Newt Gingrich and others had promised came to the House floor in March 1995, the vote split mostly along party lines, and, with 227 votes for to 204 votes against, it fell far short of the two-thirds supermajority that amendments must capture. In May of that year, the Supreme Court ruled in *U.S. Term Limits, Inc. v. Thornton* that states did not have the authority to limit the terms of members of Congress, because doing so would create an inconsistent patchwork of qualifications for office. These twin blows effectively ended the drive for federal term limits. In the states, the movement stalled after its initial burst of victories, with some of these gains eroding through the check that state courts possess on their own governments. Four state supreme courts threw out term limit initiatives, primarily on the technical grounds that they should have been passed as state constitutional amendments rather than statutes. Two state legislatures that had enacted limits, Utah and Idaho, later decided that cutting short their own terms was not such an appealing idea, after all.[16] In 2012, California voters approved a ballot measure that amended term limits by forcing legislators to spend a shorter time in the legislature overall, but allowing them to serve all of their limited time in one house of the legislature rather than trying to jump from the state Assembly to the Senate.

While their spread across the nation appears to be halted, term limits are now in effect in fifteen states ranging from Florida to Maine to Ohio to Nevada. This limited application has provided scholars and citizens alike the chance to observe and evaluate their effects. The limits did indeed bring the increased turnover that they promised, sometimes preventing as many as half of a house's members from running for reelection. Yet when they are "termed out," very few of these politicians simply disappear from politics. In every state, they run for other offices

THE HEALTH CLUB OWNERS WHO CHANGED OREGON POLITICS

strategy and choice

Although they owned competing gyms in the small town of Gresham, Oregon, Don McIntire and Frank Eisenzimmer cooperated to bring big changes to the structure of Oregon's government. In the early 1990s, each led a winning initiative drive that flexed the muscles of the potent antitax and anti-incumbent movements. Each demonstrated that everyday citizens with little record of political success could achieve big victories through smart, dedicated organizing efforts made at the right time and place.

McIntire's career had included stints as a disc jockey, an assistant city engineer, a health club owner, and a losing candidate for the Oregon state senate in 1980. When his personal candidacy failed, he became involved in initiative campaigns aimed at shrinking the size of government. After failed attempts at the state level and local successes, he ran into Eisenzimmer (who used to work out at McIntire's gym) when both were collecting signatures for ballot measures in 1990. They worked together on what became Measure 5 on that year's ballot, an initiative that proposed cutting property taxes in half, saving residents billions of dollars a year but putting funding for schools and other programs in jeopardy. McIntire took the lead, and took the brunt of criticism from political opponents who called him "a ding-aling" who "knows school financing like my dead dog does," and compared his tactics to those of Bolshevik revolutionary Leon Trotsky. But McIntire relished his role, and had the last laugh when Measure 5 passed in November.

Following this victory, Don McIntire receded from the political scene in order to spend more time running his health club, allowing Frank Eisenzimmer to take charge of the movement Measure 5 had created. After giving up his dream of becoming the next Mr. Oregon bodybuilding champion, Eisenzimmer had worked in a grocery store, in a cabinet shop, as a firefighter, and finally by running his own gym. He seemed to get the same sort of adrenaline rush from politics that he did from weightlifting, and certainly was no pushover. When Oregon's legislature voted down a term limits proposal in 1991, Eisenzimmer was waiting in the wings with his own initiative, and declared, "This is going to be a slam-dunk." He led the "LIMITS: Let Incumbents Mosey into the Sunset" campaign to victory the next year. After state legislators moved to repeal term limits five years later, Eisenzimmer reemerged to declare, "They're not only hypocritical, they're not very bright, because they're not going to pass this." He turned out to be right. In the end, Oregon's term limits law was overturned by the state supreme court, but not until after Eisenzimmer's initiative had gone into effect for two elections and ended the careers of many incumbent politicians.

On their face, these stories may seem at odds with this chapter's focus on the ways in which collective action problems can discourage individual action. That logic provides an explanation of how most people behave in the realm of politics, but gives no moral prescription for how everyone should act. Many citizens ignore their incentives to free ride, and instead put great efforts toward changing American government. A few of them succeed. Those who are passionately committed to a cause—whether or not it is one we all believe in—often provide the impetus for reforms that would otherwise be doomed by collective action dilemmas. The paradox of individual participation is that people can provide themselves with collective goods through politics only if they work for their provision for reasons other than enjoying the goods. This is why moral commitment was included as an asset in the earlier list of the advantages and disadvantages enjoyed by different groups. It is also why American politics is filled with colorful, potentially irrational, and often successful reformers such as Eisenzimmer and McIntire.

Sources: Barnes C. Ellis, "Measure 5 Triumph Converts Gadfly into Gad-Elephant," *The Oregonian,* November 8, 1990, C5; Phil Stanford, "Just Don't Call Him Late for Dinner," *The Oregonian,* November 5, 1990; Jeff Mapes, "Oregon Defeats Bid to Limit Congressional Terms," *The Oregonian,* March 19, 1991, B10; and Steve Suo, "State Senate Wants Voters to Ease Term Limits," *The Oregonian,* May 6, 1997, A1.

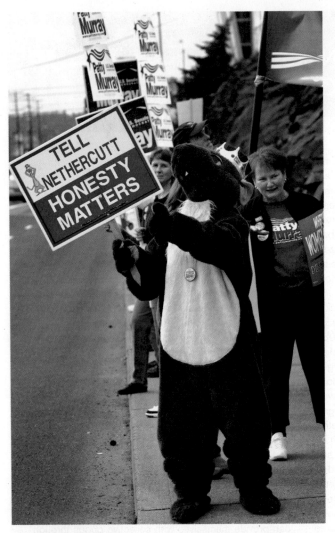

In an attempt at reforming American government through voluntary, individual actions rather than a mandatory law, some members of Congress took the "Term Limits Pledge" when they first ran for office during the 1990s, promising to step down after three or four terms. When U.S. representative George Nethercutt of Washington, a member of the "Republican Revolution" class of 1994, broke his pledge, U.S. Term Limits ran television ads attacking him as the "Weasel King." But he won reelection in 2000, demonstrating once again the ineffectiveness of voluntary reform efforts.

or seek other political jobs at surprisingly high rates. This fundamentally changes the relationship between voters as principals and legislators as agents. When politicians cannot run for reelection, they lose their incentive to serve the voters in their district, and instead have reason to please the next principal for whom they plan to work. Whether that principal is a new constituency, a governor from whom they want a job, or an interest group for which they plan to lobby, this shift in the incentives of legislators can hurt the interests of the voters who first elected them. Research shows that term-limited legislators spend less time getting to know voters in their district, working for constituent interests, or responding to their preferences on tough votes.

The steep spikes in turnover brought by the implementation of term limit laws also impose transaction costs on legislatures. Much institutional knowledge is lost at once, and the deliberative processes that houses have worked out over generations are disrupted. The most costly disruption, many studies have shown, affects the legislature's interaction with the executive branch. Power shifts greatly toward the governor and state bureaucracies, as legislatures do less to scrutinize the governor's budget proposals and oversee the administration of laws by state agencies.[17] This jeopardizes the legislature's role as a check on the executive, the mechanism for maintaining the separation of powers for which James Madison argued so forcefully in *Federalist* No. 51. Whether it was intended or not, term limits in the states have threatened the legislature's role as a coequal branch. Perhaps that is why the Framers, after observing that term limits had weakened Congress in the Articles of Confederation, kept them out of the Constitution.

Attempts to Fight Free Riding and Increase Voter Turnout

Because elections are meant to measure the desires of the electorate, and since accurately reflecting these desires is necessary for perfect representation to take place, the U.S. political system would work best if every eligible voter turned out on Election Day. Yet accomplishing this collective goal requires actions by individuals who face incentives to free ride. It is undeniably costly to take time out of one's day to cast a ballot, and the chances that any single vote swings an election are minute. Everyone certainly shares a stake in holding participatory elections; if nobody turned out, government would cease to be representative and legitimate. But because a hesitant voter can rely on others who share his views to vote, he can get away with shirking his democratic duty. As Chapter 11 notes, it is perfectly logical for a single citizen to free ride on the democratic participation of others, leading to a classic collective action problem in which individuals enjoy the benefits of everyone else's effort while failing to contribute themselves.

The classic solution would be for the government to step in and enforce behavior, just as the government does in requiring everyone who meets certain criteria to pay taxes or to register for the draft. Some countries such as Australia, Belgium, and Italy make voter turnout mandatory. The United States has never seriously moved in that direction. In fact, as Chapter 4's coverage of the civil rights movement shows, the most consequential steps taken by government for most of American history have been to suppress, rather than to increase, voter turnout. Why have there been no reform campaigns to make voting mandatory, or to offer a selective benefit by having election officials pay everyone who turns out?

At the level of theory, one might argue that this imposes high conformity costs on citizens who simply do not want to vote. But the more practical reason that these potential reforms have not been pursued with greater energy is that while full turnout might be good for the nation as a whole, it is never clearly in the interests of any faction with the organizational might to push for it. Unlike the collection of taxes, full turnout does not bring in trillions of dollars for Congress and the president to spend. Unlike the draft, full turnout does not provide the armed forces with soldiers in a time of large-scale war. Neither major party would likely benefit from full voter turnout: research on political participation indicates that although nonvoters differ from voters in their demographic characteristics, they generally share the preferences of those who turn out in major elections. Since no narrow group would derive a discrete benefit from full participation in elections, none has a direct incentive to take up the fight. In effect, a collective action dilemma lies in the way of solving the free-rider problem that plagues voter turnout.

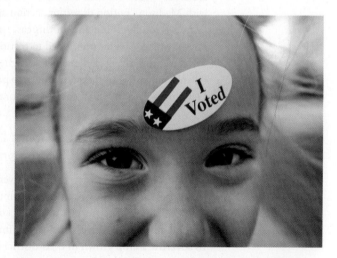

Our national and state governments have taken some relatively minor steps toward increasing voter participation. Some, such as the federal Motor Voter Law described in Chapter 11 on page 494, and the vote-by-mail elections held in Oregon, aim to discourage free riding by making registration and voting as easy as possible. The "I Voted!" stickers that many local election officials hand out are a selective benefit akin to the coffee mugs and tote bags that PBS stations give out

Voting is its own reward, but some local registrars provide an extra selective benefit by handing out stickers at the polls so that anyone who turns out can show off their democratic participation to family, friends, coworkers, and neighbors. During the 2006 election in Rhode Island, this five-year-old girl accompanied her mother to the polling place and proudly wore her sticker.

during pledge breaks, designed to reward their proud wearers individually for contributing to the collective good. While any effort to increase voter turnout is certainly laudable, American government has shied away from the sorts of larger steps, such as mandating turnout or automatically registering eligible voters, that help many European nations achieve much higher levels of participation than in the United States.

Instead, the American approach has largely been to delegate the task of turning out voters to political parties and interest groups. While none of these organizations has a stake in increasing the turnout rate overall, each has a profound incentive to bring its own supporters to the polls. The grassroots efforts of parties, labor unions, trade organizations, and ideological movements are all designed to stop their adherents from free riding. Get-out-the-vote drives decrease the costs of turnout by informing people about elections and offering rides to polls. They also increase the penalty for free riding when campaign volunteers, constantly checking the sign-in sheets at a polling place, knock on targeted voters' doors until they cast a ballot. Throughout our history, these faction-based turnout drives have been extraordinarily successful, and new technologies allow groups to be even more focused on isolating and mobilizing their followers. Major campaigns now routinely use **microtargeting** databases that combine voter rolls with credit card purchase information and even grocery store savings club records in order to identify potential supporters, then send volunteers out with smartphones directing them straight to a targeted voter's doorstep.

America's decentralized approach to voter mobilization works for those allied with a well-organized party or interest group, but what about everyone else? When the task of turning out voters is delegated to a set of agents whose incentives are not aligned with those of voters overall, there is a risk that agency loss may result. No group has an incentive to mobilize truly independent voters, making it more likely that they will free ride. If the parties or interests are evenly balanced, then each will mobilize its own supporters in equal numbers. This fits with Madison's notion of setting faction against faction, but can create problems when one faction is locally dominant. In this case, a status quo bias will emerge because the party in power, which is better positioned to recruit volunteers and raise resources for a mobilization drive, can turn out its adherents at a higher rate and capture even more political power. The reliance on parties and interest groups to pay the price of discouraging free riding on Election Day comes with potential costs to electoral equity.

Stopping "Earmarks" from Leading to the Tragedy of the Commons

Members of Congress have authority over the entire nation's budget, but each member has a direct electoral incentive to guide as much of this money as possible to his or her home district. Constituents and local groups constantly come to their representatives with pleas to fund a new post office, to widen an interstate highway, to support a museum, or to pay to advertise a crop grown in their district. If Congress **earmarks** money in the federal budget to pay for one of these projects, district voters receive a big benefit while only paying a tiny share of the costs because the price tag is spread across all districts. The problem is that because this is such a great deal for any single member of Congress, every member wants to make it happen for his or her own district. The aggregate effect of 435 representatives' and one hundred senators' individual decisions is that total spending on earmarks rises dramatically, setting up a classic tragedy of the commons. Just as herdsmen will overgraze a pasture because each pays hardly any costs for allowing one more cow to feed on it, Congress may overspend when its members are tempted to bring home one more project at little direct cost to their own districts.

Congress spent a total of $16.5 billion on 9,129 earmarked projects in 2010, according to Citizens Against Government Waste, the leading group that has taken up the crusade against such spending. Earmarks in recent years have included $3 million for The First Tee, a program designed "[t]o impact the lives of young people by providing learning facilities and educational programs that promote character development and life enhancing values through the game of golf"; $2 million for the Charles B. Rangel Center for Public Service; and $188,000 for the Lobster Institute in Maine, which maintains the "Lobster Cam" website.[18] While congressional leaders often emphasize that earmarks account for less than one-third of 1 percent of the federal budget,[19] voters are often outraged when they hear how some of their tax dollars are spent. Groups like Citizens Against Government Waste approach ending earmarks by publicizing this spending in an attempt to shame members of Congress into abstaining from it. While a handful of representatives and senators do refuse to pursue money for their districts, hoping for voluntary compliance has largely failed. The logic of the tragedy of the commons explains why. If one legislator alone abstains from spending a portion of the federal budget on his or her own district, the voters there lose out on valuable projects while only a small amount in overall spending has been saved. Because of this logic, it is rational for each individual member of Congress to pursue earmarks, even though the aggregate effect is billions of dollars in spending that many voters consider wasteful—at least, wasteful when it is spent in someone else's district.

Legislative leaders who have the collective interest of Congress in mind have intermittently attempted to solve this problem. (Of course, powerful leaders have also intermittently secured millions in funding for their own districts.) To solve it, they have reached into the Framers' tool kit of collective action solutions that we introduced in Chapter 1. Their first attempt was the mandatory, institutional approach of the **line-item veto**. This tool, also called an *item veto*, gives a chief executive the authority to cut individual items out of the budget that a legislature passes, while signing the rest of the spending bill into law. A president could use it to veto earmarks without derailing the entire federal budget. Not surprisingly, this is an example of a veto from the Framers' tool kit, a unilateral power to block new policy and preserve the status quo. In this way, it preserves the commons by giving one officeholder who is not tied to any particular district the ability to regulate how much money comes out of the federal treasury. To be sure, the line-item veto would increase the president's influence greatly. But it is also not a bad deal for members of Congress, especially compared to passing a self-imposed ban on earmarks or individually abstaining from them. When the president possesses final authority over each line of spending in appropriations bills, members of Congress are free to load them up with as many earmarks as they please, knowing that they can claim credit for fighting for their district but then blame the president when he eventually vetoes the projects.

This was part of the strategy motivating Congress's passage, under Newt Gingrich's leadership and in fulfillment of a promise contained in the "Contract with America," of a statute giving the president the line-item veto. The politics of this bill made for strange bedfellows. As Chapter 7 details, when the Republican-led Congress passed the Line Item Veto Act of 1996, President Bill Clinton happily signed it. Over the next two years, Clinton used the new authority that the opposition party had given him to veto eighty-two of the items that they sent him in eleven spending bills. Because one of these items vetoed happened to promise more Medicaid funding for New York City, Mayor Rudolph Giuliani initiated a lawsuit arguing that Congress did not have the authority to give up power in this way to presidents. The Supreme Court agreed in *Clinton v. City of New York* (1998) that because the line-item veto gave the executive branch powers not granted by the Constitution, a constitutional amendment was necessary in order to institute it. Democratic senator Robert Byrd, who had led an earlier suit against the line-item veto, joined Mayor Giuliani in celebrating the decision, while President Clinton and congressional Republicans bemoaned it.[20] These peculiar alignments demonstrate that neither party had a consistent ideological stance on the issue at that time, with positions dictated mostly by every player's institutional role.

A decade later, the parties did begin to split in their positions on earmarks, with many Republicans—and especially the Tea Party adherents within the Republican caucus—taking a public stand against district-specific spending. They did so in part because of their ideological commitment to a smaller government, but it did not hurt that their opposition to earmarks could bring electoral benefits to the party overall if they stuck together in renouncing such spending. Republican leaders recognized that while voters might like to see money coming into their districts, they hated to see it flowing elsewhere. If all of the members of one party could make a pact to forgo the temptation of earmarks, their collective frugality could indeed make an impact on overall spending, and voters would see this party as fiscally responsible. In essence, this strategy mimics one of the oldest and simplest solutions to the tragedy of the commons: privatizing the collective resource. As we saw in Chapter 1, one way for herdsmen to prevent each other from overgrazing a common pasture is to divide it up into sections, which each herdsman can control and from which each can derive the benefits. In 2010 the GOP's House leadership attempted to divide up spending patterns into "Republican earmarks" and "Democratic earmarks" in the minds of voters. If Republicans all agreed not to seek earmarks for their districts, the government could save billions, and the party could develop a clear reputation for stinginess. When Democratic legislators spent on earmarks, this would deplete the "commons" of the federal treasury, to be sure, but it would make Republicans look even better in the eyes of voters. Republicans hoped that the electoral gains from developing a national reputation for fiscal responsibility would outweigh the electoral costs of not bringing home earmarks in their individual districts and states.

The trouble was that to put their solution into practice, Republican leaders needed to keep all of their members on the fiscal austerity bandwagon. The incentives for individual representatives and senators to defect from this strategy by requesting earmarks were enormous. They could reap the rewards of their party's reputation and still bring home the bacon to their districts. Faced with this temptation as the 2010 elections approached, even most Republicans who were members of the Tea Party caucus sought earmarks. In this fifty-two-member caucus, which publicly sought spending cuts and a smaller government, only fourteen legislators refrained from asking for earmarks. The other Tea Party Republicans in Congress asked for 764 earmarks, costing over $1 billion for the 2010 fiscal year.[21] Though these accounted for just a small part of the $16.5 billion spent on earmarks that year, it was not the way to build a reputation for fiscal austerity.

When Republicans retook control of the House after the 2010 elections, party leaders were in a stronger position to crack down on any members who might request earmarks, and

A primary rationale for the line-item veto passed in 1996 was that it would allow presidents to eliminate spending on inefficient local projects championed by individual members of Congress. Because the Supreme Court struck down the line-item veto two years later, the federal budget still includes items like the $229 million originally earmarked to build the "Bridge to Nowhere" to connect Ketchikan, Alaska, pictured above, to Gravina Island, with its population of fifty residents. Public outcry over this earmark led it to be eventually dropped from the 2005 transportation spending bill, but the federal government did appropriate $2 million for the "Charles B. Rangel Center for Public Service" (named after the House Ways and Means chairman, by pure coincidence) and $500,000 for a planned Teapot Museum in Sparta, North Carolina.

members collectively agreed not to seek any.[22] Worried that a reputation for unchecked profligacy might cost them votes in 2012, Democrats in the House responded by pledging not to seek earmarks that benefited for-profit groups (thus tending to their own part of the commons). Yet neither of these strategies would work unless senators from each party followed the plans of their House colleagues. If senators continued their free-spending ways, the commons would be "overgrazed" by billions of dollars in earmarks, and party reputations would be ruined. In the immediate aftermath of the 2010 election, Senate Republicans appeared poised to band together to deny themselves earmarks. "I know the good that has come from the projects I have helped support throughout my state," said Senate Republican Leader Mitch McConnell, who had garnered many earmarks for Kentucky in the past. "But there is simply no doubt that the abuse of this practice has caused Americans to view it as a symbol of the waste and out-of-control spending that every Republican in Washington is determined to fight."[23] After President Obama pledged in his 2011 State of the Union address to veto any bill containing an earmark, senators from his own party reluctantly agreed with Republican lawmakers to institute a two-year ban on earmarks.[24] An age-old practice in Congress, it seemed, had been ended.

Yet even as the ban was being enacted, legislators driven by the inexorable local of politics set about finding creative ways to evade it. Republican senator Lamar Alexander called the earmark moratorium merely a "timeout," noting, "I reserve the right to ask Congress and the president to approve measures of urgent importance to Tennesseans." His GOP colleague from Georgia, Sen. Saxby Chambliss, explained that "there are times when crises arise or issues come forth of such importance to Georgia, such as the Port of Savannah . . . that I reserve the right to ask Congress and the president to approve funding."[25] Neither senator would commit to leaving the commons untouched, knowing how much home-state voters appreciated their own earmarks. When Republican senator Jon Kyl secured $200 million to settle a water rights claim by an American Indian tribe in his state of Arizona only three days after GOP senators renounced earmarks, the *Washington Post* reported that "Senate Republicans' ban on earmarks . . . was short-lived."[26] In 2012, legislators evaded this ban by creating "special funds," including twenty-six funds totaling $507 million within the Army Corps of Engineers' budget, that directed money to just the sorts of local projects that had been funded through earmarks in the past. Reacting to this innovation in earmarking, the leader of the budget watchdog group Taxpayers for Common Sense lamented that, "We thought we'd gotten rid of earmarks. But it looks like Congress has just moved on to other methods that are less transparent than the old way, like creating these slush funds."[27] When it comes to sending money home to their districts, it seems, Congress's appetite for overgrazing the commons is insatiable.

The temporary success but eventual failure of efforts to end earmarks underscores that reform victories can be ephemeral when they stop short of amending the Constitution. But what if the line-item veto had survived judicial review, or if Senate Republicans had remained united in their bid to ban earmarks? Would it have solved the tragedy of the commons without causing any further problems? Some scholarly works[28] on the contribution of earmarks to the smooth operation of legislatures imply that eliminating them would place high transaction costs on Congress. Including earmarks in a bill, these works argue, is a relatively cheap way to secure the support of hesitant legislators, in effect "greasing the wheels" of Congress. Earmarks serve as a selective benefit offered to members to support a bill containing policies that might cause them to take political heat in their districts. General spending bills could become even more difficult to pass if they were not loaded with concrete, district-specific projects, or if these projects were sure to be vetoed. The temptation of earmarks certainly poses a collective action problem—a tragedy of the commons that results in billions of dollars of federal spending on local projects every year—for Congress, but this problem may itself be part of the solution for Congress's higher-stakes challenge of coming to agreement on the $3.8 trillion overall federal budget.

■ **TAKE A SURVEY**

Do you support a ban on earmarks?

THE TRICKY BUSINESS OF INSTITUTIONAL REFORM

All of these stories point out problems in the American political system, the trade-offs associated with proposed solutions to them, and the challenges that must be overcome by any attempt to enact major change. Institutional shortcomings inevitably become targets for reform; some people in every generation want to "reinvent government." Those who believe that particular rules and practices or the system as a whole slights their interests or thwarts necessary changes naturally look for alternative arrangements that would redress these problems. But designing effective institutions—ones that accomplish what their designers intend—is tricky business. The political world is so densely interconnected and human beings are so clever at discovering and exploiting opportunities that the full impact of any significant institutional innovation is impossible to predict; every significant change is likely to have unintended and unwanted consequences.

What might happen if one of the reform proposals currently gaining attention comes to fruition? Getting rid of the Electoral College would ensure that whichever presidential candidate wins the popular vote is elected, and shift candidates' focus from a dozen or so "battleground states" to voters all across the nation. But note that in doing so, it would require candidates to raise vastly larger sums to run serious nationwide campaigns, all but dooming our system of voluntary public financing for presidential campaigns. And rather than conducting "retail politics" campaigns in swing states such as New Mexico, Wisconsin, and Virginia, candidates would be forced to market themselves wholesale, spreading their efforts broadly but making few deep connections. These potential side effects should be considered before backing an otherwise reasonable reform. Speculation about the potentially perverse consequences of well-intentioned reforms is important, even if perfect prediction is impossible.

Thinking hard about the logic of collective action can provide hints for anticipating some of the consequences of institutional innovations. Any reform that alters individual incentives changes behavior in predictable ways because in politics most people, most of the time, are engaged in the strategic pursuit of transparent interests—interests that can frustrate the capacity of the community to achieve desired collective goods. Yet those who design institutions can take the interests into account and structure participants' incentives so that the play of interests will yield successful collective action. Any institutional reform whose success requires political actors to routinely ignore their own interests is certain to disappoint. As James Madison observed in *Federalist* No. 51, connecting "the interest of the man . . . with the constitutional rights of the place" was an uppermost concern of the Framers as they fashioned new governmental institutions. Well-informed by both theory and experience, the Framers employed this logic well, an important reason why their work has lasted.

Thus the first task for anyone intent on redesigning institutions involves mapping out how proposed changes would alter incentives and therefore the strategic behavior of political actors. Do the revised rules and reformed institutions tempt politicians to renege on collective pursuits when citizens would want them to cooperate? Or conversely, do they invite their collusion when the citizenry's interests would be best served by healthy competition? Does the reform encourage agents to shirk or in other ways violate their responsibilities to their principals? Proposals for change that do not anticipate at least the obvious strategic responses of those who occupy new or reconfigured offices are thus fundamentally misguided and probably doomed.

Yet when reforms align the incentives of individuals with collective goals—as many have in American history, beginning with the work of the Framers—the benefits that they bring can clearly outweigh any flaws. Success is possible, even if it is not inevitable. The barriers to reform built into our system are designed to help distinguish between ideas that merely strive

TAKE A QUIZ

logic.cqpress.com

Test your knowledge of this chapter.

for laudable goals and plans that wisely harness human nature to achieve their ends. The winnowing process may not be perfect. Still, the overarching design of our political system, with its status quo bias, opportunities for state-level trials, and multiple checks and balances, seems to be suited for our national character. We can love our country and its institutions, but be unafraid of the endeavor to make them better. We can see reform ideas as worth pursuing, debating, often discarding, and sometimes deserving of an experiment. We have built enough obstacles into our political system to slow the pace of radical reforms, both bad ones and good ones, but never to stifle change completely. As long as America lasts, our brief, brilliant, and imperfect Constitution will remain the battlefield for our nation of energetic reformers.

logic.cqpress.com

■■■ Key Terms ■■■

earmarks, 686	line-item veto, 687	status quo bias, 673
King Caucus, 678	microtargeting, 686	term limits, 669
laboratories for reform, 674	nominating convention, 678	

■■■ Suggested Readings ■■■

Bernstein, Richard B., and Jerome Agel. *Amending America: If We Love the Constitution So Much, Why Do We Keep Trying to Change It?* Lawrence: University Press of Kansas, 1993. Lively discussion not only of the debates and politics that led to the twenty-seven successful constitutional amendments in American history but also of the thousands of failed attempts.

Farrar-Myers, Victoria A., and Diana Dwyre. *Limits and Loopholes: The Quest for Money, Free Speech, and Fair Elections.* Washington, DC: CQ Press, 2007. Two political scientists who have also served on congressional staffs discuss the goals and effects of campaign finance laws, with special attention given to the BCRA reforms.

Green, Donald P., and Alan S. Gerber. *Get Out the Vote! How to Increase Voter Turnout.* Washington, DC: Brookings, 2004. This book applies rigorous scientific methods to discover how well voter mobilization techniques such as door-to-door canvassing, direct mail, and phone banking actually work.

Kurtz, Karl T., Bruce Cain, and Richard G. Niemi, eds. *Institutional Change in American Politics: The Case of Term Limits.* Ann Arbor: University of Michigan Press, 2007. Also Rick Farmer, Christopher Z. Mooney, Richard J. Powell, and John C. Green, eds. *Legislating without Experience: Case Studies in State Legislative Term Limits.* Lanham, MD: Lexington Books, 2007. These companion volumes present the result of a unique cooperative study conducted in nine states by scholars and staff organizations to evaluate the impact of term limits on state legislatures.

Thompson, Hunter S. *Fear and Loathing on the Campaign Trail '72.* New York: Warner Books, 1973. The inventor of "gonzo journalism" covers the race for the Democratic presidential nomination in 1972, the party conventions, and the general election, beginning with his chance meeting with eventual nominee George McGovern in a hotel restroom.

■ Review Questions ■

1. What are some basic principles of institutional design that have been used by the Framers and others to ensure that the interests of those who make political decisions are aligned with those affected by those decisions?

2. What are the benefits of making the U.S. Constitution difficult to change? What are the disadvantages? Do these rules enhance or inhibit democracy?

3. What collective action problems do political parties and voters face in elections in which multiple candidates from each party are running? How are these problems addressed by the implementation of direct primaries? Are there any disadvantages to primaries?

4. Why do many reforms, such as campaign finance laws, fail to work as intended?

5. What role can individuals play in efforts to reform American laws and institutions? What are the benefits of engaging in political activity—be it voting for, donating to, or working for a candidate or party? Do such activities ever pay off?

Reference Material

APPENDIXES

Appendix 1

ARTICLES OF CONFEDERATION

To all to whom these Presents shall come, we the undersigned Delegates of the States affixed to our Names send greeting.

Articles of Confederation and perpetual Union between the states of New Hampshire, Massachusetts-bay Rhode Island and Providence Plantations, Connecticut, New York, New Jersey, Pennsylvania, Delaware, Maryland, Virginia, North Carolina, South Carolina and Georgia.

Article I

The Stile of this Confederacy shall be **"The United States of America".**

Article II

Each state retains its sovereignty, freedom, and independence, and every power, jurisdiction, and right, which is not by this Confederation expressly delegated to the United States, in Congress assembled.

Article III

The said States hereby severally enter into a firm league of friendship with each other, for their common defense, the security of their liberties, and their mutual and general welfare, binding themselves to assist each other, against all force offered to, or attacks made upon them, or any of them, on account of religion, sovereignty, trade, or any other pretense whatever.

Article IV

The better to secure and perpetuate mutual friendship and intercourse among the people of the different States in this Union, the free inhabitants of each of these States, paupers, vagabonds, and fugitives from justice excepted, shall be entitled to all privileges and immunities of free citizens in the several States; and the people of each State shall free ingress and regress to and from any other State, and shall enjoy therein all the privileges of trade and commerce, subject to the same duties, impositions, and restrictions as the inhabitants thereof respectively, provided that such restrictions shall not extend so far as to prevent the removal of property imported into any State, to any other State, of which the owner is an inhabitant; provided also that no imposition, duties or restriction shall be laid by any State, on the property of the United States, or either of them.

If any person guilty of, or charged with, treason, felony, or other high misdemeanor in any State, shall flee from justice, and be found in any of the United States, he shall, upon demand of the Governor or executive power of the State from which he fled, be delivered up and removed to the State having jurisdiction of his offense.

Full faith and credit shall be given in each of these States to the records, acts, and judicial proceedings of the courts and magistrates of every other State.

Article V

For the most convenient management of the general interests of the United States, delegates shall be annually appointed in such manner as the legislatures of each State shall direct, to meet in Congress on the first Monday in November, in every year, with a power reserved to each State to recall its delegates, or any of them, at any time within the year, and to send others in their stead for the remainder of the year.

No State shall be represented in Congress by less than two, nor more than seven members; and no person shall be capable of being a delegate for more than three years in any term of six years; nor shall any person, being a delegate, be capable of holding any office under the United States, for which he, or another for his benefit, receives any salary, fees or emolument of any kind.

Each State shall maintain its own delegates in a meeting of the States, and while they act as members of the committee of the States.

In determining questions in the United States in Congress assembled, each State shall have one vote.

Freedom of speech and debate in Congress shall not be impeached or questioned in any court or place out of Congress, and the members of Congress shall be protected in their persons from arrests or imprisonments, during the time of their going to and from, and attendence on Congress, except for treason, felony, or breach of the peace.

Article VI

No State, without the consent of the United States in Congress assembled, shall send any embassy to, or receive any embassy from, or enter into any conference, agreement, alliance or treaty with any King, Prince or State; nor shall any person holding any office of profit or trust under the United States, or any of them, accept any present, emolument, office or title of any kind whatever from any King, Prince or foreign State; nor shall the United States in Congress assembled, or any of them, grant any title of nobility.

No two or more States shall enter into any treaty, confederation or alliance whatever between them, without the consent of the United States in Congress assembled, specifying accurately the purposes for which the same is to be entered into, and how long it shall continue.

No State shall lay any imposts or duties, which may interfere with any stipulations in treaties, entered into by the United States in Congress assembled, with any King, Prince or State, in pursuance of any treaties already proposed by Congress, to the courts of France and Spain.

No vessel of war shall be kept up in time of peace by any State, except such number only, as shall be deemed necessary by the United States in Congress assembled, for the defense of such State, or its trade; nor shall any body of forces be kept up by any State in time of peace, except such number only, as in the judgement of the United States in Congress assembled, shall be deemed requisite to garrison the forts necessary for the defense of such State; but every State shall always keep up a well-regulated and disciplined militia, sufficiently armed and accoutered, and shall provide and constantly have ready for use, in public stores, a due number of filed pieces and tents, and a proper quantity of arms, ammunition and camp equipage.

No State shall engage in any war without the consent of the United States in Congress assembled, unless such State be actually invaded by enemies, or shall have received certain advice of a resolution being formed by some nation of Indians to invade such State, and the danger is so imminent as not to admit of a delay till the United States in Congress assembled can be consulted; nor shall any State grant commissions to any ships or vessels of war, nor letters of marque or reprisal, except it be after a declaration of war by the United States in Congress assembled, and then only against the Kingdom or State and the subjects thereof, against which war has been so declared, and under such regulations as shall be established by the United States in Congress assembled, unless such State be infested by pirates, in which case vessels of war may be fitted out for that occasion, and kept so long as the danger shall continue, or until the United States in Congress assembled shall determine otherwise.

Article VII

When land forces are raised by any State for the common defense, all officers of or under the rank of colonel, shall be appointed by the legislature of each State respectively, by whom such forces shall be raised, or in such manner as such State shall direct, and all vacancies shall be filled up by the State which first made the appointment.

Article VIII

All charges of war, and all other expenses that shall be incurred for the common defense or general welfare, and allowed by the United States in Congress assembled, shall be defrayed out of a common treasury, which shall be supplied by the several States in proportion to the value of all land within each State, granted or surveyed for any person, as such land and the buildings and improvements thereon shall be estimated according to such mode as the United States in Congress assembled, shall from time to time direct and appoint.

The taxes for paying that proportion shall be laid and levied by the authority and direction of the legislatures of the several States within the time agreed upon by the United States in Congress assembled.

Article IX

The United States in Congress assembled, shall have the sole and exclusive right and power of determining on peace and war, except in the cases mentioned in the sixth article—of sending and receiving ambassadors—entering into treaties and alliances, provided that no treaty of commerce shall be made whereby the legislative power of the respective States shall be restrained from imposing such imposts and duties on foreigners, as their own people are subjected to, or from prohibiting the exportation or importation of any species of goods or commodities whatsoever—of establishing rules for deciding in all cases, what captures on land or water shall be legal, and in what manner prizes taken by land or naval forces in the service of the United States shall be divided or appropriated—of granting letters of marque and reprisal in times of peace—appointing courts for the trial of piracies and felonies commited on the high seas and establishing courts for receiving and determining finally appeals in all cases of captures, provided that no member of Congress shall be appointed a judge of any of the said courts.

The United States in Congress assembled shall also be the last resort on appeal in all disputes and differences now subsisting or that hereafter may arise between two or more States concerning boundary, jurisdiction or any other causes whatever; which authority shall always be exercised in the manner following. Whenever the legislative or executive authority or lawful agent of any State in controversy with another shall present a petition to Congress stating the matter in question and praying for a hearing, notice thereof shall be given by order of Congress to the legislative or executive authority of the other State in controversy, and a day assigned for the appearance of the parties by their lawful agents, who shall then be directed to appoint by joint consent,

commissioners or judges to constitute a court for hearing and determining the matter in question: but if they cannot agree, Congress shall name three persons out of each of the United States, and from the list of such persons each party shall alternately strike out one, the petitioners beginning, until the number shall be reduced to thirteen; and from that number not less than seven, nor more than nine names as Congress shall direct, shall in the presence of Congress be drawn out by lot, and the persons whose names shall be so drawn or any five of them, shall be commissioners or judges, to hear and finally determine the controversy, so always as a major part of the judges who shall hear the cause shall agree in the determination: and if either party shall neglect to attend at the day appointed, without showing reasons, which Congress shall judge sufficient, or being present shall refuse to strike, the Congress shall proceed to nominate three persons out of each State, and the secretary of Congress shall strike in behalf of such party absent or refusing; and the judgement and sentence of the court to be appointed, in the manner before prescribed, shall be final and conclusive; and if any of the parties shall refuse to submit to the authority of such court, or to appear or defend their claim or cause, the court shall nevertheless proceed to pronounce sentence, or judgement, which shall in like manner be final and decisive, the judgement or sentence and other proceedings being in either case transmitted to Congress, and lodged among the acts of Congress for the security of the parties concerned: provided that every commissioner, before he sits in judgement, shall take an oath to be administered by one of the judges of the supreme or superior court of the State, where the cause shall be tried, 'well and truly to hear and determine the matter in question, according to the best of his judgement, without favor, affection or hope of reward': provided also, that no State shall be deprived of territory for the benefit of the United States.

All controversies concerning the private right of soil claimed under different grants of two or more States, whose jurisdictions as they may respect such lands, and the States which passed such grants are adjusted, the said grants or either of them being at the same time claimed to have originated antecedent to such settlement of jurisdiction, shall on the petition of either party to the Congress of the United States, be finally determined as near as may be in the same manner as is before presecribed for deciding disputes respecting territorial jurisdiction between different States.

The United States in Congress assembled shall also have the sole and exclusive right and power of regulating the alloy and value of coin struck by their own authority, or by that of the respective States—fixing the standards of weights and measures throughout the United States—regulating the trade and managing all affairs with the Indians, not members of any of the States, provided that the legislative right of any State within its own limits be not infringed or violated—establishing or regulating post offices from one State to another, throughout all the United States, and exacting such postage on the papers passing through the same as may be requisite to defray the expenses of the said office—appointing all officers of the land forces, in the service of the United States, excepting regimental officers—appointing all the officers of the naval forces, and commissioning all officers whatever in the service of the United States—making rules for the government and regulation of the said land and naval forces, and directing their operations.

The United States in Congress assembled shall have authority to appoint a committee, to sit in the recess of Congress, to be denominated 'A Committee of the States', and to consist of one delegate from each State; and to appoint such other committees and civil officers as may be necessary for managing the general affairs of the United States under their direction—to appoint one of their members to preside, provided that no person be allowed to serve in the office of president more than one year in any term of three years; to ascertain the necessary sums of money to be raised for the service of the United States, and to appropriate and apply the same for defraying the public expenses—to borrow money, or emit bills on the credit of the United States, transmitting every half-year to the respective States an account of the sums of money so borrowed or emitted—to build and equip a navy—to agree upon the number of land forces, and to make requisitions from each State for its quota, in proportion to the number of white inhabitants in such State; which requisition shall

be binding, and thereupon the legislature of each State shall appoint the regimental officers, raise the men and cloath, arm and equip them in a solid-like manner, at the expense of the United States; and the officers and men so cloathed, armed and equipped shall march to the place appointed, and within the time agreed on by the United States in Congress assembled. But if the United States in Congress assembled shall, on consideration of circumstances judge proper that any State should not raise men, or should raise a smaller number of men than the quota thereof, such extra number shall be raised, officered, cloathed, armed and equipped in the same manner as the quota of each State, unless the legislature of such State shall judge that such extra number cannot be safely spread out in the same, in which case they shall raise, officer, cloath, arm and equip as many of such extra number as they judge can be safely spared. And the officers and men so cloathed, armed, and equipped, shall march to the place appointed, and within the time agreed on by the United States in Congress assembled.

The United States in Congress assembled shall never engage in a war, nor grant letters of marque or reprisal in time of peace, nor enter into any treaties or alliances, nor coin money, nor regulate the value thereof, nor ascertain the sums and expenses necessary for the defense and welfare of the United States, or any of them, nor emit bills, nor borrow money on the credit of the United States, nor appropriate money, nor agree upon the number of vessels of war, to be built or purchased, or the number of land or sea forces to be raised, nor appoint a commander in chief of the army or navy, unless nine States assent to the same: nor shall a question on any other point, except for adjourning from day to day be determined, unless by the votes of the majority of the United States in Congress assembled.

The Congress of the United States shall have power to adjourn to any time within the year, and to any place within the United States, so that no period of adjournment be for a longer duration than the space of six months, and shall publish the journal of their proceedings monthly, except such parts thereof relating to treaties, alliances or military operations, as in their judgement require secrecy; and the yeas and nays of the delegates of each State on any question shall be entered on the journal, when it is desired by any delegates of a State, or any of them, at his or their request shall be furnished with a transcript of the said journal, except such parts as are above excepted, to lay before the legislatures of the several States.

Article X

The Committee of the States, or any nine of them, shall be authorized to execute, in the recess of Congress, such of the powers of Congress as the United States in Congress assembled, by the consent of the nine States, shall from time to time think expedient to vest them with; provided that no power be delegated to the said Committee, for the exercise of which, by the Articles of Confederation, the voice of nine States in the Congress of the United States assembled be requisite.

Article XI

Canada acceding to this confederation, and adjoining in the measures of the United States, shall be admitted into, and entitled to all the advantages of this Union; but no other colony shall be admitted into the same, unless such admission be agreed to by nine States.

Article XII

All bills of credit emitted, monies borrowed, and debts contracted by, or under the authority of Congress, before the assembling of the United States, in pursuance of the present confederation, shall be deemed and considered as a charge against the United States, for payment and satisfaction whereof the said United States, and the public faith are hereby solemnly pledged.

Article XIII

Every State shall abide by the determination of the United States in Congress assembled, on all questions which by this confederation are submitted to them. And the Articles of this Confederation shall be inviolably observed by every State, and the Union shall be perpetual; nor shall any alteration at any time hereafter be made in any of them; unless such alteration be agreed to in a Congress of the United States, and be afterwards confirmed by the legislatures of every State.

And Whereas it hath pleased the Great Governor of the World to incline the hearts of the legislatures we respectively represent in Congress, to approve of, and to authorize us to ratify the said Articles of Confederation and perpetual Union. Know Ye that we the undersigned delegates, by virtue of the power and authority to us given for that purpose, do by these presents, in the name and in behalf of our respective constituents, fully and entirely ratify and confirm each and every of the said Articles of Confederation and perpetual Union, and all and singular the matters and things therein contained: And we do further solemnly plight and engage the faith of our respective constituents, that they shall abide by the determinations of the United States in Congress assembled, on all questions, which by the said Confederation are submitted to them. And that the Articles thereof shall be inviolably observed by the States we respectively represent, and that the Union shall be perpetual.

In Witness whereof we have hereunto set our hands in Congress. Done at Philadelphia in the State of Pennsylvania the ninth day of July in the Year of our Lord One Thousand Seven Hundred and Seventy-Eight, and in the Third Year of the independence of America.

Agreed to by Congress 15 November 1777

In force after ratification by Maryland, 1 March 1781

Appendix 2

DECLARATION OF INDEPENDENCE

On June 11, 1776, the responsibility to "prepare a declaration" of independence was assigned by the Continental Congress, meeting in Philadelphia, to five members: John Adams, Benjamin Franklin, Thomas Jefferson, Robert Livingston, and Roger Sherman. Impressed by his talents as a writer, the committee asked Jefferson to compose a draft. After modifying Jefferson's draft the committee turned it over to Congress on June 28. On July 2 Congress voted to declare independence; on the evening of July 4, it approved the Declaration of Independence.

In Congress, July 4, 1776,
The Unanimous Declaration of
the Thirteen United States of America,

When in the Course of human events, it becomes necessary for one people to dissolve the political bands which have connected them with another, and to assume among the Powers of the earth, the separate and equal station to which the Laws of Nature and of Nature's God entitle them, a decent respect to the opinions of mankind requires that they should declare the causes which impel them to the separation.

We hold these truths to be self-evident, that all men are created equal, that they are endowed by their Creator with certain unalienable Rights, that among these are Life, Liberty and the pursuit of Happiness. That to secure these rights, Governments are instituted among Men, deriving their just powers from the consent of the governed. That whenever any form of Government becomes destructive of these ends, it is the Right of the People to alter or to abolish it, and to institute new Government, laying its foundation on such principles and organizing its powers in such form, as to them shall seem most likely to effect their Safety and Happiness. Prudence, indeed, will dictate that Government long established should not be changed for light and transient causes; and accordingly all experience hath shown, that mankind are more disposed to suffer, while evils are sufferable, than to right themselves by abolishing the forms to which they are accustomed. But when a long train of abuses and usurpations, pursuing invariably the same Object evinces a design to reduce them under absolute Despotism, it is their right, it is their duty, to throw off such Government, and to provide new Guards for their future security. Such has been the patient sufferance of these Colonies; and such is now the necessity which constrains them to alter their former Systems of Government. The history of the present King of Great Britain is a history of repeated injuries and usurpations, all having in direct object the establishment of an absolute Tyranny over these States. To prove this, let Facts be submitted to a candid world.

He has refused his Assent to Laws, the most wholesome and necessary for the public good.

He has forbidden his Governors to pass Laws of immediate and pressing importance, unless suspended in their operation till his Assent should be obtained; and when so suspended, he has utterly neglected to attend to them.

He has refused to pass other Laws for the accommodation of large districts of people, unless those people would relinquish the right of Representation in the Legislature, a right inestimable to them and formidable to tyrants only.

He has called together legislative bodies at places unusual, uncomfortable, and distant from the depository of their Public Records, for the sole purpose of fatiguing them into compliance with his measures.

He has dissolved Representative Houses repeatedly, for opposing with manly firmness his invasions on the rights of the people.

He has refused for a long time, after such dissolutions, to cause others to be elected; whereby the

Legislative Powers, incapable of Annihilation, have returned to the People at large for their exercise; the State remaining in the mean time exposed to all the dangers of invasion from without, and convulsions within.

He has endeavored to prevent the population of these States; for that purpose obstructing the Laws of Naturalization of Foreigners; refusing to pass others to encourage their migration hither, and raising the conditions of new Appropriations of Lands.

He has obstructed the Administration of Justice, by refusing his Assent to Laws for establishing Judiciary Powers.

He has made Judges dependent on his Will alone, for the tenure of their offices, and the amount and payment of their salaries.

He has erected a multitude of New Offices, and sent hither swarms of Officers to harass our People, and eat out their substance.

He has kept among us, in times of peace, Standing Armies without the Consent of our legislature.

He has affected to render the Military independent of and superior to the Civil Power.

He has combined with others to subject us to a jurisdiction foreign to our constitution, and unacknowledged by our laws; giving his Assent to their acts of pretended legislation:

For quartering large bodies of armed troops among us:

For protecting them, by a mock Trial, from Punishment for any Murders which they should commit on the Inhabitants of these States:

For cutting off our Trade with all parts of the world:

For imposing taxes on us without our Consent:

For depriving us in many cases, of the benefits of Trial by Jury:

For transporting us beyond Seas to be tried for pretended offences:

For abolishing the free System of English Laws in a neighbouring Province, establishing therein an Arbitrary government, and enlarging its Boundaries so as to render it at once an example and fit instrument for introducing the same absolute rule into these Colonies:

For taking away our Charters, abolishing our most valuable Laws, and altering fundamentally the Forms of our Governments:

For suspending our own Legislature, and declaring themselves invested with Power to legislate for us in all cases whatsoever.

He has abdicated Government here, by declaring us out of his Protection and waging War against us.

He has plundered our seas, ravaged our Coasts, burnt our towns, and destroyed the lives of our people.

He is at this time transporting large armies of foreign mercenaries to compleat the works of death, desolation and tyranny, already begun with circumstances of Cruelty & perfidy scarcely parallel in the most barbarous ages, and totally unworthy the Head of a civilized nation.

He has constrained our fellow Citizens taken Captive on the high Seas to bear Arms against their Country, to become the executioners of their friends and Brethren, or to fall themselves by their Hands.

He has excited domestic insurrections amongst us, and has endeavoured to bring on the inhabitants of our frontiers, the merciless Indian Savages, whose known rule of warfare, is an undistinguished destruction of all ages, sexes and conditions.

In every stage of these Oppressions We have Petitioned for Redress in the most humble terms: Our repeated Petitions have been answered only by repeated injury. A Prince, whose character is thus marked by every act which may define a Tyrant, is unfit to be the ruler of a free People.

Nor have We been wanting in attention to our British brethren. We have warned them from time to time of attempts by their legislature to extend an unwarrantable jurisdiction over us. We have reminded them of the circumstances of our emigration and settlement here. We have appealed to their native justice and magnanimity, and we have conjured them by the ties of our common kindred to disavow these usurpations, which would inevitably interrupt our connections and correspondence. They too have been deaf to the voice of justice and of consanguinity. We must, therefore, acquiesce in the necessity, which denounces our Separation, and hold them, as we hold the rest of mankind, Enemies in War, in Peace Friends.

We, therefore, the Representatives of the United States of America, in General Congress, Assembled, appealing to the Supreme Judge of the world for the rectitude of our intentions, do, in the Name, and by Authority of the good People of these Colonies, solemnly publish and declare, That these United Colonies are, and of Right ought to be Free and Independent States; that they are Absolved from all Allegiance to the British Crown, and that all political connection between them and the State of Great Britain, is and ought to be totally dissolved; and that as Free and Independent States, they have full Power to levy War, conclude Peace, contract Alliances, establish Commerce, and to do all other Acts and Things which Independent States may of right do. And for the support of this Declaration, with a firm reliance on the Protection of Divine Providence, we mutually pledge to each other our Lives, our Fortunes and our sacred Honor.

John Hancock.

New Hampshire:
Josiah Bartlett,
William Whipple,
Matthew Thornton.

Massachusetts-Bay:
Samuel Adams,
John Adams,
Robert Treat Paine,
Elbridge Gerry.

Rhode Island:
Stephen Hopkins,
William Ellery.

Connecticut:
Roger Sherman,
Samuel Huntington,
William Williams,
Oliver Wolcott.

New York:
William Floyd,
Philip Livingston,
Francis Lewis,
Lewis Morris.

Pennsylvania:
Robert Morris,
Benjamin Harris,
Benjamin Franklin,
John Morton,
George Clymer,
James Smith,
George Taylor,
James Wilson,
George Ross.

Delaware:
Caesar Rodney,
George Read,
Thomas McKean.

Georgia:
Button Gwinnett,
Lyman Hall,
George Walton.

Maryland:
Samuel Chase,
William Paca,
Thomas Stone,
Charles Carroll of Carrollton.

Virginia:
George Wythe,
Richard Henry Lee,
Thomas Jefferson,
Benjamin Harrison,
Thomas Nelson Jr.,
Francis Lightfoot Lee,
Carter Braxton.

North Carolina:
William Hooper,
Joseph Hewes,
John Penn.

South Carolina:
Edward Rutledge,
Thomas Heyward Jr.,
Thomas Lynch Jr.,
Arthur Middleton.

New Jersey:
Richard Stockton,
John Witherspoon,
Francis Hopkinson,
John Hart,
Abraham Clark.

Appendix 3

CONSTITUTION OF THE UNITED STATES

The United States Constitution was written at a convention that Congress called on February 21, 1787, for the purpose of recommending amendments to the Articles of Confederation. Every state but Rhode Island sent delegates to Philadelphia, where the convention met that summer. The delegates decided to write an entirely new constitution, completing their labors on September 17. Nine states (the number the Constitution itself stipulated as sufficient) ratified by June 21, 1788.

The Framers of the Constitution included only six paragraphs on the Supreme Court. Article III, Section 1, created the Supreme Court and the federal system of courts. It provided that "[t]he judicial power of the United States, shall be vested in one supreme Court," and whatever inferior courts Congress "from time to time" saw fit to establish. Article III, Section 2, delineated the types of cases and controversies that should be considered by a federal—rather than a state—court. But beyond this, the Constitution left many of the particulars of the Supreme Court and the federal court system for Congress to decide in later years in judiciary acts.

We the People of the United States, in Order to form a more perfect Union, establish Justice, insure domestic Tranquility, provide for the common defence, promote the general Welfare, and secure the Blessings of Liberty to ourselves and our Posterity, do ordain and establish this Constitution for the United States of America.

Article I

Section 1. All legislative Powers herein granted shall be vested in a Congress of the United States, which shall consist of a Senate and House of Representatives.

Section 2. The House of Representatives shall be composed of Members chosen every second Year by the People of the several States, and the Electors in each State shall have the Qualifications requisite for Electors of the most numerous Branch of the State Legislature.

No Person shall be a Representative who shall not have attained to the age of twenty five Years, and been seven Years a Citizen of the United States, and who shall not, when elected, be an Inhabitant of that State in which he shall be chosen.

[Representatives and direct Taxes shall be apportioned among the several States which may be included within this Union, according to their respective Numbers, which shall be determined by adding to the whole Number of free Persons, including those bound to Service for a Term of Years, and excluding Indians not taxed, three fifths of all other Persons.][1] The actual Enumeration shall be made within three Years after the first Meeting of the Congress of the United States, and within every subsequent Term of ten Years, in such Manner as they shall by Law direct. The Number of Representatives shall not exceed one for every thirty Thousand, but each State shall have at Least one Representative; and until such enumeration shall be made, the State of New Hampshire shall be entitled to chuse three, Massachusetts eight, Rhode-Island and Providence Plantations one, Connecticut five, New-York six, New Jersey four, Pennsylvania eight, Delaware one, Maryland six, Virginia ten, North Carolina five, South Carolina five, and Georgia three.

When vacancies happen in the Representation from any State, the Executive Authority thereof shall issue Writs of Election to fill such Vacancies.

The House of Representatives shall chuse their Speaker and other Officers; and shall have the sole Power of Impeachment.

Section 3. The Senate of the United States shall be composed of two Senators from each State, [chosen by the Legislature thereof,][2] for six Years; and each Senator shall have one Vote.

Immediately after they shall be assembled in Consequence of the first Election, they shall be divided as equally as may be into three Classes. The Seats of the

Senators of the first Class shall be vacated at the Expiration of the second Year, of the second Class at the Expiration of the fourth Year, and of the third Class at the Expiration of the sixth Year, so that one third may be chosen every second Year; [and if Vacancies happen by Resignation, or otherwise, during the Recess of the Legislature of any State, the Executive thereof may make temporary Appointments until the next Meeting of the Legislature, which shall then fill such Vacancies.][3]

No Person shall be a Senator who shall not have attained to the Age of thirty Years, and been nine Years a Citizen of the United States, and who shall not, when elected, be an Inhabitant of that State for which he shall be chosen.

The Vice President of the United States shall be President of the Senate, but shall have no Vote, unless they be equally divided.

The Senate shall chuse their other Officers, and also a President pro tempore, in the Absence of the Vice President, or when he shall exercise the Office of President of the United States.

The Senate shall have the sole Power to try all Impeachments. When sitting for that Purpose, they shall be on Oath or Affirmation. When the President of the United States is tried, the Chief Justice shall preside: And no Person shall be convicted without the Concurrence of two thirds of the Members present.

Judgment in Cases of Impeachment shall not extend further than to removal from Office, and disqualification to hold and enjoy any Office of honor, Trust or Profit under the United States: but the Party convicted shall nevertheless be liable and subject to Indictment, Trial, Judgment and Punishment, according to Law.

Section 4. The Times, Places and Manner of holding Elections for Senators and Representatives, shall be prescribed in each State by the Legislature thereof; but the Congress may at any time by Law make or alter such Regulations, except as to the Places of chusing Senators.

The Congress shall assemble at least once in every Year, and such Meeting shall [be on the first Monday in December],[4] unless they shall by Law appoint a different Day.

Section 5. Each House shall be the Judge of the Elections, Returns and Qualifications of its own Members, and a Majority of each shall constitute a Quorum to do Business; but a smaller Number may adjourn from day to day, and may be authorized to compel the Attendance of absent Members, in such Manner, and under such Penalties as each House may provide.

Each House may determine the Rules of its Proceedings, punish its Members for disorderly Behaviour, and, with the Concurrence of two thirds, expel a Member.

Each House shall keep a Journal of its Proceedings, and from time to time publish the same, excepting such Parts as may in their Judgment require Secrecy; and the Yeas and Nays of the Members of either House on any question shall, at the Desire of one fifth of those Present, be entered on the Journal.

Neither House, during the Session of Congress, shall, without the Consent of the other, adjourn for more than three days, nor to any other Place than that in which the two Houses shall be sitting.

Section 6. The Senators and Representatives shall receive a Compensation for their Services, to be ascertained by Law, and paid out of the Treasury of the United States. They shall in all Cases, except Treason, Felony and Breach of the Peace, be privileged from Arrest during their Attendance at the Session of their respective Houses, and in going to and returning from the same; and for any Speech or Debate in either House, they shall not be questioned in any other Place.

No Senator or Representative shall, during the Time for which he was elected, be appointed to any civil Office under the Authority of the United States, which shall have been created, or the Emoluments whereof shall have been encreased during such time; and no Person holding any Office under the United States, shall be a Member of either House during his Continuance in Office.

Section 7. All Bills for raising Revenue shall originate in the House of Representatives; but the Senate may propose or concur with Amendments as on other Bills.

Every Bill which shall have passed the House of Representatives and the Senate, shall, before it become a Law, be presented to the President of the United States; If he approve he shall sign it, but if not he shall return it, with his Objections to that House in which it shall have originated, who shall enter the Objections at large on their Journal, and proceed to reconsider it. If after such Reconsideration two thirds of that House shall agree to pass the Bill, it shall be sent, together with the Objections, to the other House, by which it shall likewise be reconsidered, and if approved by two thirds of that House, it shall become a Law. But in all such Cases the Votes of both Houses shall be determined by yeas and Nays, and the Names of the Persons voting for and against the Bill shall be entered on the Journal of each House respectively. If any Bill shall not be returned by the President within ten Days (Sundays excepted) after it shall have been presented to him, the Same shall be a Law, in like Manner as if he had signed it, unless the Congress by their Adjournment prevent its Return, in which Case it shall not be a Law.

Every Order, Resolution, or Vote to which the Concurrence of the Senate and House of Representatives may be necessary (except on a question of Adjournment) shall be presented to the President of the United States; and before the Same shall take Effect, shall be approved by him, or being disapproved by him, shall be repassed by two thirds of the Senate and House of Representatives, according to the Rules and Limitations prescribed in the Case of a Bill.

Section 8. The Congress shall have Power To lay and collect Taxes, Duties, Imposts and Excises, to pay the Debts and provide for the common Defence and general Welfare of the United States; but all Duties, Imposts and Excises shall be uniform throughout the United States;

To borrow Money on the credit of the United States;

To regulate Commerce with foreign Nations, and among the several States, and with the Indian Tribes;

To establish an uniform Rule of Naturalization, and uniform Laws on the subject of Bankruptcies throughout the United States;

To coin Money, regulate the Value thereof, and of foreign Coin, and fix the Standard of Weights and Measures;

To provide for the Punishment of counterfeiting the Securities and current Coin of the United States;

To establish Post Offices and post Roads;

To promote the Progress of Science and useful Arts, by securing for limited Times to Authors and Inventors the exclusive Right to their respective Writings and Discoveries;

To constitute Tribunals inferior to the supreme Court;

To define and punish Piracies and Felonies committed on the high Seas, and Offences against the Law of Nations;

To declare War, grant Letters of Marque and Reprisal, and make Rules concerning Captures on Land and Water;

To raise and support Armies, but no Appropriation of Money to that Use shall be for a longer Term than two Years;

To provide and maintain a Navy;

To make Rules for the Government and Regulation of the land and naval Forces;

To provide for calling forth the Militia to execute the Laws of the Union, suppress Insurrections and repel Invasions;

To provide for organizing, arming, and disciplining, the Militia, and for governing such Part of them as may be employed in the Service of the United States, reserving to the States respectively, the Appointment of the Officers, and the Authority of training the Militia according to the discipline prescribed by Congress;

To exercise exclusive Legislation in all Cases whatsoever, over such District (not exceeding ten Miles square) as may, by Cession of particular States, and the Acceptance of Congress, become the Seat of the Government of the United States, and to exercise like Authority over all Places purchased by the Consent of the Legislature of the State in which the Same shall be, for the Erection of Forts, Magazines, Arsenals, dockYards, and other needful Buildings;—And

To make all Laws which shall be necessary and proper for carrying into Execution the foregoing Powers, and all other Powers vested by this Constitution in the Government of the United States, or in any Department or Officer thereof.

Section 9. The Migration or Importation of such Persons as any of the States now existing shall think proper to admit, shall not be prohibited by the Congress prior to the Year one thousand eight hundred and eight, but a Tax or duty may be imposed on such Importation, not exceeding ten dollars for each Person.

The Privilege of the Writ of Habeas Corpus shall not be suspended, unless when in Cases of Rebellion or Invasion the public Safety may require it.

No Bill of Attainder or ex post facto Law shall be passed.

No Capitation, or other direct, Tax shall be laid, unless in Proportion to the Census or Enumeration herein before directed to be taken.[5]

No Tax or Duty shall be laid on Articles exported from any State.

No Preference shall be given by any Regulation of Commerce or Revenue to the Ports of one State over those of another; nor shall Vessels bound to, or from, one State, be obliged to enter, clear, or pay Duties in another.

No Money shall be drawn from the Treasury, but in Consequence of Appropriations made by Law; and a regular Statement and Account of the Receipts and Expenditures of all public Money shall be published from time to time.

No Title of Nobility shall be granted by the United States: And no Person holding any Office of Profit or Trust under them, shall, without the Consent of the Congress, accept of any present, Emolument, Office, or Title, of any kind whatever, from any King, Prince, or foreign State.

Section 10. No State shall enter into any Treaty, Alliance, or Confederation; grant Letters of Marque and Reprisal; coin Money; emit Bills of Credit; make any Thing but gold and silver Coin a Tender in Payment of Debts; pass any Bill of Attainder, ex post facto Law, or Law impairing the Obligation of Contracts, or grant any Title of Nobility.

No State shall, without the Consent of the Congress, lay any Imposts or Duties on Imports or Exports, except what may be absolutely necessary for executing its inspection Laws: and the net Produce of all Duties and Imposts, laid by any State on Imports or Exports, shall be for the Use of the Treasury of the United States; and all such Laws shall be subject to the Revision and Controul of the Congress.

No State shall, without the Consent of Congress, lay any Duty of Tonnage, keep Troops, or Ships of War in time of Peace, enter into any Agreement or Compact with another State, or with a foreign Power, or engage in War, unless actually invaded, or in such imminent Danger as will not admit of delay.

Article II

Section 1. The executive Power shall be vested in a President of the United States of America. He shall hold his Office during the Term of four Years, and, together with the Vice President, chosen for the same Term, be elected, as follows:

Each State shall appoint, in such Manner as the Legislature thereof may direct, a Number of Electors, equal to the whole Number of Senators and Representatives to which the State may be entitled in the Congress: but no Senator or Representative, or Person holding an Office of Trust or Profit under the United States, shall be appointed an Elector.

[The Electors shall meet in their respective States, and vote by Ballot for two Persons, of whom one at least shall not be an Inhabitant of the same State with themselves. And they shall make a List of all the Persons voted for, and of the Number of Votes for each; which List they shall sign and certify, and transmit sealed to the Seat of the Government of the United States, directed to the President of the Senate. The President of the Senate shall, in the Presence of the Senate and House of Representatives, open all the Certificates, and the Votes shall then be counted. The Person having the greatest Number of Votes shall be the President, if such Number be a Majority of the whole Number of Electors appointed; and if there be more than one who have such Majority, and have an equal Number of Votes, then the House of Representatives shall immediately chuse by Ballot one of them for President; and if no Person have a Majority, then from the five highest on the list the said House shall in like Manner chuse the President. But in chusing the President, the Votes shall be taken by States, the Representation from each State having one Vote; A quorum for this Purpose shall consist of a Member or Members from two thirds of the States, and a Majority of all the States shall be necessary to a Choice. In every Case, after the Choice of the President, the Person having the greatest Number of Votes of the Electors shall be the Vice President. But if there should remain two or more who have equal Votes, the Senate shall chuse from them by Ballot the Vice President.][6]

The Congress may determine the Time of chusing the Electors, and the Day on which they shall give their Votes; which Day shall be the same throughout the United States.

No Person except a natural born Citizen, or a Citizen of the United States, at the time of the Adoption of this Constitution, shall be eligible to the Office of President; neither shall any Person be eligible to that Office who shall not have attained to the Age of thirty five Years, and been fourteen Years a Resident within the United States.

In Case of the Removal of the President from Office, or of his Death, Resignation, or Inability to discharge the Powers and Duties of the said Office,[7] the Same shall devolve on the Vice President, and the Congress may by Law provide for the Case of Removal, Death, Resignation or Inability, both of the President and Vice President, declaring what Officer shall then act as President, and such Officer shall act accordingly, until the Disability be removed, or a President shall be elected.

The President shall, at stated Times, receive for his Services, a Compensation, which shall neither be encreased nor diminished during the Period for which he shall have been elected, and he shall not receive within that Period any other Emolument from the United States, or any of them.

Before he enter on the Execution of his Office, he shall take the following Oath or Affirmation:—"I do solemnly swear (or affirm) that I will faithfully execute the Office of President of the United States, and will to the best of my Ability, preserve, protect and defend the Constitution of the United States."

Section 2. The President shall be Commander in Chief of the Army and Navy of the United States, and of the Militia of the several States, when called into the actual Service of the United States; he may require the Opinion, in writing, of the principal Officer in each of the executive Departments, upon any Subject relating to the Duties of their respective Offices, and he shall have Power to grant Reprieves and Pardons for Offences against the United States, except in Cases of Impeachment.

He shall have Power, by and with the Advice and Consent of the Senate, to make Treaties, provided two thirds of the Senators present concur; and he shall nominate, and by and with the Advice and Consent of the Senate, shall appoint Ambassadors, other public Ministers and Consuls, Judges of the supreme Court, and all other Officers of the United States, whose Appointments are not herein otherwise provided for, and which shall be established by Law: but the Congress may by Law vest the Appointment of such inferior Officers, as they think proper, in the President alone, in the Courts of Law, or in the Heads of Departments.

The President shall have Power to fill up all Vacancies that may happen during the Recess of the Senate, by granting Commissions which shall expire at the End of their next Session.

Section 3. He shall from time to time give to the Congress Information of the State of the Union, and recommend to their Consideration such Measures as he shall judge necessary and expedient; he may, on extraordinary Occasions, convene both Houses, or either of them, and in Case of Disagreement between them, with Respect to the Time of Adjournment, he may adjourn them to such Time as he shall think proper; he shall receive Ambassadors and other public Ministers; he shall take Care that the Laws be faithfully executed, and shall Commission all the Officers of the United States.

Section 4. The President, Vice President and all civil Officers of the United States, shall be removed from Office on Impeachment for, and Conviction of, Treason, Bribery, or other high Crimes and Misdemeanors.

Article III

Section 1. The judicial Power of the United States, shall be vested in one supreme Court, and in such inferior Courts as the Congress may from time to time ordain and establish. The Judges, both of the supreme and inferior Courts, shall hold their Offices during good Behaviour, and shall, at stated Times, receive for their Services, a Compensation, which shall not be diminished during their Continuance in Office.

Section 2. The judicial Power shall extend to all Cases, in Law and Equity, arising under this Constitution, the Laws of the United States, and Treaties made, or which shall be made, under their Authority; — to all Cases affecting Ambassadors, other public Ministers and Consuls; —to all Cases of admiralty and maritime Jurisdiction; —to Controversies to which the United States shall be a Party; —to Controversies between two or more States; —between a State and Citizens of another State;[8] —between Citizens of different States; —between Citizens of the same State claiming Lands under Grants of different States, and between a State, or the Citizens thereof, and foreign States, Citizens or Subjects.[8]

In all Cases affecting Ambassadors, other public Ministers and Consuls, and those in which a State shall be Party, the supreme Court shall have original Jurisdiction. In all the other Cases before mentioned, the supreme Court shall have appellate Jurisdiction, both as to Law and Fact, with such Exceptions, and under such Regulations as the Congress shall make.

The Trial of all Crimes, except in Cases of Impeachment, shall be by Jury; and such Trial shall be held in the State where the said Crimes shall have been committed; but when not committed within any State, the Trial shall be at such Place or Places as the Congress may by Law have directed.

Section 3. Treason against the United States, shall consist only in levying War against them, or in adhering to their Enemies, giving them Aid and Comfort. No Person shall be convicted of Treason unless on the Testimony of two Witnesses to the same overt Act, or on Confession in open Court.

The Congress shall have Power to declare the Punishment of Treason, but no Attainder of Treason shall work Corruption of Blood, or Forfeiture except during the Life of the Person attainted.

Article IV

Section 1. Full Faith and Credit shall be given in each State to the public Acts, Records, and judicial Proceedings of every other State. And the Congress may by general Laws prescribe the Manner in which such Acts, Records and Proceedings shall be proved, and the Effect thereof.

Section 2. The Citizens of each State shall be entitled to all Privileges and Immunities of Citizens in the several States.

A Person charged in any State with Treason, Felony, or other Crime, who shall flee from Justice, and be found in another State, shall on Demand of the executive Authority of the State from which he fled, be delivered up, to be removed to the State having Jurisdiction of the Crime.

[No Person held to Service or Labour in one State, under the Laws thereof, escaping into another, shall, in Consequence of any Law or Regulation therein, be discharged from such Service or Labour, but shall be delivered up on Claim of the Party to whom such Service or Labour may be due.][9]

Section 3. New States may be admitted by the Congress into this Union; but no new State shall be formed or erected within the Jurisdiction of any other State; nor any State be formed by the Junction of two or more States, or Parts of States, without the Consent of the Legislatures of the States concerned as well as of the Congress.

The Congress shall have Power to dispose of and make all needful Rules and Regulations respecting the Territory or other Property belonging to the United States; and nothing in this Constitution shall be so construed as to Prejudice any Claims of the United States, or of any particular State.

Section 4. The United States shall guarantee to every State in this Union a Republican Form of Government, and shall protect each of them against Invasion; and on Application of the Legislature, or of the Executive (when the Legislature cannot be convened) against domestic Violence.

Article V

The Congress, whenever two thirds of both Houses shall deem it necessary, shall propose Amendments to this Constitution, or, on the Application of the Legislatures of two thirds of the several States, shall call a Convention for proposing Amendments, which, in either Case, shall be valid to all Intents and Purposes, as Part of this Constitution, when ratified by the Legislatures of three fourths of the several States, or by Conventions in three fourths thereof, as the one or the other Mode of Ratification may be proposed by the Congress; Provided [that no Amendment which may be made prior to the Year One thousand eight hundred and eight shall in any Manner affect the first and fourth Clauses in the Ninth Section of the first Article;

and][10] that no State, without its Consent, shall be deprived of its equal Suffrage in the Senate.

Article VI

All Debts contracted and Engagements entered into, before the Adoption of this Constitution, shall be as valid against the United States under this Constitution, as under the Confederation.

This Constitution, and the Laws of the United States which shall be made in Pursuance thereof; and all Treaties made, or which shall be made, under the Authority of the United States, shall be the supreme Law of the Land; and the Judges in every State shall be bound thereby, any Thing in the Constitution or Laws of any State to the Contrary notwithstanding.

The Senators and Representatives before mentioned, and the Members of the several State Legislatures, and all executive and judicial Officers, both of the United States and of the several States, shall be bound by Oath or Affirmation, to support this Constitution; but no religious Test shall ever be required as a Qualification to any Office or public Trust under the United States.

Article VII

The Ratification of the Conventions of nine States, shall be sufficient for the Establishment of this Constitution between the States so ratifying the Same.

Done in Convention by the Unanimous Consent of the States present the Seventeenth Day of September in the Year of our Lord one thousand seven hundred and Eighty seven and of the Independence of the United States of America the Twelfth. IN WITNESS whereof We have hereunto subscribed our Names,

George Washington, President and deputy from Virginia, and thirty-eight other delegates.

[The language of the original Constitution, not including the Amendments, was adopted by a convention of the states on September 17, 1787, and was subsequently ratified by the states on the following dates: Delaware, December 7, 1787; Pennsylvania, December 12, 1787; New Jersey, December 18, 1787; Georgia, January 2, 1788; Connecticut, January 9, 1788; Massachusetts, February 6, 1788; Maryland, April 28, 1788; South Carolina, May 23, 1788; New Hampshire, June 21, 1788.

Ratification was completed on June 21, 1788.

The Constitution subsequently was ratified by Virginia, June 25, 1788; New York, July 26, 1788; North Carolina, November 21, 1789; Rhode Island, May 29, 1790; and Vermont, January 10, 1791.]

AMENDMENTS

Amendment I

(First ten amendments ratified December 15, 1791.)

Congress shall make no law respecting an establishment of religion, or prohibiting the free exercise thereof; or abridging the freedom of speech, or of the press; or the right of the people peaceably to assemble, and to petition the Government for a redress of grievances.

Amendment II

A well regulated Militia, being necessary to the security of a free State, the right of the people to keep and bear Arms, shall not be infringed.

Amendment III

No Soldier shall, in time of peace be quartered in any house, without the consent of the Owner, nor in time of war, but in a manner to be prescribed by law.

Amendment IV

The right of the people to be secure in their persons, houses, papers, and effects, against unreasonable searches and seizures, shall not be violated, and no Warrants shall issue, but upon probable cause, supported by Oath or affirmation, and particularly describing the place to be searched, and the persons or things to be seized.

Amendment V

No person shall be held to answer for a capital, or otherwise infamous crime, unless on a presentment or indictment of a Grand Jury, except in cases arising in the land or naval forces, or in the Militia, when in actual service in time of War or public danger; nor shall any person be subject for the same offence to be twice put in jeopardy of life or limb; nor shall be compelled in any criminal case to be a witness against himself, nor be deprived of life, liberty, or property, without due process of law; nor shall private property be taken for public use, without just compensation.

Amendment VI

In all criminal prosecutions, the accused shall enjoy the right to a speedy and public trial, by an impartial jury of the State and district wherein the crime shall have been committed, which district shall have been previously ascertained by law, and to be informed of the nature and cause of the accusation; to be confronted with the witnesses against him; to have compulsory process for obtaining witnesses in his favor, and to have the Assistance of Counsel for his defence.

Amendment VII

In Suits at common law, where the value in controversy shall exceed twenty dollars, the right of trial by jury shall be preserved, and no fact tried by a jury, shall be otherwise re-examined in any Court of the United States, than according to the rules of the common law.

Amendment VIII

Excessive bail shall not be required, nor excessive fines imposed, nor cruel and unusual punishments inflicted.

Amendment IX

The enumeration in the Constitution, of certain rights, shall not be construed to deny or disparage others retained by the people.

Amendment X

The powers not delegated to the United States by the Constitution, nor prohibited by it to the States, are reserved to the States respectively, or to the people.

Amendment XI
(Ratified February 7, 1795)

The Judicial power of the United States shall not be construed to extend to any suit in law or equity, commenced or prosecuted against one of the United States by Citizens of another State, or by Citizens or Subjects of any Foreign State.

Amendment XII
(Ratified June 15, 1804)

The Electors shall meet in their respective states and vote by ballot for President and Vice-President, one of whom, at least, shall not be an inhabitant of the same state with themselves; they shall name in their ballots the person voted for as President, and in distinct ballots the person voted for as Vice-President, and they shall make distinct lists of all persons voted for as President, and of all persons voted for as Vice-President, and of the number of votes for each, which lists they shall sign and certify, and transmit sealed to the seat of the government of the United States, directed to the President of the Senate; — The President of the Senate shall, in the presence of the Senate and House of Representatives, open all the certificates and the votes shall then be counted; — The person having the greatest number of votes for President, shall be the President, if such number be a majority of the whole number of Electors appointed; and if no person have such majority, then from the persons having the highest numbers not exceeding three on the list of those voted for as President, the House of Representatives shall choose immediately, by ballot, the President. But in choosing the President, the votes shall be taken by states, the representation from each state having one vote; a quorum for this purpose shall consist of a member or members from two-thirds of the states, and a majority of all the states shall be necessary to a choice. [And if the House of Representatives shall not choose a President whenever the right of choice shall devolve upon them, before the fourth day of March next following, then the Vice-President shall act as President, as in the case of the death or other constitutional disability of the President. —][11] The person having the greatest number of votes as Vice-President, shall be the Vice-President, if such number be a majority of the whole number of Electors appointed, and if no person have a majority, then from the two highest numbers on the list, the Senate shall choose the Vice-President; a quorum for the purpose shall consist of two-thirds of the whole number of Senators, and a majority of the whole number shall be necessary to a choice. But no person constitutionally ineligible to the office of President shall be eligible to that of Vice-President of the United States.

Amendment XIII
(Ratified December 6, 1865)

Section 1. Neither slavery nor involuntary servitude, except as a punishment for crime whereof the party shall have been duly convicted, shall exist within the United States, or any place subject to their jurisdiction.

Section 2. Congress shall have power to enforce this article by appropriate legislation.

Amendment XIV
(Ratified July 9, 1868)

Section 1. All persons born or naturalized in the United States, and subject to the jurisdiction thereof, are citizens of the United States and of the State wherein they reside. No State shall make or enforce any law which shall abridge the privileges or immunities of citizens of the United States; nor shall any State deprive any person of life, liberty, or property, without due process of law; nor deny to any person within its jurisdiction the equal protection of the laws.

Section 2. Representatives shall be apportioned among the several States according to their respective numbers, counting the whole number of persons in each State, excluding Indians not taxed. But when the right to vote at any election for the choice of electors for President and Vice President of the United States, Representatives in Congress, the Executive and Judicial officers of a State, or the members of the Legislature thereof, is denied to any of the male inhabitants of such State, being twenty-one years of age,[12] and citizens of the United States, or in any way abridged, except for participation in rebellion, or other crime, the basis of representation therein shall

be reduced in the proportion which the number of such male citizens shall bear to the whole number of male citizens twenty-one years of age in such State.

Section 3. No person shall be a Senator or Representative in Congress, or elector of President and Vice President, or hold any Office, civil or military, under the United States, or under any State, who, having previously taken an oath, as a member of Congress, or as an officer of the United States, or as a member of any State legislature, or as an executive or judicial officer of any State, to support the Constitution of the United States, shall have engaged in insurrection or rebellion against the same, or given aid or comfort to the enemies thereof. But Congress may by a vote of two-thirds of each House, remove such disability.

Section 4. The validity of the public debt of the United States, authorized by law, including debts incurred for payment of pensions and bounties for services in suppressing insurrection or rebellion, shall not be questioned. But neither the United States nor any State shall assume or pay any debt or obligation incurred in aid of insurrection or rebellion against the United States, or any claim for the loss or emancipation of any slave; but all such debts, obligations and claims shall be held illegal and void.

Section 5. The Congress shall have power to enforce, by appropriate legislation, the provisions of this article.

Amendment XV
(Ratified February 3, 1870)

Section 1. The right of citizens of the United States to vote shall not be denied or abridged by the United States or by any State on account of race, color, or previous condition of servitude.

Section 2. The Congress shall have power to enforce this article by appropriate legislation.

Amendment XVI
(Ratified February 3, 1913)

The Congress shall have power to lay and collect taxes on incomes, from whatever source derived, without apportionment among the several States, and without regard to any census or enumeration.

Amendment XVII
(Ratified April 8, 1913)

The Senate of the United States shall be composed of two Senators from each State, elected by the people thereof, for six years; and each Senator shall have one vote. The electors in each State shall have the qualifications requisite for electors of the most numerous branch of the State legislatures.

When vacancies happen in the representation of any State in the Senate, the executive authority of such State shall issue writs of election to fill such vacancies: *Provided,* That the legislature of any State may empower the executive thereof to make temporary appointments until the people fill the vacancies by election as the legislature may direct.

This amendment shall not be so construed as to affect the election or term of any Senator chosen before it becomes valid as part of the Constitution.

Amendment XVIII
(Ratified January 16, 1919)

Section 1. After one year from the ratification of this article the manufacture, sale, or transportation of intoxicating liquors within, the importation thereof into, or the exportation thereof from the United States and all territory subject to the jurisdiction thereof for beverage purposes is hereby prohibited.

Section 2. The Congress and the several States shall have concurrent power to enforce this article by appropriate legislation.

Section 3. This article shall be inoperative unless it shall have been ratified as an amendment to the Constitution by the legislatures of the several States, as provided in the Constitution, within seven years from the date of the submission hereof to the States by the Congress.[13]

Amendment XIX
(Ratified August 18, 1920)

The right of citizens of the United States to vote shall not be denied or abridged by the United States or by any State on account of sex.

Congress shall have power to enforce this article by appropriate legislation.

Amendment XX
(Ratified January 23, 1933)

Section 1. The terms of the President and Vice President shall end at noon on the 20th day of January, and the terms of Senators and Representatives at noon on the 3d day of January, of the years in which such terms would have ended if this article had not been ratified; and the terms of their successors shall then begin.

Section 2. The Congress shall assemble at least once in every year, and such meeting shall begin at noon on the 3d day of January, unless they shall by law appoint a different day.

Section 3.[14] If, at the time fixed for the beginning of the term of the President, the President elect shall have died, the Vice President elect shall become President. If a President shall not have been chosen before the time fixed for the beginning of his term, or if the President elect shall have failed to qualify, then the Vice President elect shall act as President until a President shall have qualified; and the Congress may by law provide for the case wherein neither a President elect nor a Vice President elect shall have qualified, declaring who shall then act as President, or the manner in which one who is to act shall be selected, and such person shall act accordingly until a President or Vice President shall have qualified.

Section 4. The Congress may by law provide for the case of the death of any of the persons from whom the House of Representatives may choose a President whenever the right of choice shall have devolved upon them, and for the case of the death of any of the persons from whom the Senate may choose a Vice President whenever the right of choice shall have devolved upon them.

Section 5. Sections **1** and **2** shall take effect on the **15**th day of October following the ratification of this article.

Section 6. This article shall be inoperative unless it shall have been ratified as an amendment to the Constitution by the legislatures of three-fourths of the several States within seven years from the date of its submission.

Amendment XXI
(Ratified December 5, 1933)

Section 1. The eighteenth article of amendment to the Constitution of the United States is hereby repealed.

Section 2. The transportation or importation into any State, Territory, or possession of the United States for delivery or use therein of intoxicating liquors, in violation of the laws thereof, is hereby prohibited.

Section 3. This article shall be inoperative unless it shall have been ratified as an amendment to the Constitution by conventions in the several States, as provided in the Constitution, within seven years from the date of the submission hereof to the States by the Congress.

Amendment XXII
(Ratified February 27, 1951)

Section 1. No person shall be elected to the office of the President more than twice, and no person who has held the office of President, or acted as President, for more than two years of a term to which some other person was elected President shall be elected to the office of the President more than once. But this Article shall not apply to any person holding the office of President when this Article was proposed by the Congress, and shall not prevent any person who may be holding the office of President, or acting as President, during the term within which this Article becomes operative from holding the office of President or acting as President during the remainder of such term.

Section 2. This article shall be inoperative unless it shall have been ratified as an amendment to the Constitution by the legislatures of three-fourths of the several States within seven years from the date of its submission to the States by the Congress.

Amendment XXIII
(Ratified March 29, 1961)

Section 1. The District constituting the seat of Government of the United States shall appoint in such manner as the Congress may direct:

A number of electors of President and Vice President equal to the whole number of Senators and Representatives in Congress to which the District would be entitled if it were a State, but in no event more than the least populous State; they shall be in addition to those appointed by the States, but they shall be considered, for the purposes of the election of President and Vice President, to be electors appointed by a State; and they shall meet in the District and perform such duties as provided by the twelfth article of amendment.

Section 2. The Congress shall have power to enforce this article by appropriate legislation.

Amendment XXIV
(Ratified January 23, 1964)

Section 1. The right of citizens of the United States to vote in any primary or other election for President or Vice President, for electors for President or Vice President, or for Senator or Representative in Congress, shall not be denied or abridged by the United States or any State by reason of failure to pay any poll tax or other tax.

Section 2. The Congress shall have power to enforce this article by appropriate legislation.

Amendment XXV
(Ratified February 10, 1967)

Section 1. In case of the removal of the President from office or of his death or resignation, the Vice President shall become President.

Section 2. Whenever there is a vacancy in the office of the Vice President, the President shall nominate a Vice President who shall take office upon confirmation by a majority vote of both Houses of Congress.

Section 3. Whenever the President transmits to the President pro tempore of the Senate and the Speaker of the House of Representatives his written declaration that he is unable to discharge the powers and duties of his office, and until he transmits to them a written declaration to the contrary, such powers and duties shall be discharged by the Vice President as Acting President.

Section 4. Whenever the Vice President and a majority of either the principal officers of the executive departments or of such other body as Congress may by law provide, transmit to the President pro tempore of the Senate and the Speaker of the House of Representatives their written declaration that the President is unable to discharge the powers and duties of his office, the Vice President shall immediately assume the powers and duties of the office as Acting President.

Thereafter, when the President transmits to the President pro tempore of the Senate and the Speaker of the House of Representatives his written declaration that no inability exists, he shall resume the powers and duties of his office unless the Vice President and a majority of either the principal officers of the executive departments or of such other body as Congress may by law provide, transmit within four days to the President pro tempore of the Senate and the Speaker of the House of Representatives their written declaration that the President is unable to discharge the powers and duties of his office. Thereupon Congress shall decide the issue, assembling within forty-eight hours for that purpose if not in session. If the Congress, within twenty-one days after receipt of the latter written declaration, or, if Congress is not in session, within twenty-one days after Congress is required to assemble, determines by two-thirds vote of both Houses that the President is unable to discharge the powers and duties of his office, the Vice President shall continue to discharge the same as Acting President; otherwise, the President shall resume the powers and duties of his office.

Amendment XXVI
(Ratified July 1, 1971)

Section 1. The right of citizens of the United States, who are eighteen years of age or older, to vote shall not be denied or abridged by the United States or by any State on account of age.

Section 2. The Congress shall have power to enforce this article by appropriate legislation.

Amendment XXVII
(Ratified May 7, 1992)

No law varying the compensation for the services of the Senators and Representatives shall take effect, until an election of Representatives shall have intervened.

Source: U.S. Congress, House, Committee on the Judiciary, *The Constitution of the United States of America, as Amended,* 100th Cong., 1st sess., 1987, H Doc 100–94.

Notes: 1. The part in brackets was changed by section 2 of the Fourteenth Amendment.

2. The part in brackets was changed by the first paragraph of the Seventeenth Amendment.

3. The part in brackets was changed by the second paragraph of the Seventeenth Amendment.

4. The part in brackets was changed by section 2 of the Twentieth Amendment.

5. The Sixteenth Amendment gave Congress the power to tax incomes.

6. The material in brackets was superseded by the Twelfth Amendment.

7. This provision was affected by the Twenty-fifth Amendment.

8. These clauses were affected by the Eleventh Amendment.

9. This paragraph was superseded by the Thirteenth Amendment.

10. Obsolete.

11. The part in brackets was superseded by section 3 of the Twentieth Amendment.

12. See the Nineteenth and Twenty-sixth Amendments.

13. This amendment was repealed by section 1 of the Twenty-first Amendment.

14. See the Twenty-fifth Amendment.

Appendix 4

FEDERALIST NO. 10

The Same Subject Continued: The Union as a Safeguard Against Domestic Faction and Insurrection.

From the New York Packet
Friday, November 23, 1787.

Author: James Madison

To the People of the State of New York:

AMONG the numerous advantages promised by a wellconstructed Union, none deserves to be more accurately developed than its tendency to break and control the violence of faction. The friend of popular governments never finds himself so much alarmed for their character and fate, as when he contemplates their propensity to this dangerous vice. He will not fail, therefore, to set a due value on any plan which, without violating the principles to which he is attached, provides a proper cure for it. The instability, injustice, and confusion introduced into the public councils, have, in truth, been the mortal diseases under which popular governments have everywhere perished; as they continue to be the favorite and fruitful topics from which the adversaries to liberty derive their most specious declamations. The valuable improvements made by the American constitutions on the popular models, both ancient and modern, cannot certainly be too much admired; but it would be an unwarrantable partiality, to contend that they have as effectually obviated the danger on this side, as was wished and expected. Complaints are everywhere heard from our most considerate and virtuous citizens, equally the friends of public and private faith, and of public and personal liberty, that our governments are too unstable, that the public good is disregarded in the conflicts of rival parties, and that measures are too often decided, not according to the rules of justice and the rights of the minor party, but by the superior force of an interested and overbearing majority. However anxiously we may wish that these complaints had no foundation, the evidence, of known facts will not permit us to deny that they are in some degree true. It will be found, indeed, on a candid review of our situation, that some of the distresses under which we labor have been erroneously charged on the operation of our governments; but it will be found, at the same time, that other causes will not alone account for many of our heaviest misfortunes; and, particularly, for that prevailing and increasing distrust of public engagements, and alarm for private rights, which are echoed from one end of the continent to the other. These must be chiefly, if not wholly, effects of the unsteadiness and injustice with which a factious spirit has tainted our public administrations.

By a faction, I understand a number of citizens, whether amounting to a majority or a minority of the whole, who are united and actuated by some common impulse of passion, or of interest, adversed to the rights of other citizens, or to the permanent and aggregate interests of the community.

There are two methods of curing the mischiefs of faction: the one, by removing its causes; the other, by controlling its effects.

There are again two methods of removing the causes of faction: the one, by destroying the liberty which is essential to its existence; the other, by giving to every citizen the same opinions, the same passions, and the same interests.

It could never be more truly said than of the first remedy, that it was worse than the disease. Liberty is to faction what air is to fire, an aliment without which it instantly expires. But it could not be less folly to abolish liberty, which is essential to political life, because it nourishes faction, than it would be to wish the annihilation of air, which is essential to animal life, because it imparts to fire its destructive agency.

The second expedient is as impracticable as the first would be unwise. As long as the reason of man continues fallible, and he is at liberty to exercise it, different opinions will be formed. As long as the connection subsists between his reason and his self-love, his opinions and his passions will have a reciprocal influence on each other; and the former will be objects to which the latter will attach themselves. The diversity in the faculties of men, from which the rights of property originate, is not less an insuperable obstacle to a uniformity of interests. The protection of these faculties is the first object of government. From the protection of different and unequal faculties of acquiring property, the possession of different degrees and kinds of property immediately results; and from the influence of these on the sentiments and views of the respective proprietors, ensues a division of the society into different interests and parties.

The latent causes of faction are thus sown in the nature of man; and we see them everywhere brought into different degrees of activity, according to the different circumstances of civil society. A zeal for different opinions concerning religion, concerning government, and many other points, as well of speculation as of practice; an attachment to different leaders ambitiously contending for pre-eminence and power; or to persons of other descriptions whose fortunes have been interesting to the human passions, have, in turn, divided mankind into parties, inflamed them with mutual animosity, and rendered them much more disposed to vex and oppress each other than to co-operate for their common good. So strong is this propensity of mankind to fall into mutual animosities, that where no substantial occasion presents itself, the most frivolous and fanciful distinctions have been sufficient to kindle their unfriendly passions and excite their most violent conflicts. But the most common and durable source of factions has been the various and unequal distribution of property. Those who hold and those who are without property have ever formed distinct interests in society. Those who are creditors, and those who are debtors, fall under a like discrimination. A landed interest, a manufacturing interest, a mercantile interest, a moneyed interest, with many lesser interests, grow up of necessity in civilized nations, and divide them into different classes, actuated by different sentiments and views. The regulation of these various and interfering interests forms the principal task of modern legislation, and involves the spirit of party

and faction in the necessary and ordinary operations of the government.

No man is allowed to be a judge in his own cause, because his interest would certainly bias his judgment, and, not improbably, corrupt his integrity. With equal, nay with greater reason, a body of men are unfit to be both judges and parties at the same time; yet what are many of the most important acts of legislation, but so many judicial determinations, not indeed concerning the rights of single persons, but concerning the rights of large bodies of citizens? And what are the different classes of legislators but advocates and parties to the causes which they determine? Is a law proposed concerning private debts? It is a question to which the creditors are parties on one side and the debtors on the other. Justice ought to hold the balance between them. Yet the parties are, and must be, themselves the judges; and the most numerous party, or, in other words, the most powerful faction must be expected to prevail. Shall domestic manufactures be encouraged, and in what degree, by restrictions on foreign manufactures? are questions which would be differently decided by the landed and the manufacturing classes, and probably by neither with a sole regard to justice and the public good. The apportionment of taxes on the various descriptions of property is an act which seems to require the most exact impartiality; yet there is, perhaps, no legislative act in which greater opportunity and temptation are given to a predominant party to trample on the rules of justice. Every shilling with which they overburden the inferior number, is a shilling saved to their own pockets.

It is in vain to say that enlightened statesmen will be able to adjust these clashing interests, and render them all subservient to the public good. Enlightened statesmen will not always be at the helm. Nor, in many cases, can such an adjustment be made at all without taking into view indirect and remote considerations, which will rarely prevail over the immediate interest which one party may find in disregarding the rights of another or the good of the whole.

The inference to which we are brought is, that the CAUSES of faction cannot be removed, and that relief is only to be sought in the means of controlling its EFFECTS.

If a faction consists of less than a majority, relief is supplied by the republican principle, which enables the majority to defeat its sinister views by regular vote. It may clog the administration, it may convulse the society; but it will be unable to execute and mask its violence under the forms of the Constitution. When a majority is included in a faction, the form of popular government, on the other hand, enables it to sacrifice to its ruling passion or interest both the public good and the rights of other citizens. To secure the public good and private rights against the danger of such a faction, and at the same time to preserve the spirit and the form of popular government, is then the great object to which our inquiries are directed. Let me add that it is the great desideratum by which this form of government can be rescued from the opprobrium under which it has so long labored, and be recommended to the esteem and adoption of mankind.

By what means is this object attainable? Evidently by one of two only. Either the existence of the same passion or interest in a majority at the same time must be prevented, or the majority, having such coexistent passion or interest, must be rendered, by their number and local situation, unable to concert and carry into effect schemes of oppression. If the impulse and the opportunity be suffered to coincide, we well know that neither moral nor religious motives can be relied on as an adequate control. They are not found to be such on the injustice and violence of individuals, and lose their efficacy in proportion to the number combined together, that is, in proportion as their efficacy becomes needful.

From this view of the subject it may be concluded that a pure democracy, by which I mean a society consisting of a small number of citizens, who assemble and administer the government in person, can admit of no cure for the mischiefs of faction. A common passion or interest will, in almost every case, be felt by a majority of the whole; a communication and concert result from the form of government itself; and there is nothing to check the inducements to sacrifice the weaker party or an obnoxious individual. Hence it is that such democracies have ever been spectacles of turbulence and contention; have ever been found incompatible with personal security or the rights of property; and have in general been as short in their lives as they have been violent in

their deaths. Theoretic politicians, who have patronized this species of government, have erroneously supposed that by reducing mankind to a perfect equality in their political rights, they would, at the same time, be perfectly equalized and assimilated in their possessions, their opinions, and their passions.

A republic, by which I mean a government in which the scheme of representation takes place, opens a different prospect, and promises the cure for which we are seeking. Let us examine the points in which it varies from pure democracy, and we shall comprehend both the nature of the cure and the efficacy which it must derive from the Union.

The two great points of difference between a democracy and a republic are: first, the delegation of the government, in the latter, to a small number of citizens elected by the rest; secondly, the greater number of citizens, and greater sphere of country, over which the latter may be extended.

The effect of the first difference is, on the one hand, to refine and enlarge the public views, by passing them through the medium of a chosen body of citizens, whose wisdom may best discern the true interest of their country, and whose patriotism and love of justice will be least likely to sacrifice it to temporary or partial considerations. Under such a regulation, it may well happen that the public voice, pronounced by the representatives of the people, will be more consonant to the public good than if pronounced by the people themselves, convened for the purpose. On the other hand, the effect may be inverted. Men of factious tempers, of local prejudices, or of sinister designs, may, by intrigue, by corruption, or by other means, first obtain the suffrages, and then betray the interests, of the people. The question resulting is, whether small or extensive republics are more favorable to the election of proper guardians of the public weal; and it is clearly decided in favor of the latter by two obvious considerations:

In the first place, it is to be remarked that, however small the republic may be, the representatives must be raised to a certain number, in order to guard against the cabals of a few; and that, however large it may be, they must be limited to a certain number, in order to guard against the confusion of a multitude. Hence, the number of representatives in the two cases not being in proportion to that of the two constituents, and being proportionally greater in the small republic, it follows that, if the proportion of fit characters be not less in the large than in the small republic, the former will present a greater option, and consequently a greater probability of a fit choice.

In the next place, as each representative will be chosen by a greater number of citizens in the large than in the small republic, it will be more difficult for unworthy candidates to practice with success the vicious arts by which elections are too often carried; and the suffrages of the people being more free, will be more likely to centre in men who possess the most attractive merit and the most diffusive and established characters.

It must be confessed that in this, as in most other cases, there is a mean, on both sides of which inconveniences will be found to lie. By enlarging too much the number of electors, you render the representatives too little acquainted with all their local circumstances and lesser interests; as by reducing it too much, you render him unduly attached to these, and too little fit to comprehend and pursue great and national objects. The federal Constitution forms a happy combination in this respect; the great and aggregate interests being referred to the national, the local and particular to the State legislatures.

The other point of difference is, the greater number of citizens and extent of territory which may be brought within the compass of republican than of democratic government; and it is this circumstance principally which renders factious combinations less to be dreaded in the former than in the latter. The smaller the society, the fewer probably will be the distinct parties and interests composing it; the fewer the distinct parties and interests, the more frequently will a majority be found of the same party; and the smaller the number of individuals composing a majority, and the smaller the compass within which they are placed, the more easily will they concert and execute their plans of oppression. Extend the sphere, and you take in a greater variety of parties and interests; you make it less probable that a majority of the whole will have a common motive to invade the rights of other citizens; or if such a common motive exists, it will be more difficult for all who feel it to discover their own strength, and to act in unison with each other. Besides other impediments, it may be remarked that, where there is a consciousness of unjust or dishonorable purposes, communication is always checked by distrust in proportion to the number whose concurrence is necessary.

Hence, it clearly appears, that the same advantage which a republic has over a democracy, in controlling the effects of faction, is enjoyed by a large over a small republic,—is enjoyed by the Union over the States composing it. Does the advantage consist in the substitution of representatives whose enlightened views and virtuous sentiments render them superior to local prejudices and schemes of injustice? It will not be denied that the representation of the Union will be most likely to possess these requisite endowments. Does it consist in the greater security afforded by a greater variety of parties, against the event of any one party being able to outnumber and oppress the rest? In an equal degree does the increased variety of parties comprised within the Union, increase this security. Does it, in fine, consist in the greater obstacles opposed to the concert and accomplishment of the secret wishes of an unjust and interested majority? Here, again, the extent of the Union gives it the most palpable advantage.

The influence of factious leaders may kindle a flame within their particular States, but will be unable to spread a general conflagration through the other States. A religious sect may degenerate into a political faction in a part of the Confederacy; but the variety of sects dispersed over the entire face of it must secure the national councils against any danger from that source. A rage for paper money, for an abolition of debts, for an equal division of property, or for any other improper or wicked project, will be less apt to pervade the whole body of the Union than a particular member of it; in the same proportion as such a malady is more likely to taint a particular county or district, than an entire State.

In the extent and proper structure of the Union, therefore, we behold a republican remedy for the diseases most incident to republican government. And according to the degree of pleasure and pride we feel in being republicans, ought to be our zeal in cherishing the spirit and supporting the character of Federalists.

PUBLIUS.

Appendix 5

FEDERALIST NO. 51

The Structure of the Government Must Furnish the Proper Checks and Balances Between the Different Departments

From the New York Packet.
Friday, February 8, 1788.

Author: James Madison

To the People of the State of New York:

TO WHAT expedient, then, shall we finally resort, for maintaining in practice the necessary partition of power among the several departments, as laid down in the Constitution? The only answer that can be given is, that as all these exterior provisions are found to be inadequate, the defect must be supplied, by so contriving the interior structure of the government as that its several constituent parts may, by their mutual relations, be the means of keeping each other in their proper places. Without presuming to undertake a full development of this important idea, I will hazard a few general observations, which may perhaps place it in a clearer light, and enable us to form a more correct judgment of the principles and structure of the government planned by the convention.

In order to lay a due foundation for that separate and distinct exercise of the different powers of government, which to a certain extent is admitted on all hands to be essential to the preservation of liberty, it is evident that each department should have a will of its own; and consequently should be so constituted that the members of each should have as little agency as possible in the appointment of the members of the others. Were this principle rigorously adhered to, it would require that all the appointments for the supreme executive, legislative, and judiciary magistracies should be drawn from the same fountain of authority, the people, through channels having no communication whatever with one another. Perhaps such a plan of constructing the several departments would be less difficult in practice than it may in contemplation appear. Some difficulties, however, and some additional expense would attend the execution of it. Some deviations, therefore, from the principle must be admitted. In the constitution of the judiciary department in particular, it might be inexpedient to insist rigorously on the principle: first, because peculiar qualifications being essential in the members, the primary consideration ought to be to select that mode of choice which best secures these qualifications; secondly, because the permanent tenure by which the appointments are held in that department, must soon destroy all sense of dependence on the authority conferring them.

It is equally evident, that the members of each department should be as little dependent as possible on those of the others, for the emoluments annexed to their offices. Were the executive magistrate, or the judges, not independent of the legislature in this particular, their independence in every other would be merely nominal. But the great security against a gradual concentration of the several powers in the same department, consists in giving to those who administer each department the necessary constitutional means and personal motives to resist encroachments of the others. The provision for defense must in this, as in all other cases, be made commensurate to the danger of attack. Ambition must be made to counteract ambition. The interest of the man must be connected with the constitutional rights of the place. It may be a reflection on human nature, that such devices should be necessary to control the abuses of government. But what is government itself, but the greatest of all reflections on human nature? If men were angels, no government would be necessary. If angels were to govern men, neither external nor internal controls on government would be necessary. In framing a government which is to be administered by men over men, the great difficulty lies in this: you must first enable the government to control the governed; and in the next place oblige it to control itself.

A dependence on the people is, no doubt, the primary control on the government; but experience has taught mankind the necessity of auxiliary precautions. This policy of supplying, by opposite and rival interests, the defect of better motives, might be traced through the whole system of human affairs, private as well as public. We see it particularly displayed in all the subordinate distributions of power, where the constant aim is to divide and arrange the several offices in such a manner as that each may be a check on the other that the private interest of every individual may be a sentinel over the public rights. These inventions of prudence cannot be less requisite in the distribution of the supreme powers of the State. But it is not possible to give to each department an equal power of self-defense. In republican government, the legislative authority necessarily predominates. The remedy for this inconveniency is to divide the legislature into different branches; and to render them, by different modes of election and different principles of action, as little connected with each other as the nature of their common functions and their common dependence on the society will admit. It may even be necessary to guard against dangerous encroachments by still further precautions. As the weight of the legislative authority requires that it should be thus divided, the weakness of the executive may require, on the other hand, that it should be fortified.

An absolute negative on the legislature appears, at first view, to be the natural defense with which the executive magistrate should be armed. But perhaps it would be neither altogether safe nor alone sufficient. On ordinary occasions it might not be exerted with the requisite firmness, and on extraordinary occasions it might be perfidiously abused. May not this defect of an absolute negative be supplied by some qualified connection between this weaker department and the weaker branch of the stronger department, by which the latter may be led to support the constitutional rights of the former, without being too much detached from the rights of its own department? If the principles on which these observations are founded be just, as I persuade myself they are, and they be applied as a criterion to the several State constitutions, and to the federal Constitution it will be found that if the latter does not perfectly correspond with them, the former are infinitely less able to bear such a test.

There are, moreover, two considerations particularly applicable to the federal system of America, which place that system in a very interesting point of view. First. In a single republic, all the power surrendered by the people is submitted to the administration of a single government; and the usurpations are guarded against by a division of the government into distinct and separate departments. In the compound republic of America, the power surrendered by the people is first divided between two distinct governments, and then the portion allotted to each subdivided among distinct and separate departments. Hence a double security arises to the rights of the people. The different governments will control each other, at the same time that each will be controlled by itself. Second. It is of great importance in a republic not only to guard the society against the oppression of its rulers, but to guard one part of the society against the injustice of the other part. Different interests necessarily exist in different classes of citizens. If a majority be united by a common interest, the rights of the minority will be insecure.

There are but two methods of providing against this evil: the one by creating a will in the community independent of the majority that is, of the society itself; the other, by comprehending in the society so many separate descriptions of citizens as will render an unjust combination of a majority of the whole very improbable, if not impracticable. The first method prevails in all governments possessing an hereditary or self-appointed authority. This, at best, is but a precarious security; because a power independent of the society may as well espouse the unjust views of the major, as the rightful interests of the minor party, and may possibly be turned against both parties. The second method will be exemplified in the federal republic of the United States. Whilst all authority in it will be derived from and dependent on the society, the society itself will be broken into so many parts, interests, and classes of citizens, that the rights of individuals, or of the minority, will be in little danger from interested combinations of the majority.

In a free government the security for civil rights must be the same as that for religious rights. It consists in the one case in the multiplicity of interests, and in the other in the multiplicity of sects. The degree of security in both cases will depend on the number of interests and sects; and this may be presumed to depend on the extent of country and number of people comprehended under the same government. This view of the subject must particularly recommend a proper federal system to all the sincere and considerate friends of republican government, since it shows that in exact proportion as the territory of the Union may be formed into more circumscribed Confederacies, or States oppressive combinations of a majority will be facilitated: the best security, under the republican forms, for the rights of every class of citizens, will be diminished: and consequently the stability and independence of some member of the government, the only other security, must be proportionately increased. Justice is the end of government. It is the end of civil society. It ever has been and ever will be pursued until it be obtained, or until liberty be lost in the pursuit. In a society under the forms of which the stronger faction can readily unite and oppress the weaker, anarchy may as truly be said to reign as in a state of nature, where the weaker individual is not secured against the violence of the stronger; and as, in the latter state, even the stronger individuals are prompted, by the uncertainty of their condition, to submit to a government which may protect the weak as well as themselves; so, in the former state, will the more powerful factions or parties be gradually induced, by a like motive, to wish for a government which will protect all parties, the weaker as well as the more powerful.

It can be little doubted that if the State of Rhode Island was separated from the Confederacy and left to itself, the insecurity of rights under the popular form of government within such narrow limits would be displayed by such reiterated oppressions of factious majorities that some power altogether independent of the people would soon be called for by the voice of the very factions whose misrule had proved the necessity of it. In the extended republic of the United States, and among the great variety of interests, parties, and sects which it embraces, a coalition of a majority of the whole society could seldom take place on any other principles than those of justice and the general good; whilst there being thus less danger to a minor from the will of a major party, there must be less pretext, also, to provide for the security of the former, by introducing into the government a will not dependent on the latter, or, in other words, a will independent of the society itself. It is no less certain than it is important, notwithstanding the contrary opinions which have been entertained, that the larger the society, provided it lie within a practical sphere, the more duly capable it will be of self-government. And happily for the REPUBLICAN CAUSE, the practicable sphere may be carried to a very great extent, by a judicious modification and mixture of the FEDERAL PRINCIPLE.

PUBLIUS.

Appendix 6

POLITICAL PARTY AFFILIATIONS IN CONGRESS AND THE PRESIDENCY, 1789–2013*

Year	Congress	House Majority party	House Principal minority party	Senate Majority party	Senate Principal minority party	President
1789–1791	1st	AD-38	Op-26	AD-17	Op-9	F (Washington)
1791–1793	2nd	F-37	DR-33	F-16	DR-13	F (Washington)
1793–1795	3rd	DR-57	F-48	F-17	DR-13	F (Washington)
1795–1797	4th	F-54	DR-52	F-19	DR-13	F (Washington)
1797–1799	5th	F-58	DR-48	F-20	DR-12	F (John Adams)
1799–1801	6th	F-64	DR-42	F-19	DR-13	F (John Adams)
1801–1803	7th	DR-69	F-36	DR-18	F-13	DR (Jefferson)
1803–1805	8th	DR-102	F-39	DR-25	F-9	DR (Jefferson)
1805–1807	9th	DR-116	F-25	DR-27	F-7	DR (Jefferson)
1807–1809	10th	DR-118	F-24	DR-28	F-6	DR (Jefferson)
1809–1811	11th	DR-94	F-48	DR-28	F-6	DR (Madison)
1811–1813	12th	DR-108	F-36	DR-30	F-6	DR (Madison)
1813–1815	13th	DR-112	F-68	DR-27	F-9	DR (Madison)
1815–1817	14th	DR-117	F-65	DR-25	F-11	DR (Madison)
1817–1819	15th	DR-141	F-42	DR-34	F-10	DR (Monroe)
1819–1821	16th	DR-156	F-27	DR-35	F-7	DR (Monroe)
1821–1823	17th	DR-158	F-25	DR-44	F-4	DR (Monroe)
1823–1825	18th	DR-187	F-26	DR-44	F-4	DR (Monroe)
1825–1827	19th	AD-105	J-97	AD-26	J-20	DR (John Q. Adams)
1827–1829	20th	J-119	AD-94	J-28	AD-20	DR (John Q. Adams)
1829–1831	21st	D-139	NR-74	D-26	NR-22	DR (Jackson)
1831–1833	22nd	D-141	NR-58	D-25	NR-21	D (Jackson)
1833–1835	23rd	D-147	AM-53	D-20	NR-20	D (Jackson)
1835–1837	24th	D-145	W-98	D-27	W-25	D (Jackson)
1837–1839	25th	D-108	W-107	D-30	W-18	D (Van Buren)
1839–1841	26th	D-124	W-118	D-28	W-22	D (Van Buren)
1841–1843	27th	W-133	D-102	W-28	D-22	W (W. Harrison) W (Tyler)
1843–1845	28th	D-142	W-79	W-28	D-25	W (Tyler)
1845–1847	29th	D-143	W-77	D-31	W-25	D (Polk)
1847–1849	30th	W-115	D-108	D-36	W-21	D (Polk)
1849–1851	31st	D-112	W-109	D-35	W-25	W (Taylor) W (Fillmore)
1851–1853	32nd	D-140	W-88	D-35	W-24	W (Fillmore)
1853–1855	33rd	D-159	W-71	D-38	W-22	D (Pierce)
1855–1857	34th	R-108	D-83	D-42	R-15	D (Pierce)
1857–1859	35th	D-131	R-92	D-35	R-20	D (Buchanan)
1859–1861	36th	R-113	D-101	D-38	R-26	D (Buchanan)
1861–1863	37th	R-106	D-42	R-31	D-11	R (Lincoln)
1863–1865	38th	R-103	D-80	R-39	D-12	R (Lincoln)
1865–1867[1]	39th	U-145	D-46	U-42	D-10	U (Lincoln)

Year	Congress	House		Senate		President
		Majority party	Principal minority party	Majority party	Principal minority party	
1867–1869	40th	R-143	D-49	R-42	D-11	U (A. Johnson)
1869–1871	41st	R-170	D-73	R-61	D-11	R (A. Johnson)
1871–1873	42nd	R-139	D-104	R-57	D-17	R (Grant)
1873–1875	43rd	R-203	D-88	R-54	D-19	R (Grant)
1875–1877	44th	D-181	R-107	R-46	D-29	R (Grant)
1877–1879	45th	D-156	R-137	R-39	D-36	R (Grant)
1879–1881	46th	D-150	R-128	D-43	R-33	R (Hayes)
1881–1883	47th	R-152	D-130	R-37	D-37	R (Hayes)
						R (Garfield)
						R (Arthur)
1883–1885	48th	D-200	R-119	R-40	D-36	R (Arthur)
1885–1887	49th	D-182	R-140	R-41	D-34	D (Cleveland)
1887–1889	50th	D-170	R-151	R-39	D-37	D (Cleveland)
1889–1891	51st	R-173	D-159	R-37	D-37	R (B. Harrison)
1891–1893	52nd	D-231	R-88	R-47	D-39	R (B. Harrison)
1893–1895	53rd	D-220	R-126	D-44	R-38	D (Cleveland)
1895–1897	54th	R-246	D-104	R-43	D-39	D (Cleveland)
1897–1899	55th	R-206	D-134	R-46	D-34	R (McKinley)
1899–1901	56th	R-185	D-163	R-53	D-26	R (McKinley)
1901–1903	57th	R-198	D-153	R-56	D-29	R (McKinley)
						R (T. Roosevelt)
1903–1905	58th	R-207	D-178	R-58	D-32	R (T. Roosevelt)
1905–1907	59th	R-250	D-136	R-58	D-32	R (T. Roosevelt)
1907–1909	60th	R-222	D-164	R-61	D-29	R (T. Roosevelt)
1909–1911	61st	R-219	D-172	R-59	D-32	R (Taft)
1911–1913	62nd	D-228	R-162	R-49	D-42	R (Taft)
1913–1915	63rd	D-290	R-127	D-51	R-44	D (Wilson)
1915–1917	64th	D-231	R-193	D-56	R-39	D (Wilson)
1917–1919	65th	D-216	R-210	D-53	R-42	D (Wilson)
1919–1921	66th	R-237	D-191	R-48	D-47	D (Wilson)
1921–1923	67th	R-300	D-132	R-59	D-37	R (Harding)
1923–1925	68th	R-225	D-207	R-51	D-43	R (Coolidge)
1925–1927	69th	R-247	D-183	R-54	D-40	R (Coolidge)
1927–1929	70th	R-237	D-195	R-48	D-47	R (Coolidge)
1929–1931	71st	R-267	D-163	R-56	D-39	R (Hoover)
1931–1933	72nd	D-216	R-218	R-48	D-47	R (Hoover)
1933–1935	73rd	D-313	R-117	D-59	R-36	D (F. Roosevelt)
1935–1937	74th	D-322	R-103	D-69	R-25	D (F. Roosevelt)
1937–1939	75th	D-333	R-89	D-75	R-17	D (F. Roosevelt)
1939–1941	76th	D-262	R-169	D-69	R-23	D (F. Roosevelt)
1941–1943	77th	D-267	R-162	D-66	R-28	D (F. Roosevelt)
1943–1945	78th	D-222	R-209	D-57	R-38	D (F. Roosevelt)
1945–1947	79th	D-243	R-190	D-56	R-38	D (F. Roosevelt)
						D (Truman)
1947–1949	80th	R-246	D-188	R-51	D-45	D (Truman)
1949–1951	81st	D-263	R-171	D-54	R-42	D (Truman)
1951–1953	82nd	D-234	R-199	D-48	R-47	D (Truman)
1953–1955	83rd	R-221	D-213	R-48	D-46	R (Eisenhower)
1955–1957	84th	D-234	R-201	D-48	R-47	R (Eisenhower)
1957–1959	85th	D-233	R-200	D-49	R-47	R (Eisenhower)

(Continued)

(Continued)

Year	Congress	House Majority party	House Principal minority party	Senate Majority party	Senate Principal minority party	President
1959–1961	86th	D-283	R-153	D-64	R-34	R (Eisenhower)
1961–1963	87th	D-262	R-175	D-64	R-36	D (Kennedy)
1963–1965	88th	D-258	R-176	D-67	R-33	D (Kennedy)
						D (L. Johnson)
1965–1967	89th	D-295	R-140	D-68	R-32	D (L. Johnson)
1967–1969	90th	D-248	R-187	D-64	R-36	D (L. Johnson)
1969–1971	91st	D-243	R-192	D-58	R-42	R (Nixon)
1971–1973	92nd	D-255	R-180	D-54	R-44	R (Nixon)
1973–1975	93rd	D-242	R-192	D-56	R-42	R (Nixon)
						R (Ford)
1975–1977	94th	D-291	R-144	D-60	R-37	R (Ford)
1977–1979	95th	D-292	R-143	D-61	R-38	D (Carter)
1979–1981	96th	D-277	R-158	D-58	R-41	D (Carter)
1981–1983	97th	D-242	R-192	R-53	D-46	R (Reagan)
1983–1985	98th	D-269	R-166	R-54	D-46	R (Reagan)
1985–1987	99th	D-253	R-182	R-53	D-47	R (Reagan)
1987–1989	100th	D-258	R-177	D-55	R-45	R (Reagan)
1989–1991	101st	D-260	R-175	D-55	R-45	R (G. H. W. Bush)
1991–1993	102nd	D-267	R-167	D-56	R-44	R (G. H. W. Bush)
1993–1995	103rd	D-258	R-176	D-57	R-43	D (Clinton)
1995–1997	104th	R-230	D-204	R-52	D-48	D (Clinton)
1997–1999	105th	R-226	D-207	R-55	D-45	D (Clinton)
1999–2001	106th	R-223	D-211	R-55	D-45	D (Clinton)
2001–2003	107th	R-221	D-212	D-50	R-50	R (G. W. Bush)
2003–2005	108th	R-229	D-204	R-51	D-48	R (G. W. Bush)
2005–2007	109th	R-232	D-202	R-55	D-44	R (G. W. Bush)
2007–2009	110th	D-233	R-202	D-49	R-49	R (G. W. Bush)
2009–2011	111th	D-254	R-175	D-57	R-40	D (Obama)
*2011–2013	112th	D-193	R-242	D-53	R-47	D (Obama)
2013–	113th	D-232	D-200	D-53	R-45	D (Obama)

Sources: For data through the 33rd Congress, see U.S. Bureau of the Census, *Historical Statistics of the United States, Colonial Times to 1970* (Washington, D.C.: Government Printing Office, 1975), 1083–1084; for data after the 33rd Congress, see U.S. Congress, Joint Committee on Printing, *Official Congressional Directory* (Washington, D.C.: Government Printing Office, 2008), 553–554; for 2008 election data see *CQ Politics Election 2008*, www.cqpolitics.com/wmspage.cfn?parm1=2. See also http://innovation.cq.com/election_night08?tab2=f; for 2010 election data, see http://www.rollcall.com/politics/. For 2012 election data, see the Office of the Clerk of the U.S. House of Representatives, http://clerk.house.gov/member_info/cong.aspx.

Notes: Figures are for the beginning of the first session of each Congress. Key to abbreviations: AD—Administration; AM—Anti-Masonic; D—Democratic; DR—Democratic-Republican; F—Federalist; J—Jacksonian; NR—National Republican; Op—Opposition; R—Republican; U—Unionist; W—Whig.

1. The Republican Party ran under the Union Party banner in 1864.

*Numbers current as of time of publication.

Appendix 7

SUMMARY OF PRESIDENTIAL ELECTIONS, 1789–2012

Year	No. of states	Candidates		Electoral vote		Popular vote	
1789[a]	10	Fed. George Washington		Fed. 69		—[b]	
1792[a]	15	Fed. George Washington		Fed. 132		—[b]	
1796[a]	16	Dem.-Rep. Thomas Jefferson	Fed. John Adams	Dem.-Rep. 68	Fed. 71	—[b]	
1800[a]	16	Dem.-Rep. Thomas Jefferson Aaron Burr	Fed. John Adams Charles Cotesworth Pinckney	Dem.-Rep 73	Fed. 65	—[b]	
1804	17	Dem.-Rep. Thomas Jefferson George Clinton	Fed. Charles Cotesworth Pinckney Rufus King	Dem.-Rep 162	Fed. 14	—[b]	
1808	17	Dem.-Rep. James Madison George Clinton	Fed. Charles Cotesworth Pinckney Rufus King	Dem.-Rep 122	Fed. 47	—[b]	
1812	18	Dem.-Rep. James Madison Elbridge Gerry	Fed. George Clinton Jared Ingersoll	Dem.-Rep 128	Fed. 89	—[b]	
1816	19	Dem.-Rep. James Monroe Daniel D. Tompkins	Fed. Rufus King John Howard	Dem.-Rep 183	Fed. 34	—[b]	
1820	24	Dem.-Rep James Monroe Daniel D. Tompkins	—[c]	Dem.-Rep 231	—[c]	—[b]	
1824[d]	24	Dem.-Rep Andrew Jackson John C. Calhoun	Dem.-Rep John Q. Adams Nathan Sanford	Dem.-Rep 99	Dem.-Rep. 84	Dem.-Rep 151,271 41.3%	Dem.-Rep 113,122 30.9%
1828	24	Dem.-Rep. Andrew Jackson John C. Calhoun	Nat.-Rep. John Q. Adams Richard Rush	Dem.-Rep. 178	Nat.-Rep. 83	Dem.-Rep. 642,553 56.0%	Nat.-Rep. 500,897 43.6%
1832[e]	24	Dem. Andrew Jackson Martin Van Buren	Nat.-Rep. Henry Clay John Sergeant	Dem. 219	Nat.-Rep. 49 54.2%	Dem. 701,780	Nat.-Rep. 484,205 37.4%

(Continued)

(Continued)

Year	No. of states	Candidates		Electoral vote		Popular vote	
		Dem.	Whig	Dem.	Whig	Dem.	Whig
1836[f]	26	Martin Van Buren Richard M. Johnson	William H. Harrison Francis Granger	170	73	764,176 50.8%	550,816 36.6%
1840	26	Martin Van Buren Richard M. Johnson	William H. Harrison John Tyler	60	234	1,128,854 46.8%	1,275,390 52.9%
1844	26	James Polk George M. Dallas	Henry Clay Theodore Frelinghuysen	170	105	1,339,494 49.5%	1,300,004 48.1%
1848	30	Lewis Cass William O. Butler	Zachary Taylor Millard Fillmore	127	163	1,233,460 42.5%	1,361,393 47.3%
1852	31	Franklin Pierce William R. King	Winfield Scott William A. Graham	254	42	1,607,510 50.8%	1,386,942 43.9%

Year	No. of states	Candidates		Electoral vote		Popular vote	
		Dem.	Rep.	Dem.	Rep.	Dem.	Rep.
1856[g]	31	James Buchanan John C. Breckinridge	John C. Fremont William L. Dayton	174	114	1,836,072 45.3%	1,342,345 33.1%
1860[h]	33	Stephen A. Douglas Herschel V. Johnson	Abraham Lincoln Hannibal Hamlin	12	180	1,380,202 29.5%	1,865,908 39.8%
1864[i]	36	George B. McClellan George H. Pendleton	Abraham Lincoln Andrew Johnson	21	212	1,812,807 45.0%	2,218,388 55.0%
1868[j]	37	Horatio Seymour Francis P. Blair Jr.	Ulysses S. Grant Schuyler Colfax	80	214	2,708,744 47.3%	3,013,650 52.7%
1872[k]	37	Horace Greeley Benjamin Gratz Brown	Ulysses S. Grant Henry Wilson		286	2,834,761 43.8%	3,598,235 55.6%
1876	38	Samuel J. Tilden Thomas A. Hendricks	Rutherford B. Hayes William A. Wheeler	184	185	4,288,546 51.0%	4,034,311 47.9%
1880	38	Winfield S. Hancock William H. English	James A. Garfield Chester A. Arthur	155	214	4,444,260 48.2%	4,446,158 48.3%
1884	38	Grover Cleveland Thomas A. Hendricks	James G. Blaine John A. Logan	219	182	4,874,621 48.5%	4,848,936 48.2%
1888	38	Grover Cleveland Allen G. Thurman	Benjamin Harrison Levi P. Morton	168	233	5,534,488 48.6%	5,443,892 47.8%
1892[l]	44	Grover Cleveland Adlai E. Stevenson	Benjamin Harrison Whitelaw Reid	277	145	5,551,883 46.1%	5,179,244 43.0%
1896	45	William J. Bryan Arthur Sewall	William McKinley Garret A. Hobart	176	271	6,511,495 46.7%	7,108,480 51.0%
1900	45	William J. Bryan Adlai E. Stevenson	William McKinley Theodore Roosevelt	155	292	6,358,345 45.5%	7,218,039 51.7%
1904	45	Alton B. Parker Henry G. Davis	Theodore Roosevelt Charles W. Fairbanks	140	336	5,028,898 37.6%	7,626,593 56.4%

Year	No. of states	Candidates		Electoral vote		Popular vote	
		Dem.	Rep.	Dem.	Rep.	Dem.	Rep.
1908	46	William J. Bryan John W. Kern	William H. Taft James S. Sherman	162	321	6,406,801 43.0%	7,676,258 51.6%
1912[m]	48	Woodrow Wilson Thomas R. Marshall	William H. Taft James S. Sherman	435	8	6,293,152 41.8%	3,486,333 23.2%
1916	48	Woodrow Wilson Thomas R. Marshall	Charles E. Hughes Charles W. Fairbanks	277	254	9,126,300 49.2%	8,546,789 46.1%
1920	48	James M. Cox Franklin D. Roosevelt	Warren G. Harding Calvin Coolidge	127	404	9,140,884 34.2%	16,133,314 60.3%
1924[n]	48	John W. Davis Charles W. Bryant	Calvin Coolidge Charles G. Dawes	136	382	8,386,169 28.8%	15,717,553 54.1%
1928	48	Alfred E. Smith Joseph T. Robinson	Herbert C. Hoover Charles Curtis	87	444	15,000,185 40.8%	21,411,991 58.2%
1932	48	Franklin D. Roosevelt John N. Garner	Herbert C. Hoover Charles Curtis	472	59	22,825,016 57.4%	15,758,397 39.6%
1936	48	Franklin D. Roosevelt John N. Garner	Alfred M. Landon Frank Knox	523	8	27,747,636 60.8%	16,679,543 36.5%
1940	48	Franklin D. Roosevelt Henry A. Wallace	Wendell L. Willkie Charles L. McNary	449	82	27,263,448 54.7%	22,336,260 44.8%
1944	48	Franklin D. Roosevelt Harry S. Truman	Thomas E. Dewey John W. Bricker	432	99	25,611,936 53.4%	22,013,372 45.9%
1948[o]	48	Harry S. Truman Alben W. Barkley	Thomas E. Dewey Earl Warren	303	189	24,105,587 49.5%	21,970,017 45.1%
1952	48	Adlai E. Stevenson II John J. Sparkman	Dwight D. Eisenhower Richard M. Nixon	89	442	27,314,649 44.4%	33,936,137 55.1%
1956[p]	48	Adlai E. Stevenson II Estes Kefauver	Dwight D. Eisenhower Richard M. Nixon	73	457	26,030,172 42.0%	35,585,245 57.4%
1960[q]	50	John F. Kennedy Lyndon B. Johnson	Richard M. Nixon Henry Cabot Lodge	303	219	34,221,344 49.7%	34,106,671 49.5%
1964	50*	Lyndon B. Johnson Hubert H. Humphrey	Barry Goldwater William E. Miller	486	52	43,126,584 61.1%	27,177,838 38.5%
1968[r]	50*	Hubert H. Humphrey Edmund S. Muskie	Richard M. Nixon Spiro T. Agnew	191	301	31,274,503 42.7%	31,785,148 43.4%
1972[s]	50*	George McGovern Sargent Shriver	Richard M. Nixon Spiro T. Agnew	17	520	29,171,791 37.5%	47,170,179 60.7%
1976[t]	50*	Jimmy Carter Walter F. Mondale	Gerald R. Ford Robert Dole	297	240	40,830,763 50.1%	39,147,793 48.0%
1980	50*	Jimmy Carter Walter F. Mondale	Ronald Reagan George H.W. Bush	49	489	35,483,883 41.0%	43,904,153 50.7%
1984	50*	Walter F. Mondale Geraldine Ferraro	Ronald Reagan George H.W. Bush	13	525	37,577,185 40.6%	54,455,075 58.8%
1988[u]	50*	Michael S. Dukakis Lloyd Bentsen	George H.W. Bush Dan Quayle	111	426	41,809,074 45.6%	48,886,097 53.4%

(Continued)

(Continued)

Year	No. of states	Candidates		Electoral vote		Popular vote	
		Dem.	Rep.	Dem.	Rep.	Dem.	Rep.
1992	50*	William J. Clinton Albert Gore	George H.W. Bush Dan Quayle	370	168	44,909,326 43.0%	39,103,882 37.4%
1996	50*	William J. Clinton Albert Gore	Robert J. Dole Jack F. Kemp	379	159	47,402,357 49.2%	39,198,755 40.7%
2000	50*	Albert Gore Joseph I. Lieberman	George W. Bush Richard B. Cheney	266	271	50,992,335 48.4%	50,455,156 47.9%
2004	50*	John Kerry John Edwards	George W. Bush Richard B. Cheney	252	286	59,026,013 47.3%	62,025,554 50.7%
2008	50*	Barack Obama Joe Biden	John McCain Sarah Palin	365	173	69,498,459 52.9%	59,948,283 45.6%
2012	50*	Barack Obama Joe Biden	Mitt Romney Paul Ryan	332	206	62,611,250 51.5%	59,134,475 48.5%

Sources: Harold W. Stanley and Richard G. Niemi, *Vital Statistics on American Politics, 2007–2008* (Washington, D.C.: CQ Press, 2008), 26–30; *CQ Press Guide to U.S. Elections,* 5th ed. (Washington, D.C.: CQ Press, 2006), 715–719; for the 2008 election: for presidential race electoral vote data, see *CQ Politics Election 2008,* http://innovation.cq.com/election_night08?tab2=f. For presidential race popular vote data, see the *New York Times's* Presidential Big Board, http://elections.nytimes.com/2008/results/president/votes.html. 2012 election data calculated from Politico, 2012 Presidential Election, http://www.politico.com/2012-election/map/#/President/2012/.

Note: Dem.-Rep.—Democratic-Republican; Fed.—Federalist; Nat.-Rep.—National-Republican; Dem.—Democratic; Rep.—Republican.

a. Elections from 1789 through 1800 were held under rules that did not allow separate voting for president and vice president.

b. Popular vote returns are not shown before 1824 because consistent, reliable data are not available.

c. 1820: One electoral vote was cast for John Adams and Richard Stockton, who were not candidates.

d. 1824: All four candidates represented Democratic-Republican factions. William H. Crawford received 41 electoral votes and Henry Clay received 37 votes. Because no candidate received a majority, the election was decided (in Adams's favor) by the House of Representatives.

e. 1832: Two electoral votes were not cast.

f. 1836: Other Whig candidates receiving electoral votes were Hugh L. White, who received 26 votes, and Daniel Webster, who received 14 votes.

g. 1856: Millard Fillmore, Whig-American, received 8 electoral votes.

h. 1860: John C. Breckinridge, southern Democrat, received 72 electoral votes. John Bell, Constitutional Union, received 39 electoral votes.

i. 1864: Eighty-one electoral votes were not cast.

j. 1868: Twenty-three electoral votes were not cast.

k. 1872: Horace Greeley, Democrat, died after the election. In the Electoral College, Democratic electoral votes went to Thomas Hendricks, 42 votes; Benjamin Gratz Brown, 18 votes; Charles J. Jenkins, 2 votes; and David Davis, 1 vote. Seventeen electoral votes were not cast.

l. 1892: James B. Weaver, People's Party, received 22 electoral votes.

m. 1912: Theodore Roosevelt, Progressive Party, received 88 electoral votes.

n. 1924: Robert M. La Follette, Progressive Party, received 13 electoral votes.

o. 1948: J. Strom Thurmond, States' Rights Party, received 39 electoral votes.

p. 1956: Walter B. Jones, Democrat, received 1 electoral vote.

q. 1960: Harry Flood Byrd, Democrat, received 15 electoral votes.

r. 1968: George C. Wallace, American Independent Party, received 46 electoral votes.

s. 1972: John Hospers, Libertarian Party, received 1 electoral vote.

t. 1976: Ronald Reagan, Republican, received 1 electoral vote.

u. 1988: Lloyd Bentsen, the Democratic vice-presidential nominee, received 1 electoral vote for president.

* Fifty states plus the District of Columbia.

Notes

Chapter 1

1. James Harrington, *The Common-wealth of Oceana and a System of Politics* (1656; reprinted, ed. J. G. Pocock, New York: Cambridge University Press, 1992).

2. C. R. Hallpike, "Functionalist Interpretations of Primitive Warfare," *Man* (September 1973). Cited in Russell Hardin, "Hobbesian Political Order," *Political Theory* (May 1991): 168.

3. Thomas Hobbes, *Leviathan, or The matter, forme, & power of a commonwealth ecclesiasticall and civill* (1651; reprint, Oxford: Clarendon Press, 1958).

4. Ryan Lizza, "The Final Push," *New Yorker,* October 29, 2012, 67.

5. Mark Kurlansky, *Cod: A Biography of the Fish That Changed the World* (New York: Walker, 1997).

6. Nathaniel Philbrick, *Mayflower* (New York: Viking, 2006), 165.

7. Eric Schmitt, "Testing of a President: The Votes; Impeachment Doubts Erode Slim Republican Majority," *New York Times,* November 19, 1998.

8. Michael Cooper, "So How Bad Is Albany? Well, Notorious," *New York Times,* July 22, 2004, B1 and B5.

9. We will examine the Electoral College more closely in Chapter 2.

10. James Madison, *Federalist No. 51,* in Alexander Hamilton, James Madison, and John Jay, *The Federalist Papers* (see Appendix).

11. They were, among others, the French philosopher Baron de Montesquieu (1689–1755) and the English philosopher John Locke (1632–1704).

Chapter 2

1. Wayne Carp, *To Starve the Army at Pleasure: Continental Army Administration and American Political Culture, 1775–1783* (Chapel Hill: University of North Carolina Press, 1984), 197. During 1780 Washington frequently repeated this warning in correspondence with political leaders.

2. Letter from John Adams to Timothy Pickering, August 22, 1822, in John Adams, *Life and Works,* Vol. 2, ed. Charles Francis Adams (Boston: Little, Brown, 1850–1856).

3. This expression comes from Revolutionary War general Nathanael Greene—see Carp, *To Starve the Army at Pleasure,* 196. Remarkably, although the field commanders showered Congress with contempt, none ever suggested that the military could do a better job of running the government.

4. Gordon S. Wood, *The Creation of the American Republic: 1776–1787* (New York: Norton, 1969), 405–410.

5. Letter to Thomas Jefferson, October 17, 1788, in William T. Hutchinson et al., eds., *The Papers of James Madison,* Vol. 9 (Chicago: University of Chicago Press, 1962).

6. This discussion follows David P. Szatmary's treatment in *Shays's Rebellion: The Making of an Agrarian Insurrection* (Amherst: University of Massachusetts Press, 1980), 120–134.

7. John Locke, *Essay Concerning the True Original Extent and End of Civil Government. Second Treatise of Government,* ed. C. B. Macpherson (Indianapolis: Hackett, 1980).

8. William Lee Miller, *The Business of May Next: James Madison and the Founding* (Charlottesville: University Press of Virginia, 1992), 87.

9. *Marbury v. Madison,* 1 Cr. 137 (1803).

10. Quoted in James MacGregor Burns, *The Vineyard of Liberty* (New York: Vintage, 1983), 28.

11. Catherine Drinker Bowen, *Miracle at Philadelphia: The Story of the Constitutional Convention, May to September 1787* (Boston: Atlantic–Little, Brown, 1966), 278.

12. See Locke, *Essay Concerning the True Original Extent and End of Civil Government;* and David Hume, "The Perfect Commonwealth," in *Essays, Moral, Political, and Literary,* ed. Eugene F. Miller (Indianapolis: Liberty Fund, 1987). In 1776 Madison had urged fellow members of the Virginia House of Burgesses to embrace a multitude of religious sects in promoting religious reform, proposing that "all men are equally entitled to enjoy the free exercise of religion, according to the dictates of conscience." Ralph Ketcham, *James Madison: A Biography* (Charlottesville: University Press of Virginia, 1990), 72. In an essay on the "vices" of republican governments, Madison fleshed out the argument more fully and applied it to political factions. Also see Douglas Adair, "'That Politics May Be Reduced to a Science,' David Hume, James Madison and the Tenth Federalist," *Huntington Library Quarterly* (1957), reprinted in Douglas Adair, *Fame and the Founding Fathers* (New York: Norton, 1974), 93–106.

13. This argument is developed more fully in Samuel Kernell, "'The True Principles of Republican Government': Reassessing James Madison's Political Science," in *James Madison: The Theory and Practice of Republican Government,* ed. Samuel Kernell (Stanford, CA: Stanford University Press, 2003).

14. See Robert Dahl, *A Preface to Democratic Theory* (Chicago: University of Chicago Press, 1956); and E. E. Schattschneider, *Party Government* (New York: Holt, Rinehart and Winston, 1942), 18–21.

Chapter 3

1. Statistics can be found at the Oregon Health Authority's "Oregon Medical Marijuana Program Statistics" website, located at http://public.health.oregon.gov/DISEASESCONDITIONS/CHRONICDISEASE/MEDICALMARIJUANAPROGRAM/Pages/data.aspx, and details of Mr. Nelson's trial come from the June 12, 2002, press release by the U.S. Attorney's Office, District of Oregon, titled "Grants Pass Man Found Guilty of Manufacturing Marijuana and Possessing Machineguns and Silencers," as well as Jeff Barnard, "Marijuana Grower Convicted," Associated Press, June 13, 2012.

2. See Charles Lane, "Court to Hear Marijuana Case," *Washington Post*, November 29, 2004.

3. Attorney General Holder is quoted in Carrie Johnson, "US Eases Stance on Medical Marijuana," *Washington Post*, October 20, 2009. State medical marijuana laws are listed at the National Conference of State Legislatures' "State Medical Marijuana Laws" webpage, http://www.ncsl.org/issues-research/health/state-medical-marijuana-laws.aspx.

4. This definition comes directly from Parris N. Glendening and Mavis Mann Reeves, *Pragmatic Federalism,* 2nd ed. (Pacific Palisades, CA: Pacific Palisades, 1984), 11.

5. This quotation is from Howard L. McBain, *The Law and the Practice of Municipal Home Rule* (New York: Columbia University Press, 1916), 15. Dillon was an Iowa Supreme Court justice who set forth the doctrine that local governments fully subordinate to states in an 1868 decision (*Clinton v. Cedar Rapids and Missouri River R. R.,* 24 Iowa 455) and an 1872 book. It was the U.S. Supreme Court's 1907 decision in *Hunter v. Pittsburgh* (207 U.S. 161) that applied Dillon's Rule to local governments across the nation.

6. For a review of contemporary state-local relations, see Russell L. Hanson, *Governing Partners: State-Local Relations in the United States* (Boulder, CO: Westview, 1998).

7. William H. Riker, "The Senate and American Federalism," *American Political Science Review* 49 (1955): 452–469.

8. For a discussion of the Senate's special role in spawning presidential candidates, see Nelson W. Polsby, *Political Innovation in America* (New Haven, CT: Yale University Press, 1984).

9. See Article I, Section 9.

10. It also is known as the necessary and proper clause.

11. *McCulloch v. Maryland,* 4 Wheat. 316 (1819).

12. *Gibbons v. Ogden,* 22 U.S. 1 (1824).

13. This history is well told by Robert H. Wiebe in *The Search for Order, 1877–1920* (New York: Hill and Wang, 1967).

14. The case was *United States v. F. W. Darby Lumber Co.,* 312 U.S. 100 (1941). Passage cited in Lee Epstein and Thomas G. Walker, *Constitutional Law for a Changing America: A Short Course,* 3rd ed. (Washington, DC: CQ Press, 2005), 192–193.

15. The "welfare magnets" idea and the initial evidence that states raced to the bottom in welfare payments were introduced in Paul E. Peterson and Mark C. Rom, *Welfare Magnets: The Case for a National Welfare Standard* (Washington, DC: Brookings, 1990). The findings of the literature that this book inspired have been critiqued by Craig Volden in "The Politics of Competitive Federalism: A Race to the Bottom in Welfare Benefits?" *American Journal of Political Science* 46 (2002): 352–363.

16. Louis Uchitelle, "States Pay for Jobs, but It Doesn't Always Pay Off," *New York Times,* November 10, 2003.

17. MADD did meet some resistance in the low-drinking-age states that benefited economically from the commerce in alcohol.

18. *South Dakota v. Dole,* 483 U.S. 203 (1987).

19. These laws were compiled in the *2007 State Scorecard* produced by the Brady Campaign to Prevent Gun Violence, with updated scorecards accessible at www.bradycampaign.org/xshare/bcam/stategunlaws/scorecard/BradyScorecard.pdf. Many state gun control laws remain in effect, but some states have recently passed laws friendly to gun owners that attempt to relax the strict laws of other states. Utah and Florida now issue permits to carry concealed weapons to residents of other states, and these other states may decide whether or not to honor the permits. (Only thirty states currently honor the permits that Florida issues to nonresidents, according to the Florida Division of Licensing, http://licg-web.doacs.state.fl.us/news/concealed_carry.html.)

20. *Garcia v. San Antonio Metropolitan Transit Authority,* 469 U.S. 528 (1985).

21. Kenneth T. Palmer and Edward B. Laverty, "The Impact of *United States v. Lopez* on Intergovernmental Relations: A Preliminary Assessment," *Publius* 26 (Summer 1996): 109–126. This revisionism continued in a 1997 case in which the Court invalidated a provision of the 1993 Brady handgun law that required local law enforcement officials to run background checks on purchasers of handguns. Dan Carney, "Brady Decision Reflects Effort to Curb Congress' Authority," *Congressional Quarterly Weekly Report,* June 28, 1997, 1524–1525.

22. Elizabeth A. Palmer, "High Court Further Circumscribes Congress' Power in Ruling on Violence Against Women Act," *CQ Weekly,* May 20, 2000, 1188. The Court again invoked *Lopez* in 2001, ruling by a 5–4 vote that state employees could not use the federal Americans with Disabilities Act (see Chapter 4) to sue their employers.

23. John Kincaid, "Constitutional Federalism: Labor's Role in Displacing Places to Benefit Persons," *PS* (June 1993): 172.

24. Quoted on page 1127 of Wallace Oates, "An Essay on Fiscal Federalism," *Journal of Economic Literature* 37 (September 1999): 1120–1149.

25. L. Nye Stevens, *Unfunded Mandates—Reform Act Has Had Little Effect on Agencies' Rulemaking Actions, Report to the Committee on Governmental Affairs, U.S. Senate* (Washington, DC: General Accounting Office, 1998).

26. Quoted from David Brian Robertson, *Federalism and the Making of America* (New York and London: Routledge, 2012), 8.

Chapter 4

1. Sam Howe Verhovek, "Americans Give in to Race Profiling," *New York Times,* September 23, 2001.

2. "Guidance for Screeners and Other Security Personnel," U.S. Department of Transportation, Federal Aviation Administration, www.dot.gov/airconsumer.

3. Henry Weinstein et al., "After the Attack; Law Enforcement," *Los Angeles Times,* September 24, 2001.

4. Harold Sullivan proposes this distinction in *Civil Rights and Liberties: Provocative Questions and Evolving Answers* (New York: Prentice Hall, 2001), 1–2.

5. John M. Broder, "Clinton, Softening Slap at Senate, Names 'Acting' Civil Rights Chief," *New York Times,* December 16, 1997.

6. Mary B. Norton et al., *People and a Nation: A History of the United States,* Vol. 1, 5th ed. (Boston: Houghton Mifflin, 1987), 238.

7. Chaplain W. Morrison, *Democratic Politics and Sectionalism: The Wilmot Proviso Controversy* (Chapel Hill: University of North Carolina Press, 1967).

8. *Dred Scott v. Sandford,* 19 How. 393 (1857).

9. Quoted in C. Vann Woodward, *The Burden of Southern History* (Baton Rouge: Louisiana State University Press, 1968), 95.

10. Ibid.

11. C. Vann Woodward, *Reunion and Reaction: The Compromise of 1877 and the End of Reconstruction* (Boston: Little, Brown, 1966).

12. *Plessy v. Ferguson,* 163 U.S. 737 (1896).

13. Edward G. Carmines and James A. Stimson, *Issue Evolution: Race and the Transformation of American Politics* (Princeton, NJ: Princeton University Press, 1989).

14. *Brown v. Board of Education of Topeka,* 347 U.S. 483 (1954).

15. *Smith v. Allwright,* 321 U.S. 649 (1944).

16. *Sweatt v. Painter,* 339 U.S. 629 (1950).

17. *Brown v. Board of Education,* 349 U.S. 294 (1955).

18. David J. Garrow, *Bearing the Cross: Martin Luther King, Jr., and the Southern Christian Leadership Conference* (New York: Morrow, 1986), 91.

19. Dennis Chong elaborates on these issues in his *Collective Action and the Civil Rights Movement* (Chicago: University of Chicago Press, 1991).

20. Paul Burstein, "Public Opinion, Demonstrations, and the Passage of Antidiscrimination Legislation," *Public Opinion Quarterly* 43 (1979): 157–172.

21. Taylor Branch, *Parting the Waters: America in the King Years, 1954–1963* (New York: Simon and Schuster, 1988).

22. Ibid.

23. Robert M. Axelrod, "Where the Votes Come From: An Analysis of Electoral Coalitions, 1952–1958," *American Political Science Review* (March 1972).

24. From Gary Orfield, *Congressional Power: Congress and Social Change* (New York: Harcourt Brace Jovanovich, 1975), 102.

25. *Regents of the University of California v. Bakke,* 438 U.S. 265 (1978).

26. The 1987 case is *Johnson v. Transportation Agency of Santa Clara County;* the 1995 case, *Adarand Constructors, Inc. v. Peña,* 515 U.S. 200 (1995).

27. *Gratz v. Bollinger,* 539 U.S. 244 (2003), involved the undergraduate point system, while *Grutter v. Bollinger,* 539 U.S. 306 (2003), concerned the law school's consideration of race as a variable.

28. Alexander Keyssar, *The Right to Vote* (New York: Basic Books, 2000); Judith Apter Klinghoffer and Lois Elkis, "The Petticoat Electors: Women's Suffrage in New Jersey, 1776–1807," *Journal of the Early Republic* 12 (1992): 159–193.

29. Ibid., 177.

30. The rise of the abortion issue after the Supreme Court legalized abortions in its 1973 *Roe v. Wade* decision stalled the ERA. Jane Mansbridge, *Why We Lost the ERA* (Chicago: University of Chicago Press, 1986).

31. The case that triggered Congress's response was *Grove City College v. Bell,* 465 U.S. 555 (1984).

32. This estimate is based on "Charge Statistics" compiled by the EEOC and reported on its website: www.eeoc.gov/eeoc/statistics/enforcement/charges.cfm.

33. Wendy R. Weiser and Lawrence Norden, "Voting Law Changes in 2012," Brennan Center for Justice at New York University School of Law.

34. *Crawford v. Marion County Election Board,* 553 U.S. 181 (2008).

35. *Romer v. Evans,* 517 U.S. 620 (1996).

36. The list, updated in 2004, is contained in the General Accounting Office report located at www.gao.gov/new.items/d04353r.pdf.

37. *Lawrence v. Texas,* 539 U.S. 558 (2003).

Chapter 5

1. *Reno v. ACLU,* 117 S. Ct. 2329, 138 L. Ed. 2d 874 (1997).

2. From a speech to Congress, June 8, 1789. Quoted in *The Papers of James Madison,* ed. William T. Hutchinson et al. (Chicago: University of Chicago Press, 1962), 197–206.

3. *Employment Division, Department of Human Resources of Oregon v. Smith,* 494 U.S. 872 (1990).

4. *City of Boerne v. Flores,* 136 L. Ed. 2d 709 (1997).

5. Donald S. Lutz, "The State Constitutional Pedigree of the U.S. Bill of Rights," *Publius* 22 (Spring 1992): 19–45.

6. Quoted in Alpheus Thomas Mason, *The States' Rights Debate* (New York: Oxford University Press, 1972), 174. Madison informed the House of Representatives: "I will not propose a single alteration which I do not wish to see take place, as proper in itself, or proper because it is wished by a respectable number of my fellow citizens."

7. *Barron v. Baltimore,* 7 Pet. 243 (1833).

8. Andrew W. Young, *Introduction to the Science of Government,* 3rd ed. (Rochester, NY: William Alling, 1843).

9. This discussion of incorporation follows the presentation in Lee Epstein and Thomas G. Walker, *Constitutional Law for a Changing America: Rights, Liberties, and Justice,* 5th ed. (Washington, DC: CQ Press, 2004), 75–97. Indeed, this text provides a thorough review and treatment of all issues described in this chapter.

10. *The Butchers' Benevolent Association of New Orleans v. The Crescent City Livestock Landing and Slaughterhouse Co.; Esteban v. Louisiana* (The Slaughterhouse Cases), 16 Wall. 36 (1873).

11. *Hurtado v. California,* 110 U.S. 516 (1884).

12. *Tinker v. Des Moines,* 393 U.S. 503 (1969).

13. *Texas v. Johnson,* 491 U.S. 397 (1989).

14. *United States v. Eichman,* 496 U.S. 310 (1990).

15. *Schenck v. United States,* 249 U.S. 47 (1919).

16. *Gitlow v. New York,* 268 U.S. 652 (1925).

17. *Dennis v. United States,* 341 U.S. 494 (1951).

18. *Brandenburg v. Ohio,* 395 U.S. 444 (1969).

19. *Roth v. United States,* 354 U.S. 476 (1957).

20. Epstein and Walker, *Constitutional Law,* 371–372.

21. *Miller v. California,* 413 U.S. 15 (1973).

22. *Jacobellis v. Ohio,* 378 U.S. 184 (1964).

23. Epstein and Walker, *Constitutional Law,* 371–372.

24. *Reno v. ACLU.*

25. *Sheppard v. Maxwell,* 384 U.S. 333 (1966).

26. *Globe Newspaper Co. v. Superior Court,* 457 U.S. 596 (1982).

27. Ralph Ketcham, *James Madison* (Charlottesville: University Press of Virginia, 1971), 166.

28. *Bradfield v. Roberts,* 175 U.S. 291 (1899).

29. *Everson v. Board of Education,* 330 U.S. 1 (1947).

30. Frank J. Sorauf, *The Wall of Separation* (Princeton, NJ: Princeton University Press, 1976), 257.

31. *Lemon v. Kurtzman; Earley v. DiCenso,* 403 U.S. 602 (1971).

32. *Lynch v. Donnelly,* 465 U.S. 668 (1984); *County of Allegheny v. ACLU, Greater Pittsburgh Chapter,* 492 U.S. 573 (1989).

33. Leonard W. Levy, *The Establishment Clause* (New York: Macmillan, 1986), 128.

34. *Board of Education of Kiryas Joel Village School District v. Grumet,* 512 U.S. 687 (1994).

35. *Agostini v. Felton,* 521 U.S. 203 (1997); *Mitchell v. Helms,* 530 U.S. 793 (2000); *Zelman v. Simmons-Harris,* 536 U.S. 639 (2002).

36. The case is *Locke v. Davey,* 540 U.S. 712 (2004). Linda Greenhouse, "States Allowed to Avoid Subsidy of Divinity Study," *New York Times,* February 26, 2004.

37. Jeanne Cummings and Jim VandeHei, "Faith-Based Charity Initiative Takes Worldly, Rocky Path," *Wall Street Journal,* August 16, 2001, A16.

38. *Engel v. Vitale,* 370 U.S. 421 (1962).

39. *School District of Abington Township v. Schempp,* 374 U.S. 203 (1963).

40. Dan Carney, "With Barely a Prayer of Ratification, Religious Freedom Amendment Opens Perennial Election-Year Debate," *CQ Weekly,* June 6, 1998, 1530.

41. *Wallace v. Jaffree,* 472 U.S. 38 (1985).

42. *Lee v. Weisman,* 505 U.S. 577 (1992).

43. Robert Birkby, "The Supreme Court in the Bible Belt: Tennessee Reaction to the *Schempp* Decision," *American Journal of Political Science* 10 (1966): 304.

44. Kevin Sack, "In South, Prayer Is a Form of Protest: A Ruling Is Opposed in Classrooms, Courtroom and Statehouse," *New York Times,* November 8, 1997, A7.

45. *Employment Division, Department of Human Resources of Oregon v. Smith.*

46. *Church of the Lukumi Babalu Aye, Inc., et al. v. City of Hialeah,* 508 U.S. 502, 533 (1993).

47. *District of Columbia v. Heller,* 554 U.S. 570 (2008).

48. *McDonald v. Chicago,* 561 U.S. 3025 (2010).

49. *United States v. Masciandaro,* 638 F.3d 458, 475 (4th Cir. 2011).

50. Cited in Kenneth Janda, Jeffrey M. Berry, and Jerry Goldman, *The Challenge of Democracy,* 4th ed. (Boston: Houghton Mifflin, 1995), 537.

51. *Brown v. Mississippi,* 297 U.S. 278 (1936).

52. Harold W. Stanley and Richard G. Niemi, *Vital Statistics on American Politics, 2007–2008* (Washington, DC: CQ Press, 2007), 155.

53. *Katz v. United States,* 389 U.S. 347 (1967).

54. *Kyllo v. United States,* 533 U.S. 27 (2001).

55. For a full discussion of each of these conditions, see Epstein and Walker, *Constitutional Law,* 509–541.

56. *Brendlin v. California,* 551 U.S. 241 (2007); *Georgia v. Randolph,* 547 U.S. 103 (2006).

57. *Mapp v. Ohio,* 367 U.S. 643 (1961).

58. *United States v. Leon,* 468 U.S. 897 (1984); *Massachusetts v. Sheppard,* 468 U.S. 981 (1984).

59. *Hudson v. Michigan,* 547 U.S. 586 (2006).

60. *Nix v. Williams,* 467 U.S. 431 (1984).

61. *United States v. Jones,* 132 S.Ct. 945 (2012).

62. See Robert Barnes, "Supreme Court: Warrants Needed in GPS Tracking," *Washington Post,* January 23, 2012.

63. *Malloy v. Hogan,* 378 U.S. 1 (1964).

64. *Miranda v. Arizona,* 384 U.S. 436 (1966).

65. *Dickerson v. United States,* 530 U.S. 428 (2000).

66. *Gideon v. Wainwright,* 372 U.S. 335 (1963).

67. *Argersinger v. Hamlin,* 407 U.S. 25 (1972).

68. *Missouri v. Frye,* 132 S.Ct. 1399 (2012).

69. *Strickland v. Washington,* 466 U.S. 668 (1984).

70. Charles Lane, "Death Penalty of Md. Man Is Overturned," *Washington Post,* June 23, 2003.

71. Ten years after the legislation was enacted, the state had over seven thousand people incarcerated under the three-strikes law for twenty-five years or more. This number includes three hundred whose last conviction was for "petty theft." Linda Greenhouse, "Justices Uphold Long Prison Terms in Repeat Crimes," *New York Times,* March 6, 2004.

72. *Furman v. Georgia,* 408 U.S. 238 (1972). This description of the case is taken from Lee Epstein and Thomas G. Walker, *Constitutional Law for a Changing America: A Short Course,* 3rd ed. (Washington, DC: CQ Press, 2005), 573–574.

73. *Gregg v. Georgia,* 428 U.S. 153 (1976).

74. *Wiggins v. Smith,* 539 U.S. 510 (2003).

75. *Griswold v. Connecticut,* 381 U.S. 479 (1965).

76. *Eisenstadt v. Baird,* 410 U.S. 113 (1972), extended access to contraceptives to unmarried women.

77. *Planned Parenthood of Southeastern Pennsylvania v. Casey,* 505 U.S. 833 (1992).

78. *Gonzales v. Carhart,* 550 U.S. 124 (2007).

79. Charlie Savage, "Panel Approves a Bill to Safeguard E-Mail," *New York Times,* November 29, 2012.

80. Linda Greenhouse, "In New York Visit, O'Connor Foresees Limits on Freedom," *New York Times,* September 29, 2001.

Chapter 6

1. *Wesberry v. Sanders,* 376 U.S. 1 (1964).
2. *Thornburg v. Gingles,* 478 U.S. 30 (1986).
3. *Davis v. Bandemer,* 478 U.S. 109 (1986).
4. *Vieth v. Jubelirer,* 541 U.S. 267 (2004).
5. *Thornburg v. Gingles.*
6. *Shaw v. Reno,* 590 U.S. 630 (1993).
7. *Miller v. Johnson,* 515 U.S. 900 (1995).
8. Frances E. Lee and Bruce I. Oppenheimer, "Senate Apportionment: Competitiveness and Partisan Advantage," *Legislative Studies Quarterly* 22 (February 1997): 3–24.
9. Alan I. Abramowitz and Jeffrey A. Segal, *Senate Elections* (Ann Arbor: University of Michigan Press, 1992), 18.
10. The Progressive Era and its effects on U.S. politics are described more fully in Chapter 12, Political Parties.
11. Richard F. Fenno Jr., *Home Style: House Members in Their Districts* (Boston: Little, Brown, 1978), chaps. 1–5.
12. Data collected and analyzed by the authors.
13. Jerrold G. Rusk, "The Effects of the Australian Ballot Reform on Split Ticket Voting, 1876–1908," in *Controversies in Voting Behavior,* ed. Richard G. Niemi and Herbert F. Weisberg (San Francisco: W. H. Freeman, 1976), 485–486.
14. Gary C. Jacobson, *The Politics of Congressional Elections,* 7th ed. (New York: Longman, 2009), 27–45.
15. Norman J. Ornstein, Thomas E. Mann, and Michael J. Malbin, *Vital Statistics on Congress, 2008* (Washington, DC: Brookings, 2008), Tables 5-11 and 5-12.
16. Jacobson, *Congressional Elections,* 32–36.
17. David R. Mayhew, *Congress: The Electoral Connection* (New Haven, CT: Yale University Press, 1974), 37.
18. Gary C. Jacobson and Samuel Kernell, *Strategy and Choice in Congressional Elections,* 2nd ed. (New Haven, CT: Yale University Press, 1983), chaps. 2–3.
19. John Kingdon, *Congressmen's Voting Decisions,* 2nd ed. (New York: Harper and Row, 1981), 47–50.
20. John R. Johannes, *To Serve the People: Congress and Constituency Service* (Lincoln: University of Nebraska Press, 1984), 19.
21. Kerry Young, "An Earmark by Any Other Name," *CQ Weekly,* November 22, 2010, 2700.
22. The African American is Tim Scott (R-South Carolina), a congressman appointed to the Senate after his predecessor resigned following the 2012 election.
23. Roger H. Davidson, Walter J. Oleszek, and Frances E. Lee, *Congress and Its Members,* 11th ed. (Washington, DC: CQ Press, 2008), 124.
24. Mayhew, *Congress,* 87–97.
25. Sarah A. Binder, *Minority Rights, Majority Rule: Partisanship and the Development of Congress* (Cambridge: Cambridge University Press, 1997).
26. Gary W. Cox and Mathew D. McCubbins, *Legislative Leviathan: Party Government in the House* (Berkeley: University of California Press, 1993), part 2.
27. David W. Rohde, *Parties and Leaders in the Postreform House* (Chicago: University of Chicago Press, 1991), chap. 3.
28. Ibid., 31–49.

29. Jennifer Stenihauer, "Republicans Who Have Opposed Leadership See Committee Assignments Stripped," *New York Times,* December 3, 2012.
30. Diana Evans, *Greasing the Wheels: Using Pork Barrel Projects to Build Majority Coalitions in Congress* (Cambridge: Cambridge University Press, 2004).
31. George B. Galloway, *The History of the House of Representatives* (New York: Crowell, 1961), 12.
32. Barbara Hinckley, *Stability and Change in Congress,* 4th ed. (New York: Harper and Row, 1988), 155.
33. Sam Goldfarb, "Term Limits Win Out in Chairman Picks," *CQ Weekly,* December 13, 2010, 2868.
34. Richard E. Cohen, Siobhan Gorman, and Sydney J. Freedberg Jr., "National Security: The Ultimate Turf War," *National Journal,* January 4, 2003.
35. Ibid.
36. Ibid.
37. Garry Young and Joseph Cooper, "Multiple Referral and the Transformation of House Decision Making," in *Congress Reconsidered,* 5th ed., ed. Lawrence C. Dodd and Bruce I. Oppenheimer (Washington, DC: CQ Press, 1993), 212.
38. Barbara Sinclair, *Unorthodox Lawmaking: New Legislative Processes in the U.S. Congress,* 4th ed. (Washington, DC: CQ Press, 2011), Table 6.2.
39. John W. Ellwood and James A. Thurber, "The New Congressional Budget Process: The Hows and Whys of House-Senate Differences," in *Congress Reconsidered,* ed. Lawrence C. Dodd and Bruce I. Oppenheimer (New York: Praeger, 1977), 168.
40. Joseph White and Aaron Wildavsky, *The Deficit and the Public Interest: The Search for Responsible Budgeting in the 1980s* (Berkeley: University of California Press, 1989), chaps. 16–17.
41. Sinclair, *Unorthodox Lawmaking,* chaps. 2–3.
42. Mathew D. McCubbins and Thomas Schwartz, "Congressional Oversight Overlooked: Police Patrols vs. Fire Alarms," *American Journal of Political Science* 28 (February 1984): 165–179.
43. Robert Pear, "Repeal of Health Care Law Approved, Again, by House," *New York Times,* July 11, 2012.
44. Sinclair, *Unorthodox Lawmaking,* 126.
45. Kingdon, *Congressmen's Voting Decisions,* 47–54.
46. George Hager and David S. Cloud, "Democrats Tie Their Fate to Clinton's Budget Bill," *Congressional Quarterly Weekly Report,* August 7, 1993, 2212–2219.
47. Harold W. Stanley and Richard G. Niemi, *Vital Statistics on American Politics,* 6th ed. (Washington, DC: Congressional Quarterly, 1998), 252, http://en.wikipedia.org/wiki/List_of_United_States_presidential_vetoes.
48. Sinclair, *Unorthodox Lawmaking,* 5.
49. John R. Hibbing and Elizabeth Theiss-Morse, *Congress as Public Enemy: Public Attitudes toward American Political Institutions* (New York: Cambridge University Press, 1995), 46–61.

Chapter 7

1. Lawrence R. Jacobs and Robert Y. Shapiro, "Don't Blame the Public for Failed Health Care Reform," *Journal of Health Politics, Policy and Law* 20 (Summer 1995): 418.

2. Theda Skocpol, *Boomerang: Clinton's Health Security Effort and the Turn against Government in Politics* (New York: Norton, 1996).

3. Ezra Klein, "Barack Obama, Bill Clinton and Health-Care Reform," *Washington Post,* July 26, 2009.

4. Pew Research Center for People and the Press, "Death Panels Live on with Fox Viewers," August 20, 2009, http://pewresearch.org/pubs/1319/death-panels-republicans-fox-viewers.

5. Richard E. Cohen, "Help Wanted," *National Journal,* October 3, 2009.

6. Ibid.

7. Richard E. Neustadt, *Presidential Power and the Modern Presidents: The Politics of Power from Roosevelt to Reagan* (New York: Free Press, 1990), 34.

8. Marcus Cunliffe, *The Presidency* (Boston: Houghton Mifflin, 1968).

9. Quotation from David Herbert Donald, "Lincoln, the Politician," in *Lincoln Reconsidered: Essays on the Civil War Era* (New York: Random House, 1956).

10. Louis Fisher, *The Politics of Shared Power,* 3rd ed. (Washington, DC: CQ Press, 1993), 156–157.

11. Ibid., 93; and Glendon A. Schubert Jr., "Judicial Review of the Subdelegation of Presidential Power," *Journal of Politics* 12 (1950): 668.

12. Louis Fisher, *Constitutional Conflicts between Congress and the President,* 3rd ed. (Lawrence: University Press of Kansas, 1991), 103.

13. Theodore Roosevelt, *The Works of Theodore Roosevelt* (New York: Scribner, 1926), 347.

14. Sterling Denhard Spero, *Government as Employer* (Carbondale: Southern Illinois University Press, 1972), 117–143.

15. Richard E. Neustadt, "The Presidency and Legislation: The Growth of Central Clearance," *American Political Science Review* 48 (September 1954): 461–671.

16. Theodore J. Lowi and Benjamin Ginsberg, *American Government: Freedom and Power,* 4th ed. (New York: Norton, 1996), 625.

17. This figure covers presidential initiatives from 1935 through 1996. Jon R. Bond and Richard Fleisher, *Polarized Politics* (Washington, DC: CQ Press, 2000), 120.

18. Alexis de Tocqueville, *Democracy in America,* ed. J. P. Mayer (Garden City, NY: Doubleday, 1969), 122.

19. Jack Germond, *Mad as Hell: Revolt at the Ballot Box, 1992* (New York: Warner Books, 1993).

20. Glenn Kessler, "Grover Norquist's History Lesson: George H. W. Bush, 'No New Taxes,' and the 1992 Election," *Washington Post,* November 26, 2012.

21. Alison Mitchell, "Clinton Seems to Keep Running though the Race Is Run and Won," *New York Times,* February 12, 1997, A1, A12.

22. Samuel Kernell and Laurie L. Rice, "Cable and Partisan Polarization of the President's Audience," *Presidential Studies Quarterly,* 2011.

23. Noble E. Cunningham Jr., *In Pursuit of Reason: The Life of Thomas Jefferson* (Baton Rouge: Louisiana State University Press, 1987).

24. John Hart, *The Presidential Branch: From Washington to Clinton,* 2nd ed. (Chatham, NJ: Chatham House, 1995), 31.

25. Nelson W. Polsby, "Some Landmarks in Presidential-Congressional Relations," in *Both Ends of the Avenue: The President, the Executive Branch, and the Congress,* ed. Anthony King (Washington, DC: American Enterprise, 1983), cited in Charles O. Jones, *The Presidency in a Separated System,* 2nd ed. (Washington, DC: Brookings, 2005).

26. Quoted in Samuel Kernell, "New and Old Lessons on White House Management," in *Executive Leadership in Anglo-American Systems,* ed. Colin Campbell and Margaret Jane Wyszomirski (Pittsburgh: University of Pittsburgh Press, 1991), 350.

27. Terence Smith, "Carter Liaison Aide with Jews to Quit White House," *New York Times,* March 9, 1978.

28. Neustadt, *Presidential Power.*

Chapter 8

1. Richard Serrano, "Fast and Furious Weapons Were Found in Mexico Cartel Enforcer's Home," *Los Angeles Times,* October 8, 2011.

2. Richard Serrano, "Five ATF Officials Found Responsible for Fast and Furious," *Los Angeles Times,* July 30, 2012.

3. Kim Murphy, "US Gun-Tracing Operation Let Firearms into Criminal Hands," *Los Angeles Times,* March 3, 2011.

4. Ibid.

5. Kim Murphy, "Guns Tracked by Firearms Bureau Found at Firefight Scene," *Los Angeles Times,* February 2, 2011.

6. Murphy, "US Gun-Tracing Operation Let Firearms into Criminal Hands."

7. Richard Serrano, "House Panel Recommends Holder Be Found in Contempt of Congress," *Los Angeles Times,* June 20, 2012.

8. Jonathan Weisman and Charlie Savage, "House Finds Holder in Contempt Over Inquiry on Guns," *New York Times,* June 28, 2012.

9. Serrano, "Five ATF Officials Found Responsible for Fast and Furious."

10. Charlie Savage, "Guns Inquiry Urges Action Against 14 in Justice Department," *New York Times,* September 19, 2012.

11. Anthony M. Bertelli and Laurence Lynn Jr., *Madison's Managers: Public Administration and the Constitution* (Baltimore: Johns Hopkins University Press, 2006), 2.

12. Michael Nelson, "A Short, Ironic History of Bureaucracy," *Journal of Politics* 44 (1982): 750.

13. Leonard D. White, *The Jeffersonians: A Study in Administrative History, 1801–1829* (New York: Macmillan, 1961), 139–140.

14. James Q. Wilson, "The Rise of the Bureaucratic State," in *The American Commonwealth, 1976,* ed. Nathan Glazer and Irving Kristol (New York: Basic Books, 1976), 78.

15. Nelson, "A Short, Ironic History of Bureaucracy," 756.

16. Leonard D. White, *The Federalists: A Study in Administrative History* (New York: Macmillan, 1961), 427–431.

17. White, *The Jeffersonians,* 357.

18. Quoted in Leonard D. White, *The Jacksonians: A Study in Administrative History, 1829–1861* (New York: Macmillan, 1963), 318.

19. Ibid., 320.

20. Max Weber, "Bureaucracy," in *Essays in Sociology,* translated by H. H. Gerth and C. Wright Mills (New York: Oxford University Press, 1962), 196–244.

21. Matthew A. Crenson, *The Federal Machine: Beginnings of Bureaucracy in Jacksonian America* (Baltimore: Johns Hopkins University Press, 1975), 4.

22. House Ways and Means Committee, Report 641, 24th Cong., 1st sess., 1836, 2, quoted in Crenson, *The Federal Machine,* 137–138.

23. Paul P. Van Riper, *History of the United States Civil Service* (Evanston, IL: Row, Peterson, 1958), 74–75.

24. Nelson, "A Short, Ironic History of Bureaucracy," 767.

25. In 1961 President John F. Kennedy, recognizing the politically sensitive nature of the office of attorney general, entrusted it to his brother Robert.

26. Donald R. Whitnah, ed., *Government Agencies* (Westport, CT: Greenwood, 1983).

27. Ibid., 152–172.

28. Terry M. Moe, "The Politics of Bureaucratic Structure," in *Can the Government Govern?* ed. John E. Chubb and Paul E. Peterson (Washington, DC: Brookings, 1989), 276.

29. Harold Seidman and Robert Gilmour, *Politics, Position, and Power: From the Positive to the Regulatory State* (New York: Oxford University Press, 1986), 316–319.

30. Paul C. Light, *The True Size of Government* (Washington, DC: Brookings, 1999), 24.

31. Martin Kady II and Joseph C. Anselmo, "'Private Army' Blurs the Lines," *CQ Weekly,* May 8, 2004, 1067.

32. Paul C. Light, "The New True Size of Government," *Research Brief No. 2,* Robert F. Wagner Graduate School of Public Service, New York University, August, 2006, 11.

33. Paul C. Light, "Fact Sheet on the New True Size of Government," Center for Public Service, Brookings Institution (September 5, 2003), at http://www.brookings.edu/research/articles/2003/09/05politics-light.

34. Charles T. Goodsell, *The Case for Bureaucracy: A Public Administration Polemic,* 4th ed. (Washington, DC: CQ Press, 2004), 141.

35. Ibid., 84–111.

36. James Q. Wilson, *Bureaucracy: What Government Agencies Do and Why They Do It* (New York: Basic Books, 1989), 91.

37. Martin Kady II, "Security's Swelling Price Tag," *CQ Weekly,* January 11, 2003, 75.

38. Jack L. Walker, *Mobilizing Interest Groups in America: Patrons, Professions, and Social Movements* (Ann Arbor: University of Michigan Press, 1991), 30–33.

39. Kenneth R. Mayer, *The Political Economy of Defense Contracting* (New Haven, CT: Yale University Press, 1991), 158–174.

40. R. Douglas Arnold, *Congress and the Bureaucracy: A Theory of Influence* (New Haven, CT: Yale University Press, 1979), 136–137.

41. Michael Hastings, "The Runaway General," *Rolling Stone,* July 8–22, 2010.

42. Theodore J. Lowi, *The End of Liberalism: The Second Republic of the United States,* 2nd ed. (New York: Norton, 1979).

43. Mathew D. McCubbins and Thomas Schwarz, "Congressional Oversight Overlooked: Police Patrols versus Fire Alarms," *American Journal of Political Science* 28(1): 165–179, p. 166.

44. Jason A. McDonald, "Limitation Riders and Congressional Influence Over Bureaucratic Decisions, "*American Political Science Review* 104 (November 2010): 766–782.

45. David Nather, "Congress as Watchdog: Asleep on the Job," *CQ Weekly,* May 22, 2004, 1193.

46. Wilson, *Bureaucracy,* 82–83.

47. Ibid., 235.

48. B. Dan Wood and Richard W. Waterman, "The Dynamics of Political Control of the Bureaucracy," *American Political Science Review* 85 (September 1991): 801–828.

49. National Commission on the Public Service, *Leadership for America: Rebuilding the Public Service* (Washington, DC: Brookings, 1989).

50. David E. Lewis, *The Politics of Presidential Appointments: Political Control and Bureaucratic Performance,* (Princeton, NJ: Princeton University Press, 2008).

51. Ron Fournier, "FEMA Director Mike Brown Resigns," Associated Press, September 12, 2005.

52. Carl Hulse, "Mukasey Wins Vote in Senate, Despite Doubts," *New York Times,* November 9, 2007, A1.

53. Hugh Heclo, *Government of Strangers: Executive Politics in Washington* (Washington, DC: Brookings, 1977), 195–198.

54. Richard W. Waterman, *Presidential Influence and the Administrative State* (Knoxville: University of Tennessee Press, 1989), chap. 7.

55. Joseph J. Schatz, "Has Congress Given Bush Too Free a Spending Hand?" *CQ Weekly,* April 12, 2003, 858.

56. Gardiner Harris, "White House and the FDA Often at Odds," *New York Times,* April 2, 2012.

57. Martin Shapiro, *Who Guards the Guardians? Judicial Control of Administration* (Athens: University of Georgia Press, 1988), 57.

58. Douglas Cater, *Power in Washington* (New York: Vintage, 1964).

59. Hugh Heclo, "Issue Networks and the Executive Establishment," in *The New American Political System,* ed. Anthony King (Washington, DC: American Enterprise Institute, 1978), 87–124.

60. Joel D. Aberbach, "The Federal Executive under Clinton," in *The Clinton Presidency: First Appraisals,* ed. Colin Campbell and Bert A. Rockman (Chatham, NJ: Chatham House, 1996), 179.

61. Transcript of Obama's State of the Union address at www.npr.org/2011/01/26/133224933/transcript-obamas-state-of-union-address, January 25, 2011.

62. Goodsell, *The Case for Bureaucracy,* 146.

63. Ibid.

Chapter 9

1. Letter from Jefferson to John Dickinson, December 19, 1801, cited in Donald O. Dewey, *Marshall versus Jefferson: The Political Background of* Marbury v. Madison (New York: Knopf, 1970), 63.

2. *Stuart v. Laird,* 1 Cr. 299 (1803).

3. *Marbury v. Madison,* 1 Cr. (5 U.S.) 137 at 177–180 (1803); emphasis added.

4. *Pollock v. Farmers' Loan & Trust Co.,* 157 U.S. 429 (1895).

5. *McCulloch v. Maryland,* 4 Wheat. 316 (1819).

6. *Dred Scott v. Sandford,* 19 How. (60 U.S.) 393 (1857).

7. Quoted by Paul Brest and Sanford Levinson in *Processes of Constitutional Decisionmaking,* 3rd ed. (Boston: Little, Brown, 1992), 75.

8. *Fletcher v. Peck,* 6 Cr. 87 (1810).

9. *Munn v. Illinois,* 94 U.S. 113 (1877); *Mugler v. Kansas,* 123 U.S. 623 (1887).

10. *Lochner v. New York,* 198 U.S. 45 (1905).

11. *Muller v. Oregon,* 208 U.S. 412 (1908). Nine years later still, the Court disregarded *Lochner* altogether to uphold an Oregon law limiting to ten hours the workday of any person working in a "mill, factory, or manufacturing establishment." *Bunting v. Oregon,* 243 U.S. 426 (1917).

12. Robert McCloskey and Sanford Levinson, eds., *The American Supreme Court,* 2nd ed. (Chicago: University of Chicago Press, 1994); and Lawrence Baum, *The Supreme Court,* 6th ed. (Washington, DC: CQ Press, 1998), 208.

13. *West Coast Hotel Co. v. Parrish,* 300 U.S. 379 (1937).

14. *Heart of Atlanta Motel, Inc. v. United States,* 379 U.S. 241 (1964).

15. *United States v. Lopez,* 514 U.S. 549 (1995).

16. *United States v. Morrison,* 529 U.S. 598 (2000).

17. David G. Savage, "IRAs Shielded in Bankruptcy, Justices Rule," *Los Angeles Times,* April 5, 2005; and "Justices to Decide If Social Security Can Be Seized," *Los Angeles Times,* April 26, 2005.

18. Supreme Court Database, http://scdb.wustl.edu/

19. Lori Hausegger and Lawrence Baum, "Inviting Congressional Action: A Study of Supreme Court Motivations in Statutory Interpretation," *American Journal of Political Science* 43 (January 1999): 162–185.

20. *Jaffree v. Board of School Commissioners,* 554 F. Supp. 1104, 1128 (S.D. Ala. 1983).

21. *Brown v. Board of Education,* 347 U.S. 483 (1954).

22. The Chief Justice's "2011 Year-End Report on the Federal Judiciary," Public Information Office, U.S. Supreme Court.

23. J. Woodford Howard Jr., *Courts of Appeals in the Federal Judicial System* (Princeton, NJ: Princeton University Press, 1981), 76.

24. Jeffrey R. Lax, "Certiorari and Compliance in the Judicial Hierarchy: Discretion, Reputation, and the Rule of Four," *Journal of Theoretical Politics* 15 (2003): 61–86.

25. Adam Liptak, "Polarization of Supreme Court Is Reflected in Justices' Clerks," *New York Times,* September 6, 2010.

26. Peter Linzer, "The Meaning of Certiorari Denials," *Columbia Law Review* 79 (1979): 1227–1305.

27. David O'Brien, *Storm Center: The Supreme Court in American Politics,* 4th ed. (New York: Norton, 1996).

28. Gregory A. Caldeira and John R. Wright, "Organized Interests and Agenda Setting in the U.S. Supreme Court," *American Political Science Review* 82 (1988): 1109–1127.

29. *United States v. Nixon,* 418 U.S. 683 (1974).

30. *Worcester v. Georgia,* 31 U.S. (6 Pet.) 515 (1832).

31. *Immigration and Naturalization Service v. Chadha,* 462 U.S. 919 (1983).

32. Louis Fisher, "The Legislative Veto: Invalidated, It Survives," *Law and Contemporary Problems* 56 (1993): 288.

33. Mathew McCubbins, Roger G. Knoll, and Barry R. Weingast, "Political Control of the Judiciary: A Positive Theory of Judicial Doctrine and the Rule of Law," *University of Southern California Law Review* (September 1995): 1631–1683.

34. See William N. Eskridge Jr., "Overriding Supreme Court Statutory Interpretation Decisions," *Yale Law Journal* 101 (1991): 331–455; and James Meernik and Joseph Ignagni, "Judicial Review and Coordinate Construction of the Constitution," *American Journal of Political Science* 41 (April 1997): 446–467.

35. *Mobile v. Bolden,* 446 U.S. 55 (1980).

36. In 2001 the Supreme Court endorsed the federal government's authority to override a California law that allowed medicinal consumption of marijuana. Sabin Russell, "California Pot Clubs Targeted," *San Francisco Chronicle,* January 10, 1998. The 8–0 opinion overruled the decision of the Ninth Circuit in *United States v. The Oakland Cannabis Buyers' Cooperative,* 532 U.S. 483 (2001).

37. Neil A. Lewis, "Republicans Seek Greater Influence in Naming Judges," *New York Times,* April 27, 1997.

38. Baum, *The Supreme Court,* 45. Eisenhower might not have used those exact words, but the story probably is an accurate reflection of his attitude toward these two justices.

39. "The State of the Judiciary: Judicial Selection During the Remainder of President Obama's First Term." Alliance for Justice, May 7, 2012.

40. Ted Barrett, "Senate Republicans Filibuster Obama Judicial Nominee," *CNN,* July 30, 2012.

41. Lee Epstein et al., *The Supreme Court Compendium: Data, Decisions and Developments,* 2nd ed. (Washington, DC: Congressional Quarterly, 1996).

Chapter 10

1. Gallup, 2008 NES, 2008 CCES.

2. ABC News/*Washington Post,* CBS News/*New York Times,* CNN, Gallup, Ipsos, Marist, NBC News/*Wall Street Journal,* Pew Research Center for the People and the Press, Bloomberg, NPR, AP-GfK, Kaiser/PSRA, *National Journal,* and Quinnipiac Polls, http://www.huffingtonpost.com/2009/07/30/healthplan_n_725503.html.

3. See the extensive compilation of survey questions and responses at www.pollingreport.com/health.htm.

4. Gallup poll, March 26–28, 2010.

5. Pew Research Center for the People and the Press Political Survey, October 24–28, 2012.

6. Politico/George Washington University Battleground Brushfire 2012 Survey, October 22–25, 2012.

7. V. O. Key Jr., *Public Opinion and American Democracy* (New York: Knopf, 1967), 14.

8. Quoted in Susan Herbst, *Numbered Voices: How Opinion Polling Has Shaped American Politics* (Chicago: University of Chicago Press, 1993), 108.

9. Data source: Centers for Disease Control and Prevention/National Center for Health Statistics National Health Interview Survey, July–December 2011.

10. Joshua Green, "The Other War Room," *Washington Monthly,* April 2002, http://washingtonmonthly.com/features/2001/0204.green.html.

11. Sam Stein, "Obama Mocks Polls but Spends More on Them ($4.4M) Than Bush Did," July 29, 2010, www.huffingtonpost.com/2010/07/29/obama-mocks-polls-but-spe_n_663553.html.

12. Alison Mitchell, "Clinton Seems to Keep Running Though the Race Is Run and Won," *New York Times,* February 2, 1997, A1.

13. "Survey Bolsters Global Warming Fight," *Los Angeles Times,* November 21, 1997, A4.

14. Rebecca Fairly Raney, "Flood of E-Mail Credited with Halting U.S. Bank Plan," *New York Times,* March 24, 1999, http://partners.nytimes.com/library/tech/99/03/cyber/articles/24email.html.

15. William W. Lambert and Wallace E. Lambert, *Social Psychology* (Englewood Cliffs, NJ: Prentice Hall, 1964), 50.

16. Estimates from the American National Election Studies Cumulative Data File for the years 2000–2008. Data from the 2012 CCAP show similar divisions, but with 10 percent more (33 percent) people falling in the middle relative to stating "not sure" (14 percent).

17. Robert S. Erikson and Kent L. Tedin, *American Public Opinion,* 5th ed. (Boston: Allyn and Bacon, 1995), 65–78.

18. Stanley Feldman and John Zaller, "The Political Culture of Ambivalence: Ideological Responses to the Welfare State," *American Journal of Political Science* 36 (1992): 268–307.

19. Angus Campbell et al., *The American Voter* (New York: Wiley, 1960), chaps. 6 and 7.

20. Morris P. Fiorina, *Retrospective Voting in American National Elections* (New Haven, CT: Yale University Press, 1981), chap. 5.

21. Gallup/*USA Today* Poll, December 15–17, 2000, available from the Roper Center, University of Connecticut.

22. Gary C. Jacobson, "Public Opinion and the Impeachment of Bill Clinton," in *British Elections and Parties Review,* Vol. 10, ed. Philip Cowley, David Denver, Andrew Russell, and Lisa Harrison (London: Frank Cass, 2000), 1–31.

23. Gary C. Jacobson, "Barack Obama and the American Public: The First 18 Months" (paper presented at the Annual Meeting of the American Political Science Association, Washington, DC, September 2–5, 2010), 17.

24. John Sides and Lynn Vavreck, *The Gamble: The Hand You're Dealt* (Princeton, NJ: Princeton University Press, 2012), 22.

25. Annenberg Public Policy Center, "*Fahrenheit 9/11* Viewers and Limbaugh Listeners about Equal in Size Even Though They Perceive Two Different Nations," press release, August 3, 2004.

26. John Sides and Lynn Vavreck, *The Gamble: The Hand You're Dealt* (Princeton, NJ: Princeton University Press, 2012).

27. George F. Bishop, Robert W. Oldendick, and Alfred J. Tuchfarber, "Pseudo-Opinion on Public Affairs," *Public Opinion Quarterly* (1980): 189–209.

28. John Zaller and Stanley Feldman, "A Simple Theory of Survey Response: Answering Questions versus Revealing Preferences," *American Journal of Political Science* 36 (1992): 581.

29. Support was about nine points higher if "removing Saddam Hussein" replaced "the result of the war" in the question that mentioned the loss of American lives. See Gary C. Jacobson, *A Divider, Not a Uniter: George W. Bush and the American People* (New York: Pearson, 2006), 129.

30. From data reported at www.pollingreport.com/afghan.htm. The number of surveys averaged to produce these four percentages was six, fourteen, eight, and sixteen, respectively.

31. Philip E. Converse, "The Nature of Belief Systems in Mass Publics," in *Ideology and Discontent,* ed. David Apter (New York: Free Press, 1964); and Christopher Achen, "Mass Political Attitudes and Survey Response," *American Political Science Review* 69 (1995): 1218–1231.

32. Zaller and Feldman, "A Simple Theory of Survey Response," 585–586.

33. Thomas E. Nelson, Rosalee A. Clawson, and Zoe M. Oxley, "Media Framing of a Civil Liberties Conflict and Its Effect on Tolerance," *American Political Science Review* 91 (September 1977): 567–583.

34. Shanto Iyengar and Donald R. Kinder, *News That Matters* (Chicago: University of Chicago Press, 1987), 63–72.

35. Benjamin I. Page and Robert Y. Shapiro, *The Rational Public* (Chicago: University of Chicago Press, 1992), 63.

36. Ibid., 130.

37. James A. Stimson, *Public Opinion in America: Moods, Cycles, and Swings* (Boulder, CO: Westview Press, 1991), 29–31.

38. Michael B. MacKuen, Robert S. Erikson, and James A. Stimson, "Macropartisanship," *American Political Science Review* 83 (1989): 1125–1142.

39. Stimson, *Public Opinion,* 125.

40. Arthur Lupia and Mathew D. McCubbins, *The Democratic Dilemma: Can Citizens Learn What They Really Need to Know?* (New York: Cambridge University Press, 1998).

41. Paul Burstein, "The Impact of Public Opinion on Public Policy: A Review and an Agenda," *Political Research Quarterly* 56 (March 2003): 29–40.

42. Herbert McClosky and John Zaller, *The American Ethos* (Cambridge, MA: Harvard University Press, 1984), 38.

43. Pew Research Center for the People and the Press survey, December 12, 2006–January 9, 2007, www.pollingreport.com/terror.htm.

44. Herbert McClosky and Ada Brill, *Dimensions of Tolerance* (New York: Basic Books, 1983).

45. McClosky and Zaller, *The American Ethos,* 83.

46. Ibid., 84.

47. Page and Shapiro, *Rational Public,* 74; http://pollingreport.com/race.htm.

48. CNN/Opinion Research Corporation poll conducted August 22–23, 2012; *American National Election Study, 2000,* variable 000694.

49. *Los Angeles Times* poll, June 8–13, 2000.

50. Gallup poll, May 2012.

51. NBC News/*Wall Street Journal* poll, October 2009.

52. Barbara Hinkson Craig and David M. O'Brien, *Abortion and American Politics* (Chatham, NJ: Chatham House, 1993), 266–270.

53. Gallup poll, June 23–25, 2006.

54. Richard A. Brody, *Assessing the President* (Stanford, CA: Stanford University Press, 1991).

55. John E. Mueller, *War, Presidents, and Public Opinion* (New York: Wiley, 1973), 58–63.

56. Mark Peffley and Jon Hurwitz, "International Events and Foreign Policy Beliefs: Public Responses to Changing U.S.-Soviet Relations," *American Journal of Political Science* 36 (May 1992): 431–461.

57. The study can be found here: http://www.worldpublicopinion.org/pipa/pdf/may12/DefenseBudget_May12_rpt.pdf.

58. See http://pollingreport.com/terror.htm.

59. Data on the decade since 9/11 are reported in Simon Jackman and Lynn Vavreck, "Americans and Australians Compared: Ten Years after 9/11," a report prepared for the U.S. Studies Centre at the University of Sydney, Sydney, Australia. The U.S. data are from a YouGov Inc. survey of nine hundred Americans conducted during May 2011.

60. Gallup poll, June 12–15, 2003, www.pollingreport.com/race.htm.

61. "Black Americans and the 2004 Vote," BET/CBS News poll, July 6–15, 2004, http://cbsnews.com/stories/2004/07/21/opinion/polls/main630986.shtml.

62. Ninety-nine percent of black voters in the 2008 American National Election Studies and in Gallup's surveys said they had voted for Obama; in the National Exit Poll, it was 95 percent.

63. "Arizona Voters Favor Welcoming Immigration Policy, 64% Support New Immigration Law," *Rasmussen Reports,* April 28, 2010.

64. Daniel González, "SB 1070 Backlash Spurs Hispanics to Join Democrats," *The Arizona Republic,* June 8, 2010.

65. Erikson and Tedin, *American Public Opinion,* 210.

66. "Election Polls—Presidential Vote by Groups," Gallup Report, www.gallup.com/poll/139880/Election-Polls-Presidential-Vote-Groups.aspx#1.

67. Voter News Service exit poll, November 7, 2000, available from the Roper Center, University of Connecticut.

68. National Exit Poll, www.cnn.com/ELECTION/2008/results/polls/#val=USP00p2.

Chapter 11

1. More than 90 percent in some pre-election polls; see www.pollingreport.com.

2. "Palin: Obama Pals around with Terrorists," *USA Today,* October 4, 2008, www.usatoday.com/news/politics/election2008/2008-10-04-palin-obama_N.htm.

3. Gary C. Jacobson, "Legislative Success and Political Failure: The Public's Reaction to Barack Obama's Early Presidency," *Presidential Studies Quarterly* 41 (June 2011): 219–242.

4. Lynn Vavreck, *The Message Matters: The Economy and Presidential Campaigns* (Princeton, NJ: Princeton University Press, 2009).

5. See http://elections.nytimes.com/2012/results/president/exit-polls, accessed November 13, 2012.

6. Chilton Williamson, *American Suffrage: From Property to Democracy 1760–1860* (Princeton, NJ: Princeton University Press, 1960), 49.

7. Alexis de Tocqueville, *Democracy in America,* Vol. 1 (New York: Vintage, 1990), 57.

8. Quoted by David Morgan in *Suffragists and Democrats: The Politics of Women's Suffrage in America* (East Lansing: Michigan State University Press, 1972), 84.

9. Ibid., 124.

10. See, for example, Americans for a Society Free from Age Restrictions, "ASFAR Position Paper on Voting," http://asfar.org/position-papers/voting-age.

11. See Michael McDonald, "2012 General Election Turnout Rates," at http://elections.gmu.edu/Turnout_2012G.html, accessed February 18, 2013.

12. Steven J. Rosenstone and John Mark Hansen, *Mobilization, Participation, and Democracy in America* (New York: Macmillan, 1993).

13. Ibid., 150.

14. Ibid., 241.

15. Julie Pace, "Obama Wins the Way His Campaign Predicted," *SFGate,* at http://www.sfgate.com/news/politics/article/Obama-wins-the-way-his-campaign-predicted-4016946.php, accessed November 10, 2012.

16. Ibid., 214–218.

17. John Sides, Eric Schickler, and Jack Citrin, "If Everyone Had Voted, Would Bubba and Dubya Have Won?" *Presidential Studies Quarterly* 38 (September 2008): 521–539.

18. Martin P. Wattenberg, *The Decline of American Political Parties, 1952–1992* (Cambridge, MA: Harvard University Press, 1994), 155–157, 171–180.

19. Jordan Fabian, "DeMint Challenger Greene Pulls in 28 Percent in Loss," *The Hill,* November 3, 2010, http://thehill.com/blogs/blog-briefing-room/news/127421-demint-challenger-greene-pulls-in-28-percent-in-loss.

20. Samuel L. Popkin, *The Reasoning Voter: Communication and Persuasion in Presidential Campaigns,* 2nd ed. (Chicago: University of Chicago Press, 1994), 1.

21. Paul R. Abramson, John H. Aldrich, and David W. Rohde, *Change and Continuity in the 1992 Elections* (Washington, DC: CQ Press, 1994), 56–57.

22. Stephen J. Wayne, *The Road to the White House 1996: The Politics of Presidential Elections* (New York: St. Martin's, 1997), 260–261.

23. Paul S. Herrnson and Clyde Wilcox, "The 1996 Presidential Election: A Tale of a Campaign That Didn't Seem to Matter," in *Toward the Millennium: The Elections of 1996,* ed. Larry J. Sabato (Boston: Allyn and Bacon, 1997), 136.

24. Alan Ehrenhalt, "Technology, Strategy Bring New Campaign Era," *Congressional Quarterly Weekly Report,* December 7, 1985, 2559.

25. Stephen Ansolabehere et al., "Does Attack Advertising Demobilize the Electorate?" *American Political Science Review* 88 (December 1994): 829–838; and Kim Leslie Fridkin and Patrick J. Kenney, "Do Negative Messages Work?" *American Politics Research* 32 (September 2004): 570–605.

26. Nelson W. Polsby and Aaron Wildavsky, *Presidential Elections,* 9th ed. (Chatham, NJ: Chatham House, 1996), 215–216.

27. ABC News/*Washington Post* poll of likely voters taken October 17–19, 2008, www.pollingreport.com/wh08.htm.

28. Joel Bradshaw, "Strategy, Theme, and Message" (paper presented at the Conference on Campaign Management, American University, Washington, DC, December 10–11, 1992), 114.

29. Michael Cooper, "Campaigns Play Loose with Truth in Fact-Check Age," *New York Times,* August 31, 2012, at http://www

.nytimes.com/2012/09/01/us/politics/fact-checkers-howl-but-both-sides-cling-to-false-ads.html, accessed November 16, 2012.

30. *Buckley v. Valeo,* 424 U.S. 1 (1976).

31. *Colorado Republican Federal Campaign Committee v. Federal Election Commission,* 518 U.S. 604 (1996).

32. *Citizens United v. Federal Election Commission,* 130 S. Ct. 876 (2010).

33. Gary C. Jacobson, *The Politics of Congressional Elections,* 7th ed. (New York: Longman, 2009), 124–134.

34. ABC News, "Election 2012: The Campaigns by the Numbers," at http://abcnews.go.com/Politics/OTUS/election-2012-campaigns-numbers/story?id=17647443#.UKGXwmfa9hw, accessed November 12, 2012.

35. "Sheldon Adelson: Inside the Mind of the Mega-Donor," *Politico,* at http://www.politico.com/news/stories/0912/81588_Page5.html, accessed November 13, 2012.

Chapter 12

1. Larry Sabato, *The Party's Just Begun: Shaping Political Parties for America's Future* (Glenview, IL: Scott Foresman, 1988), 133.

2. See the Gallup Poll data reported at http://www.pollingreport.com/politics.htm, accessed October 15, 2012.

3. American National Election Studies, 2004 and 2008; ANES *2010–2012 Evaluations of Government and Society Study,* spring 2011 survey.

4. Martin P. Wattenberg, *The Decline of American Political Parties, 1952–1994* (Cambridge, MA: Harvard University Press, 1996); and Everett Carll Ladd, "1996 Vote: The 'No Majority' Realignment Continues," *Political Science Quarterly* 112 (Spring 1997): 1–23.

5. See exit poll results at http://elections.nytimes.com/2012/results/president/exit-polls, accessed November 9, 2012.

6. Gary C. Jacobson, *A Divider, Not a Uniter: George W. Bush and the American People,* 2nd ed. (New York: Pearson Longman, 2011), 52.

7. Gary C. Jacobson, *Barack Obama and the American Public: From Candidate to President,* paper presented at the Conference on the Early Obama Presidency, Centre for the Study of Democracy, University of Westminster, London, May 14, 2010.

8. E. E. Schattschneider, *Party Government* (New York: Holt, Rinehart, and Winston, 1942), 1.

9. Edmund Burke, *Thoughts on the Causes of the Present Discontents,* ed. W. Murison (Cambridge: Cambridge University Press, 1930).

10. Anthony Downs, *An Economic Theory of Democracy* (New York: Harper and Row, 1957), 25.

11. This conceptual trinity, originally proposed by V. O. Key Jr., is used routinely by political scientists who study parties. See *Politics, Parties, and Pressure Groups* (New York: Thomas Crowell, 1964), 163–165.

12. Maurice Duverger, *Political Parties* (New York: Wiley, 1954), 217.

13. John F. Hoadley, *The Origins of the American Party System* (Lexington: University of Kentucky Press, 1986), 51.

14. See Alexander Hamilton's discussion of the Electoral College in *Federalist* No. 68. This device is described in Chapter 7, "The Presidency."

15. Noble E. Cunningham Jr., "The Development of Parties," in *After the Constitution: Party Conflict in the New Republic,* ed. Lance Banning (Belmont, CA: Wadsworth, 1989), 104.

16. Paul Goodman, *The Democratic Republicans of Massachusetts: Politics in a Young Republic* (Cambridge, MA: Harvard University Press, 1964), 204.

17. Quoted in Richard H. Brown, "The Missouri Crisis, Slavery, and the Politics of Jacksonianism," in Banning, *After the Constitution,* 446.

18. Michael F. Holt, *Political Parties and American Political Development from the Age of Jackson to the Age of Lincoln* (Baton Rouge: Louisiana State University Press, 1992), 41.

19. James S. Chase, *Emergence of the Presidential Nominating Convention, 1798–1832* (Urbana: University of Illinois Press, 1973), 85.

20. Richard P. McCormick, "Political Development and the Second Party System," in *The American Party Systems: Stages of Political Development,* 2nd ed., ed. William Nesbit Chambers and Walter Dean Burnham (New York: Oxford University Press, 1975), 108.

21. Ibid., 8.

22. Nelson W. Polsby, *Consequences of Party Reform* (New York: Oxford University Press, 1983), chaps. 2 and 3.

23. John McCormick, "Blue and Red Don't Mix as Positions Harden among Swing-State Delegates," *Bloomberg Insider,* September 3, 2012, 4.

24. Martin P. Wattenberg, *The Decline of American Political Parties, 1952–1992* (Cambridge, MA: Harvard University Press, 1994), 174.

25. Gary C. Jacobson, *The Electoral Origins of Divided Government: Competition in U.S. House Elections, 1946–1988* (Boulder, CO: Westview, 1990), 15–19.

26. Morris P. Fiorina, *Divided Government,* 2nd ed. (Boston: Allyn and Bacon, 1996), 72–81.

27. Jacobson, *The Electoral Origins of Divided Government,* 105–120.

28. Donald C. Baumer and Howard J. Gold, *Parties, Polarization, and Democracy in the United States* (Boulder, CO: Paradigm, 2010), 32.

29. Bruce E. Keith et al., *The Myth of the Independent Voter* (Berkeley: University of California Press, 1992), chap. 4.

30. Pew Research Center for the People and the Press, "Convention Backgrounder: A Closer Look at the Parties in 2008," August 22, 2008, http://people-press.org/.

31. See www.cnn.com/ELECTION/2008/results/polls/#USP00p1.

32. See exit poll results at http://elections.nytimes.com/2012/results/president/exit-polls, accessed November 9, 2012.

33. See http://www.people-press.org/2012/08/23/a-closer-look-at-the-parties-in-2012/, accessed November 9, 2012.

34. Alan I. Abramowitz, *The Disappearing Center: Engaged Citizens, Polarization, and American Democracy* (New Haven, CT: Yale University Press, 2010), chap. 3.

35. Morris P. Fiorina, *Culture War? The Myth of a Polarized America* (New York: Pearson, 2005); Marc J. Hetherington and Jonathan D. Weiler, *Authoritarianism and Polarization in American Politics*

(New York: Cambridge University Press, 2009); and Matthew Levendusky, *The Partisan Sort: How Liberals Became Democrats and Conservatives Became Republicans* (Chicago: University of Chicago Press, 2009).

36. Mark Rozell and Clyde Wilcox, eds., *God at the Grass Roots: The Christian Right in the 1994 Elections* (Lanham, MD: Rowman and Littlefield, 1995).

37. Paul S. Herrnson, *Party Campaigning in the 1980s* (Cambridge, MA: Harvard University Press, 1988).

38. Federal Election Commission data reported by the Campaign Finance Institute, www.cfinst.org/pdf/federal/InterestGroup/Reportable_NonCandidateSpending_upd.pdf.

39. John H. Aldrich, *Why Parties? The Origin and Transformation of Party Politics in America* (Chicago: University of Chicago Press, 1995), 273.

Chapter 13

1. Edward Wyatt and Eric Lichtblau, "A Finance Overhaul Fight Draws a Lobbying Swarm," *New York Times,* April 20, 2010, A1.

2. Binyamin Appelbaum and Eric Lichtblau, "Banks Lobby to Rid Finance Bill of Ban on Trading in Derivatives," *New York Times,* May 10, 2010.

3. *New York Times,* "Editorial: Congress Passes Financial Reform," July 15, 2010.

4. James Surowiecki, "Masters of Main Street," *New Yorker,* July 12, 2010.

5. John Crawley, "Auto Dealers Press Senator for Watchdog Exemption," Reuters, May 11, 2010.

6. Alison Gilbert Olson, *Making the Empire Work: London and American Interest Groups, 1690–1790* (Cambridge, MA: Harvard University Press, 1992), 56.

7. Ibid., 146.

8. Ibid., 3.

9. Alexis de Tocqueville, *Democracy in America,* ed. Andrew Hacker (New York: Washington Square, 1964), 71.

10. Ibid., 182.

11. See Peter H. Odegard, *Pressure Politics: The Story of the Anti-Saloon League* (New York: Columbia University Press, 1928).

12. David B. Truman, *The Governmental Process* (New York: Knopf, 1951).

13. E. E. Schattschneider, *The Semi-Sovereign People: A Realist's View of Democracy in America* (Hinsdale, IL: Dryden, 1960), 34–35.

14. Mancur Olson, *The Logic of Collective Action: Public Goods and the Theory of Groups* (Cambridge, MA: Harvard University Press, 1965).

15. Jack L. Walker Jr., *Mobilizing Interest Groups in America: Patrons, Professions, and Social Movements* (Ann Arbor: University of Michigan Press, 1991), 1; and Jeffrey Birnbaum, "The Road to Riches Is Called K Street," *Washington Post,* June 22, 2005, A01.

16. *Washington Representatives,* 31st ed. (Bethesda, MD: Columbia Books, 2007).

17. James A. Thurber, "Lobbying Reform: The Importance of Enforcement and Transparency," testimony before the Senate Committee on Rules and Administration, February 8, 2006,

http://spa.american.edu/ccpsfiles/File/Thurber%20Testimony%20for%20Senate%20Rules%20Committee2006.pdf.

18. Byron Tau and Tarini Parti, "K Street Sings the Blues," *Politico,* January 23, 1013.

19. David Vogel, *Fluctuating Fortunes: The Political Power of Business in America* (New York: Basic Books, 1988), 220–227.

20. Walker, *Mobilizing Interest Groups,* 29.

21. Ibid., 31.

22. Daniel Kahneman and Amos Tversky, "Prospect Theory: An Analysis of Decision under Risk," *Econometrica* 47 (1979): 263–291.

23. William P. Browne, "Issue Niches and the Limits of Interest Group Influence," in *Interest Group Politics,* 3rd ed., ed. Allan J. Cigler and Burdett A. Loomis (Washington, DC: CQ Press, 1991), 348.

24. James Q. Wilson, *Political Organizations* (New York: Basic Books, 1973), chap. 13.

25. Browne, "Issue Niches and the Limits of Interest Group Influence," 356.

26. Kay Lehman Schlozman and John T. Tierney, *Organized Interests and American Democracy* (New York: Harper and Row, 1986), 150.

27. Unidentified lobbyist quoted in Jeffrey M. Berry, *The Interest Group Society* (Boston: Little, Brown, 1984), 117; emphasis in the original.

28. Schlozman and Tierney, *Organized Interests,* 333.

29. Kevin T. McGuire, *Understanding the U.S. Supreme Court* (Boston: McGraw-Hill, 2001), 151.

30. Karen O'Connor, "Lobbying the Justices or Lobbying for Justice?" in *The Interest Group Connection: Electioneering, Lobbying, and Policymaking in Washington,* 2nd ed., ed. Paul S. Herrnson, Ronald G. Shaiko, and Clyde Wilcox (Washington, DC: CQ Press, 2005), 319–340.

31. Gregory A. Caldeira and John R. Wright, "Lobbying for Justice: Organized Interests, Supreme Court Nominations, and the United States Senate," *American Journal of Political Science* 42 (April 1998): 510.

32. Andrew J. Polsky, "Giving Business the Business," *Dissent* (Winter 1996): 33–36.

33. Jonathan D. Salant and David S. Cloud, "To the '94 Election Victors Go the Fundraising Spoils," *Congressional Quarterly Weekly Report,* April 15, 1995, 1056.

34. Campaign Finance Institute, "PAC Fundraising Swings Democratic over the First Nine Months of 2007," November 8, 2007, www.cfinst.org/pr/prRelease.aspx?ReleaseID=167.

35. See Fredreka Schouten, "Campaign Spending by Outside Groups Skyrockets," *USA Today,* October 15, 2010.

36. See, for example, Philip Stern, *The Best Congress Money Can Buy* (New York: Pantheon, 1988); Brooks Jackson, *Honest Graft: Big Money and the American Political Process* (New York: Knopf, 1988); and Elizabeth Drew, *Politics and Money: The New Road to Corruption* (New York: Macmillan, 1983).

37. John R. Wright, *Interest Groups and Congress* (Boston: Allyn and Bacon, 1996), 136–145; Frank J. Sorauf, *Inside Campaign Finance: Myths and Realities* (New Haven, CT: Yale University Press, 1992), 163–174; Stephen Ansolabehere, John de Figueiredo, and James Snyder Jr., "Why Is There So Little

Money in U.S. Politics?" *Journal of Economic Perspectives* 17 (2003): 105–130.

38. Richard L. Hall and Frank W. Wayman, "Buying Time: Monied Interests and the Mobilization of Bias in Congressional Committees," *American Political Science Review* 84 (1990): 797–820.

39. Robert S. Salisbury, *Institutions and Interests: Substance and Structure in American Politics* (Pittsburgh, PA: University of Pittsburgh Press, 1992), 348.

40. William P. Browne, *Private Interests, Public Policy, and American Agriculture* (Lawrence: University Press of Kansas, 1988), 248–252.

41. Schlozman and Tierney, *Organized Interests,* 399–403.

42. Lester C. Thurow, *The Zero-Sum Society* (New York: Basic Books, 1980); and Mancur Olson, *The Rise and Decline of Nations* (New Haven, CT: Yale University Press, 1982).

Chapter 14

1. Timothy Cook, *Governing with the News: The News Media as a Political Institution* (Chicago: University of Chicago Press, 1998), 22.

2. Charles E. Clark, *The Public Prints: The Newspaper in Anglo-American Culture, 1665–1740* (New York: Oxford University Press, 1994), 195–196.

3. Edwin Emery, *The Press and America,* 2nd ed. (Englewood Cliffs, NJ: Prentice Hall, 1962), 107–124.

4. Richard Hofstadter, *The Idea of the Party System* (Berkeley: University of California Press, 1969), 8.

5. Thomas C. Leonard, *The Power of the Press: The Birth of American Political Reporting* (New York: Oxford University Press, 1986), 57.

6. Willard Grosvenor Bleyer, *Main Currents of the History of American Journalism* (Boston: Houghton Mifflin, 1927), 377.

7. Alfred M. Lee, *The Daily Newspaper in America* (New York: Macmillan, 1937), 214–217.

8. Paul Starr, *The Creation of the Media* (New York: Basic Books, 2004), 258.

9. *New York Journal,* May 8, 1898, 1.

10. *Historical Statistics of the United States: Colonial Times to 1970,* Vols. 1 and 2 (Washington, DC: Government Printing Office, 1975), series R104–5.

11. Erik Barnouw, *The Golden Web,* Vol. 2 (New York: Oxford University Press, 1968), 18–22.

12. Julia Angwin and Sarah McBride, "Radio's Bush-Bashing Air America Is Back in Fighting Form," *Wall Street Journal,* January 28, 2005.

13. Emery, *Press and America,* 663.

14. Figures cited in James T. Hamilton, *All the News Fit to Print* (Princeton, NJ: Princeton University Press, 2004), 284.

15. Pew Research Center for the People and the Press, "News Audiences Increasingly Politicized," June 8, 2004.

16. Brian Stetler and Richard Pérez-Peña, "Media Outlets Are Seeking a Campaign Bounce of Their Own," *New York Times,* August 4, 2008, www.nytimes.com/2008/08/04/business/media/04ratings.html.

17. *New York Times Co. v. United States,* 403 U.S. 713 (1971).

18. The Court first employed this doctrine in 1964 in *New York Times Co. v. Sullivan,* 376 U.S. 254 (1964).

19. Leon V. Sigal, *Reporters and Officials: The Organization and Politics of News Reporting* (Lexington, MA: D.C. Heath, 1973), 122.

20. Howard Kurtz of the *Washington Post,* interview on *Nightline,* ABC News, January 30, 1998.

21. Howard Kurtz said, "The White House decided the way that it could inoculate itself was to do the leaking itself, to do what they called dump dumps, to get this stuff out, take their hits early . . . [and when] Fred Thompson and other investigating senators came along, the White House could say, 'Well this is old news. This has all been in the papers. We already know all this stuff.'" Interview on *Nightline,* ABC News, March 11, 1998.

22. Stephen Hess, *Live from Capitol Hill* (Washington, DC: Brookings, 1991).

23. Joseph N. Cappella and Kathleen Hall Jamieson, *Spiral of Cynicism: The Press and the Public Good* (New York: Oxford University Press, 1997), 3–5.

24. Coverage of Congress is mostly neutral, but when it is not, it tends to be negative. Charles M. Tidmarch and John J. Pitney Jr., "Covering Congress," *Polity* 17 (1985): 463–483.

25. Transcript, presidential press conference, May 7, 1993, Washington, DC.

26. Iyengar, Shanto, and Donald Kinder, *News that Matters* (Chicago: University of Chicago Press, 1987), 63–72.

27. Richard H. Rovere, *Senator Joe McCarthy* (Cleveland, OH: Meridian, 1966), 124.

28. Paul F. Boller Jr., *Presidential Anecdotes* (New York: Penguin, 1982), 63–64.

29. James E. Pollard, *The Presidents and the Press* (New York: Macmillan, 1947), 775.

30. Cited in Worth Bingham and Ward S. Just, "The President and the Press," *Reporter* 26 (April 12, 1962): 20.

31. Marvin Kalb, "The Rise of the 'New' News: A Case Study of Two Root Causes of Modern Scandal Coverage" (discussion paper D-34, John F. Kennedy School of Government, Harvard University, October 1998).

Chapter 15

1. Tarini Parti, "DISCLOSE Act Fails Again in Senate," *Politico,* July 16, 2012.

2. This quotation, as well as all of the specifics in the preceding discussion, are taken from Anthony Corrado, "The Legislative Odyssey of BCRA," in *Life after Reform: When the Bipartisan Campaign Reform Act Meets Politics,* ed. Michael J. Malbin (Lanham, MD: Rowman and Littlefield, 2003), 38.

3. Updated figures on these types of spending are available in a report produced by the Sunlight Foundation and posted at http://reporting.sunlightfoundation.com/outside-spending/overview/, accessed by the authors on October 26, 2012.

4. Paul Blumenthal, "Citizens United Constitutional Amendment: New Jersey Legislature Seeks Reversal of Ruling," *Huffington Post,* October 18, 2012.

5. See the introduction to "Room for Debate: Amend the Constitution to Limit Political Spending?" *The New York Times*, October 24, 2012, http://www.nytimes.com/roomfor debate/2012/10/24/amend-the-constitution-to-limit-political-spending.

6. These figures were compiled using the Online Data Analysis feature at www.worldvaluessurvey.org.

7. "Flag-Burning Amendment Fails by a Vote," CNN, June 28, 2006, www.cnn.com/2006/POLITICS/06/27/flag.burning/index.html.

8. "Schwarzenegger Hints at White House Interest," February 22, 2004, www.msnbc.msn.com/id/4344297/ns/politics.

9. ABC News/*Washington Post* poll press release, "Most Oppose Same-Sex Marriage, but Balk at Amending the Constitution," January 21, 2004.

10. Frank J. Sorauf, *Inside Campaign Finance: Myths and Realities* (New Haven, CT: Yale University Press, 1992), 11.

11. Alan Ehrenhalt, *The United States of Ambition: Politicians, Power, and the Pursuit of Office* (New York: Times Books, 1991).

12. Everett S. Brown, "The Presidential Election of 1824–1825," *Political Science Quarterly* 40 (1925): 384–403.

13. All of the quotes in this paragraph are taken from C. Edward Merriam, *Primary Elections* (Chicago: University of Chicago Press, 1908), 1, 5–6.

14. V. O. Key, *Parties, Politics, and Pressure Groups*, 5th ed. (New York: Crowell, 1964).

15. Villaraigosa made this statement on the July 13, 1998, broadcast of the PBS program *NewsHour with Jim Lehrer*, and President Bartlet uttered a similar statement on Episode 20 of the *West Wing*'s first season.

16. Our discussion of the growth of the term limits movement draws mostly on Thad Kousser, *Term Limits and the Dismantling of State Legislative Professionalism* (Cambridge: Cambridge University Press, 2005); and the National Conference of State Legislatures' comprehensive record of term limit laws, www.ncsl .org/programs/legismgt/ABOUT/termlimit.htm.

17. Our discussion of the effects of term limits on the states draws from Thad Kousser, "Term Limits and State Legislatures," in *Democracy in the States: Experiments in Election Reform,* ed. Caroline Tolbert, Todd Donovan, and Bruce E. Cain (Washington, DC: Brookings, 2008), with the finding that term-limited legislators generally stay in government found in Richard J. Powell, "The Unintended Effects of Term Limits on the Career Paths of State Legislators," in *The Test of Time: Coping with Legislative Term Limits,* ed. Rick Farmer, John David Rausch Jr., and John C. Green, (Lanham, MD: Lexington Books, 2003).

18. These aggregate spending figures as well as colorful descriptions of individual projects can be found in the Citizens Against Government Waste's "2008 Congressional Pig Book Summary," http://www.cbsnews.com/htdocs/pdf/CAGW-Pig_Book_08.pdf.

19. David Herszenhorn, "McConnell to Support Earmarks Ban," *New York Times,* November 15, 2010, http://thecaucus.blogs .nytimes.com/2010/11/15/mcconnell-to-support-earmarks-ban/.

20. "Supreme Court Deletes Line-Item Veto," CNN, June 25, 1998.

21. Reid Wilson, "Tea Party Caucus Takes $1 Billion in Earmarks," *National Journal,* December 2, 2010.

22. For data on earmarks and for reporting on party policies, see the Citizens Against Government Waste's "2010 Congressional Pig Book Summary," http://cagw.org/content/pig-book-2010.

23. Herszenhorn, "McConnell to Support Earmarks Ban."

24. Scott Wong, "Senate Dems Give In On Earmark Ban," *Politico,* February 1, 2011.

25. Both senators are quoted in David Mastio, "Big Buts on Earmark Ban," *Washington Times,* November 16, 2010.

26. Andrew Taylor, "Senate Republicans' Ban on Earmarks Proves Short-Lived," *Washington Post,* November 24, 2010.

27. Steve Ellis, quoted in Ron Nixon, "Congress Appears to be Trying to Get Around Earmark Ban," *The Washington Post*, February 5, 2012.

28. See Diana Evans, *Greasing the Wheels: Using Pork Barrel Projects to Build Majority Coalitions in Congress* (New York: Cambridge University Press, 2004); and John Ellwood and Eric M. Patashnik, "In Praise of Pork," *Public Interest* 110 (1993): 19–33.

Glossary

access The ability of privileged outsiders, such as interest group representatives, to obtain a hearing from elected officials or bureaucrats.

activism When judges deliberately shape judicial doctrine to conform to their personal view of the Constitution and social policy.

ad hoc committee A congressional committee appointed for a limited time to design and report a specific piece of legislation.

affirmative action Policies or programs designed to expand opportunities for minorities and women and usually requiring that an organization take measures to increase the number or proportion of minorities and women in its membership or employment.

agency loss The discrepancy between what citizens ideally would like their agents to do and how the agents actually behave.

agenda control The capacity to set the choices available to others.

agenda setting Occurs when readers and watchers of news that relates to issues or topics are influenced by what the press covers in a very specific way—it influences what they think *about*, not what they *think*.

agent Someone who makes and implements decisions on behalf of someone else.

aggregate partisanship The distribution, or percentage, of the electorate that identifies with each of the political parties.

aggregate public opinion In a democracy, the sum of all individual opinions.

ambivalence A state of mind produced when particular issues evoke attitudes and beliefs that pull in opposite directions.

amicus curiae "Friend of the court." A brief filed in a lawsuit by an individual or group that is not party to the lawsuit but that has an interest in the outcome.

Antifederalists A loosely organized group (never a formal political party) that opposed ratification of the Constitution, which the group believed would jeopardize individual freedom and states' rights. After ratification, the efforts of the

Antifederalists led to adoption of the first ten amendments, the Bill of Rights.

Articles of Confederation The compact among the thirteen original states that formed the basis of the first national government of the United States from 1777 to 1789, when it was supplanted by the Constitution.

attitude An organized and consistent manner of thinking and feeling about people, groups, social issues, or, more generally, any event in one's environment.

attorney general The head of the Justice Department. As the nation's chief legal officer, the attorney general of the United States represents the federal government's interests in law courts throughout the nation. The attorney general is also the chief law enforcement officer.

Australian ballot A ballot prepared and distributed by government officials that places the names of all candidates on a single list and is filled out by voters in private. First adopted in the United States in 1888, the Australian ballot replaced oral voting and party-supplied ballots.

authority The right to make and implement a decision.

bargaining A form of negotiation in which two or more parties who disagree propose exchanges and concessions to find a course of acceptable collective action.

beat A regularly assigned venue that a news reporter covers on an ongoing basis.

bicameral legislature A legislature composed of two houses or chambers. The U.S. Congress (House and Senate) and every U.S. state legislature (with the exception of Nebraska's, which is unicameral) are bicameral legislatures.

Bill of Rights The first ten amendments to the U.S. Constitution.

black codes Laws enacted by southern legislatures after the Civil War that prevented former slaves from voting and holding certain jobs, among other prohibitions.

block grant A broad grant of money given by the federal government to a state government. The grant specifies the general area (such as education or health services) in which the funds may be spent but leaves it to the state to determine the specific allocations.

Brownlow report Report issued in 1937 by the President's Committee on Administrative Management that likened the president to the chief executive officer of a large corporation and concluded that the president needed a professional staff.

bureaucracy A complex structure of offices, tasks, and rules in which employees have specific responsibilities and work within a hierarchy of authority. Government bureaucracies are charged with implementing policies.

bureaucratic culture The norms and regular patterns of behavior found within a bureaucratic organization. Different agencies often develop their own norms, which shape the behavior of those who work in the agency.

cabinet The formal group of presidential advisers who head the major departments and agencies of the federal government. Cabinet members are chosen by the president and approved by the Senate.

candidate A person who is running for elected office.

casework The activity undertaken by members of Congress and their staffs to solve constituents' problems with government agencies.

caucus A closed meeting of a political or legislative group to choose candidates for office or to decide issues of policy.

central clearance A presidential directive requiring that all executive agency proposals, reports, and recommendations to Congress—mostly in the form of annual reports and testimony at authorization and appropriations hearings—be certified by the Office of Management and Budget as consistent with the president's policy.

checks and balances A constitutional mechanism giving each branch some oversight and control of the other branches. Examples are the presidential veto, Senate approval of presidential appointments, and judicial review of presidential and congressional actions.

chief of staff system The means by which a chain of command is imposed on the president's staff. The system clarifies responsibilities and shields the president from having to micromanage the staff's routine activities.

civil liberties Constitutional and legal protections from government interference with personal rights and freedoms such as freedom of assembly, speech, and religion.

civil rights The powers or privileges that are conferred on citizens by the Constitution and the courts and that entitle them to make claims upon the government. Civil rights protect individuals from arbitrary or discriminatory treatment at the hands of the government.

civil unions Allow same sex-couples to receive many of the legal benefits of married couples, but without the "marriage" classification.

clear and present danger test A rule used by the Supreme Court to distinguish between speech protected and not protected by the First Amendment. Under this rule, the First Amendment does not protect speech aimed at inciting an illegal action.

clear and probable danger test A rule introduced by Chief Justice Fred Vinson for the courts to enlist in free expression cases: "In each case [the courts] must ask whether the gravity of the 'evil,' discounted by its probability, justifies such invasion of free speech as is necessary to avoid the danger."

closed rule An order from the House Rules Committee limiting floor debate on a particular bill and disallowing or limiting amendment.

cloture A parliamentary procedure used to close debate. Cloture is used in the Senate to cut off filibusters. Under the current Senate rules, three-fifths of senators, or sixty, must vote for cloture to halt a filibuster.

coalition An alliance of unlike-minded individuals or groups to achieve some common purpose such as lobbying, legislating, or campaigning for the election of public officials.

cognitive shortcut A mental device allowing citizens to make complex decisions based on a small amount of information. For example, a candidate's party label serves as a shortcut by telling voters much about his or her positions on issues.

collective action An action taken by a group of like-minded individuals to achieve a common goal.

collective goods Goods that are collectively produced and freely available for anyone's consumption.

command The authority of one actor to dictate the actions of another.

commander in chief The title that is given to the president by the Constitution and that denotes the president's authority as the head of the national military.

commerce clause The clause in Article I, Section 8, of the Constitution that gives Congress the authority to regulate commerce with other nations and among the states.

committee and conference reports Documents submitted by committees that often instruct agencies how Congress expects them to use their "discretion." Though not legally binding, bureaucrats ignore such instructions at their peril.

community standards The Supreme Court's 1973 ruling that a work is obscene if it is "utterly without redeeming social importance" and, "to the average person, applying contemporary 'community standards,' the dominant theme of the material, taken as a whole, appeals to prurient interests."

compromise Settlement in which each side concedes some of its preferences in order to secure others.

concurring opinion A written opinion by a Supreme Court justice who agrees with the decision of the Court but disagrees with the rationale for reaching that decision.

conditional party government The degree of authority delegated to and exercised by congressional leaders; varies with and is conditioned by the extent of election-driven ideological consensus among members.

confederation A political system in which states or regional governments retain ultimate authority except for those powers they expressly delegate to a central government.

conference committee A temporary joint committee of the House and Senate appointed to reconcile the differences between the two chambers on a particular piece of legislation.

conformity costs The difference between what a person ideally would prefer and what the group with which that person makes collective decisions actually does. Individuals pay conformity costs whenever collective decisions produce policy outcomes that do not best serve their interests.

conservative In the United States, a proponent of a political ideology that favors small or limited government, an unfettered free market, self-reliance, and traditional social norms.

constitution A document outlining the formal rules and institutions of government and the limits placed on its powers.

constitutional courts Category of federal courts vested with the general judicial authority outlined in Article III of the Constitution. The most important are the Supreme Court, the courts of appeals, and the ninety-four district courts. Their authority derives from that of the Supreme Court, and they are supposed to conform to its decisions.

coordinated campaign spending Spending by the Democratic and Republican Party committees on behalf of individual congressional candidates.

coordination The act of organizing a group to achieve a common goal. Coordination remains a prerequisite for effective collective action even after the disincentives to individual participation (that is, prisoner's dilemma problems) have been solved.

core values Moral beliefs held by citizens that underlie their attitudes toward political and other issues. As integral parts of an individual's identity, these beliefs are stable and resistant to change.

court of appeals The second tier of courts in the federal judicial system (between the Supreme Court and the district courts). One court of appeals serves each of eleven regions, or circuits, plus one for the District of Columbia.

Court-packing plan An attempt by President Franklin Roosevelt, in 1937, to remodel the federal judiciary. Its purpose ostensibly was to alleviate the overcrowding of federal court dockets by allowing the president to appoint an additional Supreme Court justice for every sitting justice over the age of seventy. The legislation passed the House of Representatives but failed in the Senate by a single vote. If it had passed, Roosevelt could have added six new justices to the high bench, thereby installing a new Court majority sympathetic to his New Deal programs.

credibility gap The widespread suspicion among reporters that presidents will lie to the media when doing so serves their interest and they think they can get away with it.

cruel and unusual punishment Criminal penalties that are not considered appropriate by a society, that involve torture, or that could result in death when the death penalty had not been ordered.

cutthroat competition Competition among states that involves adopting policies that each state would prefer to avoid. For example, states engage in cutthroat competition when they underbid one another on tax breaks to attract businesses relocating their facilities.

Declaration of Independence The document drafted by Thomas Jefferson and adopted by the Second Continental Congress on July 4, 1776, declaring the independence of the thirteen colonies from Great Britain.

de facto segregation Segregation that results from practice rather than from law.

de jure segregation Segregation enacted into law and imposed by the government.

delegation The act of one person or body authorizing another person or body to perform an action on its behalf. For example, Congress often delegates authority to the president or administrative agencies to decide the details of policy.

detailed staff Staff from another government agency sent to assist the White House.

direct democracy A system of government in which citizens make policy decisions by voting on legislation themselves rather than by delegating that authority to their representatives.

discharge petition A petition that removes a measure from a committee to which it has been referred in order to make it available for floor consideration. In the House a discharge petition must be signed by a majority of House members (218).

dissenting opinion The written opinion of one or more Supreme Court justices who disagree with the ruling of the Court's majority. The opinion outlines the rationale for their disagreement.

district courts The trial courts of original jurisdiction in the federal judicial system. The ninety-four district courts are the third tier of the federal judicial system, below the Supreme Court and the courts of appeals.

divided government A term used to describe government when one political party controls the executive branch and the other political party controls one or both houses of the legislature.

dual federalism A system of government in which the federal government and state governments each have mutually exclusive spheres of action.

due process clause A clause found in both the Fifth and Fourteenth Amendments to the Constitution protecting citizens from arbitrary action by the national and state governments.

earmarks Money set aside by Congress in the federal budget to pay for projects in the home district of a member of Congress.

elastic clause Allows Congress to "make all Laws which shall be necessary and proper for carrying into Execution the foregoing Powers."

Electoral College A body of electors in each state, chosen by voters, who formally elect the president and vice president of the United States. Each state's number of electoral votes equals its representation in Congress; the District of Columbia has three votes. An absolute majority of the total electoral vote is required to elect a president and vice president.

embedding Military media strategy of putting journalists among military units in the field.

enrolled bill A bill that has been passed by both the Senate and the House and has been sent to the president for approval.

entitlement A benefit that every eligible person has a legal right to receive and that cannot be taken away without a change in legislation or due process in court.

enumerated powers The explicit powers given to Congress by the Constitution in Article I, Section 8. These include the powers of taxation, coinage of money, regulation of commerce, and provision for the national defense.

equal protection clause A Fourteenth Amendment clause guaranteeing all citizens equal protection of the laws. The courts have interpreted the clause to bar discrimination against minorities and women.

equal time A "fairness" rule established by the Federal Communications Commission to ensure that broadcasters offer balanced coverage of controversial issues. If a radio or television station sells or gives airtime to one candidate for political office, it must provide other candidates with equal time.

establishment of religion clause The first clause of the First Amendment. The establishment clause prohibits the national government from establishing a national religion.

exclusionary rule A judicial rule prohibiting the police from using at trial evidence obtained through illegal search and seizure.

executive agreement An agreement between the president and one or more other countries. An executive agreement is similar to a treaty, but unlike a treaty, it does not require the approval of the Senate.

Executive Office of the President (EOP) A collection of agencies that help the president oversee department and agency activities, formulate budgets and monitor spending, craft legislation, and lobby Congress. The major components of the EOP, established in 1939 by President Franklin Roosevelt, include the White House Office, Office of Management and Budget, National Security Council, and Council of Economic Advisers, among other agencies.

executive order A presidential directive to an executive agency establishing new policies or indicating how an existing policy is to be carried out.

externality Public goods or bads generated as a byproduct of private activity. For example, air pollution is an externality (public bad) because it is, in part, the byproduct of the private activity of driving a car.

faction A group of people sharing common interests who are opposed to other groups with competing interests. James Madison defined a faction as any group with objectives contrary to the general interests of society.

fairness doctrine Rule that assures that different points of view on controversial issues have access to the airwaves.

Federal Register A government publication listing all proposed federal regulations.

federalism A system of government in which power is divided between a central government and several regional governments. In the United States the division is between the national government and the states.

Federalists Name given to two related, but not identical, groups in late-eighteenth-century American politics. The first group, led by Alexander Hamilton and James Madison, supported ratification of the Constitution in 1787 and 1788. Subsequently, Hamilton and John Adams led the second group, the Federalist Party, which dominated national politics during the administrations of George Washington (1789–1797) and Adams (1797–1801).

filibuster A tactic used in the Senate to halt action on a bill. It involves making long speeches until the majority retreats. Senators, once holding the floor, have unlimited time to speak unless a cloture vote is passed by three-fifths (sixty) of the members.

fire alarm The type of oversight in which Congress does not act directly, but instead sets up processes that allow organized groups and private individuals to detect failures in the implementation of laws and to alert Congress.

focal point Focus identified by participants when coordinating their energies to achieve a common purpose.

focus group A method of gauging public opinion by observing a small number of people brought together to discuss specific issues, usually under the guidance of a moderator.

framing Providing a context that affects the criteria citizens use to evaluate candidates, campaigns, and political issues.

franking privilege The legal right of each member of Congress to send official mail postage-free under his or her signature.

free exercise clause The second clause of the First Amendment. The free exercise clause forbids the national government to interfere with the exercise of religion.

free-rider problem A situation in which individuals can receive the benefits from a collective activity whether or not they helped to pay for it, leaving them with no incentive to contribute.

Fugitive Slave Law The 1850 law compelling northerners to honor southerners' property claims to slaves, passed in return for the South's agreeing to admit California as a free state (and hence lose its ability to block legislation in the Senate).

fusion tickets Slates of candidates that "fused" the nominees of minor and major parties. Fusion tickets, eventually banned by state legislatures, allowed minor parties to boost their votes by nominating candidates also nominated by major parties.

gag rule An executive order prohibiting federal employees from communicating directly with Congress.

gerrymandering Drawing legislative districts in such a way as to give one political party a disproportionately large share of seats for the share of votes its candidates win.

going public Presidents "go public" when they engage in intensive public relations to promote their policies to the voters and thereby induce cooperation from other elected officeholders in Washington.

government The institutions and procedures through which people are ruled.

Government Accountability Office Office with a staff of more than five thousand that audits programs and agencies and reports to Congress on their performance.

grandfather clauses Statutes stating that only those people whose grandfather had voted before Reconstruction could vote, unless they passed a literacy or wealth test. After the Civil War this mechanism was used to disenfranchise African Americans.

grants-in-aid Funds given by Congress to state or local governments for a specific purpose.

grassroots lobbying Lobbying conducted by rank-and-file members of an interest group.

Great Compromise The agreement between large and small states at the Constitutional Convention (1787) that decided the selection and composition of Congress. The compromise stipulated that the lower chamber (House of Representatives) be chosen by direct popular vote and that the upper chamber (Senate) be selected by the state legislatures. Representation in the House would be proportional to a state's population; in the Senate each state would have two members.

gridlock A legislative "traffic jam" often precipitated by divided government. Gridlock occurs when presidents confront opposition-controlled Congresses with policy preferences and political stakes that are in direct competition with their own and those of their party. Neither side is willing to compromise, the government accomplishes little, and federal operations may even come to a halt.

hate crime A violent crime directed against individuals, property, or organizations solely because of the victims' race, gender, national origin, or sexual orientation.

hearings and investigations Meetings in which bureaucrats are called before subcommittees to explain and defend their decisions, and outsiders are sometimes invited to criticize them. Most agencies must testify annually about their activities before the House Appropriations subcommittee that has jurisdiction over their budgets.

home rule Power given by a state to a locality to enact legislation and manage its own affairs locally. Home rule also applies to Britain's administration of the American colonies.

ideology A comprehensive, integrated set of views about government and politics.

imperial presidency a presidency in which an elected monarch has a retinue of aides to do his bidding.

institutionalized presidency a set of offices and staff that assist the president.

incorporation The Supreme Court's extension of the guarantees of the Bill of Rights to state and local governments through its various interpretations of the Fourteenth Amendment.

independent campaign spending Campaign spending—by a person or organization for or against a political candidate—that is not controlled by or coordinated with any candidate's campaign.

infotainment Increasingly popular, nontraditional source of political information that combines news and entertainment. Examples include talk shows and political comedy programs.

insider tactics Interest group activity that includes normal lobbying on Capitol Hill, working closely with members of Congress, and contributing money to incumbents' campaigns. Contrasts with *outsider tactics*.

inspectors general Positions with independent offices (outside the normal bureaucratic chain of command) in virtually every government agency, who audit agency books and investigate activities on Congress's behalf.

initiative An approach to direct democracy in which a proposal is placed on an election ballot when the requisite number of registered voters have signed petitions.

institution In a democracy, an organization that manages potential conflicts between political rivals, helps them to find mutually acceptable solutions, and makes and enforces the society's collective agreements. Among the prominent federal political institutions in the United States are Congress, the presidency, and the Supreme Court.

interest groups Organized groups of people seeking to influence public policy.

iron triangle A stable, mutually beneficial political relationship among a congressional committee (or subcommittee), administrative agency, and organized interests concerned with a particular policy domain.

issue network A loose, informal, and highly variable web of relationships among representatives of various interests who are involved in a particular area of public policy.

issue publics Groups of citizens who are more attentive to particular areas of public policy than average citizens because such groups have some special stake in the issues.

issue voting Voting for candidates based on their positions on specific issues, as opposed to their party or personal characteristics.

Jim Crow laws A series of laws enacted in the late nineteenth century by southern states to institute segregation. These laws created "whites only" public accommodations such as schools, hotels, and restaurants.

joint committees Permanent congressional committees made up of members of both the House and the Senate. Joint committees do not have any legislative authority; they monitor specific activities and compile reports.

judicial doctrine The practice of prescribing in a decision a set of rules that are to guide future decisions on similar cases. Used by the Supreme Court to guide the lower courts in making decisions.

judicial review The authority of a court to declare legislative and executive acts unconstitutional and therefore invalid.

King Caucus A pejorative term used to refer to the first method of nominating presidential candidates in which party leaders elected to Congress would pick a presidential nominee. More generally, refers to the imposition of elite authority over mass action. This method of presidential nomination was retired after the presidential election of 1824.

laboratories for reform The idea that states provide their citizens with opportunities to change politics on a smaller scale, giving everyone else the chance to observe the effects of a reform without risking it themselves.

leak Strategically consequential information given to reporters on the condition that its source not be identified by name.

legislative veto A procedure that allows one or both houses of Congress to reject an action taken by the president or an executive agency. In 1983 the Supreme Court declared legislative vetoes unconstitutional, but Congress continues to enact legislation incorporating the veto.

Lemon **test** The most far-reaching of the controversial cases in which the Supreme Court specified three conditions every state law must satisfy to avoid running afoul of the establishment of religion prohibition: the statute in question "must have a secular legislative purpose," such as remedial education; the statute's "primary effect must be one that neither advances nor inhibits religion"; and the statute must not foster "an excessive government entanglement with religion."

libel A published falsehood or statement resulting in the defamation of someone's character. The First Amendment does not protect libelous statements.

liberal In the United States, a proponent of a political ideology that favors extensive government action to redress social and economic inequalities and tolerates social behaviors that conservatives view as deviant. Present-day liberals advocate policies benefiting the poor, minority groups, labor unions, women, and the environment and oppose government imposition of traditional social norms.

limitation riders Amendments, attached to appropriations bills, which forbid an agency to spend any of the money appropriated on activities specified by Congress.

line-item veto A procedure, available in 1997 for the first time, permitting a president to cancel amounts of new discretionary appropriations (budget authority), as well as new items of direct spending (entitlements) and certain limited tax benefits, unless Congress disapproves by law within a specified period of time. It was declared unconstitutional in 1998.

literacy test A legal barrier used to exclude African Americans from voting. Local white registrars would require prospective black voters to read and interpret arcane passages of the state's constitution. Since few satisfied these registrars' rigorous demands, by 1910 fewer than 10 percent of black males were voting in the South.

lobbying Activities through which individuals, interest groups, and other institutions seek to influence public policy by persuading government officials to support their groups' position.

lobbyists Professionals who work to influence public policy in favor of their clients' interests.

logroll The result of legislative vote trading. For example, legislators representing urban districts may vote for an agricultural bill provided that legislators from rural districts vote for a mass transit bill.

majority leader The formal leader of the party controlling a majority of the seats in the House or the Senate. In the Senate the majority leader is the head of the majority party. In the House the majority leader ranks second in the party hierarchy behind the Speaker.

majority rule The principle that decisions should reflect the preferences of more than half of those voting. Decision making by majority rule is one of the fundamental procedures of democracy.

mandatory reports Method by which Congress keeps its bureaucratic agents in line, in this case requiring executive agencies—even the president—to report on programs.

media bias Bias or slant in the selection of which news to report and how the news is reported.

matching grant A grant of money given by the federal government to a state government for which the federal government provides matching funds, usually between one and two dollars, for every dollar the state spends in some area.

measurement error Uncertainties in public opinion, as revealed by responses to polls, that arise from the imperfect connection between the wording of survey questions and the terms in which people understand and think about political objects.

message In a political campaign, the central thematic statement of why voters ought to prefer one candidate over others.

microtargeting The process of targeting very specific groups of potential voters. For example, using databases that combine voter rolls with credit card purchase information or grocery store savings club records to identify potential supporters.

Miranda **rule** Requirement that police inform suspects that they have a right to remain silent and a right to have counsel while being interrogated. Failure to inform suspects of their rights will result in any confession or evidence thus obtained being inadmissable against them at trial.

mobilization Also known as "getting out the vote." Mobilization occurs when activists working for parties, candidates, or interest groups ask members of the electorate to vote.

moral incentives The personal satisfactions of active self-expression through contribution or other involvement to social causes.

muckraking Journalistic investigation and exposure of scandals, corruption, and injustices, pioneered during the late-nineteenth-century Progressive Era.

multiple referral The act of sending a proposed piece of legislation to more than one committee in the same chamber.

nationalists Constitutional reformers led by James Madison and Alexander Hamilton who sought to replace the Articles of Confederation. Opposed at the Constitutional Convention (1787) by states' rights proponents, the nationalists favored a strong national legislature elected directly by the citizenry rather than the states and a national government that could veto any state laws it deemed unfit.

nationalization Shifting to the national government responsibilities traditionally exercised by the states.

national party convention A gathering of delegates to select a party's presidential and vice-presidential ticket and to adopt its national platform.

National Security Council (NSC) The highest advisory body to the president on military and diplomatic issues. Established in 1947, this agency in the Executive Office of the President helps the president coordinate the actions of government agencies, including the State and Defense Departments and the Joint Chiefs of Staff, into a single cohesive policy for dealing with other nations.

necessary and proper clause The last clause of Article I, Section 8, of the Constitution. This clause grants Congress the authority to make all laws that are "necessary and proper" and to execute those laws.

neutrality test Policy favored by justices in establishment of religion decisions. The justices used the neutrality test not so much to prevent favoritism among religious groups as to root out policies that preferred religious groups generally over non-religious groups engaged in a similar activity.

New Deal coalition An electoral alliance that was the basis of Democratic dominance from the 1930s to the early 1970s. The alliance consisted of Catholics, Jews, racial minorities, urban residents, organized labor, and white southerners.

New Jersey Plan New Jersey delegate William Patterson's proposal for reforming the Articles of Confederation. Introduced at the Constitutional Convention (1787), the New Jersey Plan was favored by delegates who supported states' rights.

news media The organizations that gather, package, and transmit the news through some proprietary communications technology.

nominating convention A political convention used to select a candidate to run in an upcoming election

obscenity Defined as publicly offensive acts or language, usually of a sexual nature, with no redeeming social value. The Supreme Court has offered varying definitions in its rulings over the years.

office Subdivision of some government departments that confers on its occupants specific authority and responsibilities.

Office of Management and Budget (OMB) Previously known as the Bureau of the Budget, OMB is the most important agency in the Executive Office of the President. The budget bureau, created in 1921 to act as a central clearinghouse for all budget requests, was renamed and given increased responsibilities in 1970. OMB advises the president on fiscal and economic policies, creates the annual federal budget, and monitors agency performance, among other duties.

open rule A provision governing debate of a pending bill and permitting any germane amendment to be offered on the floor of the House.

open seat A seat in a state or district being contested by candidates, none of whom currently holds the office. Congressional seats become "open" when the incumbent dies or does not run for reelection.

opinion leader A citizen who is highly attentive to and involved in politics or some related area and to whom other citizens turn for political information and cues.

outsider tactics Interest group activities designed to influence elected officials by threatening to impose political costs on them if they do not respond. Tactics include marches, demonstrations, campaign contributions to opponents, and electoral mobilization.

pack journalism A method of news gathering in which news reporters all follow the same story in the same way because they read each other's copy for validation of their own.

parliamentary government A form of government in which the chief executive is chosen by the majority party or by a coalition of parties in the legislature.

party identification An individual's enduring affective or instrumental attachment to one of the political parties; the most accurate single predictor of voting behavior.

party label A label carrying the party's "brand name," incorporating the policy positions and past performance voters attribute to it.

party machines State or local party organizations based on patronage. They work to elect candidates to public offices that control government jobs and contracts, which, in turn, are used by party leaders (often denigrated as "bosses") to reward the subleaders and activists who mobilize voters for the party on Election Day.

patronage The practice of awarding jobs, grants, licenses, or other special favors in exchange for political support.

penumbras Judicially created rights based on various guarantees of the Bill of Rights. The right to privacy is not explicitly stated in the Constitution, but the Supreme Court has argued that this right is implicit in various clauses found throughout the Bill of Rights.

performance voting Basing votes for a candidate or party on how successfully the candidate or party performed while in office.

pluralism A theory describing a political system in which all significant social interests freely compete with one another for influence over the government's policy decisions.

plurality A vote in which the winning candidate receives the greatest number of votes (but not necessarily a majority—over 50 percent).

pocket veto A method by which the president vetoes a bill passed by both houses of Congress by failing to act on it within ten days of Congress's adjournment.

police patrols The type of oversight in which Congress directly monitors agencies to ensure that they are implementing laws faithfully, doing this visibly so that bureaucrats will notice that they are being watched and stay in line.

policy gridlock Political paralysis in the face of pressing national problems.

political action committee (PAC) A federally registered fundraising group that pools money from individuals to give to political candidates and parties.

political party A coalition of people who seek to control the machinery of government by winning elections. Not specifically mentioned in the Constitution, political parties make mass democracy possible by, among other functions, coordinating the group activities necessary to translate public preferences into public policy.

political socialization The process by which citizens acquire their political beliefs and values.

politician Elected professional who specializes in providing compelling reasons for people with different values and interests to join in a common action.

politics The process through which individuals and groups reach agreement on a course of common, or collective, action—even as they disagree on the intended goals of that action.

poll tax A tax imposed on people when they register to vote. In the decades after the Civil War this tax was used primarily to disenfranchise black voters. With passage of the Twenty-fourth Amendment, in 1964, it became unconstitutional.

popular sovereignty Citizens' delegation of authority to their agents in government, with the ability to rescind that authority.

pork barrel legislation Legislation that provides members of Congress with federal projects and programs for their individual districts.

power An officeholder's actual influence with other officeholders, and, as a consequence, over the government's actions.

preemption legislation Laws passed by Congress that override or preempt state or local policies. The power of preemption derives from the supremacy clause (Article VI) of the Constitution. (See also *supremacy clause.*)

preferences Individuals' choices, reflecting economic situation, religious values, ethnic identity, or other valued interests.

president pro tempore In the absence of the vice president, the formal presiding officer of the Senate. The honor is usually conferred on the senior member of the majority party, but the post is sometimes rotated among senators of the majority party.

primary election An election held before the general election in which voters decide which of a party's candidates will be the party's nominee for the general election.

prime The news media's influence on how citizens make political judgments, through emphasis on particular stories.

priming Occurs when readers and watchers of news that relates to the criteria with which we evaluate candidates or elected leaders are influenced by what the press covers in a very specific way—it influences what they think *about*, not what they *think.*

principal An individual with the authority to make some decision. This authority may be delegated to an agent who is supposed to act on the principal's behalf.

prior restraint A government agency's act to prohibit the publication of material or speech before the fact. The courts forbid prior restraint except under extraordinary conditions.

prisoner's dilemma A situation in which two (or more) actors cannot agree to cooperate for fear that the other will find its interest best served by reneging on an agreement.

private goods Benefits and services over which the owner has full control of their use.

privatize To prevent a common resource from being over-exploited by tying the benefit of its consumption to its cost.

privileges and immunities clause The clause in Section 1 of the Fourteenth Amendment stipulating that "no State shall make or enforce any law which shall abridge the privileges or immunities of citizens of the United States."

procedural doctrine Principle of law that governs how the lower courts do their work.

Progressive Era A period of American history extending roughly from 1880 to 1920 and associated with the reform of government and electoral institutions in an attempt to reduce corruption and weaken parties.

proportional representation An electoral system in which legislative seats are awarded to candidates or parties in proportion to the percentage of votes received.

public goods Goods that are collectively produced and freely available for anyone's consumption.

public interest lobby A group that promotes some conception of the public interest rather than the narrowly defined economic or other special interests of its members.

public opinion "Those opinions held by private persons which governments find it prudent to heed."

quorum The minimum number of congressional members who must be present for the transaction of business. Under the Constitution, a quorum in each house is a majority of its members: 218 in the House and 51 in the Senate when there are no vacancies.

quotas Specific shares of college admissions, government contracts, and jobs set aside for population groups that have suffered from past discrimination. The Supreme Court has rejected the use of quotas wherever it has encountered them.

race to the bottom When states "race," or compete, to provide a minimum level of services (such as welfare spending) or regulation (such as tax incentives for corporations). There remains much debate over whether or not states do indeed race toward the bottom.

racial profiling Identifying the suspects of a crime solely on the basis of their race or ethnicity.

red tape Excessive paperwork leading to bureaucratic delay. The term originated in the seventeenth century, when English legal and governmental documents were bound with red-colored tape.

referendum An approach to direct democracy in which a state legislature proposes a change to the state's laws or constitution that all the voters subsequently vote on.

regulation Setting up rules limiting access to a common resource and monitoring and penalizing those who violate them.

representative government A political system in which citizens select government officials who, acting as their agents, deliberate and commit the citizenry to a course of collective action.

republic A form of democracy in which power is vested in elected representatives.

restraint The judicial action of deferring to the policies emanating from the elected branches in the absence of a clear violation of the Constitution or established doctrine.

restricted rule A provision that governs consideration of a bill and that specifies and limits the kinds of amendments that may be made on the floor of the House of Representatives.

rider An amendment to a bill that is not germane to the legislation.

roll-call vote Vote taken by a call of the roll to determine whether a quorum is present, to establish a quorum, or to vote on a question. Usually the House uses its electronic voting system for a roll call, but when the system is malfunctioning the Speaker directs the clerk to read the names. The Senate does not have an electronic voting system; its roll is always called by a clerk.

rotation in office The practice of citizens serving in public office for a limited term and then returning to private life.

rule A provision that governs consideration of a bill by the House of Representatives by specifying how the bill is to be debated and amended.

rule of four A rule employed by the Supreme Court's stating that when four justices support hearing a case the certiorari petition is granted.

scientific polling Tool developed in the twentieth century for systematically investigating the opinions of ordinary people, based on random samples.

segregation The political and social practice of separating whites and blacks into dual and highly unequal schools, hospitals, prisons, public parks, housing, and public transportation.

select committee A temporary legislative committee created for a specific purpose and dissolved after its tasks are completed.

selective incentives Private goods or benefits that induce rational actors to participate in a collective effort to provide a collective good.

selective incorporation The Supreme Court's gradual process of assuming guardianship of civil liberties by applying piecemeal the various provisions of the Bill of Rights to state laws and practices.

senatorial courtesy An informal practice in which senators are given veto power over federal judicial appointments in their home states.

seniority rule The congressional practice of appointing as committee or subcommittee chairs the members of the majority with the most years of committee service.

separate but equal doctrine The Supreme Court–initiated doctrine that separate but equivalent facilities for African Americans and whites are constitutional under the equal protection clause of the Fourteenth Amendment.

separation of powers The distribution of government powers among several political institutions. In the United States, at the national level power is divided between the three branches: Congress, the president, and the Supreme Court.

shared federalism A system in which the national and state governments share in providing citizens with a set of goods.

Shays's Rebellion Uprising of 1786 led by Daniel Shays, a former captain in the Continental army and a bankrupt Massachusetts farmer, to protest the state's high taxes and aggressive debt collection policies. The rebellion demonstrated a fundamental weakness of the Articles of Confederation—its inability to keep the peace—and stimulated interest in strengthening the national government, leading to the Philadelphia convention that framed the Constitution.

shield laws Laws that protect journalists from having to testify about their sources in court.

signing statement A statement issued by the president that is intended to modify implementation or ignore altogether provisions of a new law.

simple majority A majority of 50 percent plus one.

single-issue voters People who base their votes on candidates' or parties' positions on one particular issue of public policy, regardless of the candidates' or parties' positions on other issues.

slander Forms of false and malicious information that damage another person's reputation.

social movements Amorphous aggregates of people sharing general values and a desire for social change.

soft money Money used by political parties for voter registration, public education, and voter mobilization. Until 2002, when Congress passed legislation outlawing soft money, the government had imposed no limits on contributions or expenditures for such purposes.

solicitor general The official responsible for representing the U.S. government before the Supreme Court. The solicitor general is a ranking member of the U.S. Department of Justice.

sound bite A catchy phrase or slogan that encapsulates a politician's message, broadcast especially on television news programs.

Speaker of the House The presiding officer of the House of Representatives. The Speaker is elected at the beginning of each congressional session on a party-line vote. As head of the majority party the Speaker has substantial control over the legislative agenda of the House.

special committee A temporary legislative committee, usually lacking legislative authority.

split ticket The act of voting for candidates from different political parties for different offices—for example, voting for a Republican for president and a Democrat for senator.

spoils system A system in which newly elected officeholders award government jobs to political supporters and members of the same political party. The term originated in the saying "to the victor go the spoils."

standing The right to bring legal action.

standing committee A permanent legislative committee specializing in a particular legislative area. Standing committees have stable memberships and stable jurisdictions.

stare decisis "Let the decision stand." In court rulings, a reliance on precedents, or previous rulings, in formulating decisions in new cases.

State of the Union address A message to Congress under the constitutional directive that the president shall "from time to time give to the Congress Information of the State of the Union, and recommend to their Consideration such Measures as he shall judge necessary and expedient."

states' rights Safeguards against a too-powerful national government that were favored by one group of delegates to the Constitutional Convention (1787). States' rights advocates supported retaining those features of the Articles of Confederation that guarded state prerogatives, such as state participation in the selection of national officeholders and equal representation for each state regardless of population.

status quo bias Institutional bias that fundamentally favors continuation of current public policy.

substantive doctrine Principle that guides judges on which party in a case should prevail—akin to policymaking.

suffragists Women who campaigned in the early twentieth century for the right of women to vote.

superdelegate A delegate to the Democratic National Convention who is eligible to attend because he or she is an elected party official. The Democrats reserve a specific set of delegate slots for party officials.

supermajority A majority larger than a simple 51 percent majority, which is required for extraordinary legislative actions such as amending the Constitution or certain congressional procedures. For example, in the Senate sixty votes are required to stop a filibuster.

supremacy clause A clause in Article VI of the Constitution declaring that national laws are the "supreme" law of the land and therefore take precedence over any laws adopted by states or localities.

"take care" clause The provision in Article II, Section 3, of the Constitution instructing the president to "take Care that the Laws be faithfully executed."

Tenth Amendment The amendment that offers the most explicit endorsement of federalism to be found in the Constitution: "The powers not delegated to the United States by the Constitution, nor prohibited by it to the States, are reserved to the States respectively, or to the people."

term limits A movement begun during the 1980s to limit the number of terms both state legislators and members of Congress can serve.

ticket-splitting (See *split ticket.*)

tragedy of the commons A situation in which group members overexploit a common resource, causing its destruction.

transaction costs The costs of doing political business reflected in the time and effort required to compare preferences and negotiate compromises in making collective decisions.

trial balloon Policy announced by the president in order to test public opinion and floated either by members of Congress or the media.

two-party system A political system in which only two major parties compete for all of the elective offices. Third-party candidates usually have few, if any, chances of winning elective office.

tyranny A form of government in which the ruling power exploits its authority and permits little popular control.

unanimous consent agreement A unanimous resolution in the Senate restricting debate and limiting amendments to bills on the floor.

unitary executive When a president claims prerogative to attach signing statements to bills and asserts his/her right to modify implementation or ignore altogether provisions of a new law that encroaches on his/her constitutional prerogatives as "the chief executive" or as commander in chief.

unitary government A system of government in which a single government unit holds the power to govern the nation (in contrast to a federal system, in which power is shared among many governing units). (See also *federalism.*)

veto The formal power of the president to reject bills passed by both houses of Congress. A veto can be overridden by a two-thirds vote in each house.

Virginia Plan Constitutional blueprint drafted by James Madison that sought to reform the Articles of Confederation. Introduced at the Constitutional Convention (1787), the plan proposed a tripartite national government, but unlike the subsequent Constitution, it provided for a popularly elected legislature that would dominate national policymaking.

War Powers Act Law that requires the president to inform Congress within forty-eight hours of committing troops abroad in a military action.

whip A member of a legislative party who acts as the communicator between the party leadership and the rank and file. The whip polls members on their voting intentions, prepares bill summaries, and assists the leadership in various other tasks.

White House Office Agency in the Executive Office of the President (EOP) that serves as the president's personal staff system. Although the entire EOP does the president's business, the White House staff consists of the president's personal advisers, who oversee the political and policy interests of the administration.

white primary A practice that permitted political parties to exclude African Americans from voting in primary elections. Because historically in the South winning the Democratic primary was tantamount to winning the general election, this law in effect disenfranchised black voters in southern states.

writ of certiorari An order that is given by a superior court to an appellate court and that directs the lower court to send up a case the superior court has chosen to review. This is the central means by which the Supreme Court determines what cases it will hear.

writ of mandamus "We command." A court-issued writ commanding a public official to carry out a specific act or duty.

"yellow journalism" Style of journalism born of intense competition and characterized by screaming headlines and sensational stories. Coined at the end of the nineteenth century, the term referred to the yellow ink in which the New York World's comic strips were printed.

Photo Credits

Index

About the Authors

Samuel Kernell is professor of political science at the University of California, San Diego, where he has taught since 1977. Previously, he taught at the University of Mississippi and the University of Minnesota and served as a fellow at the Brookings Institution. Kernell's research interests focus on the presidency and American political history. His books include *Going Public: New Strategies of Presidential Leadership,* 4th Edition; an edited collection of essays, *James Madison: The Theory and Practice of Republican Government;* and *Strategy and Choice in Congressional Elections,* 2nd Edition (with Gary C. Jacobson). *Manufactured Responsiveness: The Transformation of America's Nineteenth Century Electoral Institutions* (with Erik J. Engstrom) will be published in 2014.

Gary C. Jacobson is distinguished professor of political science at the University of California, San Diego, where he has taught since 1979. He previously taught at Trinity College, the University of California at Riverside, Yale University, and Stanford University. Jacobson specializes in the study of U.S. elections, parties, interest groups, and Congress. He is the author of *Money in Congressional Elections; The Politics of Congressional Elections,* 8th Edition; *The Electoral Origins of Divided Government: Competition in the U.S. House Elections, 1946–1988;* and *A Divider, Not a Uniter: George W. Bush and the American People,* 2nd Edition; and is coauthor with Samuel Kernell of *Strategy and Choice in Congressional Elections,* 2nd Edition. Jacobson is a Fellow of the American Academy of Arts and Sciences.

Thad Kousser is associate professor of political science at the University of California, San Diego and director of the California Constitutional Reform Project at Stanford University's Lane Center for the West. He has served as a legislative aide in the California, New Mexico, and U.S. Senates. He is the author of *Term Limits and the Dismantling of State Legislative Professionalism,* and the coeditor of *The New Political Geography of California* and of *Politics in the American States,* 10th Edition. Kousser has been awarded the UCSD Academic Senate's Distinguished Teaching Award and served as coeditor of the journal *State Politics and Policy Quarterly.*

Lynn Vavreck is associate professor of political science at the University of California, Los Angeles (UCLA), where she has taught since 2001. She previously taught at Dartmouth College and has also worked at Princeton University, in the White House, and on a presidential campaign. Her research focuses mainly on the effects of campaign messaging and specifically on the impact of political advertising. She is the author of *The Message Matters: The Economy and Presidential Campaigns* and co-author of *Campaign Reform: Insights and Evidence,* and *The Gamble: Choice and Chance in the 2012 Election.* Her political commentary can be read in *The New York Times* and on broadcast outlets like MSNBC, CNN, and NPR. She serves on advisory boards for the American National Election Study and the British Election Study and has twice consulted for venture-funded start-ups interested in improving the measurement of advertising and public attitudes through innovations in technology.

SAGE researchmethods

The essential online tool for researchers from the world's leading methods publisher

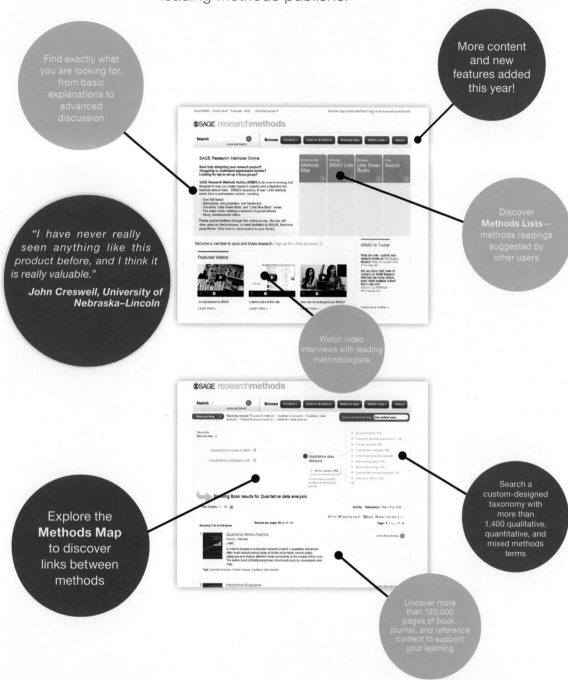

Find exactly what you are looking for, from basic explanations to advanced discussion

More content and new features added this year!

"I have never really seen anything like this product before, and I think it is really valuable."

John Creswell, University of Nebraska–Lincoln

Discover Methods Lists—methods readings suggested by other users

Watch video interviews with leading methodologists

Explore the Methods Map to discover links between methods

Search a custom-designed taxonomy with more than 1,400 qualitative, quantitative, and mixed methods terms

Uncover more than 120,000 pages of book, journal, and reference content to support your learning

Find out more at
www.sageresearchmethods.com